EIGHTH EDITION

SOCIAL PSYCHOLOGY

Robert A. Baron
Rensselaer Polytechnic Institute

Donn Byrne
University at Albany/State University of New York

Allyn and Bacon
Boston London Toronto Sydney Tokyo Singapore

To my mother Ruth and father Bernard, who taught me everything I needed to know to have a good life: The importance of work, the value of love, and the necessity of being resilient.

R.A.B.

To my cousins:

Elise Hawkins—Lago Vista, Texas
Mary Frances Kiefer—Austin, Texas
Fran Schoenvogel—Houston, Texas

Joe Singleton—Golden, Colorado
John V. Singleton—Houston, Texas
Josephine Taylor—Galveston, Texas

D.B.

Vice President and Editor-in-Chief: Sean W. Wakely
Senior Editor: Carolyn Merrill
Development Editor: Elizabeth Brooks
Cover Designer: Linda Knowles
Manufacturing Buyer: Megan Cochran
Editorial-Production Service: Colophon
Text Designer: Wendy LaChance

Photo Credits: 1.2a, Ed Kashi. 1.2b, John Coletti/Stock Boston. 1.3a, W. Hill/The Image Works. 1.3b, Robert Frerck/Odyssey. P. 14, The Archive of American Psychology. 1.5, Bob Daemmrich/ The Image Works. 2.1a, Richard Lord/The Image Works. 2.1b, Nina Berman/SIPA Press. 2.1c, S. Villeger/Photo Researchers. 2.1d, Robert Fried/Offshoot Stock. 2.1e, Bill Gallery/Stock Boston. 2.1f, David Woo/Stock Boston. 2.2a–d, Courtesy Paul Eckman, UCSF. 2.4a&b, Bonnie Kamin. 2.6a, Ed Kashi. 2.6b, Lee Snider/The Image Works. 2.7, Bob Daemmrich/The Image Works. 2.15a, Underwood Photo Archives, SF. 2.15b, Dennis Brack/Black Star. 3.2, Suzanne Opton.

(Photo credits continue on page 640 which constitutes an extension of the copyright page.)

Copyright © 1997, 1994, 1991, 1987, 1984, 1981, 1977, 1974 by Allyn and Bacon
A Viacom Company
160 Gould Street
Needham Heights, Massachusetts 02194
www.abacon.com

Library of Congress Cataloging-in-Publication Data
Baron, Robert A.
    Social Psychology / Robert A. Baron, Donn Byrne. – 8th ed.
    p.   cm.
    Includes bibliographical references and index.
    ISBN 0-205-18944-X
    1. Social psychology.   I. Byrne, Donn Erwin.   II.   Title.
HM251.B437 1996
302–dc20   96-2476
                                                                  CIP

Printed in the United States of America

10 9 8 7 6 5 4 3   00 99 98

BRIEF CONTENTS

CONTENTS

1 The Field of Social Psychology: How We Think about and Interact with Others 2

2 Social Perception: Understanding Others 36

3 Social Cognition: Thinking about Others and the Social World 74

4 Attitudes: Evaluating the Social World 110

5 Aspects of Social Identity: Establishing One's Self and Gender 150

6 Prejudice and Discrimination: Understanding Their Nature, Countering Their Effects 192

7 Interpersonal Attraction: Initial Contact, Liking, Becoming Acquainted 232

8 The Joys and Sorrows of Close Relationships: Family, Friends, Lovers, and Spouses 270

9 Social Influence: How We Change Others' Behavior—and How They Change Ours 316

10 Prosocial Behavior: Helping Other People 354

11   Aggression: Its Nature, Causes, and Control 390

12 Groups and Individuals: The Consequences of Belonging 432

13 Social Psychology and Society: Legal and Organizational Applications 474

14 Social Psychology in Action: Applications to Health and Environment 518

PREFACE

Social Psychology: An Integrated View:

WHY THE WHOLE REALLY *IS* GREATER THAN THE SUM OF ITS PARTS

IN 1979, I (BOB BARON), spent two years as a program director at the National Science Foundation. At that time there was a lot of excitement in the air at NSF, and it centered around the theme of *integration*. Boundaries that had separated different fields of science were disappearing as an increasing volume of research cut across frontiers and pulled such fields as biology, chemistry, and physics ever closer. The discussions of such integration were exhilarating, but at the time—alas!—social psychology couldn't participate in them fully. Back then, our field consisted of many discrete areas of study, each pursuing its own questions and interests in relative isolation from each other. Today, this picture has altered radically. Social psychology, we believe, is moving rapidly toward a level of integration—unity, coherence, and cross-fertilization between its various sub-fields—that it has not enjoyed since its very earliest days. Theories and principles developed in discrete areas of the field are "spilling over" more and more to other areas, and researchers who specialize in studying various topics are drawing, to an increasing degree, on the findings of colleagues working in other areas of the field.

What is the basis for this movement toward increased integration? Several factors appear to be playing a role. One, we suspect, is the atmosphere of coherence that currently pervades all fields of science. Boundaries among traditional fields have continued to weaken, and the volume of research involving collaboration between scientists from several different fields has continued to increase. Social psychology, as a scientific discipline, has been influenced by these trends, and as a result has sought greater integration within itself.

Another factor is the real and rapid progress made by social psychology during the past two decades. During these years, basic principles of social behavior and social thought have begun to emerge with startling clarity. Moreover, in contrast to conditions prevailing in the past, many of these principles are applicable to many different contexts and many forms of social interaction. Thus, they help to connect previously separate areas of our field.

Integration in the Eighth Edition

Since we view this rapid movement toward increased integration as very important, we have made strenuous efforts to represent them adequately in this book. In fact, we have made *integration* a major theme of the eighth edition. In order to bring these internal linkages into sharper focus, we have included three special features:

(1) *Integrating Principles.* At several points within each chapter, we highlight what we view as major integrating principles of social psychology—principles that have emerged out of specific lines of research but which seem to cut across many different areas of our field. As each *Integrating Principle* is presented, we also call attention to other topics in this text to which it is related. One example (from Chapter 2):

INTEGRATING PRINCIPLES

1. Because we are often interested not only in *what* other people do, but in *why* they do it, attribution is a key aspect of social perception.

2. The conclusions we reach about the causes of others' behavior can strongly influence our relations with them. Thus, attributions play an important role in many aspects of social behavior, including persuasion (Chapter 4), prejudice (Chapter 6), long-term relationships (Chapter 8), social influence (Chapter 9), and conflict (Chapter 11).

(2) *Connections: Integrating Social Psychology.* In order to illustrate how research in each area of social psychology is related to research in other areas, chapters are followed by special tables titled "Connections: Integrating Social Psychology." These *Connections* tables indicate how topics covered in the current chapter are related to topics covered in other chapters. *Connections* tables serve two major functions. First, they provide a kind of global review, reminding readers of related topics already covered in the text. Second, they emphasize the fact that many aspects of social behavior and social thought are closely *interlinked:* they do *not* occur in isolation from each other. (For examples, turn to the ends of Chapters 2 through 14.)

(3) *Thinking about Connections.* *Connections* tables are followed by what we view as a crucial additional feature: questions designed to get readers to think about the links described in the preceding table. These questions, termed "Thinking about Connections," focus on specific ways in which various aspects of social behavior and social thought are linked. In other words, they bring our claims about the importance of integration within our field into sharp, concrete focus. An example (from Chapter 5):

* Can you think of any situations in which your feelings of self-esteem influenced what you did, or of situations in which your self-esteem was affected by what happened? You might consider incidents in which someone tried to persuade you—or vice versa (Chapter 4), in which you met someone for the first time (Chapter 7), in which you were in a relationship that ended (Chapter 8), in which someone asked you to do something (Chapter 9) or to help them (Chapter 10), or of your behavior in work situations (Chapter 13) or of when you became ill (Chapter 14).

Together, the *Integrating Principles,* *Connections* tables, and *Thinking about Connections* questions help us to represent social psychology as it really is: an *integrated* field with multiple links between its diverse areas of research.

Other Features New to This Edition

In addition to *Integrating Principles, Connections* tables, and *Thinking about Connections* questions described above, the eighth edition also incorporates several other new features that we feel are consistent with important developments within social psychology.

The first of these, labeled *Cornerstones of Social Psychology,* reflects our belief that everything that happens in social psychology today has important roots in the past. Our field, like many others, has profited greatly from the work of true "giants"—founders of social psychology whose original thinking and insights put our field on the road to its modern form. In *Cornerstones* sections, we give these foundations of social psychology the attention they so richly deserve. These special sections describe truly "classic" studies in our field—ones that started major lines of research and that have exerted a lasting impact on the field. These sections call attention to the ways in which these early studies influenced subsequent thought and research in social psychology. Thus, in a sense, *Cornerstones* sections illustrate yet another kind of *integration* in our field—integration across *time*. We feel that this is important because most of the studies we describe in this text are very recent (many are from 1994 and 1995). This is as it should be, since social psychology is a rapidly changing and rapidly advancing field. But we don't want to leave readers with the impression that nothing important happened before 1990, and we believe that an effective way of countering this possibility, is by emphasizing the importance and lasting effect of classics in our field. A few examples:

- Asch's research on central and peripheral traits (Chapter 2)
- The economics of racial violence: do bad times fan the flames of prejudice? (Chapter 6)
- Festinger's social comparison theory (Chapter 7)
- Terman's investigation on husband-wife similarity and the success of the marriages (Chapter 8)
- Darley and Latané: explaining the unresponsive bystander (Chapter 10)
- Performance in the presence of others: the simplest group effect? (Chapter 12)
- Hugo Munsterberg on the inaccuracy of eyewitnesses (Chapter 13)

Social psychology has always been interested in *application*—in using the knowledge and findings it uncovers for practical purposes. This important aspect of the field is illustrated in special sections entitled *Social Psychology: On the Applied Side.* A few examples:

- Dissonance, hypocrisy, and safe sex [Chapter 4]
- What does love mean to you? [Chapter 8]
- The pique technique: preventing mindless (automatic) refusals [Chapter 9]
- When employees bite the hand that feeds them: employee theft as a response to perceived unfairness [Chapter 12]

In addition, in order to emphasize the practical nature of our field, we often draw on experiences from our own lives to illustrate the relevance, and importance, of topics and principles discussed. An example:

Friendly social interactions can begin as early as age one or two and remain stable over time. As a firsthand observation, my youngest daughter—Rebecka—met Alice at a day-care center when both were toddlers and still in diapers; they liked each other then, and they remained good friends five years later, even though they were attending different schools and lived a good many miles apart. (Chapter 7)

A third type of special section occurs near the end of each chapter and is titled *Social Diversity: A Critical Analysis*. These sections represent the growing *multicultural perspective* in social psychology to which we referred earlier. They present information concerning differences between ethnic groups within a given society, or differences across various cultures. Closely linked to the content of the chapters in which they occur, *Social Diversity* sections seek to examine key aspects of social behavior and thought from a multicultural perspective. A few examples:

- Reactions to Nonverbal Displays by Political Leaders in the United States and France (Chapter 2)
- Attitudes and Economic Growth: A Cross-National Study (Chapter 4)
- Concern about Weight: Asian versus Caucasian Women (Chapter 5)
- Physical Effects of Stereotypes: Evidence That Memory Loss in Our Later Years Is Influenced by Cultural Stereotypes about Aging (Chapter 6)
- Love and Intimacy: Individualistic versus Collectivistic Perspectives (Chapter 8)
- Evaluating the Motivation for Prosocial Behavior: Developmental and Cross-Cultural Similarities (Chapter 10)
- Cultural and Ethnic Differences in Aggression (Chapter 11)
- The Effect of Working in Another Culture: What Happens When Expatriates Come Home? (Chapter 13)

It is important to note that we have integrated many topics that were previously treated in special sections into the regular text. This, too, is consistent with our theme of greater integration both within and across topics. The result is a smaller number of special sections and, we believe, a less "busy" look for the book.

Changes in Content

When we wrote the first edition of this text, back in the early 1970s, we pledged that we would continue to keep it as up to date as possible. The eighth edition continues this strong tradition. To reflect continuing shifts in the focus of social psychology, we have made many changes in content. The most important are summarized below.

Reorganization of Several Chapters

Several chapters have undergone major reorganization:

- Chapter 9: Social Influence—The discussion of compliance has been completely reorganized so as to focus on the underlying principles that play a role in many tactics for gaining compliance.
- Chapter 11: Aggression—This chapter now includes coverage of the important topics of child maltreatment and workplace aggression.

- Chapter 12: Groups and Individuals—This chapter now includes coverage of perceived fairness in social exchange, a topic that is receiving renewed attention in many contexts.
- Chapter 13 (Social Psychology in Action: Legal and Organizational Applications) and Chapter 14 (Social Psychology in Action: Applications to Health and Environment) have been completely reorganized. Chapter 13 now includes coverage of applications of social psychology in law and business, while Chapter 14 focuses on applications in health and environmental issues.

Inclusion of Dozens of New Topics

Consistent with our commitment to reflecting social psychology as it is *now*, we have included coverage of literally dozens of new topics. Here is a partial listing of these new topics:

- Gender and publications in social psychology (Chapter 1)
- The method of converging operations (Chapter 1)
- Emotional expressiveness (Chapter 2)
- Cognitive processes in impression formation (Chapter 2)
- Rational versus intuitive processing (Chapter 3)
- The optimistic bias (Chapter 3)
- Magical thinking (Chapter 3)
- The affect infusion model (Chapter 3)
- Prototypes and safe sex (Chapter 3)
- Muscle movements and attitude formation (Chapter 4)
- Theory of planned behavior (Chapter 4)
- Attitude-to-behavior process model (Chapter 4)
- Message framing and persuasion (Chapter 4)
- Some specific components of the self-concept such as the sexual self-schema (Chapter 5)
- Self-esteem and social comparison (Chapter 5)
- Gender differences in communication styles (Chapter 5)
- Trivialization as a means of reducing cognitive dissonance (Chapter 4)
- The "new" racism (Chapter 6)
- The role of affect in stereotypic thinking (Chapter 6)
- The paradoxical effects of stereotype suppression (Chapter 6)
- The "glass ceiling" (Chapter 6)
- Acquiring a stigma through association with a stigmatized person (Chapter 7)
- Explicit and implicit affiliative needs (Chapter 7)
- The effects of anti-fat attitudes on overweight individuals (Chapter 7)
- The long-term effects of attachment style on interpersonal relations (Chapter 8)
- Predicting the success of relationships (Chapter 8)
- Descriptive and injunctive norms (Chapter 9)
- Underlying principles of compliance (Chapter 9)

- The foot-in-the-mouth technique (Chapter 9)
- The pique technique (Chapter 9)
- Responding—or not responding—to child abuse (Chapter 10)
- Genetic factors that affect empathy (Chapter 10)
- Effects of negative environmental factors on helping behavior (Chapter 10)
- Cognitive theories of aggression (Chapter 11)
- Sexual jealousy and aggression (Chapter 11)
- The "Big Five" dimensions of personality and aggression (Chapter 11)
- Child abuse; workplace aggression (Chapter 11)
- The collective effort model of social loafing (Chapter 12)
- Perceived fairness in groups (Chapter 12)
- Collective entrapment (Chapter 12)
- Organizational politics (Chapter 13)
- Expectancy confirmation in job interviews: how interviewers get the results they want (Chapter 13)
- Which teenagers are most likely to smoke? (Chapter 14)
- Disease-prone versus self-healing personalities (Chapter 14)
- Dependency and visits to a college health center (Chapter 14)

Other Learning Aids

In addition to these features, we have included many others that are specifically designed to help students learn about—and use—social psychology. These features include:

- A user-friendly writing style in which we address readers directly and often relate experiences from our own lives
- A marginal glossary in which key terms are clearly defined as they are used for the first time
- An end-of-book glossary where all key terms are defined once again
- Detailed chapter summaries that review all major points
- Annotated "For More Information" sections at the end of each chapter which describe several sources interested readers can consult.

Our own students have told us that these features are useful, and we have attempted to expand and refine them in this new edition.

Supplements

All good texts should be supported by a complete package of ancillary materials, both for the student and the instructor. This book provides ample aid for both. For the student, we offer a *Study Guide* written by Bem Allen and Gene Smith. It give students practice with short answers, definitions, matching, multiple choice, and completion questions.

For instructors, we offer an instructor's edition with bound-in teaching notes, transparencies, test bank, computerized test bank, a reader by Wayne Lesko, a new set of CNN video programs linked to topics in the text, a video library, as well as custom-published ancillaries. Please contact your Allyn and Bacon sales representative for more information on all of these, as well as related titles.

Some Concluding Comments

Now, once again, it's time to ask for *your* help. As was true of previous editions, we have spared no effort to make this one the best ever. We do realize, though, that even after twenty-five years of revisions, refinements, and—we hope—improvements, the process is not complete. In fact, we truly understand that it will never be complete—that there is *always* room for improvement. With this thought in mind, we earnestly request your comments, advice, and guidance. If there's something you feel can be improved, please let us know. Write, call, fax, or E-mail us at the addresses below. We'll be genuinely glad to receive your input, and—even more important—**we will definitely take it to heart!** Thanks in advance for your help.

Robert A. Baron
315 Lally,
Rensselaer Polytechnic Institute
Troy, NY 12180-3590
Phone: 518/276-2864
Fax: 518/276-8661
E-mail: baron94@aol.com

Donn Byrne
Department of Psychology
University of Albany, SUNY
Albany, NY 12222
Phone: 518/442-4827
Fax: 518/442-4867
E-mail: cm949cnsibm.albany.edu

ABOUT THE AUTHORS

Robert A. Baron
and Donn Byrne

ROBERT A. BARON is Professor of Psychology and Professor of Management at Rensselaer Polytechnic Institute. Former Chair of the Department of Psychology, he received his Ph.D. from the University of Iowa in 1968. Professor Baron has held faculty appointments at Purdue University, the University of Minnesota, University of Texas, University of South Carolina, and Princeton University. In 1982 he was a Visiting Fellow at Oxford University. From 1979 to 1981 he served as a Program Director at the National Science Foundation (Washington, D.C.). He has been a Fellow of the American Psychological Association since 1978.

Professor Baron has published more than ninety articles in professional journals and twenty-five chapters in edited volumes. He is the author or co-author of thirty books, including *Psychology* (3rd ed.), *Behavior in Organizations* (6th ed.), *Human Aggression* (2nd ed.), and *Understanding Human Relations* (3rd ed.). Textbooks by Professor Baron have been used by more than 1,400,000 students in colleges and universities throughout the world.

Prof. Baron is President of Innovative Environmental Products, Inc., a company engaged in the manufacture of equipment designed to enhance the physical environment of work settings and living spaces through improved air quality and elimination of distracting noise. He holds three U.S. patents, two of which apply to the P.P.S.®, a desk-top device combining air filtration, noise control, and other features. This device, and the basic psychological research behind it, were featured in the APA *Monitor* (March, 1995).

Professor Baron's research currently focuses primarily on the following topics: (1) workplace aggression, (2) impact of the physical environment (e.g., lighting, air quality, temperature) on social behavior and task performance, and (3) interpersonal conflict.

DONN BYRNE holds the rank of Distinguished Professor of Psychology and is the Director of the Social-Personality Program at the University at Albany, State University of New York. He received the Ph.D. degree in 1958 from Stanford University and has held academic positions at the California State University at San Francisco, the University of Texas, and Purdue University as well as visiting professorships at the University of Hawaii and Stanford University. A past president of the Midwestern Psychological Association and of the Society for the Scientific Study of Sex, he is a Fellow of the Society for Personality and Social Psychology, Society for the Psychological Study of Social Issues, and the Society for the Scientific Study of Sex; he is a Charter Fellow of the American Psychological Society. He has authored fifteen books, thirty-one invited chapters, one hundred and thirty-seven articles in professional journals, plus twenty-two additional publications such as book reviews and brief notes. He directed the doctoral work of forty-two Ph.D.s as well as that of several current graduate students at Albany. He has served on the Editorial Boards of *Experimental Social Psychology, Journal of Applied Social Psychology, Sociometry, Journal of Sex Research, Journal of Personality, Interamerican Journal of Psychology, Journal of Research in Personality, Psychological Monographs, Social Behavior and Personality: An International Journal,* and *Review of Personality and Social Psychology.* He was invited to deliver a G. Stanley Hall lecture at the 1981 meeting of the American Psychological Association in Los Angeles and a State of the Science Address at the 1981 meeting of the Society for the Scientific Study of Sex in New York City. He was an invited participant to Surgeon General Koop's Workshop on Pornography and Health in 1986, and received the Excellence in Research Award from the University at Albany in 1987 and the Distinguished Scientific Achievement Award from the Society for the Scientific Study of Sex in 1989. His current research interests include interpersonal attraction and the prediction of sexually coercive behavior.

ACKNOWLEDGMENTS

Some Words of Thanks

EACH TIME WE WRITE THIS BOOK, we gain a stronger appreciation of the following fact: We couldn't do it without the help of many dedicated, talented people. While we can't possibly thank all of them here, we do wish to express our appreciation to those whose help has been most valuable.

First, our sincere thanks to the colleagues listed below, who read and commented on various portions of the manuscript:

Nyla Branscombe, University of Kansas

Diana Cardova, Yale University

Donna Desforges, University of Wisconsin–Stevens Point

Christina Frederick, Southern Utah University

Grace Galliano, Kenesaw State College

Stella Garcia, University of Texas–San Antonio

Druscilla Glascoe, Salt Lake Community College

Tom Jackson, Fort Hays State University

John Harvey, University of Iowa

Herbert Leff, University of Vermont

Helen Linkey, Marshall University

Angela Lipsitz, Northern Kentucky University

Dan Sachau, Mankato State University

Delia Saenz, Arizona State University

Michael Strube, Washington University

Susan Thomas, Southern Illinois University at Edwardsville

Ann Weber, University of North Carolina–Asheville

Gary Wells, Iowa State University

Deborah Winters, New Mexico State University

In addition, of course, we are indebted to the many colleagues who kindly completed our preliminary survey; to a large degree, data from that survey guided the entire revision process:

Linda Albright, Westfield State College

Charles Alexander, Rock Valley College

Bem Allen, Western Illinois University

Tara Anthony, Syracuse University

Mark Attridge, University of Minnesota

Gordon Bear, Ramapo College

Lisa Bohon, California State University–Sacramento

Robert Bornstein, Gettysberg College

Nyla Branscombe, University of Kansas

Brad Bushman, Iowa State University

John Childers, East Carolina University

Winona Cochran, Bloomsburg University

Randolph Cornelius, Vassar College

James M. Daum, Wright State University

Lori Dawson, SUNY–Albany

Deborah Danzis, High Point University

William Delahayde, Marist College

David K. Dodd, St. Louis University

John F. Dovidio, Colgate University

Leslie Downing, SUNY–Oneonta

Karen Duffy, SUNY–Geneseo

Valerie Eastman, Drury College

Jeffrey Feinstein, Ohio State University

Phil Finney, Southeast Missouri State University

Robin Franck, Southwestern College

Grace Galliano, Kenesaw State College

Brian Gladue, University of Cincinnati/IPR

Richard Halverson, Luther College

Judith Harackiewicz, University of Wisconsin

Karen Harris, Western Illinois University

John Harvey, University of Iowa

Jay Hewitt, University of Missouri–Kansas City

Larry Hjelle, SUNY–Brockport

Matthew Hogben, University at Albany–SUNY

Blair T. Johnson, Syracuse University

J. I. Johnson, Southwest Texas State University

Robert D. Johnson, Arkansas State University

Tony Johnson, LaGrange College

Kathryn Kelley, University at Albany, SUNY

Alan Lambert, Washington University

Glenn Littlepage, Middle Tennessee State University

Charles McMullen, Tompkins Cortland Community College

Jeffrey Scott Mio, California State Polytechnic University, Pomona

Brian Mullen, Syracuse University

Mitchell Nesler, Regents College–the University of the State of New York

Bradley Olson, Northern Michigan University

Don Osborn, Bellarmine College

Robert J. Pellegrini, San Jose State University

Jacqueline Pope-Tarrence, Western Kentucky University

Jack Powell, University of Hartford

Bradley G. Redburn, Johnson County Community College

Nicholas A. Reuterman, Southern Illinois University at Edwardsville

J. G. Riggs, Eastern Kentucky University

Delia Saenz, Arizona State University

Thomas Saville, Metropolitan State College of Denver

Laura Sidorowicz, Nassau Community College

T. Smith, Iona College

Bill Snell, S.E. Missouri State University

Michael J. Strube, Washington University

James Wirth, College of the Ozarks

We also wish to thank reviewers of the seventh edition, who helped to get the entire revision process started—in the right directions.

Second—of course!—we want to offer our personal thanks to Susan Badger, our former editor at Allyn & Bacon, and former Vice President and Publisher. Her rare combination of talent, energy, and good judgment were invaluable to us, and improved the book in more ways than we can possibly mention here.

Third, our sincere thanks to Lisa Danials and Stephanie McGowan (both at the University at Albany, State University of New York) for their help with locating references needed for two important features of the book: *Foundations of Social Psychology* and *Social Diversity* sections.

Fourth, our sincere thanks to our Project Manager, Peg Latham. She oversaw many key aspects of production, and we were indeed fortunate to have her as part of the team.

Fifth, our thanks to Jay Howland for her very careful and constructive copy-editing. No author looks forward to seeing all those red marks and little yellow slips, but in this case, the extra work was well worth the effort, and helped to measurably improve the manuscript.

Sixth, our thanks to all of those others who contributed to various aspects of the production process: to Laurel Anderson for photo research; to Wendy LaChance for design work; and to Linda Knowles for the cover design.

Seventh, our thanks to the following colleagues for providing reprints and preprints of their work:

Craig Anderson, University of Missouri

Arnie Cann, University of North Carolina at Charlotte

Alan Feingold, Yale University

Joseph P. Forgas, University of New South Wales

Rick M. Gardner, University of Colorado at Denver

Jerald Greenberg, Ohio State University

Ed Hollander, Baruch College, CUNY

Saul Kassin, Williams College

Elizabeth Loftus, University of Washington

Judith Langlois, University of Texas

Ramadhar Singh, National University of Singapore

Eleanor Smith, Green Oaks at Medical City Dallas

Dolf Zillmann, University of Alabama

Finally, we wish to thank Jeanine Bloyd for her outstanding work on the Instructor's Section and Instructor's Research Manual; and to Tom Jackson for his help in preparing the Study Guide.

To all these truly outstanding people, and to many others, too, our warmest personal regards!

CHAPTER 1

THE FIELD OF SOCIAL PSYCHOLOGY: How We Think about and Interact with Others

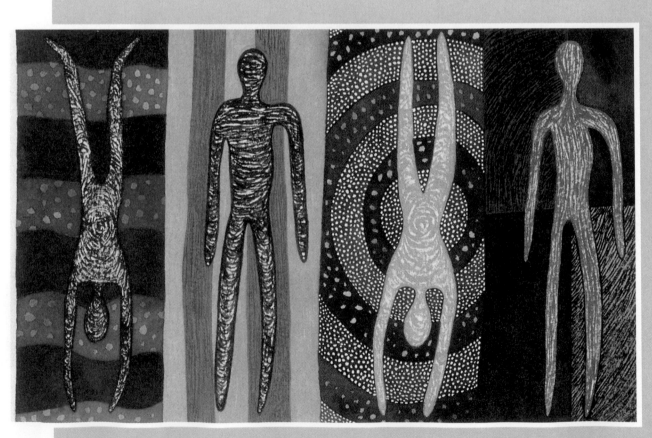

Lisa Houck, *It's Energetic*, 1996, watercolor, 6 × 9"

Chapter Outline

Why do people fall in—and out of—love? What makes relationships last—or disintegrate?

Are first impressions really as important as many people believe? And if so, what can you do to make sure that you make a good impression on others?

Are some people destined to become leaders because they possess special traits? What makes some leaders charismatic—able to exert truly amazing control over their followers?

Is aggression a built-in part of human nature, or can it somehow be reduced? Why is there so much more violence in some societies than in others?

What are the best ways of influencing other people—of changing their attitudes or their behavior? Why are we so successful at resisting efforts at persuasion most of the time?

If you've ever wondered about questions like these, welcome: you've come to the right place. These questions, and hundreds like them, form the core of social psychology—the field you are about to study.

Social psychology is a branch of psychology; and, as its name suggests, it focuses on *social behavior*—how people interact with, and think about, others. This means that every form of social behavior or social thought you can imagine—including unusual ones such as that shown in Figure 1.1—falls within its scope. Because other people and our relations with them are such an important part of our lives, we believe that social psychology, too, is very important. In fact, we don't mind stating that in many respects, we view it as the *most* central part of psychology. After all, isn't a field that investigates everything from love, cooperation, and helping on the one hand through prejudice, conflict, and violence on the other, intrinsically important?

"OK," we can almost hear you saying, "so social behavior is interesting—who could disagree? But can you tell me anything about it that I don't already

FIGURE 1.1

Social Behavior: The Focus of Social Psychology. *As shown by this cartoon, social behavior is tremendously varied in form—and often highly surprising!*

(*Source:* Drawing by Shanahan; © 1992 *The New Yorker* Magazine, Inc.)

"Don't make me get ugly, Pendleton."

know? After all, I've been interacting with other people all my life." Our answer to this question comes close to capturing the essence of modern social psychology—its fundamental nature, if you will. Two points are crucial in this respect:

1. The conclusions suggested by everyday experience, and by the accumulated wisdom of poets, philosophers, and novelists, are often insightful and informative, but also quite *inconclusive*. For example, consider the following pair of well-known sayings: "Absence makes the heart grow fonder" and "Out of sight, out of mind." Can both be true, and if so, how? Common sense often leaves us facing such dilemmas and unsolved mysteries where human social behavior is concerned.

2. Since this is so, social psychologists reason, why not use the methods of *scientific psychology* to attain answers to age-old questions about the social side of human life? These methods have worked extremely well in helping us understand other aspects of human behavior, such as how memory works and how psychological disorders like depression can be relieved; so why not apply them to social behavior, too?

Social psychologists have operated within this scientific framework since the earliest days of their field, and the results have, we feel, been very impressive. Through systematic research, social psychologists have uncovered a great deal of interesting and useful information about human social behavior. We'll be describing this work in the remaining chapters of this book. As the questions at the start of this chapter, and those in Table 1.1, suggest, social psychologists

---

TABLE 1.1 The Breadth of Social Psychology

This is a small sample of the questions currently being studied by social psychologists—questions we'll address in this text.

Question	Chapter in Which It Is Covered
How can we tell when another person is lying?	Chapter 2
Do we pay more attention to information about others that is consistent with our expectations or inconsistent with these expectations?	Chapter 3
Can our attitudes be changed by stimuli we don't consciously notice?	Chapter 4
Why do some individuals have positive self-evaluations but others negative self-evaluations?	Chapter 5
Can prejudice be reduced by preventing people from dividing the social world into "us" and "them"?	Chapter 6
What characteristics make people physically attractive?	Chapter 7
What is jealousy? What are its major causes?	Chapter 8
Can we get people to do favors for us by asking for much more than we want and then scaling back to a smaller request?	Chapter 9
Is there really "safety in numbers"—are people more likely to receive aid in emergencies when there are many other persons present?	Chapter 10
Is workplace violence increasing? If so, why?	Chapter 11
Do groups make better decisions than individuals?	Chapter 12
Are jurors influenced by the appearance and background of defendants? Or can they ignore such personal characteristics?	Chapter 13
Are optimists more resistant to the harmful effects of stress than pessimists? If so, why?	Chapter 14

seem to have taken as their motto "Let 1,000 flowers bloom," and have investigated a tremendously broad range of topics and processes. Before turning to this fascinating body of knowledge, however, it is important to provide you with some background information—some basic information about the origins, nature, and methods of social psychology. Why is such information important? Because research findings in psychology indicate that people have a much better chance of understanding, remembering, and using new information if they are first provided with a framework for organizing it. That's what this introductory chapter is all about: providing you with a framework for interpreting and understanding social psychology. Specifically, we'll use the remainder of this introductory chapter for completing three preliminary tasks.

First, we'll present a more formal and complete *definition* of social psychology. Every field has basic assumptions, and it is important to recognize these and make them explicit. Doing so will help you understand why social psychologists have chosen certain topics for intensive study and why they have studied them in certain ways.

Second, we'll offer a brief overview of social psychology's *history*—how it began and developed, where it is today, and where, we believe, it may be going in the future. No scientific activity occurs in a vacuum: on the contrary, it generally stands on the shoulders of work that went before. Social psychology is no exception to this basic rule, so knowing something about the history of the field can help you to understand the research social psychologists are conducting today.

Finally, we will examine some of the methods used by social psychologists to answer questions about social behavior. Knowledge of these *research methods* will help you to understand later discussions of specific research projects, and it will also help you to understand how the knowledge and conclusions we present throughout this text were obtained.

Social Psychology: A Working Definition

Providing a formal definition of almost any field is a complex task. In the case of social psychology, this difficulty is increased by two factors: the field's great diversity, and its rapid rate of change. Despite their diverse interests, however, most social psychologists seem to focus their attention on the following central task: Understanding how and why individuals behave, think, and feel as they do in situations involving other persons. Reflecting this fact, we will define **social psychology** as follows: *Social psychology is the scientific field that seeks to understand the nature and causes of individual behavior and thought in social situations.* In other words, social psychologists seek to understand how we think about and interact with others. We will now clarify several aspects of this definition.

Social Psychology Is Scientific in Nature

Many persons seem to believe that the term *science* refers primarily to fields such as chemistry, physics, and biology. Such persons may find somewhat puzzling our view that social psychology, too, is scientific. How can a field that seeks to investigate the nature of love, the causes of aggression, and everything in between be scientific in the same sense as astronomy, biochemistry, or geophysics? The answer is surprisingly simple. In reality, the term *science* does not

Social Psychology ■ The scientific field that seeks to understand the nature and causes of individual behavior and thought in social situations.

refer to a select group of highly advanced fields. Rather, it refers to a general set of methods—techniques that can be used to study a wide range of topics. In deciding whether a given field is or is not scientific, therefore, the crucial question is: *Does it make use of scientific procedures?* To the extent that it does, it can be viewed as scientific in orientation. To the extent that it does not, it falls outside the realm of science.

What are these techniques and procedures? We'll describe them in detail in a later section of this chapter. Here, we'll merely note that they involve efforts to gather systematic information about issues or processes of interest, plus an attitude of *skepticism*. It is a basic premise of science that *all* assertions about the natural world should be tested, retested, and tested again before they are accepted as accurate. For example, consider the following statement made by Samuel Butler, a famous English author of the nineteenth century: "We are not won by arguments that we can analyze but by tone and temper, by . . . manner. . . ." These words suggest that persuasion rests more on the *style* of would-be persuaders than on the arguments they present. Is this true? According to the basic rules of science, we can tell only by subjecting this idea to careful, systematic research. In fact, such research has been conducted, and we'll examine it in Chapter 4, where we consider the process of *persuasion* in detail.

In contrast, fields that are not generally regarded as scientific in nature make assertions about the natural world, and about people, that are *not* subjected to careful test. In such fields, intuition, beliefs, and special skills of practitioners are considered to be sufficient (see Figure 1.2).

So, is social psychology scientific? Our reply is a definite *yes*. Although the topics that social psychologists study are very different from those in the phys-

FIGURE 1.2

Science versus Nonscience: Different Methods, Different Values. In fields such as social psychology, data are gathered systematically and all hypotheses are carefully tested before being accepted as accurate. In nonscientific fields, in contrast, hypotheses and assertions are accepted at face value in the absence of any systematic tests of their accuracy.

ical or biological sciences, the methods we employ are similar in nature and orientation. For this reason, it makes sense to describe social psychology as basically scientific in nature.

Social Psychology Focuses on the Behavior of Individuals

Societies differ greatly in terms of their views concerning courtship and marriage; yet it is still individuals who fall in—and out of—love. Similarly, societies vary greatly in terms of their overall levels of violence; still, though, it is individuals who perform aggressive actions or refrain from doing so. The same argument applies to virtually all other aspects of social behavior, from prejudice to helping: the actions and cognitions in question are ultimately performed or held by individuals. Because of this basic fact, the focus, in social psychology, is squarely on individuals. Social psychologists realize, of course, that individuals do not exist in isolation from social and cultural influences—far from it. But the field's major interest lies in understanding the factors that shape the actions and thoughts of individual human beings within social settings. This contrasts sharply with the closely related field of *sociology*, which you may have studied in other courses. Sociology focuses on many of the same topics as social psychology, but its primary focus is on groups or whole societies—*not* individuals. For example, both social psychologists and sociologists study human aggression, but while social psychologists focus on factors that may cause specific individuals to engage in acts of aggression (e.g., being frustrated by another person, being in a rotten mood), sociologists tend to focus on societal causes of aggression (e.g., poor economic conditions).

Social Psychology Seeks to Understand the Causes of Social Behavior and Thought

In a key sense, the heading of this section states the most central aspect of our definition. What it means is that social psychologists are principally concerned with understanding the wide range of conditions that shape the social behavior and thought of individuals—their actions, feelings, beliefs, memories, and inferences—with respect to other persons. Obviously, a huge number of different factors play a role in this regard. It is also clear, however, that most factors affecting social interaction fall into five major categories: (1) the *actions and characteristics of others*—what others say and do; (2) basic *cognitive processes* such as memory and reasoning—processes that underlie our thoughts, beliefs, ideas, and judgments about others; (3) *ecological variables*—direct and indirect influences of the physical environment, such as temperature, crowding, privacy, and related factors; (4) the *cultural context* in which social behavior and thought occur; and (5) *biological factors* and processes that are relevant to social behavior, including certain aspects of our genetic inheritance. Perhaps a few words about each of these categories will help clarify their nature, and their importance in shaping social thought and social behavior.

The Actions and Characteristics of Others. Consider the following incidents:

You are standing in line outside a movie theater; suddenly, another person walks up and cuts in line in front of you.

The person you've been dating exclusively for six months suddenly and unexpectedly says: "I think we should see other people."

You make a presentation in one of your classes; after it is over, the professor remarks: "That was great—the best presentation I've heard in years!"

Will these actions by others have any impact on your behavior and thought? Absolutely. So it is clear that often we are strongly affected by the actions of other persons.

Now, be honest: Have you ever felt uneasy in the presence of a person with a physical disability? Do you ever behave differently toward highly attractive persons than toward less attractive ones? Toward elderly persons than toward young ones? Toward persons belonging to racial and ethnic groups different from your own? Your answer to some of these questions is probably *yes*, for we are often strongly influenced by the visible characteristics and appearance of others, too.

Cognitive Processes. Suppose that you are meeting a friend and this person is late. In fact, after thirty minutes, you begin to suspect that your friend will never arrive. Finally, your friend appears on the scene and says: "Sorry . . . meeting you just slipped my mind!" How will you react? Probably with considerable annoyance and irritation. Imagine that instead, however, your friend said: "I'm so sorry to be late. . . .There was a big accident, and the traffic was tied up for miles." Now how will you react? Probably with less annoyance, although not necessarily. If your friend is habitually late and has used similar excuses before, you may well be suspicious about whether this explanation is true. In contrast, if this is the first time your friend has been late for an appointment, or if the friend has never used such an excuse before, you may accept the explanation as true. In other words, your reactions in this situation will depend strongly upon your *memories* of your friend's past behavior, and will also involve your *inferences* concerning the true explanation for your friend's lateness. Instances like this, which are very common, call attention to the important role of *cognitive processes*—memory, inference, judgment, and so on—in social behavior and social thought. Social psychologists are well aware of the importance of such processes and realize that they must be taken into careful account in our efforts to understand many aspects of social behavior (Wyer & Srull, 1994).

Ecological Variables: Impact of the Physical Environment. Are people more prone to wild impulsive behavior during the full moon than at other times (Rotton & Kelley, 1985)? Do we become more irritable and aggressive when the weather is hot and steamy than when it is cool and comfortable (Anderson, Deuser, & DeNeve, 1995)? Does exposure to high levels of noise, air pollution, or excessive levels of crowding have any impact on our social behavior or performance of various tasks? Research findings indicate that the physical environment does indeed influence our feelings, thoughts, and behavior, so ecological variables certainly fall within the realm of modern social psychology (Baron, 1994; Bell et al., 1995). We'll consider the impact of such factors in Chapter 14.

Cultural Context. Social behavior, it is important to note, does not occur in a cultural vacuum. On the contrary, it is often strongly affected by cultural norms (social rules concerning how people should behave in specific situations), membership in various groups, and shifting societal values. Whom should people marry? How many children should they have? Should people keep their emotional reactions to themselves or demonstrate them openly? How close should they stand to others when talking to them? Is it appropriate to offer gifts to public officials in order to obtain their favorable action on various requests? These are only a small sampling of the aspects of social behavior that can be—and are—influenced by cultural factors. By *culture* we simply mean the organized system of shared meanings, perceptions, and beliefs held by persons belonging to some group (Smith & Bond, 1993).

As we'll note below, attention to the effects of cultural factors is an increasingly important trend in modern social psychology as our field attempts to take account of the growing cultural diversity that is a hallmark of the late twentieth century.

Biological Factors. Is social behavior influenced by biological processes and by genetic factors? Ten years ago, most social psychologists would have answered *no*, at least to the genetic factors part of this question. Now, however, the pendulum of scientific opinion has swung in the other direction, and many believe that our preferences, behaviors, emotional reactions, and even attitudes and values are affected to some extent by our biological inheritance (Buss, 1990; Nisbett, 1990).

The view that genetic factors play an important role in social behavior has been most dramatically stated by the field of **sociobiology.** This branch of biology suggests that many aspects of social behavior are the result of evolutionary processes in which patterns of behavior that contribute to reproduction (to getting one's genes into the next generation) are strengthened and spread throughout a population. From the sociobiological perspective, in essence, we all exist primarily to serve our genes—to ensure that our genetic material is passed on to as many offspring as possible (Barkow, 1989; Wilson, 1975). This basic assumption, in turn, is used to explain many aspects of social behavior. For example, consider how sociobiologists explain the fact that many animals that live together in herds or groups tend to issue loud warning cries when they spot a nearby predator—warning cries that focus the predator's attention on the individual issuing the warning. According to sociobiologists, animals engage in such behavior because in general, members of their herd, or those living close by, tend to be related to them. Thus, by issuing warning cries, they increase the chances of survival of these relatives, and so raise the chances of genes they share with them being passed on to the next generation.

While many social psychologists accept the view that biological and genetic factors can play *some* role in social behavior, they seriously question several of the basic assumptions of sociobiology (Brewer & Caporael, 1990; Cantor, 1990), including the key idea that our sole purpose in life is that of passing our genes to succeeding generations. For example, they reject the view that behaviors or characteristics that are affected by genetic factors cannot be altered. On the contrary, social psychologists assume that virtually every aspect of social behavior is open to potential change. An example: Many millions of people have an inherited tendency toward vision problems. Yet they readily correct this by the use of glasses or contact lenses. Similarly, social psychologists reject the view that because current tendencies in social behavior are the result of a long evolutionary process, these tendencies *should* exist.

These and other objections to the basic assumptions of sociobiology have led social psychologists who wish to study the role of biological and genetic factors in social behavior to offer another name for their field: **evolutionary social psychology** (Buss, 1990, in press). This term suggests that social behavior is indeed affected by natural selection; tendencies toward behaviors that are most adaptive from the point of view of survival often increase in strength over time within a given population. But it also recognizes the fact that such tendencies are definitely not set in stone. On the contrary, they can—and do—change in response to shifting environmental and social conditions, and they can even be altered or overridden by cognitive processes.

Although evolutionary social psychology is a relatively new field, researchers in it have already gathered intriguing evidence pointing to the potential role of genetic or evolutionary factors in human behavior. For example,

Sociobiology ■ A branch of biology that contends that many forms of behavior can be understood within the context of efforts by organisms to pass their genes on to the next generation.

Evolutionary Social Psychology ■ An area of research that seeks to investigate the potential role of genetic factors in various aspects of social behavior.

recent research on *mate preference*—the characteristics individuals seek in potential romantic partners—indicates that males and females may differ in some intriguing ways. Females tend to place greater emphasis on such characteristics as dominance and status, while males place greater emphasis on youth and physical attractiveness (Kenrick et al., 1994; see Figure 1.3). This difference is consistent with an evolutionary perspective noting that females invest greater resources in bearing children than males do in fathering them. Thus, from the standpoint of successfully passing one's genes on to the next generation, it makes sense for females to seek mates who will be able to provide the resources needed for child rearing (mates high in status or dominance). For males, in contrast, it makes sense to seek mates who are young and healthy, and so capable of bearing many offspring. We should emphasize that while findings pointing to such differences are consistent with an evolutionary approach, they do not in any way prove its accuracy. However, a growing number of social psycholo-

Figure 1.3

Mate Preference: Do Genetic Factors Play a Role? In many societies, males place greater emphasis than females on the physical attractiveness of potential romantic partners, while females place greater emphasis than males on status or dominance. Research findings suggest that such differences may stem, at least in part, from genetic predispositions.

gists believe that an evolutionary perspective is an informative one, so we'll have reason to refer to this approach at several points within this book (for instance, see our discussion of this topic in Chapter 8).

Social Psychology: Summing Up

To conclude: Social psychology focuses mainly on understanding the causes of social behavior and social thought—on identifying factors that shape our feelings, behavior, and thought in social situations. It seeks to accomplish this goal through the use of scientific methods, and it takes careful note of the fact that social behavior and thought are influenced by a wide range of social, cognitive, environmental, cultural, and biological factors.

The remainder of this text is devoted to describing some of the key findings of social psychology. This information is truly fascinating, so we're certain that you will find it of interest. We're equally sure, however, that you will find some of it to be surprising, and that it will challenge many of your current ideas about people and social relations. So please get ready for some new insights. We predict that after learning about social psychology, you'll never think about social behavior in quite the same way as before.

How We Got Here from There: The Origins and Development of Social Psychology

When, precisely, did social psychology begin? This question is difficult to answer, for speculation about social behavior stretches back to ancient times (Allport, 1985). Any attempt to present a complete survey of the historical roots of our field would quickly bog us down in more detail than is necessary. For this reason, we'll focus, in this discussion, on the emergence of social psychology as an independent field, its growth in recent decades, and current trends that appear to be shaping its present—and future—form.

The Early Years: Social Psychology Emerges

Few fields of science mark their beginnings with formal ribbon-cutting ceremonies. Instead they develop gradually, as growing numbers of scientists become interested in specific topics or develop new methods for studying existing ones. This pattern applies to social psychology: no bottles of champagne were uncorked to mark its entry on the scene, so it is difficult to choose a specific date for its official launching. Perhaps the years between 1908 and 1924 qualify as the period during which social psychology first attained status as an independent entity. In each of these years, an important text containing the words *social psychology* in its title was published. The first, by William McDougall (1908), was based largely on the view that social behavior stems from innate tendencies or *instincts*. While many modern social psychologists are willing to entertain the view that genetic factors play a role in some aspects of social behavior, almost all reject the idea of fixed, unchanging instincts as important causes of social behavior. Thus, it is clear that the field had *not* assumed its modern form in McDougall's early book.

The second volume, by Floyd Allport (1924), is a different matter. That book is much closer to the modern orientation of our field. Allport argued that social behavior stems from many different factors, including the presence of other persons and their specific actions. Further, his book emphasized the value of experimentation and contained discussions of actual research that had already been conducted on such topics as conformity, the ability to recognize others' emotions from their facial expressions, and the impact of audiences on task performance. All of these topics have been studied by social psychologists in recent years, so the following conclusion seems justified: By the middle of the Roaring Twenties, social psychology had appeared on the scene and had begun to investigate many of the topics it still studies today.

The two decades following publication of Allport's text were marked by rapid growth. New issues were studied and new methods for investigating them were devised. Important milestones in the development of the field during this period include research by two of its founders—Muzafer Sherif and Kurt Lewin. Sherif (1935) studied the nature and impact of *social norms*—rules indicating how individuals ought to behave—and so contributed basic insights to our understanding of pressures toward *conformity*. Kurt Lewin and his colleagues (e.g., Lewin, Lippitt, & White, 1939) carried out revealing research on the nature of leadership and other group processes. For a description of some of this work, which was among the earliest in social psychology on *group processes,* please see the *Cornerstones* section below. Quite apart from this research, Lewin's influence on social psychology was profound, for many of his students went on to become very prominent contributors to the field. Their names— Leon Festinger, Harold Kelley, Morton Deutsch, Stanley Schachter, John Thibaut—read like a "Who's Who" of famous social psychologists during the 1950s, 1960s, and even 1970s. In short, by the close of the 1930s, social psychology was an active, growing field that had already contributed much to our knowledge of social behavior.

Cornerstones of Social Psychology
WHAT STYLE OF LEADERSHIP IS BEST? SOME EARLY INSIGHTS

Leaders differ greatly in personal style, and these differences really matter. If you've ever been part of a group where the leader's style grated on your nerves or seemed to interfere with the group's success, you already know this fact. I (Bob Baron) discovered it for myself during the fourth and fifth grades. In the fourth grade, I had a teacher who truly "ran the show." She took firm control of all class activities and left no doubt about who was in charge. She made all the decisions and never asked for our input. She even posted a long list of rules in front of the room, telling us what to do—or not to do—in a wide range of situations. My fifth-grade teacher offered a sharp contrast to this approach. She seemed to enjoy sharing her authority with us, and let the class vote on many decisions. And while she, too, had rules, they were much more flexible and were never posted in a formal list. Which teacher did I prefer? As you can probably guess, the second one. But did I also do better work, and learn more, with this teacher than with the more directive one? In other words, was one of these contrasting styles of leadership superior to the other in terms of encouraging excellent performance?

This complex issue was the focus of a famous investigation on leader style and group performance conducted by Lewin, Lippitt, and White (1939).

Kurt Lewin. Kurt Lewin was one of many European social psychologists who came to the United States to escape from Nazi persecution. He conducted important early studies on many major topics in social psychology (e.g., leadership), and trained many students who went on to become famous social psychologists themselves.

These researchers arranged for ten- and eleven-year-old boys to meet in five-member groups after school, to engage in hobbies such as woodworking and painting. To investigate the possible effects of leader's style on the boys' behavior, the researchers arranged for each group to be led by an adult who assumed one of three contrasting styles of leadership: *autocratic, laissez-faire,* or *democratic.*

The autocratic leader was very much like my fourth-grade teacher. When playing this role, the leader gave many orders and made all the decisions for himself. He determined what activities the group would perform, and in what order, and simply assigned each boy a work partner without considering the boys' personal preferences. This autocratic leader gave many orders but remained aloof from the group, never participating in its activities. In contrast, the *democratic* leader was much more like my fifth-grade teacher. When playing this role, the leader allowed the boys to participate in reaching decisions, and often sought their input. He rarely gave orders or commands, allowed the boys to choose their own work partners, and permitted them to approach their work in whatever way they wished. The democratic leader also participated in the group's activities—he did not remain aloof as did the autocratic leader—but he did not try to dominate these activities in any way. Finally, the *laissez-faire* leader adopted a "hands-off" approach (the French words "laissez-faire" mean "let people do what they choose"). He avoided participating in group activities, and he did not intervene in them in any way. Rather, his role was primarily that of an interested observer, there to provide technical information about the hobby activities if requested to do so by the boys.

Trained observers watched the groups as they worked, and rated their behavior in several respects—for example, the amount of time spent working while the leader was present; the amount of time spent working when he left the room; and aggressive activities such as hostility among group members, demands for attention, destructiveness, and *scapegoating*—a tendency to single out one group member as the target of continuous verbal abuse.

When the behavior of the boys in the three conditions were compared, a number of differences emerged. For example, boys in the authoritarian and democratic groups spent about equal amounts of time working when the leader was present; those in the laissez-faire groups worked less. When the leader left the room, however, work dropped off sharply in the authoritarian groups, remained unchanged in the democratic groups, and actually increased slightly in the laissez-faire groups. In addition, boys in the autocratic conditions seemed more at a loss when the leader left the room: they appeared to be heavily dependent on the leader for direction and did not know how to proceed without his commands and guidance. With respect to the measures of aggressiveness, it appeared that there were more signs of such behavior in the authoritarian group than in the democratic or laissez-faire ones. For example, boys in the authoritarian groups expressed more discontent and made more aggressive demands for attention. Those in the democratic groups tended to be friendlier. (See Figure 1.4 for a summary of all these findings.) Consistent with my own experiences in school, the boys tended to prefer the democratic leaders to the other two.

What do these findings mean? Lewin and his colleagues interpreted them as suggesting that overall, a democratic style of leadership may be best. It encourages a high level of productivity, which persists even when the leader is absent. Further, it fosters positive and cooperative relations among group members. In contrast, an autocratic style of leadership produces high productivity only when the leader is present, and seems to increase both dependence on the leader and higher levels of aggression. Given that Lewin, Lippitt, and White (1939) conducted their research at a time when the world was poised on

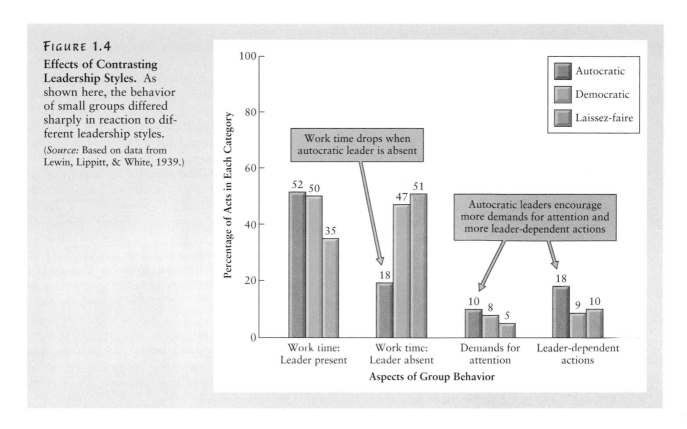

FIGURE 1.4

Effects of Contrasting Leadership Styles. As shown here, the behavior of small groups differed sharply in reaction to different leadership styles.

(*Source:* Based on data from Lewin, Lippitt, & White, 1939.)

the brink of World War II—a war that would soon pit the democracies of France, England, and the United States against the autocratic regimes of Nazi Germany and Imperial Japan—these conclusions were, and remain, somewhat comforting. However, as we'll see when we return to the topic of leadership in Chapter 12, later research has modified these conclusions to some extent (Yukl, 1989). More modern research suggests that a democratic style of leadership may indeed be preferred by group members, but is not always best from the point of group performance. For example, it can be dangerously inefficient at times when groups face imminent danger or must react quickly to changing conditions. Despite such refinements, however, the research conducted by Lewin, Lippitt, and White (1939) certainly qualifies as a cornerstone of social psychology: it added to our understanding of important topics, and it strongly shaped both the focus and the methods of much later research on leadership and related group processes. ■ ■ ■

Social Psychology's Youth: The 1940s, 1950s, and 1960s

After a pause resulting from World War II, social psychology continued its growth during the 1940s and 1950s. During this period the field expanded its scope in several directions. Social psychologists focused attention on the influence that groups and group membership exert on individual behavior (Forsyth, 1991). And they examined the link between various personality traits and social behavior—in, for example, research on the *authoritarian personality*—a cluster of traits that seem to predispose individuals toward acceptance of extreme political views such as Nazism (Adorno et al., 1950).

One of the most important events of this period was the development of the theory of **cognitive dissonance** (Festinger, 1957). This theory proposed that

Cognitive Dissonance ■ An unpleasant state that occurs when individuals discover inconsistencies between two of their attitudes or between their attitudes and their behavior.

human beings dislike inconsistency and strive to reduce it. Specifically, the theory argues that people seek to eliminate inconsistency between different attitudes that they hold, or between their attitudes and their behavior. While this theory may strike you as being quite sensible, it actually leads to many unexpected predictions. For example, dissonance theory suggests that offering individuals small rewards for stating views they don't really hold is often more effective in getting them to change these opinions than offering them larger rewards for the same actions. Why? Because when people say something they don't believe and realize that they had few reasons for engaging in such behavior, they experience strong pressure to change their views to agree with what they've just said—stronger pressure than when they are offered large rewards and, therefore, have many good reasons for stating such views. We'll examine this surprising fact, sometimes known as the *less-leads-to-more effect,* in detail in Chapter 4.

In an important sense the 1960s can be viewed as the time when social psychology came of age. During this turbulent decade of rapid social change, the number of social psychologists rose dramatically, and the field expanded to include practically every aspect of social interaction you might imagine. So many lines of research either began or expanded during these years that it is impossible to list them all here, but among the most important were these: *interpersonal attraction* and *romantic love; impression formation, attribution,* and other aspects of *social perception;* many different aspects of *social influence,* such as *obedience, conformity,* and *compliance;* and *effects of the physical environment* on many forms of social behavior.

The 1970s, 1980s, and 1990s: A Maturing Field

The rapid pace of change did not slacken during the 1970s; if anything, it accelerated. Many lines of research begun during the 1960s were expanded, and several new topics rose to prominence. Among the most important of these were *attribution* (the process through which we seek to understand the causes of others' behavior—*why* they act as they do; see Chapter 2); *gender differences* and *sex discrimination* (investigation of the extent to which the behavior of women and men actually differs, and the impact of negative stereotypes concerning the traits supposedly possessed by both genders; see Chapter 5); and *environmental psychology* (investigations of the effects of the physical environment—noise, heat, crowding, air quality—on social behavior; see Chapter 14).

In addition, two larger-scale trends took shape during the 1980s. Because these trends had a great impact on social psychology, they are worthy of special attention here.

Growing Influence of a Cognitive Perspective. As noted earlier, social psychologists have long recognized the importance of cognitive factors—attitudes, beliefs, values, inferences—in social behavior. Starting in the late 1970s, however, interest in such topics took an important new form. At this time, many social psychologists concluded that our understanding of virtually all aspects of social behavior could be greatly enhanced by attention to the cognitive processes that underlie them. The cognitive approach involves efforts to apply basic knowledge about cognitive processes such as *memory* and *reasoning* to the task of understanding many aspects of social thought and behavior. For example, within this context, social psychologists have recently sought to determine whether various forms of prejudice may stem, at least in part, from the operation of basic cognitive processes, such as the tendency to remember only information consistent with stereotypes of various groups, or tendencies to process information about one's own social group differently from information about other social groups (Forgas & Fiedler, 1996; Wegener & Petty, 1995; see Chapter 6). The results of research conducted within this cognitive perspective have been impressive, and have added greatly to our understanding of many aspects of social behavior.

Growing Emphasis on Application: Exporting Social Knowledge. Recent decades have also been marked by a second major trend in social psychology: growing concern with the *application* of social knowledge. An increasing number of social psychologists have turned their attention to questions concerning *personal health, the legal process, social behavior in work settings,* and a host of other issues. In other words, there has been growing interest in attempts to apply the findings and principles of social psychology to the solution of practical problems. This theme is certainly not new in our field; Kurt Lewin, one of its founders, once remarked, "There's nothing as practical as a good theory," by which he meant that theories of social behavior and thought developed through systematic research often turn out to be extremely useful in solving practical problems. There seems little doubt, however, that interest in applying the knowledge of social psychology to practical issues has increased greatly in recent years, with many beneficial results. We'll examine this work in detail in Chapters 13 and 14. For an indication of the great breadth of such research, and the interesting topics on which it focuses, please see Table 1.2.

Where Do We Go from Here?
The Year 2000 . . . and Beyond

James Baldwin, a noted author, once wrote: "No one can possibly know what is about to happen: it is happening, each time, for the first time, for the only time." We agree with this sentiment: predictions—especially about anything that changes as rapidly as social psychology—are a very tricky business. Still, at the risk of being proven wrong by future events, we wish to offer the following guesses about how our field will change in the coming decades.

Cognition and Application: Growing Knowledge, Growing Sophistication. The first of our predictions is the one in which we have most confidence: The two major trends described above—growing influence of a cognitive perspective and increasing interest in application—will continue. Knowledge about cognitive processes (memory, inference, reasoning) is accumulating quickly, so

---

TABLE 1.2 Applied Research in Social Psychology: A Sampling of Topics

As shown here, social psychologists are currently applying the knowledge and methods of their field to a very wide range of practical issues.

Conflict resolution tactics used by police

Bystander responses to public instances of child abuse

Returning to work after childbirth

Effects of physical attractiveness, race, and gender on the judgments of jurors

Use of child restraint devices in automobiles

Burnout among nurses

Factors affecting safe sex behavior

Alcohol use in workplaces

Effects of driver's gender on traffic citations

it seems only natural that social psychologists will use that knowledge—plus new insights into these processes that they uncover—to understand social behavior and social thought. Such work has already yielded valuable results, and we are confident it will continue to do so in the years ahead.

Similarly, we predict that interest in applying the principles and findings of social psychology will also continue. Increased concern with application appears to be a natural outgrowth of increasing maturity in almost any scientific field. Thus, we fully expect that social psychologists will expand their efforts to apply the findings of their field to practical issues.

Adoption of a Multicultural Perspective: Taking Full Account of Social Diversity. When I (Bob Baron) was in high school, my uncle gave me a book that provided an introduction to the United States for Europeans planning to visit this country for the first time. Looking back, one section was of special interest. It stated that the population of the United States was "90 percent of European descent." How the United States—and the world—has changed since the late 1950s, when that book was written! At present, the population of the United States is far more diverse than this book suggested. Consider California, the most populous state. At present, something like 55 percent of its population is of European descent, and projections indicate that in just a few years, no single group will be in the majority. And for the United States as a whole, it is projected that by the year 2050, merely 53 percent of the population will be of European descent. Such statistics indicate that multicultural diversity is a fact of life in the United States, just as it is in many other countries, too (see Figure 1.5).

This growing diversity raises some important questions for social psychology. At the present time, a large majority of the world's practicing social psychologists live and work in North America. As a result, a high proportion of all research in social psychology has been conducted in the United States and Canada. Can the findings of these studies be generalized to other cultures? In other words, are the principles established in North American research appli-

FIGURE 1.5

Cultural Diversity: A Fact of Life in the Late 20th Century. In the United States and many other countries, cultural diversity has increased rapidly. Social psychology is currently studying this diversity and the impact of cultural factors on social behavior.

cable to people all around the world? As noted by Smith and Bond (1993), this is an open question. Most social psychologists have assumed that the findings of their research are generalizable across cultures, and that the processes they study are ones operating among human beings everywhere. At first glance, this seems to be a very reasonable view. After all, why should love and attraction, conformity, persuasion, or prejudice operate differently on different continents? On closer examination, however, it seems possible that even these basic processes may be strongly affected by cultural factors (Smith & Bond, 1993). For example, some cultures do not seem to possess the notion of *romantic love* so prevalent in Western cultures. Do people in these cultures form long-term relationships in the same manner as people in cultures where the idea of romantic love is popular? Perhaps; but perhaps they do not. In any case, it is increasingly clear to social psychologists that such questions are important, and that they should be carefully investigated. Merely assuming that basic aspects of social behavior are much the same around the globe is not acceptable.

Similarly, social psychologists have increasingly recognized the fact that findings obtained with one gender may not necessarily apply to the other gender. While differences in the behavior of females and males have often been exaggerated, some differences in social behavior do seem to exist (Feingold, 1994; Oliver & Hyde, 1993). Thus, investigations that focus on only one gender may miss part of the total story. A concrete indication that social psychologists recognize this fact is suggested by the following data: In 1968, only 51 percent of studies published in the *Journal of Personality and Social Psychology* were conducted with both males and females; by 1988, this figure had risen to 82 percent (West, Newsom, & Fenaughty, 1992). Similarly, the proportion of articles in this journal for which the first (senior) author is a female has risen appreciably (see Figure 1.6).

We should add that cultural differences are now recognized as an important topic of research in their own right and, as such, are receiving increased attention from social psychologists.

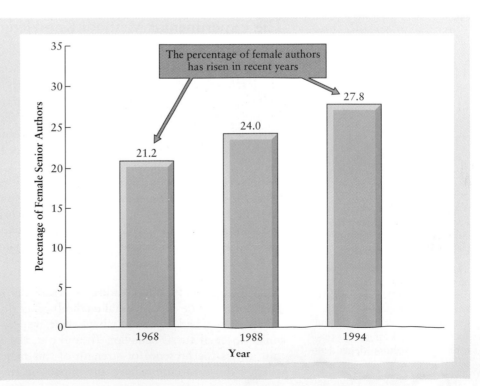

FIGURE 1.6

Publication Trends in Social Psychology: A Rising Proportion of Female-First Authors. As shown here, the proportion of articles published by females in one leading journal in social psychology (*Journal of Personality and Social Psychology*) has increased during the past three decades.

(*Source:* Based on data from West, Newsom, & Fenaughty, 1992, and data collected by R. A. Baron, 1995.)

In sum, social psychology has moved in recent years toward a **multicultural perspective**—increased recognition of the importance of cultural factors and human diversity. We believe that this trend will continue in the years ahead. To reflect this change, every chapter in this text (except this one) contains a special section titled Social Diversity. These sections highlight research dealing with cultural diversity and its effects, and relate such research to other topics covered within the chapter. They reflect our belief that interest in cultural differences, and in their origins, is a rising trend in social psychology.

Those, then, are our predictions. Will they prove to be accurate? Only time will tell. Regardless of their fate, however, there is one additional prediction we are willing to make with considerable confidence: No matter how social psychology changes in the years ahead, it will remain an active, vigorous field—one with an impressive potential for contributing to human knowledge and human welfare.

Answering Questions about Social Behavior and Social Thought: Research Methods in Social Psychology

Now that you know what social psychology is and how it developed, it is appropriate for us to turn to another essential issue: How do social psychologists attempt to answer questions about social behavior and social thought? How do they seek to expand our knowledge of these topics? To provide you with a useful overview of this process, we will examine three related issues. First, we will describe two key *methods of research in social psychology*. Next, we will consider the role of *theory* in such research. Finally, we will examine some of the complex *ethical issues* that arise in social psychological research and that, to a degree, are unique to such research.

The Experimental Method: Knowledge through Intervention

Because the subject matter of our field is so diverse, social psychologists actually use many different methods in their research (Baumeister, 1994; Murray & Holmes, 1994). Two, however, are used much more frequently than all the others: the *experimental method* of research and the *correlational method* of research. Because the experimental method is generally the one preferred by social psychologists, we'll begin with this powerful tool for understanding social behavior, then turn to the correlational method.

Experience with our own students tells us that many view the *experimental method* (or *experimentation* for short) as somewhat mysterious and complex. In fact, in its essential logic, it is surprisingly simple. To help you understand its use in social psychological research, we will first describe the basic nature of experimentation and then comment on two conditions essential for its successful use.

Experimentation: Its Basic Nature. A researcher who decides to employ **experimentation** (or the experimental method) generally begins with a clear-cut goal: to determine whether (and to what extent) a specific factor (variable) influences some aspect of social behavior. To find out, the researcher then (1) systematically varies the presence or strength of this factor, and (2) tries to determine whether those variations have any impact on the aspect of social behavior or

Multicultural Perspective ■ A focus on understanding the cultural and ethnic factors that influence social behavior.

Experimentation ■ Method of research in which one or more factors (the independent variables) are systematically changed to determine whether such variations affect one or more other factors (dependent variables).

thought under investigation. The central idea behind these procedures is this: If the factor varied does exert such effects, individuals exposed to different amounts (levels) of the factor should show different patterns of behavior. Exposure to a small amount of the factor should result in one level or pattern of behavior, exposure to a larger amount should result in another pattern, and so on.

Generally, the factor systematically varied by the researcher is termed the **independent variable,** while the aspect of behavior studied is termed the **dependent variable.** In a simple experiment, then, participants in different groups are exposed to contrasting levels of the independent variable (low, moderate, high). The researcher then carefully compares the behavior of persons in these various groups (sometimes known as *conditions*) to determine whether behavior does in fact vary with different levels of the independent variable. If it does—and if two other conditions described below are also met—the researcher can tentatively conclude that the independent variable does indeed affect the aspect of behavior or cognition being studied.

Perhaps a concrete example will help you to grasp the basic nature of this process. Let's consider an experiment designed to examine the *hypothesis* (an as yet unverified suggestion) that when people are in a good mood, they are more willing to help others. In such research, the independent variable would be some factor designed to put people into a good mood—for example, providing them with an unexpected gift. The dependent variable would be some measure of their willingness to help others—for example, the amount of time they are willing to donate to a researcher who asks for their help as an unpaid volunteer. How would such a study proceed? Something like this:

1. Participants would come to the place where the study was being conducted one at a time, and then, as part of the general procedures, would receive either a small gift (perhaps a small bag of candy) or no gift. The latter condition would serve as a *control condition*, since in it the variable expected to influence participants' behavior is absent. Control conditions provide a baseline against which the effects of different levels of an independent variable can be compared.

2. After receiving or not receiving a gift, participants would perform various activities; for instance, they might work on various puzzles or fill out questionnaires.

3. As part of these procedures, they would also be given an opportunity to help one or more other persons. For instance, they might receive a request for help from a work partner, or be asked by the researcher to donate some of their time for another study. The same opportunities to engage in helping behavior would be given to participants in both of the experimental conditions—small gift, no gift. Whether participants said yes or no, and the amount of help they offered, would then serve as *dependent variables*—measures of their willingness to help others.

4. If the hypothesis were correct, the results might look something like those in Figure 1.7 (p. 22): those receiving a gift would say yes more often and offer more of their time than those not receiving a gift (those in the control condition). In fact, research very much like this hypothetical experiment has been conducted, and results do resemble those shown in Figure 1.7 (e.g., Clark, 1991; Isen, 1987). We'll examine such research in Chapter 10.

Independent Variable ■ The factor in an experiment that is systematically varied by the researcher.

Dependent Variable ■ The variable that is measured in an experiment.

At this point, we should note that this example describes an extremely simple case—the simplest type of experiment social psychologists ever conduct. In many instances, researchers wish to examine the impact of several independent

FIGURE 1.7

Experimentation: A Simple Example. In the experiment illustrated here, participants in one group are given a small gift—a procedure designed to enhance their current mood—before receiving a request for help. In contrast, the control group does not receive the gift before receiving the request for help. Results indicate that those receiving the gift are more likely to say yes and to donate more time. This finding provides support for the hypothesis that persons in a good mood are more willing to help others.

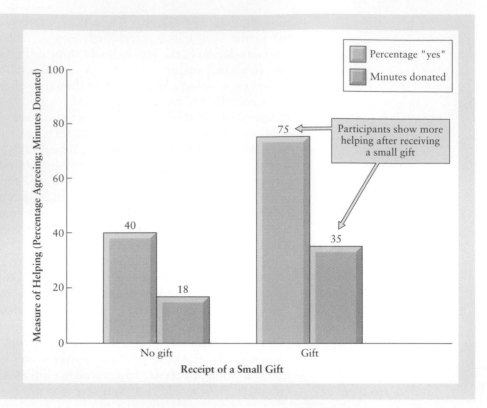

variables at once. For example, in the study just described, they might want to consider not only the effects of mood on helping, but perhaps the effects of the effort involved as well. This is because it seems possible that being in a good mood may well increase willingness to help others, but only when the effort involved is quite low. When a high degree of effort is involved, even feeling "on top of the world" may not be enough to increase overt helping. How could this possibility be studied? One possibility would involve varying the size of the request made. In a *low-effort* condition, the researcher would explain that helping would involve completing some simple questionnaires. In a *high-effort* condition, in contrast, the researcher might explain that helping would involve a more effortful (and potentially embarrassing) task, such as calling people on the phone and asking them for money. When two or more variables are included in an experiment, a larger amount of information about the topic of interest can usually be obtained. In real social situations, after all, our behavior and thought are usually influenced by many different factors acting concurrently, not simply by one factor. Even more important, potential **interactions** between variables can be examined—we can determine whether the impact of one independent variable is affected in some manner by one or more other variables. For example, consider the amount of effort involved in helping: Does being in a good mood increase helping regardless of the amount of effort involved? Or do such effects occur only when effort is fairly low? The graph in Figure 1.8 illustrates one possible *interaction* between these two variables: good mood increases helping only when a low degree of effort is involved in such behavior.

Interactions (between variables) ■ Instances in which the effects of one variable are influenced by the effects of one or more other variables.

Successful Experimentation: Two Basic Requirements. Earlier, we mentioned that before we can conclude that an independent variable has affected some form of behavior, two important conditions must be met. A basic understanding of these conditions is essential for evaluating the usefulness of any experiment.

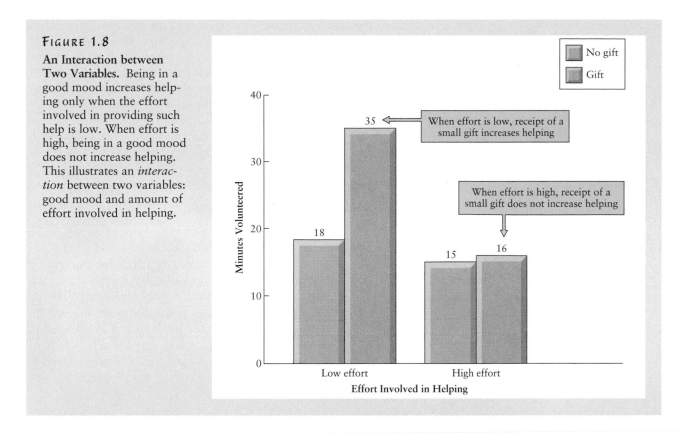

FIGURE 1.8

An Interaction between Two Variables. Being in a good mood increases helping only when the effort involved in providing such help is low. When effort is high, being in a good mood does not increase helping. This illustrates an *interaction* between two variables: good mood and amount of effort involved in helping.

The first condition involves what is usually termed the **random assignment of participants to groups.** According to this principle, each person taking part in a study must have an equal chance of being exposed to each level of the independent variable. The reason for this rule is simple: If participants are *not* randomly assigned to each group, it may prove impossible to determine whether differences in their behavior in the study stem from differences they brought with them, from the impact of the independent variable, or from both. For instance, continuing with our study of mood and helping, suppose that most of the participants who receive a small gift participate in the study late in the afternoon, when they are tired and somewhat grumpy as a result of having sat in four or five classes. In contrast, those in the no-gift condition participate in the early afternoon, right after having eaten lunch. Now, assume that results indicate that there is no difference between the two conditions in terms of helping. Does this mean that helping is *not* affected by mood? Perhaps; but it may also reflect the fact that persons who take part in the study in the late afternoon are so tired and irritable that a small gift is not sufficient to improve their mood—or at least, not sufficient to improve their mood to the point where it influences their willingness to help others. Such problems can be avoided if, instead, persons who participate early and late in the afternoon are equally distributed across the two conditions (gift, no-gift). So, as you can see, it is crucial that all participants in an experiment have an equal chance of being assigned to different experimental groups.

The second condition referred to above may be stated as follows: Insofar as possible, all other factors that might also affect participants' behavior, aside from the independent variable, must be held constant. To see why this is so, consider what would happen if, in the study on mood and helping, two different researchers who differ greatly in personal attractiveness collected data. Fur-

Random Assignment of Participants to Groups ■ A basic requirement for conducting valid experiments. According to this principle, research participants must have an equal chance of being exposed to each level of the independent variable.

ther, imagine that the highly attractive one conducted the gift condition, while the less attractive one conducted the no-gift condition. Now, assume that results indicate more helping by participants who received a small gift. What is the cause of this result? The gift? The researcher's high level of attractiveness? Both? Obviously, it is impossible to tell. In this situation, the independent variable (receipt of a small gift) is *confounded* with another variable—researcher's attractiveness. When such **confounding** occurs, it is impossible to determine the cause of any differences among the various experimental conditions. The result: findings are largely uninterpretable. (In this case, confounding could be avoided by assuring that both researchers conducted both experimental conditions.)

The Correlational Method: Knowledge through Systematic Observation

Earlier, we noted that experimentation is the preferred method of research in social psychology. (We'll see why below.) Sometimes, though, experimentation simply cannot be used. This can be true for two reasons. First, systematic variation in some factor of interest may be beyond the experimenter's control. Imagine, for example, that a researcher believes that politicians who use certain techniques of persuasion in their speeches are more likely to win elections than ones who do not. Obviously, it would be very difficult for the researchers to convince one group of candidates to use these techniques, and another to refrain from using them, so that the researchers could then see how many in each condition would win election.

Second, ethical constraints may prevent a researcher from conducting what might otherwise be a feasible experiment. In other words, it might be possible to vary some factor of interest, but doing so would violate ethical standards accepted by scientists or society. Suppose a researcher had good reason to believe that certain factors increase the likelihood of violence in intimate relationships—for example, exposure to a large number of films containing such violence. In this case, the researcher could imagine ways of testing this hypothesis, but doing so would be unethical. After all, researchers clearly do not have the right to expose individuals to conditions that might increase the chances that they, or their romantic partners, would become the victims of violent assaults. Certainly, no ethical social psychologist would consider conducting such research, and anyone who *did* perform such research would be strongly censured by his or her colleagues for doing so.

When confronted with such problems, social psychologists often adopt an alternative research technique known as the **correlational method.** In this approach, researchers make no efforts to change one or more variables in order to observe the effects of these changes on some other variable. Instead, they merely observe naturally occurring changes in the variables of interest to learn if changes in one are associated with changes in the other. Such associations are known as *correlations,* and the stronger the association, the higher the correlation. (Correlations range from −1.00 to +1.00, and the greater the departure from 0.00, the stronger the relationship between the variables in question.)

To illustrate the correlational method, let's return once again to our study of mood and helping. A researcher wishing to examine this issue by means of the correlational method might proceed as follows. The researcher might stand near persons seeking donations for charities and then might ask passersby to rate their current moods. The researcher could simply ask: "On a scale of 1 to 7, where 1 is sad and 7 is happy, how do you feel right now?" If mood is related to helping, then the researcher might find a positive correlation be-

Confounding ■ Confusion that occurs when factors other than the independent variable in an experiment vary across experimental conditions. When confounding occurs, it is impossible to determine whether results stem from the effects of the independent variable or from the other variables.

Correlational Method ■ Method of research in which a scientist systematically observes two or more variables to determine whether changes in one are accompanied by changes in the other.

tween people's self-reported moods, the likelihood that they would make a donation, and the amount given if they did choose to donate. Note that in this case, the researcher makes no effort to vary the moods of passersby; rather, the researcher obtains information about two variables—the current mood of passersby and their level of generosity—to determine if these variables are related.

The correlational method offers several advantages. For one thing, social psychologists can use it to study behavior in many real-life settings. The findings obtained can then serve as the basis for more refined laboratory research. For another, this method is often highly efficient and can yield a large amount of interesting data in a short time. Moreover, it can be extended to include many different variables at once. Thus, in the study described above, information about the age and gender of passersby, as well as whether they donate, could be obtained. Through a statistical procedure known as *regression analysis,* the extent to which each of these variables is related to—and therefore predicts—helping behavior could then be determined.

Unfortunately, however, the correlational method suffers from one major drawback: *In contrast to experimentation, the findings it yields are somewhat uncertain with respect to cause-and-effect relationships.* The fact that changes in one variable are accompanied by changes in another in no way guarantees that a causal link exists between them—that changes in the first caused changes in the second. Rather, in many cases, the fact that two variables tend to rise or fall together simply reflects the fact that both are caused by a third variable. For example, among males, yearly income is *negatively* related to the amount of hair on men's heads. Does this mean that wealth causes baldness? Hardly. Instead, it is clear, both variables are related to a third factor—*age.* As age increases, hair decreases, while experience and salary tend to increase. Perhaps this key point about correlations can best be clarified by a few additional examples. These are listed in Table 1.3. Can you identify the third factors that may underlie the relationships shown in the table? (Answers are provided.)

TABLE 1.3   Correlation Doesn't Imply Causation: Some Examples

All of the correlations shown here have been observed. However, none indicates that the two factors involved are causally linked. Can you suggest one or more additional factors that might underlie each of the relationships shown here? (Some possible answers appear below.)

Observed Correlation	Possible Underlying Cause
The more money people earn, the fewer children they tend to have.	
The greater the degree of crowding in cities, the higher their crime rates.	
The larger automobiles are, the slower their rate of travel down the highway.	

Answers:

1. The more people earn, the more education they have and the more effective methods of birth control they tend to use. *Or:* The more people earn, the more readily they can afford to purchase effective means of birth control, which often tend to be expensive.

2. The greater the degree of crowding, the greater the poverty, and poverty is related to crime. *Or:* The greater the degree of crowding, the larger the number of people out on the streets, so the greater the number of potential victims.

3. The owners of large automobiles tend to be older, and older persons tend to drive more slowly. *Or:* Large automobiles tend to be older than smaller ones, and being older they don't accelerate as well or may have engine problems that reduce their speed.

By now the main point should be clear. The existence of even a strong correlation between two factors is *not* a definite indication that they are causally related. Such conclusions are justified only in the presence of additional confirming evidence.

Social Psychologists As Perennial Skeptics: The Importance of Replication, Meta-Analysis, and Converging Operations

Let's return once again to the research question we have addressed several times already: *Does being in a good mood increase the tendency to help others?* Suppose that we conducted a very careful experiment on this topic that yielded highly significant results: Participants exposed to a treatment designed to elevate their mood did in fact offer more help than those not exposed to such a treatment. On the basis of these results, can we conclude that our hypothesis has been confirmed?

While it might be tempting to answer yes, social psychologists would take a somewhat different stand. They'd agree that we are off to a good start and that initial findings are indeed consistent with the hypothesis. However, before concluding that this hypothesis represents *truth*—an accurate description of the social world—they would require additional evidence. Social psychologists would require that many other investigators, too, *confirm* these results in subsequent studies. In other words, they would insist that the initial findings be *replicated* (reproduced) over and over again—preferably in studies employing a wide range of methods, different measures of helping, different determinants of mood, and different populations. So, for example, before accepting the hypothesis that being in a good mood increases helping, they would want to see this finding replicated not just in several laboratory studies but out in the "real world" as well—in what social psychologists often term *natural field settings*.

And here's where a serious problem enters the picture: only rarely do the results of social psychological research yield totally consistent findings. A more common pattern is for some studies to offer support for a given hypothesis while others fail to offer such support. Why is this so? In part, because different researchers may use different methods. For example, some may seek to induce a good mood by providing participants with a small gift, while others may attempt to accomplish the same goal by praising participants' work on some task. It is possible that these different procedures elevate mood to a different extent, and that only when mood is raised above some threshold does helping increase. This is only one example; there are many other reasons why research results may differ from study to study. Whatever the cause, such inconsistent results raise important questions that must be addressed.

Interpreting Diverse Results: The Role of Meta-Analysis. So, what do social psychologists do when the results of different studies designed to test the same hypothesis don't agree? In the past, they would review all existing evidence and then, on the basis of what can best be described as insight and personal judgment, would try to reach some conclusion about the meaning of these diverse results. In other words, they would try to determine, in a relatively informal manner, whether most of the studies they reviewed showed one particular pattern of results. This approach, which involved what are sometimes known as *narrative reviews* (Beaman, 1991), clearly left a lot to be desired.

Fortunately, there is now a better means of dealing with such situations—of combining the results of independent studies in order to reach conclusions about the hypotheses they all investigate. This technique is known as meta-analysis—statistical procedures for combining the results of many different studies in order to estimate the *direction* and *size* of the effects of the independent variables in these studies. In other words, after performing an appropriate meta-analysis, a social psychologist can reach conclusions about whether, and to what extent, a particular variable influenced some aspect of social behavior *across many different studies*. Because meta-analysis relies on mathematical procedures, many social psychologists believe that its results are more conclusive than those of informal narrative reviews (e.g., Eagly, Karau, & Makhijani, 1995; Feingold, 1994).

In sum, meta-analysis is an important tool for understanding the results of social psychological research, and so for understanding social behavior and social cognition. Throughout this text, therefore, we will refer to reviews of existing literature based on this procedure whenever possible.

Beyond Replication: Converging Operations in Social Psychology. Earlier, we noted that the mere fact that a research finding can be replicated—reproduced under the same conditions—is not sufficient to overcome scientific skepticism. Before social psychologists accept a finding as valid, they prefer that it be obtained in other settings and under other conditions that, while different from the original context, *are logically related to it*. This principle is known as **converging operations,** and is often used by social psychologists. Briefly, it suggests that if a particular variable affects some aspect of social behavior by influencing an underlying psychological mechanism (for example, elevations in mood), then other variables that influence the same psychological mechanism should produce similar effects *even if they seem very different from the initial variable*.

To illustrate the value of converging operations, let's return once more to the hypothesis that persons in a good mood are more helpful than those in a neutral mood. Assume that initial studies designed to test this hypothesis all seek to place some participants in a good mood by giving them a small gift. So far, so good. But if this hypothesis is really accurate, then shouldn't increased helpfulness be found in response to *any variable* that puts people in a good mood? In other words, the mood–helping relationship should not be restricted to receipt of a small gift. It should also be evident if, for example, participants are praised for their work or are shown a very funny comedy film. If research findings indicate that this is the case, then confidence in the accuracy of the hypothesis is strengthened further. Recently, I (Bob Baron) put this principle to direct use in a series of studies on a variable that has only recently entered the mainstream of social psychology: pleasant fragrances.

There's a lot of hype about fragrance in the popular press these days; but as a social psychologist, I have long suspected that there might be some scientific basis for predicting that pleasant fragrances might actually influence human behavior. Specifically, I reasoned that since people have been using fragrances in their homes for thousands of years, they may do so because pleasant smells put them in a good mood. In other words, pleasant fragrances may serve as an environmental source of pleasant moods (what social psychologists term *positive affect*) in much the same ways as pleasant temperatures, pleasant lighting, or a neat, clean environment. To test this hypothesis, I conducted several studies in which participants worked on various tasks either in the presence or in the absence of fragrances rated as very pleasant by a large group of students. (The two fragrances that received the highest ratings turned out to be lemon and a light floral aroma.) During the tasks, participants received a request for help from a partner. Would they help this person more if they worked in a room with pleasant fragrance? As you can see from Figure 1.9 (p. 28), they did. Moreover, persons who worked in the presence of pleasant fragrances showed about the same

Meta-Analysis ■ Statistical technique for combining data from independent studies in order to determine whether specific variables (or interactions between variables) have significant effects across these studies.

Converging Operations ■ A principle useful in establishing the validity of research findings. Converging operations suggests that if a particular variable affects some aspect of social behavior by influencing an underlying psychological mechanism, then other variables that influence the same mechanism should produce similar effects on behavior.

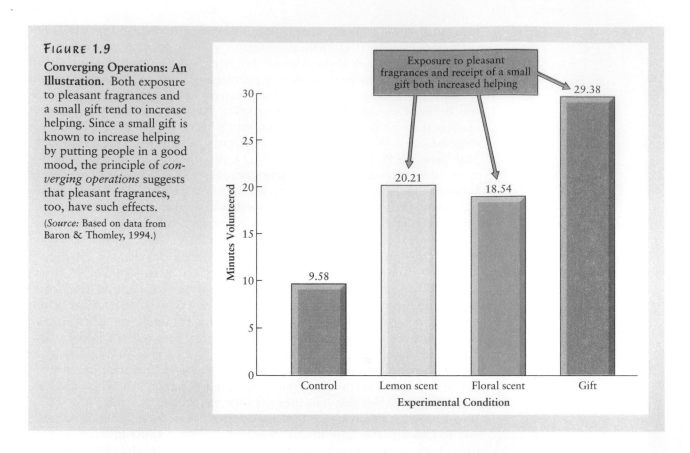

FIGURE 1.9

Converging Operations: An Illustration. Both exposure to pleasant fragrances and a small gift tend to increase helping. Since a small gift is known to increase helping by putting people in a good mood, the principle of *converging operations* suggests that pleasant fragrances, too, have such effects.

(*Source:* Based on data from Baron & Thomley, 1994.)

level of helping as other participants who were not exposed to fragrance, but who received a small gift—perhaps *the* standard way of inducing positive moods in social psychology (Baron & Bronfen, 1994; Baron & Thomley, 1994). Interestingly, the two different fragrances produced much the same effect, apparently because they were equally pleasant and produced equal, modest increments in participants' moods. Perhaps most surprising of all, I have recently replicated these findings in a large shopping mall, where passersby were more likely to help a person who dropped a pen or asked for change of a dollar when there were pleasant fragrances in the air (e.g., the smell of baking cookies or roasting coffee) than when these pleasant odors were absent (Baron, 1996).

So, in sum, the principle of converging operations is a useful tool for social psychologists, and one they often use to strengthen confidence in the accuracy of various hypotheses.

The Role of Theory in Social Psychology

Over the years, students in our classes have often asked: "How do social psychologists come up with such interesting ideas for their research?" There is no simple answer. Some research projects are suggested by informal observation of the social worlds around us. Social psychologists take note of some puzzling aspect of social behavior or social thought and plan investigations to increase their understanding of that aspect. On other occasions, the idea for a research project is suggested by the findings of an earlier study. Successful experiments in social psychology do not simply answer questions—they raise new ones as well. Indeed, as Wegner (1992) noted, studies that raise new questions are often the most valuable ones in social psychology, while "closed" series of studies that seem to answer all possible questions and all possible objections may actually work against creativity in the field. Perhaps the most important basis for research ideas in social psychology, however, is formal **theories.**

In simple terms, theories represent efforts by scientists in any field to answer the question *Why?* Theories involve attempts to understand precisely why certain events or processes occur as they do. Theories go beyond mere observation or description of aspects of social behavior; they seek to *explain* them as well. The development of comprehensive, accurate theories is a primary goal of all science (Howard, 1985; Popper, 1959), and social psychology is no exception. Thus, a great deal of research in our field is concerned with efforts to construct, test, and refine theoretical frameworks. But what are theories, and how are they used in social psychological research? Perhaps such questions are best answered in the context of a specific example—one with which you are by now quite familiar!

Imagine that a social psychologist is interested in the following question: *Why* are people in a good mood more willing to help others than people in a neutral mood? After examining existing literature, the researcher finds that several possibilities exist. For example, perhaps people in a good mood want to "keep a good thing going," and since helping others tends to make us feel good, they are more likely to help for this reason. Another possibility is that being in a good mood causes people to think positive thoughts about themselves; and because "nice people" help others when they need aid, this factor, too, may contribute to increased helping when people are in a good mood. However, the researcher may also note some findings suggesting that such effects occur only when the effort involved in helping others is not too great.

Putting these ideas together, the social psychologist now formulates a preliminary theory: *People in a good mood help others in order to maintain their good moods and to maintain their own positive self-image. However, they will do so only when the effort required is not very great.* In older fields of science such as physics or chemistry, theories are often stated as mathematical equations. In social psychology, however, they are usually phrased as verbal statements or assertions such as the ones above. Regardless of how they are expressed, theories consist of two main parts: (1) several basic concepts (in this example, mood, helping, mood maintenance, self-image, cost of helping), and (2) statements concerning relationships among these concepts ("People in a good mood try to maintain their happy state by helping others when the cost is not high").

Formulation of a theory is just the first step in a continuing process, however. Only theories that have been carefully tested and confirmed are useful; so in social psychology, as in all other fields of science, after a theory is proposed, several procedures normally follow. First, predictions are derived from the theory. These predictions are formulated in accordance with basic principles of logic and are known as *hypotheses.* For example, one hypothesis from the theory we just described is as follows: If people in a good mood can maintain their mood in some other way than by helping others and this alternative requires less effort, they will *not* be more helpful than people in a more neutral mood.

Next, hypotheses are tested in actual research. If they are confirmed, confidence in the accuracy of the theory is increased. If they are disconfirmed, however, confidence in the theory is reduced. Then the theory may be altered so as to generate new predictions. These are subjected to test, and the process continues. If the modified predictions are confirmed, confidence in the revised theory is increased; if they are disconfirmed, the theory may be modified again or, ultimately, rejected. Figure 1.10 (p. 30) summarizes this process.

Confirming evidence obtained in careful research is a crucial feature of useful theories in any field of science. In addition, however, successful theo-

Theories ■ Efforts by scientists in any field to answer the question *Why?* Theories involve attempts to understand why certain events or processes occur as they do.

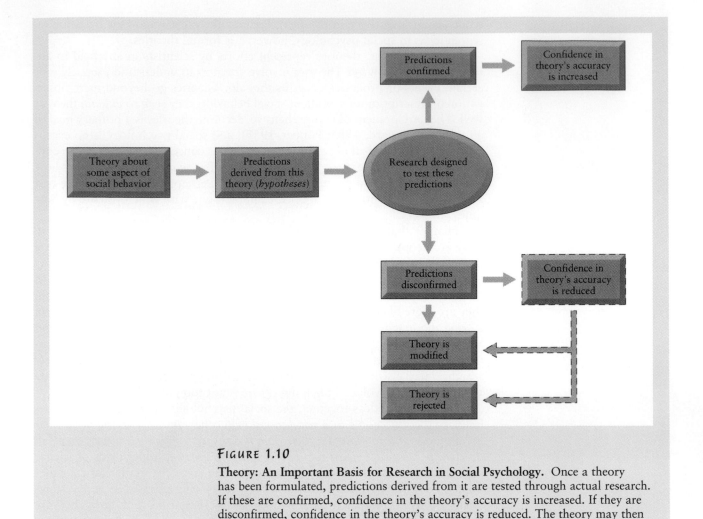

FIGURE 1.10

Theory: An Important Basis for Research in Social Psychology. Once a theory has been formulated, predictions derived from it are tested through actual research. If these are confirmed, confidence in the theory's accuracy is increased. If they are disconfirmed, confidence in the theory's accuracy is reduced. The theory may then be modified to generate new predictions or, ultimately, may be rejected

ries—ones that are viewed as useful by scientists—have several other features. First, they help to organize and explain a wide range of findings. For example, the theory above would help explain why people in a good mood are more helpful to others in some situations (when the effort required is low), but not more helpful in others (when the effort required is very high). Second, successful theories can be expanded so as to explain an increasingly broad range of phenomena. For instance, a useful theory concerned with how current moods affect helping might, ultimately, deal with the effects of bad moods as well as of good ones.

Two final points: First, theories are never *proven* in any final, ultimate sense. Rather, they are always open to test, and are accepted with more or less confidence depending on the weight of available evidence. Second, research is *not* undertaken to prove or verify a theory: it is performed to gather evidence relevant to the theory. If a researcher sets out to "prove" her or his pet theory correct, this is a serious violation of scientific skepticism!

The Quest for Knowledge and the Rights of Individuals: Seeking an Appropriate Balance

In their use of experimentation and systematic observation, and in their emphasis on theory construction, social psychologists do not differ from researchers in many other fields. One technique, however, does seem to be unique to research in social psychology: **deception.** This technique involves efforts by researchers to withhold or conceal information about the purposes of a study from participants. The reason for using this procedure is simple: Many social psychologists believe that if participants know the true purposes of an investigation, their behavior will be changed by that knowledge. Then the research will have little chance of providing valid information.

In fact, some kinds of research do seem to require the use of temporary deception. For example, imagine that in a study designed to examine the effects of physical attractiveness on first impressions, participants were informed of this purpose. Would they now react differently to a highly attractive stranger than they would have in the absence of this information? Perhaps, for now, they would lean over backwards to demonstrate that *they* are not affected by others' appearance. In this and many other cases, social psychologists feel compelled to employ temporary deception in their research (Suls & Rosnow, 1988). However, the use of deception raises important ethical issues that cannot be ignored.

First, of course, there is the chance, however slim, that deception may result in some kind of harm to the persons exposed to it (Baumrind, 1985). They may be upset by the procedures used, or by their own reactions to them. For example, in many early studies concerned with helping behavior, a topic we'll cover in detail in Chapter 10, participants were exposed to staged, but seemingly real, emergency situations. For instance, they overheard what appeared to be medical emergencies (another person having an apparent seizure; Darley & Latané, 1968), or they were exposed to an apparent fire in the laboratory (Latané & Darley, 1970). Many participants were strongly upset by these staged events; others were later disturbed by the fact that although they recognized the need to help in these situations, they failed to do so. Clearly, these procedures had powerful effects on research participants, and raise important ethical issues about just how far researchers can go when studying even very important topics such as this one.

We should hasten to emphasize that such research represented an extreme use of deception; generally, deception takes much milder and less emotion-provoking forms. For example, participants may receive a request for help from a "partner" who is actually an accomplice of the researcher; or they may be informed that most other students in their university hold certain views when in fact they do not. Still, the potential for some kind of harmful effects to participants exists, and this is a potentially serious drawback to the use of deception.

Second, there is the possibility that participants will resent being "fooled" during a study, and that as a result they will acquire negative attitudes toward social psychology and psychological research generally (Kelman, 1967). To the extent such reactions occur, they would have negative implications for the future of social psychology, which places a heavy emphasis on the value of scientific research.

Because of such possibilities, the use of deception poses something of a dilemma to social psychologists. On the one hand, it seems essential to their research. On the other, its use raises serious problems. How can this issue be resolved? At present, opinion remains divided. Some of our colleagues feel that deception, no matter how useful, is inappropriate (e.g., Baumrind, 1979). Yet many others (perhaps a large majority) believe that temporary deception *is* acceptable provided that certain safeguards are adopted (Baron, 1981). First, participants should go through an **informed consent** procedure, receiving as much information as possible about the procedures to be followed *before* making their decision to take part in a study. In this way, researchers ensure that par-

Deception ▪ Technique whereby researchers withhold information about the purposes or procedures of a study from persons participating in it.

Informed Consent ▪ Procedure in which research participants are provided with as much information as possible about a research project before deciding whether to participate in it.

ticipants know pretty much what they are getting into—what they will be asked to do in the study—before making a commitment to participate. Second, at the end of a study, participants should be provided with full **debriefing**—they should receive a full explanation of all aspects of the study, including its true goals, plus an explanation of the need for temporary deception.

Fortunately, a growing body of evidence indicates that together, informed consent and thorough debriefing can substantially reduce the potential dangers of deception (Smith & Richardson, 1985). For example, most participants report that they view temporary deception as acceptable, provided potential benefits outweigh potential costs and if there is no other means of obtaining the information sought (Rogers, 1980; Sharpe, Adair, & Roese, 1992). Further, persons who have participated in research employing deception report generally favorable attitudes about psychological research—attitudes just as favorable as those who have not participated in such research (Sharpe et al., 1992). Finally, fears that continued use of deception would "turn people off" about psychological research and make them suspicious of psychologists have *not* been confirmed; on the contrary, research participants in 1990 appeared to be just as favorable in their views about such research as those in 1970.

So, in sum, existing evidence does seem to suggest that a large majority of research participants do not react negatively to temporary deception and actually endorse its use in social psychological research. However, these findings do *not* mean that the safety or appropriateness of deception should be taken for granted (Rubin, 1985). On the contrary, the guiding principles for all researchers planning to use this procedure should be these: (1) Use deception only when it is absolutely essential to do so—when no other means for conducting a study exist; (2) always proceed with great caution; and (3) make certain that every possible precaution is taken to protect the rights, safety, and welfare of research participants.

Using This Book: An Overview of Its Special Features

Research findings show that having a framework to hold new information makes it easier to remember and use this information. Echoing that theme, we'd like to conclude this opening chapter by calling your attention to several features of this text. All are designed to increase your understanding of social psychology, and to make your studying easier.

First, each chapter begins with an outline of the major topics covered and ends with a detailed summary. Please read the outline before starting the chapter, and be sure to use the summary as a review after you have finished: both features will help you to remember the materials covered. Also, please note that key terms are printed in **boldface type** like this and are defined in the margins and in a glossary at the end of the book. Because figures and charts contained in original research reports are often quite complex, every graph and table in this text has been specially created for it. In addition, all graphs contain special labels designed to call your attention to the key findings presented (see Figure 1.8 for an example).

Second, we've included three distinct types of special sections throughout the text. These typically appear at the ends of major sections, so they *don't*

Debriefing ■ Procedure at the conclusion of a research session in which participants are given full information about the nature of the research and the hypothesis or hypotheses under investigation.

interrupt the flow of chapter content. All are designed to highlight information we feel is especially important and interesting.

The first type of special section is labeled *Cornerstones of Social Psychology*. These sections describe truly "classic" studies in our field—ones that started major lines of research and that, in this manner, exerted a lasting effect on the field. Because most of the studies we describe in this text are very recent (many are from 1994 and 1995), we feel that it is very important to emphasize the origins of this modern research and its continuity with what went before.

The second type is titled *Social Psychology: On the Applied Side*. These sections highlight the practical implications of social psychology—ways in which social psychology's knowledge and principles are being used today to help solve a wide range of practical social problems.

A third type of special section occurs near the end of each chapter and is titled *Social Diversity: A Critical Analysis*. These sections represent the growing multicultural perspective in social psychology to which we referred earlier. They present information concerning differences between ethnic groups within a given society, or differences across various cultures. *Social Diversity* sections are closely linked to the content of the chapters in which they occur, and seek to examine key aspects of social behavior and thought from a multicultural perspective.

Finally, to help you understand how research in each area of social psychology is related to research in other areas, we've included two additional features. The first involves what we term *Integrating Principles*. These are major principles of social psychology that have emerged out of specific lines of research but which seem to cut across many different areas of our field. Each *Integrating Principles* box also calls attention to other topics in this text to which it is related. Second, important links between chapters are summarized in special tables titled *Connections: Integrating Social Psychology*, which appear at the end of each chapter. These *Connections* tables indicate how topics covered in the current chapter are related to topics covered in other chapters. *Connections* tables serve two major functions. First, they provide a kind of global review, reminding you of related topics discussed elsewhere in the book. Second, they emphasize the fact that many aspects of social behavior and social thought are closely *interlinked*: they do *not* occur in isolation from each other. Finally, *Connections* tables are followed by a series of in-depth questions, called *Thinking about Connections*, designed to get you thinking about these links and how they actually operate. Together, the *Integrating Principles* and *Connections* tables help us to represent social psychology as it really is: an integrated field with multiple links between its diverse areas of research.

All of the features described above are designed to help you get the most out of your first encounter with social psychology. But in a key sense, only *you* can transfer the information on the pages of this book into your own memory—and into your own life. So please do *use* this book. Read the summaries and chapter outlines, review the *Key Terms*, and pay special attention to the *Integrating Principles*. Doing so, we truly believe, will improve your understanding of social psychology—and your grade in this course! Finally, please *do* think of this book as a reference source—a practical guide to social behavior to which you can refer over and over again in the years ahead. In contrast to some other fields you will study in college, social psychology really *is* directly relevant to your daily life: to understanding others and getting along better with them. Please consider keeping this text as part of your permanent library; we're certain that you'll find it useful long after the course is over.

To sum up: We truly hope that together, these features of our text will help to enhance your first encounter with social psychology. We also hope that they will help us communicate our own excitement with the field. Despite the fact that between us we have more than sixty years of combined teaching and research experience, we still find social psychology as fascinating as ever. To the extent we achieve these goals, and only to that extent, will we feel that as authors, teachers, and representatives of social psychology, we have succeeded.

Summary and Review

Social Psychology: A Working Definition

Social psychology is the scientific field that seeks to understand the nature and causes of individual behavior in social situations. It uses scientific methods to obtain new information about how we interact with and think about other persons.

The Origins and Development of Social Psychology

Speculation about social behavior and thought has continued since antiquity; however, a science-oriented field of social psychology emerged only during the twentieth century. Once established it grew rapidly, and social psychology currently investigates every conceivable aspect of social behavior and social thought. Two recent trends in the field have involved the growing influence of a *cognitive perspective* (efforts to apply knowledge about cognitive processes to the task of understanding social behavior), and an increasing emphasis on *applying* the principles and findings of social psychology to a wide range of practical problems. We predict that these trends will continue in the future, and that in addition, social psychology will continue its current movement toward a *multicultural perspective* that both studies and takes careful account of ethnic and cultural factors as determinants of social behavior.

Research Methods in Social Psychology

In conducting their research, social psychologists often employ *experimentation* and the *correlational method*. Experimentation involves procedures in which researchers systematically vary one or more factors (variables) to examine the impact of such changes on one or more aspects of social behavior or thought. In the correlational method scientists carefully observe and measure two or more variables to determine whether changes in one are accompanied by changes in the other.

Because their field is scientific in orientation, social psychologists are skeptical about research findings until these have been replicated many times. To compare the findings of many studies on a given topic, social psychologists often use a statistical procedure known as *meta-analysis*. Meta-analyses indicate the extent to which specific variables exert similar effects across many different studies, and also provide estimates of the magnitude of such effects. In addition to replication of research findings, social psychologists often also use the principle of *converging operations*. This suggests that if a particular variable affects some aspect of social behavior by influencing an underlying psychological mechanism, then other variables that influence the same psychological mechanism should produce similar effects.

In choosing the topics of their research and in planning specific studies, social psychologists are often guided by formal *theories*. These are logical frameworks that seek to explain various aspects of social behavior and thought. Predictions from theories are tested in research. If these predictions are confirmed, confidence in the accuracy of the theories is increased. If they are disconfirmed, such confidence is reduced.

Social psychologists often withhold information about the purpose of their studies from the persons participating in them. Such temporary *deception* is deemed necessary because knowledge of the hypotheses behind an experiment may alter participants' behavior in various ways. Although the use of deception raises important ethical issues, most social psychologists believe that it is permissible, provided that proper safeguards such as *informed consent* and thorough *debriefing* are adopted.

■ Key Terms

Cognitive Dissonance (p. 15)

Confounding (p. 24)

Converging Operations (p. 27)

Correlational Method (p. 24)

Debriefing (p. 32)

Deception (p. 31)

Dependent Variable (p. 21)

Evolutionary Social Psychology (p. 10)

Experimentation (p. 20)

Independent Variable (p. 21)

Informed Consent (p. 31)

Interactions (p. 22)

Multicultural Perspective (p. 20)

Meta-Analysis (p. 27)

Random Assignment of Participants
to Groups (p. 23)

Social Psychology (p. 6)

Sociobiology (p. 10)

Theories (p. 29)

■ For More Information

Jackson, J. M. (1993). *Social psychology, past and present.* Hillsdale, NJ: Erlbaum.

A thoughtful overview of the roots and development of social psychology. Organized around major themes in social psychological research, the book emphasizes the multidisciplinary roots of social psychology. The chapter on current trends is especially interesting.

Jones, E. E. (1985). Major developments in social psychology during the past five decades. In G. Lindzey & E. Aronson (Eds.), *Handbook of social psychology* (Vol. 1). New York: Random House.

In this chapter an eminent social psychologist describes what, in his view, have been major trends in theory and research in social psychology during the past fifty years. The author, recently deceased, contributed to the field for more than forty years, so he was actually there "on the scene" as many of these trends unfolded.

CHAPTER 2

SOCIAL PERCEPTION:
Understanding Others

Lisa Houck, *Personality Types*, 1993, watercolor, 9 × 13"

Chapter Outline

You're at a party; an attractive person glances in your direction and smiles. Is that an invitation to come over and start a conversation? Or is this person smiling because he or she has just heard an amusing remark?

You are buying a used car. You ask the owner whether there is anything wrong with it. He looks you in the eye and says, "No way! This car is in perfect shape." Do you believe him?

Imagine that you are a professor. The day after you give a midterm exam to your class, one of the students comes to see you and, with a look of pure innocence, says: "I'm sorry I missed the exam, but I was away on a field trip for one of my other classes, and we got back much later than I expected. Can I take a makeup exam?" Do you accept this story?

You are going for a job interview. You really need this job, so you want to do everything you can to make a good impression on the interviewer. How do you act? What do you say?

At first glance, these situations might seem to be totally unrelated. If you think about them for a moment, though, you'll soon realize that there's a common thread tying them together: in each, you are faced with the task of understanding other persons—deciding whether to believe what they say, and, on a more basic level, trying to figure out their intentions and their motives. As you know from your own experience, this is a complex task. Despite all our experience with other people, they sometimes remain one of the true mysteries of life. They say and do things we don't expect, have motives we don't understand, and seem to see the world through eyes very different from our own. Yet, because other persons play a such a key role in our lives, this is one mystery we can't afford to leave unsolved. Because of this basic fact, we often engage in what social psychologists describe as **social perception**—an active process (or set of processes) through which we seek to know and understand others.

Social perception is one of the most basic—and important—aspects of social life, so our efforts to understand the persons around us are truly a part of our daily lives, and take many different forms. Among these, though, two seem to be most important. First, we try to understand other persons' current feelings, moods, and emotions—how they are feeling right now. Such information is often provided by *nonverbal cues* involving facial expressions, eye contact, body posture, and movements. Was that smile a come-on (first example above)? Is that used-car owner lying (second example)? Nonverbal cues often help us reach such decisions.

Second, we attempt to understand the more lasting causes behind others' behavior—the reasons *why* they have acted in certain ways. This generally involves efforts to understand their motives, intentions, and traits. Information relating to this second task is acquired through *attribution*—a complex process in which we observe others' behavior and then attempt to *infer* the causes behind it from this basic information (Kelley, 1972). Was that student telling the truth (third example), or is the student just a slick manipulator who frequently lies like the proverbial rug? We ask ourselves questions like this every day.

Because they are important aspects of social perception, we'll examine both nonverbal communication and attribution in detail in this chapter. It's important to realize, though, that these processes are not the entire story where social perception is concerned. In addition, such perception often involves efforts to form unified *impressions* of other persons. Common sense suggests that such *first impressions* are very important; and, as we'll soon see, research findings tend to confirm this belief. But how, precisely, do we form such impressions of others? And how do these impressions change over time, in the face of new information? Recent research by social psychologists provides some intriguing answers to these questions (Ruscher & Hammer, 1994; Wyer et al., 1994). In addition, such research has focused on the opposite side of the impression-

Social Perception ■ The process through which we seek to know and understand other persons.

formation coin—the question of how we ourselves attempt to make a good first impression on others. Research on this process, known as *impression management* or *self-presentation* (Ruscher & Hammer, 1994; Wyer et al., 1994), has helped clarify which techniques work best, and why. Given the important role of impression formation and impression management in our everyday social life, we'll examine these topics, too, in the present chapter.

Nonverbal Communication: The Unspoken Language

Often, social behavior is strongly affected by temporary factors or causes. Changing moods, shifting emotions, fatigue, illness, drugs—all can influence the ways in which we think and behave. For example, most persons are more willing to do favors for others when in a good mood than when in a bad mood (Baron & Bronfen, 1994; George, 1991). Similarly, most people are more likely to lose their tempers and lash out at others in some manner when feeling irritable than when feeling pleasant (Anderson, Anderson, & Deuser, in press; Bell, 1992).

Because such temporary factors often exert important effects on social behavior and thought, we often seek knowledge about them: we try to find out how others are feeling right now. How do we go about this process? Sometimes, in a very straightforward way: We ask people directly. Unfortunately, this strategy sometimes fails, because others are often unwilling to reveal their inner feelings to us. On the contrary, they may actively seek to conceal such information, or even to mislead us about their current emotions (DePaulo, 1992). For example, negotiators often hide their reactions to offers from their opponents; and salespersons frequently show more liking and friendliness toward potential customers than they really feel.

In situations like these, we often fall back upon another, less direct method for information about others' reactions: we pay careful attention to their *nonverbal behaviors*—changes in facial expressions, eye contact, posture, body movements, and other expressive actions. As noted by DePaulo (1992), such behavior is relatively *irrepressible*—difficult to control—so that even when others try to conceal their inner feelings from us, these often "leak out" in many ways through nonverbal cues. So, in an important sense, nonverbal behaviors constitute a silent but eloquent language. The information they convey, and our efforts to interpret this input, are often described by the term **nonverbal communication**. Here, we'll examine the basic channels through which nonverbal communication takes place; then we'll turn to some interesting findings about individual differences in the extent to which people display their inner feelings in such cues—individual differences in *emotional expressiveness* (Kring, Smith, & Neale, 1994).

Nonverbal Communication: The Basic Channels

Nonverbal Communication ■ Communication between individuals that does not involve the content of spoken language but relies instead on an unspoken language of facial expressions, eye contact, and body language.

Think for a moment: do you act differently when you are feeling elated than you do when you are feeling really "down"? Most likely, you do. People do tend to behave differently when experiencing different emotional states. But precisely how do differences in your inner states—your emotions, feelings, and moods—show up in your behavior? This key question in the study of nonverbal communication focuses on the *basic channels* of such communication. Research findings indicate in fact, information about our inner states is often revealed through five basic channels: *facial expressions, eye contact, body movements, posture,* and *touching.*

Unmasking the Face: Facial Expressions As Clues to Others' Emotions. More than two thousand years ago, the Roman orator Cicero stated: "The face is the image of the soul." By this he meant that human feelings and emotions are often reflected in the face and can be read there in specific expressions. Modern research suggests that Cicero—and many other observers of human behavior— were correct in this view: it *is* possible to learn much about others' current moods and feelings from their facial expressions. In fact, it appears that six different basic emotions are represented clearly, and from a very early age, on the human face: anger, fear, happiness, sadness, surprise, and disgust (Izard, 1991; Rozin, Lowery, & Ebert, 1994). Additional findings suggest that another expression—contempt—may also be quite basic (e.g., Ekman & Heider, 1988; *1,* 1992). Because this emotion is harder to define verbally, however, it seems to be difficult to establish clear relationships between contempt and specific facial expressions. In contrast, it is easier to establish such links for other emotions— for example, smiles and happiness (Rosenberg & Ekman, in press).

It's important to realize that these findings concerning a relatively small number of basic facial expressions in no way imply that human beings can show only a small number of facial expressions. On the contrary, emotions occur in many combinations (for example, joy tinged with sorrow, surprise combined with fear), and each of these reactions can vary greatly in strength. Thus, while there may be only a small number of basic themes in facial expression, the number of variations on these themes is immense (see Figure 2.1).

Now for another important question: Do facial expressions really reflect individuals' underlying emotions? Research findings suggest that they do (e.g., Cacioppo et al., 1988). For example, in several studies participants have been asked to move various parts of their faces so as to produce configurations resembling certain facial expressions. For instance, they are asked to wrinkle their nose while opening their mouth (an expression resembling that of disgust), or to crease their brow (as in a frown). They are *not* told to show happiness, anger, fear, and so on; rather, they are merely asked to move parts of their faces in very specific ways. While they move various facial muscles, their physiological reactions (heart rate, respiration, skin conductance) are recorded. In addition, participants also report on any emotional experiences, thoughts, or memories they have while moving their facial muscles. Results indicate that different facial movements are accompanied by changes in physiological activity. The facial expression of fear, for instance, is associated with high heart rate and short periods between breaths, while facial expressions of happiness are associated with lower heart rate and longer periods between breaths. In addition—and this is a key point—the more closely the facial movements resemble expressions associated with specific emotions, the greater the tendency of participants to report experiencing those emotions (e.g., Levenson, Ekman, & Friesen, 1990; Levenson et al., 1992). Findings such as these suggest that the link between emotional experiences and certain facial expressions is a real and very basic one.

Are Facial Expressions Universal? Suppose that you traveled to a remote part of the world and visited a group of people who had never before met an outsider. Would their facial expressions in various situations resemble your own? Would they smile when they encountered events that made them happy, frown when exposed to conditions that made them angry, and so on? Further, would you be able to recognize these distinct expressions as readily as those shown by persons belonging to your own culture? Research findings generally suggest that the answer to both questions is *yes*—although, we should note, not all social

FIGURE 2.1

Basic Facial Expressions. Facial expressions such as these provide valuable information about others' emotional states. Can you identify the emotion shown on each face?

(Answers: Starting with the upper left picture, in clockwise order: Disgust, worry, sadness, happiness, surprise, anger)

psychologists accept this conclusion (e.g., Russell, 1994). In other words, people living in widely separated geographic areas do seem to show similar facial expressions in similar emotion-provoking situations, and these can be readily—and accurately—recognized by persons from outside their own cultural group (Ekman, 1989). Perhaps the most convincing evidence for such conclusions is provided by a series of cross-cultural studies conducted by Ekman and Friesen (1975).

These researchers traveled to isolated areas of New Guinea and asked persons living there to imagine various emotion-provoking events—for instance, your friend has come for a visit and you are happy; you find a dead animal that has been lying in the sun for several days, and it smells very bad. Then, participants in the research were asked to show by facial expression how they would feel in each case. As you can see from Figure 2.2 (p. 42), their expressions were very similar to ones you might show yourself in these situations. Findings such as these, which have been repeated in studies conducted in many different cultures, suggest that human beings all over the world tend to show highly similar facial expressions. Certainly, these are not identical—different cultures have contrasting rules about when and how various emotions should be expressed (these are known as *display rules*). For example, in many Asian countries, it is considered rude to show direct disagreement with or disapproval of another person's words or deeds in many situations. In European and North American

FIGURE 2.2

Facial Expressions: Much the Same around the World. The man shown here lives in an isolated part of New Guinea. When asked to show how he would feel in response to various emotion-provoking events, he demonstrated the facial expressions shown here. Can you recognize the emotions that underlie each of these expressions?

(Answers: Starting with upper left picture, in clockwise order: happiness, sadness, anger, disgust.)

(*Source:* From Ekman & Friesen, 1975, p. 27; by permission of the authors.)

cultures, in contrast, open disagreement and disapproval are considered more appropriate, and are shown during negotiations, meetings, and so on. Similarly, in many cultures, it is considered impolite to "gloat" after defeating an opponent; for this reason, expressions of pleasure may be strongly inhibited in such situations (Friedman & Miller-Herringer, 1991). When such display rules don't intervene, however, the link between specific emotions and facial expressions appears to be quite universal.

Similar conclusions have been reached with respect to recognition of such facial expressions: this, too, appears to be quite universal. Look again at the photos in Figure 2.2; do you have any difficulty in recognizing the expressions of the person shown? Probably you do not, despite the fact that he comes from a different culture and a distant geographical location. Systematic research confirms this impression: when individuals living in widely separated countries are shown photos of strangers demonstrating anger, fear, happiness, sadness, surprise, and disgust, they are quite accurate in identifying the strangers' underlying emotions (e.g., Ekman & Oster, 1979). Thus, it appears that a smile is indeed interpreted as a sign of happiness, a frown as a sign of anger, and so on, all over the world.

Having said this, however, we should note that recently there has been some controversy concerning the accuracy of these conclusions. One researcher (Russell, 1994) has called attention to the fact that in many of the studies referred to above, participants were asked to choose an emotion label from *a list of labels provided by the researchers*—a technique known as a *fixed-choice paradigm.* Russell (1994) argues that because of this procedure, we can't be sure that people would have come up with the same labels themselves. Perhaps if allowed to come up with their own labels for each facial expression they saw, participants from different cultures might have shown less consistency in identifying particular emotions. To test this possibility, Rosenberg and Ekman (in press) recently conducted a study in which participants viewed slides of strangers showing various facial expressions. Participants were then asked to identify the emotions shown by either (1) choosing one of seven emotion labels provided by the researchers (e.g., happiness, anger, surprise), (2) choosing one of seven stories provided by the researchers, or (3) providing their own description of the emotion shown. Results indicated that participants showed a high degree of accuracy in recognizing the facial expressions shown on the slides regardless of how they made these judgments (see Figure 2.3). These findings suggest that regardless of the specific research methods used, facial expressions are indeed readily recognized as reflecting specific emotions. Thus, the findings argue for the validity of the view that in contrast to spoken languages, the language of facial expressions needs no interpreter.

Gazes and Stares: Eye Contact As a Nonverbal Cue. Have you ever had a conversation with someone wearing mirror-lensed glasses? If so, you realize that this can be an uncomfortable situation. Since you can't see the other person's eyes, you are uncertain about how she or he is reacting. Taking note of the importance of cues provided by others' eyes, ancient poets often described the eyes as "windows to the soul." In one important sense, they were right: we do often learn much about others' feelings from their eyes. For example, we interpret a high level of gazing from another as a sign of liking or friendliness (Kleinke, 1986). In contrast, if others avoid eye contact with us, we may conclude that they are unfriendly, don't like us, or are simply shy (Zimbardo, 1977).

While a high level of eye contact from others is usually interpreted as a sign of liking or positive feelings, there is one important exception to this general rule. If another person gazes at us continuously and maintains such contact regardless of what we do, she or he can be said to be **staring.** A stare is often interpreted as a sign of anger or hostility—as in *cold stare*—and most people attempt to minimize their exposure to this particular nonverbal cue (Ellsworth

Staring ■ A form of eye contact in which one person continues to gaze steadily at another regardless of what the recipient does.

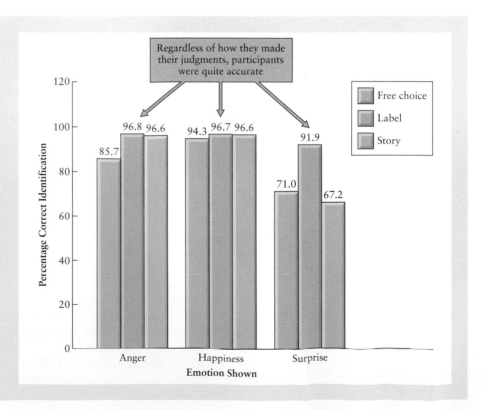

FIGURE 2.3

Accuracy in Recognizing Facial Expressions. Regardless of how they identified the emotions shown in others' facial expressions, research participants were very accurate. These findings offer further support for the view that facial expressions are quite universal.

(*Source:* Based on data from Rosenberg & Ekman, in press.)

FIGURE 2.4

Body Posture: An Important Cue to Others' Feelings. Recent findings indicate that rounded body postures such as those shown in the left photo communicate friendliness and warmth, while angular body postures communicate threat or hostility.

(*Source:* Based on findings reported by Aronoff, Woike, & Hyman, 1992.)

& Carlsmith, 1973). Thus, we may quickly terminate social interaction with someone who stares at us and may even leave the scene (Greenbaum & Rosenfield, 1978). In view of these facts, it is clear that staring is one form of nonverbal behavior that should be used with great caution in most situations.

Body Language: Gestures, Posture, and Movements. Try this simple demonstration:

First, remember some incident that made you angry—the angrier the better. Think about it for a minute.

Now, try to remember another incident, one that made you feel sad—again, the sadder the better.

Compare your behavior in the two contexts. Did you change your posture or move your hands, arms, or legs as your thoughts shifted from the first event to the second? There is a good chance that you did, for our current moods or emotions are often reflected in the position, posture, and movement of our bodies. Together, such nonverbal behaviors are termed **body language,** and they too can provide us with useful information about others.

First, body language often reveals others' emotional states. Large numbers of movements—especially ones in which one part of the body does something to another part (touching, rubbing, scratching)—suggest emotional arousal. The greater the frequency of such behavior, the higher the level of arousal or nervousness (Harrigan et al., 1991).

Larger patterns of movements, involving the whole body, can also be informative. Such phrases as "she adopted a *threatening posture*" and "he greeted her with *open arms*" suggest that different body orientations or postures can

Body Language ■ Cues provided by the position, posture, and movement of others' bodies or body parts.

indicate contrasting emotional reactions. In fact, research by Aronoff, Woike, and Hyman (1992) confirms this possibility. These researchers first identified two groups of characters in classical ballet: ones who played a dangerous or threatening role (e.g., Macbeth, the Angel of Death, Lizzie Borden) and ones who played warm, sympathetic roles (Juliet, Romeo). Then they examined examples of dancing by these characters in actual ballets to see if they adopted different kinds of postures. Aronoff and his colleagues predicted that the dangerous, threatening characters would show more diagonal or angular postures while the warm, sympathetic characters would show more rounded postures (see Figure 2.4 for examples of both types of postures). Results strongly confirmed this hypothesis. These and related findings indicate that large-scale body movements or postures can sometimes provide important information about others' emotions, and even about their apparent traits.

Further evidence for the conclusion that body posture and movements can be an important source of information about others is provided by research conducted by Lynn and Mynier (1993). These researchers chose an unusual scene for their studies: busy restaurants. In these settings, they arranged for waiters and waitresses, when taking drink orders from customers, either to stand upright or to squat down next to the customers. Lynn and Mynier (1993) predicted that squatting down would be interpreted as a sign of friendliness, because in that position the waiters and waitresses would make more eye contact with customers and would be physically closer to them (Argyle, 1988). As a result, they expected servers to receive larger tips when they squatted down than when they did not. As you can see from Figure 2.5, results offered strong support for this prediction. Regardless of servers' gender, they received larger tips when they bent down than when they did not. Also, note that male servers received larger tips than females. It is difficult to interpret this difference, however, because the males and females worked in different restaurants; this is an example of potential *confounding* between variables (see Chapter 1). We can't

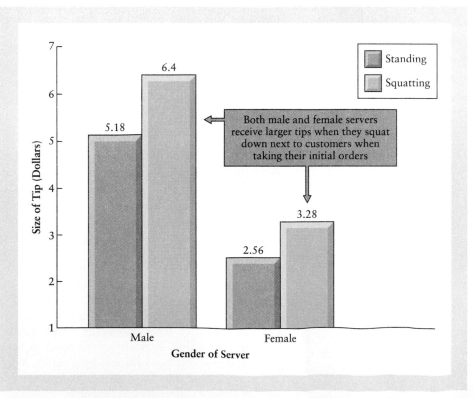

FIGURE 2.5

Body Position and Tipping. When male and female servers squatted down next to customers when taking their initial (drink) orders, they received larger tips than when they remained standing.

(*Source:* Based on data from Lynn & Mynier, 1993.)

Both male and female servers receive larger tips when they squat down next to customers when taking their initial orders

tell from these results whether males and females received different tips because of their gender or because they worked in different restaurants.

Finally, we should add that more specific information about others' feelings is often provided by gestures. These fall into several categories, but perhaps the most important are *emblems*—body movements carrying specific meanings in a given culture. For example, in several countries holding one's hand with the thumb pointing up is a sign of "OK." Similarly, seizing one's nose between the thumb and index finger is a sign of displeasure or disgust. Emblems vary greatly from culture to culture, but every human society seems to have at least some signals of this type for greetings, departures, insults, and the descriptions of many different physical states.

Touching: The Most Intimate Nonverbal Cue. Suppose that during a brief conversation with another person, she or he touched you briefly. How would you react? What information would this behavior convey? The answer to both question is, *it depends*. And what it depends upon is several factors relating to who does the touching (a friend or a stranger, a member of your own or the other gender); the nature of this physical contact (brief or prolonged, gentle or rough, what part of the body is touched); and the context in which it takes place (a business or social setting, a doctor's office). Depending on such factors, touch can suggest affection, sexual interest, dominance, caring, or even aggression. Despite such complexities, existing evidence indicates that when touching is considered acceptable, positive reactions often result (Alagna, Whitcher, & Fisher, 1979; Smith, Gier, & Willis, 1982). This fact is illustrated by yet another ingenious study performed in restaurants. The researchers (Crusco & Wetzel, 1984) arranged for waitresses working in two different restaurants to interact with customers in one of three different ways when giving them their change: they either refrained from touching these persons in any manner, touched them briefly on the hand, or touched for a somewhat longer period on the shoulder. Size of tips left for the waitresses was, again, the dependent measure. Results were clear: Both a brief touch on the hand (about 0.5 second) and a longer touch on the shoulder (1.0 to 1.5 seconds) significantly increased tipping over the no-touch condition. So, consistent with other findings, being touched in an innocuous, nonthreatening way seemed to generate positive rather than negative reactions among recipients. Of course, touching does not always produce such effects. If it is perceived as a status or power play, or if it is too prolonged or intimate, or occurs in a context where touching is not viewed as appropriate, this form of nonverbal behavior may evoke anxiety, anger, and other negative reactions (see Figure 2.6).

Gender Differences in Touching: Who Touches Whom, and When? Visit any large shopping mall, and you'll quickly notice the following fact: A lot of touching goes on in public places. People hold hands, link arms, shake hands, and touch each other in many other ways. Does one gender initiate more of such behavior than the other? Research findings (Hall & Veccia, 1990) indicate that the answer depends strongly on age. Among young couples, males are more likely to touch females than vice versa. As age increases, however, this difference shrinks, so that among older couples (those in the 40s and above) the opposite is true: Females are more likely to initiate touching than males. What is the reason for this trend? One possibility (Hall & Veccia, 1990) is that among younger couples relationships are not yet well established; and in such contexts, prevailing gender roles encourage visible gestures of possessiveness, such as touching, by males. As relationships develop, however, gender roles may require more gestures of possessiveness by females. Whatever the explanation, it is interesting to note that when all age groups are combined, there appear to be no overall gender differences in touching.

FIGURE 2.6

Touching: A Potentially Risky Nonverbal Cue. Touching can communicate many different messages. What do you think is being communicated in the left-hand photo? The right-hand photo?

Individual Differences in the Use of Nonverbal Cues: Emotional Expressiveness

Think back over the many persons you have known. Can you remember one who showed very clear facial expressions, used gestures freely, and engaged in a great deal of body movement? In contrast, can you recall someone who made little use of such nonverbal cues? Probably you have little difficulty in bringing examples of both types to mind, for informal experience suggests that human beings differ greatly along a dimension of **emotional expressiveness**—the extent to which they show outward displays of emotion (Friedman et al., 1980; Kring, Smith, & Neale, 1994).

Do such differences play a role in social behavior? Research findings suggest that they do. For example, some years ago, Friedman and his colleagues (Friedman et al., 1980) administered a test of emotional expressivity to several hundred college students. The students then answered questions about their personal lives, such as "Have you ever given a lecture?" "Have you ever been elected to office in an organization?" and "Have you ever held a major part in a play?" Friedman and his coworkers predicted that students who scored high on expressiveness would be more likely to answer "Yes" to such questions, and results confirmed this prediction. In additional research, the same team of investigators related scores on the test of expressiveness to success in several occupations. They found that among physicians, those scoring high on expressiveness were more popular with their patients than those scoring low on this dimension. And for automobile salespersons, they found that those scoring high on expressiveness actually sold more cars!

Emotional expressiveness is also related to psychological adjustment, but not in a simple or direct manner. What seems to be crucial here is not whether individuals are high or low in emotional expressiveness, but the extent to which they experience concern over expressing their emotions. Thus, persons who would like to express their emotions openly but cannot, and individuals who express their emotions openly but would prefer to hold them inside, are both high in ambivalence. Those who do not experience such feelings, in contrast, are low in such ambivalence (King & Emmons, 1991). Research findings suggest that to the extent individuals experience ambivalence over the expression

Emotional Expressiveness ■
The extent to which persons show outward expressions of their inner feelings.

of their emotions, they may experience psychological difficulties. For example, consider a recent study conducted by Katz and Campbell (1994).

In this investigation, college students first completed a measure of ambivalence over the expression of emotion. Then they kept diaries for two weeks in which they recorded their levels of stress, current moods, and current psychological and physical health. They recorded this information twice each day. Finally, participants completed yet another questionnaire on which they reported on their current psychological and physical well-being. Results indicated that the greater the ambivalence the students experienced, the more stress and negative moods they reported, and the lower their psychological well-being (for example, the more likely they were to feel depressed). These findings indicate that there is no overall "edge" to being high or low in expressiveness: both nonverbal styles can be advantageous or disadvantageous, depending on the specific social context in which they appear. However, the greater the ambivalence individuals experience over the level of expressiveness they actually do show, the more likely they are to experience negative life outcomes.

For more information about the role of nonverbal communication in social interaction, please see the *Applied Side* section below.

Social Psychology: On the Applied Side
HOW TO TELL WHEN ANOTHER PERSON IS LYING:
Nonverbal Cues and the Detection of Deception

"Of course I lie to people. But I lie altruistically—for our mutual good. . . . "
—Quentin Crisp, 1984

If all lies were told for this reason, they might (underline *might*) be more acceptable; at least, they would serve some social function. But it is a sad fact of social life that lies are *not* always told for altruistic purposes. On the contrary, lies are frequently presented for the benefit of the person who engages in deception; and if they are accepted as true, they prove costly to intended recipients. Given this fact, it is often important for us to be able to tell when another person is lying. And here is where research on nonverbal communication comes in handy. Research on what social psychologists term *detection of deception* has continued for several decades, and the results of this work provide us with several important clues that can help us determine whether another person is lying. Before turning to these specific nonverbal cues, however, we should explain *why* it's possible to use such information to recognize deception even on the part of highly skilled liars.

The answer centers around the fact that, as we've seen, there are many different channels of nonverbal communication. Because of this fact, research suggests, it's virtually impossible for individuals to monitor and control all of these separate channels at once (De Paulo, 1992; DePaulo, Stone, & Lassiter, 1985). Thus, even persons who lie frequently and are highly practiced at lying (for example, negotiators, confidence artists, some salespersons) frequently reveal that they are lying through some channel of nonverbal cues (see Figure 2.7). For example, if they focus on regulating their facial expressions and eye contact, then the fact that they are lying may be revealed through their body movements and posture, or through changes in the nonverbal aspects of speech—the tone of their voice, and related cues.

Now that we've clarified this issue, let's turn to the specific clues that can help you decide whether another person is being honest with you.

FIGURE 2.7

Detection of Deception: Often, Nonverbal Cues Are Helpful. How can we tell whether another person is lying? Nonverbal cues from others' facial expressions, eye contact, and body language often help us decide.

One nonverbal cue that can be very helpful in this respect is **microexpressions**. These are fleeting facial expressions lasting only a few tenths of a second. Such reactions appear on the face very quickly after an emotion-provoking event and are difficult to suppress (Ekman, 1985). As a result, they can be quite revealing about others' true feelings or emotions. So, when you have reason to suspect that another person may be lying, say something you think they'll find surprising or upsetting, and then *watch their face very carefully as you say it.* If you see one expression which is followed, very quickly by another, different one, watch out: they may be trying to deceive you.

A second nonverbal cue we can use is known as *interchannel discrepancies.* These are inconsistencies between nonverbal cues from different basic channels. Such inconsistencies result from the fact that, as we noted earlier, persons who are lying find it difficult to control all these channels at once. For example, a defendant who is lying on the witness stand may succeed in managing her facial expressions and in maintaining a high level of eye contact with the jury. At the same time, however, she may demonstrate postural shifts of body movements that reveal the high level of emotional arousal she is experiencing.

A third nonverbal cue involves nonverbal aspects of people's speech—what is sometimes known as *paralanguage.* When people lie, the pitch of their voices often rises (Zuckerman, DePaulo, & Rosenthal, 1981), and they tend to speak more slowly and with less fluency. In addition, they engage in more *sentence repairs*—instances in which they start a sentence, interrupt it, and then start again (Stiff et al., 1989). So listen carefully: if you observe these changes in another person's voice, the person may be lying.

Fourth, deception is frequently revealed by various aspects of eye contact. Persons who are lying often blink more frequently and show pupils that are more dilated than persons who are telling the truth. They may also show an unusually low level of eye contract or—surprisingly—an unusually high one, as they attempt to feign honesty by looking others right in the eye (Kleinke, 1986).

Finally, persons who are lying sometimes show exaggerated facial expressions. For example, they may smile more—or more broadly—than usual, or may show greater sorrow or other emotion than is typical for them in this kind

Microexpressions ■ Brief and incomplete facial expressions that occur on individuals' faces very quickly after exposure to a specific stimulus and before active processes can be used to conceal them.

of situation. A prime example: Someone says no to a request you've made and then shows exaggerated regret. This is a good sign that the reasons the person has given you for the "no" may not be accurate.

Through careful attention to these nonverbal cues, we can often tell when others are lying—or merely trying to hide their own feelings from us. Our success in this respect is far from perfect—skillful liars do often manage to deceive us. But their task will be made more difficult if you pay careful attention to the clues described above. Perfecting your own skills in this respect requires considerable effort and practice; it goes without saying, though, that the benefits of being able to cut through attempts at deception can be substantial. ■ ■■

INTEGRATING PRINCIPLES

1. Nonverbal cues often provide valuable information about others' current feelings, moods, and emotions.

2. Because of this fact, nonverbal cues play an important role in many forms of social interaction, including interpersonal attraction (Chapter 7), social influence (Chapter 9), helping (Chapter 10), aggression (Chapter 11), and doctor–patient interactions (Chapter 14).

Attribution: Understanding the Causes of Others' Behavior

Accurate knowledge of others' current moods or feelings can be useful in many ways. Yet, where social perception is concerned, this knowledge is often only the first step. In addition, we usually want to know more—to understand others' lasting traits and to know the causes behind their behavior. Social psychologists believe that our interest in such questions stems, in large measure, from our basic desire to understand cause-and-effect relationships in the social world (Pittman, 1993). In other words, we don't simply want to know *how* others have acted; we want to understand *why* they have done so, too. The process through which we seek such information is known as **attribution**. More formally, *attribution* refers to our efforts to understand the causes behind others' behavior and, on some occasions, the causes behind *our* behavior, too. Social psychologists have studied attribution for several decades, and as you'll soon see, their research has yielded many intriguing insights into this important process (e.g., Graham & Folkes, 1990; Heider, 1958; Pittman, 1993).

Theories of Attribution: Frameworks for Understanding How We Attempt to Make Sense Out of the Social World

Because attribution is complex, many theories have been proposed to explain its operation. Here, we will focus on two that have been especially influential, plus recent efforts to extend and refine them.

From Acts to Dispositions: Using Others' Behavior As a Guide to Their Lasting Traits. The first of these theories—Jones and Davis's (1965) theory of **correspondent inference**—asks how we use information about others' behavior as

Attribution ■ The process through which we seek to identify the causes of others' behavior and so gain knowledge of their stable traits and dispositions.

Correspondent Inference (theory of) ■ Theory describing how we use others' behavior as a basis for inferring their stable dispositions.

a basis for inferring that they possess various traits. In other words, the theory is concerned with how we decide, on the basis of others' overt actions, that they possess specific traits or dispositions that they carry with them from situation to situation, and that remain fairly stable over time.

At first glance, this might seem to be a simple task. Others' behavior provides us with a rich source on which to draw, so if we observe it carefully, we should be able to learn a lot about them. Up to a point this is true. The task is complicated, however, by the following fact: Often, individuals act in certain ways not because doing so reflects their own preferences or traits, but rather because external factors leave them little choice. For example, suppose you observe a woman rushing through an airport, pushing people out of the way in her haste. Does this mean that this person is impatient and rude—always in a hurry, and ready to trample bystanders to get past them? Not necessarily; this person may simply be responding to the fact that her plane is about to leave without her! In fact, this traveler may actually be quite slow-moving and polite most of the time; her behavior may be the exception, not the rule. Situations like this are very common, and when in them, using others' present behavior as a guide to their lasting traits or motives can be very misleading.

How do we cope with such complications? According to Jones and Davis's theory (Jones & Davis, 1965; Jones & McGillis, 1976), we accomplish this task by focusing our attention on certain types of actions—those most likely to prove informative.

First, we consider only behaviors that seem to have been freely chosen, while largely ignoring behaviors that were somehow forced on the person in question. Second, we pay careful attention to actions that show what Jones and Davis term **noncommon effects**—effects that can be caused by one specific factor, but not by others. (Don't confuse this word with *uncommon,* which simply means infrequent.) Why are such actions informative? Consider the following example. Imagine that one of your casual friends has just gotten engaged. Her future spouse is very handsome, has a great personality, is wildly in love with your friend, and is very rich. What can you learn about your friend from her decision to marry this man? Obviously, not much. There are so many good reasons that you can't choose among them. In contrast, imagine that your friend's fiance is very handsome, but that he treats her with indifference and is known to be extremely boring; also, he has no visible means of support and intends to live on your friend's salary. Does the fact that she is marrying him tell you anything about her personal characteristics? Now, it does; in fact, you can probably conclude that she places more weight on physical attractiveness in a husband than on personality or considerateness or wealth. As you can see, therefore, we can usually learn more about others from actions on their part that yield noncommon effects than from ones that do not.

Finally, Jones and Davis suggest that we also pay greater attention to actions by others that are low in *social desirability* than to actions that are high on this dimension. In other words, we learn more about others' traits from actions they perform that are somehow out of the ordinary than from actions that are very much like those performed by most other persons.

In sum, according to the theory proposed by Jones and Davis, we are most likely to conclude that others' behavior reflects their stable traits (that is, we are likely to reach *correspondent* inferences about them) when that behavior (1) is freely chosen; (2) yields distinctive, noncommon effects; and (3) is low in social desirability.

Attentional Resources and Trait Attribution: What We Learn—and Don't Learn—from Obscure Behavior. Jones and Davis's theory offers a useful framework for understanding how we use others' behavior to identify their key traits. However, recent research has extended the theory in several ways. Perhaps the most important of these extensions involves efforts to understand the role of

Noncommon Effects ■ Effects produced by a particular factor that could not be produced by any other apparent cause.

conscious attentional resources in trait attribution. As we'll see in more detail in Chapter 3, modern conceptions of social thought generally assume that we have limited cognitive resources—limited capacity to process social information (e.g., Gilbert & Osborne, 1989). Thus, if we devote attention to one cognitive task, we have less remaining for other tasks.

What is the relevance of this principle to Jones and Davis's theory? The answer involves the fact that when we infer others' traits from their behavior, we actually accomplish three distinct tasks (Gilbert, Pelham, & Krull, 1988). First, we *categorize* an individual's behavior—decide what it is all about. Next, we *characterize* the behavior—use it to infer specific traits. Finally, and this is crucial, we *correct* our inferences about this person's traits in the light of information about the situation in which it has occurred. For example, suppose we see a motorist talking to a state trooper who is standing next to his car. We recognize this as a specific kind of interaction: one between an officer and a driver he or she has just stopped. Suppose we also notice that the person is being very humble—he is practically groveling at the trooper's feet. At first glance, we might use this information to infer that the driver is a very meek person (characterization). Since we realize that the driver is trying to avoid a ticket, however, we may quickly correct this inference and avoid jumping to this particular conclusion.

Under normal circumstances, we generally have sufficient cognitive resources available to engage in all three tasks. But in some cases, we don't: others' behavior may be *obscure,* so that it is difficult to tell precisely what they are doing, or we simply don't have enough time to make necessary corrections. In such situations, we use up our limited resources on the first two tasks—categorization and characterization—and don't have enough left to correct our initial trait inferences. As a result, we may make errors in this respect (see Figure 2.8).

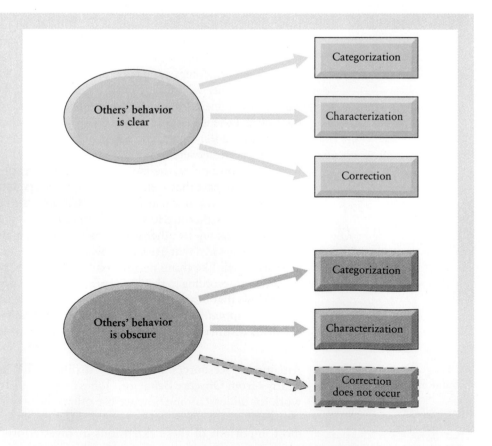

FIGURE 2.8

Information Overload and Inferring Others' Traits. If others' behavior is clear, we usually have enough cognitive resources available to categorize their behavior, to characterize it, and then to make corrections on the basis of situational information. If others' behavior is obscured in some manner, however, we may lack sufficient resources to complete the correction phase.

(*Source:* Based on suggestions by Gilbert et al., 1992.)

Gilbert and his colleagues (1992) reported direct evidence for these proposals. In this study, female participants listened to tape recordings of a "dating game" in which a woman asked a man a series of questions. The woman's comments suggested very clearly either that she preferred a man with a traditional gender-role orientation or that she preferred a man with a non-traditional sex role orientation (for instance, a man who liked being asked out by women). In both cases, the man's answers were consistent with the woman's preferences. Under these conditions, Gilbert and his colleagues proposed, listeners would be able to carry out the *correction* phase described above. They would realize that the man was trying to please the woman and would not assume that his answers were a true reflection of his own gender-role preferences. But what would happen if the man's behavior were somehow obscured? Under these conditions, the researchers predicted, listeners would have to devote more cognitive resources to the task of categorizing the behavior. As a result, they would have less available for the correction phase, and they might conclude that the man's answers were a true reflection of his views. To test this prediction, the audiotape of the "dating game" program was presented in two different forms: a normal version, in which the man's answers were easy to understand, and a *degraded* version, in which lots of noise was present on the tape. After hearing one of these tapes, participants rated the man's true gender-role attitudes. As predicted, they were more likely to assume that his statements accurately reflected his views when his answers were obscured (on the degraded tape). These findings suggest that in cases where others' behavior is obscure (difficult to observe), the effort we devote to answering the question *What?* (What are they doing or saying?) may make it more difficult for us to answer the question *Why?* (What does their behavior tell us about their traits?).

Kelley's Theory of Causal Attributions: How We Answer the Question *Why?*
Consider the following events:

> *You meet an attractive person at a party, and she or he promises to phone you the next day, but doesn't.*
>
> *You receive a much lower grade on an exam than you were expecting.*
>
> *You arrange to meet one of your friends at 5:00 p.m. You are there on time, but fifteen minutes later, your friend still hasn't arrived.*

What question would arise in our mind in each of these situations? The answer is clear: *Why?* You'd want to know *why* that person didn't call you, *why* you got a lower grade than you expected, and *why* your friend is late. In many situations, this is the central attributional task we face. We want to know why other people have acted as they have or why events have turned out in a specific way. Such knowledge is crucial, for only if we understand the causes behind others' actions can we hope to make sense out of the social world. Obviously, the number of specific causes behind others' behavior is very large. To make the task more manageable, therefore, we often begin with a preliminary question: Did others' behavior stem mainly from *internal* causes (their own traits, motives, intentions); mainly from *external* causes (some aspect of the social or physical world); or from a combination of the two? For example, you might wonder whether your received a lower grade than expected because you didn't study enough (an internal cause), because the questions were too difficult (an external cause), or perhaps because of both factors. Revealing insights into how we carry out this initial attributional task are provided by a theory proposed by Kelley (Kelley, 1972; Kelley & Michela, 1980).

According to Kelley, in our attempts to answer the question *Why* about others' behavior, we focus on information relating to three major dimensions. First, we consider **consensus**—the extent to which others react to some stimulus or

Consensus ■ The extent to which reactions by one person are also shown by others.

event in the same manner as the person we are considering. The higher the proportion of other people who react in the same way, the higher the consensus. Second, we consider **consistency**—the extent to which the person in question reacts to the stimulus or event in the same way on other occasions, that is, across time. And third, we examine **distinctiveness**—the extent to which this person reacts in the same manner to other, different stimuli or events.

How do we use such information? According to Kelley's theory, we are most likely to attribute another's behavior to *internal* causes under conditions in which consensus and distinctiveness are low, but consistency is high. In contrast, we are most likely to attribute another's behavior to *external* causes under conditions in which consensus, consistency, and distinctiveness are all high. Finally, we usually attribute another's behavior to a combination of internal and external factors under conditions in which consensus is low, but consistency and distinctiveness are high. Perhaps a concrete example will help illustrate the very reasonable nature of these suggestions.

Imagine that a student in one of your classes suddenly gets up, shouts angrily at the professor, and then throws a big, ripe tomato at her. Why did the student act this way? Because of internal causes or external causes? Is this student a weirdo with a violent temper? Or was this person responding to some external cause—something the professor did or said? According to Kelley's theory, your decision (as an observer of this scene) would depend on information relating to the three factors mentioned above. First, assume that the following conditions prevail:

1. No other student shouts or throws tomatoes *(consensus is low)*
2. You have seen this student lose his temper in this same class on other occasions *(consistency is high)*
3. You have seen this student lose his temper outside the classroom—for example, in response to slow waiters and traffic jams *(distinctiveness is low)*

In this case, Kelley's theory suggests that the student blew up because of internal causes: he is a person with a very short fuse! (Refer to the upper part of Figure 2.9.)

Now, in contrast, assume that the following conditions hold:

1. Several other students also shout at the professor *(consensus is high)*
2. You have seen this student lose his temper in this same class on other occasions *(consistency is high)*
3. You have not seen this student lose his temper outside the classroom *(distinctiveness is high)*

Under these conditions, you would probably attribute the student's behavior to external causes—perhaps arrogant or unreasonable behavior by the professor (refer to the lower part of Figure 2.9).

The basic assumptions of Kelley's theory have been confirmed in a wide range of social situations, so it seems to provide important insights into the nature of causal attributions. However, recent research on the theory also suggests the need for certain modifications, as described below.

When Do We Engage in Causal Attribution? The Path of Least Resistance Strikes Again. The kind of causal analysis described by Kelley requires considerable effort: it requires that we pay close attention to others' behavior in order to acquire information about consensus, consistency, and distinctiveness. Given this fact, it is not surprising that people tend to avoid such cognitive work whenever they can. Often, they are all too ready to jump to quick and easy conclusions about the causes behind others' actions (Lupfer, Clark, & Hutcherson, 1990). They can do this because they know from past experience that certain kinds of

Consistency ■ The extent to which an individual responds to a given stimulus or situation in the same way on different occasions (i.e., across time).

Distinctiveness ■ The extent to which an individual responds in the same manner to different stimuli or different situations.

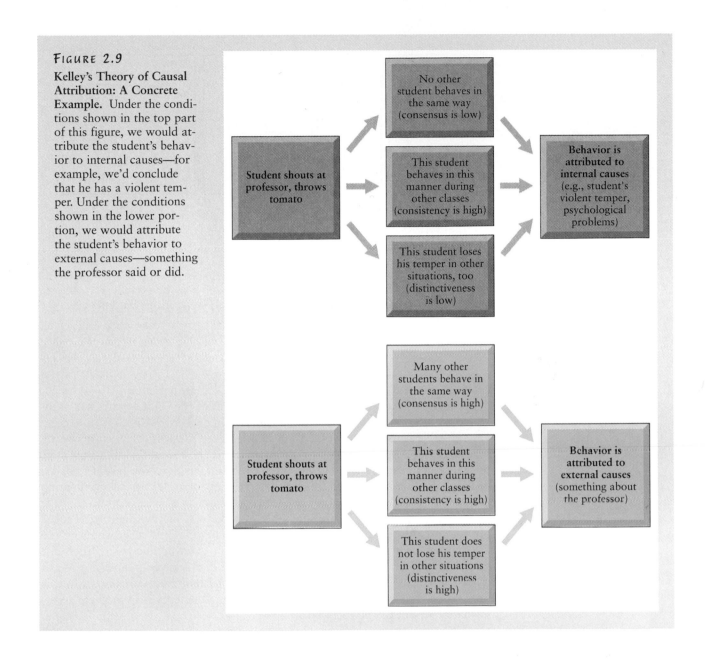

FIGURE 2.9

Kelley's Theory of Causal Attribution: A Concrete Example. Under the conditions shown in the top part of this figure, we would attribute the student's behavior to internal causes—for example, we'd conclude that he has a violent temper. Under the conditions shown in the lower portion, we would attribute the student's behavior to external causes—something the professor said or did.

behavior generally stem from internal factors, while other kinds generally derive from external ones. For example, most people believe that success is generally the result of ability and effort—two internal causes. Thus, when they encounter someone who is experiencing success, they quickly assume that this outcome derives from one or both of these internal causes. In contrast, most people assume that laughing or being amused is largely the result of external causes—exposure to a funny image or situation. Thus, when they see someone laughing, they tend to assume that she or he is doing so because of external causes.

So, when precisely, does the kind of careful analysis described by Kelley occur? Primarily under two conditions: (1) when people are confronted with unexpected events—ones they can't readily explain in terms of what they know about a specific situation or person, and (2) when they encounter unpleasant outcomes or events. In sum, Kelley's theory appears to be an accurate description of causal attribution *when such attribution occurs*. It may not describe people's behavior in many situations, though, because they simply don't want to bother.

FIGURE 2.10

Augmenting in Operation. *According to the* augmenting principle, *we assign extra weight to a factor that might facilitate a specific behavior if the behavior occurs despite the presence of other factors that tend to prevent it (inhibitory factors). The character in this cartoon is using augmenting to boost his image: by calling attention to the many factors that interfered with his game, he* augments *the importance of his own skill.*

(*Source:* King Features Syndicate.)

Augmenting and Discounting: How We Handle Multiple Potential Causes. Suppose that one day you learn that the president of the United States has nominated a certain woman for a seat on the Supreme Court. Why did he do this? One possible cause is the woman's credentials; the president may state overtly that he chose this person because she is by far the best qualified. But now suppose that you learn of another potential cause for his decision: recent polls indicate that the president can improve his chances for reelection by nominating a woman. Now that you know about this poll, you will be less certain that the president chose this candidate solely because she was highly qualified? Probably so; and this, in turn, illustrates an important principle of attribution: the **discounting principle** (sometimes known as the *subtraction rule*). Briefly, it states that we reduce (discount) the importance of any given potential cause of a person's behavior to the extent that other potential causes also exist. In this case, we reduce the importance of the candidate's credentials in the light of information about the political poll.

Now, in contrast, imagine a different situation: The president nominates the same woman for the Supreme Court, *despite* the fact that political polls indicate that this will probably cost him the election. What will you conclude about her credentials now? Probably, that they are impressive indeed. This example illustrates what is known as the **augmenting principle**, which states that when a factor that might facilitate a given behavior and a factor that might inhibit it are both present *and the behavior still occurs*, we assign added weight to the facilitative factor. We do so because that factor has succeeded in producing the behavior even in the face of an important barrier (the inhibitory factor). In this case, we give added weight to the nominee's outstanding credentials, because we realize that the president chose her despite the fact that this will harm his political career. For another, more humorous example, see Figure 2.10. In that cartoon, Silo is boosting the importance of one potential reason why he won—his skill—by calling attention to several other factors that would be expected to interfere with his game (inhibitory factors).

While discounting and augmenting seem to operate in many different contexts, one of the most important of these involves *affirmative action*—active

Discounting Principle ▪ The tendency to attach less importance to one potential cause of some behavior when other potential causes are also present.

Augmenting Principle ▪ The tendency to attach greater importance to a potential cause of behavior if the behavior occurs despite the presence of other, inhibitory factors.

efforts to hire and promote women and minorities. A growing body of evidence indicates that while affirmative action programs do increase the hiring and promotion of groups that have previously been the subject of discrimination (see Chapter 6), these programs sometimes have other, less desirable effects as well (e.g., Chacko, 1982; Summers, 1991). In particular, in situations where affirmative action policies exist and women and minorities are hired or promoted, observers—and these persons themselves!—sometimes tend to *discount* the contribution of the individuals' qualifications to these outcomes. Instead, such achievements are often attributed, both by the persons hired and promoted and by others in their company, largely to affirmative action. As you can well imagine, this is a disturbing outcome, and it suggests the need for implementing such programs in a very careful and sensitive manner.

Attribution: Some Basic Sources of Error

Our discussion of attribution so far seems to imply that it is a highly rational process in which individuals seeking to identify the causes of others' behavior follow orderly cognitive steps. In general, this is so. We should note, however, that attribution is also subject to several forms of error—tendencies that can lead us into serious errors concerning the causes of others' behavior. Several of these errors are described below.

The Fundamental Attribution Error: Overestimating the Role of Dispositional Causes. Imagine that you witness the following scene. A man arrives at a meeting one hour late. On entering, he drops his notes on the floor. While he is trying to pick them up, his glasses fall off and break. Later, he spills coffee all over his tie. How would you explain these events? The chances are good that you would reach conclusions such as "This person is disorganized and clumsy." Are such attributions accurate? Perhaps; but it is also possible that the man was late because of unavoidable delays at the airport, dropped his notes because they were printed on slick paper, and spilled the coffee because the cup was too hot to hold. The fact that you would be *less* likely to consider such potential external causes illustrates what is often termed the **fundamental attribution error**—our strong tendency to explain others' actions in terms of dispositional (internal) rather than situational (external) causes. In short, we tend to perceive others as acting as they do because they are "that kind of person," rather than because of the many external factors that may have affected their behavior.

This tendency to overemphasize dispositional causes while underestimating the impact of situational ones seems to arise from the fact that when we observe another person's behavior, we tend to focus on his or her actions; the context in which these occur often fades into the background. As a result, the potential impact of situational causes receives less attention. A second possibility is that we do notice such situational factors but tend to assign them insufficient weight (Gilbert & Jones, 1986).

Whatever the basis for the fundamental attribution error, it has important implications. For example, it suggests that even if individuals are made aware of the situational forces that adversely affect members of disadvantaged groups in a society (inadequate educational opportunities, shattered family life), they may still perceive these persons as "bad," "lazy," or "dumb," and therefore responsible for their own plight. In such cases, the fundamental attribution error can have serious social consequences.

Interestingly, our tendency to attribute others' actions to dispositional causes tends to weaken with the passage of time following the action (Burger, 1991; Frank & Gilovich, 1989). For example, consider a study by Burger and

Fundamental Attribution Error ■ The tendency to overestimate the impact of dispositional causes on others' behavior.

Pavelich (1993). These researchers analyzed people's explanations for the outcomes of presidential elections in the United States in the years 1968–1984. The researchers examined articles and columns appearing on the editorial pages of major newspapers within five days of each election and again two or three years later. They analyzed the content of these sources to determine whether the outcomes were attributed to personal characteristics of one or both candidates, or to circumstances surrounding the election or actions by people outside the candidates' control. An example of a personal cause: "Mondale made the outcome worse by the ineptitude of his campaign." An example of a situational cause: "The shadows of Watergate . . . cleared the way for Carter's climb to the presidency." Results were clear; within a few days of the elections, nearly two-thirds of the explanations for the outcome were personal. Two or three years later, however, the opposite was true: two-thirds of the explanations referred to situational factors. So, over time, the fundamental attribution error was reversed.

In sum, it appears that our attributions often shift over time, and that as a result, the tendency to explain others' actions in terms of internal causes may fade with the passage of time. When such shifts lead us to more accurate conclusions about why others acted as they did, of course, these shifts may be viewed as beneficial ones.

The Actor–Observer Effect: You Fell; I Was Pushed. Another and closely related type of attributional bias involves our tendency to attribute our own behavior to situational factors, but that of others to dispositional (internal) causes. Thus, when we see another person trip and fall, we tend to attribute this event to his or her clumsiness. If we trip, in contrast, we are more likely to attribute this event to situational causes: ice on the sidewalk or slippery shoes. This "tilt" in our attributions is known as the **actor–observer effect** (Jones & Nisbett, 1971), and has been observed in many different contexts. For example, consider a recent study by Herzog (1994). He asked participants to watch videos of common driving situations and, while watching, to play either the role of a driver or of a passive observer—a pedestrian standing nearby. After viewing the tapes, "drivers" rated the extent to which their behavior in each situation was affected by personal factors (their own personality, ability, intelligence) or by situational factors (the actions of other drivers, road conditions). "Observers" rated the extent to which the drivers' behavior was a function of personal or situational factors. Results indicated that in most of the incidents studied, drivers tended to attribute their own behavior to situational factors more than to personal factors. In contrast, passive observers showed the opposite pattern: they attributed the drivers' behavior more to personal factors.

Why does the actor–observer effect occur? In part because we are quite aware of the many situational factors affecting our own actions, but are less aware of such factors when we turn our attention to the actions of other persons. Thus, we tend to perceive our own behavior as arising largely from situational causes, but that of others as deriving mainly from their traits or dispositions.

The Self-Serving Bias: "I Can Do No Wrong, but You Can Do No Right." Suppose that you write a term paper for one of your courses. When you get it back you find the following comment on the first page: "An outstanding paper—one of the best I've seen in years. A+." To what will you attribute this success? If you are like most people, you will explain it in terms of internal causes—your high level of talent, the effort you invested in writing the paper, and so on.

Now, in contrast, imagine that when you get the paper back, *these* comments are written on it: "Horrible paper—one of the worst I've seen in years. D–." How will you interpret *this* outcome? The chances are good that you will be tempted to focus mainly on external (situational) factors—the difficulty of the

Actor–Observer Effect ■ The tendency to attribute our own behavior mainly to situational causes but the behavior of others mainly to internal (dispositional) causes.

task, your professor's inability to understand what you were trying to say, the fact that your professor is prejudiced against members of your gender, and so on.

This tendency to attribute our own positive outcomes to internal causes but negative ones to external factors is known as the **self-serving bias,** and it appears to be both general in its occurrence and powerful in its effects (Brown & Rogers, 1991; Miller & Ross, 1975).

Why does this tilt in our attributions occur? Several possibilities have been suggested, but most of these fall into two categories: cognitive and motivational explanations. The cognitive model suggests that the self-serving bias stems mainly from certain tendencies in the way we process social information (Ross, 1977). Specifically, it suggests that we attribute positive outcomes to internal causes, but negative ones to external causes, because we *expect* to succeed and have a tendency to attribute expected outcomes to internal more than to external causes. In contrast, the motivational explanation suggests that the self-serving bias stems from our need to protect and enhance our self-esteem, or the related desire to look good in the eyes of others (Greenberg, Pyszczynski, & Solomon, 1982). While both cognitive and motivational factors may well play a role in this type of attributional error, research evidence seems to offer more support for the motivational interpretation (e.g., Brown & Rogers, 1991).

Whatever the precise origins of the self-serving bias, it can be the cause of much interpersonal friction. It often leads persons who work with others on a joint task to perceive that *they,* not their partners, have made the major contributions. Similarly, it leads individuals to perceive that while their own successes stem from internal causes and are well deserved, the successes of others stem from external factors and are less merited. Also, because of the self-serving bias, many persons tend to perceive negative actions on their own part as reasonable and excusable, but identical actions on the part of others as irrational and inexcusable (Baumeister, Stillwell, & Wotman, 1990). Thus, the self-serving bias is clearly one type of attributional error with serious implications for interpersonal relations.

Applications of Attribution Theory: Insights and Interventions

Kurt Lewin, one of the founders of modern social psychology (see Chapter 1), often remarked: "There's nothing as practical as a good theory." By this he meant that once we obtain scientific understanding of some aspect of social behavior, we can, potentially, put this knowledge to practical use. Where attribution theory is concerned, this has definitely been the case. As basic knowledge about attribution has increased, so, too, has the range of practical problems to which such information has been applied (Graham & Folkes, 1990). Thus, attribution theory has served as a useful framework for understanding of issues and topics as diverse as the causes of marital dissatisfaction (e.g., Holtzworth-Munroe & Jacobson, 1985), women's reactions to miscarriage (James & Kristiansen, 1985), and the causes of interpersonal conflict (Baron & Richardson, 1994). Here, we'll examine two especially important, and timely, applications of attribution theory.

Attribution and Depression. Depression is the most common psychological disorder. In fact, estimates indicate that at any given time, more than 10 percent of the general population is suffering from this disorder to some degree (Alloy, Abramson, & Dykman, 1990). Although many factors play a role in depression, one that has received increasing attention in recent years is what might be termed a *self-defeating* pattern of attributions. In contrast to most people, who show the self-serving bias described earlier, depressed individuals tend to adopt an opposite pattern. They attribute *negative* outcomes to lasting internal causes

Self-Serving Bias ■ The tendency to attribute our own positive outcomes to internal causes (e.g., our own traits or characteristics) but negative outcomes or events to external causes (e.g., chance, task difficulty).

such as their own traits or lack of ability, but attribute *positive* outcomes to temporary, external causes such as blind good luck or special favors from others. As a result, such persons come to perceive that they have little or no control over what happens to them—that they are mere chips in the winds of unpredictable fate. Little wonder that they become depressed and tend to give up on life. Fortunately, several forms of therapy that seek to change such attributions have been developed and put to effective use (e.g., Robinson, Berman, & Neimeyer, 1990). These new forms of therapy focus on getting depressed persons to change their attributions: to take personal credit for successful outcomes, to stop blaming themselves for negative outcomes (especially ones that can't be avoided), and to view at least some failures as the result of external factors. These new forms of therapy do not explore repressed urges, inner conflicts, or traumatic events during childhood; but they seem to be more effective, in many cases, than older and more traditional forms of treatment for depression. Since attribution theory provides the basis for these innovative forms of treatment, it has certainly proved very useful in this respect.

Attribution and Rape: Blaming Innocent Victims.   It has been estimated that in the United States a rape—forced sexual intercourse—occurs every eleven minutes (Baron & Richardson, 1994). Further, in a national survey, approximately 15 percent of female college students reported that they had been raped—in most cases, by persons they knew (Koss et al., 1988). Clearly, these are frightening statistics. Perhaps even more unsettling, however, is the strong tendency of many persons to hold the victims of rape responsible for this crime (Fischer, 1986; Shotland & Goodstein, 1983). "She must have lead him on." "What was she doing in a bar or on the street at that hour of the night, anyway? She was asking for trouble!" These are the kind of comments frequently heard in conversations concerning media reports of rapes. From the perspective of attribution theory, in short, blame is often attributed to victims as much as, or even more than, to perpetrators. As you might guess, males are more likely to make such attributions than females (Cowan & Curtis, 1994); but women, too, often show some tendency to attribute responsibility for rape to its victims.

What accounts for this tendency? One possibility involves what has been termed *belief in a just world*—our desire to assume that the world is basically a fair place (Lerner, 1980). According to this reasoning, if a woman is sexually assaulted, then she "must" have done something to deserve it; thinking the opposite—that she is a completely blameless victim—is too threatening an idea for some persons to entertain. Put another way, believing that totally blameless persons can be made to suffer such degradation is very threatening, so some persons find comfort from such thoughts by concluding that rape victims are *not* blameless and must somehow have invited the assault.

Indirect support for this view is provided by the findings of a recent study conducted by Bell, Kuriloff, and Lottes (1994). These researchers asked male and female college students to read one of four descriptions of a rape. In two cases, the woman was attacked by a stranger. In two other incidents, the woman was raped by a date. After reading one of these incidents, participants were asked to rate the extent to which the victim was to blame for the crime. As you can see from Figure 2.11, both males and females blamed the victim to a greater extent when she knew the rapist (someone she dated) than when this person was a stranger. In addition, while males attributed greater blame to the victim than females, both genders seemed to hold her responsible, to some degree, for the assault.

These findings, and those of many other studies (e.g., Cowan & Curtis, 1994), have important implications with respect to rape prevention. First, they suggest that the victims of date rape—an alarmingly common event (Koss et al., 1988)—are especially likely to be blamed by other persons. Perhaps this

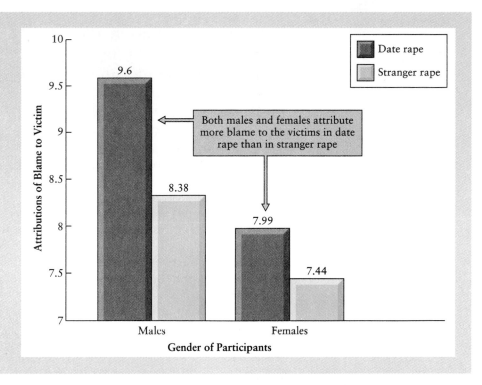

FIGURE 2.11

Attributions About Rape: Some Unsettling Findings. Both males and females blamed the victim of a rape to a greater extent when she knew the rapist (date rape) than when the rapist was a stranger.

(*Source:* Based on data from Bell, Kuriloff, & Lottes, 1994.)

is one reason why so many women who are assaulted by dates are reluctant to report this crime (Koss & Harvey, 1991). Second, the fact that men tend to blame rape victims to a greater extent than women is consistent with recent findings indicating that men—especially those who engage in sexual violence—often misinterpret female communication. Specifically, they are suspicious of, and mistrust, women's communication about sexual interest (Malamuth & Brown, 1994), so that they don't believe it when a woman says no. Obviously, such misperceptions can play a role in some instances of date rape: the woman declines sex in terms that she views as clear and definitive, but her refusals are misinterpreted by her date. To the extent such misperceptions contribute to date rape, it seems important for rape prevention programs to focus on eliminating their occurrence. In other words, programs that focus on improving communication between males and females with respect to sexual matters may prove quite effective. The development of such programs is already under way, but only time—and additional data—will reveal whether they are indeed helpful.

INTEGRATING PRINCIPLES

1. Because we are often interested not only in *what* other people do, but in *why* they do it, attribution is a key aspect of social perception.

2. The conclusions we reach about the causes of others' behavior can strongly influence our relations with them. Thus, attributions play an important role in many aspects of social behavior, including persuasion (Chapter 4), prejudice (Chapter 6), long-term relationships (Chapter 8), social influence (Chapter 9), and conflict (Chapter 11).

Impression Formation and Impression Management: The Process of Combining Social Information—and How, Sometimes, We Profit from It

First impressions, it is widely believed, are very important. Most of us assume that the initial impressions we make on others will shape the course of our future relations with them in crucial ways. Further, we believe that such impressions may be quite resistant to change once they are formed. It is for these reasons that most people prepare carefully for first dates, job interviews, and other situations in which they will meet others for the first time (see Figure 2.12). Are these assumptions about the nature of first impressions accurate? The answer provided by several decades of research is at least a qualified *yes:* first impressions *do* seem to exert a lasting effect on both social thought and social behavior (Anderson, 1981; Wyer et al., 1994).

But what, exactly, *are* first impressions? How are they formed? And what steps can we take to make sure that we make good first impressions on others? These are among the intriguing questions we'll now consider. Before turning to modern research on *impression formation* and *impression management,* however, we'll consider how this work got started, in what is without a doubt a major *Cornerstone* of social psychology.

Cornerstones of Social Psychology

ASCH'S RESEARCH ON CENTRAL AND PERIPHERAL TRAITS

As we have already seen, some aspects of social perception, such as attribution, require lots of hard mental work: it's not always easy to draw inferences about others' motives or traits from their behavior. In contrast, forming first impressions seems to be relatively effortless. As Solomon Asch (1946) put it in a classic paper on this topic: "We look at a person and immediately a certain impression of his character forms itself in us. A glance, a few spoken words are sufficient to tell us a story about a highly complex matter . . . " (1946, p. 258). How do we manage this feat? How, in short, do we form unified impressions of others in the quick (and some would say dirty!) way that we do? This is the basic question Asch investigated during a period when social psychology—like the rest of the world—attempted to pick up the pieces in the days immediately after World War II.

At the time Asch conducted his research, social psychologists were heavily influenced by the work of *Gestalt psychologists,* specialists in the field of perception. A basic principle of Gestalt psychology was "The whole is greater than the sum of its parts," which meant that what we perceive is often more than the sum of individual sensations. To illustrate this point for yourself, simply look at any painting. What you see is *not* individual splotches of paint on the canvas; rather, you perceive an integrated whole—a portrait, a landscape, a bowl of fruit—whatever the artist intended. In other words, Gestalt psychologists argued that each part of the world around us is interpreted, and understood, only in terms of its relationships to other parts or other stimuli.

FIGURE 2.12

First Impressions. *Although we use different techniques than Hagar, we too are usually concerned about making the right first impression on others.*

(*Source:* King Features, 1983.)

Asch applied these ideas to impression formation, suggesting (very tentatively, we might add) that we do *not* form impressions simply by adding together all of the traits we observe in other persons. Rather, we perceive these traits *in relation to one another*, so that the traits cease to exist individually and become, instead, part of an integrated, dynamic whole. How could these ideas—which became central to later efforts to understand impression formation—be tested? Asch, who got the ball rolling in several areas of social psychology, came up with an ingenious technique. He simply gave individuals lists of traits supposedly possessed by a stranger, and then asked them to indicate their impression of this person by checking the traits on a long list that they felt fit with their impression of the stranger. This technique was simple, but it quickly yielded some surprising results.

For example, in one study, participants read one of the following two lists:

intelligent—skillful—industrious—*warm*—determined—practical—cautious

intelligent—skillful—industrious—*cold*—determined—practical—cautious

As you can see, the lists differ only with respect to two words: *warm* and *cold*. Thus, if people form impressions merely by adding together individual traits, the impressions formed by persons exposed to these lists shouldn't differ very much. However, this was *not* the case. Persons who read the list containing *warm* were much more likely to view the stranger as generous, happy, good-natured, sociable, popular, and altruistic than were people who read the list containing *cold*. The words, *warm* and *cold,* Asch concluded, described *central traits*—ones that strongly shaped overall impressions of the stranger and colored the other adjectives in the lists. Asch obtained additional support for this view by substituting the words *polite* and *blunt* for *warm* and *cold*. When he did this, the effects on participants' impressions of the stranger were far weaker; *polite* and *blunt,* it appeared, were *not* central words with a strong impact on first impressions.

In further studies, Asch varied not the content but the *order* of adjectives on each list. For example, one group read the following list:

intelligent—industrious—impulsive—critical—stubborn—envious

Another group read:

envious—stubborn—critical—impulsive—industrious—intelligent

Here, the only difference was in the order of the words on the two lists. Yet, again, there were large differences in the impressions formed by participants. For example, while 32 percent of those who read the first list described the stranger as *happy,* only 5 percent of those who read the second list did so. Similarly, while 52 percent of those who read the first list described him as *humorous,* only 21 percent of those who read the second list used this adjective.

On the basis of many studies such as these, Asch concluded that forming impressions of others involves more than simply adding together individual traits. As he put it: "There is an attempt to form an impression of the *entire* person. . . . As soon as two or more traits are understood to belong to one person, they cease to exist as isolated traits, and come into immediate . . . interaction. . . . The subject perceives not this *and* that quality, but the two entering into a particular relation. . . ." (1946, p. 284). While research on impression formation has become far more sophisticated over the years since Asch's early work, both the methods Asch developed and many of his basic ideas about impression formation have withstood the test of time and are still reflected in studies being conducted today. Clearly, then, his research qualifies as an important *Cornerstone* of our field. ■ ■ ■

Impression Formation: A Cognitive Approach

Creative as it was, Asch's research was only the beginning where the study of **impression formation** (the process through which we form impressions of others) is concerned. Social psychologists have investigated this topic from several different perspectives for several decades. Initially, research on impression formation focused on the question of how we combine so much diverse information about others into unified impressions. One answer, suggested by early studies, was as follows: We combine this information into a *weighted average,* in which each piece of information about another person is weighted in terms of its relative importance (Anderson, 1981). Research conducted within this general framework then focused on identifying the factors

Impression Formation ■ The process through which we form impressions of others.

that influence this relative weighting. Among the most important factors identified were these: (1) the source of the input—information from sources we trust or admire is weighted more heavily than information from sources we distrust (Rosenbaum & Levin, 1969); (2) whether the information is positive or negative in nature—we tend to weight negative information about others more heavily than positive information (Mellers, Richards, & Birnbaum, 1992); (3) the extent to which the information describes behaviors or traits that are unusual or extreme—the more unusual, the greater the weight placed on information; and finally, as Asch found, (4) information received first tends to be weighted more heavily than information received later (this is known as a *primacy effect*).

While this research certainly added to our knowledge of impression formation, modern investigations of first impressions have adopted a very different approach. Drawing on basic knowledge of *social cognition*—the topic we'll consider in detail in Chapter 3—recent research has sought to understand impression formation in terms of the ways in which we notice, store, remember, and integrate social information (e.g., Wyer et al., 1994; Ruscher & Hammer, 1994). This cognitive approach has proved to be extremely productive, and has changed our basic ideas about how impressions are formed and changed. For example, it now seems clear that impressions of others involve both concrete examples of behaviors others have performed that are consistent with a given trait—*exemplars*—and mental summaries that are abstracted from repeated observations of others' behavior—*abstractions* (e.g., Klein, Loftus, & Plog, 1992; Smith & Zarate, 1992). Models of impression formation that stress the role of behavioral exemplars suggest that when we make judgments about others, we recall examples of their behavior and base our judgments—and our impressions—on these. For example, we recall that during our first conversation with a certain woman, she interrupted us repeatedly, made nasty comments about other people, and failed to hold open a door for someone whose arms were loaded with packages. The result: As we recall these pieces of information, we include the trait "inconsiderate" in our first impression of this person.

In contrast, models that stress the role of abstractions suggest that when we make judgments about others, we simply bring our previously formed abstractions to mind, and then use these as the basis for our impressions and our decisions. We recall that we have previously judged a person to be inconsiderate or considerate, friendly or unfriendly, optimistic or pessimistic, and combine these traits into an impression of this individual.

That both types of information—concrete examples of behavior and mental abstractions—play a role in impression formation is supported by a growing body of evidence (e.g., Klein and Loftus, 1993; Klein et al., 1992). In fact, it appears that the nature of impressions may shift as we gain increasing experience with others. At first, an impression consists largely of exemplars (behavioral examples); but later, as our experience with another person increases, our impression consists mainly of mental abstractions derived from observations of the person's behavior. Convincing evidence for this view is provided by research conducted by Sherman and Klein (1994).

These investigators exposed research participants either to a relatively small amount of information about another person or to a larger amount of information. In both cases, the information consisted of examples of behaviors by this person indicative of two different traits: intelligence and kindness. (An example of behavior indicative of kindness: "Bob stopped to let another car into the line of traffic"; An example of behavior indicative of intelligence: "Bob studies photography in his spare time"). After receiving this information, participants performed one of two different tasks. Some were asked to decide whether

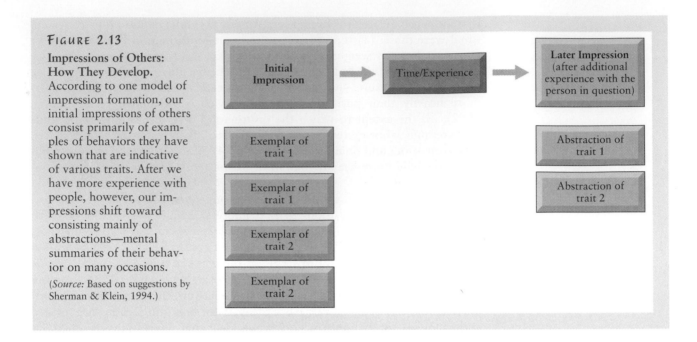

FIGURE 2.13

Impressions of Others: How They Develop.
According to one model of impression formation, our initial impressions of others consist primarily of examples of behaviors they have shown that are indicative of various traits. After we have more experience with people, however, our impressions shift toward consisting mainly of abstractions—mental summaries of their behavior on many occasions.

(*Source:* Based on suggestions by Sherman & Klein, 1994.)

various traits described the stranger (the *describe* task), while others were asked to define each trait (the *define* task). Finally, they performed a recall task in which they were asked to remember specific behaviors by the stranger. Sherman and Klein (1994) reasoned that if impressions consist largely of exemplars of behavior, then the task of deciding whether various traits described the stranger would activate these exemplars in memory and so would improve performance on the recall task: participants would recall these more quickly. However, if impressions consist largely of mental abstractions, the describe task would *not* facilitate later recall. Results indicated that for participants who received only a small amount of information about the stranger, the describe task *did* facilitate recall relative to the define task. However, for those who received a larger amount of information about the stranger, the describe task did *not* produce such effects (see Figure 2.13). These findings offer support for the view that at first, impressions of others consist mainly of concrete behavioral exemplars, but that later, they consist mainly of mental abstractions that have been extracted from experience.

In sum, existing evidence indicates that impression formation does not occur in a cognitive vacuum. On the contrary, mental frameworks representing our previous experience in many social situations, and basic cognitive processes relating to the storage, recall, and integration of social information, play a role in it. So, while the task of forming impressions often seems virtually effortless—remember Asch's words to this effect?—there's a lot going on beneath the surface as this process unfolds.

Impression Management: The Fine Art of Looking Good

Impression Management (self presentation) ■ Efforts by individuals to produce favorable impressions on others.

The desire to make a favorable impression on others is a strong one, so most of us do our best to "look good" to others when we meet them for the first time. Our efforts to make a good impression on others are known as **impression management** (or *self-presentation*), and growing evidence suggests that these efforts are well worth the trouble: persons who can perform impression management successfully do often gain important advantages in many situations (e.g., Schlenker, 1980; Wayne & Liden, 1995). What tactics do individuals use to create favorable impressions on others? And which of these are most successful? These are the issues we'll consider next.

Impression Management: Some Basic Tactics. As your own experience probably suggests, impression management takes many different forms. Most of these, however, seem to fall into two major categories: *self-enhancement*—efforts to boost our own image, and *other-enhancement*—efforts to make the target person feel good in our presence. As we'll see in Chapter 7, such positive feelings often play an important role in attraction and liking.

Specific tactics of *self-enhancement* include efforts to improve our own appearance. This can be accomplished through alterations in dress, through personal grooming (cosmetics, hairstyles, the use of perfume or cologne), and through the judicious use of nonverbal cues. Research findings indicate that all of these tactics work, at least under some conditions. For example, women who dress in a professional manner (business suit or dress, subdued jewelry) are often evaluated more favorably for management positions than women who dress in a more traditionally feminine manner (Forsythe, Drake, & Cox, 1985). Similarly, eyeglasses have been found to encourage impressions of intelligence, while long hair for women or beards for men tend to reduce such impressions (Terry & Krantz, 1993). And wearing perfume or cologne can enhance first impressions, provided this particular grooming aid is not overdone (Baron, 1983, 1986, 1989).

Most of these efforts to improve personal appearance are not potentially dangerous to the persons who use them. However, one type of effort to enhance personal appearance—developing a suntan—is potentially harmful (Broadstok, Borland, & Gason, 1991). Yet very large numbers of persons engage in such behavior, despite the fact that they are well acquainted with the risks. In fact, recent findings indicate that concern for one's appearance and the belief that having a tan enhances attractiveness appear to be the major predictors of "baking oneself in the sun"; concerns about the risk of skin cancer have much less effect on such behavior (Leary & Jones, 1993).

Other tactics of self-enhancement pose different kinds of risks. For instance, recent research by Sharp and Getz (1996) indicates that one reason why at least some young people consume alcohol is that it gives them the right "image." In other words, they engage in such behavior partly for purposes of impression management. In a carefully designed study on this topic, Sharp and Getz (1996) asked several hundred students to complete a questionnaire designed to measure their use of alcohol, their level of self-monitoring (especially, their motivation to gain others' approval), and their perceived success at impression-management. The researchers predicted that persons who used alcohol would be higher in self-monitoring and higher in perceived success at impression management than persons who did not. Their findings confirmed this. These findings offer support for the view that some people do drink alcohol as a tactic of impression management: to help look good in the eyes of others.

Turning to *other-enhancement,* individuals use many different tactics to induce positive moods and reactions in others. Among the most important of these tactics are *flattery*—heaping praise on target persons, even if they don't deserve it; expressing agreement with their views; showing a high degree of interest in them (hanging on their every word); doing small favors for them; asking for their advice and feedback (Morrison & Bies, 1991); and expressing liking for *them* either verbally or nonverbally (Wayne & Ferris, 1990). All of these tactics seem to work, at least to a degree. They cause target persons to experience positive reactions, and these, in turn, can elevate liking for, and impressions of, the persons who use such tactics.

Impression Management: To What Extent Does It Succeed?   Now for the key question: Are efforts to engage in impression management worthwhile? In other words, can they enhance the impressions we make upon others enough to make a difference in terms of their judgments of us or their behavior toward us? A large body of evidence suggests that they can: if used with skill and care, the tactics listed above can indeed be very helpful—at least to the persons who use them (Godfrey, Jones, & Lord, 1986; Kacmar, Delery, & Ferris, 1992). Convincing evidence for this conclusion—and for the view that impression management can influence important judgments based on impressions of others—is provided by a study conducted by Wayne and Liden (1995).

These researchers arranged for persons recently hired for staff positions at two large universities to complete questionnaires in which they reported on how frequently they had used various impression management tactics during their first six weeks on the job. At the same time, the supervisors of these employees completed questionnaires in which they rated their liking for and their degree of similarity to these newly hired subordinates. Then, six months later, supervisors rated the performance of the new employees. Results indicated that impression management really did pay off for this group of persons. Specifically, the greater the extent to which the new employees engaged in other-enhancement (supervisor-focused) tactics of impression management, the more their supervisors viewed them as similar to themselves. Further, the more the employees engaged in self-enhancing tactics, the more their supervisors liked them. Most important, increased liking and feeling of similarity were strong predictors of performance ratings: the more supervisors liked their subordinates and felt similar to them, the higher they rated their performance (see Figure 2.14).

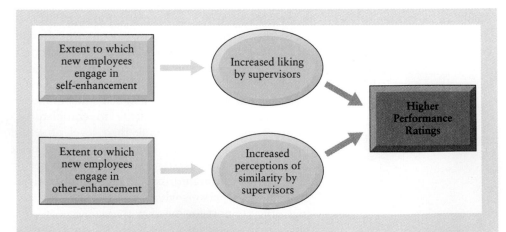

FIGURE 2.14

Impression Management: Evidence That It Really Works.   The greater the extent to which newly hired employees engaged in self-enhancing tactics, the more their supervisors liked them; and the more they engaged in other-enhancing tactics, the more their supervisors viewed them as similar to themselves. Increased liking and feelings of similarity, in turn, boosted employees' performance ratings.

(*Source:* Based on data from Wayne & Liden, 1995.)

These findings and those of many other related studies (e.g., Wayne & Kacmar, 1991; Paulhus, Bruce, & Trapnell, 1995) indicate that impression management tactics often do succeed in enhancing the appeal of persons who use them. Given this fact, should *you* resort to such procedures? In all probability, you already apply some of them in your daily life. Who does *not* try to look their best when meeting others for the first time? Whether you should seek to get ahead in life through calculated use of impression management tactics, however, depends on the extent to which you feel comfortable with such a strategy. Social psychologists can study impression management systematically and can help identify its most successful tactics; but the decision as to whether to put these tactics to use is an ethical one that individuals must reach for themselves.

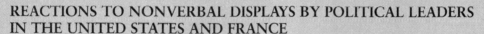

Social Diversity: A Critical Analysis

REACTIONS TO NONVERBAL DISPLAYS BY POLITICAL LEADERS IN THE UNITED STATES AND FRANCE

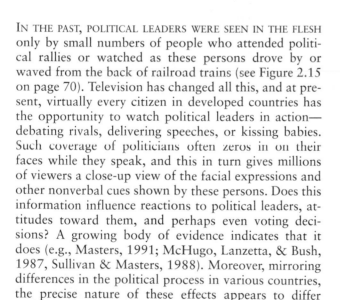

IN THE PAST, POLITICAL LEADERS WERE SEEN IN THE FLESH only by small numbers of people who attended political rallies or watched as these persons drove by or waved from the back of railroad trains (see Figure 2.15 on page 70). Television has changed all this, and at present, virtually every citizen in developed countries has the opportunity to watch political leaders in action—debating rivals, delivering speeches, or kissing babies. Such coverage of politicians often zeros in on their faces while they speak, and this in turn gives millions of viewers a close-up view of the facial expressions and other nonverbal cues shown by these persons. Does this information influence reactions to political leaders, attitudes toward them, and perhaps even voting decisions? A growing body of evidence indicates that it does (e.g., Masters, 1991; McHugo, Lanzetta, & Bush, 1987, Sullivan & Masters, 1988). Moreover, mirroring differences in the political process in various countries, the precise nature of these effects appears to differ across different cultures.

Perhaps the most revealing information on such cross-cultural differences is that reported by Masters and his colleagues (e.g., Masters, 1991; Masters & Sullivan, 1989) in a series of studies conducted in the United States and France. In these experiments, participants are shown videotapes of well-known political leaders—Ronald Reagan, Jacques Chirac—delivering speeches or debating with other candidates. These segments are carefully chosen to show the leaders demonstrating three contrasting kinds of facial expressions: happiness/reassurance, anger/threat, and fear/evasion. Before watching the tapes, participants report on their political attitudes and party affiliation. Immediately after watching each taped

excerpt, participants rate the leaders' behavior, and then report on their own emotional reactions to the leaders.

Careful analysis of these ratings indicates, first, that French and American participants distinguish between these three types of facial expression equally well, and that they tend to react to them in much the same manner. Specifically, they generally report more positive reactions to facial expression showing happiness/reassurance than to ones showing fear/evasion or anger/threat. There is one interesting difference, however: French participants react significantly more favorably to facial expressions showing anger/threat. Apparently, because of cultural differences, they find such expressions more appropriate for political candidates than do Americans.

Other intriguing cultural differences arise with respect to the extent to which political attitudes and party affiliation influence viewers' reactions to the candidates' nonverbal cues. In the United States, there are only two major political parties. As a result, both cover a wide range of political opinion. In France, in contrast, there are many parties, so each one tends to reflect a fairly specific set of views; each party, in other words, occupies a well-defined and fairly narrow location on the left–right political spectrum. These differences in the political process lead to the following intriguing predictions. In France, viewers' political attitudes would probably be more predictive of their reactions to political candidates' than the candidates' nonverbal cues, while in the United States, the opposite would be true. Why? Because in France, each candidate is identified with a specific set of positions and a particular spot on the political spectrum. Thus, viewers would pay careful attention to this information, and less attention to candidates' personal char-

FIGURE 2.15

Watching Political Leaders: Then and Now. In the past, only a relatively small number of persons could have firsthand exposure to political leaders and their nonverbal cues. Modern technology has changed all this, however, and today almost every citizen can see close-ups of the faces of political leaders as they deliver speeches or engage in debates.

acteristics or behaviors. In the United States, in contrast, political candidates go out of their way to represent many different groups, and are not so clearly linked to a specific political ideology. As a result, viewers focus to a greater extent on their personal traits and behaviors. The results of several studies (Masters & Sullivan, 1989, 1990) offer support for these predictions.

In sum, it seems clear that nonverbal cues play an important role in reactions to political leaders across different cultures. However, the precise nature of these effects varies with the political process in different countries, and with norms indicating what kinds of nonverbal displays are or are not appropriate in public settings. This finding, in turn, provides us with yet another illustration of the complex interplay between seemingly universal human tendencies and specific cultural factors in the determination of social behavior and social thought. ■ ■ ■

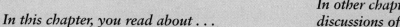

CONNECTIONS: Integrating Social Psychology

In this chapter, you read about . . .	*In other chapters, you will find related discussions of . . .*
basic channels of nonverbal communication	the role of nonverbal cues in mutual liking (Chapter 7), and in charismatic leadership (Chapter 12)
theories of attribution	the role of attribution in persuasion (Chapter 4), social identity and self-perception (Chapter 5), and the role of attribution in prejudice (Chapter 6), prosocial behavior (Chapter 10), aggression (Chapter 11), and in conflict (Chapter 11)
first impressions and impression management	the role of first impressions in interpersonal attraction (Chapter 7), and the role of impression management in job interviews (Chapter 13)

Thinking About Connections

1. As we will discuss in Chapters 4 (Attitudes) and 9 (Social Influence), influence is an important fact of social life: Each day, we attempt to change others' attitudes or behavior and they attempt to change ours. Having read about attribution in this chapter, do you think that influence attempts that conceal their true goal will be more successful than ones that do not? If so, why? If not, why?

2. In Chapter 11 (Aggression), we'll see that some persons experience much more than their fair share of aggressive encounters. Such persons, it appears, are lacking in basic social skills, such as the ability to accurately "read" other nonverbal cues. On the basis of the discussion of nonverbal cues in this chapter, can you explain how this could contribute to their problems with respect to aggression?

3. Suppose you were preparing for an important job interview (see Chapter 13). On the basis of information presented in this chapter, what steps could you take to improve your chances of actually getting the job?

4. Suppose you meet two persons for the first time and quickly conclude that you like one but don't like the other. Now, imagine you arrange to meet these people again and both are late. Will you be more annoyed with one than the other? Will you assume different possible causes for their being late? In other words, will your contrasting impressions of these persons influence your later thinking about them (Chapter 3)?

Summary and Review

Nonverbal Communication

Social perception is the process through which we attempt to understand other persons. To obtain information about the temporary causes of others' behavior (e.g., their emotions or feelings), we focus on *nonverbal cues*. These are provided by others' facial expressions, eye contact, body posture or movements, and touching. Although *display rules* concerning when and how individuals should demonstrate their emotions differ from culture to culture, evidence suggests that some aspects of nonverbal communication—for example, facial expressions—are fairly universal around the world and across many cultures. Individuals differ greatly in terms of *emotional expressiveness*—the extent to which they show outward displays of emotion; and these differences are related both to social behavior and to personal psychological adjustment. Through the use of nonverbal cues, we can often tell when others are attempting to deceive us.

Attribution: Understanding the Causes of Others' Behavior

Knowledge about the lasting causes of others' behavior is acquired through *attribution*. In this process, we infer others' traits, motives, and intentions from observation of their behavior, being careful to focus on those aspects of behavior that are most likely to be revealing in this regard. In order to determine whether others' behavior stems mainly from internal or external causes, we focus on information relating to *consensus, consistency,* and *distinctiveness*. However, we engage this kind of careful causal analysis only under some circumstances—for example, when others behave in unexpected ways. Attributions are affected by *discounting*—a tendency to discount one potential cause of behavior when other possible causes are also present, and by *augmenting*—a tendency to emphasize the importance of factors that might cause a specific behavior when that behavior actually occurs despite the presence of other factors that might prevent it. Attribution is subject to several forms of error, including the *fundamental attribution error,* the *actor–observer effect,* and the *self-serving bias*. Attribution theory has been applied to a wide range of practical problems. For example, it has proved very helpful in efforts to devise effective treatments for depression, and it has shed important light on why the victims of rape are often blamed for these assaults.

Impression Formation and Impression Management

Common sense seems to be correct in suggesting that first impressions are important. Early views of impression formation viewed this process as one in which information about others is combined into a weighted average. More recent research, however, has stressed the cognitive processes that play a role in impression formation. The findings of such research suggest, for example, that impressions of others involve memories of specific behaviors they have performed, as well as abstractions derived from observing their behavior on many occasions. Individuals engage in many tactics to make favorable impressions on others, but most of these tactics of *impression management* fall into two categories: *self-enhancement,* which includes efforts to enhance one's personal appearance, and *other-enhancement,* which involves efforts to induce positive feelings or reactions in target persons. Growing evidence suggests that impression management often succeeds in its major goal: producing a favorable impression on another person.

Social Diversity: Reactions to Nonverbal Displays by Political Leaders in the United States and France

In the past, relatively few persons could see the nonverbal cues emitted by political leaders in a firsthand manner. Modern technology, however, allows almost all citizens to see close-up views of the faces of political candidates. Studies comparing the reactions to such cues of viewers in the United States and France indicate that cultural factors play an important role in this process. For example, French viewers react more favorably than American viewers to facial expressions by candidates showing anger/threat. In addition, French viewers' reactions to candidates' nonverbal cues are more strongly affected by the viewers' political attitudes and party identification. These findings indicate that reactions to leaders' nonverbal cues involve a complex interaction between basic human tendencies and specific cultural factors.

■ Key Terms

Actor–Observer Effect (p. 58)

Attribution (p. 50)

Augmenting Principle (p. 56)

Body Language (p. 44)

Consensus (p. 53)

Consistency (p. 54)

Correspondent Inference (theory of) (p. 50)

Discounting Principle (p. 56)

Distinctiveness (p. 54)

Emotional Expressiveness (p. 47)

Fundamental Attribution Error (p. 57)

Impression Formation (p. 64)

Impression Management (self-presentation) (p. 66)

Microexpressions (p. 49)

Noncommon Effects (p. 51)

Nonverbal Communication (p. 39)

Self-Serving Bias (p. 59)

Social Perception (p. 38)

Staring (p. 43)

■ For More Information

Kenny, D. A. (1994). *Interpersonal perception: A social relations analysis.* New York: Guilford.

This well-written and relatively brief book provides an excellent overview of what social psychologists have discovered about many different aspects of interpersonal perception. The book focuses on the key questions of how we see other people, how we see ourselves, and how we think we are seen by others. All in all, a very thoughtful and useful volume.

Martin, L. L., & Tesser, B. (Eds.). (1992). *The construction of social judgments.* Hillsdale, NJ: Erlbaum.

Examines many aspects of how we make judgments about others. The chapters on impression formation and the role of moods and emotions in social judgments are especially relevant to this chapter.

Malandro, L. A., Barker, L., & Barker, D. A. (1994). *Nonverbal communication* (3rd ed). New York: Random House.

A basic and very readable text that examines all aspects of nonverbal communication. Body movements and gestures, facial expression, eye contact, touching, smell, and voice characteristics are among the topics considered.

CHAPTER 3

SOCIAL COGNITION: Thinking about Others and the Social World

Lisa Houck, *Can't Explain*, 1994, watercolor, 6 × 9"

Chapter Outline

FIGURE 3.1

Understanding the Social World: No Easy Task! *As these youngsters are beginning to realize, understanding the social world is a very complex task.*

(*Source:* Universal Press Syndicate, 1987.)

How many times each day do you think about other persons? Your answer may well be "Who can keep count?" because in fact, other persons occupy our attention many times each day—from the moment we open our eyes in the morning until we close them and go to sleep at night. And even then, people are often the focus of those private, internal videos we call dreams. What do we think about where other people are concerned? Partly, we try to understand them by identifying their major traits and the causes behind their behavior—by figuring out why they do or say what they do. As you'll certainly recall, we examined these aspects of social thought in Chapter 2. Thinking about others, however, involves much more than this. When we interact with other persons, we acquire a tremendous amount of information about them—how they look, what they say, what they do. Somehow we must sort this information and enter parts of it—those portions that seem most useful—into memory. And later, we must combine this previously stored information about others in order to make judgments about them, predict their future actions, and draw inferences about their behavior (Fiske, 1993). It is only by accomplishing these tasks that we can make sense out of the social world in which we live—a world that, we learn quite early in life, is anything but simple (see Figure 3.1).

What is such **social cognition** like? Is it accurate or subject to many errors? And how, given its obvious complexity, do we manage to accomplish social cognition so effortlessly much of the time? Research by social psychologists on these and related questions has yielded findings that are frequently as surprising as they are fascinating. A few samples, to whet your appetite for what follows:

Why are people often overoptimistic in predicting when they'll complete various tasks?

Does thinking too much get us confused and interfere with our ability to make accurate judgments?

Do our mental images of "the kind of person who . . . [smokes, takes risks, uses drugs, gets pregnant]" influence our behavior?

Do our expectations about various events or experiences shape our reactions to them when they actually occur?

After being exposed to persons we find highly attractive, do we feel more dissatisfied with our own romantic relationships?

We'll examine these and many other intriguing questions in the pages that follow. Specifically, our discussion of social cognition will proceed as follows. First, we'll examine two basic components of social thought—*schemas* and *prototypes*. These are mental structures or frameworks that allow us to organize large amounts of diverse information in an efficient manner (Fiske & Taylor, 1991). Once formed, however, these frameworks exert strong effects on social thought—effects that are not always beneficial from the standpoint of accuracy. Second, we'll turn to several shortcuts and strategies we use to help us in our ef-

Social Cognition ■ The manner in which we interpret, analyze, remember, and use information about the social world.

forts to make sense out of the social world. A basic finding of research on social cognition is that generally, we try to accomplish this task with the least amount of effort possible—in part because we often find ourselves having to deal with more information than we can readily handle (Macrae, Milne, & Bodenhausen, 1994). Mental shortcuts and strategies that we adopt allow us to cope with this state of affairs and to make sense out of the complex social world in an efficient manner. Such shortcuts often succeed—but, as we'll soon see, only to a degree and only at some cost to accuracy. Third, we'll examine several tendencies or "tilts" in social thought, tendencies that cause us to pay more attention to some kinds of input than to others and, therefore, to reach conclusions that are different, and sometimes less accurate, than would otherwise be the case. The discussion of these effects will emphasize another basic principle established by research on social cognition: while we are certainly impressive social-information processors, we are definitely *not* perfect in this respect. On the contrary, our social thought is often far less rational, reasonable, and accurate than we would like to believe (e.g., Denes-Raj & Epstein, 1994; Epstein, in press). Finally, we will examine the complex interplay between **affect**—our current feelings or moods—and various aspects of social cognition. This relationship is indeed a two-way street, with feelings influencing cognition and cognition, in turn, shaping affect (e.g., Forgas, 1994a). Please note: Another key aspect of social cognition—our efforts to understand *ourselves*—will be discussed in Chapter 5.

Schemas and Prototypes: Mental Frameworks for Holding—and Using—Social Information

Suppose that you are at a party and that you start talking to another person. As you do, you notice that she or he continues to look around the room and only half listens to what you are saying. Will it take you long to figure out what's going on? Probably not. You'll quickly realize that this person does not find you interesting or attractive and is looking for an excuse to make a quick exit. How are you able to reach such conclusions so quickly and easily? Part of the answer involves the fact that you have been in many other situations like this one; as a result of those experiences, you have built up a kind of mental framework for understanding such situations and others' behavior in them. These frameworks, or **schemas,** contain information relevant to specific situations or events and, once established, help us interpret these situations and what's happening in them. For example, in this situation, you may have a schema for "meeting people at parties," containing information on how people behave in this context, and how they signal liking—or boredom—to each other. When your schema for such encounters is activated, it lets you decide, quickly and effortlessly, that you are probably wasting your time with this person. As we'll soon see, schemas exert powerful effects on several aspects of social cognition, and therefore on our behavior as well.

Now let's consider a related concept: **prototypes.** Prototypes constitute another type of mental framework that we use to interpret the social world. Basically, prototypes involve models of the typical qualities of members of some group or category. For example, you probably have prototypes for *leaders,* for *sports heroes/heroines,* for *criminals,* and for countless other social categories. In a sense, prototypes describe the truly typical member of such categories—the "pattern" to which we compare new persons as we meet them, in order to determine if they do or do not fit into the category. When they fit quite well, we can readily place them in various categories. When they do not, the situation is more

Affect ■ Our current feelings and moods.

Schemas ■ Mental frameworks containing information relevant to specific situations or events, which, once established, help us interpret these situations and what's happening in them.

Prototypes ■ Mental models of the typical qualities of members of some group or category.

puzzling. For example, suppose you met a young woman who told you that she climbed mountains as a hobby and who was dressed in very flashy clothes. When you discovered that she was an accountant, you would probably be surprised. The reason is simple: she does not seem to fit well with the prototype of *accountant* that you have built up through past experience (see Figure 3.2). Prototypes, too, exert important effects on social thought and, as we'll see in the *Applied Side* section on p. 80, on important aspects of social behavior as well.

Now that we've defined schemas and prototypes, let's take a closer look at the role they play in social cognition.

Types of Schemas: Persons, Roles, and Events

Let's return to the party mentioned above. Suppose that the stranger you met who was so obviously bored with you had these characteristics: this person was very physically attractive, was dressed in extremely stylish clothes, and was sporting large diamonds on both ears. Would this help you to interpret his or her behavior? In all likelihood it would, because you already have a well-established *person schema* for individuals like this one: a schema for the *supercool*. Person schemas are mental frameworks suggesting that certain traits and behaviors go together and that individuals having them represent a certain *type*. Once such a schema comes into operation, you don't have to think very long or hard about why this stranger is bored with you: you aren't supercool yourself and rarely have much success with this kind of person. When the stranger walks off, therefore, you aren't very surprised.

FIGURE 3.2

Prototypes: Mental Representations of What Is "Typical." We possess many *prototypes*—mental models of the typical qualities of members of some group or category. When, as in this photo, individuals don't fit these prototypes, we are greatly surprised.

This isn't the only kind of schema we have, however. In addition, we have schemas relating to specific social roles—*role schemas*. These schemas contain information about how persons playing specific roles generally act, and what they are like. For example, consider your role schema for *professors*. You expect professors to stand in front of the room; to talk about the topic of the course; to answer questions from students, prepare exams, and so on. You *don't* expect them to try to sell you a product or to do magic tricks; such actions are definitely not part of your role schema for *professor.*

A third type of schema involves mental frameworks relating to specific situations. Such schemas relate to events, or sequences of events, and are known as *scripts.* They indicate what is expected to happen in a given setting. For example, when you walk into a restaurant, you expect someone to greet you and either lead you to a seat or put your name on a list. Then you expect a server to come to your table to offer drinks and to take your order. Next on the agenda is the appearance of the food, followed, ultimately, by the bill (see Figure 3.3). Think how surprised you'd be if instead of following this orderly and expected sequence of events, the server sat down at your table and began a friendly conversation; or if this person announced, after bringing your food, "Sorry, I've got to leave now." Scripts, like other schemas, provide us with a mental scaffold: a structure for understanding social information in the context of information we already have. Once established, scripts save us a great deal of mental effort, because they tell us what to expect, how other persons are likely to behave, and what will happen next in a wide range of social situations. (We'll consider another, and very important, type of schema—the *self-schema*—in Chapter 5.)

The Impact of Schemas on Social Cognition: Attention, Encoding, Retrieval

How do schemas influence social thought? Research findings suggest that they exert strong effects on three processes that are a basic part of social cognition—and of all cognition: attention, encoding, and retrieval. *Attention* refers to what information we notice; clearly, we are more likely to notice some things about other persons and their actions than others. *Encoding* refers to the processes through which

FIGURE 3.3

Scripts: Schemas That Tell Us "What Should Happen Next." When you go to a restaurant, you have a *script* for the events that should occur and the order in which they should take place. The activity shown here fits this schema. If a waitperson sat down at the table with you, however, this action would *not* fit your schema.

information, once it is noticed, gets stored in memory. Again, not everything we notice about the social world is stored for future use. For example, I've sometimes asked students in my own classes to name my coauthor on this book (Donn Byrne). Although they see this name every time they pick up the book, many can't answer: this information has not been entered into their long-term memory. Finally, *retrieval* refers to the processes through which we recover information from memory in order to use it in some manner—for example, in making judgments about other people, such as whether they would make a good roommate.

Schemas have been found to influence all of these basic aspects of social cognition (Wyer & Srull, 1994). With respect to attention, we often notice information or events inconsistent with existing schemas to a greater extent than information or events that are consistent with these schemas. This is not surprising, since schemas tell us what to expect, and it is usually *unexpected* events or actions that often draw our attention. For example, if your dentist tells you to sit down and open your mouth, you don't pay much attention to her actions. If she stands away from the chair and begins to sing loudly, however, you will certainly notice *that* behavior; it doesn't fit with your *script* (event schema) for this situation.

Turning to encoding, the effects of schemas are a bit more complex. Existing evidence indicates that once schemas have been formed, information consistent with them is easier to remember than information that is inconsistent. However, earlier in the process, when schemas are first being formed, information *inconsistent* with them may be more readily noticed, and thus encoded (e.g., Stangor & Ruble, 1989). Finally, schemas also influence what information is retrieved from memory. In particular, to the extent schemas are activated when we are trying to recall some information, they determine what information is actually brought to mind—in general, information that is part of these schemas or at least consistent with them (e.g., Conway & Ross, 1984).

In sum, schemas influence many aspects of social cognition. And since social thought is intimately related to social behavior, they play an important role in many forms of social interaction, too. We'll examine some of these effects in Chapter 4, where we'll see that *attitudes* often function as schemas, and in Chapter 6, where we'll examine the role of *stereotypes*, another form of schema, in prejudice and discrimination. Right now, however, we'll turn, in the *Applied Side* section below, to the impact of *prototypes* on an extremely important form of social behavior—safe sex.

Social Psychology: On the Applied Side
PROTOTYPES AND SAFE SEX: Living Up (or Down) to the Images in Our Minds

Quick: What kind of person smokes? Can you name several traits that, presumably, characterize the typical smoker? Probably you can, because many people possess a well-developed prototype for this social category. Depending on what ads you've seen and other experiences you have with the category "smokers," you might describe such persons as "cool, attractive, exciting," or "addicted, self-destructive, rash." Now, do you think that the nature of your "smoker" prototype—the traits it contains—might influence your own tendency to smoke? Growing evidence suggests that this may be the case. Apparently, the more favorable our prototypes of various social categories or groups, the more willing we are to behave like these people—for example, to smoke, if our prototype of smokers is like the first one (cool, attractive, exciting; Gibbons et al., 1991). Strong evidence for such effects has recently been reported by Gibbons, Gerrard, and McCoy (1995) in research dealing with another form of behavior with important consequences: engaging in risky sexual activity.

These researchers reasoned that many teenagers have prototypes for teenage girls who get pregnant and the males who are responsible for such pregnancies. Further, the researchers suggested that to the extent these prototypes are favorable and to the extent teenagers perceive themselves as similar to the prototypes, they may be more willing to engage in unprotected sex themselves. To test these predictions, Gibbons and his colleagues asked hundreds of thirteen- and fourteen-year-old girls and boys to rate the extent to which various adjectives described teenage girls who get pregnant or the boyfriends who get them pregnant. Some of the adjectives were favorable (sophisticated, cool, popular, intelligent), while others were unfavorable (careless, unattractive, confused). Participants' ratings indicated the favorability of their prototypes for pregnant teenagers and their boyfriends. In addition, individuals rated the extent to which they felt that they were similar to these persons—that is, to pregnant teenage girls and the fathers of their babies.

Finally, the teenagers rated their own willingness to have unprotected sex with their boyfriend or girlfriend. It was predicted that the more favorable their prototypes of pregnant teenage girls and their boyfriends, and the more similar they felt to these prototypes, the greater willingness participants would report to engage in risky sex. Results strongly confirmed these predictions, for both females and males (see Figure 3.4). Indeed, those participants who held favorable prototypes and viewed themselves as similar to the prototypes were most willing of all to engage in unprotected sex. In short, the more favorable the prototypes held by participants, the more likely they were to engage in behaviors that would convert these mental frameworks into reality in their own lives.

In our view, these findings have important practical implications. At the present time, many television shows and movies portray favorably behavior that can only be described as highly irresponsible and risky. Characters—many of them young—are shown engaging in unprotected sex with persons they have just met and about whom they know virtually nothing. Further, the negative consequences of such behavior, including the risk of serious illness and unplanned pregnancies,

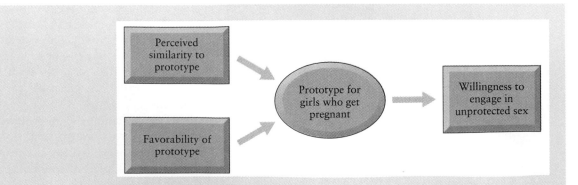

FIGURE 3.4

Prototypes and Social Behavior: The Effects Can Be Important. The more favorable individuals' prototypes for teenagers who get pregnant and the more similar they see themselves as being to these prototypes, the more likely they are to engage in unprotected sex. This is a dramatic illustration of how prototypes can exert important effects on social behavior.

(*Source:* Based on data from Gibbons, Gerrard, & McCoy, 1995.)

are minimized or ignored. To the extent such programs and movies encourage the development of favorable prototypes for risky and irresponsible behavior, they may be doing a strong disservice to young people. As we'll note again in Chapters 6 and 11, the mass media do not merely reflect societal trends: they sometimes shape them as well. And in our view, to the extent the media encourage young persons to expose themselves to serious risks that may adversely affect the rest of their lives, they are not serving as a force for positive social change. ■ ■■

INTEGRATING PRINCIPLES

1. Through experience, we acquire *schemas*—mental frameworks containing information relevant to specific situations or events, and *prototypes*—mental representations of the typical members of various groups.

2. Once formed, these mental frameworks help us to understand other persons and events occurring in social situations. They strongly affect what social information we notice (attention), store in memory (encoding), and later remember (retrieval). Thus, they have powerful effects on social behavior in many different settings.

3. Attitudes (which we'll consider in Chapter 4) and stereotypes (which we'll examine in Chapter 6) often function as schemas, and both exert strong effects on important forms of social behavior.

Heuristics: Mental Shortcuts in Social Cognition

Earlier, we called attention to a basic principle of social cognition: in general, we expend the least possible amount of effort in thinking about other persons and the social world. This is hardly surprising because as you know from your own experience, thinking is often very hard work. Our tendency to exert minimal effort in this respect, however, is also related to another basic fact of social life: we have *limited* rather than unlimited cognitive resources. In fact, we often find ourselves in the situation of having more demands on these resources than we have resources available—a situation known as **information overload.** If you've ever tried to talk on the phone while cooking, or to hold a conversation while driving in heavy traffic, you know what we mean about limited cognitive resources, and how frustrating—or even dangerous—it can be to try to do more than we can handle at one time.

To help stretch our cognitive resources, we employ many strategies. These are designed to reduce our cognitive effort and decrease the possibility of information overload. To be successful, such strategies must meet two requirements: they must provide a quick and simple way of dealing with large amounts of social information, and they must work—they must be reasonably accurate much of the time.

Many potential shortcuts for reducing mental effort exist, but among these perhaps the most useful are **heuristics**—simple rules for making complex decisions or drawing complex inferences in a rapid manner. We'll now examine two such heuristics that are used frequently in everyday life.

Representativeness: Judging by Resemblance

Suppose that you have just met your next-door neighbor for the first time. While chatting with her, you notice that she dresses in a conservative manner,

Information Overload ■ Situation in which our ability to process information is exceeded by the amount of information available.

Heuristics ■ Rules or principles that allow us to make social judgments rapidly and with reduced effort.

is very neat in her personal habits, has a very large library in her home, and has a gentle, shy manner. Later, you realize that she never mentioned what she does for a living. Is she a business executive, a physician, a waitress, an attorney, a dancer, or a librarian? One quick way of making a guess is to compare her with other members of each of these occupations. How well does she resemble persons you have in each of these fields? If you proceed in this manner, you may well conclude that she is a librarian. After all, her traits seem to resemble those that many people associate with librarians more than the traits associated with dancers, executives, or physicians. If you made your judgment about her occupation in this manner, you would be using the **representativeness heuristic.** In other words, you would make your judgment on the basis of a relatively simple rule: *The more similar an individual is to "typical" members of a given group, the more likely she or he is to belong to that group.*

Are such judgments accurate? Often they are, because belonging to certain groups does affect the behavior and mannerisms of persons in them, and because persons with certain characteristics or "styles" are attracted to particular groups in the first place. But sometimes judgments based on representativeness are wrong. Some librarians are extroverted and lead exciting social lives; some dancers are shy and read lots of books. One professor I know well is a licensed pilot and sky-dives as a hobby! Because of such exceptions, the representativeness heuristic, although useful, can lead to serious errors in at least some instances. In addition, reliance on this heuristic can cause us to overlook other types of information that may potentially be very useful. The most important type is information relating to *base rates*—the frequency with which given events or patterns occur in the general population. Our tendency to overlook such information when relying on the representativeness heuristic is illustrated quite clearly by a famous study performed by Tversky and Kahneman (1973).

Participants in this investigation were told that an imaginary person named Jack had been selected from a group of one hundred men. They were then asked to guess the probability that Jack was an engineer. Some participants were told that thirty of the one hundred men were engineers (the base rate for engineers was 30 percent). Others were told that seventy of the men were engineers. Half of the participants received no further information. The others, however, were also given a personal description of Jack that either resembled or did not resemble the common stereotype of engineers (e.g., they are practical, like to work with numbers, and so on). When participants received only information relating to base rates, their estimates of the likelihood that Jack was an engineer reflected this information. They thought it more likely that Jack was an engineer when the base rate was 70 percent than when it was 30 percent. When participants received personal information about Jack, however, they tended to ignore the important base rate information. They made their estimates primarily on the basis of whether Jack seemed to resemble their stereotype of an engineer. In sum, participants tended to overlook a valuable form of information when they operated in terms of representativeness. This tendency to ignore useful base rate information is known as the **base rate fallacy,** and we'll meet it again at several points in this chapter.

Availability: What Comes to Mind First?

Which are more common: words that start with the letter *k* (e.g., king) or words with *k* as the third letter (e.g., awkward)? In English, there are more than twice as many words with *k* in third place as there are with *k* in first place. Yet despite this fact, when asked this question a majority of persons guess incorrectly: they assume that there are more words beginning with *k* (Tversky & Kahneman, 1982). Why? In part, because of the operation of another heuristic—the **availability heuristic.** According to this heuristic, the easier it is to bring in-

Representativeness Heuristic ■ Strategy for making judgments based on the extent to which current stimuli or events resemble other stimuli or categories.

Base Rate Fallacy ■ Tendency to ignore or underutilize information relating to base rates—the relative frequency with which events or stimuli actually occur.

Availability Heuristic ■ Strategy for making judgments on the basis of how easily specific kinds of information can be brought to mind.

stances of some group, category, or event to mind, the more prevalent or important these are judged to be. This heuristic, too, makes good sense: events or objects that are common *are* usually easier to think of than ones that are less common. But relying on availability in making such judgments can also lead to errors such as the one involving words with the letter *k*. Here's another example: Two students actually participate equally in class discussions. However, one of them dresses in an unusual style, while the other does not. When the professor sits down to make up grades, the student with the unusual style of dress comes to mind more readily. On this basis, the professor concludes—falsely—that this student has contributed more during the semester. In this and many other situations, the fact that information is easy to remember does *not* guarantee that it is more important or more common. Yet our subjective feeling that something is easy to bring to mind may lead us to assume that it is important (Schwarz et al., 1991). In such cases, the availability heuristic reduces our cognitive effort but may also cause us to reach erroneous conclusions. Since information that is easier to remember *is* often more important or prevalent, however, the availability heuristic is useful in many contexts, and we do often use it—with some very interesting effects, which we'll now consider.

The False Consensus Effect: Availability and the Tendency to Assume That Others Think As We Do. The first of these effects of our reliance on availability is known as the **false consensus effect,** and relates to our tendency to assume that other persons share our views or preferences to a greater extent than is actually true. In other words, we assume that others are more like us than is actually the case. This tendency has been observed in many different contexts. For example, smokers tend to overestimate the proportion of other persons who smoke; and students overestimate the proportion of other students who share their attitudes about drugs, abortion, seat belt use, and politics (Sherman, Presson, & Chassin, 1984; Suls, Wan, & Sanders, 1988).

What is the basis for this tendency to assume that others think as we do? Two factors seem to play a role. First, most people want to believe that others agree with them, because this enhances their confidence in their own judgments, actions, or lifestyle (Marks & Miller, 1987). Second, this tendency seems to stem, at least in part, from reliance on the availability heuristic. Some people, at least, find it easier to notice and later remember instances in which others agreed with them than instances in which they disagreed. In addition, since most of us tend to choose as friends and associates others who share our views (see Chapter 7), we are actually exposed to many instances of such agreement. This, too, leads to higher availability of agreement than of disagreement and contributes to the occurrence of the false consensus effect.

While the false consensus effect is common, it is far from universal. It is comforting to assume that others share our attitudes and perhaps even our undesirable attributes (such as the inability to resist everyday temptations). For highly desirable attributes, however, people may be motivated to perceive themselves as unique (e.g., Suls & Wan, 1987). In such instances, the false consensus effect may fail to occur (Campbell, 1986).

Priming: Some Effects of Increased Availability. During the first year of medical school, many students experience what is known as the "medical student syndrome." They begin to suspect that they or their friends or families are suffering from serious illnesses. An ordinary headache may cause them to wonder if they have a brain tumor, while a mild sore throat may lead to anxiety over the possibility of some rare but fatal type of infection. What accounts for these effects? Two factors seem crucial. First, the students are exposed to descriptions of diseases day after day in their classes and in assigned readings. As a result,

False Consensus Effect ■ The tendency to assume that others behave or think as we do to a greater extent than is actually true.

such information is high in availability. Thus, when a mild symptom occurs, related disease-information is readily brought to mind, with the result that the students imagine the worst about their current health.

Such effects are termed **priming**. Specifically, priming involves any stimuli that heighten the availability of certain types or categories of information so that they come more readily to mind. Many instances of priming occur in everyday life. For example, after watching an especially frightening horror movie, many persons react strongly to stimuli that would previously have had little impact upon them ("What's that dark shape at the end of the driveway?" "What's that creak on the stairs?").

The occurrence of priming effects has been demonstrated in many studies, so it seems to be a very real aspect of social thought (e.g., Higgins & King, 1981; Higgins, Rohles, & Jones, 1977). In fact, research evidence suggests that priming may occur even when individuals are unaware of the priming stimuli—an effect known as **automatic priming** (e.g., Bargh & Pietromonaco, 1982). For example, in one study on this topic (Erdley & D'Agostino, 1989), words relating to the trait of honesty (words such as *honorable, truthful, sincere*) were flashed on a screen so briefly that participants were not aware of them. In contrast, participants in a control group were exposed to words unrelated to this trait (words such as *what, little, many, number*). After this experience, individuals in both groups read a description of an imaginary person—one that portrayed her in ambiguous terms. Finally, they rated this imaginary person on several trait dimensions, some of which were related to honesty. Results indicated that those participants exposed to the honesty-related words rated her higher on this trait than those exposed to the neutral words. That is, even though participants were unaware of them, the priming words related to honesty still affected their ratings of the stranger on this trait.

Additional studies have taken such effects still farther, demonstrating that sometimes priming effects can occur without any researcher-supplied primes. Apparently, we sometimes generate our own primes with respect to other persons. For instance, after learning that they have behaved in certain ways, we generate inferences about their traits—*spontaneous trait inferences* as they are termed. These inferences can then serve as primes, affecting our ratings of these persons on related dimensions. Such effects have actually been observed in several studies (e.g., Moskowitz & Roman, 1992) (see Figure 3.5 on p. 86).

In sum, it appears that priming is a basic fact of social thought. External events and conditions—or even our own thoughts—can increase the availability in memory of specific types of information. And increased availability, in turn, influences our judgments with respect to such information. "If I can think of it," we seem to reason, "then it must be important, frequent, or true"; and we often reach such conclusions even if they are not supported by social reality.

Priming ■ Effect that occurs when stimuli or events increase the availability of specific types of information in memory or consciousness.

Automatic Priming ■ Effect that occurs when stimuli of which individuals are not consciously aware alter the availability of various traits or concepts in memory.

Potential Sources of Error in Social Cognition: Why Total Rationality Is Scarcer Than You Think

Human beings are definitely not computers. While we can *imagine* being able to reason in a perfectly logical manner, we know from our own experience that often, we fall short of this goal. This is definitely true with respect to many aspects of social thought. In our efforts to understand others and make sense out of the social world, we are subject to a wide range of tendencies that, together, can lead us into serious error. In this section, we'll consider several of these

FIGURE 3.5

Automatic Priming: An Overview. When words relating to specific traits (e.g., honesty or arrogance) are shown so briefly that individuals cannot report being aware of them, these words can still influence ratings of a stranger. Words related to positive traits improve ratings of a stranger, while words related to negative traits worsen them. These findings indicate that priming—increased availability of specific traits or concepts in memory—can occur even when we are not aware of the priming stimuli.

"tilts" in social cognition. Before turning to these sources of potential error, however, we should carefully emphasize the following point: While these aspects of social thought do sometimes result in errors, they are also quite adaptive. They help us to focus on the kinds of information that are usually most informative, and they reduce the effort required for understanding the social world. As is true of virtually all important aspects of human behavior, then, these tendencies can be beneficial as well potentially damaging.

Rational versus Intuitive Processing: Going with Our Gut-Level Feelings Even When We Know Better

Imagine the following situation: You are shown two bowls containing red jelly beans and white jelly beans. One holds a single red bean and nine white ones, the other holds ten red beans and ninety white ones. Further, imagine that you will win money each time you select (blindfolded) a red bean. From which bowl would you prefer to draw? Rationally, it makes no difference: the chances of winning are exactly 10 percent in both cases. But if you are like most people, you'd prefer the bowl with one hundred beans. In fact, in several studies, more than two-thirds of the participants given this choice preferred the bowl with the larger number of jelly beans; and—even more surprisingly—*they were willing to pay money to guarantee this choice* (Kirkpatrick & Epstein, 1992). In a sense, it's hard to imagine a clearer illustration of the fact that our thinking is far from perfectly rational in many situations.

What accounts for this and related findings? A model of cognition proposed recently by Epstein and his colleagues (e.g., Denes-Raj & Epstein, 1994; Epstein, in press) offers one explanation. According to this model, known as **cognitive–experiential self-theory** (CEST for short), our efforts to understand the world around us proceed in two distinct ways. One of these is deliberate, rational thinking, which follows basic rules of logic. The other is a more *intuitive* system, which operates in a more automatic, holistic manner—a kind of "fly-by-the-seat-of-our-pants" approach, in which we make quick decisions according to simple heuristics we've developed through experience. CEST theory suggests that we tend to use these contrasting styles of thought in different kinds of situations. Rational thinking is used in situations involving analytical thought—for example, solving mathematical problems. Intuitive thinking is used in many other situations, including most social ones. In other words, when we try to understand others' behavior, we often revert to intuitive, gut-level thinking. So why do we tend to prefer the larger bowl of jelly beans? Because

Cognitive–Experiential Self-Theory ■ Theory suggesting that our efforts to understand the world around us involve two distinct modes of thought: *intuitive* thought and *deliberate, rational* thought.

in situations like this, the intuitive system is dominant. We *know*, rationally, that the odds of winning are the same in both cases; but *we* feel that we have a better chance of winning when there are ten red jelly beans rather than only one. Denes-Raj and Epstein (1994) suggest that this is because information in the experiential system is encoded primarily in the form of concrete representations. In other words, we can visualize one red jelly bean and nine white ones more easily than ten red and ninety white ones, so we choose the larger bowl for this reason: it seems to hold out a greater chance of winning.

The powerful effects of intuitive thought are dramatically illustrated in a recent study conducted by Denes-Raj and Epstein (1994). These researchers allowed participants to choose between two bowls of jelly beans under conditions where, if they were successful in drawing red beans from the bowl they chose, participants could win actual money. In one condition, the proportion of red beans was identical in both bowls (10 percent). In other conditions, however, the proportion of red beans in the larger bowl was actually *lower* than 10 percent: it ranged from 5 to 9 percent. In other words, there were only 5 red beans and 95 white ones (5 percent), 6 red beans and 94 white ones (6 percent), and so on. What would participants do? Rationally, they should certainly choose the small bowl, since it always contained 1 red bean (10 percent). As you can see from Figure 3.6, however, this was definitely *not* the case. Substantial proportions of persons chose the larger bowl *even when the odds of winning were lower*. Similar results were obtained in a follow-up study where the amount of money at stake was larger—participants could win as much as $35 by drawing red jelly beans. Even under these conditions, however, fully 85 percent of the participants made nonoptimal choices: they preferred to draw from the larger bowl. Interestingly, participants were well aware of the conflict between rational and intuitive modes of thought. Many reported that they *knew* the chances of winning were better with the small bowl, but went with the big one because they "felt" they had more chances of winning when there were more red beans.

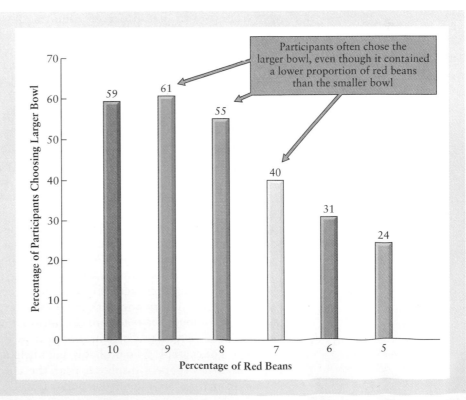

FIGURE 3.6

The Power of Intuitive Thought. When asked whether they wanted to draw jelly beans from a bowl containing one red bean and nine white ones or from a bowl containing larger numbers of red and white beans, individuals often chose the latter—*even though the odds of drawing a winning red bean were actually lower!* These findings indicate that often, we don't process information in a completely rational manner. Rather, we go with our "intuitions," even if we know these are likely to be wrong.

(*Source:* Based on data from Denes-Raj & Epstein, 1994.)

Participants often chose the larger bowl, even though it contained a lower proportion of red beans than the smaller bowl

Percentage of Participants Choosing Larger Bowl

59 61 55 40 31 24

Percentage of Red Beans

10 9 8 7 6 5

These findings, and the results of related research (e.g., Fiske & Taylor, 1991) provide convincing evidence for the conclusion we offered at the start of this section: often, we *don't* process information in a totally rational manner. On the contrary, under many conditions—especially, it appears, when we are experiencing strong emotional arousal and when we are in social situations involving other persons—we fall back upon a more intuitive mode of thought. Such thought is certainly comfortable, quick, and familiar; but as you can readily see, it doesn't always provide us with the best or most accurate answers to the puzzles of everyday life!

Dealing with Inconsistent Information: Paying Attention to What Doesn't Fit

Imagine the following situation: You are watching an evening talk show on television. One of the guests is Newt Gingrich, Speaker of the House of Representatives in the United States Congress. You only half listen as he makes several fairly extreme but, for him, not surprising comments about taxes, welfare reform, and government generally. Then, in a quiet voice, he says something totally unexpected: He has lost interest in politics, and has decided to retire to grow roses at the end of his current two-year term. You sit up straight in disbelief; can you believe your ears? Did he really say that?

This somewhat bizarre example illustrates an important fact about social cognition: In general, we tend to pay much more attention to information that is *unexpected* or somehow *inconsistent* with our expectations than to information that is expected or consistent. Thus, a statement by Newt Gingrich to the effect that he has lost interest in politics would literally leap out at you, demanding close and careful attention.

This tendency to pay greater attention to information inconsistent with our expectations than to information consistent with them is an important and basic aspect of social cognition. It is apparent in a wide range of contexts (e.g., Belmore & Hubbard, 1987; Hilton, Klein, & von Hippel, 1991), and seems to stem from the fact that inconsistent information is unexpected and surprising, with the result that we work harder to understand it (e.g., Srull & Wyer, 1989). And since the greater the amount of attention we pay to information, the better its chance of entering into long-term memory and influencing our later social judgments (Fiske & Neuberg, 1990), this tendency to notice what's inconsistent has important implications.

Although this tendency to notice what's inconsistent isn't universal (see, e.g., Srull et al., 1985), it does appear to be quite general. For example, it applies to groups as well as individuals, especially if we hold strong stereotypes about a group. In one recent study on this topic, Bardach and Park (1996) asked male and female college students to read descriptions of behaviors performed by a stranger—Mark or Marcia. Some of these behaviors were consistent with sex-role stereotypes while others were not. When the students were later asked to recall these behaviors, they remembered information inconsistent with the target person's gender (e.g., Mark was nuturant; Marcia was competitive) better than information that was consistent (e.g., Mark was adventurous, Marcia was emotional).

One final point: While it is usually the case that information to which we pay particular attention exerts stronger effects on our social thought and judgments than other information, it's important to note that this is not always so. Sometimes, although we readily *notice* information that is inconsistent with our expectations, we tend to discount it or downplay it: it's simply too unexpected to accept. For example, you probably can't help noticing the weird headlines on the tabloid newspapers displayed near the check-out lines in supermarkets ("Woman marries monster from outer space!" "Drug turns boy into fish!"

"Woman gives birth to dinosaur!"). These headlines are unexpected and inconsistent with views you already hold. But the chances of their influencing your thinking in any serious way are slight, because they are *so* bizarre that you discount them. So the fact that we often pay careful attention to information inconsistent with our current views or thinking does not mean that such information is necessarily more influential with respect to social thought.

The Optimistic Bias for Task Completion: Why We Often Think We Can Get Done Sooner Than We Can

There's a major road that I often take to get from my home to the university. Several years ago the road was greatly improved: all lanes were widened, left-turn lanes were added. When the work began, it was projected to last eighteen months. Can you guess how long it really took? *Almost three years.* And, needless to add, it cost much more than initially projected, too. This is not a rare sequence of events: almost every public project seems to take longer, and cost more, than predicted.

Why is this the case? One possibility is as follows: In predicting how long a given task will take, people tend to be overly optimistic; they predict that they can get it done much sooner than actually turns out to be the case. You can probably recognize this tendency in your own thinking. Think back to the last time you worked on a major project (for example, a term paper). Did it take more time or less time to complete than you originally estimated? In all probability, your answer is "More time . . . of course!" So this tendency to make optimistic predictions concerning how long a given task will take—a tendency known as the **planning fallacy**—seems to be both powerful and widespread, see Figure 3.7. Given that most of us have had repeated experiences with being overly optimistic in this manner, it is somewhat surprising: why don't we come to realize that tasks almost *always* take longer than we predict? According to Buehler, Griffin, and Ross (1994), several features of social thought account for this state of affairs.

Buehler, Griffin, and Ross (1994) suggest that when individuals make predictions about how long it will take them to complete a given task, they often enter a *planning* or *narrative* mode of thought, in which they focus primarily on the future: how, precisely, they will perform the task. This, in turn, prevents them from looking backward and remembering how long similar tasks took them in the past. As a result, one important "reality check" that might help them to avoid being overly optimistic in their predictions is removed. In addition, when individuals *do* consider past experiences in which tasks took longer than expected, they tend to make *attributions* that diminish the relevance of such experience. They conclude, for instance, that their past failures to get tasks done as quickly as expected were due to external factors outside their control, or to specific unforeseen events (see Chapter 2).

To find out whether these processes really play a role in the planning fallacy, Buehler and his colleagues (1994) conducted a study in which participants were asked to describe, out loud, a school project that they intended to complete within the next two weeks, and to predict just when they would complete it. The same persons were then contacted again one week after the completion target dates they had indicated, and asked whether they actually finished the projects, and if so when. In addition, they were asked to recall an occasion when they had failed to complete a similar project on schedule and to explain *why* they did not get it done on time. Results indicated that only 43.6 percent of the participants completed their projects by the times they predicted: the majority were indeed overoptimistic in this respect. Analysis of their comments also confirmed the prediction that they would be thinking primarily about planning for the project rather than

Planning Fallacy ■ The tendency to make optimistic predictions concerning how long a given task will take.

FIGURE 3.7

The Planning Fallacy in Operation. In many cases, public projects such as this one take much longer to complete than originally estimated. Such events illustrate the powerful impact of the *planning fallacy*—people's tendency to make optimistic predictions concerning how long a given task will take. This fallacy, in turn, seems to stem from basic principles of social cognition.

remembering previous experiences with similar projects; indeed, fully 71 percent of their verbal comments were related to future plans; 1 percent of these comments referred to problems in completing projects in the past. Finally, participants' attributions concerning *why* they had failed to complete past projects showed the predicted pattern: in general, they attributed such failures to external, transitory, and specific causes—factors largely outside their personal control.

In a follow-up study, Buehler et al. (1994) reasoned that if the *planning fallacy* actually stems from the fact that people fail to think about past experiences with similar projects when estimating how long a current project will take, then it might be possible to eliminate this bias by somehow inducing people to remember such experiences. To test this possibility, they asked participants in one condition to remember past experiences with similar projects (the recall condition), and those in another condition to remember such events *and* to think about how these past experiences were relevant to the present task (the recall-relevant group). Those in a control condition were not asked to think about past projects. Consistent with predictions, persons who thought about past projects and how they were relevant to the present project did *not* show the planning fallacy: their estimates about when they would complete the present project (a computer assignment) were quite accurate. In contrast, those in the other two groups were overoptimistic: they estimated that the project would take them less time to complete than it actually did. Moreover, a higher proportion of persons in the recall-relevant condition actually did complete the task within the time they predicted.

Together, these findings indicate that our tendency to be overly optimistic in predicting when we will complete various tasks does indeed stem from basic aspects of social cognition. Specifically, such misplaced optimism seems to reflect our tendency to generate our forecasts by focusing on the current project and plans for it rather than on past experiences. And even when we *do* remember previous failures to meet our own deadlines, we tend to explain these away by attributing them to unique external factors. Once again, therefore, we are brought face to face with a central fact in this chapter—perhaps *the* central fact: Where thinking about the social world is concerned, we are definitely far from perfect.

Automatic Vigilance: Noticing the Negative

Read the following information about someone named Jackie:

Jackie is a junior at State U.—a biology major with an A– grade point average. She hopes to enter medical school after graduation. She is a warm and friendly person, so most people who know her think she'll make an excellent doctor. Jackie's hobby is music, and she has a large collection of CDs. She works part time to help pay for her education and to cover the insurance on her car, which is high because of several speeding tickets. Jackie grew up in a medium-sized city and has one brother, Jason, who is a senior in high school. She is fairly neat and quite easygoing; she never has any trouble getting roommates. She is currently living with three other women in an apartment near campus.

Quick: What piece of information stands out most when you think about Jackie? If you said "those speeding tickets," you are in good company; because in general, we seem to pay more attention to negative information about others than to positive information about them. In fact, it is fair to say that we are extremely sensitive to negative social information. If another person smiles at us twenty times during a conversation but frowns once, it is the frown that we notice most. If one of our friends describes someone to us and mentions twenty positive things about the person but one negative thing, *this* is the information on which we focus and which we are later most likely to remember. So strong is this tendency to pay attention to negative information that some researchers call it **automatic vigilance**—a powerful tendency to pay attention to negative information or stimuli (e.g, Shiffrin, 1988).

In one sense, this tendency makes a great deal of sense. After all, negative information may alert us to potential danger, and it is crucial that we recognize it—and respond to it—as quickly as possible (Pratto & John, 1991). But since our attentional capacity is limited, when we direct attention to negative social information, we run the risk of overlooking or ignoring other valuable forms of input. As is true with all the tendencies in social cognition we will consider in this chapter, therefore, it is possible for automatic vigilance to cause us difficulties.

How strong is this tendency to focus on negative social information? Very strong, it appears. For example, consider what social psychologists describe as the *face-in-the-crowd effect* (Hansen & Hansen, 1988). We are especially sensitive to negative facial expressions on the part of others—so sensitive that we can very quickly pick out the angry face in a crowd of persons showing neutral or happy expressions. Interestingly, we are somewhat slower to identify a happy face in a crowd of angry faces (Hansen & Hansen, 1988). These findings are consistent with the principles of *evolutionary psychology* (Buss, in press), since angry persons do indeed represent a greater threat to our safety—or survival— than happy ones.

In any case, the findings of many different studies indicate that where social information is concerned, we are indeed especially sensitive to negative input. And since the information to which we pay most attention often exerts the strongest effects on thought and judgments about others, the *automatic vigilance* effect helps explain why, as we noted in Chapter 2, making a favorable first impression on others can be so important.

The Potential Costs of Thinking Too Much: Why, Sometimes, Our Tendency to Do As Little Cognitive Work As Possible May Be Justified

As we have already seen, there are many instances in which we adopt an intuitive approach to thinking about the social world around us. Yet there are other

Automatic Vigilance ■ The strong tendency to pay attention to undesirable or negative information.

instances in which we *do* try to be as rational and systematic as possible in our thought, despite the fact that this costs us extra effort. At first glance, such deliberate, rational thought would seem to be uniformly beneficial. But on closer examination, it appears that perhaps this is not always the case. Have you ever had the experience of thinking about some problem or decision so long and so hard that, ultimately, you found yourself becoming more and more confused? If so, you are aware of the fact that even where rational thought is concerned, there can sometimes be too much of a good thing.

Surprising as this conclusion may be, it has been confirmed by many studies conducted by social psychologists (e.g., Schooler & Engstler-Schooler, 1990; Wilson, 1990). Perhaps the most dramatic evidence for the potential downside of thinking too much is that provided by Wilson and Schooler (1991). These researchers asked college students to sample and rate several strawberry jams. Half of the participants were simply asked to taste the jams and rate them; the others were asked to analyze their reactions to the jams—to indicate why they felt the way they did about each product. Wilson and Schooler (1991) reasoned that when individuals engage in such careful introspection, the reasons they bring to mind may simply be the ones that are most prominent and accessible—the easiest to remember or put into words. However, they may *not* be the most important factors in their judgments. As a result, people may actually be misled by the reasons they report, and this may cause them to make less accurate judgments.

To determine if this is actually the case, Wilson and Schooler (1991) compared the judgments made by the participants who analyzed the reasons behind their ratings, and by those who did not, with ratings by a panel of experts—persons who make their living comparing various products. Results were clear: Participants who simply rated the jams agreed much more closely with the experts than participants who tried to report their reasons for their reactions to the various jams.

Similar findings were obtained in a follow-up study in which students were asked to read course descriptions and student evaluations of college courses, and then to indicate the likelihood that they would take these courses themselves. Some students merely rated the courses (the control condition), while those in two other conditions were asked either (1) to analyze the reasons they might want or not want to take each course, or (2) to stop and think about each piece of information as they read it and to rate the extent to which it made them more or less likely to take the course. Results indicated that those in the two "think deeply" conditions were less likely to make effective decisions—to preregister for and actually enroll in the most popular courses.

In sum, it appears that on some occasions, thinking too much can get us into serious cognitive trouble. Yes, attempting to think systematically and rationally about important matters is important; such high-effort activities do often yield better decisions or judgments than shoot-from-the-hip modes of thought. But careful thought, like anything else, can be overdone; and when it is, the result may be increased confusion and frustration rather than better and more accurate conclusions.

Finally, some food for thought—not too much thought, we hope! Very recent findings (e.g., Yost & Weary, 1996) indicate that persons who are suffering from depression are more likely to engage in effortful social thought than persons not depressed, mainly because they hope to restore their diminished feelings of personal control through greater understanding of what is happening around them. To the extent they carry these efforts too far, they may run the risk of adding to their personal problems by experiencing the harmful effects of thinking too much. No evidence on this possibility currently exists, but it does seem to be worthy of careful study.

Counterfactual Thinking and the Experience of Regret: Some Surprising Effects of Considering "What Might Have Been"

Imagine the following events:

Ms. Caution never picks up hitchhikers. Yesterday, however, she broke her rule and gave a stranger a lift. He repaid her kindness by robbing her.

Now, in contrast, consider the following events:

Ms. Risk frequently picks up hitchhikers. Yesterday she gave yet another stranger a ride. He repaid her kindness by robbing her.

Which of these two persons will experience greater regret? If you answered, "Ms. Caution, of course," your thinking in this instance is very much like that of other persons. An overwhelming majority of respondents identify Ms. Caution as experiencing more regret (Kahneman & Miller, 1986). Why is this the case? Both individuals have suffered precisely the same negative outcome: they have been robbed. Thus, from a totally rational point of view, there's no reason to expect most people to choose Ms. Caution. Why, then, do we perceive her as experiencing greater regret? The answer involves some intriguing facts about social thought and the judgments resulting from it. In the most general terms, it appears that our reactions to events depend not only on the events themselves, but also on what these events bring to mind (Miller, Turnbull, & McFarland, 1990). When we have some experience, we do not think only about the experience itself; we also engage in *mental simulation* with respect to it. This often results in what social psychologists describe as **counterfactual thinking**—bringing alternative events and outcomes to mind. In this particular instance, we think, "If only Ms. Caution had not broken her rule against picking up hitchhikers, she'd be okay." Alternatively, we may imagine that "If Ms. Risk read the papers and thought about what she was doing, she would probably act differently."

Why does such counterfactual thinking lead us to believe that Ms. Caution will experience more regret? In part, because it is easier to imagine alternatives to unusual behavior, such as Ms. Caution's picking up the hitchhiker, than it is to imagine alternatives to usual, normal behavior (e.g., Ms. Risk's picking up the hitchhiker). So we conclude that Ms. Caution will experience more regret because it is easier to imagine her acting in a different way—sticking to her standard rule—than it is to imagine Ms. Risk acting differently (see Figure 3.8 on page 94).

This reasoning leads to the interesting prediction that negative outcomes that follow unusual behavior will generate more sympathy for the persons who experience such outcomes than ones that follow usual behavior. And in fact, these predictions have been confirmed in many different studies (e.g., Miller & McFarland, 1986; Macrae, 1992). So counterfactual thinking does occur, and does influence social judgments and reactions in predictable ways.

So far, so good. But now, before you read on, try this: List the three biggest regrets in your life—the things you wish most strongly you could change. What were they? If you are like most people, you may be surprised to realize that these regrets do not relate to things you did—actions that produced negative outcomes. Rather, they probably relate to things you did not do, but wish you had: the romantic interest you didn't pursue, the job you didn't take, the trip you didn't make. These are the kinds of things most people list when asked about their biggest regrets.

At first glance, this fact seems inconsistent with a key finding of research on counterfactual thinking: in general, people express more regret for things they did—especially unusual actions—than for things they didn't do. How can this inconsistency be explained? Gilovich and Medvec (1994) offer an intrigu-

Counterfactual Thinking ■
Tendency to evaluate events by thinking about alternatives to them—"what might have been."

FIGURE 3.8

Counterfactual Thinking: Some Interesting Effects. Research findings indicate that we often feel greater sympathy for people who experience negative outcomes following *unusual* actions than for people who experience identical outcomes following *typical* actions. This seems to be the case because it is easier to imagine alternatives to unusual behavior through *counterfactual thinking*.

ing answer. They propose that initially, people may be more upset by actions they performed that yielded negative outcomes than by actions they didn't perform. The actions we perform may trigger more thoughts about "what might have been" or "should have been." Later, however, we may come to regret the things we didn't do—failures to act that led us to experience reduced or negative outcomes.

Why should our reactions in this respect change over time? Gilovich and Medvec (1994) offer several possibilities. First, they note that there are several factors that, over time, diminish our regrets for specific actions. An action that yielded negative results can sometimes be reversed. Missed opportunities stemming from failure to act, however, may never come again. Similarly, we may be better at rationalizing away actions that produced negative consequences—finding good reasons for these actions—than we are at rationalizing failures to act. Second, Gilovich and Medvec (1994) call attention to factors that, over time, tend to *increase* our regrets about things we didn't do. Often, we fail to act because of fears or lack of confidence; later, looking back, we may feel that these fears were not justified and that we *should have* acted. Similarly, once we have performed an action, we are faced with the consequences: we know what these are. In contrast, if we fail to act, we continue to speculate about what *would have* happened if we had taken some action. Such speculation is limitless, and can serve to magnify our regret. In sum, there are many reasons why the pattern of our regrets for action and inaction may shift greatly over time.

Do such shifts actually occur? To find out, Gilovich and Medvec (1994) asked individuals to describe the biggest regrets of their lives. Results indicated that a large majority reported failures to act; a smaller number listed regrets over past actions (see Table 3.1). In a follow-up study, the same researchers asked individuals to report their single most regrettable action or inaction during the past week, and from their entire lives, and to report on which they regretted more—the action or the inaction. For regrets from the past week, actions and inactions were mentioned about equally by participants. For regrets from their entire lives, however, a large majority of participants (84 percent) focused on inactions. So, consistent with what Gilovich and Medvec (1994) predicted, there was a major shift in the pattern of regrets over time.

TABLE 3.1 What People Regret

As shown here, when asked to describe the biggest regrets of their lives, individuals are more likely to describe things they didn't do rather than things they did do.

Failures to Act	Number	Actions	Number
Missed educational opportunities	21	Bad educational choice	3
Failure to seize the moment	21	Rushed in too soon	17
Not spending enough time with friends and relatives	15	Spent time badly	4
Missed romantic opportunity	13	Unwise romantic adventure	10
Not pursuing interest in something	11	Wasted time on something	0
Missed career opportunity	7	Bad career decision	3

(*Source:* Based on data from Gilovich & Medvec, 1994.)

In sum, it appears that when we think about various events in our lives, we do engage in counterfactual thinking: we imagine what might have been or should have been in these situations. Such thoughts, in turn, can strongly affect our judgments about these events or situations. However, the nature of such thinking seems to shift over time, from a focus on what we *did do* to a focus on what we *didn't do*. Whatever the focus of such thoughts, one point seems clear: we seem to torture ourselves with thoughts of possible outcomes as well as with thoughts about actual ones.

Magical Thinking: Would You Eat a Chocolate Shaped Like a Spider?

Answer truthfully:

If you think about a dangerous or harmful event, does that increase the likelihood that it will happen?

Suppose someone with AIDS bought a sweater sealed in a plastic bag and put it away in a drawer for a year; would you wear it if they gave it to you?

Imagine that someone offered you a piece of chocolate shaped like a spider—eight legs and all—would you eat it?

On the basis of purely rational considerations, you know what your answers should probably be: No, yes, and yes. But are those the answers you actually gave? If you are like most persons, perhaps not. In fact, research findings indicate that as human beings, we are quite susceptible to what has been termed **magical thinking** (Rozin & Nemeroff, 1990). Such thinking makes assumptions that don't hold up to rational scrutiny but which are compelling, nonetheless. One principle of such magical thinking is known as the *law of contagion:* it holds that when two objects touch, they pass properties to one another, and that the effects of contact may last well beyond the termination of such contact (Zusne & Jones, 1989). Another is the *law of similarity,* which suggests that things that resemble one another share fundamental properties. Still a third assumes that one's thoughts can achieve specific physical effects in a manner not governed by the laws of physics. Can you see how these assumptions relate to the questions above? The law of contagion is linked to the question about the sweater; the law of similarity has to do with the chocolate; and the third principle relates to the possibility of inviting catastrophes by thinking about them.

Surprising as it may seem, our thinking about many situations—including social ones—is often influenced by such magical thinking. For example, in one

Magical Thinking ■ Thinking involving assumptions that don't hold up to rational scrutiny—for example, the belief that things that resemble one another share fundamental properties.

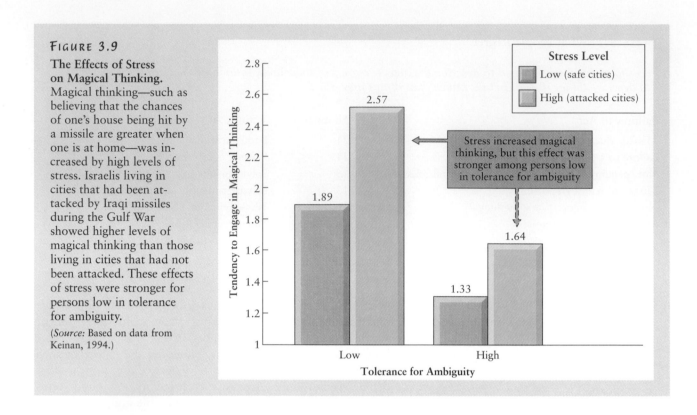

FIGURE 3.9

The Effects of Stress on Magical Thinking. Magical thinking—such as believing that the chances of one's house being hit by a missile are greater when one is at home—was increased by high levels of stress. Israelis living in cities that had been attacked by Iraqi missiles during the Gulf War showed higher levels of magical thinking than those living in cities that had not been attacked. These effects of stress were stronger for persons low in tolerance for ambiguity.

(*Source:* Based on data from Keinan, 1994.)

study, Rozin, Markwith, and Nemeroff (1992) asked individuals to rate a sweater owned either by a person with AIDS or by a healthy person, which had been left in a sealed plastic bag and never touched by the owner. Consistent with the law of contagion, participants rated the sweater less favorably when it had been owned by the person with AIDS, even though they knew that there was no chance they could catch the disease from the sweater.

Additional evidence for the operation of magical thinking is provided by a study Keinan (1994) conducted with residents of Israel during the Gulf War of 1990. Participants lived either in cities that had been attacked by Iraqi missiles or in cities that were never attacked. Persons in both groups completed a questionnaire designed to measure magical thinking—for example, agreement with items such as "If during a missile attack I had a photograph of Saddam Hussein with me, I would rip it to pieces," and "I have the feeling that the chances of being hit during a missile attack are greater if a person whose house was attacked is present . . . " It was predicted that magical thinking would be greater among those in the cities that had been attacked, and that this tendency would be stronger among persons intolerant of ambiguity—persons who tend to perceive ambiguous situations (such as the chance of being attacked) as more threatening and stressful than others do. As you can see from Figure 3.9, this is precisely what was found. Apparently, the high stress resulting from the missile attacks increased individuals' tendencies to engage in magical thinking, and this increase was greater among persons who find ambiguous situations especially threatening.

So, the next time you are tempted to make fun of someone's superstitious belief (e.g., fear of the number thirteen or of black cats crossing one's path), think again: while you may not accept such superstitions yourself, this does not imply that your own thinking is totally free from the kind of "magical" assumptions described previously.

INTEGRATING PRINCIPLES

1. We are *not* perfect information processors. On the contrary, our social thought is subject to many different sources of potential error, ranging from the tendency to be extremely sensitive to negative information (automatic vigilance), to the planning fallacy, to magical thinking.

2. These tendencies sometimes cause us to make errors in our inferences or judgments about others. Such errors are related to many aspects of social behavior, including first impressions of others (Chapter 2), persuasion (Chapter 4), and even judgments about others' innocence or guilt (Chapter 13).

Social Cognition: A Word of Optimism

The planning fallacy, automatic vigilance, the costs of thinking too much, counterfactual thinking—having read our discussions of these and other sources of error in social thought, you may be ready to despair: can we ever get it right? The answer, we believe, is *absolutely*. No, we're not perfect information-processing machines. We have limited cognitive capacities, and we can't—unfortunately—increase these by buying pop-in memory upgrades. And yes, we are somewhat lazy: we generally do the least amount of cognitive work possible in any situation. Despite these limitations, however, we frequently do an impressive job in thinking about others. Despite being flooded by truly enormous amounts of social information, we manage to sort, store, remember, and use a significant portion of this input in an intelligent and efficient manner. Certainly, we're not perfect; but we do manage to get the job done in a manner that permits us to introduce a surprising degree of order and predictability into our lives, and into our constructions of the social world around us. So, while we can imagine being better at these tasks than we are, there's no reason to be disheartened. On the contrary, it's not unreasonable to take some pride in the fact that we do accomplish quite a lot with the limited tools at our disposal.

Affect and Cognition: How Thought Shapes Feelings and Feelings Shape Thought

Look at the cartoon in Figure 3.10 (p. 98). What happened to Cathy? She was all set to be logical and assertive but then . . . she saw the chocolate candy. So long, good intentions! Her affective reactions quickly changed her cognitive processes. This cartoon actually illustrates an important area of research in social psychology: efforts to investigate the interplay between *affect*—our current moods or feelings—and *cognition*—the ways in which we process, store, remember, and use social information (Forgas, 1994a; Isen & Baron, 1991). We say *interplay*, because research on this topic indicates that in fact the relationship is very much a two-way street: our feelings and moods exert strong effects on several aspects of cognition, and cognition, in turn, exerts strong effects on our feelings and moods (e.g., Seta, Hayes, & Seta, 1994). In this section we'll

FIGURE 3.10

How Affect Influences Cognition: A Humorous Example. *When Cathy saw the chocolate candy and experienced positive affect, her thinking changed drastically. Growing evidence points to the conclusion that our affective states do often exert strong effects on many aspects of our cognition.*

(*Source:* Universal Press Syndicate, 1995.)

describe many of these effects. Before turning to these, however, we'll pause briefly to examine several contrasting views concerning the nature of emotion (e.g., Ekman, 1992; Izard, 1992). *Emotions* are complex reactions involving physiological responses, subjective cognitive states, and expressive behaviors. In general, emotions are viewed as being more intense than *affective states,* our relatively mild feelings and moods (Forgas, 1994b). However, the dividing line between *emotion* and *affect* (or *mood*) is uncertain, so it is both useful and informative to take a quick look at what modern psychology has to say about the nature of emotions.

The Nature of Emotion: Contrasting Views and Recent Advances

Cannon–Bard Theory ■ Theory of emotion suggesting that various stimuli elicit both physiological reactions and the subjective reactions we label as emotions.

Feelings, and rapid changes in them, are a central part of everyday life; so over the centuries, many different views about the nature of emotions have been proposed. Three of these, however, have been most influential. The first, generally known as the **Cannon–Bard theory** (Cannon, Lewis, & Britton, 1927), is the commonsense perspective. It suggests that when we are exposed to emotion-

FIGURE 3.11

Schachter's Two-Factor Theory of Emotion. According to Schachter's theory, when we experience arousal, we often search the external world around us for the source of such feelings. The sources we identify strongly influence the labels we then attach to our arousal. In other words, we often label our feelings in accordance with what the world around us suggests we *should* be experiencing.

We label our feelings as "love" or "sexual excitement"	3. Labeling of emotion
	External cues (presence of attractive member of opposite sex, soft lights, music, etc.)
1. Feelings of increased arousal	2. Attention to external cues
	2. Attention to external cues
We label our feelings as "anger"	3. Labeling of emotion
	External cues (near miss in traffic)

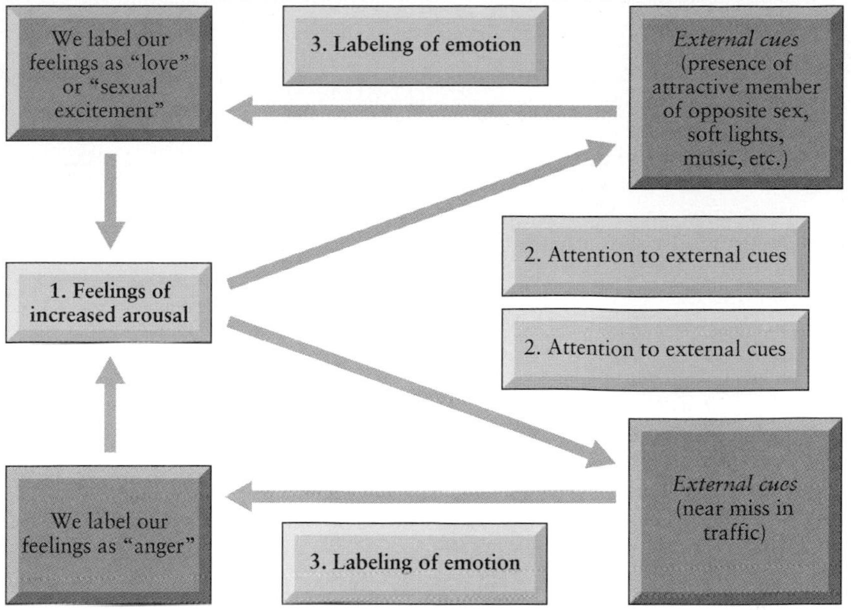

provoking events or stimuli, we quickly experience *both* the physiological signs of emotion and the subjective experiences we label as fear, anger, joy, and so on. In other words, both types of reaction occur concurrently and stem from the same stimuli or events. For example, imagine that one day you turned on the radio and learned that you had just won the lottery. Your pulse and blood pressure would leap to high levels, and you would quickly be swept by intense feelings of surprise and elation.

In contrast, the **James–Lange theory** (James, 1890) proposes that our subjective emotional experiences are actually the *result* of our relatively automatic physiological reactions to various events. According to this view, we experience anger, fear, joy, or sorrow *because* we become aware of a racing heart, tears streaming down our cheeks, and so on. Returning to the lottery example, you would experience elation *because* you quickly became aware of all the physiological signs of this emotion. As James put it, if you see a bear while in the woods, you begin to run. Then you experience fear because of the feelings of intense arousal produced by this activity.

A third view—Schachter's **two-factor theory**—suggests that any form of arousal, whatever its source, initiates a search for the causes of these feelings (Schachter, 1964; Schachter & Singer, 1962). The causes we then identify play a key role in determining the label we place on our arousal, and so in the emotion experience. Thus, if we feel aroused in the presence of an attractive person, we may label our arousal as "love" or "attraction." If we feel aroused after a near miss in traffic, we label our feelings as "fear" or perhaps "anger" toward the other driver who was—of course!—clearly at fault. In short, we perceive ourselves to be experiencing the emotion that external cues suggest we *should* be feeling (see Figure 3.11).

Which of these theories is most accurate? As we'll see in Chapter 5, the results of many studies offer support for the view proposed by Schachter, so it is clear that cognitive and situational factors do play a role in our subjective emotional reactions (e.g., Olson & Ross, 1988). But what about the Cannon–Bard and James–Lange theories: which of *these* is correct? Until recently, most evi-

James–Lange Theory ■ Theory of emotion contending that emotional experiences result from our perceptions of shifts in bodily states; we become fearful because we notice such physiological reactions as increased heart rate and so on.

Two-Factor Theory ■ Theory of emotion suggesting that in many situations we label our emotional states according to what our inspection of the world around us suggests we *should* be experiencing.

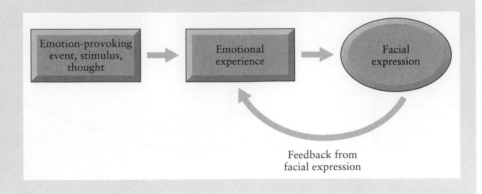

Figure 3.12
The Facial Feedback Hypothesis. The facial feedback hypothesis suggests that facial expressions can provide feedback that influences our subjective experiences of emotion. In other words, we not only show our emotions in our facial expressions; these expressions, in turn, can influence our emotions.

dence seemed to favor the Cannon–Bard approach: emotion-provoking events produce both physiological arousal and the subjective experiences we label as emotions. Now, however, the pendulum of scientific opinion has moved somewhat toward greater acceptance of the James–Lange approach—the view that we experience emotions because of our awareness of physiological reactions to various stimuli or situations. What evidence supports this view? Several lines of research point in this direction. First, studies conducted with highly sophisticated equipment indicate that different emotions are indeed associated with different patterns of physiological activity (Levenson, 1992). Not only do various emotions *feel* different, it appears, they are reflected in somewhat different patterns of bodily changes, including contrasting patterns of brain and muscle activity (Ekman, Davidson, & Friesen, 1990; Izard, 1992). Second, support for the James–Lange theory is also provided by findings indicating that changes in our facial expressions sometimes *produce* changes in our emotional experiences rather than merely reflecting them. Because it is so surprising, let's consider this research a bit more closely.

The Facial Feedback Hypothesis: Do We Feel What We Show As Well As Show What We Feel? The suggestion that changes in our facial expressions sometimes produce changes in our emotional experiences is known as the **facial feedback hypothesis** (Laird, 1984; McCanne & Anderson, 1987). Briefly, this theory suggests that there is a close association between the facial expressions we show and our internal feelings, and that in this relationship the facial expressions may themselves yield information that feeds back into our brains and influences our subjective experiences of emotion. In other words, we do not only smile because we feel happy; sometimes, when we smile, we feel happier *because* we have smiled (see Figure 3.12).

Surprising as these suggestions are, they are supported by a growing body of research evidence. For example, in one study on the facial feedback hypothesis, McCanne and Anderson (1987) asked female participants to imagine positive and negative events (e.g., "You inherit a million dollars"; "You lose a really close friendship"). While imagining these events, participants were told to either enhance or suppress tension in certain facial muscles. One of these muscles is active when we smile or view happy scenes. The other is active when we frown or view unhappy scenes. Measurements of electrical activity of both muscles indicated that after a few practice trials, most persons could carry out this task quite successfully. They could enhance or suppress muscle tension when told to do so, and they could do this without any visible change in their facial expressions.

Facial Feedback Hypothesis ■ The suggestion that changes in facial expression can induce shifts in emotions or affective states.

After imagining each scene, participants rated their emotional experiences in terms of enjoyment or distress. If the facial feedback hypothesis is correct, these ratings should be affected by participants' efforts to enhance or suppress muscle tension. For example, if they enhanced activity in muscles associated with smiling, they would report more enjoyment of the positive events. If they suppressed such activity, they would report less enjoyment. Results offered support for these predictions. Participants reported less enjoyment of the positive events when they suppressed activity in the appropriate muscle and a slight (but not significant) tendency to report less distress to the negative events when they suppressed the muscle involved in frowning. In addition, participants also reported less ability to imagine and experience scenes of both types when suppressing activity in their facial muscles.

These findings suggest that there may be a substantial grain of truth in the James–Lange theory and in modern views related to it (e.g, Zajonc, Murphy, & Inglehart, 1989). Subjective emotional experiences do often arise directly in reaction to specific external stimuli, as the Cannon–Bard view suggests. However, they can also be generated by changes in (and awareness of) our own bodily states—even, it appears, by changes in our current facial expressions. Now, let's return to the main topic of this discussion: the complex relationship between affect and cognition.

Connections between Affect and Cognition: Some Intriguing Effects

Earlier, we noted that the links between affect and cognition operate in both directions: our current moods or feelings influence the way we think, and our thoughts can influence our feelings. Some of the research findings pointing to these conclusions are summarized in the following text.

The Influence of Affect on Cognition. Suppose that you have just received some very good news—you did much better on an important exam than you expected—and are feeling great. Now, you run into one of your friends in the student union and she introduces you to someone you don't know. You chat with this person for a while and then leave for another class. Will your first impression of the stranger be influenced by the fact that you are feeling so good? Your own experience probably suggests that it will. As one old song puts it, when we are in a good mood we tend to "see the world through rose-colored glasses"—everything takes on a positive tinge. Evidence that such effects actually do occur—that our feelings do influence the way we think and our social judgments—is provided by the findings of many different studies (e.g., Bower, 1991; Clore, Schwarz, & Conway, 1993; Isen & Baron, 1991). Some of the clearest evidence for this conclusion is that reported by Mayer and Hanson (1995).

These researchers wanted to find out whether changes in mood over time are related to changes in thinking about other persons, and especially to judgments about them. To find out, they recruited the members of sororities and fraternities at a large university, and asked these persons to complete measures of their current moods and of their current social cognition. The measure of social cognition included estimates of the likelihood of positive and negative events (e.g., "What is the probability that a thirty-year-old will be involved in a happy, loving romance?" "What is the likelihood of a nuclear war?") and items relating to category judgments—for instance, "The most typical type of worker is . . . [conscientious, lazy, honest]." (Participants chose the word they thought most accurate.) Individuals completed these measures once, and then again a week later.

The major prediction was that individuals' judgments would change with their moods. Thus, their moods on the first occasion would predict their social thought and judgments at that time, but would *not* accurately predict their social thought and judgments one week later. However, their mood on the second occasion *would* predict their judgments at this later time. Results offered strong support for these hypotheses. In other words, changes in participants' moods over time were closely related to changes in their social cognition.

The results of this study also point to a general fact about the influence of affect on cognition: in general, there is a *mood-congruent judgment effect*. That is, there is often a good match between our mood and our thoughts. When we are feeling happy, we tend to think happy thoughts and retrieve happy ideas and experiences from memory; when we are in a negative mood, we tend to think *unhappy* thoughts and to retrieve negative information from memory (Seta, Hayes, & Seta, 1994). This mood-congruent judgment effect has important practical implications. For example, it has been found that when interviewers are in a good mood, they tend to assign higher ratings to job applicants (Baron, 1987, 1993). In this way, temporary fluctuations in mood can sometimes influence the course of individuals' careers.

These are not the only ways in which affect influences cognition, however. Other findings indicate, for example, that being in a happy mood can sometimes increase creativity—perhaps because being in a happy mood activates a wider range of ideas or associations, and creativity involves combining these into new patterns. A study conducted with practicing physicians by Estrada, Isen, and Young (1995) clearly illustrates such effects.

In this investigation, physicians working at a large hospital were asked to evaluate a medical case and, at the same time, to complete a test of creativity. For some participants, the packet of materials they received also contained some candy—a small, unexpected gift designed to give them a small "mood boost." The other physicians did not receive this small gift. The creativity test involved coming up with a word that was related to three other words (e.g., club, gown, mare: _____ [answer: night]); this activity has been found to provide one useful measure of creativity (Mednick et al., 1964).

Estrada and his colleagues (1995) predicted that the small gift of candy would increase the physicians' creativity; and in fact, as shown in Figure 3.13, this is what was found. Those who received the candy answered more questions correctly than those who did not. Since accurately diagnosing complex medical problems often involves recognizing links between test results and symptoms that do not at first appear to be related, these findings suggest that physicians' affective states may play some role in their success at this crucial task. Obviously, to the extent this is so, there are important implications for the quality of medical treatment.

At this point, you may be wondering about an intriguing question: Do positive and negative affect produce mirror-image effects on cognition? In other words, if being in a good mood increases creativity or raises evaluations assigned to job candidates, does being in a bad mood produce opposite effects? At the moment, there is not sufficient evidence to offer a firm answer to this question. However, a growing body of evidence points to the tentative conclusion that despite the mood-congruent judgment effect and related findings the effects of positive and negative affect are *not* always opposite in nature (e.g., Isen & Baron, 1991). For example, in one recent study, Seta, Hayes, and Seta (1994) found that individuals in a negative mood are less easily distracted from a primary task they are performing by a second, unrelated task than persons in a good mood. This may be so because being in a negative mood may signal to individuals that they are in a difficult or even dangerous environment and so should remain "on guard" or vigilant. In contrast, being in a positive mood may signal that they are in a safe and comfortable setting where they can relax. We'll return to these suggestions in the following dis-

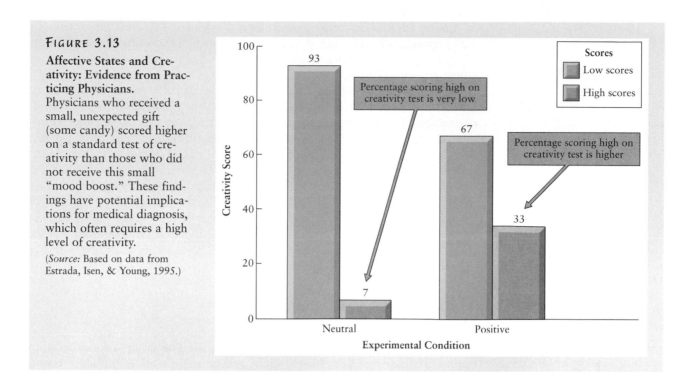

FIGURE 3.13

Affective States and Creativity: Evidence from Practicing Physicians.
Physicians who received a small, unexpected gift (some candy) scored higher on a standard test of creativity than those who did not receive this small "mood boost." These findings have potential implications for medical diagnosis, which often requires a high level of creativity.

(*Source:* Based on data from Estrada, Isen, & Young, 1995.)

cussion of the more general question "*How* does affect influence cognition?" Regardless of the mechanisms involved, however, it does seem clear that positive and negative affect do not always influence cognition in exactly opposite ways. In fact, some evidence indicates that unless they are quite intense, positive affect and negative affect may be independent of each other—not simply opposite ends of a single dimension (Goldstein & Strube, 1994). To the extent this is true, then it is not surprising that they don't always produce mirror-image effects.

The Influence of Cognition on Affect. Most research on the relationship between affect and cognition has focused on how feelings influence thought. However, there is also compelling evidence for the reverse—the impact of cognition on affect. We have already mentioned one aspect of this relationship in our earlier discussion of the two-factor theory of emotion proposed by Schachter (1964). As you may recall, their theory suggests that often, we don't know our own feelings or attitudes directly. Rather, since these internal reactions are often somewhat ambiguous, we look outward—at our own behavior or at other aspects of the external world—for clues about our feelings' essential nature. In such cases, the emotions or feelings we experience are strongly determined by the interpretation or cognitive labels we select.

A second way in which cognition can affect emotions is through the activation of schemas containing a strong affective component. For example, if we label an individual as belonging to some group, the schema for this social category may suggest what traits he or she probably possesses. In addition, it may also tell us how we *feel* about such persons. Thus, activation of a strong racial, ethnic, or religious schema or stereotype may exert powerful effects upon our current feelings or moods. (Please see Chapter 6 for more information on this topic.)

Third, our thoughts can often influence our reactions to emotion-provoking events. For example, as we'll see in our discussion of aggression in Chapter 11, anger can often be reduced by apologies and other information that helps explain why others have treated us in a provocative manner (Ohbuchi, Kameda,

& Agarie, 1989). Further, anger can often be reduced—or even prevented—by such techniques as thinking about events *other* than those that generate anger (Zillmann, 1993). In such instances, the effects of cognition on feelings can have important social consequences.

A fourth way in which cognition influences affect involves the impact of *expectancies* on our reactions and judgments. When individuals hold expectations about how they will react to a new event or stimulus, these expectations often shape their perceptions of, and feelings about, the event or stimulus when they do encounter it (e.g., Wilson et al., 1989). For example, when people expect that they will dislike a new food, they often show visible signs of displeasure even before they put it into their mouths. Conversely, when people expect to enjoy a film, joke, or story, they are very likely to do so even if they might have had weaker positive reactions in the absence of such expectations. Indeed, it appears that expectations can even shape our memories of events so that we recall them as more (or less) pleasant than they actually were, in line with our expectations (Wilson & Klaaren, 1992).

The Affect Infusion Model: How Affect Influences Cognition

Before concluding this discussion of the relationship between affect and cognition, let's address one final issue: *How,* precisely, does affect influence cognition? Through what mechanisms do our feelings influence our thought? A theory proposed by Forgas (1995), known as the **affect infusion model (AIM)**, offers some intriguing answers. According to Forgas (1995), affect influences social thought and, ultimately, social judgments through two major mechanisms. First, affect serves to *prime* (i.e., trigger) similar or related cognitive categories. In other words, when we are in a good mood, these feelings serve to prime positive associations and memories; when we are in a negative mood, in contrast, these feelings tend to prime predominantly negative associations and memories (Bower, 1991; Erber, 1991). In addition, affective states may influence attention and encoding so that we pay more attention to information congruent with our current mood, and invest more time and effort in entering mood-congruent information into memory.

Second, affect may influence cognition by acting as a *heuristic cue*—a quick way for inferring our reactions to a specific person, event, or stimulus. According to this *affect-as-information* mechanism (Clore et al., 1993), when asked to make a judgment about something in the social world, we examine our feelings and then respond accordingly. If we are in a good mood, we conclude: "I like it" or "I'm favorable toward it." If we are in a bad mood, in contrast, we conclude: "I don't like it" or "I'm unfavorable toward it." In other words, we ask ourselves, "How do I feel about it?" and use our current affective states to answer this question—*even if they are unrelated to the object, person, or event itself.*

When do such effects occur? Forgas (1994) suggests that affective states influence cognition through the first mechanism, priming, in situations where we engage in *substantive* thought—where we attempt to interpret new information and relate it to existing knowledge. In contrast, affective states influence cognition primarily through the second mechanism, affect-as-information, in situations where we think *heuristically*—situations where we try to get away with as little cognitive effort as possible. Evidence from many studies offers support for these suggestions (e.g., Clore et al., 1993; Forgas, 1992). Consider an ingenious field study conducted recently by Forgas (1994).

In this investigation, people were approached on the street either immediately after seeing a sad or happy film, or (in the control group) *before* seeing one of these films. They were asked to complete a questionnaire dealing with

Affect Infusion Model ■ Theory explaining how affect influences social thought and social judgments.

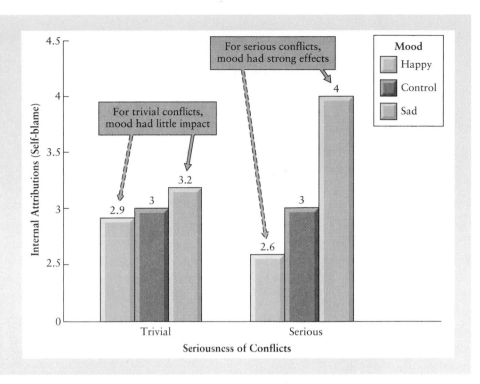

FIGURE 3.14

Evidence for the AIM Model: How Affect Influences Our Interpretations of Interpersonal Conflicts. As predicted by the *affective infusion model* (AIM), individuals in a sad mood (who had just seen a sad movie) blamed themselves for serious conflicts to a greater extent than persons who were in a happy mood (who had just seen a happy movie). These effects were much weaker in the case of trivial conflicts.

(*Source:* Based on data from Forgas, 1994.)

six trivial and six serious conflicts in their personal relationships. (Examples of trivial conflicts: which TV channel to watch, what music to play. Examples of serious conflicts: jealous behavior, amount of time spent with partner.) For each conflict, participants rated the extent to which they and their partner were responsible for the conflict. Forgas (1994) predicted that because individuals would be more likely to engage in substantive processing about serious conflicts, the effects of mood would be stronger for such conflicts than for trivial conflicts. This would be so because priming effects would be stronger for serious conflicts. As you can see from Figure 3.14, results offered support for these predictions. Persons in a sad mood were much more likely to blame themselves for serious conflicts than those who were in a happy mood. However, such effects were much weaker with respect to the trivial conflicts, about which, presumably, individuals thought less carefully.

These and other findings provide evidence for the affect infusion model and help us to understand precisely *how* our current moods or feelings can influence our thoughts and judgments. Apparently, several different mechanisms can underlie the important links between affect and cognition, and which is most important in a given situation depends on the kind of social thought in which we engage—substantive or heuristic—plus several additional factors. Contrary to what our everyday experience suggests, therefore, there is considerably more to the interplay between feelings and thought than at first meets the eye.

INTEGRATING PRINCIPLES

1. A large body of research evidence indicates that affect and cognition are intimately—and complexly—linked. Our feelings influence many aspects of our cognition, and cognition, in turn, can strongly shape our moods and feelings.

2. These connections rest on several basic mechanisms, including *priming* of affect-related associations and memories and our tendency to use our moods as a quick basis for formulating social judgments.

3. Links between affect and cognition play an important role in many forms of social behavior, including prejudice (Chapter 6), attraction (Chapter 7), helping (Chapter 10), and effects of the physical environment on social behavior (Chapter 14). In addition, they also play a role in social judgments in important practical situations such as job interviews (Chapter 13).

Social Diversity: A Critical Analysis

TRUST AS A COGNITIVE BIAS: A Cross-National Study

QUICK: WHO DO YOU THINK ARE MORE TRUSTING—JAPANESE or Americans? Given media reports of much lower crime rates in Japan and the emphasis in Japanese culture on stable, long-term relationships (in business as well as personal life), it is tempting to conclude, "Japanese, of course." But in fact, several studies designed to measure levels of trust in Japan and the United States have reported precisely the opposite result: Americans turn out to be more trusting than Japanese (Yamagishi & Yamagishi, 1989).

How can this be so? According to two Japanese researchers (Yamagishi & Yamagishi, 1994), the answer lies in the definition of *trust* and in the distinction between *trust* and *assurance*. Trust, they contend, can be viewed as another tendency or bias in social cognition: a tendency to infer more benign intentions on the part of

others than may actually be justified by the incomplete social information at our disposal. In other words, when we trust someone else, we may overestimate the extent to which their actions stem from desirable traits and positive intentions, and therefore tend to overestimate, too, the predictability of their future actions: the likelihood that they'll continue to behave in a benign and trustworthy manner. In contrast, *assurance* relates only to the belief that others will continue to act in a predictable manner because of incentives that make it worth their while to do so. There is no assumption that their intentions are good—or that they should be trusted.

Going farther, Yamagishi and Yamagishi (1994) propose that what is often mistaken for a high level of trust in Japanese society is really a high level of assurance: Since

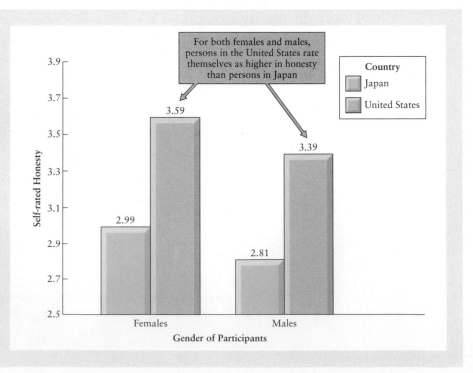

FIGURE 3.15

American and Japanese: Contrasting Self-Perceptions. Americans perceive themselves as honest and fair more than do Japanese. These findings are consistent with other evidence indicating that Americans have higher levels of trust in others than do Japanese.

(*Source:* Based on data from Yamagishi & Yamagishi, 1994.)

long-term relationships are a central part of Japanese culture, and acting in accordance with them is highly valued, individuals know that others will continue to honor these relationships. At the same time, though, Japanese individuals do not attribute such predictability to others' good intentions or positive traits. On the contrary, they recognize that these outcomes stem mainly from the structure of the relationships rather than from personal characteristics such as being honest or trustworthy. In the United States, in contrast, long-term relationships are less prevalent, so predictability tends to stem, instead, from personal trust. The conclusion: Americans will actually be more trusting than Japanese—they will be more subject than Japanese to this particular form of cognitive bias.

To test these intriguing predictions, Yamagishi and Yamagishi (1994) had hundreds of individuals in the United States and Japan complete a questionnaire designed to measure trust, assurance, and related concepts such as the importance of personal reputations. Results obtained with this questionnaire were very revealing. First, as predicted, Americans were indeed higher in general trust than Japanese—they more strongly agreed with such statements as "Most people are basically honest" and "Most people are basically good and kind." Moreover, this was the case whether the other persons involved were strangers or personal acquaintances. Second, Japanese reported perceiving more value in dealing with others through personal relations than did Americans. Third, Americans rated one's personal reputation as more important than did Japanese. Finally, and perhaps most surprising of all, Americans rated themselves as honest and fair more than did the Japanese participants (see Figure 3.15).

In sum, results offered support for the view that what are often mistaken for high levels of *trust* in Japanese society are really high levels of mutual *assurance*—the perception that others will act in predictable ways because they are involved with the perceiver in long-term, stable relationships. Outside of the context of such relationships, Americans are actually more trusting than Japanese; they assume that other persons, strangers as well as friends, are likely to behave in an honest manner and out of good intentions.

Is the tendency to trust others really a form of bias in social cognition? It is, but only to the extent that levels of trust exceed those that reflect reality. In any case, it is our view that too much trust—too much faith in others' motives and intentions—may be a far less serious social error than the opposite tendency, to perceive malevolence in others' motives and behavior when none actually exists. We'll have more to say about this tendency, known as the *hostile attributional bias*, in Chapter 11. ■ ■■

CONNECTIONS: Integrating Social Psychology

In this chapter, you read about . . .	In other chapters, you will find related discussions of . . .
schemas and prototypes	the effects of schemas and prototypes on other aspects of social behavior, such as attitudes (Chapter 4) and prejudice (Chapter 6)
potential sources of error in social cognition	the role of these errors in first impressions (Chapter 2) and persuasion (Chapter 4)
the interplay between affect and cognition	the role of such interplay in many forms of social behavior, including prejudice (Chapter 6), attraction (Chapter 7), helping (Chapter 10), and effects of the physical environment on social behavior (Chapter 14)

Thinking about Connections

1. As we noted in this chapter, we possess cognitive frameworks known as *schemas* that help us interpret many social situations. Do you think such frameworks play a role in intimate relationships? (See Chapter 8.) Do you believe that we possess relatively clear frameworks suggesting, for instance, that relationships should change in various ways over time, and even *when* such changes should occur? If so, what are these frameworks like?

2. Suppose that one day, you met someone who seemed to be the boldest, most adventurous person you had ever encountered; no risk seemed to be too great for this person, and she was truly ready for "action" of every conceivable kind.

(continued)

Then, much to your surprise, you learned that this individual was a professor of English literature. Drawing on what you now know about social cognition, how would you handle this information? Would it influence your first impression of this new acquaintance? (See Chapter 2.)

3. Suppose that you help another person in need of assistance (see Chapter 10), and by doing to, you improve your own mood. Would this "soft glow of

kindness" now influence your impression of this person? What about your future behavior toward her or him?

4. Commercials often seek to associate positive images (e.g., attractive places or people) with specific products (see Chapter 4). Drawing on what you've learned in this chapter about social thought, do you think this strategy is effective? If so, why? If not, why?

Summary and Review

Schemas and Prototypes

Social cognition involves the processes through which we notice, interpret, remember, and later use information about the social world. *Schemas* are mental frameworks containing information relevant to specific traits, situations, or events. They are formed through experience and, once developed, exert strong effects on many aspects of social cognition, including attention, encoding, and retrieval of social information. *Prototypes* are mental models of the typical qualities of members of some group or category. They, too, exert strong effects on social cognition once formed. Moreover, recent findings indicate that individuals are more likely to engage in various high-risk behaviors, such as smoking or unprotected sex, if they hold favorable prototypes of persons who engage in such actions or perceive themselves as similar to these prototypes.

Heuristics: Mental Shortcuts in Social Cognition

Because we have limited capacity to process social information, we often use mental shortcuts. *Heuristics* are mental rules of thumb that permit us to make rapid decisions or judgments about complex social stimuli. According to the *representativeness heuristic,* the more similar an individual is to typical members of a given group, the more likely she or he is to belong to that group. Another important heuristic is *availability,* according to which the more readily information can be brought to mind, the more important or frequent it is judged to be. *The false consensus effect*—our tendency to assume that others are more similar to us than they actually are—also stems in part from the availability heuristic. *Priming* involves procedures that increase the availability of specific information in consciousness. External conditions can serve as primes,

but in many cases we seem to generate our own primes on the basis of our inferences about others' traits.

Potential Sources of Error in Social Cognition

We are not perfect information-processing mechanisms. On the contrary, social cognition is subject to several tendencies and biases that can reduce its accuracy. We often engage in *intuitive* rather than *rational* thought. We tend to pay more attention to information that is inconsistent with our expectations than to information consistent with them. Another important tilt in social perception involves the *planning fallacy*— our tendency to be overoptimistic in predicting how long it will take us to complete tasks. We also tend to notice and emphasize negative social information— the *automatic vigilance* effect. Thinking too much about a particular problem or decision can sometimes prove counterproductive and lead to reduced rather than increased accuracy.

We often engage in *counterfactual thinking,* imagining "what might have been"; this can affect our judgments about events that actually did take place. In addition, we tend to experience greater regrets over actions we didn't take than over ones we did take that yielded negative outcomes. Finally, we often engage in *magical thinking,* in which, for example, we assume that when two objects are in contact, one passes properties to the other, or that thinking about various events can increase their likelihood.

Affect and Cognition

Sharply contrasting views of the nature of emotions have been proposed. The *Cannon–Bard theory* suggests that emotion-provoking stimuli evoke both physiological reactions and subjective emotional states. In contrast, the *James–Lange theory* suggests that emotional experiences stem primarily from our recognition of changes in our bodily states. Schachter's *two-factor theory* proposes that it is the cognitive label we attach to physiological arousal that is crucial.

Affective states have been found to influence memory, creativity, and many forms of social judgment, including evaluations of job applicants. Recent evidence indicates that changes in mood are often reflected in changes in social judgments. Also, cognition often influences affect. The emotions we experience are determined, at least in part, by the labels we attach to arousing events, and our emotional reactions to provocative actions by others depend in part on our interpretation of the causes behind these actions. If we expect to like or dislike some stimulus or event, our affective reactions to it will usually be consistent with such expectations.

The *affect infusion model* explains how our affective states influence cognition. According to this model, such effects occur because affect primes related associations, memories, and thoughts, and because we use our affective states as a basis for inferring our judgments about social stimuli. The model also predicts that affect will have a stronger impact upon cognition at times when we engage in careful, substantive thought.

Social Diversity: Trust As a Cognitive Bias

Trust can be viewed as a form of bias in social cognition—a tendency to attribute benign intentions and motives to others to a greater extent than may be justified by available information. Recent evidence indicates that, contrary to popular belief, Americans are actually more trusting than Japanese. This seems to stem from the fact that in Japanese culture, predictability in social interactions derives primarily from confidence that people will behave in accordance with the requirements of long-term, committed social relationships. Such relationships are less common in American culture, resulting in greater cultural emphasis on trust.

■ Key Terms

Affect (p. 77)

Affect Infusion Model (p. 104)

Automatic Priming (p. 85)

Automatic Vigilance (p. 91)

Availability Heuristic (p. 83)

Base Rate Fallacy (p. 83)

Cannon–Bard Theory (p. 98)

Cognitive–Experiential Self-theory (p. 86)

Counterfactual Thinking (p. 93)

Facial Feedback Hypothesis (p. 100)

False Consensus Effect (p. 84)

Heuristics (p. 82)

Information Overload (p. 82)

James–Lange Theory (p. 99)

Magical Thinking (p. 95)

Planning Fallacy (p. 89)

Priming (p. 85)

Prototypes (p. 77)

Representativeness Heuristic (p. 83)

Schemas (p. 77)

Social Cognition (p. 76)

Two-Factor Theory (p. 99)

■ For More Information

Forgas, J. P. (Ed.). (1991). *Emotion and social judgments*. Elmsford, NY: Pergamon Press.

Chapters in this volume deal with the complex relationship between affect and cognition. In particular, the many ways in which our feelings can influence our social judgments are carefully examined by experts in this field.

Fiske, S. T., & Taylor, S. E. (1991). *Social cognition* (2nd ed.). New York: McGraw-Hill.

A clear and thorough review of research on social cognition. Many basic aspects of our thinking about others (e.g., attribution, memory for social information) are examined in an insightful manner.

Kahneman, D., Slovic, P., and Tversky, A. (Eds.). (1982). *Judgment under uncertainty: Heuristics and biases*. Cambridge, England: Cambridge University Press.

A collection of articles and chapters focused on heuristics, biases, and fallacies. If you want to learn more about the ways in which we make use of mental shortcuts and err in our efforts to understand the social world, this is must reading.

Martin, L. L., & Tesser, A. (Eds.). (1992). *The construction of social judgments*. Hillsdale, NJ: Erlbaum.

In this book researchers who have studied how we make social judgments report their major findings. The chapters on the influence of mood states on judgments and on different cognitive processes underlying social judgments are directly relevant to discussions in this chapter.

CHAPTER 4

ATTITUDES:
Evaluating the Social World

Lisa Houck, *A Likely Story,* 1992, watercolor, 9 × 13"

Chapter Outline

FIGURE 4.1

What Are Your Reactions to This Person? You may have strong feelings about and reactions to this person. Social psychologists refer to such reactions as *attitudes*.

What are your views about abortion? Affirmative action? Capital punishment? Welfare? How do you feel about Newt Gingrich, O. J. Simpson, President Clinton (see Figure 4.1)? We doubt that you are neutral toward all of these issues and people. In fact, the chances are good that you have strong views and reactions to at least some of them. You may be passionately against—or for—abortion; you may believe that affirmative action is mainly beneficial—or harmful—in its effects. You may have strong positive or negative feelings and beliefs about Newt Gingrich, O. J. Simpson, and Bill Clinton. The fact that you have such reactions is hardly surprising. As human beings, we are usually not neutral toward important aspects of the social world around us—aspects that affect us in some manner. And of course, all the issues and people named here do have an impact upon many of us. (If you don't live in the United States, just insert the issues and names that are most important in your own society; the basic principle remains the same.)

Social psychologists have long been interested in such reactions, which they term **attitudes.** There are many definitions of this term, but most center in the fact that we tend to evaluate many aspects of the social world. Thus, a good working definition of attitudes is as follows: *Attitudes are associations between attitude objects (virtually any aspect of the social world) and evaluations of those objects* (Fazio & Roskos-Ewoldsen, 1994). More simply, attitudes are lasting evaluations of various aspects of the social world—evaluations that are stored in memory (Judd et al., 1991).

Why are attitudes important? For two basic reasons. First, they strongly influence social thought—the way in which we think about and process social information. Attitudes often function as *schemas*—cognitive frameworks that hold and organize information about specific concepts, situations, or events (Wyer & Srull, 1994). As we saw in Chapter 3, these "mental scaffolds" strongly influence the way in which we process social information—what we notice, enter into memory, and later remember. To the extent attitudes operate as schemas, they, too, exert such effects. For example, imagine two people who hold very dif-

Attitudes ■ Lasting evaluations of various aspects of the social world.

ferent attitudes about capital punishment: one is strongly in favor of the death penalty for convicted criminals, the other is just as passionately against it. Both now read a newspaper article describing a recent study indicating that murder rates are no lower in countries that have the death penalty than in ones that do not. Will the two people interpret this information differently? The chances are good that they will. The person who is against the death penalty may reason: "See, it's just what I thought all along. Executing people is useless; it doesn't deter others from committing similar crimes." In contrast, the person in favor of capital punishment may think: "So what? The death penalty isn't designed to deter other criminals; its main function is eliminating dangerous people so they won't hurt other victims." In this and many other ways, attitudes can strongly influence our social thought and the conclusions and inferences we reach.

That's not the only reason why social psychologists have been interested in attitudes for several decades, however. Attitudes have also been a focus of research because, it has been assumed, they often influence behavior. Do you believe that abortion is wrong and should be outlawed? Then you may take part in a demonstration against it. Do you hold a negative attitude toward the President? Then you may vote against him in the next election. If attitudes influence behavior, then knowing something about them can help us to predict people's behavior in a wide range of contexts. As we'll see in Chapters 7 and 8, we also hold attitudes toward specific persons—for example, we like them or dislike them. Clearly, such attitudes can play a key role in our relations with these persons.

For these and other reasons, attitudes have been a central concept—and a major focus of research—in social psychology since its earliest days (e.g., Thurstone, 1928). In this chapter, we'll provide you with an overview of what social psychologists have discovered about these evaluations of the social world and their effects. Beginning at what is, logically, the beginning, we'll first consider the ways in which attitudes are *formed* or developed. Obviously, attitudes don't come from nowhere, but be ready for some surprises: many factors seem to play a role in attitude formation. Next, we'll consider a basic and crucial question: *Do attitudes actually influence behavior?* As we'll soon see, they do; but this link is much more complex than you might at first assume, and the correct question is not "Do attitudes influence behavior?" but "When and how do they exert such effects?" Third, we'll turn to the question of how, sometimes, attitudes are changed—the process of *persuasion.* Please emphasize the word "sometimes," because as we'll discover, changing attitudes is trickier than advertisers, politicians, salespersons, and many others seem to assume. Fourth, we'll examine some of the reasons why attitudes are usually difficult to change—why people are often so resistant to persuasion. Finally, we'll consider the intriguing fact that on some occasions, our actions shape our attitudes rather than vice versa. The process that underlies such effects is known as *cognitive dissonance,* and it has fascinating and unexpected implications for many aspects of social behavior.

Forming Attitudes: How We Come to Hold the Views We Do

Were the people shown in Figure 4.2 (p. 114) born with the attitudes they are demonstrating so clearly? Few persons would answer yes. On the contrary, most would agree that these and many other attitudes are acquired through experience. In a word, attitudes are *learned.* Social psychologists, too, accept this position. But please take note: We would be remiss if we did not mention the fact that a small but growing body of evidence suggests that attitudes may be influenced by

FIGURE 4.2

Attitudes: Born or Made?
Social psychologists believe that attitudes, such as the ones shown by the people in this photo, are acquired during life through learning and related processes.

genetic factors, too. We'll describe some of the evidence pointing to this surprising conclusion after we examine the major ways in which attitudes are learned.

Social Learning: Acquiring Attitudes from Others

One source of our attitudes is obvious: we acquire them from other persons through the process of **social learning**. In other words, many of our views are acquired in situations where we interact with others or merely observe their behavior. Such social learning occurs through several processes.

Classical Conditioning: Learning Based on Association. It is a basic principle of psychology that when one stimulus regularly precedes another, the one that occurs first may soon become a signal for the one that occurs second. In other words, when the first stimulus is presented, individuals expect that the second will follow. As a result, they may gradually acquire the same kind of reactions to the first stimulus as they show to the second stimulus, especially if the second is one that induces fairly strong and automatic reactions. Consider, for example, a woman whose shower emits a low hum just before the hot water runs out and turns into an icy stream. At first, she may show little reaction to the hum. After it is followed by freezing water on several occasions, though, she may well experience strong emotional arousal (fear!) when it occurs. After all, it is a signal for what will soon follow—something that is quite unpleasant.

What does this process—known as **classical conditioning**—have to do with attitude formation? Potentially, quite a bit. Many studies indicate that when initially neutral words are paired with stimuli that elicit strong negative reactions—for instance, electric shocks or loud sounds—the neutral words acquire the capacity to elicit favorable or unfavorable reactions (Staats & Staats, 1958; Staats, Staats, & Crawford, 1962). Since evaluative reactions lie at the very core of attitudes, these findings suggest that attitudes toward initially neutral stimuli can be acquired through classical conditioning. To see how this process might work under real-life conditions, imagine the following situation. A young child sees her mother frown and show other signs of displeasure each time the

Social Learning ■ The process through which we acquire new information, forms of behavior, or attitudes from other persons.

Classical Conditioning ■ Basic form of learning in which one stimulus, initially neutral, acquires the capacity to evoke reactions through repeated pairing with another stimulus.

mother encounters members of a particular racial group. At first, the child is quite neutral toward members of this group and their visible characteristics (skin color, style of dress, accent). After these visible characteristics are paired (associated) with the mother's negative emotional reactions, however, classical conditioning occurs; gradually, the child comes to react negatively to these stimuli, and so to members of this racial group (see Figure 4.3). We'll consider such *racial prejudice* in detail in Chapter 6.

Interestingly, studies indicate that classical conditioning can occur below the level of conscious awareness—even when people are not aware of the stimuli that serve as the basis for this kind of conditioning. For example, in one study (Krosnick, et al., 1992) students saw photos of a stranger engaged in routine daily activities such as shopping in a grocery store or walking into her apartment. While these photos were shown, other photos, known to induce either positive or negative feelings, were exposed for very brief periods of time—so brief that participants in the study were not aware of their presence. One group of participants was exposed to photos that induced positive feelings (e.g., a bridal couple, people playing cards and laughing) while another was exposed to photos that induced negative feelings (open-heart surgery, a werewolf). Later, both groups expressed their attitudes toward the stranger. Results indicated that even though participants were unaware of the photos, these stimuli significantly affected their attitudes toward the stranger. Those exposed to the positive photos reported more favorable attitudes toward this person than those exposed to the negative photos. These findings suggest that attitudes can be influenced by

FIGURE 4.3

Classical Conditioning of Attitudes. A young child sees her mother show signs of emotional discomfort when she encounters members of a minority group. Initially, the child has little or no emotional reaction to the characteristics of these people. After repeated pairing of her mother's emotional upset with these characteristics, however, she acquires negative emotional reactions to the characteristics herself.

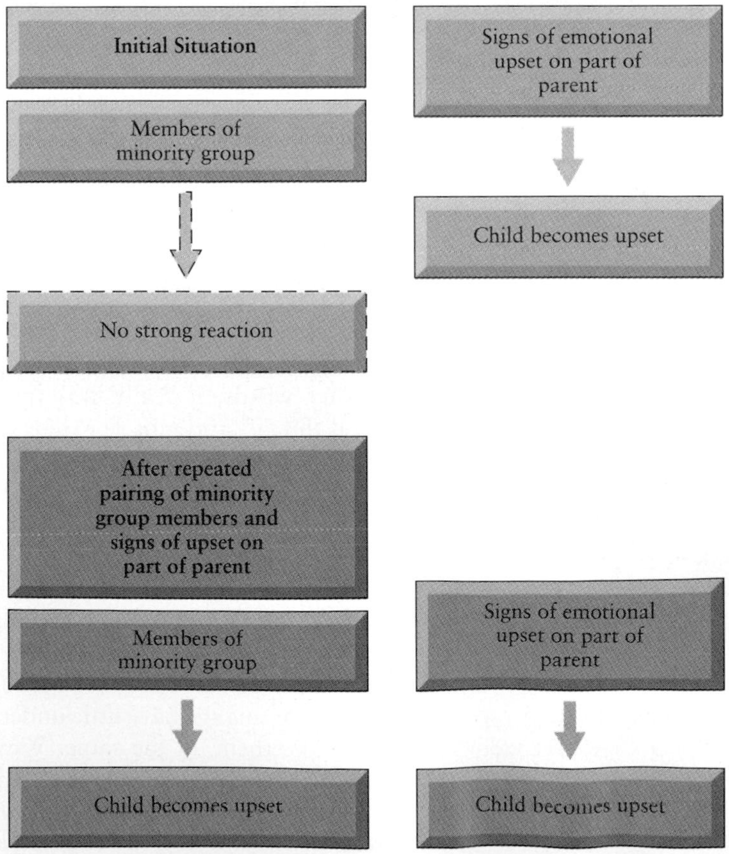

FIGURE 4.4

FIGURE 4.4

Attitudes and Muscle Movements. In research by Cacioppo and his colleagues (1993), individuals acquired attitudes toward stimuli such as the ones shown here simply because the stimuli were presented while the participants either flexed or extended their arms. These findings indicate that attitudes can be shaped by subtle processes that we can't describe verbally.

(*Source:* Courtesy Dr. John T. Cacioppo.)

subliminal conditioning—classical conditioning that occurs in the absence of conscious awareness of the stimuli involved.

Muscle Movements and Attitude Formation. If you found our brief description of subliminal conditioning of attitudes surprising, hold onto your seat: other studies indicate an even more surprising mechanism for the conditioning—and hence formation—of attitudes. This mechanism involves the movement of certain muscles and appears to involve a very basic fact: We draw things we like toward ourselves by flexing our arm muscles, but push things we don't like away by extending our arm muscles. Apparently, the association between these muscle movements and positive and negative feelings can serve as the basis for attitude conditioning. Such effects have been demonstrated very convincingly by Cacioppo, Priester, and Berntson (1993) in a series of skillfully conducted studies.

In these investigations, participants were asked to flex their arm muscles (by pushing up on the bottom of a table) or to extend them (by pushing down on the top of a table) while looking at a series of unfamiliar ideographs—Chinese symbols that stand for various words (see Figure 4.4). Then they were asked to rate these ideographs along a dimension ranging from extremely unpleasant to extremely pleasant. Results indicated that the participants rated the ones they saw while flexing their arms as more pleasant than the ones they saw while extending their arms. Further studies indicated that, consistent with the reasoning presented by Cacioppo and his colleagues, arm flexion induced positive reactions among participants to a greater extent than arm extension. But participants did not find flexion more pleasant in and of itself than extension; in other words, it really was the associations between muscle flexions and "good things" and muscle extensions and "bad things" that underlay these results. The reason this research is important is that it provides additional evidence for the role of classical conditioning in attitude formation. Our attitudes, it appears, can indeed be shaped by subtle processes of which we are largely unaware and which we can't describe verbally.

Instrumental Conditioning: Learning to State the "Right" Views. Have you ever heard a three-year-old state, with great conviction, that she is a Republican or a Democrat? Or that Fords (or Hondas) are superior to Chevrolets (or Toyotas)? Children of this age have little understanding of what these statements mean. Yet they make them all the same. Why? The answer is obvious: They have been praised or rewarded in various ways by their parents for stating such views. As we're sure you know, behaviors that are followed by positive outcomes are strengthened and tend to be repeated. In contrast, behaviors that are followed by negative outcomes are weakened, or at least suppressed. Thus, another way in

Subliminal Conditioning (of attitudes) ■ Classical conditioning of attitudes by exposure to stimuli that are below the threshold of conscious awareness.

which attitudes are acquired from others is through the process of **instrumental conditioning.** By rewarding children with smiles, approval, or hugs for stating the "right" views—the ones they themselves favor—parents and other adults play an active role in shaping youngsters' attitudes. It is for this reason that until they reach their teen years, most children express political, religious, and social views highly similar to those held by their families. Given the power of positive reinforcement to influence behavior, it would be surprising if they did not.

Modeling: Learning by Example. Still another process through which attitudes are formed can operate even when parents have no desire to transmit specific views to their children. This process is **modeling,** in which individuals acquire new forms of behavior merely through observing the actions of others. And where attitude formation is concerned, modeling appears to play an important role. In many cases children hear their parents say things not intended for their ears, or observe their parents engaging in actions the parents tell them not to perform. For example, parents who smoke often warn their children against smoking, even as they light up a cigarette. What message do children acquire from such instances? The evidence is clear: they learn to do as their parents *do*, not as they *say*.

Social Comparison and Attitude Formation

While many attitudes are formed through social learning, this is not the only way in which they are acquired. Another mechanism involves **social comparison**— our tendency to compare ourselves with others in order to determine whether our view of social reality is or is not correct (Festinger, 1954). To the extent our views agree with those of others, we conclude that our ideas and attitudes are accurate; after all, if others hold the same views, the views *must* be right! Because of the operation of this process, we often change our attitudes so as to hold views closer to those of others. On some occasions, moreover, the process of social comparison may contribute to the formation of new attitudes, ones we didn't previously hold. For instance, imagine that you heard others you know, like, and respect expressing positive views about some product you've never tried. Do you think you'd acquire a positive attitude toward it, and be more likely to try it yourself? Probably you would. In this case, you've acquired an attitude, or at least an *incipient* attitude, from social information and social comparison. The same processes may operate with respect to attitudes directed toward various social groups. For example, imagine that you heard individuals you like and respect expressing negative views toward a group with whom you've had no contact. Would this influence your views? While it's tempting to say, "Of course not! I wouldn't form any opinions without seeing for myself!" research findings indicate that hearing others state negative views might actually influence you to adopt similar attitudes—without ever meeting a member of the group in question (e.g., Shaver, 1993). Such effects are clearly demonstrated in a study by Maio, Esses, and Bell (1994).

These researchers presented Canadian visitors to a large science center with information about a fictitious group that was, supposedly, about to immigrate to Canada. Some persons received favorable information about this imaginary group (the Camarians): they learned that people in England had assigned them high ratings in terms of personality traits (friendliness, industriousness, honesty, intelligence) and values (education, equality, family, freedom, law and order). In contrast, others received unfavorable information about the Camarians: they learned that people in England assigned them low ratings on the same dimensions. After receiving this information, individuals rated their attitudes toward the Camarians (on an unfavorable–favorable dimension), and also indicated whether Camarians should be allowed to immigrate to Canada. As expected, par-

Instrumental Conditioning ■ Basic form of learning in which responses that lead to positive outcomes or that permit avoidance of negative outcomes are strengthened.

Modeling ■ Basic form of learning in which individuals acquire new forms of behavior through observing others.

Social Comparison ■ The process through which we compare ourselves to others in order to determine whether our view of social reality is or is not correct.

ticipants who received the favorable social information about this fictitious group expressed more favorable attitudes toward them than those who received negative information, and showed greater willingness to allow them to immigrate to Canada. Remember: these differences were based entirely on social information received by participants; they had never met a Camarian. Indeed, because this group is fictitious, they never could meet one. Findings such as these indicate that often our attitudes are shaped by social information, coupled with our own desire to hold the "right" views—those held by people we admire or respect.

Genetic Factors: Some Surprising Recent Findings

Can we inherit our attitudes, or at least a tendency to develop certain attitudes about various topics or issues? At first glance, most people—and most social psychologists—would answer *no*. While we readily accept the fact that genetic factors can influence our height, eye color, and other physical characteristics, the idea that they might also play a role in our thinking seems strange, to say the least. Yet if we remember that thought occurs within the brain and that brain structure, like every other part of our physical being, is certainly affected by genetic factors, the idea of genetic influences on attitudes becomes, perhaps, a little easier to imagine. In fact, a small but growing body of empirical evidence indicates that genetic factors may play some small role in attitudes (e.g, Arvey et al., 1989; Keller et al., 1992).

Most of this evidence involves comparisons between identical (monozygotic) and nonidentical (dizygotic) twins. Because identical twins share the same genetic inheritance while nonidentical twins do not, higher correlations between the attitudes of the identical twins would suggest that genetic factors play a role in shaping such attitudes. This is precisely what has been found: the attitudes of identical twins *do* correlate more highly than those of nonidentical twins (e.g, Waller et al., 1990). Of course, such findings are open to an important criticism: perhaps the environments of identical twins are more similar than those of nonidentical twins—for example, perhaps people treat them more similarly. Thus, the finding that identical twins hold more similar attitudes than nonidentical twins may stem from environmental factors. To deal with such complexities, other studies have focused on identical and nonidentical twins separated very early in life (see Figure 4.5). Even though these twin pairs were raised in very different environments, identical twins' attitudes still correlate more highly than those of nonidentical twins, and more highly than the attitudes of unrelated persons (Waller et al., 1990). Moreover, these findings hold true for several kinds of attitudes, ranging from interest in religious occupations and activities through job satisfaction (Bouchard et al., 1992). For example, consider a recent study conducted by Hershberger, Lichtenstein, and Knox (1994).

These researchers contacted hundreds of twin pairs living in Sweden (both identical and nonidentical twins), and asked them to complete several measures of attitudes toward the organizations where they worked. These measures assessed the twins' job satisfaction and their attitudes about the work climate in their organizations. Results indicated that the impact of genetic factors on job satisfaction was relatively weak. However, significant evidence was found for effect on the twins' assessments of work climate. Identical twins were more similar in their perceptions of work climate than nonidentical twins, and identical twins reared apart and those reared together were more similar to each other in these attitudes than was true for nonidentical twins reared together and apart. Together, these findings offer additional evidence for the view that even complex attitudes such as those toward one's job or work can be influenced by genetic factors.

Needless to add, twin research, like any other kind of research, can be questioned on several grounds. Twins are an unusual group, so results obtained with them may not generalize to other groups of people. Further, even when separated

FIGURE 4.5

Identical Twins Separated Very Early in Life: Often, Their Attitudes Are Very Similar. The attitudes of identical twins separated very early in life correlate more highly than those of nonidentical twins or unrelated persons. This finding provides support for the view that attitudes are influenced by genetic factors, at least to some extent.

early in life, identical twins may be assigned by adoption agencies to more similar environments than nonidentical twins. This could falsely inflate the apparent role of genetic factors in shaping their attitudes. Still, given the many safeguards and controls built into these studies, it is hard to ignore their findings.

But how, we can almost hear you asking, can such effects occur—how can genetic factors influence attitudes? One possibility is that genetic factors influence more general dispositions, such as the tendency to experience positive or negative affect—to be in a positive or negative mood much of the time (George, 1990). Such tendencies, in turn, could then influence evaluations of many aspects of the social world. For instance, an individual who tends to be in a positive mood much of the time might tend to express a high level of job satisfaction, no matter where the person works; in contrast, someone who tends to be in a negative mood might tend to express more negative attitudes in the same settings. Only time, and further research, will allow us to determine whether, and how, genetic factors influence attitudes. But at present, social psychologists are giving this possibility serious consideration, so an answer seems likely to emerge very soon.

INTEGRATING PRINCIPLES

1. Attitudes are acquired from other persons through *social learning*—a process that plays a role in many aspects of social behavior, such as helping (Chapter 10) and aggression (Chapter 11).

2. Attitudes are also shaped by *social comparison*—a basic process that influences many aspects of social behavior, including attraction (Chapter 7), relationships (Chapter 8), and perceptions of fairness (Chapter 12).

3. Genetic factors, too, may influence some kinds of attitudes, just as such factors influence other aspects of social behavior, such as mate selection (Chapters 1 and 7) and aggression (Chapter 11).

Do Attitudes Influence Behavior?
And If So, *When* and *How*?

Do our attitudes influence our behavior? Your first reaction is probably to say, "Of course!" Before you leap to this tempting conclusion, however, let me (Bob Baron) tell you about one of my own experiences concerning this issue. Last year, my village had a paint-collection day. Everyone who had old oil-based paint in their garage or basement was supposed to bring it to a collection point on Saturday morning so that it could be safely destroyed without contaminating the environment. I have strong proenvironment attitudes, so on Saturday morning, my wife and I drove to the designated spot. As we approached, we could see a line of cars stretching almost a mile. "There goes our Saturday!" I remarked, and I was right: we sat in line for more than two hours before getting a chance to give our paint to the people doing the collecting. So far, so good: my strong proenvironment attitudes did indeed predict my behavior. But here's where things get tricky. Two weeks later, the village announced another paint-collection day, this time for latex-based paint. I had three cans of this type of paint in my basement, so I put them aside with the intention of taking them to the collection point. But then I began to think about that long line, and another ruined Saturday. . . . Guess what I did? Shame on me, but I left the cans where they were and conveniently "forgot" all about the collection day. So much for my proenvironment attitudes!

While you may never have experienced events exactly like these, we're willing to bet that you, too, have had plenty of opportunities to observe a sizable gap between your attitudes and your behavior. To the extent that such a gap exists, of course, social psychologists find themselves facing a disturbing question: Have they been wasting their time studying attitudes for so many years? That an attitude–behavior gap *does* sometimes exist is clear. In fact, as described in the *Cornerstones* section below, the fact that attitudes do not always predict behavior was uncovered in some of the earliest research in our field (LaPiere, 1934) and was repeatedly confirmed during the 1960s and 1970s (e.g., Wicker, 1969). But it is equally clear that attitudes often do exert important effects on behavior. So our conclusion is: *No*, social psychologists have definitely *not* wasted their time by studying attitudes. The key question, however, is not "Do attitudes influence behavior?" but rather "When and how do they exert such effects?" These issues have been very central to modern research on the attitude–behavior link, so we'll focus on them in this discussion. Before turning to modern research on this issue, however, let's take a look at the first study that called the possibility of a gap between attitudes and behavior to the attention of social psychologists.

Cornerstones of Social Psychology

ATTITUDES VERSUS ACTIONS: "No, We Don't Admit That Kind of Person—Unless They Show Up at the Door!"

It was 1930, and all over the world, the bottom had dropped out of the economy. But Richard LaPiere, a social psychologist at Stanford University, wasn't interested in economics: he was concerned, in his research, with the link between attitudes and behavior. At the time, social psychologists generally defined attitudes largely in terms of behavior—as a set of tendencies or predispositions to behave in certain ways in social situations (Allport, 1924). Thus, they as-

Richard T. LaPiere.
Richard T. LaPiere, a social psychologist at Stanford University during the 1930s, conducted unique research demonstrating that people's attitudes are not always reflected in their overt behavior. His study initiated research on the link between attitudes and behavior that continues up to the present time.

sumed that attitudes were generally reflected in overt behavior. LaPiere, however, was not so certain. In particular, he wondered whether persons holding various prejudices—negative attitudes toward the members of various social groups (see Chapter 6)—would demonstrate these actions in their overt behavior. To find out, he adopted a novel technique. For more than two years, LaPiere traveled around the United States with a young Chinese couple. During these travels, they stopped at 184 restaurants and 66 hotels and "tourist camps" (predecessors of the modern motel). In the overwhelming majority of the cases, they were treated with courtesy and consideration. In fact, they were refused service only once; and in most cases they received what LaPiere (1934) described as an average to above-average level of treatment.

Now, however, the study gets really interesting. After the travels were complete, LaPiere wrote to all the businesses where he and the Chinese couple had stayed or dined, and asked whether they would offer service to Chinese visitors. The results were nothing short of astonishing: Out of the 128 establishments that responded, 92 percent of the restaurants and 91 percent of the hotels said no. In short, there was a tremendous gap between the attitudes expressed by these businesses (generally, by their owners or managers), and what they had done when confronted with live, in-the-flesh Chinese guests (see Figure 4.6). Similar attitudes were expressed by hotels and restaurants LaPiere did not visit, so the sample appears to have been a representative one.

What accounts for these findings? LaPiere himself noted that the young couple with whom he traveled spoke English well and—as he put it—were "skillful smilers." In other words, they were attractive and friendly. Faced with such persons, the owners of businesses ignored their own prejudiced attitudes and, far from rejecting such guests, welcomed them with courtesy. In fact, LaPiere reported that in the only "yes" letter he received from motels they had visited, the owner noted that she would be glad to accept Chinese guests, since

FIGURE 4.6

Evidence That Attitudes Don't Always Influence Behavior. Virtually all restaurants, hotels, and motels visited by LaPiere and a young Chinese couple offered courteous service. When asked through the mail whether they would serve Chinese visitors, however, more than 90 percent said *no*. These findings provide evidence for the view that often there is a sizable gap between attitudes and behavior.

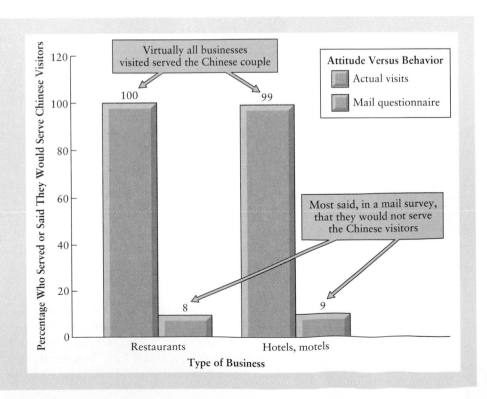

she had enjoyed a pleasant visit from a Chinese gentleman and his sweet wife the previous summer!

Putting such factors aside, however, LaPiere (1934) interpreted his results as indicating that there is often a sizable gap between attitudes and behavior—between what people say and what they actually do. Because of this fact, he concluded, it was important for social psychologists to study actual behavior, not just verbally reported attitudes. In the years since this ingenious research, social psychologists have taken LaPiere's suggestion to heart and, as you'll see in the rest of this section, have focused a great deal of attention on the questions of *when* and *how* attitudes predict behavior. So this study, conducted many years ago and in a manner so different from the rigorous methods used in modern research, has continued to exert a lasting impact on our field and the topics we study. ■■■

When Do Attitudes Influence Behavior? Specificity, Strength, Accessibility, and Other Factors

Research on the question of *when* attitudes influence behavior has uncovered several different factors that serve as what social psychologists term *moderators*—they influence the extent to which attitudes affect behavior. While many of these moderators exist, most seem to be related to aspects of the *situation*, aspects of *attitudes* themselves, and aspects of *individuals* (Fazio & Roskos-Ewoldsen, 1994).

Aspects of the Situation. Dress on campuses is very casual these days, so I don't usually pay much attention to the way students in my classes are dressed. Once in a while, though, someone comes to class looking so dirty and sloppy that I can't help but notice. I'd like to say something about it, because I do feel that college is important and that it's worth maintaining some minimal standards of appearance. But I never say a word. Why? Because I realize that the *norms* in this situation are dead set against me. *Norms,* as we'll see in Chapter 9, are rules indicating how people are supposed to behave in a given situation; and for faculty, the norm is clearly "How students dress is *not* your concern." This kind of incident illustrates one important factor that moderates (influences) the relationship between attitudes and behavior: *situational constraints.* Sometimes, people can't express their attitudes because doing so would be contrary to the norms in a given social situation. Much research provides support for this view (e.g., Ajzen & Fishbein, 1980; Fazio & Roskos-Ewoldsen, 1994), so it is clear that gaps between attitudes and behavior often involve such factors.

Another aspect of situations that influences the attitude–behavior link is *time pressure.* Attitudes, as we noted, often function as cognitive frameworks for processing social information. When individuals are under time pressure and have to decide to act very quickly, they tend to fall back upon their attitudes as quick-and-easy guides. Thus, in situations in which time pressure is great, the attitude–behavior link tends to be stronger than in situations in which such pressures are lacking, and in which individuals have the time to consider available information more carefully (Jamieson & Zanna, 1989).

Situational factors can influence the link between attitudes and behavior in one additional way. Think for a moment: whom are you likely to find at a rally against abortion—people in favor of personal choice where abortion is concerned, or people in favor of outlawing abortion? The answer is obvious: Except perhaps for a few hecklers, most people attending such a meeting will be opponents of abortion. The same principle holds for many other situations, and this points to an important fact: In general, we tend to prefer situations that allow us to maintain a close match between our attitudes and our behavior. In other words, we often choose to enter and spend time in situations in which what we say and what we do can coincide (Snyder & Ickes, 1985).

Recently, DeBono and Snyder (1995) have reasoned that because individuals tend to choose situations where they can engage in behaviors consistent with their attitudes, the attitudes themselves are strengthened and so become better predictors of behavior. To obtain evidence on this possibility, DeBono and Snyder conducted several studies. In one, they asked students who were strongly in favor of affirmative action to indicate the extent to which they had previously engaged in such attitudinally consistent behaviors as attending meetings or lectures about affirmative action, joining discussion groups at their dorms concerning this policy, and so on. Later, the same persons were telephoned and asked whether they would be willing to volunteer for a study dealing with affirmative action. As predicted, it was found that the more frequently participants reported entering pro–affirmative action situations, the more willing they were to volunteer for the study. In a second experiment, participants again indicated the extent to which they had previously chosen to enter situations that allowed them to express their attitudes on several issues (e.g., affirmative action, religion). In addition, the same persons performed a task in which they indicated, as quickly as possible, whether they agreed or disagreed with statements relating to these attitudes. DeBono and Snyder (1995) predicted that the more often participants had chosen to enter situations relating to their attitudes, the stronger the attitudes would be, and so the more quickly participants would respond to statements about them. Again, these predictions were confirmed.

These findings indicate that the relationship between attitudes and situations may be a two-way street. Situational pressures shape the extent to which attitudes are expressed in overt actions; but in addition, attitudes determine whether individuals choose to enter various situations. So, in order to understand the link between attitudes and behavior, we must take careful account of both sets of factors.

Aspects of Attitudes Themselves.   Years ago, I witnessed a very dramatic scene. A large timber company had signed a contract with the government allowing the company to cut trees in a national forest. Some of the trees scheduled to become backyard fences and patios were ancient giants, hundreds of feet tall. A group of conservationists objected strongly to plans to cut these magnificent trees, and they quickly put their money where their mouths were. They joined hands and formed a human ring around each of the largest trees, thus preventing the chain saw–wielding workers from cutting them. The tactic worked: there was so much publicity that soon the contract was revoked, and the trees were saved.

Why did these people take such drastic action? The answer is obvious: They were passionately committed to saving the trees. In other words, they held powerful attitudes that strongly affected their behavior. Incidents like this one are far from rare. For example, persons who are passionately against abortion demonstrate outside abortion clinics—and even physically assault doctors who perform abortions. And in 1995, one or more persons who held strong antigovernment attitudes blew up a federal building in Oklahoma City, killing hundreds of innocent persons through this violent expression of their views (see Figure 4.7 on page 124). Incidents like these call attention to the fact that the link between attitudes and behavior is strongly moderated by several aspects of attitudes themselves. Let's consider several of these factors.

Attitude Origins.   One has to do with how attitudes were formed in the first place. Considerable evidence indicates that attitudes formed on the basis of direct experience often exert stronger effects on behavior than ones formed indi-

FIGURE 4.7

Strong Attitudes in Action: A Tragic Example. When individuals hold certain attitudes passionately, they often express these in relatively extreme forms of behavior. In 1995, one or more persons holding powerful antigovernment attitudes blew up this building to express their views, killing hundreds of innocent victims in the process.

rectly through hearsay (refer to our earlier discussion of attitude formation; e.g., Regan & Fazio, 1977). Apparently, attitudes formed on the basis of direct experience are easier to bring to mind, and this magnifies their impact on behavior.

Attitude Strength.   Another factor—and obviously one of the most important—involves what is typically termed the *strength* of the attitudes in question. The stronger attitudes are, the greater their impact on behavior (Petkova, Ajzen, & Driver, 1995). By the term *strength,* social psychologists mean several things: the extremity or intensity of an attitude (how strong is the emotional reaction provoked by the attitude object?), its *importance* (the extent to which an individual cares deeply about and is personally affected by the attitude); *knowledge* (how much an individual knows about the attitude object), and *accessibility* (how easily the attitude comes to mind in various situations). Recent findings indicate that all these components play a role in attitude strength, but that, as you can probably guess, they are all related (Krosnick et al., 1993). Not only do strong attitudes exert a greater impact on behavior, they are also more resistant to change, are more stable over time, and have a greater impact on several aspects of social cognition. Thus, attitude strength is truly an important factor in the attitude–behavior link—so important that it's worth taking a closer look at some of the components that influence it (Kraus, 1995).

Let's start with attitude *importance*—the extent to which an individual cares about the attitude (Krosnick, 1988). Growing evidence indicates that the greater the importance of various attitudes, the greater individuals' tendency to make use of such attitudes in processing information; making decisions; and, of course, taking specific actions (Kraus, 1995). What factors influence attitude importance—in other words, why are some attitudes so important to specific persons? Research conducted by Boninger, Krosnick, and Berent (1995) provides some important clues.

These researchers reasoned that three factors may play a key role in determining attitude importance. One is *self-interest*—the greater the impact on an individual's self-interest, the more important the attitude. Another is *social identification*—the greater the extent to which an attitude is held by groups

FIGURE 4.8

Major Components of Attitude Importance. As shown here, attitude importance appears to stem from three major factors: self-interest, social identification, and value relevance.

(*Source:* Based on suggestions by Boninger, Krosnick, & Berent, 1995.)

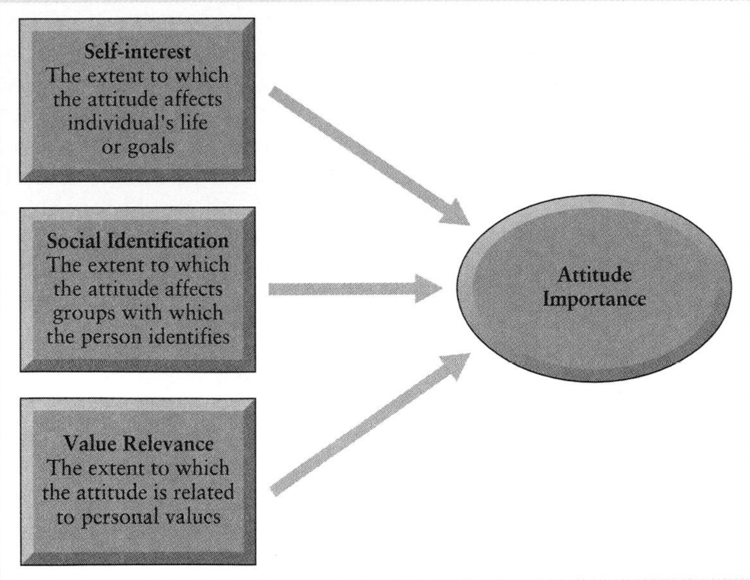

with which an individual identifies, the greater its importance. Finally, attitude importance also stems from *value relevance*—the more closely an attitude is connected to an individual's personal values, the greater its importance. To test this reasoning, Boninger and his colleagues (1995) called persons chosen randomly from the telephone book of a large city, and asked them to express their views about one current issue in the United States—gun control. Participants were asked to indicate how much the issue affected their lives (self-interest), how much it affected members of the social group to which they felt most similar and close (social identification), and how much their opinions on gun control were related to their own personal values (value relevance). Consistent with predictions, results indicated that all of these factors played an important role in overall attitude importance (Figure 4.8). So, in sum, it appears that what makes an attitude important is its relationship to basic social and individual needs and values.

Another, and somewhat different, aspect of attitude strength is **attitude accessibility**—the strength of the attitude object–evaluation link in memory. The stronger this link, the more quickly or readily an attitude can come to mind; and, as we saw in Chapter 3, the more readily social information comes to mind, the stronger, in general, its impact on our thought, decisions, and actions. Do you remember the research conducted by DeBono and Snyder (1995), dealing with people's tendencies to choose situations that permit them to behave in ways congruent with their attitudes? These researchers found that the more often people had been in such situations, the more quickly they responded to questions about their attitudes. These findings illustrate the effects of attitude accessibility: in general, the stronger an attitude, the more readily it comes to mind. Similar results have been obtained in many other studies (Bargh et al., 1992; Fazio, 1989), so it appears that attitude accessibility is indeed another component—or at least a clear reflection—of attitude strength.

Attitude Accessibility ▪ The ease with which specific attitudes can be remembered and brought into consciousness.

Attitude Specificity. Finally, we should mention *attitude specificity*—the extent to which attitudes are focused on specific objects or situations rather than general ones. For example, you may have a general attitude about religion (e.g., it is important for everyone to have some religious convictions) but much more specific attitudes about the importance of attending services every week (it's important—or unimportant—to go every week) or about wearing a religious symbol (it's something I like to do—or don't want to do). Research findings indicate that the attitude–behavior link is stronger when attitudes and behaviors are measured at the same level of specificity. For instance, we'd probably be more accurate in predicting whether you'll go to services *this* week from your attitude about weekly attendance than from your attitude about religion generally. On the other hand, we'd probably be more accurate in predicting your willingness to take action to protect religious freedoms from your general attitude toward religion than from your attitude about wearing religious jewelry (Fazio & Roskos-Ewoldsen, 1994). So attitude specificity, too, is an important factor in the attitude–behavior link.

We could go on to describe many other studies, because social psychologists have focused a great deal of attention on attitude strength and related concepts. The basic conclusion of this research, however, is straightforward: The stronger attitudes are, the greater the impact on overt behavior (Kraus, 1995).

Aspects of Individuals: Is the Attitude–Behavior Link Stronger for Some Persons Than for Others? So far, we've discussed the attitude–behavior link in general terms—as it exists for all individuals. In other words, we've ignored individual differences in this respect—the possibility that the link between attitudes and behavior is stronger for some persons than for others. Is this the case? Growing evidence suggests that it is. Some persons, it appears, use their attitudes as an important guide to behavior: they look inward when trying to decide how to behave in a given situation. Others, in contrast, focus their attention outward—they see what others are doing or saying, and try to behave in the manner that will be viewed most favorably by the people around them. This dimension is known as **self-monitoring,** and the strength of the attitude–behavior link does seem to differ for persons at its high and low ends—high and low self-monitors, respectively. Specifically, it appears that attitudes are indeed a better predictor of behavior for low self-monitors—people who use their attitudes as important guides to behavior. In contrast, this link is weaker for high self-monitors (e.g., Azjen, Timko, & White, 1982; DeBono & Snyder, 1995). We'll return to self-monitoring in more detail in Chapter 5; for the moment, we simply want to note that individuals do differ in the extent to which their attitudes predict their behavior, and that self-monitoring appears to play an important role in such differences.

How Do Attitudes Influence Behavior?

Understanding *when* attitudes influence behavior is an important topic. But as we noted in Chapter 1, social psychologists are interested not only in the *when* of social thought and social behavior, but in the *why* and *how* as well. So it should come as no surprise that researchers have also tried to understand *how* attitudes influence behavior. Work on this issue points to the conclusion that in fact, there may be two basic mechanisms through which attitudes shape behavior.

Attitudes, Reasoned Thought, and Behavior. The first of these mechanisms seems to operate in situations where we give careful, deliberate thought to our attitudes and their implications for our behavior. For example, in their **theory of planned behavior,** Ajzen & Fishbein (1980) suggest that the best predictor of how we will act in a given situation is the strength of our intentions with respect to that situation (Ajzen, 1987). Perhaps a specific example will help illustrate the eminently reasonable nature of this assertion. Suppose a student is

Self-Monitoring ■ Personality characteristic involving willingness to change one's behavior to fit situations, awareness of one's effects on others, and the ability to regulate one's nonverbal cues and other factors to influence others' impressions.

Theory of Planned Behavior ■ A theory of how attitudes guide behavior suggesting that individuals consider the implications of their actions before deciding to perform various behaviors.

considering body piercing—for instance, wearing a nose ornament. Will he actually engage in body piercing? According to Ajzen and Fishbein, the answer depends on his intentions; and these, in turn, are strongly influenced by three key factors. The first factor is the person's attitudes toward the behavior in question. If the student really dislikes pain and resists the idea of someone sticking a needle through his nose, his intention to engage in such behavior may be weak. The second factor relates to the person's beliefs about how others will evaluate this behavior (this factor is known as *subjective norms*). If the student thinks that others will approve of body piercing, his intention to perform it may be strengthened. If he believes that others will disapprove of it, his intention may be weakened. Finally, intentions are also affected by *perceived behavioral control*—the extent to which a person perceives a behavior as hard or easy to accomplish. If it is viewed as difficult, intentions are weaker than if it is viewed as easy to perform. Together, these factors influence *intentions;* and these, in turn, are the best single predictor of the individual's behavior.

Attitudes and Immediate Behavioral Reactions. The model described above seems to be quite accurate in situations where we have the time and opportunity to reflect carefully on various actions. But what about situations in which we have to act quickly—for example, when a panhandler approaches on a busy street? In such situations, attitudes seem to influence behavior in a more direct and seemingly automatic manner. According to one theory—Fazio's **attitude-to-behavior process model** (Fazio, 1989; Fazio & Roskos-Ewoldsen, 1994)—the process goes something like this. Some event activates an attitude; the attitude, once activated, influences our perceptions of the attitude object. At the same time, our knowledge about what's appropriate in a given situation (our knowledge of various social norms) is also activated. Together, the attitude and this stored information about what's appropriate or expected shape our definition of the event; and this definition or perception, in turn, influences our behavior. Let's consider a concrete example.

Imagine that a panhandler does approach you on the street. What happens? This event triggers your attitudes toward panhandlers and also your understanding about how people are expected to behave on public streets. Together, these factors influence your definition of the event, which might be "Oh no, another one of those worthless bums!" or "Gee, these homeless people really have it rough!" Your definition of the event then shapes your behavior (refer to Figure 4.9 on page 128). Several studies provide support for this model, so it seems to offer a reasonable description of how attitudes influence behavior in some situations.

In short, it appears that attitudes affect our behavior through at least two mechanisms, and that these operate under somewhat contrasting conditions. When we have time to engage in careful, reasoned thought, we can weigh all the alternatives and decide, quite deliberately, how to act. Under the hectic conditions of everyday social life, however, we often don't have time for this kind of deliberate weighing of alternatives; in such cases, our attitudes seem to shape our perceptions of various events, and hence our immediate behavioral reactions to them.

To recap: Contrary to what early research suggested, attitudes are related to behavior. Indeed, in many cases—when they are strong and important, were acquired through direct experience, influence individuals' self-interest, and come readily to mind—attitudes can exert strong effects on behavior (Kraus, 1995). So social psychologists have definitely *not* wasted their time by studying attitudes, because these evaluations of the social world turn out to be an important determinant of social behavior in many contexts.

Attitude-to-Behavior Process Model ■ A model of how attitudes guide behavior that emphasizes the influence of attitudes and stored knowledge (of what is appropriate in a given situation) on one's definition of the present situation; this definition, in turn, influences overt behavior.

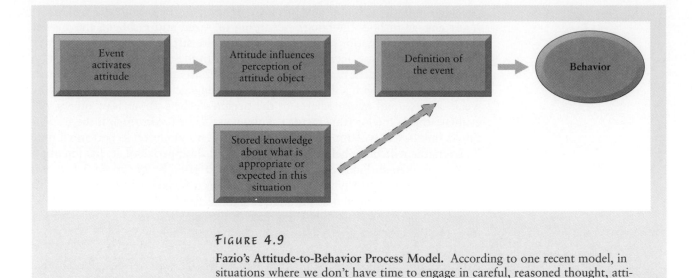

FIGURE 4.9
Fazio's Attitude-to-Behavior Process Model. According to one recent model, in situations where we don't have time to engage in careful, reasoned thought, attitudes guide behavior in the manner shown here.
(*Source:* Based on suggestions by Fazio, 1989, and Fazio & Roskos-Ewoldsen, 1994.)

INTEGRATING PRINCIPLES

1. Contrary to early findings, recent evidence indicates that attitudes do indeed influence behavior. Such effects are readily apparent with respect to several forms of social behavior, including prejudice (Chapter 6), attraction (Chapter 7), and helping (Chapter 10).

2. The strength of the attitude-to-behavior link, however, is moderated by several factors relating to the situation in which attitudes are activated, aspects of attitudes themselves (such as their strength), and personal characteristics of the individuals who hold them.

3. Attitudes appear to influence behavior through at least two different mechanisms; which of these operates depends on whether individuals have the time and opportunity to engage in careful thought, or must act quickly. These two modes of behavior—reflecting careful thought or impulsive action—are also apparent in many other aspects of social behavior, such as helping (Chapter 10) and aggression (Chapter 11).

Persuasion: The Process of Changing Attitudes

How many times during the past day has someone, or some organization, tried to change your attitudes? If you stop and think for a moment, you may be surprised at the answer, for it is clear that each day we are literally bombarded with many efforts of this type. Newspaper and magazine ads, radio and television commercials, political speeches, appeals from charities—the list seems almost endless. To what extent are such attempts at **persuasion**—efforts to change our

Persuasion ■ Efforts to change others' attitudes.

attitudes—successful? And what factors determine whether they succeed or fail? These are the issues we'll consider next.

Persuasion: The Traditional Approach

In most cases, efforts at persuasion involve the following elements: Some *source* directs some type of message (the *communication*) to those whose attitudes the source wishes to change (the *audience*). Taking note of this fact, much early research on persuasion focused on these key elements, addressing various aspects of the following question: *Who* says *what* to *whom* and with what effect? This traditional approach to the study of persuasion is known in social psychology as the *Yale Approach,* since much of the early research within this framework was conducted at Yale University. Such research sought to identify those characteristics of communicators (sources), communications (persuasive messages), and audiences that together influence persuasion (Hovland, Janis, & Kelley, 1953). The findings of this research were complex and not always entirely consistent. Among the results that have generally withstood the test of time—and additional research—however, are these:

1. Experts are more persuasive than nonexperts (Hovland & Weiss, 1951). The same arguments carry more weight when delivered by people who seem to know what they are talking about and to have all the facts than when made by people lacking expertise. This is why television commercials often show laboratory-coated "experts."

2. Messages that do not appear to be designed to change our attitudes are often more successful in this respect than ones that seem intended to reach this goal (Walster & Festinger, 1962). In other words, we generally don't trust—and generally refuse to be influenced by—persons who deliberately set out to persuade us. This is one reason why the soft-sell is so popular in advertising—and in politics.

3. Attractive communicators (sources) are more effective in changing attitudes than unattractive ones (Kiesler & Kiesler, 1969). This is one reason why the models featured in many ads are highly attractive, and why advertisers engage in a perpetual search for new faces.

4. People are sometimes more susceptible to persuasion when they are distracted by some extraneous event than when they are paying full attention to what is being said (Allyn & Festinger, 1961). We'll explain why this is so later in the chapter.

5. Individuals relatively low in self-esteem are often easier to persuade than those high in self-esteem (Janis, 1954). However, because persons low in self-esteem are often withdrawn, they may fail to pay attention to some persuasive messages, so this relationship is far from straightforward (Wood & Stagner, 1994).

6. When an audience holds attitudes contrary to those of a would-be persuader, it is often more effective for the communicator to adopt a *two-sided approach,* in which both sides of the argument are presented, than a *one-sided approach.* Apparently, strongly supporting one side of an issue while acknowledging that the other side has a few good points in its favor serves to disarm the audience and makes it harder for them to resist the source's major conclusions.

7. People who speak rapidly are often more persuasive than persons who speak more slowly (Miller et al., 1976). So, contrary to popular belief, people do not always distrust fast-talking politicians and salespersons.

FIGURE 4.10

Fear Appeals: One Effective Technique for Changing Attitudes. Persuasive messages that arouse strong emotions—especially fear—are often effective in changing attitudes and behavior relating to these attitudes.

One reason rapid speech is more persuasive is that it seems to convey the impression that the communicator knows what he or she is talking about.

8. Persuasion can be enhanced by messages that arouse strong emotions (especially fear) in the audience, particularly when the communication provides specific recommendations about how a change in attitudes or behavior will prevent the negative consequences described in the fear-provoking message (Leventhal, Singer, & Jones, 1965). Such fear-based appeals seem to be especially effective in changing health-related attitudes and behavior, and you've probably seen them yourself in many magazines and on television (Robberson & Rogers, 1988; see Figure 4.10).

At this point we should insert a note of caution: While most of these findings appear to be accurate, some have been modified by more recent evidence. For instance, while fast talkers are often more persuasive than slow ones, recent findings indicate that this is true only when the speakers present views different from those held by their audience (Smith & Shaffer, 1991). When they present views consistent with those of their audience, fast talkers may actually be less persuasive, in part because the speed of their speech prevents listeners from thinking about and elaborating the message while it is being presented. Such exceptions aside, however, the findings summarized previously represent useful generalizations about persuasion gained through decades of systematic research. Thus, they form an important part of our knowledge about this process.

Persuasion: The Cognitive Approach

The traditional approach to understanding persuasion has certainly provided a wealth of information about the *when* and *how* of persuasion—when such attitude change is most likely to occur, and how, in practical terms, it can be produced. It did not, however, address the *why* of persuasion—why people change their attitudes in response to persuasive messages or other information.

This issue has been brought sharply into focus by a more modern approach to understanding the nature of persuasion—an approach that rests firmly on social psychology's increasingly sophisticated understanding of the nature of social thought. This **cognitive perspective** on persuasion (Petty et al., 1994) does not concentrate on the question of "Who says what to whom and with what effect?" Rather, it focuses on the cognitive processes that determine how individuals are actually persuaded. In other words, this newer perspective focuses on what many researchers term a *cognitive response analysis*—efforts to understand (1) what people think about when they are exposed to persuasive messages, and (2) how these thoughts and basic cognitive processes determine whether, and to what extent, people experience attitude change (Petty & Cacioppo, 1986; Petty, Unnava, & Strathman, 1991). Let's examine what is, perhaps, the most influential cognitive theory of persuasion.

The Elaboration Likelihood Model of Persuasion: Where Persuasion Is Concerned, "To Think or Not to Think" Is Indeed a Crucial Question. What happens when individuals receive a persuasive message? According to Petty, Cacioppo, and their colleagues (Petty & Cacioppo, 1986; Petty et al., 1994), they think about the message, the arguments it makes, and (perhaps) the arguments it has left out. It is these thoughts—not the message itself—that then lead either to attitude change or to resistance to such change.

But how does persuasion actually occur? According to the **elaboration likelihood model** (ELM for short), two different processes, reflecting different amounts of cognitive effort on the part of message recipients, can occur. The first—known as the **central route**—occurs when recipients find a message interesting, important, or personally relevant, and when nothing else (such as distraction or prior knowledge of the message) prevents them from devoting careful attention to it. In such cases, they may examine the message in a careful and thoughtful manner, evaluating the strength or rationality of the arguments it contains. If their reactions are favorable, their attitudes and other existing cognitive structures may be changed, and persuasion occurs (refer to Figure 4.11 on page 132).

In contrast, if recipients find the message uninteresting or uninvolving, they are not motivated to process it carefully. This doesn't mean that it can't affect them, however. On the contrary, persuasion can still occur, but this time through what is known as the **peripheral route** (see Figure 4.11). Why would individuals change their attitudes in response to such messages? Perhaps the message contains something that induces positive feelings, such as a very attractive model or a scene of breathtaking natural beauty. Or perhaps the source of the message is very high in status, prestige, or credibility. Under these conditions, attitude change may occur in the absence of a critical analysis of the con-

Cognitive Perspective (on persuasion) ■ An approach that attempts to understand persuasion by identifying the cognitive processes that play a role in its occurrence.

Elaboration Likelihood Model (of persuasion) ■ A theory suggesting that persuasion can occur in either of two distinct ways, differing in the amount of cognitive effort or elaboration they require.

Central Route (to persuasion) ■ Attitude change resulting from systematic processing of information presented in persuasive messages.

Peripheral Route (to persuasion) ■ Attitude change that occurs in response to persuasion cues such as the attractiveness, expertise, or status of would-be persuaders.

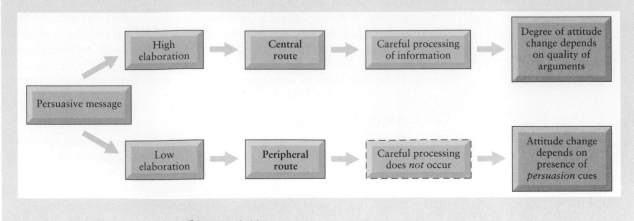

FIGURE 4.11

The Elaboration Likelihood Model. According to the elaboration likelihood model, persuasion can occur in either of two distinct ways. Individuals can engage in systematic processing of the information contained in persuasive messages, in which case persuasion occurs through the central route. Alternatively, they can respond largely to persuasion cues such as the source's apparent status or attractiveness. In this case, persuasion occurs through the peripheral route.

tents of the message. Needless to say, advertisers, politicians, salespersons, and others wishing to change our attitudes are well aware of this alternate route to persuasion, and often try to use it when they realize that the arguments they can marshal in support of their product or candidate are not strong or convincing. In such situations, they try to wow you with beautiful people, clever slogans, or catchy tunes. As you probably know from your own experience, such appeals can be quite effective—at least in the short run.

Is the ELM accurate? A large body of evidence indicates that it is. For example, it has been found that when persuasive messages are not interesting or relevant to individuals, the amount of persuasion they produce is *not* strongly influenced by the strength of the arguments they contain. However, when such messages are highly relevant to individuals, they are much more successful in inducing persuasion when the arguments they contain *are* strong and convincing (e.g., Petty & Cacioppo, 1979, 1990). Can you see why this is so? According to the ELM, when relevance is low, individuals are not motivated to process messages carefully, so any attitude change that occurs is probably produced through the peripheral route. When relevance is high, however, individuals are motivated to process messages carefully—with the result that they are persuaded to a much greater degree by strong than weak arguments.

Many other predictions based on the ELM have been confirmed. For example, the ELM predicts that if weak arguments are added to strong ones in a persuasive appeal, they may actually *reduce* the amount of persuasion produced, especially for issues that are important or involving individuals. For such issues, individuals tend to scrutinize message arguments very carefully. Such careful processing leads to unfavorable thoughts in response to weak arguments—thoughts that might not occur if the message contained only strong arguments. The result: Persuasion is reduced by the presence of the weak arguments (e.g., Friedrich, Fethersonbaugh, Casey, & Gallagher, 1996). Several other predictions based on the ELM have been verified, too (e.g., DeBono, 1992; Roskos-Ewoldsen & Fazio, 1992), so it appears that this model does indeed provide important insights into the nature of persuasion, and the cognitive processes that underlie it.

Effects of Persuasion through the Two Kinds of Routes. Since it is more difficult to come up with convincing arguments than it is to find gorgeous models, it might seem, at first glance, that would-be persuaders shouldn't waste their time on the central route. They should concentrate, instead, on producing persuasion through the peripheral route. However, research findings suggest that there are some definite disadvantages to such a strategy. First, attitudes changed through the central route seem to last longer than ones changed through the peripheral route (Petty & Cacioppo, 1986). Initially, both routes to persuasion may produce similar levels of attitude change; but later, change produced through the peripheral route tends to disappear. Given that persuasion via the central route involves careful thought and changes in cognitive structures, this finding is hardly surprising.

Second, it appears that attitude change produced by means of the central route is more resistant to later attempts at persuasion than change produced through the peripheral route (Petty et al., 1994). And finally, attitudes changed by the central route are more closely related to behavior than attitudes changed via the peripheral route. All these differences seem to be related to the fact that change induced through the central route represents a real shift in the way people think about a particular attitude object—a reorganization of the cognitive structure relating to this object. In contrast, change induced through the peripheral route seems to reflect a response to current conditions or stimuli—a whim of the moment if you will; once these current stimuli are gone, the change they induce, too, may disappear. So the message for would-be persuaders is clear: short-term results *can* be attained through flash and sizzle; but if the goal is that of producing lasting change in recipients' attitudes, then there may be no substitute for well-reasoned arguments presented in a clear and forceful manner.

Other Factors Affecting Persuasion: Attitude Functions, Reciprocity, and Message Framing

While most recent research on persuasion has focused on cognitive aspects of this process, we do not want to leave you with the impression that this is the entire story where such research is concerned. In fact, persuasion is a central topic in social psychology, so it continues to be studied from several different perspectives. In this section, we'll provide you with an overview of some of this recent work.

Attitude Functions. Attitudes can, and often do, serve several different functions for the persons who hold them. Sometimes they help the attitude holders to organize and interpret diverse sets of information (a *knowledge function*). Sometimes they permit individuals to express their central values or beliefs (a *self-expression* or *self-identity function*). And in other instances, attitudes help the persons who hold them to maintain or enhance their self-esteem (a *self-esteem function*) by, for example, allowing them to compare themselves favorably with others.

The functions served by attitudes are important from the point of view of persuasion. Persuasive messages containing information relevant to specific attitudes—and especially information relevant to the functions served by those attitudes—will be processed differently (perhaps more carefully) from persuasive messages that do not contain such information. For example, if an attitude helps people boost their self-esteem, then efforts to change this attitude should focus on the benefits to one's image from adopting this change. Similarly, if an attitude helps individuals to express their central values, then persuasive appeals should focus on how the recommended change will assist the target person in attaining *this* goal. The results of several studies offer support for this reasoning (e.g., Shavitt, 1989, 1990); so it appears that where persuasion is concerned, the functions served by attitudes are important to consider. Messages that draw a bead on these functions may be processed more carefully, and so exert greater impact, than ones that do not.

Reciprocity: Attitude Change As a Two-Way Street. Where social behavior is concerned, *reciprocity* appears to be a guiding principle. With few exceptions, we like others who like us, cooperate with others who cooperate with us, help others who help us, and aggress against others who treat us harshly (e.g., Cialdini, 1994). Given the strength and generality of this principle, it seems possible that reciprocity might play a role in persuasion, too; and recent evidence suggests that it does. In other words, we tend to change our attitudes—or at least our public expression of them—in response to persuasion from others who have previously changed *their* views in response to our own efforts at persuasion. This principle has been supported by the findings of careful research (e.g., Cialdini, Green, & Rusch, 1992), so it seems that reciprocity does indeed play an important role in at least some instances of attitude change.

Message Framing: Should Would-Be Persuaders Give People the Good News or the Bad News? Earlier, we saw that would-be persuaders often use emotional appeals as a tool of persuasion: they try to frighten people into changing their attitudes by telling them about the negative effects that will result unless their recommendations are accepted. Is this always a useful tactic? Or are there occasions when it is better to emphasize the positive outcomes that may result if we change our attitudes and our behavior? Recent research on this issue points to the following conclusion: Whether to emphasize the bad news (harmful effects that will occur if persuasion is *not* accepted) or the good news (beneficial outcomes that will occur if it is accepted) depends on who is the intended audience. Some persons are more influenced by the bad-news approach—known as *negative framing*—while others are more influenced by the "good-news" approach—known as *positive framing*. Research conducted recently by Tykocinski, Higgins, and Chaiken (1994) provides valuable insights into this relationship.

These researchers reasoned that which of these approaches will be most effective depends, in part, on certain aspects of individuals' self-concept. Specifically, they noted that most of us are aware of discrepancies between our current self-concept and the kind of person we'd like to be. However, the nature of such discrepancies differs across individuals. Some people focus on discrepancies between their current self and their ideal self (actual:ideal discrepancies), while others focus on discrepancies between their current self and how other important persons in their life think they should be (actual:ought discrepancies). Tykocinski, Higgins, and Chaiken (1994) reasoned that persons in the first category would be very disturbed by information about positive outcomes—this would remind them of how much they fall short of their ideal. Thus, they would engage in more counterarguing in response to positively framed messages. The result: They would be more influenced by *negatively* framed messages. In contrast, persons in the second category (those who experience actual:ought discrepancies) would be more disturbed by information about negative outcomes—this would remind them of instances in which they fell short of others' (e.g., their parents') ideals. Thus, such persons would engage in more counterarguing to negatively framed messages and would therefore be influenced to a greater extent by *positively* framed messages.

To test these complex but intriguing predictions, the researchers presented persons who were identified as falling into these two groups (actual:ideal and actual:ought discrepancies) and who didn't currently eat breakfast to persuasive messages designed to get them to eat this meal every morning. For both groups,

FIGURE 4.12

Message Framing and Persuasion. Positively framed messages that emphasized the benefits of eating breakfast were more effective than negatively framed messages that emphasized the costs of not eating breakfast for individuals with actual:ought discrepancies in their self-concept. The opposite was true for individuals with actual:ideal discrepancies.

(*Source:* Based on data from Tykocinski, Higgins, & Chaiken, 1994.)

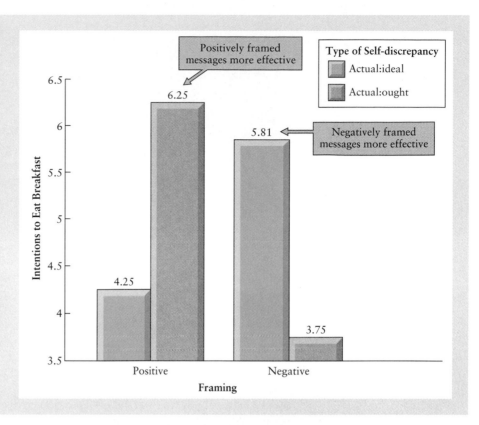

some participants were exposed to negatively framed messages emphasizing the negative outcomes that would result if they continued to skip breakfast (e.g., low glucose level, poor performance and concentration). Others, in contrast, were exposed to positively framed messages—ones emphasizing the benefits of eating breakfast (e.g., high glucose levels, increased performance and concentration). After receiving the persuasive messages, participants indicated their intentions about eating breakfast. As shown in Figure 4.12, the two types of messages did indeed have contrasting effects on the two groups of participants. Those with actual:ideal discrepancies were more strongly influenced by the negatively framed message, while those with actual:ought discrepancies were more strongly influenced by the positively framed message.

These findings serve to emphasize two important points about persuasion that should be considered carefully by all would-be persuaders: (1) Personal characteristics of target persons often strongly influence their reactions to persuasive appeals, and (2) carefully matching such appeals to their intended audiences is often a useful strategy for increasing persuasion.

INTEGRATING PRINCIPLES

1. The success of efforts at persuasion is strongly influenced by the characteristics of communicators, aspects of the messages they send, and the characteristics of persons who receive these persuasive appeals.

2. In addition, the impact of persuasion is strongly influenced by cognitive processes—the ways in which recipients think about persua-

sive messages. Thus, persuasion is closely linked to basic aspects of social perception (Chapter 2) and social thought (Chapter 3).

3. Persuasion is also related to other forms of social influence (Chapter 9), to personal characteristics of recipients, and to the functions served by attitudes (Chapter 3).

When Attitude Change Fails: Resistance to Persuasion

Given the frequency with which we are exposed to persuasive messages, one point is clear: If we changed our attitudes in response to even a small fraction of these messages, we would soon be in a pitiful state. Our views on a wide range of issues would change from day to day or even from hour to hour; and reflecting these shifts, our behavior, too, would show a pattern of shifts and reversals as we responded to one persuasive message after another. Obviously, this does not happen. Despite all the charm, talent, and expertise would-be persuaders can muster, our attitudes remain remarkably stable. Rather than being pushovers where persuasion is concerned, we are a tough sell; like the character in Figure 4.13, we can fend off even powerful efforts to change our attitudes. Why? What factors provide us with such impressive ability to resist? We'll now examine several of these.

Reactance: Protecting Our Personal Freedom

Have you ever had an experience like this? Someone exerts mounting pressure on you to get you to change your attitudes. As they do, you experience increasing levels of annoyance and resentment. The final outcome: You not only

FIGURE 4.13

Resistance to Persuasion: A Fact of Social Life. *Like the individual in this cartoon, most of us are definitely a tough sell where persuasion is concerned.*

(*Source:* Drawing by C. Barsotti; © 1984 *The New Yorker* Magazine, Inc.)

resist; you actually lean over backward to the *opposite* of what the would-be persuader wants. This behavior reflects what social psychologists term **reactance**—a negative reaction to efforts by others to limit our personal freedom by getting us to do what *they* want us to do. Research findings indicate that in such situations, we really do often change our attitudes (or behavior) in a direction exactly opposite to that being urged on us—an effect known as *negative attitude change* (Brehm, 1966; Rhodewalt & Davison, 1983). Indeed, so strong is the desire to resist excessive influence that in some cases individuals shift away from a view someone else is advocating even if it is one they would otherwise normally accept!

The existence of reactance is one principal reason why hard-sell attempts at persuasion often fail. When individuals perceive such appeals as direct threats to their personal freedom (or their image of being an independent person), they are strongly motivated to resist. And such resistance, in turn, virtually assures that many would-be persuaders are doomed to fail.

Forewarning: Prior Knowledge of Persuasive Intent

When we watch television, we fully expect commercials to interrupt most programs (except if we are watching public television). We know full well that these messages are designed to change our views—to get us to buy various products, for instance. Similarly, we know, when we listen to a political speech, that the politician delivering it has an ulterior motive: she or he wants our vote. Does the fact that we know in advance about the persuasive intent behind such messages help us to resist them? Research evidence on such advance knowledge—known as **forewarning**—indicates that it does (e.g., Cialdini & Petty, 1979; Petty & Cacioppo, 1981). When we know that a speech, taped message, or written appeal is designed to alter our views, we are often less likely to be affected by it than if we do not possess such knowledge. Why is this the case? Because forewarning influences several cognitive processes that play a role in persuasion. First, forewarning provides us with a greater opportunity to formulate *counterarguments* that can lessen the message's impact. In addition, forewarning also provides us with more time in which to recall relevant facts and information—information that may prove useful in refuting a persuasive message (Wood, 1982). The benefits of forewarning are more likely to occur with respect to attitudes we consider important (Krosnick, 1989), but they seem to occur to a smaller degree even for attitudes we view as fairly insignificant. In many cases, then, it appears that to be forewarned is indeed to be forearmed where persuasion is concerned.

Selective Avoidance

Still another way in which we resist attempts at persuasion is through **selective avoidance,** a tendency to direct our attention away from information that challenges our existing attitudes. As we explained in Chapter 3, selective avoidance is one of the ways in which schemas guide the processing of social information, and attitudes often operate as schemas. A clear illustration of the effects of selective avoidance is provided by television viewing. People do not simply sit in front of the tube and absorb whatever the media decide to dish out. Instead, they channel surf, mute the commercials, engage in many other activities, or cognitively tune out when confronted with information contrary to their views. The opposite effect occurs as well. When we encounter information that *supports* our views, we tend to give it our full attention. These tendencies to ignore or avoid information that contradicts our attitudes while actively seeking information consistent with them constitute the two sides of what social psychologists term *selective exposure,* and such selectivity in what we make the focus of our

Reactance ■ Negative reaction to threats to one's personal freedom; often increases resistance to persuasion.

Forewarning ■ Advance knowledge that one is about to become the target of an attempt at persuasion; often increases resistance to the persuasion that follows.

Selective Avoidance ■ Tendency to direct attention away from information that challenges existing attitudes; increases resistance to persuasion.

attention helps ensure that our attitudes remain largely intact for long periods of time. Incidentally, these tendencies play a role in our preference for friends who share our attitudes—a topic we'll examine in detail in Chapter 7.

To conclude: Because of the operation of reactance, forewarning, and selective avoidance, our ability to resist persuasion is impressive. Of course, attitude change *does* occur in some cases; to deny that it does would be to suggest that all forms of advertising, propaganda, and political campaigning are worthless—a conclusion that few would accept. But the opposite conclusion, that we are helpless pawns in the hands of all-powerful persuaders, is equally false.

Cognitive Dissonance: How We Sometimes Change Our Own Attitudes

Do you remember my experience with "paint collection day" in my village? I went to the first one because doing so was consistent with my strong proenvironmental attitudes. But after learning that I'd have to wait more than two hours to get rid of my old paint cans, I didn't go to the next one. That's bad enough, but there's more to the story. After a while, I got so tired of looking at those half-filled cans of paint and thinking to myself "I should have gotten rid of them," that I *did* get rid of them: I put them in with our regular trash. That's not strictly forbidden in my town, but I certainly looked around to be sure my neighbors didn't see me the day I did it! In fact, I still feel a little uncomfortable about it now, more than six months later. Why? Because in this situation, my behavior was clearly inconsistent with my attitudes. Social psychologists term the kind of discomfort I experienced **cognitive dissonance**—an unpleasant state that occurs when we notice that various attitudes we hold, or our attitudes and our behavior, are somehow inconsistent (Festinger, 1957).

Unfortunately, cognitive dissonance is an all-too-common experience. Any time you say things you don't really believe, make a tough decision, or discover that something you've purchased isn't as good as you expected, you may well experience dissonance. In all these situations, there is a gap between your actions and your attitudes, and it tends to make us quite uncomfortable. Most important from the present perspective, cognitive dissonance can sometimes lead us to change our attitudes—to shift them so that they are consistent with other attitudes we hold or with our overt behavior. Put another way, because of cognitive dissonance and its effects, *we sometimes change our own attitudes,* without any outside pressure to do so. Let's take a closer look at the theory of cognitive dissonance, which has been one of the most influential views in the history of social psychology, and at the role of cognitive dissonance in the process of attitude change.

Cognitive Dissonance: What It Is and How It's Reduced

Cognitive Dissonance ■ Internal state that results when individuals notice inconsistency between two or more of their attitudes or between their attitudes and their behavior.

Dissonance theory, we've already noted, begins with a very reasonable idea: people don't like inconsistency, and are uncomfortable when it occurs. In other words, when we notice that two or more of our attitudes are inconsistent with each other ("I'm against prejudice" but "I don't want minority people living in my neighborhood"), or that our attitudes and behavior are inconsistent ("I'm on a diet because I want to be slim" but "I'm sitting here eating a huge, rich dessert"), we experience an uncomfortable state known as *cognitive dissonance.*

When we do, the theory continues, we experience motivation to reduce that unpleasant state. In short, we are motivated to reduce dissonance. How can we accomplish this goal? The theory focuses on three basic mechanisms.

First, we can change our attitudes or behavior so that these are more consistent with each other. For instance, in the first example above, the person in question can become more favorable toward having minority persons as neighbors. In the second example, in contrast, the individual can actually push the dessert away before finishing it, thus reducing the inconsistency between present behavior and his underlying attitudes. Second, we can acquire new information that supports our attitude or our behavior. For instance, persons who smoke may search for evidence suggesting that the harmful effects of this habit are minimal or far from conclusive. Third, we can decide that the inconsistency actually doesn't matter; in other words, we can engage in *trivialization*—concluding that the attitudes or behaviors in question are not important ones, so any inconsistency between them is insignificant (Simon, Greenberg, & Brehm, 1995; see Figure 4.14).

Which of these various modes of dissonance reduction do we use? In general, the one requiring least effort. In other words, we are pragmatic where dissonance reduction is concerned; we take whatever steps will reduce this unpleasant state and at the same time require the least effort. When we experience dissonance, something has to give, and this something is generally the cognitive element that is easiest or most open to change.

Now that we've examined the basic nature of cognitive dissonance, we'll turn to its role in attitude change. Before doing so, however, let's briefly consider recent evidence concerning the accuracy of certain key aspects of dissonance theory.

Is Dissonance Really Unpleasant? Do people really experience discomfort when they notice that their attitudes and their behavior are inconsistent? This is a basic and important assumption of dissonance theory, because it is presumably the unpleasantness of dissonance that motivates people to try to reduce

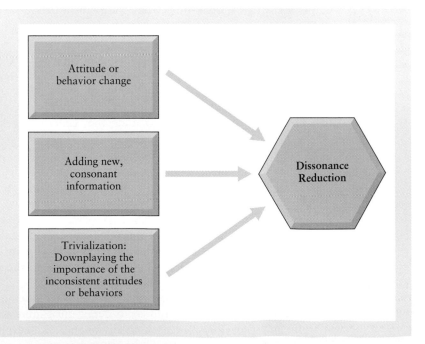

FIGURE 4.14

Major Ways of Reducing Cognitive Dissonance. Individuals experiencing cognitive dissonance can reduce it in several different ways. The three mechanisms shown here are the most important of these.

it. That dissonance is arousing in a physiological sense has been well established (e.g., Elkin & Leippe, 1986; Losch & Cacioppo. 1990). When people are placed in a situation where their attitudes and behavior don't agree, they do show increased levels of arousal. But is such arousal also unpleasant? Until recently, there was no direct evidence on this suggestion. Research by Elliot and Devine (1994), however, has now filled this gap.

To determine whether dissonance is indeed an unpleasant state, these researchers asked students at a large university to write essays favoring a large tuition increase. In other words, they wrote essays arguing *against* their own views. (Many studies indicate that engaging in such behavior induces strong cognitive dissonance; e.g., Cooper & Scher, 1994.) In contrast, other students were asked to write essays against the tuition increase—essays supporting their own views. To find out whether dissonance produces feelings of psychological discomfort, some of the individuals who wrote the essay arguing against their own views were asked to report on their current feelings immediately after writing it, and then on their attitudes toward the tuition increase. Those in another group, in contrast, reported on their attitudes first and then on their feelings after writing the essay. Finally, those in a baseline control group reported on their current feelings *before* agreeing to write the essay, and then reported on their attitudes after completing it; another control group wrote an essay expressing their own real attitudes. Elliot and Devine predicted that those who rated their current feelings immediately after writing the essay would experience dissonance, and so would report high levels of discomfort—higher than those in the other groups. In contrast, those who wrote the essay, then reported on their attitudes, and only then rated their current feelings would show relatively low levels of discomfort; after all, they had an opportunity to change their attitudes and so to reduce dissonance before rating their current moods. However, these individuals would show the largest shift in attitudes toward the tuition increase. Those in the two control conditions (the baseline group and those who wrote essays consistent with their attitudes) would also show relatively low levels of discomfort. As you can see from Figure 4.15, all these predictions were confirmed. Together, these results provide clear support for the view that dissonance *is* an unpleasant state, and that it is individuals' efforts to reduce this discomfort that motivate attitude change when people engage in attitude-discrepant behavior.

Modes of Dissonance Reduction: Tactics for Eliminating That Uncomfortable Feeling. "Whenever possible, take the path of least resistance." As we saw in Chapter 3, this seems to be a guiding principle for many aspects of human behavior, including social thought. So it is not surprising that when individuals experience dissonance, they generally seek to reduce it in the easiest possible way. Since changing one's overt behavior is often very difficult, most studies on the effects of dissonance have focused on attitude change. And as we'll see in the next section, a large amount of evidence indicates that this is indeed one important way in which people eliminate inconsistencies between their attitudes and their actions. But another strategy may be even less effortful in some situations: **trivialization**—perceiving the attitudes or behaviors involved as relatively unimportant. "True, I didn't take those cans of paint to the recycling center; but after all, a few cans of paint aren't very important, and I'm only one out of almost six billion people in the world. . . ." That's the kind of thinking involved in trivialization.

Although this method for reducing dissonance seems to be a useful one, it was not studied in detail until quite recently, so this was another gap in our knowledge about dissonance. Research conducted by Simon, Greenberg, and Brehm (1995), however, has now provided the missing information.

Trivialization ■ A technique for reducing dissonance in which the importance of attitudes or behavior that are inconsistent with each other is cognitively reduced.

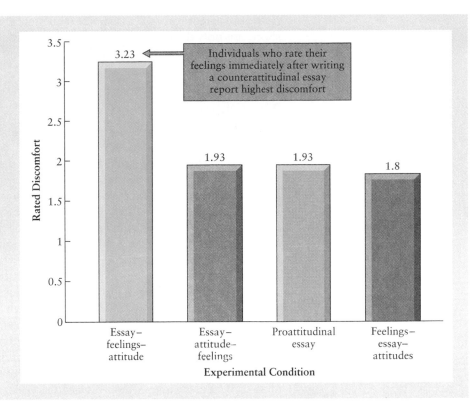

FIGURE 4.15

Evidence That Dissonance Is Indeed an Unpleasant State. Individuals who rated their current feelings immediately after engaging in counterattitudinal behavior (writing an essay against their own views) expressed the highest levels of discomfort. Those who wrote the essay, reported their attitudes, and only then reported their feelings showed lower levels of discomfort—apparently because they had changed their attitudes to reduce dissonance.

(*Source:* Based on data from Elliot & Devine, 1994.)

These researchers reasoned that individuals would tend to use trivialization as a means for reducing dissonance when changing their attitudes was made relatively difficult. To make it harder for some individuals to change their attitudes, Simon and her colleagues asked them to think about their attitudes concerning an important issue—comprehensive final exams for students—before writing an essay in support of such exams. As you can readily guess, virtually all students were opposed to such exams. Other participants, in contrast, were not asked to think about their attitudes in this manner. Since thinking about an attitude makes it more obvious (salient), Simon and her colleagues (1995) reasoned that it would be more difficult for individuals to change their attitudes in this condition. Another aspect of the study involved whether participants freely chose to write the counterattitudinal essays or were simply assigned to do so. Previous findings indicated that dissonance is much greater when individuals freely choose to engage in actions contrary to their actual beliefs than when they are simply told to do so and are given little choice in the matter. After writing their essays, participants expressed their attitudes toward comprehensive final exams and also answered several questions designed to assess trivialization—their tendencies to perceive the issue of comprehensive exams or the writing of a counterattitudinal essay as unimportant. As predicted, students in the high-choice condition who had been asked to think about their attitudes before writing the essay (high-salience condition) were most likely to engage in trivialization. They rated the essay and the issue of comprehensive final exams as less important than those in any of the other conditions. In a follow-up study, conditions were changed so that individuals either expressed their attitude first or rated the importance of the issue and the essay first. Interestingly, participants were less likely to engage in trivialization if they first expressed their attitude—apparently because under these conditions, they reduced their dissonance by changing their views. Taken together, the studies conducted by Simon, Greenberg, and Brehm (1995) point to the overall conclusion that once individuals choose the easiest or most convenient form of dissonance reduction, they tend to ignore all others. In short, not only do we choose the path of least resistance; once we head down it, we don't bother to glance, cognitively, at the alternatives.

Dissonance and Attitude Change: The Effects of Forced Compliance

There are many occasions in everyday life when we must say or do things inconsistent with our real attitudes. For example, your friend buys a new car and proudly asks you how you like it. You have just read an article indicating that this model is such a lemon that the manufacturer puts a free ten-pound bag of sugar in the trunk. But what do you say? Probably something like "Nice, really nice." Similarly, imagine that you have just started dating someone you really like and that he or she has invited you over for dinner. One bite, and you can tell you are in trouble: the food is awful. But when your date asks, "How do you like it?" what do you say? In all probability, "Great!" "Delicious!" or something to that effect. Social psychologists refer to such situations as ones involving **forced compliance**—situations in which we are forced to say or do something contrary to our real views. And by now you can probably guess what social psychologists predict will happen in such situations: often, when we can't change our behavior, we'll change the attitudes that are inconsistent with it. You may conclude that your friend's car must be better than the article says, or that the food really *is* good; it's just that you are unfamiliar with this combination of tastes and can't appreciate it—yet. In short, dissonance theory suggests that sometimes we really do change our own attitudes in order to bring them into closer alignment with our overt actions. And, of course, we are especially likely to do this when other techniques for reducing dissonance require greater effort.

Dissonance and the Less-Leads-to-More Effect. So far, so good. Predictions derived from dissonance theory seem straightforward and make good sense. But now consider this question: Will the reasons why you engaged in behavior inconsistent with your attitudes matter? Obviously, we can engage in attitude-discrepant behavior for many reasons, and some of these are stronger or more compelling than others. For instance, if you expect your friend with the new car to give you a lift to school every day, you have strong reasons for concealing your true reactions to it. But if your friend is about to move to another town, your reasons for saying that you like it when you think it's a lemon are somewhat weaker. Now for the key question: When will dissonance be stronger—when we have many good reasons for engaging in attitude-discrepant behavior, or when we have few such reasons? The answer is surprising: Dissonance will be stronger when we have few reasons for engaging in attitude-discrepant behavior. This is so because under these conditions, we can't explain away our actions to ourselves; we performed them even though there was no compelling reason for doing so. The result: Dissonance looms large in our consciousness.

In other words, as shown in Figure 4.16, predictions derived from dissonance theory suggest that it may be easier to change individuals' attitudes by getting them to engage in attitude-discrepant behavior under conditions where they have just barely enough reasons to engage in such behavior. Social psychologists sometimes refer to this surprising prediction as the **less-leads-to-more effect**—less reason leads to more attitude change—and it has been confirmed in many different studies (e.g., Riess & Schlenker, 1977). For example, in the first and most famous of these experiments (Festinger & Carlsmith, 1959), participants were offered either a small reward ($1) or a large one ($20) for telling another person that some dull tasks they had just performed were very interesting.

Forced Compliance ■ Situations in which individuals are somehow induced to say or do things inconsistent with their true attitudes.

Less-Leads-to-More Effect ■ The finding that offering individuals small rewards for engaging in counterattitudinal behavior often produces more dissonance, and so more attitude change, than offering larger rewards.

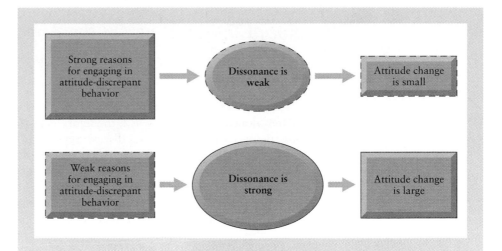

FIGURE 4.16

Why Less (Smaller Inducements) Often Leads to More (Greater Attitude Change) after Attitude-Discrepant Behavior. When individuals have strong reasons for engaging in attitude-discrepant behavior, they experience relatively small amounts of dissonance and relatively weak pressure to change their attitudes. However, when individuals have weak reasons for engaging in attitude-discrepant behavior, they experience larger amounts of dissonance and stronger pressure to change their attitudes. The result: Less (smaller rewards) leads to more (greater amount of attitude change).

One of these tasks consisted of placing spools on a tray, dumping them out, and repeating the process over and over again. After engaging in the attitude-discrepant behavior—telling another person that the dull tasks were interesting—participants were asked to indicate their own liking for these tasks. As predicted by the less-leads-to-more effect, those given the small reward for misleading a stranger actually reported liking the tasks to a greater extent than those given the large reward.

While this effect has been confirmed in many studies, we should note that it does not occur under all conditions. Rather, it seems to happen only when several circumstances exist (Cooper & Scher, 1994). First, the less-leads-to-more effect occurs only in situations in which people believe that they have a choice as to whether or not to perform the attitude-discrepant behavior. Second, small rewards lead to greater attitude change only when people believe that they were personally responsible for both the chosen course of action and any negative effects it produced (Goethals, Cooper, & Naficy, 1979). And third, the less-leads-to-more effect does not occur when people view the payment they receive as a bribe rather than as a well-deserved payment for services rendered. These and related findings indicate that there are definite limits on the impact of forced compliance: it doesn't lead to attitude change on all occasions. Still, the conditions just outlined often do exist—often people do have (or think they have) freedom of action; they accept responsibility for their own behavior and its consequences; and they tend to view inducements they receive as well-earned rewards. As a result, the strategy of offering others just barely enough to induce them to say or do things contrary to their true attitudes can often be an effective technique for inducing attitude change—and self-generated change at that.

For information on the practical—and beneficial—uses of dissonance theory, please see the Applied Side section on the following page.

Social Psychology: On the Applied Side
DISSONANCE, HYPOCRISY, AND SAFE SEX

By the mid-1990s, more than 100,000 persons had died of AIDS in the United States alone; around the world, the figure is in the millions. Even more alarming, the incidence of this fatal disease appears to be rising rapidly among adolescents. AIDS can be transmitted in several different ways (through blood transfusions, contaminated needles), but it is primarily a sexually transmitted disease, so in order to reverse these devastating trends, it will be necessary to change the sexual practices of many millions of persons. Specifically, sexually active individuals must somehow be induced to adopt the use of condoms, because this is the only procedure that has been proven to be highly reliable in preventing the spread of AIDS.

How can this goal be attained? How can we induce vast numbers of persons to change both their attitudes and their sexual behavior? Forced compliance by itself does not seem to be an effective procedure, because most persons, whether they use condoms or not, already agree with the suggestion that they *should* use these devices to combat the risk of AIDS. Thus, if they do use them, this is consistent, rather than inconsistent, with their underlying attitudes. Despite this fact, however, Aronson and his colleagues believe that dissonance can still be used to promote safe sex and other beneficial changes in social behavior (Aronson, Fried, & Stone, 1991; Dickerson et al., 1992). Specifically, they suggest that this can be accomplished through the use of a procedure that points out *hypocrisy*—(1) inducing individuals to make a public commitment to some course of action (e.g., use of condoms), and (2) reminding them that sometimes they have failed to behave in accordance with this commitment. Under these conditions, individuals are made to recognize their hypocrisy: the inconsistency between their public commitment (and the attitudes underlying this) and their actual behavior. The result is a high degree of dissonance and—it is hoped—subsequent change in the relevant behaviors.

This technique has been tested in many different settings and has been found to be quite effective (e.g., Dickerson et al., 1992). That it can also be successful in encouraging safe sex is indicated by the results of a study conducted by Stone and his colleagues (Stone et al., 1994). In this investigation, sexually active students were exposed to one of four conditions. One group—the *commitment* condition—was asked to prepare a videotape urging others to engage in safe sex. Another—the *mindfulness* condition—was asked to recall situations in which they had failed to use condoms; in other words, they were reminded of their failure to behave in a manner consistent with their own attitudes. A third group—the *hypocrisy* condition—received both of these treatments. Finally, a control group—the *information only* condition—made no public commitment about safe sex and were not asked to recall times when they failed to follow such practices.

After these procedures were completed, participants were asked to complete questionnaires on which they indicated their intentions to engage in safe sex in the future. In addition, they were given an opportunity to purchase condoms at a reduced price with the money they were paid for participating in the study. This opportunity was a private one: the experimenter left the room supposedly to run an errand, leaving participants alone in the room with the condoms and money for making change.

It was predicted that participants in the hypocrisy condition would express the greatest intentions of engaging in safe sex in the future, and would also be the

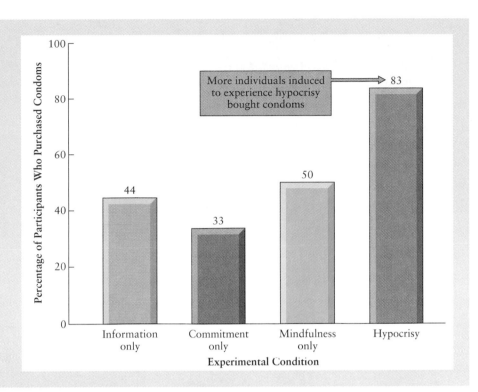

FIGURE 4.17

Hypocrisy As a Means of Encouraging Safe Sex. Individuals induced to experience hypocrisy bought more condoms than individuals who did not experience hypocrisy. They also expressed stronger intentions of engaging in safe sex in the future. These findings indicate that dissonance can be used to change socially important attitudes and behavior.

(*Source:* Based on data from Stone et al., 1994.)

most likely to buy condoms. Both predictions were confirmed: in fact, as shown in Figure 4.17, fully 83 percent of the participants in the hypocrisy condition purchased condoms; this was significantly higher than in any other conditions.

These findings, and those of several other studies (e.g, Aronson, 1992; Thibodeau & Aronson, 1992), indicate that inducing individuals to experience hypocrisy—and the strong levels of dissonance this generates—can be an effective means for changing both attitudes and behavior in a desirable direction. Moreover, it appears that it is not necessary for individuals to engage in attitude-discrepant behavior for such effects to occur. On the contrary, merely being reminded of certain attitudes one holds and one's own failure to live up to them can be helpful. In short, we can sometimes change our own attitudes by saying or doing things we believe as well as by saying or doing things we don't believe. ■■■

Social Diversity: A Critical Analysis

ATTITUDES AND ECONOMIC GROWTH: A CROSS-NATIONAL STUDY

THAT THE ECONOMIC FORTUNES OF NATIONS RISE AND FALL with the passage of time is obvious. When I (Bob Baron) took high school economics in the late 1950s, our teacher showed us many graphs suggesting that the United States was truly the dominant economic power: This nation accounted for a majority of the world's output of steel, automobiles, and electricity, to name just a few important items. Today, of course, such graphs tell a very different story. The United States no longer accounts for most of the world's production in these areas; and in recent years, its rate of growth has been much lower than that of several Asian countries. What factors contribute to such trends? Most persons (including trained economists) would quickly list such variables as the price and availability of natural resources, labor costs, and government policies that encourage or discourage growth.

TABLE 4.1 Attitudes Potentially Related to Economic Growth

Furnham, Kirkcaldy, and Lynn (1994) related attitudes to economic trends in forty-one different countries. They found that several of these attitudes (e.g., importance of money, competitiveness) were related to nations' economic growth and economic wealth.

Attitude	Description; Sample Items
Work ethic	Attitudes toward the moral value of work. "I like hard work."
Achievement motivation	The desire to attain excellent standards of performance. "I am an ambitious person."
Mastery	The need for mastery over problems and events. "If I am not good at something, I would rather keep struggling to master it than move on to something I may be good at."
Competitiveness	The motive to outperform others. "I feel that winning is important in both work and games."
Money beliefs	The importance attached to money. "I would do practically anything legal for money if it were enough."
Attitudes to saving	The value attached to saving. "I do financial planning for the future."

(*Source:* Based on information in Furnham, Kirkcaldy, & Lynn, 1994.)

To this list we'd add another, and uniquely social psychological, factor: *attitudes*. Growing evidence indicates that people in different countries do indeed hold sharply contrasting attitudes about the importance of work, achievement, competitiveness, saving, and the importance of personal wealth (Furnham, 1990; McClelland, 1976). And these attitudes, it appears, play a role in the economic fortunes of their countries.

Direct evidence for such links between attitudes and economic trends has been reported in several studies (e.g., Lynn, 1991). Perhaps the most comprehensive of these, however, is a massive study conducted by Furnham, Kirkcaldy, and Lynn (1994) involving more than 12,000 participants in forty-one different countries. These researchers examined the relationship between a wide range of attitudes and two economic indicators: gross domestic product (the amount of annual income per person in the country), and growth rate (rate of increase in economic output from year to year). The attitudes investigated are described in Table 4.1, and included attitudes toward work, achievement, competitiveness, money, and saving.

When scores on measures of these attitudes were related to the two economic indicators, significant relationships emerged. First, the researchers found that across all countries, attitudes toward competitiveness were a significant predictor of economic growth: the stronger these attitudes, the greater the rate of growth. Second, attitudes about the importance of money or personal wealth were a significant predictor of gross domestic product: the stronger these attitudes, the greater the wealth in the countries studied. In addition, interesting differences emerged among the countries with respect to economic attitudes. Participants from countries in North and South America scored highest on belief in the work ethic, mastery, and savings. On the other hand, Asian/Eastern countries (Bangladesh, China, Hong Kong, India, Iraq, Israel, Japan, Jordan, Korea, Singapore, Syria, Taiwan, Turkey, United Arab Emirates) scored highest on competitiveness and money beliefs (favorable attitudes toward the importance of personal wealth). Interestingly, persons from European countries scored lowest on most of the dimensions studied.

What do these findings mean? One possible interpretation is as follows: Certain attitudes are related to economic growth because they lead individuals to behave in ways that contribute to their countries' wealth. For instance, note that persons from Asian and Eastern countries scored highest on competitiveness and money beliefs—attitudes that were found to be significant predictors of economic growth. Of course, it is a large leap from attitudes held by individuals to the economic well-being of entire nations. Yet it should be noted that in the final analysis, economic trends reflect actions by large numbers of individuals. To the extent this is so, it is not really very surprising that attitudes relevant to economic activity may well play a role in shaping the destiny of national economies. The economic whole, after all, is indeed the sum of its parts—and these parts consist of thinking, feeling, behaving human beings. ■ ■ ■

CONNECTIONS: Integrating Social Psychology

In this chapter, you read about . . .	*In other chapters, you will find related discussions of . . .*
the role of social learning in attitude formation	the role of social learning in several forms of social behavior—attraction (Chapter 7), helping (Chapter 10), and aggression (Chapter 11)
persuasion and resistance to persuasion	other techniques for changing attitudes and behavior and why they are effective or ineffective (Chapter 9); the use of persuasive techniques in health-related messages (Chapter 14)
cognitive dissonance	the role of cognitive dissonance in various attitudes and forms of social behavior; for example, in job satisfaction (Chapter 13)

Thinking about Connections

1. Suppose that you wanted to launch a campaign to prevent teen-agers from starting to smoke (a major threat to their future health; see Chapter 14). What specific features would you build into this program in order to maximize its effectiveness?

2. Suppose that shortly after graduation, you receive two job offers. After a lot of painful thought, you choose one and reject the other. Do you think that your satisfaction with the job you chose (i.e., your job satisfaction [see Chapter 13]) will be greater because the decision was so difficult? Would your job satisfaction be lower if the decision were an easy one?

3. As noted in Chapter 3, we often tend to notice, and remember, information that is inconsistent with our views to a greater extent than information that is consistent with these views. Do you think that politicians and advertisers can put this fact to use in their efforts to change our attitudes? How?

4. If attitudes are indeed learned, this implies that important aspects of social behavior that involve attitudes—for instance prejudice (see Chapter 6)—are open to change. Drawing on our discussion of attitude change in this chapter, what steps could a society that wishes to reduce prejudice take in order to reach this important goal?

Summary and Review

Forming Attitudes

Attitudes are enduring evaluations of various aspects of the social world—evaluations that are stored in memory. Attitudes are acquired through experience or from other persons through *social learning*. This involves three basic forms of learning: classical conditioning, instrumental conditioning, and modeling. Recent evidence indicates that *subliminal conditioning* of attitudes is also possible and may play a role in their development. Attitudes can also be formed through *social comparison*, a process in which we compare ourselves with others. Recent evidence indicates that genetic factors, too, may play a role in the formation of attitudes.

Do Attitudes Influence Behavior?

Contrary to early findings, growing evidence indicates that attitudes do indeed influence behavior. However, this relationship is far from simple. Numerous factors influence (moderate) the strength of the attitude-to-behavior link. These include aspects of the situation, such as the operation of social norms and time pressure; aspects of attitudes themselves, such as their strength, importance, and accessibility; and aspects of individuals, such as *self-monitoring*.

Attitudes seem to guide behavior through two distinct processes. If we have enough time to engage in careful thought about our attitudes and our behavior, then attitudes guide behavior primarily by affecting our intentions. When we do not have the opportunity to engage in such reasoned thought, in contrast, attitudes seem to influence behavior in a more automatic manner involving our perceptions of the attitude object and our knowledge about what is appropriate or expected in a given situation.

Persuasion

Persuasion is the process of changing attitudes. The traditional view of persuasion focused on identifying crucial characteristics of communicators, communications, and audiences. A newer *cognitive perspective* focuses on the cognitive processes that underlie persuasion. The *elaboration likelihood model,* an influential cognitive model of persuasion, suggests that attitude change can occur either through careful processing of attitude-relevant information (the central route), or in a relatively automatic manner in response to various persuasion cues (the peripheral route). Attitude change produced through the central route is more lasting and has a stronger impact upon overt behavior. The effectiveness of persuasion is also influenced by the functions played by attitudes, by the principle of reciprocity, and by the framing of persuasive messages.

Resistance to Persuasion

Several factors play a role in our strong ability to resist persuasion. These include *reactance*—efforts to protect or restore our personal freedom; *forewarning*—

advance knowledge of persuasive intent on the part of others; and *selective avoidance* of information inconsistent with our attitudes.

Cognitive Dissonance

When individuals notice inconsistency between attitudes they hold or between their attitudes and their behavior, they experience *cognitive dissonance*. Dissonance motivates persons experiencing it to attempt to reduce it. They can accomplish this in several ways: by changing the attitudes in question, by acquiring information to support the behavior, or by means of trivialization—downplaying the importance of the attitudes or the behavior. Recent evidence indicates that dissonance is indeed an unpleasant state. The fewer good reasons people have for engaging in attitude-discrepant behavior, the greater the dissonance and the stronger the pressure for attitude change. This is known as the *less-leads-to-more effect*. Individuals also experience dissonance when they experience *hypocrisy*—when they recognize that they have not lived up to attitudes that they have stated publicly. Recognition of hypocrisy can induce individuals to change their behavior in order to match their attitudes. Recent findings indicate that it can even be effective in encouraging individuals to engage in safe sex, thereby helping prevent the spread of AIDS.

Social Diversity: Attitudes and Economic Growth

Growing evidence indicates that attitudes held by individuals in various countries are related to the wealth and economic growth of these nations. For example, it appears that individuals in many Asian countries that have recently had very high rates of economic growth have more favorable attitudes toward competitiveness and toward acquiring personal wealth than persons in many Western countries.

■ Key Terms

Attitude Accessibility (p. 125)

Attitude-to-Behavior Process Model (p. 127)

Attitudes (p. 112)

Central Route (to persuasion) (p. 131)

Classical Conditioning (p. 114)

Cognitive Dissonance (p. 138)

Cognitive Perspective (on persuasion) (p. 131)

Elaboration Likelihood Model (of persuasion) (p. 131)

Forced Compliance (p. 142)

Forewarning (p. 137)

Instrumental Conditioning (p. 117)

Less-Leads-to-More Effect (p. 142)

Modeling (p. 117)

Peripheral Route (to persuasion) (p. 131)

Persuasion (p. 128)

Reactance (p. 137)

■ For More Information

Eagly, A., & Chaiken, S. (1993). *The psychology of attitudes*. San Diego, CA: Harcourt Brace & Jovanovich.

A comprehensive review of the vast existing literature on attitudes. The book is written by two expert researchers and contains much valuable information about the nature of attitudes, how they can be changed, and their effects on behavior.

Petty, R. E., & Krosnick, J. A. (1995). *Attitude strength: Antecedents and consequences*. Hillsdale, NJ: Erlbaum.

This book focuses on what is perhaps the most important factor determining the extent to which attitudes influence behavior—*attitude strength*. Chapters explore various aspects of attitude strength, such as attitude ex-

tremity, attitude accessibility, and resistance to change. If you want to know more about the nature of attitudes and their relationship to behavior, this is an excellent source to consult.

Shavitt, S., & Brock, T. C. (1994). *Persuasion: Psychological insights and perspectives*. Boston: Allyn & Bacon.

Explores all aspects of persuasion. The chapters on when and how attitudes influence behavior, cognitive dissonance (when our actions affect our attitudes), and the cognitive perspective on persuasion are all outstanding. The book is written in an interesting style that undergraduates should find easy to understand.

CHAPTER 5

ASPECTS OF SOCIAL IDENTITY: Establishing One's Self and Gender

Lisa Houck, *A Recent Find in a French Cave*, 1995, watercolor, 6 × 9"

Chapter Outline

Who are you? If you suddenly found yourself in radio contact with beings on another planet, and that question were asked, what would you say in the next thirty seconds? Who are you?

Think about a very pleasant experience that you have had. Maybe the day you first fell in love, the day you received an unexpected A on a test, the day you bought your first car, or whatever. How did you feel about yourself? How did you react to the people you met? Were you optimistic about the future? Now think about a very unpleasant experience that you have had and consider the same questions about your feelings, reactions, and optimism. Assuming that you reacted differently to the two experiences—why?

Can you remember how old you were when you first realized that people were divided into boys and girls, men and women? Even if you can't precisely recall having such a realization, what did you think about the other gender when you were little, and what do you think now? How different are men and women?

Very early in our lives, each of us begins learning who we are. We develop a **social identity,** or a self-definition, that includes how we conceptualize ourselves, including how we evaluate ourselves (Deaux, 1993a; Ellemers, Wilke, & van Knippenberg, 1993). For each person, this identity includes unique aspects such as one's name and self-concept, and aspects shared with others (Sherman, 1994). Familiar categories include one's gender and relationships (such as woman, man, daughter, son, divorced person); vocation or avocation (such as student, musician, psychologist, salesperson, athlete); political or ideological affiliation (feminist, environmentalist, Democrat, Republican); attributes that at least some people dislike (such as being homeless, overweight, homosexual, a drug user); and ethnicity or religion (such as Catholic, Southerner, Hispanic, Jewish, African American) (Deaux et al., 1995).

These various categories are closely tied to our interpersonal world, and they indicate ways in which we are like and unlike other individuals. Note that when a person's social context changes, this places a strain on his or her social identity that requires some degree of coping. For example, when Hispanic students enter a primarily Anglo university, one response is to become increasingly involved in Hispanic activities and groups, thus strengthening identification with this aspect of themselves. The opposite reaction—becoming less identified with Hispanics and seeking other ties—is also a familiar way to deal with the new situation (Ethier & Deaux, 1994).

In this chapter, we will concentrate on just two of the major components of social identity. First, we describe some of the crucial elements of the *self,* including self-concept, self-esteem, self-focusing, self-monitoring, and self-efficacy. Second, we examine *gender,* especially the social determinants of gender identity, gender roles, and the way behavior is influenced by these attributes.

Social Identity ■ A person's definition of who he or she is; includes personal attributes (self-concept) along with membership in various groups (aspects shared with others).

Self-Concept ■ One's self-identity, a schema consisting of an organized collection of beliefs and feelings about oneself.

The Self: Components of One's Identity

We humans spend a lot of time and effort thinking about *ourselves.* To some extent, we tend literally to be self-centered. That is, the self is the center of each person's social universe. Your self-identity, or *self-concept,* is acquired primarily through social interactions that begin with your immediate family and continue with the other people you meet throughout life. The **self-concept** is an organized collection of beliefs and feelings about oneself—in other words, it is a schema that functions like other schemas as discussed in Chapter 3. Thus, the

FIGURE 5.1

The Self-Concept Includes All Self-Relevant Information, Including Possessions. *The schema that is the self-concept includes all of the information and feelings relevant to our past, present, and future selves. Even our possessions become incorporated as self-relevant information.*

(*Source:* Drawing by W. Steig; © 1991 *The New Yorker* Magazine, Inc.)

Possessions are part of the self.

self-concept is a special framework that influences how we process information about the social world around us along with information about ourselves—such as our motives, emotional states, self-evaluations, abilities, and much else besides (Klein, Loftus, & Burton, 1989; Van Hook & Higgins, 1988). As in Figure 5.1, even possessions are perceived as part of oneself; have you ever spoken of "my dog," "my clock," "my room" and so forth?

Self-Concept: The Central Schema

At the beginning of this chapter, we asked, "Who are you?" Beginning with William James (1890) more than a century ago, several variations of this question (such as "Who am I?") have been used to measure self-concept (Bugental & Zelen, 1950; Gordon, 1968; Ziller, 1990).

Most recently, Rentsch and Heffner (1994) brought this measure up to date by instructing each of more than two hundred college students to give twenty different answers to that question. (You might want to try it yourself before reading any farther.) The researchers then subjected the responses to statistical analysis in order to determine the basic content categories that constituted the self-concepts of these students. The investigators assumed that each person possesses a unique self-concept with *specific content,* but that the *overall structure* of the self-concept is the same for all individuals. As shown in Figure 5.2 (p. 154), these research participants described themselves in terms of eight categories or factors. You may notice that some of these include the aspects of social identity described earlier, while others refer to personal attributes. If you answered the question for yourself, which of these factors appeared in your responses? By repeating this investigation in quite different samples, social psychologists can determine the generality of this "blueprint" of the self.

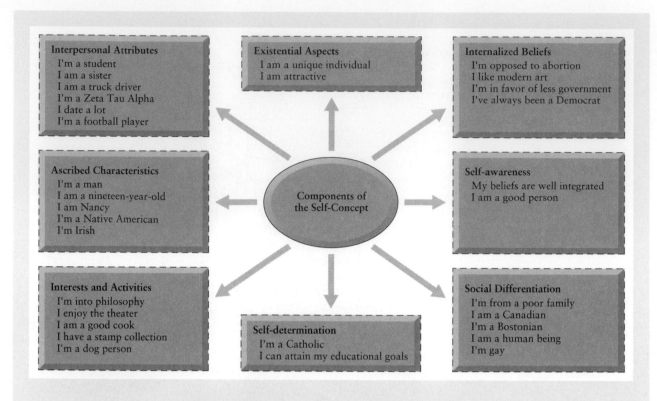

FIGURE 5.2

Components of the Self-Concept: Who Am I? More than two hundred college students were asked to respond to the question, "Who am I?" with twenty different answers. Statistical analysis of their responses indicated eight distinct categories. The investigators suggested the category labels shown in the figure. Though different people tend to use the same categories in describing themselves, the specific content of each category varies from person to person.

(*Source:* Based on data from Rentsch & Heffner, 1994.)

The Cognitive Effects of a Person's Self-Schema. Self-schemas are probably much more complex than the responses to "Who am I?" would suggest. Beyond the overall framework, such a schema would also reflect all of your relevant past experiences, all of your memories about what happened in your past, your knowledge about what you are like now, and your beliefs about what you will be like in the future. In other words, a self-schema is the sum of everything a person knows and can imagine about herself or himself.

Because the self is the center of each person's social world and because self-schemas are very well developed, it follows that we are able to do a better job of processing self-relevant information than any other kind of information—the **self-reference effect.** For example, because my last name is Byrne, I can easily remember that Gabriel Byrne is an Irish actor, Jane Byrne was mayor of Chicago, and Brendan Byrne was governor of New Jersey—even though I've never seen any of these individuals in person. In a similar way, if you participate in an experiment, are shown a series of words, and are asked, "Does this word describe you?" after each one, you will be able to recall the words better than if you are shown the same words and asked after each, "Is this word printed in big letters?" Self-relevant information is most likely to catch your attention, to be retained in memory, and to be recalled easily (Higgins & Bargh, 1987).

Self-Reference Effect ■ The greater efficacy of cognitive processing of information relevant to the self compared to processing of other types of information.

Psychologists have pursued the question of just *how* information relevant to the self is processed more efficiently. Klein and Loftus (1988) reasoned that recall of self-relevant information could be facilitated in one of two ways. First, you are likely to spend more time thinking about words or events if they are relevant to yourself than if they are not. Such mental activity connects the new material to existing information that is already stored in your memory—a phenomenon known as *elaborative processing*. Second, self-relevant material is likely to be better organized in your memory and placed in categories that are already present there—a phenomenon known as *categorical processing*.

Klein and Loftus devised a very clever experiment to determine whether either or both of these types of processing is involved when people deal with self-relevant material. In effect, they compared recall of material relevant to the self with recall of material that was primarily processed elaboratively or primarily processed categorically. Research participants were shown a series of words and asked either to think of a definition of each (to encourage elaborative processing), to place each word in one of five categories (to encourage categorical processing), or to think about whether each word reminded them of an important personal experience (to encourage self-relevant processing). Afterward, individuals in each group were asked to write down as many of the words as they could remember. By comparing performance on different word lists and the different kinds of processing cues, the investigators were able to show that recall of self-relevant material is most efficient because it is based on *both* elaborative and categorical processing. We think deeply about anything that is relevant to ourselves, and we also categorize it effectively. As a result, we can recall self-relevant information better than information unrelated to ourselves. These processes are summarized in Figure 5.3.

FIGURE 5.3

The Self-Reference Effect: Efficient Processing of Information about the Self. The *self-reference effect* refers to the fact that self-relevant information is more effectively processed than information about other topics. Research indicates that this occurs because self-relevant information is likely to be better organized in memory (categorical processing) *and* more fully related to other information stored in memory (elaborative processing).

(*Source:* Based on data from Klein & Loftus, 1988.)

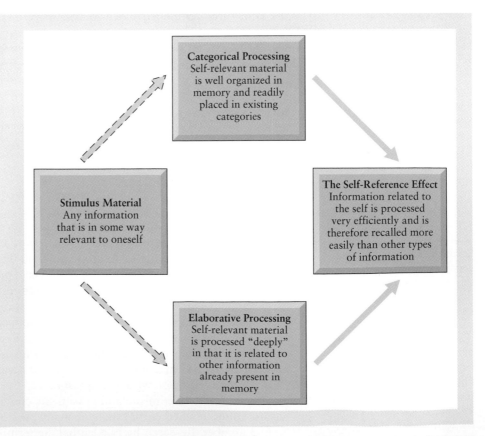

Categorical Processing
Self-relevant material is well organized in memory and readily placed in existing categories

Stimulus Material
Any information that is in some way relevant to oneself

The Self-Reference Effect
Information related to the self is processed very efficiently and is therefore recalled more easily than other types of information

Elaborative Processing
Self-relevant material is processed "deeply" in that it is related to other information already present in memory

The Affective, Evaluative, and Behavioral Effects of the Sexual Self-Schema. In addition to affecting cognitive processes, a person's self-schema presumably affects his or her behavior. Andersen and Cyranowski (1994) suggest that these effects can best be investigated with respect to *specific aspects* of the self-schema rather than the overall schema. They focused on **sexual self-schema**—the cognitive representations of the sexual aspects of oneself that originate in past experience, are manifested in current experience, influence the processing of sexual information, and guide sexual behavior.

Because the study of cognitive schemas has not generally dealt with sexuality and because the study of sexuality has not generally included cognitive schemas, these investigators first had to develop a measure of the sexual self-schema. A sample of undergraduate women (mean age of 20) and two samples of older women (mean ages of 34 and 49) took part in a series of investigations. Fifty adjectives were identified as describing relevant aspects of a woman's sexual self-concept, and the research participants were asked to rate each adjective on a scale ranging from 0 ("not at all descriptive of me") to 6 ("very much descriptive of me"). As summarized in Figure 5.4, three major components of sexual self-schema were identified: passionate–romantic, open–direct, and embarrassed–conservative. Also assessed were several aspects of self-reported sexual attitudes and sexual behavior, as shown in the figure.

These and other findings indicated clearly that women who differ in sexual self-schema also respond differently to sexual cues emotionally, attitudinally, and behaviorally. Andersen and Cyranowski (1994) emphasize the importance of further research on the cognitive representations of sexual self as a central aspect of the self-concept. For example, they are exploring the possible origins of different sexual self-schemas and the effect of one's sexual self-schema on more general views of oneself. Further research is also needed to determine the extent to which the sexual self-schemas of men can be categorized according to the same three components identified in women.

One Self-Concept or Many? People ordinarily speak of themselves as though the self were a stable and unchanging entity. Even so, we are aware that we can and do change over time. You are not the same person you were ten years ago, and you are not likely to be the same person ten years from now that you are today. Sometimes you may imagine what your life will be like after college—entering the job market, getting married, having children, earning more money, living somewhere else. In effect, you have a self-concept, but you are also aware of other **possible selves,** as well.

Markus and Nurius (1986) suggest that a self-concept at any given time is actually just a *working self-concept,* one that is open to change in response to new experiences, new feedback, and new self-relevant information. The existence of alternative possible selves affects us in several ways. The image of a future self may have an effect on one's *motivation,* as when a decision is made to spend more time studying or to stop smoking. Though you may have a clear image of your future self, others tend to perceive only your present self, and the *discrepancy* can be a source of discomfort. Even more upsetting is a discrepancy between the person we are and the person we want to be (Higgins, 1990).

College students who were either characteristically optimistic or generally pessimistic were asked to describe their future selves (Carver, Reynolds, & Scheier, 1994). Both types of students could imagine positive futures, but the optimistic ones had higher expectations about actually attaining a positive possible self than did those who were pessimistic.

In addition to optimistic and pessimistic conceptions of a future self, people also differ in whether they imagine many possible alternatives or only a very limited number. Research by Niedenthal, Setterlund, and Wherry (1992) indi-

Sexual Self-Schema ■ The cognitive generalizations about the sexual aspects of oneself that originate in past experience, become manifested in current experience, influence the processing of sexual information, and guide sexual behavior.

Possible Selves ■ Mental representations of what we might become, or should become, in the future.

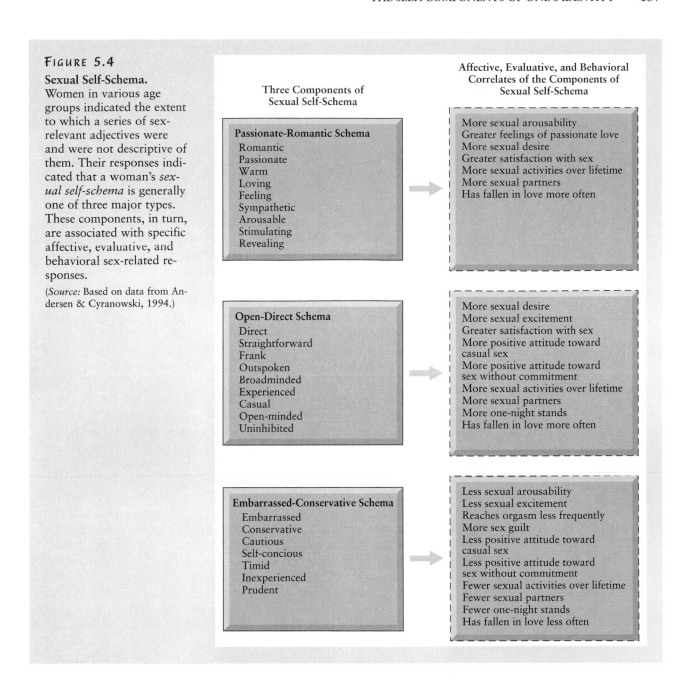

FIGURE 5.4

Sexual Self-Schema. Women in various age groups indicated the extent to which a series of sex-relevant adjectives were and were not descriptive of them. Their responses indicated that a woman's *sexual self-schema* is generally one of three major types. These components, in turn, are associated with specific affective, evaluative, and behavioral sex-related responses.

(*Source:* Based on data from Andersen & Cyranowski, 1994.)

Three Components of Sexual Self-Schema

Passionate-Romantic Schema
Romantic
Passionate
Warm
Loving
Feeling
Sympathetic
Arousable
Stimulating
Revealing

Open-Direct Schema
Direct
Straightforward
Frank
Outspoken
Broadminded
Experienced
Casual
Open-minded
Uninhibited

Embarrassed-Conservative Schema
Embarrassed
Conservative
Cautious
Self-concious
Timid
Inexperienced
Prudent

Affective, Evaluative, and Behavioral Correlates of the Components of Sexual Self-Schema

More sexual arousability
Greater feelings of passionate love
More sexual desire
Greater satisfaction with sex
More sexual activities over lifetime
More sexual partners
Has fallen in love more often

More sexual desire
More sexual excitement
Greater satisfaction with sex
More positive attitude toward casual sex
More positive attitude toward sex without commitment
More sexual activities over lifetime
More sexual partners
More one-night stands
Has fallen in love more often

Less sexual arousability
Less sexual excitement
Reaches orgasm less frequently
More sex guilt
Less positive attitude toward casual sex
Less positive attitude toward sex without commitment
Fewer sexual activities over lifetime
Fewer sexual partners
Fewer one-night stands
Has fallen in love less often

cated that people who have a very limited number of possible future selves are emotionally vulnerable to relevant feedback. For example, if you are considering twenty different possible future careers, information that you don't have the necessary ability for one of them is of relatively limited importance—there are nineteen other possibilities. If you have only one career goal, however, information indicating a lack of ability may be devastating. In a similar way, the more strongly and the more exclusively a person identifies with the role of athlete, the more emotionally upsetting is an athletic injury (Brewer, 1993). More broadly, research indicates that adjustment following various sorts of traumatic events is best for those who can envision many different positive selves (Morgan & Janoff-Bulman, 1994). Further, self-complexity actually serves as a cognitive buffer against depression and stress-related illness (Linville, 1987).

It seems that having a complex view of one's possible selves (assuming that they are realistically grounded) is more emotionally beneficial than having a very simple view. This general finding raises the possibility that people could be helped by learning to imagine additional possible selves, as described in the following *Applied Side* section.

Social Psychology: On the Applied Side
INCREASING THE NUMBER OF POSSIBLE SELVES

Can children be taught to conceptualize an increased number of possible selves? Day and her colleagues (1994) concentrated on bringing about just such changes in young Mexican American children. These youngsters were targeted for study because academic achievement among Hispanic students is lower than among Anglo students, beginning in elementary school and persisting through high school. The investigators proposed that this negative pattern could potentially be altered by a planned intervention designed to produce an expanded view of future possibilities.

The investigators worked with Mexican Americans in the third, fourth, and fifth grades. These children were tested before and after the intervention program concerning such things as the jobs they hoped to have when they grew up and the relevance of school performance to these jobs. Before the program, most of the boys and girls simply expressed gender stereotypes about occupations (boys expected to be policemen or athletes, and girls expected to be teachers or nurses), as shown in Figure 5.5. Also, any relationship between schoolwork and a person's future career was not at all obvious to these children.

The program itself consisted of eight one-hour sessions over a four-week period. Specifically, in groups of five to ten, the children were taught to listen to others without making fun of them and to ask any questions they wished. The sessions included material on the youngsters' present selves as well as thinking about the past and future, making connections between school assignments and future selves ("possible me"), understanding what is involved in owning a house and a fancy car, and role-playing both enjoyable jobs and boring ones. One exercise involved the Me Tree, in which the participants were instructed to think of themselves as a tree that represented what they are now as well as what they would grow into when they were older. They constructed a tree of felt material with a strong trunk (representing knowledge, skills, personality, and values) and sturdy branches (representing education, relationships with others, and ways to spend leisure time). On each branch were green leaves (representing hopes and goals) and red leaves (representing fears). In other "lessons" the children examined the differences between good learners and poor learners, played with a time machine in which they examined their past actions and future possibilities, considered future selves (house, family, a red Corvette, money, and the way in which doing well in school and getting a good job made these goals possible), and role-played different future occupations.

Compared to similar children in a no-intervention control group, those who went through the eight sessions significantly improved in their understanding of what it means to be a good student and the relevance of that to future job opportunities; and these children also showed greater interest in the possibility of becoming a physician, a judge, or a pilot. The authors propose that such interventions, along with exposure to multiple role models, can have a beneficial effect in helping all children develop possible selves.

FIGURE 5.5

Increasing Possible Selves Leads to More Occupational Options. When Hispanic children in the third, fourth, and fifth grades were asked about their future occupations, they tended to respond with possibilities that were gender-stereotyped and limited. After taking part in a program designed to help the youngsters increase the number of possible selves and to provide information about how to reach different goals, the participants became interested in exploring much more varied occupational opportunities (Day et al., 1994).

It seems very important for children to be encouraged to think about their future lives and to make connections between alternative futures and what they are currently doing in school. ■ ■ ■

Changes in Self-Concept. We have suggested that the self-concept slowly changes over time, as we grow older. Other factors, however, can change our beliefs about who we are in a very short period of time. One example is the negative effects on a person's self-concept when he or she loses a job and suddenly has a new social identity—*unemployed* (Sheeran & Abraham, 1994). The opposite experience—entering a new occupation—also leads to changes in the self-concept; for example, new police officers are found to develop new views of themselves (Stradling, Crowe, & Tuohy, 1993). Even greater changes occur when an individual joins the armed forces and is thrust into combat. This experience can lead to many self-relevant problems, including confusion about "Who am I? ("Am I a civilian or a military person?"), confusion about time perspective ("I was too young to feel so old"), interpersonal and work-related problems, and the development of a negative self-identity (Silverstein, 1994).

It appears, then, that the self-concept is far from a fixed aspect of a person, and that external events can bring about changes. McNulty and Swann (1994) examined what happens to the self-concept in an ongoing interpersonal context. They investigated the self-perceptions and interpersonal perceptions of same-sex college roommates over several weeks. The participants were asked to rate themselves and the other person on various characteristics, including academic ability, social skills, athletic ability, attractiveness, and agreeableness. The findings suggest a negotiation process in which self-perceptions influence the other person's perceptions, and those perceptions in turn have an effect on self-perceptions. The investigators suggest that the self acts as an "architect" in shaping and determining the reactions of others, but that the self also is altered by how others react. If these interactive effects between self and others operate in pairs of roommates, it seems likely that they are even more important in close relationships such as friendships and marriage.

A different way of viewing such findings is to take the view of William James (1890) that while we have a central core self ("set like plaster" by age thirty), we also have many different *social selves* that we express to different people in different social interactions. To pursue this conception, Roberts and Donahue (1994) studied a sample of middle-aged women and assessed their *role-specific self-concepts* as well as their *general self-concepts*. The role-specific concepts for each individual were worker, wife, friend, and daughter (see Figure 5.6). The women were asked to describe themselves in these different roles with respect to positive affect, competence, and dependability. As hypothesized, each participant's self-conceptions differed across roles; but there was also a high degree of consistency for individuals from role to role. For example, two women could each describe affect as a function of social role (both might indicate more positive feelings in the role of friend than in the role of daughter), thus indicating role-*specific* self-concepts. But the two women could also differ from each other in that one experienced more positive affect in both situations than the other. Because this difference between them is consistent across roles, it indicates the operation of a *general* self-concept.

Self-Esteem: Evaluating Oneself

Perhaps the most important attitude each person holds is his or her attitude about self, an evaluation that we label **self-esteem** (James, 1890). A person with high self-esteem perceives himself or herself as better, more capable, and of greater worth than does someone with low self-esteem. Self-evaluations are based in part on the opinions of others and in part on how we perceive specific experiences. Interestingly, negative self-perceptions lead to more predictable behavior than positive self-perceptions. Presumably, this happens because negative self-views involve more tightly organized schemas than positive ones (Malle & Horowitz, 1995); as a result, someone with generally high self-esteem can interpret a success in a variety of ways, but someone with low self-esteem tends to overgeneralize the implications of a failure (Brown & Dutton, 1995).

Though most of the research on self-esteem is focused on a global indication of self-evaluation, it is also clear that people subdivide aspects of their self. For example, I rate myself very high on being able to make delicious lasagne and very low on being able to speak French. Because of such subdividing, you can have very positive attitudes about some aspects of yourself and very negative attitudes about other aspects. Your overall, global self-esteem can be conceptualized as the combination of the relative number and relative intensity of these positive and negative self-evaluations (Marsh, 1993).

A slightly different approach to assessing self-esteem is to compare a person's self-concept with his or her conception of an ideal self. The greater the dis-

Self-Esteem ■ The self-evaluation made by each individual; one's attitude toward oneself along a positive–negative dimension.

FIGURE 5.6

Self-Concept: Role-Specific Self-Concepts. When Roberts and Donahue (1994) asked women to describe themselves with respect to several characteristics, they produced different self-descriptions in different roles (worker, wife, friend, daughter), indicating role-specific self-concepts. In other words, one's self-concept differs to some extent in different interpersonal situations. The women nevertheless showed some consistency from role to role, indicating some continuity of the self-concept.

crepancy, the lower the self-esteem. That is, the more you perceive that your characteristics fail to measure up to what you feel they should be, the more negative your attitude about yourself. Credible feedback indicating that one has some of the characteristics of his or her ideal self is a positive experience, while feedback indicating the presence of undesired characteristics is negative (Eisenstadt & Leippe, 1994). It also matters whether one's "good" and "bad" qualities are common or rare. The lowest level of self-esteem is found among those who perceive their liked characteristics to be quite common and their unliked characteristics to be relatively rare (Ditto & Griffin, 1993). For example, I (Donn Byrne) know a seventh grader who is an outstanding writer, though she is barely average in dance class; she sometimes feels bad about herself because she (mistakenly) believes that everyone can write well while almost no one dances poorly.

Self-Esteem and Social Comparison. As we'll see in Chapter 7, we tend to make self-evaluations by comparing ourselves to others. These comparisons are a major determinant of how we evaluate ourselves (Brown et al., 1992). This fact explains some research findings that might otherwise seem surprising. For example, given the very real problems of racism and sexism (see Chapter 6), you might expect women and minority group members to be low in self-esteem. Instead, women and minorities tend to express *higher* self-esteem than white males (Crocker & Major, 1989). Clearly, social comparisons must differ for these different groups of people.

Depending on your comparison group, specific successes and failures may contribute to high or low self-evaluations or be completely irrelevant. For example, Osborne (1995) points out that despite better academic performance among whites than among African Americans in U.S. schools, global self-esteem is significantly higher for the latter group. The apparent reason: Among whites academic success and failure are related to self-evaluation more than they are among African Americans. In the earliest grades, both racial groups indicate a connection between grades and self-esteem; but by the tenth grade, the relationship tends to drop dramatically for African Americans, especially males (Steele, 1992). For them, the comparison groups affecting self-esteem seem to involve not classmates engaging in academic activities, but other people and different activities.

Several lines of research help clarify some of the ways in which these complex social comparisons operate. When you compare yourself to others, your esteem goes up when you perceive some inadequacy in them—a *contrast effect*. This kind of comparison with someone who is worse off (a downward comparison) arouses positive feelings and raises your self-esteem (Reis, Gerrard, & Gibbons, 1993). When, however, the comparison is with someone to whom you feel close, your esteem goes up when you perceive something very good about them—an *assimilation effect* (Brown et al., 1992). In a similar way, a person who compares unfavorably with ingroup members experiences lower self-esteem and increased depression much more than if the unfavorable comparison is with outgroup members (Major, Sciacchitano, & Crocker, 1993). In effect, social comparison with others in the ingroup is the most self-relevant comparison. It follows that doing well within one's own, relatively unsuccessful group—like a big frog in a little pond—can be a much bigger boost to self-esteem than performing equally well in a larger and more successful group—like a little frog in a big pond (McFarland & Buehler, 1995).

One theme of these various findings is that self-esteem can be raised by identifying with a group, because *social identity* can help compensate for problems involving *personal identity* (Crocker et al., 1994). Consider someone who is the target of prejudice in society at large—a member of a stigmatized group. Rather than accepting prejudicial evaluations as an accurate assessment of self-worth, it is possible to identify with those similar to oneself (in terms of race, sexual orientation, religion, disability, or whatever) and to feel pride in this ingroup. As one example, Bat-Chava (1994) investigated the positive effects of group identification on self-esteem among deaf adults. As hypothesized, those who identified with other deaf individuals expressed higher self-esteem than those who lacked this group identification. For those who are deaf, identification is enhanced by having deaf parents who communicate in sign language at home and by attending a school for the deaf rather than a regular school. This and related findings point to the beneficial effects of group identity.

Why Do We Engage in Self-Evaluation? Sedikides (1993) suggests three motives for evaluating oneself: *self-assessment* (seeking accurate self-knowledge, whether positive or negative), *self-enhancement* (seeking favorable self-knowledge), and *self-verification* (seeking fairly obvious self-knowledge that is probably true). When research participants are given the opportunity to select questions whose answers would provide various kinds of knowledge about themselves, self-enhancement is most often sought, while self-assessment is the least popular type of knowledge. Despite what they may believe to be true, most people do not really want to know more about themselves; rather, they want either positive information or information that simply confirms what they already know.

If we want only positive information about ourselves, it follows that self-esteem can readily be enhanced by external events. For example, any experience that creates a positive mood tends to raise self-esteem—we feel good and so feel good about ourselves (Esses, 1989). Even dressing in clothes you like can increase self-esteem (Kwon, 1994). For this reason, self-esteem can be raised quite easily in an experimental setting; for example, when research participants are given fake feedback that they did well on a personality test, their self-esteem goes up (Greenberg et al., 1992).

People with very low self-esteem are most apt to focus on self-protection (Wood et al., 1994). They, too, want positive information and self-enhancement, but only when it is not risky to seek such information. That is, they seek social comparison only after they have already received feedback indicating success on a task. People with high self-esteem seek social comparison even after receiving failure feedback, possibly to determine how to perform better in the future, but also to make themselves feel better by concentrating on the negative performance of others (Crocker, 1993). In other words, one coping strategy to maintain a positive view of oneself is to focus on the shortcomings of others.

The Consequences of Positive versus Negative Self-Evaluations. Research consistently indicates that high self-esteem is beneficial while low self-esteem has many negative consequences. For example, a negative self-evaluation is associated with less adequate social skills (Olmstead et al., 1991); depression (Pillow, West, & Reich, 1991)—especially among women (Jex, Cvetanovski, & Allen, 1994; Russo, Green, & Knight, 1993); and adverse reactions to job insecurity (Orpen, 1994). It has even been suggested that *unrealistically* positive self-evaluations and *unrealistic* optimism are associated with good mental health (Taylor & Brown, 1988); but more recent research suggests that in the long run, accurate self-evaluation seems to be essential to healthy mental functioning (Colvin, Block, & Funder, 1995).

There is evidence of specific physiological correlates of self-esteem. For example, experimental procedures that induce a negative self-evaluation (and associated negative emotions) lead to a weakening of the immune system and, presumably, greater susceptibility to disease (Strauman, Lemieux, & Coe, 1993). More complex associations are also being discovered. *Serotonin* is a biochemical contained in various fruits and nuts as well as in the venom of wasps and scorpions. In mammals, serotonin is found in blood serum, the brain, and the stomach. It is involved in constricting blood vessels, stimulating the smooth muscles, and transmitting impulses between nerve cells. Studies of male monkeys indicate that social success (high dominant status and affiliative interactions with females) is associated with higher levels of serotonin; low serotonin levels, in turn, are associated with impulsivity and aggressiveness (Raleigh et al., 1991). Though still quite speculative, the intriguing possibility has been raised that in humans, as self-esteem goes up, so does the level of serotonin (Wright, 1995). This further suggests that any factor that influences self-esteem may also have biochemical effects *and* that biochemicals might be used to raise self-esteem and decrease aggressiveness.

Does self-esteem influence how well people perform unfamiliar tasks or just how well they *believe* they perform? Martin and Murberger (1994) investigated the effects of self-esteem on both the perceived and actual performance of undergraduates who had previously been tested for low and high self-esteem. The task was to sort 200 cards (each having the name of a color printed on it) into small bags. Each bag was also labeled with the name of a color. The students

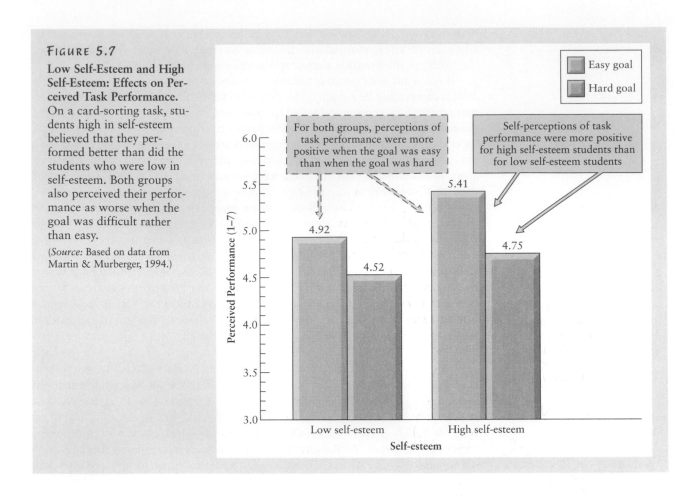

FIGURE 5.7

Low Self-Esteem and High Self-Esteem: Effects on Perceived Task Performance. On a card-sorting task, students high in self-esteem believed that they performed better than did the students who were low in self-esteem. Both groups also perceived their performance as worse when the goal was difficult rather than easy.

(*Source:* Based on data from Martin & Murberger, 1994.)

had to match the color name on each card with the name on each bag; this task was complicated by the fact that the word on a card (for example, RED) might be written in ink of a different color (for example, blue); nevertheless, the card had to be placed in the bag labeled RED. The experimenters also varied the performance pressure by telling half the students simply to do their best in sorting cards for five minutes (easy goal); the other half were told to sort at least 175 cards in five minutes (hard goal). As illustrated in Figure 5.7, both low- and high-self-esteem groups thought that they did less well when the goal was a hard one; but, overall, those high in self-esteem had more positive perceptions of how well they did than those low in self-esteem.

Given the generally negative effects of low self-esteem (or high self–ideal self discrepancy), attempts to bring about lasting increases in esteem or decreases in discrepancy are potentially very important. An early attempt to attain this goal is described in the following *Cornerstones* section.

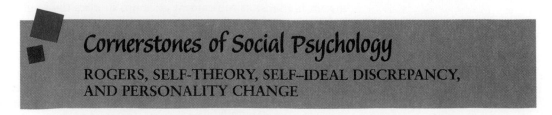

Cornerstones of Social Psychology
ROGERS, SELF-THEORY, SELF–IDEAL DISCREPANCY, AND PERSONALITY CHANGE

Though Carl Rogers was a clinical psychologist, his theorizing about self became an integral part of the field of personality, and his research findings on the

Carl Rogers. Carl Rogers was born in 1902 in Illinois and died in 1987 in California. His distinguished career was somewhat unusual in that he worked in clinical settings for the first decade after receiving the Ph.D. degree, and then entered academia with the rank of full professor. At Ohio State, Chicago, Wisconsin, and the Western Behavioral Sciences Institute in La Jolla, he developed a theory of personality based on the self, devised a new method of psychotherapy, and established a rigorous research program to evaluate both his theoretical constructs and his therapeutic procedures. Late in his career, I (DB) had the privilege of spending an afternoon in informal conversation with him and one of his former students. Carl Rogers was as impressive in person as in his written work; he struck me as the kind of man anyone would very much like to have as a favorite uncle.

origins of the self-concept and on changing self-perceptions are directly relevant to the current interests of many social psychologists.

Rogers (1951) emphasized that the self is the most important aspect of each person's world. He believed that, in addition to maintaining and enhancing the self, everyone needs to receive positive regard. That is, from infancy on, we need love, and parents are most often the original source of affection. From the beginning, each person needs love so strongly, in fact, that a child's self-concept is more dependent on what the parents and others declare it to be than on the child's actual feelings and perceptions. If, for example, the parents insist that their little girl is pleased to have a new baby brother, she incorporates that reaction as part of her self-concept even though her actual feelings include anger, resentment, jealousy, and other negative emotions. The greater the difference between one's learned self-concept and what one truly experiences, the greater the need to distort perceptions and defend against threat.

Rogers believed that the way to correct a maladaptive self-concept is a therapeutic interaction (called "client-centered") in which the therapist acts as an interested, accepting, and nonjudgmental parent figure who does not impose his or her external viewpoint on what the client is feeling. In this positive atmosphere, clients are free to explore their actual feelings and perceptions and—as a result—to change.

Rogers was very much interested in conducting research to test both his self-theory and his therapeutic method. The investigations carried out by his research group focused on the difference between a person's *self* and the person's *ideal self*—a difference known as self–ideal discrepancy—as an indicator of maladjustment. The higher the discrepancy (and hence the lower the person's self-esteem), the less well adjusted, more unhappy, and more defensive the individual. Note that quite different kinds of change are equally effective in reducing the discrepancy. For example, the client can become convinced (correctly or incorrectly) that the self is really much closer to the ideal than was initially thought (a change in self-perception); the self can become more like the ideal (a change in self-concept); the ideal standards can be lowered because they are unreasonably high (a change in ideal–self); or more than one kind of change can occur simultaneously.

In a pioneering book, Rogers and Dymond (1954) described many of the research projects that were undertaken. For example, one relatively basic study compared measures of self–ideal discrepancy for clients before and after they took part in therapy. The control group consisted of volunteers for a research project who were not seeking therapeutic help. Measures of self and ideal–self were taken at the beginning of the project and six to twelve months after the clients had completed therapy.

Figure 5.8 (p. 166) compares the clients who were rated as "definitely improved" by the therapists and outside observers, the clients who showed less clear improvement, and the nontherapy control participants. Both therapy groups showed a significant decrease in self–ideal discrepancy, with the greatest drop for the "definitely improved" clients. As would be expected, the volunteers in the control group had less self–ideal discrepancy than the clients at both time periods, and no changes in discrepancy were observed. Still another control involved clients who were tested and then asked to wait sixty days before beginning therapy. Their discrepancy scores remained high during the waiting period, indicating that the passage of time was not the crucial factor in bringing about a beneficial change in self–ideal discrepancy—client-centered therapy was the key.

Among many applied psychologists, Rogers's emphasis on therapy as a way to raise self-esteem and on research as a way to validate therapeutic effectiveness continues as an influential guide (Shechtman, 1993). ■ ■ ■

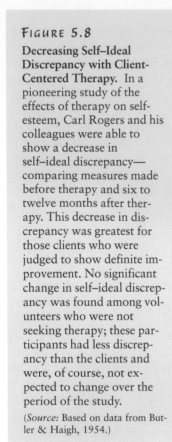

FIGURE 5.8

Decreasing Self–Ideal Discrepancy with Client-Centered Therapy. In a pioneering study of the effects of therapy on self-esteem, Carl Rogers and his colleagues were able to show a decrease in self–ideal discrepancy—comparing measures made before therapy and six to twelve months after therapy. This decrease in discrepancy was greatest for those clients who were judged to show definite improvement. No significant change in self–ideal discrepancy was found among volunteers who were not seeking therapy; these participants had less discrepancy than the clients and were, of course, not expected to change over the period of the study.

(*Source:* Based on data from Butler & Haigh, 1954.)

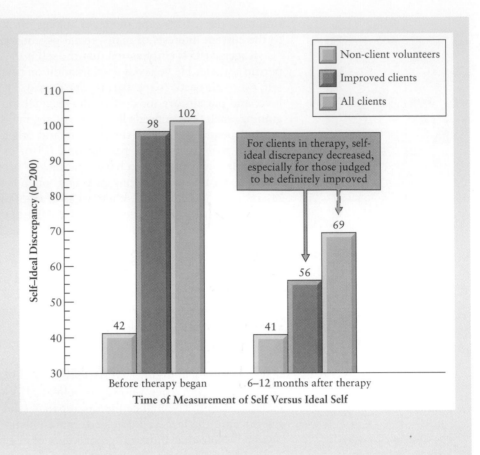

Variable Self-Esteem. We pointed out earlier that depression is associated with *low self-esteem,* but negative emotions are also associated with *variable self-esteem.* That is, people whose self-esteem fluctuates up and down in response to changes in their situation are the ones most likely to become depressed (Roberts & Monroe, 1992). The explanation is that anyone whose self-esteem is strongly affected by minor occurrences has a less stable source of self-worth compared to people whose esteem remains relatively constant (Kernis et al., 1993). High self-esteem acts as a helpful buffer when negative events are encountered (Wiener, Muczyk, & Martin, 1992).

Which is a better predictor of depression, consistently low self-esteem or variable self-esteem? By comparing undergraduates who were currently depressed, had previously been depressed, or had never been depressed, Butler, Hokanson, and Flynn (1994) were able to show that variable self-esteem is a better index of who becomes depressed than is low self-esteem.

INTEGRATING PRINCIPLES

1. The self-concept is a schema (Chapter 3) consisting of an organized collection of self-oriented beliefs, memories, feelings, and conceptions of possible future selves. This all-important schema influences how we process social and personal information that is relevant to our own identities.

2. For most people, the most influential attitude (Chapter 4) they hold is the one concerning self—the complex set of evaluations known as self-esteem. A person's self-esteem is based on direct evaluations made by other people and on social comparisons between oneself and others (Chapter 7).

Additional Aspects of Self-Functioning: Focusing, Monitoring, and Efficacy

Though self-concept and self-esteem have been the central concerns of research on the self, several other aspects of self-functioning are also of interest. We will now examine three of these: *self-focusing, self-monitoring,* and *self-efficacy.*

Self-Focusing: Attending to Oneself or to the Environment

At any given moment, a person's attention can be directed inward toward the self or outward toward the environment (Fiske & Taylor, 1991). **Self-focusing** is defined as the extent to which attention is directed toward oneself.

Cognitive and Affective Aspects of Focusing on Self. Self-focusing is associated with memory and cognition. Recall of relevant past events and processing of relevant current information is required for self-focusing to occur. Self-focus affects the accuracy of biographical recall (retrieving factual information about yourself) and the complexity of self-descriptive judgments (Dixon & Baumeister, 1991; Klein, Loftus, & Burton, 1989). A question such as "Where were you born?" directs you toward the retrieval process. A question such as "How would you describe your relationship with your parents?" can elicit relatively simple or relatively complex judgments about yourself.

Self-focusing increases between childhood and adolescence (Ullman, 1987), and some adults consistently self-focus more than others. Nevertheless, situational influences have a great effect, and self-focusing is easily induced by simple instructions (Right now, please think about the most positive aspects of yourself!) or by environmental cues such as the presence of a video camera or a mirror (Fenigstein & Abrams, 1993).

To some extent, a brief period of self-focusing improves self-insight. When research participants are instructed to spend a few minutes thinking about themselves, they are more accurate in judging social feedback than other participants who are not asked to self-focus (Hixon & Swan, 1993). On a long-term basis, however, self-focused attention (among depressed individuals, for example) may simply reflect a continuing *attempt* to understand oneself rather than increased awareness (Conway et al., 1993). If one is depressed, external focusing helps relieve the negative affect (Lyubomirsky & Nolen-Hoeksema, 1995); the direction of focus has no effect on the feelings of nondepressed individuals, however (Nix et al., 1995).

One's self-concept is complex and contains a great many discrete elements. As a result, the focusing process involves only a small fraction of the total at any given time—much like a flashlight pointed at various objects in a very large, dark room. Where one's focus is directed is determined in part by the *framing* of the

Self-Focusing ■ The act of directing attention inward toward oneself as opposed to outward toward the environment.

question (see Chapters 3 and 13). This affects not only retrieval but what specifically is retrieved (Kunda et al., 1993). For example, if your knowledge about your social life contains both positive and negative elements, you might give a positive response to the question, "Are you happy with your social life?" and a negative response to the question, "Are you unhappy with your social life?"

We are not always aware of exactly when we pay attention to ourselves (Epstein, 1983); but self-focusing is more likely in a familiar, comfortable situation than in an unfamiliar, threatening one. For example, if you are driving in daylight along a road you know well, you may well begin thinking about yourself. In contrast, you tend to focus on the environment when driving on an unfamiliar road on a stormy night.

Storing Positive and Negative Information about Self in Memory. It appears that many people file positive and negative aspects of themselves separately in memory (Showers, 1992a). A person's mood, in turn, is affected by whether the focus is on positive or negative elements. This interrelationship between affect and cognition was also discussed in Chapter 3. If you think about only the negative aspects of yourself, you can easily become unhappy. Not only does self-focusing influence mood (Sedikides, 1992); mood also affects self-focusing. As a result, any external event that affects mood also tends to direct self-focusing (Salovey, 1992). For example, if you are unhappy following an argument with a close friend, you are more likely to focus on and recall negative things about yourself and to be pessimistic about the future. Figure 5.9 outlines these interconnections.

Showers (1992b) has also found that *some* people store positive and negative self-knowledge together. When this is the case, self-focusing can't ever involve purely negative elements, and the overall result is less negative affect and higher self-esteem. Despite this benefit of having positive and negative information intermixed, when you are confronted by extremely stressful negative events, it is better to have some clearly differentiated (compartmentalized) aspects of the self that are *very positive* and *very important*. The presence of separate, positive elements of the self on which you can fall back is a protection against becoming depressed when stress occurs (Showers & Ryff, 1993).

Self-Monitoring: Guiding Behavior on the Basis of Internal versus External Factors

One person I (DB) know fairly well behaves in exactly the same friendly and jolly way in every setting in which I've observed him—with his employees, with fellow professionals, with his wife, with close friends at a party, with strangers at a restaurant, and so on. At the opposite extreme, I also know someone else whom I've seen acting in an authoritative way with employees, conducting herself as a serious and concerned colleague at work, exchanging teasing insults with her husband, being a bubbly flirt at parties, and remaining totally distant and silent with strangers. The first individual is solidly predictable, while the second could be described as a "social chameleon."

Self-Monitoring ■ Regulation of one's behavior on the basis of the external situation and the reactions of others (high self-monitoring) or on the basis of internal factors such as beliefs, attitudes, and values (low self-monitoring).

Self-monitoring refers to the relative tendency of individuals to regulate their behavior on the basis of external events such as the reactions of others (high self-monitoring) or on the basis of internal factors such as their own beliefs, attitudes, and interests (low self-monitoring). Low self-monitors tend to respond more consistently across differing situations than do high self-monitors (Koestner, Bernieri, & Zuckerman, 1992).

Conceptualizing Differences in Self-Monitoring. The formulation of self-monitoring was first developed by Snyder (1974) and his colleagues (Gangestad & Snyder, 1985; Snyder & Ickes, 1985). You may have noted that there are

FIGURE 5.9

The Interrelationship of External Events, Mood, Self-Focusing, and Expectancies. Many people store positive and negative self-information separately in memory. When attention is focused on positive information, this results in a positive mood and optimistic expectancies. Positive external events also can lead to positive mood, self-focusing on positive information, and optimism. In just the same way, self-focusing on negative information, a negative mood, negative external events, and pessimistic expectancies are also interrelated.

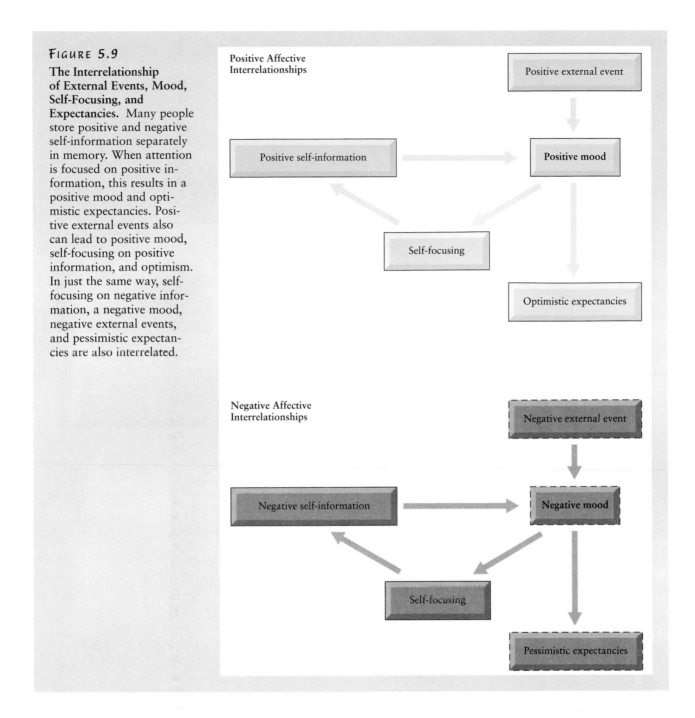

some similarities between self-monitoring and self-focusing (attending to internal versus external cues), but the major emphasis of work on self-monitoring is the way a person's *behavior* is regulated by these attentional differences.

Hoyle and Sowards (1993) have further described self-monitoring in terms of differences in responses to social situations. As shown in Figure 5.10 (p 170), high self-monitors analyze a social situation by referring to the public self, compare this self to social standards of behavior, and strive to alter the public self to match the situation. In contrast, low self-monitors analyze a social situation by referring to the private self, compare this self to their personal standards of behavior, then strive to alter the situation to match their private self.

Snyder proposed that high self-monitors engage in role-playing because they are striving to receive positive evaluations from other people. In other

FIGURE 5.10

Self-Monitoring and Behavior in Social Situations. In a social situation, a high self-monitor compares his or her public self to social demands, then attempts to alter the public self to match the situation. A low self-monitor, in contrast, compares his or her private self to personal standards of behavior, then attempts to alter the situation to match the private self.

(*Source:* Based on information from Hoyle & Sowards, 1993.)

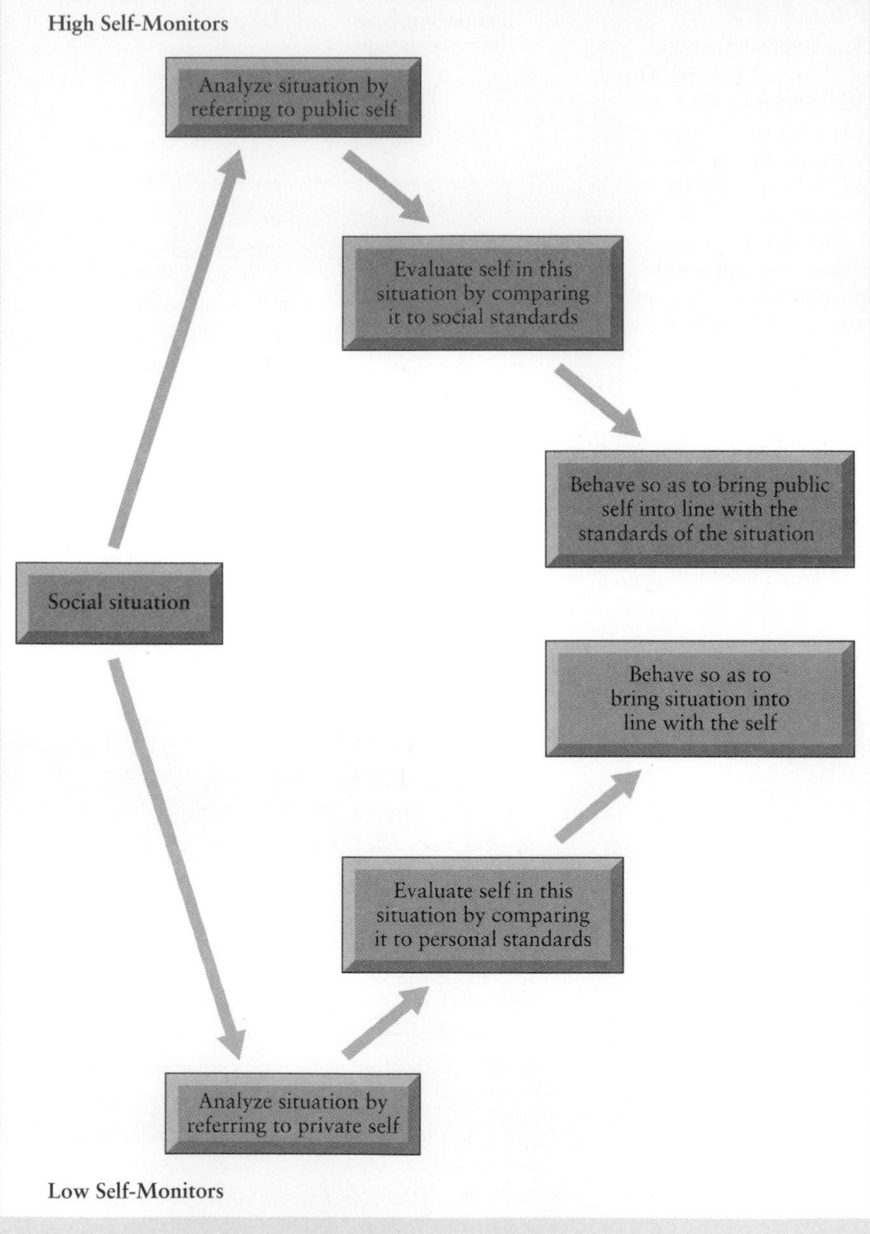

High Self-Monitors

Analyze situation by referring to public self

Evaluate self in this situation by comparing it to social standards

Behave so as to bring public self into line with the standards of the situation

Social situation

Behave so as to bring situation into line with the self

Evaluate self in this situation by comparing it to personal standards

Analyze situation by referring to private self

Low Self-Monitors

words, they mold their behavior to fit their audience—a useful characteristic for politicians, salespeople, and actors. The description of Lieutenant General George S. Patton in the April 9, 1945, issue of *Time* magazine seems appropriate to this concept:

> *Patton the General is also Patton the Actor. Showmanship is instinctive in him. Like all practiced actors he can manage a deft touch of corn or a flight of oratory. He fits his act to his audience's mood.*

Self-monitoring is measured by a true–false scale (Snyder, 1974) in which some of the items reflect high self-monitoring ("In different situations and with different people, I often act like very different persons"), and others reflect low self-monitoring ("My behavior is usually an expression of my true inner feelings, attitudes, and beliefs"). The validity of this measure is indicated by studies such as that of Lippa and Donaldson (1990). Students were given the Self-Monitoring Scale and asked to keep a detailed diary over a ten-day period about their interactions with others. As predicted, high self-monitors reported tailoring their behavior to specific situations and audiences, but low self-monitors reported behaving in the same way, regardless of the situation.

Because differences in self-monitoring behavior are assumed to be based in part on genetic differences, Gangestad and Simpson (1993) engaged in an unusual test construction procedure to identify items that tap the genetic component of self-monitoring. Using pairs of identical and fraternal twins, the researchers compared the relative similarity of the two groups in responding to questions that were associated with self-monitoring behavior. The resulting measure, labeled Genic Expressive Control, consists of items answered in a much more similar way by identical than by fraternal twins. Future research should benefit from the use of a technique that distinguishes acquired self-monitoring behavior from similar behavior that is linked to genes. The self-monitoring items in this scale (and the scoring key for high self-monitors) include:

"I find it hard to imitate people." (false)

"I guess I put on a show to impress or entertain people." (true)

"I have never been good at games like charades or improvisational acting." (false)

"I can look anyone in the eye and tell a lie with a straight face (if for a right end)." (true)

Differences between High and Low Self-Monitors. Many behaviors have been identified that are different for high versus low self-monitors. For example, Ickes, Reidhead, and Patterson (1986) found that high self-monitors, when they speak, more often use the third person (he, she, his, her, their, etc.) while low self-monitors use the first person (I, me, my, mine, etc.). DeBono and Packer (1991) found that highs respond best to advertising that is image-based ("Heineken—you're moving up") and lows to quality-based ads ("Heineken—you can taste the difference"). Because people who are confident about their decisions tend to be liked and respected, Cutler and Wolfe (1989) correctly predicted that the higher the self-monitoring tendency, the greater the confidence in one's decisions, regardless of whether a decision was right or wrong.

High self-monitors make interpersonal choices on the basis of their external qualities (for example, selecting a tennis partner on the basis of how well he or she plays), while low self-monitors make choices based on how much they like the other person (Snyder, Gangestad, & Simpson, 1983). Even in romantic relationships, low self-monitors are more committed to the other individual (and so have fewer and longer-lasting relationships), while high self-monitors are attuned to the situation and to a variety of partners (Snyder & Simpson, 1984).

Such findings led Jones (1993) to investigate motivational differences in the dating behavior of high and low self-monitors. She administered the self-monitoring scale and a test that assesses dating motivation to undergraduate men and women. Intrinsic motives for dating are indicated by such items as "We share the same interests and concerns" and "We have the same attitudes and values." Intrinsic motivation means that an individual enjoys being with the partner. Extrinsic motives are indicated by such items as "He (she) has the right connections" and "His (her) friends and relatives could be of benefit to my career and future aspirations." Extrinsic motivation means that the partner is selected on the basis of expected rewards beyond the relationship—see Figure 5.11 (p. 172). Low self-monitors tended to emphasize intrinsic dating motivation more than highs, while high self-monitors stressed extrinsic dating motives more than lows. Once

FIGURE 5.11

Intrinsic versus Extrinsic Dating Motives: Low versus High Self-Monitors. When asked about their motivation in selecting a dating partner, low self-monitors tend to stress intrinsic motives (such as similarity) more than high self-monitors do, while high self-monitors stress extrinsic motives (such as the helpfulness of the partner's connections) more than low self-monitors do.

(*Source:* Based on data from Jones, 1993.)

again, low self-monitors appear to be oriented toward the other person, while high self-monitors are oriented toward satisfying their own broader needs.

A very different interpretation of the interpersonal relationships of those high and low in self-monitoring has been provided by Howells (1993). He found that high self-monitors had more positive personality characteristics than lows. Students scoring high on the self-monitoring scale were more sociable, affectionate, energetic, sensitive, intellectually curious, and open than students scoring low. Some of the previous interpersonal findings could simply indicate that low self-monitors are less socially competent and less confident about taking risks in social situations. An independent but consistent proposal by Leary and colleagues (1995) is that self-esteem serves as a "sociometer" that is a necessary element in the monitoring of interpersonal relations. People with high self-esteem (presumably high self-monitors) interpret the positive reactions of others as indicating they are liked and included; if self-esteem begins to dip in a social situation, this indicates the possibility of social rejection and exclusion, so behavior is altered to correct the problem.

In thinking about the differences that have been found between high and low self-monitors, you may have concluded that lows are better adjusted than highs. That is, lows are consistent, honest in expressing their actual beliefs, and committed to their romantic partners, while highs are inconsistent, eager to please others, and happy with multiple relationships. Yet the same findings, of course, could be described as showing that lows are self-centered, closed-minded, insensitive to the opinions of others, and lacking in social skills, while highs are sensitive to the feelings of others, open-minded, and socially skillful. Research indicates, in fact, that greater maladjustment (neuroticism) is more characteristic of individuals falling at both extremes of the dimension than of those who score in the middle (Miller & Thayer, 1989).

Self-Efficacy: "I Think I Can, I Think I Can . . ."

Self-Efficacy ■ A person's evaluation of his or her ability or competency to perform a task, reach a goal, or overcome an obstacle.

Self-efficacy refers to a person's evaluation of his or her ability or competency to perform a task, reach a goal, or overcome an obstacle (Bandura, 1977). Can you succeed in a calculus course? Can you learn to drive a car? Can you overcome your fear of heights? Your answer may differ from question to question because feelings of self-efficacy vary as a function of the task. I (DB) am confident that I can eventually put together any toy or piece of furniture for which "some assembly is required," and equally confident that I cannot fill out my tax forms correctly each year. Research confirms such differences in feelings of efficacy—after the severe 1989 earthquake in California, college students there expressed low self-efficacy about their ability to cope with natural disasters; but in unrelated aspects of their lives (such as school performance), self-efficacy was unaffected (Burger & Palmer, 1992).

Self-Efficacy and Performance. Performance in both physical and academic tasks is enhanced by the appropriate type of self-efficacy. For example, those high in athletic self-efficacy are able to continue longer at exercise requiring physical endurance than those low in such self-efficacy (Gould & Weiss, 1981). One reason for this ability is that feelings of high self-efficacy for physical tasks stimulates the body to produce *endogenous opioids,* and these function as natural painkillers that make it possible for a person to continue a physical task (Bandura et al., 1988). Also, high self-efficacy concerning physical ability leads to perceived success at an exercise task and attributions of personal control over this behavior (Courneya & McAuley, 1993).

In academics, self-efficacy is equally beneficial. When college students were given the task of writing test questions for a class, questions written by those high in self-efficacy were rated as better than those written by low self-efficacy individuals (Tuckman & Sexton, 1990). These same research participants were also asked to estimate how well they would do at this task. The high-self-efficacy students did better than they expected, and those who were low failed to meet their expectancies. In related research, Sanna and Pusecker (1994) found that when students expect to perform well, they also expect a positive self-evaluation, and the result is improved performance. Expectations of a poor performance are associated with expectations of a negative self-evaluation and impaired performance.

Among college professors, academic success (defined by rank and salary) is predicted in part by self-efficacy (Taylor et al., 1984). The higher the professors' self-efficacy, the more they engaged in many projects simultaneously and set goals for completing articles and books. These behaviors, in turn, resulted in their producing more publications and having these publications cited by others in their field. The end results were more promotions and higher salary levels.

Self-Efficacy in Social Situations. Interpersonal behavior is also affected by feelings of self-efficacy with respect to social interactions. Among the reasons for low social self-efficacy is the lack of social skills, and the consequences include anxiety and avoidance of such situations (Morris, 1985).

Attributions about social failure are affected by social self-efficacy (Alden, 1986). When provided with negative feedback about the outcome of a given social behavior, high-efficacy individuals perceive the cause as external (something unique to a given situation), while those low in efficacy make internal attributions (lack of ability).

Increasing a Person's Feelings of Self-Efficacy. Self-efficacy is by no means fixed and unchanging. When a person receives positive feedback about his or her skills (even false feedback), self-efficacy is likely to rise (Bandura, 1986). In a pioneering experiment, Bandura and Adams (1977) were able to show that a phobia such as fear of snakes can be interpreted in cognitive terms as a reaction based on low self-efficacy—on a lack of confidence in one's ability to cope with a snake. In a program of behavioral therapy (*systematic desensitization*), snake-phobic individuals learned to relax while viewing a snake photograph, then a toy snake, then a small snake in a glass cage, and so on, over a period of time. Eventually, they could deal comfortably with a large, uncaged snake. As the phobia decreased, physiological arousal to a snake stimulus decreased, and self-efficacy increased.

The effect of such therapy on self-efficacy is quite specific and does not generalize to other situations. Nevertheless, analogous desensitization procedures can have parallel results, decreasing other phobias (such as fear of spiders or of open places) and raising self-efficacy about one's ability to cope with such previously feared cues (Bandura, Adams, & Hardy, 1980).

More recently, Riskind and Maddux (1993) have examined additional elements of a frightening situation and the ways in which external cues and self-efficacy interact in determining the strength of fear. These investigators point out that two models of fear have been proposed. The *harm-looming model* describes fear as a function of the closeness of the feared object to the individual and whether it is moving. You have probably seen many horror movies in which you become increasingly uncomfortable as some dreaded creature comes closer and closer to the potential victim. The *self-efficacy model* focuses on the individual's perception that he or she has the ability to prevent harm. An experimental test provided evidence that both models are correct and that they can be integrated. Male and female undergraduates looked at video presentations in which tarantulas either moved toward the camera, moved backward, or were still. Before viewing the tarantulas, the research participants either were asked to imagine one of two situations: in one situation, they see a large spider in the room and can choose to smash it with a magazine or leave the room (inducing feelings of high self-efficacy); in the other situation, they are helpless, strapped to a chair in a locked soundproofed room with a large spider (inducing feelings of low self-efficacy). As shown in Figure 5.12, both the "looming" object and the level of self-efficacy influenced fear. The still or retreating tarantula was less frightening, regardless of self-efficacy. The advancing tarantula aroused more fear, but only for those low in self-efficacy.

INTEGRATING PRINCIPLES

1. Self-functioning is associated with many specific aspects of cognition, affect, and overt physical behavior. For example, one's attention can be focused on positive or on negative elements of oneself—or of the external world. As discussed in Chapter 3, the result is an interaction of cognitive and affective factors.

2. Attentional focus is also involved in individual differences in monitoring of overt behavior—whether to conform to fixed internal standards or to adapt to the situationally specific reactions of other people in order to gain popularity and acceptance (Chapter 7). As a result of differences in such monitoring behavior, some people behave in the same, unchanging way in quite different social situations, while others are social chameleons.

3. A third important type of self-functioning involves the relative strength of feelings of efficacy about one's ability to perform a task or to cope with a particular stressful event. Feelings of high self-efficacy affect not only task performance but also such broad realms as interpersonal behavior (Chapter 8) and the body's ability to maintain good health through effective coping responses (Chapter 14).

FIGURE 5.12

Effects of a Harm-Looming Stimulus and Self-Efficacy on Fear. Fear is aroused by aspects of the feared stimulus (*harm-looming* means moving toward the individual) and by perceptions of self-efficacy (ability to deal effectively with the feared stimulus). Feelings of high or low self-efficacy in responding to spiders were induced in research participants, and they were then shown video presentations of a tarantula that was harm-looming (moving toward the viewer) or not (standing still or moving away). The importance of harm-looming was shown by the fact that little fear was aroused by a still or retreating tarantula. The importance of self-efficacy was shown by the greater fear among low- than among high-self-efficacy individuals when the tarantula was moving toward them.

(*Source:* Based on data from Riskind & Maddux, 1993.)

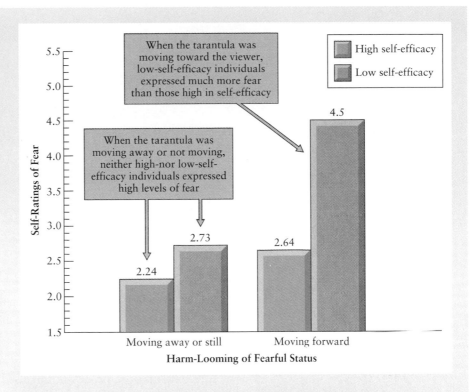

High self-efficacy

Low self-efficacy

When the tarantula was moving toward the viewer, low-self-efficacy individuals expressed much more fear than those high in self-efficacy

When the tarantula was moving away or not moving, neither high-nor low-self-efficacy individuals expressed high levels of fear

Self-Ratings of Fear

2.24   2.73   2.64   4.5

Moving away or still   Moving forward

Harm-Looming of Fearful Status

Gender: Maleness or Femaleness As a Crucial Aspect of Identity

Sex ■ Maleness or femaleness as determined by genetic factors present at conception that result in anatomical and physiological differences.

Gender ■ The attributes, behaviors, personality characteristics, and expectancies associated with a person's biological sex in a given culture; may be based on biology, may be learned, or may represent a combination of biological and cultural determinants.

Perhaps the most pervasive element of personal identity is that portion of social identity in which each of us is assigned to one of two categories: male or female.

The terms *sex* and *gender* are often used to mean the same thing. In our discussion, however, we follow the lead of others (e.g., Beckwith, 1994) and define **sex** in biological terms—in terms of the anatomical and physiological differences that develop on the basis of genes present at conception (see Figure 5.13 on page 176). **Gender** refers to everything else associated with one's sex, including the roles, behaviors, preferences, and other attributes that define what it means to be a male or a female in a given culture. Until research provides unambiguous answers, we can simply assume that many of these attributes are probably learned while others may very well be based in whole or in part on biological determinants. An example of the interaction of genetics and learning occurs when physical attributes are interpreted as indications of masculinity or femininity. Presumably as the result of learned stereotypes, a muscular build and a deep voice are perceived as attributes of masculinity while long hair and a high voice are perceived as feminine (Aube, Norcliffe, & Koestner, 1995).

FIGURE 5.13

Sex versus Gender. Though terminology is still a matter of debate, psychologists most often speak of *sex* when they are referring to anatomical and physiological differences between males and females that are based on genetic differences present at conception. *Gender* is used in describing other attributes and behaviors associated with sex that are acquired on the basis of cultural expectations or a combination of biological and cultural factors—or whose determinants are unknown.

Please note that the specific definitions used here are not universally accepted by those actively working in this field (e.g., Deaux, 1993b; Gentile, 1993; Unger & Crawford, 1993).

Gender Identity and Stereotypes Based on Gender

Each of us has a **gender identity;** that is, we label ourselves as male or female. Except in relatively rare instances, a person's biological sex and gender identity correspond.

Developing a Gender Identity. Adults usually react to a newborn baby's sex as the all-important defining characteristic. It appears that the initial task of parents, relatives, friends, and strangers is to determine the infant's sex ("Is it a boy or a girl?"). Parents must quickly attach a boy name or a girl name, and often provide additional cues to the baby's sex by selecting pink versus blue clothing, decorating the newborn's room in a masculine or feminine style, and selecting "gender-appropriate" toys and clothing.

Despite all of this emphasis on gender differentiation, young children are not ordinarily aware of sex or gender until they are about two years old. At this point, they begin to identify themselves as a "girl" or a "boy"—though without a clear understanding of what such terms mean. Gender identity occurs when gender becomes part of one's self-concept; the individual develops a sense of self that includes maleness or femaleness (Grieve, 1980)—though not ordinarily in the way suggested in Figure 5.14.

Between the ages of four and seven, children gradually acquire the concept of **gender consistency.** They begin to accept the principle that gender is a basic attribute of each person. As soon as these cognitions are firmly in place, our perceptions are affected by what we believe about gender. For example, when children (aged five to nine) and adolescents (fifteen-year-olds and college students) are shown videotapes of four nine-month-old infants, both age groups agree that the babies identified as being female (Mary and Karen) appear to be smaller, more beautiful, nicer, and softer than those identified as being male

Gender Identity ■ The sex (male or female) that a person identifies as his or her own; usually, though not always, corresponds corresponds to the person's biological sex.

Gender Consistency ■ The concept that gender is a basic, enduring attribute of each individual, a concept ordinarily acquired by children between the ages of four and seven.

FIGURE 5.14

Gender Identity. *Gender identity refers to the sex that a person identifies as his or her own—a subjective self-perception as being a male or a female that usually corresponds to the person's biological sex. Though social psychologists are not totally sure of how this self-perception originates, the conscious process suggested in this cartoon is, of course, only a joke.*

(*Source:* Drawing by Manhoff; © 1995 *The New Yorker* Magazine, Inc.)

"We don't believe in pressuring the children. When the time is right, they'll choose the appropriate gender."

(Stephen and Matthew). In fact, for different research participants, the experimenters assigned a male or a female name to infants of both sexes. Thus, each male baby was identified correctly as a boy for half the participants and incorrectly as a girl for the remaining participants; similarly, each female baby was identified for half the participants as a girl and for half as a boy. As a result, it is clear that gender stereotypes determined how the infants were perceived (Vogel et al., 1991).

The Origin of Gender Identity. Though all observed differences in the behavior of men and women were long assumed to be biological givens, it seems increasingly likely that many "typical" masculine and feminine characteristics are in fact acquired (Bem, 1984). *Gender schema theory* was formulated by Bem (1981, 1983). She suggested that children have a "generalized readiness" to organize information about the self in a way that is based on cultural definitions of what is appropriate behavior for each sex. Once a young child learns to apply the label "girl" or "boy" to herself or himself, the stage is set for the child to learn the "appropriate" roles that accompany these labels. As childhood progresses, **sex typing** occurs when children learn in detail the stereotypes associated with maleness or femaleness in their culture. Though recent studies provide some evidence of widely held stereotypes (for example, compared to men, women are perceived as more sociable and happier), such effects are small and often different for male and female observers (Feingold, 1995). In contrast to gender schema theory, Spence (1993) favors a multifactorial gender identity theory in which the gender-relevant aspects of self are composed of many factors rather than a simple division into male and female.

Part of what children learn about gender is based on observing their parents and trying to be like them. Generally, children are rewarded for engaging in gender-appropriate behavior and discouraged (or ridiculed) when they engage in gender-inappropriate behavior. Consider, for example, the probable response to a little girl who requests a doll for Christmas versus the response to a little boy who makes the same request. In an analogous way, do you think parents respond differently to a little boy who wants boxing gloves and a

Sex Typing ■ Acquisition of the attributes associated with being a male or a female in a given culture.

punching bag for his birthday versus a little girl who expresses the same desire? On the basis of how adults, older siblings, and others respond, a little girl learns that wanting a doll is acceptable but wanting boxing gloves is not, while a little boy learns that for him boxing gloves are cute but a doll is unacceptable. Even when parents reject the stereotypes and try to teach their children to be less role-bound, they may find themselves in a losing battle when their offspring respond to advertising and to what their friends have. A couple in my neighborhood were determined to "do things differently," but they nevertheless ended up buying their daughter Barbie dolls and their son G.I. Joe action figures. In countless ways, a culture's gender stereotypes are learned. Girls can cry and boys can fight. Boys can play football and girls can play jacks. Boys and girls are given different clothes to wear, have their hair cut differently, are assigned different chores around the house, are encouraged to identify with different fictional characters, and so on.

As the years pass, the lessons are well learned, and by the time they reach the sixth grade, the overwhelming majority of children in the United States have learned the prevailing gender stereotypes (Carter & McCloskey, 1984), even if they do not personally agree with them. They know what is considered suitable for each gender and what constitutes out-of-role behavior. This developmental progression is outlined in Figure 5.15.

The specific content of these stereotypes about masculinity and femininity in our culture and the possibility of nonstereotyped behavior are presented in the following *Cornerstones* section.

Cornerstones of Social Psychology
BEM'S CONCEPT OF PSYCHOLOGICAL ANDROGYNY AS AN ALTERNATIVE TO MASCULINITY VERSUS FEMININITY

In introducing this particular cornerstone, we want to point out that it represents part of a very important revolution within social psychology. Our field, like most scientific fields, was historically dominated by men. Among the many implications of this state of affairs was a seemingly automatic emphasis on "masculine" issues (aggression, leadership, conflict, achievement, etc.) combined with a neglect of now familiar "feminine" issues such as sex differences, gender stereotypes, sexism, harassment, and many other topics that constitute a major aspect of today's mainstream social psychology.

Why the change? No one can speak with certainty, but a possible explanation includes some combination of changing societal views, the rise of feminism, a more widespread comprehension of gender issues, and the dramatic increase in the proportion of women entering doctoral programs. Whatever the ultimate explanation, in the 1970s much more research was suddenly devoted to issues relevant to woman, and many female social psychologists challenged the old order by introducing creative new lines of research. Included among these are Janet Spence (e.g., Spence, Helmreich, & Stapp, 1973), Eleanor Maccoby (e.g., Maccoby & Jacklin, 1974), Kay Deaux (e.g., Deaux, 1976), Alice Eagly (e.g., 1978), and many others—along with Sandra Bem, whose work we will now describe.

In two articles published in the mid-1970s, Bem (1974, 1975) outlined a theoretical framework and developed a measuring device that profoundly affected the study of gender. More than two decades later, this work plus her newer contributions continue to influence how gender issues are conceptualized.

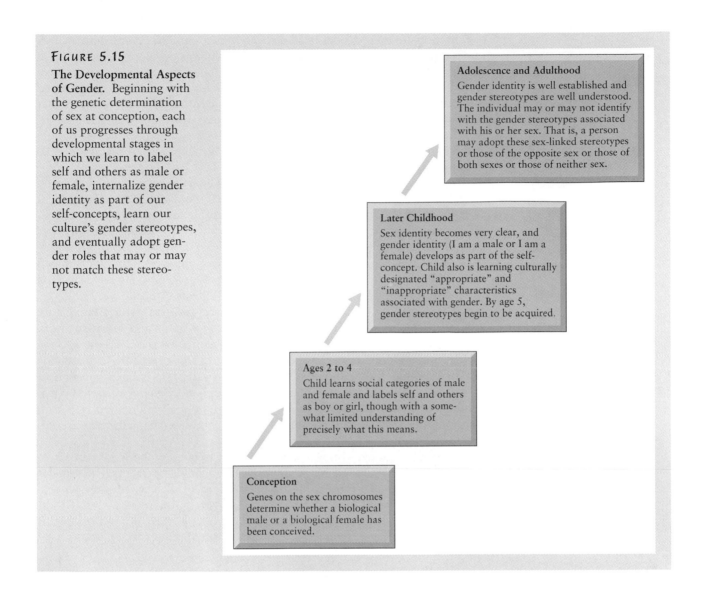

FIGURE 5.15

The Developmental Aspects of Gender. Beginning with the genetic determination of sex at conception, each of us progresses through developmental stages in which we learn to label self and others as male or female, internalize gender identity as part of our self-concepts, learn our culture's gender stereotypes, and eventually adopt gender roles that may or may not match these stereotypes.

Adolescence and Adulthood
Gender identity is well established and gender stereotypes are well understood. The individual may or may not identify with the gender stereotypes associated with his or her sex. That is, a person may adopt these sex-linked stereotypes or those of the opposite sex or those of both sexes or those of neither sex.

Later Childhood
Sex identity becomes very clear, and gender identity (I am a male or I am a female) develops as part of the self-concept. Child also is learning culturally designated "appropriate" and "inappropriate" characteristics associated with gender. By age 5, gender stereotypes begin to be acquired.

Ages 2 to 4
Child learns social categories of male and female and labels self and others as boy or girl, though with a somewhat limited understanding of precisely what this means.

Conception
Genes on the sex chromosomes determine whether a biological male or a biological female has been conceived.

Bem pointed out that up to the 1970s, psychologists, along with people in general, tended to think of masculinity and femininity as lying at the two endpoints of a single continuum. Each individual was thus either masculine or feminine, and there was no way to be both highly masculine *and* highly feminine.

Bem—along with Kagan (1964) and Kohlberg (1966)—acknowledged that many people *do* fit the gender stereotypes of masculine and feminine. Those who are highly stereotyped are motivated to behave in a way consistent with the gender role acquired from the culture and internalized. Any "inappropriate" gender behavior must be suppressed to avoid disturbing a narrowly masculine or narrowly feminine self-concept.

What if, however, the varied personal characteristics associated with masculinity and femininity lie on independent continuums that range from low to high masculinity and from low to high femininity? In that case, many individuals might actually be high on characteristics associated with both genders (for example, a person could be both competitive and sensitive to the needs of others) and thus characterized by psychological **androgyny.** An androgynous person is one who combines traditional masculine and traditional feminine behavioral characteristics.

Androgyny ■ In studies of gender, the tendency to report having both traditionally "masculine" and traditionally "feminine" characteristics.

Sandra Bem. Sandra Bem obtained the Ph.D. degree in 1968 at the University of Michigan. A few years later, while at Stanford University, she developed the Bem Sex-Role Inventory and undertook research that investigated the effects of identifying with gender stereotypes versus adopting characteristics of the opposite gender, both genders, or neither. Since 1981, she has held the rank of professor at Cornell University. Along with several of her contemporaries in the 1970s, Bem was at the forefront of social psychology's new emphasis on gender issues.

Bem Sex-Role Inventory (BSRI) ■ Bem's measure of the extent to which an individual's self-description is characterized by traditional masculinity, traditional femininity, a mixture of the two (androgyny), or neither (undifferentiated).

Gender-Stereotype Identification ■ The extent to which an individual identifies with the culture's gender stereotypes; masculinity or femininity, as measured by the BSRI.

To measure these gender-related characteristics and to pursue this new formulation, the **Bem Sex-Role Inventory** (or **BSRI**) was developed. (Note that in today's terminology, we would label this the Bem Gender-Role Inventory.) Bem started with about two hundred positive personality characteristics that seemed to be either masculine or feminine in tone along with two hundred others that did not appear to be gender-related. Masculinity was defined in terms of attributes associated with an instrumental orientation ("getting the job done") and femininity with attributes associated with an expressive orientation ("affective concern for the welfare of others").

Undergraduates rated each characteristic as to whether it would be socially desirable for a man and/or socially desirable for a woman. The final instrument contains twenty characteristics judged to be desirable for a male but not for a female, twenty characteristics judged to be desirable for a female but not for a male, and twenty gender-neutral characteristics (no more desirable for one gender than the other). Table 5.1 lists examples of the three types of items contained in the BSRI. It is interesting to note that these gender stereotypes have changed very little with the passage of time (Martin, 1987; Raty & Snellman, 1992).

In taking Bem's test, a person responds to all sixty items by indicating how accurate each one is as part of his or her self-description on a scale ranging from "never or almost never true" to "always or almost always true." Based on these responses, the individual is classified as sex-typed (gender-typed) as a masculine man or feminine woman, sex-reversed (gender-reversed) as a masculine woman or feminine man, androgynous (a person of either gender having relatively equal numbers of masculine and feminine attributes), or undifferentiated (a person who indicates that most of the masculine and feminine characteristics are *not* self-descriptive).

Based on research samples, it is estimated that only about 30 percent of males adhere to the masculine gender type and a similar percentage of females to the feminine gender type, while about one-third of each sex is androgynous. Undifferentiated and cross-gender categories make up the rest.

Despite signs of declining adherence to the details of these concepts or this measuring instrument, the influence of Bem's contribution is clear. ■ ■ ■

The various terms used by those studying sex and gender can become confusing, and it may be helpful in keep in mind Beckwith's (1994) differentiation of *sex* (biological maleness or femaleness), *gender* (social categorization as female or male), *gender identity* (one's self-perception as male or female), and **gender-stereotype identification** (self-reported masculinity or femininity as measured by the BSRI).

Gender-Role Behavior and the Reactions of Others to Gender-Role Behavior

Once people acquire a specific pattern of gender-relevant characteristics, they tend to behave in ways that are consistent with their assumptions about appropriateness (Chatterjee & McCarrey, 1991). That is, they behave in ways identified as masculine, feminine, androgynous, or none of the above.

Androgynous versus Gender-Typed Behavior. Much of the research on gender and gender roles has focused on androgyny, and the assumption is often made that an androgynous role is preferable to either male or female gender-typed roles. Many would quarrel with this assumption, however, and we might benefit from considering adherence to gender roles as falling along a continuum from androgyny to relatively traditional masculinity and femininity to *extreme*

TABLE 5.1 Gender Stereotypes Identified by Bem

A person taking the Bem Sex-Role Inventory rates a series of characteristics in terms of how well they describe him or her. Those items shown here are the ones that are perceived as more characteristic of males than of females or vice versa. That is, they represent pervasive gender stereotypes in our culture.

Self-Descriptions on the Bem Sex-Role Inventory That Correspond to Masculine and Feminine Stereotypes

Characteristics of the Male Stereotype	Characteristics of the Female Stereotype
acts as a leader	affectionate
aggressive	cheerful
ambitious	childlike
analytical	compassionate
assertive	does not use harsh language
athletic	eager to soothe hurt feelings
competitive	feminine
defends own beliefs	flatterable
dominant	gentle
forceful	gullible
has leadership abilities	loves children
independent	loyal
individualistic	sensitive to the needs of others
makes decisions easily	shy
masculine	soft-spoken
self-reliant	sympathetic
self-sufficient	tender
strong personality	understanding
willing to take a stand	warm
willing to take risks	yielding

(*Source:* Based on information in Bem, 1974.)

gender-role ideology (Hamburger et al., 1995; Mosher, 1991; Murnen & Byrne, 1991).

Many past studies were consistent with the proposition that "androgyny is good." For example, compared to gender-typed individuals, androgynous men and women were found to be: better liked (Major, Carnevale, & Deaux, 1981); better adjusted (Orlofsky & O'Heron, 1987; Williams & A'lessandro, 1994); more adaptable to situational demands (Prager & Bailey, 1985); more flexible in coping with stress (McCall & Struthers, 1994); more comfortable with their sexuality (Garcia, 1982); more satisfied interpersonally (Rosenzweig & Daley, 1989); and, in an elderly sample, more satisfied with their lives (Dean-Church & Gilroy, 1993). Spouses report happier marriages when both partners are androgynous than is true for any other combination of roles (Zammichieli, Gilroy, & Sherman, 1988). Further, sexual satisfaction is greater if one or both partners is androgynous than if both are sex-typed (Safir et al., 1982).

Strong adherence to traditional gender roles is often found to be associated with problems. For example, men who identify with the extreme masculine role behave more violently and aggressively than men who perceive themselves as having some feminine characteristics (Finn, 1986). Among adolescent males, high masculinity is associated with having multiple sexual partners, the view that men and women are adversaries, low condom use, and the belief that getting a partner pregnant is a positive indication of one's masculinity (Pleck, Sonenstein, & Ku, 1993). Both men and women who endorse a purely feminine role are lower in self-esteem than either masculine or androgynous individuals (Lau, 1989). In interpersonal situations, high femininity is associated with feeling depressed after failing at an interpersonal task (Sayers, Baucom, & Tierney, 1993). Most of these findings suggest that some gender roles are better than others. Among the few neutral results—regardless of their sex, people high in femininity place more importance on Valentine's Day than low-femininity individuals; femininity also predicts the likelihood of wearing red on that day (Ogletree, 1993).

Aube and her colleagues (1995) point out the importance of studying not just the self-reports of research participants in gender-role studies but also the way these individuals are viewed by others. For example, in one study men high in masculinity described their relationships with roommates and romantic partners as more positive than did those low in masculinity; but this association was not confirmed when the roommates and partners were asked for their views about the relationship.

The Effects of Gender Roles on Behavior at Home and in the Workplace. Keep in mind that there is consensus about which characteristics are preferred for each gender and that these stereotypes influence interpersonal behavior in many ways. (See Chapter 6 for additional information about how gender stereotypes can lead to prejudice and discrimination.)

Gender roles still influence what men and women do within the home (Major, 1993). Even when both partners are employed in demanding and high-paying jobs, work around the house is most often divided along traditional gender lines (see Chapter 8). That is, men often take out the garbage, make repairs, and do the yard work, while women clean the house, cook, and engage in child care. Altogether, women spend more time doing housework than men, whether they personally are gender-typed or androgynous (Gunter & Gunter, 1991). When it comes time to clean the bathroom or paint the garage, the culturally prescribed gender roles seem to be more powerful than one's self-description on the BSRI.

In the workplace, gender and gender roles also remain of central importance. For example, when women are chosen to do a task and then told that gender constituted the primary reason for their selection, they evaluate their performance as being less adequate than women told that the assignment was based on merit (Turner, Pratkanis, & Hardaway, 1991). Men might well react the same way, but research has not been conducted to find out how men react to being chosen primarily because of their gender.

Gender also affects expectancies. For example, Subich and colleagues (1986) presented to undergraduates information about three unfamiliar occupations—administrative assistant, information analyst, and traffic coordinator. The research participants were asked to indicate how interested they were in these occupations. Compared to women, men expressed more interest in the relatively unknown fields, had higher expectations of succeeding, and placed more stress on salary. Men stressed extrinsic motives for choosing a job; women, in contrast, were more concerned about whether the jobs would be personally satisfying, thus stressing intrinsic motives for job selection. There is no reason to label either motivation as somehow "better" than the other, but they are clearly different.

Despite a vast increase in the percentage of women in the workforce (Norwood, 1992; Uchitelle, 1994) and federal laws against discrimination based on gender, gender-related occupational restrictions still operate in the labor market

(Kelley & Streeter, 1992). In academia, for example, U.S. women remain at a disadvantage compared to men with respect to doctorates granted, salaries, and professorships (Callaci, 1993). One reason is that women are more likely than men to believe that they *deserve* to earn a lower salary than others (Moore, 1994), presumably because they have been taught to evaluate themselves in a less egotistical way.

Though sexism and gender stereotypes may well play a major role in differential male–female success, Tannen (1994) stresses the additional importance of gender differences in communication styles. For example, women are not as likely as men to brag about their accomplishments, and one result is a failure to receive the appropriate credit when their work is exceptionally good (Tannen, 1995). Women are expected to express positive emotions about the successes of others but not about their own accomplishments (Stoppard & Gruchy, 1993). Tannen (1994) also points out that the promotion of women to management positions is hindered because the men in charge of deciding who gets promoted misinterpret female communication styles as indicating "indecisiveness, inability to assume authority and even incompetence." Managers need to know that modest self-descriptions versus bragging self-descriptions represent an aspect of interpersonal style rather than actual worth.

When women are able to obtain high-level positions in an organization, they differ from men in ways that go beyond how they communicate. Female leadership style tends to be *connective* and *interactive*. That is, women prefer to collaborate, consult, and negotiate while men tend to stress competition, make demands, and reward individual achievement (Lipman-Blumen, 1988; Rosener, 1990). Self-esteem is associated with these different managerial styles. For men, self-esteem is linked to personal achievement; for women, self-esteem is a function of positive interpersonal attachments (Josephs, Markus, & Tafarodi, 1992). Even in childhood, girls are more concerned about the success of interpersonal relationships than are boys (Manolis & Milich, 1993).

When women overcome various obstacles and succeed in "masculine" fields, they are often patronized or criticized. In the O. J. Simpson trial, prosecutor Marcia Clark's change of hairstyle was front-page news, and she was described by male defense attorneys as "an attractive lady" with "great legs" but also as "shrill" and "a little hard" (Toobin, 1995). Try to imagine an analogous interest in the hair of a male prosecutor, his physical attractiveness, or his being too shrill or too hard.

What happens when women catch up to men in a given occupation? A common reaction is, "There goes the neighborhood." That is, when barriers are overcome in a specific job and a higher and higher percentage of women engage in that occupation, the job is then viewed as less prestigious (Johnson, 1991). It is as if negative reactions to the feminine role are so pervasive that the only way to explain newfound female success in an occupation is to devalue the work itself.

Why Do Traditional Gender Roles Remain Powerful? The concept of male–female differences and of male superiority has a long history. In the Judeo-Christian tradition, men were originally identified as the owners of their families (Wolf, 1992). In the Jewish Talmud, categories of property included cattle, women, and slaves. In the New Testament, Ephesians (5:22–24) instructs Christian women as follows: "Wives, be subject to your husbands as you are to the Lord. For the husband is the head of the wife just as Christ is the head of the Church."

Despite the passage of many centuries, gender differences still have strong cultural support. For example, in children's books and stories, stereotypes of boys and girls and of men and women have been generally accepted until fairly recently (McArthur & Eisen, 1976; Weitzman et al., 1972). That is, men and boys tended to play active, initiating roles while women and girls either tagged along as followers or needed to be rescued when they found themselves in danger. As the artificiality of these stereotypes became increasingly obvious in the 1970s, different books came along. In *He Bear, She Bear* the Berenstains informed their readers in 1974 that fatherhood is reserved for boy bears and motherhood for girl bears, but that otherwise gender isn't tied to activities or occupations—"There's *nothing* that we cannot try. We can do all these things you see, whether we are he OR she."

Despite this new consciousness, the old stories still remain popular. Lurie (1993) points out that traditional fairy tales were deliberately designed to teach children various moral and behavioral lessons. A familiar story line is that a rule is given to a child, the child disobeys, and negative consequences then occur; for example, Little Red Riding Hood should have followed her mother's advice about how best to get to grandma's house. The threatened punishment was provided by the hungry wolf. Luckily, a male with an ax was able to save her from the consequences of her reckless independence.

In countless old stories and the modern movies based on them, heroines such as Snow White, the Sleeping Beauty, Cinderella, the Little Mermaid, and all the rest get into serious trouble, and their only hope is the love of a handsome prince who will kiss them and/or fight the evil ones so that the couple can live happily ever after. When a male character has the lead (in *Bambi, The Lion King, The Jungle Book, Dumbo,* etc.), the traditional role for a female is simply to give birth to the hero or to serve as a sex object who will bear his offspring. Studies of prime-time television, soap operas, advertising, and even *Sesame Street* indicate that just such traditional gender roles are still portrayed (Helman & Bookspan, 1992). An informal survey of movies playing in New York's capital district in summer 1995 revealed that of the thirteen films rated G, PG, and PG-13, males had the leading roles in ten (including *A Kid in King Arthur's Court, The Indian in the Cupboard, Free Willy 2,* and *Dumbo Drop*); the three with female leading roles were *Clueless,* about a high school girl who thinks Kuwait is located somewhere in the San Fernando Valley; *Congo,* boasting Amy the talking gorilla; and *The Net*—in which the heroine was, refreshingly, both human and smart. The ten R-rated movies split evenly between those with male and female leading characters; this may appear to be an encouraging sign, until you discover that the males were all action heroes (*Batman Forever, Under Siege 2, Virtuosity,* etc.) while three of the five female leads involved a part-time prostitute (*Belle du Jour*), young lesbians (*Two Girls in Love*), and a rapacious creature whose genes were partly extraterrestrial (*Species*). So far, there seems to be no compelling evidence that the entertainment industry is being overwhelmed by concerns about gender equality.

Leaving aside books, television, and the movies for the moment—what about the new world of computers with games and learning devices on hard drives, floppy disks, and CD-ROMs? The story is not much different. Most students in the sixth, seventh, and eighth grades react with stress to stereotypical opposite-gender computer software (Cooper, Hall, & Huff, 1990). Possibly because most educational software is based on male stereotypes, boys greatly outnumber girls in computer courses, use of computer labs, enrollment in computer camps, and expressed interest in the field of computer science.

Moving beyond Gender Stereotyping: Signs of Progress. There is still hope for a gradual move away from gender stereotypes in our culture. For one thing, despite assumptions that most individuals personally hold these stereotypes, research participants are, in fact, much more likely to think nonstereotypically or to underestimate gender differences than to overestimate them (Swim, 1994); under threatening conditions, however, stereotypes and gender differences be-

FIGURE 5.16

Depicting Nontraditional Gender Roles in Advertisements. Though ads are one of the many places where traditional gender stereotypes are regularly presented, an increasing percentage are now attracting attention by reversing male and female roles. Here, a man is depicted as a sex object.

come accentuated (Grant, 1993). Also, some stories are now published in which brave and intelligent heroines fight when necessary, rescue male victims, and otherwise engage in nontraditional feminine behavior (Phelps, 1981). In the movies, it may be that heroines such as Pocahontas, Sandra Bullock as a computer whiz (*The Net*), and Michelle Pfeiffer as an ex-Marine who teaches in a tough inner-city school (*Dangerous Minds*) represent a new and different tradition. As shown in Figure 5.16, even advertising has begun occasionally to present men and women in nontraditional ways (Kilbourne, 1994). Do such role models matter? Keep in mind that when small children are exposed to stories in which the traditional male and female roles are reversed, their expectancies about possible female accomplishments rise (Scott & Feldman-Summers, 1979). Maybe exposure to Roseanne, Mrs. Doubtfire, and the equal-opportunity-for-violence Mighty Morphin Power Rangers will have some positive lasting effects.

When Differences Are Found between Males and Females, Are They Based on Sex, Gender, or Both?

Studies of gender identity clearly show that social factors determine the ways in which maleness and femaleness are defined. Cross-cultural research also provides evidence that the characteristics associated with each gender differ when cultural influences differ. Such findings do not, however, rule out the possibility of some built-in, genetically linked differences between the sexes in personality, ability, response tendencies, or whatever (Diamond, 1993; Wright, 1994). *Some* behavioral differences between men and women are important; but the question is whether the differences are based on biology, learning, or some combination of the two (Eagly & Steffen, 1986). How this question is answered sometimes involves a clash between scientific data and a feminist political agenda, according to Eagly (1995); but others argue that there is *no* uniform feminist agenda (Hyde & Plant, 1995). Interestingly, among undergraduates both men and women believe that social and biological factors each play a role, but that socialization is the more important determinant (Martin & Parker, 1995).

Interpersonal Behavior. In interacting with other people, women are more likely than men to share rewards (Major & Deaux, 1982) or to deprive themselves in order to help someone else (Leventhal & Anderson, 1970).

Many investigators assume that these male–female differences are based on learned expectancies associated with gender roles (Major & Adams, 1983). It should come as no surprise that women whose lives have been spent experiencing social pressure to accept second place in assertive and aggressive situations may deal with people in a way different from men (Nadkarni, Lundgren, & Burlew, 1991). Perhaps women have better social skills than men (Margalit & Eysenck, 1990) because they *have* to.

Other investigators stress the importance of biochemical differences. The male hormone—*testosterone*—has a limited effect on sexual behavior, but it strongly affects the tendency to dominate and control others. Presumably, among our distant ancestors those males who produced the most testosterone were combative and dominant, thus enabling them to subdue rival males, obtain mates, and so pass on their genes, including some that controlled high testosterone production among their male descendants. Modern men have higher testosterone levels than women and behave in more aggressive and dominant ways (Berman, Gladue, & Taylor, 1993), especially with male strangers (Moskowitz, 1993). Perhaps men are more likely than women to initiate sexual contact because they tend to behave dominantly rather than because of differences in sexual needs (Anderson & Aymami, 1993).

Also, those males with the highest testosterone levels tend to choose dominant and controlling occupations such as trial lawyer, actor, politician, or criminal (Dabbs, 1992). Hormone level is also affected by the situation, such as participating in competitive athletics or even just watching from the sidelines. Dabbs (1993) reported that before a basketball game, testosterone rises for those on the team and for male fans, and the levels go even higher if one's team wins.

Given these investigations of how testosterone affects behavior, you might wonder about the behavioral effects of the female hormone—*estrogen*. Strangely enough, research on estrogen effects has tended to concentrate on physical consequences, such as skin tone, vaginal lubrication, and the risk of cancer.

Self-Perception. Gender differences in self-perception are commonly found. Compared to men, women are much more likely to be concerned about their body image (Pliner, Chaiken, & Flett, 1990), to express dissatisfaction about their bodies (Heinberg & Thompson, 1992) and about physical appearance in general (Hagborg, 1993), to develop eating disorders (Forston & Stanton, 1992; Hamilton, Falconer, & Greenberg, 1992), and to become depressed (Strickland, 1992). Obesity is a special issue for women. When males blame them for being overweight ("It's your own fault"), women are likely to accept this evaluation. When an overweight woman is viewed as an unacceptable date by a male, instead of being mad at him and attributing the problem to his prejudice, she is more likely to blame herself (Crocker, Cornwell, & Major, 1993). Even though obese women tend to attribute rejection in the workplace as caused by unfair biases, romantic rejection is perceived to be justified (Crocker & Major, 1993).

Why is appearance a major problem for women? Possibly because from infancy on, others respond to appearance differently on the basis of gender. College women report a high frequency of childhood experiences in which they were teased by peers and by brothers about such characteristics as facial appearance and weight (Cash, 1995). Even parents discriminate against overweight daughters (but not overweight sons) with respect to providing financial support for college (Crandall, 1995). Figure 5.17 only mildly exaggerates male–female differences in concerns about body image. To the extent that young men express any appearance anxiety, it is a relatively mild dissatisfaction

FIGURE 5.17

Female versus Male Concern with Body Image. *Presumably because of societal pressures, women are much more concerned with body image than men, especially with respect to weight. This cartoon ridicules the gender stereotypes that result in insensitivity among egocentric men and oversensitivity and self-depreciation among women. Interestingly, some reviewers perceived this particular strip as a sexist attack on women, whereas cartoonist Cathy Guisewite had exactly the opposite intention.*

(*Source:* Cathy Guisewite, May 26, 1991.)

about not measuring up to the body-builder muscular ideal of male attractiveness (Davis, Brewer, & Weinstein, 1993).

Consider for a moment the day-to-day negative effects of the special emphasis our society places on the physical attractiveness of women in general and on specific anatomical details such as breast size (Thompson & Tantleff, 1992). One consequence is that women often are vulnerable and easily upset when their appearance becomes an issue (Mori & Morey, 1991). For example, after looking at magazine pictures showing ultrathin models, undergraduate women respond with feeling of depression, stress, guilt, shame, insecurity, and dissatisfaction with their own bodies (Stice & Shaw, 1994). As they age, women are perceived as increasingly less feminine, though men are not viewed as becoming less masculine with age (Deutsch, Zalenski, & Clark, 1986).

Beyond appearance, other self-perceptions also differ for men and women. On self-report measures, women describe themselves as more anxious, gregarious, trusting, and nurturing than men, while men describe themselves as more assertive than women (Feingold, 1994). Compared to men, women respond with greater emotional intensity, as indicated by self-reports and by physiological assessment (Grossman & Wood, 1993). Some evidence suggests that the explanation for such gender differences rests on differences in the specific areas of the brain used by men and women in thinking and responding to emotional cues (Gur, 1995; Kolata, 1995; Shaywitz & Shaywitz, 1995).

At this time, no one can sensibly come to a grand conclusion about the reason for differences between men and women. We understand that you probably feel frustrated when we say that, but such uncertainty reflects the reality of current scientific research. It is easy enough to find certainty among people who rely on their opinions rather than on objective data. Some probably still agree with Queen Victoria (1881) who was convinced that "God created men and women different" and that any attempt to change things and speak of women's rights was a "mad, wicked folly." Happily, more than a hundred years have passed since such views were common. Today, many of us are convinced that men and women differ primarily because they have learned to differ. The final answer will almost certainly lie in the specifics as to which differences are biologically based, which are acquired, and which reflect both kinds of influence.

INTEGRATING PRINCIPLES

1. An extremely important aspect of one's personal identity includes a complex gender schema that is the result of being categorized from infancy on as either a male or a female. Beyond biological differences, we acquire attitudes, beliefs, emotions, and prejudices (Chapters 2, 3, 4, and 6) that are associated with gender—both our own and that of others.

2. Once we learn the gender-role behavior "appropriate" for our culture, much of our behavior and many of our reactions to others are guided by our conceptions of masculinity and femininity. Male–female differences are influenced in part by the prevailing beliefs of parents and others and are reinforced by images provided by the media. The effects of these gender roles extend to interpersonal relationships (Chapter 8) and the workplace (Chapter 13).

Social Diversity: A Critical Analysis
CULTURAL DIFFERENCES IN CONCERN ABOUT WEIGHT

WE DESCRIBED THE GREATER CONCERN AMONG WOMEN than among men about appearance, including a special dissatisfaction with weight. Because this is a strong gender difference, a cross-cultural comparison of weight concern should be helpful in showing the possible power of societal influences in shaping differential male–female reactions.

One consequence of wanting to be thinner is to take dieting to an extreme; sometimes the result is death. Wardle and her colleagues (1993) point out that eating disorders are much less common in developing nations than in Western society. Also, within the United Kingdom and

North America, African American and Asian women have fewer eating disorders than Caucasian women. Similar ethnic comparisons indicate that Caucasian women are the most likely to judge themselves as being overweight and to evaluate their bodies negatively.

To examine these cultural differences more precisely, Wardle and her colleagues studied white and Asian schoolgirls (aged fourteen to fifteen) and female college students (aged nineteen to twenty-two) in London. The first question was whether racial differences were associated with differential concern about weight. A higher percentage of white than of Asian females at each of the

FIGURE 5.18

Female Concern about Weight: Young Asians versus Young Whites. Young women enrolled in various schools in London were asked about their desire to lose weight and about their active attempts to do so. A higher percentage of white females than of Asians wanted to lose weight and were trying to lose weight. These and other findings suggest the role of cultural factors in specific gender differences in body image and appearance anxiety, but the mechanisms are far from clear.

(*Source:* Based on data from Wardle et al., 1993.)

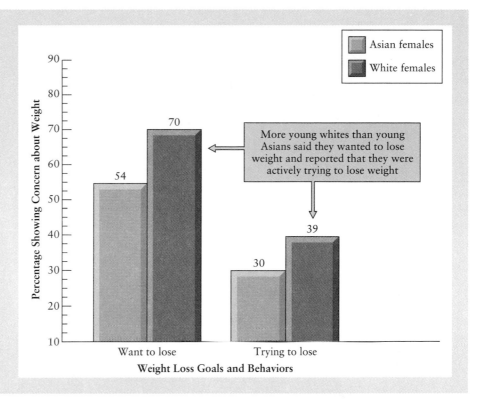

two age levels wanted to lose weight and were actively trying to do so. The summary data are shown in Figure 5.18. Also, among those with access to scales, Asians reported weighing themselves significantly less often than whites. Clearly, female concern with weight seems to be different for whites and Asians.

Unexpectedly, however, the difference was not based on racial differences in concepts of ideal body weight. Both groups agreed that it was best to be thin and that men prefer a woman who is slim.

Alternatively, it seemed possible that differences in actual body characteristics accounted for the findings. The investigators noted that, compared to the white research participants, the Asians were shorter and lighter, and had a smaller body mass. When these differences are taken into account statistically, however, whites still reported feeling larger than Asians, even when their size was the same. Among those who were the thinnest, more white than Asian females said they felt "fat."

Altogether, then, cultural differences in female concern about weight were confirmed, but the underlying reason is still not known. One hypothesis is that white men reject overweight women to a greater extent than is true among Asian men. Further research will be required to explain what it is about these two cultures that creates the difference. ■ ■ ■

CONNECTIONS: Integrating Social Psychology

In this chapter you read about . . .	*In other chapters, you will find related discussions of . . .*
self-schemas	schemas and information processing (Chapter 3); attitudes as schemas (Chapter 4); and stereotypes as schemas (Chapter 6)
self-esteem	effects of self-esteem in persuasion (Chapter 4); self-esteem after receiving help (Chapter 10)

(continued)

self-monitoring	effects of self-monitoring in persuasion (Chapter 4)
self-efficacy	effects of self-efficacy on health (Chapter 14)
gender stereotypes	prejudice and stereotypes (Chapter 6)

Thinking about Connections

1. In this chapter we discuss attitudes about self (self-esteem) as one aspect of self-schemas. In Chapter 4, we presented a more general discussion of attitudes as schemas. Consider some widely known situation, such as the O. J. Simpson trial, and try to determine whether your attitudes about race, spouse abuse, gender, or whatever else influenced the way you processed information about the trial as it progressed. Did such schemas influence who you liked and believed among the attorneys on each side and among the witnesses? Do you think you were best at remembering information and events that fit your schemas?

2. Can you think of any situations in which your feelings of self-esteem influenced what you did, or situations in which your self-esteem was affected by what happened? You might consider incidents in which someone tried to persuade you—or vice versa (Chapter 4); in which you met someone for the first time (Chapter 7); in which you were in a relationship that ended (Chapter 8); in which

someone asked you to do something (Chapter 9) or to help them (Chapter 10); or in work situations (Chapter 13) or when you became ill (Chapter 14).

3. We each have different degrees of self-efficacy in different situations. Think about yourself with respect to various tasks or goals and whether you felt confident and sure of your ability or felt a lack of confidence and unsureness. Why the difference? What did you do in these situations? When you lacked self-efficacy, was there any possible way to change your self-perception?

4. What do you believe are the most common stereotypes about men and women? Do you (or some of your friends) hold these stereotypes? Do you think they are accurate or inaccurate? Do you know people who don't fit gender stereotypes? If so, what do you think of them? Either in your own experience or for someone you know, do you believe that gender stereotypes have had any effect (good or bad) on your behavior?

Summary and Review

Social identity refers to the way we conceptualize ourselves. Two of the major components of social identity are self and gender.

The Self: Components of One's Identity

Each person's self-identity, or *self-concept,* is acquired through interaction with others. The self operates as a schema that determines how we process information about the world around us and about ourselves. The *self-reference effect* means that we process information about ourselves better than any other kind of information. The self-concept is not a fixed entity. We are aware of other *possible selves* that we could become; self-concept changes with age and in response to situational changes. The evaluation of oneself is known as *self-esteem.* In general, high self-esteem is preferable to low self-esteem, and self-esteem can

increase in response to positive experiences and to therapy.

Additional Aspects of Self-Functioning

Self-focusing refers to directing one's attention toward self as opposed to the external world. Self-focusing (on positive versus negative memories), mood, external events, and expectancies about future success and failure are interconnected. *Self-monitoring* behavior refers to whether a person's behavior is guided by external or internal factors. High and low self-monitors respond differently in many situations, and those who are extremely high or extremely low in self-monitoring tend to be less well adjusted than those whose self-monitoring is intermediate. *Self-efficacy* refers to a person's evaluation of his or her ability to perform a task, reach a goal, or overcome an obstacle. High self-efficacy enhances many kinds of performance, from athletics to academics.

Gender: Maleness or Femaleness As a Crucial Aspect of Identity

Sex refers to anatomical and physiological differences based on genetic determinants, and *gender* refers to all of the attributes associated with being a male or a female, whether determined by biology or by culture. In the developmental process, we acquire *gender identity* when we learn to label ourselves as female or male and include this as part of our self-concept. Gender characteristics can involve stereotypic masculine or feminine qualities, some combination of the two (*androgyny*), or neither. The gender role that we adopt affects what we do and the way that other people respond to us. Gender stereotypes tend to be supported by many aspects of the culture, but these currently seem to be weakening in our culture. A central question in the study of gender differences is whether such differences are based on physiology, learning, or a combination of factors.

Social Diversity: Cultural Differences in Concern about Weight

For reasons that are not clear, Western societies are characterized by female concerns about appearance in general and body weight in particular more than other societies. A comparison of young Asian and Caucasian females indicates differential concern about weight, but this concern is not based on different images of ideal weight. More white than Asian females feel fat, desire to lose weight, and actively try to lose weight, though both groups agree that a thin body is ideal.

■ Key Terms

Androgyny (p. 179)

Bem Sex-Role Inventory (BSRI) (p. 180)

Gender (p. 175)

Gender Consistency (p. 176)

Gender Identity (p. 176)

Gender-Stereotype Identification (p. 180)

Possible Selves (p. 156)

Self-Concept (p. 152)

Self Efficacy (p. 172)

Self-Esteem (p. 160)

Self-Focusing (p. 167)

Self-Monitoring (p. 168)

Self-Reference Effect (p. 154)

Sex (p. 175)

Sex Typing (p. 177)

Sexual Self-Schema (p. 156)

Social Identity (p. 152)

■ For More Information

Baumeister, R. F. (Ed.). (1993). *Self-esteem: The puzzle of low self-regard.* New York: Plenum.

This collection of chapters by active investigators provides a comprehensive view of the last two decades of research and theory on self-esteem. Among the many topics covered are the origins of low self-esteem, fluctuations in self-esteem, and how esteem is defended in response to threat.

Bordo, S. (1993). *Unbearable weight: Feminism, Western culture, and the body.* Berkeley, CA: University of California Press.

The author, a philosopher, describes how women are regularly provided images of an ideal feminine body that is young, slim, and muscular. She traces the different responses to male and female bodies to ancient Greece, where the virtues of the mind were attributed to men and the vices of the body were attributed to women. Much of the book centers on eating disorders, such as anorexia, which are assumed to represent the attempt of some women to achieve the ideal body image that has been provided for them.

Hattie, J. (1992). *Self-concept.* Hillsdale, NJ: Erlbaum.

This book concentrates on presenting a model of the self-concept based on empirical research. The author deals with the development of self-concept and discusses intervention programs such as therapy that attempt to enhance the self-concept.

Oskamp, S., & Costanzo, M. (Eds.). (1993). *Gender issues in social psychology.* Newbury Park, CA: Sage.

Research and theory on gender and gender differences are discussed by leading psychologists. Included are such topics as a feminist perspective on research methodology, gender-role development in childhood and adolescence, masculine ideology, gender differences in marital conflict, gender stereotypes, and job issues ranging from salary discrepancies to sexual harassment.

CHAPTER 6

PREJUDICE AND DISCRIMINATION: Understanding Their Nature, Countering Their Effects

Lisa Houck, *No Two Alike*, 1996, watercolor, 6 × 9"

Chapter Outline

People who know me well (Bob Baron) say that I'm usually in a hurry. Where getting my career started was concerned, that was definitely the case. I worked hard to complete my Ph.D. by June so I could get right to work teaching that summer. My first job was at a large Southern university; and like all new professors, I wanted very badly to succeed. I was pleased, therefore, when most of the ratings and comments I received from my students were favorable. Mixed in among these, though, were a few that literally sent me reeling. The words varied, but all said something to this effect: *"What makes you think you're better than we are? We're proud of our heritage, too."* I was truly floored; what had I said or done to give a few of my students the impression that I was prejudiced against them—that I held negative views about their Southern culture? I racked my brain, but at first I couldn't figure it out: I wasn't aware of any negative views or feelings about the South. Gradually though, a glimmer of light began to emerge. Social psychologists often have assistants who help them with their research by pretending to be one of the participants; and often, social psychologists refer to these people as . . . *confederates!* That was it! The word *confederate* had a special meaning for some students in my classes, and I had totally missed this connection. So, unaware of what I was doing, I had spouted this word repeatedly while describing various studies. Some of my students must have perceived my use of a word with sensitive connotations for them as careless at best, or—even worse—as a deliberate effort to be condescending. No wonder they were annoyed at me. Right then and there, I made a vow never to refer to experimental assistants as *confederates* again, either in class or in anything I wrote. (You won't see that word in *this* book!) This change did the trick: I never received another one of those angry comments from my students.

Why do we start with this incident? Mainly, to call a key fact to your attention: *At some time or other in our lives, virtually every one of us comes face to face with prejudice.* It may not be the malignant form that leads to dangerous riots, crimes of violence, or horrible atrocities such as Nazi death camps and "ethnic cleansing," but meet it we do. And even when prejudice takes relatively subtle or mild forms, its effects can be very damaging both to the victims of prejudice and to the persons who hold it. To mention just one example, recent findings indicate that many persons harbor prejudice toward overweight individuals. For example, overweight persons receive lower ratings in job interviews than persons of normal weight (Pingitore et al., 1994). And nurses report feeling less empathy toward overweight patients, and greater reluctance to care for them (Maroney & Golub, 1992; Figure 6.1, p. 195). Certainly, no one would equate these mild aversions toward overweight persons with the strong racial or ethnic bigotry that has caused so much suffering throughout human history. Yet even these mild forms of prejudice can have important consequences for the persons toward whom they are directed.

Social psychologists have long recognized the pervasive impact of prejudice on human behavior and human societies. Thus, they have used the impressive tools of their field to study this topic for several decades. In this chapter, we'll review the major findings of their research efforts. We'll start by examining the nature of *prejudice* and *discrimination,* two words that are often used as synonyms but which in fact refer to very different concepts. Second, we'll consider the causes of prejudice and discrimination—why they occur and what makes them so intense and persistent. Third, we'll explore various strategies for reducing prejudice and discrimination. Finally, because it has been the subject of an especially large amount of research and because it influences the lives of more than half of all human beings, we will focus on the nature and effects of *sexism*—prejudice based on gender.

FIGURE 6.1

Prejudice: Even Subtle Forms Can Be Harmful. Recent findings indicate that many nurses hold mild prejudice toward overweight persons: they are more reluctant to care for them than for persons of normal weight.

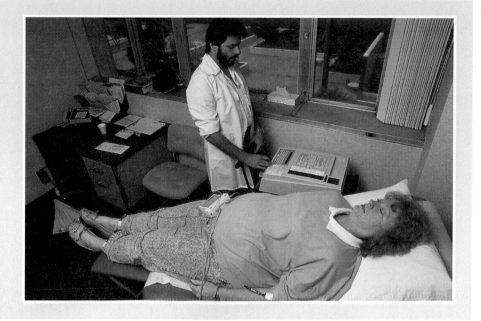

Prejudice and Discrimination: What They Are, How They Differ

In everyday speech, the terms *prejudice* and *discrimination* are used interchangeably. Are they really the same? Most social psychologists draw a clear distinction between them. *Prejudice* refers to a special type of *attitude*—generally, a negative one—toward the members of some social group. In contrast, *discrimination* refers to negative *actions* toward those individuals—attitudes translated into actions, if you will. This is an important distinction, so let's consider it more closely.

Prejudice: Choosing Whom to Hate

We'll begin with a more precise definition: **Prejudice** is *an attitude (usually negative) toward the members of some group, based solely on their membership in that group.* In other words, a person who is prejudiced toward some social group tends to evaluate its members in a specific manner (usually negatively) merely because they belong to that group. Their individual traits or behaviors play little role; they are disliked (or, in a few cases, liked), simply because they belong to a specific social group. When prejudice is defined as a special type of attitude, two important implications follow. First, as we saw in Chapters 3 and 4, attitudes often function as *schemas*—cognitive frameworks for organizing, interpreting, and recalling information (e.g., Fiske & Taylor, 1991). Thus, individuals who are prejudiced toward particular groups tend to process information about these groups differently from the way they process information about other groups. For example, information that is consistent with their prejudiced views often receives more attention, is rehearsed more frequently, and as a result tends to be remembered more accurately than information that is not consistent with these views (e.g., Fiske & Neuberg, 1990; Judd, Ryan, & Parke, 1991). To the extent this happens, prejudice becomes a kind of closed

Prejudice ■ Negative attitudes toward the members of specific social groups.

cognitive loop and, in the absence of events or experiences that shatter this self-confirming effect, can only grow stronger over time.

Second, if prejudice is a special kind of attitude, then it may involve more than negative evaluations of the groups toward whom it is directed: it may also include negative feelings or emotions on the part of prejudiced persons when they are in the presence of, or merely think about, members of the groups they dislike (Bodenhausen, Kramer, & Susser, 1994). Prejudice may also involve beliefs and expectations about members of these groups—specifically, *stereotypes* suggesting that all members of these groups demonstrate certain characteristics and behave in certain ways. As we'll soon discuss, stereotypes—which can be defined, most generally, as people's beliefs about the members of some social group (e.g., Jussim et al., 1995)—play a central role in many aspects of prejudice. Finally, prejudice may involve tendencies to act in negative ways toward those who are the object of prejudice.

One additional—and central—point: When most people think about prejudice, they tend to focus on its emotional or evaluative aspects. They emphasize the strong negative feelings and irrational hatreds that so often characterize racial, religious, or ethnic prejudice. Such reactions are important; and as we'll see in a later section, there are important links between the affective (feeling) and cognitive components of prejudice, just as there are important links between affect and cognition generally (see our discussion of this topic in Chapter 3). Yet it is crucial to note that prejudice is also related to, and involves, certain aspects of *social cognition*—the ways in which we notice, store, recall, and later use information about others in various ways, for example, in making judgments about them. Because we have only limited capacity to perform these tasks, we often adopt various cognitive shortcuts in our efforts to make sense out of the social world (Gilbert & Hixon, 1991). We are especially likely to do this at times when our capacity for handling social information is pushed to the limits; it is at such times that we are most likely to fall back upon *stereotypes* as mental shortcuts for understanding others or making judgments about them (e.g., Macrae, Hewstone, & Griffiths, 1993). As Gilbert and Hixon (1991) put it, stereotypes are tools that "jump out" of our cognitive toolbox when we realize that we are being exposed to more information than we can readily handle.

We'll return to a detailed examination of stereotypes and their role in prejudice in a later section. Here, however, we want to note that there is a large and growing amount of evidence pointing to the conclusion that the tendency to stereotype others, and to think about them in terms of stereotypes, does indeed stem—at least in part—from the fact that this strategy saves us cognitive effort. Strong support for this view is provided by research conducted recently by Macrae, Milne, and Bodenhausen (1994).

In the first of a series of carefully executed studies, the researchers asked participants to perform simultaneously two unrelated tasks: (1) an impression formation task, in which participants were to form impressions of fictitious persons whose names were paired on a computer screen with adjectives describing their supposed traits, and (2) an unrelated listening task, in which they heard a tape describing the geography and economy of Indonesia. After these tasks were completed, participants were asked to remember as many of the traits of each person shown as possible, and also to answer a series of questions about the information on the tape about Indonesia. Macrae, Milne, and Bodenhausen reasoned as follows: If stereotypes serve as mental shortcuts, freeing up cognitive resources for other tasks, then persons in whom stereotypes were activated during the impression formation task would do better on both tasks. This would be so because the stereotypes, once activated, would free resources for use in both simultaneous tasks. But how could stereotypes be activated? Macrae and his colleagues accomplished this by showing not only the strangers' names but

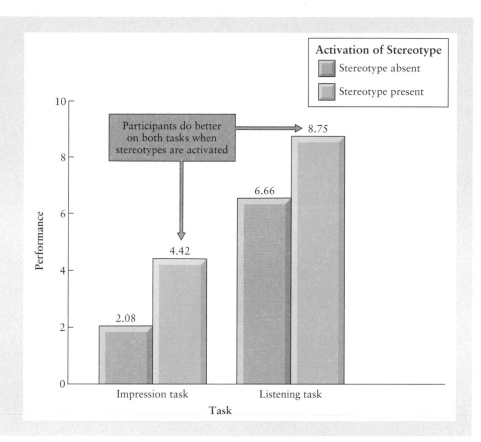

FIGURE 6.2

Stereotypes As a Means of Saving Cognitive Effort. As shown here, the activation of stereotypes increased performance on two different tasks performed simultaneously. These findings suggest that stereotypes do indeed save precious cognitive resources. This is one reason why they are so prevalent—and so resistant to change.

(*Source:* Based on data from Macrae, Milne, & Bodenhausen, 1994.)

also labels about them (e.g., doctor, artist) to half of the participants; the remainder did not see these labels. If labels evoke stereotypes and stereotypes free up cognitive resources, then participants exposed to them should do better on both tasks than those not exposed to these labels. As you can see from Figure 6.2, this is precisely what happened.

In an ingenious follow-up study, Macrae, Milne, and Bodenhausen (1994) presented the labels so quickly that participants could not even recognize them or report their presence. Despite this fact, however, performance was still better in the group who were exposed to these stereotype-inducing labels than in the control condition. These findings suggest that stereotypes can serve as an "energy-saving tactic" where cognition is concerned, even when people are not aware of their presence Combined with the findings of related studies (e.g., Bodenhausen, 1993), the findings also suggest that one reason stereotypes are so pervasive, and so resistant to change, is that, in one sense, they "work": they do succeed in saving cognitive resources for the persons who use them. Of course, such stretching of cognitive resources comes at the cost of reduced accuracy—a kind of trade-off in life with which all of us are very familiar.

INTEGRATING PRINCIPLES

1. Prejudice can be viewed as a special type of attitude (see Chapter 4)— a negative attitude toward the members of specific social groups, based solely on their membership in these groups.

2. As an attitude, prejudice involves not only negative evaluations but beliefs about others which are often reflected in *stereotypes*. Stereotypes, in turn, influence the processing of social information in ways that make them self-confirming (see Chapter 3).

3. Stereotypes also serve as mental shortcuts, reducing the cognitive effort we must exert to understand others, form impressions of them (Chapter 2), or make judgments about them (see Chapter 3).

Discrimination: Prejudice in Action

Attitudes, we noted in Chapter 4, are not always reflected in overt actions, and prejudice is definitely no exception to this rule. In many cases, persons holding negative attitudes toward the members of various groups cannot express these views directly. Laws, social pressure, fear of retaliation—all serve to deter people from putting their prejudiced views into open practice. In addition, many persons who hold prejudiced views do feel that overt discrimination is wrong, and perceive such actions on their own part as a violation of personal standards. When such individuals observe that they *have* shown discrimination, they experience considerable discomfort, in the form of guilt and related feelings (Devine & Monteith, 1993). This, in turn, may reduce their tendency to behave in similar ways again. Unfortunately, people don't always notice such inconsistencies between how they behave and how they feel they *should* behave, but when they do, overt discrimination may indeed be reduced (Monteith, 1996).

For several reasons, blatant forms of **discrimination**—negative actions toward the objects of racial, ethnic, or religious prejudices—have decreased in recent years in the United States and many other countries (e.g., Swim et al., 1995). Such actions as restricting members of various groups to certain seats on buses or in movie theaters, or barring them from public restaurants, schools, or neighborhoods—all common practices in the past (see Figure 6.3)—have now largely vanished in many countries. Of course, they have not disappeared completely: anyone who watches the evening news well knows that open expressions of prejudice, and violent confrontations stemming from them, still occur throughout the world with disturbing frequency. For the most part, though, the expression of prejudice in social behavior has become increasingly subtle in recent decades. What are these *subtle* or *disguised* forms of discrimination like? Research by social psychologists points to several interesting conclusions.

The New Racism: More Subtle, but Just As Deadly.   At one time, many people felt no qualms about expressing openly racist beliefs. They would state that they were against school desegregation, that they viewed members of minority groups as inferior in various ways, and that they would consider moving away if persons belonging to these groups took up residence in their neighborhoods (Sears, 1988). Now, of course, very few persons would openly state such views. Does this mean that racism, a particularly virulent form of discrimination, has disappeared? While many social psychologists would argue that this is the case (e.g., Martin & Parker, 1995), others would contend that in fact, all that has happened is that "old-fashioned" racism (read "blatant" for "old-fashioned") has been replaced by more subtle forms, which these researchers term *modern racism*. What is such racism like? Swim and her colleagues (Swim et al., 1995) have recently gathered data indicating that this new variety of racism focuses on three major components: (1) denial that there is continuing discrimination against minorities

Discrimination ■ Negative behaviors directed toward people who are the object of prejudice.

FIGURE 6.3

FIGURE 6.3

Discrimination in the Past. In the past, members of various minority groups (especially African Americans) were barred from many public places in the United States. Fortunately, such open forms of discrimination have now totally vanished.

(e.g., "Discrimination against African Americans is no longer a problem in the United States"); (2) antagonism to the demands of minorities for equal treatment (e.g., "African Americans are getting too demanding in their push for equal rights"); and (3) resentment about special favors for minority groups (e.g., "Over the past few years, the government and news media have shown more respect to African Americans than they deserve"). As you can readily see, such views are certainly different from those involved in "old-fashioned" racism, but they can still be very damaging to the victims. For example, as noted by Swim et al. (1995), modern racism may influence the likelihood of voting for a minority candidate to an even stronger extent than "old-fashioned" racism. So—and we want to emphasize this point strongly—despite the fact that blatant forms of racism have all but vanished from public life in the United States and many other countries, this especially repulsive and damaging form of prejudice is still very much alive and represents a serious problem in many societies.

Tokenism: Small Benefits, High Costs. Imagine that you are hired for a job you really want and at a higher starting salary than you expected. At first, you are happy about your good fortune. Now assume that one day you learn that you got the job mainly because you belong to a specific group—one whose members the company must hire in order to avoid charges of discrimination. How will you react? And how will other members of your company, who know that you were hired for this reason, perceive you? With respect to the first of these questions, research indicates that many persons find this kind of situation quite disturbing. They are upset to realize that they have been hired or promoted solely because of their ethnic background, gender, or some other aspect of their personal identity (e.g., Chacko, 1982). Further, they may object to being hired as a token member of their gender or of their racial, ethnic, or religious group.

Turning to the second question raised above, growing evidence indicates that persons who are hired as token representatives of their groups are perceived quite negatively by fellow employees (Summers, 1991). For example, Heilman, Block, and Lucas (1992) found that job applicants who were identified as "affirmative action hirees" were perceived as less competent by persons who reviewed their applications than applicants who were *not* identified in this manner.

Hiring persons as token members of their groups is just one form of **tokenism;** it occurs in other contexts as well. In its most general form, tokenism involves performing trivial positive actions for the targets of prejudice and then using these as an excuse or justification for later forms of discrimination. "Don't bother me," persons who have engaged in tokenism seem to say; "I've done enough for those people already!" (Dutton & Lake, 1973; Rosenfield et al., 1982). Wherever it occurs, tokenism seems to have at least two negative effects. First, it lets prejudiced people off the hook; they can point to tokenistic actions as public proof that they aren't really bigoted. Second, it can be damaging to the self-esteem and confidence of the targets of prejudice, including those few persons who are selected as tokens or who receive minimal aid. Clearly, then, tokenism is one subtle form of discrimination worth preventing.

Reverse Discrimination: Giving with One Hand, Taking with the Other. A second type of subtle discrimination occurs in situations in which persons holding at least some degree of prejudice toward the members of a social group lean over backward to treat members of that group favorably—more favorably than they treat other persons. At first glance, such **reverse discrimination** might appear to be beneficial for persons it affects (Chidester, 1986). On one level, this is certainly true: people exposed to reverse discrimination do receive raises, promotions, and other benefits. On another level, however, such favorable treatment may prove harmful, especially over the long run. For example, consider what may happen if well-intentioned teachers lean over backwards to assign inflated grades or ratings to minority children (Fajardo, 1985). To the extent they do so, they run the risk of setting these youngsters up for severe disappointment later. After all, at some point, a clash between falsely raised expectations and reality may be inevitable.

Another possibility is that teachers may assign higher-than-deserved ratings to minority children because by doing so, they minimize their contact with these youngsters. Students who receive good grades don't need special help, so when teachers assign inflated evaluations to minority students' work, they also avoid having to work closely with them. In this and other ways, reverse discrimination can be as harmful as the more obvious forms of discrimination it sometimes replaces.

While the effects of reverse discrimination on the persons who are its targets can sometimes be harmful, there have recently been strong objections to such practices on quite another basis: the suggestion that reverse discrimination harms other groups, who suffer because of the special help given to minorities. In the United States, increasingly strong objections to reverse discrimination—for example, to admission of members of minority groups to schools even if their credentials are weaker than those of majority group applicants—have been voiced by white males (see Figure 6.4). Some persons in this category feel that now they are the victims of discrimination: *they* are rejected from schools and jobs even though they may be better qualified than the minority persons accepted for these positions. Clearly, this is a complex issue, and one that will be resolved only slowly and painfully in many different countries.

Subtle Forms of Discrimination: A Note of Optimism. In sum, while overt discrimination has indeed decreased in many societies, it seems possible that it has been replaced to some degree by other, somewhat more subtle forms. Having said this, however, we want to close this discussion on an optimistic note. While subtle forms of discrimination are both real and damaging, it is our personal conviction that several forms of prejudice, and the discrimination stemming from them, have in fact decreased in recent decades in the United States and

Tokenism ■ Instances in which individuals or groups perform trivial positive actions for people toward whom they feel prejudice, then use these actions as an excuse for refusing more meaningful beneficial behavior.

Reverse Discrimination ■ Tendency to evaluate or treat persons belonging to certain groups (especially ones that are the object of ethnic or racial prejudice) more favorably than members of other groups.

FIGURE 6.4

Reverse Discrimination: A Growing Backlash. In recent years, white males in the United States have raised increasing objections to *reverse discrimination,* noting that they are often the victims of such practices.

elsewhere. Several forms of evidence point to this conclusion, but for us the most convincing is this: When asked to indicate the extent to which differences between social groups (e.g., between different racial groups or between males and females) stem from various sources, young persons report views that are both sophisticated and relatively free from obvious prejudice (Martin & Parker, 1995). For example, they view racial differences as stemming primarily from social factors such as childhood experiences and contrasting opportunities—not from inherited biological factors. Similarly, they express a fairly high degree of optimism with respect to eliminating such group differences, regardless of their origins. Together, these views seem to suggest that something important has indeed happened in recent decades where prejudice is concerned. No, these negative attitudes have not vanished; indeed, as we noted above, racism is still present to an alarming degree in many societies and continues to harm the groups toward whom it is directed (e.g., African Americans in the United States). But we do feel that existing evidence indicates that several subtle forms of prejudice are neither as intense nor as prevalent as they were in the past. We're not pie-in-the-sky optimists, and we realize that there's still a long way to go; but maybe, just maybe, the incidence of persons like the one shown in Figure 6.5 (p. 202) *has* begun to decrease.

FIGURE 6.5

Prejudice: On the Wane? While many forms of prejudice are still present throughout the world, some evidence indicates that extreme forms, such as that shown here, have decreased in many countries. (*Source: The New Yorker*, 1977.)

FIGURE 6.5

Prejudice: On the Wane? While many forms of prejudice are still present throughout the world, some evidence indicates that extreme forms, such as that shown here, have decreased in many countries.
(*Source: The New Yorker*, 1977.)

The Origins of Prejudice: Contrasting Perspectives

Why does prejudice exist? Why, even today, do so many people hold negative views about the members of specific social groups—attitudes that sometimes lead to tragic results? Many different answers to these questions have been offered. Here, we will consider several perspectives on prejudice that have proved influential.

Direct Intergroup Conflict: Competition As a Source of Prejudice

It is sad but true that the things people want and value most—good jobs, nice homes, high status—are always in short supply. This fact serves as the foundation for what is perhaps the oldest explanation of prejudice—**realistic conflict theory** (e.g., Bobo, 1983). According to this view, prejudice stems from competition among social groups over valued commodities or opportunities. In short, prejudice develops out of the struggle over jobs, adequate housing, good schools, and other desirable outcomes. The theory further suggests that as such competition continues, the members of the groups involved come to view each other in increasingly negative terms (White, 1977). They label each other as "enemies," view their own group as morally superior, and draw the boundaries between themselves and their opponents more and more firmly. The result is that what starts out as simple competition relatively free from hatred gradually develops into full scale, emotion-laden prejudice.

   Evidence from several different studies confirms the occurrence of this process. As competition persists, individuals come to perceive each other in increasingly negative ways. Even worse, such competition often leads to direct, and sometimes violent, conflict. A very dramatic demonstration of this princi-

Realistic Conflict Theory ▪
The view that prejudice sometimes stems from direct competition between various social groups over scarce and valued resources.

ple in operation is provided by a well-known field study conducted by Sherif and his colleagues (Sherif et al., 1961).

For this unusual study, the researchers sent eleven-year-old boys to a special summer camp in a remote area where, free from external influences, the nature of conflict and its role in prejudice could be carefully studied. When the boys arrived at the camp (named *The Robber's Cave* in honor of a nearby cave that was once, supposedly, used by robbers), they were divided into two separate groups and assigned to cabins located quite far apart. For one week, the campers in each group lived and played together, engaging in such enjoyable activities as hiking, swimming, and other sports. During this initial phase, the boys quickly developed strong attachments to their own groups. They chose names for their teams (*Rattlers* and *Eagles*), stenciled them onto their shirts, and made up flags with their groups' symbols on them.

At this point the second phase of the study began. The boys in both groups were told that they would now engage in a series of competitions. The winning team would receive a trophy, and its members would earn prizes (pocket knives and medals). Since these were prizes the boys strongly desired, the stage was set for intense competition. Would such conflict generate prejudice? The answer was quick in coming. As the boys competed, the tension between the groups rose. At first it was limited to verbal taunts and name-calling, but soon it escalated into more direct acts—for example, the Eagles burned the Rattlers' flag. The next day the Rattlers struck back by attacking the rival group's cabin, overturning beds, tearing out mosquito netting, and seizing personal property. Such actions continued until the researchers intervened to prevent serious trouble. At the same time, the two groups voiced increasingly negative views of each other. They labeled their opponents "bums" and "cowards," while heaping praise on their own group at every turn. In short, after only two weeks of conflict, the groups showed all the key components of strong prejudice toward each other.

Fortunately, the story had a happy ending. In the study's final phase, Sherif and his colleagues attempted to reduce the negative reactions described above. Merely increasing the amount of contact between the groups failed to accomplish this goal; indeed, it seemed to fan the flames of anger. But when conditions were altered so that the groups found it necessary to work together to reach *superordinate goals*—ones they both desired—dramatic changes occurred. After the boys worked together to restore their water supply (previously sabotaged by the researchers), pooled their funds to rent a movie, and jointly repaired a broken-down truck, tensions between the groups largely vanished. In fact, after six days of such experiences the boundaries between the groups virtually dissolved, and many cross-group friendships were established.

There are, of course, major limitations to this research. The study took place over a relatively short period of time; the camp setting was a special one; all participants were boys; and perhaps most important, the boys were quite homogeneous in background—they did not belong to different racial, ethnic, or social groups. Despite these restrictions, however, the findings reported by Sherif and his colleagues are compelling. They offer a chilling picture of how what begins as rational competition over scarce resources can quickly escalate into full-scale conflict, which then in turn fosters the accompanying negative attitudes toward opponents that form the core of prejudice.

The research reported by Sherif and his colleagues is viewed as a classic in the study of prejudice. Yet it was not the first, nor the most dramatic, study of the relationship between conflict and prejudice conducted by social psychologists. That honor goes to a much earlier, and much more disturbing, investigation conducted by Hovland and Sears (1940)—a study described in detail in the *Cornerstones* section on the next page.

Cornerstones of Social Psychology

THE ECONOMICS OF RACIAL VIOLENCE: Do Bad Times Fan the Flames of Prejudice?

Carl I. Hovland and Robert R. Sears. Carl Hovland and Robert Sears conducted many important studies during the 1940s and 1950s. Their research on prejudice, based in part on the famous *frustration–aggression hypothesis*, had a major impact on subsequent research in this area. In addition, they made important contributions to the study of attitudes and persuasion.

In 1939 several psychologists published an influential book entitled *Frustration and Aggression* (Dollard et al., 1939). In this book, they suggested that aggression often stems from *frustration*—interference with goal-directed behavior. In other words, aggression often occurs in situations where people are blocked or prevented from getting what they want. As we'll see in Chapter 11, this hypothesis is correct, but only up to a point. Frustration *can* sometimes lead to aggression, but it is definitely not the only, or the most important, cause of such behavior.

In any case, the frustration–aggression hypothesis stimulated a great deal of research in psychology, and some of this work was concerned with prejudice. The basic reasoning was as follows: When groups are competing with each other for scarce resources, they come to view one another as potential or actual sources of frustration. After all, if "they" get the jobs, the housing, and other benefits, then "we" don't. The result, it was reasoned, is not simply negative attitudes toward opposing groups; in addition, strong tendencies to aggress against them may also be generated.

Although this possible link between conflict, prejudice, and aggression was studied in several different ways, the most chilling findings were reported by Carl Hovland and Robert Sears (1940)—two psychologists who made important contributions to social psychology in several different areas (including the study of attitudes and persuasion; see Chapter 4). These researchers hypothesized that economic conditions provide a measure of frustration, with bad times being high in frustration for many people and good times somewhat lower. They reasoned that if this is so, then racially motivated acts of violence such as lynchings should be higher when economic conditions are poor than when they are good. To test this unsettling hypothesis, Hovland and Sears obtained data on the number of lynchings in the United States in each year between 1882 and 1930. Most of these lynchings (a total of 4,761) occurred in fourteen Southern states, and most (but not all) of the victims were African Americans. Next, Hovland and Sears (1940) related the number of lynchings in each year to two economic indexes: the farm value of cotton (the total value of cotton produced that year) and the per-acre value of cotton. Since cotton played a major role in the economies of the states where most lynchings occurred, Hovland and Sears assumed that these measures would provide a good overview of economic conditions in those states. As you can see from Figure 6.6, results were both clear and dramatic: the number of lynchings rose when economic conditions declined, and fell when economic conditions improved. Hovland and Sears (1940, p. 307) interpreted these findings as reflecting *displaced aggression*: since farmers could not aggress against the economic factors that were causing their frustration (e.g., a lack of rainfall), they aggressed against African Americans—a group they disliked and who were, at that time, relatively defenseless. Today, most social psychologists prefer a somewhat different interpretation—one suggesting that competition for scarce economic resources increases when times are bad, and that this increased competition intensifies racial prejudice. Lynchings and other violence then result from this increased prejudice rather than from displaced aggression. Regardless of the precise mechanism involved, however, Hovland and Sears's study was important for several reasons.

First, it demonstrated an important link between economic conditions and racial violence—a finding that has been confirmed with more sophisticated

FIGURE 6.6

Racial Violence and Economic Conditions. As shown here, the number of lynchings in the United States—primarily of African Americans and mainly in Southern states—varied with economic conditions. Lynchings increased when times were bad, but decreased when economic conditions improved. These findings provide indirect support for the direct conflict model of prejudice.

(*Source:* Based on data from Hovland & Sears, 1940.)

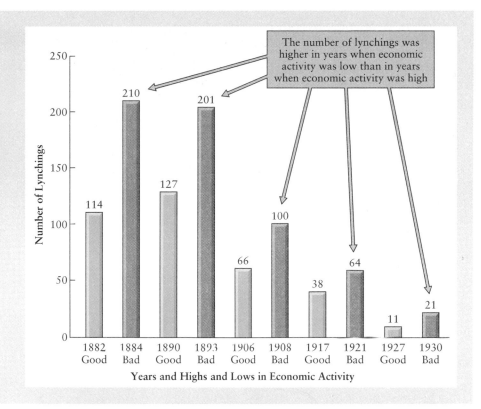

modern research methods (Hepworth & West, 1988). Clearly, this relationship is relevant to government programs designed to improve economic conditions for disadvantaged persons—many of whom are the victims of racial or ethnic prejudice. Second, this research provided a dramatic illustration of the value of applying psychological theory to important real-life events. Finally, it showed how important social problems can be investigated by means of *archival data*—existing records of social events. In these and other ways, Hovland and Sears's research paved the way for further and more sophisticated investigations of the roots of prejudice—research that has continued without interruption ever since. ▪ ▪ ▪

Early Experience: The Role of Social Learning

A second explanation for the origins of prejudice is straightforward: it suggests that prejudice is *learned* and that it develops in much the same manner, and through the same basic mechanisms, as other attitudes (refer to our discussion in Chapter 4). According to this **social learning view**, children acquire negative attitudes toward various social groups because they hear such views expressed by parents, friends, teachers, and others, and because they are directly rewarded (with love, praise, and approval) for adopting these views. In addition to direct observation of others, *social norms*—rules within a given group suggesting what actions or attitudes are appropriate—are also important (Pettigrew, 1969). As we will see in Chapter 9, most persons choose to conform to most social norms of groups to which they belong. The development and expression of prejudice toward others often stems from this tendency. "If the members of my group dislike them," many children seem to reason, "then I should too!"

The mass media also play a role in the development of prejudice. Until recently, members of various racial and ethnic minorities were shown infrequently

Social Learning View (of prejudice) ▪ The view that prejudice is acquired through direct and vicarious experience in much the same manner as other attitudes.

FIGURE 6.7

The Changing Image of African Americans on American Television. During the 1980s the presence of African Americans in many popular television programs increased substantially, although their representation in product commercials did not show a similar increase.

(*Source:* Based on data from Weigel, Kim, & Frost, 1995.)

in movies or on television. And when they did appear, they were often cast in low-status or comic roles. Given repeated exposure to such materials for years or even decades, it is not surprising that many children came to believe that the members of these groups must be inferior. After all, why else would they be shown in this manner?

Fortunately, this situation has changed greatly in recent years in the United States and elsewhere. Members of various racial and ethnic minorities now appear more frequently and are shown in a more favorable manner than was true in the past. Such changes are clearly documented by a recent study conducted by Weigel, Kim, and Frost (1995). These researchers systematically examined prime-time television programming and prime-time product commercials appearing during 1989 in order to determine whether African Americans were shown more frequently, and in different ways, than was true in 1978, when another major survey of this kind was conducted (Weigel, Loomis, & Soja, 1980). Results indicated that in terms of appearance in actual programs, there had indeed been significant change. As shown in Figure 6.7, African Americans appeared more frequently in regular programming in 1989 than was true in 1978, and the percentage of cross-racial interaction time in these shows also increased significantly. (Surprisingly, there were *not* similar changes in product commercials, perhaps because these commercials are aimed primarily at the majority group.) The programming picture was not entirely rosy, however. While the frequency with which African Americans was shown did increase, further analyses indicated that cross-racial interactions in these television programs showed a lower level of intimacy and were rated as less intense and multifaceted than within-race interactions. So, while there was considerable change during the period studied, there were still differences in the treatment of whites and African Americans in television programs even in 1989. Of course, it seems possible that an analysis of current programming might indicate even more progress toward comparable presentation of all ethnic and racial groups in popular shows. Until such treatment is equal, the possibility remains that the mass media are contributing, to some degree, to the persistence of various forms of prejudice.

Social Categorization: The Us-versus-Them Effect and the "Ultimate" Attribution Error

A third perspective on the origins of prejudice begins with a basic fact: People generally divide the social world into two distinct categories—*us* and *them*. In short, they view other persons as belonging either to their own group (usually termed the **ingroup**) or to another group (the **outgroup**). Such distinctions are based on many dimensions, including race, religion, gender, age, ethnic background, occupation, and income, to name just a few.

If the process of dividing the social world into "us" and "them"—**social categorization**—stopped there, it would have little bearing on prejudice. Unfortunately, however, it does not. Sharply contrasting feelings and beliefs are usually attached to members of one's ingroup and members of various outgroups. Persons in the former ("us") category are viewed in favorable terms, while those in the latter ("them") category are perceived more negatively. Outgroup members are assumed to possess more undesirable traits, are perceived as being more alike (i.e., more homogeneous) than members of the ingroup, and are often disliked (Judd, Ryan, & Parke, 1991; Lambert, 1995; Linville & Fischer, 1993). The ingroup–outgroup distinction also affects *attribution*—the ways in which we explain the actions of persons belonging to these two categories. Specifically, we tend to attribute desirable behaviors by members of our ingroup to stable, internal causes (e.g., their admirable traits), but attribute desirable behaviors by members of outgroups to transitory factors or to external causes. For example, when students in Hong Kong were asked to explain why students from one university tend to receive better starting jobs than those from another university, those at the favored school attributed their success to better preparation. Those at the school whose graduates received less desirable jobs, however, attributed this outcome to better personal connections on the part of the students at the other school (Hewstone, Bond, & Wan, 1983). This tendency to make more favorable and flattering attributions about members of one's own group than about members of other groups is sometimes described as the **ultimate attribution error,** since it carries the self-serving bias we described in Chapter 2 into the area of intergroup relations—with potentially devastating effects.

That strong tendencies exist to divide the social world into "us" and "them" has been demonstrated in many studies (e.g., Stephan, 1985; Tajfel, 1982). But how, precisely, does this tendency translate into prejudice? Why do we view others in biased and negative ways once we define them as being different from ourselves? An intriguing answer has been provided by Tajfel and his colleagues (e.g., Tajfel, 1982). These researchers suggest that individuals seek to enhance their self-esteem by identifying with specific social groups. This tactic can succeed, however, only to the extent that the persons involved perceive these groups as somehow superior to other, competing groups. Since all individuals are subject to the same tendencies, the final result is inevitable: each group seeks

Ingroup ■ The social group to which an individual perceives herself or himself as belonging ("us").

Outgroup ■ Any group other than the one to which individuals perceive themselves belonging.

Social Categorization ■ The tendency to divide the social world into two separate categories: our ingroup ("us") and various outgroups ("them").

Ultimate Attribution Error ■ The tendency to make more favorable and flattering attributions about members of one's own group than about members of other groups.

to view itself as somehow better than its rivals, and prejudice rises out of this clash of social perceptions.

Support for the accuracy of these suggestions has been obtained in several experiments (e.g., Meindl & Lerner, 1985). Thus, it appears that our tendency to divide the social world into two opposing camps often plays a role in the development of important forms of prejudice.

Cognitive Sources of Prejudice: The Role of Stereotypes

Next, we come to sources of prejudice that are, in some ways, the most unsettling of all. These involve the possibility that prejudice stems, at least in part, from basic aspects of *social cognition*—the ways in which we think about other persons, integrate information about them, and then use this information to make social judgments or decisions. Because this has clearly been the focus of most recent research on prejudice in social psychology, we'll divide our discussion of this topic into two parts. First we'll examine what appears to be the central cognitive component in prejudice—*stereotypes*. Then we'll examine other cognitive mechanisms that also play a role in the occurrence of prejudice.

Stereotypes: What They Are and How They Operate. Consider the following groups: Korean Americans, homosexuals, Jews, Cuban Americans, African Americans. Suppose you were asked to list the traits most characteristic of each. Would you find this to be a difficult task? Probably you would not. You would be able to construct a list for each group—and, moreover, you could probably do so *even for groups with whom you have had limited personal contact*. Why? The reason involves the existence and operation of **stereotypes**—cognitive frameworks consisting of knowledge and beliefs about specific social groups. As noted by Judd, Ryan, and Parke (1991) stereotypes involve generalizations about the typical or "modal" characteristics of members of various social groups. In other words, they suggest that all members of such groups possess certain traits, at least to a degree. Once a stereotype is activated, these traits come readily to mind; and it is this fact that explains the ease with which you can probably construct lists like the ones mentioned above. You may not have had much direct experience with Korean Americans, Cuban Americans, or Jews, for instance; but you do have stereotypes for them, so you can readily list their supposed traits.

Like other cognitive frameworks we have considered, stereotypes exert strong effects on how we process social information. For example, information relevant to an activated stereotype is processed more quickly than information unrelated to it (e.g., Dovidio, Evans, & Tyler, 1986). Similarly, stereotypes lead persons holding them to pay attention to specific types of information—usually, information consistent with the stereotypes. And when information *inconsistent* with stereotypes does manage to enter consciousness, it may be actively refuted or even simply denied (O'Sullivan & Durso, 1984). For example, recent evidence indicates that when individuals encounter persons who behave in ways contrary to stereotypes they hold, they often perceive these persons as a new "subtype," rather than changing their stereotype (Kunda & Oleson, 1995). In sum, stereotypes exert powerful effects on our thinking about others.

Given the potential errors that can occur as a result of stereotype-driven thinking, what accounts for the persistence of these cognitive frameworks? As we noted earlier, part of the answer lies in the fact that stereotypes operate as a labor-saving device where social cognition is concerned (Macrae et al., 1994). When activated, stereotypes allow us to make quick-and-dirty judgments about others without engaging in complex, and more effortful, thought. Of course,

Stereotypes ■ Beliefs to the effect that all members of specific social groups share certain traits or characteristics; stereotypes are cognitive frameworks that strongly influence the processing of incoming social information.

the conclusions we reach on the basis of stereotypes are often wrong; but the saving of cognitive effort is so great that we tend to rely on stereotypes in many different contexts.

As you can probably already see, stereotypes are closely related to prejudice. Once an individual has acquired a stereotype about some social group, she or he tends to notice information that fits readily into this cognitive framework and to remember "facts" that are consistent with it more readily than "facts" that are inconsistent. As a result, the stereotype becomes, to a large degree, self-confirming. Even exceptions to it make it stronger, for they simply induce the person in question to bring more supporting information to mind. Evidence for the role of stereotypes in social thought have been reported in many different studies (e.g., Bodenhausen, 1988; Fiske & Neuberg, 1990; Monteith, 1993). Moreover, additional findings indicate that stereotypes are activated quite readily in most social situations. Doing so requires cognitive resources (Gilbert & Hixon, 1991); but again, once they are activated, stereotypes seem to provide such handy mental shortcuts that they are an integral part of everyday social thought. We'll have more to say about the profound effects of stereotypes not only on social thought, but on personal health as well, in the Social Diversity section at the end of this chapter. Now, however, we'll turn to another intriguing question regarding stereotypes: the relationship of *affective states* (moods, positive and negative feelings) to stereotypes and their role in prejudice.

The Role of Affect in Stereotypic Thinking: The Interface between Feelings and Thought Revisited. Do you remember our discussion of the relationship between affect and cognition in Chapter 3? If so, you may recall our key conclusion: Feelings (for example, our current moods) often exert strong effects upon cognitive processes; and cognitive processes, in turn, often exert powerful effects upon our feelings. Here, we will return to this important issue as it relates to stereotypes and their role in prejudice.

Do Stereotypes Involve an Affective Component? Let's begin with a very basic question: Do stereotypes operate in a purely cognitive manner, or do they also involve an emotional component? We know that they strongly influence our thinking about others and our judgments of them, but do they exert such effects solely because they provide mental shortcuts—quick-and-dirty ways of perceiving the complex social world? Until quite recently, most social psychologists would have replied *yes*. Stereotypes were viewed primarily as cognitive mechanisms or structures, and most research attention was focused on just how they functioned and on their relationship to other aspects of social cognition, such as schemas, expectations, and *base rates*—our estimates of the frequency of occurrence of various traits or outcomes (e.g., Hamilton et al., 1990; Jussim, 1991).

Now, however, a growing number of social psychologists are investigating the possibility that stereotypes also contain an affective component or, at least, are influenced by affective states to an important extent (e.g., Bodenhausen, Kramer, & Susser, 1994; Jussim et al., 1995). Research in this area is very new, but convincing evidence for the role of affect in stereotypic thinking has already been reported. For example, consider a series of studies conducted by Jussim and his colleagues (1995).

These researchers conducted several studies in which participants received background information on various strangers, who were described to them either as child abusers or rock musicians. Then they read word definitions supposedly written by these persons. On the basis of these definitions, participants were then asked to rate the strangers on dimensions relating to creativity and degree of mental illness. In addition, they indicated their *feelings* about each of the two groups (child abusers, rock musicians), and their *beliefs* (cognitions) about them—for example, the ambitiousness, intelligence, and susceptibility to drug and alcohol abuse of persons belonging to these groups. Not surprisingly, the effects of stereotypes relating to child abusers and to rock musicians were obvious in participants' ratings of the strangers: they rated the rock musicians as significantly more creative and less mentally ill than the child abusers. But the key question was this: What would happen to these results if the effects of participants' feelings about these two groups or of their beliefs (cognitions) about them were held constant statistically? If stereotypes exert their effect entirely through cognition (beliefs), then holding feelings constant would not change the results; liking for these groups would have little impact on the extent to which stereotypes affected participants' ratings. On the other hand, if stereotypes exert their effect at least in part through feelings, then holding feelings constant would reduce the impact of stereotypes on the ratings. In fact, this latter pattern is precisely what the researchers found. Thus, it appeared that stereotypes were operating, if anything, more through feelings than through cognitions.

Similar results were obtained when homosexuals and heterosexuals were substituted for the original two groups; again, when feelings toward these groups were held constant, the impact of stereotypes about them vanished. In this case, however, beliefs were also found to play a role: when these were held constant statistically, the impact of stereotypes decreased, too, although not as consistently as was true for feelings.

Together, these findings seem to offer support for a model of the effects of stereotypes that emphasizes the role of feelings. However, given the large body of evidence indicating that stereotypes do involve beliefs, base rates, and other aspects of cognition, it seems likely that a model like the one shown in Figure 6.8 may turn out to be more accurate. As you can see, this model suggests that when stereotypes are activated by, for example, group names or labels (Native Americans, Mexicans, Catholics, engineers, senior citizens), they influence several aspects of cognition *and*, simultaneously, affective reactions. Together, these processes influence our evaluations or judgments of others, and our overt actions toward them. Of course, only time—and additional data—will tell whether such a model is accurate. It is consistent with existing evidence, however, and in this respect, it seems to be a reasonable first guess.

Stereotypes and Mood: One Potential Downside to Being in a Good Mood. Suppose that you are in an especially good mood when you encounter another person belonging to a widely stereotyped social group (e.g., an African American, a person of Hispanic descent). Do you think you will be more likely or *less* likely to engage in stereotypic thinking about this person than would be true at

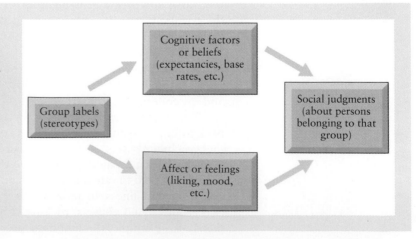

FIGURE 6.8

A Model of the Impact of Stereotypes on Social Evaluations. Recent evidence indicates that stereotypes may exert their impact on evaluations of others through both affective and cognitive factors.

(*Source:* Based on suggestions by Jussim et al., 1995.)

other times? Common sense, and some research findings, suggest that you will be less likely to engage in stereotypic thinking. After all, if you are feeling good, you may be less likely to attribute negative characteristics to this stranger; and as we saw in Chapter 3, you may tend to make judgments about this person that are consistent with your current mood (Forgas, 1994; Stroessner & Mackie, 1993). But there are other findings that point to the opposite possibility—findings suggesting that when we are in a good mood, we are especially unwilling to engage in hard cognitive work. It's almost as though we don't want to do anything that will disrupt our pleasant feelings, and we know from past experience that thinking hard and deep will do just that (Mackie & Worth, 1989; Schwarz, Bless, & Bohner, 1991). In fact, research carried out recently by several investigators (e.g., Forgas & Fiedler, 1996), indicates that this is actually what tends to happen when a good mood runs head-on into the temptation to think stereotypically. For example, consider a study by Bodenhausen, Kramer, and Susser (1994) that indicates that this is actually what tends to happen when a good mood runs head-on into the temptation to think stereotypically.

To investigate the relationship between mood and stereotypes, Bodenhausen and his colleagues (1994) conducted a series of studies in which participants read one of two cases involving disciplinary hearings for students. One incident involved an alleged assault; the other, a case of alleged cheating. Before reading one of these cases, some participants were asked to remember and think about an event that made them especially happy; the others were asked to remember and describe ordinary, routine events of the previous day. In order to activate stereotypes, participants who read about the case of assault learned either that the defendant was of Hispanic descent (he was named Juan Garcia) or that he did not have a strong ethnic identity (he was named John Garner). For the cheating case, the target either was described as a "well-known athlete on campus" or was not described in any special terms. Presumably, these treatments would activate stereotypes of Hispanic persons and athletes in participants exposed to them. Finally, participants rated the guilt of the defendant in the case they read. As you can see from Figure 6.9 (p. 212), results offered strong support for the view that being in a happy mood *increases* the tendency to think stereotypically. Among participants placed in a happy mood by memories of happy events, those whose stereotypes were activated assigned much higher guilt ratings to the defendant than those whose stereotypes had not been activated. In contrast, among participants in a neutral mood, there was little effect of stereotype activation.

In a follow-up study Bodenhausen, Kramer, and Susser (1994) obtained evidence indicating that the reason for the greater stereotypic thinking among happy persons was not that they were incapable of cognitive effort; rather, they simply had lower motivation to engage in hard cognitive work than those in a neutral mood. The researchers showed this by telling participants in a happy mood that they would be held accountable for their judgments—in other words, that it was important to do a good job in evaluating the defendant's guilt. Under these conditions, persons in a happy mood were not more likely to fall back on stereotypes than those in a neutral mood. So, consistent with other findings, it appears that being in a happy mood does not necessarily reduce our *capacity* for rational thought; rather, it merely reduces our *motivation* to do this hard cognitive work (Smith & Shaffer, 1991).

Other Cognitive Mechanisms in Prejudice: Illusory Correlations and Outgroup Homogeneity

Consider the following set of information: (1) There are one thousand members of Group A but only one hundred members of Group B; (2) one hundred members of Group A were arrested by the police last year, and ten members of

FIGURE 6.9

Effects of Mood on the Tendency to Think Stereotypically. Activation of a negative stereotype greatly increased guilt ratings assigned to a defendant by persons in a good mood. However, activation of a negative stereotype did not increase such ratings by persons in a neutral mood. These findings suggest that persons in a good mood may be more likely to think stereotypically than ones in a neutral mood.

(*Source:* Based on data from Bodenhausen et al., 1994.)

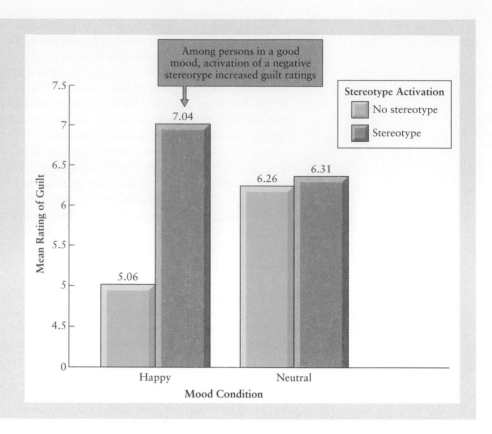

Group B were arrested. Suppose you were asked to evaluate the criminal tendencies of these two groups. Would your ratings of them differ? Your first answer is probably "Of course not—why should they? The rate of criminal behavior is 10 percent in both groups, so why rate them differently?" Surprisingly, though, a large body of evidence suggests that you might actually assign a less favorable rating to Group B (Hamilton & Gifford, 1976; Hamilton & Sherman, 1989; Mullen & Johnson, 1990). Social psychologists refer to this tendency to overestimate the rate of negative behaviors in relatively small groups as **illusory correlation.** This term makes a great deal of sense, because such effects involve perceiving links between variables that aren't really there—in this case, links between being a member of a Group B and the tendency to engage in criminal behavior.

As you can readily see, illusory correlations, to the extent they occur, have important implications for prejudice. In particular, they help explain why negative behaviors and tendencies are often attributed by majority group members to the members of various minority groups. For example, some social psychologists have suggested that illusory correlation effects help explain why many white persons in the United States overestimate crime rates among African American males (Hamilton & Sherman, 1989). For many complex reasons, young African American men are, in fact, arrested for various crimes at higher rates than young white men or men of Asian descent (U.S. Department of Justice, 1994). But white Americans tend to *overestimate* the size of this difference, and this can be interpreted as an instance of illusory correlation. Why do such effects occur? One explanation is based on the *distinctiveness* of infrequent events or stimuli. According to this view, infrequent events are distinctive—readily noticed. As such, they are encoded more extensively than other items when they are encountered, and so become more accessible in memory. When we make judgments

Illusory Correlation ■ Perception of a stronger association between two variables than actually exists; occurs because each variable is distinctive and their apparent correlation is readily entered into and retrieved from memory.

about the groups involved at later times, therefore, the distinctive events come readily to mind, and this leads us to overinterpret their importance.

Consider how this explanation applies to the tendency of white Americans to overestimate crime rates among African Americans. African Americans are a minority group (they make up about 12 percent of the total population); thus, they are high in distinctiveness. Many criminal behaviors, too, are highly distinctive (relatively rare), despite the fact that their incidence has increased greatly in recent decades. When news reports show African Americans being arrested for such crimes, therefore, this information is processed extensively and becomes highly accessible in memory. Thus, it is readily available at later times and may lead to the tendency to overestimate crime rates among minority groups—an instance of illusory correlation

A large number of studies offer support for this *distinctiveness-based interpretation* of illusory correlation (Hamilton & Sherman, 1989; Stroessner, Hamilton, & Mackie, 1992). However, recent findings indicate that this theory should be modified in at least one important respect. Apparently, it is not crucial that information be distinctive when it is first encountered; rather, information can *become* distinctive at later times and produce illusory correlations when this occurs (McConnell, Sherman, & Hamilton, 1994). It seems that we review and reconsider social information again and again in the light of new information. As a result of this process, information that was not highly distinctive when it was first encountered may become distinctive at a later time. And if it is, it may then exert unduly strong effects on judgments relating to it; in other words, it may serve as a source of illusory correlation. In practical terms, this means that even if individuals don't extensively encode negative information about minority group members when they first receive it, they may go back and do so in the light of new, and perhaps even more attention-getting, news coverage of violent crimes. Then such information may produce an illusory correlation: the tendency to overestimate the rate of such behaviors among minority groups. In this respect, it is interesting to speculate about the consequences of the massive news coverage of the O. J. Simpson trial. Did this coverage serve to make negative information about African Americans more distinctive in the minds of other Americans? Only systematic research can provide an answer, but even the question itself is quite unsettling.

Ingroup Differentiation, Outgroup Homogeneity: "They're All the Same"—or Are They? Persons who hold strong prejudice toward some social group often make remarks like these: "You know what *they're* like; they're all the same," or "If you've met one, you've met them all." What such comments imply is that the members of an outgroup are much more similar to one another (are more homogeneous) than the members of one's own group. This tendency to perceive persons belonging to groups other than one's own as all alike is known as the **illusion of outgroup homogeneity** (Linville et al., 1989). The mirror image of this tendency is known as **ingroup differentiation**—the tendency to perceive members of our own group as showing much larger differences from one another (as being more heterogeneous) than those of other groups.

Existence of the illusion of outgroup homogeneity has been demonstrated in many different contexts. For example, individuals tend to perceive persons older or younger than themselves as more similar to one another in terms of personal traits than persons in their own age group—an intriguing type of "generation gap" (Linville, Fischer, & Salovey, 1989). Perhaps the most disturbing example of the illusion of outgroup homogeneity, however, appears in the context of *cross-racial facial identification*—the tendency for persons belonging to one racial group to be more accurate in recognizing differences among the faces

Illusion of Outgroup Homogeneity ■ The tendency to perceive members of outgroups as more similar to one another (more homogeneous) than members of one's own ingroup.

Ingroup Differentiation ■ The tendency to perceive members of our own group as much more different from one another (more heterogeneous) than members of other groups.

of strangers in their own group than in another racial group (e.g., Bothwell, Brigham, & Malpass, 1989). In the United States, this tendency has been observed among both African Americans and whites, although it appears to be somewhat stronger among whites (Anthony, Cooper, & Mullen, 1992).

What accounts for the tendency to perceive members of other groups to be more homogeneous than members of our own group? One explanation involves the fact that we have a great deal of experience with members of our own group, and so are exposed to a wider range of individual variation within that group. In contrast, we generally have much less experience with members of other groups, and hence less exposure to *their* individual variations (e.g., Linville et al., 1989). As noted recently by Lee and Ottati (1993), however, several other factors may play a role as well.

First, it is possible that some groups are actually more homogeneous than others. For example, as Lee and Ottati (1993) note, Americans are less homogeneous than Chinese in terms of several physical characteristics (e.g., hair color, eye color). Thus, if an American perceives greater heterogeneity among Americans than among Chinese, this perception may be related to reality, at least to a degree. Second, it is possible that perceptions of outgroup homogeneity may be related to more basic tendencies to evaluate other groups in an evaluatively consistent manner. Americans, for example, tend to value individuality. Thus, to the extent they dislike another group, they would tend to perceive its members as homogeneous: this would be consistent with their overall negative evaluation of the group. If, instead, they *liked* another group, they might tend to perceive its members as relatively heterogeneous; in this case, perceiving heterogeneity (individuality) in the group would be consistent with positive feelings toward it.

In fact, research conducted by Lee and Ottati (1993) provides evidence for both of these suggestions. They asked both Americans and citizens of mainland China to rate the extent to which people in their own culture and the other culture were heterogeneous, to indicate the amount of contact they had with people from the other culture, and to report their evaluations of the other culture. Perhaps the most interesting finding was that both Americans *and* Chinese did perceive greater heterogeneity among Americans (see Figure 6.10). Moreover, the greater the contact Chinese participants reported having with Americans, the stronger their tendency to rate Americans as heterogeneous. Among Americans, in contrast, increasing contact with Chinese did not lead to increased ratings of heterogeneity. These findings, of course, suggest that the illusion of outgroup homogeneity is not always an illusion, and that sometimes it stems from factors other than limited contact with such persons.

Finally, confirming the tendency to evaluate outgroups in a consistent manner, it was found that among Americans, the more they reported positive evaluations of Chinese people, the greater the degree of heterogeneity they perceived for these people. Since Chinese culture does not value individuality or heterogeneity as strongly, it was not surprising that similar results were not obtained for the Chinese participants: their liking for Americans was not significantly related to the amount of heterogeneity they perceived among Americans.

Together, these findings suggest that in some instances the tendency to perceive other groups as more homogeneous than our own may stem from sources other than prejudice—factors such as actual differences along this dimension and our tendency to evaluate outgroups in a consistent manner. However, it is equally clear that on many other occasions the illusion of outgroup homogeneity *is* an illusion: we tend to perceive members of outgroups as more homogeneous than they really are. This perception saves us a great deal of cognitive effort, but once we conclude that "they're all alike," there is little reason to seek

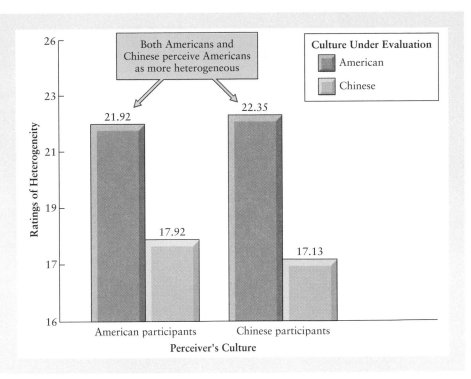

FIGURE 6.10

Potential Sources of the Illusion of Outgroup Homogeneity. Both Chinese and Americans perceived greater heterogeneity among Americans. These findings indicate that sometimes the tendency to perceive greater homogeneity among groups other than one's own may have a basis in social reality.

(*Source:* Based on data from Lee & Ottati, 1993.)

contact with members of various outgroups. This, in turn, lessens the probability that we will ever learn that they really *do* differ. For this reason alone, the illusion of outgroup homogeneity is another cognitive source of prejudice we should make every effort to avoid.

INTEGRATING PRINCIPLES

1. Prejudice seems to derive, in part, from basic aspects of social thought. Once they are established, *stereotypes* strongly affect important aspects of social thought (Chapter 3). Stereotypes involve beliefs about various social groups, but are also influenced by affective states and reactions (Chapters 3, 4). Thus, the effects reflect the complex interaction between affect and cognition discussed at several points in this book (e.g., Chapter 3).

2. Illusory correlations—the tendency to overestimate the rate of negative behaviors in small groups—seem to stem primarily from the fact that both minority group members and negative behaviors are high in distinctiveness and so are more accessible in memory (Chapters 2, 3).

3. We tend to perceive greater heterogeneity among members of our own group than among members of various outgroups. These effects reflect the fact that we have less experience with members of other groups than with members of our own group, but may also reflect actual differences in heterogeneity across groups. Several aspects of group functioning are examined in Chapter 12.

Striking Back against Prejudice: Techniques That Can Help

Given that prejudice is common in all human societies and exerts damaging effects both on its victims and on those who hold such views, the next question is obvious: What steps can be taken to reduce the impact of prejudice? In this section, we'll summarize the major findings of social psychological research with respect to this issue.

Breaking the Cycle of Prejudice: On Learning *Not* to Hate

Few persons would argue that children are born with prejudices firmly in place. Rather, most would contend that bigots are *made,* not born. Social psychologists share this perspective: they believe that children acquire prejudice from their parents, other adults, their peers, and—as we noted earlier—the mass media. Given this fact, one useful technique for reducing prejudice follows logically: somehow, we must discourage parents and other adults who serve as models for children from providing training in bigotry.

Having stated this principle, we must now admit that putting it into practice is far from simple. How can we induce parents who are prejudiced to encourage unbiased views among their children (see Figure 6.11 on page 218)? One possibility involves calling parents' attention to their own prejudiced views. Few persons are willing to describe themselves as prejudiced; instead, they view their own negative attitudes toward various groups as entirely justified. A key initial step, therefore, is somehow convincing parents that the problem exists. Once they come face to face with their own prejudices, many people do seem willing to modify their words and behavior so as to encourage lower levels of prejudice among their children. True, some extreme fanatics actually *want* to turn their children into hate-filled copies of themselves. Most people, however, recognize that we live in a world of increasing diversity and that this environment calls for a higher degree of tolerance than ever before.

Another argument that can be used to shift parents in the direction of teaching their children tolerance rather than prejudice lies in the fact that prejudice harms not only those who are its victims, but those who hold such views as well (Dovidio & Gaertner, 1993; Jussim, 1991). Persons who are prejudiced, it appears, live in a world filled with needless fears, anxieties, and anger. They fear attack from presumably dangerous social groups; they worry about health risks stemming from contact with such groups; and they experience anger and emotional turmoil over what they view as unjustified incursions by these groups into *their* neighborhoods, schools, or offices. In other words, their enjoyment of everyday activities and life itself is reduced by their own prejudice. Of course, offsetting such costs is the boost in self-esteem prejudiced persons sometimes feel when they derogate or scapegoat outgroup members (Branscombe & Wann, 1994; Grau, 1985). Overall, though, it is clear that persons holding intense racial and ethnic prejudices suffer many harmful effects from these intolerant views. Since most parents want to do everything in their power to further their children's well-being, calling these costs to parents' attention may help discourage them from transmitting prejudiced views to their offspring.

Direct Intergroup Contact: The Potential Benefits of Acquaintance

At the present time many American cities resemble a doughnut in one respect: a disintegrating and crime-ridden core inhabited primarily by minority groups is surrounded by a ring of relatively affluent suburbs inhabited mainly by whites and minority group members who have made it economically. Needless to say, contact between the people living in these different regions is minimal.

This state of affairs raises an intriguing question: Can communities reduce prejudice by somehow increasing the degree of contact between different groups? This idea is known as the **contact hypothesis,** and there are several good reasons for predicting that such a strategy might prove effective (Pettigrew, 1981). First, increased contact between persons from different groups can lead to a growing recognition of similarities between them. As we will see in Chapter 7, perceived similarity can enhance mutual attraction. Second, while stereotypes are resistant to change, they *can* be altered when sufficient information inconsistent with them is encountered, or when individuals meet a sufficient number of "exceptions" to their stereotypes (Kunda & Oleson, 1995). Third, increased contact may help counter the illusion of outgroup homogeneity described earlier. For these reasons, it seems possible that direct intergroup contact may be one effective means of combating prejudice. Is it? Existing evidence suggests that it is, but only when the following conditions are met:

> *The groups interacting must be roughly equal in social, economic, or task-related status.*
>
> *The contact situation must involve cooperation and interdependence so that the groups work toward shared goals (as in the Robber's Cave experiment described earlier).*
>
> *Contact between the groups must be informal so that they can get to know one another as individuals.*
>
> *Contact must occur in a setting in which existing norms favor group equality.*
>
> *The groups must interact in ways that permit disconfirmation of negative stereotyped beliefs about one another.*
>
> *The persons involved must view one another as typical of their respective groups.*

When contact between initially hostile groups occurs under these conditions—which are, unfortunately, quite rare—prejudice between them does seem to decrease (Cook, 1985; Riordan, 1978). Such effects have been observed in the United States, where increased contact between African Americans and whites has been found to reduce prejudice between them (Aronson, Bridgeman, & Geffner, 1978), and in many others nations as well. For example, increased school contact between Jews of Middle Eastern origin and Jews of European or American origin tends to reduce intergroup bias among Israeli soldiers (Schwarzwald, Amir, & Crain, 1992).

In sum, when used with care, direct intergroup contact *can* be an effective tool for combating cross-group prejudice. When people get to know one another, it seems, many of the anxieties, stereotypes, and false perceptions that have previously kept them apart can melt in the face of new information and the warmth of new friendships.

Recategorization: Redrawing the Boundary between "Us" and "Them"

Think back to your high school days. Imagine that your school's basketball team was playing an important game against a rival high school from a nearby town or neighborhood. In this case, you would certainly view your own school as "us" and the other school as "them." But now imagine that the other school's team won, and went on to play against a team from another state or province in a national tournament. Now how would you view them? The chances are good that under these conditions, you would view the other school's team as

Contact Hypothesis ■ Theory that increased contact between members of various social groups can be effective in reducing prejudice between them; seems to be valid only when contact takes place under specific favorable conditions.

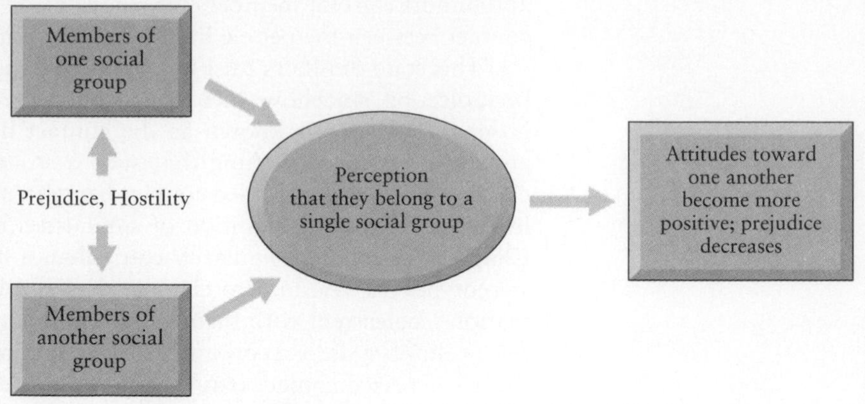

FIGURE 6.11

The Common Ingroup Identity Model. The common ingroup identity model suggests that when individuals belonging to different groups come to perceive themselves as members of a single group, their attitudes toward each other become more positive. This increases contact between members of the groups, which reduces intergroup bias still further.

(*Source:* Based on suggestions by Gaertner, Dovidio, et al., 1990, 1993.)

Recategorizations ■ Shifts in the boundary between an individual's ingroup ("us") and various outgroups ("them"), causing persons formerly viewed as outgroup members now to be seen as belonging to the ingroup.

Common Ingroup Identity Model ■ Theory suggesting that to the extent individuals in different groups view themselves as members of a single social entity, positive contacts between them will increase and intergroup bias will be reduced.

"us"; after all, it represents your area. And of course, if a team from a state or province other than your own was playing against teams from other countries, you might now view it as "us" relative to those foreigners.

Situations like this, in which we shift the boundary between "us" and "them," are quite common in everyday life, and they raise an interesting question: Can such shifts—or **recategorizations,** as they are termed by social psychologists—be used to reduce prejudice? A theory proposed by Gaertner, Dovidio, and their colleagues (1989, 1993) suggests that it can. This theory, known as the **common ingroup identity model,** suggests that when individuals belonging to different social groups come to view themselves as members of a *single social entity,* their attitudes toward each other—toward former outgroup members—become more positive. These favorable attitudes then promote increased positive contacts between members of the previously separate groups, and this in turn reduces intergroup bias still further. In short, weakening or eliminating initial us–them boundaries starts a process that carries the persons involved toward major reductions in prejudice and hostility (see Figure 6.11).

How can this process be launched? In other words, how can we induce people belonging to different groups to perceive each other as members of a single group? Gaertner and his colleagues (1990) suggest that one crucial factor in this process is the experience of working together cooperatively. When individuals belonging to initially distinct groups work together toward shared goals, they come to perceive themselves as a single social entity. Then feelings of bias or hostility toward the former outgroup—toward "them"—seem to fade away, taking prejudice with them. Such effects have been demonstrated in several laboratory studies (e.g., Brewer et al., 1987; Gaertner et al., 1989, 1990). In addition, they have been observed in a field study carried out by Gaertner, Dovidio, and their associates (1993).

This investigation was conducted in a multicultural high school in the United States. Students in the school came from many different backgrounds— African American, Chinese, Hispanic, Japanese, Korean, Vietnamese, and Caucasian. More than 1,300 students completed a survey designed to measure their perceptions of factors that had been shown in previous research to influence the effects of increased intergroup contact (e.g., equal status, cooperative interdependence, norms supportive of friendly intergroup contact). Other items on the survey measured students' perceptions of the extent to which the student body at the school was a single group, consisted of distinct groups, or was composed of separate individuals. Finally, students also completed items designed to measure their feelings toward both their ingroup and various outgroups.

Results offered strong support for the common ingroup identity model. First, as predicted, perceptions of cooperative interdependence between students from different groups were positively related to the students' belief that the student body was a single group. In other words, the more students reported experiencing cooperative interactions with persons from other groups, the weaker the us-versus-them boundaries they reported. Similarly, the greater the extent to which the students felt as though they belonged to a single group, the more positive their feelings toward outgroup members.

When combined with the results of laboratory studies, these findings suggest that efforts to induce persons belonging to different groups to engage in *recategorization*—to shift the boundary between "us" and "them" so as to include persons previously excluded—can be an important step toward the reduction of many forms of prejudice. We should hasten to add, however, that broadening the "us" category to include groups that were previously excluded does *not* eliminate the human tendency to enhance our own self-identity by cognitively boosting our own group while belittling others (Tajfel, 1982). This seems to be a basic tendency that cannot be entirely eliminated. However, recategorization can certainly reduce prejudice in some contexts, and any reduction in such blanket negative reactions is a definite plus in ongoing social life.

Cognitive Interventions: When Stereotypes Shatter— Or At Least Become Less Compelling

Throughout this chapter, we have noted that stereotypes play an important role in prejudice. The tendency to think about others in terms of their membership in various groups or categories (known as *category-driven processing*) appears to be a key factor in the occurrence and persistence of several forms of prejudice. If this is so, then interventions designed to reduce the impact of stereotypes may prove highly effective in reducing prejudice and discrimination. How can this goal be attained? Several techniques seem to be effective.

First, the impact of stereotypes can be reduced if individuals are encouraged to think carefully about others—to pay attention to their unique characteristics rather than to their membership in various groups. Research findings indicate that such *attribute-driven processing* can be encouraged even by such simple procedures as informing individuals that their own outcomes or rewards in a situation will be affected by another's performance, or telling them that it is very important to be accurate in forming an impression of another person. Under these conditions, individuals are motivated to be accurate, and this reduces their tendency to rely on stereotypes (Neuberg, 1989).

Second, and more surprising, the impact of stereotypes can sometimes be reduced by techniques based on principle of attribution (see Chapter 2; Mackie et al., 1992). How do such procedures work? Several are based on the fact that often, we make inferences about others on the basis of their outcomes, while ignoring factors that might have produced these outcomes (Allison, Worth, & King, 1990). For example, suppose that you learn that a stranger scored 70 on a certain exam and that 65 was passing. Thus, the outcome is "Passed." In contrast, suppose that you learn that 75 was passing and the person scored 70; here the outcome is "Failed." If you were asked to rate this person's intelligence or motivation, the chances are good that you would assign higher ratings in the first instance than in the second, despite the fact the stranger's performance is identical in both cases. This illustrates our strong tendency to base inferences about others on their outcomes.

Now let's apply this to prejudice, and to the task of countering stereotypes. Suppose that you learned that a woman was promoted to a high-level managerial job in a large company. The outcome is clear: she was promoted. Would this outcome influence your estimations of her talent or motivation? Again, the chances are good that it would—and crucially, that this would be the case *even if you learned that her company has a strong affirmative action program and actively seeks to promote women and minorities.* In cases such as this, our tendency to base our inferences about others on their outcomes can lead us to conclusions that are *counterstereotypic* in nature; and the result may be a weakening of the stereotypes involved. Effects of this type have been reported in several different studies (e.g., Mackie et al., 1992), and they suggest a complex, but effective, means of weakening various stereotypes.

This technique, of course, has important implications for efforts to counter the effects of prejudice through *affirmative action programs.* These programs are designed to improve the outcomes of various disadvantaged groups by increasing the chances that they will obtain such benefits as jobs and promotions. To the extent that such outcomes improve, perceptions of the characteristics of these groups, too, may improve although, as we noted earlier, this is not always the case. In other words, our tendency to base inferences about others on the outcomes they receive may lead us to perceive members of these groups as higher in talent, motivation, and intelligence than was the case before they received these good outcomes. Truly, this is a case of "fighting fire with fire"—using a basic tilt in our attributions to reduce the impact of harmful social stereotypes.

For information about another cognitive technique for countering prejudice, please see the *Applied Side* section below.

Social Psychology: On the Applied Side

THE PARADOXICAL EFFECTS OF STEREOTYPE SUPPRESSION: When Thoughts We Don't Want Come Back to Haunt Us

In many social situations, people actively attempt to suppress stereotypic thinking. The reason for doing so is obvious; we don't want to run the risk of offending members of various social groups by saying or doing things suggesting that we hold negative stereotypes of them, and we know quite well that our overt actions often reflect what we think. At first glance, this would seem to be a useful technique for countering the effects of stereotypes; after all, what we don't think can't hurt us, right? The answer, it appears, is "Wrong!" Recent findings indicate that while efforts to suppress stereotypes and drive them from consciousness may work temporarily, this suppression may be followed by a strong *rebound* effect, in which stereotypes come back to haunt us—and shape our thinking—with a vengeance. Clear evidence for such effects has been reported by Macrae, Bodenhausen, and their colleagues (Macrae et al., 1994).

Extending previous work by Wegner and his colleagues (Wegner, 1992; Wegner & Erber, 1992), these researchers reasoned that when individuals attempt to suppress stereotypic thinking, two processes are initiated: an intentional process that drives stereotypic thoughts from consciousness, and an automatic process that monitors thoughts for any appearance of the unwanted stereotypes. The result of this second process is paradoxial, in that it actually serves to activate or prime the unwanted thoughts over and over again (although, of course, at a very low intensity). The result? When the intentional

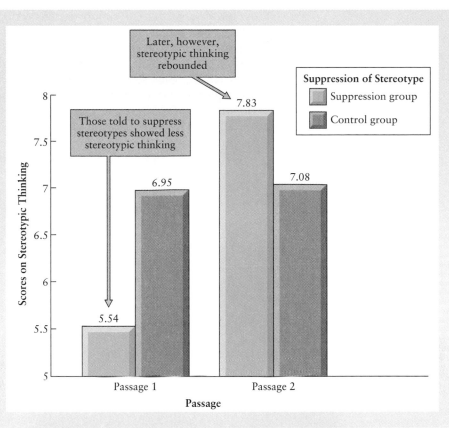

FIGURE 6.12

Stereotype Suppression and the Rebound Effect. Individuals told to suppress stereotypes showed less stereotypic thinking while actively suppressing such thoughts. Later, however, they actually showed more stereotypic thinking than persons not previously told to suppress stereotypes. In other words, stereotyped thinking showed a *rebound* effect following suppression.

(*Source:* Based on data from Macrae et al., 1994.)

process is stopped, stereotypic thoughts flood back into consciousness; in other words, they rebound strongly.

To test this reasoning, Macrae and his colleagues (1994) exposed participants to a color photo of a skinhead, then asked them to write a passage describing a typical day in the life of this person. Before writing the passage, half of the participants were warned to avoid thinking about this person in terms of the stereotype for skinheads, while the others were not given this warning. Then participants saw another photo of a different skinhead, and were asked to perform the same task; this time, none of the participants were warned to avoid thinking stereotypically. The passages written by participants were then scored for the presence of stereotypic thinking.

Macrae and his colleagues (1994) reasoned that on the first passage, participants told to suppress stereotypes would show less stereotypic thinking than those not told to suppress such thoughts. As you can see from Figure 6.12, this is what they found. For the second passage, however, they predicted that stereotypes would *rebound* among participants previously told to suppress them; thus, these persons would actually show as much or even more stereotypic thinking as persons not previously told to suppress such thoughts. Again, as shown in Figure 6.12, results offered support for this prediction.

In a follow-up study, Macrae and his colleagues (1994) measured the rebound effect in terms of actual behavior. After writing their passages about the skinhead, participants were brought to a second room where, supposedly, they would meet this person. He was not present, but his jacket and bookbag indicated that he was sitting in the first seat of a row of eight chairs. Participants could sit anywhere they wished, and the presence of stereotypic thinking was measured in terms of how close they chose to sit to the skinhead. As expected, those previously told to suppress stereotypic thoughts chose to sit farther away—evidence that their negative stereotypes had rebounded and were now affecting their behavior.

Together, the findings reported by Macrae, Bodenhausen, and their colleagues (1994), plus research on the effects of thought suppression generally (see Chapter 3), suggest that active efforts to suppress stereotypic thinking may sometimes backfire. True, they may prevent us from making social blunders when we encounter members of groups we stereotype. But suppressing stereotypes now may lead to their stronger recurrence later; and this, of course, can actually increase our overall risk of offending others. ■ ■ ■

INTEGRATING PRINCIPLES

1. Techniques for reducing prejudice have been derived from basic principles of social psychology. Efforts to reshape prejudiced attitudes through altered socialization practices and persuasion (Chapter 4) can sometimes be effective. Similarly, increased contact often enhances liking (Chapter 7) and can reduce prejudice if the contact occurs under appropriate conditions.

2. Breaking down the us–them boundary by inducing individuals to perceive themselves and others as belonging to a single group is also successful in reducing prejudice and intergroup conflict (Chapter 12).

3. Prejudice-reducing techniques based on cognitive mechanisms have also been developed. These include inducing individuals to think about others' personal attributes rather than their membership in specific groups (Chapter 3) and procedures based on principles of attribution (Chapter 2). Active suppression of stereotypic thinking, however, seems to produce only temporary beneficial effects (Chapter 3).

Prejudice Based on Gender: Its Nature and Effects

More than half of the world's population is female. Yet despite this fact, in many cultures females have been treated like a minority group. They have been excluded from economic and political power; they have been the subject of strong negative stereotypes; and they have faced overt discrimination in many areas of life—work settings, higher education, government (Fisher, 1992; Heilman, Block, & Lucas, 1992). In the late 1990s, this situation is changing, at least in some countries and to some degree. Overt discriminatory practices have been banned by laws in many nations, and there has been at least some weakening of negative gender-based stereotypes. Yet such progress has been spotty at best, and **sexism**—prejudice based on gender—continues to exert harmful effects upon females in many countries (e.g., Kanekar, Kolsawalla, & Nazareth, 1988). Because prejudice based on gender affects more individuals than any other single kind (more than half the human race) and produces negative outcomes for males as well as females, we will consider it here in detail.

Sexism ■ Prejudice based on gender.

FIGURE 6.13

The Exaggeration of Gender Differences. *Some gender differences do exist with respect to social behavior; but, as in this cartoon, gender stereotypes exaggerate the differences.*

(*Source:* Drawing by Handelsman; © 1995 *The New Yorker* Magazine, Inc.)

"*That was a fine report, Barbara. But since the sexes speak different languages, I probably didn't understand a word of it.*"

Gender Stereotypes: The Cognitive Core of Sexism

Females have often been the object of strong, persistent stereotypes. To an extent, so have males: they too are perceived as being "all alike" with respect to certain traits—and in many cultures, woe to the male who fails to live up to these stereotypes (Aube & Koestner, 1992). By and large, however, stereotypes about females are more negative in content than those about males. For example, in many cultures, males are assumed to possess such desirable traits as *decisiveness, forcefulness, confidence, ambition,* and *rationality.* In contrast, the corresponding assumptions about females include less desirable traits such as *passivity, submissiveness, indecisiveness, emotionality,* and *dependence* (Deaux, 1993; Unger, 1994).

Are such **gender stereotypes** accurate? Do men and women really differ in the ways these stereotypes suggest? This question is complex, for differences between the sexes, even if observed, may be more a reflection of the impact of stereotypes and their self-confirming nature than of basic differences between females and males. Existing evidence, however, points to these conclusions: (1) There are indeed some differences between females and males with respect to several aspects of social behavior—the ability to send and "read" nonverbal cues (DePaulo, 1992), aggression (Bettencourt & Miller, in press), and the nature of same-sex friendships (Elkins & Peterson, 1993), to name just a few; *but* (and this is an important *but*) (2) the magnitude and scope of these differences are far smaller than gender stereotypes suggest (see Figure 6.13; Feingold, 1992; Oliver & Hyde, 1993). Unfortunately, though, the fact that gender stereotypes are quite inaccurate does not prevent them from exerting harmful effects—for example, from preventing females from obtaining some jobs (Van Vianen & Willemsen, 1992), some promotions (Stroh, Brett, & Riley, 1992), and equal

Gender Stereotypes ■ Stereotypes concerning the traits supposedly possessed by females and males, which distinguish the two genders from each other.

pay for the jobs they do obtain (Lander, 1992). How do the stereotypes exert these negative effects? This is the question to which we turn next.

Discrimination against Females: Subtle but Often Deadly

In the late 1990s, overt discrimination on the basis of gender is illegal in many countries. As a result, businesses, schools, and social organizations no longer reject applicants for jobs or admission simply because they are female (or male). Despite this fact, females continue to occupy a relatively disadvantaged position in many societies in certain respects. They are concentrated in low-paying, low-status jobs (Fisher, 1992), and their average salary remains lower than that for males, even in the same occupations. Why is this the case? One possibility is that sufficient time has not passed for women to realize the full benefits of the changes that occurred during the 1970s and 1980s. Another possibility—one supported by a large body of research evidence—is that while overt barriers to female advancement have largely disappeared, other, more subtle forces continue to operate against women in many contexts. We'll now review several of these.

The Role of Expectations. One factor impeding the progress of females involves their own expectations. In general, women seem to hold lower expectations about their careers than men. They expect to receive lower starting and peak salaries (Jackson, Gardner, & Sullivan, 1992; Major & Konar, 1984). And they view lower salaries for females as being somehow fair (Jackson & Grabski, 1988). Why do females hold these lower expectations? Research findings (e.g., Jackson, Gardner, & Sullivan, 1992) indicate that several factors play a role.

First, females expect to take more time out from work (for example, to spend with their children); this tends to lower their expectations for peak career salaries. Second, women place somewhat less importance on job outcomes generally, including salary, than men do. To the extent this is the case, they may find lower pay relatively acceptable. Third, women realize that females do generally earn less than males. Thus, their lower expectations may simply reflect their recognition of current reality and its likely impact on their own salaries. Fourth, as we noted earlier, women tend to perceive relatively low levels of pay as more fair than males do (Jackson et al., 1992). Finally, and perhaps most important, women tend to compare themselves with other women, and since women earn less than men in many instances, this leads them to conclude that they aren't doing too badly after all (Major, 1995). Whatever the specific basis for women's lower salary expectations, it is a fact of life that, in general, people tend to get what they expect or what they request. Thus, females' lower expectations with respect to such outcomes may be one important factor operating against them in many organizations.

The Role of Self-Confidence. Confidence, it is often said, is the single best predictor of success. People who expect to succeed often do; those who expect to fail find *that* prediction confirmed. Unfortunately, women tend to express lower self-confidence than men in many achievement-related situations. This may be one reason why almost 10 percent of the executives who responded to a survey in *Business Week* reported believing that females are not as aggressive or determined to succeed as males (Lander, 1992). In short, women are less self-confident than men in at least some situations, and people notice these differences. This, in turn, may contribute to the fact that women have not yet attained full equality with men in many work settings.

Negative Reactions to Female Leaders. In the late 1990s, most people agree that females can definitely be effective leaders. Women have been elected to major offices (prime minister, senator); have been appointed as senior judges (e.g., to the Supreme Court of the United States); hold high ranks in the military, and—in a few cases—head major companies and organizations. But how do people react to female leaders? Do they hold them in equally high regard and evaluate them as favorably as men? The answer to both questions appears to be no. First, although subordinates often *say* much the same things to female and male leaders, research findings indicate that they actually demonstrate more negative *nonverbal behaviors* toward female leaders (Butler & Geis, 1990). Moreover, such differences occur even when individuals strongly deny any bias against females. Apparently, many persons still find women in leadership roles to be somewhat disturbing, perhaps because leadership on the part of women runs counter to prevailing gender stereotypes.

Perhaps even more disturbing, however, is the fact that when they serve as leaders, females tend to receive lower evaluations from subordinates than males do. In a meta-analysis of existing evidence on this issue, Eagly, Makhijani, and Klonsky (1992) found that overall, female leaders received slightly lower evaluations than male leaders. Since earlier findings had indicated that females received much lower evaluations than males (e.g., Butler & Geis, 1990), this finding, on the face of it, was somewhat encouraging: it suggested that perhaps bias against female leaders was decreasing. However, the same researchers also found that the tendency to down-rate female leaders was considerably stronger when the female leaders adopted a style of leadership viewed as stereotypically masculine (autocratic, directive), when the persons who evaluated them were males, and when the females occupied leadership roles in fields where most leaders were males. Together, these findings and those of other studies (e.g., Kent & Moss, 1994) suggest that females continue to face subtle disadvantages even when they do manage to obtain positions of leadership and authority.

The Glass Ceiling: Why Women Don't Rise to the Top. Between 1970 and 1992, the proportion of managers who are female rose from 16 percent to more than 42 percent (U.S. Department of Labor, 1992). Yet the proportion of top executives who are women increased only from 3 percent to 5 percent (Fisher, 1992). These facts have led many authors to suggest the existence of a **glass ceiling**—a final barrier that prevents females, as a group, from reaching the top positions in many companies (see Figure 6.14 on page 226). More formally, the U.S. Department of Labor has defined the glass ceiling as "those artificial barriers based on attitudinal or organizational bias that prevent qualified individuals from advancing upward in their organization" (U.S. Department of Labor, 1992).

Is this barrier real? And if so, why does it exist? Research evidence on these issues is just beginning to accumulate, so we can't offer any definitive answers here. However, recent studies seem to point to these conclusions: Yes, there is a glass ceiling in terms of the share of top jobs that go to females—this number is much lower than would be predicted on the basis of the proportion of females in the workplace. But no, the glass ceiling does not appear to result from a conscious effort on the part of male executives to keep women out of their domain (Powell & Butterfield, 1994). Rather, more subtle factors seem to produce this effect. Clear evidence on what some of these may be is provided by a field study conducted recently by Ohlott, Ruderman, and McCauley (1994).

These researchers reasoned that in order to advance their careers, managers must have a wide range of *developmental opportunities*—job-related experiences that help prepare them for top-level jobs (Van Velsor & Hughes, 1990). Ohlott and her colleagues then hypothesized that perhaps women receive fewer of these opportunities than men and that this accounts, at least in part, for their underrepresentation in top-level jobs. To test this reasoning, they had nearly 600 men and women working in many different organizations complete a survey de-

Glass Ceiling ■ Barriers based on attitudinal or organizational bias that prevent qualified females from advancing to top-level positions.

FIGURE 6.14

The Glass Ceiling: Another Barrier to Female Achievement. Although females fill 42 percent of all managerial jobs, they constitute only 5 percent of top-level executives. This fact has lead some researchers to conclude that a *glass ceiling* operates to prevent females from moving into the highest positions in many organizations.

signed to measure the extent to which participants had experienced a wide range of developmental opportunities in their jobs. These opportunities included *job transitions* (being given new responsibilities different from their previous ones); being asked to create change (start something new or solve existing problems); dealing with external pressures, such as unions or government agencies or working in a foreign culture; and being given tasks that involve high levels of *visibility* and *responsibility*. In addition, participants in the study reported on the extent to which they encountered obstacles in their job—such factors as lack of support from top management, lack of personal support, or a difficult boss.

Results indicated that in general, males and females did not appear significantly different in terms of the developmental opportunities measured. However, a few differences did emerge, and these were ones that the researchers viewed as especially costly to women. Specifically, females reported fewer developmental opportunities than males that increased their visibility or widened the scope of their responsibilities. In short, they were *not* given key assignments perceived as crucial by their companies—assignments that would teach them the skills they needed and, at the same time, allow them to demonstrate their competence. In addition, females reported encountering more obstacles in their jobs: they reported that it was hard to find personal support, that they felt left out of important networks, and that they had to fight to be recognized for the work they did.

Taken together, these findings suggest that the glass ceiling is indeed real, and that it stems from factors suggestive of lingering, if subtle, forms of prejudice toward females. While other findings indicate that the glass ceiling is not present in all organizations—for example, it has been found to be entirely lacking in government agencies (Powell & Butterfield, 1994)—its presence in at least some work settings appears to be an additional subtle barrier to female achievement.

Sexual Harassment ■ Unwelcome sexual advances, requests for sexual favors, and other verbal or physical conduct of a sexual nature.

Sexual Harassment: When Discrimination Hits Rock Bottom

Teresa Harris was a manager at Forklift Systems, Inc., in Nashville, Tennessee, when she encountered **sexual harassment**—defined in the United States as unwelcome sexual advances, requests for sexual favors, and other verbal or physical conduct of a sexual nature—from her boss, Charles Hardy. During Harris's two and a half years with the company, he often made remarks such as "You're a woman, what do you know?" and "We need a man as the rental manager." He suggested to her in front of other employees that they go to a nearby motel to "negotiate her raise." Occasionally, he asked Harris to remove coins from his pants pocket and would drop items on the floor and ask her to pick them up. The last straw came when, after Harris had negotiated a deal with a customer, Harris remarked, in front of other employees: "What did you promise the guy . . . some sex Saturday night?" At this point Harris quit her job and filed suit against Hardy and her former company. It took several years, but she took her case to the Supreme Court and, in 1993, finally won.

Unfortunately, sexual harassment is far from rare in many work settings. For example, in one recent poll fully 31 percent of employed women indicated that they had been the object of such harassment on at least one occasion (*BNA's Employee Relations Weekly,* 1994). In contrast, only 7 percent of male respondents to the same survey indicated that they had been the victim of such actions. It's important to note, by the way, that sexual harassment is not restricted to the kind of extreme and unpleasant actions encountered by Teresa Harris; under U.S. law it can involve any actions of a sexual nature that create a hostile work environment for employees—such actions as posting offensive pinups, staring at portions of coworkers' anatomy, or making repeated remarks about their appearance. In short, a boss or fellow employee doesn't have to request sexual favors or make these a condition of employment to commit sexual harassment: many other forms of behavior meet the legal definition.

Fortunately, recognition of sexual harassment as a problem in many work settings has increased greatly in recent years. Perhaps the most famous case involving sexual harassment involved the charges brought by Professor Anita Hill against Justice Clarence Thomas when he was being reviewed by the United States Senate Judiciary Committee for a seat on the Supreme Court. The committee concluded that there was not enough evidence to bar Clarence's nomi-

TABLE 6.1 Reducing the Incidence of Sexual Harassment: Some Useful Steps

The steps shown here can often be useful in reducing the frequency of sexual harassment in work settings.

Step or Policy	Description
Develop a clear policy prohibiting sexual harassment.	This policy should describe in detail what is meant by sexual harassment. It should also note that the company will not tolerate such behavior.
Train all employees to understand what sexual harassment is and how to avoid it.	Employees should receive training that will help them become sensitive to the possible ways in which they may be offending others.
Keep the workplace free of sexually offensive materials.	Posters, calendars, and slogans of a sexual nature may seem innocent, but they offend some persons and should not be permitted.
Set up clear grievance procedures with respect to sexual harassment.	The persons to whom employees should bring complaints should be clearly identified and readily available.
Specify in advance how the company will treat offenders, then strictly enforce this policy.	The consequences of engaging in sexual harassment should be stated clearly and enforced vigorously.

(*Source:* Based on suggestions by Bohren, 1993.)

nation, but many women did not agree with that decision and objected to his appointment to this important position.

In any case, as recognition of the frequency and harmful effects of sexual harassment has grown, many organizations have moved to establish clear policies against such behavior, and have taken other steps to lessen its occurrence. Several of these steps are summarized in Table 6.1 (Bohren, 1993). Growing evidence suggests that together, such steps can be quite effective in reducing the incidence of this detestable form of discrimination, and in so doing protecting the psychological and physical welfare of tens of millions of employees—men as well as women.

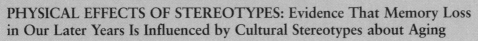

Social Diversity: A Critical Analysis

PHYSICAL EFFECTS OF STEREOTYPES: Evidence That Memory Loss in Our Later Years Is Influenced by Cultural Stereotypes about Aging

THROUGHOUT THIS CHAPTER, WE'VE EMPHASIZED THE importance of stereotypes in prejudice. These mental frameworks exert powerful effects on social thought, and so on our reactions to, and judgments about, persons belonging to various social groups. But now get ready for a surprise: recent findings indicate

that stereotypes can do more than shape social thought—they can actually affect our physical well-being as well. Dramatic evidence for this conclusion has been reported by Levy and Langer (1994) in a study concerned with the effects of aging on memory.

FIGURE 6.15

Stereotypes and Memory Loss with Aging. Young persons from three different cultural groups did not differ with respect to their scores on tests of memory. Among older persons, however, those from American nondeaf culture—which has negative stereotypes of older persons—showed larger declines in memory than those from Chinese and American deaf cultures, which have more positive stereotypes of older persons.

(*Source:* Based on data from Levy & Langer, 1994.)

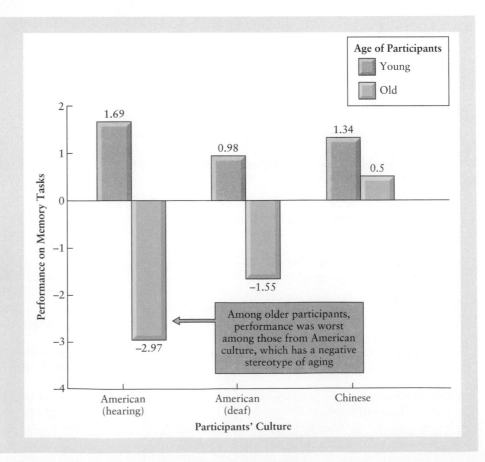

Do you think that your own memory will decline with age? Many Americans believe that this is so. In fact, the stereotype of "the elderly" in the United States is largely negative: it suggests that aging is associated with unavoidable declines in appearance, health, and mental abilities. Growing old, in other words, is viewed as no fun. Other cultures, however, have a very different view of older persons. In China, for example, older persons are revered for their wisdom and accumulated knowledge; moreover, Chinese culture does *not* assume that older persons will lose their memories or show other declines in cognitive functions. Similar views are held among deaf persons in the United States; they, too, have relatively positive views of older persons, and do not assume that they will experience reduced cognitive capacities as they age. In short, stereotypes about older persons differ sharply in different cultures.

But how, you are probably wondering, can stereotypes influence physical well-being? Levy and Langer (1994) suggest that they can exert such effects through premature *cognitive commitments*—beliefs that people accept unconditionally. Once such beliefs are formed, they are never reexamined; on the contrary, they are accepted in a largely unconscious manner and often remain unchanged throughout life. Levy and Langer (1994) argue that such beliefs can be incorporated into stereotypes and then, since they are strong and unchanging, can contribute to the powerful self-fulfilling effects that stereotypes so often exert. In other words, if, in a given culture, the prevailing stereotype of older people suggests that they will show a decline in cognitive abilities, then older people probably will. If, in contrast, such declines are not part of prevailing stereotypes, then they will occur to a lesser degree.

To test these intriguing predictions, Levy and Langer (1994) studied three groups of subjects: American deaf individuals, American persons who were not deaf, and Chinese. In each group, half of the participants were young (in their twenties) while the remainder were older adults (from their late fifties to their nineties). All participants then performed several tasks designed to measure their memory—for example, reproducing patterns of dots shown on a computer screen for ten seconds, or remembering which sentences accompanied photos of eight different strangers. As shown in Figure 6.15, the young persons from the three different groups did not differ significantly in their performance. Among the older participants, however, those from the Chinese and American deaf groups performed significantly better than those from the normal hearing group. Additional findings indicated that culture did indeed affect participants' stereotypes about aging—these were more favorable among Chinese and American deaf participants than among the American participants with normal hearing. Further, the more positive these views, the better participants' performance on the memory tasks.

These results provide dramatic evidence for the powerful self-confirming impact of stereotypes. Not only do they act as filters for new social information; they can also influence our performance on various tasks and our physical well-being. It is difficult to think of a more convincing illustration of the crucial interface between social thought and social behavior that is one of the major themes of modern social psychology—and of this book. ■ ■ ■

CONNECTIONS: Integrating Social Psychology

In this chapter, you read about . . .	In other chapters, you will find related discussions of . . .
stereotypes as mental shortcuts—one means of saving cognitive effort	heuristics and other mental shortcuts (Chapter 3)
the role of economic factors (frustration) in prejudice and racism	the role of frustration in aggression and conflict (Chapter 11)
the tendency to divide the social world into "us" and "them" and its effects	other effects of group membership (Chapter 12)
the effects of suppressing stereotypic thoughts	the causes and effects of other kinds of thought suppression (Chapter 3)
sexual harassment in work settings	other aspects of social behavior in work settings (Chapter 13)

(continued)

Thinking About Connections

1. Some observers suggest that as open forms of discrimination have decreased, more subtle forms have increased. Do you think that's true? And if so, do you think these new forms of discrimination are condoned or accepted by various groups (Chapter 12), and by more widespread social norms (Chapter 9)?

2. Stereotypes, it appears, save us considerable cognitive effort. And we've noted repeatedly in this book, as human beings, we usually seek to hold such effort to a minimum (Chapters 2, 3). Given this fact, do you think that the tendency to think about others in terms of stereotypes can really be reduced? And if not, are we doomed to continuing cycles of prejudice, discrimination, and violence (Chapter 11)?

3. Many people seem to take great pride in belonging to various groups (Chapter 12). As we've seen in this chapter, however, this often leads them to divide the social world into "us" and "them"—people belonging to their group and all others. Can you suggest steps that might be successful in reducing this tendency? For example, can groups themselves introduce norms (Chapter 9) tending to discourage such social categorization?

4. The fact that relatively few women have made it to the top in the world of business may indicate the existence of prejudice against them—for example the glass ceiling. However, it may also reflect other factors, such as different career orientations on the part of women and men, contrasting approaches to intimate relationships (Chapter 8), or persisting gender stereotypes. What factors do *you* think are the most important in this situation? Can they be changed or overcome?

Summary and Review

Prejudice and Discrimination

Prejudice is a negative attitude toward the members of some social group that is based solely on their membership in that group. *Discrimination* refers to harmful actions directed toward the persons or groups who are the targets of prejudice. Because overt discrimination is now illegal in many countries, such behavior now frequently takes more subtle forms. These include attitudes described as *the "new" racism and sexism, tokenism,* and *reverse discrimination.* Unfortunately, these newer and more subtle forms of prejudice—especially disguised forms of racism—are still present, and continue to exert extremely harmful effects on the persons and groups who are their targets.

The Origins of Prejudice

Prejudice stems from a number of different sources. According to *realistic conflict theory,* it derives from competition between social groups for scarce resources. The *social learning view* suggests that children acquire prejudice from parents, teachers, friends, and mass media. *Social categorization* suggests that prejudice stems from our strong tendencies to divide the social world into "us" and "them."

Much recent evidence supports the view that prejudice stems from certain aspects of *social cognition*—the ways in which we think about others and make judgments about them. *Stereotypes,* cognitive frameworks involving beliefs about the typical characteristics of members of social groups, play an especially important role in this regard. Once stereotypes are activated, they exert profound effects on social thought. Stereotypes serve as mental shortcuts, reducing cognitive effort; for this reason, they are very difficult to change. Recent findings indicate that stereotypes contain an affective component, and that persons in a good mood are more likely to engage in stereotypic thinking than those in a more neutral mood. Other aspects of social cognition that play a role in prejudice include *illusory correlations*—perceptions of stronger relationships between distinctive events than actually exist; and the illusion of *outgroup homogeneity,* which involves the tendency to perceive lower variability among outgroup members than among ingroup members.

Striking Back against Prejudice

One way to reduce prejudice is to encourage parents and others to transmit tolerant rather than prejudiced attitudes to children. *Direct intergroup contact* can be helpful, provided that the contact occurs under appropriate conditions. Another useful technique involves recategorization—somehow inducing individuals to shift the boundary between "us" and "them" so that outgroup members are now included as part of the ingroup. Cognitive interventions, such as inducing individuals to think about others in terms of their individual attributes rather than in terms of their group membership and inducing them to form *counterstereotypic inferences,* can also be effective in reducing prejudice. Actively *suppressing* stereotypic thinking is effective while such suppression is occurring, but is followed by a rebound effect in which the influence of stereotypes on social thought returns.

Prejudice Based on Gender

Sexism, prejudice based on gender, involves acceptance of *gender stereotypes* suggesting that males and females possess sharply different traits. In fact, gender differences are smaller than these stereotypes suggest. Overt discrimination against females is now illegal in many countries, but several subtle forces continue to operate against female achievement. These include lower expectations and low self-confidence on the part of females, negative reactions to and evaluations of female leaders, and the *glass ceiling*—barriers that prevent women from attaining the highest-level jobs in many organizations. Recent findings indicate that the glass ceiling is real, but that it stems from such factors as lower developmental opportunities in organizations for females than for males. *Sexual harassment* involves unwelcome sexual advances, requests for sexual favors, and other verbal or physical conduct of a sexual nature. Females are much more likely than males to be the victims of such treatment, but its incidence can be reduced in work settings through the establishment of appropriate policies and guidelines.

Social Diversity: Physical Effects of Stereotypes

Recent evidence indicates that stereotypes can influence not only social thought but also important aspects of physical well-being. Declines in mental abilities such as memory are greater in cultures that possess negative stereotypes about "the elderly" than is true in cultures that possess more positive stereotypes of the elderly. These findings suggest that the self-confirming nature of stereotypes can extend to task performance and physical well-being.

■ Key Terms

Common Ingroup Identity Model (p. 218)

Contact Hypothesis (p. 217)

Discrimination (p. 198)

Gender Stereotypes (p. 223)

Glass Ceiling (p. 225)

Illusion of Outgroup Homogeneity (p. 213)

Illusory Correlation (p. 212)

Ingroup (p. 207)

Ingroup Differentiation (p. 213)

Outgroup (p. 207)

Prejudice (p. 195)

Realistic Conflict Theory (p. 202)

Recategorization (p. 218)

Reverse Discrimination (p. 200)

Sexism (p. 222)

Sexual Harassment (p. 226)

Social Categorization (p. 207)

Social Learning View (of prejudice) (p. 205)

Stereotypes (p. 208)

Tokenism (p. 200)

Ultimate Attribution Error (p. 207)

■ For More Information

Dovidio, J. F., & Gaertner, S. L. (Eds.). (1986). *Prejudice, discrimination, and racism.* Orlando, FL: Academic Press.

This book contains chapters prepared by various experts on the topics of prejudice and discrimination. Several argue that racial prejudice has not actually decreased or disappeared in recent years—it has simply shifted into more subtle forms.

Knopke, H., Norrell, & Rogers, R. (Eds.). (1993). *Opening doors: An appraisal of race relations in contemporary America.* Tuscaloosa: University of Alabama Press.

A valuable overview of the current state of race relations in the United States. Chapters by social psychologists who have studied racial prejudice in their research provide valuable insights on this important and timely topic.

Oksamp, S., & Costanzo, M. (Eds.). (1993). *Gender issues in contemporary society.* Newbury Park, CA: Sage.

Chapters by leading experts on all aspects of gender. The unit on gender stereotyping and discrimination is directly related to topics covered in this chapter.

CHAPTER 7

INTERPERSONAL ATTRACTION: Initial Contact, Liking, Becoming Acquainted

Lisa Houck, *Nightlife in the Bird World*, 1993, watercolor, 6 × 9"

Chapter Outline

Some time in your life, you probably moved into a new neighborhood, apartment complex, or dormitory where you didn't know anyone. During the first several days, however, some of the people you passed on the sidewalk, in the hallway, or wherever began to seem familiar. You didn't know them, but you recognized them. Eventually, you probably became acquainted with some of these former strangers. Why? On what basis did a few of them become acquaintances while others remained strangers?

Think of a day when you woke up feeling really great about yourself and then had nothing but good experiences the rest of the day. Can you remember how you reacted to the people you encountered that morning, afternoon, and evening? You might also think about the worst day of your life—when everything went wrong. How did you react to people then? Do you suppose there is a connection between your emotional state and your interpersonal perceptions?

You are planning to see a movie this weekend because one of your favorite actors and one of your favorite actresses are costarring for the first time. You mention your plans to someone you know, and that person begins describing those two performers as the two dullest performers in the entertainment industry. It is suggested that you would have more fun spending the evening having your cavities drilled. After a few minutes of listening to this individual's opinions, how do you feel? Do you like or dislike the person more than before you had the conversation? Why?

All through our lives, we make judgments about people, objects, and events. Recent laboratory experiments provide evidence that we instantly evaluate every word, sound, picture, and person as soon as the perception registers, and this occurs before we are actually conscious of having perceived anything (Bargh, 1995). Some things we like, some we dislike, but we seldom if ever have a neutral reaction. We instantly evaluate even nonsense words—for example, English-speaking research participants tend to like "juvalamu" and to dislike "chakaka" (Goleman, 1995). With respect to how we feel about other people, is it possible that our selection of friends, romantic partners, and spouses is also based on relatively automatic processes that are predictable and understandable? Many social psychologists strongly believe that the answer is *yes*. In the pages to follow (including Chapter 8), we will describe some of the reasons for this answer.

The very human tendency to evaluate almost everything and everyone was discussed in Chapter 4; we form *attitudes* about the people, objects, and events that we encounter. As we encounter other individuals at school, at work, or in our neighborhoods, we develop attitudes about each of them. These interpersonal evaluations fall along a dimension ranging from like to dislike, as shown in Figure 7.1.

Our attitudes about other people are the specific target of investigation in research on **interpersonal attraction**. Attraction research consists of identifying in detail the factors responsible for interpersonal evaluations. As you read about the research on the effects of each factor, it is easy to lose sight of the forest, because we tend to focus on the trees. It may be helpful to keep in mind from the very beginning a simple but all-important concept: Some social psychologists propose that *we make positive evaluations when our feelings are positive and negative evaluations when our feelings are negative.* That is, our interpersonal likes and dislikes are determined by emotions. Any factor that affects emotions also affects attraction. As you read this chapter, the reasons for that assertion will become much more clear. Beyond simple positive–negative emotions, additional factors can also affect interpersonal behavior, and as a consequence our

Interpersonal Attraction ■
Our evaluation of other people with respect to how much we like or dislike them.

FIGURE 7.1

FIGURE 7.1

Interpersonal Attraction: Liking and Disliking. *Interpersonal attraction* refers to the evaluation one person makes of another. Such evaluations are made along an attitudinal dimension that includes strong liking (toward a friend), mild liking (toward a close acquaintance), neutral feelings (toward a superficial acquaintance), mild dislike (toward an annoying acquaintance), and strong dislike (toward someone considered undesirable). Attraction research involves the attempt to identify the factors responsible for these evaluations and to create formulations that explain the phenomena.

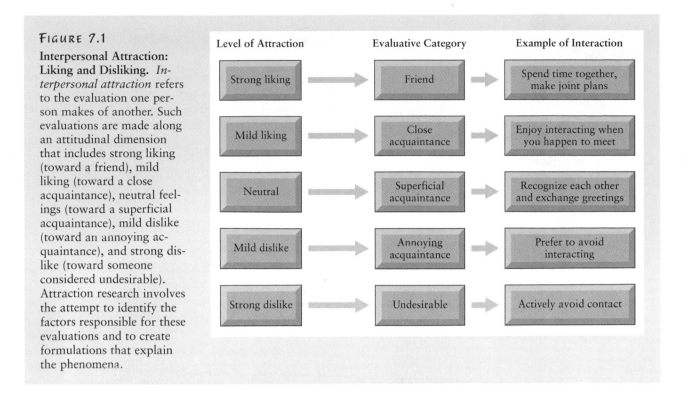

Level of Attraction	Evaluative Category	Example of Interaction
Strong liking	Friend	Spend time together, make joint plans
Mild liking	Close acquaintance	Enjoy interacting when you happen to meet
Neutral	Superficial acquaintance	Recognize each other and exchange greetings
Mild dislike	Annoying acquaintance	Prefer to avoid interacting
Strong dislike	Undesirable	Actively avoid contact

evaluations are likely to become more extreme—as you will see when you read about *love* in Chapter 8 and *hate* in Chapter 11.

Let's quickly preview the subject matter of this chapter. Attraction begins when people come into contact with one another. We most often make such contacts by accident—based on such impersonal determinants as the locations of streets and sidewalks in one's neighborhood, seats in a classroom, room assignments in a dormitory, or the physical arrangements at work. Simply because of where we sit, live, or earn a living, we come into repeated contact with some people more than with others. As a result, *physical proximity* very often constitutes the first step in our becoming attracted to another person. A very important factor influencing whether or not you like those you encounter is your *affective state* at the time. It is simple, but true, that we tend to like others when our emotions are positive and to dislike them when we are experiencing negative feelings, no matter what caused the emotions. Your affect may be based on something the other person says or does (an amusing remark versus an insulting comment) or on something unrelated to that person (receiving an obscene gesture from a rude driver shortly before you meet the other person). Even with repeated contacts and positive emotions, attraction may not develop unless both individuals are *motivated to establish a relationship* and unless each responds positively to the *observable characteristics* of the other. That is, two strangers must desire to form a relationship and not be turned off by their initial responses to the other person's physical appearance, skin color, age, or any other factor that can activate stereotypes and prejudice (as described in Chapter 6). If two people do begin to interact, liking versus disliking is strongly determined by whether they are *similar* (rather than dissimilar) in their attitudes, beliefs, values, and other characteristics. A relationship can become increasingly positive if two people indicate mutual liking through *positive evaluations* of the other person in words or deeds.

Meeting Strangers: Proximity and Emotions

Though we each have about six billion potential friends and acquaintances on this planet, we are likely to interact with only a very small percentage of them. Among those, some become acquaintances and some remain strangers. Why? Our physical surroundings exert a critical influence on who we are (or are not) likely to meet. Simply stated, two people will most probably become acquainted if they are brought into regular contact through physical **proximity** (closeness; sometimes labeled *propinquity*) and if each of them is experiencing positive rather than negative *affect* (feelings or mood) at the time.

Physical Surroundings: Repeated Interpersonal Contact Leads to Attraction

When two strangers regularly pass one another in the corridor of a dormitory, sit in adjoining classroom seats each day, or wait together every morning at the bus stop, these casual and unplanned contacts soon lead to mutual recognition. Next, they may well begin exchanging a brief greeting when they meet ("Hi") and maybe a word or two about the weather or some newsworthy event. In other words, a familiar face evokes positive feelings. Even infants tend to smile at a photograph of someone they have seen before, but not at a photograph of someone they are seeing for the first time (Brooks-Gunn & Lewis, 1981). On a college campus, employees are better able to identify buildings close to the one in which they work than more distant buildings; they also express a preference for nearby buildings (Johnson & Byrne, 1996). How can such responses be explained?

Why Does Repeated Contact Increase Interpersonal Attraction? In a monograph that initiated a large body of research, Zajonc (1968) proposed that **repeated exposure** to a new stimulus—frequent contact with that stimulus—leads to a more and more positive evaluation of the stimulus. Whether that stimulus is a drawing, a word in an unknown foreign language, a new product being advertised, a political candidate, or a stranger in a classroom, the more frequent the exposure, the more positive the response (Moreland & Zajonc, 1982). The general idea is that we often respond with at least mild discomfort to anything or anyone new. With repeated exposure, the feelings of anxiety decrease, and the *new* something or someone gradually becomes *familiar*. That is, you begin to feel friendly toward the stranger sitting next to you in class because you see that individual over and over again. In the same class, you are much less likely to see someone sitting three rows back on the other side of the room, so familiarity and friendliness don't develop.

To show just how this process operates, Moreland and Beach (1992) asked one female research assistant to attend a college class fifteen times during the semester, another to attend ten times, another five times, and one not to attend at all. Then, at the end of the semester, all four individuals came to the classroom, and the experimenters asked the students to indicate how much they liked each one on a rating scale. The assistants were fairly similar in appearance, and none interacted with any of the class members during the semester. Nevertheless, attraction increased as the number of classroom exposures increased—see Figure 7.2. Clearly, repeated exposure affected liking.

As you might expect from our discussion of the subliminal conditioning of attitudes in Chapter 4, repeated exposure operates even when one is not consciously aware that a stimulus is present. Actually, the effect is *stronger* under these conditions. Bornstein and D'Agostino (1992) presented stimuli to some

Proximity ■ In attraction research, the closeness between two individuals' residences, classroom seats, work areas, and so on; the closer the physical distance, the greater the probability of the individuals' coming into regular contact.

Repeated Exposure ■ Frequent contact with a stimulus; according to Zajonc's theory, with repeated exposure to any mildly negative, neutral, or positive stimulus, the evaluation of that stimulus becomes increasingly positive.

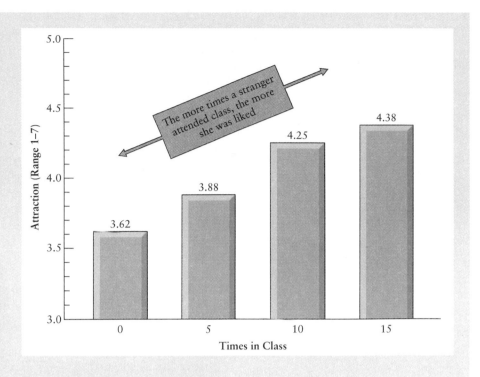

Figure 7.2

Classroom Contacts Lead to Attraction. Four female research assistants pretended to be students in a large college class. One did not attend class at all, another attended class five times, a third attended ten times, and a fourth, fifteen times; those who came to class sat quietly in the classroom and did not interact with the professor or with fellow students. At the end of the semester, the attraction of the students toward all four assistants was assessed. Attraction increased as the number of exposures to the strangers increased.

(*Source:* Based on data from Moreland & Beach, 1992.)

research participants at a normal speed—and to others at a sufficiently rapid speed that they afterward were not aware of having seen anything. In both conditions, the more frequently the stimulus was presented, the more positive the ratings; but the effect was greater when the stimuli were subliminal than when they were shown slowly enough to be perceived at the conscious level. In the normal viewing condition, the reason for familiarity with a repeatedly exposed stimulus is clear, and such a stimulus is liked because it is familiar. Why should that reaction increase with subliminal stimuli? R. F. Bornstein (personal communication, February 1993) points out that the rapidly exposed stimulus, in fact, *is perceived* at some level of awareness, and so it too becomes increasingly familiar. When research participants are asked afterwards to rate the picture that has been presented subliminally, however, they aren't aware that the stimulus is familiar, so the positive reaction is attributed to liking.

One caution about the repeated exposure effect is that it does not apply to a new stimulus if the initial reaction is very negative. For example, several years ago the song "Copacabana" came out and was quite popular. I (Donn Byrne) disliked it the first time I heard it and liked it less and less with repeated exposure. Research confirms the fact that repeated exposure to something or someone that evokes quite negative feelings does *not* result in increased liking (Swap, 1977). Additional contact with a disliked stimulus can actually *maximize* the initial feeling of dislike.

In most interpersonal situations the initial reaction to a stranger tends to be neutral or mildly positive, so what are the effects of repeated exposure to others in real-life settings?

Residential Proximity: Friendships and Marriage. Studies of many kinds of residences over the past few decades are consistent in finding that as the distance between residences decreases, random contact between the residents becomes more frequent, and positive relationships develop.

For example, studies of multistoried undergraduate dormitories showed that two-thirds of friendships develop among people living on the same floor, and only rarely do students get to know those living more than one floor away (Evans & Wilson, 1949; Lundberg & Beazley, 1948). Almost fifty years after those studies were conducted, Whitbeck and Hoyt (1994) found that the choice of dating partners among undergraduates is in part a function of the distance between the partners' college residences.

Beyond the college campus, very similar effects are found among adult families in suburbia (Ebbesen, Kjos, & Konecni, 1976), as illustrated in Figure 7.3. And in a housing project for the elderly, friendship patterns are determined by the distance between rooms in much the same way as in college dormitories (Nahemow & Lawton, 1975).

To illustrate the long-range effects of such findings, we'll jump ahead for a moment to the kinds of relationships discussed in Chapter 8. Proximity not only results in people becoming acquainted, it even influences dating and marriage. Two of the oldest studies showing a relationship between the physical environment and attraction were conducted in the 1930s. In Philadelphia, Bossard (1932) examined the first 5,000 marriages performed in 1931 and then determined where the bride and groom lived before the wedding. About a third of the couples lived within five blocks of one another before they married, and more than half lived within a twenty-block radius. A few years later, the study was repeated in New Haven with the records of 1,000 marriages in 1931, and almost identical results were obtained (Davie & Reeves, 1939). The closer the residences of a man and a woman, the greater the probability they will marry.

Please note that in the proximity studies we have described, the investigators reported a *correlation* between distance and attraction. Presumably, proximity led to the relationship, but this could not be concluded with any certainty using the correlational approach. Perhaps people who share other characteristics (religion, race, social class, or whatever) prefer to live near one another. If so, these other factors may have influenced both proximity and attraction,

FIGURE 7.3

Proximity and Attraction: The Importance of Environmental Factors. Studies of neighborhoods and other residential settings such as dormitories and apartment buildings indicate that physical proximity is a major determinant of which individuals become acquainted.

(*Source:* FPG International Corporation, *The New Yorker,* February 20 & 27, 1995, p. 150.)

rather than proximity influencing attraction. Researchers have turned to the experimental method to clarify this issue.

Manipulating Proximity to Determine Its Effects. Though it is obviously not possible or reasonable for an experimenter to manipulate where people live or work in order to study interpersonal attraction, such manipulation often does occur in the college setting. When administrators or instructors make random assignments of housing or seating, for example, they create the necessary conditions for an experiment.

Thus, when couples assigned to random apartments in married student housing become acquainted on the basis of proximity, this provides strong evidence that proximity leads to attraction. As distance varies, attraction varies. For example, couples whose apartments are located within twenty-two feet of one another are quite likely to become acquainted; in contrast, such relationships are quite *un*likely if the apartments are more than eighty-eight feet apart (Festinger, Schachter, & Back, 1950).

In a similar way, whenever students are randomly assigned to classroom seats at the beginning of a semester and relationships develop during the semester as a function of the distance between seats, it indicates that proximity influences which students become acquainted. This is precisely what has been found. For example, students assigned to a middle seat in a row are much more likely to become acquainted with the two students sitting closest to them (those sitting to their left and right) than to get to know any other students in the class (Byrne & Buehler, 1955). When a student is assigned a seat on the end of a row, fewer relationships develop than if the seat is elsewhere in the row (Maisonneuve, Palmade, & Fourment, 1952). If the random seat assignments are made alphabetically, friendships form between those whose last names begin with the same or a nearby letter (Segal, 1974). Finally, if the instructor makes new seat assignments at various times during the semester, more students will become acquainted than if they must remain in one location all semester (Byrne, 1961a).

Note that when you are are free to choose your own classroom seat, you may want to apply what you have just learned about proximity effects. For example, if you want to make new friends, you should obviously avoid seats on the ends of rows; and if it is possible to change seats from day to day, you should do so and increase the number of potential new acquaintances. If you *don't* want new friends because you prefer to maintain your privacy (Larson & Bell, 1988), select a seat in the back of the room, as far from others as possible (Pedersen, 1994).

Positive and Negative Affect: The Basis of Liking and Disliking

We experience and express emotions throughout our daily lives, and our emotional state at any given moment influences perception, cognition, motivation, *and* interpersonal judgments (Erber, 1991; Forgas, 1993; Zajonc & McIntosh, 1992). As you may remember from Chapter 3, psychologists often use the term *affect* when referring to emotions or feelings. The two most important characteristics of affect consist of *intensity* (the weakness or strength of the emotion) and *direction* (whether the emotion is positive or negative). Positive emotions such as excitement and happiness were once thought to fall at one end of a continuum with negative emotions such as anxiety and depression falling at the opposite end. It now appears, however, that positive and negative emotions involve two separate and independent dimensions (Smeaton & Byrne, 1988). For example, when emotions are measured before and after students receive feedback indicating that they did well on an exam, positive affect is aroused by the good news but negative affect remains unchanged; also, receiving feedback that they did badly on an exam arouses negative affect but has no influence on positive feelings (Goldstein & Strube, 1994).

Experiments consistently indicate that positive feelings lead to positive evaluations of others—liking—while negative feelings lead to negative evaluations—dislike (Dovidio et al., 1995). Affect can influence attraction in two ways. First, another person can do something to make you feel good or bad; you tend to like people or events that make you feel good and to dislike them if they make you feel bad (Downey & Damhave, 1991; Shapiro, Baumeister, & Kessler, 1991). It is obvious that you will prefer someone who brightens your day by giving you a sincere compliment to someone who brings you down with an unfair criticism. Second, and less obvious, is that anyone or anything *simply present* when your positive or negative feelings are aroused (by something else entirely) is also liked or disliked as a consequence. It may seem a little odd, but you evaluate others more positively when waiting to get into a movie than when waiting to see your dentist. Let's consider research involving both kinds of affect–attraction research.

A Person Who Does Something That Arouses Positive or Negative Affect Is Liked or Disliked Accordingly. We have suggested that proximity influences attraction because repeated exposure to a stranger leads to a more positive affective response to that individual. In later sections of this chapter, we will show how your attraction to another person is strongly influenced by affective reactions to his or her appearance, attitudes, and other attributes. But before getting to those topics, let's consider a special sort of social interaction: attempts to initiate a conversation with a stranger. What are the affective and evaluative consequences of different kinds of "opening lines"?

Kleinke, Meeker, and Staneski (1986) investigated the kinds of things people say when they try to interact with someone they don't know. Many people—especially men—attempt to be amusing by saying something cute or flippant, presumably hoping to elicit positive affect and to be liked. One example from Kleinke and colleagues' research is, "Hi. I'm easy, are you?" The most common emotional response to such attempted cleverness was negative, the opposite of what was intended. In contrast, a positive affective response is much more common when the opening line is either innocuous ("Where are you from?") or direct ("Hi. I'm a little embarrassed about this, but I'd like to get to know you"). Some additional liked and disliked opening lines from this research appear in Table 7.1.

The relationship between opening lines and attraction toward the person using them was investigated in a subsequent laboratory experiment (Kleinke & Dean, 1990). The most positive response was toward a person saying something simple and direct, and the most negative was toward someone using a cute or flippant line, as illustrated in Figure 7.4. Expanding this research to a real-life setting, research assistants were sent to a singles bar to use these different kinds of openers on strangers to determine their effects, and the same results were obtained in a bar as in the laboratory (Cunningham, 1989). Those who try to be too cute manage to turn other people off.

A Person Who Is Simply Associated with Positive or Negative Affect Is Liked or Disliked Accordingly. Besides what someone may say that is affect-arousing, our positive and negative feelings are also aroused by events having nothing directly to do with the other person (Johnston & Short, 1993). Your immediate affective state is influenced by recent experiences, thoughts, physical sensations,

TABLE 7.1 Opening Lines: Making a Good (or Bad) First Impression

In a social situation, how one initiates a conversation with a stranger of the opposite sex can be crucial in creating a favorable first impression. Research indicates that the best strategy is to avoid cute or flippant openers. Women are especially negative in evaluating men's attempts to be amusing.

Setting	Most Preferred Opening Line	Least Preferred Opening Line
General	Hi.	Your place or mine?
Bar	Do you want to dance?	Bet I can outdrink you.
Restaurant	I haven't been here before. What's good on the menu?	I bet the cherry pie jubilee isn't as sweet as you are.
Supermarket	Can I help you to the car with those things?	Do you really eat that junk?
Laundromat	Want to go have a beer or a cup of coffee while we're waiting?	Those are some nice undies you have there.
Beach	Want to play frisbee?	Let me see your strap marks.

(*Source:* Based on data from Kleinke, Meeker, & Staneski, 1986.)

and much else besides. If another person just happens to be there when your feelings are good, you tend to like him or her; if that person is present when your feelings are bad, you tend to feel dislike (Byrne & Clore, 1970). The general idea is based on classical conditioning, as outlined in Figure 7.5 (p. 242). In Chapter 4 we described how attitudes in general can be acquired through classical conditioning; whenever an attitude object is paired with a stimulus that evokes positive or negative affect, the observer develops positive or negative attitudes toward the object. In the same way, researchers have prompted attraction or dislike toward a stranger by pairing the stranger's photograph with pleasant or unpleasant pictures presented subliminally (Krosnick et al., 1992).

FIGURE 7.4

Opening Lines Influence Liking. Experimental subjects watched videotapes of a man or a woman approaching an opposite-sex stranger and beginning a conversation using an opening line that was one of three types. Consistent with other research, subjects rated those using a cute or flippant approach as least likable and those using a direct approach as most likable.

(*Source:* Based on data from Kleinke & Dean, 1990.)

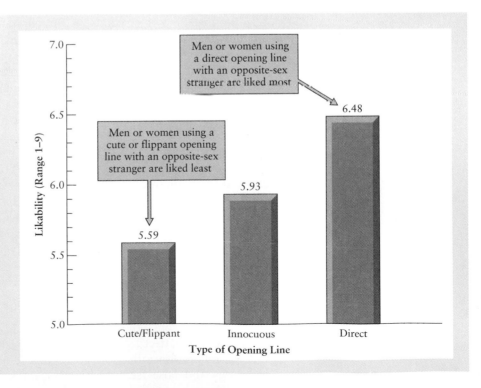

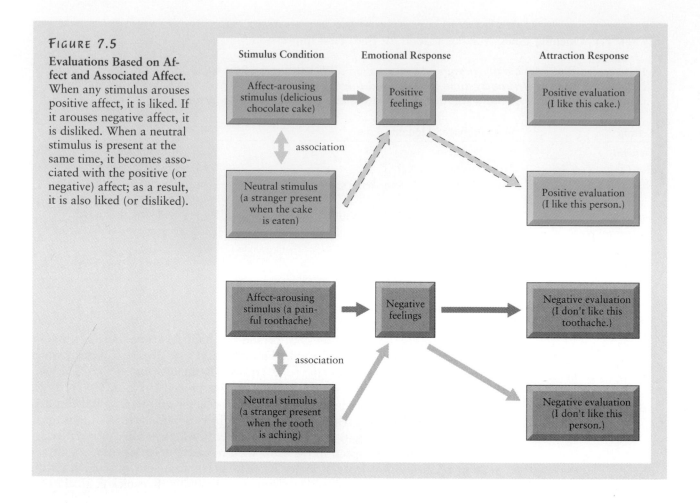

Figure 7.5

Evaluations Based on Affect and Associated Affect. When any stimulus arouses positive affect, it is liked. If it arouses negative affect, it is disliked. When a neutral stimulus is present at the same time, it becomes associated with the positive (or negative) affect; as a result, it is also liked (or disliked).

To test the effect of emotions on attraction, numerous experimenters have manipulated the affective state of research subjects and then asked them to indicate their attraction toward a stranger (someone simply associated with the affect, and not in any way responsible for it). The results are quite consistent. For example, May and Hamilton (1980) aroused affect with background music that had been rated by undergraduates as pleasant or unpleasant. When other female undergraduates made judgments about male strangers based on their photos, the researchers played either no music, pleasant music (rock), or unpleasant music (avant-garde classical) in the background. The women were asked to indicate how much they liked each man on the basis of his photograph. Compared to the no-music condition, students listening to the pleasant rock music liked the strangers better and even thought they were more physically attractive. The most negative evaluations were made by subjects listening to the unpleasant advant-garde music. The same photographs were used in each condition, so the different responses were obviously based on affect and not on the appearance of the strangers.

In much the same way, emotions have been aroused by good versus bad news on the radio (Kaplan, 1981), happy versus sad movies (Gouaux, 1971), and pleasant versus unpleasant room lighting (Baron, Rea, & Daniels, 1992). In these and numerous other experiments, positive affect results in liking others while negative affect leads to dislike. Beyond a verbal response indicating attraction, mood also influences interpersonal behavior. Cunningham (1988) used movies and false feedback to cause male research participants to feel

FIGURE 7.6

The Affect-Centered Model of Attraction. In this theoretical model of attraction, affective responses play a central role in determining who is liked or disliked. Positive and negative affect can be aroused directly by the acts of another person (and by that person being associated with some other source of affect), or by that person's words or observable characteristics. In the latter instance, the words or characteristics must be cognitively processed before resulting in an affective response. The cumulative affective response leads to an evaluation of the other person and/or to relevant overt acts.

(*Source:* Based on concepts from Byrne, 1992.)

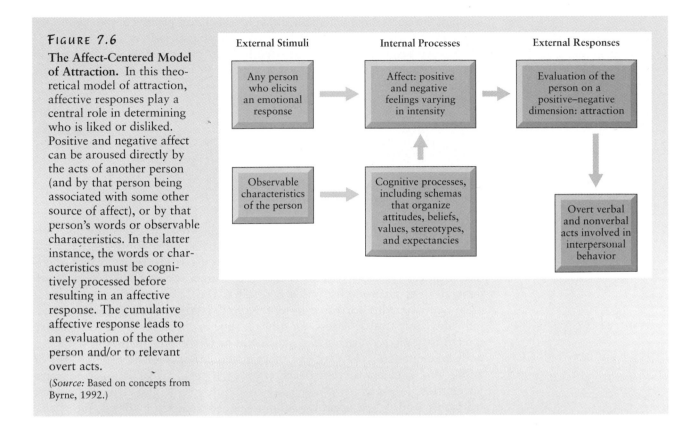

either happy or sad. They then were shown into a waiting room where a female assistant was seated. Males who felt happy communicated more with the assistant and disclosed more about themselves than did those with negative feelings.

The Affect-Centered Model of Attraction. The proposal that attraction is based on affective responses is known as the **affect-centered model of attraction** (Byrne, 1992). The emphasis on affect does not mean, however, that cognitive processes are irrelevant, as shown in Figure 7.6. The top row of boxes illustrates what we have just been discussing. An individual's affective state—whether or not the target person is the direct cause of the affect—has a direct effect on evaluative responses such as attraction and on subsequent interpersonal behavior. In addition, any available information about the target person must be processed, and this information can be affectively arousing, thus contributing to the evaluative response. This cognitive pathway to emotions is involved when the perceiver's schemas include positive, or negative information relevant to another person's attitudes, gender, race, clothing style, sexual orientation, or any other information about him or her.

When you consider the importance of affect and the ease with which it is conditioned to previously neutral targets, you can see that interpersonal behavior is often quite predictable, even though it is not always entirely reasonable. For example, Rozin, Millman, and Nemeroff (1986) point out that even a brief contact between a neutral object and something that arouses affect can transfer the emotional response to the neutral object. In one study of this process, a laundered shirt that had been worn by a disliked person was rated as less desirable than a laundered shirt that had been worn by a liked person.

Affect-Centered Model of Attraction ■ Theoretical model of interpersonal attraction proposing that positive and negative interpersonal evaluations are based on positive versus negative emotions, including emotions elicited by cognitive processes.

Though the shirts did not actually differ, one elicited a positive response and the other a negative response on the basis of learned associations.

Do we respond positively or negatively to other people on the basis of similar associations? As evidence that we do just that, consider the following *Applied Side* section.

Social Psychology: On the Applied Side
STIGMA BY ASSOCIATION

In the 1950s, I was part of a marketing research project in which the goal was to sell a new brand of relatively cheap, sweet wine. Our job was to interview liquor store customers in several large cities to determine their favorite entertainer. Singer Nat King Cole was the clear winner; he was hired to do commercials, and the wine became a best-seller. You have probably witnessed a great many similar efforts to transfer the positive affect associated with a given individual (a popular actress, an athletic star, or an unknown but attractive model) to some product such as sunglasses or to some other person such as a political candidate. You may find these manipulations ridiculously obvious or mildly annoying, but they are clearly effective. If positive reactions can be transferred from person to person, you can be sure that the same is true for negative reactions. And, when negative emotions and dislike are involved, the consequences are more disturbing.

If negative emotions lead us to dislike other people, and if affect is easily associated with any given person, do we also transfer our negative feelings about person A to person B just because we observe them at the same time? For example, if I very much dislike John and see him talking to Bill—someone I barely know—do I then dislike Bill as a consequence? The answer seems to be yes. In this example, my response may be at least partly reasonable. That is, if Bill is friendly with someone as unpleasant as John, we probably wouldn't like each other anyway. But—what if my dislike for John was based on prejudice? What would you think then about my subsequent transfer of negative affect to Bill?

Research on *stigmas* indicates that just such negative associations occur as easily as positive ones. A **stigma** is any characteristic of a person that some observers perceive negatively—race, age, a foreign accent, physical disability, or whatever. As is true of prejudice in general (see Chapter 6), a person perceived as having a stigma tends to elicit a negative stereotype (Frable, 1993). The stigmatized person may even arouse fear or disgust; but at the very least such an individual tends to be disliked and avoided. Even if a stigma is overcome, the negative affect associated with a past stigma does not necessarily go away. For example, Rodin and Price (1995) presented research participants with information about individuals who had removed a stigma (unattractiveness by having plastic surgery, overweight by dieting, loneliness by learning social skills, etc.). Despite the removal of the stigma, a person with a past stigma was viewed as less acceptable than the same individual without such a history. You receive credit for having improved yourself, but you are nevertheless perceived as less acceptable socially. "Once-damaged goods" are less valued than never-damaged goods. A possible implication of such research is that a person who wants to be liked, to be hired for a job, or to win an election would do well *not* to reveal past stigmas. Honesty may be the best policy, but not necessarily the best interpersonal strategy.

Stigma ■ Any characteristics of a person that some observers perceive negatively.

However unjustified it may be to respond negatively to a person on the basis of a stigma, it seems even less justified to respond negatively to someone who is simply associated with that individual. Neuberg and his colleagues (1994) point out that many people are unfairly disliked and avoided (stigmatized) because of their race, physical appearance, and a wide variety of other characteristics, including sexual orientation. Consider the latter characteristic. If someone reacts negatively to (stigmatizes) a man on the basis of his being gay, will there also be a negative reaction to a heterosexual friend of the gay man? Research was designed to answer that question (Neuberg et al., 1994).

The experimenters videotaped a conversation between two men who were friends in real life. They were each above average in attractiveness, physically fit, and casually dressed; they discussed classes, cars, and other common topics. The research participants were male undergraduates who did not know the men on the tape. They were provided with fictional "background information" dealing with each man's supposed grades, majors, hobbies, and so forth. Also, one of men on the tape was described as being active in the Gay Student Association, while the other indicated being romantically involved in a heterosexual relationship. In other conditions, both men were identified as gay or both were identified as heterosexual. After the participants viewed the taped conversation, they indicated how much they liked each of the two men and judged each one on several personality traits.

The male undergraduates responded negatively to the gay target *and* also to the heterosexual target if he was conversing with a gay friend. Thus, there was strong evidence for a transfer of affect and evaluation from the stigmatized target to the neutral one—"stigma by association." Based on this finding, do you think a political candidate would lose votes if he or she reported having a homosexual friend? President Bill Clinton's poll ratings declined when he tried to remove the ban on homosexuals in the military. In our daily lives, each of us could benefit from being more aware of the basis for our interpersonal evaluations and more cautious about our judgments. ■ ■ ■

INTEGRATING PRINCIPLES

1. Repeated contacts between any two strangers are facilitated by the arrangement of their physical surroundings, and the repeated exposure that occurs in these contacts most often results in positive affect and thus in positive evaluations (Chapter 3).

2. Attraction (as well as other evaluations) is influenced by affect, whether the positive and negative emotions are directly aroused by the target person or simply associated with the target. Affect also is a crucial factor in attitude formation (Chapter 4), prejudice (Chapter 6), love (Chapter 8), and decisions made in the courtroom (Chapter 13).

Becoming Acquainted: Needing to Affiliate and Responding to Observable Characteristics

Once two people come into contact and experience relatively positive affective responses, they are at a transition point. They may remain *superficial acquain-*

tances who nod and say a word or two whenever they happen to see one another. A second possibility is that they may begin to talk, learn each other's names, and exchange bits and pieces of information; that is, they can become *close acquaintances.* Which alternative occurs depends on two factors—the extent to which each individual is motivated by *affiliation need,* and how each reacts to the *observable characteristics* of the other.

The Need to Affiliate: Dispositional Differences and External Events

Most of us spend a large portion of our free time interacting with other people, perhaps because such affiliation improved the chances of survival for our prehistoric ancestors (Wright, 1984). People differ in the strength of this **need for affiliation**; such differences constitute a relatively stable affiliative *trait* or *disposition.* Those whose affiliative needs are weak often prefer being alone, while those with strong needs interact with other people whenever possible. The stronger the need, the more likely people are to make an effort to become closely acquainted with those they meet. In addition to individual differences in affiliation motivation, specific situations can also affect the strength of this motive; such influences arouse a relatively temporary affiliative *state.* We will describe the effects of both types of affiliation need.

Affiliation Need As a Trait. Beginning with the pioneering work of Murray (1938), psychologists have measured the affiliative trait or disposition by constructing one of two types of personality test. Self-report questionnaires ask about relevant desires and activities directly, measuring the self-attributed (or explicit) motivation to affiliate. To measure unconscious (or implicit) motives, researchers analyze the stories people write in response to pictures (Craig, Koestner, & Zuroff, 1994). Explicit and implicit affiliation needs represent different aspects of this disposition and result in different behaviors. For example, Craig and her colleagues (1994) used both types of measures with college students who had been asked to maintain a record of their social interactions for a week. Those with high explicit affiliative motivation were very sociable and interacted with many people, while those with high implicit motivation were more likely to interact in two-person situations involving close relationships. It seems that we can meet affiliation needs by having many friendly interpersonal contacts or a few, very close ones.

It also appears that different people have different reasons to want to affiliate. Hill (1987) has proposed four basic motives. Two of these resemble the explicit and implicit motives that were just described: people may want to be with others to have interesting, lively interactions (*positive stimulation*) or to have companionship when problems arise (*emotional support*). In addition, affiliation can be motivated by the desire to reduce uncomfortable feelings of uncertainty about what is going on (*social comparison*) or to receive praise and attention (*attention*). Table 7.2 describes these four somewhat different motives to affiliate.

Affiliation Need As a State. External events can also arouse affiliation needs. On November 3, 1994, President Clinton came to our Albany campus. For security reasons, the exact times and travel routes were kept secret. That day, most of the students, faculty, and staff went from place to place on the campus trying to get a glimpse of our visitor. Rumors and inside tips were plentiful and often wrong. Strangers talked to strangers, including police officers and newspeople from the local TV stations. After several fruitless hours, I had almost

Need for Affiliation ■ The motive to seek interpersonal relationships.

TABLE 7.2 Four Different Types of Affiliation Need

Four different types of motivation to affiliate have been identified, as indicated here. Also shown are sample items from a test designed to measure them and a typical college situation in which specific needs might arise.

Type of Affiliation Need

Positive Stimulation

Sample Test Item	Just being around others and finding out about them is one of the most interesting things I can think of doing.
Typical Situation	After several hours of studying in the library.

Emotional Support

Sample Test Item	One of my greatest sources of comfort when things get rough is being with other people.
Typical Situation	After receiving a very low grade on an exam.

Social Comparison

Sample Test Item	When I am not certain about how well I am doing at something, I usually like to be around others so I can compare myself to them.
Typical Situation	When class papers are returned to students.

Attention

Sample Test Item	I like to be around people when I can be the center of attention.
Typical Situation	When the opportunity arises to make the class laugh.

(*Source:* Based on information from Hill, 1987.)

given up, when my twelve-year-old daughter and I passed Senator Moynihan on the sidewalk. I asked him if the president had left. He indicated that the presidential limousine would be passing by in a few minutes. The senator was right, and we got a quick glimpse and a wave as Clinton rode past. Without the unusual circumstances, few of us would have talked to strangers, much less to a U.S. senator. How common is such an experience?

Newspaper stories quite often describe situations in which strangers are brought together by out-of-the-ordinary occurrences, including natural disasters such as a flood or forest fire or a special public celebration such as Mardi Gras or Woodstock II (Byrne, 1991). Humphriss (1989) described the aftereffects of a California earthquake—a dreadful destruction of property that led neighbors to unite in an unusually friendly atmosphere. Even in New York, when a blizzard left commuters and tourists no way to get out of the city, the stranded individuals "swapped life stories and passed around pictures of their children as snow swirled down upon the metropolitan area" (Daley, 1983, p. 1). These special occurrences somehow bring people together.

The psychological basis of these affiliative reactions was first identified by Schachter (1959) in his investigations of the effect of fear on affiliation. Some participants in an experiment were led to expect painful electric shocks, while others expected to receive only mild, tickling electrical stimulation. While waiting for the experiment to begin, many of those expecting pain preferred to spend the time with other participants, while those expecting a nonpainful experience wanted to wait alone or had no preference. Presumably, affiliation need is aroused by this laboratory manipulation, and by real-life events, because people seek out other people—even strangers—in order to talk about what is going on, to compare perceptions, and to decide what to do next.

This kind of interpersonal behavior is one example of how *social comparison* processes operate—remember that "social comparison" was the name given to one of the four types of affiliation motives. This term refers to our tendency to evaluate what we think and do by comparing our reactions with those of others, thus reducing negative feelings of uncertainty and anxiety. In our everyday lives, with familiar occurrences, we don't feel uncertain and anxious and therefore have no special reason to interact with strangers. With unexpected and unusual events, however, we usually are puzzled and often worried about what is going on. We feel better if we can affiliate and discover how others perceive what is happening. The origin of the concept of social comparison is outlined in the following *Cornerstones* section.

Cornerstones of Social Psychology
FESTINGER'S SOCIAL COMPARISON THEORY

Leon Festinger is probably best known for proposing the theory of cognitive dissonance (discussed in Chapters 1 and 4), but his **social comparison theory** was equally creative and influential. We will summarize the portion of this theory that has had the greatest effect on attraction research.

An early version of his formulation (Festinger, 1950) dealt with how group members alter their opinions in response to the opinions of others in the group. Festinger's more general theory of social comparison (1954) expanded these earlier ideas to include abilities, and he proposed additional theoretical implications.

Festinger first hypothesized that each human being has a drive to evaluate his or her opinions and abilities. Behavior is affected by a person's cognitions concerning the situation and by his or her capacity to deal with that situation. These cognitions include opinions and self-perceived abilities (you might recognize a hint of the concept of self-efficacy here). If the opinions are incorrect or if the abilities are misjudged, the result can be punishing or even fatal. For example, if you mistakenly believe that wearing blue jeans and a sweatshirt to a job interview at a bank is acceptable, you are unlikely to be hired. If you overestimate your ability at mountain climbing, you may be seriously injured—or worse. To avoid negative outcomes, we want to make accurate self-evaluations.

The problem is *how* to make such evaluations. Festinger hypothesized that we will turn to objective criteria whenever possible. For example, if you believe a meter is longer than a yard (or vice versa), you can either look in a table showing metric and English equivalents for linear measures or simply place a yardstick next to a meter stick and see which one is longer. If you believe that you can run a mile in four minutes, you can try it and find out. But when an objective approach is not possible—and it very often is not—the theory's second hypothesis states that people evaluate their opinions and abilities by comparing them with the opinions and abilities of others. For example, there is no objective physical test to determine which political candidate will be a better president or whether you have the talent to become a concert pianist. The best any of us can do when objective criteria are not available is to compare ourselves with others. That is, we make social comparisons.

Social Comparison Theory ■
Festinger's influential theory of our tendency to evaluate our opinions and abilities based on comparison with other people and our preference for making comparisons with others similar to ourselves.

Leon Festinger. Leon Festinger (1919–1989) was born in New York City, and his distinguished career as a social psychologist included work on friendship formation in married student housing, social comparison processes, cognitive dissonance, and perception. In informal contacts at Stanford and Texas, I (DB) found him to be a consistently creative, challenging, and amusing colleague.

Festinger's third hypothesis states that we prefer to make comparisons with others who are similar to ourselves. You cannot evaluate yourself very accurately if you compare yourself with someone who is very different. For example, if you were leaning toward the moderate Republican candidate in the next presidential election, you wouldn't try to evaluate your judgment by discussing the matter with a terrorist or with a neo-Nazi (unless you, by chance, are a terrorist or a neo-Nazi). In a similar way, you could not determine your musical ability by comparing your piano skills with those of a toddler banging on the keys or with a professional pianist. Your best bet is to make comparisons with someone pretty much like yourself.

These three hypotheses, as well as additional ones in the theory, have been extremely important in the study of interpersonal attraction. In investigations of situational effects on affiliation, for example, people are found to seek out similar others when unexpected situations arise in order to compare what they think is happening and what should be done (Morris et al., 1976). In general, an individual prefers the company of a similar person, whether as a friend, coworker, or spouse; later in this chapter and in Chapter 8, we will provide evidence supporting this prediction. Beyond attraction and close relationships, this cornerstone theory makes equally useful predictions about conformity pressures, attempts to persuade others to change their opinions, self-efficacy, hostility toward those whose opinions differ greatly from the norm, and the tendency to divide society into subgroups consisting only of similar people. ■ ■ ■

Responding to Observable Characteristics

When we like—or dislike—someone at first sight, it probably means that our response is based on something we observe about that person that may or may not provide accurate information about him or her. For example, if a stranger resembles someone we have known, the positive or negative characteristics of the person we know tend to be transferred to the new person (Andersen & Baum, 1994). However different the new person may be from the one in our past, our evaluations are strongly affected by this association.

As described earlier in this chapter and in Chapter 6, stereotypes are poor predictors of behavior, but we very often react to other people on the basis of incorrect beliefs stemming from their superficial characteristics. The characteristic most studied has been physical attractiveness (Albright, Kenny, & Malloy, 1988).

Physical Attractiveness: A Major Determinant of Liking. Despite much cultural wisdom telling us that "beauty is only skin deep" and "you can't judge a book by its cover," people respond strongly to the **physical attractiveness,** or aesthetically appealing outward appearance, of others (Collins & Zebrowitz, 1995; Hatfield & Sprecher, 1986); this is especially true when a person tries to judge someone's desirability as a date (Sprecher & Duck, 1994). Sometimes attractiveness can outweigh other considerations. For example, in an experiment undergraduate men were sufficiently eager to be liked by an attractive female stranger that they tried to ingratiate themselves by expressing false attitudes in order to agree with her; in response to an unattractive woman, they did the opposite and expressed false disagreements (Plesser-Storr, 1995). Men and women differ to some degree; men are affected more by female attractiveness than women are by male attractiveness (Feingold, 1990; Pierce, 1992).

Why should physical attractiveness lead to attraction? According to the affect-centered model described earlier, good-looking individuals arouse positive affect (Kenrick et al., 1993), and we have seen that affect is an all-important determinant of attraction. A possible explanation as to why men overemphasize female attractiveness is provided by evolutionary theory. In responding to the op-

Physical Attractiveness ■ Combination of facial and bodily characteristics perceived as aesthetically appealing (for example, beautiful or handsome) by others.

posite sex, men have been reproductively successful most often when they have favored females whose appearance was associated with youth and fertility. More specifically, Singh (1993) presents evidence that men respond to a woman's waist-to-hip ratio. The lower a woman's ratio (the more small-waisted she is, in other words), the more men prefer her and rate her as attractive, healthy, and reproductively valuable. Women, in contrast, have been more reproductively successful when they have reacted positively to a male's character and abilities more than to his looks; because such a mate can provide resources and protection for a woman and her offspring (Kenrick et al., 1994), as discussed in Chapter 1.

Reactions to various observable characteristics are based on learned stereotypes, and attractiveness is no exception (Calvert, 1988). Research findings show that people tend to believe that attractive men and women are also more poised, interesting, sociable, independent, dominant, exciting, sexy, well adjusted, socially skilled, and successful than those who are unattractive (Dion & Dion, 1987; Moore, Graziano, & Miller, 1987). Handsome men are perceived as more masculine and beautiful women as more feminine than their less attractive counterparts (Gillen, 1981). Attractiveness even affects judgments about a stranger who is HIV-positive; attractive individuals are assumed to have contracted the infection in a heterosexual relationship, while unattractive ones are assumed to have acquired the virus in a homosexual relationship or through sharing a needle (Agnew & Thompson, 1994). Essays identified as the work of attractive students are evaluated more positively than those whose authors were identified as unattractive (Cash & Trimer, 1984). Attractiveness among adults aged sixty to ninety-three is also assumed to indicate positive personality traits (Johnson & Pittenger, 1984). Altogether, as social psychologists discovered more than two decades ago, people assume that "what is beautiful is good" (Dion, Berscheid, & Hatfield, 1972).

Most of the stereotypes based on appearance are quite wrong (Feingold, 1992; Kenealy et al., 1991). The only characteristics actually associated with attractiveness are those related to popularity (Johnstone, Frame, & Bouman, 1992; Reis, Nezlek, & Wheeler, 1989) and good interpersonal skills (O'Grady, 1989). Further, the more positive a person's self-rating of attractiveness, the stronger his or her feelings of subjective well-being (Diener, Wolsic, & Fujita, 1995). Presumably, these differences based on appearance develop primarily because attractive individuals are liked and treated nicely by others from their earliest years, while those who are unattractive receive less-favorable treatment.

Though most of the attractiveness studies have concentrated on adolescents and young adults in the context of dating, elderly men respond to the attractiveness of young women just as young men do (Singh, 1993). And attractive babies are assumed to have more positive characteristics (such as sociability and competence) than unattractive ones (Karraker & Stern, 1990).

More surprising than adult reactions to attractive infants is the fact that infants respond to the attractiveness of adults. Langlois, Roggman, and Rieser-Danner (1990) conducted an experiment in which an attractive or unattractive female assistant interacted briefly with a series of twelve-month-olds. In a very carefully conducted study, the researchers varied the stranger's attractiveness by having the same person wear either an attractive or unattractive theatrical mask molded to her face. To guard against the possibility that she might behave differently depending on her appearance, the experimenters did not tell the assistant which mask was being applied for each experimental session. She then entered the room where a baby was with its mother, talking briefly to the mother and then to the infant. She picked the child up and played with some of the nearby toys. These very young boys and girls responded quite differently to the attractive versus the unattractive stranger, as you can see in Figure 7.7. As rated by observers, the infants expressed more positive affect and were more involved

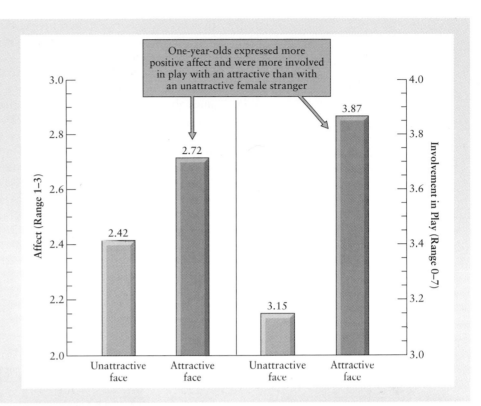

FIGURE 7.7

Attractiveness: Infants' Responses to Adult's Appearance. The physical attractiveness of an adult female stranger affected how infants reacted to her. One-year-olds expressed more positive affect and became more involved in playing with the stranger when she wore an attractive mask than when she wore an unattractive mask. The positive response to physical attractiveness clearly begins very early.

(*Source:* Based on data from Langlois, Roggman, & Rieser-Danner, 1990.)

in their play activity (accepting an offered toy, vocalizing) when the woman wore the attractive mask than when she wore the unattractive one. Additional research (Langlois et al., 1991) found that infants prefer attractive to unattractive adults regardless of the adult's gender, race, or age. Even when the stimulus is a doll, children spend more play time with attractive than with unattractive ones.

People are not at all accurate in estimating their own attractiveness as judged by others, and men (but not women) overestimate how good they look (Gabriel, Critelli, & Ee, 1994). Because of the many biases favoring attractiveness, it is not surprising that many people worry about their appearance. This concern about one's attractiveness and fear of negative judgments by others is known as **appearance anxiety.** Dion, Dion, and Keelan (1990) designed a test to measure appearance anxiety, using items such as "I enjoy looking at myself in the mirror" (answered false) and "I feel that most of my friends are more physically attractive than myself" (answered true). Women score higher on appearance anxiety than men. For both genders, the higher the score on this measure, the greater the person's social anxiety, the fewer dates he or she has, and the more discomfort in interpersonal interactions (K. L. Dion, personal communication, March 1993).

Despite the overwhelmingly positive effects of being attractive, a few negative attributes are also associated with good looks. For example, beautiful women are often perceived as vain and materialistic (Cash & Duncan, 1984). Though attractive male political candidates receive more votes than unattractive ones, beauty is not helpful to female candidates (Sigelman et al., 1986), possibly because an elected official who is "too feminine" is assumed to be ineffective.

Searching for the Physical Details that Constitute Attractiveness. Research shows that people tend to agree extremely well about who is or is not attractive, even across racial and ethnic lines and with respect to targets whose race

Appearance Anxiety ■ Apprehension or worry about the adequacy of one's physical appearance and about how others evaluate it.

or ethnicity matches or does not match the participants' own (Cunningham et al., 1995). Nevertheless, it is difficult to identify the precise cues that determine judgments of relative attractiveness.

One approach is to identify individuals who are perceived by others as attractive and then determine what these attractive people have in common. For example, Cunningham (1986) asked male college students to look at photographs of young women and rate their attractiveness. The "most attractive" pictures were of women who had either childlike features (large, widely spaced eyes and a small nose and chin) or "mature" features (prominent cheekbones, narrow cheeks, high eyebrows, large pupils, and a big smile), as shown in Figure 7.8. These same two facial types were perceived as equally attractive among white, African American, and Asian women. Another finding is that women with the childlike features are stereotyped as "cute" (McKelvie, 1993a).

Langlois and Roggman (1990) took a very different approach to determine what is meant by attractiveness. They began with photographs of faces, then produced computer-generated pictures that combined several faces into one. That is, the image in each photo was transformed into a series of numbers representing shades of gray, the numbers were averaged across the group of pic-

FIGURE 7.8

Women's Faces Rated Most Attractive by Men. When male undergraduates examined pictures of young women and rated their attractiveness, two distinct types were identified. Women with "childlike" or "mature" features were the ones rated most attractive.

tures, and the result was translated back into a photo. The process is shown in Figure 7.9. For both men and women, a composite face was rated as more attractive than most of the individual faces that went into making it. Further, the more faces that were used to make the composite, the more attractive the result. These investigators concluded that, for most people, an attractive face is simply one whose components represent the arithmetic mean of the details of many faces (Langlois, Roggman, & Musselman, 1994). Why? Because the average of multiple individual faces is perceived as more *familiar* than any of the actual faces, the investigators assume that they are *representative* of the total sample of faces. Even though we don't ordinarily see a truly average face (or an average apple or an average anything), our experiences lead us to define what we mean by "face" by using an informal averaging process; that is, we construct a mental prototype from our many experiences with faces. This cognitive construction—a schema for the concept of face—makes it possible to process a face

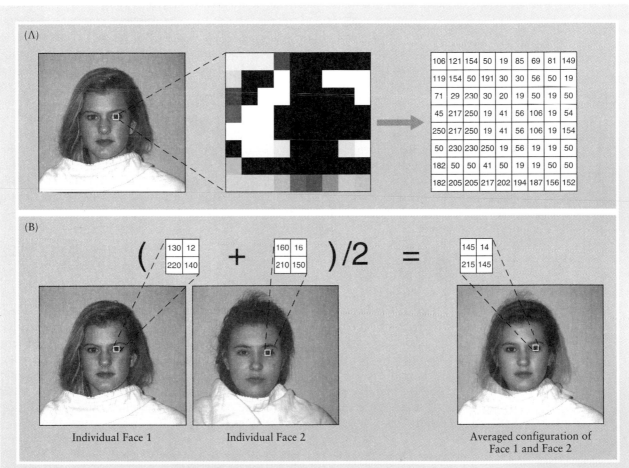

Figure 7.9

Digitizing and Averaging Faces. In research on attractiveness, a black-and-white photograph of a face is transformed into a series of numbers that represent shades of gray or *gray-values*, a process known as *digitizing*, shown in A. These gray-values from different faces can then be averaged and the result turned back into a photograph, as shown in B. An averaged face is perceived as more "familiar" and more attractive than the individual faces that go into it. Further, the more faces that are combined, the more attractive the resulting face; quite possibly it becomes more and more typical so that it resembles one's schema for the concept "face."

(*Source:* Langlois, Roggman, & Musselman, 1994).

easily and readily whenever we encounter one. The computer-average faces presented in the experiment resemble one's own cognitive schema for what is meant by "face," and that is why they are familiar. And, as in the proximity studies, that which is familiar elicits a positive response.

Situational Effects on Perceived Attractiveness. Judgments of attractiveness are not entirely a matter of the physical details of the target person. Also important are situational factors that influence the viewer. In many studies of attractiveness, a research participant simply responds to one stranger and judges his or her attractiveness. What if, just before viewing an individual of ordinary attractiveness, the participant had looked at several other extremely attractive individuals? Kenrick and his colleagues (1993) found that in that situation the target person is rated as *less* attractive. The difference between the target and the comparison others changes how the target is perceived—there is a "contrast effect." This effect generalizes beyond the experimental situation; when men view photographs of very attractive women, they also report being less attracted to their own romantic partners (Kenrick & Gutierres, 1980).

Attractiveness ratings are also affected by the opinions of same-sex peers, at least for women. Graziano and his colleagues (1993) asked male and female undergraduates to rate—in private—the attractiveness of opposite-sex individuals based on their yearbook photographs. Each photo was accompanied either by information that same-sex peers of the participants had rated the person in the photo as relatively attractive or relatively unattractive, or by no information about peer ratings. Women's ratings of men were influenced by what they believed to be the opinions of other women, but men ignored the opinions of other men when they rated women. Among several possible explanations, the investigators proposed that when men evaluate women, they simply respond to physical cues of maximum fertility, and they don't care what others think. Women rating men, in contrast, are looking for cues as to male resources and reliability; because there is not much to go on in yearbook photos, they are receptive to additional information and opinions from other women.

A different sort of situational effect was suggested by the Mickey Gilley song in which he tell us that in bars "the girls all get prettier at closing time." Social psychological research has confirmed such an effect and extended it to boys as well (Nida & Koon, 1983; Pennebaker et al., 1979). In one study conducted at a college bar at night, Gladue and Delaney (1990) asked the patrons to rate same- and opposite-sex fellow drinkers at 9:00, 10:30, and midnight. Those of the opposite sex were rated as being increasingly attractive as closing time approached. Because those of the same sex were not rated as more attractive later in the evening, the results don't seem to be based on a warm alcoholic glow. Instead, the effect is believed to occur because the number of unattached potential partners decreases over the course of the evening, and the resulting scarcity leads to more positive evaluations.

Other Observable Cues That Influence Attraction. In addition to general attractiveness, several other observable cues elicit stereotypes and emotional responses, which can result in instant likes and dislikes based on superficial factors.

One physical characteristic to which people respond is physique. Both men and women stereotype strangers on the basis of their bodily shape. A once-popular theory proposed that personality traits are associated with physique, or *somatotype.* Sheldon, Stevens, and Tucker (1940) classified people into three categories: *endomorphs,* who are round and fat; *mesomorphs,* who are muscular; and *ectomorphs,* who are thin and angular. Ryckman and his colleagues

(1989) asked students to describe strangers differing in these somatotypes. The participants were in fairly good agreement. Endomorphs were perceived as ugly, sloppy, sad, dirty, and slow. Mesomorphs were described as not very smart or kind, but as popular, healthy, brave, and attractive. Ectomorphs were seen as average on most traits, but as more fearful, intelligent, and neat than nonectomorphs. Stereotypes about physique seem to develop in childhood. Brylinsky and Moore (1994) found, for example, that negative reactions to a chubby body build first appear between the first and second grade.

Examining physique stereotypes in still greater detail, Ryckman and his colleagues (1995) found subtypes within each somatotype that are perceived somewhat differently. Among endomorphs, for example, there are very favorable responses to endomorphic clowns, housewives, motherly figures, and Santa Claus. For mesomorphs, very positive reactions were elicited by female athletes; male athletes received mixed ratings, as did jocks, bodybuilders, and studs. Negative ratings were given to mesomorphic males in the subtypes identified as steroid users, bullies, and showoffs. Among ectomorphs, male scholars were perceived favorably, "brains" and fashion models elicited mixed ratings, and very unfavorable ratings were given to males who were ectomorphic because of AIDS.

When you read about these various findings, keep in mind that somatotype research has *not* found that fat people are sloppy, muscular people stupid, thin people fearful, and so on—these are mere stereotypes.

Using the kind of computer simulation described earlier in the study of physical attractiveness, Gardner and Tockerman (1994) created different somatotypes for each of several male and female target persons, as illustrated in Figure 7.10. The actual target persons were of normal weight, average physical attractiveness, and in their mid-twenties. Undergraduates rated the depicted strangers on a series of personality traits, and typically differentiated the endomorphic images from the other two. That is, the stranger whose image had been made to appear overweight was perceived as less sincere, honest, intelligent, friendly, humorous, pleasant, ambitious, talented, neat, and so on—and as more aggressive, lonely, envious, obnoxious, and cruel—than the same stranger shown either normally or as an ectomorph.

FIGURE 7.10

Creating Different Somatotypes for the Same Individual. When researchers distorted the same person's image on video to create a narrow and a wide version, more negative personality characteristics were attributed to the image of the wide individual than to the other two. As in other studies, observers' evaluations were affected by a stranger's physique.

(*Source:* Gardner & Tockerman, 1994.)

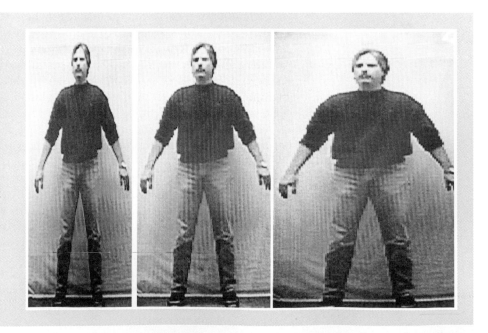

TABLE 7.3   Antifat Prejudice

A negative reaction to people who are overweight is very much like racial prejudice—a negative attitude based on stereotypes. Shown here are sample items from the Antifat Attitudes Questionnaire.

Type of Antifat Attitude	Sample Test Item
Dislike	I really don't like fat people much.
	If I were an employer looking to hire, I might avoid hiring a fat person.
Fear of Fat	I feel disgusted with myself when I gain weight.
	I worry about becoming fat.
Willpower	People who weigh too much could lose some part of their weight through a little exercise.
	Fat people tend to be fat pretty much through their own fault.

(*Source:* Based on information from Crandall, 1994.)

Clearly, in terms of personality traits, the least valued somatotype includes excess body fat. It comes as no surprise, then, that people who are overweight are generally perceived as less attractive (Harris, Harris, & Bochner, 1982; Larkin & Pines, 1982). As in the somatotype experiment just described, when subjects are rating the attractiveness of fat, thin, and actual versions of the same stimulus person, the overweight version is rated lowest (Lundberg & Sheehan, 1994).

Negative evaluations of attractiveness are often followed by social rejection. Crandall (1994) compares the prejudice against fat people to racial prejudice and has developed a measure of antifat attitudes, shown in Table 7.3. The rejection indicated by such attitudes not unreasonably causes the overweight individual to experience social anxiety and to develop low self-esteem. Could these reactions, in turn, have secondary negative effects, in that the obese person would be at a disadvantage in learning how to deal with social situations? Miller and her colleagues (1990) examined this question by having obese and nonobese college women engage in telephone conversations with students who did not know anything about their appearance or their weight. Presumably because of differences in past social experiences, the obese women were judged—sight unseen—as less likable, less socially skilled, and less attractive than those who were not overweight.

Follow-up research indicates, however, that obese women often do develop strong social skills and overcome the prejudices of others (Miller et al., 1995). When obese and nonobese women were compared, obesity was *unrelated* to social anxiety, social competence, or the size of an individual's social networks—as reported either by the women themselves or by their friends and coworkers.

Adults who look or sound very young are also perceived in stereotypic ways. They are judged to be weak, naive, and incompetent, but warm and honest (Berry & Brownlow, 1989; Berry & Zebrowitz-McArthur, 1988). Those who sound very "mature" are perceived as more dominant and attractive but less warm and agreeable (Zuckerman, Miyake, & Elkin, 1995). No matter how inaccurate most such assumptions about observable characteristics may be as cues to personality, they nevertheless influence first impressions, affective responses, and interpersonal attraction.

Behavioral cues also affect perceptions. People react more positively to a person whose walking style is youthful than to one whose gait seems elderly, regardless of the individual's gender or actual age (Montepare & Zebrowitz-McArthur, 1988). An individual who expresses emotions openly and acts in an extraverted way creates a positive first impression (Friedman, Riggio, & Casella, 1988).

Some research has found men with a dominant style—gesturing, authoritative, competitive—to be preferred to men who behave submissively—looking downward, nodding in agreement, and engaging in sports just for fun (Sadalla, Kenrick, & Vershure, 1987). More recently, however, male dominance seemed to have no effect on attraction (Jensen-Campbell, West, & Graziano, 1995); instead, women reported a preference for men with prosocial tendencies. It seems possible that with limited information, a man who fits a traditional masculine role is liked better than a less masculine man. When women have additional information, however, they place greater weight on niceness and sensitivity. A similar explanation could be applied to a finding that competitive men are liked better than noncompetitive men (Riskind & Wilson, 1982). When Morey and Gerber (1995) also provided information about the kind of competitiveness, a more complex picture emerged. Both men and women are liked if they express *goal competitiveness*—doing their best to win and attain a goal—but not if they express *interpersonal competitiveness*—trying to do better than others in order to beat them.

Stereotypes are also associated with specific visible characteristics of a person such as clothing (Cahoon & Edmonds, 1989), grooming (Mack & Rainey, 1990), height (Pierce, 1992), disabilities (Fichten & Amsel, 1986), age (McKelvie, 1993b; Perdue & Gurtman, 1990), and many other things as well. Interpersonal judgments are even influenced by what a person eats (Stein & Nemeroff, 1995). With all other background data the same (weight, height, physical fitness, etc.), research participants received information about a man or a woman who supposedly ate either "good food" (such as oranges, salad, whole-wheat bread, and chicken) or "bad food" (such as steak, hamburgers, French fries, doughnuts, and double-fudge sundaes). The participants rated the "good food" eaters as morally superior, more attractive, more likable, more feminine, and less masculine that the "bad food" eaters. The students who took part in this research seem to have accepted wholeheartedly the adage, "You are what you eat."

Another example of the effect of an observable cue on evaluative judgments is provided by the much studied effect of eyeglasses (Terry & Macy, 1991). When the same stimulus persons are presented wearing or not wearing glasses, both men and women are perceived as more attractive without than with them (Hasart & Hutchinson, 1993). Though some past research has indicated that a person wearing glasses is perceived to be intelligent (Edwards, 1987; Harris, Harris, & Bochner, 1982), Lundberg and Sheehan (1994) provide evidence that this particular stereotype seems to be fading away.

One final, and perhaps most surprising, aspect of a stranger that elicits positive and negative stereotypes is that person's first name. For example, Mehrabian and Piercy (1993a) found that a man with a nickname such as Bill is perceived as more cheerful and popular, though less successful and moral, than a man with the given name of William, in part because longer names are perceived differently than shorter ones. These researchers next investigated other personality characteristics that are assumed by college students to be associated with specific male and female names (Mehrabian & Piercy, 1993b). Some of that study's findings are summarized in Table 7.4. Name length again played some role in determining how men (but not women) were perceived.

Table 7.4 Personality Characteristics Attributed to Men and Women
on the Basis of Their First Names

*One of many observable characteristics to which others respond is a
person's first name. As a result, one element determining first impressions
is the name your parents gave you. Once again, stereotypes seem to
operate.*

Attributions	Male Names	Female Names
Successful	Alexander	Elizabeth
Unsuccessful	Otis	Mildred
Moral	Joshua	Mary
Immoral	Roscoe	Tracy
Popular	Mark	Jessica
Unpopular	Norbert	Harriet
Warm	Henry	Ann
Cold	Ogden	Freida
Cheerful	Scott	Brittany
Not Cheerful	Willard	Agatha
Masculine	Taylor	Rosalyn
Feminine	Eugene	Isabella

(*Source:* Based on information from Mehrabian & Piercy, 1993b.)

INTEGRATING PRINCIPLES

1. People differ in their motivation to affiliate with others because of trait differences and because of state differences based on the situation. As predicted by social comparison theory, people affiliate in arousing, confusing situations in order to evaluate their perceptions and judgments. Social comparison also plays a key role in social influence (Chapter 9) and among bystanders who witness an emergency (Chapter 10), as well as in other contexts.

2. First impressions of others are determined in part by stereotypes that are associated with observable characteristics (see Chapter 2). These stereotypes elicit positive or negative affect and hence result in liking or in dislike. Stereotypes are also important in understanding prejudice (Chapter 6), romantic relationships (Chapter 8), and courtroom decisions (Chapter 13).

Similarity and Reciprocal Positive Evaluations: Becoming Close Acquaintances and Moving toward Friendship

So far we have learned that once two people are brought together by physical proximity or any other means, the probability of their liking each other and establishing a relationship is greatest if each (1) is in a positive emotional state, (2) is strongly motivated to affiliate, and (3) responds positively to the appearance and other observable characteristics of the other. The next steps involve communication, in which the two people seek areas of *similarity* and indications of *mutually positive evaluations*.

Similarity: Birds of a Feather Really Do Flock Together

More than two thousand years ago, Aristotle wrote about the characteristics of friendship. Among other things, he hypothesized that people who agree with one another become friends, while those who disagree do not. Throughout the twentieth century, social psychological research has consistently confirmed this ancient prediction. A friendly relationship is often based on the discovery of **attitude similarity.** As we will show shortly, the importance of similarity to attraction goes far beyond attitudes. In the words of radio "shock jock" Howard Stern, "If you're not like me, I hate you" (Zoglin, 1993).

Attraction and Attitude Similarity. The proposed association between attitude similarity and attraction was first documented in correlational studies. For example, Schuster and Elderton (1906) studied over more than four hundred families and reported significant agreement between spouses about such topics as politics and religion. Many such studies were conducted during the early 1900s; pairs of friends as well as married couples were found to express greater than chance similarity of attitudes, beliefs, values, and interests. Most of these studies, however, acknowledged uncertainty about cause and effect. That is, these findings could mean that similarity leads to attraction, or that two people were attracted for various other reasons but then developed similar attitudes as they spent time together. One approach to clarifying that issue is described in the following *Cornerstones* section.

Cornerstones of Social Psychology
NEWCOMB AND THE EFFECT OF SIMILARITY ON ATTRACTION

Theodore (Ted) Newcomb actively investigated many aspects of social behavior; in one well-known investigation, for example, he studied the effect of a liberal college on the political attitudes of students from conservative families. He nevertheless maintained a lifelong interest in attraction. Newcomb and Svehla (1937) examined the similarity–attraction relationship in a study of almost two hundred married couples, reporting the usual substantial similarity between husbands and wives in their attitudes about church, war, and Communism. To get at the question of causality, the investigators then turned to a separate group of younger couples who had been married for a relatively short period of time. Their attitudinal similarity was as great as that of the older couples, even though the older pairs had been together for many more years. These findings suggest that attitude similarity was present from the beginning of the relationship rather than developing after a long period of togetherness. The issue was not conclusively settled, however, until Newcomb undertook additional research in the second half of this century.

In 1956 Newcomb was able to conduct a much needed longitudinal investigation. He reasoned that if attitudes were measured before people had even met one

---

Attitude Similarity ■ The extent to which two individuals share the same attitudes about a series of topics.

Theodore M. Newcomb. Ted Newcomb (1903–1984) was born in Ohio, and conducted early work on political attitudes at Bennington College. During his long career he developed *balance theory,* and his work on interpersonal relationships was a strong influence on the field. While in graduate school, I (DB) read Newcomb's American Psychological Association presidential address on attraction. It was interesting, but when he described similar attitudes as "reinforcing," a guiding formulation for my future research was instantly created. I later felt quite fortunate to meet and interact with someone whose research strongly influenced my career.

Proportion of Similar Attitudes ■ The number of topics on which two individuals hold the same views in relation to the total number of topics on which they compare their views, expressed as a percentage or proportion.

---

another, the finding of a subsequent relationship between similarity and attraction would clearly indicate that similar attitudes *were responsible* for attraction.

His research participants consisted of two different samples of seventeen male transfer students who entered the University of Michigan in two consecutive years. These men were given a rent-free semester in a cooperative housing unit in return for taking part in the research. Attitudes about such issues as sex and the family, religion, public affairs, and race relations were assessed by mail before the students reached the campus and had an opportunity to meet. Once they arrived at the housing unit, each student's attraction toward the other sixteen students was determined weekly.

Attitude similarity did *not* predict the initial attraction between pairs, of course, because the students had no way to know one another's attitudes until they interacted over time. Other determinants of attraction, such as proximity, determined mutual liking fairly quickly. Before the end of fifteen weeks of living together in the same housing unit, however, similarity began to influence attraction: the more agreements about important issues existed between two individuals, the more they liked each other.

For the first time, then, it was clearly established that attraction between two people is based, at least in part, on the attitudes they hold at the time they meet. Newcomb explained the relationship between attraction and similarity in terms of *balance theory*—which will be discussed shortly. Beyond research testing the implications of that theory, Newcomb's work also aroused considerable interest in the effect of attitude similarity on attraction. Attraction research has expanded far beyond simple questions about similar attitudes, but Newcomb's interests served as an important catalyst to today's efforts. ■ ■ ■

Numerous experiments conducted in the 1950s and 1960s added further support to Newcomb's conclusion that similar attitudes lead to attraction. For example, a research participant learns about the attitudes of a stranger (either a real person, an experimental assistant, or a nonexistent person who has supposedly responded to an attitude scale) and then indicates his or her attraction toward that stranger. The greater the similarity, the greater the attraction (e.g., Byrne, 1961b; Schachter, 1951; Smith, 1957).

What is involved in this similarity effect? When people interact, various topics are likely to come up (school, work, music, television, politics, or whatever), and each person is very likely to express his or her likes and dislikes (Hatfield & Rapson, 1992). The effects of these expressions of attitude are surprisingly precise. Each person in the interaction evaluates the other on the basis of the **proportion of similar attitudes** that are expressed, regardless of the total number of topics (Byrne & Nelson, 1965). To determine proportion, you simply divide the number of topics on which two people express similar views by the total number of topics about which they exchange information. Attraction is the same if two people agree on three out of four issues ($3 \div 4 = .75$) or on 75 out of 100 ($75 \div 100 = .75$). The higher the proportion of similar attitudes, the greater the liking. This cause-and-effect relationship can be expressed in mathematical terms as a linear (straight-line) function, as depicted in Figure 7.11. The wide-ranging generality of the similarity–attraction relationship has been shown in studies of people across different age groups, different socioeconomic levels, and different cultures. Even on the information superhighway, it has been noted that those using e-mail exchange lists are most likely to seek out others who share their views and to exclude those who disagree (Schwartz, 1994).

Many behavioral scientists have no doubts that the similarity–attraction effect is extremely well established. For example, Cappella and Palmer (1990,

FIGURE 7.11

Attraction Increases As Proportion of Similar Attitudes Increases: A Linear Function. The effect of proportion of similar attitudes (number of similar attitudes divided by the total number of similar and dissimilar attitudes) on attraction is found among people differing in age, social class, and culture. As shown here, the higher the proportion of similar attitudes expressed by one person, the more positive the attraction response of a second person.

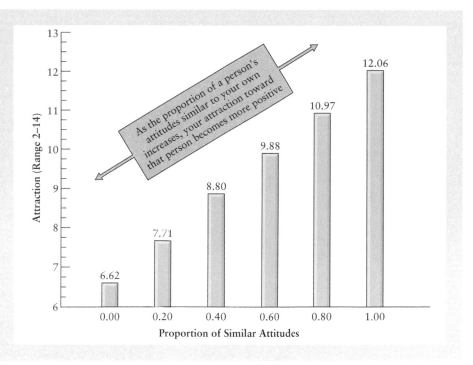

p. 161) state that "perhaps the most well known and well established finding in the study of interpersonal relations is that attitude similarity creates attraction." Any phenomenon described as "well established" is likely to be challenged by critics eager to overturn a false conclusion, and the effect of attitudes on attraction is no exception. Some challenges are easily dismissed. When Sunnafrank (1992) suggests that similarity between partners has little effect on relationships, the cumulative findings over the past century in both field studies and laboratory experiments indicate quite the reverse.

A more cogent criticism was offered by Rosenbaum (1986) with his **repulsion hypothesis.** Simply stated, he proposed that dissimilar attitudes decrease attraction but that similar attitudes have no effect. He pointed out that in most studies participants respond to a stranger who expresses both similar and dissimilar attitudes. Though it has been assumed that each type of attitude influences attraction, Rosenbaum suggested otherwise. In effect, he assumed that people like whomever they meet, but are gradually *repulsed* if the other person expresses dissimilar attitudes. His hypothesis that similar attitudes are irrelevant was, however, shown to be incorrect in an experiment in which the number of dissimilar attitudes remained the same in each of three conditions, while the number of similar attitudes varied (Smeaton, Byrne, & Murnen, 1989). The repulsion hypothesis predicts no difference in attraction across the conditions, because their only difference consisted of varying numbers of similar attitudes. The proportion hypothesis, in contrast, predicts that attraction will differ across conditions, because the proportion of similar attitudes varies. As Figure 7.12 (p. 262) indicates, the repulsion hypothesis was found to be incorrect, and the proportion hypothesis was confirmed.

Rosenbaum's dramatic but flawed proposal was of value, however, in leading to additional research. And this research does indicate a slightly greater effect for dissimilar attitudes than for similar ones (Chapman, 1992), in part because most people assume that a stranger, especially an attractive one (Miyake & Zuckerman, 1993), holds attitudes similar to their own (Hoyle,

Repulsion Hypothesis ■ Rosenbaum's proposal that attraction is not enhanced by similar attitudes; instead, people initially respond positively to others but are repulsed by the discovery of dissimilar attitudes.

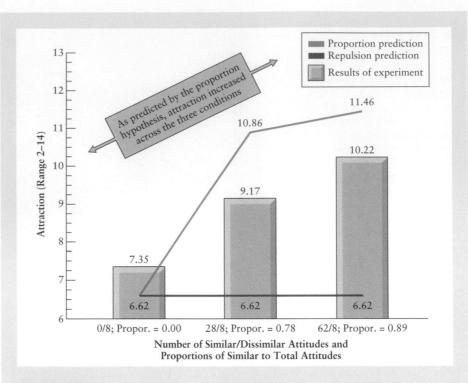

FIGURE 7.12

Repulsion Hypothesis versus Proportion of Similar Attitudes Hypothesis: An Experimental Test. The *repulsion hypothesis* states that people respond only to dissimilar attitudes and that similar attitudes have no effect on attraction. The *proportion of similar attitudes hypothesis* states that *both* similar and dissimilar attitudes have an effect on attraction. In an experimental test of the opposing hypotheses, the number of dissimilar attitudes in each of three conditions was held constant (8) while the number of similar attitudes varied (0, 28, and 62). The repulsion hypothesis predicts a flat line, because the varying number of similar attitudes should be irrelevant. The proportion hypothesis predicts an increase in attraction, because both similar and dissimilar attitudes should be relevant. The results of the experiment clearly were consistent with the prediction of the proportion hypothesis rather than that of the repulsion hypothesis.

(*Source:* Based on data from Smeaton, Byrne, & Murnen, 1989.)

1993; Krueger & Clement, 1994). This assumption of widespread agreement with one's own views—sometimes labeled the false consensus effect (Alicke & Largo, 1995)—applies to both important and unimportant topics and occurs not only among college students but among representatives of the general population (Fabrigar & Krosnick, 1995). In research conducted at the National University of Singapore, children aged seven and eleven were found to assume that others were like themselves to an even greater extent than did adolescents and adults (Tan & Singh, 1995).

An implication of assuming a false consensus, among all age groups, is that agreement is expected while disagreement is surprising (Singh & Tan, 1992). Disagreement can have a greater effect, because this negative information "stands out" (remember the automatic vigilance effect discussed in Chapter 3?). The reverse can also occur. If, on some specific issues, an individual believes that he or she holds a minority view and that most people disagree, disagreement is expected and has less effect than an unexpected agreement (Smeaton et al., 1995).

As Duck and Barnes (1992) point out, the similarity–attraction relationship resembles the history of the *Titanic* in reverse; many are sure it will sink, but it remains afloat.

Why Do Similar and Dissimilar Attitudes Influence Attraction? The simplest explanation for the effect of attitudes on attraction is that similar attitudes arouse positive affect while dissimilar attitudes arouse negative affect, and we have already described how affect leads to attraction. As accurate as that may be, it is still not entirely clear *why* the attitudes of another person are emotionally pleasing or displeasing.

The oldest explanation, described by Newcomb and also by Fritz Heider among others, is **balance theory** (Hummert, Crockett, & Kemper, 1990). The proposal is that people naturally organize their likes and dislikes in a symmetrical way. **Balance,** a pleasant emotional state, exists when two people like each other and agree about some topic (Newcomb, 1961). When people like each other but disagree, an unpleasant state occurs because of **imbalance** (Orive, 1988). In response, each person strives to restore balance by changing his or her attitudes in order to reach agreement, convincing the other person to change attitudes for the same reason, minimizing the disagreement through misperception, or deciding to dislike rather than like the other person (Monsour, Betty, & Kurzweil, 1993). When two people dislike each other, they are in a state of **nonbalance,** and each is indifferent about the other's attitudes.

Though balance theory appears to be accurate, and though it leads to many interesting predictions about how two interacting people will respond to agreements and disagreements, it doesn't really explain why attitudinal information matters in the first place. One answer is provided by Festinger's (1954) social comparison theory, discussed earlier. In effect, you turn to other people to obtain **consensual validation** of your opinions: agreement provides "evidence" that you are correct. It is pleasing to discover that your judgment is sound, your intelligence is high, and so forth. Disagreement suggests the reverse, and it is uncomfortable to find that you have poor judgment, low intelligence, and so on. As discussed in Chapter 5 (with respect to seeking information relevant to one's self-concept), this formulation suggests that we are interested in the views of other people not because we are seeking accuracy, but only because we want to verify what we already believe.

More recently, Rushton (1989) has offered an evolution-based genetic explanation of the similarity–attraction effect. He hypothesizes that people use attitude similarity, as well as other cues, to detect those who are genetically similar to themselves (Rushton, 1990). Research has demonstrated, for example, that friends are more similar than chance would predict on several inherited characteristics, such as blood type and Rh factor. If you like a genetically similar other, become friends, and assist one another when help is needed, you are unconsciously acting in ways that increase the odds that your kind of genes will be protected and eventually passed on to the next generation. If so, attraction should be facilitated by many sorts of similarity; and just such findings are described in the following section.

The Matching Hypothesis: Liking Others Who Are Like Yourself. Whether or not the evolutionary explanation for a similarity effect is the basic one, it *is* true that attraction is affected by many types of interpersonal similarity. Though it is commonly believed that "opposites attract," research overwhelmingly indicates that similarity is the rule.

Sir Francis Galton first determined that "like marries like" in 1870, but the **matching hypothesis** became a matter of interest to social psychologists in the context of research on physical attractiveness (Berscheid et al., 1971). The idea

Balance ■ In Newcomb's theory, the pleasant emotional state that results when two people like each other and agree about a topic of discussion.

Balance Theory ■ Newcomb's cognitively oriented theory of the relationships among (1) an individual's liking for another person, (2) his or her attitude about a given topic, and (3) the other person's perceived attitude about the same topic.

Imbalance ■ In Newcomb's theory, the unpleasant emotional state that results when two people like each other but disagree about a topic of discussion; each is motivated to change some element in the interaction in order to achieve *balance* or *nonbalance*.

Nonbalance ■ In Newcomb's theory, the indifferent emotional state that results when two people dislike each other and don't care whether they agree or disagree about a topic of discussion.

Consensual Validation ■ The perceived "validation" of one's views about any aspect of the world that is provided whenever someone else holds the same views.

Matching Hypothesis ■ The proposal that individuals are attracted to one another as friends, romantic partners, or spouses on the basis of similar attributes—physical attractiveness, age, race, personality characteristics, or social assets such as wealth, education, or power.

is that romantic partners tend to pair off on the basis of being *similar* in physical attractiveness. Not only are dating couples similar in attractiveness, but married couples are, too (Zajonc et al., 1987). Observers usually react negatively when they perceive couples who are "mismatched." The dissimilar couples are rated as having less ability, being less likable, and having a less satisfactory relationship than couples who are similar in attractiveness (Forgas, 1993).

It is perhaps more surprising, but matching for attractiveness also occurs in same-sex friendships, for men as well as women (Cash & Derlega, 1978; McKillip & Reidel, 1983). Also surprising is the fact that two individuals assigned as college roommates will be less satisfied if they are dissimilar in attractiveness than if they are similar (Carli, Ganley, & Pierce-Otay, 1991). The dissatisfaction is expressed by the more attractive of the two, apparently because the less attractive roommate is believed to be unacceptable to outside friends and hence an obstacle to the attractive student's social life.

Beyond attitude and appearance similarity, numerous studies have reported that similarity and perceived similarity on a wide variety of specific characteristics are associated with attraction (Hogg, Cooper-Shaw, & Holzworth, 1993). For example, college students who choose their roommates do so in part because the two individuals are similar in sociability (Joiner, 1994). Among other similarity findings are the positive effects on attraction of being alike in expressing emotions (Alliger & Williams, 1991); smoking marijuana (Eisenman, 1985); belonging to a given religion (Kandel, 1978); having similar self-concepts (LaPrelle et al., 1990); smoking, drinking, and engaging in premarital sex (Rodgers, Billy, & Udry, 1984); accepting traditional gender roles (Smith, Byrne, & Fielding, 1995); and being morning versus evening people (Watts, 1982).

Some of these other areas of similarity have even greater effects than attitudes. For example, Cann, Calhoun, and Banks (1995) provided research participants with the attitudes of a fellow student on ten topics, and, as expected, attraction was greater toward a similar (.90) than a dissimilar (.10) stranger. The investigators also asked participants to select the funniest joke out of a series and then read it to the "stranger"; this was actually a research assistant, who either laughed or responded with indifference. Agreement that the joke was funny also had a positive effect on attraction—surprisingly, in fact, it had a greater effect on attraction than did the similar attitudes. A dissimilar stranger who laughed at the participant's joke was liked more than a similar stranger who was indifferent to the joke. The most positive response, of course, was to a stranger who agreed about the attitude topics *and* about the joke.

Opposites may not attract, but birds of a feather most certainly do flock together.

Reciprocity: Mutual Liking

Once two individuals discover enough areas of similarity to move toward friendship, one additional step is all-important. Each individual must somehow indicate that the other person is liked and evaluated positively (Byrne & Griffitt, 1966; Condon & Crano, 1988). Almost everyone is extremely happy to receive such positive feedback and is quite displeased to be evaluated negatively (Coleman, Jussim, & Abraham, 1987). It is not unusual for even an inaccurate positive evaluation (Swann et al., 1987) or an obvious attempt at flattery (Drachman, DeCarufel, & Insko, 1978) to be well received, even from a total stranger, as Figure 7.13 suggests. One exception is that individuals with negative self-concepts (see Chapter 5) sometimes respond well to accurate negative evaluations (Swann, Stein-Seroussi, & Giesler, 1992), presumably because such evaluations are consistent with their self-schema.

FIGURE 7.13

A Positive Evaluation by Another Person Elicits Positive Affect and Attraction toward That Person. *Positive evaluations, or any other indications that another person likes you and approves of you, constitute a positive emotional experience resulting in feelings of attraction. We all enjoy receiving compliments, positive feedback, and a pat on the back, as suggested in this cartoon.*

(*Source:* Drawing by R. Chast; © 1987 *The New Yorker* Magazine, Inc.)

A positive or negative evaluation affects attraction, and interpersonal behavior as well. Curtis and Miller (1986) led some research participants to believe that a stranger liked them and others to believe that they were disliked by a stranger. Participants interacted with a fellow participant who was falsely identified as the stranger who had made the evaluation, and their behavior was strongly influenced by whether they believed the other person had given a positive or a negative evaluation. Those who believed they had been evaluated positively were more self-disclosing, expressed more positive attitudes, made more eye contact, and spoke in a warmer tone than those who believed the other person gave negative evaluations. Expecting to be liked leads to positive interpersonal behavior; when two students each received the false information about positive evaluations from the other, greater reciprocal liking was expressed afterward.

Though mutual liking is often expressed in words, the first signs of attraction may be nonverbal cues (discussed in Chapter 2). For example, when a woman maintains eye contact while conversing with a man and leans toward him, these acts tend to be interpreted (sometimes incorrectly) to mean that she likes him; his response is then attraction toward her (Gold, Ryckman, & Mosley, 1984).

In brief, we like those who like us or who we believe like us.

INTEGRATING PRINCIPLES

1. Similarity on a wide variety of verbal and nonverbal attributes leads to attraction. Similarity also affects the selection of a romantic partner (Chapter 8) and whether or not help is provided to a person in need (Chapter 10).

2. We like people who like us and evaluate us positively and dislike people who dislike us and evaluate us negatively. Indicating a positive reaction to others is important in close relationships (Chapter 8) and in the workplace (Chapter 13).

Social Diversity: A Critical Analysis

THE SIMILARITY–ATTRACTION RELATIONSHIP AS A CROSS-CULTURAL PHENOMENON

THOUGH PROPORTION OF SIMILAR ATTITUDES AFFECTS ATtraction in a very consistent fashion, most of the initial research was conducted in the United States. How general is this relationship? As with a lot of psychological research, the question arises as to whether we are observing behavior that is characteristic of a single culture or whether it is a general human tendency found in many different cultures. It has been argued, for example, that peaceful coexistence in pluralistic societies is threatened by a preference for similarity but would be enhanced by secure ingroups who accept dissimilar others (Moghaddam & Solliday, 1991). While that may be a positive goal, the immediate question is whether most people like similar better than dissimilar others.

FIGURE 7.14

Cross-Cultural Comparisons: Attraction and Proportion of Similar Attitudes. Students in five different parts of the world took part in an experiment in which they responded to a stranger who expressed one of several possible levels of attitude similarity. Attraction in each instance increased as proportion of similar attitudes increased. The only difference across cultures was that students in Texas and Japan expressed less attraction toward a stranger at each level of similarity than did students in Mexico, India, and Hawaii. In this and other investigations, the similarity–attraction effect appears to be universal.

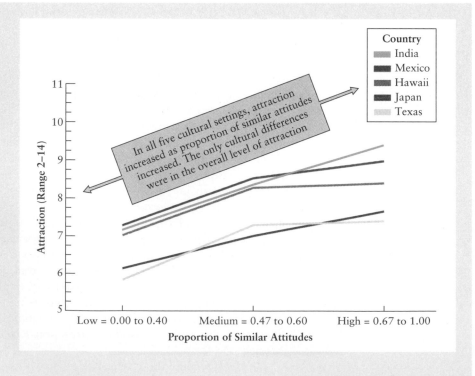

In all five cultural settings, attraction increased as proportion of similar attitudes increased. The only cultural differences were in the overall level of attraction

The first investigation of attitudes and attraction across diverse cultures compared college students in Texas, Japan, Hawaii, India, and Mexico (Byrne et al., 1971). Each respondent filled out a fifteen-item attitude scale (in the appropriate language) and then examined the attitudes (on the same fifteen items) of someone described as another student; next, each respondent's attraction toward the other person was assessed. As shown in Figure 7.14, the five samples each responded to proportion of similar attitudes in the familiar linear fashion. The only significant cultural differences were in the overall positiveness or negativeness of the attraction response. Students in Japan and Texas were relatively less attracted to the stranger while those in Hawaii, India, and Mexico were relatively more attracted.

Why the culture-based differences in overall attraction level? The finding was unexpected, but it is possible after the fact to make a tentative guess. One suggestion was that Japan and Texas each represent a unique and somewhat exclusive culture in which outsiders are only barely tolerated. In contrast, Hawaii, India, and Mexico are each composed of a mixture of diverse people with a history of welcoming outsiders. Only in future research can such hypotheses be tested. ■ ■ ■

CONNECTIONS: Integrating Social Psychology

In this chapter, you read about . . .	*In other chapters, you will find related discussions of . . .*
the role of associated affect in determining attraction	the roles of affect in attitude formation (Chapter 4), prejudice (Chapter 6), love (Chapter 8), and courtroom decisions (Chapter 13)
social comparison theory	social comparison as a factor in social influence (Chapter 9), in emergency situations (Chapter 10),
stereotypes based on observable characteristics	stereotypes as they operate in prejudice (Chapter 6), in spouse selection (Chapter 8), and in response to defendants in trials (Chapter 13)

Thinking about Connections

1. Imagine yourself in a very bad mood. You don't feel good, several unpleasant things have happened to you in the past few weeks, you have a lot of studying to do, and you don't have anything planned for the near future that promises to be fun. Now—make a list of the kinds of decisions and judgments that might be affected by your emotional state. Consider how you might react to other people, to events, and to specific factors in your environment. Next, imagine yourself in a very good mood, and start over. Can you remember any actual experiences in which your decisions and judgments differed because you were experiencing negative or positive affect?

2. Think of some situation in your life in which an unusual and disrupting event occurred—a power failure, a blizzard, a hurricane, an earthquake, a flood, or whatever. What did you do?

Were there other people around? What did you talk about? What was going through your mind? Can you think of other events, large or small, that might have aroused your need for social comparison?

3. In the past week, try to recall an instance in which you reacted to someone you didn't know (in real life, on TV, or wherever) on the basis of their appearance, their accent, or something about their behavior. What did you assume about this person, what feelings were aroused, and what kind of evaluation did you make? What are some of the stereotypes you hold about specific observable characteristics of others, and how much do they influence you?

4. Select a recent example in which someone (perhaps a professor in class, a politician on tele-

(continued)

vision, or someone you just met) expressed an opinion with which you totally disagree. How did you react? What feelings were aroused? How did you evaluate that individual? Why do you think you responded as you did? Try to recall other, quite different situations in which you reacted to other people (positively or negatively) on the basis of their attitudes and beliefs.

Summary and Review

Our attitudes about other people range from strong liking to strong dislike, and research on *interpersonal attraction* deals with the factors that determine such interpersonal attitudes.

Proximity and Emotions

Attraction between two strangers often begins with unplanned encounters that depend on the physical details of their shared environment. When dormitory assignments, classroom seating arrangements, neighborhood layouts, or the structure of the workplace bring two people into repeated contact, they are likely to become acquainted. Research in many settings over a long period indicates that *proximity* leads to repeated interpersonal contact and hence repeated exposure to specific individuals. The result is familarity and the increased likelihood of a friendly interaction.

The central determinant of attraction is *affect*—a person's emotional state during an interpersonal interaction. Positive affect leads to liking, while negative affect causes dislike. Such effects occur whether the other person is responsible for the emotion or is simply present at the same time as the emotional arousal. Through simple conditioning, we associate our positive or negative emotional state with anyone (or anything) we encounter while aroused.

Needing to Affiliate and Responding to Observable Characteristics

A positive relationship is most likely to form between two people if they each are high in *need for affiliation*. This motivation differs from person to person as a dispositional variable, and there are specific motives (emotional support, attention, etc.) that underlie affiliation. In addition, the need to affiliate can be aroused by an exciting or confusing situation that brings people together—in part because they are seeking *social comparison,* as a way to verify their opinions and perceptions.

Initial attraction or avoidance is often based on stereotypes about the *observable characteristics* of others—race, sex, age, height, physique, clothing, and so on. Social psychologists have focused a great of research on the effects of *physical attractiveness* at all age levels. For both males and females, it is generally beneficial to be physically attractive. Judgments of this attribute are influenced not only by a person's physical appearance but also by situational and interpersonal factors.

Similarity and Reciprocal Positive Evaluations

For more than two thousand years, observers have noted the importance of *attitude similarity* in determining interpersonal likes and dislikes. In this century, correlational studies supported the observations. In the last fifty years, both longitudinal field research and laboratory experimentation have established the causal effect of similarity on attraction. Theoretical explanations of the response to attitudes include balance theory, the need for consensual validation, and the sociobiological importance of genetic similarity. Though attitudinal similarity and dissimilarity have been investigated extensively, many other types of similarity (physical attractiveness, personality, intelligence, age, etc.) also influence who likes whom.

In order to move beyond being acquaintances or casual friends toward a closer relationship, two individuals need to express mutual liking and other mutual positive evaluations (reciprocity) either in words or overt acts.

Social Diversity: The Similarity–Attraction Relationship As a Cross-Cultural Phenomenon

Despite the importance of mutual respect and tolerance in making a peaceful world a real possibility, cross-cultural research suggests a seemingly universal human tendency to respond positively to similarity and negatively to dissimilarity. Until or unless we develop ways to modify this intolerance, diversity will continue to be a potential source of conflict.

■ Key Terms

Affect-Centered Model of Attraction (p. 243)

Appearance Anxiety (p. 251)

Attitude Similarity (p. 259)

Balance (p. 263)

Balance Theory (p. 263)

Consensual Validation (p. 263)

Imbalance (p. 263)

Interpersonal Attraction (p. 234)

Matching Hypothesis (p. 263)

Need for Affiliation (p. 246)

Nonbalance (p. 263)

Physical Attractiveness (p. 249)

Proximity (p. 236)

Proportion of Similar Attitudes (p. 260)

Repeated Exposure (p. 236)

Repulsion Hypothesis (p. 261)

Social Comparison Theory (p. 248)

Stigma (p. 244)

■ For More Information

Erwin, P. (1993). *Friendship and peer relations in children.* Chichester, England: Wiley.

This book focuses on peer relationships among young children. Social and cognitive processes are discussed in relation to the effect of childhood friendships on later development.

Hatfield, E., & Sprecher, S. (1986). *Mirror, mirror . . . : The importance of looks in everyday life.* Albany, NY: SUNY Press.

A well-written and extremely interesting summary of research dealing with the effects of physical attractiveness on interpersonal relationships. The scientific literature is well covered, and the findings are illustrated throughout with anecdotes, photographs, and drawings that consistently enliven the presentation.

Newcomb, T. M. (1961). *The acquaintance process.* New York: Holt, Rinehart and Winston.

This slim volume contains a description of balance theory and presents Newcomb's pioneering field study of strangers becoming acquainted in a natural setting.

CHAPTER 8

THE JOYS AND SORROWS OF CLOSE RELATIONSHIPS: Family, Friends, Lovers, and Spouses

Lisa Houck, *Landscape with Signs of Human Habitation*, 1995, watercolor, 24 × 62"

Chapter Outline

271

Do you have at least one sibling? What kind of relationship do you have? Most of us have mixed feelings about siblings—love, resentment, jealousy, pleasant memories that we share, envy, and so forth. Try to imagine what your future relationship might be, ten years from now or after thirty years have passed. It can be deeply satisfying to be in this kind of close relationship—yet sometimes quite annoying, because neither of you had a choice in the matter.

Falling in love is one of the most intense experiences that anyone can have, and the topic seems to have an endless fascination for us—in real life, in songs, on television, and in movies and books. What do we mean by love? When you are strongly attracted to another person, how can you know whether the feelings are genuine or based in part on fiction and on what you have learned to expect about love and romance?

For most people, marriage is the ultimate goal of close interpersonal relationships. A husband and wife can be emotionally and physically close, raise sons and daughters, and face the good and the bad aspects of life as a close-knit unit. The dark side of the picture is that marriages all too often lead to unhappiness, bickering (or worse), and a deteriorating relationship that culminates in a broken family. What goes wrong, and what can people do to avoid an unhappy ending?

Though the study of interpersonal attraction (Chapter 7) has been a major research focus of social psychologists for most of this century, the broader topic of interpersonal *relationships* received much less attention. In recent years, however, social psychologists have begun concentrating on love and intimacy (Hatfield & Rapson, 1993b) and also on the cognitive representation of social relationships (Baldwin, 1992; Haslam, 1994). Given the importance of family, friendship, love, and marriage to most people, it would seem to be a crucial goal for behavioral scientists to learn as much as possible about interpersonal success and failure.

We will first describe what is known about two important kinds of *interdependent relationships*—those within families and those involving close friendships—as well as the consequences of not being able to establish lasting interdependent relationships and thus having to deal with *loneliness*. We next examine *intimate relationships* and the factors involved in romance, love, and sexual intimacy. The final topic is *marital relationships*, including how individuals respond to the problems that arise between partners and the effects of dissolving a relationship.

Initial Interdependent Relationships: Family Interactions and Close Friendships versus Loneliness

Interdependence ■ The characteristic common to all close relationships—an interpersonal association in which two people influence one another's lives and engage in many joint activities.

The common element of all close relationships is **interdependence,** an interpersonal association in which two people consistently and reciprocally influence one another's lives, focus their thoughts and emotions on one another, and—if possible—regularly engage in joint activities. Such interdependence occurs across age groups and among individuals representing many quite different relationships. Studies of families, for example, include the traditional two-parent household (Cook, 1993), families in which either the father or the mother is a stepparent (Fine & Kurdek, 1994), and lesbian and gay families (Patterson, 1994).

According to college students (Berscheid, Snyder, & Omoto, 1989), the *one person* in the world to whom they feel closest is a romantic partner (reported by almost half of the respondents), a friend (mentioned by a third), or a family member (more than 10 percent). We will first discuss relatives and friends and then turn to romantic partners (and spouses) in the following sections.

Close Relatives: It All Begins in the Family

We pointed out in Chapter 5 that the basic aspects of the self-concept develop within the family through the social interactions that occur there. Who we are and what we think of ourselves result in large part from the perceptions and evaluations of our closest relatives. The potential lifelong effects of these early relationships are suggested in Figure 8.1.

Attachment Style: The Infant's Experience with Its Mother. In addition to the family's role in molding one's self-concept, a growing body of research also suggests that the nature of each person's interpersonal relationships is established

FIGURE 8.1

The Lifelong Effects of Early Family Relationships. *Though this statue's inscription is amusing, research actually does indicate that we are influenced throughout our lives by our earliest relationships within the family.*

(*Source:* Drawing by Richter; © 1984 *The New Yorker* Magazine, Inc.)

SOLDIER
STATESMAN
AUTHOR
PATRIOT
BUT STILL
A
DISAPPOINTMENT
TO HIS MOTHER

FIGURE 8.2

The First Interpersonal Relationship. The interaction between mother and infant appears to be a critical determinant of the infant's *attachment style*—avoidant, secure, or ambivalent. The attachment style, in turn, is reflected in later interpersonal relationships throughout life.

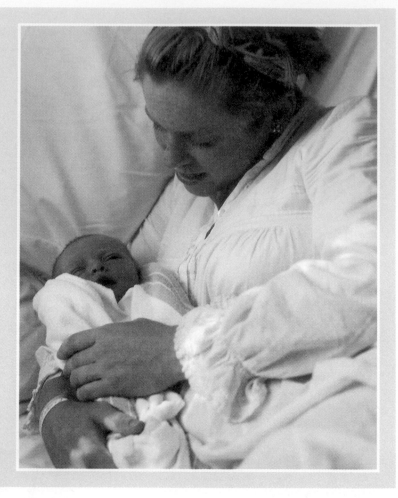

in the interaction between an infant and the primary caregiver—usually the mother (Ainsworth et al., 1978; Bartholomew & Horowitz, 1991; see Figure 8.2). Bowlby (1982) proposed that the way a mother interacts with her infant results in one of three major types of **attachment style:** either *secure* or one of two insecure styles, *avoidant* and *ambivalent,* based on whether the infant feels secure or insecure in this relationship. In effect, the infant learns to trust and to love another person, to mistrust and avoid, or a mixture of the two.

Attachment style refers to temperamental differences stemming from the infant's affective response to these early interactions; but it is recognized that a reciprocal relationship is also possible—that is, built-in differences in an infant's temperament may in part influence how the mother responds to her offspring (Goldsmith & Harman, 1994). It is believed that sensitive, responsive parenting during the child's first year leads to secure attachment. To the degree that parenting is lacking in sensitivity or responsiveness, one of the two insecure attachment styles develops.

What specific behaviors differentiate mothers who foster secure versus insecure feelings in their infants? Becker and Becker (1994) studied emotional bonding by examining the behavior of mothers, and they developed an observational measure that refers to amount of physical contact, visual contact, verbal contact, and the mother's awareness of and responsiveness to the infant's needs. The investigators expect to be able to predict infant attachment style on

Attachment Style ■ An infant's degree of security in mother–infant interactions, believed to result in a secure, avoidant, or ambivalent attachment style—which affects interpersonal behavior throughout life.

TABLE 8.1   A Behavioral Measure of Mother's Interaction with Her Infant

To help investigators study the role of maternal behavior in mother–infant attachment, a behavioral measure has been developed. Observers note degrees of closeness involved in the mother's touching the baby, looking at the baby, talking to the baby, and being aware of and responsive to the baby's needs. It is proposed that the infant's attachment style is based on the amount of closeness and security provided by the mother.

Mother's Tactile Contact with Infant	*Low Security*	touches infant only with fingertips
	Medium Security	holds infant in arms away from chest
	High Security	presses infant to chest
Mother's Visual Contact with Infant	*Low Security*	actively avoids visual contact with infant
	Medium Security	briefly looks at infant, without comment
	High Security	positions and maintains face-to-face contact
Mother's Verbal Contact with Infant	*Low Security*	few or no verbalizations to or about infant
	Medium Security	positive and negative verbalizations to or about infant
	High Security	mostly positive verbalizations to or about infant *and* statements about the infant's care and well-being
Mother's Awareness of and Responsivity to Infant's Needs	*Low Security*	appears to be unaware of infant's needs
	Medium Security	aware of infant's needs but responds inappropriately
	High Security	is aware of and responds promptly and appropriately to infant's needs

(*Source:* Based on material from Becker & Becker, 1994.)

the basis of the degree of security provided by the mother. Some of the details of different maternal behaviors are presented in Table 8.1.

Psychologists measure an infant's attachment style by observing its behavior during a twenty-minute laboratory session in which the investigators arrange two separations and reunions of infant and mother. Secure infants are mildly upset by the mother's absence but quickly soothed by her return. The avoidant pattern includes rejecting the mother and showing emotional control and restraint in her presence. An ambivalent infant indicates conflict—crying when separated from its mother but also crying when the mother returns—tending to be angry and unsoothable.

Though the empirical data are not totally consistent, there is evidence that secure attachment is associated with such later characteristics as positive affect, empathy, high self-esteem, and unconflicted interactions with peers and with adults. The insecure avoidant children are hostile and distant in social relationships, and they resist seeking adult help when problems arise. The insecure ambivalent children tend to be both dependent on adults and angry at them, as well as being noncompliant, unenthusiastic, and unsociable.

To jump ahead just a bit, what do these mother–infant relationships and youthful behavior patterns have to do with the social behavior of adults? For one thing, after a woman gives birth, her own attachment style is related to the way in which she interacts with her infant (Scher & Mayseless, 1994). Hazan and Shaver (1990) hypothesize that when an adult enters a relationship, the attachment style formed in infancy determines the nature of that relationship. Specifically, secure individuals seek closeness, are comfortable in having to depend on the partner, and are not constantly worried about losing the partner. In contrast, avoidant individuals are uncomfortable about intimacy and closeness;

they don't trust other people. The ambivalent person wants a relationship but also fears it, because a partner is often perceived as distant, unloving, and likely to break off the relationship. Of these three styles, only secure individuals would seem to be able to form long-lasting, committed, satisfying relationships (Shaver & Brennan, 1992). Because it is possible for a close adult relationship to alter one's attachment style (Shaver & Hazan, 1994), infant attachment style does not mean that the person's interpersonal future is etched in stone.

Still other research with adults indicates that secure individuals report warm parental relationships, while avoidant and ambivalent individuals describe interactions with their parents as cold or inconsistent (Bringle & Bagby, 1992). We will return to the topic of attachment styles in our later discussions of relationships.

Additional Aspects of Relationships between Parents and Their Offspring. Though studies of attachment emphasize the importance of mother–child interactions in infancy, how parents deal with toddlers, young children, and adolescents are also crucial factors in how people develop and in what they learn about relationships. For example, O'Leary (1995) emphasizes the importance of discipline—how and how effectively children are taught to follow rules. The behavioral consequences of specific child-rearing techniques include delinquency and aggression among those whose parents are either harsh, excessively lenient, or inconsistent.

When children approach adolescence, parents are often apprehensive because they fear being rejected by rebellious teenagers. To document the association between age and parent–offspring conflict, Flannery and his colleagues (1993) observed girls and boys (grades five to nine) as they held two conversations with each parent (they talked about an enjoyable shared activity and about a topic on which they disagreed or were in conflict). As hypothesized, this developmental period was found to be associated with problems—the more physically mature the youngsters, the less positive and the more negative was any affect expressed by parents and their offspring during their interactions, and the more conflict in the relationship. It seems that as puberty arrives, the typical parent–offspring relationship becomes less pleasant.

Nevertheless, most adolescents report very positive feelings about their parents, despite feeling less close and dependent than in childhood (Galambos, 1992). Jeffries (1987, 1990, 1993) has explored the love felt by adolescents for their mother and father. He proposes that love of parents is based on *attraction* and *virtue*. Incidentally, we don't often hear the word "virtue," but it refers to a person being good in the sense of behaving in a moral and ethical way. Both attraction and virtue consist of five factors, as outlined in Figure 8.3. An adolescent who *likes* his or her parents and who is also a *good* person feels loved in return, is happy and satisfied with the relationship, has high self-esteem (see Chapter 5), trusts other people, and exhibits prosocial behavior (see Chapter 10).

Interestingly, data consistent with this model of parent–offspring relationships are reported in other cultures as well. An investigation of Chinese people living in Hong Kong (aged sixteen to seventy-eight) indicated that people who were raised in a cohesive family were most likely to develop feelings of empathy and to assume responsibility for the well-being of their parents (Cheung, Lee, & Chan, 1994). In the United States, to an increasing degree, grown offspring take responsibility for their parents. For example, when I (Donn Byrne) recently faced some difficult problems with moving and storing several heavy items of furniture, my son Keven spontaneously volunteered to drive from Indiana in order to do what was necessary. The little boy who wanted Dad to read him the funnies or take him to Six Flags over Texas was now a man whose help

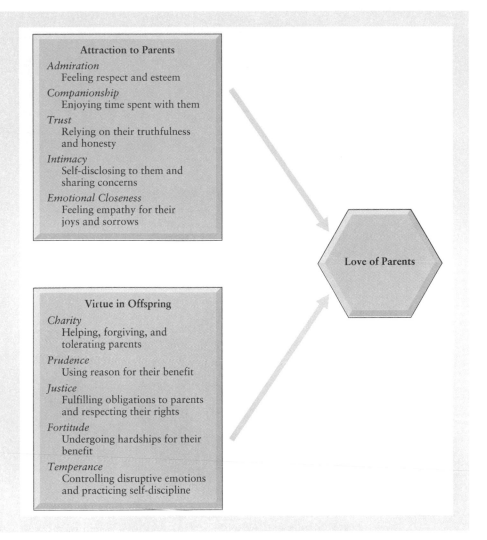

FIGURE 8.3

Loving One's Parents = Liking Them plus Being Virtuous. In studying adolescents and the love they often feel for their parents, Jeffries concluded that this parental love stems from two basic components: attraction toward them and the adolescent's personal virtue. Young people who genuinely like their parents and are themselves virtuous are able to experience parental love and to treat their mothers and fathers lovingly.

(*Source:* Based on concepts from Jeffries, 1987, 1990, 1993.)

Attraction to Parents

Admiration
Feeling respect and esteem

Companionship
Enjoying time spent with them

Trust
Relying on their truthfulness and honesty

Intimacy
Self-disclosing to them and sharing concerns

Emotional Closeness
Feeling empathy for their joys and sorrows

Virtue in Offspring

Charity
Helping, forgiving, and tolerating parents

Prudence
Using reason for their benefit

Justice
Fulfilling obligations to parents and respecting their rights

Fortitude
Undergoing hardships for their benefit

Temperance
Controlling disruptive emotions and practicing self-discipline

Love of Parents

was both needed and appreciated. Once again it is clear that a positive relationship between parents and their sons and daughters constitutes an extremely important basis for later interpersonal behavior.

Relationships between and among Siblings. The great majority of children (about 80 percent) grow up in a household with at least one sibling, and sibling interactions provide a way to learn and to practice interpersonal skills (Dunn, 1992); see Figure 8.4 (p. 278). Brothers and sisters very often experience a mixture of feelings—including affection, rivalry, and hostility. An affectionate relationship between siblings is most likely if each sibling has a warm relationship with each parent (Stocker & McHale, 1992). The emotions aroused in response to siblings recur throughout one's life in other relationships, because friendships, love affairs, and marriages tend to bring forth the kind of reactions originally associated with siblings (Klagsbrun, 1992).

Siblings tend to be closest in childhood, but they begin to grow apart in adolescence and young adulthood (Rosenthal, 1992). By the time they reach middle age, the vast majority once again establish positive relationships. Some do not. About 10 percent express only indifference to their siblings, and another 10 percent actively dislike one another.

FIGURE 8.4

Siblings: Learning and Practicing Interpersonal Skills. The complex emotional relationships between and among siblings provide a way to learn and to practice ways of getting along with other people. In many respects, sibling relationships are reflected in later friendships and romantic relationships.

As with parent–child relationships, how a person relates to siblings also appears to affect interactions with those outside of the family. For example, an English study of middle school children found that bullies had low cohesion with the other members of their families, especially siblings (Bowers, Smith, & Binney, 1994). An interesting—and hopeful—study across generations reveals that women who report having had negative sibling relationships in childhood tend to be concerned about preventing such conflicts among their own children and promoting positive interactions instead (Kramer & Baron, 1995).

Close Friendships: Establishing Relationships beyond the Family

Beginning in childhood, most of us establish casual friendships with several others of about the same age who share common interests (see Chapter 7), and also form a **close friendship** with just one person. A close friendship, compared to a casual one, involves spending more time together, interacting in more varied situations, excluding others from the relationship, and providing mutual emotional support (Hays, 1989; Kenny & Kashy, 1994). A casual friend is someone who is "fun to be with," while a close friend is valued for such qualities as generosity, sensitivity, and honesty (Urbanski, 1992).

Close Friendship ■ A relationship in which friends spend a great deal of time together, interact in a variety of situations, exclude others from the relationship, and provide emotional support to one another.

Childhood Friendships. The essential element in the friendship of children seems to be the desire to share activities that they both enjoy (Enright & Rawlinson, 1993), as in Figure 8.5. These social interactions can begin as early as age one or two and remain stable over time (Howes, 1989; Whaley & Rubenstein, 1994). As a firsthand observation, my (Donn Byrne's) youngest daughter—Rebecka—met Alice at a day-care center when both were toddlers and still in diapers; they liked each other then, and they remained good friends five years later, even though they attended different schools and lived a good many miles apart.

In reviewing a great many studies of children's friendships, Schneider, Wiener, and Murphy (1994) identified the major determining factors that are consistently reported by investigators. If you think for a minute about what determines attraction—as discussed in Chapter 7—you probably won't be surprised to find that two children are likely to become friends if *proximity* brings them into close contact; if they engage in pleasant activities together (*positive affect*); and if they are *similar* in interests, abilities, age, race, attitudes, and behavior (Boivin, Dodge, & Coie, 1995; Kupersmidt, DeRosier, & Patterson, 1995). Much like adolescents and adults, childhood friends help one another, engage in self-disclosure, and express mutual trust (Bernath & Feshbach, 1995). The behavior of friends changes somewhat with age; for example, children gradually acquire appropriate social norms, and third-grade friends divide rewards more equally than do first-grade friends (Pataki, Shapiro, & Clark, 1994).

Attachment style influences how children interact and, as a result, affects childhood relationships. For example, preschoolers with secure attachment to mother and to father are more likely to interact positively with their peers and to be involved in interactive play (Kerns & Barth, 1995). Among four- and five-year-olds, friendship pairs consisting of two secure children interact in a more positive fashion than pairs in which one child is secure and the other insecure (Kerns, 1994). Also, we noted earlier that insecure avoidant children tend to be hostile and aggressive; as you might expect, highly aggressive children tend to be rejected by their peers (Coie & Cillessen, 1993).

Several measures have been developed to assess friendship quality among children, preadolescents, and early adolescents (Bukowski, Hoza, & Boivin, 1994; Sharabany, 1974, 1994). These measures tend to stress such elements as

FIGURE 8.5

Childhood Friendships. When two children find that they enjoy engaging in the same activities, they often form friendships. Even toddlers as young as one and two years of age can establish lasting relationships.

frankness, mutual liking, exclusiveness, sharing, enjoying common activities, trust, spending time together, and mutual helping.

The continuing importance of attachment style has been found in the friendships of preadolescents. Shulman, Elicker, and Stroufe (1994) observed how friendships were formed over a four-week period among boys and girls enrolled at two summer day camps. These children averaged ten years of age, and they had been part of a long-term study beginning in their infancy, so their attachment styles had previously been determined. Among other findings, *close friendships* (often described by the campers as having a "special friend") were more common among those with secure than with insecure attachment styles, but the majority of insecure children at least *perceived* that they, too, had special friends. Careful observation of the interactions of these youngsters led the psychologists to propose a three-stage model of preadolescent friendship growth. Figure 8.6 shows the three stages as well as the observed differences among secure, avoidant, and ambivalent children in interactions with peers. One conclusion is that young people with secure attachment histories have better social skills than those with insecure histories. Attachment style is clearly related to differences in the friendship behaviors of preadolescents.

Close Friendships among Adolescents and among Adults. In adolescence and young adulthood, friendships tend to be more intimate than in childhood, and women report having more close friends than men do (Fredrickson, 1995). Being involved in an intimate friendship most often has positive effects on the two individuals forming the pair (Berndt, 1992). For example, having a good friend where one works is associated with greater job satisfaction (Winstead et al., 1995). Close friends frequently interact, and they become increasingly accurate in describing the characteristics of one another (Paulhus & Bruce, 1992) and in inferring what the other person is thinking and feeling (Stinson & Ickes, 1992). When events such as college graduation interrupt close friendships, this poses an emotional threat to which the friends must adapt (Fredrickson, 1995). As a result, graduating seniors (compared to students not approaching a time of separation) reported more intense emotional involvement in their contacts with close friends.

Among friends of the same or of the opposite sex, an "intimate relationship" means that the two individuals feel free to engage in self-disclosing behavior, express their emotions, provide support and receive it, experience trust, engage in physical contact, and generally relax with one another (Monsour, 1992; Planalp & Benson, 1992).

Bartholomew and her associates (Bartholomew, 1990; Bartholomew & Horowitz, 1991) have formulated a model of adult attachment that grew out of Bowlby's original theories about interactions between mothers and infants. As shown in Figure 8.7 (p. 282), four attachment patterns are proposed, and they are based on two underlying dimensions: positive versus negative evaluation of self and positive versus negative evaluation of other people (Griffin & Bartholomew, 1994a, 1994b). These two evaluative dimensions consist of a person's sense of self-worth and the person's perception of others as trustworthy or unreliable.

Consider for a moment some of the implications of this model and how it relates to the original concept of attachment style. A person with a positive self-image tends to assume that others will respond positively; the individual expects to be liked and treated well and for that reason should ordinarily feel comfortable in close relationships. A negative self-image is associated with the expectation that others will be rejecting, and therefore close relationships tend to

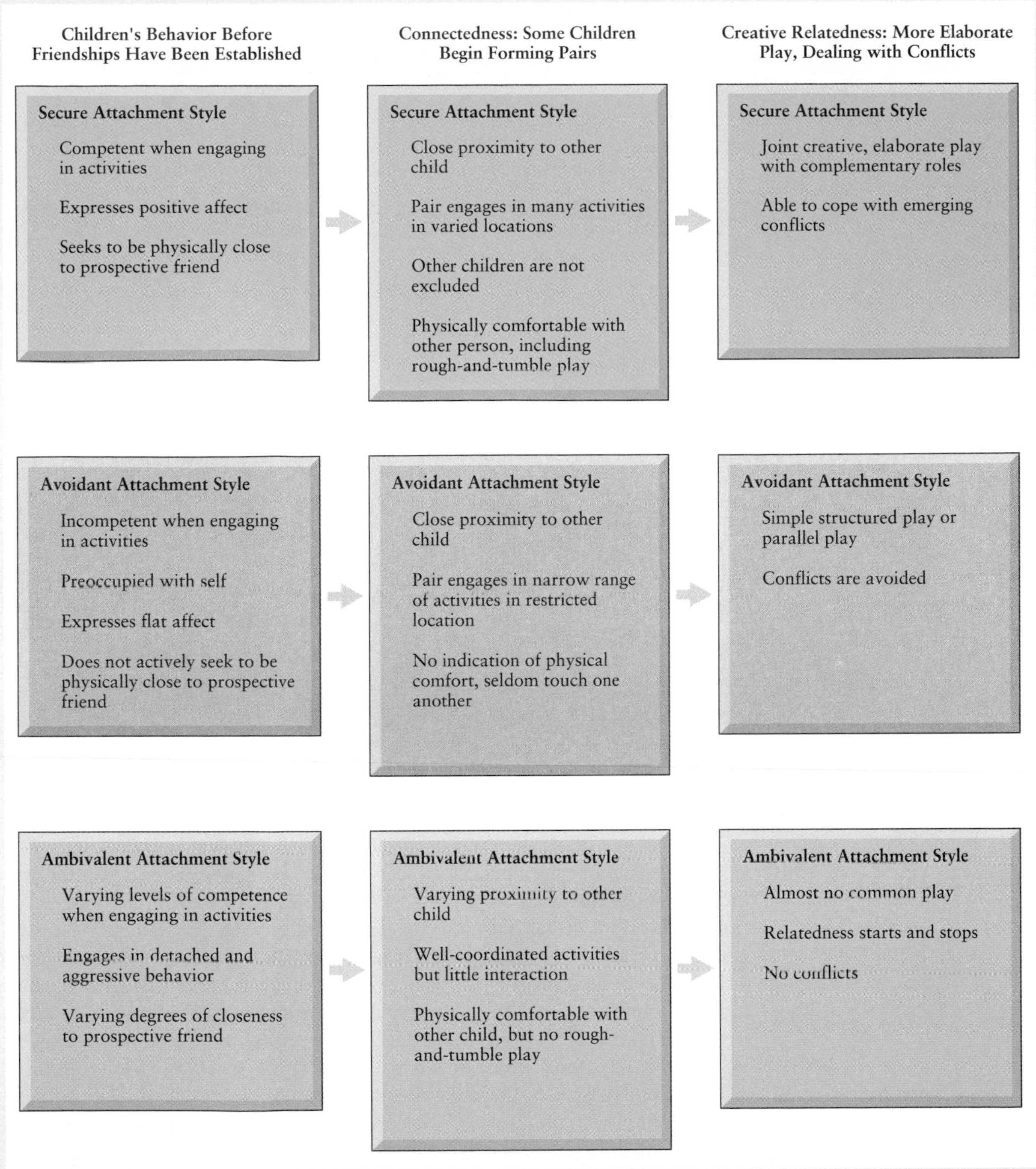

Children's Behavior Before Friendships Have Been Established	Connectedness: Some Children Begin Forming Pairs	Creative Relatedness: More Elaborate Play, Dealing with Conflicts
Secure Attachment Style Competent when engaging in activities Expresses positive affect Seeks to be physically close to prospective friend	**Secure Attachment Style** Close proximity to other child Pair engages in many activities in varied locations Other children are not excluded Physically comfortable with other person, including rough-and-tumble play	**Secure Attachment Style** Joint creative, elaborate play with complementary roles Able to cope with emerging conflicts
Avoidant Attachment Style Incompetent when engaging in activities Preoccupied with self Expresses flat affect Does not actively seek to be physically close to prospective friend	**Avoidant Attachment Style** Close proximity to other child Pair engages in narrow range of activities in restricted location No indication of physical comfort, seldom touch one another	**Avoidant Attachment Style** Simple structured play or parallel play Conflicts are avoided
Ambivalent Attachment Style Varying levels of competence when engaging in activities Engages in detached and aggressive behavior Varying degrees of closeness to prospective friend	**Ambivalent Attachment Style** Varying proximity to other child Well-coordinated activities but little interaction Physically comfortable with other child, but no rough-and-tumble play	**Ambivalent Attachment Style** Almost no common play Relatedness starts and stops No conflicts

FIGURE 8.6

A Three-Stage Model of Preadolescent Friendship and Effects of Attachment Style. Preadolescents in a summer day camp setting were observed as they formed friendships. The process was described as consisting of three stages: behavior prior to friendship formation, connectedness (forming pairs), and creative relatedness (relating to one another as friends). Behavior at each stage was influenced by the child's attachment style.

(*Source:* Based on information from Schulman, Elicker, & Stroufe, 1984.)

FIGURE 8.7

Four Adult Attachment Patterns Based on Evaluations and Expectancies with Respect to Self and Other People. Bartholomew has extended Bowlby's work on attachment by identifying four adult attachment styles or patterns. The two underlying dimensions are the extent to which an individual (1) has a positive self-image and expects others to respond accordingly, and (2) has a positive image of other people and expects others to be available and supportive. Depending on where one falls on these two dimensions, the result is one of four attachment patterns: *secure, preoccupied, dismissing,* or *fearful.*

(*Source:* Based on information from Griffin & Bartholomew, 1994a, 1994b.)

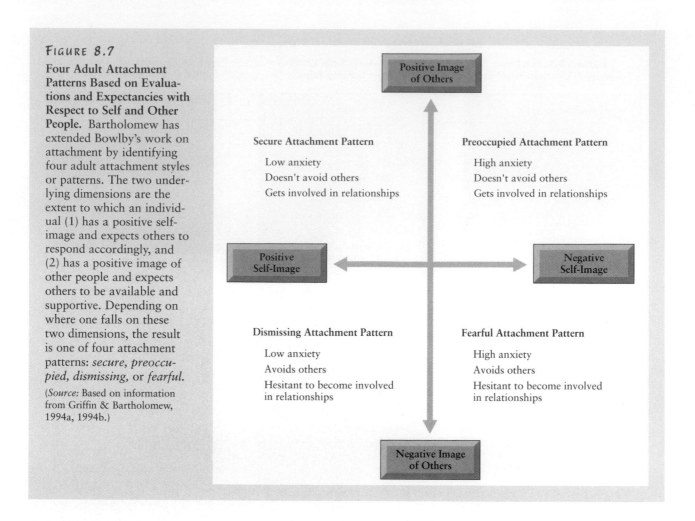

arouse feelings of anxiety, unworthiness, and dependency. Individuals with a positive image of other people expect them to be available and supportive, so close relationships tend to be sought; but people with a negative image of others are motivated to avoid close relationships because they expect others to be unavailable and nonsupportive. It is possible to fall on the positive or negative end of each dimension, so four basic patterns of adult attachment are possible—as shown in the figure. Two of the patterns are very clear: those who are self-positive and other-positive (*secure*) seek closeness with others, while those who are self-negative and other-negative (*avoidant* or *fearful*) avoid rejection by avoiding closeness. That is, they regulate the possible threat of a close relationship by simply staying away. Relationships are also potentially threatening to those falling into the other two patterns. Each involves emotional conflict, and they represent two aspects of what we have previously labeled as the *ambivalent* attachment style. A *preoccupied* person has a negative self-view along with the belief that other people will be loving and accepting; as a result, the individual seeks closeness in relationships (sometimes excessive closeness) but experiences distress whenever emotional needs are not met. *Dismissing* individuals avoid genuine closeness because they expect the worst from others, but they maintain a positive self-image, stress their independence, and perceive the world through egocentric glasses.

Current theorizing about attachment style is very interesting; but keep in mind that it may be too easy to assume that the expectancies developed in infancy are perfect predictors of attachment patterns expressed in childhood, adolescence, and adulthood. That seems to be at least partially true, but all we can be reasonably sure of at this point is that evaluations of self and evaluations of others are important determinants of interpersonal behavior at all ages.

An increasing amount of research in social psychology is now concentrating on relationships, including adult friendships (Adams & Blieszner, 1994), friendships through the lifespan and into old age (Matthews, 1986), cross-sex friendships (Gaines, 1994; McWilliams & Howard, 1993), and the role of friendship in the lives of gays and lesbians (Nardi & Sherrod, 1994).

Loneliness: Life without a Close Relationship

Though most people place a high value on establishing relationships, many have difficulty in achieving that goal. The outcome is likely to be **loneliness**—the feeling a person has whenever the quantity and quality of desired relationships is higher than the quantity and quality of actual relationships (Archibald, Bartholomew, & Marx, 1995; Peplau & Perlman, 1982). Note, however, that many people prefer solitude; they may be alone, but not lonely (Burger, 1995). Much of the research on loneliness has dealt with the consequences of loneliness, why some people have trouble forming relationships, and what can be done to overcome the problem (Marangoni & Ickes, 1989).

What Is It Like to Be Lonely? Much of the research on loneliness has used the *UCLA Loneliness Scale* (Russell, Peplau, & Cutrona, 1980). Test respondents indicate how frequently ("never" to "often") they feel or do various things; for example, "I feel left out" or "I have a lot in common with the people around me." The lonely individual is likely to feel left out and not to have a lot in common with others. We pointed out in Chapter 7 that there is a general tendency for people to believe that others share their attitudes and beliefs, but the false consensus effect is *not* characteristic among those who are lonely (Bell, 1993). Besides feeling that others are relatively dissimilar, the greater one's loneliness, the less one trusts other people (Rotenberg, 1994). As you would expect, the interpersonal behavior of people scoring high in loneliness is consistent with their test responses. That is, a person who *feels* lonely tends to spend his or her leisure time in solitary activity, to have very few dates, and to have only casual friends or acquaintances rather than a close friend (R. A. Bell, 1991; Berg & McQuinn, 1989; Williams & Solano, 1983).

Loneliness is associated with negative emotions such as depression, anxiety, unhappiness, dissatisfaction, and shyness (Jones, Carpenter, & Quintana, 1985; Neto, 1992). Those who know lonely individuals tend to evaluate them as maladjusted (Lau & Gruen, 1992; Rotenberg & Kmill, 1992).

Why Are Some People Lonely? The question of why some people desire relationships but are unable to establish them has been answered in several ways. For example, Duggan and Brennan (1994) trace the problem to Bartholomew's attachment patterns, noting that both "dismissing" and "fearful" individuals are hesitant to become involved in relationships.

Others propose that loneliness begins in childhood, if a child fails to develop appropriate social skills—for whatever reason, he or she simply doesn't know how to interact successfully with other children (Braza et al., 1993). For example, a child who is either withdrawn or aggressive is very likely to be rejected as a playmate (Johnson, Poteat, & Ironsmith, 1991). Unless something is done to change the inappropriate behavior, interpersonal difficulties typically continue through childhood and into adolescence and adulthood—they don't just go away (Asendorpf, 1992).

Loneliness ■ The emotional state that results from desiring close interpersonal relationships but being unable to attain them.

Because peer relationships become crucial in adolescence, when young people begin to distance themselves from parents and family, this is the time when *social phobia* is most likely to develop (Herbert, 1995). This is a debilitating anxiety disorder in which social situations become sufficiently frightening that a person totally avoids them as a way to protect herself or himself from embarrassment and humiliation. An extremely lonely and fearful teenager may decide that life is *hopeless*. At its worst, this feeling of despair can sometimes lead to suicide (Page, 1991).

Some of the specific details of good and bad social skills have been identified in research (Segrin & Kinney, 1995). For example, a socially skilled adolescent is friendly, possesses high self-esteem, seldom responds angrily, and makes conversation easily (Reisman, 1984). A socially unskilled individual tends to be shy, to have low self-esteem, and to be self-conscious when interacting with a stranger (Bruch, Hamer, & Heimberg, 1995).

When college students are observed interacting with a peer, a socially unskilled individual is generally insensitive to the other person—referring primarily to herself or himself, failing to follow up on what the other individual says, asking no questions that would indicate an interest in the other, and misinterpreting the other person's sexual intentions (Kowalski, 1993). Socially unskilled persons also show insensitivity by either disclosing very little about themselves or making inappropriate disclosures (B. Bell, 1991; Jones, Hobbs, & Hockenbury, 1982). This interpersonal style tends to drive potential friends away (Meleshko & Alden, 1993); being rejected further confirms a person's existing expectancies about interpersonal failure as well as the person's pessimism, depression, and belief that life is uncontrollable (Davis et al., 1992; Johnson, Johnson, & Petzel, 1992). Such reactions add to the problem, in that negative emotions and a pessimistic outlook increase the individual's social unacceptability (Carver, Kus, & Scheier, 1994).

Socially unskilled people are often very much aware of their interpersonal problems. When shown a videotape of themselves interacting with someone they know, socially unskilled students evaluate their own performance negatively (Duck, Pond, & Leatham, 1994).

What sort of cognitions might underlie socially skillful versus socially unskillful behavior? Langston and Cantor (1989) studied the interpersonal successes and failures of college students for several months. As outlined in Figure 8.8, the investigators found that students who were socially successful perceived interpersonal tasks differently from those who failed. Consistent with other research, the two groups of students also were found to use different strategies in interacting with others. Specifically, unskilled students appraise a social situation negatively and react with *social anxiety*. Given this negative perception of the situation, the socially unskilled person develops a restrained and conservative social strategy, attempting to avoid the risk of being rejected. This tendency to hold back and "play it safe" interpersonally makes a negative impression on others. In contrast, a socially successful student is more likely to perceive a new social situation as an interesting challenge and an opportunity to make new friends. The resulting strategy is to be open and informative, with the result that other people respond positively.

What Can Be Done to Reduce Loneliness? Because loneliness is not something that will simply improve with the passage of time, most investigators agree that some kind of active intervention is needed to help the lonely individual. Without such intervention, loneliness can motivate a retreat into wish-fulfilling fantasies, total involvement in work, or reliance on alcohol and drugs to ease the pain (Revenson, 1981). Music can sometimes serve as a substitute for interper-

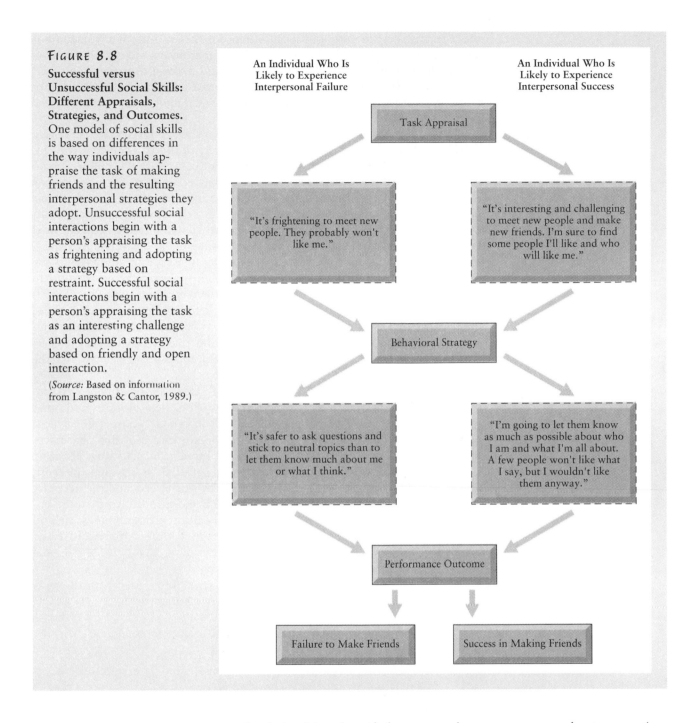

FIGURE 8.8

Successful versus Unsuccessful Social Skills: Different Appraisals, Strategies, and Outcomes. One model of social skills is based on differences in the way individuals appraise the task of making friends and the resulting interpersonal strategies they adopt. Unsuccessful social interactions begin with a person's appraising the task as frightening and adopting a strategy based on restraint. Successful social interactions begin with a person's appraising the task as an interesting challenge and adopting a strategy based on friendly and open interaction.

(*Source:* Based on information from Langston & Cantor, 1989.)

An Individual Who Is Likely to Experience Interpersonal Failure

An Individual Who Is Likely to Experience Interpersonal Success

Task Appraisal

"It's frightening to meet new people. They probably won't like me."

"It's interesting and challenging to meet new people and make new friends. I'm sure to find some people I'll like and who will like me."

Behavioral Strategy

"It's safer to ask questions and stick to neutral topics than to let them know much about me or what I think."

"I'm going to let them know as much as possible about who I am and what I'm all about. A few people won't like what I say, but I wouldn't like them anyway."

Performance Outcome

Failure to Make Friends

Success in Making Friends

sonal relationships, but if the person focuses on songs about separation, heartache, and sadness, feelings of loneliness increase (Davis & Kraus, 1989).

Among the more successful intervention techniques—often used simultaneously—are *cognitive therapy* and *social skills training* (Hope, Holt, & Heimberg, 1995).

The typical cognitions of lonely and nonlonely people usually differ. For a lonely person, the self-schema (see Chapter 5) is usually quite negative, which results in selective attention being paid to negative information about self, especially information relevant to interpersonal relationships. As a result, the person's negative self-concept is repeatedly confirmed in its negativity (Frankel & Prentice-Dunn, 1990). In cognitive therapy, procedures are designed to alter these negative cognitions about social situations. For example, if a woman finds social gatherings stressful because she believes that others are continually paying attention to her, looking at her "funny," and making negative evaluations (Asendorpf, 1989), she can gradually be convinced that she really isn't the center of everyone else's attention. Other people, in fact, tend to be most concerned about themselves.

Along with changes in maladaptive cognitions, behavioral changes are also necessary. As we have seen, loneliness characteristically is associated with inadequate social skills and with worries about not being socially skillful (Solano & Koester, 1989). How can these skills be taught? One approach is to provide a lonely individual with the chance to observe interpersonally successful role models on videotape. He or she can then practice social skills in a nonthreatening situation while being taped and afterward view the results. Sometimes it is necessary to instruct the socially unskilled individual about very specific acts (for example, initiating a conversation, showing interest and animation when interacting with another person, giving compliments), which the person can then try out and "rehearse" before attempting them in actual situations. The effects of such training can be remarkable, even in a short period of time. Once a lonely person learns to think about social situations in a new way, learns precisely how best to interact with other people, and changes his or her interpersonal style, the result is likely to be a series of success experiences and the subsequent elimination of loneliness.

Within the last decade, those suffering from extreme social anxiety or social phobia have also been treated with drugs such as beta blockers and other medications used in treating hypertension and depression (Garcia-Borreguero & Bronisch, 1992; Liebowitz et al., 1992). The advantage of this pharmacologic approach is that behavioral changes occur rapidly, and the drugs are more cost-effective than either cognitive therapy or social skills training (Herbert, 1995). The disadvantages include problems with side effects and the necessity that the person continue on the medication to avoid a return to the pretreatment emotional state. It seems possible that medication may be most helpful when the problem is severe and when the drug is used along with cognitive and behavioral therapy.

INTEGRATING PRINCIPLES

1. All close relationships involve interdependence—when two people influence one another's lives, thoughts, and emotions, and behaviors. Family relationships seem to form the basis for all later relationships. The first and perhaps most important interpersonal experience is that between mother and infant, generating basic attitudes about self (Chapter 5) and about other people (Chapter 7)—attitudes that are reflected in one's attachment style.

2. Close friendships can begin at a very young age, and the ability to form these relationships in childhood, adolescence, and adulthood appears to be strongly influenced by the individual's attachment style.

3. When a person desires a close relationship but fails to attain this goal, loneliness results. Relationship problems (and hence loneliness) are believed to occur because of negative attachment patterns, the absence of good social skills, and maladaptive interpersonal cognitions.

Romantic Relationships, Love, and Physical Intimacy

Among the more puzzling phenomena in the study of human interactions are those that differentiate an intimate relationship from a close friendship. We will examine what social psychologists have discovered about romantic relationships, love, and the role of sexual intimacy in these relationships. Note that as relationships develop, romance, love, and sex each may occur or not, and they can occur either simultaneously or in any order.

Romantic Relationships

Some degree of physical intimacy is one of the defining characteristics of romantic relationships, as suggested by Figure 8.9. Intimacy may involve simply kissing, holding hands, or embracing, or it may also involve a variety of interpersonal sexual acts. Rapid cultural changes over the past several decades have made it difficult to know precisely what is implied by terms such as "hanging out together," "dating," "going steady," "living together," and "becoming engaged"; but each suggests romantic attraction, possible feelings of love, the strong likelihood of sexual interest, and marriage as something that may occur at some future date.

Similarities between Romantic Relationships and Close Friendships. In some respects the attraction between a male and a female is much like other close relationships. For example, similarity influences who is likely to date whom (Whitbeck & Hoyt, 1994).

FIGURE 8.9

Physical Intimacy: One Indicator of a Romantic Relationship. One of the differences between a friendship and a romantic relationship is that romance usually includes some degree of physical intimacy. Cultural influences define what kind of contact is suitable.

Attachment style is once again an important aspect of interpersonal behavior. In a four-month study of heterosexual relationships among Canadian undergraduates, Keelan, Dion, and Dion (1994) found that those with a secure attachment style expressed more satisfaction with and greater commitment to the relationship, and that they trusted the partner more, than students whose attachment styles were avoidant or ambivalent. Among undergraduates involved in a romantic relationship, there is a also a weak but significant tendency to be attracted to someone with an attachment style like one's own (Brennan & Shaver, 1995). Thus, some aspects of interpersonal style that can be traced to infant experiences continue to be reflected in adult romantic interactions.

Differences between Romantic Relationships and Close Friendships. Some aspects of a romantic interaction differ from other relationships. For example, Swann, De La Ronde, and Hixon (1994) indicate that among friends, college roommates, and even married couples, the preference is for a partner who can validate one's self-concept. That is, we generally want to be with someone who knows us well enough to understand our best and our worst characteristics. Dating, however, is different. Early in such a relationship, at least, two people are not committed to one another and aren't looking for self-validation. Rather, they are looking for acceptance and want to like and to be liked, hoping most of all for compliments and praise. In effect, people go out to have fun, and they are on their best behavior. We "test drive" potentially acceptable models—but our judgments are often unrealistic, because of this search for uncomplicated *positivity feedback*.

Consistent with the general conceptualization of romantic relationships as built in part on fantasy are findings in both the United States and the Netherlands that couples judge their own relationships to be better (more positive) than the relationships that other people have (Van Lange & Rusbult, 1995). The hidden (and sometimes not so hidden) agenda of sexual motivation also differentiates romantic relationships from other types. Simpson and Gangestad (1991, 1992) have found that people differ in whether their primary motivation in seeking a romantic partner is sex or closeness. This difference falls along a personality dimension labeled **sociosexuality**. At one extreme are individuals who have an *unrestricted sociosexual orientation*; they are willing to engage in sexual interactions with partners in the absence of either closeness, commitment, or emotional bonding. At the other extreme are people who have a *restricted sociosexual orientation*; they believe that a sexual relationship *must* be based on closeness, commitment, and emotional bonding. In addition, restrictive sociosexuality is associated with having a secure attachment style (Brennan & Shaver, 1995).

An unrestricted orientation is more characteristic of men than of women, but either gender can be restricted or unrestricted. Compared to those who are restricted, unrestricted people engage in sex earlier in a relationship, are less interested in love, and are more likely to be involved with two or more partners at the same time. Sociosexual orientation is not related to sex drive, sexual satisfaction, or sex guilt, but it *is* related to the kind of romantic partner that the person finds attractive—as summarized in Figure 8.10.

Besides sexuality, dating can involve another type of interaction that is rare in friendships: One of the partners (usually the male) may physically abuse the other. There is, in fact, more intense physical violence in close relationships than in any other kind of relationship. Sugarman and Hotaling (1989) report that 40 percent of U.S. women experience violence from a person they are dating. As with spouse abuse, many abused dates continue their relationship with a violent male until they are somehow convinced to stop putting up with it. That is,

Sociosexuality ■ Personality dimension ranging from an *unrestricted* orientation (willingness to engage in casual sexual interactions) to a *restricted* orientation (willingness to engage in sex only with emotional closeness and commitment).

FIGURE 8.10

Reactions to a Romantic Partner: Effects of Sociosexuality. *Sociosexuality* is a personality dimension that ranges from restricted to unrestricted extremes. Those whose orientation is restricted (more women than men) feel that sexual interactions are appropriate only when there is emotional closeness, love, and commitment to a relationship. Those whose orientation is unrestricted (more men than women) are quite willing to engage in sexual interactions in the absence of emotional closeness, love, or commitment. As indicated in the figure, restricted and unrestricted individuals (regardless of gender) differ in their romantic preferences, criteria for attraction, nonverbal behavior with a potential partner, and type of relationship with current partner.

(*Source:* Based on information from Simpson & Gangestad, 1991, 1992; Simpson, Gangestad, & Biek, 1993.)

(*continued on p. 290*)

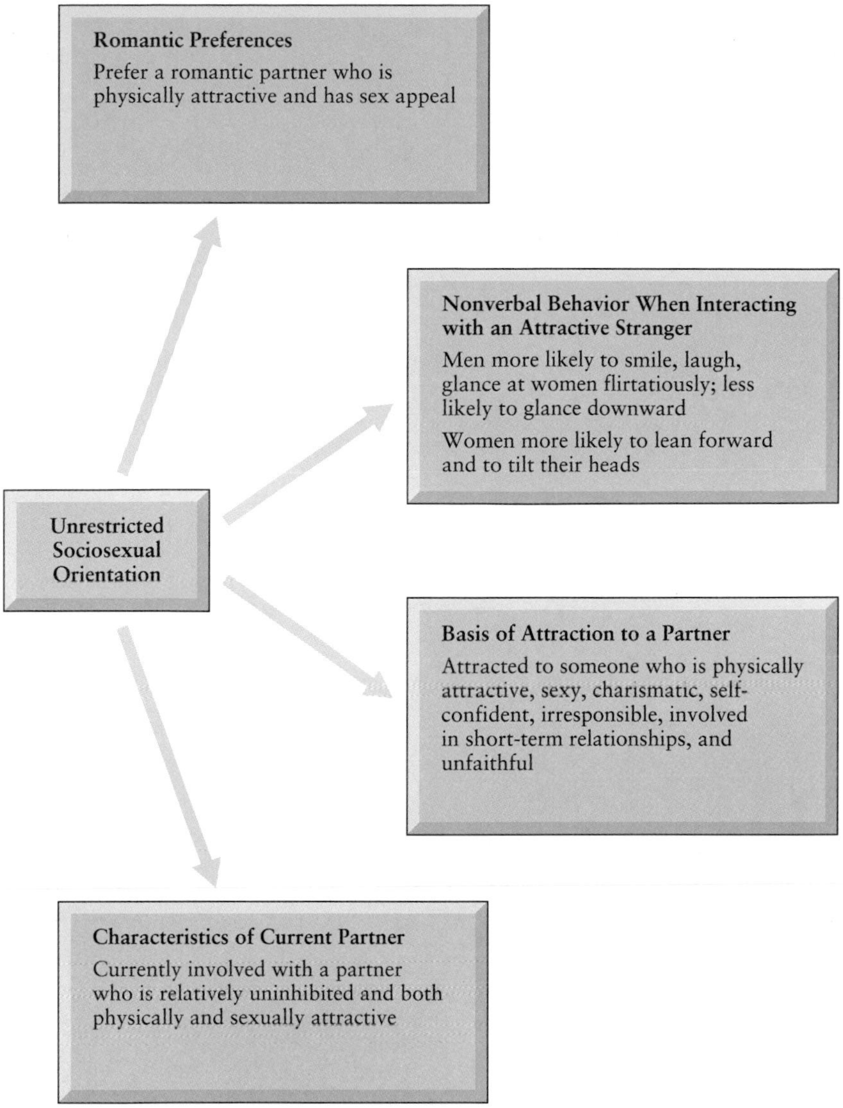

Romantic Preferences
Prefer a romantic partner who is physically attractive and has sex appeal

Unrestricted Sociosexual Orientation

Nonverbal Behavior When Interacting with an Attractive Stranger
Men more likely to smile, laugh, glance at women flirtatiously; less likely to glance downward
Women more likely to lean forward and to tilt their heads

Basis of Attraction to a Partner
Attracted to someone who is physically attractive, sexy, charismatic, self-confident, irresponsible, involved in short-term relationships, and unfaithful

Characteristics of Current Partner
Currently involved with a partner who is relatively uninhibited and both physically and sexually attractive

a woman stops dating an abusive partner when she begins to define the relationship as unhealthy and unlikely to improve, or when she reappraises what is going on and decides to take control of her own life, or when she has an experience that she perceives as "the last straw" (Rosen & Stith, 1995).

Do You Love Me? And What Does That Mean?

Love is one of the most common themes in our songs, movies, and everyday lives, as suggested by the nightclub performer in Figure 8.11 (p. 291). Data support the proposition that most people perceive love as a very common experience. A 1993 poll of 1,000 American adults revealed that almost three out of four say that they are currently "in love." What do they mean when they say that? One possibility is that a friendship between a man and a woman is redefined as a loving relationship when the two people begin to perceive themselves as potential sexual partners. As we shall see in the following section, a

Love ■ Several quite different combinations of emotions, cognitions, and behaviors that can be involved in intimate relationships.

FIGURE 8.10
(continued)

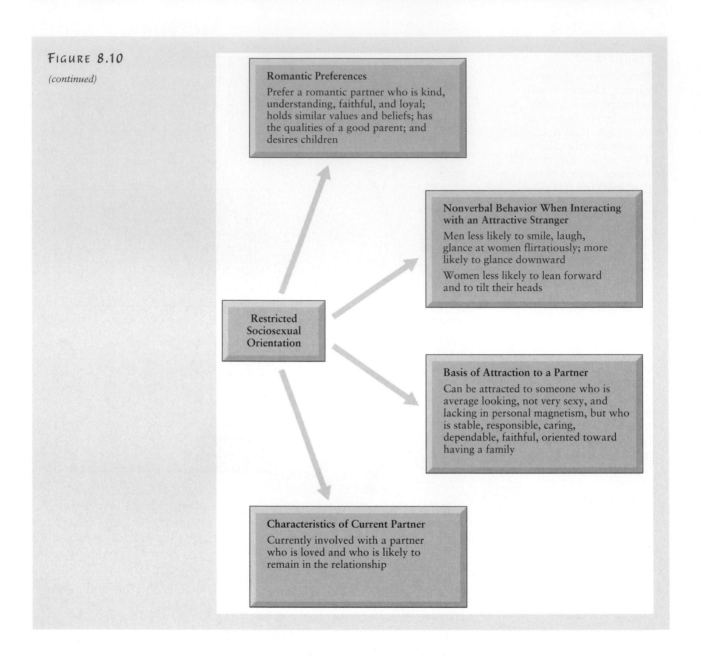

quarter century of social psychological research and theory indicates that love is more complex and much less straightforward than that.

Passionate Love Is Not Like Friendship. Aron and colleagues (1989) point out that many people fall in love, but no one ever reports "falling in friendship." In Chapter 7, we discussed many factors—from propinquity to similarity—that gradually facilitate the establishment of a friendship. In contrast, **passionate love** (an intense and often unrealistic emotional reaction to a potential romantic partner) seems to occur suddenly and to depend primarily on specific observable cues provided by the other person, as well as on what one believes and expects about love. McClelland (1986) suggests that a person can talk about (and write about) love or friendship as a logical process when using the left brain, but the often illogical experience of falling in love occurs only when a person is using the right brain.

Passionate Love ■ Intense and often unrealistic emotional response to another person; the individuals involved often interpret their feelings as "true love," while observers often label their response as "infatuation."

FIGURE 8.11

Love As a Pervasive Part of Our Experience. *In our songs and movies, and in our lives (past, present, and future), love seems to be one of the most common and most popular of themes.*

(*Source:* Drawing by B. Grace; © 1982 *The New Yorker* Magazine, Inc.)

"And now, for all of you out there who are in love, or if you've ever been in love, or if you think you'll be in love someday, or even if you only think you might like to be in love someday, this song is for you."

The person you love may not even love you; *unrequited love* refers to this one-way flow of affection. Both the one who loves and the one who does not love feel distressed—one is rejected and undergoes a loss of self-esteem, while the other feels guilty about hurting the would-be lover (Baumeister, Wotman, & Stillwell, 1993). Surveying more than four hundred respondents, Bringle and Winnick (1992) found that most (60 percent) said they had experienced unrequited love at least once in the past two years.

Most social psychological research dealing with love has focused on the more common situation, in which two people fall in love with each other. What have we learned so far?

Why and How Do People "Fall in Love"? When people say they are in love, they tend to mean passionate love (Hatfield, 1988); but love also can take several other forms—and we will discuss these variations shortly. Passionate love usually begins as a sudden, overwhelming, all-consuming reaction to another person—something that feels as if it's beyond your control, an unpredictable accident—"falling head over heels." I remember having this reaction when I was ten years old and too shy even to talk to this beautiful red-haired preadolescent girl who was in my class. I saw her, and that was it. Later, in high school, we became good friends, but I wasn't ever able to tell her about the impact she had once had on me. A person experiencing such love is preoccupied with the loved one—who has no faults or imperfections ("love is blind"). It is even possible to convince yourself that your lover's faults are really virtues (Murray & Holmes, 1993, 1994).

Passionate love seems to be a mixture of sexual attraction, physiological arousal, the desire to be physically close, an intense need to be loved as much as you love, and the constant fear that the relationship might end. A measure of this emotional state, the *Passionate Love Scale,* includes items such as "I would feel deep despair if _____ left me" and "For me, _____ is the perfect romantic partner" (Hatfield & Sprecher, 1986). These emotions are sufficiently intense that simply thinking about a past experience of falling in love creates a positive mood, while thinking about a failed love affair in one's past has the opposite effect (Clark & Collins, 1993).

More often than you might think, passionate love can arise without warning—literally, love at first sight (Averill & Boothroyd, 1977). In Chapter 3, we described how facial feedback influences your emotional response (smile and you feel happier, etc.). Somewhat surprisingly, an emotion such as love can also be aroused by what you are doing. When two opposite-sex strangers are simply asked to gaze into each other's eyes for two minutes, each is then more likely to express affectionate feelings toward the other (Kellerman, Lewis, & Laird, 1989). The positive effect of physical acts such as gazing at and holding hands with an opposite-sex stranger is most likely for research participants who strongly believe in romantic ideals: love at first sight, love conquers all, and love as the major foundation for relationships (Williams & Kleinke, 1993).

How is it that something as basic as passionate love can be generated so easily? Increasingly, many psychologists, anthropologists, and others believe that love is a universal phenomenon (Hatfield & Rapson, 1993a), though its specific meaning can vary greatly from culture to culture and in different eras (Beall & Sternberg, 1995). One reason that love is found throughout the world may be based on its association with attachment style. As discussed earlier, an infant interacts with its mother (or other primary caregiver) and develops basic attitudes about self and other people. What each of us learns in this interaction is reflected not only in parent–child relationships but also in the kind of affectional bonds we tend to form in adolescence and adulthood with those to whom we are attracted (Bowlby, 1969, 1979). Indirect evidence consistent with this proposal was reported by Hazan and Shaver (1987), who found that the percentages of adults indicating secure (56 percent), avoidant (25 percent), and ambivalent (19 percent) attachment styles in a romantic relationship were approximately the same as the percentages of each attachment style found in studies of infant–mother interactions (Campos et al., 1983).

A completely different explanation of passionate love's universal presence is based on evolutionary theory (Buss & Schmitt, 1993; Fisher, 1992). About four or five million years ago, our ancestors began to walk in an upright position and forage for whatever food could be carried back to a safe shelter. The survival of our species depended on reproductive success—on men and women (1) engaging in sexual intercourse and (2) investing the time and effort required to feed and protect their offspring until the young ones, in turn, were old enough to seek partners and reproduce. These two different but equally crucial aspects of reproductive success—lust and commitment—were enhanced among those humans whose biochemistry led them to seek and enjoy not only sexual satisfaction but also male–female bonding and parent–child bonding. Note that animal research provides evidence of the effect of brain chemistry on pair bonding (Rensberger, 1993). With emotional attachments motivated by physiological underpinnings, early human male–female pairs became more than just sex partners—they also liked and trusted one another and divided up the necessary tasks into hunting and gathering food versus caring for the children. Humans who behaved in this fashion were more likely to pass on their genes than humans who were not motivated to seek intercourse *and* also to establish strong interpersonal bonds. As a result, today's humans have been genetically primed to seek sex, fall in love, and care for their children (Trivers, 1972). While it is difficult—perhaps impossible—to provide a definitive test of this kind of theoretical formulation, evolutionary pressures nevertheless provide a convincing explanation of some of our interpersonal behavior. If you are deeply in love with someone at this moment, you may not want to think of yourself as driven by genetics and biochemistry; but it seems quite possible that such factors could help explain why you feel the way you do.

Keep in mind that human behavior is influenced by many factors other than genetics (Allgeier & Wiederman, 1994). Even if the evolutionary scenario just described turns out to be totally accurate, cultural influences can still overcome these tendencies, guide them into quite specific forms, or even add to them, by way of the stories we tell our children (and ourselves), our religious practices, and the laws we enact. In any event, Hatfield and Rapson (1993b) conclude that the major cultural groups in today's world are more similar than dissimilar in their views about love and intimacy.

Given the widespread cultural support of love, marriage, and parenthood, Hatfield and Walster (1981) have proposed that for most individuals, passionate love is easily aroused if three simple conditions are present.

First, you must be exposed to romantic images and role models that lead you to expect that you will someday find the right person and fall in love. Consider how, since childhood, each of us has repeatedly learned that life includes love, marriage, and living happily ever after from fairy tales (*Snow White, Cinderella, Sleeping Beauty,* and hundreds of others) not to mention unlimited later exposure to love songs and love stories.

Second, you must come in contact with an appropriate person to love. Who you believe is "appropriate" is likely to be strongly influenced by what you have learned from your culture—for example, the potential love object should be of the opposite sex, physically attractive, unmarried, a member of the same religious faith, and on and on. Besides these criteria based on cultural rules, evolutionary psychologists suggest that we are also strongly influenced by unconscious factors that direct us toward a love object who is able to reproduce and to take care of our future offspring (Buss, 1988). Because men can reproduce daily from puberty until they die, while a woman's reproductive capability is more limited; and because pregnancy and child care create longer pauses during her fertile years, and thus interfere with a woman's ability to seek food and other necessities, the sexes are genetically selected to differ in the attributes they seek in a partner. A man is attracted to women younger than himself (making them more likely to be capable of reproducing), whereas a woman is often attracted to older men who offer the material resources and character she and her offspring will need (Bailey et al., 1994; Feingold, 1992; Kenrick & Keefe, 1992; Kenrick et al., 1993; Sprecher, Sullivan, & Hatfield, 1994; see also the discussion in Chapter 1). These male–female differences are outlined in Figure 8.12 on page 294. Evolutionary psychologists further propose that physical similarity (skin color, etc.) is preferred (Bailey & Czuchry, 1994), because mating with a similar partner increases the odds that your kind of genes will be passed on to future generations (Rushton, 1990; Rushton & Nicholson, 1988). As convincing as evolutionary principles may be, they are seemingly difficult to apply in some situations, including those of homosexual couples (Metz, Rosser, & Strapko, 1994), heterosexual couples who decide never to have children, or couples who mate in later life. In such circumstances, do men and women employ similar strategies? If so, do genetics play *any* role?

The *third* condition for experiencing passionate love is strong emotional arousal. Schachter's two-factor theory (see Chapter 3) states that we interpret

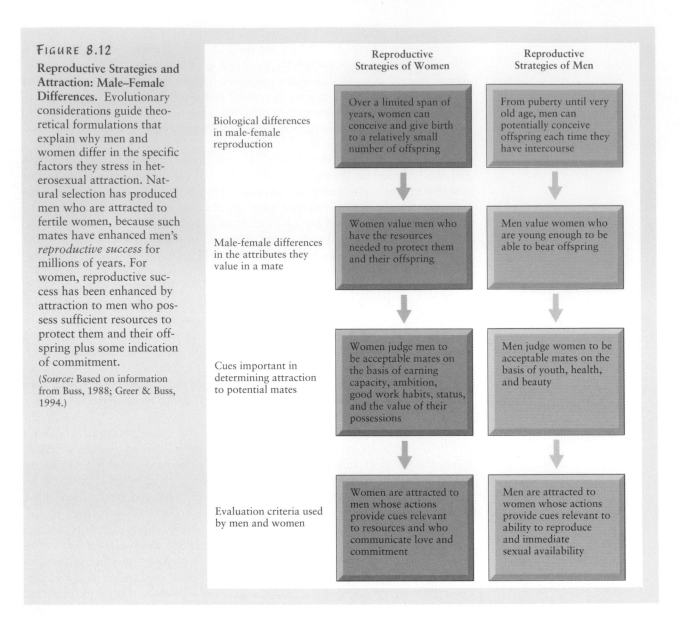

FIGURE 8.12

Reproductive Strategies and Attraction: Male–Female Differences. Evolutionary considerations guide theoretical formulations that explain why men and women differ in the specific factors they stress in heterosexual attraction. Natural selection has produced men who are attracted to fertile women, because such mates have enhanced men's *reproductive success* for millions of years. For women, reproductive success has been enhanced by attraction to men who possess sufficient resources to protect them and their offspring plus some indication of commitment.

(*Source:* Based on information from Buss, 1988; Greer & Buss, 1994.)

	Reproductive Strategies of Women	Reproductive Strategies of Men
Biological differences in male-female reproduction	Over a limited span of years, women can conceive and give birth to a relatively small number of offspring	From puberty until very old age, men can potentially conceive offspring each time they have intercourse
Male-female differences in the attributes they value in a mate	Women value men who have the resources needed to protect them and their offspring	Men value women who are young enough to be able to bear offspring
Cues important in determining attraction to potential mates	Women judge men to be acceptable mates on the basis of earning capacity, ambition, good work habits, status, and the value of their possessions	Men judge women to be acceptable mates on the basis of youth, health, and beauty
Evaluation criteria used by men and women	Women are attracted to men whose actions provide cues relevant to resources and who communicate love and commitment	Men are attracted to women whose actions provide cues relevant to ability to reproduce and immediate sexual availability

an aroused state on the basis of whatever cues are present. If you expect to fall in love and if you perceive an appropriate love object, you may well interpret arousal of any kind as indicating love. Research consistently shows that arousal based on emotions as different as fear (Dutton & Aron, 1974), frustration and anger (Driscoll, Davis, & Lipetz, 1972), or sexual excitement (Istvan, Griffitt, & Weidner, 1983) can easily be attributed to "love." Altogether, these factors based on culture, genetics, and emotional attributions make it very easy for most people to experience the often irrational and overpowering feelings of passionate love.

Love Can Take Many Forms. Passionate love occurs frequently, but it is too intense to be maintained indefinitely. Emotion-based love is sufficiently fragile that simply being asked to think about one's relationship or to answer questions about it can change relationship-relevant attitudes (Wilson & Kraft, 1993). Passionate love may thrive best when our fantasies are not interrupted by close, rational inspection.

There are, however, other kinds of love that *can* be long-lasting and thoughtful. Hatfield (1988, p. 205) describes **companionate love** as "the affec-

Companionate Love ■ Love based on friendship, mutual attraction, common interests, mutual respect, and concern for one another's happiness and welfare.

tion we feel for those with whom our lives are deeply entwined." Unlike passionate love, companionate love represents a very close friendship in which two people are attracted, have a great deal in common, care about one another's well-being, and express mutual liking and respect (Caspi & Herbener, 1990). This is a kind of love that can sustain a relationship over time—even though it does not lend itself to emotionally stirring songs and movies.

Before reading any further, you might find it interesting to examine the following *Applied Side* section and consider your own perceptions of love.

Social Psychology: On the Applied Side
WHAT DOES LOVE MEAN TO YOU?

If you want to try this exercise, please write a personal account or a story about a romantic relationship. It doesn't matter whether the events really happened in your life or are simply a fictional creation. When you have finished, read about love styles in the text and then come back to this section.

Hendrick and Hendrick (1993) asked male and female undergraduates to write about a romantic relationship just as you did, and then read the stories carefully to determine which of the six love styles seemed to be most important to each participant (many of the students stressed two styles rather than just one). In Table 8.2 are some examples from the students' stories that expressed each of the six styles, along with the percentage of students who expressed each theme.

Obviously, you can't classify your story with the same accuracy as the Hendricks', but you may be able to decide whether your story fits one or two of the love styles better than the others. In other words, do you think your approach to love fits any of the descriptions of these different approaches to love?

One of the findings that surprised the investigators was that their participants stressed friendship more than any other love style, including passionate love. Do you believe that friendship is the most important aspect of a relationship? One intriguing possibility raised by Hendrick and Hendrick is that relationships may be different in the 1990s than they were in the 1970s, when the initial research on passionate love was conducted. The Hendricks note that marriages now take place at a later age, divorce rates are high, AIDS and other sex-related infections are a focus of concern, and gender roles are slowly changing. They suggest that romantic relationships could be evolving toward a more realistic foundation. Instead of falling in love first and (if they're lucky) developing a friendship afterward, perhaps couples today are more likely to establish a friendship *before* they experience a feeling labeled as "love." If so, romantic relationships may have a more solid base and be more stable than ever before. ■ ■ ■

Several other formulations of love and relationships have also been developed (for example, Hecht, Marston, & Larkey, 1994; Jacobs, 1992; Rusbult, Onizuka, & Lipkus, 1993; Snell & Finney, 1993). Most of this research has concentrated on a model containing passionate and companionate love plus four additional "love styles" (Borrello & Thompson, 1990; Hendrick & Hendrick, 1986; Lasswell & Lobsenz, 1980). Table 8.3 indicates the components of this six-part description of love along with examples of test items designed to measure each type.

TABLE 8.2   Love Styles Expressed by Undergraduates in Accounts of Real or Fictional Romantic Relationships

When students were asked to write a personal account or a story about a romantic relationship, each participant tended to stress one or two of the six love styles. Clearly, friendship love is described most frequently, followed by passionate love. How do your own views of romance match these styles?

Love Styles and Excerpts from Student Accounts of a Romantic Relationship

EROS	When we first met, we ended up dancing and talking all night. It was sort of a case of "love at first sight." *This theme was stressed by 34 percent of the participants.*
STORGE	We were very close friends—virtually inseparable—but we were not dating. . . . I'm not sure where our friendship turned to love. *This theme was stressed by 66 percent of the participants.*
LUDUS	I find myself being attracted to other girls. I don't want to hurt her, but I feel so tied down and prevented from being the social, flirtatious person that I really am. *This theme was stressed by 2 percent of the participants.*
MANIA	During the time we were together, I would do practically anything to be with her. . . . But eventually my jealousy and insecurity made our relationship impossible. *This theme was stressed by 2 percent of the participants.*
PRAGMA	When I met him, I began to realize he was everything I wanted in a man. He matched everything I had on my "list," plus things I hadn't realized were important. *This theme was stressed by 17 percent of the participants.*
AGAPE	We are both unselfish and giving with each other, and we make sure to look out for one another's needs. . . . It is as if our souls were connected. *This theme was stressed by 2 percent of the participants.*

(*Source:* Based on information from Hendrick & Hendrick, 1993.)

TABLE 8.3   How Do I Love Thee? Six Styles from Which to Choose

In addition to passionate love and companionate (friendship) love, some theorists have suggested four additional love styles. The resulting six styles are shown in the table along with their Greek names and sample items from a scale designed to measure each. Because people differ in how they approach love, a relationship between two people with very different styles is likely to pose problems.

Basic Love Styles	Sample Test Items
EROS: Passionate Love	My lover and I were attracted to each other immediately after we first met.
STORGE: Friendship Love	Love is really a deep friendship, not a mysterious, mystical emotion.
LUDUS: Game-Playing Love	I have sometimes had to keep two of my lovers from finding out about each other.
MANIA: Possessive Love	I cannot relax if I suspect that my lover is with someone else.
PRAGMA: Logical Love	It is best to love someone with a similar background.
AGAPE: Selfless Love	I would rather suffer myself than let my lover suffer.

(*Source:* Based on material from Hendrick & Hendrick, 1986.)

Research on the six love styles has provided considerable information about their effect on relationships. For example, compared to women, men are higher in both passionate (*eros*) and game-playing (*ludus*) love. Women are higher than men in friendship (*storge*), logical (*pragma*), and possessive (*mania*) love (Hendrick et al., 1984). Women high in possessive love also report more verbal and physical aggression in their dating relationships (Bookwala, Frieze, & Grote, 1994). Game-playing love is characteristic of individuals who are concerned primarily with themselves and their independence (Dion & Dion, 1991). Game-playing is considered the least satisfactory style, because it is associated with unhappy relationships and, for males, sexually coercive behavior (Kalichman et al., 1993). Very religious individuals are likely to be highest in friendship, logical, and selfless love (Hendrick & Hendrick, 1987). As you might guess on the basis of the research discussed in Chapter 7, people who become romantic partners tend to have similar love styles (Hendrick, Hendrick, & Adler, 1988; Morrow, Clark, & Brock, 1995). Unlike some personality traits, love styles seem to be unrelated to genetics; they are based instead on environmental effects such as parent–child interactions (Waller & Shaver, 1994).

Another major conceptualization is Sternberg's (1986, 1988b) **triangular model of love,** which is depicted in Figure 8.13 (p. 298). This model suggests that—instead of different styles—each love relationship contains three basic components that are present in varying degrees for different couples. One component is **intimacy**—the closeness two people feel and the strength of the bond holding them together. Partners high in intimacy are concerned with each other's welfare and happiness, and they value, like, count on, and understand one another. The second component, **passion,** is based on romance, physical attraction, and sexual intimacy. **Decision/commitment** is the third component, representing cognitive factors such as the decision that you love the other person and are committed to maintaining the relationship. A scale was developed to assess these components in specific relationships (Sternberg, 1988a); couples who have all three components tend to have lasting relationships (Whitley, 1993).

Premarital Sexuality

Despite centuries of religious and legal sanctions against premarital sex in many parts of the world, dramatic changes in sexual attitudes and behavior have occurred during the second half of the twentieth century. Increasingly, sexual interactions have become a common and widely accepted part of romantic relationships.

Patterns of Sexual Behavior. The United States, Western Europe, Australia, and Canada have witnessed the greatest sexual changes. Surveys taken before and after World War II provide evidence of a steady and consistent shift toward more permissive sexual expression. By the 1960s, these changes had been labeled as the beginning of a "sexual revolution." To take one example, oral sex was considered to be a perversion in the first half of this century. By the 1990s, most American adults said they liked to give and to receive oral sex (Michael et al., 1994).

Similar changes did not even begin to occur in China until about 1988—and that nation's response has been to ban all written, audio, and visual material describing sexual behavior; to arrest those who produce it; and to execute those who sell it (Pan, 1993). The power of culture to influence sexuality is demonstrated by studies of Chinese American students, whose attitudes about premarital sex as well as their actual practices are much more permissive than is true for students in China; the more acculturated they are, the more their sexuality is like that of other American students (Huang & Uba, 1992).

Triangular Model of Love ■ Sternberg's conceptualization of love relationships as encompassing three basic components: intimacy, passion, and decision/commitment.

Intimacy ■ In Sternberg's triangular model of love, the closeness the two partners feel—the extent to which they are bonded.

Passion ■ In Sternberg's triangular model of love, the sexual motives and sexual excitement associated with a couple's relationship.

Decision/Commitment ■ In Sternberg's triangular model of love, the cognitive elements involved in the decision to form a relationship and in expressions of continuing commitment to it.

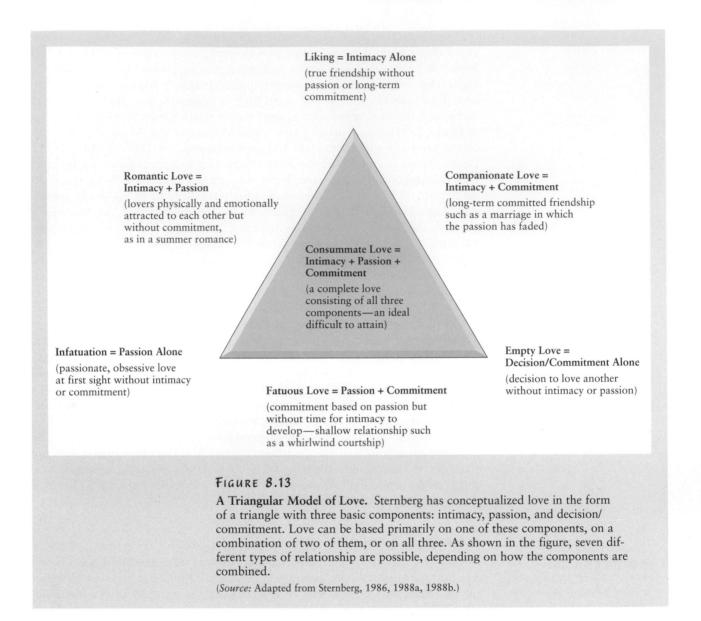

FIGURE 8.13

A Triangular Model of Love. Sternberg has conceptualized love in the form of a triangle with three basic components: intimacy, passion, and decision/commitment. Love can be based primarily on one of these components, on a combination of two of them, or on all three. As shown in the figure, seven different types of relationship are possible, depending on how the components are combined.

(*Source:* Adapted from Sternberg, 1986, 1988a, 1988b.)

In the Western world, before about 1950 a typical finding in sex surveys was that most men were sexually active before marriage while most women were not (Kinsey, Pomeroy, & Martin, 1948; Kinsey et al., 1953). This gender difference was possible because men had intercourse with women who *were* sexually active (possibly those who were sociosexually unrestricted) or with prostitutes. Though the 1950s are perceived as the last decade of sexual innocence (see Figure 8.14), during that decade premarital sex became an increasingly common experience among couples involved in a close relationship (Coontz, 1992).

With a few exceptions, such as Northern Ireland (Sneddon & Kremer, 1992), by the early 1980s, women in the Western world were as likely as men to engage in premarital intercourse (Breakwell & Fife-Schaw, 1992; Clement, Schmidt, & Kruse, 1984; McCabe, 1987; Weinberg, Lottes, & Shaver, 1995), though men still play a traditional role in initiating sexual activity (O'Sullivan & Byers, 1992). Both male and female undergraduates say they offer token resistance when sexual activity is suggested by the partner; the reasons given by both genders include maintaining their image, teasing and game playing, trying

FIGURE 8.14

The 1950s: The End of Sexual Innocence? Though the 1950s are often portrayed as the last decade before the sexual revolution, that decade was actually a time of transition in which sexual attitudes and behaviors were beginning to undergo dramatic changes in much of the Western world.

to gain control in the relationship, and wanting to slow things down (O'Sullivan & Allgeier, 1994). In serious relationships, sexuality has become both expected and widely accepted. In one sample of college couples, only 17 percent reported *not* having had intercourse (Christopher & Cate, 1985). Among young adults in the United States, only 5 percent of the women and 2 percent of the men have intercourse for the first time on their wedding night (Laumann et al., 1994; Michael et al., 1994).

In some respects, the choice of sexual partners resembles other interpersonal choices, in that 90 percent of all sexual relationships involve partners of the same ethnic group, and 84 percent involve people who have the same educational background (McDonald, 1995).

Some gender differences are still found. College men and women differ in how long they believe they must know the other person before it's acceptable to consent to intercourse. As shown in Figure 8.15 (p. 300), men more than women say that sex with a relative stranger is something they would do, while women say that they prefer to know the other person for a longer period of time (Buss & Schmitt, 1993). Of course, it is possible that both genders are trying to impress the investigators—men want to appear macho, and women want to appear selective. Perhaps people's verbal reponses to a survey do not reflect their real attitudes, behavioral intentions, or actions. Another gender difference has continued in this new sexual era—male adolescents want and actually have more sexual partners than female adolescents (Buss & Schmitt, 1993; Traeen, Lewin, & Sundet, 1992). Also, in an ongoing relationship, women want their partners to express more love and intimacy, while men want more arousing and more varied sexual activity (Hatfield et al., 1989). Many of these findings could be based on gender differences in sociosexuality.

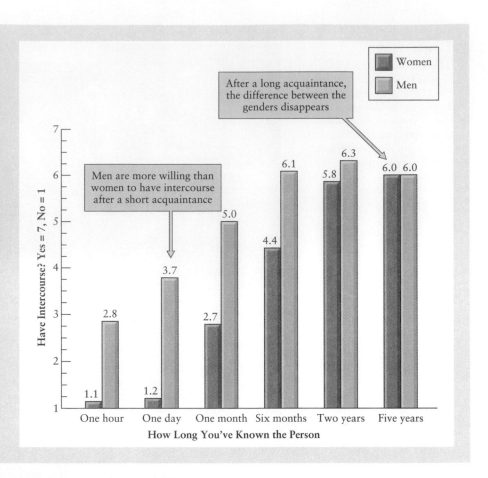

FIGURE 8.15

How Long Should You Know a Person before Having Sex? Men and Women Differ. College students were asked, "If the conditions were right, would you consider having sexual intercourse with someone you viewed as desirable if you had known that person for one hour? One day?" (etc. up to five years). The students answered on a seven-point scale ranging from "definitely not" to "definitely yes." While both men and women were more likely to say yes as the time period increased, men were more inclined than women to agree to sex at every acquaintance level through two years. Once the person had been known for five years, gender differences disappeared.

(*Source:* Based on data from Buss & Schmitt, 1993.)

Earlier, it was pointed out that physical intimacy is a defining characteristics of romantic relationships. The more intimate the touch, the more it is perceived as an indication that the partners are committed to the relationship (Johnson & Edwards, 1991). Men and women agree about the meaning of holding hands, kissing on the lips, and hugging as indicators of increased commitment, but there is considerable ambiguity and misperception between men and women about the meaning of such acts as indicators of an eventual sexual interaction (Abbey, 1982). As touches become more intimate and the couple moves toward petting and intercourse, both genders perceive greater commitment, but women interpret intimate contact as communicating *much more* about relationship commitment than men do.

Has the Sexual Revolution Stalled—or Even Gone into Reverse?   Though the "flower children" of the 1960s and 1970s had high hopes that the world would be a better place if people "made love, not war," there were warning signs by the end of that time period that permissive sexuality was not an all-purpose solution to the problems of love and relationships.

It soon became fairly obvious that engaging in sex was not necessarily always a deliberate choice; sometimes sexual activity occurred because of a partner's insistence or in response to a general belief that those who abstained were uptight, repressed, and generally out of it (DeLamater, 1981). When asked, women said they felt vulnerable, guilty, and anxious about being exploited by men (Townsend, 1995; Weis, 1983). For both genders, sexual activity was perceived as something disapproved of by one's parents (Moore & Rosenthal, 1991); even their peers viewed persons who were

vorce, two-parent families are still much more common than one-parent families; more than three-fourths of American households with children also contain both a father and a mother (Burrell, 1995). Still, there are millions of families that are blended (remarried parents with a child or children from another marriage), single-parent families, children being raised by grandparents, and so on. We will now describe some of the research that deals with what it means to live as husband and wife, including what is known about maintaining (or failing to maintain) a satisfying relationship.

Moving from a Romantic Relationship to a Married Relationship

As you might expect, much of what we said about interpersonal attraction in Chapter 7 and about attachment, friendship, romance, and love earlier in this chapter is also directly relevant to married partners.

Similarity and Marriage. Not surprisingly, almost a century of research consistently indicates that spouses are similar in their attitudes, values, interests, and other attributes (for example, Pearson & Lee, 1903; Schuster & Elderton, 1906; Smith et al., 1993). Further, a longitudinal study of couples from the time they first became engaged until they had been married for two decades indicated a relatively unchanging degree of similarity over the entire period (Caspi, Herbener, & Ozer, 1992). In other words, similarity is characteristic of those who marry, and it neither increases nor decreases over time.

Though similarity is an important factor in our choice of a spouse, two complicating factors should be considered. (1) It is easy enough to find a potential mate who is much more similar to us than chance, but practically impossible to find one who is exactly similar. (2) Many factors other than similarity influence our choice of a partner; as a result, we can easily "overlook" or discount areas of dissimilarity because of attributes such as physical attractiveness, the possession of material resources, and so forth. So we make compromises, trying to find someone with more positive than negative qualities; but we inevitably settle for less than perfect mates. As a result, the negative attributes (such as dissimilar attitudes) that didn't seem all that important at first can later have a negative effect on marital success. To take a simple example, will the positive effect of your partner's dazzling smile begin to fade over time, while the fact that you disagree about religion becomes an increasing source of discomfort? One of the first attempts to approach such questions is described in the following *Cornerstones* section.

Cornerstones of Social Psychology

TERMAN'S INVESTIGATION OF HUSBAND–WIFE SIMILARITY AND THE SUCCESS OF THE MARRIAGE

Though Lewis M. Terman's major contributions to psychology center on his lifelong work in the field of intelligence testing, Terman was also interested in discovering some of the factors that predicted marital compatibility. In the 1930s, following up what was already known about the association between similarity and attraction, he and a colleague examined the differences between happy and unhappy married couples (Terman & Buttenweiser, 1935a, 1935b).

Lewis M. Terman.
Lewis Terman was born in 1877 in Indiana. Much of his professional career was spent in developing and using the Stanford–Binet Intelligence Test. Terman had retired when I (DB) entered graduate school at Stanford, but I caught glimpses of him in the hallway once or twice before his death in 1956. His many interests included studying gifted children, helping to develop the first group intelligence test for use in the armed services during World War I, and investigating some of the factors responsible for happy versus unhappy marriages. It is the latter work that constitutes his major contribution to social psychology.

The investigators proposed that if similarity results in mutual attraction, highly similar spouses should be more satisfied with their marriage than less similar (and especially dissimilar) spouses. A test of marital happiness was given to hundreds of couples, and 100 of the most happy, 100 of the most unhappy, and 100 divorced pairs were matched for factors such as age, education, and occupational status. These couples were then given psychological inventories consisting of more than 500 items on which each respondent independently indicated whether he or she felt positively or negatively about various activities, occupations, kinds of people, and famous individuals.

The first finding was that across all couples, people tended to marry someone similar to themselves, at least with respect to their responses to this heterogeneous group of test items. The second—and more crucial—finding was that the relative similarity–dissimilarity of couples was associated with the happiness of the marriage. A summary of some of these findings is presented in Table 8.4. You might note that—as in attraction research—the importance of similar attitudes is just as strong for issues that seem to be irrelevant to the married couple (such as attitudes about Thomas Edison) as for seemingly central concerns within the marriage (such as attitudes about avoiding arguments).

Though we cannot draw firm conclusions about the role of specific items on the basis of a single study such as this, the general finding that marital success is more likely for similar than for dissimilar pairs has been confirmed numerous times in subsequent investigations. Terman's cornerstone study was the initial step that has led to many decades of continuing research on the factors that influence marital relationships. ■ ■ ■

Relationships among Young Married Couples. Just how do two people interact in their day-to-day lives as married partners? Johnson and his associates (1992) studied couples who had been married about two years and asked them to describe in detail what was involved when they engaged in household tasks, leisure pursuits, interactions, conflicts, and conversations. Based on their descriptions, the researchers identified four distinct marital patterns. As described in Figure 8.16, relationships tend to be either symmetrical, parallel, differentiated, or reversed.

Symmetrical marriages were the most common type (about two out of five couples): Both spouses work outside of the home and hold egalitarian beliefs about gender roles. They divide household chores in ways not based on traditional sex typing (see Chapter 5); these couples tend not to have much leisure time to spend together. About one marriage in four is categorized as *parallel*— once the most typical husband–wife relationship. The husband is the primary wage earner, work in the home is divided according to gender stereotypes, and the partners have different and separate ways of spending leisure time—the man with his friends, and the woman with her relatives. Couples who are *differentiated* (about one out of five) both work, but the husband is more involved in his job. They divide the household work along traditional lines and spend their leisure time together with both friends and relatives. The smallest group (one out of ten) have a *reversed* relationship. The husband is unemployed, the wife is involved in her job, and the housework doesn't reflect gender typing. These couples tend to be companionate, and the husband is more involved than the wife with friends and relatives.

Despite their differences in job patterns, division of household chores, and how leisure time is spent, couples in each group are equally satisfied with their marriages. They differ a great deal, however, in parenthood. After two years, both the parallel and differentiated couples are very likely to have children, but only half of the reversed and about a third of the symmetrical couples have become parents.

TABLE 8.4 Husband–Wife Similarity in Happy versus Unhappy and Divorced Couples

A pioneering study of marital compatibility found a general tendency for happily married couples to be more similar in responding to a variety of test items than were unhappily married or divorced couples.

Items on Which Happily Married Couples Were More Similar Than Unhappy or Divorced Couples

Attitudes about One's Own Behavior	Avoiding arguments
	Earning a definite salary versus a commission
	Getting attention from acquaintances when ill
	Contributing to charity
	Looking at a collection of antique furniture
	Having a pet canary
	Being alone at times of emotional stress
Attitudes about Other People	Life insurance salesmen
	Dentists
	Men who use perfume
	Energetic people
	General Pershing
	Thomas Edison
	Ranchers
	Conservative people

(*Source:* Based on data from Terman & Buttenweiser, 1935a, 1935b.)

FIGURE 8.16

Four Types of Marriage. When couples who had been married about two years described their daily lives, their responses indicated four quite different relationship patterns. These four patterns differed with respect to jobs outside of the home, the way in which household duties were divided, how leisure time was spent, and the probability of having children—but they did not differ in marital satisfaction.

(*Source:* Based on data from Johnson et al., 1992.)

Type of Marriage	Characteristics of Marriage
Symmetrical 42%	• Husband and wife both have jobs. • Household tasks are not sex-typed. • Sex role ideology is egalitarian. • Spouses spend little leisure time together. • 35.7% have children.
Parallel 27%	• Husband is primary wage earner. • Housework is divided in sex-typed way. • Spouses spend little time together. • Husband spends time with friends. • Wife spends time with relatives. • 77.8% have children.
Differentiated 21%	• Both work; husband's job emphasized. • Housework is divided in sex-typed way. • Spouses spend most leisure time together and are equally involved with friends and relatives. • 71.4% have children.
Reversed 10%	• Wife is involved with outside job. • Household jobs are not sex-typed. • Relationship is highly companionate. • Husband spends time with friends and relatives. • 50% have children.

Marital Sex, Parenthood, and General Satisfaction. Surveys of married partners consistently indicate that sexual interactions become less frequent over time, and the most rapid decline occurs during the first four years of marriage (Udry, 1980). Nevertheless, 41 percent of all married couples have sex twice a week or more often, while only 23 percent of single individuals have sex that frequently. Cohabiting singles are the most sexually active of all, however, in that 56 percent have sex at least twice a week (Laumann et al., 1994; Michael et al., 1994).

It is not surprising that passionate love tends to decrease over the years (Tucker & Aron, 1993), but Aron and Henkemeyer (1995) found that women who still felt passionate love after the passage of several years were more satisfied with their marriages than women who no longer had these feelings. Male satisfaction with the marriage was unrelated to feelings of passionate love. For both men and women, satisfaction is related to behavior that suggests companionate love—sharing activities, exchanging ideas, laughing together, and working together on projects. It appears that companionate love is a key to a satisfying marriage, but that women are happier if they also continue to feel sparks of passionate love.

With respect to the relationship in general and to sexuality specifically, parenthood can create multiple problems (Alexander & Higgins, 1993; Hackel & Ruble, 1992). For example, becoming a parent is accompanied by a decrease in feelings of passionate love (Tucker & Aron, 1993). Perhaps knowledge of these difficulties is a factor influencing an increasing number of women not to have children; according to the U.S. Census Bureau, in 1965 only 11 percent of American women aged thirty-five to thirty-nine were childless, but that figure rose to 18 percent in 1990. Nevertheless, both men and women who have children say that they enjoy being parents (Feldman & Nash, 1984).

Further, while people who are married consistently report being happier and healthier than those who are single (Steinhauer, 1995), the gap is not as great as it used to be—because unmarried men are happier now than in the past, while married women are less happy (Glenn & Weaver, 1988). A possible explanation for these changes may lie in the availability of sexual relationships for unmarried men (Reed & Weinberg, 1984) and the conflicts women face in pursuing a career while simultaneously having the role of mother (Batista & Berte, 1992). A Norwegian study also indicates that married individuals are better off than those who are unmarried—a lower suicide rate and higher self-reported feelings of well-being—up until age thirty-five to forty, but that after that, the advantages of being married rapidly decline (Mastekaasa, 1995).

A major task for both spouses is discovering how best to adjust to the demands of a two-career family (Gilbert, 1993; Helson & Roberts, 1992). For one thing, as discussed in Chapter 5, even when they have an active career, women still do much more than 50 percent of the housework (Hochschild, 1989). In fact, compared to heterosexual and gay couples, only lesbian pairs seem able to share household labor in a fair manner (Kurdek, 1993). A day in the life of Hi and Lois (Figure 8.17) depicts some of the interrelated problems associated with dual careers, parenthood, and attempts to maintain a sexual relationship.

Troubled Relationships: Problems and the Effects of Failure

Each year, about 2.4 million American couples marry and another 1.2 million get divorced, most often after two to six years of marriage (Glick, 1983). More than one-third of the children in the United States have had to go through the painful experience of their parents' divorce (Bumpass, 1984). Among the consequences for these children are negative long-term effects on their health and their lifespans (Friedman et al., 1995).

FIGURE 8.17
Trying to Meet the Conflicting Demands of Dual Careers, Parenthood, and Romance. Living happily ever after isn't easy, as Hi and Lois have discovered.
(*Source:* Reprinted with special permission from King Features Syndicate.)

What happens to turn a loving, romantic relationship into one characterized by unhappiness, dissatisfaction, and—often— hate? At times, even an originally positive attribute of the other person becomes a primary reason for dislike (Felmlee, 1995).

Some problems are universal in that being in an intimate relationship involves some degree of compromise. For example, two people have to decide what to have for dinner, what show to watch on TV, what to do in bed; and hundreds of other major and minor decisions must continually be made. Neither individual can do exactly what she or he wants, and a conflict between the desire for independence and the need for closeness is inevitable (Baxter, 1990). Other problems are specific, and some can be avoided. We will describe a sample of the common difficulties that arise in marriage and the painful effects of relationship failure.

Problems: General and Specific. Because any partner (including oneself) is less than perfect, spouses who initially believe they are ideally suited for one another inevitably come to realize that there are negative elements in the relationship. Only 1.2 percent of married couples say that they *never* have any disagreements, and most report that conflicts arise monthly or more often (McGonagle, Kessler, & Schilling, 1992). Because spouses greatly overestimate how much they agree about most matters (Byrne & Blaylock, 1963), they often don't realize that their views differ even when they believe they are communicating (Sillars et al., 1994).

Partners who are similar in the way they cope with stress are more satisfied with their relationship than those whose coping strategies differ (Ptacek & Dodge, 1995), and men more than women tend to believe that avoiding a conflict is a legitimate way to deal with it (Oggins, Veroff, & Leber, 1993). One of the greatest problems is the tendency to respond to the negative words or deeds of one's partner in an equally negative and destructive way; when people have time to consider the long-term consequences for the relationship, a constructive response is more likely to occur (Yovetich & Rusbult, 1994).

Individual differences in characteristics such as hostility, defensiveness, and depression are important determinants of how partners interact (Newton et al., 1995; Thompson, Whiffen, & Blain, 1995). In general, those who are best able to express their emotions are happiest in their marriages (King, 1993). Gender roles (Chapter 5) also matter (Bradbury, Campbell, & Fincham, 1995; Peplau, Hill, & Rubin, 1993). Women who describe themselves as feminine or expressive are most likely to report marital satisfaction, as are men who describe themselves as instrumental or expressive (Langis et al., 1994).

Buss (1989) proposes that many difficulties arise because of built-in differences between men and women. Remember the differences in the qualities sought by each gender in a mate? Look back at Figure 8.12—these same qualities in reverse can cause conflict between partners. That is, a woman becomes upset by any indication that her partner is not loving and protective, while a man becomes upset if his partner rejects him sexually. Jealousy is also a common problem in relationships (Buunk, 1995; Sharpsteen, 1995). Presumably because of our evolutionary history, a man becomes most jealous when his partner is sexually unfaithful, but a woman becomes most jealous when her partner becomes emotionally committed to someone else (Buss et al., 1992).

Other conflicts arise because partners slowly discover (or at least begin to attend to the fact) that they are dissimilar in various respects (Byrne & Murnen, 1988). Her compulsive neatness, for instance, may have seemed cute when they were dating, but it becomes annoying in their marriage. Other dissimilarities don't arise until later, when one of the partners changes in some way (Levinger, 1988). For example, I (DB) knew a young couple who both expressed left-wing views during the Vietnam War; but as the years went by, his attitudes moved increasingly to the political right, while hers did not. They eventually divorced.

Still other sources of conflict may be irrelevant when the couple is dating but become central later on. Two people can belatedly discover that they are very different in their views about saving versus spending money, about how best to respond to a child's misbehavior, or about what to say when an aging parent asks to move into their home.

For some, a long-term relationship begins to be uncomfortable simply because it has become *boring* (Hill, Rubin, & Peplau, 1976; Skinner, 1986). Married couples are very likely to develop unchanging routines in their daily interactions (sexual and otherwise) and then gradually perceive themselves to be in a rut. If one person wants variety and excitement while the other prefers regularity and predictability, these dissimilar goals create stress, and each spouse blames the difficulty on the other (Fincham & Bradbury, 1992, 1993).

Considering the importance of affect in relationships (see Chapter 7), it is not surprising that sexual satisfaction is closely associated with the perception of marital well-being for both women and men (Henderson-King & Veroff, 1994). Sex is obviously not the only source of positive or negative affect, however. Negative emotions aroused on the job can spill over to one's home life, and vice versa (Chan & Margolin, 1994; Geller & Hobfoll, 1994). Interestingly, mothers feel more positively when they are away from the home (including on the job), while fathers are happier at home than elsewhere (Larson, Richards, & Perry-Jenkins, 1994).

Further, negative affect caused by conflicts and disagreements can add greatly to the couple's dissatisfaction (Margolin, John, & O'Brien, 1989). Instead of trying to solve a given problem, unhappy partners may simply express their mutually negative evaluations as they blame one another and express their anger (Bradbury & Fincham, 1992; Kubany et al., 1995). Miller (1991, p. 63) observes that some of the "most hateful, caustic, and abusive interactions take place with those we say we love." Videotaped interactions of satisfied and dissatisfied couples reveal much more negative verbal and nonverbal behavior between partners whose relationship is deteriorating than between satisfied partners (Halford & Sanders, 1990). Unhappy couples express less positive affect and more negative affect than those who are satisfied (Levenson, Carstensen, & Gottman, 1994). All expressions of positive affect—including nicknames such as "sweet pea" and "pussycat"—are more common in satisfied than in dissatisfied marriages (Bruess & Pearson, 1993).

Though much of the research focuses on problems, it should be remembered that as many marriages succeed as fail. One secret seems to involve placing an emphasis on friendship, commitment, similarity, and efforts to create positive affect (Lauer & Lauer, 1985). Older couples who remain married express more positive affect than younger and middle-aged couples (Levenson, Carstensen, & Gottman, 1994), perhaps because people get smarter and mellower about relationships as they grow older (Locke, 1995).

Relationship Failure: When Dissatisfaction Leads to Dissolution. Though it is possible for friends simply to drift apart, the partners in an intimate relationship are more likely to feel intense distress and anger when the relationship fails (Fischman, 1986), in part because they have invested a great amount of time, exchanged powerful rewards, and expressed a lasting commitment to one another (Simpson, 1987). Men and women differ in how they cope with a failed relationship: women tend to confide in their friends, whereas men tend to start a new relationship as quickly as possible (Sorenson et al., 1993).

Rusbult and Zembrodt (1983) point out that people respond either actively or passively to an unhappy partnership. To summarize the Rusbult and Zembrodt typology, an active response can involve ending the relationship (*exit*—"I talked to a lawyer, and I'm filing for divorce") or working to improve it (*voice*—"I believe we should give marital counseling a try"). Passively, one can simply wait for improvement (*loyalty*—"I'll stand by my man until things get better") or simply wait for the inevitable breakup (*neglect*—"I know things are bad, but I won't do anything until she becomes totally impossible"). These alternatives are depicted in Figure 8.18 (p. 310). If the goal is to maintain a relationship, *exit* and *neglect* are clearly the least constructive and *voice* the most constructive choice. *Loyalty* tends to go unnoticed or to be misinterpreted; people report themselves as having responded with loyalty but not their partners (Drigotas, Whitney, & Rusbult, 1995).

FIGURE 8.18

Four Alternative Responses to a Troubled Relationship. When a relationship is beginning to fail, the partners can respond in either an *active* or a *passive* way. Within each of these alternatives, the response can be *positive* or *negative*. The decision to end the relationship is an active–negative response ("exit"), and the decision to work on improving the relationship is an active–positive response ("voice"). Simply waiting for the problems to get worse is a passive–negative response ("neglect"), and simply waiting for improvement to occur is a passive–positive response ("loyalty").

(*Source:* Based on information from Rusbult & Zembrodt, 1983.)

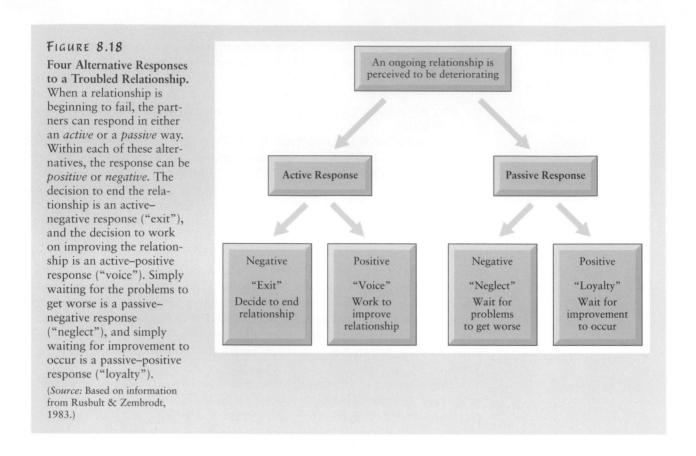

Among quite different kinds of couples (college students, older couples, gays, and lesbians), men and women with high self-esteem respond to relationship failure by exiting, while low self-esteem is associated with passive neglect (Rusbult, Morrow, & Johnson, 1990). It is very difficult to reverse a deteriorating relationship, but sometimes problems can be solved and the couple can reconcile if (1) the partnership satisfies the needs of each individual, (2) each remains committed to staying together, and (3) alternative lovers are not available (Rusbult, 1983; Simpson, 1987). The more dependent a person is on the relationship, the less he or she is motivated to dissolve it (Drigotas & Rusbult, 1992), even in response to physical abuse (Rusbult & Martz, 1995).

It is interesting to note that most divorced individuals remarry, especially men; in the United States, more than two million people have been married three or more times (Brody, Neubaum, & Forehand, 1988). The desire for love and happiness in a relationship seems to have a greater influence on behavior than negative past experiences.

Returning to the concept of attachment styles, only those in the secure category seem to be able to form long-lasting, committed, satisfying relationships. In Bartholomew's model (see Figure 8.7), verbal and physical abuse were least likely for those with a secure attachment style, most likely for those with a fearful style, and less so for those with a preoccupied style; a dismissing style was unrelated to abusiveness (Dutton et al., 1995). Without a warm, secure, consistent relationship with one's parents early in life, future relationships are very likely to suffer (Radecki-Bush, Farrell, & Bush, 1993).

INTEGRATING PRINCIPLES

1. As with other types of interpersonal relationships, marriage is most likely between two relatively similar individuals (Chapter 7). Married couples face an array of potential conflicts, challenges, and compromises as they interact in areas as diverse as sexual intimacy, the division of household chores (Chapter 5), dealing with two careers, and raising children—marital satisfaction depends in part on how well couples deal with such interactions.

2. In the United States about half of all marriages fail. Among the reasons are the discovery or development of dissimilarities, boredom, differences in ways of coping with stress (Chapter 14), attachment style, gender roles and gender differences in perceiving threat (Chapter 5), and a shift from positive to negative affect in the couple's interactions (Chapter 7). Unfortunately, we know more about why relationships fail than about how to prevent the emotional trauma of a breakup.

Social Diversity: A Critical Analysis

LOVE AND INTIMACY: Individualistic versus Collectivistic Perspectives

MUCH OF THE CROSS-CULTURAL RESEARCH IN SOCIAL psychology is based on the differences between individualistic societies—most Western nations—and collectivistic societies—most Eastern nations (Triandis, 1995). Simply, individualism places central importance on personal goals, while collectivism stresses group goals. These orientations can be applied at the level of individuals or at the cultural level (Dion & Dion, 1991). Psychological individualism and collectivism can occur anywhere, and societal individualism or collectivism refers to a situation in which one of these value orientations is characteristic of most of a society's citizens (Hui & Triandis, 1986). Some of the differences between these orientations are indicated in Table 8.5 (p. 312).

Dion and Dion (1993) suggest that these different orientations strongly affect how people conceptualize love and intimacy. These researchers offer three specific propositions, supported by relevant data from two individualistic societies (Canada and the United States) and three collectivistic societies (China, India, and Japan).

(1) Romantic love is more likely to be considered an important basis for marriage in individualistic societies than in collectivistic ones.

For North Americans, it seems natural and even self-evident to say that two people meet, fall in love, decide to get married (or live together), and hope to

live happily ever after. Marriage provides an opportunity for two individuals to explore and share their real selves, and to experience personal growth through the relationship. In contrast, in many Asian societies the person getting married is supposed to take into account the wishes of others, especially of parents and other family members. It is not unusual for marriages to be arranged by the respective families on the basis of such factors as occupation and status, not on the basis of love and the lovers' free choice. The intense feelings of passionate love and the self-absorption of two lovers would be disruptive to the functioning of the group.

(2) Psychological intimacy in marriage is more basic to marital satisfaction and personal well-being in individualistic than in collectivistic societies.

In Canada and the United States, for example, much of the research on marriage deals with how the partners evaluate one another, how well they know one another, and how satisfied each person feels in the relationship. In China, India, and Japan, there is less concern about this kind of marital happiness or satisfaction—because the primary ties of intimacy and the source of well-being are rooted in family relationships with parents, siblings, and other relatives. One example of the difference is that marital satisfaction in the

TABLE 8.5 Differences between Individualistic and Collectivistic Societies

Cross-cultural research often focuses on the differences between societies that stress individualism and societies that stress collectivism—as defined by elements such as those listed here. Dion and Dion (1993) point out the relevance of these differences between societies (and related differences between individuals) to love, intimacy, marriage, and the breakup of relationships.

Individualistic Societies	Emphasis on promoting the self-interest of oneself and one's immediate family
	Stress on rights, not duties, of the individual
	Personal autonomy
	Privacy
	Self-realization
	Individual initiative
	Independence
	Decision making
	Personal identity = the attributes of the individual
	Less concern about the needs and interests of others
	Typical individualistic societies = Australia, Great Britain, Canada, United States
Collectivistic Societies	Emphasis on loyalty to the group; the group in turn looks after the interests and well-being of the individual
	Emotional dependence on groups and organizations
	Less personal privacy
	Belief that group decisions are superior to individual decisions
	Interdependence
	Personal identity = one's place in the group
	Concern about the needs and interests of others
	Typical collectivistic societies = China, Hong Kong, India, Japan, Pakistan, Taiwan, Singapore

United States is based on the couple's interaction; in Japan, socioeconomic factors determine satisfaction (Kamo, 1993). At a more general level, those in individualistic societies express more unrealistic optimism than those in collectivistic ones (Heine & Lehman, 1995). So, when expectations are not fulfilled, Westerners react with surprise and disappointment.

(3) Although individualism values romantic love as the basis for marriage, some aspects of psychological individualism make it difficult to develop and maintain intimacy.

Earlier, we pointed out the problems faced by married partners who must make compromises in their everyday interactions. This issue is all-important in individualistic societies, which emphasize the value of autonomy, personal control, and independence. It is clearly difficult to strive simultaneously for intimacy and for independence, and Dion and Dion suggest that this conflict may account for the high divorce rate in the United States and Canada—a relationship simply ends when either partner

feels sufficiently dissatisfied. The strongly individualistic person finds it difficult to care for, need, and trust his or her partner. In collectivistic societies, in contrast, dependency on others is not something to be avoided but a highly valued aspect of relationships.

Given these societal differences, what can we conclude? It seems that individualistic societies place us in an unavoidable conflict between wanting freedom and independence and striving for love and intimacy. One result is unhappiness in relationships, a booming business in marital advice and marital counseling, and a high divorce rate. No one can foresee the future; but changes that have been documented seem to indicate that North Americans are becoming even more individualistic than previously and that collectivistic societies are slowly shifting toward an individualistic orientation (Dion & Dion, 1993). If so, the future prospects for relationship satisfaction do not seem especially good.

CONNECTIONS: Integrating Social Psychology

In this chapter, you read about . . .	*In other chapters, you will find related discussions of . . .*
the effects of self-esteem on parental love and on responding to a relationship in trouble	self-esteem (Chapter 5)
prosocial behavior and parental love	the characteristics of prosocial individuals (Chapter 10)
the role of similarity in friendships, romantic relationships, and marriage	similarity and attraction (Chapter 7)
the self-schemas of those who are lonely	self-schemas (Chapter 5)
effects of your behavior on feelings of love	the effect of facial feedback on emotional responses (Chapter 3)
love based on emotional attributions	Schachter's two-factor theory of emotions (Chapter 3)
affect and relationships	affect and attraction (Chapter 7)

Thinking about Connections

1. How would you describe your relationship with your parents? Do you feel that you really know your mother and father as people, and do they know you? Do you feel comfortable talking to them? We each have our own sets of experiences and memories involving parents—some very good and some very bad. In what way is your self-perception affected by your past or present relationship with each parent?

2. Is it easy or difficult for you to establish relationships? Who is the earliest friend you can remember? What was it about this individual that attracted you? Did such factors as proximity, similarity, affect, and observable characteristics play any role? What did the two of you do together? Are you still friends or do you no longer see each other? Are there any parallels between this friendship and later relationships in your life?

3. Think about yourself in a close romantic relationship—either in the past, in the present, or in an imaginary romance. Is your partner at all like your ideal? How did the two of you meet, and what attracted you to this individual? Are there aspects of this person that you would like to change? Are there things about you that he or she would like to change? Would you say that you love this person? What do you mean by "love"? Is it possible that feelings of love—at least at the beginning— were based on misattributed emotions, genetically related reproductive strategies, or expectancies based on stories about love? In other words, does the research and theory dealing with relationships and emotions connect at all with your own life?

4. Have you gone through the experience of a romance that breaks up or a divorce—your own or your parents'? If so, why do you think it happened, and what were the aftereffects? Could anything have prevented the breakup? Current research focuses a lot on attachment styles; can you apply attachment concepts to your own experience?

Summary and Review

All close relationships involve *interdependence*—when two people influence one another's lives and engage in joint activities.

Family Interactions and Close Friendships versus Loneliness

A major concept in research on relationships is the importance of the interactions between an infant and the primary caregiver—usually the mother. The resulting *attachment style* has to do with the person's self-esteem and the way other people are evaluated. All subsequent relationships (friendships, romantic attachments, and marriage) seem to be influenced in part by one's attachment style. Sibling relationships are also important, primarily as a way to learn how to interact with peers. Some individuals fail to develop close friendships, and the result is likely to be a feeling of *loneliness*. This negative state seems to be based on several factors: insecure attachment patterns, the failure to learn interpersonal skills, and faulty cognitions about social situations and about other people. Loneliness and social anxiety can be helped by cognitive therapy, social skills training, and to some extent by specific prescription drugs.

Romantic Relationships, Love, and Physical Intimacy

Some degree of physical intimacy is a defining characteristic of an *intimate relationship*. Romantic relationships are like close friendships with respect to the importance of similarity and attachment style, but different in other respects—the desire for positivity feedback and for sexual contact. *Love* is a common experience and a common theme in songs and stories. It is manifested in multiple forms, including *passionate love* based on cultural influences, genetics, and emotional misattributions. *Companionate love* is the other major variety, much like a close, caring friendship. Widespread changes in sexual attitudes and behaviors in the Western nations after World War II have resulted in premarital intercouse becoming normative behavior in romantic relationships. The newfound sexual freedom has also led to many problems, including unwanted pregnancies and the spread of sexually transmissible diseases.

Marital Relationships

Most people seek marriage as a major life goal. People tend to select a marriage partner on the basis of some of the same factors (such as similarity) that determine friendships. Spouses must work out how best to interact while dealing with daily decisions about such diverse issues as household tasks, careers, leisure time, sex, and parenthood. The challenge of this task is shown by the fact that about half of the marriages in the United States and Canada end in divorce. Dissatisfaction is common because of such factors as stress, dissimilarities, boredom, and the presence of more negative than positive affect. Relationship failure is a frequent, though emotionally traumatic, occurrence.

Social Diversity: Love and Intimacy: Individualistic versus Collectivistic Perspectives

A comparison of intimate relationships in individualistic and collectivistic societies suggests that, compared with collectivism, individualism results in romantic love being seen as a more important basis for marriage and psychological intimacy as a more important determinant of marital satisfaction; a built-in conflict between independence and intimacy often leads to relationship failure.

■ Key Terms

Attachment Style (p. 274)

Close Friendship (p. 278)

Companionate Love (p. 294)

Decision/Commitment (p. 297)

Interdependence (p. 272)

Intimacy (p. 297)

Loneliness (p. 283)

Love (p. 289)

Passion (p. 297)

Passionate Love (p. 290)

Sociosexuality (p. 288)

Triangular Model of Love (p. 297)

■ For More Information

Duck, S. (1994). *Meaningful relationships: Talking, sense, and relating*. Thousand Oaks, CA: Sage.

A leading investigator and theorist in the field of interpersonal behavior, Professor Duck describes how relationships are a continual challenge because of the need to think about and to respond to what the other person says and does. Relationships are never a "done deal," but rather require constant effort to maintain.

Gottman, J. M. (1993). *What predicts divorce? The relationship between marital processes and marital outcomes*. Hillsdale, NJ: Erlbaum.

This book covers research on marriage and divorce from that of Terman to current studies. The emphasis is on predicting marital success and failure, but the author also presents a theory of marital stability and recommendations about how to achieve a stable marriage.

Weber, A. L., & Harvey, J. H. (Eds.). (1994). *Perspectives on close relationships*. Boston: Allyn & Bacon.

Chapters by a series of active investigators, who examine research and theory relevant to most of the topics in this chapter—including close relationships, attachment, love, commitment, sexuality, jealousy, and the need to cope with relationship dissolution.

CHAPTER 9

SOCIAL INFLUENCE:
How We Change Others'
Behavior—and How
They Change Ours

Lisa Houck, *Studying Fish Behavior on the Ocean Floor*, 1993, watercolor, 9 × 13"

Chapter Outline

How many times each day does someone try to influence you—to get you to think, feel, or act in ways that they want? If your life is like mine, the answer is probably "Who can keep count?!" Like the character in Figure 9.1, most of us are on the receiving end of a large number of attempts at **social influence** every day—efforts by others to change our attitudes, beliefs, perceptions, or behaviors (Cialdini, 1994). Consider the number of radio and television commercials, magazine and newspaper ads, and billboards you encounter each day: All involve efforts to influence you in some manner. Now add to this the number of direct requests you receive from people you know—friends, relatives, co-workers, and even total strangers such as panhandlers, salespersons, or politicians. When you do, you'll quickly realize that social influence is a basic fact of social life.

But we are not merely the passive targets or recipients of such influence: We also seek to exert it on others. Consider my own day. Often, it begins with gentle efforts on my part to wake my wife and get her out of bed; she truly hates getting up in the morning, so I have to start applying my knowledge of social influence early on. As the hours pass, I usually find myself engaging in conversations where I make various requests to try to persuade other people do something I'd like them to do: I ask the waiter in the restaurant to hold the mayonnaise on my sandwich; I try to convince the clerk at the dry cleaners' to get my coat back by Tuesday instead of Thursday; I ask one of my colleagues if she'll take over my class on a day when I have to be out of town; I plead with

Social Influence ■ Efforts by one or more individuals to change the attitudes, beliefs, perceptions, or behaviors of one or more others.

FIGURE 9.1

Social Influence: A Fact of Daily Life.
Each day, we are exposed to many different forms of social influence—efforts by others to change our attitudes, beliefs, perceptions, or behaviors.

(*Source:* Reprinted with special permission of King Features Syndicate.)

my daughter to drive carefully when she goes to visit her boyfriend . . . and so it goes, throughout the day. In short, like you, I definitely get my turns at bat where social influence is concerned.

From the standpoint of sheer frequency, then, social influence is clearly an important part of social interaction. Its importance doesn't rest on frequency alone, however; social influence is also important because it plays a key role in many forms of social interaction, including *leadership* (Chapter 12), *aggression* (Chapter 11), *prejudice* (Chapter 6), and *helping* (Chapter 10); please see the *Connections* table at the end of this chapter. Indeed, in one sense we began the discussion of social influence back in Chapter 4, where we examined the nature of *persuasion*. Because of its role in many forms of social behavior, social influence has long been the subject of careful study by social psychologists. This research has added greatly to our knowledge of this process, and we'll summarize much of this information for you in the remainder of this chapter. We'll begin by focusing on **conformity**—pressures to go along with the crowd, to behave in the same manner as other persons in one's group or society. Next, we'll turn to **compliance**—efforts to get others to say "yes" to direct requests. As we'll soon see, a wide range of tactics, many of them quite ingenious, are used to induce compliance—to increase the likelihood that others really will say "yes" (Cialdini, 1994). Finally, we'll examine **obedience**—a form of social influence in which one person simply orders one or more others to do what they want. Usually, the persons who issue commands have some means of enforcing submission to them—they have *power* over those on the receiving end (Yukl & Tracey, 1992). Research findings indicate, however, that direct orders can often be effective in inducing obedience even in situations where the persons who issue these commands have little or no means for backing them up.

Conformity: Group Influence in Action

Have you ever found yourself in a situation in which you felt that you stuck out like the proverbial sore thumb? If so, you have already had direct experience with pressures toward *conformity*. In such situations, you probably experienced a strong desire to "get back into line"—to fit in with the other people around you. Such pressures toward conformity stem from the fact that in many contexts, there are explicit or unspoken rules indicating how we *should* or *ought to* behave. These rules are known as **social norms**. In some instances, social norms are both detailed and precise. For example, governments generally function through constitutions and written laws; athletic contests are usually regulated by written rules; and signs in many public places (e.g., along highways, in parks, at airports) frequently describe expected behavior in considerable detail.

In contrast, other norms are unspoken or implicit. Most of us obey such unwritten rules as "Don't stand too close to strangers on elevators if you can help it" and "Don't arrive at parties exactly on time." Similarly, we are often influenced by current and rapidly changing standards of dress, speech, and personal grooming. Regardless of whether social norms are explicit or implicit, one fact is clear: *Most people obey them most of the time.* For example, few persons visit restaurants without leaving a tip for their server. And virtually everyone, regardless of personal political beliefs, stands when the national anthem of their country is played at sports events or other public gatherings.

At first glance, this strong tendency toward conformity—toward going along with society's expectations about how we should behave in various situations—

Conformity ■ A type of social influence in which individuals change their attitudes or behavior in order to adhere to existing social norms.

Compliance ■ A form of social influence involving direct requests from one person to another.

Obedience ■ A form of social influence in which one person obeys direct orders from another to perform some action(s).

Social Norms ■ Rules indicating how individuals are expected to behave in specific situations.

FIGURE 9.2

Conformity: Often, It Serves a Useful Function. In many situations, conformity to existing social norms makes life simpler, less stressful, and safer for large numbers of persons.

may strike you as objectionable. After all, it does place restrictions on personal freedom. Actually, though, there is a strong basis for the existence of so much conformity: without it, we would quickly find ourselves facing social chaos. Imagine what would happen outside movie theaters or voting booths or at supermarket checkout counters if people did *not* obey the norm "Form a line and wait your turn." And consider the danger to both drivers and pedestrians if there were not clear and widely followed traffic regulations. In many situations, then, conformity serves a useful function (see Figure 9.2). But this in no way implies that it is always helpful. Some norms governing individual behavior appear to have no obvious purpose; they simply exist. For example, although dress codes have weakened or vanished in recent years, they still prevail in some settings—especially in the business world, where many companies still require that their male employees wear neckties and that their female employees wear skirts or dresses. While such clothing can be attractive, it is often unrelated to performance of various jobs and may be a cause of personal discomfort when temperatures are very high (neckties) or very low (short skirts). I remember my own experience with one dress code when I was a graduate student at the University of Iowa. In those days (the mid-1960s), female students were required to wear skirts or dresses to class, even in the winter. Since the fashion at that time was for very short skirts, and since temperatures in Iowa City often went below zero Fahrenheit, this particular dress code certainly caused female students a lot of unnecessary misery!

Given that strong pressures toward conformity exist in many social settings, it is surprising to learn that conformity, as a social process, received relatively little attention from social psychologists until the 1950s. At that time Solomon Asch (1951), whose research on impression formation we considered in Chapter 2, carried out a series of experiments with dramatic results. In fact, the results were so clear and so surprising that they quickly captured the attention of both social psychologists and the general public. This research is described in the following *Cornerstones* section.

Cornerstones of Social Psychology

ASCH'S RESEARCH ON CONFORMITY: Social Pressure—the Irresistible Force?

Suppose that just before an important math exam, you discover that your answer to a homework problem is different from that obtained by one of your friends. How do you react? Probably, with mild concern. Now imagine that you learn that a second person's answer, too, is different from yours. Moreover, to make matters worse, it agrees with the answer reported by the first person. How do you feel *now*? The chances are good that your anxiety will be considerable. Next, you discover that a third person agrees with the other two. At this point, you know that you are in big trouble. Which answer should you accept? Yours or the one obtained by your three friends? There's no time to find out, because at this moment the exam starts. Sure enough, the first question relates to this specific problem. Which answer should you choose? Can all three of your friends be wrong while you are right?

Life is filled with such dilemmas—instances in which we discover that our own judgments, actions, or conclusions are different from those reached by other persons. What do we do in such situations? Important insights into our behavior in such cases was provided by a series of studies conducted by Solomon Asch (1951, 1955)—studies that are considered to be true classics in social psychology. In his research, Asch asked participants to respond to a series of simple perceptual problems such as the one in Figure 9.3 (p. 322). On each problem they indicated which of three comparison lines matched a standard line in length. Several other persons (usually six to eight) were also present during the session; but, unknown to the real participant, all were accomplices of the experimenter. On certain occasions known as critical trials (twelve out of the eighteen problems) the accomplices offered answers that were clearly wrong: they unanimously chose the wrong line as a match for the standard line. Moreover, they stated their answers before the participant responded. Thus, on these critical trials, the participants faced the type of dilemma described above. Should they go along with the other persons present or stick to their own judgments? A large majority of the participants in Asch's research opted for conformity. Indeed, in several different studies, fully 76 percent of those tested went along with the group's false answers at least once; in fact, they voiced their agreement with these errors about 37 percent of the time. In contrast, only 5 percent of the subjects in a control group, who responded to the same problems in the absence of any accomplices, made such errors.

Of course, there were large individual differences in this respect. Almost 25 percent of the participants *never* yielded to the group pressure. At the other extreme were persons who went along with the majority nearly all the time. When Asch questioned them, some of these persons stated "I am wrong, they are right"; they had little confidence in their own judgment. Others, however, said they felt that the other persons present were the victims of some sort of optical illusion, or were merely sheep following the responses of the first person. Nevertheless, when it was their turn to speak, these participants still went along with the group.

In further studies, Asch (1951, 1956) investigated the effects of shattering the group's unanimity by having one of the accomplices break with the others. In one study, this person gave the correct answer, becoming an "ally" of the real participant; in another, he chose an answer in between the one given by the

FIGURE 9.3

Asch's Line Judgment Task: An Example. Participants in Asch's research were asked to report their judgments on problems such as this one. On each problem, they indicated which of the comparison lines (1, 2, or 3) best matched the standard line in length.

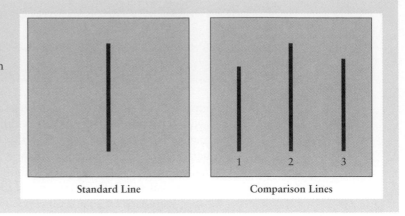

Standard Line   Comparison Lines

group and the correct one; and in a third, he chose an answer that was even more incorrect than that chosen by the majority. In the latter two conditions, in other words, he broke from the group but still disagreed with the real participant. Results indicated that conformity was reduced under all three conditions. However, somewhat surprisingly, this reduction was greatest when the dissenting accomplice expressed views even more extreme (and wrong) than the majority (see Figure 9.4). Together, these findings suggest that it is the unanimity of the group that is crucial: it is much easier to resist group pressure when such unanimity is lacking.

There's one more aspect of Asch's research it is important to mention. In later studies, he repeated his basic procedure, but with one important change: Instead of stating their answers out loud, participants wrote them down on a piece of paper. As you might guess, conformity dropped sharply. This finding

FIGURE 9.4

Breaking Group Unanimity: An Effective Means of Reducing Conformity. When another person present broke with the majority, whether by becoming the participant's ally (giving the correct answer), by giving a compromise answer, or by giving an answer even more inaccurate than that chosen by the majority, conformity was greatly reduced.

(Based on data from Asch, 1956.)

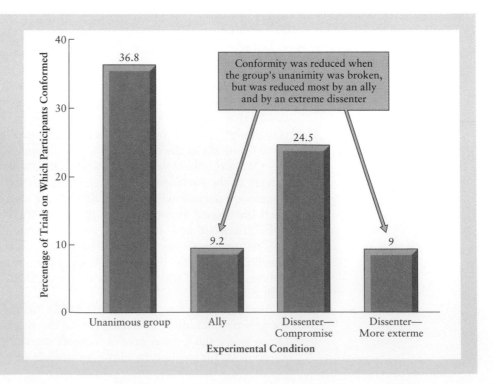

points to the importance of distinguishing between *public conformity*—doing or saying what others around us say or do—and *private acceptance*—actually coming to feel or think as others do. Often, it appears, we follow social norms overtly, but don't actually change our private views (Maas & Clark, 1984). This distinction between public conformity and private acceptance is an important one, and we'll have reason to comment on it at several points in this book.

Asch's research was the catalyst for a flurry of activity in social psychology, as many other researchers rushed to investigate the nature of conformity, to identify factors that influence its impact, and to establish its limits (e.g., Crutchfield, 1955; Deutsch & Gerard, 1955). Indeed, such research is still continuing today, and is still adding to our understanding of this crucial form of social influence (e.g., Buehler & Griffin, 1994; Reno, Cialdini, & Kallgren, 1993). Clearly, then, Asch's early studies of conformity constitute an important cornerstone of social psychology—one with a lasting impact upon the field. ■ ■ ■

Factors Affecting Conformity: Cohesiveness, Group Size, and Type of Social Norm

Asch's research demonstrated the existence of powerful pressures toward conformity. Even a moment's reflection indicates, however, that conformity does not occur to the same degree in all settings. This fact raises an intriguing question: What factors determine the extent to which individuals yield to conformity pressure or resist it? Many variables play a role, but among these, two have received most attention: (1) *cohesiveness*—the target person's degree of attraction to the group exerting influence, and (2) *group size*—the number of persons exerting social influence. In addition, research by Cialdini and his colleagues indicates that a third factor, which might be termed *type of social norm*, also plays an important role in this regard (Cialdini, Reno, & Kallgren, 1990; Cialdini, Kallgren, & Reno, 1991). We'll consider evidence relating to this factor, and to the suggestion that there are at least two different kinds of social norms, below.

Cohesiveness and Conformity: Accepting Influence from Those We Like. Consider the following situation. You move in with a new group of roommates. You knew them slightly before, and liked them—that's why you accepted their offer to move into their apartment. After you are there for a few weeks, you begin to realize that they hold political views considerably more conservative than your own. They repeatedly state their opposition to various government programs and criticize judges who, in their view, are too lenient toward criminals. Will your own views change as a function of living with these new friends? Perhaps. You may find yourself agreeing with them more and more as time passes.

Now, in contrast, imagine that you have signed up for an evening course in personal self-defense. During these sessions, you hear other members of the class express conservative views about law and order, the right to own guns, and punishment of criminals. Will you be influenced by these statements? Probably not; you may refrain from disagreeing with them openly in order to avoid trouble, but it is unlikely that your private views will change. Why do you react differently in these two contexts—why are your views more likely to be influenced by your roommates than by the strangers in your evening class? One answer involves what social psychologists term **cohesiveness**—your degree of attraction to a group. Clearly, you like your roommates and want to gain their approval and acceptance, but you are more neutral toward the people in your self-defense class. A classic finding of social psychology is that when cohesiveness (attraction) is high, pressures toward conformity are magnified. After all,

Cohesiveness ■ With respect to conformity, the degree of attraction felt by an individual toward an influencing group.

if you want to be liked and accepted by others, it is best to share their views—or at least to express acceptance of these (that distinction between private acceptance and public conformity again). This is a basic reason why most persons are more willing to accept social influence from friends or persons they admire than from others.

How strong is the impact of cohesiveness on conformity? A unique study by Crandall (1988) indicates that it is very strong indeed. In this investigation, members of two different sororities completed two questionnaires: one designed to measure patterns of friendship within these social organizations (i.e., who was friends with whom); the other to measure tendencies toward binge eating, an eating disorder in which individuals usually alternate periods of huge food consumption with purging—forcing themselves to throw up. Both questionnaires were completed by members of the sororities twice: at the start of the academic year and again when it was nearly over. The purpose was to allow Crandall to find out whether shifts in friendship patterns over time would be related to changes in tendencies toward binge eating. Specifically, Crandall hypothesized that the young women who participated in the study would report becoming more like their friends with respect to binge eating as time passed and bonds of friendship (cohesiveness) strengthened. Results offered strong support for this prediction: groups of friends did become increasingly like one another over time in terms of binge eating.

These findings provide a compelling illustration of the fact that the more we like others and wish to gain their approval, the more we tend to be influenced by them. Moreover, they also underscore the fact that pressures toward conformity can affect virtually any aspect of behavior—even something as basic as eating habits.

Conformity and Group Size: Why More Isn't Always Better with Respect to Social Influence. A second factor that exerts important effects on the tendency to conform is the size of the influencing group. Asch (1955) found that conformity increases with group size up to about three members, but then seems to level off; and this finding has been confirmed by several other studies (e.g., Gerard, Wilhelmy, & Conolley, 1968). Why is this the case? One possibility is that as group size rises beyond three or four members, individuals exposed to social pressure begin to suspect collusion: they conclude that group members are not expressing individual views but are actually working together to influence them (Wilder, 1977). This makes a great deal of sense; after all, it is rare to find all the people around us agreeing unanimously with one another. Usually, people hold varying opinions and engage in many kinds of behavior, reflecting their individual preferences. When too many people agree, therefore, this may be a signal that it's time to be on guard.

Descriptive and Injunctive Norms: The Difference between What People Do in a Given Situation and What They Feel Is Right. Social norms, we have already seen, can be formal or informal in nature—as different as rules printed on large signs for all the world to see and informal guidelines such as "Say excuse me if you bump into someone." This is not the only way in which norms differ, however. Cialdini (one of social psychology's true experts on social influence) and his coworkers have called attention to another important distinction—the difference between what they term *descriptive norms* and *injunctive norms* (Cialdini, Kallgren, & Reno, 1991; Reno, Cialdini, & Kallgren, 1993). Descriptive norms are ones indicating what most people do in a given situation. They influence behavior by informing us about what is generally seen as effective or adaptive behavior in that situation. In contrast, injunctive norms specify what *ought* to be done—what is approved or disapproved behavior in a given situation. Both norms can influence behavior, but Cialdini and his colleagues believe that in certain situations—especially ones where antisocial behavior (behavior not approved of by a given society) is likely to occur—injunctive norms may exert somewhat stronger effects. This is true for two reasons. First, such norms tend to shift attention away from the fact that many people are acting in an undesirable manner in a particular situation—for example, littering when they should be putting trash into appropriate containers. Second, such norms may activate the social motive to do what's right in a given situation regardless of what others have done.

To test this prediction, Reno, Cialdini, and Kallgren (1993) conducted a series of studies in which individuals crossing a parking lot encountered an accomplice walking toward them. In one condition, this person carried a bag from a fast-food restaurant and dropped it on the ground. In another, this person was not carrying anything, but actually picked up the fast-food bag. The researchers suggested that seeing another person drop a bag on the ground would call pedestrians' attention to the state of the environment (whether it was clean or already full of litter); this, in turn, would activate a *descriptive* norm—information about whether most other people littered or did not litter in this area. In contrast, seeing another person actually pick litter up from the ground would remind them of society's disapproval of such behavior—an *injunctive* norm. Another variable involved the existing state of the environment: the ground was either littered with trash, or newly cleaned by the researchers. The researchers measured people's own tendency to litter in each of these conditions by observing what they did with a handbill that had been placed on their windshield. Reno and his colleagues (1993) reasoned that activating the descriptive norm would reduce people's tendency to litter (throw the handbill on the ground) when the environment was clean, but not when it was dirty. In contrast, however, they predicted that activating the injunctive norm would reduce littering regardless of the environment's present condition. As you can see from Figure 9.5, this is precisely what was found.

In additional studies, Reno and his colleagues (1993) found that making pedestrians aware of the injunctive norm against littering reduced their tendency to litter even in other environments—ones different from that in which they observed the accomplice picking up some litter. The researchers accomplished this by having some pedestrians encounter this person on a path that led to the parking lot, while others encountered the accomplice in the parking lot itself. (Remember: The parking lot was the location where people found the handbill on their car and could engage in littering themselves.) Results again underscored the importance of injunctive norms: people were much less likely to litter in both conditions if they had seen the accomplice pick up some litter than if they did not see the accomplice engage in such behavior.

Taken together, these findings and those of related studies (e.g., Cialdini et al., 1991) indicate that there are indeed two distinct types of social norms. Moreover, it appears that these two types of norms may influence our behavior through somewhat different mechanisms, and may operate in somewhat different settings. As noted by Reno and his colleagues (1993, p. 111), understanding the difference between descriptive and injunctive norms can also be of practical value. In situations where most people already behave in a beneficial manner, such behavior can be further strengthened by activation of descriptive norms—calling people's attention to the fact that most persons do indeed behave in a prosocial manner. In situations where many people do not behave in a socially beneficial way, however, activating *injunctive* norms, and so reminding people of how they *should* behave, may be more effective. In both cases,

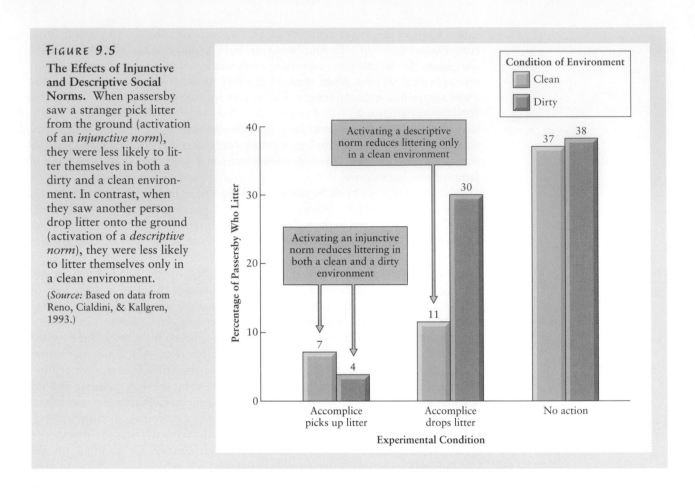

FIGURE 9.5

The Effects of Injunctive and Descriptive Social Norms. When passersby saw a stranger pick litter from the ground (activation of an *injunctive norm*), they were less likely to litter themselves in both a dirty and a clean environment. In contrast, when they saw another person drop litter onto the ground (activation of a *descriptive norm*), they were less likely to litter themselves only in a clean environment.

(*Source:* Based on data from Reno, Cialdini, & Kallgren, 1993.)

knowledge of social norms and how they operate provides us with important tools for enhancing many aspects of our society. (We will consider another variable that was once assumed to strongly influence conformity—*gender*—in the *Social Diversity* section later in this chapter.)

The Bases of Conformity: Why We Often Choose to "Go Along"—and What Happens after We Do

As we have just seen, several factors determine whether and to what extent conformity occurs. Yet this does not alter the essential point: Conformity is a basic fact of social life. Most people conform to the norms of their groups or societies much, if not most, of the time. Why is this so? Why do people often choose to go along with these social rules or expectations instead of resisting them? The answer seems to center primarily on two powerful needs possessed by all human beings—the desire to be liked or accepted by others and the desire to be right (Deutsch & Gerard, 1955; Insko, 1985)—plus cognitive processes that lead us to view conformity as fully justified after it has occurred (e.g., Griffin & Buehler, 1993).

The Desire to Be Liked: Normative Social Influence. How can we get others to like us? This is one of the eternal puzzles of social life. As we saw in Chapter 7, many tactics can prove effective in this regard. One of the most successful of these is to appear to be as similar to others as possible. From our earliest days, we learn that agreeing with the persons around us, and behaving as they do, causes them to like us. Parents, teachers, friends, and others often heap praise and approval on us for demonstrating such similarity (see our discussion of attitude formation in Chapter 4). One important reason we conform, therefore, is simple: we have learned that doing so can yield the approval and acceptance we crave. This source of social influence—and especially of conformity—is known as **normative social influence**, since it involves altering our behavior to meet others' expectations.

The Desire to Be Right: Informational Social Influence. If you want to know your weight, you can step onto a scale. If you want to know the dimensions of a room, you can measure them directly. But how can you establish the accuracy of your own political or social views or decide which hairstyle suits you best? There are no simple physical tests or measuring devices for answering these questions. Yet most of us have just as strong a desire to be correct about such matters as about questions relating to the physical world. The solution is obvious: to answer these questions, we must turn to other people. We use *their* opinions and their actions as guides for our own. Obviously, such reliance on others can be another source of conformity, for in an important sense, other people's actions and opinions define social reality for us. This source of social influence is known as **informational social influence**, since it is based on our tendency to depend upon others as a source of information about many aspects of the social world.

Together, normative and informational social influence provide a strong basis for our tendency to conform—to act in accordance with existing social norms. In short, there is nothing very mysterious about the pervasive occurrence of conformity; it stems directly from basic needs and motives that can be fulfilled only when we do indeed decide to "go along" with others.

Justifying Conformity: The Cognitive Consequences of Going Along with the Group. Asch reported that some people who conform do so without any reservations: they conclude that they are wrong and the others are right. For these people, conforming poses only a very temporary dilemma, at most. But for many persons, the decision to yield to group pressure and do as others do is more complex. Such persons feel that their own judgment is correct, but at the same time they don't want to be different; so they behave in ways that are inconsistent with their private beliefs. What are the effects of conformity on such persons? Recent findings (e.g., Griffin & Buehler, 1993; Buehler & Griffin, 1994) suggest that one may involve a tendency to alter their perceptions of the situation so that conformity appears, in fact, to be justified. As John Kenneth Galbraith stated, "Faced with the choice between changing one's mind and proving that there is no need to do so, almost everyone gets busy on the proof!" (cited in Buehler & Griffin, 1994, p. 993). Convincing evidence for such effects is provided by a series of studies conducted recently by Buehler and Griffin (1994).

In these studies, participants read a story in which a stranger faced an important decision: whether to go to medical school or to a conservatory of music. Then participants were asked to indicate to lowest probability of the stranger's being successful as a concert performer they would require before recommending that he choose the conservatory. Before making their decision, participants in one experimental condition learned that three other participants who were also present had chosen a low chance of success (20 percent). In contrast, those in another experimental condition did not receive this information.

Both before and after making their decisions, participants indicated their interpretation of the facts of the story. Buehler and Griffin (1994) predicted that among persons who conformed—those who went along with the group judgment—these interpretations would change in the direction of offering more support for the group's risky choice (20 percent). In contrast, among persons who resisted social influence, the opposite would be true. As you can see from Figure 9.6 (p. 328), both predictions were confirmed. After conforming, participants did indeed

Normative Social Influence ■ Social influence based on individuals' desire to be liked or accepted by other persons.

Informational Social Influence ■ Social influence based on individuals' desire to be correct (i.e., to possess accurate perceptions of the social world).

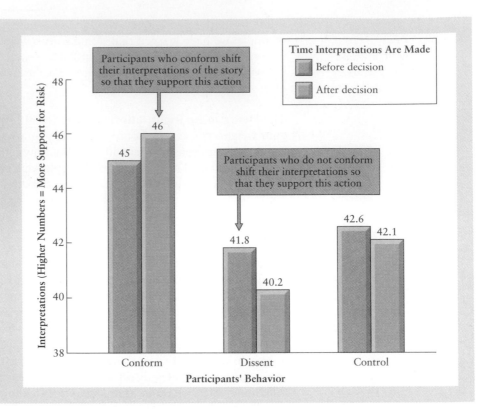

FIGURE 9.6

Cognitive Justification of Conformity and Dissent. After conforming to a group judgment, participants changed their interpretation of a story so as to provide more support for their decision. Similarly, after dissenting from a group judgment, they changed their interpretation of the story to provide more support for *this* decision.

(*Source:* Based on data from Buehler & Griffin, 1994.)

come to perceive more support for the group's choice—and their own conformity; after resisting, they perceived more support for *this* behavior.

These findings, and those in several related studies (Griffin & Buehler, 1993; Buehler & Griffin, 1994, Studies 2, 3), suggest that the decision to conform may be followed by changes in perceptions of the facts—changes that tend to justify conformity. It is interesting to speculate on whether this would be equally true in all cultures. In cultures such as that of the United States, which value individual choice backed by rational analysis, it is not surprising that such effects occur: people feel the need to explain why they conformed. In cultures that place greater value on group judgments and on avoiding actions that rock the social boat, however, the pressure toward such cognitive justification may be weaker. As noted by Buehler and Griffin (1994, p. 994), this is an intriguing issue for further study.

INTEGRATING PRINCIPLES

1. Social influence—efforts by one or more persons to change the attitudes, behaviors, or perceptions of one or more others—is a very common and important form of social behavior. As such, it plays a key role in many other forms of social behavior, including attitude formation and change (Chapter 4), prejudice (Chapter 6), helping (Chapter 10), aggression (Chapter 11), and group decision making (Chapter 12).

2. Our willingness to conform stems from several basic social motives, including the desire to be right and the desire to be liked. These motives play a role in other forms of social behavior, too. For example, the desire to be liked is important in many relationships (Chapter 8) and underlies at least some efforts at impression management (Chapter 2).

FIGURE 9.7
The Need to Be Unique.
Why do individuals behave
in the unusual or strange
ways shown here? Partly
because they wish to establish their uniqueness as individuals. In other words,
such behavior may stem, in
part, from the need for *individuation*.

FIGURE 9.7
The Need to Be Unique.
Why do individuals behave
in the unusual or strange
ways shown here? Partly
because they wish to establish their uniqueness as individuals. In other words,
such behavior may stem, in
part, from the need for *individuation*.

The Need for Individuality and the Need for Control: Why, Sometimes, We Choose *Not* to Go Along

Having read our discussion of normative and informational social influence, you may now have the distinct impression that pressures toward conformity are all but impossible to resist. If so, take heart. In many cases, individuals—or groups of individuals—decide to dig in their heels and say *no*. This was certainly true in Asch's research, where, as you may recall, most of the participants yielded to social pressure, but *only part of the time*. On many occasions they stuck to their own judgments, even in the face of a unanimous disagreeing majority. What accounts for this ability to resist even powerful pressures toward conformity? Research findings point to two key factors.

First, as you probably already realize, most of us have a strong desire to maintain our uniqueness or individuality. We want to be like others, but not to the extent that we lose our personal identity. In other words, along with the needs to be right and to be liked, most of us possess a desire for **individuation**— for being distinguished from others in some respects (e.g., Maslach, Santee, & Wade, 1987; Snyder & Fromkin, 1980). The result is that most people want to be similar to others *generally,* but don't want to be *exactly* like the people around them. In short, they want to hold on to at least a pinch of individuality (e.g., Snyder & Endelman, 1979). It is partly because of this motive that individuals sometimes choose to disagree with others or to act in unusual or even bizarre ways (see Figure 9.7). They realize that such behavior may be costly in terms of gaining the approval or acceptance of others, but their desire to maintain a unique identity is simply stronger than various inducements to conformity.

A second reason why individuals often choose to resist group pressure involves their desire to maintain control over the events in their lives (e.g., Burger, 1992; Burger & Cooper, 1979). Most persons want to believe that they can determine what happens to them, and yielding to social pressure sometimes runs counter to this desire. After all, going along with a group implies behaving in ways one might not ordinarily choose, and this can be interpreted as a restriction of personal freedom and control.

Individuation ■ The desire to differentiate oneself from others by emphasizing one's uniqueness or individuality.

While everyone seems to have a desire for personal control, there appear to be large individual differences in this respect, and these can be measured by a special questionnaire known as the *Desirability of Control Scale* (Burger & Cooper, 1979). One social psychologist (Burger, 1992) has reasoned that persons high in the desire for personal control may be especially sensitive to situations in which it is unclear as to whether other persons are trying to influence them. Presumably, persons high in the desire for personal control find such situations highly unsettling because they resent subtle attempts by others to influence them more than do persons low in the desire for personal control.

One type of situation in which it is often difficult to tell whether others are trying to influence us involves instances in which people offer us unrequested help. Sometimes such assistance is offered freely, without any obvious strings attached. But at other times it is truly the entering wedge for influence: it is often followed by requests for a return of the favor. Thus, it seems possible that persons high in desire for control might react more negatively to being helped by a stranger than persons low in desire for control.

To test these predictions, Daubman (1993) conducted a study in which pairs of participants who had previously completed the *Desirability of Control Scale* worked independently on a set of puzzles. Each participant then received feedback suggesting that he or she had done only average work, while the other person in the pair had done quite well. (Both persons received the same information.) At this point, participants either received or did not receive a helpful hint from the other person on how to solve the problems. Daubman reasoned that persons low in desire for control would feel better after receiving help, while those high in desire for control would feel worse; and this prediction was confirmed. In addition, more than half of the participants high in desire for control said that receiving the help was irritating; only 22 percent of those low in desire for control had such reactions.

These findings, and those of related research, lend support to Burger's (1992) contentions. Persons high in the desire for control do tend to perceive others' behavior as threatening to their personal freedom and often take active steps to resist such incursions. In short, they tend to go about their daily lives with the proverbial chip on their shoulder, ever ready to say to those who attempt to influence them: "Oh, yeah?"

Minority Influence: Does the Majority Always Rule?

As we have just noted, individuals can—and often do—resist group pressure (Wolfe, 1985). Lone dissenters or small minorities can dig in their heels and refuse to go along. Yet even this is not the total story; in addition, there are cases in which such persons or groups can turn the tables on the majority and exert rather than merely receive social influence. History provides numerous examples of such events. Many giants of the scientific world—Galileo, Pasteur, Freud—faced virtually unanimous majorities who rejected their views in harsh terms. Yet over time, they won growing numbers of colleagues to their side, until ultimately their views prevailed. More recent examples of minorities influencing majorities are provided by the successes of environmentalists. Initially, such persons were viewed as wild-eyed radicals operating at the fringes of society. Over time, however, they have succeeded in changing strongly held attitudes and laws so that society itself has been altered through their efforts. I (RAB) vividly remember the jokes I endured when, back in the early 1960s, I bought a small, fuel-efficient car, partly because of my concern with air pollution (see Figure 9.8). It took another ten years before the people who laughed at me came around to my way of thinking—but come around they finally did. Today even my father, a big-car fanatic if ever there was one, drives a small four-cylinder import.

FIGURE 9.8
A Minority View in 1963. When I (RAB) bought a small, fuel-efficient car in 1963, I was the butt of many jokes from my friends. Gradually, however, more and more people came to share my views, until today concern with protecting the environment is a *majority* view.

When do minorities succeed in exerting social influence on majorities? Research findings suggest that they are most likely to succeed under certain conditions (Kruglanski & Mackie, 1991; Moscivici, 1985). First, the members of such groups must be *consistent* in their opposition to majority opinions. If they waffle or show signs of yielding to the majority view, their impact is reduced. Second, members of the minority must avoid appearing to be rigid and dogmatic (Mugny, 1975). A minority that merely repeats the same position over and over again is less persuasive than one that demonstrates a degree of flexibility. Third, the general social context in which a minority operates is important. If a minority argues for a position that is consistent with current social trends (e.g., conservative views at a time of growing conservatism), its chances of influencing the majority are greater than if it argues for a position that is out of step with such trends.

Of course, even when minorities are consistent, flexible, and in line with current social trends, they face a tough uphill struggle. The power of majorities is great, partly because, in ambiguous or complex social situations, people view majorities as providing more information about correctness—in other words, majorities function as an important source of both informational and normative social influence (Mugny & Perez, 1991). Why, then, are minorities sometimes able to get their message across?

One possibility is that when people are confronted with a minority stating views they don't initially accept, they are puzzled, and exert cognitive effort to understand why these people hold these views, and why they are willing to depart so visibly from widely accepted views (Nemeth, 1986). Similarly, individuals exposed to minority views may devote more, or more careful, scrutiny to the minority's ideas.

This possibility has recently been investigated by Baker and Petty (1994). They used the *elaboration likelihood model,* discussed in Chapter 4, to determine whether individuals pay more attention to messages when they come from majorities or when they come from minorities. Results were somewhat surprising: messages from neither majorities nor minorities automatically receive more attention from recipients. Rather, both the source and the message—the position taken—combine to determine how carefully messages are examined. It is when the source and the message are somehow *imbalanced*—for example, a majority endorsing an unexpected or disagreeable position, or a minority endorsing an agreeable position—that messages receive especially careful scrutiny. When, in contrast, the source and message are *balanced* (a majority endorsing an agreeable position, or a minority endorsing an unpopular one), recipients expend less cognitive effort. Put another way, it is when the combination of the message and the source is somehow *surprising* that people are willing to spend extra effort in processing the information they receive. Since minorities do often express views that people find surprising or unexpected—even for the minority—it seems possible that this is one reason why minorities often exert considerable influence.

A related possibility is that minorities lead individuals to consider ideas and alternatives they would otherwise have ignored. Would large numbers of people have paid any attention to the hole in the ozone layer or the possibility of the greenhouse effect during the 1980s and 1990s if vocal minorities had not started them thinking about environmental issues during preceding decades? It seems unlikely. So, in sum, even when minorities fail to sway majorities initially, they may initiate processes that lead to eventual social change. In this sense, as well as in several others, there is much truth to Franklin Roosevelt's remark that "No democracy can long survive which does not accept as fundamental to its very existence the recognition of the rights of minorities" (June 15, 1938).

Compliance: To Ask—Sometimes—Is to Receive

Suppose that you wanted someone to do something for you, how would you go about getting them to do it? If you think about this question for a moment, you'll quickly realize that you—like me!—have quite a few tricks up your sleeve for gaining *compliance*—for inducing others to say yes to your requests. What are these techniques like? Which ones work best—and when? These are among the basic questions studied by social psychologists in their efforts to understand this, the most frequent form of social influence. In the discussion that follows, we'll examine a number of different tactics for gaining compliance. Before turning to these, however, let's briefly examine one basic framework for understanding all of these procedures.

Compliance: The Underlying Principles

Some years ago, one well-known social psychologist (Robert Cialdini), decided that the best way to find out about compliance was to study what he termed *compliance professionals*—people whose success (financial or otherwise) depends on their ability to get others to say yes. Who are such persons? They include salespeople, advertisers, political lobbyists, fund-raisers, con artists and—one might argue—trial attorneys, professional negotiators, and politicians. Cialdini's technique for learning from these people was straightforward: he temporarily concealed his true identity and took jobs in various settings where seeking compliance is a way of life. In other words, he worked in advertising, direct (door-to-door) sales, fund-raising organizations, and other settings. On the basis of these firsthand experiences, he concluded that although techniques for gaining compliance take many different forms (see Figure 9.9), they all rest to some degree on six basic principles (Cialdini, 1994):

FIGURE 9.9
One of the Many Techniques for Gaining Compliance. *As illustrated by this cartoon, efforts to gain compliance take many different forms.*
(*Source:* Reprinted with special permission of King Features Syndicate.)

Friendship/Liking: In general, we are more willing to comply with requests from friends or from people we like than with requests from strangers or people we don't like.

Commitment/Consistency: Once we have committed ourselves to a position or action, we are more willing to comply with requests for behaviors that are consistent with that position. We generally want to behave in a consistent manner, so once we are committed to a position or view, we try to say or do things that fit with it in various ways.

Scarcity: In general, we value, and try to secure, opportunities that are scarce or decreasing. As a result, we are more likely to comply with requests that focus on "disappearing opportunities" than on ones that make no reference to such changes.

Reciprocity: We are generally more willing to comply with a request from someone who has previously provided a favor or concession to *us* than to someone who has not. In other words, we feel obligated to pay people back in some way for what they have done for us.

Social Validation: We are generally more willing to comply with a request for some action if this action is consistent with what we believe persons similar to ourselves are doing (or thinking). We want to be correct, and one way to do so is to act and think like others.

Authority: We value authority, so we are usually more willing to comply with requests from someone who is a legitimate authority—or simply looks like one.

According to Cialdini (1994), these basic principles—which are well-known to social psychologists—underlie many techniques professionals use for gaining compliance. We'll now examine specific techniques based on these principles, plus a few others as well.

Tactics Based on Friendship or Liking: Ingratiation

We've already considered several techniques for increasing compliance through liking in our discussion of *impression management* (Chapter 2). As you may recall, impression management involves various procedures for making a good impression on others. While this can be an end in itself, impression management techniques are often used for purposes of **ingratiation**: getting others to like us so that they will be more willing to agree to our requests (Jones, 1964; Liden & Mitchell, 1988).

What ingratiation techniques are effective? Virtually all of the ones we described in Chapter 2. Under the heading of *self-enhancing tactics* are such procedures as improving one's appearance, emitting many positive nonverbal cues (e.g., smiling, a high level of eye contact), and associating oneself with positive events or people the target person already likes. In contrast, *other-enhancing tactics* include flattery, agreeing with target persons, showing interest in them, and providing them small gifts or favors. Research findings indicate that all of these tactics can be successful, at least to a degree, in increasing others' liking for us (e.g., Wayne & Liden, 1995). And increased liking, in turn, can lead to greater compliance.

Tactics Based on Commitment or Consistency: The Foot in the Door, the Lowball, and Others

As observed by Cialdini (1994), experts in compliance—salespersons, advertisers, fund-raisers—often start their campaigns for gaining compliance with a trivial request. For example, a salesperson may ask potential customers to accept a free sample or to answer a few questions about products they use. Only after these small requests are granted do the experts move on to the requests they really want—ones that can prove quite costly to the target persons. In all such instances, the basic strategy is much the same: somehow induce another person to comply with a small initial request and so increase the chances that he or she will agree to a much larger one. What is the basic principle behind this technique—which is often known as the **foot-in-the-door technique?** Briefly, the desire to be *consistent*. Once the target person says yes to the small request, it is more difficult for that person to say no to a larger, subsequent request, because doing so would be somewhat inconsistent with the first response. It's almost as if by saying yes to the small request, the target has indicated that "I'm a helpful person who does try to help others." Refusing the second request is inconsistent with this flattering self-perception, so the pressure is on to agree to the second, larger request.

The results of many studies indicate both that the foot-in-the-door technique really works (Beaman et al., 1983) and that its effectiveness stems, at least in part, from the operation of the consistency principle. The first of these conclusions—that the foot in the door really works—is supported in a fairly dramatic way by a famous study conducted by Freedman and Fraser (1966).

These researchers had a male experimenter phone homemakers, to whom he identified himself as a member of a consumers' group. Then he asked participants to answer a few simple questions about the kinds of soap they used at home. Several days later, the same person called again and made a much larger request: could he send a crew of five or six persons to the participant's home to conduct a thorough inventory of all the products he or she had on hand? It was explained that this survey would take about two hours and that the crew would require freedom to search in all closets, cabinets, and drawers. This was a truly gigantic request, yet fully 52.8 percent of the persons exposed to this "one-two" pattern of requests agreed. In contrast, only 22.2 percent of persons called only once and presented "cold" with the large request agreed. Similar results have been obtained in many other studies, in which requests involved everything from signing a petition (Baron, 1973) through contributing to charity (Pliner et al., 1974); so the foot in the door does appear to be an effective technique for gaining compliance. That it actually operates through people's tendency to be

Ingratiation ■ A technique for gaining compliance in which requesters first induce target persons to like them, then attempt to change their behavior in some desired manner.

Foot-in-the-Door Technique ■ A procedure for gaining compliance in which requesters begin with a small request and then, when this is granted, escalate to a larger one (the one they actually desired all along).

FIGURE 9.10

The Lowball Technique in Action. Auto dealers sometimes use the *lowball* technique. This involves offering an attractive deal to customers but then, after they accept, changing it in some way. Rationally, customers should refuse; but in fact, they often accept the less attractive deal because they feel committed to buying the car.

consistent is suggested by the findings of several additional studies (e.g., DeJong & Musilli, 1982).

In one of these, for instance, it was found that the foot-in-the-door effect occurs among children down to the age of about seven, but does not operate below that age. Since children above the age of seven possess the capacity for such reasoning as "I was helpful before; therefore, I should be helpful again to be consistent," but those below this age do not, these findings offer support (although indirect) for the consistency explanation outlined above.

The foot-in-the-door technique is not the only one based on the consistency/commitment principle, however. Another is the **lowball procedure.** In this technique, which is often used by automobile salespersons, a very good deal is offered to a customer. After the customer accepts, however, something happens that makes it necessary for the salesperson to change the deal and make it less advantageous for the customer—for example, an "error" in price calculations is found, or the sales manager rejects the deal. The totally rational reaction for customers, of course, is to walk away. Yet often they agree to the changes and accept the less desirable arrangement (see Figure 9.10).

Such informal observations have been confirmed by carefully conducted studies. In one, for example, students first agreed to participate in a psychology experiment. Only after making this commitment did they learn that it started at 7:00 a.m. (Cialdini et al., 1978). Despite the inconvenience of this early hour, however, almost all persons in this *lowball* condition appeared for their appointments. As you can probably guess, a much lower proportion of students who learned in advance about the 7:00 a.m. starting time agreed to take part in the study. In instances such as this, an initial commitment seems to make it more difficult for individuals to say no, even though the conditions under which they said yes are now changed.

A third, and closely related, technique is the notorious **bait-and-switch tactic** (Cialdini, 1994). Here, retailers may advertise some item at a special low price. When customers arrive, they find that the items are sold out, or are of very low quality. Since they have already made an initial commitment to buy, however, it is now much easier to sell them something else—a more expensive

Lowball Procedure ■ A technique for gaining compliance in which an offer or deal is changed to make it less attractive to the target person after this person has accepted it.

Bait-and-Switch Tactic ■ A technique for gaining compliance in which items offered for sale are unavailable or of very low quality. This leads customers to buy a more expensive item that *is* available.

FIGURE 9.11

The Door in the Face: An Example. *Mr. Dithers is using the door-in-the-face technique: he starts with relatively large requests and, when these are rejected, moves to the one he wanted all along. But Dagwood is aware of what he's doing, and this may reduce this tactic's effectiveness.*

(*Source:* Reprinted with special permission of King Features Syndicate.)

item—than would otherwise be the case. Why? Because changing one's mind and reversing an initial commitment requires hard work, and many people, it appears, would rather pay a higher price than change their minds.

In sum, several tactics for gaining compliance take full advantage of our desire to be consistent and to stick to initial commitments. So beware of situations in which you are asked to do something trivial, or are asked to make a commitment to a course of action early on: in such cases, the persons with whom you are dealing may be laying the groundwork for something entirely different.

Tactics Based on Reciprocity: The Door in the Face, the Foot in the Mouth, and the "That's-Not-All" Approach

Reciprocity is a basic rule of social life. When someone does something for us, we generally feel an obligation to do something for them in return. While this makes a great deal of sense and is viewed by most persons as being only fair and just, the principle of reciprocity also serves as the basis for several important techniques for gaining compliance. One of these is, on the face of it, the opposite of the foot-in-the-door technique: instead of beginning with a small request and then escalating to a larger one, persons seeking compliance sometimes start with a very large request and then, after this is rejected, shift to a smaller request—the one they wanted all along (see Figure 9.11). This tactic is known as the **door-in-the-face technique** (because the first refusal seems to slam the door in the face of the requester), and several studies indicate that it can be quite effective. For example, in one well-known experiment, Cialdini and his colleagues (1975) stopped college students on the street and presented a huge request: Would the students serve as unpaid counselors for juvenile delinquents two hours a week for the next *two years*? As you can guess, none agreed. When the experimenters then scaled down their request to a much smaller one—would the same students take a group of delinquents on a two-hour trip to the zoo—fully 50 percent agreed. In contrast, less than 17 percent of those in a control group agreed to this smaller request when it was presented cold, rather than after the larger request.

Door-in-the-Face Technique ■ A procedure for gaining compliance in which requesters begin with a large request and then, when this is refused, retreat to a smaller one (the one they actually desired all along).

The same tactic is often used by negotiators, who may begin with a position that is extremely advantageous to themselves but then back down to a position much closer to the one they really hope to obtain. Similarly, sellers often begin with a price they know that buyers will reject, and then lower the price to a more reasonable one—but one that is still quite favorable to themselves. In all these cases, the persons using the *door-in-the-face tactic* appear to make a concession after their first request or proposal is rejected; then target persons feel obligated to make a matching concession in return—a concession that may end up giving the requester what she or he wanted all along.

A related procedure is known as the **that's-not-all technique.** Here, an initial request is followed, before the target person can make up her or his mind to say yes or no, by something that sweetens the deal—a small extra incentive from the person using this tactic. For example, auto dealers sometimes decide to throw in a small additional option to the car in the hope that this will help them close the deal; and often, it really does! Persons on the receiving end of the *that's-not-all technique* view this small extra as a concession on the part of the other person, and so feel obligated to make a concession themselves. Several studies indicate that this technique, too, really works: throwing in a small "extra" before people can say no does indeed increase the likelihood that they will say yes (e.g., Burger, 1986).

A third procedure for increasing compliance involves a more subtle use of the reciprocity principle. When people feel that they are in a relationship with another person—no matter how trivial—they often feel that they owe this person some consideration simply because the relationship exists. For example, friends help friends when they need assistance, and persons who perceive themselves as similar in some manner may feel that they should help one another when the need arises. This subtle use of the reciprocity principle underlies what social psychologists term the **foot-in-the-mouth technique** (e.g., Howard, 1990). Briefly, this involves a requester establishing some kind of relationship, no matter how trivial, with the target person, and so increasing the target's feelings of an obligation to comply with reasonable requests. By admitting the existence of this relationship (for example, "We're all human beings, right?")—which may be a very tenuous one—the target person give the requester an important edge. In a sense, then, the target person "puts his or her foot in his or her mouth" by agreeing that the relationship exists. A clear demonstration of the power of this tactic is provided by research conducted recently by Aune and Basil (1994).

These researchers had female accomplices stop students on a university campus and ask them to contribute to a well-known charitable organization. In a control condition, they simply made this request without providing additional information. In another condition (which used the foot-in-the-mouth technique), they asked passersby if they were students, and then commented, "Oh, that's great, so am I." Then they made their request for funds. Results indicated that a much larger percentage of the persons approached made a donation in the foot-in-the-mouth condition (25.5 percent) than in the control group (9.8 percent). These findings, and those of a follow-up study by the same authors, suggest that the reciprocity principle can be stretched even to such tenuous relationships as "We're both students, right? And students help students, right? So how about a donation?"

Tactics Based on Scarcity: Playing Hard to Get and the Fast-Approaching-Deadline Technique

It's a general rule of life that things that are scarce, rare, or difficult to possess are viewed as being more valuable than those that are easy to obtain. Thus, we are often willing to expend more effort, or go to greater expense, to obtain items

That's-Not-All Technique ■ A technique for gaining compliance in which a requester offers additional benefits to target persons before they have decided whether to comply with or reject specific requests.

Foot-in-the-Mouth Tactic ■ A procedure for gaining compliance in which the requester establishes some kind of relationship, no matter how trivial, with the target person, thereby increasing this person's feeling of obligation to comply.

or outcomes that are scarce than to obtain ones that are common. This principle, too, serves as the basis for several techniques for gaining compliance. One of the most intriguing of these is **playing hard to get.**

Many people know that this can be an effective tactic in the area of personal romance: by suggesting that it is difficult to win their affections or that there are many competitors for their love, they can greatly increase their desirability (e.g., Walster, Walster, Piliavin, & Schmidt, 1973; see Figure 9.11). This tactic is not restricted to interpersonal attraction, however; research findings indicate that it is also sometimes used by job candidates to increase their attractiveness to potential employers, and hence to increase the likelihood that the employers will offer them a job. For example, consider a study carried out by Williams and her colleagues (1993).

These researchers arranged for professional recruiters who were interviewing students at large universities to review information about potential job candidates. This information, which was presented in folders, indicated either that the job candidate already had two job offers (a hard-to-get candidate) or no other job offers (easy-to-get candidate), and was either highly qualified (very high grades) or less well-qualified (low average grades). After reviewing this information, the interviewers then rated the candidates in terms of their qualifications and desirability, the company's likelihood of inviting them to interview, and the likelihood of considering them for a job. Results were clear: The hard-to-get candidates were rated more favorably than the easy-to-get candidates regardless of their grades. However, the hard-to-get candidate who was also highly qualified received by far the highest ratings of all. Since it is persons who receive high ratings that usually get the interviews—and the jobs—these findings indicate that creating the impression of being a scarce and valuable resource (being hard to get) can be another effective means for gaining compliance.

A related technique based on the same "what's-scarce-is-valuable" principle is one frequently used by retailers. Ads using this **deadline technique** state a specific time limit during which an item can be purchased for a specific price. After the deadline runs out, the ads suggest, the price will go up. Of course, in many cases the sale is not a real one, and the time limit is bogus. Yet many persons reading ads such as the ones in Figure 9.12 believe them and hurry down to the store in order to avoid missing out on a great opportunity. I encountered this recently myself, when ads proclaiming "Closeout of Winter Merchandise" in several major department stores appeared in our local newspaper. When I questioned salesclerks, they confirmed the claims in the ads: winter merchandise would be removed from the stores to make way for spring fashions when the sale ended. However, a week after the proclaimed deadline, the sale was still going on in several of the stores that ran these ads. So when you encounter an offer that suggests that "the clock is ticking," be cautious: it may be based more on good sales techniques than on reality.

Other Tactics for Gaining Compliance: Complaining and Putting Others in a Good Mood

While many techniques for inducing compliance seem to rest on the basic principles described by Cialdini (1994), others seem to involve other mechanisms. One of the most interesting of these involves an action in which most of us engage every day: **complaining.** Complaining involves expressions of discontent or dissatisfaction with oneself or some aspect of the external world, and often such statements are simple expressions of personal states ("I feel lousy!") or comments on the external world ("Wow, is it cold today!"). Sometimes, however, complaining is used as a tactic of social influence: "Why didn't you take

Playing Hard to Get ■ Efforts to increase compliance by suggesting that a person or object is scarce and hard to obtain.

Deadline Technique ■ A technique for increasing compliance in which target persons are told that they have only limited time to take advantage of some offer or to obtain some item.

Complaining ■ In the context of compliance, expressing discontent, dissatisfaction, resentment, or regret as a means of exerting social influence on others.

FIGURE 9.12

The Deadline Technique in Advertising. Advertisers often use the *deadline technique* to convince customers to buy—now, before it's too late!

out the garbage like you promised?" "We always see the movie you want; it's not fair," or the classic *"You don't love me anymore!"* Statements such as these are directed toward the goal of getting the recipient to change his or her attitudes or behavior in some manner, and recent studies conducted by Alicke and his colleagues (1992) indicate that they are often successful in this respect.

These researchers asked college students to keep diaries in which they recorded their daily complaints over a three-day period. Each time they complained, participants recorded the complaint and indicated when and where it occurred, the reason for the complaint, and the response of the other person or persons involved. Results indicated that most complaints fell into several distinct categories, including (1) global statements expressing attitudes or feelings about a person, object, or event ("Those fraternity brothers are so vain"); (2) specific complaints about others' behavior or one's own actions ("You forgot to pay the phone bill"); (3) one's physical state ("My head is really pounding"); (4) falling below achievement expectations ("My roommate thinks I let him down last night"); (5) obligations ("I wish I didn't have to pick up my sister after work"); and (6) obstacles to goal achievement ("I am getting really sick of school").

The reasons for complaining, too, varied widely, with the desire to vent or express frustration being by far the most common (50.0 percent). However, participants indicated that they also complained to get advice (9.6 percent), sympathy (6.1 percent), or information (3.8 percent). Most important to the present discussion, many complaints (7.5 percent) involved direct efforts to change others' attitudes or behavior, and such efforts often worked: others agreed with complaints or tried to resolve them more than 25 percent of the time. So, in sum, complaining to others did seem to be at least a moderately effective technique for gaining compliance in some situations.

In follow-up research, Klotz and Alicke (1993) asked same-sex friends, opposite-sex friends, and dating couples to report on the frequency and content of complaints in their relationships. Results revealed some intriguing gender differences. Female friends made fewer complaints about their partners than did male friends or romantic partners. In addition, female friends made more complaints about *themselves* (e.g., "I really dislike my hair"). Finally, female friends made more supportive reactions to partner's complaints. They offered more suggestions for dealing with the topic of the complaints, and more supportive emotional responses ("I'm sorry to hear that," "I know just how you feel"). In contrast, males made more nonresponsive comments in response to partner's complaints (changing the subject, saying nothing), or overtly *nonsupportive* statements ("Big deal," "Tough!").

One additional finding of interest is that females were generally more accurate than males in reporting others' complaints: their reports of their friends' or romantic partners' complaints more accurately reflected these complaints than did males' reports. All in all, a picture emerges in which females are less likely to complain than males, are more responsive to the complaints of their friends and lovers, and recognize these more accurately than males. Thus, it appears that this is one technique of social influence used somewhat differently— and perhaps with differential success—by the two genders. We'll return to the topic of possible gender differences in social influence in the *Social Diversity* section at the end of this chapter.

Before concluding, we should mention one additional tactic for gaining compliance: putting others in a good mood. As we noted in Chapters 2 and 7, people's moods often exert a strong effect on their behavior. And, it seems, this principle also holds with respect to compliance. When individuals are in a good mood, they tend to be more willing to say "Yes" to various requests than when they are in a neutral or negative mood (cf., Cunningham, 1979). This is one reason why individuals seeking to influence others often "wine and dine" them before making their request. They realize that when the target persons feel good or happy, they are less likely to refuse.

Intriguing evidence for this relationship between mood and helping has recently been reported by Rind (1996). He arranged for a server in a large hotel in Atlantic City to describe the weather outside to guests as he served them food in their rooms. The windows of the hotel made it impossible for guests to tell what the weather was like outside, so this information could be systematically varied. Four groups were told that it was "cold and rainy," "cold and sunny," "warm and rainy," or "warm and sunny." The size of the tips given to the server by guests was then recorded. Results indicated that information about temperature had no effect, but that tips were significantly larger when the weather was described as sunny (23.65%) than when it was described as rainy (18.67%). Other findings, such as differences in guests' facial expressions, indicated that mood did play an important role in these findings: individuals told it was sunny appeared to be considerably happier or more cheerful than those told it was rainy. So, as our informal experience suggests, putting others in a good mood increases their willingness to say "Yes" to implicit requests (e.g., for a tip) as well as to more explicit ones. For information on another technique for gaining compliance that may have practical implications for many charitable organizations, please read the *Applied Side* section below.

Social Psychology: On the Applied Side

THE PIQUE TECHNIQUE: Preventing Mindless (Automatic) Refusals

Quick: What's your typical reaction to panhandlers, or even to people soliciting funds for charitable organizations? If you are like most individuals, you

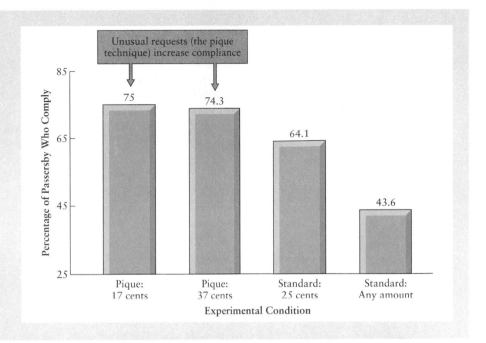

FIGURE 9.13

The Pique Technique in Operation. Passersby were more likely to give money to a panhandler when she asked for an unusual amount of money (17 cents or 37 cents) than when she made a more standard appeal for funds. This happened because the unusual nature of the request prevented potential donors from refusing the request in an automatic "mindless" manner.

(*Source:* Based on data from Santos, Leve, & Pratkanis, 1994.)

probably look away, avoid eye contact with these persons, and don't even think about responding favorably to their requests. Is this because you are hardhearted and callous? Not at all. Many social psychologists would offer a kinder interpretation of your actions in such situations: You ignore these requesters because you are operating on "automatic pilot"—you are following an automatic refusal script. This interpretation relates to a basic fact about social thought we mentioned in Chapter 3: In general, people follow the path of least resistance in social cognition, just as they do in many other areas of life. And where compliance is concerned, we are faced with so many requests each day that we tend to react to such requests—especially when they come from strangers—in a nonthinking, automatic manner. We reject such requests in an automatic manner because we don't want to bother thinking about them. Social psychologists refer to our actions in such cases as "mindless," to reflect the fact that we are proceeding with a minimum of cognitive effort or thought (Langer, Blank, & Chanowitz, 1978; Pratkanis & Aronson, 1992).

If our tendency to ignore many requests from strangers is indeed due to such "mindlessness" (or to automatic refusal scripts that we follow), then anything that shocks people out of this "mindless" state and gets them to think about a request, might increase compliance with it. This reasoning is the basis for the **pique technique**—a procedure for increasing compliance based on *piquing* (stimulating) target persons' interest. Evidence that the *pique technique* really works is provided by several studies (e.g., Langer et al., 1978). Recently, for example, Santos, Leve, and Pratkanis (1994) conducted an experiment in which female accomplices played the role of panhandlers and asked passersby for money. In two standard conditions not expected to pique interest, they asked, "Can you spare any change?" or "Can you spare a quarter?" In two other pique conditions, in contrast, they made unusual requests: "Can you spare 17 cents?" or "Can you spare 37 cents?" As you can see from Figure 9.13, results indicated that the pique technique was quite effective: a higher proportion of passersby donated in the pique conditions (especially when asked for 17 cents) than in the nonpique control groups.

Pique Technique ■ A technique for gaining compliance that focuses on gaining target persons' attention and so preventing them from engaging in automatic (mindless) refusal.

In a follow-up experiment, Santos and his colleagues (1994) asked another group of participants to imagine their own reactions to the pique and nonpique conditions used in the first study, and to describe any thoughts they had as they considered these requests. Results indicated that as expected, those in the two pique conditions reported more thoughts, such as "What does the person need the money for?" or "How did this person come to be needy?" These findings lend support to the view that the pique technique is effective because it gets targets' attention and disrupts the automatic tendency to refuse requests from panhandlers.

These findings have important practical implications for charitable organizations seeking to raise funds. Briefly, they suggest that such organizations might often increase the amount they collect by doing something that makes their requests unusual and attention-getting. In fact, some organizations already use this procedure. On my own campus, faculty are "arrested" once a year by students representing a charity drive; they can be released from jail only if they—or others—pay their "bail" by making sufficient contributions to the campaign. This humorous technique is highly successful, and I have always suspected that it works, at least in part, because of the props it uses—students dressed as sheriffs, large cages holding faculty members, official-looking "Bail Requests." All these capture people's attention and cause them to stop in their tracks, then to donate. Clearly, this is one example of how the findings of social psychology can be put to practical—and prosocial—use. ■ ■ ■

INTEGRATING PRINCIPLES

1. Many different techniques for increasing the likelihood that others will say yes to various requests—for increasing compliance—exist.

2. Many of these tactics are based on fundamental principles of social behavior, such as *reciprocity, the desire to be consistent,* and *liking* or *friendship.*

3. These principles also play an important role in other forms of social behavior. For example, we tend to like persons who like us (Chapter 7) and to aggress others who have aggressed against us (Chapter 11). Similarly, we sometimes change our own attitudes because we want them to be consistent with other attitudes we hold or with our overt behavior (Chapter 4).

Obedience: Social Influence by Demand

In discussing compliance, we noted that often, we are more willing to agree to requests from persons with *authority*—persons whose position in an organization or social system seems to give them the right to make such requests—than to requests from persons lacking in authority. This principle also underlies another major form of social influence: obedience. Obedience occurs when people obey commands or orders from others to do something. Obedience is less frequent than conformity or compliance, because even persons who possess authority and power generally prefer to exert it through the *velvet glove*—through requests rather than direct orders (e.g., Yukl & Falbe, 1991). Still, obedience is far from rare. Business executives sometimes issue orders to their subordinates;

military officers shout commands that they expect to be followed without question; and parents, police officers, and sports coaches, to name just a few, seek to influence others in the same manner. Obedience to the commands of persons who possess authority is far from surprising; they usually have some means of enforcing their orders. More surprising is the fact that often, persons lacking in such power can also induce high levels of submission from others. The clearest and most dramatic evidence for the occurrence of such effects was reported by Stanley Milgram in a series of famous—and controversial—studies (Milgram, 1963, 1965a, 1974).

Destructive Obedience: Some Basic Findings

In his research, Milgram wished to learn whether individuals would obey commands from a relatively powerless stranger requiring them to inflict what seemed to be considerable pain on another person—a totally innocent stranger. Milgram's interest in this topic derived from the occurrence of tragic events in which seemingly normal, law-abiding persons actually obeyed such directives. For example, during World War II, troops in the German army frequently obeyed commands to torture and murder unarmed civilians—millions of them. In fact, the Nazis established horrible but highly efficient death camps designed to eradicate Jews, Gypsies, and other groups they felt were inferior or a threat to their own racial purity (see Figure 9.14 on p. 344). In the United States these events—known as the *holocaust*—are depicted in a new museum that is part of the famous Smithsonian Institution (refer to Figure 9.14).

In an effort to gain insights into the nature of such events, Milgram designed an ingenious, if unsettling, laboratory simulation. The experimenter informed participants in the study (all males) that they were taking part in an investigation of the effects of punishment on learning. Of each pair of participants, one would serve as a "learner," and would try to perform a simple task in which the learner would supply the second word in pairs of words after hearing the first. The other, the "teacher," would read these words and would punish errors by means of electric shock, delivered by the device shown in Figure 9.15 (p. 345). This apparatus contained thirty numbered switches, with the first labeled "15 volts," the second "30 volts," and so on, up to 450 volts. The two persons present—a real participant and an accomplice—then drew slips of paper from a hat to determine who would play each role; as you can probably guess, the drawing was fixed so that the real participant always became the teacher. The teacher was then instructed to deliver a shock to the learner each time he made an error on the task. Moreover—and this is crucial—teachers were instructed to *increase the strength of the shock each time the learner made an error.* This meant that if the learner made many errors, he would soon be receiving strong jolts of electricity. It's important to note that this was bogus information: in reality, the accomplice (the learner) *never received any shocks* during the experiment. The only real shock ever used was a mild demonstration pulse from one button (number three) to convince participants that the equipment was real.

During the session, the learner (following prearranged instructions) made many errors. Thus, participants soon found themselves facing a dilemma: Should they continue punishing this person with what seemed to be increasingly painful shocks? Or should they refuse to go on? If they hesitated, the experimenter pressured them to continue with a series of graded prods presented one after the other: "Please continue"; "The experiment requires that you continue"; "It is absolutely essential that you continue"; "You have no other choice; you *must* go on."

Since participants were all volunteers and were paid in advance, you might predict that most would quickly refuse the experimenter's orders. In reality,

FIGURE 9.14

The Holocaust: Destructive Obedience Carried to the Extreme. During World War II, the Nazis established death camps where soldiers and even prisoners obeyed commands to systematically murder millions of innocent victims. These tragic events are the focus of a new museum in Washington, D.C.

though, fully *65 percent showed total obedience*—they proceeded through the entire series to the final 450-volt level (see Figure 9.16). In contrast, persons in a control group who were not given such commands generally used only very mild shocks during the session. Many participants, of course, protested and asked that the session be ended. When ordered to proceed, however, a majority yielded to the experimenter's influence and continued to obey. Indeed, they continued doing so even when the victim pounded on the wall as if in protest against the painful shocks (at the 300-volt level), and then *no longer responded.* The experimenter told participants to treat failures to answer as errors; so from this point on, "teachers" believed that they were actually delivering dangerous shocks to someone who might, perhaps, be unconscious!

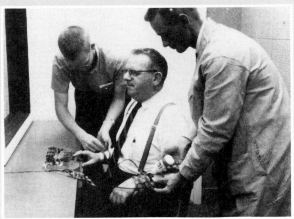

FIGURE 9.15

Studying Obedience in the Laboratory. The left-hand photo shows the apparatus Stanley Milgram used in his famous experiments on obedience. (It has recently been displayed in a special exhibit at the Smithsonian Institution in Washington, D.C.) The right photo shows the experimenter (right front) and a participant (rear) attaching electrodes to the learner's (accomplice's) wrist.

(*Source:* From the film *Obedience,* distributed by the New York University Film Library, Copyright 1965 by Stanley Milgram. Reprinted by permission of the copyright holder.)

FIGURE 9.16

Obedience to the Commands of a Powerless Authority. As shown here, 65 percent of the participants in Milgram's research were fully obedient: they obeyed the experimenter's commands to continue delivering shocks to the victim throughout the entire series—including the final, 450-volt shock! (Remember, there were no actual shocks in the study; participants were merely told that the learner was receiving these painful stimuli.)

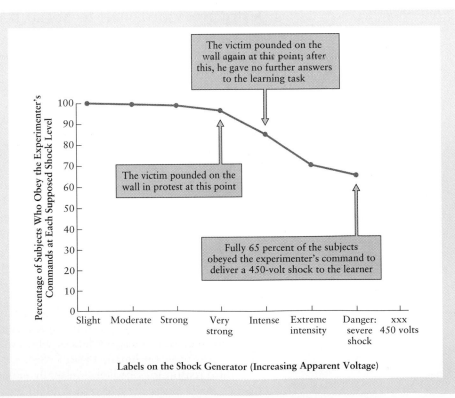

In further experiments, Milgram (1965b, 1974) found that similar results could be obtained even under conditions that might be expected to reduce such obedience. When the study was moved from its original location on the campus of Yale University to a run-down office building in a nearby city, participants' level of obedience remained virtually unchanged. Similarly, a large proportion continued to obey even when the accomplice complained about the painfulness of the shocks and begged to be released. Most surprising of all, many (about 30 percent) obeyed even when they were required to grasp the victim's hand and force it down upon a metal shock plate! That these chilling results are not restricted to a single culture is indicated by the fact that similar findings were soon reported in studies conducted in several different countries (e.g., Jordan, Germany, Australia) and with children as well as adults (e.g., Kilham & Mann, 1974; Shanab & Yahya, 1977). Thus, Milgram's findings seemed to be alarmingly general in scope.

I (Bob Baron) went to high school with Milgram's niece, and I can remember the shock with which students in my class reacted when she told us about her uncle's findings, several years before they were published. Yet I was dismayed again when, as a college student, I read the actual report of his study. Psychologists, too, found Milgram's findings highly unsettling. On the one hand, many wondered whether it was appropriate to conduct such research; many participants experienced extreme stress when confronted with the dilemma of either harming an innocent stranger or disobeying an authority figure. Milgram conducted a complete and thorough debriefing after each session; but still, important ethical issues remained that could not be readily dismissed. On the other hand, psychologists were shaken by the actual results: Milgram's studies seemed to suggest that ordinary people are willing, albeit with some reluctance, to harm an innocent stranger if ordered to do so by someone in authority. This led to an important question: Why does such destructive obedience occur?

Destructive Obedience: Its Social Psychological Basis

One reason why the results reported by Milgram are so disturbing is that they seem to parallel many real-life events involving atrocities against innocent victims (for example, the willingness of Chinese troops to fire on unarmed civilians during the Tiananmen Square demonstrations in 1989; the willingness of Saddam Hussein's troops to murder unarmed citizens of their own country). Why does such *destructive obedience* occur? Why were subjects in these experiments—and many persons in tragic situations outside the laboratory—so willing to yield to this powerful form of social influence? Several factors appear to play a role.

First, in many situations, the persons in authority relieve those who obey of the responsibility for their own actions. "I was only carrying out orders" is the defense many offer after obeying harsh or cruel directions. In life situations this transfer of responsibility may be implicit. In Milgram's experiments, in contrast, it was explicit. Participants were told at the start that the experimenter (the authority figure), not they, would be responsible for the learner's well-being. In view of this fact, it is not surprising that many tended to obey; after all, they were completely off the hook.

Second, persons in authority often possess visible badges or signs of their status. These consist of special uniforms, insignia, titles, and similar symbols. Faced with such obvious reminders of who's in charge, most people find it difficult to resist (e.g., Bushman, 1984, 1988).

A third reason for obedience in many situations where the targets of such influence might resist involves the gradual escalation of the authority figure's orders. Initial commands call for relatively innocuous actions. Only later do directives increase in scope and come to require behavior that is dangerous or objectionable. For example, police or military personnel may at first be ordered to question, threaten, or arrest potential victims. Gradually, demands are increased to the point where these personnel are commanded to beat, torture, or even kill unarmed civilians. In a similar manner, participants in the laboratory research on obedience were first required to deliver only mild and harmless shocks to the victim. Only as this person continued to make errors on the learning task did the intensity of punishments rise to harmful levels.

Finally, events in many situations involving destructive obedience move very quickly: demonstrations turn into riots, or arrests turn into mass beatings—or murder—suddenly. The fast pace of such events gives participants little time for reflection: people are ordered to obey and—almost automatically—they do so. Such conditions prevailed in Milgram's research; within a few minutes of entering the laboratory, participants found themselves faced with commands to deliver strong electric shocks to the learner. This fast pace, too, operates to increase obedience.

In sum, several factors contribute to the high levels of obedience witnessed in laboratory studies and in a wide range of real-life contexts. Together, these pressures merge into a powerful force—one that many persons find difficult to resist. Unfortunately, the consequences of this compelling form of social influence can be disastrous for innocent and largely defenseless victims.

Destructive Obedience: Resisting Its Effects

Now that we have considered some of the factors responsible for the strong tendency to obey sources of authority, we will turn to a related question: How can this type of social influence be resisted? Several strategies seem to help to reduce tendencies to obey.

First, individuals exposed to commands from authority figures can be reminded that they—not the authorities—are responsible for any harm produced. Under these conditions sharp reductions in the tendency to obey have been observed (e.g., Hamilton, 1978; Kilham & Mann, 1974).

Second, individuals can be provided with a clear indication that beyond some point, unquestioning submission to destructive commands is inappropriate. One procedure that is highly effective in this regard involves exposing individuals to the actions of *disobedient models*—persons who refuse to obey an authority figure's commands. Research findings indicate that such models can greatly reduce unquestioning obedience (Milgram, 1965b; Powers & Geen, 1972).

Third, individuals may find it easier to resist influence from authority figures if they question the expertise and motives of these figures. Are authority figures really in a better position to judge what is appropriate and what is not? What motives lie behind their commands—socially beneficial goals or selfish gains? By asking such questions, persons who might otherwise obey may find support for independence rather than submission.

Finally, simply knowing about the power of authority figures to command blind obedience may be helpful in itself. Some research findings (e.g., Sherman, 1980) suggest that when individuals learn about the results of social psychological research, they sometimes change their behavior to take account of this new knowledge. With respect to destructive obedience, there is some hope that knowing about this process can enhance individuals' ability to resist. To the extent this is so, then even exposure to findings as disturbing as those reported by Milgram can have positive social value. As they become widely known, they may produce desirable shifts within society.

FIGURE 9.17

Refusing to Obey Authority: Sometimes, It Changes the World. When Boris Yeltsin (who later became president of Russia) defied the Soviet government, he helped bring about its downfall—and the downfall of many other totalitarian communist regimes throughout the world.

To conclude: The power of authority figures to command obedience is certainly great, but it is definitely *not* irresistible. Under appropriate conditions, it *can* be countered or reduced (see Figure 9.17). As in many other areas of life, there *is* a choice. Deciding to resist the commands of persons in authority can, of course, be highly dangerous. Those holding power have tremendous advantages in terms of weapons and other resources. Yet, as events in Russia, Eastern Europe, and elsewhere in the late 1980s and early 1990s indicate, the outcome is by no means certain when committed groups of citizens choose to resist. Ultimately, victory may go to those on the side of freedom and decency rather than to those who possess the guns and tanks and who wish to control and repress their fellow citizens.

Social Diversity: A Critical Analysis

GENDER DIFFERENCES IN SOCIAL INFLUENCE: More Apparent Than Real

SUPPOSE THAT YOU APPROACHED ONE HUNDRED PEOPLE AT random in some public place (e.g., a large shopping mall) and asked them the following question: "Do women and men differ in their tendencies to conform or accept social influence from others?" What would you find? Even today, the chances are good that a majority of individuals would suggest that females are higher in conformity than males. In support of this supposed difference, such persons might note that women are more likely than men to follow changing fashions, and that women are more concerned with being liked or being pleasing to others.

In short, they would call attention to contrasting gender-role stereotypes for females and males.

Are such views accurate? Are women really more susceptible to conformity pressure or to other forms of social influence than men? Early studies on this issue seemed to indicate that they are (e.g., Crutchfield, 1955). The results of these investigations indicated that women show greater yielding to social pressure than men. More recent studies, however, point to very different conclusions (e.g., Eagly & Carli, 1981). They suggest that, in fact, there are no significant differences between males and females in this respect, at least in most situations. Why did the findings of these two groups of studies differ so sharply? Several factors may have played a role.

One of these involves the nature of the tasks and materials used in the early experiments (those conducted in the 1950s and 1960s). In many of these studies, the tasks employed were ones more familiar to males than to females. Since individuals of both genders yield more readily to social influence when they are uncertain about how to behave than when they are more confident, it is hardly surprising that females demonstrated higher levels of conformity. After all, the dice were strongly loaded against them.

That this factor was indeed responsible for the gender differences obtained in early research is indicated by the findings of an experiment carried out by Sistrunk and McDavid (1971). These researchers found that when females were less familiar with the items used than males, they did in fact show greater yielding to group pressure. However, when the tables were turned so that the items were less familiar to males, it was they who showed greater conformity. So, in efforts to compare females and males in terms of susceptibility to social pressure, we must be on guard against confounding gender with an additional, unrelated factor—familiarity with the items or tasks used in the research.

Another reason for the disagreement between early and more recent studies involves major shifts in gender roles and gender-role stereotypes during the 1970s and 1980s (Steffen & Eagly, 1985). An ever increasing number of women have moved into jobs and fields once occupied solely by men; and stereotypes suggesting that women are less ambitious, less competent, and less independent than males have weakened. It seems reasonable to suggest that one result of such changes has been a fading of any tendency for females either to be, or simply to be perceived as being, more susceptible to social influence than males (Maupin & Fisher, 1989).

Gender and Status: Additional Evidence Indicating That Gender Differences in Conformity Are More Illusory Than Real

Additional evidence pointing to the conclusion that males and females do not actually differ with respect to conformity has focused on the following possibility. In general, females have lower status than males (Eagly, 1987). Since persons holding low status are often easier to influence than those holding higher status, this difference between females and males may account, at least in part, for the popular view that females are more easily influenced than males. Support for this reasoning has been obtained in several studies conducted by Eagly and her colleagues (e.g., Steffen & Eagly, 1985). For instance, in one such study, Eagly and Wood (1982) asked men and women to read a brief story in which one business employee attempted to influence the views of another employee of the opposite sex. In half the cases the would-be influencer was male and the target was female; in the

remainder, the reverse was true. In half of the stories, job titles were included, thus informing participants of the status of the persons involved. In the remaining instances, information of this type was omitted.

After reading the story, participants were asked to indicate the extent to which the target person would be influenced. It was predicted that when no information on status was provided, participants would tend to assume that females were lower in this regard than males. Thus, they would predict greater compliance by female targets than by male targets. When information on status was provided, however, this factor—not gender—would affect their judgments. Both predictions were confirmed. In the absence of any information about relative status, participants predicted greater yielding by females. When information on status was present, they predicted greater yielding by low-status than by high-status targets, *regardless of their gender*. Findings such as these add further support to the view that in general, all other things being equal, there are no appreciable differences between females and males in terms of susceptibility to social pressure.

A Possible Exception to the "No Difference" Rule: Judgments of Physical Attractiveness

While females and males do not appear to differ in overall susceptibility to social influence, this does not mean that they may not differ in this respect in some situations. In fact, research findings indicate that modest gender differences in susceptibility to social influence may exist with respect to one specific kind of judgment—ratings of others' physical attractiveness. For example, in a series of studies on this issue, Graziano and his colleagues (Graziano et al., 1993), asked male and female students to rate the attractiveness of opposite-sex strangers shown in photographs. The strangers had previously been rated as being average in attractiveness; but before making their own ratings, participants in the study received information suggesting that other students had rated the persons in some of the photos as attractive and other as unattractive. For other photos no ratings were provided, so these served as no–social influence (control) stimuli. Results indicated that males' judgments of the attractiveness of female strangers was not significantly affected by the ratings supposedly provided by other persons. In contrast, females' ratings of males were influenced by information indicating that these persons had been rated as unattractive by other women (see Figure 9.18 on page 350). Similar results were found in additional studies, so these results appeared to be quite stable.

What accounts for this difference? Graziano and his colleagues (1993) suggest that it may stem, at least to some degree, from the fact that men base their judgments of attractiveness largely on observable physical characteristics while women base such judgments on such characteristics *plus* information about behavioral dispositions, especially ones relevant to a man's being a cooperative, responsible parent and provider (Jensen-

FIGURE 9.18

Gender Differences in Judgments of Physical Attractiveness. As shown here, female students were influenced, in their judgments of males' attractiveness, by ratings supposedly assigned to these persons by other students. In contrast, males were not influenced in a similar manner in their judgments of females' attractiveness. These findings suggest that there may be some modest gender differences in susceptibility to social influence in at least one situation.

(*Source:* Based on data from Graziano et al., 1993.)

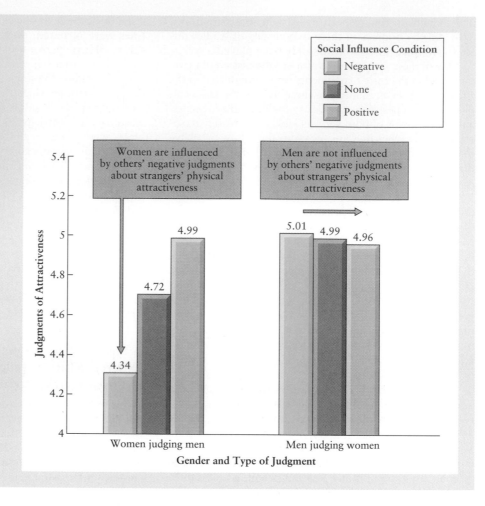

Campbell & Graziano, 1992). Since such traits are hard to see in a photo, there would be good reason for females to pay attention to—and be influenced by—the judgments of other women with respect to males' attractiveness. As you can see, this reasoning is related to the *evolutionary perspective* we discussed in Chapter 1, which contends that in the realm of mate selection, females tend to place greater emphasis on such various traits or characteristics (for example, *dominance* and *status*), while males place greater emphasis on physical

traits such youth and physical beauty (Kenrick et al., 1994). Regardless of the precise basis for the findings reported by Graziano and his colleagues, however, they call attention to the fact that while males and females do not differ in susceptibility to social influence across many situations, such differences may exist in a few restricted instances. Overall, however, our basic conclusion remains the same: With few if any exceptions, there are no important differences between females and males in terms of susceptibility to social influence. ■ ■ ■

CONNECTIONS: Integrating Social Psychology

In this chapter, you read about . . .	*In other chapters, you will find related discussions of . . .*
the role of social norms in conformity	the role of social norms in attraction (Chapter 7), helping (Chapter 10), aggression (Chapter 11), and group decision making (Chapter 12)

the basic principles underlying many different techniques for gaining compliance

the role of these principles in other aspects of social behavior:

... the role of reciprocity in attraction (Chapter 7), aggression (Chapter 11), and cooperation (Chapter 12)

... the role of the desire to be consistent in attitude change (Chapter 4), the self-concept (Chapter 5), and helping (Chapter 10)

... the role of liking or friendship in social perception (Chapter 2), social relationships (Chapter 8), leadership (Chapter 12), and the legal process (Chapter 13)

obedience to the commands of authority figures

the role of power and conflict in racial prejudice (Chapter 6), in various forms of social groups (Chapter 12), in charismatic leadership (Chapter 12), and in politics (Chapter 14)

Thinking about Connections

1. Some observers have suggested that a "culture of violence" has developed in the United States (see Chapter 11). By this, they mean that the norms governing aggression have changed in recent decades, becoming more permissive about such behavior. While assaults against others were once strongly censured, they are now viewed as more appropriate and acceptable by many persons. Do you agree? If so, what factors do you think may have been responsible for this shift in social norms?

2. Charismatic leaders are often viewed as masters of social influence: They seem to possess an uncanny ability to bend others to their will (Chapter 12). Do you think they use the principles and tactics for gaining compliance described in this chapter? And which of these do you feel might be most important to such leaders in their efforts to control their followers?

3. In many situations, we can tell when another person is trying to influence us. What may be harder to determine, at least sometimes, is the reasons why they wish to influence us (see our discussion of persuasion in Chapter 4). Are they engaging in such tactics for selfish reasons, purely for their own benefit? Or do they have our best interests at heart, too? On the basis of our discussion of attribution in Chapter 2, how do you think we try to determine others' motives in such situations? And how successful do you think we are at this important task?

4. It has sometimes been argued that social influence is the most basic and important aspect of social behavior. Do you agree? Can you think of any forms of social behavior in which influence does *not* play a role?

Summary and Review

Conformity

Conformity occurs when individuals change their attitudes or behavior to comply with *social norms*—rules or expectations about how they should behave in various situations. Conformity increases with *cohesiveness*—liking for the sources of such influence—and with the number of persons exerting pressure, but only up to a point. Conformity is reduced in the presence of *social support*—one or more persons who share the target person's views, or who depart from the majority's position in some manner. Two distinct types of social norms exist: *descriptive norms,* which describe how most people behave in a given situation, and *injunctive norms,* which indicate which behaviors are approved or disapproved in a given situation. Both types of norms can influence behavior, but the impact of injunctive norms appears to be broader or more powerful in some respects.

We tend to conform because of two basic social motives: the need to be liked and the need to be right. The first motive leads us to accept influence from others so that we will be liked by others whose acceptance we desire (*normative social influence*), while the second leads us to accept social influence so that we can be correct in our judgments or actions (*informational social influence*). In addition, recent evidence indicates that after we decide to conform or resist such pressure, we change our perceptions of the situation so as to justify our previous behavior.

While there are strong tendencies to conform, individuals often resist social pressure. One reason for this is that they wish to maintain their unique identity as individuals. Minorities can sometimes influence larger majorities, especially when they appear to be deeply committed to the views they support. We do not automatically pay more attention to information from majorities or minorities; rather, we tend to pay special attention to information that is *imbalanced*— for example, when majorities support disagreeable positions or minorities support agreeable ones.

Compliance

Compliance involves efforts by one or more individual to change the behavior of others. Many techniques can be used to gain compliance, but most of these seem to rest on six basic principles: *friendship/liking, commitment/consistency, scarcity, reciprocity, social validation,* and *authority.* Ingratiation is one major technique based on friendship and liking. Techniques based on commitment or consistency include the *foot in the door* and the *lowball.* Several tactics are based on reciprocity, including the *door in the face,* the *foot in the mouth,* and the *"that's-not-all"* approach. Techniques based on scarcity include *playing hard to get* and the *fast-approaching deadline* technique. Additional procedures for gaining compliance involve *complaining* and the *pique technique.* In the latter, re-

quests are made surprising in order to capture (pique) the attention of target persons.

Obedience

The most direct form of social influence is *obedience*— yielding to direct orders from another person. Research findings indicate that we often obey commands from authority figures even when such persons have little power to enforce their orders. These tendencies toward obedience stem from several causes (e.g., authority figures gradually escalate the scope of their orders; they have visible signs of power; there is little time for target persons to consider their actions in detail). Several procedures can help individuals resist obedience. These include reminding target persons that they, not the authority figures, will be responsible for any harmful outcomes and exposing target persons to disobedient models.

Social Diversity: Gender Differences in Social Influence

Early investigations suggested that females are more susceptible to conformity pressures and other forms of social influence than males. More recent investigations, however, have called these conclusions into question. It now appears that early studies used materials and tasks more familiar to males than to females and so placed females at a disadvantage in terms of susceptibility to conformity pressure. In addition, other findings suggest that many persons continue to believe that females are more conforming than males, because females generally occupy lower-status positions in society, and low-status persons tend to conform to a greater degree than high-status persons. But, there appear to be no overall gender differences in susceptibility to social influence among equal-status persons. However, recent evidence indicates that females and males may differ in this respect in a few situations; for example, females appear to be influenced to a greater degree than males by others' judgments concerning the attractiveness of opposite-sex strangers.

■ Key Terms

■ For More Information

Cialdini, R. B. (1988). *Influence: Science and practice* (2nd ed.). New York: HarperCollins.

An insightful account of the major techniques people use to influence others. The book draws both on the findings of systematic research and on informal observations made by the author in a wide range of practical settings (e.g., sales, public relations, fund-raising agencies, organizations). This is the most readable and informative account of knowledge about influence currently available.

Milgram, S. (1974). *Obedience to authority.* New York: Harper & Row.

More than twenty years after it was written, this book remains the definitive work on obedience as a social psy-

chological process. The untimely death of its author only adds to its value as a lasting contribution to our field.

Shavitt, S., & Brock, T. C. (1994). *Persuasion: Psychological insights and perspectives.* Boston: Allyn & Bacon.

In this excellent book, experts on persuasion and other aspects of social influence summarize existing knowledge about many fascinating topics. Among the chapters you are sure to find of interest are ones on how our actions affect our attitudes, on cognitive processes in persuasion, on many forms of interpersonal influence, and on subliminal persuasion.

CHAPTER 10

PROSOCIAL BEHAVIOR:
Helping Other People

Lisa Houck, *Interesting Ecosystem*, 1994, watercolor, 6 × 9"

Chapter Outline

You are driving along a nearly deserted country road when you notice a car that appears to have skidded across the shoulder and into a ditch. An elderly man is standing beside the vehicle, seemingly bewildered. You are in a hurry to meet someone in town, but you can see that the man needs help. What do you do?

You've just finished lunch at a cafeteria, and when you step outside, there is a surprising sight. Two couples seem to be arguing. They shout back and forth, and one of the women begins shoving the other. You wonder whether they are joking or really angry, whether you should do something or mind your own business. How do you make a decision?

In a grocery store, you notice a small child sitting in a shopping cart, crying. A woman, probably his mother, slaps him in the face and yells, "Shut up crying or you'll get worse than that!" You feel sorry for the child, but will you just make things worse if you say something?

On the news, you watch a segment about a civil war taking place on the other side of the world. You see unbelievably thin men, women, and children in a refugee camp, staring blankly at the TV camera. The voice-over says there is an immediate need for donations to provide food and medicine for these refugees before the death toll rises. Do you feel sorry for them? Will you do anything?

As you read about research dealing with just such situations throughout this chapter, think back to these examples and about the factors that might make you likely to help—or to hold back and not get involved.

It is not unusual to find yourself in a situation in which a stranger requires help and you happen to be a bystander, or in a situation in which *you* require help from strangers who happen to be nearby. A major segment of social psychological research has concentrated on the many factors that determine whether help will or will not be given to someone in need. Though most of the investigations deal with what people do in a sudden, unexpected emergency— for example, a car accident—help can sometimes be required over a long time period when the need is continuing, as in a chronic illness.

Psychologists want to be able to understand and to predict **prosocial behavior:** actions that provide benefit to others but that have no obvious benefits for the person who carries them out. Prosocial behavior can sometimes involve risk for the one who helps. An example is provided in Figure 10.1. Other terms, such as *helping behavior, charitable behavior,* and *volunteerism* are also used to describe the "good" things that people do to provide needed assistance to others.

Prosocial behavior became a topic of major interest to social psychologists in the 1960s. As this chapter will describe, a widely publicized event helped motivate a number of social psychologists to create theories and design experiments to explain why bystanders sometimes do and sometimes do not *respond to an emergency.* We'll see how this initial work led to a large body of research that expanded far beyond the concerns of the initial investigations. In a variety of situations, research has dealt with *external factors that influence prosocial behavior.* We will also explore *additional theoretical explanations of prosocial motivation.*

Prosocial Behavior ■ Actions that benefit others but have no obvious benefits for the person carrying them out, and which sometimes involve risk for the prosocial person.

Responding to an Emergency: Are Bystanders Helpful or Indifferent?

The daily news provides many examples of people helping one another, sometimes even acting as heroes who risk their lives to aid a stranger in distress. Consider the following newspaper stories:

FIGURE 10.1

Prosocial Behavior Can Be Risky. *Despite the good intentions of the individual providing help, prosocial behavior can result in harm to the helper, as this kindly gentleman discovers.*

(*Source:* Drawing by Booth; © 1980 *The New Yorker* Magazine, Inc.)

1. A sixty-six-year-old man was driving a delivery truck on a highway in upstate New York when he had a cardiac arrest. His heart had stopped beating and his lungs were no longer functioning when two passing motorists stopped and began cardiopulmonary resuscitation on this stranger. An ambulance came and took the truck driver to the hospital, and he survived (Conlon, 1995).

2. Early one morning in New York City, a man stopped at a newsstand to help a friend untie newspapers. As they worked, they saw someone being stabbed after obtaining money from an ATM in the lobby of a bank that was not yet open. The wounded victim stumbled out of the door calling for help as the criminal gathered the bills that were scattered on the floor. The two men at the newsstand rushed over and blocked the door so the criminal could not get out. Other strangers stopped to help, and one of them called the police. The assailant was ar-

rested, and the victim was rushed to the hospital, where he received treatment (Perez-Pena, 1994).

3. There are sometimes serious risks associated with being a Good Samaritan. In the state of Washington, a man had a car wreck, and three strangers in a pickup stopped to help. They took the man home. As they were helping him enter his house, the man's frightened thirteen-year-old son saw the strange truck parked outside and assumed that burglars were breaking in. He opened fire with a .22-caliber semiautomatic rifle, hitting one of the helpful strangers in the chest, face, and shoulder; the man died almost instantly (Esser, 1995).

Another actual emergency took place more than thirty years ago. A murderous attack in which no one helped the victim, served as the starting point for two social psychologists who wanted to understand why bystanders sometimes fail to help. The case of the seemingly indifferent bystanders, and the research it inspired, are described in the following *Cornerstones* section.

Cornerstones of Social Psychology
DARLEY AND LATANÉ—EXPLAINING THE UNRESPONSIVE BYSTANDER

The event that launched the research occurred in the early morning hours of March 13, 1964, in New York. Catherine (Kitty) Genovese was returning home from her job as the manager of a bar. As she crossed the street from her car to her apartment building, a man with a knife approached. She ran; he chased, caught, and stabbed her. Genovese screamed for help, and lights came on in the windows of several apartments overlooking the street. The attacker retreated briefly, and then came back to his bleeding victim. She screamed again, but he continued stabbing her until she died. It was later determined that this horrifying forty-five-minute interaction was viewed by thirty-eight witnesses, but no one came to Kitty Genovese's rescue or even called the police (Rosenthal, 1964).

Following the news stories about this incident, there was widespread debate about why no one helped. Were people apathetic, cold, indifferent to the problems of others? Was something wrong with our society? Did urban life make people callous? Professors John Darley and Bibb Latané have described how their own discussion of the event over lunch led them to propose quite different reasons as to why the bystanders failed to respond. As the two psychologists talked, they began sketching proposed experimental designs on their tablecloth (Krupat, 1975).

The first of Darley and Latané's studies dealt with **diffusion of responsibility** as the explanation for why bystanders sometimes fail to respond. These psychologists hypothesized that when one person sees someone in need of help, the bystander's responsibility is clear; but with multiple witnesses to an emergency, as in Kitty Genovese's murder, any one of the 38 individuals *could* have acted. In effect, each had only ⅛ of the total responsibility, and that was not enough to motivate any one of them to act. The general hypothesis, then, is that as the number of bystanders increases, the likelihood of prosocial behavior decreases.

The experimenters devised a very clever way to test this proposition. Male students took part in what was supposed to be a study of student life, but they were suddenly confronted by what seemed to be a fellow student's emergency medical problem. The situation was designed so that the research participant

Diffusion of Responsibility ■ Decrease in individual sense of responsibility for taking action in an emergency because of the presence of other bystanders; the greater the number of bystanders, the less likely each individual is to act.

would be either the only one who was aware of the problem, one of two bystanders, or one of five bystanders. The crucial question was whether helpfulness would be most likely to occur with only one bystander, though inhibited by the presence of additional bystanders.

When each participant arrived to take part in the experiment, it was explained that various students would be asked to discuss some of the problems they experienced in attending college in a high-pressure urban setting. Each participant was to sit in a separate room, and they could communicate only over an intercom. The students could hear one another, but the experimenter would not be listening—presumably to avoid embarrassment, but actually to avoid serving as an additional bystander. Some subjects were told that they were one of two discussants, others that they were part of a group of three, and still others that their group consisted of six students. Each was to talk for two minutes; afterward, the others would be commenting about what had been said. In fact, only one student was a "live" participant, because the others were prerecorded on tape. The taped person who was soon to have an emergency stated at the beginning of the interaction that he was ashamed to say so, but he sometimes had seizures in a stressful situation. After the actual student (and—in some conditions—other taped "participants") had each talked about college problems, the victim spoke again.

> I er I think I need er if if could er er somebody er er help because I er I'm er h-h-having a a a real problem er right now and and I er if somebody could help me out it would er er s-s-sure be good . . . because er there er er a thing's coming on and and I could really er use some help so if somebody here er help er uh uh uh (choking sounds) . . . I'm gonna die er er I'm gonna die er help er er seizure (chokes, then is quiet). (Darley & Latané, 1968, p. 379)

What would you do? The only way to help in this situation was to leave the experimental room and try to find the person who was having a seizure. Bystander responsiveness was measured in two ways: (1) the percentage of individuals in each condition who tried to help and, if they did make an effort, (2) how much time passed before they did something. As shown in Figure 10.2 (p. 360), Darley and Latané predicted correctly that the more bystanders present in an emergency, the less helping there would be. Further, when someone did help, the more bystanders present, the longer was the delay in coming to the victim's assistance.

Darley and Latané labeled the inhibiting effect of additional witnesses to an emergency the **bystander effect.** This insight about the effect of multiple bystanders makes it clear why the newspaper stories of helpfulness most often involve only one or two bystanders, and also why thirty-eight bystanders could be expected not to respond when Kitty Genovese was being assaulted.

This experiment also provided evidence that bystanders are not at all apathetic or indifferent. In the condition in which only one student was aware of the supposed problem, 85 percent cared enough to take action within the first 60 seconds. When more bystanders were present, helpfulness was inhibited, but the witnesses nevertheless were concerned, upset, and confused.

Though Darley and Latané may not have fully foreseen where their work would lead, we know now that it was the first of many social psychological investigations, providing considerable understanding of prosocial behavior (Darley, 1991). ■ ■ ■

Bystander Effect ■ The finding that as the number of bystanders increases, the likelihood of any one bystander helping decreases and more time passes before help does occur.

To Help or Not to Help? Five Choice Points

When one is sitting in a comfortable chair and reading about emergencies, there is no ambiguity about what should be done. The witnesses to Genovese's murder should have shouted at the attacker and called the police. The subjects in

FIGURE 10.2

The Bystander Effect: More Bystanders = Less Help. In the initial experiment designed to explore the *bystander effect,* students heard what seemed to be a fellow student having a seizure. The research participant was supposedly either the only bystander to this emergency, one of two bystanders, or one of five. As the number of bystanders increased, the percentage of individuals who tried to help the "victim" decreased. In addition, among those who *did* help, as the number of bystanders increased, the more time passed before help began. This effect was initially explained on the basis of *diffusion of responsibility.*

(*Source:* Based on data from Darley & Latané, 1968.)

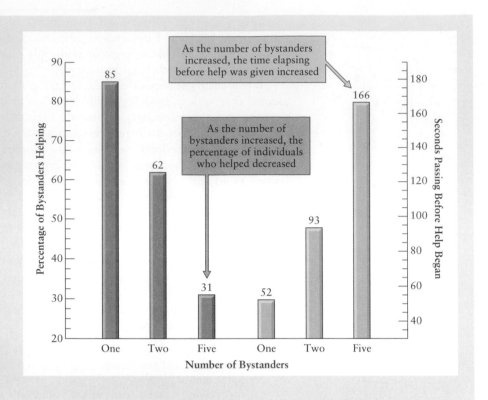

the seizure experiment should have rushed out to provide help to a fellow student. Things are different, however, when *you* are actually confronted by such situations. It is not that easy to do the right thing. Latané and Darley (1970) outlined a series of choices that a bystander must make (often unconsciously) before help can occur. These decision points are shown in Figure 10.3. Notice that at each point, the simplest choice is the path of least resistance—doing nothing, and thus failing to provide help.

Step 1. The Bystander Must Perceive the Emergency. We don't spend our lives standing idly around, waiting for an emergency to occur. Instead, we tend to be engaged in some activity and thinking about our own concerns when an emergency event intrudes. To take the first step toward helping, we must shift our attention away from personal matters and toward the unexpected happening. Much of the time we screen out passing sights and sounds because they are personally irrelevant. As a result, it is easy to ignore an emergency.

Darley and Batson (1973) investigated how preoccupation can inhibit prosocial acts. The experimenters gave seminary students the task of going to a nearby building to present a talk about Luke's parable of the Good Samaritan or about jobs. To manipulate preoccupation, the investigators created different degrees of time pressure for different research participants. They told some that they were ahead of schedule and had plenty of time to get to their talk, others that they were right on schedule, and a third group that they were already late for the speaking engagement. Presumably, the first group would be the least preoccupied and the third group the most preoccupied.

FIGURE 10.3

Five Steps: Prosocial Action or Failure to Help? Latané and Darley conceptualized prosocial behavior as the end point of a series of five steps, representing choice points. At each step in the process, the choices (whether conscious or unconscious) result in either (1) no help being given or (2) movement to the following step in a progression toward possible helping.

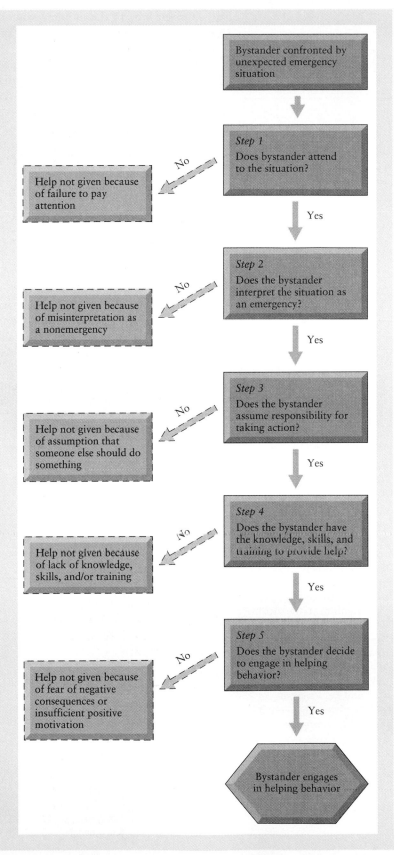

On the way to the building where the talk was to be given, each seminary student encountered a research assistant who was slumped in a doorway, coughing and groaning. Would they notice this seemingly sick or hurt individual and help him? Though the topic of the upcoming talk (jobs or the Good Samaritan) had no effect on the seminarians' behavior, preoccupation (time pressure) did. You can see in Figure 10.4 that 63 percent of those with plenty of time provided help. Helping dropped to just 45 percent among those who were on time, and even lower (only ten percent) among those in a hurry. Many of the most preoccupied seminarians simply stepped over the victim and rushed along to their appointment. Clearly, if you don't notice the problem, you won't help.

Step 2. Correctly Interpreting the Situation As an Emergency. In our daily contact with passing strangers, we usually don't know what they are doing or why. If we wonder why a man is running past us down the sidewalk, it is much easier to imagine a routine, everyday explanation than a highly unusual and unlikely one (Macrae & Milne, 1992). That is, he might be hurrying to catch a bus, to find his dog, to get some exercise, or—least likely—to grab a thief who has just robbed him. Surely a dramatic chase following a daylight robbery is not the first possibility that would occur to you. The difficulty with interpreting an ordinary event as an extraordinary emergency is that you can look foolish, as suggested in Figure 10.5. Unless you conclude that you are really witnessing an emergency, you won't help, because there is no reason to help and you want to avoid making stupid mistakes.

When there is any ambiguity about what is going on, potential helpers hold back and wait for more information. If the signals are mixed—some indicating

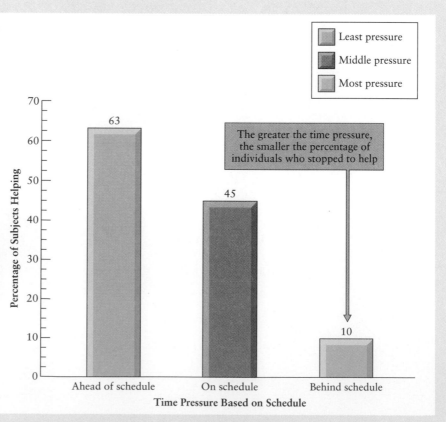

FIGURE 10.4

Preoccupation with Time Pressure Interferes with Perception of Emergency. When potential helpers are preoccupied with other concerns, they are much less likely to help a person in need. Among other factors, they are too busy to pay attention to the victim. Research participants who believed they had plenty of time to reach the room in which they were giving a talk were most likely to stop and help a stranger who was slumped, coughing and groaning, in a doorway. Those who believed they were running behind schedule were least likely to help.

(*Source:* Based on data from Darley & Batson, 1973.)

Least pressure
Middle pressure
Most pressure

The greater the time pressure, the smaller the percentage of individuals who stopped to help

Percentage of Subjects Helping

63
45
10

Ahead of schedule   On schedule   Behind schedule

Time Pressure Based on Schedule

FIGURE 10.5

Fear of Looking Foolish. *Bystanders can inhibit one another from taking action in an emergency. Engaging in prosocial behavior is safe when there are no observers, because no one can judge your actions as foolish. In the cartoon, the unusual act of building an ark and gathering pairs of animals would lead to ridicule if the expected flood failed to occur. The fear of ridicule and other negative interpersonal responses is one reason that a single bystander is more likely to respond to an emergency than multiple bystanders are.*

(*Source:* Drawing by Modell; © 1983 *The New Yorker* Magazine, Inc.)

"We're going to look like damn fools if this is just a shower."

Pluralistic Ignorance ■ Bystanders' misinterpretation of an event, caused by reliance on what others do or say even though no one is sure what is happening; all hold back and act as if there is no problem, then each individual uses this "information" to justify failure to act.

that everything is OK and others indicating that a serious problem exists—people are inclined to give more weight to the information indicating that nothing need be done (Wilson & Petruska, 1984). Among the several reasons for the bystander effect is the fact that additional witnesses to the scene constitute an audience who may evaluate your behavior as a dumb or silly overreaction. In addition, when the situation is unclear, you will probably engage in social comparison (see Chapter 7) to validate your impressions by finding out what the other people say and do. This isn't a problem when the bystanders are friends, because they are likely to communicate with one another, greatly reducing the bystander effect (Rutkowski, Gruder, & Romer, 1983). If, however, fellow bystanders are strangers and the others fail to react, the inhibition against helping is very strong. A victim should not expect help from a group of uninformed bystanders who incorrectly interpret the situation and also hold back to avoid being embarrassed by losing their cool.

This group reaction, called **pluralistic ignorance,** was documented in an experiment involving a smoke emergency (Latané & Darley, 1968). The research participants were each given a questionnaire to fill out. Some did so in a room by themselves, while others were in a room with two other participants. After a few minutes, the experimenters pumped smoke into the room through a vent. Do you think the number of bystanders would affect whether students would react to the smoke as indicating an emergency? Among other possibilities, their building might be on fire! Of those who were alone in the room, 75 percent left to tell someone about the smoke, half of them in the first two minutes. In contrast, with three people in the room, only 38 percent reacted, while 62 percent did absolutely nothing—even when the smoke became so thick that it was hard to see. And, of the minority who responded, only one did so in the first *four* minutes. It seems that an unreactive group can be a powerful inhibiting force.

Both fear of making a blunder and social inhibitions about communicating with strangers are reduced if a bystander has consumed alcohol. Even a mod-

FIGURE 10.6

Who Has the Responsibility to Act? In some situations, the responsibility for providing help is clear. In this instance, trained firefighters are expected to take charge and deal with the problem. In many other situations, there is confusion because no one has obvious responsibility; the result is delay in providing help.

est amount of alcohol increases the tendency to help, and additional drinking further enhances the likelihood of prosocial acts (Steele, Critchlow, & Liu, 1985). Steele and his colleagues hypothesized that when an inebriated person perceives a victim's need, he or she is unaware of possible ambiguities in the situation and unworried about potential negative consequences that might result from helping. Steele says, "Now you may not want the help of a drunk. . . . I don't know about the quality of the help you'd get, but they're more likely to do it" (quoted in Kent, 1990, p. 13).

Step 3. Assuming Responsibility to Act. At the third choice point in the model, the bystander either does or does not assume responsibility for doing something. In many situations, responsibility is clear, as in Figure 10.6. If a house is burning, help is the responsibility of firefighters. If a store is being robbed, help is the responsibility of police officers. If someone is injured, medical personnel take responsibility.

When, however, responsibility is less clear, we tend to assume that someone in a leadership role is the one to act (Baumeister et al., 1988). That is, a professor should deal with an emergency in a classroom, a bus driver is responsible for dealing with an emergency on his vehicle, and an adult assumes responsibility among a group of children.

One of the reasons that a lone bystander is most likely to act is that there is no one else who *could* take responsibility. As we discussed earlier, multiple bystanders are much less likely to act because of *diffused responsibility*—in this situation, *no one* is clearly responsible. Even with just two bystanders, helping becomes less likely unless one of them (for whatever reason) *feels personally responsible* for providing help.

Step 4. Knowing What to Do. At the fourth choice point, the bystander must ponder whether he or she knows *how* to be helpful. Some emergencies are simple. If you see someone slip on an icy sidewalk, you help the person up. If you see two rough-looking men trying to break into a parked car, pick up the phone and call 911. Other emergencies require special knowledge and skills. In one of the news stories cited earlier, the motorists who stopped to help the driver of the delivery truck had previously been trained to administer cardiopulmonary resuscitation. In a similar way, if you don't know how to swim, you are unable to provide immediate help to someone who is drowning.

Whenever a bystander possesses the necessary knowledge, experience, or skills, he or she tends to assume responsibility and to provide help whether or not other bystanders are present. For example, with two bystanders present at an accident, registered nurses offer help more than nonnurses; with only one bystander, nurses and nonnurses are equally helpful (Cramer et al., 1988).

Step 5. Making the Final Decision to Help.   Even though a bystander has passed through each of the first four choice points with a yes, helping behavior still may not occur.

On the one hand, helping may be inhibited by fears about negative consequences. If you try to help a person who slipped on the ice, you may fall down yourself. If you help a person who is coughing and groaning on the sidewalk, you may get your clothes dirty or catch a disease. And most serious of all, remember the man who helped an accident victim and then was mistakenly shot to death by the victim's son. Altogether, unless one is especially motivated to provide help, helping may not occur because the potential costs simply appear too great (McGuire, 1994).

All five of these decisions or choices are illustrated in the following *Applied Side* section. The research involves a common situation that you probably encounter from time to time—while shopping, you observe an adult interacting with a crying child. If you perceive the adult's behavior as inappropriate, what do you do?

Social Psychology: On the Applied Side
RESPONDING TO AN ABUSED CHILD

Imagine that you hear the sounds of a fight in a neighboring apartment, and a woman yells, "I hate you! I don't ever want to see you again!" Will you do anything? In this kind of situation, most people tend to assume that they are overhearing a lovers' quarrel or a marital spat, which is defined as none of their business. But what if the woman shouts, "Whoever you are, just get out of my apartment!"? Shotland and Strau (1976) found that three times as many interventions take place in response to the second shouted message, which is interpreted as an interaction between strangers, than to the first, which appears to involve a couple who have some kind of relationship. The problem may be equally serious in the two instances, but most people feel that a dispute between lovers or spouses is simply not the responsibility of an outsider.

Consider a different situation. What if a child is being abused by a person who is, or is perceived to be, a family member? How will a bystander react? If you were shopping and saw a small boy complaining about being led outside by two slightly older children—who could well be his older brothers—what would you do? Make them stop? Try to find the parents? Call the authorities? Decide to mind your own business? In 1993, a chilling event occurred in a shopping center in Liverpool, England. A two-year-old boy wandered away from his mother and then was dragged outside, crying, by two ten-year-old boys, who were seen by many witnesses shoving and kicking the little one. Soon afterward, the older boys took the younger one to a deserted railroad track, spent some time tormenting the little boy—and then murdered him. As with Kitty Geno vese, a widely asked question in the United Kingdom was, why didn't the bystanders intervene? The answers are no different in the 1990s in England than in the 1960s in New York City.

Christy and Voigt (1994) report a high incidence of child abuse in the United States. About two and a half million cases are reported annually, of which 1,200 result in the child's death. Given this serious problem, you probably would not want to ignore a case of abuse if you encountered one. Let's say you are in a grocery store and happen upon a mother hitting her pre-school-age daughter. First, do you pay attention to what is happening? Depending on your time schedule that day and on how unusual the interaction, you may easily walk past the unpleasant scene on your way to the frozen food section without even noticing.

Second, do you interpret this as an emergency involving abuse? Technically, abusive behavior is defined by such acts as whipping, slapping, kicking, poking, punching, and hair pulling—especially if these acts result in bruises, welts, cuts, scratches, dislocations, fractures, or burns (Milner, Robertson, & Rogers, 1990). People differ, however, in their definitions of acceptable and unacceptable physical punishment; and in the grocery, you will not be able to determine whether bodily injury has occurred. To cite an extreme example of defining abuse, a judge in Amarillo, Texas, declared that a mother who spoke only Spanish at home to her five-year-old daughter was "abusing" her (Associated Press, August 29, 1995).

Third, if you feel that you are truly witnessing child abuse, is it *your* responsibility? Many people assume that only very specific individuals (clinical psychologists, social workers, police, etc.) have any right to take action when abuse is observed.

Fourth, do you know what to do? You might decide to notify the store manager or to call the police, but the abusive interaction is likely to end before help arrives.

Fifth, do you act? Given the difficulties just presented, you may not. Among other considerations, the abusing mother might very well believe—loudly and angrily—that you are interfering in a matter that is none of your business. She might later bring legal action against you; or she might blame the child for creating the problem and become even more abusive in retaliation.

A study of response to child abuse in public places indicates that most bystanders, in fact, report doing nothing. Christy and Voigt (1994) surveyed almost three hundred college students and faculty members. About half reported witnessing instances of child abuse in public places. Among those who observed abuse, only 26 percent intervened. Of those who intervened, most (70 percent) said something or engaged in some act to help the child; the remainder either encouraged someone else to intervene or reported the incident to someone else. It appears that witnessing child abuse is a fairly common experience, but that intervention is most often avoided.

It is interesting to note that these investigators found no bystander effect; being the only witness or one of many had no influence on intervention in this type of emergency. People who intervened and those who failed to do so differed in several respects, however. It seems that having personal experience with abuse, feeling responsible, being a parent, and knowing what to do are the most crucial aspects of this kind of prosocial act. Among the characteristics *unrelated* to intervention were gender, race, occupation, political affiliation, religion, socioeconomic status, marital status, and education.

Having read about and (we hope) thought about this specific situation, how do you think you will respond to future incidents? Intervention is obviously not an easy decision to make. Because most respondents feel strongly that child abuse is intolerable (National Committee for Prevention of Child Abuse, 1990), and because even those who failed to intervene in the Christy and Voigt (1994) sample said they felt very uncomfortable and wanted to stop the abuse, one suggestion proposes widespread training in intervention. Such training could focus on what constitutes abuse, emphasize personal responsibility to stop it, and explain the appropriate actions to take. This kind of educational effort would seem to constitute a useful application of our present knowledge. ■ ■ ■

In the following section we'll consider some of the factors that are most characteristic of people who help.

Who Are the Helpers? Dispositional Influences on Prosocial Behavior

The research described so far has emphasized aspects of the *situation* that increase or decrease the probability of prosocial acts. We have also indicated some factors that cause certain individuals to be more likely to help in specific situations. Examples are drinking enough alcohol to reduce anxiety about experiencing negative consequences, having past experiences as a victim of child abuse, and possessing the necessary knowledge and skills in a medical emergency.

Some general *dispositional characteristics* also influence prosocial behavior across different situations. Some investigators have examined the effects of single characteristics, while others have looked at multiple characteristics, that contribute to prosocial behavior.

Influence of Specific Dispositions on Prosocial Behavior. You might try to answer the question, "Is any prosocial act *truly* unselfish?" That is, do people ever help someone in need on the basis of **altruism** (an unselfish concern for the welfare of others), or are they always motivated by **egoism** (an exclusive concern with one's own personal welfare)? We will return to that issue from time to time. In the search for the characteristics of those who help, it appears that self-centered motives may be operating. For example, people who have a strong *need for approval* are more likely to help others, presumably because they are especially gratified when they receive appreciation and praise. Their helpfulness is most apparent if they have previously been rewarded for such behavior (Deutsch & Lamberti, 1986). If you are the one in need of help, of course, you may not quibble about the possibly selfish motives of the person who provides you with assistance.

More research has concentrated on the apparently *altruistic* motives of bystanders (Clary & Orenstein, 1991; Grusec, 1991), and most of the emphasis has been on **empathy**—responding to another person's affective state with a vicarious emotional reaction that resembles whatever emotion is experienced by the other individual (Darley, 1993; Eisenberg et al., 1991). For example, an empathic person perceives that someone else is unhappy and as a consequence experiences unhappiness. In the words of President Clinton, "I feel your pain."

Showing distress in response to the distress of others has been observed in children as young as twelve months (Brothers, 1990) and also among monkeys and apes (Ungerer et al., 1990). As suggested in Figure 10.7 (p. 368), human beings differ dramatically in empathy, ranging from people who are deeply concerned about any distress experienced by others to sociopathic individuals who are totally indifferent to and unaffected by the emotional state of those around them.

Besides *feeling personal distress at the distress of others*, the empathic individual is also described as having three other characteristics. One is *feeling sympathetic*—feeling a kind concern for another person's needs. Others are *perspective taking*—being able to "put oneself in someone else's shoes"; and *fantasy—*

Altruism ■ Unselfish concern with the welfare of others.

Egoism ■ Exclusive concern with one's own personal welfare.

Empathy ■ Basically, tendency to respond to another's emotional state with vicarious feelings resembling the emotions of the other; definition has been broadened to include sympathizing, taking the perspective of the other person, and being able to empathize with fictional characters.

FIGURE 10.7

Individual Differences in Empathy. The capacity for empathy appears to play a crucial role in differentiating those who engage in prosocial behavior and those who do not. Clearly, human beings span a wide range in this characteristic.

feeling empathy for a fictional character, shown by such behavior as crying at a sad movie (Eisenberg et al., 1991; Trobst, Collins, & Embree, 1994). People who are most empathic on these dimensions respond emotionally when someone else has a problem and generally do their best to provide help. This ability to empathize is associated with the secure attachment style described in Chapter 8.

Either because of genetic differences or because of differential cultural experiences, women tend to score higher than men on measures of empathy (Trobst et al., 1994). Studies of non-Jewish Germans who rescued Jews from the Nazis in World War II also report consistent sex differences, with a two-to-one ratio of female to male rescuers (Anderson, 1993).

The role of hereditary factors in dispositional empathy was investigated by Davis, Luce, and Kraus (1994), who compared the responses of more than eight hundred sets of identical and fraternal twins on a measure of empathy. The affective components of empathy (sympathetic concern and personal distress) were found to be based in part on inherited factors. The investigators estimated that 28 percent of the differences among individuals in empathic concern and 32 percent of the differences in personal distress are genetic.

Combining Dispositional Variables to Predict Prosocial Behavior. Knight and his colleagues (1994) point out that any given dispositional variable is only a weak behavioral predictor. The reason, they suggest, is that a prosocial act is complex and may occur only when several different dispositional variables operate in conjunction. In other words, any single variable may not predict very well because a combination of relevant variables must be taken into account. Knight and his colleagues predicted that children between the ages of six and eight would contribute money to someone in need if, and only if, they were high in sympathy, *and* in affective reasoning (correctly identifying the emotions associated with facial expressions in a story), *and* in money knowledge (knowing how many quarters make a dollar, etc.). The children were paid $5 for taking part in the study. After watching a videotape of a girl who had been burned in a fire, they were asked to contribute money to a local hospital's burn unit. As predicted, all three characteristics were relevant to the amount of money donated: only children who were high on all three factors made substantial donations.

TABLE 10.1 Identifying Aspects of the Altruistic Personality

To identify some of the basic factors making up the altruistic personality, *investigators compared citizens who witnessed a traffic accident and provided first aid to the victim with comparable citizens who witnessed such an accident and did* not *provide first aid. As indicated here, the two groups were found to differ on five personality characteristics. Together, these characteristics identify altruistic individuals.*

Those Who Administered First Aid	Those Who Failed to Administer First Aid
reported self-concepts high in empathy as a component	reported self-concepts low in empathy as a component
believed more strongly in a just world	believed less strongly in a just world
felt more socially responsible	felt less socially responsible
tended to be high in internal locus of control	tended to be low in internal locus of control
were less egocentric	were more egocentric

(*Source:* Based on data from Bierhoff, Klein, & Kramp, 1991.)

A broader attempt to identify the *altruistic personality* was undertaken by Bierhoff, Klein, and Kramp (1991). They obtained several personality variables identified in previous prosocial research and compared the scores of people at the scene of an accident who had and had not administered first aid before the ambulance arrived. These two groups were matched with respect to sex, age, and social class, and then were compared on the personality measures. On five of the tests, those who helped accident victims and those who did not help were significantly different, as summarized in Table 10.1.

The five components of the **altruistic personality** are described as follows:

1. Among those who helped, *empathy* was an important part of the self-concept. Helpers also described themselves as responsible and socialized, and as having self-control, wanting to make a good impression, and being conforming and tolerant.

2. Those who provided first aid expressed a strong *belief in a just world*. They assume that giving first aid is the right thing to do and that the person who helps will benefit from doing so. Altogether, they perceive the world as a fair and predictable place in which good behavior is rewarded and bad behavior punished—people get what they deserve.

3. *Social responsibility* also differentiated the helpers from the nonhelpers. A person high on this dimension believes that we should all do our best to help others.

4. Altruistic individuals were characterized as assuming an *internal locus of control*. This is the belief that one can behave in such a way as to maximize good outcomes and minimize bad ones—that the individual can make a difference and is not helplessly at the mercy of luck, fate, and other uncontrollable forces.

5. The helpers were *lower* than the nonhelpers on the measure of egocentrism. Those who failed to help tended to be self-absorbed and competitive.

Altruistic Personality ■ Combination of empathic self-concept, belief in a just world, feelings of social responsibility, internal locus of control, and low egocentrism increases likelihood of prosocial behavior.

Interestingly, these same five dispositional variables were found to be characteristic of people throughout Europe who were active during the 1940s in rescuing Jews from Nazi persecution (Oliner & Oliner, 1988).

INTEGRATING PRINCIPLES

1. Bystanders who fail to help a stranger in distress are not cold and indifferent. Rather, prosocial behavior can be inhibited by preoccupation, failure to interpret an ambiguous situation as an emergency, lack of clarity about who should take responsibility, absence of appropriate knowledge and skills, and fear of potential consequences. Among the processes involved are the interpretation of nonverbal cues and attributions (Chapter 2), cognition (Chapter 3), and social comparison (Chapter 7).

2. Prosocial behavior is facilitated by the presence of relevant dispositional variables. Though several personality characteristics are important, the most crucial component of the altruistic personality is empathy, which is also associated with a secure attachment style (Chapter 8). Also playing a role are self-concept (Chapter 5) and locus of control (Chapter 14).

Additional Factors That Influence Prosocial Behavior

In addition to aspects of the external situation and different personality dispositions, other factors that affect a person's likelihood of engaging in prosocial behavior are *exposure to appropriate social models,* various *characteristics of the victim,* and specific *motivations* to provide help. In other words, the crucial final step in the sequence of choices (actually to provide or not to provide help) can be influenced toward or away from a prosocial act by several additional situational and dispositional factors.

The Role of Social Models

If you are out shopping and encounter someone collecting money to purchase shelter for the homeless, winter coats for needy children, or food for destitute families, do you reach in your pocket or purse to make a contribution? That is, assume you are paying attention to the request, the need is clear, you are as responsible as anyone else, and you have the skills needed to deposit money in the bucket; what about the final step? Do you help? An important determinant of your behavior at this final choice point is whether you see someone else make a contribution: if others give money, then you are more likely to do so (Macauley, 1970). Even the presence of paper money and coins in the collection box encourages a charitable response. The various compliance techniques discussed in Chapter 9 are directly relevant to this kind of helping behavior. In other words, collecting money for charity, selling a product, and panhandling involve many of the same psychological processes.

In emergency situations, we have already seen that the presence of fellow bystanders who fail to respond tends to inhibit helpfulness. It is equally true that the presence of a helpful bystander provides a *social model* encouraging helpfulness. In effect, what others do in the situation helps to create a social norm. An example of modeling is provided by a field experiment in which a young woman (a research assistant) was parked by the side of a road with a flat tire. Male motorists were much more likely to stop and help if they had previously passed a staged scene in which another woman with car trouble was receiving help (Bryan & Test, 1967).

Even television presentations of helpful models can create a social norm that encourages prosocial behavior among the viewers (see Figure 10.8). To study the effects of a TV model on six-year-olds, investigators let some youngsters view an episode of *Lassie* in which there was a rescue scene, while others viewed the same show without such a scene, and still others watched a humorous episode of *The Brady Bunch* (Sprafkin, Liebert, & Poulous, 1975). After seeing one of the shows, the children played a game in which the winner could receive a prize. In the midst of the game, they came in contact with a group of puppies who were whining unhappily. Despite the fact that stopping to help the puppies would interfere with winning, the children who had viewed the *Lassie* rescue episode spent much more time trying to comfort the little animals than did those seeing either of the other two TV programs.

Other experiments have confirmed the positive role that TV models can play. When preschool children watch prosocial programs such as *Mister Rogers' Neighborhood* or *Sesame Street*, they are much more likely to engage in proso-

FIGURE 10.8

Prosocial Models on TV and in Movies Influence Prosocial Acts. Television programs and movies that depict prosocial models are found to increase the incidence of children's prosocial behavior.

cial behavior than children who do not watch the shows (Forge & Phemister, 1987). These and other studies consistently demonstrate that appropriate social models exert a very positive influence on prosocial responding.

Some Victims Are More Likely to Receive Help Than Others

You are walking down the sidewalk in a large city and see a man lying unconscious next to the curb. Would you be more likely to stop and help (a) if a wine bottle were clutched in his hand and his clothes were stained and torn or (b) if he were neatly dressed and had a bruise on his forehead? The odds are that you would be more strongly motivated to help the second man than the first. Why? Victim characteristics are important determinants of helping: we are inclined to help those we *like*, including those who are most *similar* to ourselves (Chapter 7), and those who are *not responsible* for their plight.

Helping a Liked Victim. On the basis of the discussion in Chapter 7 about the effect of attraction on our evaluations of other people, you might assume that the more we like a person, the stronger our tendency to provide needed assistance. You would be right (Clark et al., 1987; Schoenrade et al., 1986). Whatever factors increase attraction also increase prosocial responses. For example, a physically attractive victim receives more help than an unattractive one (Benson, Karabenick, & Lerner, 1976).

Also discussed in Chapter 7 was the fact that many people see homosexuality as a stigma. Given this widespread prejudice based on a person's sexual orientation, Shaw, Borough, and Fink (1994) predicted that a homosexual stranger in need would receive less help than a comparable heterosexual stranger. To test this proposal, they used the "wrong number technique." A research assistant dials a random telephone number and, if an adult answers, says that he was trying to call for assistance from a pay phone using his last quarter but made a mistake in dialing; he then asks the stranger to make the call for him. The number given is actually that of the assistant, who can thus determine whether or not the stranger in fact dials the number as requested.

To suggest a heterosexual relationship, the caller ("Mike") asked to speak to his girlfriend, Lisa. In the homosexual condition, he asked to speak to his boyfriend, Rick. In both conditions, finding that he had the "wrong number," Mike apologized for his mistake, then explained that he had a flat tire and would be late for the first-anniversary celebration with his opposite-sex or same-sex companion. Because Mike had no more change, he asked the stranger to please call Lisa or Rick for him. Help by the stranger consisted of actually making the phone call within the next three minutes. Nonhelp consisted of hanging up on the caller, refusal to write down Lisa's or Rick's number, refusal to make the call, or failure to call within the next three minutes.

As shown in Figure 10.9, slightly more than half of the forty men and forty women Mike called helped by making the requested call, but such help was given much less frequently to the homosexual stranger than to the heterosexual one. The investigators plan to conduct a follow-up study with a female caller, because they hypothesize that attitudes about lesbians are less negative than attitudes about gays; if so, a homosexual female caller should not inhibit helping behavior to the same extent.

Because similarity generally has a positive effect on attraction, it is reasonable to expect people to help those who are like themselves. This is often the case, and the response to homosexual versus heterosexual phone requests may in part reflect greater helpfulness of heterosexual respondents toward a similar stranger (that is, by chance the great majority of the random calls would have been to het-

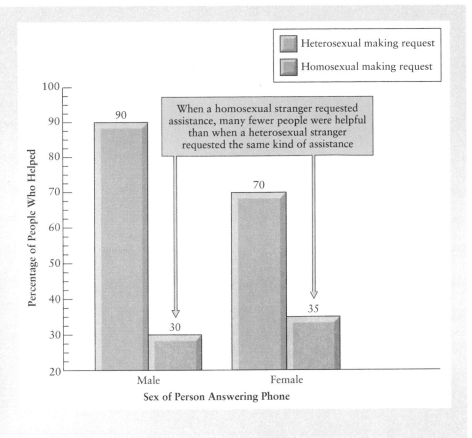

FIGURE 10.9

Helping a Heterosexual versus a Homosexual Stranger. Using the "wrong number technique," a male experimental assistant called a telephone number at random and asked for his girlfriend or his boyfriend by name. Discovering that he had the "wrong number," he apologized, said that he had a flat tire and would be late for their anniversary celebration but had no more change for the pay phone, and asked the stranger please to call Lisa or Rick to explain. When the caller was identified as heterosexual, most people helped out by making the requested telephone call. When the caller was identified as homosexual, most people did not help. It seems clear that a negative attitude about the person in need can inhibit prosocial behavior.

(*Source:* Based on data from Shaw, Borough, & Fink, 1994.)

erosexuals). There are additional factors at work in some situations, however, and we will now examine why similarity may not always lead to helping.

For example, in some situations similarity seems to be irrelevant. Bornstein (1994) conducted a meta-analysis of twenty-three investigations that studied the effect of the victim's dependency. The more the victim is dependent on others for help, the greater the likelihood that others actually *will* help. With a very dependent victim, similarity or lack of similarity to the person providing assistance ceases to matter.

In certain situations being dissimilar is actually an advantage, as indicated in the following *Applied Side* section.

Social Psychology: On the Applied Side

DOES GENDER MATTER? MALE AND FEMALE POLICE OFFICERS RESPONDING TO MALE AND FEMALE TRAFFIC OFFENDERS

In some interactions being the opposite gender from a potential helper is an advantage (Piliavin & Unger, 1985). Think about a familiar scene in many old movies (as in Figure 10.10 on page 374): a male traffic officer stops a car driven

FIGURE 10.10

Are Police Officers More Helpful to Opposite-Gender Drivers? A familiar interaction in old movies depicted a male police officer giving a kindly warning to an attractive female driver rather than issuing a citation. Research indicates that police officers (both men and women) actually are more helpful to drivers of the opposite gender.

by an attractive woman, she responds in an exaggeratedly stereotyped feminine way ("Poor little old me, was I really going that fast?"), and he then offers her kindly advice rather than giving her a citation.

Koehler and Willis (1994) suggest that giving a warning to an offending driver is a more prosocial response than issuing a citation. They investigated whether real-life male officers actually react more helpfully to the opposite sex, as laboratory research *and* old movies indicate. Do officers issue more citations to fellow men and more warnings to women? These investigators also wanted to find out, because women today are increasingly employed in a formerly male occupation, whether female officers respond differently to men and women.

The social psychologists obtained data from almost two dozen municipal police departments in Kansas and Missouri and determined how many citations were issued for speeding, driving under the influence of alcohol, and other offenses. The overall finding in each state was that both male and female officers were more likely to issue citations to drivers of the same gender than to drivers of the opposite gender. That is, male officers issued a higher percentage of citations to male drivers than did female officers, and female officers issued a higher percentage of citations to female drivers than did male officers.

In deciding whether or not to issue a citation, both male and female officers seem to be more lenient with drivers whose gender is different from their own. In this specific situation, then, dissimilarity is an advantage. If you ever exceed the speed limit and then are pulled over by a police officer, wish for one who is not your same gender. ■ ■ ■

Similarity of Victim to Bystander and Attributions of Victim Responsibility.
When we are making the final choice to help or not help a victim, attribution

processes (see Chapter 2) are of considerable importance. According to Weiner (1980), if we make the attribution that the victim is *responsible* for his or her problem, we often respond with disgust and tend not to help—because, after all, "the victim is to blame." If, however, the attribution is that the problem was caused by circumstances beyond the victim's control, we are more likely to feel empathy and to provide help.

What is the relationship between the victim's similarity to self and blaming the victim? Consider a crime such as rape. Most sexual assaults are committed by men against women. As a result, women are more likely than men to perceive themselves as similar to the victim, while men are more likely than women to perceive themselves as similar to the rapist (Bell, Kuriloff, & Lottes, 1994). Further, the more similar a person feels to the female victim, the *less* the victim is blamed for the attack; whereas the more similar the person feels to the male rapist, the *more* the female victim is blamed. See Chapter 2 for additional information about rape attributions.

What if someone "just like you" (same gender, same age, same race, etc.) is in trouble and needs help? Perhaps you will very much want to help this similar other—but the opposite reaction can also occur. That is, what happened to the victim may be especially threatening to you, because if it happened to that person and that person is similar to you, *it could happen to you, too!* One way to control your uncomfortable emotions is to misperceive a victim as being dissimilar to yourself (Drout & Gaertner, 1994). An alternate solution is to try to distance yourself from a similar victim by attributing responsibility to that person. Blaming the victim is one way of restoring your own sense of perceived control over events (Murrell & Jones, 1993).

People differ in their readiness to assign blame and responsibility to a victim. Thornton (1992) hypothesized that whenever we encounter a victim, we feel threatened, because it reminds us that we too could be injured, robbed, or whatever. In dealing with this kind of threat, we often use one of two kinds of defenses. One is **repression,** the tendency to avoid or deny the threat, and the other is **sensitization,** the tendency to worry about the threat and try to control it by focusing on why it occurred (Byrne, 1964). Thornton predicted that those who use sensitizing defenses would be more likely to blame the victim than those who repress. He reasoned that repressers can easily reduce the threat by denying that the problem is serious, forgetting about it, and suppressing any feelings of discomfort. Sensitizers, in contrast, tend not to deny, forget, or suppress; so they are more likely to reduce the threat by placing blame on the victim. "That person is not *really* like me, because I would have avoided the situation by being smarter or more careful."

To test this hypothesis, Thornton categorized undergraduate women as repressers or sensitizers. The participants then read about an event in the life of a twenty-year-old unmarried fellow student at their university. According to the scenario, she encountered a young man in the campus library one evening and had a casual conversation with him. Then, as she was returning to her dorm, the man followed her, caught up to her, and committed rape. The research participants were then asked questions about how responsible the victim was for what happened (she shouldn't have talked to a stranger, she shouldn't have walked alone at night, etc.). As predicted, sensitizing women assigned more responsibility to the woman for the rape than did repressing women, as shown in Figure 10.11 (p. 376). It was also interesting that when the research participants were asked four weeks later to describe the details of the experiment, the repressers remembered less about the rape story than did the sensitizers. Faced by a threat, repressers dealt with their fears by forgetting as much as possible, while sensitizers did so by blaming the person who was harmed.

Repression ■ A defensive response to threat in which the person attempts to control anxiety by using avoidance mechanisms such as denial and forgetting.

Sensitization ■ A defensive response to threat in which the person attempts to control anxiety by using approach mechanisms such as rumination and intellectualization.

FIGURE 10.11

Blaming a Rape Victim: Sensitizers versus Repressers. Undergraduate women were asked to read about a fellow student who had been raped. The threat of learning about an attack on a stranger similar to themselves was handled differently by participants using different types of defense mechanisms. Sensitizers more than repressers felt that the victim was responsible for what happened to her. Repressers more than sensitizers forgot the details of the crime after a few weeks.

(*Source:* Based on data from Thornton, 1992.)

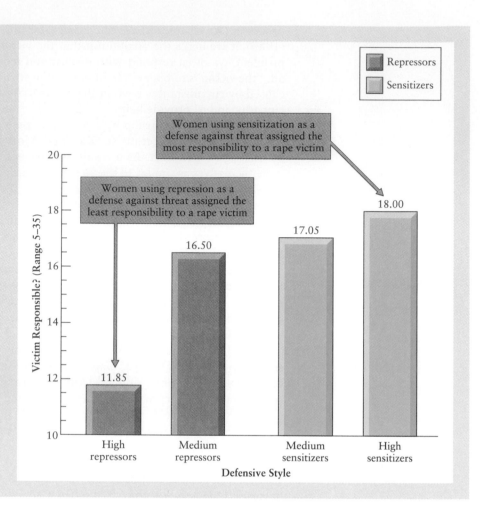

Volunteering to Help: Responding to the AIDS Epidemic

Most of the research on prosocial behavior involves emergencies in which helping involves short-term interaction with a stranger. Quite different helping behavior is required in situations in which someone (including a relative) has a chronic, continuing problem (Williamson & Schulz, 1995). The one who helps must volunteer to commit time, special skills, and money over a period of time, often with long-term interactions with people who are initially strangers. Almost one hundred million adult Americans volunteer 20.5 billion hours each year, averaging 4.2 hours of prosocial activity each week (Moore, 1993).

The five choice points remain relevant in such situations. Think of the men, women, and children in a distant country who are the innocent victims of a war. If you are going to help, you must become aware of the problem—newspaper, magazine, and television stories inform you that they don't have sufficient food, medical supplies, or shelter. You need to interpret the difficulty correctly—they need something to eat, medicine, and money. You next have to assume responsibility to help. Then you decide what to do—volunteer your time or make a donation. Finally, you either act or fail to do anything. What factors inhibit or encourage that crucial last step? Let's look at a specific long-term problem.

One example of a continuing problem in which help is needed is the HIV epidemic. In 1981 the Centers for Disease Control first reported on the then-

TABLE 10.2 Motives for Volunteerism: Helping Those with Aids

People who volunteer to help in the AIDS epidemic do so on the basis of different motives. The same pro-social act can satisfy quite different needs. Interestingly, volunteers who continue such work over a long period of time (compared to those who drop out) are most likely to be motivated by "self-centered" needs such as a desire to increase understanding, a wish to enhance self-esteem, and/or a quest for personal development.

Motivation for Volunteering to Help in the AIDS Epidemic	Sample Reason
Desire to Increase Understanding	"Because I want to learn how people cope with AIDS"
Enhancement of Self-Esteem	"I want to feel better about myself"
Personal Development	"I want to challenge myself and test my skills"
Community Concern	"Because of my concern and worry about the gay community"
Personal Values	"Because of my humanitarian obligation to help others"

(*Source:* Based on data from Omoto & Snyder, 1995; Snyder & Omoto, 1992a.)

unknown disease that is now familiar as AIDS (see Chapter 8). There is still no effective way to immunize against the HIV virus, which interferes with one's immune system, or to cure the disease. As a result, a steadily increasing number of people continue to develop AIDS, and they require assistance. Volunteers can provide emotional support, help with household chores and transportation, staff hotlines, raise funds, become political activists, and so on.

There are many reasons not to help, of course. One popular excuse is that most of those who become infected "have only themselves to blame," because they were engaging in immoral sexual or drug-related behavior. Pullium (1993) found that people are less empathetic and less willing to help an AIDS patient who had control over the source of the disease (engaging in a homosexual interaction or injecting drugs with a contaminated needle) as opposed to one who had no control (becoming infected after having a blood transfusion). Even if they don't blame those with AIDS, some people report that the costs of working with AIDS patients are too high; they feel uncomfortable and embarrassed, fearing that the stigma of the disease may "rub off on them" by association (see the discussion of stigma by association in Chapter 7).

Even if these negative considerations are not operating, one still must be *motivated to help.* Snyder and Omoto (1992a, 1992b) identified five different basic motivations that lead volunteers to engage in a prosocial response to the AIDS epidemic, and these are listed in Table 10.2. The decision to help AIDS patients can be based on personal values, the need to understand the phenomenon, concern about the community, the desire for personal development, and/or a need to enhance self-esteem. Volunteers may work side by side doing the same job, but for quite different underlying reasons.

One implication of the existence of multiple motives to help is that efforts to recruit volunteers will be most successful if recruiters stress multiple reasons to participate rather than just one. Omoto and Snyder (1995) also examined the problem of retaining volunteers, because about half quit over a twelve-month period. Interestingly, people who engage in sustained volunteer work over a two-and-a-half-year period are most likely to be motivated by the need to gain understanding, enhance self-esteem, and help their own personal development. These seemingly "selfish" needs are more likely to be associated with continuing volunteer work than the seemingly "selfless" motives emphasizing community concern and the value of helping others.

Prosocial Acts from the Viewpoint of the Person Who Needs Help

Most of our focus has been on the person who provides or doesn't provide help to someone in need. The behavior of the person who is in need of assistance also plays a role in the interaction, both before and after help is given.

Asking for Help. In research on the bystander effect, we saw how ambiguity in a situation can inhibit prosocial responding. Perhaps the most direct way to reduce ambiguity is for the victim to *ask for help*. This doesn't always happen. For example, shy people are very reluctant to seek help from a member of the opposite sex (DePaulo et al., 1989). Also, women find it easier to request help than men, young adults ask for help more than the elderly, and individuals of high socioeconomic status seek help more than do those of low status (Nadler, 1991).

A major reason not to ask for aid is the belief that others will perceive the request as an indication of incompetence (DePaulo & Fisher, 1980). The greater the similarity between victim and potential helper, the greater the reluctance to seek help (Nadler, 1987; Nadler & Fisher, 1986). The explanation is that similarity emphasizes the possible incompetence of the one needing help. It's OK to ask for aid from someone different from yourself (older, younger, richer, poorer, etc.), because they may have some skill or resource that you lack. But to ask someone just like yourself for help suggests that the other person must be smarter, stronger, or otherwise more competent than you.

In a more general way, A. Nadler (personal communication, March 1993) finds that it can be stigmatizing to seek help. Western culture places a high value on independence and self-reliance as indicating personal strength and adequacy. If you seek help, you may be perceived as dependent, unable to take care of yourself, and weak. The reaction is more negative when the request itself implies dependence ("Help me because I can't do it by myself") rather than independence ("Help me because I want to learn how to do it"). When Nadler examined how a person requesting help is perceived, he found that someone from a low socioeconomic background is viewed most negatively, because the request confirms a stereotype that those who are low in status and monetary resources have failed because they are dependent and incompetent.

In face-to-face interactions, the victim may be viewed by others as overreacting; the victim's emotional response may be perceived as inappropriate and an indication of character faults (Yates, 1992). Perhaps this is one reason for the popularity of radio programs that offer psychological advice to callers: it is possible to remain anonymous while seeking help. The effect on those who listen but do not actively participate is also relevant. Raviv (1993) interviewed regular listeners (and nonlisteners) to such shows and concluded that the radio audience in part engages in social comparison with the callers as a preliminary step to seeking help themselves.

How Does It Feel to Be Helped? Though it might seem that receiving help would generate gratitude and positive emotions, most people grasp the fact that in our culture needing help suggests incompetence; and therefore, help often elicits a negative rather than a positive reaction. Self-esteem (see Chapter 5) decreases when you receive help, especially if a friend or someone similar to yourself is the helper (DePaulo et al., 1981; Nadler, Fisher, & Itzhak, 1983). For example, help from a sibling can be unpleasant. Help from an older sister is least threatening, but it is very uncomfortable to be helped by a younger brother (Searcy & Eisenberg, 1992). Because threats to self-esteem arouse negative affect, the helper can easily be resented and disliked (see Chapter 7). Because help from a dissimilar or disliked other doesn't threaten self-esteem, such help does *not* evoke negative affect (Cook & Pelfrey, 1985).

If receiving help, particularly on an important task, is a sufficiently negative experience, the person may be motivated to engage in self-help in the future (Fisher, Nadler, & Whitcher-Alagna, 1982; Lehman et al., 1995). Help that doesn't arouse negative feelings does not motivate future self-help. These various reactions are summarized in Figure 10.12.

Consider a possible implication of this research. A business goes bankrupt and many people lose their jobs. The newly unemployed victims need support of various kinds. If the help comes from friends, family, and neighbors, the victims feel inadequate, resent those who help them, and will be strongly motivated to avoid the need for future assistance. If the help comes from strangers, such as a government agency, the victims feel deserving, appreciate the help, but have no motivation to avoid the need for future assistance. Which outcome do you think is preferable? And how would you go about structuring assistance programs to maximize the most desirable outcomes?

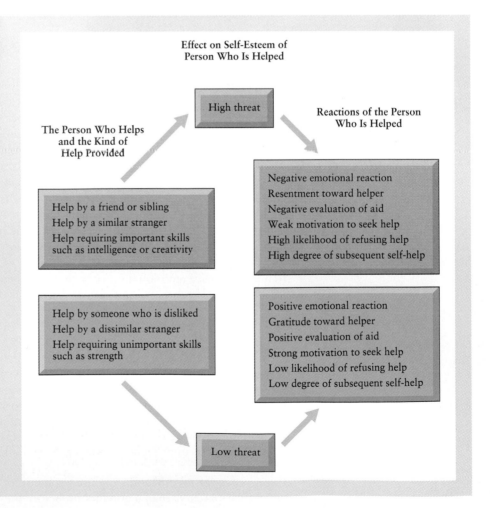

FIGURE 10.12

Reactions to Being Helped: Effects of Helper and Type of Aid. A person who receives help sometimes responds negatively and sometimes positively. According to Fisher, Nadler, and Whitcher-Alagna (1982), being helped by a friend or a similar other on important tasks is threatening, lowers one's self-esteem, and evokes other negative reactions *but* may lead to more self-help in the future. Being helped by a non-friend or a dissimilar other on unimportant tasks is not threatening, does not lower self-esteem, and evokes various positive reactions *but* leads to less self-help in the future.

Effect on Self-Esteem of Person Who Is Helped

High threat

The Person Who Helps and the Kind of Help Provided

Reactions of the Person Who Is Helped

Help by a friend or sibling
Help by a similar stranger
Help requiring important skills such as intelligence or creativity

Negative emotional reaction
Resentment toward helper
Negative evaluation of aid
Weak motivation to seek help
High likelihood of refusing help
High degree of subsequent self-help

Help by someone who is disliked
Help by a dissimilar stranger
Help requiring unimportant skills such as strength

Positive emotional reaction
Gratitude toward helper
Positive evaluation of aid
Strong motivation to seek help
Low likelihood of refusing help
Low degree of subsequent self-help

Low threat

INTEGRATING PRINCIPLES

1. Exposure to prosocial models, either within the emergency situation or in past exposure in the media, has a positive effect on prosocial behavior. Chapter 11 also discusses the effects of aggressive social models.

2. Volunteering to provide help over an extended time period can be inhibited by fear of a perceived stigma by association (Chapter 7) or encouraged by the opportunity to enhance one's self-esteem (Chapter 5).

3. Victims are most likely to receive help if the bystander likes them, for any of the reasons described in Chapter 7. Similarity between the victim and the bystander tends to promote helpfulness, but too much similarity can sometimes be threatening and cause potential helpers to blame the victim.

Additional Theoretical Explanations of Prosocial Motivation

We have described a variety of explanations of prosocial behavior based on factors in the situation, reactions to the behavior of others, dispositional differences among potential helpers, and aspects of the persons needing help. Other theories of prosocial motivation have been formulated, and most of them involve an interaction between the potential helper's emotional state and specific aspects of the emergency situation. The most general assumption is that people respond so as to maximize positive affect and minimize negative affect. In other words, prosocial behavior can be viewed as egoism rather than pure altruism.

From the perspective of prediction, it is crucial to determine precisely which characteristics of the bystander and which aspects of the situation lead to positive versus negative feelings. Presumably, the greater the amount of positive affect relative to the amount of negative affect, the more likely an individual is to behave in a prosocial way. In a slightly oversimplified summary, a bystander will help a victim if the helpful act is perceived as leading to a *more positive* or to a *less negative* emotional outcome for the bystander. Consider the following formulations of prosocial motivation.

The Effect of a Positive versus a Negative Mood on Helping

Before getting into how the emergency situation can arouse affect, let's consider the general effects of mood on prosocial behavior. It might seem obvious that being in a good mood would encourage one to be helpful while a bad mood would discourage altruism. Actually, research indicates that the effects of mood on helping are more complicated than that, because additional variables must be taken into account (Salovey, Mayer, & Rosenhan, 1991).

Effects of a Positive Mood. Children sometimes wait for the magic moment when their parents are in a good mood before they ask for something. They assume that a happy parent is more likely to grant their requests than an unhappy parent. Research provides support for this idea, at least under the right circumstances. For example, experimenters have created a positive mood by having research participants listen to a Steve Martin comedy album (Wilson, 1981), find money in the coin return slot of a pay phone (Isen & Levin, 1972), or go outside on a sunny day (Cunningham, 1979); in each instance, positive emotions led to prosocial behavior.

In controlled experiments, a pleasant odor—either a floral or a lemon fragrance—has the same positive effect on emotions and on prosocial acts (Baron & Thomley, 1992). The effects of pleasant fragrances extend to our everyday world. For example, in a large shopping mall, Baron (1995) arranged for a research assistant to drop a pen or to request change for a dollar when a same-sex shopper approached. These encounters took place near a pleasant-smelling business (bakery or coffee shop) or a relatively odorless business (clothing store). Helping was considerably more likely to occur when a pleasing smell was present than when it was not.

Consider the role of positive emotions in a somewhat different situation. What if the bystander is in a positive mood when he or she encounters an ambiguous emergency situation, or what if helping involves possible unpleasantness such as embarrassment or danger (Rosenhan, Salovey, & Hargis, 1981)? A person who is very happy has a sense of power, including the power to say no to a request for help and then to walk away. Whenever being helpful means that one's good mood will possibly be spoiled, positive emotions actually result in *less* helpfulness (Isen, 1984).

It is a general finding, then, that *if the need for help is clear* and if helping *doesn't involve negative consequences*, positive emotions result in prosocial behavior. If however, the need is ambiguous and/or consequences may occur, positive emotions inhibit helping.

Effects of a Negative Mood. Again, a common belief is that someone in a negative mood will be unhelpful, and this effect has also been confirmed by research. When you are experiencing negative affect through no fault of your own and concentrating on your own needs and concerns, it is unlikely that you will be helpful to someone in need (Amato, 1986; Rogers et al., 1982; Thompson, Cowan, & Rosenhan, 1980). A study of helping in thirty-six U.S. cities suggests that negative environmental factors such as high population density, high cost of living, and unemployment reduce prosocial responding to a stranger needing help (Levine et al., 1994). If you are curious, the residents of Rochester, Houston, and Nashville were the most helpful, while the least help was offered in Los Angeles, New York, and Patterson, New Jersey.

Negative affect can sometimes have the opposite influence, though. If the helping behavior itself promises to make you *feel good,* negative emotions actually increase the frequency of prosocial acts (Cialdini, Kenrick, & Bauman, 1982). Such a response is likely to occur only if your *negative feelings are not too intense,* if *the emergency is obvious,* and if *the act of helping is interesting or fun rather than difficult and unpleasant* (Berkowitz, 1987; Cunningham et al., 1990).

Possible Alternative Motives Underlying Prosocial Behavior

Positive or negative affect can be aroused not only by events external to the emergency situation but also by the bystander's perception of the victim and that person's needs. The theoretical explanations of *why* one might provide help for a stranger in distress tend to stress either selfish or selfless motives for altruism (Campbell & Specht, 1985). As you might guess, people tend to attribute their own helpful behavior to selfless motives ("It was the right thing to do") while observers are equally likely to attribute selfless or selfish motives ("He wanted to make a good impression") when someone else helps (Doherty, Weigold, & Schlenker, 1990).

Four somewhat different theoretical proposals relative to the motives underlying prosocial behavior are shown in Figure 10.13, and you may find it helpful to examine the basic elements in these models as you read the details below.

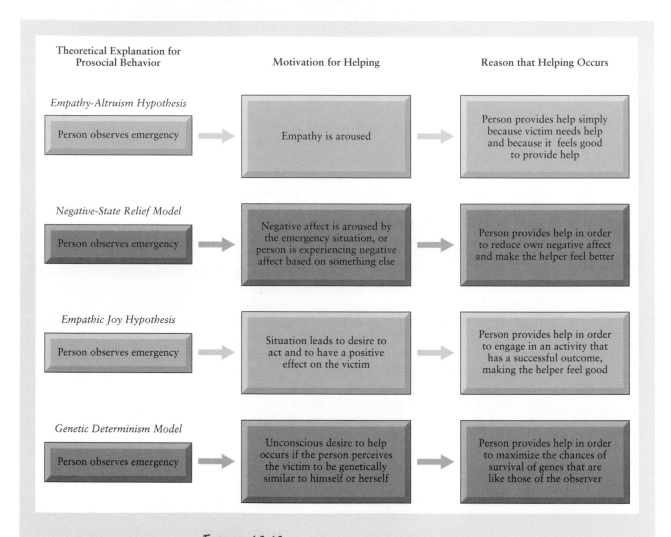

FIGURE 10.13

Four Alternative Proposals to Explain Why People Help. Four somewhat different explanations have been proposed to explain the motivation underlying prosocial behavior. The *empathy–altruism hypothesis* suggests that people help because someone needs help and because it is satisfying to provide help. The *negative state relief model* suggests that people help in order to reduce their negative affect. The *empathetic joy hypothesis* suggests that people help in order to have a successful influence on the person in need. The *genetic determinism model* suggests that people help others like themselves because of an unconscious desire to maximize the odds that their common genes will survive in subsequent generations. Supporting data have been generated for each proposal, and it is possible that each is correct. That is, helping may be based on more than one motive, depending on the situation and the individual who helps.

Unselfish Motivation: Empathy Leads to Helpfulness. We discussed empathy earlier as the tendency to experience the other person's emotional state, to feel sympathy for him or her, and to perceive the situation from that person's perspective. Based on this conception, Batson et al. (1981) proposed the **empathy–altrusim hypothesis.** The proposal is that at least some prosocial behavior is motivated entirely by the unselfish desire to help someone who needs help (Batson & Oleson, 1991). This motivation to help someone in need can even be at the expense of oneself and of the group as a whole (Batson, Batson, et al., 1995). That is, feelings of compassion may outweigh such considerations as fairness and justice (Batson, Klein, et al., 1995). A cognitive component enhances the emotional effect—the experience of empathy provides information that one *values* the other person's welfare and therefore must want to provide help (Batson, Turk, et al., 1995).

To test this altruistic view of helping behavior, Batson and colleagues devised an experimental procedure to manipulate a bystander's empathy and provide an opportunity for that individual to be helpful (Batson et al., 1983; Toi & Batson, 1982). Each participant served as the "observer" as another student performed a task while (supposedly) receiving random electric shocks. The female student being shocked was actually a research assistant recorded on videotape. After the task began, she indicated she was in pain and confided that, as a child, she had had a traumatic experience with electricity. Though she said she was able to continue, the experimenter asked whether the participant was willing to trade places. Empathy was manipulated by means of information indicating that the person being shocked was quite similar to (high empathy) or dissimilar from (low empathy) the participant. When empathy was low and it was easy to get out of the experiment, participants tended to leave rather than engage in a prosocial act. When empathy was high, the participants volunteered to take the victim's place and receive the shocks, whether or not it was easy to leave. It was concluded that their altruism was motivated by empathic concern.

Notice that people will gladly leave such a situation if empathy is not high. After all, the cost of helping is high—the observers believe they will receive electric shocks. What would happen if a person had a choice about whether to feel empathy? Shaw, Batson, and Todd (1994) asked college students to take part in a new program to help a homeless man—a program with either a low cost (spending an hour preparing letters to solicit contributions) or a high cost (meeting with the homeless person on three occasions for an hour and a half or two hours each time). The students then had a choice of getting additional information involving either an unemotional, factual description of the homeless man or an emotional, empathy-arousing message about what he is going through and how it affects his life. When the cost of helping was low, most students wanted to hear the emotional message. When the cost of helping was high, most wanted to hear the informational message. In other words, they engaged in *empathy avoidance* so they would not be motivated to engage in high-cost helping.

Selfish Motivation: Helping in Order to Feel Better. In describing the effect of negative moods on helping, we pointed out that people sometimes act in a prosocial way simply in order to make themselves feel better. In a more general form, this is known as the **negative state relief model** (Cialdini, Baumann, & Kenrick, 1981). This model assumes that prosocial behavior is motivated primarily by the desire to improve one's own emotional state.

Note that it doesn't matter whether the negative emotions are already present when the emergency is encountered or if they are aroused by the emergency itself. You may have unpleasant feelings because you argued with a friend

Empathy–Altruism Hypothesis
■ The proposal that at least some prosocial behavior is motivated solely by the desire to help someone who is in need.

Negative State Relief Model ■ The proposal that prosocial behavior is motivated by the desire to reduce uncomfortable negative emotions.

earlier in the day or because you are upset about seeing a stranger on crutches trip and fall. Either way, you engage in a prosocial act because you want to make yourself feel better (Fultz, Schaller, & Cialdini, 1988).

According to this theoretical model, the only role of empathy is as an additional source of negative affect. For example, Cialdini and his colleagues (1987) found that when empathy for a victim is aroused, one of the accompanying emotions is sadness. When the experimenters were able to separate empathic feelings from sad ones, they found that sadness alone leads to increased helping but that empathy alone does not.

Selfish Motivation: Helping Because It Feels Good to Have an Impact. Another interpretation of the role of empathy has been offered by Smith, Keating, and Stotland (1989). According to the **empathic joy hypothesis,** empathy leads to helping because the helper anticipates feeling good about accomplishing something.

What difference does it make whether you feel good because you helped or because you know your helping has an impact on the victim? Smith, Keating, and Stotland (1989) point out that with purely empathic motivation, the helper would not need feedback about the success of his or her actions. The empathic joy hypothesis predicts that empathy alone is not enough; altruism must be followed by information about one's success—an egoistic reward. These investigators designed an experiment in which the research participants saw a videotape of a female student who expressed feelings of isolation and stress and said she was considering withdrawing from college. The viewers had the opportunity to offer advice. Some were told they would get feedback about the effectiveness of their advice, and others were told that they would receive no further information about the woman. Participants' empathy was aroused by means of information about the woman's similarity to themselves; non-empathy was created by dissimilarity information. Under these conditions, empathy led to helping (the giving of advice) only when the research participants thought they would receive feedback about the effect of their advice. In other words, empathy alone was not enough to produce prosocial behavior; rather, knowledge of one's impact was necessary so that empathic joy could be felt.

It is possible, of course, to label any act of altruism as selfish simply because it feels good to help someone in need (Williamson & Clark, 1989; Yinon & Landau, 1987). The positive emotion that accompanies prosocial behavior is known as *helper's high*—a feeling of calmness, self-worth, and warmth (Luks, 1988). In fact, it sometimes feels so good to be helpful that if a victim refuses help when it is offered, the frustrated prosocial person becomes angry (Cheuk & Rosen, 1992).

Selfish Motivation: Helping Similar Others to Preserve Your Common Genes. While the previous explanations of prosocial motivation are based on the role of emotions, the **genetic determinism model** is based on a more general theory of human behavior. Rushton (1989) and other evolutionary psychologists stress that we are not conscious of why we respond to genetic influences; but they hypothesize we do so in many situations, including those that involve prejudice (Chapter 6), attraction (Chapter 7), mate selection (Chapter 8), aggression (Chapter 11)—and helping.

Archer (1991) points out that all sociobiological theories are based on the theory of natural selection. As with physical attributes, any behavior that increases an individual's ability to reproduce successfully (known as *fitness*) will be represented in subsequent generations more frequently than a behavior that is irrelevant to reproductive success or that interferes with reproduction.

Studies of other species indicate that the greater the genetic similarity between two animals, the more likely it is that one will help the other when help

Empathic Joy Hypothesis ■ The proposal that prosocial behavior is motivated by the positive empathetic feelings that result from helping a person in need feel better.

Genetic Determinism Model ■ The proposal that prosocial behavior is unconsciously motivated by genetic factors that evolved because they enhanced the ability of our ancestors to survive and reproduce; for example, genetic similarity.

is needed (Ridley & Dawkins, 1981). Such behavior is said to be the result of the "selfish gene"; because when one helps a genetically similar other, genes like one's own are more likely to survive and be passed on—even if the helper dies in the process (Rushton, Russell, & Wells, 1984). The assumption is that each individual is unconsciously motivated not only to live long enough to reproduce his or her own individual genes but also to enhance the reproductive odds of anyone else who shares those genes (Browne, 1992).

Much the same conclusion is reached by Burnstein, Crandall, and Kitayama (1994), who approach the role of evolution in prosocial behavior in a slightly different way. They assume that helping another person is not in one's self-interest, and that natural selection favors nonhelping. In other words, any primitive humans who were inclined to rush forth to help others who were drowning, being attacked, or otherwise in serious trouble would put themselves at risk and thus decrease their odds of surviving and passing on their genes. The exception occurs when the person in need is a relative. In that case, natural selection favors those who tend to help others on the basis of *how closely they are related* plus the likelihood that the person in need will be *able to reproduce*. Burnstein and his colleagues conducted several studies based on hypothetical decisions to help. As predicted, research participants are more likely to indicate they would offer help to someone closely related than to someone more distantly related or unrelated. In life-or-death situations, especially, help is given to close relatives more than to distant relatives. Reproductive ability is also a factor, in that help is given to young relatives more than to old ones, and to women young enough to reproduce more than to women past menopause.

The evolutionary perspective not only suggests why we would help anyone related to ourselves but also why we help similar others. By helping people like ourselves, we are actually behaving so as to preserve whatever genes we are likely to have in common.

In reviewing the literature on altruism, Buck and Ginsburg (1991) conclude that there is no evidence of a gene that determines prosocial behavior. Among humans, however, there *are* genetically based capacities to communicate one's emotional state and to form social bonds. These inherited aspects of social behavior make it likely that we will help one another when the need arises. In other words, people are inherently sociable, and when they interact in social relationships, "they are always prosocial, usually helpful, and often altruistic" (Fiske, 1991, p. 209).

You would probably find it more satisfying if we were able to declare one of these explanations entirely correct and the other three totally wrong, but that is not the case. In fact, it seems quite possible that prosocial behavior is based on a variety of motives; and it seems that little is gained by labeling some of them as selfless and others selfish. Regardless of the underlying reason for being helpful, it is good to help and good to receive help when you need it.

INTEGRATING PRINCIPLES

1. Most theoretical explanations of the motivation for prosocial behavior involve the emotional state of the potential helper and the emotional effect of engaging in helping behavior. Though there are debates about the ultimate selflessness or selfishness of the resulting behavior, it is generally agreed that altruistic reactions occur because they enhance positive affect and/or decrease negative affect. Affect is given an equally important emphasis in the study of cognition (Chapter 3), attitudes (Chapter 4), prejudice (Chapter 6), attraction (Chapter 7), relationships (Chapter 8), and aggression (Chapter 11).

Social Diversity: A Critical Analysis

EVALUATING PROSOCIAL MOTIVATION ACROSS AGE GROUPS AND ACROSS NATIONS

DESPITE WHAT WE SUGGESTED ABOUT THE POSSIBLE WISDOM of downplaying the importance of selfless versus selfish motives for prosocial behavior, most people do value some motivations more than others.

Reykowski (1982) suggests that prosocial actions are goal-oriented and that people engage in such behavior on the basis of how much they value a given goal and the perceived relationship between the specific behavior and attaining the goal. He suggests that each individual evaluates a given prosocial goal on the basis of cognitive schemas involving standards. The three basic standards are *hedonism* (maximizing pleasure and minimizing pain—self-interest), *conformity* (responding to the demands of external authority or of one's peers), and *conceptual reasoning* (responding affectively on the basis of cognitive processing—orientation toward the task or toward someone's needs).

Developmental research has generally indicated that as individuals grow from childhood to adolescence and then to adulthood, hedonism tends to decrease while reasoning based on the needs of others tends to increase. Boehnke and his colleagues (1989) investigated the generality of this age-related pattern among children and adolescents in four countries: Germany, Italy, Poland, and the United States. While age groups were expected to differ, the investigators did not expect cross-cultural differences in prosocial motivation.

Using the *Prosocial Motivation Questionnaire* (Silbereisen, Boenke, & Reykowski, 1986), Boehnke and his colleagues assessed the standards preferred by research participants who read twenty-four stories in which "you" helped or refrained from helping. As an example of one of the scenarios:

> It's a nice day. After school you go to visit a friend. He's helping his parents to clean up the house. Because it's going to take some time before they get done, you decide to help your friend clean up.

The participants were asked why they would have behaved in that way, and several choices were provided:

1. After sitting all day in school, I thought it would do me good to do some work and get into the groove (*hedonism*).

2. I remembered that I still had to clean up our basement and figured that my friend would help me too (*self-interest*).

3. Since everyone was pitching in, I didn't want to just sit there and do nothing (*conformity*).

4. Because I know that if I helped, the work would get done more quickly (*conceptual reasoning oriented toward task*).

5. I take it for granted that friends help each other; if they didn't, they wouldn't really be friends (*conceptual reasoning oriented toward the needs of others*).

Across the four countries, preferences were consistent, with the hedonic standards being least preferred and the conceptual standards being most preferred. As in previous research, preference for hedonistic motives declined somewhat with age, while reliance on conceptual standards increased somewhat. The ordering of the motives was remarkably similar within age groups, however, regardless of gender or nationality.

There appears, then, to be widespread agreement that prosocial behavior is most valued if done purely in response to the needs of someone else and least valued if based on one's own personal welfare. ■ ■ ■

CONNECTIONS: Integrating Social Psychology

In this chapter, you read about . . .	*In other chapters, you will find related discussions of . . .*
bystanders' response to the nonverbal cues provided by other bystanders	interpretation of nonverbal cues (Chapter 2)

social comparison among bystanders in emergency situations	social comparison as a factor in affiliative behavior (Chapter 7) and as a factor in social influence (Chapter 9)
attribution processes in perceptions of emergency situations	theories of attribution (Chapter 2)
self-concept of those helping and self-esteem of those receiving help	research and theory dealing with self-concept and self-esteem (Chapter 5)
locus of control as an aspect of the altruistic personality	locus of control and health-related behavior (Chapter 14)
social models and prosocial behavior	social models and aggressive behavior (Chapter 11)
similarity of victim and bystander	similarity and attraction (Chapter 7)
genetics and helping	the roles of genetics in prejudice (Chapter 6), attraction (Chapter 7), mate selection (Chapter 8), and aggression (Chapter 11)
affect and helping	the roles of affect in attitudes (Chapter 4), prejudice (Chapter 6), attraction (Chapter 7), and relationships (Chapter 8)

Thinking about Connections

1. At least once you have probably observed a stranger who possibly needed help. For example, on our campus a letter to the student newspaper described a scene near the student union late one cold Saturday evening. A student lay on a bench—apparently unconscious. Many students walked past him as they left the building. If you were one of them, how would you react? Make a list of the nonverbal cues possibly provided by other bystanders. How would social comparison processes operate in this instance? What possible attributions would you make about the stranger who might (or might not) need help? How would these nonverbal cues, social comparisons, and attributions influence your behavior?

2. There was a news story not long ago in which a car hung precariously on the edge of a bridge over a flooded river with the passengers still inside. They had to be helped out of the car one by one, carefully enough that the car did not become jarred loose and crash into the water. Imagine that you are on the scene in such a situation and that you have to decide which of four strangers should be helped out first, which second, and so on. One passenger is an elderly lady, two are very young boys (one of your race, one of another race), and the driver is a young woman in her twenties. Keep in mind that the first one out is very likely to be rescued, and that the risk of a fatal accident is greatest for the fourth passenger you attempt to rescue. In what order would you remove these individuals? Why?

3. You are hurrying toward a movie theater in a busy mall a few minutes before your film is scheduled to begin when a woman in front of you slips and drops several small packages that she is carrying. Make of list of all the factors that might determine whether you stop and help or continue toward the movie.

Summary and Review

Prosocial behavior refers to acts of helping others that have no obvious benefits for the person who helps.

Responding to an Emergency

Latané and Darley proposed that a bystander responds or fails to respond to an emergency as a function of choices made (often unconsciously) in a series of five steps. A prosocial act will not occur unless the bystander pays attention to the situation, interprets it as an emergency, assumes responsibility for taking action, knows what must be done to provide help, and decides to engage in the helping behavior. In addition to various aspects of the situation that encourage or discourage helping, dispositional factors are also involved, and a combination of traits make up the *altruistic personality*.

Additional Factors That Influence Prosocial Behavior

Helping behavior is enhanced by the presence of helpful models, including exposure to such models in the media. A victim is most likely to receive help if he or she is liked by the bystander and is similar to that person. When similarity is too great, however, the situation can be threatening, because it suggests to the bystander that "this could happen to you." One way to control this threat is to attribute responsibility to the victim, blaming the victim for the problem. Not all helping involves emergencies, and long-term volunteering is motivated by both selfless and selfish needs. A victim who asks for help is most likely to receive it, though the need for help can constitute a stigma. Receiving help is often uncomfortable and threatening to one's self-esteem, especially when the helper is a sibling or otherwise similar to oneself.

Additional Theoretical Explanations of Prosocial Motivation

Most explanations of helpfulness assume that the final motivation to act is based on whether the perceived outcome for the bystander is increased positive affect or decreased negative affect. The more specific proposals include the idea that at least some prosocial behavior is based on *empathy* and the unselfish desire to be helpful, that helping is based on *relieving a negative emotional state,* and that helping is done to make the helper *feel good.* From an evolutionary perspective, we have inherited the tendency to help those most like ourselves because their survival increases the odds that our shared genes will be passed on to future generations.

Social Diversity: Evaluating Prosocial Motivation across Age Groups and across Nations

People evaluate prosocial goals according to whether they are based on maximizing one's own pleasure and minimizing pain, on conformity to authority figures or to peers, or on conceptual reasoning about the task or the needs of the other person. Research indicates that motives based on cognitive processing increase with age, while the self-centered hedonistic motives decrease. Relatively positive evaluations of cognition-based motives and negative evaluations of self-centered motives are extremely consistent within age groups and across different nations.

■ Key Terms

Altruism (p. 367)

Altruistic Personality (p. 369)

Bystander Effect (p. 359)

Diffusion of Responsibility (p. 358)

Egoism (p. 367)

Empathic Joy Hypothesis (p. 384)

Empathy (p. 367)

Empathy–Altruism Hypothesis (p. 383)

Genetic Determinism Model (p. 384)

Negative State Relief Model (p. 383)

Pluralistic Ignorance (p. 363)

Prosocial Behavior (p. 356)

Repression (p. 375)

Sensitization (p. 375)

■ For More Information

Clark, M. S. (Ed.). (1991). *Prosocial behavior.* Newbury Park, CA: Sage.

An encompassing review of current research on prosocial behavior, with chapters written by active investigators.

Included are such topics as empathy, volunteerism, mood, and help-seeking.

Schroeder, D. A., Penner, L. A., Dovidio, J. F., & Piliavin, J. A. (1995). *The social psychology of helping and altruism: Problems and puzzles.* New York: McGraw-Hill.

The first text entirely devoted to the topic of prosocial behavior. The authors cover much of the material contained in this chapter, plus such topics as the developmental aspects of helping, cooperation, and collective helping. Their concluding chapter is designed to integrate the research material into an affective and cognitive model and to suggest future research.

Spacapan, S., & Oskamp, S. (Eds.). (1992). *Helping and being helped.* Newbury Park, CA: Sage.

This collection of chapters grew out of a symposium at which the contributors presented research and theories dealing with helping behavior in our everyday lives. Included are studies of people who donate kidneys, self-help groups, and helping behavior within families.

Wright, R. (1994). *The moral animal: The new science of evolutionary psychology.* New York: Pantheon.

A readable and creative exposition of the way evolutionary influences affect human genetics, and how genes affect behavior. Wright's discussion includes prosocial behavior and feelings of compassion but also covers many other aspects of human social behavior.

CHAPTER 11

AGGRESSION:
Its Nature, Causes, and Control

Lisa Houck, *Landscape with Active Volcano*, 1990, watercolor, 29 × 54"

Chapter Outline

FIGURE 11.1

Violence: A Worldwide Problem. As this scene from war-ravaged Somalia indicates, the costs of aggression in terms of human suffering are often very high—too high, most social psychologists would contend.

Are you feeling comfortable and relaxed? Then consider the following statistics:

In the United States there were 6,621,140 crimes of violence in one recent year (1992; U.S. Department of Justice, 1994).

In that same year, there were 140,930 forcible rapes and 657,550 assaults that resulted in injury to the victim (U.S. Department of Justice, 1994)— more than one rape every 5 minutes and one assault every 28 seconds.

Nearly 1,400 cases of fatal child abuse are reported in the United States each year (Daro & McCurdy, 1992); tens of thousands of children are treated medically for what are termed "unintended injuries," and recent findings suggest that many of these injuries are actually the result of abuse by parents or other adults (Peterson & Brown, 1994).

Each year, more than 1.8 million wives are beaten by their husbands (Straus & Gelles, 1988); many incidents involving abuse of husbands by their wives also occur, although such actions appear to be much less likely to result in serious injury to the victim (e.g., Holtzworth-Munroe & Stuart, 1994).

Homicide is the leading cause of death among African American males ages 15–34 in the United States (Butterfield, 1992).

Before you jump to the conclusion that violence is an American monopoly, consider the following facts: In Bosnia tens of thousands of civilians have been killed—many of them as part of a conscious policy of "ethnic cleansing" (translation: genocide); in Somalia continuing struggles between warlords during the 1990s resulted in the deaths of at least 500,000 persons in that war and famine-ravaged country (see Figure 11.1); and new waves of wholesale violence seem likely.

Do these facts make you uncomfortable? They should, because these numbers, plus conditions existing in many places around the globe today, confirm a basic lesson of human history: **aggression**—the intentional infliction of some form of harm on others—is an all-too-common form of social behavior (Huesmann, 1994).

Because of its alarming frequency and devastating consequences, aggression has long been a topic of careful research in social psychology (Baron &

Aggression ■ Behavior directed toward the goal of harming another living being.

Richardson, 1994). Such research has added significantly to our current understanding of human aggression—what it is, why it occurs, and how, perhaps, it can be prevented. To provide you with an overview of this important research, we'll proceed as follows.

First, we'll describe several different *theoretical perspectives* on aggression—contrasting views about the nature and origins of such behavior. Next, we'll review important *social determinants* of aggression—aspects of others' behavior that play a role in the initiation of aggressive outbursts. To balance the picture, we'll then turn to several *personal causes* of aggression—characteristics or traits that seem to predispose specific persons toward more than their fair share of aggressive actions. Fourth, we'll turn to two forms of aggression that occur within the context of long-term relationships: *child maltreatment* (Peterson & Brown, 1994), and *workplace violence* (Baron, 1995). Finally, to conclude on an optimistic note, we'll examine various techniques for the *prevention and control* of human aggression.

Theoretical Perspectives on Aggression: In Search of the Roots of Violence

Why do human beings aggress against others? What makes them turn, with brutality unmatched by even the fiercest of predators, against their fellow human beings? Scientists and scholars from many different fields have pondered these questions for centuries and have proposed many contrasting explanations for the paradox of human violence. Here, we'll examine several that have been especially influential, plus some newer theories based on modern ideas about human cognition and human behavior (e.g., Anderson, 1995; Huesmann, 1994).

Instinct Theories: Aggression As an Innate Tendency

The oldest and probably best known explanation for human aggression centers on the view that human beings are somehow "programmed" for violence by their basic nature. According to this view, which was initially known as the **instinct theory** of aggression, people aggress because, quite simply, it is part of their essential human nature to do so. The most famous supporter of this perspective was Sigmund Freud, who held that aggression stems mainly from a powerful *death wish* or instinct (thanatos) possessed by all persons. According to Freud, this instinct is initially aimed at self-destruction but is soon redirected outward, toward others. Freud believed that the hostile impulses it generates increase over time and, if not released, soon reach high levels capable of generating dangerous acts of violence.

A related view was proposed by Konrad Lorenz, a Nobel Prize–winning scientist. Lorenz (1966, 1974) proposed that aggression springs mainly from an inherited *fighting instinct* that human beings share with many other species. Presumably, this instinct developed during the course of evolution because it yielded important benefits—for example, dispersing populations over a wide area. In addition, Lorenz contended, it is often closely related to mating: fighting helps assure that only the strongest and most vigorous individuals will pass their genes on to the next generation. Very similar views have been proposed by other scientists, especially by *sociobiologists,* who, as we mentioned in Chapter 1, contend that many aspects of social behavior are the result of evolutionary processes favoring patterns of behavior that contribute to reproduction (to getting one's genes into the next generation; e.g., Ardrey, 1976; Barkow, 1989).

Instinct Theory ■ View suggesting that aggression stems from innate tendencies that are universal among members of a given species.

Sociobiologists argue that because aggression aids males of many species in obtaining mates, principles of natural selection will favor increasing levels of aggression, at least among males.

Is there any basis for the views just described? Do inherited tendencies toward aggression actually exist among human beings? Most social psychologists doubt that they do, primarily for two important reasons. First, critics note that proponents of instinct views such as those of Freud and Lorenz use somewhat circular reasoning. These theorists start by observing that aggression is a common form of behavior. On the basis of this fact, they then reason that such behavior must stem from universal, built-in urges or tendencies. Finally, they use the high incidence of aggression as support for the presence of such instincts and impulses! As you can see, this is questionable logic.

Second, and perhaps more important, several findings argue against the existence of universal, innate human tendencies toward aggression. Comparisons among various societies indicate that the levels of at least some forms of aggression vary tremendously. In many developed countries, rates of violent crimes are much lower than those we reported earlier for the United States; while in many developing nations, rates are even higher (Osterman et al., 1994). These huge differences in the incidence of aggression suggest that such behavior is strongly influenced by social and cultural factors, and that even if it stems in part from innate tendencies, these are literally overwhelmed by social conditions. For these and other reasons, an overwhelming majority of social psychologists reject instinct theories of aggression. Such theories should be viewed primarily as intriguing, but largely unverified, proposals concerning the origins of human violence.

Biological Theories

While social psychologists overwhelmingly reject instinct views of aggression, this does not imply that they also reject any role of biological factors in such behavior. On the contrary, there is increasing recognition by social psychologists of the importance of biological factors in many forms of social behavior (e.g., Buss, in press; Nisbett, 1990), and aggression is no exception to this general pattern. Indeed, growing evidence points to the conclusion that biological factors do predispose some individuals toward aggression (e.g., Gladue, 1991). For example, consider a study by Marazzitti and his colleagues (Marazzitti, et al., 1993).

These researchers conducted careful analyses of the blood chemistry of three groups of persons: ones who had attempted suicide, ones who had been institutionalized since childhood because of extremely high levels of aggression, and a group of healthy volunteers. Results indicated that both of the clinical groups (the attempted suicides and highly aggressive patients) differed from the control group with respect to measures reflecting reduced levels of *serotonin*—an important neurotransmitter in the nervous system. The researchers interpreted these findings as suggesting that both suicide attempters and highly aggressive persons suffer from reduced ability to control their aggressive impulses. In the case of would-be suicides, these impulses are directed at themselves, while in the case of highly aggressive persons, they are directed outward, at others. Regardless of whether this is indeed the case, the findings reported by Marazzitti and her colleagues (1993) lend support to the view that biological factors do indeed play an important role in at least some forms of aggression.

Perhaps even more dramatic evidence in this regard is provided by a recent investigation conducted with female transsexuals: female who decided to change their gender from female to male (Van Goozen, Frijda, & de Poll, 1994). As part of their medical treatment, these individuals received regular, large doses of male sex hormones (testosterone) either by injection or orally. During the study, these

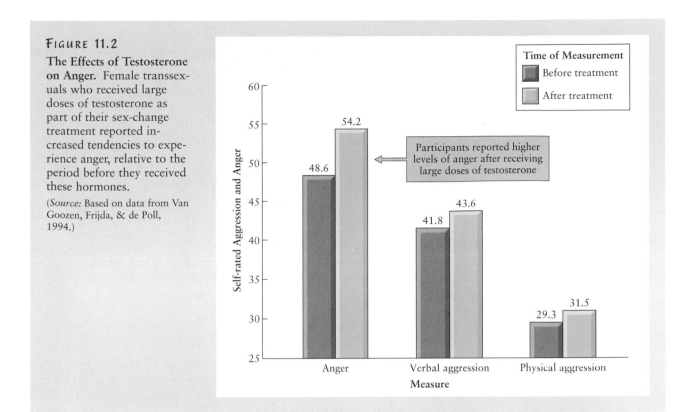

FIGURE 11.2

The Effects of Testosterone on Anger. Female transsexuals who received large doses of testosterone as part of their sex-change treatment reported increased tendencies to experience anger, relative to the period before they received these hormones.

(*Source*: Based on data from Van Goozen, Frijda, & de Poll, 1994.)

transsexuals completed questionnaires designed to assess their level of overt aggression and their tendency to become angry in various situations (anger-proneness); these measures were completed both before the women began receiving male sex hormones and three months later. Results showed little change in reports of overt aggression, either physical or verbal. However, as shown in Figure 11.2, participants did report higher tendencies to become angry after receiving these hormones.

These findings, plus other evidence suggesting, for example, that extreme aggression may be linked to disorders in neural mechanisms that regulate our emotions (e.g., Patrick, Bradley, & Lang, 1993), point to the conclusion that biological factors may indeed play a role in aggressive behavior. It's important to note, however, that none of this evidence indicates that aggressive tendencies are inherited in a simple or direct manner or that biological factors are overwhelmingly important as determinants of human aggression. On the contrary, existing evidence suggests that biological processes exert their effect against a rich backdrop of social and cognitive factors. So, just as human beings are not pushed to harm others by irresistible aggressive instincts, they are not driven to engage in such behavior by all-powerful biological forces. Where human aggression is concerned, biology may be important, but it is definitely *not* destiny.

Drive Theories (of aggression)
■ Theories suggesting that aggression stems from external conditions that arouse the motive to harm others; the most famous of these is the frustration–aggression hypothesis.

Drive Theories: The Motive to Harm Others

When psychologists rejected instinct views of aggression, they countered with an alternative of their own: the view that aggression stems mainly from an externally elicited *drive* to harm others. This approach is reflected in several different **drive theories** of aggression (e.g., Berkowitz, 1989; Feshbach, 1984).

FIGURE 11.3

Aggression: It Takes Many Different Forms. *As shown here, there are many ways to hurt another person, and some of them are extremely subtle!*
(*Source:* Reprinted with special permission of King Features Syndicate, Inc.)

Drive theories propose that external conditions such as *frustration*—any interference with goal-directed behavior—arouse a strong motive to harm others. This aggressive drive, in turn, leads to overt acts of aggression. By far the most famous of these theories is the well-known *frustration–aggression hypothesis* (Dollard et al., 1939). According to this view, frustration leads to the arousal of a drive whose primary goal is that of harming some person or object— primarily the perceived cause of frustration (Berkowitz, 1989).

Because drive theories suggest that external conditions rather than innate tendencies are crucial in the occurrence of aggression, they seem to offer somewhat more hope about the possibility of preventing such behavior. Since frustration is a common experience of everyday life, however, drive theories, too, seem to leave human beings facing continuous—and often unavoidable— sources of aggressive impulses.

Social Learning Theory: Aggression As Learned Social Behavior

Another, and sharply contrasting, perspective on aggression is known as the **social learning view.** This approach emphasizes the idea that aggression, like other complex forms of social behavior, is largely *learned* (Bandura, 1973, 1986; Baron & Richardson, 1994). Human beings, this perspective contends, are *not* born with a large array of aggressive responses at their disposal. Rather, they must acquire these in much the same way that they acquire other complex forms of social behavior: through direct experience or by observing the actions of others. Thus, depending on their past experience, people in different cultures learn to attack others in contrasting ways—by means of kung fu, blowguns, machetes, guns—or in more subtle ways, such as that shown in Figure 11.3.

But this is not all that is learned where aggression is concerned. Through direct and vicarious experience, individuals also learn (1) which persons or groups are appropriate targets for aggression, (2) what actions by others either justify or actually require aggressive retaliation, and (3) what situations or contexts are ones in which aggression is appropriate or inappropriate.

Social Learning View ■ Theory emphasizing that aggressive behaviors are learned either through direct experience and practice or through observation of others.

In short, the social learning perspective suggests that whether a specific person will aggress in a given situation depends on a vast array of factors, including that person's past experience, the current reinforcements (rewards) associated with aggression, and many variables that shape the person's thoughts and perceptions concerning the appropriateness and potential effects of such behavior. Since most if not all of these factors are open to change, the social learning approach is quite promising with respect to the possibility of preventing or controlling overt aggression. Needless to say, this makes it an appealing theory for social psychologists.

Cognitive Theories of Aggression: The Roles of Scripts, Appraisals, and Affect

Imagine that you are in a busy supermarket when suddenly another shopper rams you with her cart. How do you react? Certainly, with surprise and pain. But do you retaliate in kind, shoving your cart into *her*? Or do you swallow your annoyance and proceed with your shopping? Obviously, this depends on many different factors: the size and apparent ferocity of the shopper, who else is present on the scene, and so on. According to several modern theories of aggression, though, *cognitive factors* play a crucial role in determining how you will react (e.g., Anderson, 1995; Berkowitz, 1989; Huesmann, 1988, 1994). One of these involves what social psychologists term *scripts*—cognitive "programs" for the events that are supposed to happen in a given setting. Since your script for visiting a supermarket doesn't include getting into a battle with another shopper, this factor would probably operate *against* retaliation on your part in this setting.

Another cognitive factor that will influence your behavior is your interpretation of the situation—your *appraisal* of *why* the other shopper bumped you. Did she do it on purpose? Was it totally an accident? You will do a quick assessment of available information (for instance, is the other shopper smiling in glee or apologizing profusely?) and then, very quickly, decide whether there was malice on the other person's part or not (Anderson, 1995). This initial appraisal may then be followed by *reappraisal*, in which you take a little more time to consider the situation and assess such factors as what may happen if you act in various ways. If you ram the other shopper, you may get momentary satisfaction but may not be able to finish your shopping. She may retaliate, and ultimately you may both be thrown out of the store. Thoughts such as these clearly influence aggression in situations where people take the time to consider their actions and the possible results these will produce.

Finally, it's important to consider your current mood. Aversive (unpleasant) experiences, such as being rammed by another shopper, produce *negative affect*. As we noted in Chapter 3, our current moods exert strong effects on our cognitive processes. Thus, as suggested by Berkowitz (1989, 1994), the pain you experience may lead you to experience not only immediate tendencies to either retaliate or withdraw ("fight or flight") but also thoughts and memories related to other painful or annoying experiences. These, in turn, could trigger an aggressive reaction (Berkowitz, 1989).

In sum, **cognitive theories** of aggression suggest that such behavior stems from a complex interplay between our current moods and experiences, the thoughts and memories these elicit, and our cognitive appraisals of the current situation (see Figure 11.4 on page 398). Clearly, this kind of framework for understanding the roots of aggression is more complex than the early ones offered by Freud and Lorenz, or even than the famous *frustration–aggression hypothesis* proposed by Dollard and his colleagues (1939). But as you can readily see, it is much more likely to be accurate and useful than these earlier frameworks.

Cognitive Theories (of aggression) ■ Modern theories suggesting that aggression stems from a complex interplay between cognitive factors, affective states, and additional variables.

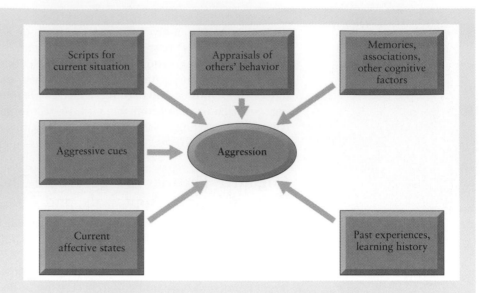

FIGURE 11.4

Cognitive Theories of Aggression. Modern theories suggest that aggressive behavior is influenced by complex interactions between cognitive factors (scripts, appraisals of others' behavior, memories and associations elicited by aggressive cues) and our current affective states.

(*Source:* Based on suggestions by Anderson, Anderson, & Deuser, in press; Berkowitz, 1989; Zillmann, 1994; and others.)

Social Determinants of Aggression: How Others' Actions, or Our Understanding of Them, Influence Aggression

Think back to the last time you lost your temper. What made you blow your cool? The chances are quite good that your anger stemmed from the actions of another person. In fact, when asked to describe situations that made them angry, most people refer to something another person said or did (Harris, 1993; Torestad, 1990). They are much less likely to mention purely physical events such as a flat tire, bad weather, or the like. In short, aggression often stems from various *social* conditions that either initiate its occurrence or increase its intensity. In this section we'll examine some of the most important of these factors. Before doing so, however, we will first consider a critical preliminary question: *How can human aggression—especially physical aggression—be studied in a systematic manner without the risk of harm to the participants in such research?* One important answer was provided by Arnold Buss (1961), in research that many social psychologists consider to be as creative as it was controversial. We'll examine this work, which provided the basis for much of the research we'll describe in this chapter, in the *Cornerstones* section below.

Cornerstones of Social Psychology

THE BUSS TECHNIQUE FOR STUDYING PHYSICAL AGGRESSION: "Would You Electrocute a Stranger?" Revisited

Creative minds, it seems, often run in the same circles. Do you remember our description of Stanley Milgram's research on obedience in Chapter 9? If so, you recall that the procedures he devised involved ordering research participants to deliver stronger and stronger electric shocks to an innocent victim. The key

Arnold Buss. Arnold Buss devised a technique for studying physical aggression under safe laboratory conditions. He developed this technique at almost precisely the same time that Stanley Milgram was devising *his* procedures for studying obedience to authority. I first met Arnie Buss when I was a visiting professor at the University of Texas, and have remained friends with him ever since. He is a true *bon vivant,* and one of the most energetic persons I have ever known.

question was: Would participants obey? At the same time that Milgram was developing these procedures for investigating an important form of social influence, Arnold Buss was working on a different but related question—the one we posed above. *How could researchers wishing to study human aggression do so in a way that would eliminate the risk of actual harm to participants?* The solution he formulated seems, on the surface, to be quite similar to the technique devised by Milgram. However, I (Bob Baron) knew both Stanley Milgram and Arnold Buss (I say "knew" because Milgram passed away several years ago), and they both confirmed what I suspected all along: they developed their similar-seeming research techniques simultaneously, but in a totally independent manner.

How do the procedures developed by Buss differ from those devised by Milgram? Let's take a closer look at them to see. In the approach designed by Buss, research participants are told that they are taking part, along with another person, in a study concerned with the effects of punishment on learning. One of the two persons present serves as a *teacher* and the other as a *learner*. The teacher (always the actual participant) presents various materials to the learner (an accomplice), who attempts to learn them. Each time the learner makes a correct response, the teacher rewards the learner with a signal indicating "Correct." Each time the learner makes an error, however, the teacher delivers an electric shock to this person, using apparatus like that shown in Figure 11.5 (p. 400).

So far, all this sounds very much like the procedures we described in Chapter 9. But here is where they differ: *The teachers in Buss's study were given free choice as to how strong the shocks should be.* In fact, they were told that they could choose any button on the apparatus, and hold it down for as long as they wished. The higher the number on the button, the stronger, supposedly, was the shock delivered to the learner; and as in Milgram's procedures, teachers (real participants) were given several sample shocks to convince them that the equipment really worked.

During each session the learner (accomplice) made many errors, thus providing participants with numerous opportunities on which to deliver electric shocks. Buss reasoned that since participants *were free to choose any shock level they wished,* these procedures would, in fact, measure participants' desire to hurt the accomplice: after all, if they wished, they could stick to the mildest shock (from button 1), which was described as being so mild that the learner would probably not even feel it.

Social psychologists interested in studying human aggression quickly seized on Buss's experimental apparatus, sometimes known as the **aggression machine,** as a valuable new research tool. Before its appearance, studies of aggression were largely limited to asking individuals how they would respond in various imaginary situations or measuring their *verbal* reactions to provocations or frustrations from others (that is, from experimental accomplices). Here, it seemed, was a means of studying not what people guessed they would do in such situations, but what they actually *would* do in terms of aggressing against another person. Thus, the Buss technique, and related procedures such as one devised by Stuart Taylor (1967), were soon used in a large number of studies designed to examine many different aspects of aggression. The results of these studies seemed to support the validity of Buss's procedures. For example, as expected, persons who were angered in some manner by the accomplice did choose to deliver more or stronger shocks than persons who were not angered (Baron, 1971; Geen, 1968). But questions concerning the ultimate validity of Buss's procedures were quickly raised. Critics noted that some participants, at least, might doubt that they could really hurt the victim by pushing buttons on the aggression machine. To the extent this was true, then the Buss procedures would fail in their attempt to measure aggressive intentions.

Aggression Machine ■ Apparatus used to measure physical aggression under safe laboratory conditions.

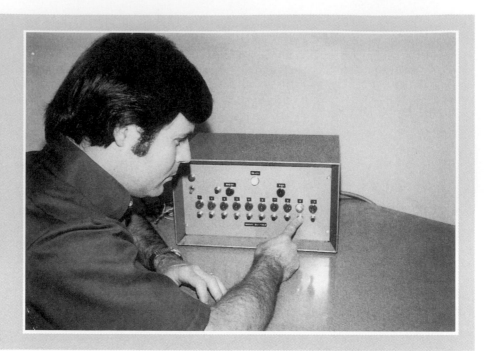

FIGURE 11.5

An Aggression Machine Similar to the One Devised by Arnold Buss. The apparatus shown here is used to study physical aggression without risk of harm to research participants. Participants are told that they can deliver shocks of varying intensities to another person by pushing buttons on this machine: the higher the number of the button pushed, the stronger the shock.

In response to such criticisms, researchers who used these procedures noted that in fact, most participants *did* believe that they could hurt the accomplice (Berkowitz & Donnerstein, 1982). Further, they called attention to the finding, repeated in several studies, that people with a prior history of aggressive behavior often chose stronger shocks or behaved more aggressively in other ways, than persons without such a history (e.g., Cherek et al., 1996; Gully & Dengerink, 1983; Wolfe & Baron, 1971).

Together, this evidence suggests that the method devised by Buss does provide a means of measuring aggression, or at least aggressive intent. Certainly this method, and ones based on it, are far from perfect: some people probably *don't* believe that they can deliver painful stimuli to the victim, and this situation is, of course, very different from real-life situations in which aggression occurs—for example, there is no opportunity for the victim to retaliate. If used with care, however, this method does seem to provide at least a rough index of the central concept we wish to measure in research on aggression: people's willingness to inflict harm—physical or otherwise—on another human being. ■ ■ ■

Frustration: Why Not Getting What You Want (or What You Expect) Can Sometimes Lead to Aggression

Suppose that you asked twenty people you know to name the single most important cause of aggression. What would they say? The chances are good that most would reply *frustration*. And if you asked them to define frustration, many would state, "The way I feel when something—or someone—prevents me from getting what I want or expect to get in some situation." This widespread belief in the importance of frustration as a cause of aggression stems, at least in part, from the famous **frustration–aggression hypothesis** first proposed by Dollard and his colleagues on the eve of World War II (Dollard et al., 1939). In its original form, this hypothesis made the following sweeping assertions: (1) Frustration *always* leads to some form of aggression, and (2) aggression *always* stems from frustration. In short, the theory held that frustrated persons always engage

Frustration–Aggression Hypothesis ■ The suggestion that frustration is a very powerful determinant of aggression.

in some type of aggression and that all acts of aggression, in turn, result from frustration. Bold statements like these are appealing, but this doesn't imply that they are necessarily accurate. In fact, existing evidence suggests that both portions of the frustration–aggression hypothesis go too far with respect to the importance they assign to frustration.

First, it is clear that frustrated individuals do not always respond with aggressive thoughts, words, or deeds. On the contrary, they show many different reactions to frustration, ranging from despair or depression on the one hand, to direct attempts to overcome the source of their frustration on the other.

Second, it is equally clear that not all aggression results from frustration. People aggress for many different reasons and in response to many different factors. For example, professional boxers hit their opponents because they wish to win valued prizes—not because of frustration. Similarly, during wars, air force pilots report that flying their planes is a source of pleasure, and that they bomb enemy targets while feeling elated, not frustrated. In these and many other cases, aggression definitely stems from factors other than frustration. We'll consider many of these other causes of aggression below.

In view of these considerations, few social psychologists now accept the idea that frustration is the only, or even the most important, cause of aggression. Instead, most believe that it is simply one of many factors that can potentially lead to aggression. Along these lines, Berkowitz (1989) has proposed a revised version of the frustration–aggression hypothesis that seems consistent with a large amount of evidence about the effects of frustration. According to this view, frustration is an aversive, unpleasant experience, and frustration leads to aggression because of this fact. In short, frustration sometimes produces aggression because of a basic relationship between negative affect and aggressive behavior—a relationship that has been confirmed in many different studies (e.g., daGloria Pahlavan, Duda, & Bonnet, 1994).

These suggestions help explain why *unexpected* frustration and frustration that is viewed as *illegitimate* or unjustified produce stronger aggression than frustration that is expected or legitimate. Presumably, this is so because unexpected or illegitimate frustration generates greater amounts of negative affect that frustration that is expected or viewed as legitimate.

In sum, while it appears that frustration can, indeed, be one potential cause of aggression, it is definitely not the only factor leading to such behavior, and does not play the very central role in human aggression that many people believe.

Direct Provocation: When Aggression Breeds Aggression

Remember the shopping cart episode described above? Suppose that when you looked at the shopper who rammed her cart into you, she gave you a dirty look and muttered "That'll teach you to get in my way!" How would you react? Probably with anger, and perhaps with some kind of retaliation. You might make a biting remark, such as "Who do you think *you* are?" or "What's wrong with you—are you crazy?" Alternatively, you might, if you were angry enough, push *your* cart into hers, or even aim at her directly.

Provocation ■ Actions by others that tend to trigger aggression in the recipient, often because they are perceived as stemming from malicious intent.

This incident illustrates an important point about aggression: Often, it is the result of physical or verbal **provocation** from others. That is, when we are the victims of some form of aggression from others, we rarely turn the other cheek, at least not if we can help it. Instead, we tend to reciprocate, returning as much aggression as we have received—or perhaps even slightly more, especially if, as in this incident, we are quite certain that the other person *meant* to harm us in some way (Dengerink, Schnedler, & Covey, 1978; Ohbuchi &

Ogura, 1984). This latter finding—that we often return a bit more aggression than we have received—helps explain why aggression often spirals upward from mild taunts to stronger insults, and from pushing or shoving to kicks, blows, or worse.

But what actions, precisely, do people find provoking? Several studies have investigated this issue (e.g., Torestad, 1990). One that provides especially clear evidence in this respect, and that also points to important gender differences in responses to provocation, has been conducted by Harris (1993). She asked several hundred students (both males and females) to describe the most anger-provoking behavior that a man or woman of their own age could display toward them. As shown in Table 11.1, physical and verbal aggression by another person were identified by both males and females as the most anger-provoking behaviors they could encounter. However, interesting gender differences emerged with respect to several other potential causes of anger. For example, females reported being much more likely than males to be angered by condescending actions—ones in which the other person showed arrogance or suggested that he or she was superior in some manner. Similarly, females reported being more likely than males to be angered by actions in which someone hurt someone else, and by actions involving insensitivity—behaviors in which their feelings were ignored by another person. In sum, while both females and males reported being angered by various forms of provocation from others, they did seem to differ somewhat in terms of the specific forms of provocation they find most anger-inducing. As noted by Harris (1993), these differences seem to reflect prevailing gender stereotypes such as the ones we described in Chapter 6. Such stereotypes suggest that females should be kind, nurturant, and sensitive to others' feelings; in view of such stereotypes, it is not surprising that they find behavior contrary to these supposed traits to be especially annoying.

Exposure to Media Violence: The Effects of Witnessing Aggression

List several films you have seen in recent months. Now, answer the following question: How much aggression or violence did each of these contain? How

---

TABLE 11.1 Anger-Provoking Actions by Others

As shown here, both females and males find physical and verbal aggression by another person to be the most anger-provoking. However, interesting gender differences occur with respect to other potential sources of anger. For instance, females report being angered to a greater extent than males by condescending actions, or by ones showing insensitivity.

Type of Behavior	Males	Females
Physical Aggression	45	55
Verbal Aggression	25	34
Insensitivity	9	37
Condescension	18	48
Dishonesty	2	5
Inefficiency	1	1

(*Source:* Based on data from Harris, 1993.)

FIGURE 11.6

The Prevalence of Media Violence. Many popular films contain large amounts of violence—more violence, and in more graphic forms, than was true in the past. Does exposure to such materials increase the likelihood of aggression by persons who are exposed to them? This important question has received a great deal of attention in ongoing research by social psychologists.

often did characters in these movies, hit, shoot at, or otherwise attempt to harm others? Unless your moviegoing habits are somewhat unusual, you probably recognize that many popular films contain a great deal of violence—much more than you are ever likely to see in real life. Careful analyses of the contents of television programs, films, and televised sports events indicate that all contain a great deal of violence (Reiss & Roth, 1993; Waters et al., 1993). Indeed, one recent study that analyzed the content of commercials for food products—for example, milk, soups, and dry and hot cereals—found that even *these* often contained themes of violence (Rajecki et al., 1994; see Figure 11.6).

These findings have lead many social psychologists to pose the following question: Does exposure to such materials increase aggression among children or adults? This is an important issue, so it is not surprising that it has been the subject of literally hundreds of research projects (e.g., Huesmann & Miller, 1994). The findings of these studies have not been entirely consistent, but taken together, they point to the following conclusion: *Exposure to media violence may indeed be one factor contributing to high and rising levels of violence in the United States and elsewhere.*

Evidence for the Effects of Media Violence on Aggression. Several different lines of research, conducted in very different ways, are consistent with this conclusion. First, researchers have conducted many *short-term laboratory experiments*—studies in which individuals are exposed to films or television programs showing either a high or a low level of violence, followed by observations of the viewers' own tendencies to aggress against others (e.g., Bandura, Ross, & Ross, 1963; Geen, 1991). In general, the results of these experiments indicate that even very young children can acquire new ways of aggressing against others from exposure to media violence, and that exposure to such materials can also increase their tendency to put such behaviors into practice.

A second group of studies have used a different approach, sometimes described as *static observation* (Huesmann & Miller, 1994). In such studies, information on two factors—children's current level of aggression (as rated, for example, by teachers or peers), and the amount of television and film violence children are currently watching—is obtained. Researchers then correlate these variables to determine whether they are related in any manner. The results of such studies indicate that these factors are, indeed, positively correlated: the more aggressive television programs and films children watch, the more aggressive their behavior tends to be (e.g., Bachrach, 1986; Huesmann & Eron, 1986; Leyens et al., 1975).

Perhaps the most convincing evidence for an important link between exposure to media violence and aggression, however, is provided by *long-term (longitudinal) research* in which participants have been studied for many years (e.g., Huesmann & Eron, 1984, 1986). For example, in one of the best-known of these investigations, all third-graders in one county of upstate New York were questioned about their favorite television programs. In addition, ratings of the children's aggression were obtained from their classmates. Results indicated that there was a link between these variables, at least among boys: the more violence these eight-year-olds watched, the higher the ratings of their aggression by other children. Ten years later, the same participants were studied again, and this relationship was confirmed: the more violence they had watched as children, the higher their level of aggression as teenagers. Finally, the same persons were studied once more when they were about thirty years old. Again, the amount of aggression viewed by participants as children predicted their level of aggression—both their self-ratings of such behavior and state records of arrests for aggressive actions. These dramatic results have been replicated in several other long-term studies conducted in many different countries—for example, Australia, Finland, Israel, Poland, and South Africa (Botha, 1990; Huesmann & Eron, 1986). In all these studies, too, the greater the amount of violent television watched by participants, the greater their subsequent levels of aggression. Moreover, in these later studies, these findings have been obtained for females as well as for males.

While these studies are impressive, and have been very carefully conducted, it's important to remember that they are still only correlational in nature. As we pointed out in Chapter 1, the fact that two variables are correlated does *not* imply that one necessarily causes the other. Further, as we noted earlier, not all studies on the potential effects of media violence have yielded consistent findings. Still, when all types of research evidence are considered, and when the findings of all these studies are subjected to meta-analysis (refer to Chapter 1; Comstock & Paik, 1991; Wood, Wong, & Chachere, 1991), results do point to the conclusion we stated at the outset: Exposure to media violence can contribute, along with many others factors, to the occurrence of overt aggression.

Heightened Arousal: Emotion, Cognition, and Aggression

Suppose that you are driving to the airport to meet a friend. On the way there, another driver cuts in front of you so suddenly that you almost have a collision. Your heart pounds wildly and you feel your blood pressure shoot through the roof; but fortunately, no accident occurs. Now you arrive at the airport. You park and rush inside, because it's almost time for your friend's flight to arrive. When you get to the security check, there's an elderly man in front of you. As he walks through, the buzzer sounds and he becomes confused. The security guard can't make him understand that he must empty his pockets and walk through again. You are irritated by this delay. In fact, you feel yourself growing extremely angry. "What's wrong with him?" you think to yourself. "Hasn't he ever been to an airport before?" As the delay continues, you feel yourself sorely tempted to shout at the elderly man or even to push your way by him.

Now for the key question: Do you think that your recent near miss in traffic may have played any role in your sudden surge of anger? In short, could the emotional arousal from that incident have somehow transferred to the totally unrelated situation at the security gate? Growing evidence suggests that it could (Zillmann, 1988, 1994). Under some conditions, heightened arousal—whatever its original source—can enhance aggression in response to frustration or provocation. In fact, in various experiments arousal stemming from such diverse sources as participation in competitive games (Christy, Gelfand, & Hartmann, 1971), vigorous exercise (Zillmann 1979), and even some types of music (Rogers & Ketcher, 1979) has been found to facilitate subsequent aggression. Why is this the case? A compelling explanation is offered by **excitation transfer theory** (Zillmann, 1983, 1988).

Excitation Transfer Theory. This theory begins by noting that physiological arousal, however produced, tends to dissipate slowly over time. As a result, some portion of such arousal may persist as a person moves from one situation to another. In the example above, some portion of the arousal you experienced as a result of a near miss in traffic may still be present as you approach the security gate in the airport. Now, when you encounter minor annoyance, that arousal intensifies your emotional reactions to the annoyance. The result: You become enraged rather than just mildly irritated. Excitation theory further suggests that such effects are most likely to occur when the persons involved are relatively unaware of the presence of residual arousal—a common occurrence, since small elevations in arousal are difficult to notice (Zillmann, 1988, 1994). Excitation transfer theory also suggests that such effects are likely to occur when the persons involved recognize their residual arousal but attribute it to events occurring in the present situation (Taylor et al., 1991). In the incident we have been describing, for instance, your anger would be intensified if you recognized your feelings of arousal but attributed them to the elderly man's actions (see Figure 11.7 on page 406).

Emotion, Cognition, and Aggression: The Complex Interplay among Them. Recently, Zillmann (1988, 1994) has expanded excitation transfer theory to help explain how emotion (arousal) and cognition can interact in shaping aggressive reactions. First, let's consider the impact of cognition on emotion—a topic we considered in another context in Chapter 3. How can our thoughts influence arousal and so our tendencies to aggress? One answer involves the fact that our thoughts can lead us to *reappraise* various emotion-provoking events. For example, consider the delay at the security gate described above. Suppose that after a few seconds, you realize that the elderly gentleman is a foreigner who doesn't speak English. Now the reason for his confusion will be clear, and the result may well be a lower level of anger on your part. In other words, this new information will lead you to reinterpret the situation, and this cognitive activity, in turn, may well influence your emotional reactions. Evidence for precisely such effects has been obtained in many different studies (Zillmann, 1994). For example, if persons are warned in advance that someone with whom they will soon interact is very upset, they experience less anger in response to rudeness by this individual than if they do not receive such information, or if they receive it only *after* the person has provoked them (Zillmann & Cantor, 1976). In such situations, cognition exerts strong effects on our emotional reactions.

What about the impact of arousal on cognition? Do our levels of arousal influence our thoughts about others' behavior, and so our tendencies to aggress against them? Again, the answer appears to be *yes*. In fact, as noted by Zillmann (1994), strong emotional arousal sometimes produces what he describes as *cognitive deficit*—reduced ability to formulate rational plans of action, or re-

Excitation Transfer Theory ∎ Theory suggesting that arousal produced in one situation can persist and intensify emotional reactions occurring in later situations.

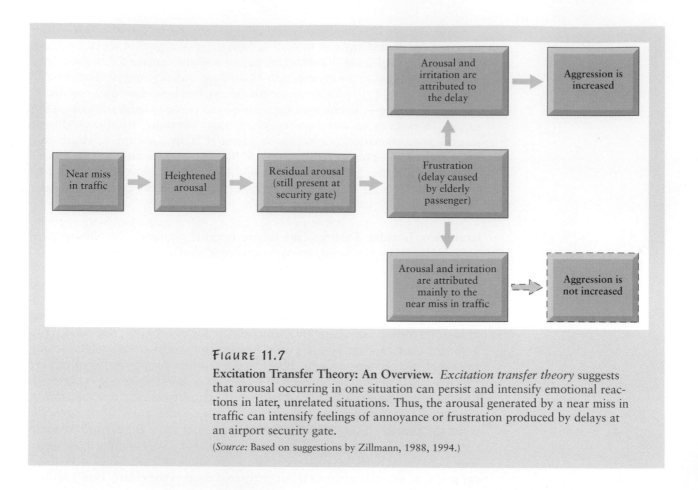

FIGURE 11.7

Excitation Transfer Theory: An Overview. *Excitation transfer theory* suggests that arousal occurring in one situation can persist and intensify emotional reactions in later, unrelated situations. Thus, the arousal generated by a near miss in traffic can intensify feelings of annoyance or frustration produced by delays at an airport security gate.

(*Source:* Based on suggestions by Zillmann, 1988, 1994.)

duced ability to evaluate the possible outcomes of various behaviors. Or, as I (RAB) sometimes describe this principle to my classes, "When emotions run high, reason flies out the window." The result, then, may be an impulsive lashing out at others, with all the risks this implies. We'll return to the role of cognition in aggression in our later discussion of the prevention and control of aggression; for as we'll see then, reestablishing cognitive control over behavior can be highly effective in reducing the likelihood of interpersonal violence (Zillmann, 1993).

Sexual Arousal and Aggression: Are Love and Hate Really Two Sides of the Same Behavioral Coin?

Love and hate, it is often contended, are closely related. For example, consider the following quotation: *"I hated her now with a hatred more fatal than indifference because it was the other side of love"* (J. August Strindberg, 1900). Are such observations concerning potential links between love and hate accurate? If *love* is interpreted primarily in terms of sexual arousal or excitement, research by social psychologists offers some support for this age-old idea.

First, it appears that relatively mild levels of sexual arousal can reduce overt aggression. In several studies the following procedures were followed: Participants were first annoyed by a stranger. Then they examined stimuli that were either mildly sexually arousing (e.g., pictures of attractive nudes) or neutral (e.g., pictures of scenery, abstract art). Finally, they had an opportunity to retaliate against their provoker (e.g., Baron, 1974, 1979; Ramirez, Bryant, & Zillmann, 1983). Results indicated that those exposed to mildly arousing materials showed lower levels of aggression than those exposed to the neutral stimuli.

The word *mild* should be emphasized, however. Because in subsequent studies in which participants were exposed to more arousing sexual materials, such arousal was found to *increase* rather than reduce aggression (e.g., Jaffe et al., 1974; Zillmann, 1984). Together, these findings suggest that the relationship between sexual arousal and aggression is *curvilinear* in nature. Mild sexual arousal reduces aggression to a level below that shown in the absence of such arousal, while higher arousal actually increases it above this level. Why is this so? A *two-component model* proposed by Zillmann (1984) offers one useful answer.

According to this model, exposure to erotic stimuli produces two effects: It increases arousal and it influences current *affective states*—negative and positive feelings. Whether sexual arousal will increase or reduce aggression, then, depends on the overall pattern of such effects. Mild erotic materials generate weak levels of arousal but high levels of positive affect. As a result, exposure to such materials tends to reduce overt aggression. In contrast, explicit sexual materials generate stronger levels of arousal—but also, since many people find some of the acts shown to be disturbing or even repulsive, such explicit materials also generate considerable negative affect. As a result, materials of this type may increase aggression. The findings of several studies support this two-factor theory (e.g., Ramirez, Bryant, & Zillmann, 1983), so it appears to offer important insights into the relationship between sexual arousal and aggression. Taken together, research findings suggest that while sexual arousal and aggression do seem to be related, the nature of this relationship is somewhat more complex than was initially believed.

Sexual Jealousy and Aggression: Do We Want to Hurt the Ones We Love If They Have Been Unfaithful?

Observers of human behavior from Shakespeare to Freud have contended that **sexual jealousy**—perception of a threat to a romantic relationship by a rival for one's partner—can be a potent cause of aggression. Systematic research on this topic confirms this view. Individuals who feel that their lover has "done them wrong" by flirting—or worse—with another person often experience strong feelings of anger, and frequently think about or actually engage in actions designed to punish their lover, the rival, or both (Buss et al., 1992; Parrott, 1991; Sharpsteen, 1991). Interestingly, and perhaps contrary to what informal observation suggests, most of the anger and blame in such situations seems to fall on the partner rather than on the rival (Paul, Foss, & Galloway 1993). Perhaps the most intriguing findings of research on sexual jealousy, however, are those pointing to the conclusion that females experience stronger feelings of anger at both the partner and the rival than males do (Paul et al., 1993), and are more likely to react aggressively to such betrayals. Clear evidence for this suggestion is provided by a study conducted by de Weerth and Kalma (1993).

These researchers asked a large number of students enrolled in a social psychology course at a university in the Netherlands to indicate how they would react if they learned that their current lover was having an affair with another person. As you can see from Figure 11.8 (p. 408), females reported they would be more likely to respond with verbal and physical abuse of their lover, or to demand an explanation. In contrast, males indicated that they would be more likely to get drunk!

Similar results have been obtained in several other studies (e.g., Paul et al., 1993), so this gender difference appears to be a real one. What accounts for its existence? One possibility is suggested by the perspective of *evolutionary psychology*, which we described in Chapter 1 (e.g., Buss, in press). According to

Sexual Jealousy ■ Perception of a threat to a romantic relationship by a rival for one's partner.

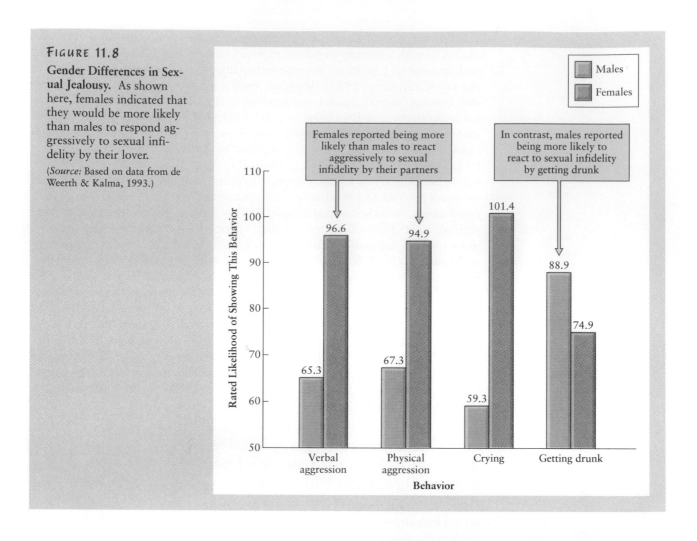

this perspective, contrasting biological forces may underlie male and female sexual jealousy. For females, such jealousy may focus primarily on the potential loss of resources needed for child rearing. Throughout most of human history, females were dependent on males for the resources needed to raise children. In this context, a wandering mate might ultimately decide to wander off, taking these precious resources with him. The result: Females react very strongly to male sexual infidelity. For males, in contrast, sexual jealousy may rest primarily on concern over paternity. If their mate has sexual relations with other men, they may find themselves in the situation of raising other men's children. In the past, this was a strong basis for male sexual jealousy. However, the advent of effective contraceptives has made it much less likely that men's mates will become pregnant by other men, even if they have affairs with them. As a result, de Weerth and Kalma (1993, p. 275) contend, men may now have weaker reasons for reacting aggressively to sexual jealousy than was true in the past. For women, however, the basis for such reactions may be largely unchanged. The overall result? More aggressive reactions to sexual infidelity on the part of women than on the part of men. Of course, given the fact that men are generally stronger, physically, than women, women's aggressive reactions to sexual jealousy usually take a less serious form than that by men. For example, women may shout at their mates or attempt to slap or scratch them. In contrast, males' aggressive reactions to sexual jealously often result in serious injuries to the targets—the kind of violent wife abuse we mentioned at the start of this chapter (Holtzworth-Munroe & Stuart, 1994).

We should hasten to add that this is only one, highly speculative possibility; many other explanations for recent findings pointing to more aggressive jealousy among females than among males also exist—for example, norms suggesting that males should not aggress against females, even when strongly provoked (see our later discussion of gender differences in aggression). Whatever the precise explanation, however, it is clear that sexual jealousy is a strong impetus to aggression for both women and men, and that in this respect the green-eyed monster continues to live up to its fearful reputation.

For information on another potential cause of aggression, please see the *Applied Side* section below.

Social Psychology: On the Applied Side
VIOLENT PORNOGRAPHY: A Potential Cause of Rape?

In recent decades, restrictions against explicit sexual materials have all but disappeared in many Western nations. This fact, coupled with the huge sale of videocassette recorders, has resulted in a situation where access to print and video pornography is as close as the nearest shopping center. Moreover, some of the explicit sexual material available contains scenes that offer a potentially volatile mixture of sex and violence. In such materials, women are generally the victims, and they are shown being raped, tortured, and brutalized in many ways. Given—as we have seen—that exposure to media violence can encourage aggressive behavior among viewers and that high levels of sexual arousal (coupled with negative affect) can also increase aggression, it seemed possible to social psychologists that violent pornography, as it is often termed, can be quite dangerous. What do research findings reveal?

As was the case with studies of the effects of media violence, social psychologists have adopted several different research methods to study this topic. One of these involves the conduction of short-term laboratory experiments in which individuals are exposed either to violent pornography, to pornography that involves sexual behavior without any overt violence, or to other, neutral materials (e.g., Linz, Donnerstein, & Penrod, 1984; Zillmann & Bryant, 1984). The results of these studies indicate that exposure to violent pornography seems to encourage callous attitudes toward sexual violence among both males and females—for example, a tendency to perceive rape as less serious and to report less sympathy toward rape victims. In addition, exposure to such materials exerts a *desensitizing effect,* in which viewers react less negatively to the violence in these films as they watch more and more of them. These findings suggest that exposure to scenes of violence against women may well exert adverse effects upon viewers, making them more callous about sexual violence and—in the case of males—potentially increasing their willingness to engage in such behavior themselves (e.g., Linz, Donnerstein, & Penrod, 1988).

Other research employing different methods, however, points to somewhat different conclusions, at least with respect to the very serious crime of rape (e.g., Baxter et al., 1984). In one group of studies, for instance, researchers did a content analysis of pornographic magazines, films, and videotapes in order to determine what proportion of these materials fall under the heading of *violent pornography.* While this research is far from conclusive, it suggests that only a relatively small proportion of such materials contain violent content. Estimates vary across different studies, but most find that only 4 to 7 percent of pornographic materials contain aggressive content in which the persons shown are

FIGURE 11.9

Pornography: Is It Related to Rape? After pornography became readily available in Denmark, Sweden, and Germany, the incidence of rape did not increase. Rape *did* increase in the United States after pornography became readily available; however, assaults also increased in the United States during the same period. Together, these findings seem to argue against the suggestion that pornography stimulates rape.

(*Source:* Based on data from Kutchinsky, 1991.)

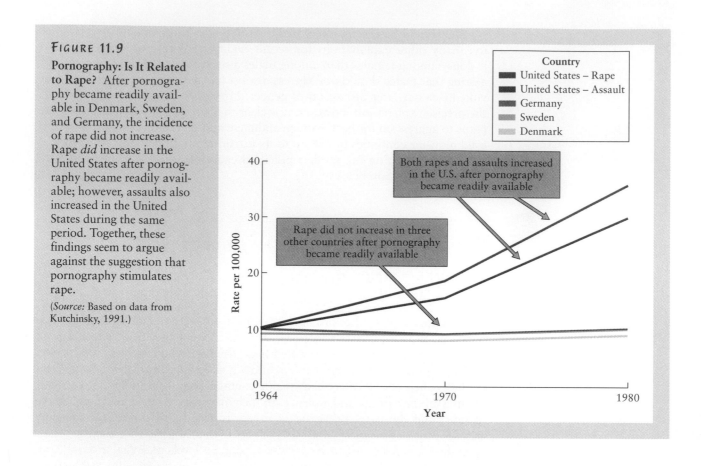

hurt in some manner. Further, in only 0.4 percent of these films and tapes do the women present show strongly negative reactions to the activities performed (Palys, 1984). So, in sum, violent pornography does not appear to constitute a large proportion of available pornographic materials.

But what about the possibility that, as some feminists have contended, "Pornography is the theory—rape is the practice" (Morgan, 1980)? Does the ready availability of pornographic materials contribute to the violent crime of rape? While there is no definitive answer to this disturbing question, a study reported by Kutchinsky (1991) provides some thought-provoking data. Kutchinsky reasoned as follows: If pornography is related to rape, then the incidence of this crime should rise after such materials are legalized, or at least after they become readily available. To test this possibility, he gathered crime statistics for a twenty-year period from four countries: the United States, Denmark, Sweden, and Germany. Pornography was legalized in Denmark, Sweden, and Germany in 1969, 1970, and 1973, respectively, and became widely available, although not explicitly legalized, in the United States during roughly the same period. Did rape increase in these countries after pornography became readily available? As you can see from Figure 11.9, rape rose only in the United States; and in this respect, it mirrored a very similar increase in other assaults. These findings seem to suggest that the increased availability of pornography did *not* contribute to an increase in rape, as some critics had feared.

Of course, these findings are far from conclusive. Although rape did not increase in Denmark, Sweden, or Germany after pornographic materials were legalized, it is possible that such materials *did* exert negative effects in this respect, but that these were countered by other changes in these societies. In other words, since this research is correlational in nature, we cannot rule out the possibility that other factors, not included in the analysis, somehow concealed or masked any adverse effects of pornography. But as Kutchinksy (1991, p. 61) notes, the fact that both rape and other assaults increased in the United States during this period offers support for the view that rape is primarily an act of violence, not of sexual arousal. If this is indeed the case, then perhaps we should be more concerned about the potential effects of films and television programs containing scenes of explicit violence than about the effects of materials portraying explicit sexual behavior. Only further research can resolve this complex issue; but one fact *is* clear: The media have powerful effects upon viewers' attitudes, values, and behavior. Thus, they may do much more than merely mirror society: they may shape and influence it as well. ■ ■ ■

INTEGRATING PRINCIPLES

1. Contrary to earlier beliefs, human aggression does not stem from a single, all-important cause such as frustration. In fact, it is influenced by many different social factors, including provocations from others, exposure to aggressive models, heightened arousal, and sexual jealousy.

2. Several of these factors play important roles in other forms of social behavior as well as in aggression. For example, modeling influences prosocial behavior (Chapter 10); heightened arousal affects many aspects of social behavior, such as attraction (Chapter 7); and sexual jealousy influences the course of many relationships (Chapter 8).

Personal Causes of Aggression

Are some persons "primed" for aggression by their personal characteristics? Informal observation suggests that this is so. While some individuals rarely lose their tempers or engage in aggressive actions, others seem to be forever blowing their tops, often with serious consequences. In this section, we will consider several personal traits or characteristics that seem to play an important role in aggression.

The Type A Behavior Pattern: Why the *A* in Type A Could Well Stand for *Aggression*

Do you know anyone you could describe as (1) extremely competitive, (2) always in a hurry, and (3) especially irritable and aggressive? If so, this person shows the characteristics of what psychologists term the **Type A behavior pattern** (Glass, 1977; Strube, 1989). At the opposite end of the continuum are persons who do not show these characteristics—individuals who are not highly competitive, who are not always fighting the clock, and who do not readily lose their temper; such persons are described as showing the **Type B behavior pattern.**

Given the characteristics mentioned above, it seems only reasonable to expect that Type A's would tend to be more aggressive than Type B's in many situations. In fact, the results of several experiments indicate that this is actually the case (Baron, Russell, & Arms, 1985; Carver & Glass, 1978). For example, consider a study by Berman, Gladue, and Taylor (1993). These researchers ex-

Type A Behavior Pattern ■ Pattern consisting primarily of high levels of competitiveness, time urgency, and hostility.

Type B Behavior Pattern ■ Pattern consisting of the absence of characteristics associated with the Type A behavior pattern.

posed young men known to be Type A or Type B to increasing provocation from a stranger: this person set increasingly strong shocks for them in a competitive reaction time task where the slower-to-respond person (the loser on each trial) received the shock set for him by his opponent. (This is the method for studying aggression devised by Stuart Taylor that we mentioned in the *Cornerstones* section.)

Another feature of the study involved measurement of participants' testosterone level; testosterone is an important male sex hormone. Testosterone was measured from participants' saliva before the start of the reaction time task. Results indicated that during the competitive task, Type A's who also had a high level of testosterone set the highest level of shocks for their opponent. In addition, Type A's with high testosterone levels were much more likely than other participants to use the highest shock setting available. These findings indicate that two different personal characteristics—the Type A behavior pattern and testosterone level—both play a role in determining aggressive behavior.

Additional findings indicate that Type A's are truly hostile people: they don't merely aggress against others because this is a useful means for reaching other goals, such as winning athletic contests or furthering their own careers. Rather, they are more likely than Type B's to engage in what is known as **hostile aggression**—aggression in which the prime objective is inflicting some kind of harm on the victim (Strube et al., 1984). In view of this fact, it is not surprising to learn that Type A's are more likely than Type B's to engage in such actions as child abuse or spouse abuse (Strube et al., 1984), topics we'll soon examine in more detail. In contrast, Type A's are *not* more likely to engage in **instrumental aggression**—aggression a person performs not primarily to harm the victim but to attain other goals, such as control of valued resources or praise from others for behaving in a "tough" manner.

Perceiving Evil Intent in Others: Hostile Attributional Bias

Remember the shopping cart example we considered above? In discussing that example, we pointed out that often, our *attributions* concerning others' behavior—our interpretation of *why* people acted as they did—play an important role in the occurrence of aggression. If we decide that someone's actions, such as bumping us with a shopping cart, were done on purpose, we are much more likely to retaliate than if we conclude that the actions were unintentional or accidental. In many situations, however, interpreting others' actions is not a simple task: their behavior is ambiguous, and we can't easily determine whether they meant to harm us or not. In such situations, another personal factor known as **hostile attributional bias** becomes relevant. This is the tendency to perceive hostile intentions or motives in others' actions when these are ambiguous. In other words, persons high in hostile attributional bias rarely give others the benefit of the doubt: they simply *assume* that any provocative actions from others are intentional, and react accordingly—often, with strong retaliation (Dodge et al., 1986).

The results of many studies offer support for the potential impact of this factor. For example, in one especially revealing experiment, Dodge and Coie (1987) measured boys' tendencies to attribute hostile intentions to others and then observed the boys' behavior while playing with other children. Results indicated that the greater the boys' tendency to demonstrate hostile attributional bias, the greater their tendency to engage in aggression.

Similar results have also been obtained with adolescents and adults. In one study on this topic, Dodge and his colleagues (1990) examined the relationship

Hostile Aggression ■ Aggression in which the prime objective is to inflict some kind of harm on the victim.

Instrumental Aggression ■ Aggression in which the primary goal is not to harm the victim but rather attainment of some other goal, such as access to valued resources.

Hostile Attributional Bias ■ Tendency to perceive others' actions as stemming from hostile intent even when this is not clearly the case.

between hostile attributional bias and aggression among a group of male adolescents confined to a maximum security prison for juvenile offenders. These young men had been convicted of a wide range of violent crimes, including murder, sexual assault, kidnapping, and armed robbery. The researchers hypothesized that hostile attributional bias among these youths would be related to the number of violent crimes they had committed, as well as to trained observers' ratings of the prisoners' tendencies to engage in aggression in response to provocation from others. Results offered support for both predictions. In sum, it appears that the tendency to perceive malice in the actions of others, even when it doesn't really exist, is one personal characteristic closely related to high levels of aggression against others.

Irritability, Rumination, and the "Big Five" Dimensions of Personality

In recent years, research on personality has converged on a startling conclusion: While people differ in a very large number of ways, many of these are related to only five underlying basic dimensions (Costa & McCrae, 1994; Funder & Sneed, 1993). These are shown in Table 11.2, and many studies indicate that they are, indeed, very basic dimensions of personality. For example, where individuals stand on several of these dimensions is readily apparent to strangers meeting them for the first time (Funder & Colvin, 1991; Watson, 1989). And standing on several of the "Big Five" dimensions is closely linked to satisfaction in and performance of many different jobs (Barrick & Mount, 1993). Are these dimensions also related to aggression? Research carried out by Caprara and his colleagues (e.g., Caprara et al., 1994) indicates that they are.

In these studies—most of which were conducted in European countries such as Italy—Caprara and his associates found that several traits, including *irritability* (the tendency to react impulsively or rudely to even slight provocations), *emotional reactivity* (the tendency to overreact emotionally to frustration), and *rumination* (the tendency to think about provocations and seek

---

TABLE 11.2   The "Big Five" Dimensions of Personality

A growing body of research findings indicate that the dimensions shown here are very basic ones with respect to human personality.

Dimension	Description
Extraversion	A dimension ranging from sociable, talkative, fun-loving, affectionate, adventurous at one end to retiring, sober, reserved, silent, and cautious at the other.
Agreeableness (**Related to Aggression**)	A dimension ranging from good-natured, gentle, cooperative, trusting, and helpful at one end to irritable, ruthless, suspicious, uncooperative, and headstrong at the other.
Conscientiousness	A dimension ranging from well-organized, careful, self-disciplined, responsible, and scrupulous at one end to disorganized, careless, weak-willed, and unscrupulous at the other.
Emotional Stability (**Related to Aggression**)	A dimension ranging from poised, calm, composed, and not hypochondriacal at one end to nervous, anxious, excitable, and hypochondriacal at the other.
Openness to Experience	A dimension ranging from imaginative, sensitive, intellectual, and polished at one end to down-to-earth, insensitive, crude, and simple at the other.

revenge for them), are all related to aggression (e.g., Caprara, 1986, 1987). These characteristics, in turn, have been found to be closely linked to two aspects of the "Big Five" dimensions of personality: *agreeableness* and *emotional stability*. In other words, persons who are high in irritability and emotional reactivity tend to fall toward the hostile end of the agreeableness–hostility "Big Five" dimension, while those who are high in rumination tend to fall toward the unstable end of the emotional stability dimension. So, in short, aggression appears to be related to two basic dimensions of personality—dimensions that have been found to be linked to many other aspects of social behavior as well. Moreover, these dimensions are ones that seem closely related to our own experiences with highly aggressive persons: often, these persons *do* seem to be disagreeable, suspicious, and hostile, as well as emotionally over-reactive and unstable.

Gender Differences in Aggression: Are They Real?

Are males more aggressive than females? Folklore suggests that they are, and research findings suggest that in this case, such informal observation is correct: when asked whether they have ever engaged in any of a wide range of aggressive actions, males report a higher incidence of many aggressive behaviors than do females (Harris, 1994, in press; see Figure 11.10). On closer examination, however, the picture regarding gender differences in aggression becomes more complex. On the one hand, males are generally more likely both to perform aggressive actions and to serve as the target for such behavior (Bogard, 1990; Harris, 1992, 1994)—although, as we noted earlier, incidents involving sexual jealousy appear to represent an important exception to this rule (de Weerth & Kalma, 1993; Harris, 1994). On the other hand, however, the size of these differences appears to vary greatly across situations.

First, gender differences in aggression are much larger in the absence of provocation than in its presence. In other words, males are significantly more likely than females to aggress against others when these persons have *not* pro-

FIGURE 11.10

Gender Differences in Aggression: More Complex Than You Might Guess. *Research evidence indicates that, as shown here, males are more likely to engage in* physical *aggression than females. However, females are more likely than males to engage in other forms of aggression, especially verbal and* indirect *forms.*

(*Source:* Reprinted with special permission of King Features Syndicate.)

voked them in any manner (Bettencourt & Miller, in press). In situations where provocation *is* present, in contrast, gender differences in aggression tend to shrink or even disappear. Further, the size—and even the direction—of gender differences in aggression seems to vary greatly with the *type* of aggression in question. While males are more likely than females to engage in various forms of *physical* aggression—hitting, punching, kicking, use of weapons—the opposite seems to be true with respect to verbal aggression and various *indirect* forms of aggression. Females actually seem to be more likely to engage in forms of aggression that make it difficult for victims to identify the aggressor, or even to realize that they have been the target of aggressive behavior (Bjorkqvist, Lagerspetz, & Kaukiainen, 1992). Among children, such indirect forms of aggression include telling lies or spreading rumors behind the target's back, replacing the person as a friend with a rival, and ignoring the target person. Research findings indicate that these gender differences are present among children as young as eight and increase through age fifteen (Bjorkqvist et al., 1992). And they seem to persist into adulthood as well. In fact, recent findings (Bjorkqvist, Osterman, & Hjelt-Back, 1994) can be interpreted as suggesting that although males show increased use of indirect forms of aggression as they mature, females continue to "outshine" them in this respect.

In sum, there do appear to be some differences between females and males with respect to aggression, but these are more subtle and complex than informal observation might suggest. If such differences do exist, though, the next question about them is obvious: *Why* do they occur? This is the issue we'll examine next.

The Origins of Gender Differences in Aggression: Genetics, Hormones, or Social Roles? As we've seen throughout this book, gender differences, when they occur, often appear to be smaller in magnitude and more restricted in scope than folklore suggests. Moreover, most social psychologists believe that when such differences occur, they are largely the result of social factors—contrasting expectations or stereotypes in a given society about what behavior is "appropriate" for females and males. You should not be surprised to learn, therefore, that many social psychologists explain gender differences in aggression in similar terms. For example, Eagly and her colleagues (Eagly, 1987; Eagly & Wood, 1991) offer a *social-role interpretation* for gender differences in aggression. According to this view, many societies expect males to be more assertive and masterful—and aggressive—than females, but also expect females to be more nurturant, more emotional, and more concerned for the well-being of others than males. It is these contrasting expectations, these researchers argue, that account for gender differences in aggression.

While such arguments are compelling and are supported by the findings of many studies (e.g., Eagly & Steffen, 1986), some evidence points to the conclusion that biological or genetic factors, too, play a role in the greater tendency of males to engage in at least some forms of aggression. Perhaps most convincing in this regard is the evidence suggesting that among males, the higher the level of testosterone (an important male sex hormone), the higher the level of aggression either reported or shown by research participants (e.g., Christiansen & Knussman, 1987; Olweus, 1986). We have already described one study reporting such results (Berman, Gladue, & Taylor, 1993), but a related investigation by Gladue (1991) adds some interesting facets to these findings.

In this study, male and female participants completed a measure of sexual orientation (heterosexual or homosexual) and a measure of the frequency with which they engaged in various forms of aggression—physical, verbal, impulsive. Samples of their blood were also taken and were analyzed for levels of various hormones, including testosterone. Results indicated that for males, the higher the concentration of testosterone in their blood, the greater their self-reported tendencies to engage in physical, verbal, and impulsive aggression. For females, in contrast, the higher the levels of testosterone, the *lower* their tendencies to engage in various forms of aggression.

Gladue (1991) also reasoned that if social factors and gender roles play a dominant part in differences between males and females with respect to aggression, then perhaps such differences might be larger among heterosexuals, because societal gender roles would apply to heterosexuals more than to homosexuals. If biological factors play an important role, however, the size of such differences should be the same for both groups. In other words, males should report higher levels of aggression than females, regardless of sexual orientation. Results supported this latter prediction. In addition, although levels of testosterone were much higher among males than females, there were no differences between homosexual and heterosexual males or females in testosterone levels.

Taken together, these findings and those of several other studies (e.g., Olweus, 1986) suggest that biological factors may indeed play a role in gender differences in aggression. It's important to realize, however, that even if hormonal and genetic factors play some role in gender differences in aggression, this in no way implies either (1) that males *must* show higher levels of aggression than females, or (2) that social factors such as gender stereotypes are unimportant in this regard. On the contrary, it seems clear that gender differences in aggression, like other gender differences we have considered, stem from a complex interplay of many different factors and are definitely *not* an unchangeable given where social behavior is concerned.

INTEGRATING PRINCIPLES

1. Several personal characteristics influence aggression. These include the Type A behavior pattern, the hostile attributional bias, and traits relating to the "Big Five" dimensions of personality.

2. These same characteristics also influence many other aspects of social behavior. For example, the Type A behavior pattern plays a role in behavior in work settings (Chapter 13), while the "Big Five" dimensions of personality are related to self-perceptions (Chapter 5) and behavior in groups (Chapter 12).

Child Abuse and Workplace Violence: Aggression in Long-Term Relationships

Reports of random acts of violence in which persons are attacked by total strangers are disturbing. Even more unsettling, however, are descriptions of instances in which individuals are harmed by persons they know or with whom they have long-term, intimate relationships. While such aggression takes many different forms, we'll focus here on what psychologists and others have discovered about two important forms of such aggression: child abuse (or *maltreatment;* Peterson & Brown, 1994) and workplace violence (Baron, 1995b).

Child Maltreatment: Harming the Innocent

Children, most adults would strongly agree, are to be cherished, protected, and loved. Yet a total of 2.7 million cases of **child maltreatment**—actions that harm children either physically or psychologically—occur each year in the United States alone (Children's Defense Fund, 1992). Such maltreatment takes many different forms, but most cases involve: (1) physical abuse (attacks that produce physical injuries); (2) sexual abuse (fondling, intercourse, and other forced sexual contacts); (3) physical neglect (living conditions in which children do not receive sufficient food, clothing, medical attention, or supervision); (4) emotional neglect (failure of parents or other adults to meet children's need for affection and emotional support); and/or (5) psychological abuse (actions that damage children emotionally, such as rejection and verbal abuse) (see Figure 11.11).

Who are the persons who commit such acts? At first glance, you might assume that they are some kind of monsters—seriously deranged persons who, perhaps, were abused themselves as children and are now perpetuating the cycle with their own youngsters. However, research findings indicate that while many persons who engage in child maltreatment were indeed mistreated themselves, many were not; many persons who mistreat children appear to be quite "normal" psychologically in other respects (e.g., Emery, 1989). In short, there does not appear to be a single "abusive personality type" against which we must be carefully on guard.

What, then, are the roots of this disturbing problem? Taking account of existing evidence on this issue, Peterson and Brown (1994) have recently offered a model of the factors responsible for many forms of child maltreatment. As shown in Figure 11.12 (p. 418), this model assumes that instances of child maltreatment involve *sociocultural variables*—factors such as poverty, crowded living conditions, frequent moves, and isolation from others; and *caregiver-based variables*—factors relating to caregivers, such as having been abused themselves as youngsters, emotional disturbances, substance abuse, being young and sin-

Child Maltreatment ■ Actions that harm children either physically or psychologically.

FIGURE 11.11

The Tragedy of Child Abuse. Each year, large numbers of children are physically abused by their parents or other adults. This is a form of aggression most people find especially abhorrent.

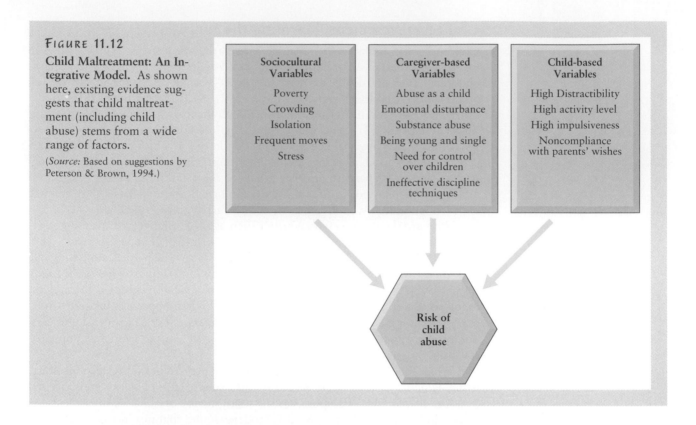

FIGURE 11.12

Child Maltreatment: An Integrative Model. As shown here, existing evidence suggests that child maltreatment (including child abuse) stems from a wide range of factors.

(*Source:* Based on suggestions by Peterson & Brown, 1994.)

gle, and intense needs for exerting control over their children. Finally, the model calls attention to the importance of *child-based variables*—characteristics of children that seem to be related to maltreatment. These include being highly distractible, showing a high activity level, being impulsive, and being resistant to parental control and discipline. In short, this model, which is based on the results of many different studies, suggests that child maltreatment arises out of a complex interplay among many different variables. The overall portrait that emerges is one in which parents living in disadvantaged backgrounds must cope with overactive, resistant children, and must do so under the burdens of their own emotional problems, youth, inexperience, and (often) dependence on drugs. This is not a pretty picture, but it does help explain why some parents and other caregivers, who should be delivering love and support to the children in their care, deliver something very different instead.

Do some of the variables shown in Figure 11.2 sound familiar? They should, because in a sense, we have examined many of these in earlier sections of this chapter, where we examined factors that have been shown to play important roles in human aggression. Poverty, crowding, and stress are all related to high levels of frustration, and as we saw earlier, this is one important trigger for human aggression. Emotional disturbances on the part of caregivers relate closely to the "Big Five" dimensions of emotional reactivity, irritability, and emotional instability—characteristics that have been found to be linked to outbursts of aggression. And high impulsiveness and disobedience on the part of children may serve as direct provocations to their caregivers—provocations that induce strong anger in these adults. In sum, the roots of child abuse are not in themselves mysterious: many of the factors that lead to this repulsive behavior also play a role in human aggression generally. What is unique is not the variables themselves, but rather the fact that they occur together, in a devastating combination.

Can anything be done to reduce the incidence of tragic instances of child maltreatment? We'll consider techniques for reducing aggression generally in a later section. Here, though, we should note that several procedures aimed specifically at child maltreatment have indeed been developed. Mirroring the model proposed by Peterson and Brown (1994), these procedures target the *environment,* the *caregivers,* and the *children.* With respect to the environment, interventions aimed at providing economic assistance and job training to disadvantaged families may prove effective (Willett, Ayoub, & Robinson, 1991). With respect to caregivers, programs designed to equip young, single parents with improved parenting skills—with better techniques for controlling their children than physical force—have been developed and found to be useful (e.g., Wolfe, 1991). Finally, in terms of child-related factors, efforts have been made to alert children to potential dangers (for example, of sexual abuse), and to teach them better self-control so that they will not push their parents or others over the edge (Peterson & Brown, 1994). Together, these and other procedures currently being developed may help to lessen the incidence, and hence the tragic consequences, of child maltreatment.

Familicide: Extreme Violence Within Families. While physical and psychological abuse of children are certainly disturbing, there are instances in which such behavior takes even more extreme forms. In these tragic cases, parents actually murder their own children. Such actions are often part of a larger pattern known as **familicide**—instances in which an individual kills his or her own spouse and one or more of his or her children. We say "his or her," but in fact, the vast majority of such actions are perpetrated by males. Indeed, in a recent study that examined all the cases of familicide in several countries during a sixteen-year period (Wilson et al., 1995), it was found that between 93% and 96% of these crimes were committed by males.

What factors lead individuals to perform such ghastly actions? Research on this issue suggests that two patterns are common. In the first, the killer expresses great anger against his wife, especially with respect to real or imagined sexual infidelities, or the wife's intention to leave the marriage. "If I can't have her, no one else will!" is how many of these murderers put it.

The second pattern involves suicide by the individual who has murdered his spouse and children, and seems to stem from deep depression. Such persons often state in their suicide notes that "this is the only way out," and they perform such actions when their personal lives become too painful to bear—for example, when illegal business activities are about to be revealed, or when they have experienced major failures. Whatever the precise reasons behind familicide, it is a truly frightening instance of aggression in the context of intimate relationships.

Workplace Violence: Aggression on the Job

Newark, N.J.—An ex–postal employee has confessed to slaughtering two of his former colleagues and two customers inside a Montclair, N.J., post office during a robbery for rent money, officials charged Wednesday. "He ordered them to lie down and he just shot them," said New Jersey U.S. Attorney Ruth Hochberg (Newsday, March 12, 1995).

New York—A young woman worked a blue-collar job alongside a young man who repeatedly asked her out. She told him she wasn't interested, and when he persisted, she filed a harassment claim. When he still didn't stop, she wrote a letter to the plant manager saying she feared for her safety. While the manager procrastinated, the man shot and killed the woman in

Familicide ■ Instances in which an individual kills his or her spouse and one or more of his or her children.

front of 125 other employees, then turned the gun on himself (Associated Press, June 12, 1994).

Reports of incidents such as these have appeared with alarming frequency in recent years, and appear to reflect a rising tide of violence in workplaces. In fact, an average of fifteen people are murdered at work each week in the United States alone, a total of more than 7,600 from the early 1980s through the early 1990s (National Institute for Occupational Safety and Health, 1993). During 1992, the last year for which complete data are available, the Bureau of Labor Statistics reports that 1,004 employees were killed on the job—a rate more than one-third higher than the annual average during the 1980s.

While these statistics seem to suggest that workplaces are becoming truly violent locations where disgruntled employees frequently shoot or otherwise attack one another, two facts should be carefully noted: (1) A large majority of violence occurring in work settings takes place in connection with robberies and related crimes; it does *not* generally involve instances in which angry employees suddenly open fire on coworkers or supervisors. And (2) recent surveys indicate that threats of physical harm or actual harm in work settings are actually quite rare—only 7 percent and 3 percent of employees of companies in one large-scale study reported such experiences (Northwestern National Life Insurance Company, 1993).

In sum, growing evidence suggests that while overt *violence* in workplaces is certainly an important topic worthy of careful study, it is actually only the dramatic tip of a much larger problem—what might more appropriately be termed **workplace aggression** (Neuman & Baron, in press). In other words, while some employees are indeed the victims of murderous attacks, vastly larger numbers are on the receiving end of less dramatic forms of aggression (see, e.g., Bjorkqvist, Osterman, & Hjelt-Back, 1994). What is such aggression like? Growing evidence suggests that it is largely covert in nature. In other words, it is designed to inflict harm on the intended victim while preventing this person from identifying the source of aggression—or, perhaps, even from knowing that she or he has been the victim of intentional harm-doing. This type of aggression is strongly preferred for two reasons. First, in work settings there are many potential witnesses to acts of aggression, and in general they disapprove of such behavior. Covert aggression, of course, avoids such problems. Second, since would-be aggressors in workplaces usually expect to interact with their intended victims in the future, they prefer covert forms of aggression because these lessen the likelihood of retaliation.

What is *covert* aggression like? A framework developed by Arnold Buss (whose research we discussed in the *Cornerstones* section on page 398), suggests that it would tend to be *verbal* rather than *physical*, passive rather than *active*, and *indirect* rather than *direct*. Verbal forms of aggression involve efforts to inflict harm on others through words rather than deeds, while physical forms of aggression involve overt actions intended to harm the victim in some manner. Direct forms of aggression are delivered directly to the victim while indirect forms are delivered through the actions of other agents or through assaults on persons or objects valued by the victim (e.g., damage to the victim's property, family, or friends; Lagerspetz and Bjorkqvist, 1994). Finally, active aggression produces harm through the performance of some action while passive aggression produces harm through the withholding of some action. Examples of each of the eight forms of aggression suggested by Buss's (1961) framework are presented in Table 11.3, which suggests that covert aggression in workplaces takes many different forms.

Evidence that verbal, indirect, and passive forms of aggression are actually more common in work settings than other types has recently been reported by

Workplace Aggression ■
Aggression occurring in work settings.

TABLE 11.3 Aggression in Workplaces

As shown here, aggression in workplaces can take many different forms, and can be either physical or verbal, active or passive, and direct or indirect.

Type of Aggression	Examples
Verbal–Passive–Indirect	Failing to deny false rumors about the target. Failing to transmit information needed by the target.
Verbal–Passive–Direct	Failing to return the target's phone calls. Giving the target the silent treatment.
Verbal–Active–Indirect	Spreading false rumors about the target. Belittling the target's opinions to others.
Verbal–Active–Direct	Yelling, shouting, making insulting remarks. Flaunting status or authority; acting in a condescending, superior manner.
Physical–Passive–Indirect	Causing others to delay action on matters of importance to the target. Failing to take steps that would protect the target's welfare or safety.
Physical–Passive–Direct	Purposely leaving a work area when target enters. Reducing targets' opportunities to express themselves (e.g., scheduling them at the end of a session so that they don't get their turn).
Physical–Active–Indirect	Theft or destruction of property belonging to the target. Needlessly consuming resources needed by the target.
Physical–Active–Direct	Physical attack (e.g., pushing, shoving, hitting). Negative or obscene gestures toward the target.

Baron and Neuman (in press). These researchers asked advanced business students to rate (on five-point scales) the frequency with which they had witnessed or experienced forty different forms of aggression. These forms were chosen to represent all eight combinations within the Buss framework. As shown in Figure 11.13 (p. 422), results indicated that participants reported witnessing verbal more frequently than physical forms of aggression. In addition, they reported witnessing passive more frequently than active forms of aggression, and indirect more often than direct forms of aggression. Thus, there was some support for the view that much of the aggression occurring in workplaces is indeed covert rather than overt in nature.

Is Workplace Aggression Increasing, and If So, Why? The growing number of media reports of violence in workplaces seems to suggest that such behavior is increasing; is this actually so? And what about workplace *aggression*—is it increasing as well? Existing evidence does not yet provide clear answers to these questions, but there do appear to be grounds for suggesting that such an increase has already occurred, or is currently taking place. The basis for this suggestion is straightforward: in recent years, many organizations have undergone far-reaching changes, and several of these changes appear to be ones that may have set the stage for increased aggression by generating conditions known to facilitate such behavior. Among the most important of these changes are *downsizing and layoffs,* which have increased frustration and uncertainty for millions of employees, and *increased diversity in the workforce,* which offers fertile ground for the operation of negative stereotypes such as those we discussed in Chapter 6. In addition, because of large budget cuts, the physical conditions present in many work settings have worsened, thus exposing many employees

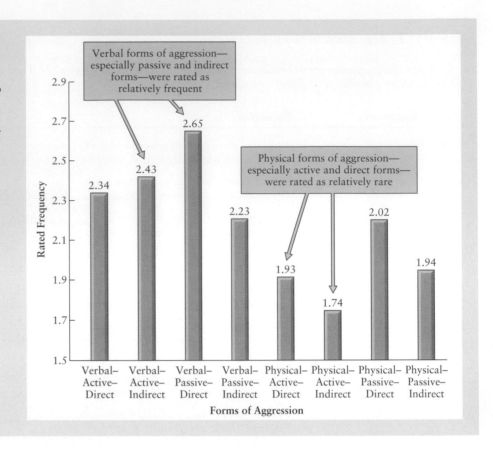

FIGURE 11.13

Relative Frequency of Different Types of Workplace Aggression. When asked to rate the frequency of a wide range of aggressive actions in work settings, individuals reported witnessing verbal, passive, and indirect aggressive behaviors more frequently than physical, active, or direct aggressive actions.

(*Source:* Based on data from Baron & Neuman, in press.)

to environmentally generated sources of negative affect (Baron, 1994; Hammer & Champy, 1993). Together, these changes may have created conditions in many workplaces that are known to encourage aggressive behavior. We should hasten to add that as yet there is no conclusive evidence that workplace changes have led to such effects, although in one recent study (Baron & Neuman, in press), the amount of aggression reported by employees did correlate positively with the magnitude of such changes in their organizations. In any case, uncovering the causes of workplace violence and aggression is essential, because only when these factors are identified can effective procedures for preventing and controlling such aggression be developed.

What would these procedures be like? For some ideas, please turn to the next section, where we cover several steps for the prevention and control of aggression.

The Prevention and Control of Aggression: Some Useful Techniques

If there is one idea in this chapter we hope you'll remember in the years ahead, it is this: Aggression is *not* an inevitable or unmodifiable form of behavior. On the contrary, since it stems from a complex interplay between external events, cognitions, and personal characteristics, it *can* be prevented or reduced. In this final section, we'll consider several procedures that, when used appropriately, can be effective in this regard.

FIGURE 11.14

Capital Punishment: A Continuing Controversy. Many states in the United States, and many other countries, execute persons convicted of murder and other crimes of violence. Whether this serves as a useful deterrent to other potential criminals remains an open question.

Punishment: An Effective Deterrent to Violence?

In New York state, where we both live, a key issue in the election for governor in 1994 was *capital punishment*—the death penalty for certain crimes of violence (see Figure 11.14). Former Governor Mario Cuomo was resolutely against capital punishment; in fact, he vetoed it twelve years in a row when it was passed by the state legislature. The new governor, George Pataki, favored capital punishment and quickly signed it into law when it was passed once again by the state legislature. Although these two governors had many reasons for opposing or favoring the death penalty, one that was emphasized in the election was its potential value as a *deterrent*. Governor Cuomo felt that capital punishment would *not* deter criminals from engaging in aggressive acts, while Governor Pataki felt that it would. As we'll explain below, this is a complex issue, and evidence relating to it is mixed. Thus, we can't hope to resolve it here (Baron & Richardson, 1994). What we *can* do, however, is point out a few pertinent facts about the use of **punishment**—delivery of aversive consequences in order to decrease some behavior—as a technique for reducing overt aggression.

First, we should note that existing evidence points to the conclusion that punishment *can* succeed in deterring individuals from engaging in many forms of behavior. However, such effects are neither automatic nor certain. Unless punishment is administered in accordance with basic principles, it can be totally *ineffective* in this respect. What conditions must be met for punishment

Punishment ■ Delivery of aversive consequences in order to decrease some behavior.

to succeed? First, it must be prompt—it must follow aggressive actions as quickly as possible. Second, it must be *certain*—the probability that punishment will follow aggression must be 100 percent. Third, it must be *strong*—it must be of sufficient magnitude to be highly unpleasant to potential recipients. Finally, it must be seen as *justified;* if, in contrast, it is perceived by recipients as random or unrelated to their past actions, its deterrent effects will be greatly reduced.

Unfortunately, as you can readily see, these conditions are often *not* present in the criminal justice systems of many nations. In many societies, the delivery of punishment for aggressive actions is delayed for months or even years; many criminals avoid arrest and conviction; the magnitude of punishment itself varies from one courtroom or jurisdiction to another; and punishment *is* often perceived as unjustified or unfair by those who receive it. In view of these facts, it is hardly surprising that punishment often seems to fail as a deterrent to violent crime. The dice, so to speak, are heavily loaded against it. Would punishment prove effective as a deterrent to violence if it were used more effectively? While we can't say for certain, existing evidence does suggest that it could, potentially, exert such effects. But again, this would be so only if it were used in accordance with the principles noted above.

Now, before concluding, let's return briefly to the issue of capital punishment. Putting aside the complex ethical issues it raises, we can ask: Is it an effective deterrent to crimes of violence? As currently used, we doubt it. So few people are ever executed that everyone—potential criminals included—realizes the probability of experiencing this fate is close to nonexistent. Under these conditions, it is difficult to see how capital punishment could be expected to exert any measurable effects. But there may be another justification for such punishment—one that is rarely mentioned in debates of this issue. While capital punishment may not deter others from performing aggressive acts, it does indeed make it impossible for those who receive it to harm additional defenseless victims. This may be an important consideration, because sad to relate, many crimes of violence are performed by repeat offenders—persons who were previously convicted of violent crimes but are now back on the street. We should hasten to add that all forms of punishment, and capital punishment especially, raise important ethical issues that neither we nor any other psychologists can resolve. However, given the rising tide of violence in the United States and elsewhere, it does seem important to examine carefully every available means for protecting innocent victims.

Catharsis: Does Getting It Out of Your System Really Help?

When I (RAB) was a little boy, my grandmother used to greet my temper tantrums with the following comment: "That's right, Bobby, get it out . . . don't keep it inside or it will make you sick!" She truly believed in the **catharsis hypothesis**—the view that if individuals give vent to their anger and hostility in some relatively nonharmful way, their tendencies to more dangerous forms of aggression may be reduced (Dollard et al., 1939).

Is this actually true? Existing evidence offers a mixed picture (Feshbach, 1984; Geen, 1991). On the one hand, participation in various activities that are not harmful to others (e.g., vigorous sports activities, attacking a photo of one's archenemy, shouting obscenities into an empty room) can reduce emotional arousal stemming from frustration or provocation (Zillmann, 1979). Unfortunately, though, such effects appear to be temporary. Arousal stemming from

Catharsis Hypothesis ■ Theory that if angry persons can express their aggressive impulses in relatively safe ways, they will be less likely to engage in more harmful forms of aggression.

provocation may reappear as soon as individuals think once again about the incidents that made them angry (Caprara et al., 1994; Zillmann, 1988).

What about the idea that performing "safe" aggressive actions reduces the likelihood of more harmful forms of aggression? Results in this respect are even less encouraging. Overt aggression, it appears, is not reduced by (1) watching scenes of filmed or televised violence (Geen, 1978), (2) attacking inanimate objects (Mallick & McCandless, 1966), or aggressing verbally against others. Indeed, there is some evidence that aggression may actually be *increased* by these activities.

In short, contrary to popular belief, catharsis does not appear to be a very effective means for reducing aggression. Participating in "safe" forms of aggression or merely in vigorous, energy-draining activities may produce temporary reductions in arousal; but feelings of anger may quickly return when individuals meet, or merely think about, the persons who previously annoyed them. For this reason, catharsis may be less effective in producing lasting reductions in aggression than has often been assumed.

Cognitive Interventions: Apologies and Overcoming Cognitive Deficits

Let's return once again to our shopping cart example. This time, imagine that immediately after ramming you, the other shopper apologizes profusely. "Excuse me!" she says, obviously upset. "Are you hurt? I'm so sorry!" Will you get angry? Probably not. Her apology—an admission of wrongdoing plus a request for forgiveness—will go a long way toward defusing your emotional reaction. Of course, your reactions will depend strongly on the nature of her excuses—and on the apparent sincerity of her apologies. Research findings suggest that excuses that make reference to causes beyond the excuse-giver's control are much more effective than ones that refer to events within this person's control (Weiner et al., 1987). And we are much less likely to get angry when apologies seem to be sincere than when they appear to be an attempt to conceal true malicious intent (Baron, 1989; Ohbuchi, Kameda, & Agarie, 1989). So both excuses and apologies can be effective as cognitive strategies for reducing aggression.

Other cognitive techniques are related to the concept of *cognitive deficit* that we discussed earlier. As you may recall, this refers to the fact that when we experience strong anger, our ability to evaluate the consequences of our own actions may be reduced. As a result, the effectiveness of restraints that normally serve to hold aggression in check (e.g., fear of retaliation) may be reduced. Any procedures that serve to overcome this cognitive deficit, then, may help reduce overt aggression (Zillmann, 1993). One such technique involves *preattribution*—attributing annoying actions by others to *unintentional* causes before the provocation actually occurs. For example, before meeting with someone you know can be irritating, you could remind yourself that she or he doesn't mean to make you angry—it's just the result of an unfortunate personal style. Another technique involves preventing yourself—or others—from ruminating about previous real or imagined wrongs (Zillmann, 1993). You can accomplish this by participating in pleasant, absorbing activities that have no connection to anger and aggression—anything from watching a funny movie or television program to solving interesting puzzles. Such activities allow for a cooling-off period during which anger can dissipate, and also help to reestablish cognitive controls over behavior—controls that play a key role in inhibiting overt aggression.

Other Techniques for Reducing Aggression: Exposure to Nonaggressive Models, Training in Social Skills, and Incompatible Responses

Many other techniques for reducing overt aggression have been suggested. Here, we'll briefly consider three that appear to be quite effective.

Exposure to Nonaggressive Models: The Contagion of Restraint. If exposure to aggressive actions by others in films or on television can increase aggression, it seems possible that exposure to *non*aggressive actions might produce opposite effects. In fact, the results of several studies indicate that this is so (e.g., Baron, 1972; Donnerstein & Donnerstein, 1976). When individuals who have been frustrated or provoked are exposed to others who either demonstrate or urge restraint, the tendency of potential aggressors to lash out is reduced. These findings suggest that it may be useful to plant restrained, nonaggressive models in tense and potentially dangerous situations. Their presence may well serve to tip the balance against the occurrence of violence.

Training in Social Skills: Learning to Get Along with Others. One reason why many persons become involved in aggressive encounters is that they are sorely lacking in basic social skills. They don't know how to respond to provocations from others in a way that will soothe these persons rather than inflame them. Similarly, they don't know how to make their wishes known to others, and they grow increasingly frustrated when people don't take account of these wishes. Persons lacking in basic social skills seem to account for a high proportion of violence in many societies (Toch, 1985). Thus, equipping these individuals with the social skills they so sorely lack may go a long way toward reducing the incidence of aggression.

Fortunately, systematic procedures for teaching individuals such skills do exist, and they are not very complex. For example, both adults and children can rapidly acquire improved social skills from watching *social models*—people who demonstrate both effective and ineffective behaviors (Schneider, 1991). Moreover, such gains can be obtained through just a few hours of treatment (Bienert & Schneider, 1993). These findings serve to underscore the following points: (1) Highly aggressive persons—children and adults—are not necessarily "bad" individuals who attack others because of uncontrollable hostile impulses; (2) their aggression often stems from deficits in basic social skills; and (3) such deficits can readily be overcome.

Incompatible Responses: Positive Affect As a Means of Reducing Anger. Suppose that you were in a situation where you felt yourself growing angry, and then suddenly someone told a joke that made you laugh. Would you remain angry? Or would the likelihood that you'd lose your temper be reduced? A growing body of evidence suggests that your laughter, and the positive feelings associated with it, might well help to counter both anger and overt aggression (see Figure 11.15; Baron, 1993). This is because it is extremely difficult, if not impossible, to engage in two **incompatible responses** or experience two incompatible emotional states at once.

What stimuli or experiences are incompatible with aggression? Research findings indicate that humor, mild sexual arousal, and feelings of empathy toward the victim are all effective in reducing overt aggression (e.g., Baron, 1983, 1993). For example, consider a recent study on the aggression-inhibiting effects of empathy conducted by Richardson and her colleagues (Richardson et al., 1994). These researchers had male college students participate in the kind of competitive reaction time task we described earlier—the task in which the per-

Incompatible Responses ■ In relation to aggression, responses that are incompatible with anger or overt aggression against others.

FIGURE 11.15

Incompatible Responses in Action. *As suggested by this cartoon, it is difficult (if not impossible) to remain angry and experience feelings of amusement at the same time. This basic fact provides the basis for the incompatible response technique for reducing aggression.*

(*Source:* Drawing by C. Barsotti; © 1989 *The New Yorker* Magazine, Inc.)

"Well, darn, Ted, I just can't stay mad at you."

son slower to respond receives an electric shock from his opponent. Before performing this task, half of the participants were told to try to understand how the other person was feeling on each trial; the others were not given these empathy-inducing instructions. Results indicated that as expected, those told to imagine how the other person was feeling delivered weaker shocks to their opponent. So, as predicted, empathy toward the potential victim did tend to reduce aggression. These findings, and those of many other studies (e.g., Baron, 1993) suggest that when angry persons are induced to experience feelings or emotions incompatible with aggression, their tendency to engage in overt aggression is often reduced. Thus, incompatible responses, too, can be a useful strategy for reducing overt aggression.

INTEGRATING PRINCIPLES

1. Several different techniques useful in preventing or reducing human aggression are suggested by basic principles of social psychology.

2. These include inducing individuals to attribute provocative actions to causes other than personal malice (attributions; see Chapter 2), equipping them with improved social skills (modeling; see Chapters 6 and 10), and exposing them to stimuli that induce emotional states incompatible with anger or aggression (the interplay between affect and cognition; see Chapter 3).

Social Diversity: A Critical Analysis
CULTURAL AND ETHNIC DIFFERENCES IN AGGRESSION

EARLIER IN THIS CHAPTER, WE REFERRED TO THE FACT THAT levels of aggression vary greatly across different cultures.

This conclusion is supported by many studies in which the frequency of various forms of aggression—for instance, physical and verbal—in various cultures have been compared (e.g., Huesmann & Eron, 1986; Fraczek, 1985). In one of these studies, for example, levels of aggression in 137 different societies were examined (Burbank, 1987), and findings indicated that truly huge differences existed.

That such differences are present among adults, on whom most of these investigations have focused, is not surprising. By the time they are adults, individuals have been immersed in the norms of their culture for many years and have had ample time to learn what their culture has to say about aggression: when it's appropriate, what forms it should take, who are suitable targets. But what about children? Do they reflect these cultural norms and values even at a young age? A recent study conducted by Ostermann and her colleagues (Ostermann et al., 1994) suggests that in fact, they do.

In this investigation, the researchers studied the incidence of three types of aggression (verbal, physical, and indirect) among eight-year-old children in several different cultural and ethnic groups. The groups included children from Poland, two groups from Finland (Finnish-speaking and Swedish-speaking children), and two groups from the United States (African American children and Caucasian children). Several hundred children were interviewed individually, and the researchers asked a series of questions about physical, verbal, and in-

direct forms of aggression. Some examples: "Who hits when they get angry with others?" (physical). "Who yells when they get angry with others?" (verbal). "Who tells bad or false stories about others when they get angry?" (indirect). In addition, the children were also asked to indicate how often the person or persons named engaged in each behavior. They were shown photos of all the students in their class while being asked these questions, and answered by pointing to the appropriate persons. Their own photo was included, so they could also nominate themselves.

Results indicated that very large differences in aggression existed across the groups studied. As you can see from Figure 11.16, the African American youngsters stood out as the most aggressive, followed by the Caucasian American children. This pattern was true both for peer estimations of aggression (the average ratings given to each child by other members of her or his class) and for self estimations of aggression (when the children named and rated themselves). An additional finding of interest was that across all cultures, the children rated others as being more aggressive than themselves. In other words, they showed the typical *self-serving attributional bias* we discussed in Chapter 2—the tendency to attribute negative actions or outcomes to others and positive actions or outcomes to oneself.

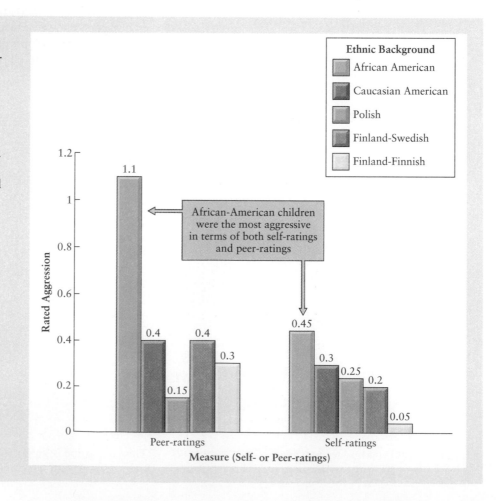

FIGURE 11.16

Cultural and Ethnic Differences in Aggression. As shown here, African American children in the United States were more aggressive (both in self-ratings and in ratings by peers) than Caucasian children in the United States and children in Poland and Finland. Such differences stem from many different factors, including different cultural norms concerning aggression.

(*Source:* Based on data from Ostermann et al., 1994.)

What accounts for the difference in aggression levels among children of different cultures? Ostermann and her colleagues didn't focus specifically on this important question. However, the fact that the African American participants—the children who were most aggressive—came from inner-city neighborhoods of Chicago is suggestive. Such youngsters are exposed to a great deal of aggression; indeed, some studies indicate that by the time they are twelve or thirteen, almost half of all inner-city African American children have actually seen someone shot (Shakook & Chalmers, 1991). Given the powerful impact of modeling on behavior, it seems possible that being raised in an environment filled with violence may contribute to the higher level of aggression shown by these youngsters. Further, social norms in such environ-

ments—and perhaps in American society generally—seem to offer more support for settling interpersonal differences aggressively than do corresponding norms in other cultures (e.g., Hammond & Yung, 1993). Pending the completion of additional research, such suggestions are mainly speculative in nature; but they are consistent with what we know about the various social factors that contribute to human aggression (e.g., Baron & Richardson, 1994).

In sum, large ethnic or cultural differences in aggression appear to be present even among young children. Culture, it seems, sets the "ground rules" for aggression early in life, and once established, these rules exert strong effects on such behavior throughout the remainder of adult life.

CONNECTIONS: Integrating Social Psychology

In this chapter, you read about . . .

cognitive theories of aggression

social factors that play a role in aggression

personal characteristics that influence aggression

In other chapters, you will find related discussions of . . .

cognitive theories relating to other forms of social behavior: attitude change (Chapter 4), prejudice (Chapter 6), helping (Chapter 10)

the effects of these factors on other forms of social behavior: attributions (Chapter 2), arousal (Chapter 7), social models (Chapter 10)

the roles of these characteristics in several other forms of social behavior: gender differences in mate selection (Chapters 1, 7, 8), susceptibility to social influence (Chapter 9), and leadership (Chapter 12), Type A behavior pattern and organizational conflict (Chapter 13)

Thinking about Connections

1. Attorneys sometimes defend individuals who commit violent acts—including murder—by suggesting that these persons were "overwhelmed" by emotions beyond their control. In view of our discussions in other chapters (e.g., Chapter 3, Chapter 10) of the effects of emotions on social thought and social behavior, what are your reactions to such defenses? And do you think that such reactions, if they occur, excuse the persons who commit such acts from personal responsibility for them?

2. As we noted in Chapter 8, intimate relationships are complex. They involve many different aspects of social thought and social behavior. What aspects of intimate relationships do you think

might determine how the persons in them react to sexual jealousy? In other words, what facets of intimate relationships might determine whether such jealousy would result in overt aggression?

3. Violence, and perhaps other forms of aggression, too, appears to be increasing in many workplaces. Do you think it would be possible to screen potential employees, so as to reduce the frequency or intensity of such behavior? In other words, on the basis of our discussions of personality throughout this book, as well as in this chapter, do you think there might be some traits it would be best to avoid in potential employees, and others that it would be desirable to seek?

Summary and Review

Theoretical Perspectives on Aggression

Aggression—the intentional infliction of harm on others—has been attributed to many different causes. *Instinct theories,* such as the ones proposed by Freud and Lorenz, suggest that aggression stems from innate urges. *Biological theories* suggest that aggression is influenced, at least to some degree, by biological factors such as sex hormones and various neural disorders. *Drive theories* suggest that aggression stems from externally generated motives. The *social learning view,* in contrast, emphasizes the role of learning, calling attention to the fact that human beings learn how to aggress against others through both direct and vicarious experience. Finally, *cognitive theories* of aggression suggest that aggression stems from a complex interplay among cognitive factors, past experiences, and current moods.

Social Determinants of Aggression

Many acts of aggression are triggered by the words or deeds of persons with whom the aggressor interacts, or by social conditions generally. *Frustration*—interference with goal-directed behavior—can facilitate aggression, perhaps because of the negative feelings it generates; but frustration is *not* the only or the strongest determinant of aggression. *Direct provocations* from others are important causes of aggression, especially when such actions appear to stem from malevolent intent. Exposure to *media violence* (in films or television shows) can increase aggression on the part of viewers.

Heightened arousal can increase aggression. However, the impact of arousal on aggression depends on the complex interplay between emotions and cognitions. Cognitions—for example, our interpretations of the motives behind others' behavior—can strongly influence our emotional reactions to provocation. Similarly, strong emotions can interfere with our ability to formulate rational plans or to assess the likely results of our behavior—an effect known as *cognitive deficit.*

Sexual jealousy—perception of a threat to a romantic relationship from a rival for one's partner—often plays an important role in aggression. Interestingly, recent research suggests that such reactions may often be stronger among women than men. Exposure to violent forms of pornography may also increase aggression, although growing evidence suggests that such effects are due to the violent content of such films or tapes rather than their explicit sexual content.

Personal Causes of Aggression

Persons showing the *Type A behavior pattern* are more aggressive in many situations than persons showing the *Type B behavior pattern.* Individuals who perceive hostile intent behind others' actions, even when this does not really exist, are more aggressive than those who do not show this *hostile attributional bias.* Recent findings indicate that several traits related to aggression—for example, *irritability* and *rumination* (the tendency think about real or imagined provocations)—are closely related to the "Big Five" dimensions of personality. Specifically, aggression-related traits appear to be linked to the dimensions of *agreeableness* and *emotional stability.*

Males are more aggressive overall than females. However, these differences occur primarily in situations where provocation is lacking; when provoked, males and females do not differ appreciably in level of aggression. In addition, while males tend to show higher levels of physical aggression than females, females demonstrate higher levels of *indirect* aggression than males. Both cultural and biological factors may be involved in these gender differences in aggression.

Child Abuse and Workplace Violence: Aggression in Long-Term Relationships

Child maltreatment takes many different forms, including *child abuse*—instances in which children are physically harmed by adults. Child abuse stems from many different factors. These include: *sociocultural variables,* such as poverty, crowded living conditions, and isolation from others; *caregiver-based variables,* including caregivers' having been abused as youngsters themselves, having emotional disturbances, and/or being young and single; and *child-based variables,* such as high levels of activity, high impulsiveness, and being resistant to parental control. Intervention techniques focused on these causes may be effective in reducing this tragic form of aggression.

Workplace violence is alarmingly frequent, but careful analysis of such incidents indicates that most occur in the context of other crimes (e.g., robberies). Thus, workplace violence may constitute only the disturbing tip of a larger problem—*workplace aggression.* Such aggression is usually *covert* in nature—it takes forms that allow aggressors to disguise their identity and the aggressive nature of their actions from victims. Recent changes in many work settings—for instance, downsizing, and increasing ethnic diversity, and increasingly unpleasant physical conditions—may be setting the stage for increased levels of workplace aggression by generating high levels of frustration and negative affect among employees.

The Prevention and Control of Aggression

Several techniques are effective in reducing aggression. *Punishment* can be effective if it is delivered swiftly and surely, is intense, and is perceived as justified. *Capital punishment* does not appear to be an effective deterrent to aggression by other potential criminals, but does prevent highly aggressive persons from harming additional victims. Participation in *cathartic activities* (e.g., vigorous nonaggressive behaviors) can sometimes lower arousal and anger. Such reductions are only temporary, however, and anger may quickly reappear when individuals think about events that previously made them angry.

Direct *apologies* can sometimes deter aggression. In addition, several techniques help to overcome the *cognitive deficits* produced by intense anger. These include *preattribution*—attributing provocative actions by others to causes other than malice *before* these provocations occur—and participation in activities that divert attention away from anger-producing events or situations. Additional techniques for reducing aggression include exposure to *nonaggressive models*, training in basic *social skills*, and the induction of *incompatible responses*—reactions incompatible with anger or overt aggression.

■ Key Terms

Aggression (p. 392)

Aggression Machine (p. 399)

Catharsis Hypothesis (p. 424)

Child Maltreatment (p. 417)

Cognitive Theories (of aggression) (p. 397)

Drive Theories (of aggression) (p. 395)

Excitation Transfer Theory (p. 405)

Familicide (p. 419)

Frustration–Aggression Hypothesis (p. 400)

Hostile Aggression (p. 412)

Hostile Attributional Bias (p. 412)

Incompatible Responses (p. 426)

Instinct Theory (p. 393)

Instrumental Aggression (p. 412)

Provocation (p. 401)

Punishment (p. 423)

Sexual Jealousy (p. 407)

Social Learning View (p. 396)

Type A Behavior Pattern (p. 411)

Type B Behavior Pattern (p. 411)

Workplace Aggression (p. 420)

■ For More Information

Baenninger, R. (Ed.). (1991). *Targets of violence and aggression.* Amsterdam: Elsevier/North-Holland.

Deals with aggression toward targets that are either helpless or unable to retaliate. Separate chapters (each written by a different expert) explore such important and timely topics as human aggression toward other species, child abuse, athletes as targets of aggression, aggression toward homosexuals, and aggression along roadways. A comprehensive overview of what we currently know about several especially distressing forms of violence.

Baron, R. A., & Richardson, D. R. (1994). *Human aggression,* (2nd ed.). New York: Plenum.

This book provides a broad introduction to current knowledge about human aggression. Separate chapters focus on the biological, social, environmental, and personal determinants of aggression. Additional chapters examine the development of aggression and the incidence of aggression in many natural settings.

Geen, R. G. (1991). *Human aggression.* Pacific Grove, CA: Brooks/Cole.

A well-written and relatively brief overview of research findings concerning aggressive behavior. One unique chapter integrates laboratory research on aggression with findings in behavioral medicine concerning potential links between hostility and heart disease.

Felson, R. B., & Tedeschi, J. T. (Eds.). (1993). Washington, DC: *Aggression and violence: Social interactionist perspectives.* American Psychological Association.

Distinguished researchers from several fields (psychology, sociology, criminology) consider aggression from several different perspectives. Intriguing hypotheses concerning the causes of aggression, and the roles of such factors as social power and the self-serving effects of conflict, are examined.

Huesmann, L. R. (Ed.). (1994). *Aggressive behavior: Current perspectives.* New York: Plenum.

A collection of chapters by well-known researchers, dealing with many different aspects of aggression. The chapters on gender differences, the long-term effects of exposure to media violence, and delinquent gangs are especially interesting, and expand on topics covered in this book.

CHAPTER 12

GROUPS AND INDIVIDUALS:
The Consequences of Belonging

Lisa Houck, *Studying Fish Behavior in the Mid-Atlantic*, 1991, watercolor, 23 × 46"

Chapter Outline

Suppose you were sitting in a dentist's office, waiting your turn, when a very attractive person entered and sat down opposite you. Would your behavior change in any way?

Have you ever felt that you were being treated unfairly by other persons—for example, by one of your professors or by a company for which you worked?

Imagine that you were part of a group that had to make an important decision. Suppose that later, after making it, your group learned that its decision had been a bad one. Would you and the other members feel any pressure to stick with it anyway?

Quick: Can you name any current leaders (political, spiritual, military, or otherwise) that you consider to be truly great?

These are intriguing questions, and although they seem diverse, social psychologists would argue that they are actually related: all refer to various aspects of *group influence*—the effects of being part of (or belonging to) social groups. As you'll soon see, group influence is a pervasive and powerful force. All of us belong to many different social groups, and the effects of such membership can be profound. To provide you with an overview of the scope and impact of group influence, we'll focus in this chapter on five important topics. First, we'll consider the basic nature of groups: what they are and how they exert their effects on individuals. Second, we'll examine the impact of groups on *task performance*—how our performance on various tasks can be affected by working with others, or merely by their presence on the scene (as in the first question above). Third, we'll turn to the question of *fairness* in groups. As we'll soon see, individuals' beliefs that they are, or are not, being treated fairly can influence many aspects of their behavior. Fourth, we'll examine *decision making* in groups, focusing on the ways in which groups can affect, and sometimes distort, this important process. Finally, we'll conclude with a discussion of *leadership*—why certain individuals become leaders and how they influence other group members.

Groups: Their Nature and Function

Look at the photos in Figure 12.1. Which show social groups? Probably you would identify the two top photos as involving groups, but the one in the bottom as showing a mere collection of persons. Why? Because implicitly, you already accept a definition of the term **group** close to the one adopted by social psychologists: *A group consists of two or more interacting persons who share common goals, have a stable relationship, are somehow interdependent, and perceive that they are in fact part of a group* (Paulus, 1989). Let's examine this definition more closely.

First, the definition suggests that to be part of a group, individuals must usually *interact* with each other, either directly or indirectly. Second, they must be *interdependent* in some manner—what happens to one must affect what happens to the others. Third, their relationship must be relatively *stable*; it must persist over appreciable periods of time (days, weeks, months, or even years). Fourth, the individuals involved must share at least some goals that they all seek to attain. Fifth, their interactions must be *structured* in some manner so that, for instance, each group member performs the same or similar functions each time they meet. Finally, the persons involved must recognize that they are part of a group.

Are all these conditions really necessary before we can describe several persons as belonging to a group? While all are important, it's crucial to note that

Group ■ Two or more persons who interact with one another, share common goals, are somehow interdependent, and recognize that they belong to a group.

FIGURE 12.1

What Makes a Group a Group? In order for two or more persons to be termed a *group*, several criteria must be met. The left photo shows an actual social group; the right photo shows a mere collection of individuals who are *not* part of a group.

there are varying degrees of groupness. At the high end, for instance, are groups consisting of persons who have worked together for many years. Clearly, they meet all requirements of the definition. At the low end are persons who have only a fleeting relationship with one another—for example, the passengers on an airplane. They are interdependent to a degree: if one blocks the aisle, others can't pass. They share certain basic goals, such as getting safely to their destination. But they don't expect to interact in the future and usually don't perceive themselves as part of a group—unless there is an emergency in flight, which can change this picture radically. In between these extremes are many social entities that we might be more or less inclined to describe as *groups*. So, in brief, deciding whether a collection of persons constitute a true group is a complex matter, one of degree, rather than a simple yes/no decision. Having said this, we should note that many social psychologists feel that the key issue is whether the persons involved perceive themselves as part of a group. Only to the extent they do does it make sense to talk about a social group (Moreland, 1987).

Group Formation: Why Do People Join Groups?

Think about all the groups to which you belong at present: clubs, student associations, religious groups, informal groups consisting of the people with whom you hang out. Why did you join them in the first place? Social psychologists who have studied this issue have reached the conclusion that people join social groups for several different reasons (Paulus, 1989). First, groups help us to satisfy important psychological or social needs, such as those for giving and receiving attention and affection, or for attaining a sense of belonging. These are subtle, but very real: imagine what it would be like to live in total social isolation. You might not mind it much at first, but after a while, you'd probably get very lonely. Second, groups help us achieve goals that we could not attain as individuals. By working with others, we can often perform tasks we could not perform alone. Third, group membership often provides us with knowledge and information that would otherwise not be available to us. Fourth, groups help meet our need for security; in many cases there is safety in numbers, and belonging to various groups can provide protection against common enemies (see Figure 12.2).

Finally, group membership also contributes to establishment of a positive *social identity*—it becomes part of our self-concept (see Chapter 5). And the greater the number of prestigious, restrictive groups to which an individual is admitted, the more her or his self-concept is bolstered. Groucho Marx—a famous comedian of the 1930s, '40s, and '50s—once remarked: "I wouldn't want to belong to any club that would accept me." As you can see, he was well aware of the value of joining prestigious groups—ones that would *not* accept someone such as himself!

How Groups Function: Roles, Status, Norms, and Cohesiveness

That groups often exert powerful effects upon their members is obvious: that will be a basic theme of this entire chapter. Before turning to such group influence, however, we should address a basic issue: How, precisely, do groups af-

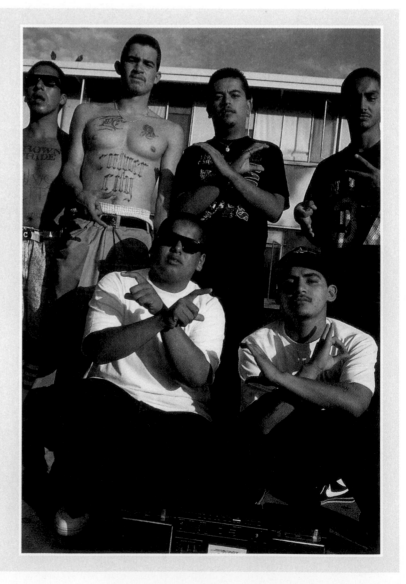

FIGURE 12.2

Mutual Defense: One Reason Why People Join Groups. Young people join gangs for many reasons. One of these is to gain protection against real or imagined enemies.

fect their members? A complete answer to this question involves many processes we have examined in previous chapters (e.g., conformity, persuasion, attraction). In addition, though, four aspects of groups themselves play a key role in this regard: *roles, status, norms,* and *cohesiveness.*

Roles: Differentiation of Function within Groups. Think of a group to which you belong or have belonged—anything from the scouts to a professional association relating to your career. Now consider the following question: Did everyone in the group act in the same way or perform the same functions? Your answer is probably *no.* Different persons performed different tasks and were expected to accomplish different things for the group. In short they fulfilled different **roles.** Sometimes roles are assigned in a formal manner; for instance, a group may choose an individual to serve as its leader, secretary, or bouncer. In other cases, individuals gradually acquire certain roles without being formally assigned to them. However roles are acquired, people often *internalize* them: they link their roles to key aspects of their self-concept and self-perceptions (see Chapters 2 and 5). When this happens, a role may exert profound effects on a person's behavior, even at times when the individual interacts with others who are not part of the group. For example, a high-powered attorney may find herself behaving toward her children in the same confrontational "Oh yeah?" manner she adopts in the courtroom.

Roles help to clarify the responsibilities and obligations of the persons belonging to a group. In addition, they provide one important way in which groups shape the behavior and thoughts of their members. They do have a potential downside, however. Group members sometimes experience *role conflict*—stress stemming from the fact that two roles they play are somehow incompatible. A very common example of role conflict involves the pressures experienced by new mothers and fathers who find the obligations of one role— *parent*—inconsistent with the obligations of the role of *student* or *employee.* Recent findings indicate that this kind of role conflict can be extremely stressful (Williams et al., 1991). So, while roles serve an important function in the effective functioning of groups, they can sometimes exert negative as well as positive effects.

Status: The Prestige of Various Roles. Have you ever met someone like the character in Figure 12.3 (p. 438)? If so, you know that **status**—social standing or rank within a group—is a serious matter for many persons. In fact, as we'll see later in this chapter, status may play a key role in our perceptions of whether we are being treated fairly by others (Tyler, 1994). If we feel we are getting treatment that is appropriate to our status, we feel that we are being treated fairly, and all is fine. If our treatment falls short of what we feel we deserve in this respect, however, watch out!—we may take strong steps to rectify the situation.

In any case, status is another important factor in the functioning of groups. Different roles or positions in a group are associated with different levels of status, and people are often exquisitely sensitive to this fact. Moreover, since status is linked to a wide range of desirable outcomes—everything from one's salary to perks such as the size of one's office or the use of a reserved parking spot—it is something individuals frequently seek. Thus, groups often confer or withhold status as a means of influencing the behavior of their members. And as you know from your own experience, such tactics can be highly effective.

Norms: The Rules of the Game. A third factor responsible for the powerful impact of groups upon their members is one we considered in Chapter 9: **norms.** Norms are rules, implicit or explicit, established by groups to regulate the

Roles ■ The sets of behaviors that individuals occupying specific positions within a group are expected to perform.

Status ■ Social standing or rank within a group.

Norms ■ Rules within a group indicating how its members should (or should not) behave.

FIGURE 12.3

Status: An Important Feature of Groups. *Like the person shown here, most of us are deeply concerned with our* status *in the groups to which we belong.*

(*Source:* Drawing by Gahan Wilson; © 1985 *The New Yorker* Magazine, Inc.)

"Didn't they tell you on the way in that I'm important?"

behavior of their members. They tell group members how to behave (*prescriptive norms*) or how *not* to behave (*proscriptive norms*) in various situations. Most groups insist upon adherence to their norms as a basic requirement for membership. Thus, it is not surprising that individuals wishing to join or remain in specific groups generally follow these rules of the game quite closely. If they do not, they may soon find themselves on the outside looking in.

Cohesiveness: The Glue that Binds.   Consider two groups. In the first, members like one another very much, strongly desire the goals their group is seeking, and feel that they could not possibly find another group that would better satisfy their needs. In the second, the opposite is true: members don't like one another, they do not share common goals, and they are actively seeking other groups that might offer them a better deal. Which group would exert stronger effects upon its members? The answer is obvious: the first. The reason for this difference involves **cohesiveness,** which has traditionally been defined in social psychology as all the forces (factors) that cause members to remain in the group such as liking for the other members and the desire to maintain or increase one's status by belonging to a high-status group (Festinger et al., 1950). At first glance, it might seem that cohesiveness involves primarily liking or attraction between group members. However, recent analyses of cohesiveness suggest that it involves what has been termed *depersonalized attraction*—liking for other group members stemming from the fact that they belong to the group and embody or represent its key features. The individual characteristics of the group members play little role in such attraction (Hogg & Hains, 1996).

In the past, cohesiveness was viewed as a unitary dimension ranging from low to high. Now, however, it is often viewed in *multidimensional terms*—in other words, it actually involves several factors, and these can vary independently of one another (Zaccaro & McCoy, 1988). For example, Cota and his

Cohesiveness ■ All forces (factors) that cause group members to remain in the group.

colleagues (1995) suggest that cohesiveness involves two primary dimensions: *task–social* and *individual–group*. The task–social dimension relates to the extent to which individuals are interested in the goals of the group (task) or in social relationships within it (social). The individual–group dimension has to do with the extent to which members are committed to the group or to other members. In addition, Cota and his colleagues (1995) suggest that group cohesiveness involves *secondary dimensions* as well—dimensions relating to particular kinds of groups. For example, in military groups, cohesiveness may relate to status (ranks), with higher-ranking persons having higher cohesiveness than lower-ranking ones. In sports teams, the roles individuals play may be more important in determining cohesiveness.

Additional factors that influence cohesiveness include (1) the amount of effort required to gain entry into the group—the greater the costs of joining the group in the first place, the higher members' attraction to it (see our discussion of dissonance theory in Chapter 4); (2) external threats or severe competition (Sherif et al., 1961); and (3) size—small groups tends to be more cohesive than large ones.

In sum, several aspects of groups—roles, status, norms, and cohesiveness—determine the extent to which groups can, and do, influence their members. Since these factors play an important role in group influence, keep them in mind as we consider some of the specific ways in which groups shape the behavior and thought of their members. You'll certainly see them in operation at several points.

INTEGRATING PRINCIPLES

1. Individuals join groups to satisfy many of their basic social motives—to enjoy recognition and affection, to acquire information, and to bolster their self-esteem. These same motives play important roles in many forms of social behavior and social thought; for example, in attraction, Chapter 7; in social cognition, Chapter 3; and in self-identity, Chapter 5.

2. Groups influence the behavior of their members through roles, status, norms, and cohesiveness. Norms are of special importance and, as we saw in Chapter 9, influence many forms of social behavior.

Groups and Task Performance: The Benefits—and Costs—of Working with Others

Some activities, such as reading, solving complex mathematical problems, or writing love letters, are best carried out alone. Most tasks we perform, however, are done in cooperation with others, or at least in their presence. This raises an intriguing question: What impact, if any, do groups exert upon task performance? In order to answer this question, we'll consider two separate but related issues: (1) What are the effects on performance of the presence of others, even if we are not actively coordinating our efforts with them? And (2) do individuals exert more effort or less when working with others in a group?

Social Facilitation: Performance in the Presence of Others

Imagine that you are a young athlete—an ice-skater, for example—and that you are preparing for your first important competition. You practice your routines alone for several hours each day, month after month. Finally, the big day arrives, and you skate out onto the ice in a huge arena filled with the biggest crowd you've ever seen. How will you do? Better or worse than was true when you practiced alone, or in front of your coach? This was one of the first topics of research in social psychology; so before we turn to modern findings concerning this issue, let's consider a very early series of studies on it by Floyd Allport (1920), one of the true founders of modern social psychology.

Cornerstones of Social Psychology

PERFORMANCE IN THE PRESENCE OF OTHERS: The Simplest Group Effect?

Floyd H. Allport. In many ways, Floyd H. Allport was the first truly modern social psychologist. He wrote the first textbook that defined social psychology as a scientific field of study, and his own research on social facilitation, attitudes, and other topics, shaped later research on these topics in important ways. In short, he was one of the true founders of our field.

Social psychology was literally struggling for its existence as an independent field when Floyd Allport decided to study what, in his opinion, was a very basic question: What are the effects of working on a task in the presence of other persons who are working on the same, or even a different, task—persons who are *not* competing with each other? Allport felt that this was an important question and—more to the point—one that would allow the new field to replace speculation with scientific data. To study the effects of the presence of others on task performance, he used several different but related methods.

In one study, for example, he asked participants to write down as many associations as they could think of for words printed at the top of an otherwise blank sheet of paper (e.g., "building," "laboratory"). The participants were allowed to work for three one-minute periods, and they performed this task both alone and in the presence of two other persons. (In other words, Allport used what social psychologists describe as a *within-subjects* design: the same persons worked under both experimental conditions.) Results were clear: Ninety-three percent of the participants produced more associations when working in the presence of others than when working alone.

Allport was encouraged by these findings, but he realized that in many cases participants could think of more words than they could actually write down. This, he reasoned, might be affecting the results. To eliminate this problem, he asked them to write down every third or every fourth word they thought of—not all of them. Again, results indicated that performance was increased in the presence of others. But still Allport was not satisfied: he wondered whether the same effect would be found with a more complex task—one requiring high levels of thought. To find out, he asked participants to read short passages from ancient Roman authors, and then to write down all the arguments they could think of that would tend to *disprove* the points made in these passages. Once more, they performed this task while alone and while in the presence of several other persons. Once more, results indicated that performance was increased when individuals worked in groups. Not only did they come up with more arguments; the quality of their ideas was better, too (see Figure 12.4).

While results generally supported a facilitation of performance in the presence of others, Allport was careful to note that this was not true for all

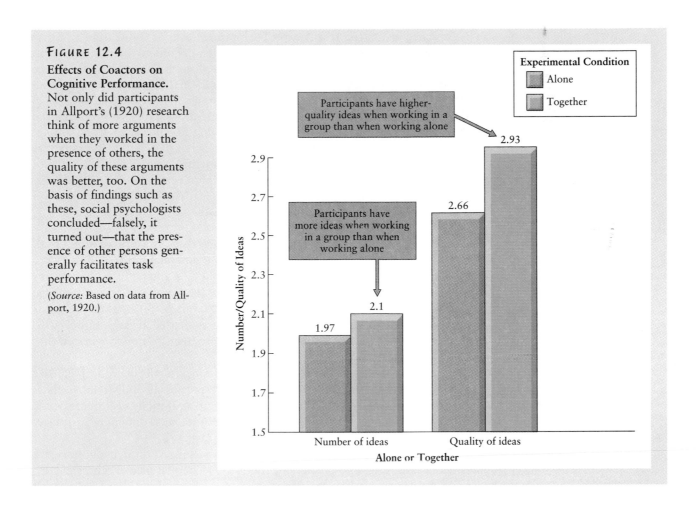

FIGURE 12.4

Effects of Coactors on Cognitive Performance. Not only did participants in Allport's (1920) research think of more arguments when they worked in the presence of others, the quality of these arguments was better, too. On the basis of findings such as these, social psychologists concluded—falsely, it turned out—that the presence of other persons generally facilitates task performance.

(*Source:* Based on data from Allport, 1920.)

individuals: some actually did worse in the presence of others than when alone. In other words, there were large individual differences even with respect to this very basic form of group influence. Although he lacked the sophisticated methodology available to modern social psychologists, Allport also concluded that the presence of others shifts individuals' thought processes toward what he described as a more "expansive" style. If you recall our discussion of the relationship between affect and cognition in Chapter 3, you will note that this is one of the effects of positive affect uncovered in modern research on this issue. In this and many other ways, Allport demonstrated that he was a keen observer of social behavior, and far ahead of his time in some of his insights about the cognitive processes that underlie such behavior.

Allport's research paved the way for the study of what soon came to be known in social psychology as **social facilitation**. Early researchers defined this term as improvements in performance produced by the mere presence of others, either as audience or as coactors—persons performing the same task, but independently. As we'll now see, this term turned out to be premature: the presence of others does not always enhance performance, and social psychologists now understand why this is the case. There can be little doubt, however, that although some of his conclusions were later shown to be false, Allport's early studies were in many respects a model for the young field of social psychology— a model that is still reflected in its scientific orientation today. ■ ■ ■

Social Facilitation ■ Effects upon performance resulting from the presence of others.

The Presence of Others: Is It Always Facilitating? Allport's research, and that conducted by other early social psychologists (e.g., Triplett, 1898), seemed to indicate that the presence of others is a definite plus—it improves performance on many different tasks. As the volume of research on this topic increased, however, puzzling findings began to appear: sometimes the presence of others, as audience or as coactors, facilitated performance; but sometimes it produced the opposite effect (Pessin, 1933). So social facilitating was not always *facilitating*; indeed, it appeared as though this term was somewhat misleading. But *why* was this the case? Why did the presence of others sometimes enhance and sometimes impair performance? Believe it or not, this question remained unresolved until the mid-1960s, when a famous social psychologist, Robert Zajonc, offered an insightful answer. Let's take a closer look at his ideas.

The Drive Theory of Social Facilitation: Other Persons As a Source of Arousal. The basic idea behind Zajonc's **drive theory of social facilitation** is simple: the presence of others produces increments in arousal. As you can readily see, this suggestion agrees with our informal experience: the presence of other persons, especially when they are paying close attention to our performance as an interested audience, does seem to generate feelings of increased arousal. But how do such increments in arousal then affect our performance? Zajonc suggested that the answer involves two facts.

First, it is a basic principle of psychology that increments in arousal increase the occurrence of *dominant responses*—the responses an individual is most likely to make in a given situation. Thus, when arousal increases, the tendency to make dominant responses, too, increases. Second, such dominant responses can be either correct or incorrect for any given task.

When these two facts are combined with the suggestion that the presence of others is arousing, two predictions follow: (1) The presence of others will facilitate performance when an individual's dominant responses are the correct ones in a given situation; but (2) the presence of others will impair performance when a person's dominant responses are incorrect in a given situation. (Please see Figure 12.5 for a summary of these points.) Another implication of Zajonc's reasoning is that the presence of others will facilitate performance in situations where individuals are highly skilled in performing the task in question; this is because under these conditions, their dominant responses are correct ones. In contrast, the presence of others will impair performance in situations where individuals are not highly skilled—for example, when they are learning to perform a new task. Here, their dominant responses are likely to be errors.

Initial studies designed to test Zajonc's predictions generally yielded positive results (e.g., Matlin & Zajonc, 1968; Zajonc & Sales, 1966). Individuals were more likely to emit dominant responses in the presence of others than when alone, and performance on various tasks was either enhanced or impaired depending on whether these responses were correct or incorrect in each situation (Geen, 1989; Geen & Gange, 1977).

Additional research, however, soon raised an important question: Does social facilitation stem from the mere physical presence of others? Or do other factors, such as concern over others' evaluations, also play a role? Support for the latter possibility was provided by the results of several ingenious studies indicating that social facilitation occurred only when individuals believed that their performance could be observed and evaluated by others (e.g., Bond, 1982; Cottrell et al., 1968). Such findings led some social psychologists to propose that social facilitation actually stems either from **evaluation apprehension**—concern over being judged by others (which is often arousing), or from related concerns over *self-presentation*—looking good in front of others (see our dis-

Drive Theory of Social Facilitation ■ A theory suggesting that the mere presence of others is arousing and increases the tendency to perform dominant responses.

Evaluation Apprehension ■ Concern over being evaluated by others, which can increase arousal and so contribute to social facilitation.

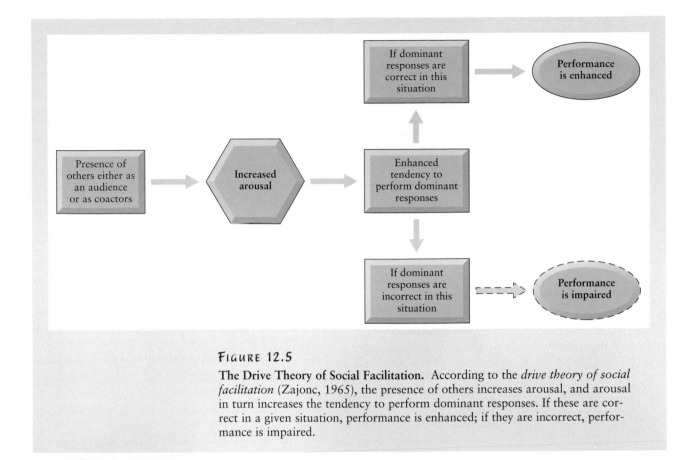

FIGURE 12.5

The Drive Theory of Social Facilitation. According to the *drive theory of social facilitation* (Zajonc, 1965), the presence of others increases arousal, and arousal in turn increases the tendency to perform dominant responses. If these are correct in a given situation, performance is enhanced; if they are incorrect, performance is impaired.

cussion of this topic in Chapter 2). Thus, it may be these factors, not the mere physical presence of others, that are crucial in determining the impact of an audience or coactors upon task performance.

These conclusions make good sense; after all, would your performance be affected by the presence of someone who was sleeping soundly while you worked on a task? Probably not. But we must note that other evidence points to the conclusion that sometimes social facilitation effects occur in situations where concern over looking good to others, or over their evaluations of our work, do *not* seem to play a role (e.g., Schmitt et al., 1986). For example, it has been found that animals—even insects—perform simple tasks better in the presence of an audience than when alone (Zajonc, Heingartner, & Herman, 1969). Since it is difficult to assume that insects are concerned about the impressions they make on others, these findings raise serious questions about an interpretation of social facilitation based solely on evaluation apprehension. Corresponding effects have also been found in studies with human participants. For instance, Schmitt and his colleagues (Schmitt et al., 1986) found that performance on a simple task (typing one's own name) was improved by the presence of others who wore blindfolds and earphones, and so could not possibly observe participant's performance. However, when the audience did not wear blindfolds and earphones, performance was increased even more. These findings suggest that the mere presence of others is arousing and influences performance, but that the possibility of being evaluated by others increases arousal even more, and produces even stronger social facilitation effects. Before you give up in despair, read on: a resolution to all these confusing and seemingly contradictory results has begun to emerge from recent experiments.

One Potential Resolution: Distraction–Conflict Theory. Does social facilitation stem from the mere presence of others? From evaluation apprehension? From both factors? From other causes? A resolution to all these confusing possibilities has been provided by Robert S. Baron (not the Bob Baron whose name appears on the cover of this book) and his colleagues (e.g., R. S. Baron, 1986; Sanders, 1983).

Like other explanations of social facilitation, this theory—known as **distraction–conflict theory**—assumes that audiences and coactors increase arousal. In contrast to earlier views, however, distraction–conflict theory suggests that such arousal stems from conflict between two tendencies: (1) the tendency to pay attention to the task being performed, and (2) the tendency to direct attention to an audience or coactors. Such conflict is arousing, and such arousal, in turn, enhances the tendency to perform dominant responses. If these are correct in a given situation, performance is enhanced; if they are incorrect, performance is impaired.

Several findings offer support for this theory. For example, audiences produce social facilitation effects only when directing attention to them conflicts in some way with task demands (Groff, R. S. Baron, & Moore, 1983). When paying attention to an audience does not conflict with task performance, social facilitation fails to occur. Similarly, individuals experience greater distraction when they perform various tasks in front of an audience than when they perform them alone (R. S. Baron, Moore, & Sanders, 1978). Finally, when individuals have little reason to pay attention to others present on the scene (e.g., when these persons are performing a different task), social facilitation fails to occur; when they have strong reasons for paying attention to others, social facilitation occurs (Sanders, 1983).

One major advantage of distraction–conflict theory is that it can explain why animals, as well as people, are affected by the presence of an audience. Briefly, since animals can experience conflicting response tendencies of the kind described above, it is not surprising that they are susceptible to social facilitation. Obviously, any theory that can explain similar patterns of behavior among organisms ranging from the lowly cockroach through human beings is powerful indeed, and worthy of very careful attention. So, while distraction–conflict theory may not provide a final answer to the persistent puzzle of social facilitation, it has certainly added substantially to our understanding of this process. Our final conclusion: Social facilitation—once viewed by social psychologists as the "simplest type of group influence"—has turned out to be far from simple. But systematic research has certainly helped to clarify its possible roots and to explain why the presence of others is not always facilitating.

Social Loafing: Letting Others Do the Work in Group Tasks

Suppose that you and several other people are helping a friend to move. In order to lift the heaviest pieces of furniture, you all pitch in. Will all of the people helping exert equal effort? Probably not. Some will take as much of the load as possible, while others will simply hang on, appearing to help more than they really do.

This pattern is quite common in situations where groups of person perform what are known as **additive tasks**—ones in which the contributions of each member are combined into a single group product. On such tasks, some persons work hard while others goof off, doing less than their share, and less than they might do if they were working alone. Social psychologists refer to such effects as **social loafing**—reductions in motivation and effort when individuals

Distraction–Conflict Theory ■ Theory suggesting that social facilitation stems from the conflict produced when individuals attempt simultaneously to pay attention to a task and to other persons.

Additive Tasks ■ Tasks for which the group product is the sum or combination of the efforts of individual members.

Social Loafing ■ Reductions in motivation and effort when individuals work collectively in a group compared to when they work individually or as independent coactors.

FIGURE 12.6

Social Loafing: A Fact of Social Life. When individuals work together with others on some task, they often experience reductions in motivation, make less effort, and do less (as individuals) than they would when working alone. Such effects are known as *social loafing*.

work collectively in a group compared to when they work individually or as independent coactors (Karau & Williams, 1993; see Figure 12.6).

That social loafing occurs has been demonstrated in many experiments. For example, in one of the first of these studies, Latané, Williams, and Harkins (1979) asked groups of male students to clap or cheer as loudly as possible at specific times, supposedly so that the experimenter could determine how much noise people make in social settings. Participants engaged in clapping and cheering either alone or in groups of two, four, or six persons. Results were clear: The magnitude of the sounds made by each person decreased sharply as group size rose. In other words, each participant put out less and less effort as the number of other group members increased. And this was *not* due merely to increasing lack of coordination between group members; on the contrary, it stemmed from actual reductions in effort in the group condition. Additional research suggests that such social loafing is quite general in scope. It occurs among both males and females; among children as well as adults (Williams & Williams, 1981); in several different cultures—although it is stronger in Western than in Asian cultures (Yamaguchi, Okamoto, & Oka, 1985); under a wider variety of work conditions (e.g., Brickner, Harkins & Ostrom, 1986; Harkins, 1987); and for cognitive tasks as well as ones involving physical effort (Weldon & Mustari, 1988; Williams & Karau, 1991). In short, social loafing appears to be a basic fact of social life. As noted by Karau and Williams (1993), this has important implications, because many crucial tasks can only be accomplished in groups—sports teams, committees, juries, and government task forces, to mention just a few (e.g., Russell, 1993). The prevalence of social loafing has lead social psychologists to focus their attention on two important issues: *Why* do such effects occur? And what steps can be taken to reduce social loafing?

The Collective Effort Model: An Expectancy Theory of Social Loafing. Many different explanations for the occurrence of social loafing have been proposed. For example, one view—*social impact theory*—has related social loafing to a topic we examined in Chapter 10, *diffusion of responsibility* (Latané, 1981). According to social impact theory, as group size increases, each member feels less and less responsible for the task being performed. The result: Each person exerts decreasing effort on it. In contrast, other theories have focused on the fact that in groups, members' motivation decreases because they realize that their contributions can't be evaluated on an individual basis—so why work hard? (Harkins & Szymanski, 1989). Perhaps the most comprehensive explanation of social loafing offered to date, however, is the **collective effort model** proposed by Karau and Williams (1993).

These researchers suggest that we can understand social loafing by extending a basic theory of individual motivation—*expectancy–valence theory*—to situations involving group performance. Expectancy–valence theory suggests that individuals will work hard on a given task only to the extent that the following conditions exist: (1) They believe that working hard will lead to better performance (*expectancy*); (2) they believe that better performance will be recognized and rewarded (*instrumentality*); and (3) the rewards available are ones they value and desire (*valence*). In other words, individuals working alone will exert effort only to the extent that they believe that doing so will yield the outcomes they want.

According to Karau and Williams (1993), these links are often weaker when individuals work together in groups than when they work alone. First, consider *expectancy*—the perception that increased effort will lead to better performance. This may be high when individuals work alone, but lower when they work together in groups, because people realize that other factors aside from their own effort will determine the group's performance; for instance, the amount of effort exerted by other members. Similarly, *instrumentality*—the belief that good performance will be recognized and rewarded—may also be weaker when people work together in groups. They realize that valued outcomes are divided among all group members, and that as a result, they may not get their fair share, given their level of effort. Therefore, social loafing occurs; and within the framework of the collective effort model, this is not surprising. After all, when individuals work together with others, the relationship between their own effort and performance and rewards is more uncertain than when they work alone. See Figure 12.7 for a summary of the collective effort model, or CEM for short.

Is the collective effort model accurate? To find out, Karau and Williams performed a meta-analysis of dozens of studies of social loafing. The CEM makes several predictions concerning the conditions under which social loafing should be most and least likely to occur. For example, it predicts that social loafing will be weakest (1) when individuals work in small rather than large groups; (2) when they work on tasks that are intrinsically interesting or important to them; (3) when they work with respected others (friends, teammates, etc.); (4) when they perceive that their contributions to the group product are unique rather than redundant; (5) when they expect their coworkers to perform poorly; and (6) when they come from cultures that emphasize individual effort and out-

Collective Effort Model ■ An explanation of social loafing suggesting that perceived links between individuals' effort and their outcomes are weaker when they work together with others in a group.

FIGURE 12.7

The Collective Effort Model. According to the *collective effort model* (Karau & Williams, 1993), social loafing occurs because when individuals work together with others, the links (1) between their effort and the group's performance and (2) between the group's performance and their own rewards are weaker than when individuals work alone.

(*Source:* Based on suggestions by Karau & Williams, 1993.)

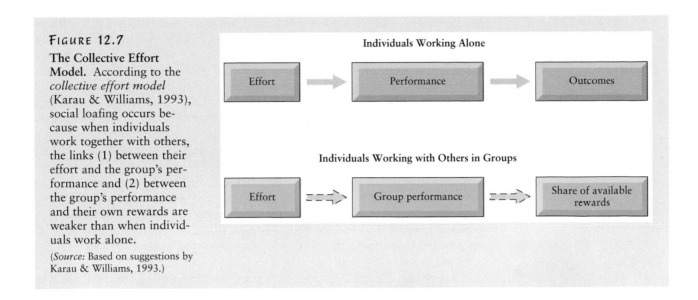

comes rather than group outcomes (Western versus Asian cultures, for instance). The results of the meta-analysis offered support for all the CEM's predictions. In others words, social loafing was weakest and strongest under conditions predicted by the theory. In addition, the meta-analysis confirmed that social loafing was a very reliable and pervasive effect: it occurred across many different studies conducted with many different kinds of participants and many different kinds of tasks.

On the basis of these findings, Karau and Williams (1993) concluded that the CEM provides a useful framework for understanding social loafing. Moreover, they also noted that the results of their meta-analysis indicate that social loafing is a potentially serious problem: it is most likely to occur under conditions in which individuals' contributions can't be evaluated, when people work on tasks they find boring or uninspiring, and when they work with others they don't greatly respect or don't know very well. Unfortunately, precisely these conditions exist in many settings where groups of persons work together—for instance, in many manufacturing plants and government offices. If social loafing poses a threat to performance in many settings, the next question is obvious: What steps can be taken to reduce it? It is to this important issue that we turn next.

Reducing Social Loafing: Some Useful Techniques. As we'll see in the next section of this chapter, no one likes to feel that they are getting the short end of the stick—less than they deserve, given their contributions to a task or relationship. It's not surprising, therefore, that many people react negatively to social loafing by others: they experience anger and resentment when they feel that others are goofing off, and may ultimately decide to leave a group rather than be exploited in this manner (Yamagishi, 1988). For this reason, it seems important to hold social loafing to a minimum in many situations. What steps can be taken to attain this goal? Research on social loafing offers some useful suggestions.

The most obvious tactic involves making the output or effort of each participant readily identifiable (e.g., Williams, Harkins, & Latané, 1981). Under these conditions, people can't sit back and let others do their work, so social loafing is in fact reduced. Second, groups can reduce social loafing by increasing group members' commitment to successful task performance (Brickner et al., 1986). Pressures toward working hard will then serve to offset temptations to engage in social loafing. Third, social loafing can be reduced by increasing the apparent importance or value of a task (Karau & Williams, 1993). Fourth, social loafing is reduced when individuals view their contributions to the task as unique rather than merely redundant with those of others (Weldon & Mustari, 1988). And finally, social loafing can be reduced by strengthening group cohesiveness. This increases the extent to which members care about the group's outcomes, and hence their level of individual effort. We should add that one's role in a task-performing group may also have an important effect on social loafing: persons who hold high-status positions—for instance, leaders—may perceive a closer link between their effort and the group's performance than do other members; as a result, they may be less likely to engage in social loafing. This prediction is based on CEM theory but has not, as yet, been systematically tested (Karau & Williams, 1993). However, it underscores the importance of *roles* in the functioning of many groups—a point we made in our earlier discussion of roles.

Together, these steps can sharply reduce the magnitude of social loafing in many situations. Social loafing, it appears, is *not* an unavoidable feature of task-performing groups. It can be reduced if appropriate safeguards are built into the situation. When they are, individuals will perceive strong links between their effort, the group's performance, and their own outcomes. And then the tendency to goof off at the expense of others may be greatly reduced.

Perceived Fairness in Groups: Getting What We Deserve—or Else!

Group membership, we have already noted, is a two-way street. On the one hand, groups demand—and generally receive—contributions from their members: adherence to the group's norms, effort on group tasks, support of the group and its goals. On the other hand, individuals expect to get something back for these investments: satisfaction of their basic needs, information, boosts to their self-concept. In addition, they usually want something else, too: *fair treatment* by the group and other group members. In other words, individuals want to feel that what they receive from any group to which they belong is a fair reflection of what they have contributed to the group (Greenberg, 1993a; Tyler, 1994). How important is this desire for fairness? If you've ever been in a situation where you felt that you were being shortchanged by others, you already know the answer: very strong indeed. In situations where we feel that we are being treated unfairly, we often experience anger, resentment, and a strong desire to even the score (Croponazno, 1993). Such feelings, in turn, often exert strong effects on our behavior: unfair treatment calls for action—attempts to rectify the situation. So when faced with unfairness, we engage in a wide range of behaviors, ranging from loud protest through withdrawal from the group or relationship.

Social psychologists have long been aware of the important role of perceived fairness in the functioning of groups (Adams, 1965) and in interpersonal behavior generally. Thus, they have investigated this topic from several different perspectives. To acquaint you with what we've learned about perceived fairness, we'll focus here on two issues: the factors that lead individuals to conclude that they have been treated fairly or unfairly, and the ways in which individuals attempt to deal with—and hopefully eliminate—unfairness.

Judgments of Fairness: Outcomes, Procedures, and Courtesy

The summer before I (Bob Baron) entered college, I worked in the finance office of a large labor union. I was a summer fill-in, so the work was BORING almost beyond belief. My hours were long, and I had to punch a time clock when I arrived and when I left. I had only forty minutes for lunch, and my supervisor insisted that I be back right on time. I needed the money, so I could have stood the job without any difficulty except for one thing: the favored treatment given to another summer employee. His name was Tom, and he was a year ahead of me in school. Tom arrived late every morning and often left early. He often disappeared for long periods of time during the day, and he often took two-hour lunches. Worst of all, he was given the most interesting jobs to do. The final blow came when, by mistake, I received Tom's paycheck one week. It was for 50 percent more than mine! My head nearly exploded. "How unfair!" I thought. "Who is this guy anyway?" I soon found out: he was the nephew of the president of the union. End of mystery—but not of my feelings of being treated unfairly.

This situation provides a clear illustration of one major type of circumstance that leads individuals to perceive that they are being treated unfairly: a special kind of imbalance between the *contributions* individuals make to a relationship or group, and the *outcomes* they receive in return—their share of available rewards (Adams, 1965). In general, we expect these to be proportional: the more we, or anyone else, contributes, the larger the share of available reward we, or they, should receive. Thus, if someone who makes a large contribution to a group receives the lion's share of the rewards, while someone who makes a small contribution receives a much smaller share, everything is fine: contributions and outcomes are in balance, and we perceive that fairness or **equity** exists. In situations like the one I experienced, however, this kind of balance is missing: my contributions to the job were fairly large, yet my rewards were small. In contrast, Tom's contributions were small (he was almost never there!), yet he received larger rewards—a higher salary, more privileges, and so on. Under these circumstances, I experienced feelings of *inequity* or unfairness. A large body of research findings indicate that in fact, we do base many of our judgments of fairness on this kind of cognitive equation (see Figure 12.8 on page 450). We compare the ratio of our inputs and outcomes to those of other persons to determine whether we are being treated fairly. Because such comparisons involve our assessment of whether we are getting a fair share of available rewards, social psychologists describe them as focusing on **distributive justice** (Adams, 1965; Greenberg, 1993a).

Two more points are worth carefully noting. First, judgments about distributive justice are very much in the eye of the beholder: we do the comparing, and we decide whether our share of available rewards is fair relative to that of others. Second, as you can probably guess, we are much more sensitive about receiving less than we feel we deserve than to receiving *more* than we feel we deserve (Greenberg, 1986). In other words, the *self-serving bias* that we described in Chapter 2 operates strongly in this context.

Procedural and Interpersonal Justice: It's Not Just What You Get; *Why* You Get It Matters Too. Distributive justice plays a key role in shaping perceptions of fairness. It is not all there is, however. In addition to concern over how much we receive relative to others, we are also interested in other things as well. In particular we are interested in (1) the *procedures* followed in the allocation of available rewards—**procedural justice;** and (2) the *considerateness and courtesy*

Equity ■ Fairness in social exchange. Judgments of equity relate to distributive justice, and involve comparisons, by individuals, of their own outcomes and contributions to those of other persons.

Distributive Justice ■ Refers to individuals' judgments about whether they are receiving a fair share of available rewards—shares proportionate to their contributions to the group or any social relationship.

Procedural Justice ■ Judgments concerning the fairness of the procedures used to distribute available rewards among group members.

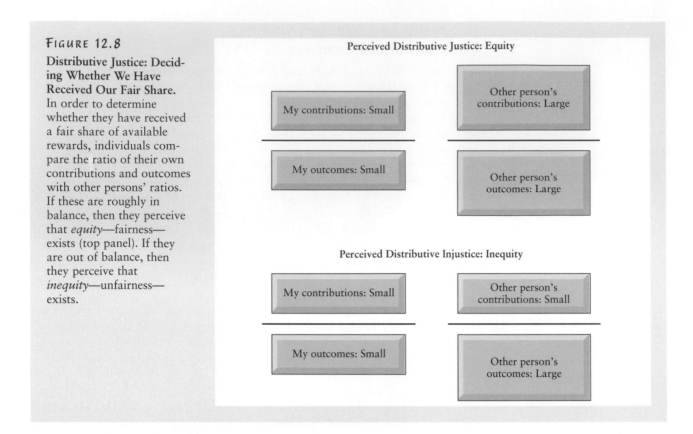

FIGURE 12.8

Distributive Justice: Deciding Whether We Have Received Our Fair Share. In order to determine whether they have received a fair share of available rewards, individuals compare the ratio of their own contributions and outcomes with other persons' ratios. If these are roughly in balance, then they perceive that *equity*—fairness—exists (top panel). If they are out of balance, then they perceive that *inequity*—unfairness—exists.

Interpersonal Justice ■ Refers to judgments concerning the considerateness and courtesy individuals are shown by parties responsible for distributing available rewards to members of a group.

shown to us by the parties responsible for dividing the available rewards—**interpersonal justice** (Folger & Bies, 1989; Shapiro, Buttner, & Barry, 1995). In other words, in reaching conclusions about whether we have been treated fairly, we do not focus solely on our actual outcomes; we also care about how the decisions to distribute rewards in a specific way were reached (the procedures followed), and about how we were treated throughout the process—especially when being informed about our share (interpersonal factors).

What factors influence judgments concerning the fairness of procedures? Research findings point to several that are important (Brockner et al., 1994). First, individuals view procedures as fair to the extent that they are consistent—applied in the same manner across all the persons involved. Second, they tend to view procedures as fair when they are based on accurate information about how much each person contributed. Third, they view procedures as fair when the interests of all concerned parties are represented. Additional determinants of procedural justice include opportunities to correct any errors in distributions, and the extent to which decisions about distributions are based on widely accepted moral and ethical standards (Brockner et al., 1994; Leventhal, Karuza, & Fry, 1980). To the extent these conditions exist, individuals perceive their treatment as fair: after all, correct, reasonable procedures have been used, and who can argue with these?

What about *interpersonal justice*—what factors play a role with respect to this type of fairness? Research on this topic is quite recent, but already two important factors have been identified. The first is the extent to which individuals feel that they were given clear and rational reasons for the division of rewards that was adopted (Bies, Shapiro, & Cummings, 1988). In other words, people want to *understand* why they received what they did, and will perceive they have been treated fairly to the extent such information is provided.

A second factor that influences perceptions of interpersonal justice involves the courtesy and sensitivity with which reward allocations are presented. Have we been treated with the respect we deserve? Or have the people in charge of distributing rewards acted in a high-handed and insensitive manner? These are the kind of questions we ask ourselves in deciding whether we have been treated in an interpersonally fair manner. As you probably know from your own experience, such fairness is not always present. For example, some professors refuse to discuss grades with students; the professors' attitude is "*I* make the grades; if you don't like it, that's tough." (Needless to say, only a small number of professors *we* know would dream of acting in this manner!) Similarly, some bosses see no reason for presenting their decisions about raises, promotions, or other rewards in a courteous manner sensitive to employees' feelings: they just lay down the law, so to speak.

Evidence for the important role of both these factors—clear explanations for the reasons behind reward distributions and sensitive treatment of group members—has been obtained in several recent studies (e.g., Brockner et al., 1994; Shapiro, Buttner, & Barry, 1995). An especially clear illustration of the impact of these variables, however, is provided by a study conducted by Greenberg (1994). In this investigation, a large financial services company planned to ban all smoking by its employees. The ban was a fact: it was going to happen no matter what. But how should it be presented to employees? Greenberg reasoned that reactions would be most favorable when employees were given a clear explanation for the ban and when the company's president —who announced the ban—did so in a sensitive, sympathetic manner. To test this prediction, Greenberg arranged for the president to announce the ban to different groups of employees in four different ways: with or without a clear explanation for its necessity, and with or without expressions of personal sensitivity. He predicted that when later asked to indicate their acceptance of the ban, those who were treated in an interpersonally fair manner would indicate greater acceptance than those treated in a less fair manner. As you can see from Figure 12.9 (p. 452), results confirmed these predictions. However, as you might expect, the benefits of interpersonal fairness were stronger for heavy smokers, who were directly affected by the ban, than for light smokers and nonsmokers.

Taken together, recent research on perceived fairness in groups, whether at work or in other contexts, indicates that such judgments are indeed influenced by many different factors. Distributive justice—how much one receives relative to others—is important, but it is not the entire story. In addition, judgments of fairness are influenced by factors relating to procedures and to what might best be described as the "style" in which information about reward allocations is communicated. Perceived fairness is indeed in the eye of the beholder, but as is true with all aspects of social perception, many factors shape our conclusions about others' behavior.

Reactions to Perceived Unfairness: Tactics for Dealing with Injustice

If dissonance is unpleasant (see Chapter 4), then inequity—the perception that one has been cheated or shortchanged by others—is downright obnoxious. As we noted earlier, most people react quite strongly to such treatment. But what, precisely, do they do? What steps do they take to restore fairness, or at least to reduce perceptions of unfairness? Here are some of the most important strategies people adopt.

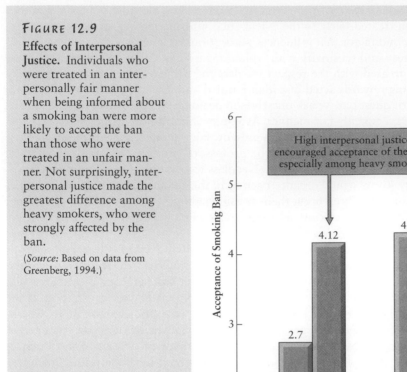

FIGURE 12.9

Effects of Interpersonal Justice. Individuals who were treated in an interpersonally fair manner when being informed about a smoking ban were more likely to accept the ban than those who were treated in an unfair manner. Not surprisingly, interpersonal justice made the greatest difference among heavy smokers, who were strongly affected by the ban.

(*Source:* Based on data from Greenberg, 1994.)

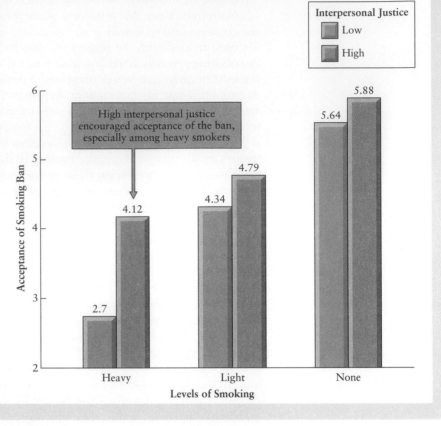

Alterations in Contributions or Outcomes. First, individuals who conclude that they have been treated unfairly often attempt to restore fairness either by *changing their contributions* or by *changing their outcomes*. Since most people are far more sensitive to receiving *less* than they feel they deserve than they are to receiving *more* than what is fair, these alterations generally involve reductions in their contributions or efforts to increase their outcomes.

Turning to contributions first, employees who feel that they are getting less than they deserve relative to others (as I did in my summer job) may reduce their effort on the job, arrive late, and leave early. In addition, they may refuse to perform any task not specifically included in their job description. Since many individuals *do* perform activities beyond the call of duty, adhering strictly to one's job description is more than an idle threat: it can be quite costly for one's organization (George & Brief, 1992). Evidence for such effects has been observed in many different studies. For instance, in one well-known investigation, Pritchard, Dunnette, and Jorgenson (1972) hired people for actual jobs and then led them to believe that they were being underpaid relative to other persons performing the same work, or that they were being fairly paid. Not surprisingly, those who felt they were being underpaid reduced their output on a tedious record-keeping task, relative to those led to believe that they were being fairly paid.

Efforts to reduce inequity by altering one's outcomes are also quite common. If you've ever seen angry strikers picketing outside a business, you are already well aware of this fact: the strikers' goal is to increase their outcomes and so to reduce what they perceive to be unfair treatment by their company. Individuals don't have to go out on strike to demand greater rewards, however: they can seek to accomplish this by asking for a raise; for greater recognition; for more perks, such as a larger office; or even for various honors. For information on a much more dramatic way in which employees seek to increase their outcomes, please see the *Applied Side* section below.

Other Techniques for Coping with Unfairness. In addition to increasing their outcomes or reducing their contributions, individuals also use several other means for dealing with perceived unfairness. For example, they can decide to withdraw from the relationship altogether—to leave the group, quit their job, or leave a romantic relationship in which they feel they are somehow being shortchanged (see Chapter 8).

More common, and less drastic, than these moves are several related techniques involving changes in perceptions of the situation. In these techniques, individuals alter their perceptions of social reality so that the illusion of justice—if not justice itself—is restored. Persons who find themselves receiving the short end of the stick, for instance, may rationalize this unpleasant state of affairs by concluding that others actually *deserve* to receive more than they do because they possess something special—extra talent, greater experience, a bigger reputation than the perceiver (Walster, Walster, & Berscheid, 1978). Or, in an even more bizarre manner, individuals may conclude that they are actually benefiting in some strange way from the unfair treatment they receive: a little suffering is good for the soul! While such thinking may seem strange, it does allow individuals to eliminate the intense discomfort generated by perceptions of unfairness. Thus, in this respect, it can be adaptive for the persons who engage in it.

INTEGRATING PRINCIPLES

1. Persons belonging to groups want to be treated fairly by the group and by other members. In particular, they want to feel that their share of available rewards accurately reflects their contribution to the group.

2. When such *distributive justice* is lacking, or when individuals conclude that the procedures used to divide rewards were not fair, or when they perceive that they were treated in an insensitive manner, they may experience strong feelings of unfairness.

3. These, in turn, can have strong effects on many forms of social behavior, ranging from reduced willingness to help others or the company (see Chapter 10) through various forms of aggression against the company or other employees (e.g., theft, vandalism; see Chapter 1).

Social Psychology: On the Applied Side
WHEN EMPLOYEES BITE THE HAND THAT FEEDS THEM:
Employee Theft As a Response to Perceived Unfairness

Have you ever taken pencils or paper home from an office where you worked? How about some "overripe" fruit if you worked in a supermarket? Don't be upset if you answered yes. Recent evidence indicates that more than 75 percent of all employees engage in such activities (Delaney, 1993). Is this stealing? Many employees would deny it, but from a legal standpoint, it is; after all, employees are taking company property for their own use. Employee theft is very costly for businesses. The United States Chamber of commerce, for example, suggests that employee theft is ten times more costly to American companies than street crime (Govoni, 1992). As one expert on such theft put it: "Shoplifting will steal your profits; employees will steal your business" (Snyder & Blair, 1989).

Why do employees steal from their companies? One answer is: They are selfish and dishonest. Another answer, however, is closely linked to our discussion of perceived fairness: Many individuals report that they steal from their companies because they believe this is justified. In their eyes, their companies are not providing them with fair outcomes—outcomes proportionate to their contributions. So, to even the score, they simply take company property (Clarke, 1990). And what they take is often far more than a stray pencil or two: employees steal merchandise in retail stores, tools in manufacturing companies, and valuable drugs or supplies in hospitals. In short, they take anything and everything they can get away with; and all, it often appears, in the total absence of guilt. They view such thefts as simply getting even. Consider the following statement, made by one employee after learning that the typical person in his company was stealing about $300 worth of merchandise a year. "Heck, I'm behind schedule . . . there's only three months left in the year and I don't have my $300!" (Altheide et al., 1978, p. 108).

Can anything be done to change this situation? Research by Greenberg and his colleagues (Greenberg, 1990; Greenberg & Scott, in press) indicates that this is an area where *interpersonal justice* plays a crucial role. In one study, for example, Greenberg (1990) arranged for information about a pay cut to be presented in strikingly different ways to employees at two different plants within the same company. In one plant, the reasons for the pay cut were carefully explained, and the announcement was made with repeated expressions of regret over the hardships this would produce. In the other plant, in contrast, limited information was supplied about the reasons for the pay cut, and no effort was made to soften the blow. Over the next few months, the amount of theft at the two plants was recorded. As predicted, theft was much higher in the plant where no effort had been made to produce interpersonal fairness.

While the results of this study are dramatic, there is one serious problem: we can't tell whether the results stemmed from the amount of information provided, the statements of regret, or both. To separate these factors, Greenberg (1993b) conducted a laboratory study in which students who had been promised $5 per hour for working in a study were told either that they would receive this pay, or that they would receive a much lower rate—$3 per hour. The experimenter announced this cut in pay and provided either a full explanation for why the cut was necessary, or no explanation. Then this person either expressed a great deal of regret about the pay cut, or made no such statements. To find out whether these variables would influence participants' willingness to engage in employee theft, the researcher then departed, leaving a pile of money on the table. As the experimenter left, he said, "I don't how much is here, but . . . just take the amount you are supposed to be paid and leave the rest." As expected, those paid the amount of money they were promised ($5) did not engage in theft. However, with participants who were paid less than expected, both aspects of interpersonal fairness had an effect. Those given no explanation and no statements of regret stole the most; those given information or statements of regret stole less; and those given both these treatments stole the least (see Figure 12.10).

Together, these findings have important practical implications. They suggest that companies *can* reduce the amount of theft by their employees, and that

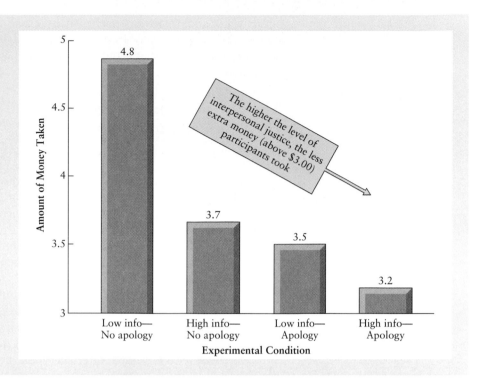

FIGURE 12.10

Theft As One Reaction to Perceived Unfairness. Individuals who were given a full explanation for why they were paid less than they expected stole less money than those who were not given such an explanation. Similarly, those who received apologies for the reduced pay stole less than those who did not. These findings indicate that both factors—information and apologies or statements of regret—influence perceived fairness.

(*Source:* Based on data from Greenberg, 1993b.)

to do so, they do not have to increase rates of pay and other employee benefits. Just as important as these factors, it appears, is the interpersonal treatment they provide to employees. As Greenberg and Scott (in press) note, managers should always treat employees with dignity, respect, and trust—not simply because this is the right thing to do, but also because it's far more difficult to steal from a friend than from someone who doesn't care about you. This may sound like enlightened self-interest, but it is also a means of increasing interpersonal fairness in work settings; and that, as we've already seen, can be very beneficial. ■ ■ ■

Decision Making by Groups: How It Occurs and the Pitfalls It Faces

Groups are called upon to perform a wide range of tasks—everything from conducting surgical operations through harvesting the world's crops. One of the most important activities they perform, however, is **decision making**—combining and integrating available information in order to choose one out of several possible courses of action. Governments, large corporations, military units, sports teams—virtually all social entities entrust key decisions to groups. As a result, most of the laws, policies, and business practices that affect our daily lives are determined by committees and other groups. There are several reasons for this fact, but perhaps the most important is this: Most people believe that groups, by pooling the expertise and knowledge of their members and by avoiding extreme courses of action, usually reach better decisions than individuals.

Are such beliefs accurate? Do groups actually make better or more accurate decisions than individuals? In their efforts to answer this practical question, social psychologists have focused on three major topics: (1) How do groups

Decision Making ■ The processes through which individuals or groups combine and integrate available information in order to choose one out of several possible courses of action.

actually go about moving toward consensus? (2) Do decisions reached by groups differ in any way from those reached by individuals? And (3) what accounts for the fact that groups sometimes make truly disastrous decisions—ones so bad that they are, in retrospect, hard to explain?

The Decision-Making Process: How Groups Attain Consensus

When groups first begin to discuss any issue, their members rarely voice unanimous agreement. Rather, they support a wide range of views and favor competing courses of action. After some period of discussion, however, they usually reach a decision. This does not always happen—juries, for instance, sometimes become hung, and other decision-making groups, too, may deadlock. In most cases, though, some decision is reached. Is there any way of predicting the final outcome from information about the views initially held by a group's members? Growing evidence suggests that there is (e.g., Kaplan & Miller, 1987).

Social Decision Schemes: Blueprints for Decisions. To summarize briefly some very complex findings, it appears that the final decisions reached by groups can often be predicted quite accurately by relatively simple rules known as **social decision schemes**. These rules relate the initial distribution of members' views or preferences to the group's final decisions. For example, one scheme—the *majority-wins rule*—suggests that in many cases the group will opt for whatever position is initially supported by most of its members. According to this rule, discussion serves mainly to confirm or strengthen the most popular view; it rarely reverses it, no matter how strongly the minority argues for its position. In contrast, a second decision scheme—the *truth-wins rule*—indicates that the correct solution or decision will ultimately come to the fore as its correctness is recognized by a growing number of members. A third decision scheme, adopted by many juries, is the *two-thirds majority rule*. Here, juries tend to convict defendants if two-thirds of the jurors initially favor this decision (Davis et al., 1984). Finally, some groups seem to follow a *first-shift rule*. They tend, ultimately, to adopt a decision consistent with the direction of the first shift in opinion shown by any members.

Surprising as it may seem, the results of many studies indicate that these straightforward rules are quite successful in predicting even complex group decisions. Indeed, they have been found to be accurate up to 80 percent of the time (e.g., Stasser, Taylor, & Hanna, 1989). Of course, different rules seem to be more successful under some conditions than under others. The majority-wins scheme, for instance, predicts decisions best in *judgmental tasks*—ones that are largely a matter of opinion. In contrast, the truth-wins rule seems best in predicting group decisions on *intellective tasks*—ones for which there *is* a correct answer (Kirchler & Davis, 1986).

Procedural Processes: When Decisions Are Influenced by the Procedures Used to Reach Them. While the decisions reached by groups can often be predicted from knowledge of members' initial positions, it is clear that many other factors play a role in this complex process. Among the most important of these are several aspects of the group's *procedures*—the rules it follows in addressing its agenda, managing interactions among members, and so on. One procedure adopted by many decision-making groups is the **straw poll,** in which members indicate their present positions or preferences in a nonbinding vote. While straw polls are nonbinding and thus allow group members to shift to other positions, research findings indicate that these informal votes often exert strong effects on members. Apparently, simply learning about the current distribution of opin-

Social Decision Schemes ■ Rules relating the initial distribution of member views to final group decisions.

Straw Poll ■ Procedure in which group members indicate their current preferences regarding a decision in a nonbinding vote.

FIGURE 12.11

Straw Polls: Sometimes, They Can Affect Group Decisions. *As suggested by this cartoon, when influential members of a group state their positions in a* straw poll, *this can exert strong effects upon the decision ultimately reached by the group.*

(*Source:* Drawing by C. Barsotti; © 1989 *The New Yorker* Magazine, Inc.)

ions within a group—or about the opinions of especially influential members (see Figure 12.11)—may cause some persons to join the majority, thus tilting the decision in this direction (Davis et al., 1988; MacCoun & Kerr, 1988).

Research on the effects of straw polls and several other procedures adopted by groups indicate that such procedures can strongly influence the decisions they reach, quite apart from information relating to these decisions.

The Nature of Group Decisions: Moderation—or a Tendency to Go Straight off the Deep End?

Truly important decisions are rarely left to individuals. Instead, they are usually assigned to groups—and highly qualified groups at that. Even kings, queens, and dictators usually consult with groups of skilled advisers before taking major actions. As we mentioned earlier, the major reason behind this strategy is the belief that groups are far less likely than individuals to make serious errors—to rush blindly over the edge. Is this really true? Research on this issue has yielded surprising findings. Contrary to popular beliefs, a large body of evidence indicates that groups are actually *more* likely to adopt extreme positions than individuals making decisions alone. In fact, across many different kinds of decisions and in many different contexts, groups show a pronounced tendency to shift toward views more extreme than the ones with which they initially began (Burnstein, 1983; Lamm & Myers, 1978). This is known as **group polarization,** and its major effects can be summarized as follows: Whatever the initial leaning or preference of a group prior to its discussions, it is strengthened during the group's deliberations. The result: Not only does the *group* shift toward more extreme views—*individual* members, too, often show such a shift. (Please note: The term *group polarization* does not refer to a tendency of groups to split apart into two opposing camps or poles; on the contrary, it refers to a strengthening of the group's initial preferences.)

Why does this effect occur? Research findings have helped provide an answer. Apparently, two major factors are involved. First, it appears that *social comparison*—a process we examined in Chapter 4—plays an important role. Everyone, it seems, wants to be "above average." Where opinions are concerned, this implies holding views that "better" than those of most other persons, and, especially, better than those of other group members. What does "better" mean? This depends on the specific group. Among a group of liberals,

Group Polarization ■ The tendency of group members to shift toward more extreme positions than those they initially held as a result of group discussion.

"better" would mean "more liberal." Among a group of conservatives, it would mean "more conservative." Among a group of racists, it would mean "even more bigoted." In any case, during group discussions, at least some members discover—to their shock!—that their views are *not* "better" than those of most other members. The result: After comparing themselves with these persons, they shift to even more extreme views, and the group polarization effect is off and running (Goethals & Zanna, 1979).

A second factor involves the fact that during group discussion, most arguments presented are ones favoring the group's initial leaning or preference. As a result of hearing such arguments, persuasion occurs (presumably through the *central route* described in Chapter 4), and members shift increasingly toward the majority view. This, of course, increases the proportion of arguments favoring this view, and ultimately members convince themselves that this is the "right" view and shift toward it with increasing strength. The result: Group polarization occurs (Vinokur & Burnstein, 1974).

While both of these factors seem to play a role in group polarization, research evidence (Zuber, Crott, & Werner, 1992) suggests that social comparison may be somewhat more important, at least in some contexts.

Regardless of the precise basis for group polarization, it definitely has important implications. The occurrence of polarization may lead many decision-making groups to adopt positions that are increasingly extreme, and therefore increasingly dangerous. In this context, it is chilling to speculate about the potential role of such shifts in disastrous decisions by political, military, or business groups who should by all accounts have known better—for example, the decision by the hard-liners in the now dissolved Soviet Union to stage a coup to restore firm communist rule. This backfired so badly that the government fell within a matter of days. Did group polarization influence this and other disastrous decisions—the decision by President Johnson to escalate the Vietnam war, the decision by IBM to refuse to buy a new operating system created by a struggling young technician named Bill Gates (now president of Microsoft, Inc.; see Figure 12.12)? It is impossible to say for sure. But the findings of many experiments on group polarization suggest that this is a real possibility.

Potential Dangers of Group Decision Making: Groupthink and the Tendency of Group Members to Tell Each Other What They Already Know

The drift of many decision-making groups toward polarization is a serious problem—one that can interfere with their ability to make accurate decisions. Unfortunately, this is not the only process that can exert such negative effects. Several others, too, seem to emerge out of group discussions and can lead groups to make costly, even disastrous, decisions (Hinsz, 1995). Among the most important of these are (1) groupthink, and (2) groups' seeming inability to share and use information held by some, but not all, of their members.

Groupthink: When Too Much Cohesiveness Is a Dangerous Thing. Earlier, we suggested that tendencies toward group polarization may be one reason why decision-making groups sometimes go off the deep end—with catastrophic results. However, another, even more disturbing factor may also contribute to such outcomes. This is a process known as **groupthink**—a strong tendency for decision-making groups to close ranks, cognitively, around a decision, assuming that the group *can't* be wrong, that all members must support the decision strongly, and that any information contrary to it should be rejected (Janis,

Groupthink ■ The tendency of highly cohesive groups to assume that their decisions can't be wrong: that all members must support the group's decision and ignore information contrary to it.

FIGURE 12.12

Disastrous Group Decisions: Why Do They Occur? In 1980, Bill Gates, president of Microsoft, tried to sell his computer operating system to IBM. A committee of IBM executives considered this offer, then refused. This was one of the worst business decisions of all time, and IBM soon paid the price for its mistake.

1982). Once this collective state of mind develops, it appears, groups become unwilling—and perhaps *unable*—to change their course of action, even if external events suggest very strongly that their original decision was a poor one. In fact, according to Janis (1982), the social psychologist who originated the concept of *groupthink,* norms soon emerge in the group that actively prevent its members from considering alternative courses of action. The group is viewed as being incapable of making an error, and anyone with lingering doubts is quickly silenced, both by group pressure and by their own desire to conform.

Why does groupthink occur? Research findings (e.g., Kameda & Sugimori, 1993; Tetlock et al.,1992) suggest that two factors may be crucial. The first is a very high level of *cohesiveness* among group members. Decision-making groups that fall victim to groupthink tend to consist of persons who share the same background and ideology. The second factor is the kind of *emergent group norms* mentioned above—norms suggesting that the group is infallible and morally superior, and that therefore there should be no further discussion of the issues at hand: the decision has been made, and the only task now is to support it as strongly as possible. Once groupthink takes hold in a decision-making group, Janis (1982) argues, pressure toward maintaining high levels of group consensus—*concurrence seeking* is his term for it—overrides the motivation to evaluate all potential courses of action as accurately as possible. The result: Such groups shift from focusing on making the best decisions possible to focusing on maintaining a high level of consensus and the belief that the group is right, no matter what.

Research on groupthink indicates that it is real, and that it does play an important role in at least some disastrous decisions (e.g., Tetlock et al., 1992). For example, consider a revealing study by Kameda and Sugimori (1993). These researchers suggested that groupthink may be closely linked to another important pitfall in group decision making—one known as **collective entrapment**. This is the tendency for groups to cling stubbornly to unsuccessful decisions or policies even in the face of overwhelming evidence that the decisions are bad ones. Entrapment (sometimes known as *sunk costs* or *escalation of commitment*) also occurs at the individual level (Bobocel & Meyer, 1994; Brockner, 1992). Here's an example: I once owned a used car that seemed to have one thing wrong with it after another. The more money I spent repairing it, the harder it became for me to sell it; I simply had too much invested to quit—to admit that I had made a mistake and cut my losses. Situations like this are very common, and they are entrapping: the longer we stick with a bad decision, the harder it is to admit our error and reverse it.

Collective entrapment involves similar tendencies on the part of decision-making groups. They, too, find it difficult to admit that they made a mistake, and according to Kameda and Sugimori (1993), this is an important element in groupthink. To test this reasoning, these researchers conducted a study in which Japanese students were asked to decide which of two job applicants to hire for their companies. The participants worked in three-person groups, and were, in two different conditions, to make this decision by reaching either a unanimous consensus or a simple majority. The groups were formulated so that in some, initial opinions about promoting the employee were split, while in others, all members agreed. After making their decisions, all the groups learned that the person they hired had done very poorly during a probationary period. They were then asked whether to fire this person or to promote her to full employee status. In making this second decision—the crucial one for purposes of the study—participants were told to reach a unanimous decision.

Kameda and Sugimori (1993) reasoned that the greater the effort groups had to expend in reaching their initial decision, the more strongly they would stick to it, and thus the more likely they would be to promote the poorly performing employee. When would effort be greatest? When the groups were told to make the initial decision unanimously and when opinions were split in the group; under these conditions, the groups would have to work hard to resolve differences between members. Kameda and Sugimori (1993) reasoned that as a result, cohesiveness would be high and emergent norms supporting the group's decision would be strong—in other words, key elements of groupthink would emerge. Thus, the groups would be most likely to stick to their poor decision under these conditions. As you can see from Figure 12.13, this is precisely what happened. Groups in which opinion was initially split and which originally reached a unanimous decision about whom to hire were much more likely to promote the employee than those in the other conditions. These findings indicate that groupthink is indeed closely related to collective entrapment: similar factors play a role in both processes.

When it develops, groupthink can be a powerful force serving to lock decision-making groups into bad choices or policies. Can anything be done to prevent its occurrence? Several procedures seems useful. First, groups wishing to avoid groupthink should promote open inquiry and *skepticism* among their members. Group leaders should encourage careful questioning of each alternative or policy and should, if necessary, play the role of devil's advocate, intentionally finding faults with various options. Second, once a decision is reached, *second-chance* meetings, in which group members are asked to express any lingering doubts, can be extremely valuable. Third, it is often helpful to ask different groups of persons than those who made the initial decision to decide whether to continue with it. Since the second group did not make the initial decision, it does not experience strong pressures to justify the original choice; in this way, pressures toward collective entrapment are reduced, and one important ingredient in groupthink may

Collective Entrapment ■ Tendency of some groups to cling stubbornly to unsuccessful decisions or policies even in the face of evidence that they are bad ones.

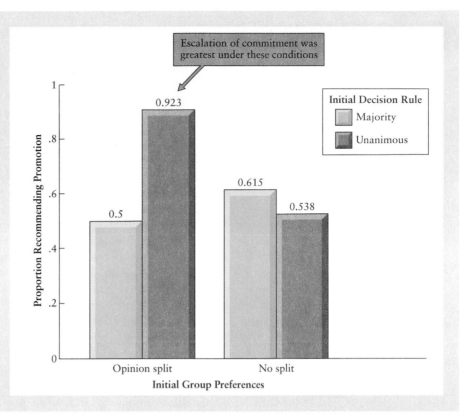

FIGURE 12.13

Groupthink and Collective Entrapment. Groups in which opinion was initially split and which originally had to reach a unanimous decision about whom to hire showed the strongest tendencies toward escalation of commitment—promoting the employee even though she had performed very poorly. These findings indicate that groupthink is indeed closely related to collective entrapment: Similar factors play a role in both processes.

(*Source:* Based on data from Kameda & Sugimori, 1993.)

be eliminated. In sum, while groupthink is a real danger faced by decision-making groups, several steps can reduce the likelihood of its occurrence—and hence the risk that groups will adopt, and stick to, failing courses of action.

Why Groups Often Fail to Pool Their Resources: Information Sampling and the Common Knowledge Effect. One reason why many key decisions are entrusted to groups is the belief that members will pool their resources—share information and ideas unique to each individual. In this way, the decisions they reach will be better, it is reasoned, than those that would be reached by individuals working in isolation. Is this actually the case? Do groups really share the knowledge and expertise brought to them by their individual members? Research on this issue (Gigone & Hastie, 1993; Stasser, 1992; Stasser & Titus, 1985) suggests that in fact, such pooling of resources may occur less often than common sense predicts.

Several of these studies were undertaken to test a theory of group discussion known as the **information sampling model** (Stasser & Titus, 1985). This model suggests that information shared by many members is more likely to be mentioned during group discussion than information held by only a single member. Why? Because since many members have this information, the probability is high that at least one will call it to the group's attention. As a result, decision-making groups are more likely to discuss—and discuss again—information already known to most members, whereas information known to only one or a few members is much less likely to come to the fore. The model further predicts that the larger the group, the greater the advantage of shared over unshared information. Perhaps even more discouraging, the information sampling model also suggests that leaders' efforts to increase the pooling of information by

Information Sampling Model
■ A theory of group decision making suggesting that group members are more likely to discuss shared than unshared information; this tendency increases with group size.

urging groups to discuss all information before reaching a decision may actually backfire: these efforts *increase* the tendency for members to discuss information already known to most of them (Stasser, Taylor, & Hanna, 1989).

Fortunately, at least one technique does seem effective in countering this tendency to discuss shared information over and over again. When group members are told that there is a correct solution or decision and that their task is to find it, the tendency to discuss *unshared* information is increased (Stasser & Stewart, 1992). This appears to be an exception to the general rule, however: in most cases, group discussions tend to focus on information already known to most members.

This is not the only problem that gets in the way of the hoped-for pooling of resources in decision-making groups, however. In addition, research findings indicate the existence of a **common knowledge effect**—the tendency for information held by most members to exert a stronger impact on the group's final decision than information that is not held by most members (Gigone & Hastie, 1993). This seems to occur because such information shapes members' views prior to the group discussion, and also because such information *is* discussed more often than unshared information. So not only does shared information tend to gain the floor during group discussions, it is also more influential in determining the group's decision.

Additional findings indicate that as groups continue to work together, they may come to recognize what information most members share and what information is unique. Then the likelihood of a pooling of resources may tend to increase (Stasser & Hinkle, 1994). However, taken as a whole, existing evidence indicates that decision-making groups do not automatically benefit from the fact that various individual members have unique knowledge and skills.

INTEGRATING PRINCIPLES

1. Contrary to popular belief, groups tend to make more extreme decisions than individuals, in part because of social comparison and persuasion (see Chapter 4).

2. Groups are sometimes subject to *groupthink*, a strong tendency to assume that the group *can't* be wrong and to ignore information inconsistent with the group's decisions. Groupthink stems, in part, from strong pressures toward conformity with the group's norms (Chapter 9).

3. Groups often fail to pool the resources of their members: they discuss information already known by most members rather than information held by only one or a few members. Since only information presented can influence a group's decision (Chapter 4), this is another potential pitfall facing decision-making groups.

Common Knowledge Effect ■
The tendency for information held by most members of a group to exert a stronger impact on the group's final decision than information not held by most members.

Leadership: Patterns of Influence within Groups

Try this simple demonstration with your friends. Ask each one to rate themselves, on a seven-point scale ranging from 1 (very low) to 7 (very high), in terms of *leadership potential*. What do you think you will find? Probably, that most people rate themselves as average or above on this characteristic. This suggests that people view leadership in very favorable terms. But what, precisely, *is* **leadership?** Social psychologists define it as *the process through which one member of a group (its leader) influences other group members toward the attainment of specific group goals* (Yukl 1994). In other words, leadership has to do with *influence*—who influences whom in various groups. The assumption, of course, is that leaders do most of the influencing; but as we'll soon see, leadership, like all social relationships, is reciprocal in nature—leaders are influenced by, as well as exert influence over, their followers.

Research on leadership has been a part of social psychology since its very earliest days; and in recent decades, this research has spilled outside social psychology to the closely related fields of *industrial/organizational psychology* and *organizational behavior* (Fiedler, 1994; Greenberg & Baron, 1995). In this discussion, we'll provide you with an overview of what social psychologists and others have discovered about leadership. We'll start by examining the question of *who* becomes a leader. We'll turn next to the various *styles* of leadership—how leaders exert their influence over others. And we will conclude with some comments on what is perhaps the most dramatic form of leadership—*charismatic* or *transformational* leadership.

Who Becomes a Leader: Traits, Situations, or Both?

Are some people born to lead? Common sense suggests that this is so. Eminent leaders of the past such as Alexander the Great, Queen Elizabeth I, and Abraham Lincoln seem to differ from ordinary human beings in several respects. Such observations led early researchers to formulate a view of leadership known as the **great person theory.** According to this theory, great leaders possess certain traits that set them apart from most human beings. Further, the theory suggests that these traits remain stable over time and across different cultures so that *all* great leaders, no matter when or where they lived, resemble one another in certain respects.

These are intriguing ideas, but up until about 1890 research designed to test the theory generally failed to yield positive findings. Try as they might, researchers could not formulate a short, agreed-upon list of the key traits shared by all leaders (Geier, 1969; Yukl, 1981). In recent years, however, this situation has altered greatly. More sophisticated research methods, coupled with a better understanding of the basic dimensions of human personality, have led many researchers to conclude that leaders do indeed differ from other persons in several important respects (Kirkpatrick & Locke, 1991).

What, then, are the key traits of leaders—the characteristics that suit them for this important role? The findings of research on this topic are summarized in Table 12.1 (p. 464). As you can see from this table, leaders appear to be higher than other persons in terms of such characteristics as *drive*—the desire for achievement coupled with high energy and resolution; *self-confidence; creativity;* and *leadership motivation*—the desire to be in charge and exercise authority over others. Perhaps the most important single characteristic of leaders, however, is a high level of *flexibility:* the ability to recognize what actions or approaches are required in a given situation, and then to act accordingly (Zaccaro, Foti, & Kenny, 1991).

While certain traits do seem to be related to leadership, however, it is also clear that leaders do *not* operate in a social vacuum. On the contrary, different groups, facing different tasks and problems, seem to require different types of leaders—or at least, leaders who demonstrate different styles. This basic fact is recognized in all modern theories of leadership, which take careful note of the fact that leadership is a complex role, involving not only influence but many

Leadership ■ The process through which leaders influence other group members toward attainment of specific group goals.

Great Person Theory (of leadership) ■ Theory suggesting that all great leaders share key traits that suit them for positions of authority.

Table 12.1 The Characteristics of Successful Leaders

Research findings indicate that successful leaders show the traits listed here to a greater extent than other persons.

Trait	Description
Drive	Desire for achievement; ambition; high energy; tenacity; initiative
Honesty and Integrity	Trustworthiness; reliability; openness
Leadership Motivation	Desire to exercise influence over others to reach shared goals
Self-Confidence	Trust in own abilities
Cognitive Ability	Intelligence; ability to integrate and interpret large amounts of information
Creativity	Originality
Flexibility	Ability to adapt to needs of followers and to changing situational requirements
Expertise	Knowledge of the group's activities; knowledge of relevant technical matters

(*Source:* Based on suggestions by Kirkpatrick & Locke, 1991.)

other kinds of interaction between leaders and followers as well (Bass, 1990; House & Podsakoff, 1994; Locke, 1991). So *yes*, traits do matter where leadership is concerned, but they are only part of the total picture. Leadership, like all forms of social behavior, can be understood only in terms of complex interactions between social situations and individual characteristics. Approaches that focus entirely on one of these aspects are appealing in their simplicity, but decades of research indicate that they are also inaccurate.

How Leaders Operate: Contrasting Styles and Approaches

All leaders are definitely *not* alike. On the contrary, they differ greatly in terms of personal *style* or approach to leadership (e.g., George 1995). Do you remember how I learned this fact myself through the contrasting styles of my fourth-grade and fifth-grade teachers (see Chapter 1)? As you may recall, my fourth-grade teacher truly ran the show: she took charge of *everything*. In contrast, my fifth-grade teacher took a much more democratic approach: she let the class vote on many decisions, and let us do our own thing to a much greater extent. A very large volume of research suggests that such differences in leadership style are both real and important. Early research, such as that by Lewin and his colleagues, presented in Chapter 1, described leaders' style in terms of a single dimension ranging from *democratic* on one end through *autocratic* on the other. More modern research, however, suggests that there are actually several key dimensions along which leaders differ in terms of their style.

One of these is, in fact, the *autocratic–democratic* dimension first noted by Lewin, Lippitt, and White (1939). Autocratic leaders make decisions unilaterally, while democratic leaders invite input and participation in decision making from their followers. Another important dimension, however, is one involving the extent to which leaders dictate how followers should carry out their assigned tasks versus giving them the freedom to work in any way they wish. This is referred to as the *directive–permissive* dimension, and it cross-cuts the autocratic–democratic dimension; thus, leaders tend to show one of the four different patterns summarized in Figure 12.14 (Muczyk & Reimann, 1987).

FIGURE 12.14

Basic Dimensions of Leadership Style.
Leaders differ greatly along the two dimensions shown here: democratic–autocratic and directive–permissive.

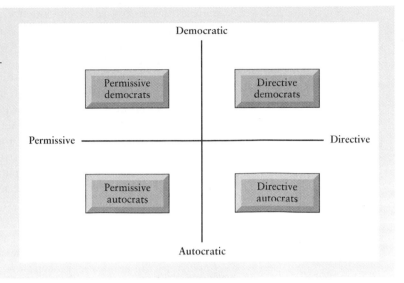

Finally, we should note that leaders' styles also differ along two other important dimensions, sometimes known as *task orientation* and *person orientation*. Task orientation refers to the extent to which a given leader focuses on getting the task done—whatever it happens to be. Person orientation, in contrast, refers to leaders' interest in maintaining good, friendly relations with their followers. Leaders can be high or low on each of these dimensions; for instance, a given leader can be high on both, low on both, high on one and low on the other, or moderate on both. These dimensions of leader style appear to be very basic ones: they have been observed among thousands of different leaders in many different contexts (e.g., business groups, military groups, and sports teams), and in several different countries (Bass, 1990). Interestingly, no single style seems to be best; rather, which one is most effective depends on the specific circumstances. For example, when leaders are high on person orientation, they often have friendly relations with their followers—who may then be reluctant to give them any bad news. The result: The leaders may get into serious trouble because they are not receiving vital feedback from followers. In contrast, leaders high in task orientation often do wring high levels of performance out of their followers. These people may feel that the leader has no interest in them, though, and this may weaken their commitment to the group.

In sum, leaders do appear to differ greatly with respect to personal style—how they go about fulfilling the role of leader—and these differences have important effects on their groups. However, because leaders' style is only one of many factors influencing leadership, it would be misleading to suggest that one style is always—or even usually—best.

Gender Differences in Leadership

Do male and female leaders differ in their styles of leadership? While there is a widespread belief that they do, systematic research on this issue suggests that in general, they actually do not (Powell, 1990). Female and male leaders appear to differ in only a few respects, and even these are far smaller in magnitude than gender-role stereotypes suggest. Evidence pointing to these conclusions has been collected by Eagly and her colleagues in a series of careful meta-analyses of existing research evidence. (See our discussion of meta-analysis in Chapter 1.)

In the first of these reviews, Eagly and Johnson (1990) examined the results of more than 150 studies in order to determine whether female and male leaders actually differ in terms of leadership style. They focused on several dimensions of leadership style described above: task orientation versus person orientation, and autocratic versus democratic styles of decision making. Gender-role stereotypes suggest that female leaders might show more concern with persons than male leaders and might make decisions in a more democratic manner. However, results offered support only for differences with respect to the autocratic–democratic dimension. Female leaders were slightly more likely to adopt a democratic style than male leaders. They were not, however, more person-oriented than male leaders.

In a follow-up investigation, Eagly and her colleagues (Eagly, Makhijani, & Klonsky, 1992) focused on a related issue: Are female and male leaders evaluated differently by others? Because serving as a leader is in some respects contrary to the gender stereotype for females, the researchers predicted that female leaders might receive lower ratings than male leaders, even when their performance was identical. Moreover, Eagly and her colleagues also expected that such down-rating of female leaders would be greater among male evaluators than among female evaluators, and that it would be more likely to occur in fields where most employees were male, and in situations in which the female leaders adopted a directive, autocratic style of leadership—a traditionally "masculine" leadership approach. Results provided support for all of these predictions. There was a small, but significant, tendency for female leaders to be rated lower than male leaders. However, this down-rating of female leaders was stronger when they adopted a style of leadership viewed as stereotypically masculine (autocratic, directive), when the evaluators were male, and when the female leaders were working in fields where most other leaders were male.

Combining the findings reported by Eagly and her associates with those of others studies, it appears that female leaders continue to face disadvantages in many settings. While their behavior or style differs from that of male leaders in only a few relatively minor respects, female leaders continue to receive lower ratings than their male counterparts. We can only hope that this situation will change in the years ahead, as gender stereotypes weaken and as the number of females in leadership positions continues to increase.

Transformational Leadership: Leadership through Vision and Charisma

Transformational Leaders ■ Leaders who exert profound influence over followers by proposing an inspiring vision and through several other techniques. (See also *charismatic leaders*).

Charismatic Leaders ■ Leaders who induce high levels of loyalty, respect, and admiration among their followers. (See also *transformational leadership*).

Have you ever seen films of John F. Kennedy? Franklin D. Roosevelt? Martin Luther King Jr.? If so, you may have noticed that there seemed to be something special about these leaders. As you listened to their speeches, you may have found yourself being moved by their words and stirred by the vigor with which they delivered their messages. If so, you are not alone: these leaders exerted such effects on many millions of persons and, by doing so, changed their society—and perhaps even the entire world. Leaders who accomplish such feats are often termed **transformational** or **charismatic leaders,** and the terms (which are used interchangeably) seem fitting. Such persons do indeed transform social, political, or economic reality; and they do seem to possess special skills that equip them for this task. (The word *charisma* by the way, means *gift* in Greek.) What personal characteristics make certain leaders charismatic?

And how do such leaders exert their dramatic influence on large numbers of followers? Systematic research on this issue has begun to yield some intriguing answers.

The Basic Nature of Charisma: Traits or Relationships? At first glance, it is tempting to assume that transformational leaders are special because they possess certain traits; in other words, that such leadership can be understood in terms of the *great person theory* described earlier. While traits may play a role in transformational leadership, there is growing consensus that it makes more sense to understand such leadership as involving a special type of *relationship* between leaders and their followers (House, 1977). Charismatic leadership, it appears, rests more on specific types of reactions by followers than on traits possessed by charismatic leaders. Such reactions include: (1) high levels of devotion, loyalty, and reverence toward the leader; (2) enthusiasm for the leader and the leader's ideas; (3) a willingness by followers to sacrifice their own personal interests for the sake of a larger group goal; and (4) levels of performance beyond those that would normally be expected. In short, transformational or charismatic leadership involves a special kind of leader–follower relationship, one in which the leader can, in the words of one author, "make ordinary people do extraordinary things in the face of adversity" (Conger, 1991).

The Behavior of Transformational Leaders. But what, precisely, do transformational leaders do to generate this kind of relationship with followers? Studies designed to answer this question point to the following conclusion: Such leaders gain the capacity to exert profound influence over others through many different tactics. One of the most important of these involves the fact that such leaders propose a *vision* (Howell & Frost, 1989). They describe, usually in vivid, emotion-provoking terms, an image of what their nation or group can—and should—become. Consider the following words, uttered by Martin Luther King Jr. in his famous "I Have a Dream" speech:

> So I say to you, my friends, that even though we must face the difficulties of today and tomorrow, I still have a dream. It is a dream deeply rooted in the American dream that one day this nation will rise up and live out the true meaning of its creed—we hold these truths to be self-evident, that all men are created equal. This will be the day when all of God's children will be able to sing with new meaning "My country, 'tis of thee, sweet land of liberty."

But transformational leaders do more than merely describe a dream or vision; in addition, they offer a route for attaining it. They tell their followers, in straightforward terms, how to get from here to there. This, too, seems to be crucial, for a vision that seems perpetually out of reach is unlikely to motivate people to try to attain it.

Third, transformational leaders engage in what Conger (1991) terms *framing:* they define the purpose of their movement or organization in a way that gives meaning and purpose to whatever actions they are requesting from followers. Perhaps the nature of framing is best illustrated by the well-known story of two stonecutters working on a cathedral in the Middle Ages. When asked what they were doing, one replied, "Why cutting this stone, of course." The other answered, "Building the world's most beautiful temple to the glory of God." Which person would be more likely to expend great effort on his task? The answer is obvious.

Other tactics shown by transformational leaders include high levels of self-confidence and confidence in their followers, a high degree of concern for their followers' needs, excellent communication skills, and a stirring personal style (House, Spangler, & Woycke, 1991). Finally, transformational leaders are often masters of *impression management,* engaging in many actions designed to enhance their appeal to others (see Chapter 2). When these forms of behavior are added to the exciting visions they promote, the tremendous impact of transformational leaders loses most of its apparent mystery. In fact, it rests firmly on principles and processes well understood by social psychologists.

The Effects of Transformational Leaders: A Very Mixed Bag.   Are transformational or charismatic leaders always a plus for their groups or societies? As you probably already realize, definitely not. Many charismatic leaders use their skills for what they perceive to be the good of their group or society—people like Martin Luther King Jr., Franklin D. Roosevelt, and Indira Gandhi, to name just a few (see Figure 12.15). But others use this leadership style for purely selfish ends (Howell & Avolio, 1992). For example, Michael Milken, former head of the brokerage firm Drexel Burnham Lambert, was described by followers as being extremely charismatic. Yet he used the trust and loyalty he inspired for illegal ends: stock fraud that cost innocent investors millions of dollars. Similarly, David Koresh, leader of a religious cult in Waco, Texas, used his position to reserve all females in the group for himself—including girls as young as ten years old—while insisting that the other males remain celibate. Ultimately, Koresh's charismatic style of leadership resulted in the death of many of his followers, who set fire to their compound when it was besieged by federal agents (refer to Figure 12.15).

In short, charismatic or transformational leadership is definitely a two-edged sword. It can be used to promote beneficial social change consistent with the highest principles and ethical standards; or it can be used for selfish, illegal, and immoral purposes. The difference lies in the personal conscience and moral code of the persons who wield it.

FIGURE 12.15

Charismatic Leaders: Good and Evil. Some charismatic leaders like Martin Luther King (left) use their powerful impact on followers for what they view as prosocial ends: changing their societies for the better. However, others such as David Koresh (right), use their impact on followers for purely selfish purposes—or worse!

INTEGRATING PRINCIPLES

1. Leadership involves the exercise of influence by one group member over other members. In exerting such influence, leaders use many different tactics (see Chapter 9).

2. Leaders appear to differ from followers in terms of several traits, but not all leaders are alike. On the contrary, they adopt very different styles.

3. Transformational or charismatic leaders are masters of impression management (Chapter 2) and use techniques such as framing (see Chapter 3) and a vision to exert profound effects upon their followers.

Social Diversity: A Critical Analysis

SOCIAL LOAFING: An International Perspective

IN OUR EARLIER DISCUSSION OF SOCIAL LOAFING, WE NOTED that the collective effort model proposed by Karau and Williams (1993) predicts that such behavior will be less prevalent in cultures that value group outcomes more than individual outcomes. In fact, many such cultures exist. They are typically described as *collectivistic* in orientation, because they place a high value on shared responsibility and the collective good of all. In such cultures, it is often viewed as bad form to stand out from the group by exceeding others in terms of performance. Rather, it is group performance that is important. In *individualistic* cultures such as those in many Western countries, in contrast, the emphasis is on individual accomplishments and success.

Is social loafing actually less frequent in collectivistic cultures? To find out, Earley (1993) asked individuals from the United States, Israel, and the People's Republic of China to complete a task that simulated the daily activities of managers—for example, writing memos, filling out forms, and rating job applicants. They were asked to perform these tasks for one hour either alone or as part of a group of ten persons. In the *alone* condition, participants simply wrote their names on each item as they completed it and turned it in. In the *group* condition, however, participants were told that their group's overall performance would be assessed at the end of the session.

Earley (1993) predicted that for persons from the United States, performance would be lower in the group than in the alone condition; in other words, social loafing would occur. In contrast, for persons from Israel and China—two cultures that are more collectivistic than the United States—performance would be better in the group than in the alone condition. In other words, social loafing would not occur; on the contrary, participants would actually work *harder* when part of a group. As you can see from Figure 12.16 (p. 470), results offered clear support for these predictions.

These results indicate that culture plays an important role in shaping individuals' willingness to engage in social loafing. In societies where individual accomplishment is highly valued, people seem to experience reduced motivation when they feel that their performance will not be evaluated on an individual basis. The result: They engage in social loafing. In societies where greater emphasis is placed on group outcomes, working together with others does not lead to reductions in motivation. On the contrary, people may actually work harder when they are part of a group. The moral is clear: Social loafing, like many other aspects of social behavior, occurs against a background of complex cultural factors. Thus, taking careful account of these can add significantly to our understanding of many social processes.

FIGURE 12.16

Social Loafing in Three Different Countries. As shown here, Americans performed far better on a task when they worked alone than when they worked with others. In contrast, persons from Israel and China performed better when they worked as part of a group. These findings are consistent with the prediction that social loafing will be greater in *individualistic* cultures such as the United States than in *collectivistic* cultures such as Israel and China.

(*Source:* Based on data from Earley, 1993.)

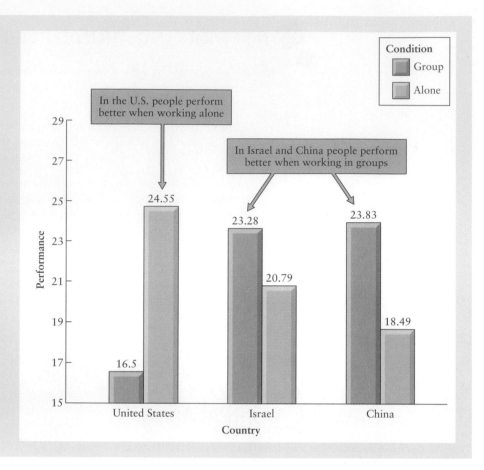

CONNECTIONS: Integrating Social Psychology

In this chapter, you read about . . .	*In other chapters, you will find related discussions of . . .*
the role of norms in the functioning of groups	the nature of norms and their role in social influence (Chapter 9)
individuals' concern with others' evaluations of their performance	the effects of others' evaluations on our self-concept (Chapter 5) and on our liking for others (Chapter 7)
perceived fairness	the effects of perceived fairness on many other forms of social behavior, such as helping (Chapter 10) and aggression (Chapter 11), and its role in close relationships (Chapter 8)
the role of persuasion and other forms of social influence in group decision making	the nature of persuasion (Chapter 4) and various forms of social influence (Chapter 9)

the role of personal characteristics in leadership

gender and leadership

the role of personal characteristics in many other forms of social behavior, such as helping (Chapter 10) and aggression (Chapter 11)

the role of gender in many other aspects of social behavior: persuasion and conformity (Chapters 4, 9), attraction and close relationships (Chapters 7, 8), helping (Chapter 10), and aggression (Chapter 11)

Thinking about Connections

1. Suppose that despite high wages and access to excellent equipment, a work team in a large company is performing far below expectations. Do you think that social norms (see Chapter 9) might be playing a role in this surprising outcome? How could this be so?

2. As we noted in this chapter, some group members do less than their fair share with respect to the group's work—they engage in *social loafing*. Drawing on what you know about the impact of norms (Chapter 9), interpersonal attraction (Chapter 7), and long-term relationships (Chapter 8), what steps could a group take to minimize such "goofing off" among its members?

3. Some leaders, such as those of religious cults, exert incredibly powerful effects on their followers. Drawing on what you know about social influence (see Chapter 9), what are your views on how these leaders attain such power? In other words, what tactics or procedures do they use to gain an amazing degree of control over their follower?

4. Decision making by groups is a complex process. Drawing on previous discussions of gender throughout this book (e.g., Chapters 6, 7, 10, 11), do you think that decision making would be different in groups consisting of males than in groups consisting of females? If so, in what ways, and why would these differences exist?

Summary and Review

Groups: Their Nature and Function

A *group* consists of two or more persons who share common goals, whose fates are interdependent, who have a stable relationship, and who recognize that they belong to a group. Groups influence their members through *roles*—members' assigned functions in the group; *status*—their relative standing in the group; *norms*—rules concerning appropriate behavior for members; and *cohesiveness*—all the factors that cause members to remain in the group.

Groups and Task Performance

Individuals' performance of various tasks is often affected by the presence of others or by the potential evaluation of their work by these persons. Such effects are known as *social facilitation*, although they can involve reduced as well as enhanced task performance. According to *distraction–conflict theory*, social facili-

tation effects stem from the arousal induced by conflict between two incompatible tendencies: paying careful attention to others, and paying careful attention to a task.

When individuals work on a task with others, they may show *social loafing*—reduced motivation and effort. Social loafing appears to be influenced by several different factors. One recent theory of social loafing, the *collective effort model*, suggests that social loafing occurs because when individuals work with others in a group, relationships between their effort and their outcomes become less certain. Several techniques are effective in reducing social loafing. These include making the output or effort of each group member readily identifiable, increasing members' commitment to successful performance, increasing the apparent importance of the task being performed, and strengthening group cohesiveness.

Perceived Fairness in Groups

Individuals want to be treated fairly by others and by groups to which they belong. More specifically, they are concerned that the ratio of their contributions to a group and the outcomes they receive be approximately equal to the same ratio for other members (*distributive justice* or *equity*). In addition, they are concerned that the procedures used to allocate rewards be fair (*procedural justice*), and that they be treated in a considerate manner (*interpersonal justice*). When individuals conclude that they have not been treated fairly, they experience strong negative feelings and generally engage in various tactics to restore perceived fairness. These include altering their actual outcomes or contributions, withdrawing from the relationship, or changing their perceptions of the situation so that it no longer seems quite so unfair.

Decision Making by Groups

Many important decisions are entrusted to groups. Group decisions can sometimes be predicted by *social decision schemes*—simple rules relating the initial views held by members to the group's final decision. Procedures such as *straw polls* can influence group decisions. Group discussions often result in a shift toward more extreme positions—the *group polarization effect*. Thus, contrary to popular belief, groups may tend to make more extreme decisions than individuals. Decision-making groups also face other potential pitfalls. One of these is *groupthink*: tendencies for a group to assume that it is infallible coupled with refusal to examine relevant information. Recent evidence indicates that groupthink may be related to *collective entrapment*—the tendency to stick to bad decisions even in the face of increasing evidence that they are wrong. Another important problem faced by decision-making groups is their apparent inability to pool the resources of members. Groups tend to discuss information shared by all members rather than information held by only one or a few members. Moreover, such shared information exerts stronger effects on group decisions than other information; this is known as the *common knowledge effect*.

Leadership

Leadership involves the exercise of influence by one group member over other group members. According to the *great person theory*, all great leaders share similar traits. Recent evidence indicates that in fact, leaders do seem to differ from followers with respect to several characteristics. However, successful leadership involves a complex interplay between these characteristics, many aspects of the situation faced by the group, and leaders' relations with group members. Leaders differ greatly in terms of personal style. Important dimensions of leadership style include the autocratic–democratic and directive–permissive dimensions, and two dimensions relating to leaders' degree of emphasis on task performance or personal relationships with followers. Male and female leaders do not differ in most respects. However, female leaders appear to adopt a more democratic leadership style than males.

Transformational or *charismatic* leaders exert profound effects on their followers. They do this by establishing a special kind of relationships with followers, by proposing an inspiring vision, and by the expert use of many tactics of influence.

Social Diversity: Social Loafing

The *collective effort model* predicts that social loafing will be less common in collectivistic cultures—ones that emphasize the importance of group performance and outcomes—than in individualistic cultures—ones that emphasize the importance of individual performance and success. Research findings have confirmed this prediction, indicating that social loafing is more common in the United States than in Israel and China.

■ Key Terms

Group Polarization (p. 457)

Groupthink (p. 458)

Information Sampling Model (p. 461)

Interpersonal Justice (p. 450)

Leadership (p. 463)

Norms (p. 437)

Procedural Justice (p. 449)

Roles (p. 437)

Social Decision Schemes (p. 456)

Social Facilitation (p. 441)

Social Loafing (p. 444)

Status (p. 437)

Straw Poll (p. 456)

Transformational Leaders (p. 466)

■ For More Information

Castellan, N. J. Jr. (Ed.). (1993). *Individual and group decision making: Current issues.* Hillsdale, NJ: Erlbaum.

This book contains chapters prepared by many experts on the topic of decision making by both individuals and groups. It is an excellent source to consult if you want to learn more about this fascinating topic.

Paulus, P. B. (Ed.). (1989). *Psychology of group influence.* Hillsdale, NJ: Erlbaum.

Deals with many of the topics considered in this chapter (e.g., social facilitation, social loafing, leadership). If

you'd like to know more about these aspects of behavior in group settings, this is an outstanding source.

Simonton, D. K. (1994). *Greatness: Who makes history and why?* New York: Guilford Press.

A social psychologist who has conducted extensive research on leadership offers his perspective on why certain persons become great leaders and on how these leaders exert powerful effects on large numbers of people. A must if you are interested in transformational or charismatic leadership.

CHAPTER 13

SOCIAL PSYCHOLOGY AND SOCIETY: Legal and Organizational Applications

Lisa Houck, *An Ancient Living Situation*, 1993, watercolor, 22 × 30"

Chapter Outline

In recent years the U.S. public has discovered the courtroom as a source of seemingly endless fascination. Have you watched any portion of the trials involving Lorena Bobbitt (accused of severing her husband's penis with a knife), the Menendez brothers (accused of murdering their parents), several Los Angeles policemen (accused of using excessive violence against Rodney King), or O. J. Simpson (accused of murdering his former wife and one of her friends)? If so, did you observe anything in the proceedings that reminded you of the social psychological research you read about in this book?

In a trial, members of the jury face a complex information-processing task, and they are usually instructed by the judge not to take notes and not to discuss the case with anyone until the end of the proceedings. You might try this yourself during any trial that is broadcast on Court TV, CNN, or other outlets. How well do you think you will do in keeping an open mind until all of the evidence is in?

Have you ever held a job that you hated, or one that you truly enjoyed? What are some of the factors that created these two different kinds of experience? Was your performance on the job affected by your feelings and attitudes? If you owned a business, which reaction would you prefer among your employees, and what could you do to increase the likelihood of such an outcome?

When social psychologists apply their theories and research skills in real-life settings such as the legal system and the organizations in which we work, the relevance of our field to societal concerns becomes obvious. In the following pages, we first describe the way in which social psychology has been applied to numerous aspects of the *legal system*, one of the original applied interests of the early social psychologists. Cognitive and emotional processes are crucial at each step in the legal process, from police interrogations and pretrial publicity to the behavior of the participants in the courtroom. We then turn to applications of social psychology to business, focusing on several areas of research that rest directly on basic principles of our field: *work-related attitudes* (job satisfaction and organizational commitment), social aspects of *job interviews, organizational politics,* and *conflict* in work settings.

The Application of Social Psychology to the Interpersonal Aspects of the Legal System

If the real world lived up to our ideals, the judicial process would provide an elaborate and totally fair set of procedures to reach objective, unbiased decisions about violations of criminal and civil laws. At the other extreme, our worst nightmares would be realized if the judicial process functioned in the way depicted in Figure 13.1. In fact, the legal system is neither as perfect as our ideal nor as terrible as our nightmares. Research in **forensic psychology** (the psychological study of legal issues) repeatedly indicates that the human participants in the judicial process usually try their best to do what is right but are inevitably affected by many factors other than objectivity and the unbiased search for truth and justice (Davis, 1989). As you know from the previous chapters, social psychological research shows clearly that our perceptions, attributions, recollections, and interpersonal behaviors are influenced by cognitions and emotions. Among the many consequences are biased judgments, reliance on stereotypes, faulty memories, and incorrect or unfair decisions. Those same influences operate as strongly in the courtroom as in the laboratory, and the consequences clearly affect the outcome of legal proceedings, as we shall see.

Forensic Psychology ■ Psychological research and theory dealing with legal proceedings and the law.

FIGURE 13.1

The Importance of Safeguards in a Judicial System. *The judicial behavior shown here seems ridiculous only because we are familiar with a different kind of courtroom procedure. Throughout history, and even today in many totalitarian societies, there are many examples of what can happen in the absence of courtroom safeguards. In U.S. courts we have procedures designed to insure objectivity, fairness, and the use of factual evidence. Social psychological research indicates that we often fail to live up to these standards, but the goal remains an all-important one.*

(*Source:* Drawing by Handelsman; © 1995 *The New Yorker* Magazine, Inc.)

"In the interest of streamlining the judicial process, we'll skip the evidence and go directly to sentencing."

The Initial Steps: Police Interrogation and Pretrial Publicity

Before a case reaches the courtroom, two major factors influence the testimony that will be presented and the preliminary attitudes of the jurors: police interrogation and publicity about the case in the media.

Interrogation: Seeking the Truth or Seeking a Confession? Williamson (1993) points out that each nation's criminal justice system tends to emphasize either an adversarial approach (attempting to prove the guilt of the person who is accused of the crime) or the inquisitorial approach (attempting to discover the truth). Despite differences across nations, both approaches are commonly represented in interrogations conducted by specific detectives. The social interaction between interrogator and suspect thus can have either the biased goal of confirming what the interrogator already believes to be true, or the impartial goal of accuracy.

Most citizens—who are neither detectives nor suspects—indicate that they prefer that interrogators simply search for the truth. This widespread preference led to legislation in the United Kingdom that provides training for police officers to convince them of the value of "investigative interviewing"—obtaining accurate evidence in a cooperative way. A major reason for this emphasis is that court rulings in both Great Britain and the United States have repeatedly

FIGURE 13.2

Police Interrogation: Contrasting Goals and Contrasting Styles. A study of Scotland Yard detectives indicated that interrogations can be classified according to the goal of the questioning (to obtain evidence or to obtain a confession) and the style of the encounter (cooperative or confrontational). Despite official attempts to institute a policy that stresses the gathering of evidence, about half of the detectives studied remain oriented toward obtaining a confession.

(*Source:* Based on data from Williamson, 1993.)

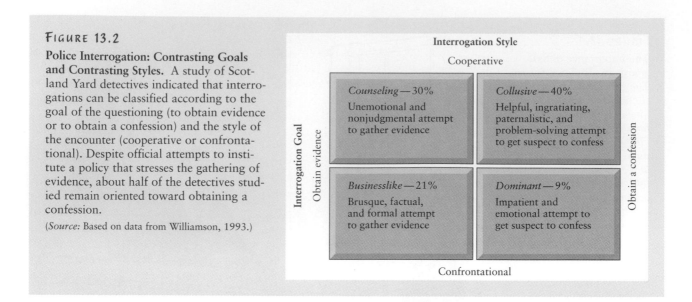

stressed the unreliability and inadmissibility of confessions obtained in a coercive confrontation with an interrogator (Gudjonsson, 1993).

In a Scotland Yard study of the actual practices of detectives, Williamson (1993) found evidence that many of these officers have adopted the desired investigative methods of interrogation, though about half are still oriented toward obtaining a confession. As shown in Figure 13.2, the questioning of a suspect falls along two dimensions. One dimension relates to the goal of the interrogation: getting the suspect to confess (adversarial) versus gathering evidence (inquisitorial). The other dimension involves how the interrogator seeks to achieve this goal: whether in a friendly, cooperative style or in angry confrontation. This second dimension is sometimes known as good cop–versus–bad cop.

The four styles resulting from the combination of these two dimensions are shown in the figure. Of the British detectives studied, 40 percent were identified as *collusive*—using an approach that was helpful, ingratiating, paternalistic, and problem-solving as a way to elicit a confession. Thirty percent used the *counseling* style—a friendly, unemotional, and nonjudgmental attempt to obtain evidence. The *businesslike* style was endorsed by 21 percent of the detectives—a brusque, factual, and formal attempt to gather evidence. Only 9 percent were classified as *dominant*—behaving impatiently and emotionally as a way to get the suspect to confess.

Despite this promising indication that about half of the British officers studied have learned to seek evidence rather than a confession, Moston and Stephenson (1993) raise doubts about the genuineness of this apparent shift in police goals. They suggest that a great many officers still seek confessions but have simply learned to carry out their most persuasive questioning when recording equipment is not present to document what they do. Members of the Los Angeles Police Department have experienced problems with such documentation in recent years.

Less Obvious Techniques to Elicit Confessions. Instead of evading the rules in an illegal and heavy-handed manner, interrogators who want a confession can turn to a more subtle approach (Kassin & McNall, 1991). Rather than *maximization*—exaggerating the strength of the evidence and the magnitude of the crime—an interrogator can utilize *minimization*—playing down the evidence and the seriousness of the charge. The minimizing interrogator may go so far as to blame the victim and thus provide an excuse for what the suspect did. When a questioner downplays the seriousness of the crime and seems supportive, the implicit promise is that punishment will be relatively light. Not only is this ingratiating compliance technique effective (see Chapter 9), it avoids the legal problems raised by threatening the suspect. Further, it helps the police convince jurors. In an experiment that compared interrogation approaches, Kassin and McNall (1991) found that mock jurors tended to discount a confession obtained by threats of punishment, whereas conviction rates were significantly higher when the interrogator used minimization. The experimenters point out that while this soft-sell technique may seem noncoercive, such impression management simply provides a less obvious way to elicit compliance by lulling the suspect into a false sense of security. If you were a suspect, you would probably prefer a minimizing to a maximizing interrogation, but keep in mind that the goal remains the same: persuading you to confess.

Another commonly used indirect technique to obtain the desired answer from the person being interrogated is to ask **leading questions,** questions worded so as to suggest what the answer should be. For example, an unbiased question might be "Could you describe Mr. Jones's appearance when he returned to the car on the night of the murder?" A leading question, in contrast, could be "How much blood did you see on Mr. Jones's clothing when he returned to the car on the night of the murder?" A witness is much more likely to "remember" and to testify about bloody clothing in response to the second question than to the first. As with minimization, leading questions subtly draw the respondent into a role-playing interaction in which the interrogator is writing the script.

Experimental studies of the interrogation process show these effects quite clearly. For example, Smith and Ellsworth (1987) presented research participants with a videotape of a bank robbery, and then asked them questions about the crime. The questioner was a research assistant who was described to half of the participants as very *knowledgeable* about the robbery and to the other half as *relatively uninformed.* Also, half of the participants were asked unbiased questions such as "Was there a getaway car?" while the other half were asked leading questions such as "Where was the getaway car parked?" You can see in Figure 13.3 (p. 480) that the unbiased questions led to the most accurate answers, whether or not the questioner was supposedly well informed. Accuracy decreased when leading questions were asked, especially when the questioner had been described as being knowledgeable about the crime.

The effectiveness of leading questions depends in part on the person who is being questioned—for example, some individuals are more responsive to such suggestions and more eager to please. For almost anyone, however, the setting in which a formal interrogation takes place tends to enhance the impact of this technique (Schooler & Loftus, 1986). The usual interrogation is carried out in an intimidating location such as a police station, and it is conducted by a designated representative of the government (local, state, or federal). The location and the authority of the questioner reinforce the ordinary citizen's belief that the person asking the questions is an expert who possesses detailed knowledge about the case (Gudjonsson & Clark, 1986). Almost always, the officer is in charge of what happens during the proceedings, and the person being questioned is not supposed to interrupt or to argue about what is said.

Under the coercive circumstances just described, three factors encourage compliance with the interrogator's indirect and sometimes subtle suggestions. When a leading question is asked, the witness usually feels (1) some *uncertainty* about the "right" answer, (2) some degree of *trust* in the officer asking the question, and (3) an unspoken *expectation* that he or she is supposed to know the answer. As a result, rather than saying, "I don't know" or "I don't remember"

Leading Questions ■ Questions asked of witnesses or suspects by police or by attorneys that are worded so as to suggest specific answers.

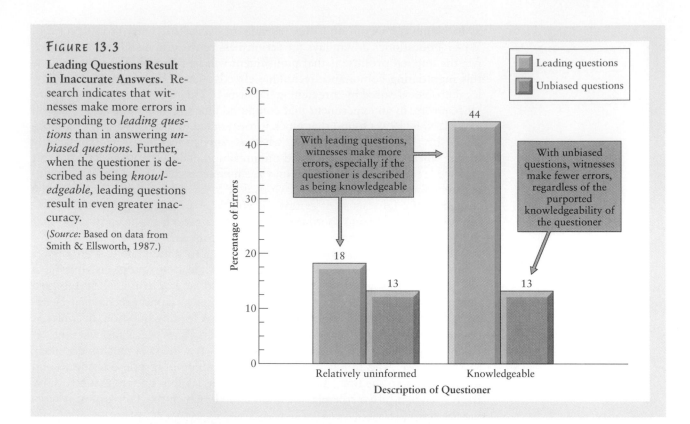

FIGURE 13.3

Leading Questions Result in Inaccurate Answers. Research indicates that witnesses make more errors in responding to *leading questions* than in answering *unbiased questions*. Further, when the questioner is described as being *knowledgeable,* leading questions result in even greater inaccuracy.

(*Source:* Based on data from Smith & Ellsworth, 1987.)

or "I'm not sure," most people tend to provide an answer, even if it is offered tentatively. Once an answer is given, no matter how tentative it was initially, the person is inclined to believe what he or she just said, especially if the interrogator indicates approval (nodding or saying "good," etc.). The respondent's memory quickly incorporates whatever has been stated and afterward reinforced by the interrogator. This process is sufficiently convincing that innocent individuals are sometimes led to confess committing crimes and genuinely to believe themselves to be guilty (Kassin & Kiechel, 1995).

Effects of the Media: General Perceptions about Crime. In newspapers, on television and radio, and in other media sources, we are routinely exposed to information about crimes and criminals (Henry, 1991). Crime information is so pervasive that people easily develop a distorted view of this aspect of our world. On a daily basis, the media suggest to us that crime is a widespread problem that threatens each of us, and the availability heuristic clearly applies (see Chapter 3) when we make assumptions about the crime rate and its dangers. For example, polls show that U.S. citizens believe criminal activity has reached epidemic proportions. Polls also indicate that crime is ranked as one of the two or three greatest problems faced by U.S. society (Blonston, 1993).

In fact, record highs for violent crime in the United States, including homicide and burglary, were set in the early 1980s and have been dropping ever since. According to the U.S. Bureau of Justice Statistics, the total number of crimes dropped from 41.2 million in 1981 to 34.4 million in 1991. FBI statistics indicate that the rates of seven major offenses (including violent crime) continued to drop in 1994—for the third consecutive year. One explanation is that most violent crimes are committed by young males, and the baby boomer generation (including violent boomers) is now reaching middle age. The bad news—and one reason that we perceive more rather than less violence—is that the rate of gun murders by teenage boys is rapidly increasing (Crime rate down . . . , 1995). In fact, the number of juvenile murderers has tripled over the last decade (Number of young . . . , 1996). Who are these young people shooting? The U.S. Bureau of Justice Statistics indicates that youngsters aged 12 to 15 have a 1 in 8 chance of being a crime victim in the 1990s, whereas the chance is only 1 in 179 for those 65 and older (Teens top . . . , 1995). Thus, the facts about crime are complicated. Altogether, violent crime is decreasing while teenage crime (especially against other teenagers) is increasing; but our perceptions tend to simplify the issue by leaving out specific details. It is easier to take what information is easily available and believe that criminal violence is worse than ever.

Even a very specific, and very frightening, crime such as the abduction of children is widely misperceived. The missing children that you see on posters and on milk cartons are most often youngsters taken away by one of the parents involved in a custody battle during or after a divorce. According to the FBI, the total number of missing children abducted by strangers in the United States is no more than about seven at any given time (Dunn, 1993). This doesn't mean that a parent has no reason to be extremely upset when an ex-spouse takes a child unlawfully or that even one kidnapping by a stranger is not a truly terrible event. The point is that we magnify the overall problem on the basis of the amount of media attention devoted to each tragic instance in which a child is harmed by a stranger. Remember the story in Chapter 10 of the small boy taken from a mall and killed? We find such stories easy to remember, and it becomes easy to believe that similar events are everyday occurrences.

Effects of the Media: Pretrial Publicity and Perceptions of a Specific Crime and a Specific Suspect. If distortions about the general incidence of crime are common, what happens when a specific case is widely publicized? With events as traumatic as the bombing of the federal office building in Oklahoma City, there is detailed coverage of the event and background news about the victims and their families. When a suspect is arrested, we are provided information about that individual, most dramatically in the form of a photo or videotape of the suspect in handcuffs surrounded by law enforcement officials. We each form an impression of the suspect, and primacy effects (see Chapter 2) are likely to create an impression of guilt. Because most people are horrified by the crime and eager to convict whoever committed it, the guilt of the arrested suspect is immediately assumed by most of the general public: "Why else would the police have arrested him and put him in handcuffs?" Think of the reactions to Lee Harvey Oswald being led through the Dallas police station after President Kennedy was shot and to O. J. Simpson being led to a squad car after the murder of Nicole Simpson and Ron Goldman. Remember—these assumptions are created *before* we know anything about the evidence or the legal basis of the suspect's defense. Because all subsequent information is influenced by this first impression, wouldn't you guess that such publicity would have a major effect?

Using actual criminal investigations in Florida, Moran and Cutler (1991) surveyed potential jurors and found that exposure to news about a crime and about the accused criminal was associated with potential jurors' reaching the pretrial conclusion that the defendants were in fact guilty. Other research also indicates that the greater the publicity about a crime, the more prone are jurors to convict whoever has been accused of committing it (Linz & Penrod, 1992).

Given such biasing effects, why would pretrial publicity be as common as it is? Moran (1993) suggests that government representatives (the police, the district attorney, etc.) purposely provide pretrial crime information to newspapers and television stations *because* they want the public (and potential jurors) to form a negative impression of the accused person. The attempt to identify and excuse prospective jurors who have been exposed to and influenced by media coverage appears hopeless. Even when jury prospects are questioned about how much exposure they have had to news of a specific crime, warned about media inaccuracies, and told the importance of remaining impartial until hearing all of the evidence, the biasing impact of pretrial publicity remains the same (Dexter, Cutler, & Moran, 1992). Potential jurors either don't realize or are unwilling to admit that the publicity has caused them to reach premature conclusions about a defendant. According to O'Connell (1988), asking prospective jurors whether they can be fair and impartial is "as useless as asking an alcoholic if he can control his drinking." In either instance, a yes response is essentially meaningless.

Among the reasons for the power of the media's effects on our perception of crime and criminals is the very strong tendency for people to believe what they have read in print, heard on the radio, or viewed on television; if we can comprehend whatever assertions are made, we are also very likely to believe them (Gilbert, Tafarodi, & Malone, 1993). It's almost as if we automatically assume that "They wouldn't have put it on television if it weren't true."

Still another reason for the impact of crime news is that when we make morality judgments (good versus bad, innocent versus guilty), negative information has a greater impact than positive information (Skowronski & Carlston, 1989). This "automatic vigilance" effect was discussed in Chapter 3. To learn that Congressman X is a good legislator and a devoted family man makes only a minor impression. The news that the congressman is accused of ties to organized crime and has been engaged in an intimate relationship with his secretary affects our evaluation of him in a much stronger and more lasting way.

In the United States many of us are exposed to publicity not only before a trial but also *during* a trial. Canadian law, in contrast, imposes restrictions designed to insure a fair trial and to avoid "polluting" the jury. One Canadian reporter summed up the difference as follows: "In the States, we sequester the jury; in Canada we sequester the public" (Farnsworth, 1995, p. E-8). Similarly, neither pretrial publicity nor live broadcasts of trials is permitted in the United Kingdom. Citizens of Great Britain were thus intrigued by the extraordinary U.S. coverage of O. J. Simpson, beginning with the murder and the travels of the white Bronco and continuing through very popular nightly satellite presentations of the sensational trial (Lyall, 1995).

The American public was clearly not "sequestered" or subjected to a news blackout before or during the Simpson trial. What effects might the pretrial information blitz have had on the beliefs of the public in general and—more importantly—on those who eventually served on the jury? The following *Applied Side* section deals with this very important question along with the role of racial prejudice (Chapter 6) in evaluations of guilt and innocence.

Social Psychology: On the Applied Side
BELIEFS ABOUT O. J. SIMPSON: Prejudice and Pretrial Publicity

In addition to media publicity, racial and ethnic prejudice also influence response to crime suspects. For example, the mother who drowned her two young children in South Carolina at first concocted a story about a black man stealing her car and driving off with the boys in the back seat. This false accusation was widely believed until she confessed that there was no black man; instead, she was responsible for propelling the car and her small sons to the bottom of a lake. Immediately after the Oklahoma City bombing, one of the first assumptions was that Middle Eastern terrorists were responsible, and at least one national radio personality proposed that all Islamic fundamentalists be rounded up immediately. If one's stereotypes about members of a particular racial or ethnic group include the likelihood of wrongdoing, it is easy to assume guilt in a specific instance. What happens when both prejudice and publicity are focused on a given suspect? The O. J. Simpson case provides an instructive example—see Figure 13.4.

In the United States, crime news and trial broadcasts have become a popular form of "entertainment." For those residents of California who were called for jury duty in the Simpson case, the daily news could very well have affected the final verdict. In order to examine some of the factors responsible for the opinions formed by the general public (including potential jurors) before a trial begins, Page and Gropp (1995) examined attitudes and beliefs about O. J. Simpson prior to the trial in which he was accused of a double murder.

From the very beginning of the Simpson case, several surveys indicated that most African Americans believed him to be innocent while most white Americans believed in his guilt. By midtrial, a Harris poll revealed that 60 percent of whites believed that Simpson was guilty, compared to 12 percent of African Americans who thought so (Toobin, 1995). Similar racial differences were found among college students (Mixon, Foley, & Orme, 1995). For this reason, Page and Gropp (1995) studied the effects of prejudice and of pretrial publicity. The investigators administered a measure of racial prejudice to more than one hundred white adults (aged twenty to seventy) and also questioned

FIGURE 13.4

Pretrial Publicity about a Crime and about a Suspect: First Impression = Guilty. There is abundant evidence that pretrial publicity about a crime generates interest and a general desire to punish the perpetrator. When a suspect is identified, the information tends to focus on his or her arrest, the presence of handcuffs, and other details that suggest guilt. Because of primacy effects, the general public often concludes that the accused individual is guilty long before the trial even begins.

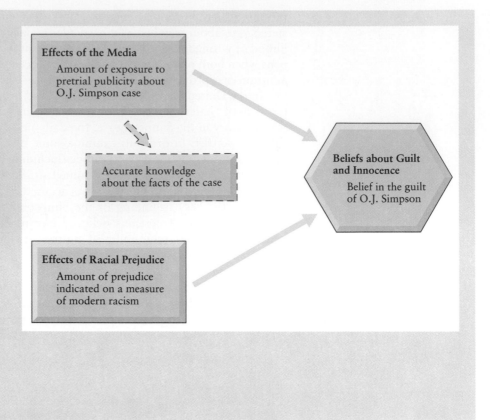

FIGURE 13.5

The Effects of Prejudice and Pretrial Publicity on Beliefs about the Guilt of O. J. Simpson. Two factors were found to influence pretrial beliefs about the guilt or innocence of O. J. Simpson. Belief in the defendant's guilt was greater among those whites who were the most prejudiced against blacks, and among those who had the greatest exposure to pretrial publicity about the case. (Amount of exposure was unrelated to prejudice.) Those with the greatest media exposure possessed more knowledge about the facts of the case; nevertheless, knowledge of the facts was unrelated to belief in the defendant's guilt or innocence.

(*Source:* Based on data from Page & Gropp, 1995.)

them about their exposure to media accounts of the crime, their knowledge of various facts associated with the case, and their beliefs about the defendant's guilt.

As shown in Figure 13.5, exposure to pretrial publicity was found to be associated with believing that the evidence indicated Simpson's guilt as well as with the personal belief that he actually *was* guilty. Interestingly, the more exposure to pretrial publicity, the more accurate a person's knowledge of the facts in the case; but knowledge of the facts was unrelated to beliefs about guilt. Racism was unrelated to how much individuals had been exposed to the media publicity, but such prejudice *was* associated with perceptions of guilt.

Altogether, then, the belief that this defendant was guilty was predicted by exposure to pretrial publicity and (independently) by racism. Though accurate knowledge about the facts of the case was greater among those with the most exposure, knowledge alone was unrelated to beliefs about guilt. If those individuals who served as jurors in the trial were at all like these research participants, it seems very likely that many of them were convinced of the defendant's guilt or of his innocence long before the months of testimony began and before the detailed evidence was presented.

One explanation of such findings is that exposure affects beliefs about a defendant on the basis of emotional arousal rather than on the basis of cognitive information about factual details. Supporting this suggestion is the finding that when individuals read about serious crimes, they afterward indicate more negative reactions not only toward the individuals accused of these crimes but also toward defendants in other, completely unrelated crimes (Roberts & Edwards, 1989). When race and racial stereotypes are also involved, it seems that judgments about a defendant can be strongly affected by emotional reactions to the individual even though these reactions may have little or nothing to do with the facts. ■ ■ ■

Eyewitness Testimony: How Accurate Is It?

Anyone who witnesses a crime or who has observed something relevant to the case may be asked to testify about what was seen or heard. Each year witnesses provide crucial evidence relevant to 75,000 suspects in U.S. courtrooms (Goldstein, Chance, & Schneller, 1989). These witnesses frequently make mistakes, in part because intense emotions can interfere with information processing (see Chapter 3). A related factor is Zillmann's "cognitive deficit" hypothesis (see Chapter 11). Despite the danger of errors, eyewitness testimony has a major impact on jurors (Wolf & Bugaj, 1990). Studies of mistakes (wrongful convictions) indicate that inaccurate eyewitness identification is the single most important reason that innocent defendants are convicted (Wells, 1993; Wells, Luus, & Windschitl, 1994).

Even when the eyewitness is the victim of the crime, errors can occur, as indicated by a case reported in the state of Washington (Goleman, 1995; Loftus, 1992a). Early one evening a young woman was hitchhiking on a highway near Seattle when a bearded man picked her up. Soon afterward, he drove off of the highway and onto a deserted dirt lane, raped her, and then drove away, leaving her beside the road. A day later, detectives showed the woman several photographs (see Figure 13.6), and she identified a man named Steve Titus as the person who assaulted her.

Mr. Titus was quickly picked up, charged with the crime, tried, and, on the basis of the victim's sworn testimony, convicted. A few months later, a different man was arrested as a suspect in a series of other rapes. When she saw the photograph of this new suspect, the woman who had identified Titus realized her mistake. Upset, she cried out, "What have I done to Mr. Titus?" But her discovery of the error came too late to avoid damage to the innocent suspect. Even though he was released from prison, he had lost his job; his savings were reduced to nothing by attorney fees; and his fiancée had broken off their relationship. Mr. Titus spent the next four years trying to sue the authorities to make restitution for the damages he suffered, but he died of a heart attack before his case came to trial.

FIGURE 13.6

Which One Committed the Crime? In a typical photo lineup, crime victims or witnesses are shown pictures of several possible suspects and asked to identify the one they believe committed the crime. In an actual case, a rape victim mistakenly identified an innocent man as the one who assaulted her. He was convicted, but the charges were later dropped when the real criminal, shown in the photograph, was apprehended. Procedures that increase the accuracy of identification are crucial in helping to prevent this kind of tragic mistake.

(*Source:* Loftus, 1992a.)

This is a dramatic example of a common problem that has long been of concern to legal experts and, as described in the following *Cornerstones* section, to psychologists as well.

Cornerstones of Social Psychology
HUGO MUNSTERBERG ON THE INACCURACY OF EYEWITNESSES

Hugo Munsterberg
Hugo Munsterberg (1863–1916) was born in Danzig, Germany, and earned a Ph.D. degree at Leipzig and afterward an M.D. degree at Heidelberg. His doctoral dissertation so impressed William James that James invited Munsterberg to join the faculty at Harvard. Munsterberg was one of the founders of the field of psychology. Spillman and Spillman (1993) point out that his contributions fall into two categories: his early work on sensory psychology and philosophy, and his later work on applied social psychology, which included books dealing with the legal system, prohibition, patriotism, industrial/organizational psychology, and the effects of war and peace on America. He died in Cambridge, Massachusetts.

Basic psychological research dealing with memory and with the effect of emotions on perception led Hugo Munsterberg (1907) to become interested in the relevance this research to actual witnesses in the courtroom. In studies with Harvard undergraduates in his experimental laboratory, he found that these participants were unreliable judges of even very simple events, such as how many seconds passed between the presentation of two signals or how many spots were on a card that was shown briefly. Munsterberg found that the arousal of emotions such as fear and anger lead to even greater inaccuracy. As a result, he concluded, witnesses to a crime were likely to be even less reliable than his college students.

Despite their inability to give an accurate report, people tend to reconstruct their experiences and to believe that their memories are accurate. Munsterberg (1907, pp. 39–40) described his personal experience with false memories following a burglary when he and his family were on vacation:

> . . . I was called upon to give an account of my findings against the culprit whom they had caught with a part of the booty. I reported under oath that the burglars had entered through a cellar window, and then described what rooms they had visited. To prove, in answer to a direct question, that they had been there at night, I told that I had found drops of candle wax on the second floor. To show that they intended to return, I reported that they had left a large mantel clock, packed in wrapping paper, on the dining-room table. Finally, as to the amount of clothes which they had taken, I asserted that the burglars did not get more than a specified list which I had given to the police.
>
> Only a few days later I found that every one of these statements was wrong. They had not entered through the window, but had broken the lock of the cellar door; the clock was not packed by them in wrapping paper, but in a tablecloth; the candle droppings were not on the second floor, but in the attic; the list of lost garments was to be increased by seven more pieces; and while my story under oath spoke always of two burglars, I do not know that there was more than one.

In addition to his laboratory research and his personal experiences, Munsterberg involved himself in field studies that confirmed his beliefs about the inaccuracy of witnesses. Once, during a meeting in Göttingen of a scientific association attended by forty legal experts, psychologists, and physicians, a surprise interruption was staged. A street carnival was in progress during one of their evening sessions, and a clown in a bright costume suddenly burst into the room, excitedly followed by a black man carrying a gun. The two individuals shouted at each other, one fell down, the other jumped on him, a shot was fired, and then both men ran out of the room. Only the president of the association knew that this thirty-second scene had been planned, rehearsed—and photographed. The assembled witnesses were told that, because the police would undoubtedly be asking for their testimony, it was important for them to write down exactly what had just happened in the meeting room.

Despite the professional expertise of those attending the meeting, and despite their writing about the experience immediately after it happened, only one of the forty was found to be very accurate in recording the facts (he correctly recalled more than 80 percent of the details). As shown in Figure 13.7, the remaining witnesses were classified as moderately accurate (recalling 60 to 80 percent of the details), inaccurate (recalling 50 to 60 percent), or very inaccurate (recalling less than 50 percent).

These individuals not only failed to remember much of what had just occurred, they also made up many totally false details. For example, the black man who came into the room did not wear anything on his head but was "seen" in a derby, a top hat, and other headgear. He wore white trousers, a black jacket, and a red tie, but was "seen" as wearing a red suit, a brown suit, and a striped suit, and also as being in shirtsleeves. Other details of the event were equally distorted.

Munsterberg concluded that most observers to an unexpected and disturbing event leave out or falsely remember about half of what occurred. His documentation of the inaccuracy of witnesses and his attempts to overcome that problem constituted the beginning of psychological research on the legal system, an enterprise that has continued actively throughout this century. ■ ■ ■

Eyewitness Accuracy and Inaccuracy. After many decades of research, it is now very clear that even the most honest, intelligent, and well-meaning witnesses to an event very often make mistakes. As Loftus (1992b) has pointed out, a major obstacle to accuracy in a great many instances is that an extended time period passes between the event that was witnessed and the task of presenting testi-

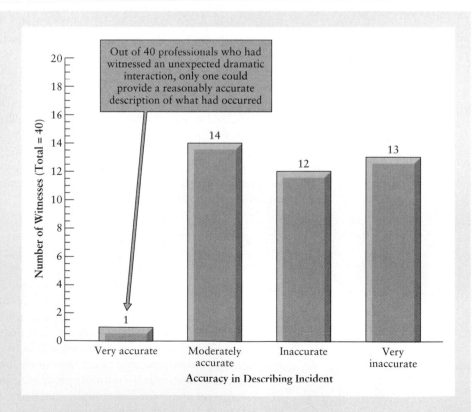

FIGURE 13.7

Accuracy in Describing Incident That Had Just Occurred. In the early part of this century, psychologists began conducting research relevant to legal issues. Professor Hugo Munsterberg described one such study. At a meeting of psychologists, physicians, and lawyers, a surprise interruption was staged—two men burst into the room, interacted for less than a minute, and then left. When the forty professionals present were then asked to write down everything that had occurred, only one witness was classified as very accurate (reporting about 80 percent of the facts), while the remainder omitted many details and "remembered" details that were incorrect.

(*Source:* Based on data from Munsterberg, 1907.)

Out of 40 professionals who had witnessed an unexpected dramatic interaction, only one could provide a reasonably accurate description of what had occurred

mony in court. During this interval, numerous potential sources of *misleading postevent information* (including police questions, media stories, and statements made by others) are responsible for additions to memory that tend to be incorporated as subjective "truth," thus reducing accuracy. It becomes difficult to distinguish what one remembers of the original event from what has subsequently been learned about it.

Despite the doubts cast by research on eyewitness memory, Yuille and Cutshall (1986) found a high level of accuracy among witnesses to an actual shooting incident that occurred one afternoon on a busy street in Burnaby, British Columbia. Stress level during the shooting had no negative effects on witnesses' memory; the witnesses' recollections remained accurate five months later; and these witnesses were unaffected by leading questions.

There is *some* relationship between the certainty of a witness and his or her accuracy, but only if the memory hasn't been contaminated by intervening events (Bothwell, Deffenbacher, & Brigham, 1987). As in Munsterberg's testimony about the burglary, people genuinely believe that their memory is accurate (Lindsay, 1993). Nevertheless, the confidence of eyewitnesses can be manipulated (Luus & Wells, 1994). For example, an eyewitness who falsely identifies a suspect can become highly confident if positive feedback is given by the investigating detective—"Another witness picked out the same one you did." This confidence remains high (a persistence effect) even if the choice is later discredited.

A variety of other factors interfere with witness accuracy (Wells & Luus, 1990; Yuille & Tollestrup, 1990). For example, accuracy decreases if the suspect is holding a weapon (Tooley et al., 1987), if the suspect and the witness belong to different racial or ethnic groups (Platz & Hosch, 1988), and if misleading suggestions are offered to the witness (Ryan & Geiselman, 1991).

What influences members of the jury to believe or not to believe a given witness? The more sure the witness appears and the more details he or she can provide, the greater the impact on the jury (Bell & Loftus, 1988; Whitley & Greenberg, 1986). Also, a nervous witness tends not to be believed (Bothwell & Jalil, 1992). A special problem arises when children are the witnesses, as in cases of alleged sexual abuse. As you might expect, the credibility of children on the witness stand is lower than that of adults (Leippe & Romanczyk, 1987). Nevertheless, when observers view the actual testimony of children—in their own words—this bias can be erased (Luus, Wells, & Turtle, 1995). Other research indicates that children are more likely to be perceived as credible to the extent that they are younger rather than older, if there is corroboration by other witnesses, if the defendant's character is sufficiently negative, and if the jurors are women (Bottoms & Goodman, 1994).

Attempts to Increase Eyewitness Accuracy. Even in Munsterberg's (1907) early research, he worked to devise techniques to increase witness accuracy. It was once thought that hypnosis might solve the problem of lost memories; but this approach creates more problems than it solves, because inaccurate details can easily be suggested under hypnosis and then "remembered." Orne and his colleagues (1984) conclude that it is dangerous to rely on *hypnotically refreshed* memories unless there is other evidence that provides independent corroboration. There is simply no way to distinguish between accurate memories recovered under hypnosis and inaccurate memories suggested during hypnosis.

The police lineup is a common procedure in which the suspect is mixed in with several innocent individuals; the witness looks over this group and is asked to pick out the guilty individual. Wells and Luus (1990) suggest that the lineup is analogous to a social psychological experiment. For example, the officer conducting the lineup is the *experimenter*, the eyewitnesses are the

TABLE 13.1   Police Lineups and Psychological Experiments As Analogous Attempts to Obtain Reliable and Objective Information

Wells and Luus (1990) suggest a number of parallels between police lineups and social psychological experiments. They also indicate that police officers can improve the accuracy of lineups by following a variety of well-established experimental procedures that provide safeguards against ending up with contaminated data. Both in experiments and in lineups, it is important to avoid nonindependent data, demand characteristics, and so forth.

Recommended Procedures for Police Lineups and Photo Lineups	Analogous Procedures in Psychological Experiments
Witnesses should be separated and not permitted to interact.	Participants cannot communicate with one another before responding; otherwise, their data are not independent.
A witness should not be told or led to believe that the actual perpetrator is in the lineup.	Experimental instructions should be worded so as not to create demands that the participants respond in a given way.
The officer conducting the lineup should not know the identity of the suspected perpetrator.	The experimental assistants who interact with the participants should be kept "blind" as to both the hypothesis and the experimental condition to which the participant is assigned.
If there is more than one witness, the position of the suspect in the lineup should be different for each witness.	The order in which stimuli are presented should be randomized or counterbalanced across participants.
Not until the lineup procedure is totally concluded should cues of any kind be given to a witness with respect to whether or not the person he or she identified is actually the suspect in the case.	Not until the experiment is concluded and all dependent measures collected should a participant be debriefed and told the experimenter's hypothesis.

research participants, the suspect is a *stimulus,* and the other people in the lineup and the placement of the suspect constitute the *design.* Consider also that the police have a *hypothesis* as to the guilt of the suspect; the identification made by a witness provides the *data* that may be evaluated by the police, prosecutor, judge, and jury; and in both experiments and testimony the data are stated in terms of *probability,* because neither procedure provides absolute certainty.

In Chapter 1 you read about factors that can interfere with researchers' obtaining accurate results, such as demand characteristics, experimenter bias, or the absence of a control group. The same factors can interfere with the accuracy of a witness examining a lineup. For example, do you see anything wrong with a lineup in which the suspect is a tall, fat man while the nonsuspects in the lineup are all short and thin?

Using the same analogy, police can improve the validity of lineups by using common experimental procedures such as a *control group.* One procedure is the **blank-lineup control**—witnesses are first shown a lineup in which each "suspect" is really an innocent volunteer (Wells, 1984). No matter who is identified, the witness is wrong. (Or if the witness identifies no one, confidence in that witness's accuracy is increased.) This control experience tends to induce caution and increase later accuracy, especially when information is then provided about the serious consequences of making a mistake. The analogy between lineups and experiments leads to several other examples of possible ways to improve eyewitness identification procedures, as shown in Table 13.1.

Blank-Lineup Control ■ A procedure in which a witness is shown a police lineup that does *not* contain the suspect; helps police ascertain the accuracy of the witness and/or point up the importance of caution.

Can anything be done directly to improve witnesses' memory concerning the person who was observed committing the crime? One technique is to "reinstate the context" just before the identification is made (Cutler, Penrod, & Martens, 1987). That is, the witness is first shown pictures of the crime scene and of the victim before seeing the suspects. Accuracy is also increased if a witness looks at one suspect at a time rather than at a lineup of several suspects (Leary, 1988).

The U.S. Supreme Court has ruled that using a "show-up" in which only one suspect is seen is unfair; because this procedure suggests that the suspect is guilty, as opposed to a lineup, in which the suspect (or the suspect's photograph) is mixed in with other individuals. Nevertheless, research finds no evidence that one-person show-ups lead to more inaccurate identifications than do multiple-person lineups (Gonzalez, Ellsworth, & Pembroke, 1993).

A different approach is to identify accurate and inaccurate witnesses and then to look for ways in which they differ. Dunning and Stern (1994) presented research participants with a videotape of a staged crime and then asked them to identify the criminal from a photo lineup. Accurate witnesses were found to say that their judgments were "automatic"—"His face just 'popped out' at me." In contrast, inaccurate witnesses went through an elimination process, comparing photos to each other and narrowing the choices. Why the difference? Dunning suggests that faces are stored in memory in a visual pattern rather than in words. Witnesses who make an instant and accurate identification are using a nonverbal process and often do not know exactly what influenced the decision. When people are informed that giving a first impression is a better strategy than going through an elimination process, they can change their approach. As a result, accuracy increases.

How Attorneys and Judges Can Affect the Jury's Verdict

The outcome of a trial is in part influenced by what is said and done by the opposing attorneys and by the judge. We will describe some of the ways that this influence has been documented.

Attorneys: Adversaries with Opposite Goals. Lawyers obviously play a major role in the courtroom, but their effect is not entirely limited to matters of evidence and legal technicalities. For example, the prosecutor in the O. J. Simpson trial, Marcia Clark, was advised to change her behavioral style, her wardrobe, and her hair because research with mock jurors revealed that she needed to be "warmer, fuzzier, and more juror-friendly" (Margolick, 1994).

The first problem faced by attorneys, however, is not their image but jury selection. Who does and does not serve on the jury can be critical (Hans & Vidmar, 1982). Jurors are selected (and rejected) during a pretrial procedure known as **voir dire,** in which attorneys for each side (as well as the judge) can "see and speak" with potential jurors to determine which individuals are most and least suitable to serve. Despite the stated goal of choosing the most competent citizens to serve on the panel, the goal of the opposing attorneys is in reality somewhat different from that. They, of course, try very hard to select those jurors who are perceived as being most likely to favor their side, and to eliminate jurors most likely to favor the other side. To facilitate this process, the opposing sides may each use a certain number of *peremptory challenges,* which permit a potential juror to be dismissed without the attorney having to state any reason for the dismissal. Abramson (1994) suggests that jury trials have become a game in which each side attempts to load the jury with members who will show bias in a given direction.

Voir Dire ■ A French term used in law to mean the examination of prospective jurors to determine their competence to serve; both the judge and the opposing attorneys may dismiss certain prospects for specific reasons or for no stated reason.

TABLE 13.2 Both Prosecutors and Defense Attorneys Seek Jurors Who Favor Their Position in the Trial

Before a trial begins, the jury selection process (known as voir dire) *technically involves selecting jurors who are competent to serve. In fact, attorneys for both the prosecution and the defense seek information about the characteristics of prospective jurors that may indicate a tendency to favor one side or the other. Shown here are the characteristics rated as most important by attorneys and the questions they ask most often in the attempt to identify biasing attitudes and experiences.*

Characteristics Identified by Attorneys As Important in Jurors	intelligence	age	appearance
	occupation	open-mindedness	gender
	attentiveness	impressibility	race
Questions Asked Most Often by Attorneys During Voir Dire Process	What is your attitude about this kind of crime?		
	What is your general reaction to police officers?		
	How much have you heard about this case in the media?		
	Were you ever the victim of this kind of crime?		
	How do you feel about someone who has been arrested?		
	Do you have any racial bias?		
	Have any of your acquaintances ever been arrested or convicted?		
	Do you have any relationship with any of the individuals connected with this case?		

(*Source:* Based on data from Olczak, Kaplan, & Penrod, 1991.)

Olczak, Kaplan, and Penrod (1991) investigated this process. They asked lawyers to indicate which juror characteristics provide the most important information and which questions they usually ask to determine these characteristics—shown in Table 13.2. The investigators next asked practicing lawyers to rate prospective jurors as to whom they would select to be on a jury, and compared their ratings with those of introductory psychology students. The lawyers and the undergraduates made almost identical decisions. A third study compared lawyers and students in their guesses about several jurors who had actually served in courtroom trials: the question was whether the jurors would favor the prosecution or the defense. Both groups were more often wrong than right, and neither did better than the other at guessing what jurors would do. It seems that even experienced attorneys use stereotypes in selecting jurors and that their expert decisions are no different from those of inexperienced college students.

In our discussion of police interrogations, we described the effect of *leading questions.* Leading questions are not permitted when lawyers examine their own witnesses in court; but lawyers are permitted to ask leading questions during cross-examination and—as a result, responses may be biased. Thus, attorneys ask their own witnesses unbiased questions, whereas witnesses on the other side are asked leading questions. Interestingly, jurors are found to perceive a witness as more competent and more credible when he or she is responding to unbiased questions than when he or she is responding to leading ones (McGaughey & Stiles, 1983).

The Judge: Bias from the Bench. Though the ideal judge in a trial is totally objective, judges are human beings who sometimes make mistakes or hold biases. These mistakes and these biases are likely to determine how jurors respond. For example, when a judge allows the jury to hear evidence that is later ruled inadmissible (Cox & Tanford, 1989) or when the judge attacks the credibility of a witness (Cavoukian & Doob, 1980), the final verdict is affected. Many of the cognitive processes described in Chapter 3 (such as priming) obviously apply to how the judge's statements can influence the jurors.

In a trial, the judge instructs the jury to form impressions about guilt and innocence, but to refrain from making a final decision about the verdict until the trial ends and the panel can deliberate as a group (Hastie, 1993). Despite this goal of suspending judgment, the judge often forms his or her own private impression and concludes what the verdict is likely to be. These expectations, in turn, influence the judge's verbal and nonverbal behavior, and thus the final decision of the jurors—however unintentional the influence may be (Blanck et al., 1990).

Hart (1995) studied the effect of a judge's unstated opinions about the defendant in an experiment using citizens who had been summoned for jury duty. These prospective jurors were shown videotapes of judges made while the judges were reading the identical standard instructions to juries in various trials. Before reading the instructions, each judge had privately indicated to those conducting the research whether he or she expected a verdict of guilty or not guilty. The individuals taking part in the research were shown the tape of a single trial (not one involving any of the taped judges). Then they were shown a tape of judicial instructions (falsely described as coming from the trial they had just viewed). As summarized in Figure 13.8, these research participants were significantly more likely to give a "verdict" of guilty when the judge expected a guilty vote than when the judge expected the outcome to be not guilty. It seems that beliefs about guilt and innocence must have influenced the judge's nonverbal behavior (Chapter 2), and this in turn influenced the decisions of these mock jurors.

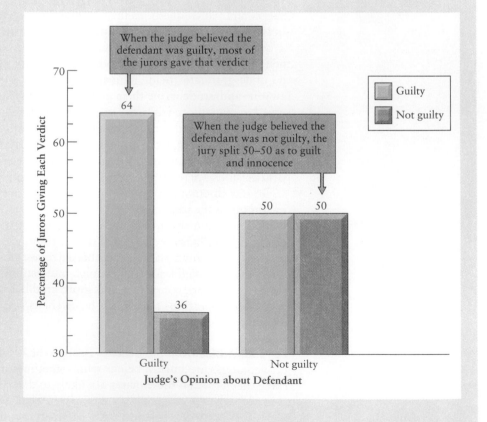

FIGURE 13.8

Judge's Opinion about Guilt and Innocence and Jury's Verdict. Jurors were shown videotapes of a trial and of a judge giving standard instructions to the jury. The tape showing the instructions was actually from a different trial, in which the judge had privately given the investigators his or her opinion that the defendant was guilty or not guilty. When the judge believed the defendant to be guilty, the jurors overwhelmingly returned a guilty verdict. When the judge believed the defendant to be not guilty, the jurors split 50–50 in their verdict. Evidently the judge's opinion (apparently communicated through nonverbal cues) influenced the jurors' decision.

(*Source:* Based on data from Hart, 1995.)

Many people believe that some judges are soft on crime and biased toward protecting the rights of criminals while others ("hanging judges") give maximum sentences. Carroll and colleagues (1987) found that it *is* in fact possible to classify judges into one of two categories. Judges tend either to emphasize the social and economic causes of crime and therefore stress rehabilitation, or to blame the criminal for breaking the law and therefore stress punishment and retribution. Public support for "hard" or "soft" judges depends, in turn, on what each individual believes about the causes of crime. Among university students, for example, relatively liberal social science majors blame society, while relatively conservative business and engineering majors blame the criminal (Guimond & Palmer, 1990).

How Decisions Are Influenced by Characteristics of the Defendants and the Jurors

Social psychological research on prejudice (Chapter 6) and interpersonal attraction (Chapter 7) indicates that people respond to one another on the basis of such characteristics as race, gender, and physical attractiveness. In the courtroom, a defendant's likability is an important determinant of how much he or she is blamed for causing harm (Alicke, 1994). Stereotypes and liking should of course be irrelevant in a trial, but they nevertheless *do* influence the outcome of both real and simulated trials (Dane, 1992). For most crimes, it is to the defendant's advantage to be physically attractive, a female, and of high rather than low socioeconomic status (Mazzella & Feingold, 1994).

Each of these positive attributes can, however, have negative effects under specific circumstances. For example, attractiveness is a disadvantage if it appears to have helped the suspect commit the crime—such as when a swindler is attractive (Sigall & Ostrove, 1975). In an assault case, a female defendant is more likely than a male defendant to be found guilty (Cruse & Leigh, 1987), presumably because an assaultive woman is engaging in unacceptable gender-role behavior (see Chapter 5), while an assaultive man is not. Also, high status becomes a liability if the crime is related to the defendant's profession; an example would be a therapist who rapes a client (Skolnick & Shaw, 1994).

In addition to broad characteristics such as appearance, gender, and occupation, the defendant's behavior affects decisions about punishment. LaFrance and Hecht (1995) examined reactions to an accused individual as a function of whether that person smiles or fails to smile. The investigators asked research participants to act as members of a college disciplinary panel in a case of a student accused of cheating on an exam. Besides information relevant to the charge, participants saw a smiling or a nonsmiling photograph of a female student who supposedly was the accused cheater, and they were asked to judge her probable guilt and to recommend what action should be taken. Though smiling had no effect on judgments of guilt, both male and female panel members who saw a smiling picture of the accused recommended greater leniency than did those who saw a picture in which she was not smiling. Why? Further analysis revealed that leniency was related to the belief that the accused person was trustworthy (basically honest and good); judgments of trustworthiness, in turn, were influenced by smiling.

Are All Defendants Equal under the Law?   One of the more consistent findings is that attractive defendants are at an advantage compared to unattractive ones with respect to being acquitted, receiving a light sentence, and gaining the sympathy of the jurors (Esses & Webster, 1988; Stewart, 1980; Wuensch, Castellow, & Moore, 1991; see Figure 13.9 on page 494). This attractiveness effect is strongest with serious but nonfatal crimes such as burglary, and with

FIGURE 13.9

What Is Beautiful Is Good Revisited: Effect of Defendant's Physical Attractiveness on Judicial Decisions. Though the physical appearance of a defendant is obviously unrelated to his or her guilt, a great many studies indicate a general tendency for jurors to respond more favorably to an attractive than to an unattractive defendant.

female defendants (Quigley, Johnson, & Byrne, 1995). Because attorneys are well aware of the importance of the bias toward attractiveness, they usually advise a client to do everything possible to enhance his or her appearance before entering the courtroom.

You might assume that even if the attractiveness of a defendant could influence the responses of a juror, judges surely would be unaffected by how a defendant looks. In fact, as Downs and Lyons (1991) discovered, judges are as susceptible to the effects of appearance as the rest of us. These investigators collected data on the dollar amounts assigned by forty judges for bail and for fines in more than 1,500 court cases involving misdemeanors. The attractiveness of each defendant was rated by police officers who were not involved in the arrest and who did not know the purpose of the study. The results clearly indicated that the more attractive a defendant, the lower the amount of bail or the fine set by the judge. The seriousness of the crime also influenced the amount of the bails and fines (the more serious, the higher the dollar amount), but the attractiveness effect was evident at each level of seriousness. A similar analysis of still more serious cases—felonies—revealed that attractiveness becomes irrelevant when extremely serious crimes are involved, and other research supports this finding (McKelvie & Coley, 1993).

Does the *victim's* attractiveness have any effect on judgments about the *defendant*? The answer is, sometimes. When, for example, the case is one of alleged sexual harassment, the attractiveness of *both* the plaintiff and the defendant influence decisions about guilt and innocence (Castellow, Wuensch, & Moore, 1990). In a test of these effects, research participants read the trial summary of a case in which a young secretary/receptionist accused her employer of repeatedly making suggestive remarks, attempting to kiss and fondle her, and letting her know in detail what sexual activities he would enjoy with her. The participants saw two photographs that were identified as the plaintiff and the defendant. Some saw two attractive individuals, some saw two unattractive ones, and still others saw either an attractive male defendant and an unattractive female plaintiff or the reverse. As shown in Figure 13.10, guilty judgments were most likely when the plaintiff was an attractive woman and the defendant was an unattractive man (83 percent) and least likely when the plaintiff was unattractive and the defendant attractive (41 percent).

FIGURE 13.10

Sexual Harassment: Attractiveness of Plaintiff and of Defendant. Mock jurors deliberated a sexual harassment case in which a female plaintiff brought charges against a male defendant. The jurors read a court summary based on actual trials, and they were shown photographs of a woman and a man who were supposedly the plaintiff and the defendant. The pictures were either of two attractive individuals, two unattractive individuals, an attractive plaintiff and an unattractive defendant, or an unattractive plaintiff and an attractive defendant. Both male and female jurors were most likely to give a guilty verdict when an attractive woman charged an unattractive man with harassment, and least likely to vote guilty when an unattractive woman charged an attractive man with harassing her.

(*Source*: Based on data from Castellow, Wuensch, & Moore, 1990.)

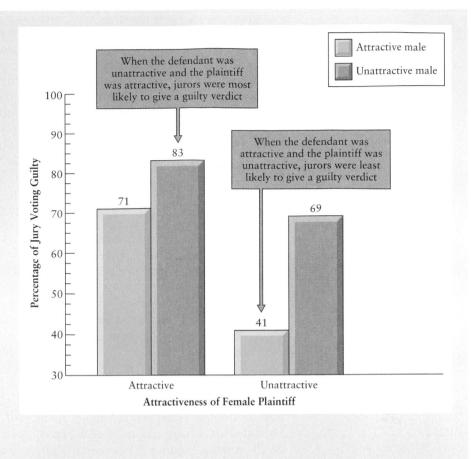

Though the attractiveness effects in sexual harassment cases seem clear and convincing, subsequent research suggests that an additional factor is involved. Because attractiveness leads to positive judgments about various other personal characteristics—"what is beautiful is good" (see Chapter 7)—Egbert and colleagues (1992) conducted the sexual harassment experiment again; but instead of varying attractiveness, they presented positive and negative information about the plaintiff and the defendant. Analogous to the findings when attractiveness was manipulated, the largest percentage of guilty decisions were found when the defendant was described negatively (uncaring, low-achieving, dishonest) and the plaintiff described positively (friendly, likable, pleasant), and the smallest percentage of guilty decisions occurred when the defendant was positive (respected, honest, churchgoing) and the plaintiff negative (grumpy, unpleasant, unprofessional). This finding suggested to the investigators that attractiveness has an effect, but only because attractiveness is associated with inferences about character. But this explanation is slightly complicated by the fact that participants assumed positively described individuals were more attractive than those described in negative terms—"what is good is beautiful." The question is whether attractiveness influences judgments because of assumptions about character or whether character influences judgments because of assumptions about physical attractiveness (or possibly both).

To determine directly whether the basic determinant of the effect was attractiveness or character, Moore and his colleagues (1994) conducted a follow-up experiment varying *both* physical attractiveness and character of the defendant and of the plaintiff. With both types of information present, character influenced juror decisions while physical attractiveness did not. It seems quite possible, then, that the attractiveness effect in legal decisions is real but that it operates only because of its effect on assumptions about character.

In the United States, African American defendants have generally been found to be at a disadvantage. For example, they are more likely than whites to be convicted of homicide and to receive the death penalty (Sniffen, 1991). Of the prisoners awaiting execution at any given time, about 40 percent are black, a much higher figure than the proportion of blacks in the total population (about 11 percent). The explanation for this black overrepresentation on death row is not a simple one. The most obvious—but not necessarily correct—hypothesis is that white judges and jurors tend to be racially biased. The reason may not be that straightforward. We noted earlier that young males tend to commit a high proportion of crimes of violence; and a higher proportion of blacks than of whites are involved in such offenses. The suggested reasons for black over-representation include the pervasive effects of poverty and unemployment on young black males, and the influence of a subculture in which violent social models are readily available to these young men. Still another explanation is that white defendants have an economic advantage and can afford more skillful attorneys. Racism, however, seems the most likely explanation for another black–white finding: A study of American trials revealed that regardless of a criminal's race, 11.1 percent who kill a white victim receive a death sentence, but only 4.5 percent of those killing a black victim are sentenced to die (Henderson & Taylor, 1985).

In addition to attractiveness and race, what a defendant says in court can also influence judgments. When defendants deny guilt, this has little effect on whether observers believe the statement to be true. When, however, defendants deny accusations that have not been made ("I am not a crook"), they are perceived as being less trustworthy, more nervous, more responsible for what happened, and more likely to be guilty (Holtgraves & Grayer, 1994). When defendants do not speak English, and the testimony must be translated, they are more likely to be found guilty than if precisely the same testimony is simply given in English (Stephan & Stephan, 1986).

Who Is Sitting in the Jury Box?   A joke among lawyers describes the difference between jury trials in England and in the United States. In England the trial starts once the jury is selected, while in the United States the trial is actually over once the jury is selected (Goleman, 1994). Adler (1994) believes that the American jury system is failing, because those selected often miss key points, focus on irrelevant issues, are influenced by their prejudices, and fail to recognize that attorneys sometimes blatantly manipulate their feelings of sympathy or of hate. Adler's suggestions for improving the situation include the elimination of peremptory challenges by each side during jury selection, the elimination of exemptions for some of the best-educated members of the community (such as physicians, professors, and the clergy), and changes in the rules so that jurors would be allowed to make notes and even to ask questions approved by the judge.

Research suggests that one cause of jury incompetence is based on individual differences in cognitive processing. About a third of all individuals serving on juries make up their minds about which story to believe (prosecution or defense) at the time of opening arguments (if not before). Once this decision is made, a schema is in place. Thus, all of the evidence and testimony that follows is interpreted in such a way as to fit that schema, or is simply ignored if it can't be made to fit (Kuhn, Weinstock, & Flaton, 1994). More competent jurors, in contrast, process trial information by constructing alternative schemas so that, as evidence is presented, it can be examined with respect to alternative cognitive constructions. Jurors who quickly conclude that one story is the true one also tend to be very certain about their beliefs, to give extreme verdicts, and to create hung juries because they are unwilling to change their minds. As you might guess, the more complex and technical the evidence, the greater difficulty jurors have in processing whatever information they receive (Bourgeois, Horowitz, & Lee, 1993).

Even seemingly irrelevant differences among jurors can determine a trial's outcome. For example, the more previous jury experience a juror has had, the more likely that person is to vote to convict the defendant (Werner et al., 1985).

Just as there are hard and soft judges, jurors also hold attitudes that range from blaming society to blaming the accused criminal. For example, those with a **leniency bias** (a general tendency to favor a defendant) are least likely to vote guilty (MacCoun & Kerr, 1988). At the opposite extreme is **legal authoritarianism** (a general tendency to assume the worst about a defendant), and jurors with this attitude are most likely to vote guilty (Narby, Cutler, & Moran, 1993).

In states having a death penalty, potential jurors in a murder trial who oppose such executions are routinely eliminated. This is not to the defendant's advantage, because those who favor the death penalty are more likely to vote in favor of conviction than those who oppose it (Bersoff, 1987).

Some very specific attitudes—such as respecting psychiatry or judging it to be unscientific nonsense—can be crucial when a psychiatrist testifies about the defendant's mental state (Cutler, Moran, & Narby, 1992). In cases of a battered woman who kills her abuser, jurors who are well informed about the dynamics of such abuse are more likely to believe the woman's version of what happened than are jurors who know little about the topic (Schuller, Smith, & Olson, 1994).

Altogether, research on the legal system provides ample evidence that considerable effort is needed to create judicial fairness and objectivity. The elimination of all biases is an important goal, but a difficult (perhaps impossible) one to achieve.

INTEGRATING PRINCIPLES

1. Before a case comes to trial, the evidence gathered from suspects and from witnesses can be biased by specific methods of interrogation. Pretrial publicity in the media can shape public opinion, including the opinions of those who will eventually serve as jurors, negative media coverage yields negative first impressions of the suspect, and these effects tend to persist as a function of primacy (Chapter 2).

2. In providing accurate eyewitness testimony, an individual must retrieve material from memory, but the efficiency of such cognitive processing (Chapter 3) can be subject to interference from both internal and external factors. When the police present witnesses with a lineup, the situation closely resembles a social psychological experiment (Chapter 1), and accurate results require similar safeguards.

Leniency Bias ▪ Among some jurors, a general tendency to make favorable assumptions about a person accused of a crime.

Legal Authoritarianism ▪ Among some jurors, a general tendency to assume the worst about a person accused of a crime.

3. In our legal system, attorneys act as adversaries who seek to influence the attitudes and judgments (Chapter 4) of the jury by selecting individuals they believe to be biased toward their position. Lawyers on each side attempt to manipulate the affective responses (Chapter 7) of those who must reach a verdict.

4. Jury members reach conclusions about a given defendant on the basis of processes familiar to social psychologists. Included are nonverbal communication, attributions, and impression formation (Chapter 2), social cognition (Chapter 3); attitudes about specific crimes and their causes (Chapter 4); prejudices based on race and gender (Chapter 5 and 6); interpersonal attraction and therefore numerous characteristics that should be irrelevant to judgments about guilt and innocence (Chapter 7); and social influence in the courtroom and in the deliberations of the jurors (Chapter 9).

Social Psychology and Business: Work-Related Attitudes, Impression Management in Job Interviews, and Conflict

What single activity fills more of most persons' time than any other? The answer is simple: work. Unless we are fortunate enough to be born with or to acquire vast wealth, most of us spend a majority of our waking hours doing some type of job. And we don't work alone; on the contrary, most of us work together with other persons in what, from the point of view of social psychology, are certainly social situations. It's not surprising, then, that the principles and findings of social psychology have often been applied to the task of understanding what goes on in work settings—mainly with an eye toward making this central part of life more satisfying and productive. In many cases, social psychologists themselves have used the knowledge of their field to address important questions and to solve practical problems relating to work. In other cases, however, the findings and principles of social psychology have been put to use by **industrial/organizational psychologists**—psychologists who specialize in studying all aspects of behavior in work settings (Murnighan, 1993). Regardless of who has applied social psychology in this manner, the results have been rewarding: social psychology *does* provide many insights into the complex world of work.

In this section, we'll consider some of the valuable contributions made by social psychology in this respect. Specifically, we'll examine four major topics: *work-related attitudes*—employees' attitudes toward their jobs and their organizations; the role of impression management in *job interviews*—how job applicants attempt to look good to interviewers; *organizational politics*—tactics used by individuals to further their own ends, often at considerable costs to others and their company; and the nature and causes of interpersonal *conflict* in work settings.

Work-Related Attitudes: Job Satisfaction and Organizational Commitment

As we saw in Chapter 4, we are rarely neutral to the social world around us: on the contrary, we hold strong *attitudes* about many aspects of it. Jobs are no exception to this general rule. In fact, if asked, most persons can readily report

Industrial/Organizational Psychologists ■ Psychologists who investigate all aspects of behavior in work settings.

their attitudes toward their work and also toward their organization. Attitudes concerning one's own job or work are generally referred to by the term **job satisfaction**. Don't let this term confuse you: not everyone likes their job. So *job satisfaction* actually refers to a dimension of reactions ranging from very positive (high job satisfaction) to very negative (low job satisfaction or high job *dis*satisfaction) (Hulin, 1991).

In contrast, attitudes toward one's company are known as **organizational commitment**. This term refers to the extent to which an individual identifies with his or her company and is unwilling to leave it (e.g., Hackett, Bycio, & Hausdorf, 1994). Let's take a closer look at the factors that influence both kinds of work-related attitudes.

Factors Affecting Job Satisfaction. Despite the fact that many jobs are repetitive and boring in nature, large scale surveys of employees' attitudes toward their jobs indicate that for most, job satisfaction is quite high (e.g., Page & Wiseman, 1993). In part, this may reflect the operation of *cognitive dissonance,* a process we discussed in Chapter 4. Briefly, since most persons know that they have to go on working and that there is often considerable effort—and risk—involved in changing jobs, stating that they are not satisfied with their current jobs tends to generate dissonance. To avoid or reduce such reactions, then, many persons report relatively high levels of job satisfaction—and may actually come to believe their own ratings in this respect (e.g., Greenberg & Baron, 1995).

Individuals do report a wide range of job satisfaction, though, so the question remains: What factors influence such attitudes? Research on this issue indicates that two major groups of factors are important: *organizational factors*—ones related to a company's practices or the working conditions it provides—and *personal factors*—ones related to the traits of individual employees.

Among organizational factors, a very important one is the company's *reward system*—the way in which raises, promotions, and other rewards are distributed. As we saw in Chapter 12, *fairness* is an extremely important value for most persons, and this value comes into full operation with respect to job-related rewards. Job satisfaction is higher when individuals believe that rewards are distributed fairly and impartially than when they believe they are distributed unfairly (Miceli & Lane, 1991). Another organizational factor that plays an important role in job satisfaction is the *perceived quality of supervision*—the extent to which employees believe that their bosses are competent, have employees' best interests at heart, and treat them with respect. A third factor influencing job satisfaction is the extent to which individuals feel that they can participate in decisions that affect them. The greater such participation, the higher the reported job satisfaction (Callan, 1993). Finally, as you can readily guess, the nature of jobs themselves plays an important role in job satisfaction. Individuals who must perform boring, repetitive jobs report much lower levels of job satisfaction than ones whose jobs provide a degree of variety (Fisher, 1993). In fact, recent findings indicate that not only do boring, monotonous jobs reduce job satisfaction—they may undermine psychological and even physical health, too. A study conducted by Melamed and his colleagues (Melamed et al., 1995) provides important insights into this relationship.

These researchers reasoned that repetitive work, and work that exposes individuals to *underload*—jobs that do not give people enough to do or that are beneath their capacities—would cause strong feelings of monotony, and that these, in turn, would produce low job satisfaction, psychological distress, and even physical illness. Melamed as his associates further reasoned that repetitive jobs that are also *hectic*—jobs requiring individuals to repeat the same task over and over again very quickly (see Figure 13.11 on page 500)—would have especially negative effects. To test these predictions, they analyzed the work performed by

Job Satisfaction ■ Attitudes held by individuals about their jobs.

Organizational Commitment ■ Attitudes held by individuals toward their organization, reflecting the extent to which they identify with the company and are unwilling to leave it.

FIGURE 13.11

Monotonous, Hectic Jobs: One Source of Low Job Satisfaction. Individuals performing jobs in which they must repeat the same task over and over again very quickly often report low levels of job satisfaction.

almost 1,300 blue-collar workers working in manufacturing plants to see how monotonous and hectic the jobs were. Then they asked these individuals to complete questionnaires designed to measure their subjective feelings of monotony, their job satisfaction, and their psychological distress (feelings of depression, anxiety, irritability). Finally, they obtained records of sickness-related absences for these employees. Results offered support for the key predictions. The more monotonous the jobs were, the lower employees' job satisfaction, the higher their psychological distress, and the greater their absences from work (although the last of these findings was stronger for women than for men). And these negative effects were especially pronounced for jobs classified as *hectic* in nature.

Turning to personal factors that influence job satisfaction, several interesting findings have been uncovered. Job satisfaction is related to several personal traits, such as the Type A behavior pattern, which we discussed in Chapter 11 (Day & Bedian, 1991): Type A's tend to be more satisfied than Type B's, despite their greater overall irritability. Job satisfaction is also related to *status* and *seniority.* The higher a person's position within a company, the greater his or her reported satisfaction. Also, the longer an individual has been on the job, the greater his or her job satisfaction (Zeitz, 1990). Fourth, the greater the extent to which jobs are *congruent* with people's interests, the greater their satisfaction (Fricko & Beehr, 1992). Indeed, very low levels of satisfaction are often reported by persons working in fields that do not interest them. Finally, job satisfaction is related to people's *general life satisfaction*. The more individuals are satisfied with aspects of their lives outside work, the higher the levels of job satisfaction they report (Judge & Watanabe, 1993). In sum, many different factors seem to influence job satisfaction. Given that job satisfaction is an important type of attitude, this is far from surprising.

The Effects of Job Satisfaction: Weaker Than You Might Guess. In Chapter 4, we stressed the fact that attitudes are not always reflected in overt behavior. (Do you recall LaPiere and his travels throughout the United States?) Thus, there is no reason to expect that individuals' level of job satisfaction would necessarily influence important aspects of their behavior at work. In fact, this is precisely what research has found. Research on the effects of job satisfaction has generally reported weak relationships between job satisfaction and task performance (Iffaldano & Murchinsky, 1985) and between job satisfaction and voluntary turnover—decisions by individuals to quit their jobs (Judge, 1993; Tett & Meyer, 1993).

Why aren't these relationships stronger? Shouldn't people who are happy with their jobs be more productive and less likely to quit? Not necessarily. Let's consider the job satisfaction–task performance relationship first. One reason this link may be relatively weak is that many jobs leave little room for variations in performance. If individuals fall below certain minimum levels, they can't retain their jobs. Similarly, they can't exceed these minimum standards by much, because their work depends on input from others—for example, they can't proceed with *their* work until they receive input from other persons with whom they work. Because of this limited range of possible performance, job satisfaction cannot exert a strong influence on task performance.

Another reason for the relatively weak link between job satisfaction and task performance is that many other factors also determine performance: working conditions, the availability of required materials and tools, the extent to which the task is structured. In many situations, the effects of these factors may be more important, as determinants of performance, than job satisfaction.

Having pointed out these complexities, we should note that research has found a somewhat stronger relationship between job satisfaction and performance on the level of *organizational performance* than on that of individual task performance. For instance, in one very revealing study, Ostroff (1992) measured the level of job satisfaction among more than 13,000 high school and junior high school teachers. In addition, she also obtained several measures of the performance of the schools in which they worked: the percentage of students graduating, academic performance on standardized national tests, levels of vandalism. Ostroff found that most of these measures of *school performance* were significantly related to teachers' job satisfaction: in fact, the mean correlation across all measures was +.28. This correlation was considerably higher than the correlation between *individual performance* and job satisfaction found in many other studies (e.g., Iffaldano & Murchinksy, 1985). So, in sum, job satisfaction does influence performance, but we must search for this link at the appropriate level of analysis.

Now, what about job satisfaction and voluntary turnover: why is *this* relationship relatively weak? Research findings indicate that the answer involves the fact that the decision to leave one's job is actually affected by many different factors, and job satisfaction is only one of these. For example, consider economic conditions. When times are good and there are many jobs available, individuals who are unhappy with their jobs may decide to quit and look for another one: they are confident that they can get a better position. When times are bad, however, even people who are very dissatisfied with their jobs may stay put: they can't risk being unemployed. A study by Carsten and Spector (1987) confirms this reasoning. They found that the relationship between job satisfaction and voluntary turnover was stronger at times when unemployment was low than when it was high. Several other factors, too, have been found to influence the decision to leave one's job—factors ranging from personal characteristics (Judge, 1993) and the perceived probability of finding another job through cognitive mechanisms involving thoughts about quitting and intentions to search for a new job (Mobley, Horner, & Hollingsworth, 1978). Given this fact, it is far from surprising that the relationship between job satisfaction and quitting—like the relationship between job satisfaction and performance—is not as simple or as strong as you might expect.

Organizational Commitment: Attitudes toward One's Company. Do you know anyone who constantly knocks your college or university, criticizing it constantly and harshly? What about the opposite: do you know anyone who frequently praises your college, telling others what a great place it is and how nice all the professors are? Our own experience tells us that the second pattern is much more rare than the first one; but in any case, you probably do know people with contrasting reactions to their school or the organization in which they work. This range of reactions indicates that people hold attitudes not only toward their jobs, but toward their companies as well. Such attitudes are known as *organizational commitment,* because they refer to the extent to which individuals identify with, are involved with, and are unwilling to leave their organizations—whether these are universities, small businesses, or giant corporations (Meyer & Allen, 1991; Dunham, Grube, & Castaneda, 1994). In fact, a model proposed by Allen and Meyer (1990) suggests that such attitudes involve three different components.

First, there is what Meyer and Allen (1991) term the *affective component.* This involves emotional attachment to and identification with the organization. A person high on this component feels good about her or his company and has made working for it a part of her of his self-concept. "I'm an IBM person," or "I'm a Marine!" such a person might state, with pride. Second, there is what Allen and Meyer describe as the *continuance component.* This relates to the potential costs involved in leaving the company. For example, after working for a company for several years, an individual may have a considerable sum built up in its pension fund; if the employee leaves, a part (or even all) of these funds many be lost. Similarly, an individual may realize that it will be difficult to find another comparable job. Third, there is what Meyer and Allen describe as a *normative component.* This refers to feelings of obligation to stay with the company—mainly because of norms and values indicating that loyalty is desirable, that it's wrong to jump from job to job, or that the individual owes the company allegiance. According to Meyer and Allen (1991), these three components combine to generate an individual's level of organizational commitment (see Figure 13.12 for an overview of this process).

This model has been tested in many recent studies (e.g., Dunham, Grube, & Castaneda, 1994; Hackett, Bycio, & Hausford, 1994), and in general results have supported its accuracy. Thus, it appears that organizational commitment

FIGURE 13.12

Organizational Commitment: One Influential Model. According to a model proposed by Allen and Meyer (1990), organizational commitment involves the three separate components shown here.

(*Source:* Based on suggestions by Meyer & Allen, 1991.)

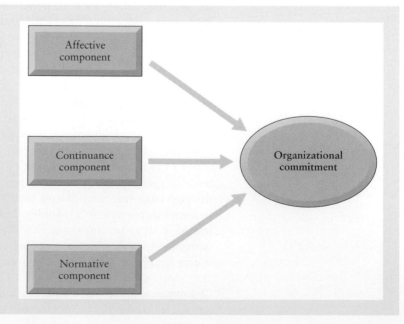

does involve the three components shown in Figure 13.12. What factors influence such commitment? Recent findings suggest that somewhat different conditions play a role in each of the three components (e.g., Dunham et al., 1994). For example, with respect to affective commitment, the following variables seem to be important: quality of supervisory feedback, autonomy (freedom to structure one's own work), task identity (being able to complete a whole piece of work from beginning to end), and skill variety (working on a job that requires a number of different activities). Tenure (length of time with the company) also plays a role; the longer the tenure, the higher affective commitment tends to be. Tenure plays an even more important role with respect to continuance commitment: the longer people have been with a given company, the more they have to lose, in many cases, if they leave. Finally, normative commitment is influenced by such factors as commitment on the part of one's coworkers and the extent to which individuals are allowed to participate in decisions relating to their jobs: being able to participate in decisions creates a sense of obligation to stay with a company that has treated the individual fairly and with respect. In short, many different factors influence organizational commitment, and these seem to differ for each of the components of such commitment.

Effects of Organizational Commitment. What are the effects of organizational commitment? First, as you might well expect, persons who are high on such commitment show lower levels of absenteeism and voluntary turnover (Lee et al., 1992). Second, the higher individuals' organizational commitment, the greater their willingness to make sacrifices for their company (Randall, Fedor, & Longenecker, 1990). In other words, the greater their willingness to do what's good for the company even at some cost to themselves. Such actions are sometimes described as **organizational citizenship behavior,** and they are closely related to the kinds of prosocial behavior we discussed in Chapter 10 (Konovsky & Pugh, 1994; Van Dyne, Graham, & Dienesch, 1994). Finally, organizational commitment often has effects on individuals' life away from work. When employees are strongly committed to their organizations, they may be more willing to devote large amounts of time to it and to engage in activities that are not officially part of their job (again, such actions are sometimes described as citizenship behaviors). This necessarily leaves less time for relationships and activities outside work, so a high level of organizational commitment may be one aspect of the *workaholic* syndrome that afflicts some ambitious persons. However, some evidence suggests that persons high in organizational commitment actually report more enjoyable lives outside work than do persons low in organizational commitment (Romzek, 1989). Are they deluding themselves in this respect, or does being committed to one's organization actually yield increased personal happiness? Only further research can answer these intriguing questions. What we can conclude with certainty, though, is that work-related attitudes, like other attitudes, do often exert important effects on overt behavior. This relationship is often complex and far from perfect, but it is both real and important.

Organizational Citizenship Behavior ■ Voluntary behaviors by individuals that aid their organizations and that are not related to the formal reward system of their job.

Job Interviews ■ Interviews conducted with applicants for various jobs in order to choose the best job candidates.

Job Interviews: Impression Management Revisited

Do you remember our discussion of *impression management* in Chapter 2? At that time, we pointed out the importance of first impressions and described some of the tactics individuals employ to look good to others they are meeting for the first time (Wayne & Liden, 1995). One important context where such tactics are often used is during **job interviews**—interviews organizations conduct with applicants for various jobs in order to choose the best candidates. Think about it: Wouldn't *you* try your best to make a good first impression on an interviewer if you were applying for a job? Actually, you've probably already had experience in doing just this—in trying to look your best during an interview. Taking a cue from research on first impressions and impression management conducted by social psychologists, industrial/organizational psychologists have studied these processes as they occur during interviews. The results of this research are somewhat unsettling; for it has been found that interviewers' ratings of job applicants are influenced by a wide range of factors that, most persons would agree, should *not* play a role in the selection of employees (e.g., Dipboye, 1992). These factors include applicants' physical appearance, which we discussed earlier in this chapter in connection with jurors' reactions to defendants; through the mood of interviewers (Baron, 1993a); and many tactics of *impression management* that can be used, with varying success, by applicants (Wayne & Liden, 1995). Since job interviews remain one of the most widely used procedures for choosing employees (McDaniel et al., 1994), these findings have important implications. Let's take a closer look at some of the social factors that can influence the judgments of even experienced interviewers who are trying hard to choose the best applicants.

Applicants' Appearance. Almost without exception, people preparing for job interviews dress and groom themselves as carefully as possible. After all, everyone "knows" that appearance really matters where first impressions are concerned. Systematic research suggests that such beliefs are well-founded: interviewers' ratings of job applicants are indeed sometimes influenced by the applicants' appearance and factors relating to this. For example, attractive persons often have an edge over less attractive ones, and persons who dress for interviews in a manner considered appropriate by interviewers—a manner consistent with the style of dress adopted in their companies—often receive higher ratings than persons who dress in a less appropriate manner (Forsythe, Drake, & Cox, 1985). Similarly, interviewers often assign higher ratings to applicants who emit high levels of nonverbal cues—persons who smile, nod, and lean forward frequently during an interview (Riggio & Throckmorton, 1988).

In short, the outcome of interviews is often influenced by aspects of applicants' appearance over which they exert direct control. Perhaps even more unsettling is evidence indicating that such effects also occur for variables over which individuals have relatively little control—factors such as gender (Heilman, Martell, & Simon, 1988) and being overweight (Klesges et al., 1990). The strong impact of this latter factor is clearly illustrated in a study by Pingitore and her colleagues (1994).

These researchers prepared eight different videotapes of simulated job interviews in which three factors were systematically varied: (1) nature of the job (either sales—a job for which personal appearance is relevant—or systems analysis, for which it is not relevant); (2) gender of the applicants (male or female); and (3) weight of the applicants (normal-weight or considerably overweight). Professional actors were hired to play the roles of job applicants in the videotapes, and these persons wore special makeup and padding under their clothes to make themselves appear overweight or of normal weight in the appropriate conditions. After watching one of the eight tapes, participants rated the extent to which they would hire the job applicant they saw. In addition, they reported on their own level of satisfaction with their own bodies and weight. It was predicted that participants would assign lower ratings to the applicants when they appeared to be overweight, and that this tendency might be stronger for female than for male applicants. As you can see from Figure 13.13, these predictions were confirmed. The overweight applicants received significantly lower ratings, and this effect was indeed stronger for female applicants than for male applicants. Interestingly, the nature of the job made no difference: Overweight applicants received lower ratings even for the systems analyst job, one

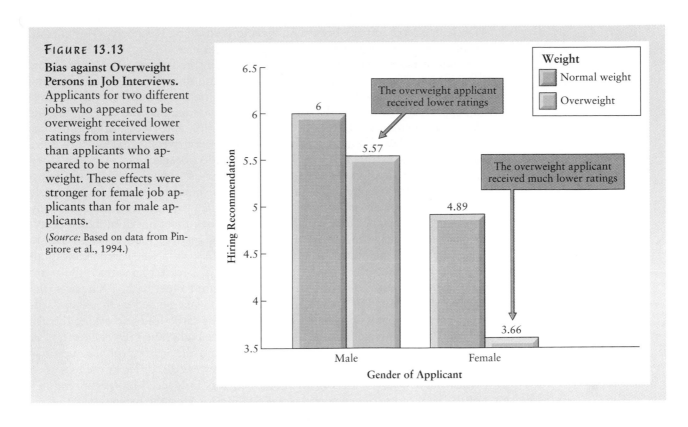

FIGURE 13.13

Bias against Overweight Persons in Job Interviews. Applicants for two different jobs who appeared to be overweight received lower ratings from interviewers than applicants who appeared to be normal weight. These effects were stronger for female job applicants than for male applicants.

(*Source:* Based on data from Pingitore et al., 1994.)

for which appearance is largely irrelevant. Finally, individuals who were themselves pleased with their own bodies and weight—especially women—were somewhat harsher in their evaluations of the overweight applicants. It was as though they reasoned, "If I'm so slim, why aren't you?"

In sum, the findings reported by Pingitore and her colleagues (1994) indicate that there is indeed a bias against overweight job applicants and that such bias is especially strong for females. Clearly, these are unsettling findings, which serve to underscore a point we made in Chapter 3: as human beings, we are definitely *not* perfectly rational information-processing machines. On the contrary, we are often influenced, in our social judgments, by factors that, we would be quick to agree, should not play a role in such decisions.

How Interviewers Sometimes Get the Results They Want: Expectancy Confirmation in Job Interviews. In Chapters 2 and 3, we noted that expectancies often exert a strong effect on our thoughts and our behavior. Often, we perceive—and actually get—what we *expect* to get. Do such effects play a role in job interviews? A growing body of evidence indicates that they do (Dipboye, 1992; McCannan & Dipboye, 1990). In many cases, it appears, interviewers form expectancies about job applicants before actually meeting them, from applicant personnel and human resource forms, letters of recommendation, and other input. Then they engage in behaviors that tend to confirm these expectations. For example, if they expect to like a particular applicant or to evaluate this person highly, they may do such things during the interview as ask supportive questions, agree with the applicant, emit positive nonverbal cues to this person, and focus on selling their company to the applicant rather than on asking the applicant to explain why she or he would be suited for the job in question. In contrast, if they expect to dislike the applicant or to evaluate this person poorly, they may ask more searching and fewer supportive questions, may emit negative nonverbal cues, and may focus on examining applicant qualifications.

Do such effects actually occur? An ingenious study by Dougherty, Turban, and Callender (1994) indicates that they do.

These researchers received permission from three professional interviewers to make audiotapes of their interviews with real job applicants. Before meeting each applicant, the interviewers received information about them (test scores, an application form). On the basis of this information, they rated the applicants on their apparent qualifications. The key question addressed in the study was this: Would these ratings be reflected in the interviewers' behavior during the actual interviews? To find out, Dougherty and colleagues (1994) had trained coders use the audiotapes to rate the interviewers' behavior during the interviews. Results indicated that the interviewers' behavior was indeed strongly influenced by their initial ratings of the applicants, and that they generally behaved in a manner that would tend to *confirm* these initial ratings. For example, the higher the ratings interviewers assigned to the applicants before meeting them, the more they adopted a positive style when interacting with these persons and the more positive nonverbal cues they emitted (the more friendly, outgoing, and cheerful the coders found them to be). Similarly, the higher their ratings of the applicants, the more they tended to focus on "selling" their company and the job to these persons rather than on asking the applicants for job-related information. Further, the higher the ratings interviewers assigned to the applicants before meeting them, the fewer probing questions they asked of these persons. The three interviewers did differ in the extent to which their behavior during the interviews was influenced by their preratings of the applicants, but such effects were found for all three persons.

In sum, the findings obtained by Dougherty and his colleagues (1994) indicate that expectancies play an important role in job interviews, just as they do in many other social situations. Applicants who look good on paper before the interview may find themselves facing an interviewer who is largely on their side and who engages in actions that help them do their best. In contrast, applicants whose records are unimpressive may find themselves facing an interviewer who acts as an adversary—one who seems to say, in many different ways, "OK—show me why I should recommend you for this job."

Organizational Politics: Tactics for Getting Ahead—Whatever the Cost to Others

Do you recall our comments about *organizational citizenship behavior*—actions taken by individuals that benefit fellow employees or their company, even at some cost to themselves? In some ways, *organizational politics*—actions taken by individuals to further their own goals, often at considerable costs to others or their organization—represents the opposite pattern (Drory & Romm, 1990; Ferris & Kacmar, 1992). Viewed from the perspective of social psychology, such behavior represents various forms of social influence applied to purely selfish ends (see Chapter 9). What specific tactics do individuals use in organizational politics? Here are some of the most important:

Controlling access to information. In an important sense, information is power in many organizations: those who have information, and know how to use it, can get pretty much what they want. Being aware of this basic fact, persons engaging in organizational politics manipulate information for their own purposes. They attempt to withhold information needed by others so that these persons flounder around without a clue as to what's happening. Similarly, they conceal information that makes them look bad, thus protecting their own image. In addition, they sometimes attempt to overwhelm others with too much information—more than they can handle. The primary goal of all these related tactics is much the same: controlling the flow of information in ways that benefit the politician and, at the same time, harm others (Feldman, 1988).

Cultivating a good image. Persons who engage in organizational politics also frequently use tactics designed to make them look good—better than their potential rivals. They do this by associating themselves with successful persons and with successful projects, by drawing attention to their own accomplishments, and by ingratiating themselves to powerful persons in their organization (Ferris & King, 1991). Persons who engage in such tactics are sometimes described as being *organizational chameleons*—they do or say whatever it takes to make a favorable impression on others and build their own reputation.

Developing a base of support. Another set of tactics often used in organizational politics involves building a base of political support within the company. In other words, persons skilled at organizational politics go out of their way to ensure that others are committed to them and will support them when push comes to shove. They often do this by using the principle of *reciprocity* to their own advantage (see Chapter 9). This involves doing small favors for others and collecting their IOUs. Persons involved in organizational politics then call in these debts—and others' support—at just those times when it will do them most good. The result: They get what they want, often at very little cost.

Dirty tricks. If the tactics we have described so far sound somewhat unprincipled, get ready for worse—much worse. Persons engaging in organizational politics also often engage in what are known as *dirty tricks*—actions that most persons would view as downright unethical. Many of these exist, but one that is especially common is the *hidden agenda*. In this tactic, an agenda for a meeting is announced. When the meeting actually occurs, however, new issues that were *not* on the agenda are raised. This catches many persons unprepared, and the individual using this tactic can then often exert strong influence over the outcome. Another dirty trick involves spreading false rumors about another organization member. These can range from rumors about office romances (Pierce, Byrne, & Aguinis, in press) through rumors that the person in question is actively seeking another job. The result, of course, is unfair damage to the target person. Several other dirty tricks are described in Table 13.3 (p. 508).

When are organizational politics most likely to occur? Research findings indicate that such actions tend to be most frequent when the stakes are high—when there is a lot to be gained by winning; when individuals or groups within organizations have conflicting interests; and when the parties involved have roughly equal power, so that one party can't simply demand—and get—what it wants (Pfeffer, 1992). Additional findings indicate that such behavior is especially likely to occur with respect to *human resource issues*—decisions about raises, promotions, and the like (Ferris & Kacmar, 1992). This is so because these issues are ones where the conditions mentioned above—high stakes, conflicting interests, and equal power—tend to exist.

Protecting Yourself and Others against Organizational Politics. Politics is a fact of life in most organizations: there is simply too much at stake for it to be otherwise. This doesn't mean that you must fall victim to such tactics, however. There are means for reducing organizational politics and for blunting their potentially harmful effects. Here are several countermeasures suggested by careful research (e.g., Velasques, Moberg, & Cavanaugh, 1983):

1. *Clarify job expectations.* Before you undertake a job, be sure that you fully understand what it involves and what, precisely, is expected of you. Doing so can make it much more difficult for politicians to manipulate you, or to demand more than is fair.

TABLE 13.3 Dirty Tricks: Extreme Forms of Organizational Politics

The tactics shown here are sometimes described as dirty tricks. *They represent extreme forms of organizational politics, and are generally viewed as being unethical.*

Tactic	Description
Hidden Agenda	Announcing one agenda but then following another
Spreading False Rumors	Spreading false information about another person's behavior or intentions
Using Up Needed Resources	Consuming resources needed by another person to complete an important job
Withholding Information	Preventing other persons from getting information they need; destroying messages, erasing files
Back-Stabbing	Convincing another person that you are their ally, but speaking against them or their ideas behind their back
Falsifying Records	Changing recorded information so as to put others in a bad light or cover up your own actions

2. *Insist on (or at least encourage) open communication.* As we noted earlier, control over the flow of information is a favorite tactic of organizational politicians. By insisting that communication be as open as possible—that it be open to public scrutiny, for instance—you can reduce the opportunities for such manipulation.

3. *Be on the lookout for, and do not tolerate, political game players.* The biggest mistake you can make, in many cases, is to stand by while someone uses political tactics against others. You may not be involved now, but there's always next time! So, by being a socially responsible member of your organization and refusing to let unethical behavior pass, you may well protect your own interests.

Through these and related actions, you can make it more difficult for would-be politicians to manipulate you and others for their own selfish purposes. By doing so, not only will you protect your own career and well-being, but you may also help to make any organization where you work a more ethical social setting (see Chapter 10).

Conflict in Work Settings: A Social Psychological Perspective

In several important respects, all persons working in the same organization are *interdependent*. Their individual fates are linked, to some degree, at least while they remain in that organization. If the enterprise prospers, they can all share in a growing pie. If it fails, their individual outcomes may be sharply reduced or may even come to an end. Given these basic facts, it seems reasonable to assume that *cooperation*—working together to attain various benefits—would be the dominant mode of interaction in work settings. In fact, however, this is often not the case. Instead of working together in a coordinated fashion, individuals and groups often engage in **conflict**—they work against each other and attempt to block one another's interests. Unfortunately, conflict is far from rare in many work settings. In surveys, managers in a wide range of companies have reported that they spend more than 20 percent of their time dealing with conflict and its effects (e.g., Baron, 1989; Kilmann & Thomas, 1977). Moreover, it is clear that grudges, the desire for revenge, and other ill effects of intense conflicts can persist for months or even

Conflict ■ Actions taken by individuals to block or interfere with others' interests, because of perceptions of incompatible interests and the belief that others may be interfering with the perceiver's interests.

FIGURE 13.14

Causes of Conflict in Work Settings. As shown here, conflict in work settings stems from both organizational causes (e.g., competition over scarce resources, ambiguity over responsibility) and interpersonal causes (grudges, stereotypes, faulty attributions).

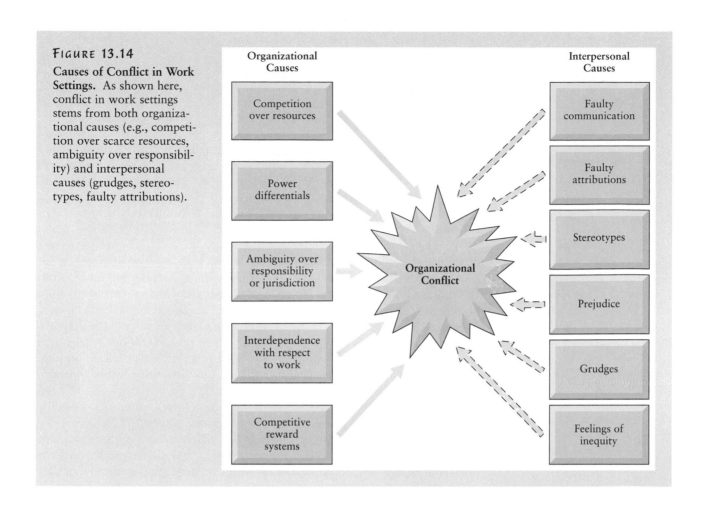

years, exacting a toll both on individuals and on their companies. As you can readily see, such conflicts are clearly related to *aggression,* a topic we examined in detail in Chapter 11. But the two concepts are not identical. While aggression refers to intentional efforts to harm one or more persons, conflict is defined as behavior resulting from two perceptions: (1) One's own and another person's interests are incompatible; and (2) the other person is about to interfere—or already has interfered—with the perceiver's interests (e.g., van de Vliert & Euwema, 1994). As you can readily see, these perceptions may sometimes lead to aggressive acts; but in other situations, they may lead to actions that are definitely not aggressive in nature—for example, trying to resolve the conflict through negotiation (see below). What are the causes of conflict? How do people actually behave in conflict situations? And what steps can be taken to reduce the potentially harmful effects of conflict? These are the questions on which we'll now focus.

The Causes of Conflict at Work: Organizational and Interpersonal. Suppose that you asked a large number of people to describe the factors that contribute to conflict in their work settings. How would they answer? The chances are good that most would refer to what have been described as *organizational causes* of conflict (Baron, 1993b). That is, they would describe factors such as those shown on the left side of Figure 13.14—causes relating to the structure and functioning of their companies, such as *competition over scarce resources,* or *ambiguity over responsibility* (who's in charge here, anyway?). Such answers reflect a traditional approach to organizational conflict—one that dominated the study of this topic in the past.

More recently, however, another perspective—one deriving directly from social psychology—has emerged. According to this point of view, conflict in work settings, like conflict in many other contexts, stems, at least in part, from *interpersonal factors*—factors related to individuals, their social relationships, and the ways in which they think about others (e.g., Baron, 1990; Hammock & Richardson, 1992; Kabanoff, 1991). As shown on the right side of Figure 13.14, such factors include stereotypes, prejudice, faulty styles of interpersonal communication, grudges stemming from loss of face and other factors, and faulty attributions—assuming that others are out to get us even if they are not (see Chapter 11). A growing body of evidence offers support for this perspective (e.g., Baron, 1988; 1990; Bies, Shapiro & Cummings, 1988; Ohbuchi & Takahashi, 1994), so it appears to be a useful one for understanding the causes of conflict.

Strategies for Dealing with Conflict: Contrasting Patterns, Underlying Dimensions. When I (Bob Baron) was the chair of my department, I often faced a conflict situation like this one. At a meeting of department chairs, the dean would announce that he had some funds he could distribute to individual departments. We would then discuss the division of these funds—often in a very heated manner. As you can see, this was basically a "win–lose" situation: if one department received some funds, the others could not. So it was clearly a conflict situation. I soon observed that different chairpersons reacted differently in this situation. Most, as you can guess, were quite competitive: they tried to convince the dean and the rest of us that they needed the money most. I must admit that I usually behaved in this manner myself. In contrast, a few chairpersons recommended dividing the money equally—equal shares for all. Surprisingly, there was one chair who often made comments to this effect: "My department needs the money, but let's give it to [another department], because I'm convinced that they need it more; and our real goal is to strengthen the entire school, right?"

These actions represent very different modes of responding to conflict. In fact, a large amount of research on conflict indicates that most people tend to adopt one of five distinct patterns: *competition*—get as much as possible for oneself or one's group; *compromise*—split everything down the middle or equally; *accommodation*—give up and let the others take all the benefits; *avoidance*—avoid conflict in any way possible, including withdrawal from the situation; and *collaboration*—attempt to maximize everyone's gains. As you can see, most department chairs (me included) chose competition; a few selected compromise; and one actually pushed for collaboration. (No one could avoid this situation; the dean expected us all to be at the meeting.)

If you think about these contrasting patterns—which have been confirmed in many studies (e.g., Thomas, 1988; Putnam, 1990)—you may quickly realize that they seem to relate to two basic dimensions: concern for one's own outcomes and concern for others' outcomes. Competition is high on concern for one's own outcomes and low on concern for others' outcomes, while accommodation (surrender) is high on concern for others' outcomes but low on concern for one's own outcomes. Compromise, of course, is in the middle on both dimensions. Interestingly, large individual differences seem to exist with respect to preferences among these patterns (e.g., Rahim, 1983). In other words, across many situations, some individuals tend to prefer confrontation (competition), while others tend to prefer less confrontating modes of resolving conflicts (compromise, collaboration, avoidance). Please see Figure 13.15 for the placement of all five patterns on these two dimensions.

Are any of the various modes for handling conflict we have discussed most effective? As you can see, this is a complex question, because what works in one situation may be inappropriate in another. Collaboration, which focuses on

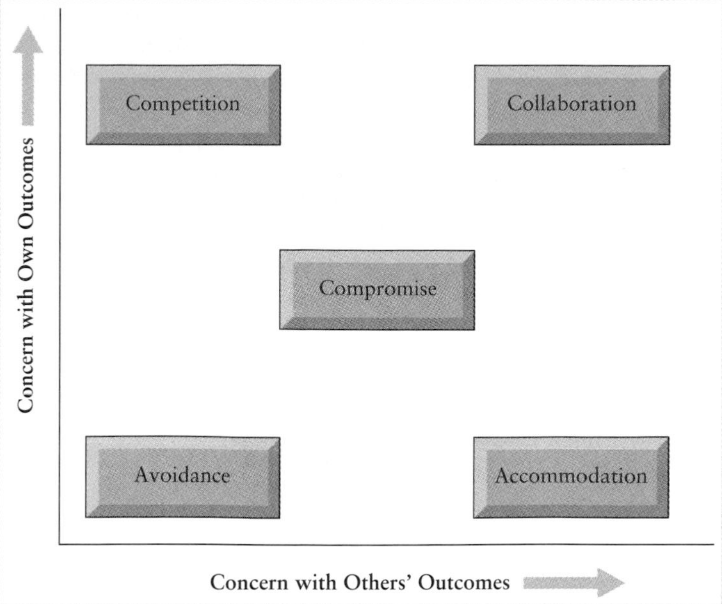

FIGURE 13.15

Reactions to Conflict: Five Basic Patterns. When faced with conflict situations, individuals often adopt one of the five patterns shown here: competition, compromise, accommodation, avoidance, collaboration. These reactions, in turn, are related to two underlying dimensions: concern with one's own outcomes and concern with others' outcomes.

maximizing the outcomes of both sides, is often very useful. However, if one is faced with an opponent who sticks rigidly to competition, collaboration can't be used. Similarly, there are some conflicts that are best avoided—ones in which there is virtually no chance of obtaining an acceptable outcome or in which the conflict seems likely to escalate to ever more intense levels. Recent research by van de Vliert, Euwema, and Huismans (1995), however, suggests that across a wide range of situations, some strategies may be especially useful.

In this research, Dutch police officers interacted with a professional actor trained to show different patterns of behavior in a conflict situation involving unauthorized use of a police vehicle. (The actor played the role of another police officer who had engaged in this conflict-inducing action.) During the conversation with the real police officer, the accomplice began by trivializing the situation (indicating that it was unimportant), then switched to stating that what he did was consistent with underlying policy. Finally, he resorted to personal attacks: "Blame yourself!" "It was really your fault!" The researchers videotaped and then analyzed the conversations between the trained actor and the police officers to determine what actions the officers took, and how effectively the conflict was handled. These ratings were made by trained judges who viewed the tapes.

Results indicated that the less the police officers engaged in *competition* (termed *forcing* in this study) and the more they engaged in *collaboration* (termed *problem solving*), the higher the judges' ratings of effectiveness. The strongest effects, however, were produced by another pattern termed *process controlling*, a procedure in which the officers tried to structure the situation so that it "stayed on track" and did not escalate into stronger conflicts. Overall, van de Vliert and his colleagues (1995) interpreted their results as suggesting that in actual life situations individuals combine several different modes of handling conflict, and that some of these combinations—especially low levels of competition combined with some collaboration and a moderate level of process control—may turn out to be most effective.

Techniques for Reducing the Harmful Effects of Conflict. As we noted earlier, conflict is often a costly process for both individuals and organizations. The effects are not always negative—conflict sometimes encourages both sides to examine the issues more carefully and, as a result, to formulate more creative solutions or decisions (e.g., Amason, 1996). This is especially true in cases where participants focus on issues and ideas, and emotions such as anger do not rise to high levels (Baron, in press). In many instances, however, conflict *is* disruptive, and generates negative outcomes. For this reason, it seems important to develop practical techniques for reducing its negative effects. Many different procedures for attaining this goal have been developed, and several of them rest firmly on the principles and findings of social psychology.

By far the most widely used procedure for resolving conflicts, and therefore for heading off their adverse effects, is **negotiation** or bargaining (e.g., Johnson, 1993; Sheppard, Bazerman, & Lewicki, 1990). In this process, opposing sides to a dispute exchange offers, counteroffers, and concessions, either directly or through representatives. If the process is successful, a solution acceptable to both sides is attained and the conflict is resolved (see Figure 13.16). If, instead, bargaining is unsuccessful, a costly deadlock may result, intensifying the conflict. What factors tip the balance toward favorable or unfavorable outcomes? Research findings offer some intriguing answers.

One group of factors that strongly affect the outcomes of negotiation involves the tactics adopted by each side. Many of these are designed to lower opponents' aspirations—to convince opponents that they have little chance of reaching their goals. One of the specific strategies used for this purpose is the suggestion by one side that it has an "out" (another potential partner with whom to make a deal). Another is the *big lie* technique—claims that one's break-even point is much higher or lower than it really is. A third tactic often used by negotiators involves making "tough" or extreme initial offers. Relatively extreme offers seem to put strong pressure on opponents to make concessions, often to their own detriment.

A second group of factors that determine the nature and outcomes of bargaining involves the perceptions of the persons involved in the process. Studies by Thompson and her colleagues reveal that negotiators often enter negotiations with important misperceptions about the situation (Thompson, 1990). In particular, they seem to begin with the view that their own interests and those of the other side are totally incompatible—the **incompatibility error.** This causes them to overlook interests that are actually compatible. Research findings indicate that this incompatibility error stems from the tendency of negotiators to perceive (falsely) that the quantity of available outcomes is fixed and that they must seize the largest possible share of this amount (Thompson, 1993).

A second important technique for resolving conflicts, aside from bargaining, rests firmly on social psychological foundations. It involves the induction of the kind of **superordinate goals** we discussed in Chapter 6—goals that are shared by both sides. Do you remember our discussion of the Robber's Cave experiment? If so, you already know that when opposing sides recognize the fact that they share certain goals, conflicts between them may be greatly reduced. In fact, this technique underlies several practical programs for resolving costly conflicts (e.g., Blake & Mouton, 1984; Kolb & Bartunek, 1992).

Finally, we should note that one strategy useful in reducing aggression, the incompatible response strategy, has also been found to be useful in reducing interpersonal conflicts (Baron, 1984, 1993b). Since intense conflicts often generate strong anger, and since strong emotions, in turn, interfere with cognitive efficiency (Zillmann, 1994), getting people to lower the volume by exposing them to events or stimuli that induce feelings incompatible with anger can be a useful means for getting negotiations back on track, and hence for resolving serious conflicts.

Negotiation ■ A process in which two or more parties to a conflict exchange offers, counteroffers, and concessions in an effort to attain a mutually acceptable agreement.

Incompatibility Error ■ Mistaken perception by negotiators that their own interests and those of the other side are totally incompatible.

Superordinate Goals ■ Goals shared by the parties in a conflict or dispute.

FIGURE 13.16

Negotiation: A Key Technique for Resolving Conflicts. In order to resolve conflicts occurring in work settings, the two sides often engage in negotiation—an exchange of offers, counteroffers, and concessions. If this process is successful, a solution acceptable to both sides is attained.

In sum, the findings, principles, and theories of social psychology serve as the basis for several techniques for reducing or resolving conflicts. In this respect, as in many others, our field has made valuable contributions to understanding human behavior in work settings and to making such environments more pleasant and productive for large numbers of persons.

INTEGRATING PRINCIPLES

1. Work-related attitudes influence several aspects of behavior in work settings (e.g., job performance, voluntary turnover), although this relationship is not a very strong one. This illustrates, once again, the complexities in the attitude–overt behavior link (see Chapter 4).

2. Even professional job interviewers are influenced by factors that, rationally, should not affect their judgments—factors such as the appearance of applicants, tactics of impression management used by applicants, and even the interviewers' moods (see Chapter 2). These findings illustrate a basic principle of social thought to which we've referred many times throughout this book: Human beings are definitely not perfect information-processing mechanisms (see Chapter 3).

3. Organizational politics involves tactics that rest, in part, on basic principles of social influence (see Chapter 9).

4. Conflicts often stem from the fact that opposing sides have incompatible interests. However, they are also influenced by many social factors—stereotypes, grudges, attributions, and so on. This fact underscores the import role of social factors and processes in business settings; refer to earlier discussions of social cognition (Chapter 3), prejudice (Chapter 6), attraction (Chapter 7), and aggression (Chapter 11).

Social Diversity: A Critical Analysis

THE EFFECTS OF WORKING IN ANOTHER CULTURE:
What Happens When Expatriates Come Home?

ONCE, MOST COMPANIES OPERATED WITHIN A SINGLE COUNTRY or, perhaps, in a few countries in one region of the world. Now, however, business has become truly international in scope. Many organizations have branches, factories, and offices in dozens of different countries; and many do business around the world even if they don't have offshore facilities. One result of this change is that increasing numbers of employees are assigned to jobs in cultures other than their own. For example, several Japanese automobile companies have opened large plants in the United States. While the production-line employees in these plants are Americans, many of the managers are Japanese, at least initially (see Figure 13.17). Similarly, many American managers have been assigned to jobs in European, Asian, African, and Latin American countries. In fact, it is estimated that currently more than 80,000 American managers are working in other cultures (Arvey, Bhagat, & Salas, 1991). What are the effects of these experiences? And what happens to these individuals when they return home? These questions have been investigated by industrial/organizational psychologists—again, often using principles and findings from social psychology (Gregersen & Black, 1992). A recent study by Guzzo, Noonan, and Elron (1994) provides some revealing insights into the experiences of these *expatriate* managers.

In this study, about 150 managers who had worked for their companies in other cultures responded to a survey containing questions about their companies' practices with respect to expatriates, and about the extent to which these actions met their expectations. In other words, they indicated what steps their companies had taken to ease the difficulties of working abroad, both for themselves and their families, and whether these steps were adequate. In addition, the managers completed a standard measure of organizational commitment and indicated their intentions to remain with the company. Six months later, the researchers obtained information on whether the managers were still employed by their companies or had left.

Results indicated that most companies did indeed take steps to ease the burden of working abroad. For example, they provided expatriates with financial benefits (increased salary, supplemental pay to cover higher housing expenses, reimbursement for extra taxes), general support (a company car or driver, access to high-quality health care), and family support (language training for family members, child-care providers). So companies did offer a wide range of services to their employees. The key question, however, was this: Did these services live up to the managers' expectations? Guzzo and his associates (1994) predicted that to the extent they did, managers' commitment to their organizations would be high, and this prediction was confirmed. In addition, it was also found that the greater the extent to which managers felt their companies had met their

FIGURE 13.17

Working in Another Culture: An Increasingly Common Experience. As international trade has expanded, an increasing number of individuals have been sent by their companies to jobs in other cultures. Depending on the amount of support provided by their organizations, such expatriate employees can find this experience rewarding or disturbing.

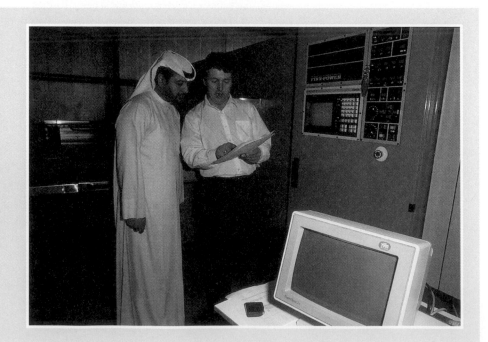

expectations, the stronger their intentions to remain with their companies.

In sum, it appears that the experience of working in another culture can be a positive one, strengthening one's career and commitment to one's company, or a negative one with a serious downside. A crucial determinant of which of these outcomes individuals experience is the extent to which their companies provide the support they promise, and which expatriates believe they deserve. ■ ■ ■

CONNECTIONS: Integrating Social Psychology

In this chapter, you read about . . .	In other chapters, you will find related discussions of . . .
forming attitudes about a suspect based on pre-trial publicity	first impressions (Chapter 2); attitude formation (Chapter 4)
accuracy of eyewitness testimony	information processing and retrieving information from memory (Chapter 3)
the similarity of police lineups and experiments	designing experiments to maximize objectivity of results (Chapter 1)
nonverbal communication from judge to jury	basic channels of nonverbal communication (Chapter 2)
attraction toward and evaluation of defendants	factors influencing interpersonal attraction (Chapter 7)
stereotypes and prejudice in judgments about defendants	stereotypes and prejudice based on race and gender (Chapter 6)
work-related attitudes	attitudes as a basic aspect of social thought (Chapter 4)
effects of impression management on job interviews	impression management as a basic aspect of social perception (Chapter 2)

Thinking about Connections

1. Sometime in the past few months a major crime has probably captured the attention of the media either nationally or in the community in which you live. Try to remember what information about the crime you obtained from the newspaper, radio, and television. Once a suspect was arrested, what is your memory of the images that were published or broadcast? What impressions did you form about the suspect (Chapter 2), and what were your attitudes (Chapter 4) about the crime and the person accused of committing it? To what extent do you believe you were influenced by the media presentations?

2. You are in charge of setting up and conducting a police lineup. Following a bank robbery, ten eyewitnesses have agreed to come to the police station in order to help identify the thief they saw at the crime scene. Think of your task as that of devising an objective psychological experiment (Chapter 1). Exactly what would you do in arranging the lineup that would be analogous to what you would do in designing an experiment?

3. You have been arrested and will be tried for a relatively minor violation, but you know that you are absolutely innocent. Beyond your own testimony and that of any relevant witnesses, what could you do that would increase the chances that the judge and members of the jury would form a positive impression of you? Consider what you have learned about impression management (Chapter 2), attitude formation (Chapter 4), stereotypes and prejudice (Chapter 6), and interpersonal attraction (Chapter 7).

(continued)

4. Suppose that a manager discovered that job satisfaction among the employees working under her supervision was low. Drawing on what you know about attitudes (Chapter 4) and social influence (Chapter 9), what steps could she take to improve these attitudes?

5. Imagine that an ambitious person wanted to advance his career by eliminating his competition—by sabotaging the careers of rivals for promotions and raises. Drawing on our previous discussions of influence (Chapter 9) and aggression (Chapter 11), what kinds of actions could this person take to reach his goal? Which of these do you think would be most effective?

Summary and Review

The findings and principles of social psychology have been applied to many of our social institutions and have provided an improved understanding of how institutions function and suggestions as to how they can be changed for the better. The legal process and the workplace have each been the focus of a great deal of psychological research.

The Legal System

Forensic psychology has produced extensive evidence that the reality of our legal system often fails to live up to its stated ideals. For example, the testimony of witnesses and defendants is influenced by interrogation procedures, and judgments about the defendant by the general public and by potential jurors are influenced by pretrial publicity in the media. Eyewitness testimony may be inaccurate, and the behavior (both deliberate and accidental) of attorneys and judges can influence verdicts. Jurors respond in part on the basis of emotional biases for and against specific defendants, as well as on the basis of their own general attitudes, cognitive processing skills, and assumptions about various physical and behavioral attributes of the person on trial.

Social Psychology and Business

The principles of social psychology have been applied to the understanding of behavior in work settings, especially within the field of industrial/organizational psychology. *Work-related attitudes* include employees' evaluations of their jobs (*job satisfaction*) and of their organizations (*organizational commitment*). Many factors influence such work-related attitudes, and these attitudes, in turn, have been found to play a role in important aspects of work-related behavior, such as performance and turnover.

Organizations frequently use job interviews to choose employees. Because these interviews involve social interactions between applicants and interviewers, they are influenced by many social factors. Applicants' appearance—including whether they are overweight—and their use of nonverbal cues influence the ratings they receive. Interviewers' expectancies, too, play a role. Interviewers tend to behave differently toward applicants they expect to evaluate highly or poorly, and these differences in behavior serve to confirm their expectation.

Organizational politics—tactics used by individuals to further their own selfish ends—are all too common in many work settings. The most disturbing of these are clearly unethical, and are known as *dirty tricks*. Several countermeasures can be effective in reducing organizational politics, or at least their harmful effects. These involve clarifying job expectations, insisting on open communication, and refusing to tolerate political game players.

A common problem in organizations is *conflict,* which results from perceptions of incompatible interests between groups or individuals. Conflict stems from organizational causes, such as competition over scarce resources, and from interpersonal causes, such as stereotypes, prejudices, grudges, and ineffective communication styles. Individuals react to conflict in several different ways; among the most common patterns are competition, compromise, accommodation, avoidance, and collaboration. These contrasting patterns reflect underlying dimensions: concern with one's own outcomes versus concern with others' outcomes. Conflicts can be reduced or resolved by several techniques based on social psychological principles and findings, including negotiation, superordinate goals, and the induction of responses incompatible with anger and conflict.

■ Key Terms

Blank-Lineup Control (p. 489)

Conflict (p. 508)

Forensic Psychology (p. 476)

Incompatibility Error (p. 512)

Industrial/Organizational Psychologists (p. 498)

Job Interviews (p. 503)

Job Satisfaction (p. 499)

Leading Questions (p. 479)

Legal Authoritarianism (p. 497)

Leniency Bias (p. 497)

Negotiation (p. 512)

Organizational Citizenship Behavior (p. 503)

Organizational Commitment (p. 499)

Superordinate Goals (p. 512)

Voir Dire (p. 490)

■ For More Information

Adler, S. J. (1994). *The jury.* New York: Times Books.

This book provides many details about the current breakdown of the American jury system and specific suggestions as to how this very serious problem might be solved. Mr. Adler is the legal editor of the *Wall Street Journal.*

Greenberg, J., & Baron, R. A. (1995). *Behavior in organizations* (5th ed.). Englewood Cliffs, NJ: Prentice-Hall.

A broad introduction to what research by psychologists and others tells us about behavior in work settings. The chapters on work-related attitudes, conflict, and perception are closely related to topics covered in this book.

Johnson, R. A. (1993). *Negotiation basics: Concepts, skills, exercises.* Thousand Oaks, CA: Sage.

A useful guide to basic negotiating skills and tactics. Anyone who must deal with conflicts—either at work or in their personal life—will find this book informative and helpful.

Loftus, E. F. (1992). *Witness for the defense.* New York: St. Martin's Press.

A comprehensive summary of a great deal of research in forensic psychology by one of the leading researchers in this field.

Wrightsman, L. S. (1991). *Psychology and the legal system.* Pacific Grove, CA: Brooks/Cole.

This volume uses psychological concepts to examine the legal system and is directed at students of both law and psychology. It is meant to serve as a bridge between social science issues and methods on the one hand and the law and criminal justice system on the other. Topics include moral judgment, children's rights, and the role of psychologists in the legal system.

CHAPTER 14

SOCIAL PSYCHOLOGY IN ACTION:
Applications to Health and Environment

Lisa Houck, *Exit, Stage Left*, 1995, watercolor, 6 × 9"

Chapter Outline

On the morning news you hear a story about a new finding related to health. Someone conducted a survey and reported that people who eat food high in beta carotene have a lower risk of several kinds of cancer than people who do not eat such food. You don't particularly like any of the vegetables that the newscaster mentions as being high in this substance. She also mentions that it is possible to take beta carotene in pill form. Are the pills as effective as the vegetables? Because you want to avoid cancer, what do you do with this information? Would it be best to change your diet, buy some pills, consult your doctor, wait to see if other studies confirm the findings or contradict them, or just ignore the whole thing? You probably won't develop cancer anyway. Right?

You wake up in the middle of the night, feeling sick. There is a sharp pain in your lower abdomen, and you also realize that you are about to throw up. When you return to your bed, you lie there wondering what to do. Should you take some over-the-counter remedy in the medicine cabinet? Should you wait a day or so because the problem may just go away? Should you call a doctor first thing in the morning? Whenever symptoms of illness develop, we have to make just such decisions.

Driving along an interstate highway, you approach a large city, but it is hard to make out many details because the buildings are obscured by a dark haze. As you drive closer, your visibility becomes more limited and you notice an unpleasant chemical odor. The freeway traffic slows to a crawl; your eyes water, your nose becomes stuffy, and it is harder and harder to see. On the car radio you hear something about a smog alert. How could things get so messed up?

Among the many applications of social psychology, a major interest is research that deals with the interaction between psychological processes and those physical processes involving health versus illness. In this chapter we will first discuss *health psychology* and how emotions, cognitions, and behavior are relevant to many aspects of human health, from the way we process relevant information to our ability to cope with medical treatment. Next, we'll turn to *environmental psychology;* we'll look at research that indicates some of the ways we are affected by aspects of our physical and interpersonal surroundings as well as research indicating how our attitudes and behavior have positive and negative effects on the environment.

Health Psychology: Maintaining a Healthy State and Coping with Illness

When we speak of good health or of illness, we are clearly referring to a person's physical state. And whether a person is well or sick might seem to involve purely medical issues unrelated to the concerns of psychologists. Over the years, however, it has become very clear that psychological factors affect all aspects of our physical well-being (Rodin & Salovey, 1989). Work on these problems is labeled **health psychology**—the research specialty focusing on the psychological processes that affect the development, prevention, and treatment of physical illness (Glass, 1989). How are psychological and physiological processes interconnected?

Dealing with Health-Related Information

One obstacle to taking the necessary steps that help prevent physical disorders is our understandable confusion in processing the large quantity of relevant in-

Health Psychology ■ The study of how psychological factors influence the origin, prevention, and treatment of physical illness.

FIGURE 14.1

Processing Health-Related Information. *We frequently are overwhelmed by information about how to maximize health and prevent illness. Even when the scientific facts are clear (and they sometimes are not), product advertising can be misleading, as in this example of "salt-free sugar."*

(*Source:* Drawing by Ed Arno; © 1982 *The New Yorker* Magazine, Inc.)

formation that bombards us daily (Thompson, 1992)—see Figure 14.1 for a fictional example. For an actual example, consider a recent article in *The British Medical Journal*: a Danish study over a twelve-year period reported a lower death rate among those who drank three to five glasses of wine each day than among those who drank beer, liquor, or no alcoholic beverages. One explanation for the finding that alcohol has a positive effect on longevity is its tendency to raise the blood level of "good" HDL cholesterol—a substance that reduces the risk of death from cardiovascular disease. Does that mean you should stock up on wine and drink it often to prolong your life? Wait. Almost immediately, other researchers issued cautions about consuming any alcohol, including wine, because the Danish results might have been based on special genetic factors among Danes, high-quality medical care in that country, the possibility that the extremely straight roads in Denmark decrease the accident rate among drunk drivers, or the fact that wine drinkers tend to be more health-conscious than most other individuals. Whatever the explanation, Dr. Charles Hennekens of Harvard Medical School concludes that "People shouldn't change their habits on the basis of one study" (Brody, 1995, p. A18). Meanwhile, while ordinary citizens wait for competing explanations to be sorted out, they must decide whether to avoid alcohol altogether, drink only wine, or move to Denmark. In relation to this and many other relevant research findings, a final answer is simply not yet available.

A second obstacle, even when all of the research data are in and experts agree as to precisely which information is valid, is our extreme reluctance to alter major aspects of our behavior. For example, there is little doubt that cigarette smoking is harmful and that exercise is beneficial; but many smokers resist giving up the habit, and many couch potatoes resist strenuous physical activity.

What Information Is Most Available? In Chapter 13, we described the discrepancy between what people believe about crime and the actual crime rate.

Similar discrepancies are found with respect to health. When news reports inform us about the AIDS epidemic, a drug-resistant strain of tuberculosis, Lyme disease, and outbreaks of "flesh-eating bacteria," you might reasonably conclude that health problems are overwhelming us. It may come as a surprise to learn from the U.S. Centers for Disease Control and Prevention that people are living longer than ever before (the average is 76 years), that the annual death rate is at a record low (504.5 deaths per 100,000 people in 1992), and that the death rates for the six leading causes of death (heart disease, cancer, stroke, lung disease, accidents, and pneumonia–influenza) all are dropping (Latest figures . . . , 1994). As in overestimating the seriousness of crime, people also overestimate threats to health on the basis of the *availability heuristic* that was discussed in Chapter 3 (Eisenman, 1993). In any event, things are better than they seem.

What Information Do We Accept? A basic question facing those who provide information about health to the general public is whether to emphasize factual details or to make an emotional appeal. The emotion most commonly manipulated is fear—the consequences of engaging in certain behavior (for example, smoking) or not engaging in certain behavior (for example, not going to the dentist) are often described in horrifying detail. Though the results are not entirely consistent across studies, there is evidence that when fear is induced, people actually process a health message more carefully than when fear is absent (Baron et al., 1994). Rothman and his colleagues (1993) propose that a *positively framed* message (see Chapter 4) is best for facilitating preventive behavior ("Eat high-fiber foods to promote good health and prevent disease"), while a *negatively framed* message is best for facilitating detection behavior ("Get a Pap smear annually to avoid the pain and suffering associated with uterine cancer").

Whatever the message, it might seem obvious to predict that people would be most receptive to information personally relevant to them. This is not, however, always true—we often defend ourselves against threat, and this defensiveness can be maladaptive. For this reason, Liberman and Chaiken (1992) proposed that the more relevant a health threat is to an individual, the less likely that person is to accept the truth of a message about the threat. These experimenters created a fictitious article, supposedly from the *New England Journal of Medicine*, that described a link between amount of caffeine consumed and fibrocystic breast disease. The reported study was either highly threatening (follow-up studies supposedly confirmed the original finding) or low in threat (follow-up studies were described as yielding inconsistent results). The personal relevance of this information to the female research participants differed in that some did not drink coffee (low relevance) while some drank two to seven cups a day (high relevance). Regardless of how threatening the message was, it was believed *less* by those for whom it was highly relevant than by those for whom it had little relevance, as shown in Figure 14.2. Clearly, a common response to a message about a self-relevant health problem is to reduce anxiety by rejecting the information. A person feels better if the information is processed as "untrue." A second "benefit" of rejecting the information is that there is no need to alter one's current behavior.

Because different people defend themselves against threat in different ways, Millar and Millar (1993) proposed that response to a relevant health message would depend on an individual's characteristic defense mechanisms (repressing versus sensitizing; see Chapter 10), the nature of the health message (emotional versus cognitive), and the content of the individual's self-focused attention (on affect or on cognition). The experimenters selected the topic of breast cancer, the leading cause of death among American women, as highly relevant to their female research participants; and they focused on messages about the impor-

FIGURE 14.2

A Threatening Health Message: If It's Relevant, Don't Believe It. Information about possible health threats can arouse fear and anxiety, and the more relevant such messages are to oneself, the greater the tendency to reduce the threat by not believing the message. In an experiment, women received either a low-threat or a high-threat message about the health dangers of coffee. The high-threat message was more believable, but at both levels of threat, the coffee drinkers (high relevance) were less likely to believe the message than those who did not drink coffee (low relevance).

(*Source*: Based on data from Liberman & Chaiken, 1992.)

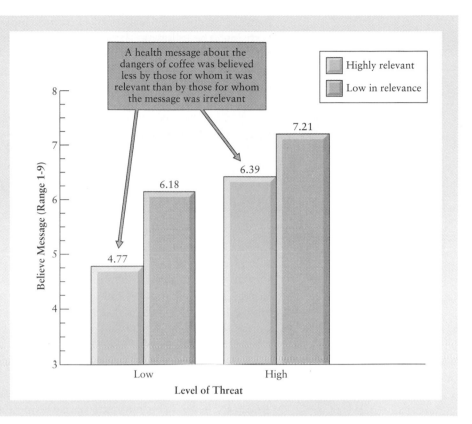

tance of breast self-examination for early detection of a potential problem, because fewer than 25 percent of American women regularly engage in this procedure. Defense mechanisms function to reduce anxiety; people who use *sensitization* attempt to control threat by thinking about it and seeking relevant information, while those who use *repression* attempt to control threat by avoiding and denying it.

In the experiment testing the effects of breast cancer information, the female research participants were divided into sensitizers and repressers, and they were given instructions designed to create an affective focus ("think about your feelings during and after performing a breast examination") or a cognitive focus ("think about your reasons for liking or disliking a breast self-examination"). They were then exposed to either an emotional or an informational message about breast self-examination and afterward asked to indicate how much they agreed or disagreed with the message. All three variables (type of defense mechanism, content of self-focusing, and nature of the health message) had an effect on acceptance of the message. Repressers agreed with the message more if they were given a cognitive focus and received an emotional message or if they were given an affective focus and received an informational message. Sensitizers were just the opposite, agreeing more if they were given an affective focus and received an emotional message or if they were given a cognitive focus and received an informational message. The participants followed the same pattern in reporting whether they intended actually to engage in breast self-examination in the future. The general point is that the effectiveness of a health message depends on message content, the way an individual characteristically defends himself or herself against threat, and how attention is focused at the time the message is received.

Of all the messages directed toward us on a regular basis, the most consistent and broadly applied health campaign over the past four decades has been to warn against the dangers of cigarette smoking and to curtail cigarette advertising. The following *Applied Side* section examines the successful effects of this antismoking effort along with the reasons for its failure among some segments of the population.

Social Psychology: On the Applied Side
SUCCESS IN ENCOURAGING PEOPLE NOT TO SMOKE CIGARETTES AND THE REASONS THAT MANY TEENAGERS DO SO ANYWAY

In the United States alone, approximately 1,200 people die each day as the result of cancer brought about by smoking tobacco (Sunstein, 1993); and the smoking rate in most other nations (for example, China, Indonesia, Japan, Korea, Thailand, and the United Kingdom) is much higher than in the United States (Jarvis, 1991; Shenon, 1994; Smolowe, 1992). When a pregnant woman smokes, her offspring has an increased risk of such problems as low birth weight, prematurity, and long-term behavioral difficulties. We know that nonsmokers run health risks caused by the smoke of others—"passive smoking." Toxins from such smoke can also reach the fetus of nonsmoking pregnant women, and the nicotine and other harmful contents of tobacco also show up clearly in their newborn infants (Passive smoking . . . , 1994).

In the United States, the federal government's response to the smoking problem has been a consistent series of steps to discourage the tobacco habit. This program began with a warning label on cigarette packages and continued with the imposition of higher taxes and the banning of cigarette advertising on radio and television. Many communities now target passive smoking exposure by restrictive rules about smoking in public settings.

However you personally feel about this kind of government action, the result has been a startling decrease in the percentage of Americans who smoke. According to the U.S. Centers for Disease Control and Prevention, smoking dropped from 42 percent of the population in 1955 to only 25 percent of the population in 1992. Many of those who still smoke are older people who have smoked throughout their lives and will not or cannot give up the habit. Of greater concern to the health field is the 3,000 teenagers who begin smoking each day, according to the Surgeon General (Gleick, 1995). While the percentage of adult smokers has dropped, youthful smoking is increasing—especially among young white women, according to the U.S. Centers for Disease Control and Prevention (More young white . . . , 1994). The major questions are: Why do they smoke? And what can be done to prevent it?

One answer to "Why?" is that advertising in the print media and on billboards is subtly directed toward a youthful market, with Joe Camel as a prominent example. Altogether, the tobacco industry spends $6 billion yearly on advertising. Gender and race also play a role; while white men and black teenagers of both genders continue to show declines in smoking, the percentage of white women who smoke is actually *increasing* each year (Black teens . . . , 1995; Smoking rate . . . , 1993). Studies suggest a possible causal link between the introduction of cigarette brands for women in 1967 (Virginia Slims, Silva Thins, and Eve) and dramatic increases in smoking by teenage girls. During the first six years during which "women's" cigarettes were promoted for the first time (see Figure 14.3), the rate of twelve-year-old girls who started smoking increased by 110 percent, thirteen-year-olds by 55 percent, fourteen-year-olds by

FIGURE 14.3

Cigarette Advertising Encouraged Young Women to Smoke. In 1967, tobacco companies began producing and advertising cigarette brands specifically designed for women. During the first six years that such brands were promoted, cigarette smoking among girls aged twelve to seventeen increased dramatically.

70 percent, fifteen-year-olds by 75 percent, sixteen-year-olds by 55 percent, and seventeen-year-olds by 35 percent (Brody, 1994).

Beyond the social influence (see Chapter 9) of advertisers, additional psychological factors are found to play a major role. A major reason for smoking, according to evidence from many types of research, is that tobacco helps one cope with negative affect—simply stated, smoking makes you feel better (Brandon, 1994). Consistent with this proposition is the finding that seventh graders who express low positive affect are more likely than those expressing high positive affect to use tobacco—in addition to alcohol and marijuana (Wills, DuHamel, & Vaccaro, 1995).

A very common explanation of teenage smoking blames pressure from the peer group, but Ennett and Bauman (1994) found that most adolescent smokers don't tend to belong to peer groups. Some studies indicate that smokers like smokers and nonsmokers like nonsmokers, but that the explanation is the selection of similar friends (see Chapter 7) rather than the pressure of peers to smoke or not to smoke.

A more complex explanation of adolescent smoking is provided by De Vries and colleagues (1995) in a study of 401 high school students in the Netherlands over an eighteen-month period. To enhance the validity of the students' self-reports about smoking, the investigators pretended to be able to measure the truthfulness of the self-report responses with a sort of lie detector—a procedure known as the *bogus pipeline technique* (Aguinis, Pierce, & Quigley, 1993, 1995). Measures of carbon monoxide levels were also used to verify smoking. As summarized in Figure 14.4, three types of social influence (Chapter 9), specific attitudes and beliefs (Chapter 4) about the consequences of smoking, and

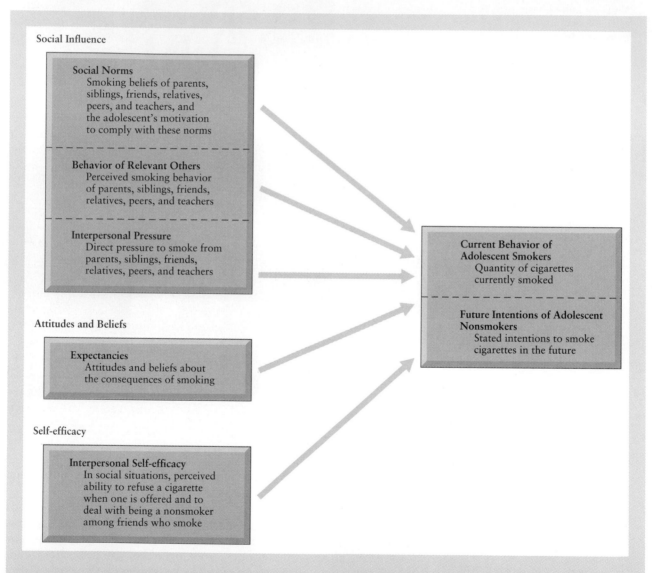

Figure 14.4

Predicting Adolescent Smoking and Intention to Smoke. In a longitudinal study of high school students conducted in the Netherlands, adolescent smoking and intention to begin smoking were found to be associated with three types of social influence, attitudes and beliefs about the consequences of smoking, and feelings of low self-efficacy in being able to refuse cigarettes in a social situation. It seems likely that intervention programs aiming to prevent adolescent smoking would benefit from focusing simultaneously on multiple factors.

(*Source:* de Vries et al., 1995.)

feelings of self-efficacy (Chapter 5) about one's ability to resist smoking each independently influenced students' current smoking behavior and intentions to smoke in the future.

One implication of these findings is that smoking prevention programs should not rely totally on assertiveness training aimed at enhancing resistance to supposed peer pressure ("Just say no") but instead should address each of the identified causative factors. Thus, attempts to convince teenagers not to smoke should (1) make it explicit that nonsmoking is the norm; (2) explain how modeling effects can occur; (3) teach young people to recognize direct interpersonal pressures to smoke from peers, family, and the media; (4) present accurate evidence about the consequences of smoking; and (5) provide instruction on how to experience self-efficacy in resisting any type of pressure to smoke. Have such recommendations influenced large-scale prevention programs? Not yet.

What is actually being done to discourage teenage smoking? The Philip Morris company voluntarily added a message to its cigarette packages—UNDERAGE SALE PROHIBITED—and President Clinton recommended cracking down on sales to young people, banning vending machines, restricting billboard advertising near playgrounds and schools, and adding further restrictions to magazine advertising. His final recommendation—requiring those who manufacture cigarettes to spend $150 million on public education campaigns—*could* conceivably incorporate the recommendations that stem from research on teenage smoking. ■ ■ ■

Stress and Illness

At least since World War II, psychologists have been interested in *stress* and its effects on human behavior (Lazarus, 1993). The original focus of research and theory was on the physical causes of stress (Selye, 1956), but interest soon broadened to include psychological factors (Lazarus, 1966). We now use the word **stress** to indicate negative responses to physical or psychological events that are perceived by the individual to cause physical harm or emotional distress.

When confronted by perceived danger, the individual feels threatened and tries to cope with the situation (Bar-Tal & Spitzer, 1994). Such **coping** behavior is considered successful if it reduces or eliminates the threat (Taylor, Buunk, & Aspinwall, 1990). Of special interest has been the connection between stress and physical illness.

Illness As a Consequence of Stress. Research consistently indicates that as stress increases, illness becomes more likely. And we encounter a great many sources of stress.

For example, work-related stress is commonly found, and both depression and health complaints increase with continued stress. These effects have been demonstrated among auto workers, medical residents working in emergency rooms, hospital staff, social workers, psychiatric health-care staff, railroad workers, and steel pipe mill workers. Examples of stress include negative reactions to colleagues and superiors involving such issues as inequity (Buunk et al., 1993), confusion about one's role on the job (Revicki et al., 1993), perceived demands and lack of support (Parkes & Rabenau, 1993), work overload (Marshall & Barnett, 1993; Perrewe & Anthony, 1990), low job involvement and lack of control in the work environment (Schaefer & Moos, 1993), and the worst work-related stress—unemployment (Hamilton et al., 1993; Schwarzer, Jerusalem, & Hahn, 1994).

College students encounter their own array of stress-inducing events, such as low grades, unwanted pregnancies, and parents who get divorced; again, the

Stress ■ The response to physical or psychological events perceived by the individual as potentially causing harm or emotional distress.

Coping ■ Responding to stress in a way that reduces the threat and its effects; includes what a person does, feels, or thinks in order to master, tolerate, or decrease the negative effects of a stressful situation.

greater the stress a person experiences, the more likely that physical illness will occur (Brody, 1989). For each of us, everyday hassles such as interacting with a rude or indifferent spouse (Hendrix, Steel, & Schultz, 1987) or driving an automobile in heavy traffic on a regular basis (Weinberger, Hiner, & Tierney, 1987) can increase the probability of catching a cold or developing the flu. With a more serious problem such as the death of a loved one, the likelihood of becoming ill is even greater (Schleifer et al., 1983).

When several negative events occur in the same general time period, they have a cumulative effect (Seta, Seta, & Wang, 1991); that is, as the total number of stressful experiences increases, the probability of illness increases (Cohen, Tyrrell, & Smith, 1993).

How could stress cause physical illness? Two factors are involved. First, in times of stress, the resulting depression (Whisman & Kwon, 1993), worry, and anxiety can interfere with health-related behaviors such as eating a balanced diet, exercising, and getting enough sleep (Wiebe & McCallum, 1986). Second, and more directly, the body's immune system functions less well when stress is high (Stone et al., 1987). Work on *psychoneuroimmunology* examines the interrelationships among stress, emotional and behavioral reactions, and the immune system (Ader & Cohen, 1993). For example, it is frequently reported that college students show an increase in upper respiratory infections when exams are approaching (Dorian et al., 1982). To understand just how this might occur, Jemmott and Magloire (1988) obtained samples of students' saliva over several weeks in order to assess the presence of *secretory immunoglobulin A*—the body's primary defense against infections. The level of this substance dropped during final exams and then returned to normal levels when the exams were over. Thus, the psychological stress of finals brought about a change in body chemistry, and this in turn increased susceptibility to disease.

Individual Differences in Vulnerability to Stress. When exposed to the same objectively stressful conditions, some people experience a high level of stress and become ill, while other people experience much less stress and remain well. For example, men who are perfectionists ("I feel that I must do things perfectly, or not do them at all") are more depressed than nonperfectionists when stress is high (Joiner & Schmidt, 1995).

Though genetic factors explain some of the differences in the effects of stress (Kessler et al., 1992), Friedman, Hawley, and Tucker (1994) present evidence from a large number of studies indicating a difference between **disease-prone personalities** and **self-healing personalities.** People who are disease-prone respond to stressful situations with negative emotions and unhealthy behavior patterns, resulting in illness and a shorter life span. At the opposite extreme are self-healing individuals, who deal effectively with stress and resist illness. They are found to be enthusiastic about life, emotionally balanced, alert, responsive, energetic, curious, secure, and constructive—"people one likes to be around." Research on *subjective well-being* indicates the many benefits of interpreting daily life in positive terms, being engaged in your work and in leisure activities, feeling a sense of purpose, and hoping for positive future outcomes (Myers & Diener, 1995). What specific personality characteristics differentiate disease-prone versus self-healing individuals?

People with disease-prone personalities are often characterized as neurotic (Booth-Kewley & Vickers, 1994), maladjusted (Bernard & Belinsky, 1993), pessimistic (Scheier & Carver, 1987), and having low self-esteem (Campbell, Chew, & Scratchley, 1991) and an external locus of control (Birkimer, Lucas, & Birkimer, 1991). In contrast, self-healing individuals are described as hardy (Priel, Gonik, & Rabinowitz, 1993), optimistic (Scheier & Carver, 1993), ex-

Disease-Prone Personality ■ Personality type in which the individual responds to stress with negative affect and unhealthy behavior patterns, resulting in physical illness and a shortened life span.

Self-Healing Personality ■ Personality characterized by enthusiasm, emotional balance, extraversion, alertness, and responsiveness; the individual tends to be energetic, curious, secure, and constructive, and have a relatively lower incidence of physical illness and longer life span.

traverted (Amirkhan, Risinger, & Swickert, 1995), conscientious (Friedman et al., 1993, 1995), and as having an internal locus of control (Quadrel & Lau, 1989) and believing in a just world (Tomaka & Blascovich, 1994).

Other factors also differentiate those most and least vulnerable to stress. The importance of perceived control is repeatedly emphasized (Thompson, Nanni, & Levine, 1994). Stressful events have negative effects in part because they make us realize that sometimes we cannot control such unpleasant occurrences as accidents, bad grades, and failed love affairs. When events are beyond our control, we are likely to feel depressed (Brown & Siegel, 1988) and to become physically ill (Larsen & Kasimatis, 1991). An extremely important step in reducing such stress is to identify your possible options and then to choose among them (Paterson & Neufeld, 1995). To take a simple but personally unpleasant example, I (Donn Byrne) recently had to move from my home of sixteen years to an apartment. Just contemplating the move was extremely stressful, and I quickly began reading classified ads and making a list of the apartment complexes that sounded attractive. I spent several weeks looking at the best-sounding apartments, then ranked them in terms of location, appearance, price, size, availability of a swimming pool and tennis courts, and so on. Once I identified the apartments I liked best, I felt much less anxious; and by the time I made a final decision, the stress had disappeared.

Oddly enough, positive events can sometimes cause problems, because they too can suggest a lack of control. Anyone who has planned a complicated trip or a big party or a wedding knows what it means to be caught up in a seemingly joyful but nevertheless stressful situation. Langston (1994) reports that you can increase positive affect in such situations by expressing your emotions (telling others about the event, celebrating) and doing your best to maintain control of what is happening. In general, any activity that lets you feel in charge of what happens rather than perceiving yourself as helpless is beneficial. In either a crisis or a good but complex event, it is much better to do *something* actively that increases perceived control rather than to drift passively, caught up in uncontrollable ongoing events.

Self-efficacy was discussed in Chapter 5, and one of the characteristics of high efficacy is an increase in physical endurance because of the body's production of a natural painkiller. As you might expect, then, self-efficacy also is a key factor in how well we deal with stress. Bandura (1993) has described several kinds of research that are relevant to health. A relatively basic finding involves how a person's perceived self-efficacy in coping with stressors affects bodily reactions that are essential to maintaining health. Volunteer research participants are subjected to physical stress until they reach a point that is beyond their ability to cope. For example, a familiar procedure is to place the participant's hand in a bowl containing water and ice until the pain becomes too great for the participant to continue. This experience causes a series of negative physiological reactions, including activation of the autonomic nervous system. In ordinary life, when such bodily reactions continue over time, the immune system is weakened and the body is less able to defend itself against disease. In the experiments with the ice-cold water, the participants are given a guided procedure that increases their confidence in being able to cope—thus raising their perceived self-efficacy. When self-efficacy is at a maximum, they are again subjected to the stressful experience. Because of the increase in perceived self-efficacy, the stressors that had previously been biologically disruptive now cause very little physiological activation. Simply stated, uncontrollable stressors impair the immune system, but controllable stressors do not.

What do we ordinarily do when confronted by threat? Compas and colleagues (1991) proposed a two-level process. As outlined in Figure 14.5 (p. 530),

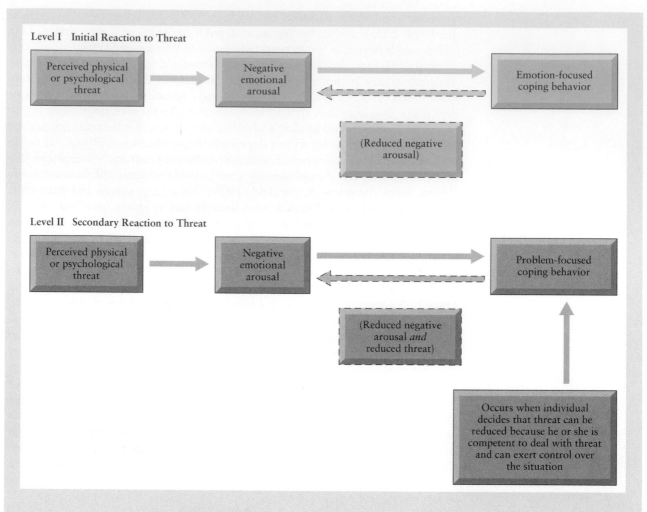

Level I   Initial Reaction to Threat

Level II   Secondary Reaction to Threat

FIGURE 14.5

Two Levels of Response to Threat. We respond to threat in two ways. The initial reaction is an emotional one (level 1), and we must cope with our feelings of distress (emotion-focused coping). If a situation is truly uncontrollable, this is the best that anyone can do. If the situation can be modified, a second type of response (level 2) is possible. Attempts to solve the stressful difficulty (problem-focused coping) occur if the individual feels competent and able to control the situation.

(*Source:* Based on information in Compas et al., 1991.)

the response at the first level is emotional distress and an attempt to deal with your feelings—emotion-focused coping. At the second level you examine your possible options and assess how competent you are to deal with them. As you start to perceive some degree of control, problem-focused coping occurs (Tomaka et al., 1993).

Gender differences have frequently been found—some researchers report that women use emotion-focused coping, while men use problem-focused coping (Ptacek, Smith, & Zanas, 1992). Some have suggested that these differences are based on the different ways men and women are taught to cope with stress (Ptacek, Smith, & Dodge, 1994). Both conclusions about gender differences have been strongly challenged by Porter and Stone (1995). Over a twelve-week period, these investigators asked married couples to fill out a daily questionnaire dealing with events, mood, coping, and so forth. The researchers found no gender differences in *coping;* instead, it became clear that men and women report different *problems.* Women describe difficulties relevant to the self, parenting, and interactions with others, while men report work-related difficulties. It was concluded that men and women differ very little in the amount of stress they face or in how they cope with the stress—the difference is in the content of their respective problems.

Health is also affected by the nature of the goals for which we strive. Emmons (1992) studied the goals of undergraduates and also of older married couples. Some people reported high-level, abstract goals for which they were striving (wanting a deeper relationship with God, wanting to be totally honest, wanting increased knowledge of the world). Others reported low-level, concrete goals (wanting to be well-groomed, wanting to make others laugh, wanting to be organized and neat). Individuals with high-level strivings experienced more negative emotions but less physical illness, while those with low-level strivings reported less negative emotions and more illness. Emmons's explanation is that high, difficult goals require commitment and effort—among the components of **hardiness** (that also involves the perception that a difficulty is a challenge, and a sense of control over one's life) and the self-healing personality described earlier; nevertheless, these broad goals are seldom met, so there is unpleasant affect. The low-level goals are easy to reach, and thus pleasant; but individuals who set easy goals generally tend to repress negative feelings such as anxiety (R. A. Emmons, personal communication, March 2, 1993)—a characteristic of the disease-prone personality.

The *Type A* behavior pattern was discussed in Chapter 11 as a personality disposition associated with aggression. The original interest in Type A individuals (and their more placid opposites, Type B's) centered on increased risk for heart disease. Research indicates that people classified as Type A, compared to Type B individuals, have higher blood pressure (Contrada, 1989), produce less HDL—the "good cholesterol" (Type A's lack . . . , 1992), and are twice as likely to suffer from heart disease (Weidner, Istvan, & McKnight, 1989). It now appears that anger is the critical component that leads to coronary disease and other health problems (Fekken & Jakubowski, 1990; Smith & Pope, 1990), so the term *hostile* Type A is increasingly used by health psychologists.

Taking Active Steps to Cope with Stress

Because some stress is almost inevitable in our lives and because not everyone is blessed with a self-healing personality, what can we do to cope with stress and/or to ward off its negative effect on health? Three strategies have been identified: becoming physically fit; increasing positive affect by altering our cognitions, behaviors, and environmental surroundings; and seeking social support.

Increasing Physical Fitness. Perhaps the simplest coping strategy is to stay as healthy as possible through a sensible pattern of diet, sleep, and regular physical exercise. The result is increased *fitness*—the maintenance of a good physical condition as indicated by one's endurance and strength. For example, just thirty-five minutes of aerobic dancing has immediate positive effects, with increased feelings of well-being and decreased feelings of distress (Lox & Rudolph, 1994).

Brown (1991) conducted research that provided convincing evidence of the long-term beneficial effects of exercise (see Figure 14.6 on page 532). More than one hundred undergraduates participated in a study of fitness, which was assessed by the students' self-reports of engaging in physical exercise and by objective measures of each student's heart rate before, during, and after riding an

Hardiness ■ Includes such characteristics as commitment, defining difficulties as challenges, and perceiving oneself as having control over one's life.

FIGURE 14.6

Exercise As a Strategy to Cope with Stress and Prevent Illness. Research indicates that *fitness* (endurance and strength) is an important element in resisting the negative effects of stress. Regular exercise results in fitness, and people who are fit are less likely to become ill in response to stress than those who are not fit.

exercise bike under standard conditions. Frequency of illness was determined by self-reports and also by objective data indicating number of visits to the college health center over a period of two semesters. Finally, stress was determined by the number and severity of negative events in each student's life over the previous year. As in previous research, the role of stress was again quite clear. Students who experienced very little stress in their lives had very few illnesses, regardless of their physical fitness. When stress was high, however, fitness became very important, in that low-fitness students made significantly more visits to the health center than did high-fitness students.

Altogether, the students who were physically fit were much less vulnerable to the negative health effects of stress in their lives than the unfit students. Keep in mind that the personality dispositional variables discussed previously are equally important. A combination of fitness and hardiness provides the greatest protection against illness (Roth et al., 1989).

Creating Positive Affect. A second strategy for dealing with stress and maintaining good health is to discover how to create more positive affect for oneself. Some people, for whatever reason, are better able than others to regulate their emotions—for example, to optimize happiness (Mayer & Salovey, 1995).

By its very nature, stress creates negative affect; and negative affect, in turn, interferes with the body's immune system. A common response to an unpleasant event is to engage in *counterfactual thinking* (see Chapter 3), dwelling on alternative behavior that might have prevented the event's occurrence—and these thoughts add to one's negative and distressed feelings (Davis et al., 1995).

A much more adaptive response to a stressful event is to engage in acts that will generate positive affect. Research by Stone and his colleagues (1994) indicates that positive events (such as a family celebration or getting together with friends) enhance the immune system over a longer time period than a negative event (such as being criticized) weakens it. We have already described how an increase in negative events leads to illness, but Stone's research found that a *decrease* in positive events had an even greater adverse effect on health (Goleman, 1994).

What are some of the other things you can do to promote positive feelings? An ideal activity is to engage in work that is enjoyable (Csikszentmihalyi, 1993). Positive cognitions also help; women diagnosed as having breast cancer reported less distress if they accepted the situation and used humor as a coping device than if they denied the problem and thus attempted to avoid the threat (Carver et al., 1993).

Environmental factors influence affect, and we can utilize this knowledge to make ourselves feel happier. For example, in Chapter 10 we described the beneficial effects of pleasant fragrances on positive affect (and on prosocial responding as well). In a similar way, when research participants are working on a stressful task in a laboratory setting, the introduction of such fragrances results in a more positive emotional state *and* improved performance on the task (Baron & Bronfen, 1994). It is quite possible that we could each alleviate the negative effects of stress by manipulating our own surroundings to include pleasant music, fragrances, lighting, art, and anything else that helps improve our mood.

Seeking Social Support. The third important coping strategy is to seek **social support**—physical and psychological comfort provided by friends and family (Sarason, Sarason, & Pierce, 1994). Even among monkeys, stress leads to an increase in affiliative behavior, and affiliation in turn enhances the immune system (Cohen et al., 1992).

In general, people who interact closely with others are better able to avoid illness than those who remain isolated from interpersonal contact. When illness does occur, people who receive social support recover more quickly than those who do not. The negative effects of stressors in a work setting can be lessened if the employee receives support from coworkers and from the organization itself (Shinn et al., 1993). Studies of real-life stress in Israel—during combat training for the military and during Iraqi missile attacks on civilians in the Gulf War—indicate that people who differ in attachment style (Chapter 8) also differ in their ability to seek and thus benefit from social support (Mikulincer & Florian, 1995; Mikulincer, Florian, & Weller, 1993). Individuals whose attachment pattern is secure are more likely to cope effectively with stress through support seeking than are those with ambivalent or avoidant attachment patterns.

The utilization of social support is also associated with fewer sports injuries among young people (Smith, Smoll, & Ptacek, 1990), less postpartum depression (and higher-birth-weight babies) among women (Collins et al., 1993), and decreased risk of heart disease among the elderly (Uchino, Kiecolt-Glaser, & Cacioppo, 1992).

One of the reasons for the positive effects of interpersonal support is that talking to someone else (especially about ways to solve one's problems) reduces stress and the incidence of both major and minor health problems (Clark, 1993; Costanza, Derlega, & Winstead, 1988; Pennebaker, Hughes, & O'Heron, 1987). Interestingly enough, there are also positive emotional, physiological, and health benefits associated with simply writing about one's negative experi-

Social Support ■ Physical and psychological comfort provided by friends and relatives to people facing stress; with social support, people tend to be in better physical health and better able to cope with stress.

ences (Greenberg & Stone, 1992; Hughes, Uhlmann, & Pennebaker, 1994; Pennebaker & Beall, 1986) instead of talking about them (Mendolin & Kleck, 1993). The more an individual is secretive and conceals from others any personal information that is negative or distressing, the greater the feelings of anxiety and depression and the more likely the development of physical symptoms (Larson & Chastain, 1990). It appears that "confession" is good not only for the soul but for the body as well.

Though comparatively little research has concentrated on the effects of being the *provider* of social support, Perrine (1993) reports that trying to help another person who is facing problems can result in anger and sadness. These reactions are especially likely when the other person does not show improvement and when the listener is providing emotional support rather than engaging in problem solving. Probably because of gender-role expectations (see Chapter 5), women are more likely than men to receive social support and to provide it to others (Barbee et al., 1993). Beyond gender differences, people who are ambivalent about expressing their emotions and who are afraid of intimacy tend not to receive much social support (Emmons & Colby, 1995).

Responding to Health Problems

Offhand, it might seem that even though psychological factors might influence the probability of becoming ill, only physical factors would be relevant once illness strikes. Actually, the person who becomes ill must process the incoming information, attend to whatever physical symptoms are present, and correctly interpret them. Next, a series of critical decisions and choices must be made—whether to do nothing and simply wait for improvement, to rely on self-diagnosis, or to seek some type of formal or informal treatment. Psychological processes are central to these perceptions, cognitions, attributions, and decisions.

Attending to Symptoms—Noticing That Something Is Wrong. A sudden and dramatic symptom of a health problem such as fainting or vomiting can be expected to grab the attention of almost anyone. The same cannot be said about gradual and less obvious changes in your physical state. Considerable time may pass before you notice a slight pain in your lower back, a light rash on your chest, or a gradual change in how your gastrointestinal system is functioning. Some people pay less attention to internal sensations than others; for them, a physical problem has to become fairly intense before it is noticed (Mechanic, 1983). At the opposite extreme are *hypochondriacs*—sometimes characterized as the "worried well"—who focus on and overestimate the seriousness of every perceived symptom and thus unnecessarily seek medical advice (Wagner & Curran, 1984). In order to evaluate a symptom accurately, we have to acquire specific knowledge, and people differ in their motivation to seek medical information.

Attending to symptoms is also affected by external events that can *prime* (see Chapter 3) the individual to attend to such input or not. For example, when people take part in an experimental task exposing them to words such as "pain" and "pill," they afterward report more symptoms than do others who didn't receive health priming (Skelton & Strohmetz, 1990). Such findings suggest that exposure to health-relevant material in the media may prime us to attend to and report physical symptoms. Even more directly, have you ever learned about some new disease or medical problem and then found yourself wondering whether you have some of those same symptoms? When Lyme disease first became newsworthy, I (DB) remember looking carefully at my arms and legs each time I returned from a walk in the woods. When the media focus on this disease decreased, my search for tick bites also decreased.

A person's emotional state also influences response to symptoms. For example, mood affects how much attention you pay to symptoms. When college students were shown a movie that made them feel sad or depressed, they reported having more medical problems than other students whose affective state was made positive by a pleasant movie (Croyle & Uretsky, 1987). The importance of affect in responses to health problems was even more clearly demonstrated by Cohen et al. (1995). Healthy volunteers were exposed to a respiratory virus. Negative affect (anxiety) had been measured before the illness was induced; and the greater an individual's usual anxiety level, the more disease-specific complaints the person expressed once the respiratory infection developed.

The importance of perceived control was emphasized earlier with respect to the effects of stress. There is more than one type of control, however. Basso, Schefft, and Freedman (1994) differentiate a general need to control one's physical and social environment and the specific need to control other people. Among the various components of the Type A personality pattern, the need for both types of control are found. These investigators hypothesized, however, that an exaggerated need for interpersonal control—trying to dominate social interactions, acting bossy, and making arbitrary and unilateral decisions—is of greater importance in health functioning than the general need for control. Among a research group of almost two hundred undergraduates, those who reported the greatest need for interpersonal control also reported the greatest number of physical complaints and highest level of affective distress; in contrast, a higher general need for control was related to reporting *fewer* symptoms.

Among possible physical symptoms, pain is the most obvious—and the most difficult to ignore or overlook. More than 80 percent of all visits to physicians' offices are prompted by the presence of pain (Turk, 1994). The traditional medical view of pain has been quite straightforward: the greater the pain, the worse the physical problem must be (tissue damage, infection, or whatever). The difficulty with this seemingly sensible model is that there is not a simple relationship between physical disorders and subjective experiences of pain. The reason for the discrepancy is that such psychological factors as cognitive distortions, coping strategies, and perceived self-efficacy have a direct influence on how much pain is experienced (Reesor & Craig, 1988; Turk & Rudy, in press). Perceived pain is also influenced by a person's view of his or her general physical health—both in the past and in the future (Idler, 1993). That is, the perception that one has been healthy and will be healthy in the future is associated with minimizing current pain symptoms, whereas viewing oneself as being in generally poor health is associated with reporting many current pain symptoms.

Deciding What the Symptom Means. Once you notice a pain, a lump, a stiffness, or whatever, you must decide what—if anything—is wrong. If you conclude that there is no problem, you do nothing. Self-attributions were discussed in Chapter 2, and people tend to use a commonsense attributional model when engaging in self-diagnosis (Leventhal, Nerenz, & Steele, 1984).

When my son was about ten, he woke up one night with an abdominal pain, nausea, and fever. He had spent much of the previous afternoon at an amusement park playing on an enormous slide. He assumed that the repeated sliding had made him sick. My wife and I made a different assumption—that he had probably picked up some intestinal virus that would go away in a day or two. If either assumption were true, there would be no pressing reason to seek treatment. But what if such attributions were *not* true? Luckily, we considered another possibility. His symptoms might indicate appendicitis, and failure to contact a physician could result in a ruptured appendix, a serious and sometimes fatal complication. We did contact a physician, our son did have appendicitis, he was hospitalized the next morning, and he recovered nicely. It is obvious that mislabeling a symptom can sometimes be a very dangerous mistake (Routh & Ernst, 1984).

Another common instance of mislabeling occurs when elderly people attribute every ache and pain to "old age"; this attribution means that there is no need to bother a doctor about it (Prohaska et al., 1987). If such a self-diagnosis is wrong, of course, needed medical treatment will be needlessly delayed.

Mistaken self-diagnosis is also a problem when a disease has no symptoms. A great many people take prescription drugs to control high blood pressure, but they sometimes decide to stop their daily pills because they feel fine without them. The difficulty is that hypertension has no symptoms, and if one's blood pressure rises when the medication is stopped, the risk of coronary disease increases (Meyer, Leventhal, & Gutman, 1985).

In sum, when we make an incorrect decision about symptoms, we risk either overreacting to a minor symptom or dangerously neglecting a major one. There is no simple guideline about what to do, but it is important for each of us to know as much as we can about the meaning of possible symptoms and what to do if they occur.

If You Decide It's a Medical Problem, Do You Contact a Physician? Once a given symptom has been noticed and self-diagnosed as a health problem, what is the next step? The person must either engage in self-treatment or seek professional help—see Figure 14.7.

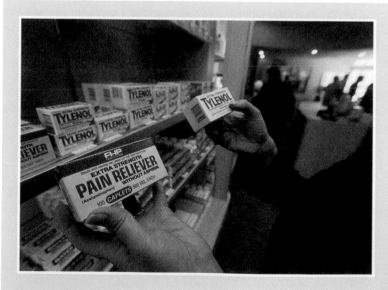

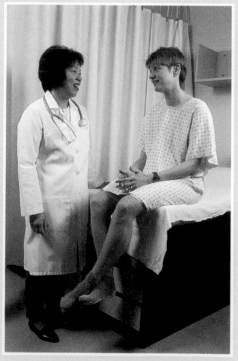

FIGURE 14.7

Once a Symptom Is Identified As a Problem: Self-Treatment or Medical Treatment? To respond to a health problem, an individual must first become aware of a physical symptom and then arrive (correctly or incorrectly) at some kind of diagnosis. The next step is to decide between treating oneself or seeking professional help. That decision is determined in part by the specifics of the problem and in part by personality characteristics.

Though self-treatment can be a mistake, there are many health-related actions that do not require the help of a professional. You can, for example, brush and floss your own teeth regularly, stop smoking, and eat more fresh fruits and vegetables. A sense of self-efficacy includes the ability to control one's behavior in ways that enhance or cause harm to health (Bandura, 1993). When self-efficacy enhances control over one's lifestyle, one can then assume responsibility for his or her diet, exercise, and other behaviors that are crucial to good health. Benefits include lowering the risk of cardiovascular disorders and lessening the negative effects of chronic diseases such as arthritis.

Sometimes, of course, medical expertise is required. According to Bishop (1987), four factors enter into most people's decision to contact or not to contact a physician. If the self-diagnosis labels the symptom as being caused by a virus and/or if it involves the upper half of the body, the most common response is to avoid a medical expert and attempt to deal with the difficulty by means of over-the-counter remedies. On the other hand, if the symptom is interpreted as a nonviral problem and/or if it involves the lower half of the body, the person is most likely to seek professional help.

The decision to seek or not to seek medical help is also influenced by personality dispositions. *Monitoring* is one example. High monitors are constantly on the lookout for threatening information of any kind, and they are more likely to make a doctor's appointment in response to a mild problem than are low monitors (Miller, Brody, & Summerton, 1988). Other dispositional and attitudinal characteristics can deter a person from contacting a physician. For example, women who are anxious about social interactions or who are concerned about their physique are much less inclined to make an appointment for an embarrassing gynecological examination and a Pap test (Kowalski & Brown, 1994)—despite the importance of early diagnosis in treating cervical cancer and the effectiveness of the Pap test in detecting it.

A longitudinal study of college students identified interpersonal *dependency* as a major determinant of visits to college health centers (Bornstein et al., 1993). The dependency measure included such factors as emotional reliance on other people, lack of social self-confidence, and low sense of autonomy and independence. The investigators determined the number of health center visits made by each student per month—both early in the semester and toward the end. As summarized in Figure 14.8 (p. 538), male and female students high in dependency sought medical help more frequently than low-dependency students. As the semester progressed (and, presumably, the stress of exams and grades increased), the high-dependency students increased their visits to the health center, while low-dependency students did not. Also, some students sought out their own doctors rather than using the student health center, and dependency and time during the semester had the same effect on visits to private physicians.

These various lines of research suggest that the decision to seek expert medical help is influenced by several different factors. Two of the major factors were described by Wills and DePaulo (1991):

> In some cases, seeking help may be construed as a form of direct-action coping . . . which [is] aimed at resolution of the problem. In certain other cases the help-seeking may be dependency based . . . where requests for help are part of self-presentation concerns, used as a way of eliciting sympathy from others.

Coping with Medical Care

Even after you decide that your health problem requires professional treatment, you still face potential difficulties when you interact with a physician, undergo diagnostic tests, and receive the necessary treatment.

FIGURE 14.8

Dependency and Visits to College Health Center During Semester. On a college campus, students low in dependency made significantly fewer visits to the health center during the semester than did students high in dependency. Toward the end of the semester (as the stress of grades and examinations increased), the high-dependency students increased their visits to the health center even more.

(*Source:* Based on data from Bornstein et al., 1993.)

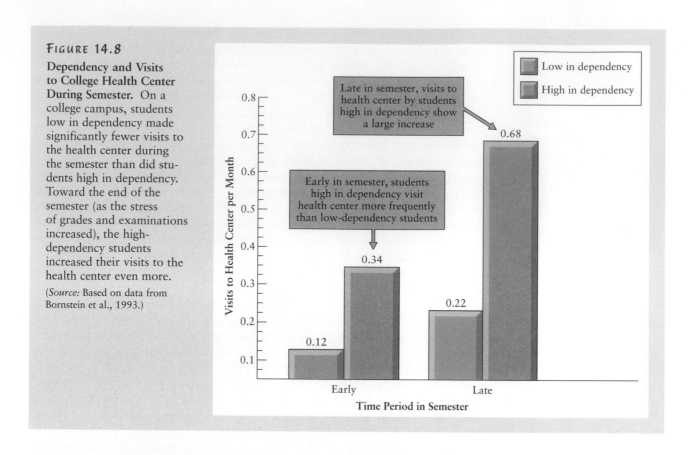

Patient–Physician Interactions. The moment you make an appointment, you are likely to feel a mounting sense of anxiety and uncertainty—feelings that increase in intensity when you enter the doctor's waiting room. These negative emotions can make it very difficult to inform the busy physician about all of the symptoms that brought you there and to remember all of the questions you wanted answered. It helps to rehearse or even to write down what you want to say and what you need to find out (Roter, 1984). A patient who is prepared in this way says more and learns more than when someone who just plays it by ear.

The physician also has a crucial role to play. A basic element is for the patient to find out enough about the doctor beforehand to be able to trust him or her as an expert. No one wants to discover a problem with medical competence when it is too late. Think of how you might react if you were on a public elevator in a hospital and overheard one of the following remarks. These are actual statements made by doctors, nurses, and other hospital staff members that were secretly recorded by investigators riding up and down in elevators in five Pennsylvania hospitals (Marchione, 1995):

"He must have been on drugs last night; he couldn't even read a chart."

"That's it. I'm getting out of here. I'm going where I can make big bucks. No more running after patients."

"I worked sixteen hours yesterday, went home, had some beer, and before I knew it, I was back here. I don't think I can make it all night."

Such comments were made on 14 percent of the elevator rides, and the conversations also included derogatory remarks about patients and breaches of patient confidentiality. As unsettling as such conversations may be, media accounts of the wrong limb being amputated or the wrong medication being administered are far worse.

Beyond competence and discretion, a physician's personal qualities are also very important. A doctor who behaves in an abrupt manner, seems uninterested, or maintains total control of the interaction can discourage patients from describing and discussing their major concerns (Goleman, 1991; Street & Buller, 1987). Not only must patients be prepared with what they want to say, they also must learn to be assertive with medical personnel. It's *your* health and *your* money.

You may have discovered for yourself that not all doctors are able to communicate very well. Not surprisingly, a physician who answers the patient's questions and discusses the diagnosis is liked better and perceived as more competent than one who overlooks questions and lets a nurse communicate the diagnosis (Rall, Peskoff, & Byrne, 1994). Other research indicates that patients are most satisfied if the physician is skilled at sending and at interpreting the kind of nonverbal messages discussed in Chapter 2 (DiMatteo, Hays, & Prince, 1986). When a medical practitioner cannot control his or her nonverbal communications (for example, feelings of anxiety or uncertainty), the patient is likely to assume the worst. The physician may actually be upset about something in his or her own life, but the patient is likely to assume that something personal is involved—"I'm in such bad shape that the doctor is afraid to tell me the truth!" I (Donn Byrne) once visited a doctor who left the room several times during the examination without explanation. I began to think that he had discovered a terrible problem and was trying to contact specialists or arrange for my admission to a hospital. In fact, he was calling his broker about which shares to sell during a rapid drop in stock prices. Physicians can be taught communication skills and thus avoid these problems (Hays & DiMatteo, 1984).

Physicians also need to be sensitive about the way medical information is presented. Consider the effects of **framing** (see Chapter 12)—the words that are used to describe the patient's condition or the prescribed treatment. Consider, for example, the effects of providing information in positive rather than negative terms. For example, a couple can be told that a pregnancy has a 50 percent chance of producing a normal offspring or that there is a 50 percent chance of producing an abnormal child. The information is the same, but the negative framing of the second statement results in more decisions to abort the fetus than the positive framing of the first statement (Wilson, Kaplan, & Schneiderman, 1987). You can think of similar examples. If you were to have an operation, which would you find more frightening: (1) "There is a 10 percent chance that you will die," or (2) "There is a 90 percent chance that you will recover"?

Dealing with Diagnosis and Treatment. Medical procedures designed to reveal the source of a patient's symptoms and to treat the underlying problem are often intrusive, sometimes painful, and occasionally dangerous. Diagnostic tests and medical treatment are thus stressful, and patients must somehow cope with this very specific type of stress. What can be done by medical personnel and what can be done by the patient to reduce this kind of medical threat?

Early in an illness episode, it is important to notice symptoms and to make accurate attributions about their cause. At that point, coping mechanisms such as avoidance and denial can be very dangerous. When, however, you are undergoing a medical examination or treatment, those same defenses can be quite beneficial (Suls & Fletcher, 1985): You will experience less stress if you can mentally avoid and deny what is being done to you. The next time you are in a dentist's office having your teeth cleaned or a cavity drilled, try concentrating on something else—past experiences, future plans, a movie you liked. To a surprising extent, these incompatible thoughts (see Chapter 11) actually prevent or at least greatly reduce pain and discomfort.

Framing ■ The specific wording of information, which can influence decision making.

Mood also is important. For example, Stalling (1992) found that inducing a positive mood leads to a decrease in self-reports of pain. In related research Zillmann et al. (1993) found, as expected, that exposure to humorous video-tapes such as stand-up comedy (*A Night at the Improv*) or a situation comedy (*Married with Children*) reduced physical discomfort compared to a control tape involving cooking instructions (*The Frugal Gourmet*). Unexpectedly, how-ever, tragic material in which a dying mother says good-bye to her three small children (from *Terms of Endearment*) had the same effect. It appears that either positive or negative material buffers the effects of a painful stimulus, presum-ably because it is helpful to become emotionally involved with something other than your immediate situation.

These various effects all seem to involve *distraction*—thinking about some-thing else. You can make a painful experimental task (leaving your hand in ice-cold water as long as possible) less painful by engaging in distracting thoughts such as thinking about your room at home (Cioffi & Holloway, 1993). Less ob-viously, the opposite strategy—paying careful attention to the painful sensa-tions—also can have a beneficial effect. When receiving a shot or having blood withdrawn for a test, some people look away and think about something else, while others watch the needle very closely. Both approaches are more effective as coping strategies than trying to deal with pain by suppressing awareness ("Just empty your mind").

The Role of Perceived Control in Coping with Treatment. Earlier, in discussing how people cope with stress, we noted the importance of *perceived control*. Per-ceived control is also of crucial importance when you are dealing with the stress of medical care (Affleck et al., 1987). As a simple example, it is much less stress-ful to remove a splinter from your own finger than to have another person re-move it. In situations that are not actually controllable, it is still helpful to *believe* that you can determine the outcome. Studies of patients with heart dis-ease, cancer, and AIDS indicate that those who believe themselves able to con-trol symptoms, health care, and treatment make a much better adjustment than do patients who believe that what happens is totally beyond their control (Tay-lor et al., 1991; Thompson et al., 1993). When one's beliefs about control are entirely fictional, the benefits cannot continue indefinitely. Optimal medical ad-justment occurs when threat is high and the perception of control has at least *some basis in reality* (Helgeson, 1992).

A different kind of control has been introduced in some medical settings by means of an interactive laser-disc player, a touch-screen terminal, and a key-board (Freudenheim, 1992). The process works as follows. A physician informs a patient that, for example, he has an enlarged prostate gland and surgery is one of his options. At this point, the patient becomes directly involved in the deci-sion process. Using the laser-disc player, he enters his own health data (age, weight, symptoms, etc.) and then requests information about the pros and cons of having the surgery, being treated with drugs, or simply doing nothing at pre-sent and waiting to see whether the condition improves or worsens. After he considers the pluses and minuses of each option, it's up to the patient to make a final decision.

Still another type of control is provided by accurate information about what is happening to you and what is going to happen next (Jay et al., 1983). Knowledge—even knowledge about unpleasant procedures—is less stressful than ignorance and the resulting fear of the unknown (Suls & Wan, 1989). For a patient hospitalized for surgery, it helps to have a roommate who has already undergone the same kind of operation. Kulik and Mahler (1987) found that patients with a postoperative roommate (compared to those whose roommate had not yet had the operation) were less unhappy and anxious, needed less medication for their pain, and were able to be discharged from the hospital more quickly. Information provides a kind of cognitive road map that keeps the patient knowledgeable and thus able to avoid fearful surprises.

Note that perceived control has little benefit for patients who don't want to have control of the situation (Baron & Logan, 1993; Law, Logan, & Baron, 1994). For those of us who prefer control, however, it is all-important.

INTEGRATING PRINCIPLES

1. Psychological factors affect each aspect of one's physical well-being. When we process information dealing with health risks, preventive measures to help maintain good health, or medical procedures, the cognitive functions described in Chapters 2, 3, and 12 (including the availability heuristic, priming, attributional processes, and framing) are clearly relevant. Information designed to improve our health-related behaviors relies on what is known about attitude change and persuasion (Chapter 4).

2. A central concept in health psychology is the effect of stress (and our ability to cope with stress) on our risk of developing major and minor illnesses. Stress both interferes with health-promoting activities and, at the physiological level, decreases the efficiency of the immune system. Coping with stress (both in everyday life and in medical settings once an illness develops) is based on such psychological characteristics as possessing feelings of self-efficacy (Chapter 5), having a secure attachment style (Chapter 8), avoiding a hostile Type A behavior pattern (Chapter 11), being physically fit, and increasing positive affect (Chapter 7).

Environmental Psychology: How Environmental Factors Affect Human Behavior and How Human Behavior Affects the Environment

In Chapter 1 we indicated that one of the five major factors that influence social behavior consists of ecological variables—the direct and indirect influences of the physical environment. The study of such variables has developed into the field known as **environmental psychology**—the study of the interaction between human behavior and our physical surroundings. Much of the initial research in this field dealt with how the presence of other people influences us—studies of crowding, for example. During the 1960s and 1970s, interest broadened to include a variety of negative behavioral effects caused by environmental variables such as noise, heat, and air pollution. In the 1980s and 1990s, research increasingly concentrated on how human behavior negatively impacts the environment and on how best to change this behavior.

Environmental Psychology ■
The research area that concentrates on the interaction between the physical world and human behavior.

Environmental Effects on Human Behavior

In discussing the effects of stress on health, we pointed out that researchers' initial focus centered on physical threats. Throughout human history, people have been threatened by floods, earthquakes, and other natural disasters. In more recent times, technological advances have brought us new potential dangers. We are regularly exposed to health-related messages about environmental threats such as increased cancer risk caused by living or working near power lines (Gorman, 1992) or talking on cellular telephones (Angier, 1993), often followed by research reports assuring us that our fears are unfounded (Broad, 1995). Other environmental dangers seem to be quite real; an example is the association between living or working close to a hazardous waste site and higher cancer rates (Harmon & Coe, 1993). Some people react to repeated warnings about microwave ovens, computer terminals, pesticides, and much else by developing a general dislike of living in a technological society—*technophobia* (Pilisuk & Acredolo, 1988). One result is that *perceived* exposure to toxic factors in the environment sometimes causes attribution of normal bodily sensations to the presence of serious illness (Williams & Lees-Haley, 1993). It sometimes seems that we are in the helpless position of Ziggy in Figure 14.9.

Because environmental threats are stressful, people must find ways to cope, as discussed earlier in the section on health psychology. Perhaps the least effective coping strategy is wishful thinking—doing nothing but hoping that the problem will simply go away (Hallman & Wandersman, 1992). Another ineffective response is to attribute environmental problems to the evil motives of industrial firms or of government agencies and then to resort to violence against individuals associated with these organizations. The Unabomber is a prime example. This anonymous individual has sent mail bombs that killed or injured a series of people as a way to attain his aim: "the complete and permanent destruction of modern industrial society in every part of the world" (The Unabomber speaks, 1995).

FIGURE 14.9

Avoiding Environmental Threats? *Because many aspects of our natural and technological environment are potentially threatening and stressful, the suggestion to "avoid the environment for awhile" sounds tempting. That is, of course, impossible, so we must reduce threats whenever it is possible to do so and learn how best to cope with the threats that remain.*

(*Source:* Universal Press Syndicate, September 11, 1982.)

The most adaptive approach is to take steps to alter the behavior of individuals (for example, prohibiting smoking in public buildings) or of organizations (for example, regulating automobile emission standards). Until the most harmful negative environmental features are brought under control, what do we know about their effects?

Noisy Environments: Unpleasant and Unpredictable Sounds. **Noise** is defined as unwanted sound—in other words, sounds that create a negative affective response (Baron, 1994). Loudness is one of the major reasons that a given sound is evaluated as unpleasant. We tend to react negatively to loudness, whether it is a natural occurrence (such as a loud clap of thunder) or artificial (such as a jet taking off).

Unpredictability is the other major reason for a negative response to sound. We can adapt more easily to a regular, predictable sound, such as birds that start singing each morning at sunrise or a clock that chimes on the hour, than to unexpected and unpredictable sound. Glass, Singer, and Friedman (1969) found that it is very difficult to adapt to an unpredictable sound—quite possibly because one has less perceived control when a stimulus occurs at unknown intervals (Worchel & Shackelford, 1991). Glass and colleagues (1969) tested these propositions by giving research participants a proofreading task; while they worked, half of the participants were exposed to predictable and half to unpredictable noise. Both groups were able to complete the proofreading, but those in the unpredictable condition made more mistakes and showed less tolerance for frustration. The negative effects of unpredictable noise on performance have since been found for many tasks, including reading comprehension and anagram solving (Nagar & Pandey, 1987). The negative effects of noise are reduced when individuals perceive that they have control over it. When research participants are told they can press a switch and turn off the noise, they perform better and feel less upset—even though most of them do not actually press the switch (Glass et al., 1969). As you might guess, loud, unpredictable noise generates a great deal of negative affect, including anger (Donnerstein & Wilson, 1976), and it is a major source of environmental stress (Bell et al., 1990).

Noise interferes with behavior in daily life as well as in the laboratory. As a mild example, recently the two authors of this book were participating in an oral examination of a graduate student when the very loud and very unpredictable noise of construction work began in the hallway outside of the meeting room. It was sufficiently disrupting to the student and to the faculty members that we called a halt to the formal meeting until we could locate a new, quieter place to hold the orals. Much more serious is the finding that children who live where they are regularly exposed to the noise of highway traffic or airplanes taking off and landing have impaired reading ability (Cohen, Glass, & Singer, 1973). Daily exposure to the sounds of a busy airport causes adults to be less able to find items in a supermarket, to have memory loss, and even to be more likely to drop things (Smith & Stansfeld, 1986). Still more serious are the health threats caused by noise as an environmental stressor (Topf, 1989). Examples include hearing loss (Cohen, Glass, & Singer, 1973), hypertension (Cohen et al., 1986), and a higher incidence of fatal strokes (Dellinger, 1979).

Despite its many negative effects, it is possible to take active steps to avoid noise. Several devices on the market—including the one shown in Figure 14.10 (p. 544), which was invented by Bob Baron—are very effective in reducing room noise that originates elsewhere. They perform this function by producing a soothing sound made up of many different sound frequencies. Such devices not only block outside noise, they increase feelings of personal privacy as well.

Noise ■ An unwanted sound, one that brings about a negative affective response.

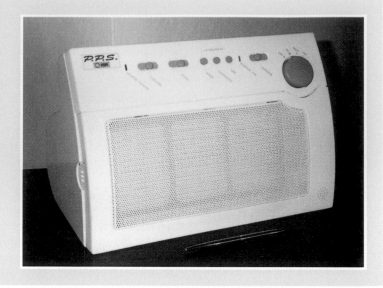

FIGURE 14.10

A Device to Reduce Stressful Noise. Noise, especially unpredictable noise, has negative effects on affect, work performance, reading ability, and health. Several devices (including the one shown here, which was invented by Bob Baron) are effective in reducing this source of environmental stress.

High Temperatures: Negative Affect and Negative Interpersonal Behavior. Research has made it very clear that when the temperature rises to a point where it is uncomfortably hot, people interact with one another in less positive ways. Note that discomfort is not simply a matter of air temperature—it is also affected by humidity and by air movement (Sundstrom & Sundstrom, 1986). Most of the research, however, has simply focused on temperature as a rough index of discomfort.

Why should an uncomfortably hot environment bring about negative interpersonal behavior? Anderson, Deuser, and DeNeve (1995) studied college students who played a Pac Man sort of video game or engaged in aerobic exercise under either comfortable, warm, or hot conditions. Hot temperatures resulted in hostile affect, hostile thoughts, and physiological arousal; any one of these responses to heat (as well as their combined effect) can increase the likelihood of negative interpersonal responses.

What sort of negative responses? We know that when the heat is sufficiently intense, both interpersonal attraction (Chapter 7) and prosocial behavior (Chapter 10) decrease (Bell, 1990). In a study of automobile drivers at an intersection in Phoenix, Arizona, the higher the temperature, the more the drivers angrily honked their horns if the car in front of them remained stationary after the light turned green (Kenrick & McFarlane, 1986).

Some negative reactions to heat involve more harmful interpersonal behavior. One example is provided by sports "accidents." In major-league baseball, it is not unusual for a batter to be hit by the ball. Are such pitches always simply accidents, or do they in part represent aggressiveness by the pitcher? If negative affect is involved, Reifman, Larrick, and Fein (1991) hypothesized that the number of batters getting hit would increase as the temperature rose. They analyzed data from 826 major-league games played over two seasons. As shown in Figure 14.11, the hypothesis was strongly confirmed. The higher the temperature, the greater the mean number of batters hit by a ball.

Temperature level has also been linked to still more serious interpersonal aggression (Anderson & DeNeve, 1992). For example, Anderson and Anderson (1984) found that murders and rapes in two large American cities occurred more frequently as the temperature increased. Other research on criminal violence in other cities indicates the same association between heat and aggressive

FIGURE 14.11

Odds of Getting Hit by a Pitch: It Depends on the Temperature. Data from hundreds of major-league baseball games indicate that as the temperature rises, there is an increase in the average number of times batters get hit by the ball. This finding provides additional support for the proposition that heat results in an increase in aggressive behavior.

(*Source:* Based on data from Reifman, Larrick, & Fein, 1991.)

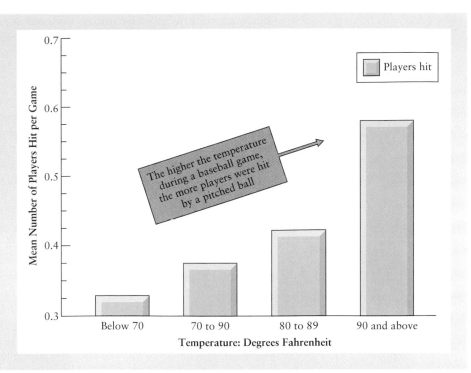

crimes (Cohn, 1990; Simpson & Perry, 1990). Interestingly, the relationship between temperature and crimes that do *not* involve interpersonal aggression (such as burglary and car theft) is much weaker (Anderson, 1987).

Not only does heat affect aggressive crimes, it also increases the aggressiveness of police officers toward suspected offenders. Dutch police officers of both sexes took part in a video and laser-disc experiment in which a realistic crime scene was presented—life size and in color (Vrij, van der Steen, & Koppelaar, 1994). Each participant was asked to imagine himself or herself as the officer sent to investigate suspicious activity at a shed where a burglar alarm had sounded. In the presentation, after arriving at the scene, the officer enters, and a male suspect suddenly appears with a crowbar in his hand, threatening the officer. The participants watched this scene in either comfortable or hot conditions. When questioned afterward (in a comfortable room) about the scene, those officers who had watched it while experiencing uncomfortably hot conditions expressed more negative affect, believed the suspect was more aggressive and more dangerous, and said they were more likely to fire a shot at the man than did officers who had watched the tape in comfortable conditions.

Despite general agreement that negative interpersonal acts increase as the temperature increases, there is some disagreement about the effect of *extremely* high temperatures. While Anderson (1989) and others argue that aggressiveness continues to rise no matter how high the temperature, the *negative affect escape model* (Baron, 1978; Baron & Bell, 1976; Bell, 1992) proposes that when the discomfort in response to heat is sufficiently high, aggression begins to decline. The explanation is that extreme discomfort motivates the individual to escape the situation and seek relief by sipping a cold drink, sitting beside a fan or air conditioner, going for a swim, or whatever. Research evidence seems to indicate that negative affect continues to rise with higher and higher temperature, whereas aggressive behavior begins to decrease at extremely high levels (Bell & Fusco, 1986, 1990).

The Negative Effects of Breathing Polluted Air. Though worldwide concern about air quality was expressed at the Rio Conference on the global environment in 1992, pollution remains a problem, as shown in Figure 14.12. On the job, more than half of all factory workers are exposed to hazardous polluted air (Quinn & Staines, 1979). How much of a problem is air pollution? Data released by the Environmental Protection Agency and by the Harvard School of Public Health indicate that 50,000 to 60,000 deaths are caused each year in the United States by particles in the air we breathe (Hilts, 1993). The victims are primarily children with respiratory illnesses, individuals of all ages who have asthma, and elderly citizens who have upper respiratory illnesses. Most of the particles are released into the air by industrial plants—a smaller proportion originate in the exhausts of vehicles powered by diesel engines. In countries that have less restrictive environmental laws, these problems are even worse.

Pollution is dangerous, but people who are exposed to it on a regular basis learn to accept dirty air as normal. For example, newcomers to a heavily polluted area such as southern California, northwest Indiana, or eastern New Jersey complain about the terrible condition of the air; but those who have lived in the area for a period of time seldom even notice the pollution and do not consider it to be an important community issue (Evans, Jacobs, & Frager, 1982).

In addition to particles, odor is also involved in our response to impure air. In general, bad smells evoke negative feelings and less-friendly interpersonal behavior (Rotton et al., 1979). The negative emotional effects of bad air are assumed to be responsible for the association between pollution level and the frequency of family disturbances reported to the police (Rotton & Frey, 1985).

Air that has a pleasant smell has the opposite effect—positive emotions and friendly behavior (see Chapter 10). Baron (1990) found that research participants exposed to the scent of an air freshener while working on a clerical task set higher goals, used more efficient work strategies, and were friendlier than other participants who worked without the air freshener. It seems likely that adding

FIGURE 14.12

Air Pollution: Discomfort, Illness, and Death. Polluted air is one of several factors in the environment that have a negative effect on humans. Impure air causes negative emotional reactions, increases various health risks, and is responsible for thousands of deaths annually.

FIGURE 14.13

The Effects of Atmospheric Electricity on Human Behavior. Natural atmospheric phenomena such as lightning cause air molecules to split into positively and negatively charged ions, and these ions affect behavior. For example, after a thunderstorm, the level of negative ions rises; as a consequence, people experience an increase in positive affect and show improved task performance.

pleasant smells such as peppermint to a work setting could improve both morale and performance (Baron, 1990; Warm, Dember, & Parasuraman, 1991).

Electrical Ions in the Atmosphere. Natural environmental phenomena can also influence behavior. Lightning, strong winds, and other atmospheric disturbances cause air molecules to split into positively and negatively charged particles called *ions*. The result is *atmospheric electricity,* which affects social behavior in several ways. How?

Positive ions are generated by hot, dry winds blowing from mountain ranges down across the plains below. If you have ever lived or vacationed in such an area, you may have noticed the negative reactions associated with several days of winds such as the hot Santa Ana that blows down from the Rocky Mountains. As the positive ion level rises, the frequency of suicides, traffic accidents, industrial accidents, and several types of crime also increases (Sulman et al., 1974).

In contrast, the level of negative ions rises after a thunder storm, as in Figure 14.13. You may have gone outdoors after such a storm and experienced a rush of positive feelings. Research, in fact, indicates that negative ions increase positive affect (DeSanctis, Halcomb, & Fedoravicius, 1981) and improve work performance (Baron, 1987a). We have repeatedly pointed out the influence of positive versus negative affect on behavior, and environmental factors such as noise, high temperatures, bad-smelling air, and positive ions lead to negative behavior in part because they create negative affect, while a quiet atmosphere, comfortable temperatures, fragrant smells, and negative ions arouse positive affect and have beneficial behavioral effects. Note that numerous other environmental factors, such as room lighting, also influence our behavior because of their effect on emotions (Baron, Rea, & Daniels, 1992).

Besides positive affect, negative ions increase general arousal level. When negative ions arouse and activate people, the affected individuals are more likely to do something that they were already inclined to do. This has been demonstrated in laboratory experiments in which special equipment generates high levels of atmospheric electricity. As the negative ion level increases, the activation level of the participants rises, adding to the strength of each person's ordinary responses. For example, such ions increase the aggressiveness of Type A individuals (see Chapter 11)—presumably because they already possess a strong tendency to aggress; this tendency is simply activated by the ions (Baron, Russell, & Arms, 1985). As you might guess from the work described in Chapter 7, activation caused by the presence of these ions also increases the strength of positive responses to similar strangers and of negative responses to dissimilar strangers (Baron, 1987b).

The Effects of Human Behavior on the Environment

At the beginning of this section, we defined environmental psychology in terms of the *interaction* between our behavior and our physical surroundings. It really is a two-way street, with the environment affecting our actions and our actions affecting the environment.

How do human activities affect the environment? In fact, almost everything that humans do has a small but cumulative effect on the world around us. Whenever someone becomes a parent, drives a car, uses hair spray, buys a product, sends garbage to a landfill, lights a fire, uses salt on icy sidewalks, or plants a tree, the environment is affected. Anything that you personally do probably has very little effect, of course; but what you plus the other billions of people living on our planet do can be sufficiently great so as to alter the environment, and this alteration in turn can influence the lives of all of us (Stern, 1992).

The More People, the More Effect They Have on the Environment. We know that "overpopulation" can quickly become a controversial issue. It should be easy to agree that the actions of two people have a greater effect on the environment than the actions of one, that four have more effect than two, and so on. There is, however, no agreement with respect to how many people are *too many,* how many are *just enough,* or how many *years remain* before the earth's resources finally become overextended (Daily, Ehrlich, & Ehrlich, 1994). Nevertheless, we must all realize that the land and the water and the air on Earth cannot support an infinite number of human beings.

An old real estate saying that encourages customers to buy acreage applies here—"They're making more people, but they're not making any more land." According to the World Bank, they're not making any more water, either. At least eighty countries now have serious water shortages with a consequent threat to their agriculture (Lekic, 1995). The threatened areas include the Middle East, North Africa, northern China, southern India, western South America, and large parts of Pakistan and Mexico. New usable water *can* be created by a fairly expensive procedure that purifies ocean water, but even this source is not infinite.

As this chapter is written, the world's population is approximately 5.6 billion people (Hollingsworth, 1995)—and growing. A world population conference was held in Cairo in 1994 in an attempt to deal with the issues involved in continued growth. During the nine-day meeting, there was a *net increase in the world's population of almost two million human beings,* according to estimates made by the Population Division of the United Nations.

Because of our intellectual ability, human beings can and do affect the planet more than any other living creatures. The amazing growth of world population is a positive indication of how well we are succeeding as a species and also an indication of how great our potentially negative effects can be (Jolly, 1994). It may help you to picture our planet's population growth if you consider a few points in time. In 8000 B. C., only about five million people existed—imagine what it would be like if the population of Philadelphia and its suburbs today were spread out across all the continents. It took almost 10,000 years for these small bands of people to increase in size to a population of one billion in the year 1800 (Demeny, 1974). The second billion took only another 130 years, and those two billion living in 1930 doubled to four billion by the late 1970s, taking less than 50 years to do so. By the year 2000, the world's population is expected to be about six billion (Dumanoski, 1990). It is crucial to understand that, over time, the population grows at a faster and faster pace (Stycos, 1995). To most of us, however, this growth is not obvious, because it takes place over decades and centuries. For example, I (DB) was born in Austin, Texas, and I'm willing to bet that I would not have noticed Austin's remarkable growth had I spent the rest of my life there. Instead, I've lived many years in California, Indiana, and New York. A brief visit to Austin in 1990 revealed startling changes. The small town I first left shortly after the bombing of Pearl Harbor had "suddenly" become a city. Thus, the pace of growth is hard to comprehend when you remain in a given location. It may be easier to envision the birth of about five thousand more humans than die—*every thirty minutes* (Haub, 1991).

Note that the birth rate varies considerably across different countries. For example, in Kenya, the relatively high birth rate results in a 4 percent annual increase in population—and this means that the number of Kenyans doubles every eighteen years (Kaplan, 1992). In the United States, the relatively low birth rate is dropping, and population growth in 1994 was less than 1 percent (including over 800,000 immigrants); if that figure remains constant, the number of Americans will double in seventy-six years (U.S. birth rate . . . , 1995).

Whether at a relatively low or at a relatively high annual rate, is growth a cause for celebration or a cause for concern? This is where the major disagreement lies. People known as "cornucopians" argue that continued population growth is essential to our overall well-being. They assume that short-term misery is beneficial in the long run because it acts as an incentive for us to devise new and better ways to feed and house and educate people (Umpleby, 1990), with the end result being a rise in everyone's standard of living (Simon, 1989; Wattenberg, 1989). The opposite argument is made by others (sometimes labeled "neo-Malthusians") who view human beings as analogous to a cancer spreading across the earth's surface—a malignancy that will continue to grow until it destroys its environment and itself (Hern, 1990). A third view agrees with the cornucopians and points out that human ingenuity is not automatic—some countries will develop ways to overcome the shortages, but others will not, and the discrepancies will cause regional crises characterized by poverty, interpersonal violence, and environmental destruction (Stevens, 1994a).

Which view is closer to your own attitudes and beliefs? Actually, both the optimists and the pessimists agree that at some point growth must stop, either because we rationally decide that the number of people simply cannot exceed the available resources required to live a good life (Daly, 1991) or because we more or less ignore the question until catastrophe strikes in the form of famine,

FIGURE 14.14

Trash: One Effect of Human Beings on the Environment. Perhaps the most obvious by-product of human activity is waste material, ranging from sewage to garbage. As the population grows, the amount of waste increases and the problem of how to dispose of it becomes more difficult.

regional wars fought to control drinkable water and arable land, and/or the spread of fatal diseases (Heilbroner, 1974; Luten, 1991).

Note that the decision to halt growth need not involve political control and the use of coercion; the most effective way to lower birth rates is by increasing educational opportunities and raising the level of personal income (Emery, 1994), making family planning services available (FitzGerald, 1994), and using the media to increase the general awareness of options (Ryerson, 1994).

If we prefer choice to catastrophe, the task of persuading people to change their behavior, convincing people to change their attitudes, and teaching billions of people to interact in mutually beneficial ways will obviously require the knowledge and skills of applied social psychologists (Katzev & Wang, 1994).

Some of the Effects of Our Actions: Producing Waste, Altering the Climate, and Causing the Spread of New Diseases. Even though most people place a high value on a clean environment (Simmons, Binney, & Dodd 1992), a growing population necessarily means the creation of more and more waste products. The United States alone produces about 180 million tons of waste each year, and more than 70 percent of America's trash is buried in 5,500 landfills throughout the country (Rathje, 1991); see Figure 14.14. Most of these sites are becoming filled to capacity, and few communities are eager to have new ones located in their vicinity.

There are no easy solutions to the growing problem of waste, but *recycling* is one promising approach (De Young et al., 1995). To the extent that paper, glass, plastic, and metal can be saved and reused, there is obviously less trash (and a decreased need to use additional raw resources to manufacture new products). How can recycling be encouraged? Among the possibilities: Persuade citizens to become concerned about the problem and committed to doing their share (Vining & Ebreo, 1990), develop communications that encourage such activity (Burn & Oskamp, 1986), and legislate perceived rewards such as the return of deposits on bottles and cans (Kahle & Beatty, 1987). The latter approach has proved very successful, in that people not only return their containers but, over time, also come to have more favorable general attitudes about recycling and other proenvironmental activities.

People clearly create waste, but do human activities alter such large-scale factors as climate and the ozone layer? Though there is some dispute about the answer to that question, the evidence is gradually becoming less easy to dismiss (Broad, 1994; Browne, 1994). There is reason to believe that **global warming** is gradually taking place: temperature increases in the atmosphere and in the oceans, attributable in part to human activity (Stevens, 1995a). Among the consequences are an increase in storms and other weather extremes (Stevens, 1995b), plus a melting of the ice caps at the North and South Poles that will raise the sea level two to three feet during the next century (Sullivan, 1995).

These effects have already been observed in several parts of the world, because the oceans are rising about one inch every five years. Three of the islands of the Republic of Maldives are now under water, and the gradual loss of land has been documented in Bermuda and in several islands of the Caribbean (Crossette, 1990). Among the additional effects of a warmer climate will be changes in the plants and animals now living in temperate zones; for example, the sugar maple and the deer mouse will have to migrate toward the poles. Some animals—for example, polar bears and monarch butterflies—may cease to exist (Schneider, 1991; Stevens, 1992).

The cause of this change in climate is known as the **greenhouse effect**—that is, heat is trapped in our atmosphere because of an increase in the levels of three gases that began about the middle of the 1800s. The gases are *carbon dioxide*—produced in greater and greater amounts once people began burning coal and oil to produce energy (Price, 1995); *methane*—produced in rice paddies, forest fires, landfills, and the digestive tracts of the cattle and other animals we raise for milk, food, and hides (Heilig, 1994); and *chlorofluorocarbons* or *CFCs*—used in refrigerators, air conditioners, and many aerosol cans (Lemonick, 1992). An added problem with CFCs is the gradual thinning of the ozone layer; as a result, we are less protected from the most intense and dangerous of the sun's rays. According to the U.S. National Oceanic and Atmospheric Administration, the thickness of the ozone layer has decreased between 1985 and 1995, and more so at higher latitudes (for example, Edmonton) than at lower ones (for example, Miami).

Can global warming be stopped or reversed? The only natural force that can change the trend is an equally fearful disaster such as the onset of the next ice age (Olivenstein, 1992). To the extent that human behavior brought on the problem, however, changes in behavior can solve the problem. It will not be enough simply to stop further increases of carbon dioxide emissions (Stevens, 1994b); it will be necessary to *reduce* the amount of this gas we produce by developing energy technology that doesn't require the burning of organic matter—solar and wind power are examples (Greenwald, 1993)—and by planting more trees than we

Global Warming ■ The probable increase in the temperature of the earth's atmosphere and its oceans brought about partly as a result of various human activities.

Greenhouse Effect ■ The basis of global warming: Gases released into the atmosphere (carbon dioxide, methane, and chlorofluorocarbons) trap the sun's heat, turning the earth into a vast "greenhouse."

cut down (Grondahl, 1989). We can reduce methane by feeding our cud-chewing domestic animals a diet low in fiber and by eating less beef. Chlorofluorocarbons have been banned in fifty nations and replaced with alternatives, and several international agreements are designed to bring about improvement (Ozone depletion . . . , 1995). The result has been a surprisingly rapid drop in CFCs in the atmosphere; if the trend continues, the ozone layer should return to its normal thickness in fifty to one hundred years (Stevens, 1993b).

Though the problems of waste and global warming are deadly serious, a third effect of people on the environment (and vice versa) is more immediately terrifying—the development of new diseases (Garrett, 1995). Some occur as infectious agents mutate and become resistant to antibiotics. A second and less certain cause of disease is the destruction of rain forests to provide lumber and to increase the amount of land available for agriculture (Linden, 1992). Despite the warnings sounded by scientists and environmentalists (Angier, 1994), the rate of deforestation is rapidly increasing in places such as the Amazon region of Brazil (Stevens, 1993a).

Why should the destruction of rain forests be a problem? This activity has two major consequences. One is the destruction of millions of as yet unknown species of plants and animals that live in these forests. In the past, just such species have provided disease-resistant crops such as Jalisco maize and medicines such as aspirin (Thernstrom, 1993). The other, more immediate danger is the transfer of viral infections that were once confined to tropical animals to the humans who venture into these once isolated habitats (Wade, 1995). Among the diseases believed to originate in the rain forests are HIV infections that result in AIDS, dengue (or "break-bone") fever, and the Ebola virus.

Ebola was first discovered near the Ebola river in northern Zaire in 1976 when the residents of fifty-five villages experienced a dreadful new illness. Ebola begins with headache and fever and progresses to hemorrhaging of the internal organs and bleeding from every bodily orifice (Preston, 1995). Only 10 percent of patients survive, and the only "good" news is that the virus kills so quickly that

FIGURE 14.15
New Viral Diseases from the Rain Forests: Fiction and Fact. The emergence of new and deadly diseases such as the Ebola virus has resulted in interesting fictional presentations, but the diseases and the dangers are real. When humans invade and destroy isolated natural habitats such as a rain forest, organisms that once infected the animal inhabitants can adapt to the threat by transferring to human hosts.

victims have little time to spread it beyond where they live (Lemonick, 1995). The fear of this destructive new disease was the impetus for two fictional movies (*Outbreak* and *Virus;* see Figure 14.15); but reality is even more frightening than fiction, in that Ebola broke out again in Zaire almost two decades after it first struck (Gibbs, 1995), and continues to break out from time to time. Except for HIV and rabies, Ebola is the deadliest virus ever to infect humans. Though there is a vaccination for rabies, there are no vaccines for the other two viruses. Still others that have yet to emerge from their natural habitats or have yet to be identified can presumably be prevented only if we protect the rain forests.

Clearly, what we do can alter our environment, and changes in the environment—in turn—can affect the lives of each of us.

INTEGRATING PRINCIPLES

1. Among the sources of environmental stress are the threats caused by modern technology and unpredictable noise. People must avoid or learn to cope with such stressors or risk illness. Negative affect is elicited by uncomfortably hot and humid surroundings, bad-smelling air, and atmospheric electricity containing positive ions; negative feelings, in turn, result in less-positive interpersonal reactions (Chapter 7), less prosocial behavior (Chapter 10), and more aggression (Chapter 11). Positive behavioral effects result from environmental factors such as perceived control of noise, comfortable temperatures, pleasant fragrances, and atmospheric electricity with a high level of negative ions.

2. The growing world population directly contributes to the negative effects of human behavior on our physical environment. Among the effects of overpopulation are the annual creation of tons of waste, global warming and a thinning ozone layer, and the accidental introduction of new diseases. Among the positive steps to reverse the effects are persuasive efforts (Chapter 4) to promote family planning, recycling, control of gases that have a negative impact on the atmosphere, and the protection of once isolated habitats.

Social Diversity: A Critical Analysis
DIFFERENCES BETWEEN ASIANS AND AMERICANS IN RESPONDING TO ILLNESS

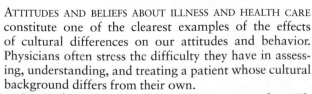

ATTITUDES AND BELIEFS ABOUT ILLNESS AND HEALTH CARE constitute one of the clearest examples of the effects of cultural differences on our attitudes and behavior. Physicians often stress the difficulty they have in assessing, understanding, and treating a patient whose cultural background differs from their own.

Research interest in this question arose for Nilchaikovit, Hill, and Holland (1993) when two of these in-

dividuals (one Asian and the other American) were each involved in assessing the depression of a twenty-four-year-old Korean woman who was a leukemia patient at a New York hospital. After examining her independently, the two professionals had very different perceptions of this woman and recommended very different ways to help her. The American believed that the patient's mother and father were overinvolved with their daughter, and

TABLE 14.1 Cultural Differences Affect One's Self-Concept, and Self-Concept Affects Illness Behavior and Medical Care

Observations of Western versus Eastern family patterns and the resulting differences in self-concept suggest that individual reactions to illness and medical care are quite different in individualistic and collectivistic cultures. When a physician and a patient come from different cultures, it is especially necessary to be sensitive to these variations.

Differences between Americans and Asians

Ideal Self	*American*—values individualism, freedom, perfection, assertiveness, self-confidence, youth as a sign of vigor
	Asian—values self in a social context, duties, harmony, modesty, moderation, maturity as a sign of wisdom
Communication and Emotional Expression	*American*—verbal, direct, expressive; openly communicates love and affection
	Asian—nonverbal, indirect, suppressive; communicates love and affection by fulfilling obligations and tending to needs
Physician–Patient Relationship	*American*—equality; contractual agreements; physician professional and competent; patient participates in decision making
	Asian—hierarchical; mutual obligations; physician virtuous and concerned; patient defers to physician's authority
Meanings of Life, Illness, and Death	*American*—life is happiness and under one's control; illness and death indicate failure and must be fought
	Asian—life is suffering and uncontrollable; illness and death indicate normal bad luck, or they are the result of past deeds and are unavoidable

(*Source:* Based on information from Nilchaikovit, Hill, & Holland, 1993.)

that the young woman needed to distance herself from her family in order to gain independence and control. The Asian disagreed, indicating that the patient wanted even *more* involvement with her family; indeed, it was suggested that her depressed symptoms developed because the hospital staff failed to understand what was involved in effective health care in a culture unlike their own. The attempts of these two practitioners to understand why their perceptions and recommendations differed led them to explore cultural differences in (1) aspects of the self-concept, (2) the effects of self-concept on communication and interpersonal behavior, and (3) how very different worldviews affect how an individual responds to illness and to medical care.

Nilchaikovit, Hill, and Holland (1993) suggest that Eastern and Western concepts of self constitute the basic reasons for different responses to a medical setting. Each of us acquires our self-concept within the context of our family, and our culture plays a central role in determining how the self is defined. As described in several earlier discussions of cross-cultural comparisons, the central contrast is between a society's emphasis on collectivism versus individualism. In Asian countries, for example, the self tends to be conceived as interdependent and centered on family so that the individual is part of an inter-connected group. In many Western nations, such as the United States, the self is usually conceived as independent, and there is a sharp distinction between "I" or "me" and other people. Americans and Asians typically differ in the way they conceptualize family and the individual's role in that group. Americans tend to define family in terms of those now living, and the husband and wife constitute the core relationship. This small unit is financially independent; the family is oriented toward feelings; and the overall goal is individual happiness. In contrast, Asians tend to define family in terms of past, present, and future generations, and the core relationship is parent–child. In addition, people have an economic obligation to all of their relatives; they are task-oriented; and the overall goal is the welfare of the family.

Some of the factors identified as different for Americans and Asians are outlined in Table 14.1. As summarized in the table, these different self-perceptions lead to different communication styles and different ways of expressing emotion, differences in the relationship between a patient and a physician, and quite different perceptions of the meanings of illness and death.

Nilchaikovit and his colleagues (1993) also point out specific ways in which Asian–American differences influence health-related behavior. One example is suicide.

An American may take his or her own life, but the decision is made by the individual. On this topic, an Asian woman expressed her collective sense of the self:

> "Your life is not yours as many people like to think. You cannot grow up without the help of others, your family, your friends, the society, and many others. You owe your life to others and you cannot take it away without affecting and hurting other people. Thus you have no right to take your own life without the consent of the others involved." (p. 42)

The most general conclusion to be drawn from this type of research is that a physician must understand how a patient views herself or himself, what the patient is communicating, how the individual conceptualizes illness, and what kind of patient–physician relationship is considered appropriate. Such understanding and sensitivity are extremely important in diverse cultures—such as Canada and the United States—where patient and physician very often come from different cultural backgrounds. ■ ■ ■

CONNECTIONS: Integrating Social Psychology

In this chapter, you read about . . .	In other chapters, you will find related discussions of . . .
processing health-related information	use of the availability heuristic and the resulting distortions (Chapter 3) and persuasive appeals (Chapter 4)
self-efficacy in responding to stress	the general effects of self-efficacy (Chapter 5)
self-healing personality	the altruistic personality, which has many similar characteristics (Chapter 10)
hostile Type A behavior as a health risk	Type A behavior and aggression (Chapter 11)
the negative affect caused by thinking about alternatives to stressful events	counterfactual thinking (Chapter 3)
seeking social support as a coping strategy	the importance of affiliation (Chapter 7) and the effects of loneliness (Chapter 8)
attachment style as a determinant of social support behavior	attachment style in interpersonal relationships (Chapter 8)
the effects of the wording of information leading to health-related decisions	framing (Chapter 12)
the effects of external factors on attending to symptoms	priming (Chapter 3)
interpreting the meaning of a physical symptom	attribution processes (Chapter 2)
nonverbal cues given by physicians	nonverbal communication (Chapter 2)
effects of mood on perceptions of pain	affect, cognition, and feelings (Chapter 3 and Chapter 7)
environmental effects on mood and interpersonal behavior	affect and attraction (Chapter 7)
heat and aggression	determinants of aggression (Chapter 11)

Thinking about Connections

1. In the past few years you have probably experienced at least one stressful situation. How did you respond? Did you seek social support from anyone, or did you feel that you would rather handle the problem by yourself? List any parallels you see between your use (or nonuse) of social support and how you see yourself with respect to affiliation need (Chapter 7) and your opinion about your attachment style (Chapter 8).

2. Think about your most recent experience with illness. When did you first notice any symptoms, and do you believe that priming factors (Chapter 12) were involved? What attributions did you make about the symptoms (Chapter 2)? Did you decide to treat yourself or to depend on professional help? Why?

3. List any aspects of your environment that have positive or negative effects on your emotional state. Can you think of incidents in which the way you responded to other people was influenced by

the affect you were experiencing (Chapters 7, 10, and 11)? Assuming that you prefer positive to negative affect, what might you do to change your personal environment so as to produce more pleasant feelings?

4. What, if anything, should be done to control population growth? This is a very controversial issue, and there is obviously no consensus as to a "right" answer. Try to think about the consequences of your position. If you believe that overpopulation is not a problem, how would you deal with such consequences as increasing amounts of human waste and a decreasing share per person of land, water, and other resources? If you believe that overpopulation is a problem, what would you do to change the parenting practices of people throughout the world? What techniques of persuasion (Chapter 4) or social influence (Chapter 9) would you employ in attempting to change attitudes, beliefs, and behaviors?

Summary and Review

Among the many applications of social psychology are those that concentrate on the interaction between psychological processes and (1) the physical aspects of health and illness and (2) the physical environment.

Maintaining a Healthy State and Coping with Illness

Health psychology is concerned with the effect of emotions, cognitions, and behavior on preventing physical illness, maintaining good health, and responding to medical problems. An important topic is how we process relevant health information—and sometimes reject it because it is perceived as threatening. A great deal of research has dealt with the effects of *stress* on susceptibility to illness and with the personality factors that make some individuals better than others at *coping* with physical and psychological threats. Beyond dispositional variables, coping with stress is aided by being physically fit, maintaining high levels of *positive affect*, and receiving *social support*. When a health problem arises, the individual must make a series of critical choices and decisions—noticing and interpret-

ing the symptoms, deciding what action to take, and coping with medical procedures.

Environmental Psychology

Environmental psychology is the field that deals with the interaction between the physical world and human behavior. Among the many environmental factors that influence one's emotional state, ability to work effectively, interpersonal behavior, and health are *perceived technological threats, noise, heat and humidity, polluted air,* and *atmospheric electricity.* The negative effects of humans on the physical environment are based in part on the rapid growth of population—the greater the number of people on the planet, the greater the effects of their actions on the world around them. Attention has been focused on such issues as the creation of *waste* material, alterations of the world's *climate,* and the disruption of isolated habitats that results in the spread of *new diseases.* In each instance, there are steps than can be and have been taken by individuals and by governments to halt the destructive behavior and to repair the damage.

Social Diversity: Differences between Asians and Americans in Responding to Illness

Differences between Asian and American patients in medical settings led to an examination of the way self-concept is shaped by cultural factors. In Asian countries, the self-concept is tied to other people and centered on one's extended family. In the United States and other Western societies, the self-concept is individualistic and independent. Among the consequences are very different ways of expressing emotions and communicating with others, and doctor–patient relationships differ as a result. Another difference is the American belief that life should involve happiness and be controllable; illness and death constitute failure and must be fought. In contrast, a typical Asian belief is that life involves suffering and is beyond one's control; illness and death are the normal result of bad luck or of your past deeds, and they must be accepted.

■ Key Terms

Coping (p. 527)

Disease-Prone Personality (p. 528)

Environmental Psychology (p. 541)

Framing (p. 539)

Global Warming (p. 551)

Greenhouse Effect (p. 551)

Hardiness (p. 531)

Health Psychology (p. 520)

Noise (p. 543)

Self-Healing Personality (p. 528)

Social Support (p. 533)

Stress (p. 527)

■ For More Information

Preston, R. (1994). *The hot zone*. New York: Random House.

This is the book that first made the general public aware of the existence of the Ebola virus and its horrendous effects. When the disease first struck in Zaire and Sudan in 1976, 600 people died—90 percent of those who were infected. Only when it broke out again in 1989 in an American laboratory housing African monkeys did scientists begin to speculate about the origins of this deadly killer and about the potential danger that it could spread beyond Africa. Though Preston's account reads like a science fiction thriller, it is based on a real threat that has yet to be conquered.

Radley, A. (1994). *Making sense of illness: The social psychology of health and disease*. Thousand Oaks, CA: Sage.

This book cuts across the fields of health psychology, sociology, and medicine to describe the importance of psychological factors that influence response to stress, ways of coping with acute and chronic health problems, and behavior that helps promote good health and prevent disease.

Worster, D. (1993). *The wealth of nature: Environmental history and the ecological imagination*. Oxford, England: Oxford University Press.

Traces the truly revolutionary change in the public's perception of the environment that began to occur only very recently. Before the twentieth century, it was generally assumed that people could do whatever they liked with our physical world. The earth's resources were there to be used for any purpose we desired and then discarded when we were through. Worster outlines the history of the growing awareness of the importance of caring for the environment and not destroying it—from John Muir and the Sierra Club to today's worldwide concern with environmental issues that were once literally inconceivable.

REFERENCES

Abbey, A. (1982). Sex differences in attributes for friendly behavior: Do males misperceive females' friendliness? *Journal of Personality and Social Behavior, 42,* 830–838.

Abramson, J. (1994). *We, the jury.* New York: Basic Books.

Adams, J. S. (1965). Inequity in social exchange. In L. Berkowitz (Ed.), *Advances in experimental social psychology* (Vol. 2, pp. 267–299). New York: Academic Press.

Adams, R. G., & Blieszner, R. (1994). An integrative conceptual framework for friendship research. *Journal of Social and Personal Relationships, 11,* 163–184.

Ader, R., & Cohen, N. (1993). Psychoneuroimmunology: Conditioning and stress. *Annual Review of Psychology, 44,* 53–85.

Adler, S. J. (1994). *The jury.* New York: Times Books.

Adorno, T. W., Frenkel-Brunswick E., Levinson, D. J., & Sanford, R. N. (1950). *The authoritarian personality.* New York: Harper & Row.

Affleck, G., Tennen, H., Pfeiffer, C., & Fifield, J. (1987). Appraisals of control and predictability in adapting to a chronic disease. *Journal of Personality and Social Psychology, 53,* 273–279.

Agnew, C. R., & Thompson, V. D. (1994). Causal inferences and responsibility attributions concerning an HIV-positive target: The double-edged sword of physical attractiveness. *Journal of Social Behavior and Personality, 9,* 181–190.

Aguinis, H., Pierce, C. A., & Quigley, B. M. (1995). Enhancing the validity of self-reported alcohol and marijuana consumption using a bogus pipeline procedure: A meta-analytic review. *Basic and Applied Social Psychology, 16,* 515–527.

Aguinis, H., Pierce, C. A., & Quigley, B. M. (1993). Conditions under which a bogus pipeline procedure enhances the validity of self-reported cigarette smoking: A meta-analytic review. *Journal of Applied Social Psychology, 23,* 352–373.

Ainsworth, M. D. S., Blehar, M. C., Waters, E., & Wall, S. (1978). *Patterns of attachment.* Hillsdale, NJ: Erlbaum.

Ajzen, I., & Fishbein, M. (1980). *Understanding attitudes and predicting social behavior.* Englewood Cliffs, NJ: Prentice-Hall.

Ajzen, I., Timko, C., & White, J. B. (1982). Self-monitoring and the attitude–behavior relation. *Journal of Personality and Social Psychology, 52,* 426–435.

Alagna, F. J., Whitcher, S. J., & Fisher, J. D. (1979). Evaluative reactions to interpersonal touch in a counseling interview. *Journal of Counseling Psychology, 26,* 465–472.

Albright, L., Kenny, D. A., & Malloy, T. E. (1988). Consensus in personality judgments at zero acquaintance. *Journal of Personality and Social Psychology, 55,* 387–395.

Alden, L. (1986). Self-efficacy and causal attributions for social feedback. *Journal of Research in Personality, 20,* 460–473.

Alexander, M. J., & Higgins, E. T. (1993). Emotional trade-offs of becoming a parent: How social roles influence self-discrepancy effects. *Journal of Personality and Social Psychology, 65,* 1259–1269.

Alicke, M. D. (1994). Evidential and extra-evidential evaluations of social conduct. *Journal of Social Behavior and Personality, 9,* 591–615.

Alicke, M. D., & Largo, E. (1995). The role of the self in the false consensus effect. *Journal of Experimental Social Psychology, 31,* 28–47.

Alicke, M. D., Braun, J. C., Glor, J. E., Klotz, M. L., Magee, J., Sederhold, H., & Siegel, R. (1992). Complaining behavior in social interaction. *Personality and Social Psychology Bulletin, 18,* 286–295.

Allgeier, E. R., & Wiederman, M. W. (1994). How useful is evolutionary psychology for understanding contemporary human sexual behavior? Annual Review of Sex Research, 5, 218–256.

Alliger, G. M., & Williams, K. J. (1991). Affective congruence and the employment interview. *Advances in Information Processing in Organizations, 4,* 31–43.

Allison, S. T., Worth, L. T., & King, M. C. (1990). Group decisions as social inference heuristics. *Journal of Personality and Social Psychology, 58,* 801–811.

Alloy, L. B., Abramson, L. Y., & Dykman, B. M. (1990). Depressive realities and nondepressive optimistic illusions: The role of the self. In R. E. Ingram (Ed.), *Contemporary psychological approaches to depression: Treatment, research and theory.* New York: Plenum Press.

Allport, F. H. (1920). The influence of the group upon association and thought. *Journal of Experimental Psychology, 3,* 159–182.

Allport, F. H. (1924). *Social psychology.* Boston: Houghton Mifflin.

Allport, G. W. (1985). Attitudes. In C. Murchison (Ed.), *Handbook of social psychology.* Worcester, MA: Clark University Press.

Allyn, J., & Festinger, L. (1961). The effectiveness of unanticipated persuasive communications. *Journal of Abnormal and Social Psychology, 62,* 35–40.

Altheide, D. L., Adler, P. A., Adler, P., & Altheide, D. A. (1978). The social meanings of employee theft. In J. M. Johnson & J. D. Douglas (Eds.), *Crime at the tip: Deviance in business and the professions* (pp. 90–124). Philadelphia: J. B. Lippincott.

Amason, A. C. (1996). Distinguishing the effects for functional and dysfunctional conflict on strategic decision making: Resolving a paradox for top management teams. *Academy of Management Journal, 39,* 123–148.

Amato, P. R. (1986). Emotional arousal and helping behavior in a real-life emergency. *Journal of Applied Social Psychology, 16,* 633–641.

Ambuel, B. (1995). Adolescents, unintended pregnancy, and abortion: The struggle for a compassionate social policy. *Current Directions in Psychological Science, 4,* 1–5.

Amirkhan, J. H., Risinger, R. T., & Swickert, R. J. (1995). Extraversion: A "hidden" personality factor in coping? *Journal of Personality, 63,* 189–212.

Andersen, B. L., & Cyranowski, J. M. (1994). Women's sexual self-schema. *Journal of Personality and Social Psychology, 67,* 1079–1100.

Andersen, S. M., & Baum, A. (1994). Transference in interpersonal relations: Inferences and affect based on significant-other representations. *Journal of Personality, 62,* 459–497.

Anderson, C. A. (1987). Temperature and aggression: Effects on quarterly, yearly, and city rates of violent and nonviolent crime. *Journal of Personality and Social Psychology, 46,* 91–97.

Anderson, C. A. (1989). Temperature and aggression: The ubiquitous effects of heat on the occurrence of human violence. *Psychological Bulletin, 106,* 74–96.

Anderson, C. A., & Anderson, D. C. (1984). Ambient temperature and violent crime: Tests of the linear and curvilinear hypotheses. *Journal of Personality and Social Psychology, 46,* 91–97.

Anderson, C. A., & DeNeve, K. M. (1992). Temperature, aggression, and the negative affect escape model. *Psychological Bulletin, 111,* 347–351.

Anderson, C. A., Anderson, K. B., & Deuser, W. E. (1995). Hot temperatures, hostile affect, hostile cognition, and arousal: Test of a general model of affective aggression. *Personality and Social Psychology Bulletin, 21,* 434–448.

Anderson, C. A., Anderson, K. B., & Deuser, W. E. (in press). A general framework for the study of affective aggression: Tests of effects of extreme temperatures and of viewing weapons on hostility. *Personality and Social Psychology Bulletin.*

Anderson, C. A., Deuser, W. E., & DeNeve K. M. (1995). Hot temperatures, hostile affect, hostile cognition, and arousal: Tests of a general model of affective aggression. *Personality and Social Psychology Bulletin, 21,* 434–448.

Anderson, N. H. (1981). *Foundations of information integration theory.* New York: Academic Press.

Anderson, P. B., & Aymami, R. (1993). Reports of female initiation of sexual contact: Male and female differences. *Archives of Sexual Behavior, 22,* 335–343.

Anderson, V. L. (1993). Gender differences in altruism among holocaust rescuers. *Journal of Social Behavior and Personality, 8,* 43–58.

Angier, N. (1993, February 2). Cellular phone scare discounted. *New York Times,* pp. C1, C3.

Angier, N. (1994, November 29). Redefining diversity: Biologists urge look beyond rain forests. *New York Times,* pp. C1, C6.

Anthony, T., Cooper, C., & Mullen, B. (1992). Cross-racial identification: A social cognitive integration. *Personality and Social Psychology Bulletin, 18,* 296–301.

Archer, J. (1991). Human sociobiology: Basic concepts and limitations. *Journal of Social Issues, 47*(3), 11–26.

Archibald, F. S., Bartholomew, K., & Marx, R. (1995). Loneliness in early adolescence: A test of the cognitive discrepancy model of loneliness. *Personality and Social Psychology Bulletin, 21,* 296–301.

Ardrey, R. (1976). *The hunting hypothesis.* New York: Atheneum.

Argyle, M. (1988). *Bodily communication.* New York: Methuen.

Aron, A., & Henkemeyer, L. (1995). Marital satisfaction and passionate love. *Journal of Social and Personal Relationships, 12,* 139–146.

Aron, A., Dutton, D. G., Aron, E. N., & Iverson, A. (1989). Experiences of falling in love. *Journal of Social and Personal Relationships, 6,* 243–257.

Aronoff, J., Woike, B. A., & Hyman, L. M. (1992). Which are the stimuli in facial displays of anger and happiness? Configurational bases of emotion recognition. *Journal of Personality and Social Psychology, 62,* 1050–1066.

Aronson, E. (1992). The return of the repressed: Dissonance theory makes a comeback. *Psychological Inquiry, 3*(4), 303–311.

Aronson, E., Bridgeman, D. L., & Geffner, R. (1978). Interdependent interactions and prosocial behavior. *Journal of Research and Development in Education, 12,* 16–27.

Aronson, E., Fried, C., & Stone, J. (1991) Overcoming denial: Increasing the intention to use condoms through the induction of hypocrisy. *American Journal of Public Health, 18,* 1636–1640.

Arvey, R. D., Bhagat, R. S., & Salas, E. (1991). Cross-cultural and cross-national issues in personnel and human resources management: Where do we go from here? In G. R. Ferris & K. M. Rowland (Eds.), *Research in personnel and human resources management* (Vol. 9, pp. 367–407). Greenwich, CT: JAI Press.

Arvey, R. D., Bouchard, T. J. Jr., Segal, N. L., & Abraham, L. M. (1989). Job satisfaction: Genetic and environmental components. *Journal of Applied Psychology, 74,* 187–192.

Asch, S. (1946). Forming impressions of personality. *Journal of Abnormal and Social Psychology, 41,* 258–290.

Asch, S. E. (1951). Effects of group pressure upon the modification and distortion of judgment. In H. Guetzkow (Ed.), *Groups, leadership, and men.* Pittsburgh: Carnegie.

Asch, S. E. (1955). Opinions and social pressure. *Scientific American, 193*(5), 31–35.

Asch, S. E. (1956). Studies of independence and conformity: A minority of one against unanimous majority. *Psychological Monographs, 70* (Whole No. 416).

Asendorpf, J. B. (1989). Shyness as a final common pathway for two different kinds of inhibition. *Journal of Personality and Social Psychology, 57,* 481–492.

Asendorpf, J. B. (1992). A Brunswickean approach to trait continuity: Application to shyness. *Journal of Personality, 60,* 55–77.

Aube, J., & Koestner, R. (1992). Gender characteristics and adjustment: A longitudinal study. *Journal of Personality and Social Psychology, 63,* 485–493.

Aube, J., Norcliffe, H., Craig, J.-A., & Koestner, R. (1995). Gender characteristics and adjustment-related outcomes: Questioning the masculinity model. *Personality and Social Psychology Bulletin, 21,* 284–295.

Aube, J., Norcliffe, H., & Koestner, R. (1995). Physical characteristics and the multifactorial approach to the study of gender characteristics. *Social Behavior and Personality, 23,* 69–82.

Aune, R. K., & Basil, M. C. (1994). A relational obligations approach to the foot-in-the-mouth effect. *Journal of Applied Social Psychology, 24,* 546–556.

Averill, J. R., & Boothroyd, P. (1977). On falling in love: Conformance with romantic ideal. *Motivation and Emotion, 1,* 235–247.

Azjen, I. (1987). Attitudes, traits, and actions: Dispositional prediction of behavior in personality and social psychology. In L. Berkowitz (Ed.), *Advances in experimental social psychology* (Vol. 20). San Diego, CA: Academic Press.

BNA's *Employee Relations Weekly.* (1994, April 6). Survey finds 31 percent of women report having been harrassed at work. pp. 111–112.

Bachrach, R. S. (1986). The differential effect of observation of violence on kibbutz and city children in Isreal. In L. R. Huesmann & L. D. Eron (Eds.), *Television and the aggressive child: A cross-national comparison* (pp. 201–238). Hillsdale, NJ: Erlbaum.

Bailey, J. M., Gaulin, S., Agyei, Y., & Gladue, B. A. (1994). Effects of gender and sexual orientation on evolutionarily relevant aspects of human mating psychology. *Journal of Personality and Social Psychology, 66,* 1081–1093.

Bailey, R. C., & Czuchry, M. (1994). Psychological kinship fulfillment and dating attraction. *Social Behavior and Personality, 22,* 157–162.

Baker, S. M., & Petty, R. E. (1994). Majority and minority influence: Source–position imbalance as a determinant of message scrutiny. *Journal of Personality and Social Psychology, 67,* 5–19.

Baldwin, M. W. (1992). Relational schemas and the processing of social information. *Psychological Bulletin, 112,* 461–484.

Bandura, A. (1973). *Aggression: A social learning analysis.* Englewood Cliffs, NJ: Prentice-Hall.

Bandura, A. (1977). Self-efficacy: Toward a unifying theory of behavior change. *Psychological Review, 84,* 191–215.

Bandura, A. (1986a). The explanatory and predictive scope of self-efficacy theory. *Journal of Social and Clinical Psychology, 4,* 359–373.

Bandura, A. (1986b). *Social foundations of thought and action: A social cognitive view.* Englewood Cliffs, NJ: Prentice-Hall.

Bandura, A. (1993). Self-efficacy mechanisms in psychobiological functioning. *Stanford University Psychologist, 1,* 5–6.

Bandura, A., & Adams, N. E. (1977). Analysis of self-efficacy theory of behavioral change. *Cognitive Therapy and Research, 1,* 287–310.

Bandura, A., Adams, N. E., & Hardy, A. B. (1980). Tests of the generality of self-efficacy theory. *Cognitive Therapy and Research, 4,* 39–66.

Bandura, A., Cioffi, D., Taylor, C. B., & Brouillard, M. E. (1988). Perceived self-efficacy in coping with cognitive stressors and opioid activation. *Journal of Personality and Social Psychology, 55,* 479–488.

Bandura, A., Ross, D., & Ross, S. (1963). Imitation of film-mediated aggressive models. *Journal of Abnormal and Social Psychology, 66,* 3–11.

Bar-Tal, Y., & Spitzer, A. (1994). Coping use versus effectiveness as moderating the stress–strain relationship. *Journal of Community and Applied Social Psychology, 4,* 91–100.

Barbee, A. P., Cunningham, M. R., Winstead, B. A., Derlega, V. J., Gulley, M. R., Yankeelov, P. A., & Druen, P. B. (1993). Effects of gender role expectations on the social support process. *Journal of Social Issues, 49*(3), 175–190.

Bardach, A. L. (1995, June 5). The white cloud. *New Republic,* 27–28, 30–31.

Bardach, L., & Park, B. (1996). The effect of in-group/out-group status on memory for consistent and inconsistent behavior of an individual. *Personality and Social Psychology bulletin, 22,* 169–178.

Bargh, J. A. (1995, August). *Before you know it: The preconscious of everyday life.* Paper presented at the meeting of the American Psychological Association, New York.

Bargh, J. A., & Pietromonaco, P. (1982). Automatic information processing and social perception: The influence of trait information presented outside of conscious awareness on impression formation. *Journal of Personality and Social Psychology, 43,* 437–449.

Bargh, J. A., Chaiken, S., Govender, R., & Pratto, F. (1992). The generality of the automatic attitude activation effect. *Journal of Personality and Social Psychology, 62,* 893–912.

Barkow, J. H. (1989). *Darwin, sex, and status.* Toronto: University of Toronto Press.

Barnett, R. C., Marshall, N. L., Raudenbush, S. W., & Brennan, R. T. (1993). Gender and the relationship between job experiences and psychological distress: A study of dual-earner couples. *Journal of Personality and Social Psychology, 64,* 794–806.

Baron, R. A. (1971). Magnitude of victim's pain cues and level of prior anger arousal as determinants of adult aggressive behavior. *Journal of Personality and Social Psychology, 17,* 236–243.

Baron, R. A. (1972). Reducing the influence of an aggressive model: The restraining effects of peer censure. *Journal of Experimental Social Psychology, 8,* 266–275.

Baron, R. A. (1973). The "foot-in-the-door" phenomenon: Mediating effects of size of first request and sex of requester. *Bulletin of the Psychonomic Society, 2,* 113–114.

Baron, R. A. (1974). The aggression-inhibiting influence of heightened sexual arousal. *Journal of Personality and Social Psychology, 30,* 318–322.

Baron, R. A. (1976). The reduction of human aggression: A field study of the influence of incompatible responses. *Journal of Applied Social Psychology, 6,* 95–104.

Baron, R. A. (1977). *Human aggression.* New York: Plenum.

Baron, R. A. (1978). Aggression and heat: The "long hot summer" revisited. In A. Baum, S. Valins, & J. E. Singer (Eds.), *Advances in environmental research* (Vol. 1). Hillsdale, NJ: Erlbaum.

Baron, R. A. (1979). Aggression, empathy, and race: Effects of victim's pain cues, victim's race, and level of instigation on physical aggression. *Journal of Applied Social Psychology, 9,* 103–114.

Baron, R. A. (1981). The "costs of deception" revisited: An openly optimistic rejoinder. *IRB: A Review of Human Subjects Research, 3,* 8–10.

Baron, R. A. (1983). The "sweet smell of success"? The impact of pleasant artificial scents (perfume or cologne) on evaluations of job applicants. *Journal of Applied Psychology, 68,* 709–713.

Baron, R. A. (1983). The control of human aggression: An optimistic perspective. *Journal of Social and Clinical Psychology, 1,* 97–119.

Baron, R. A. (1984). Reducing organizational conflict: An incompatible response approach. *Journal of Applied Psychology, 69,* 272–279.

Baron, R. A. (1986). Self-presentation in job interviews: When there can be "too much of a good thing." *Journal of Applied Social Psychology, 16,* 16–28.

Baron, R. A. (1987). Interviewers' moods and reactions to job applicants: The influence of affective states on applied social judgments. *Journal of Applied Social Psychology, 16,* 16–28.

Baron, R. A. (1987a). Effects of negative ions on cognitive performance. *Journal of Applied Psychology, 72,* 131–137.

Baron, R. A. (1987b). Effects of negative air ions on interpersonal attraction: Evidence for intensification. *Journal of Personality and Social Psychology, 52,* 547–553.

Baron, R. A. (1988). Attributions and organizational conflict: The mediating role of apparent sincerity. *Organizational Behavior and Human Decision Processes, 41,* 111–127.

Baron, R. A. (1988). Negative effects of destructive criticism: Impact on conflict, self-efficacy, and task performance. *Journal of Applied Psychology, 73,* 199–207.

Baron, R. A. (1989). Applicant strategies during job interviews. In G. R. Ferris & R. W. Eder (Eds.), *The employment interview: Theory, research, and practice* (pp. 204–216). Newbury Park, CA: Sage.

Baron, R. A. (1989). Personality and organizational conflict: The Type A behavior pattern and self-monitoring. *Organizational Behavior and Human Decision Processes, 44,* 281–297.

Baron, R. A. (1990). Attributions and organizational conflict. In S. Graha & V. Folkes (Eds.), *Attribution theory: Applications to achievement, mental health, and interpersonal conflict* (pp. 185–204). Hillsdale, NJ: Erlbaum.

Baron, R. A. (1990). Environmentally induced positive affect: Its impact on self-efficacy, task performance, negotiation, and conflict. *Journal of Applied Social Psychology, 20,* 368–384.

Baron, R. A. (1993). Effects of interviewers' moods and applicant qualifications on ratings of job applicants. *Journal of Applied Social Psychology, 23,* 254–271.

Baron, R. A. (1993). Reducing aggression and conflict: The incompatible response approach, or why people who feel good usually won't be bad. In G. C. Brannigan & M. R. Merrens (Eds.), *The undaunted psychologist* (pp. 203–218). Philadelphia: Temple University Press.

Baron, R. A. (1993a). Effects of interviewers' moods and applicant qualifications on ratings of job applicants. *Journal of Applied Social Psychology, 23,* 254–271.

Baron, R. A. (1993b). Criticism (informal negative feedback) as a source of perceived unfairness in organizations: Effects, mechanisms, and countermeasures. In R. Cropanzano (Ed.), *Justice in the workplace: Approaching fairness in human resource management* (pp. 155–170). Hillsdale, NJ: Erlbaum.

Baron, R. A. (1994). The physical environment of work settings: Effects of task performance, interpersonal relations, and job satisfaction. In M. Staw & L. L. Cummings (Eds.), *Research in organizational behavior* (Vol. 16, pp. 1–46). Greenwich, CT: JAI Press.

Baron, R. A. (1995). The sweet smell of . . . helping: Effects of pleasant ambient odors on prosocial behavior in shopping malls. Manuscript submitted for publication.

Baron, R. A. (1995b). *Workplace violence and workplace aggression: Insights and integrations from basic research.* Paper presented at the Meetings of the Academy of Management, Vancouver, British Columbia.

Baron, R. A. (1996). The sweet smell of . . . helping: Effects of pleasant ambient odors on helping in a shopping mall. Manuscript submitted for publication.

Baron, R. A. (in press). Positive effects of conflict: A cognitive perspective. In C. K. W. deDreu & V. deVliert (Eds.), *Conflict escalation and organization performance.* Thousand Oaks, CA: Sage.

Baron, R. A., & Bell, P. A. (1973). Effects of heightened sexual arousal on physical aggression. *Proceedings of the American Psychological Association, 81st Annual Convention,* 171–172.

Baron, R. A., & Bell, P. A. (1976). Aggression and heat: The influence of ambient temperature, negative affect, and a cooling drink on physical aggression. *Journal of Personality and Social Psychology, 33,* 245–255.

Baron, R. A., & Bronfen, M. I. (1994). A whiff of reality: Empirical evidence concerning the effects of pleasant fragrances on work-related behavior. *Journal of Applied Social Psychology, 23,* 1179–1203.

Baron, R. A., & Neuman, J. H. (in press). Workplace violence and workplace aggression: Evidence on their relative frequency and potential causes. *Aggressive Behavior.*

Baron, R. A., & Richardson, D. R. (1994) *Human Aggression* (2nd ed.). New York: Plenum.

Baron, R. A., & Thomley, J. (1994). A whiff of reality: Positive affect as a potential mediator of the effects of pleasant fragrances on task performance and helping. *Environment and Behavior, 26,* 766–784.

Baron, R. A., & Thomley, J. E. (1992). Positive affect as a potential mediator of the effects of pleasant fragrances on task performance and helping. *Environment and Behavior, 26,* 766–784.

Baron, R. A., Russell, G. W., & Arms, R. L. (1985). Negative ions and behavior: Impact on mood, memory, and aggression among Type A and Type B persons. *Journal of Personality and Social Psychology, 48,* 746–754.

Baron, R. S. (1986). Distraction–conflict theory: Progress and problems. In L. Berkowitz (Ed.), *Advances in experimental social psychology* (Vol. 20). New York: Academic Press.

Baron, R. S., & Logan, H. (1993). Desired control, felt control, and dental pain: Recent findings and remaining issues. *Motivation and Emotion, 17,* 181–204.

Baron, R. S., Moore, D., & Sanders, G. S. (1978). Distraction as a source of drive in social facilitation research. *Journal of Personality and Social Psychology, 36,* 816–824.

Barrick, M. R., & Mount, K. (1993). Autonomy as a moderator of the relationships between the Big Five personality dimensions and job performance. *Journal of Applied Psychology, 78,* 111–118.

Barringer, F. (1993, April 1). 1 in 5 in U.S. have sexually caused viral disease. *New York Times,* pp. A1, B9.

Bartholomew, K. (1990). Avoidance of intimacy: An attachment perspective. *Journal of Social and Personal Relationships, 7,* 147–178.

Bartholomew, K., & Horowitz, L. M. (1991). Attachment styles among young adults: A test of a four category model. *Journal of Personality and Social Psychology, 61,* 226–244.

Bass, B. M. (1990). *Bass and Stogdill's handbook of leadership* (3rd ed.). New York: Free Press.

Basso, M. R., Schefft, B. K., & Freedman, R. (1994). Interpersonal control and health complaints in the context of the Type A behavior pattern. *Journal of Social Behavior and Personality, 9,* 811–822.

Bat-Chava, Y. (1994). Group identification and self-esteem of deaf adults. *Personality of Social Psychology Bulletin, 20,* 494–502.

Batista, S. M., & Berte, R. (1992). Maternal behavior and feminine work: Study with Belgian mothers with infants. *Interamerican Journal of Psychology, 26,* 143–157.

Batson, C. D., & Oleson, K. C. (1991). Current status of the empathy–altruism hypothesis. In M. S. Clark (Ed.), *Prosocial behavior* (pp. 62–85). Newbury Park, CA: Sage.

Batson, C. D., Batson, J. G., Todd, R. M., Brummett, B. H., Shaw, L. L., & Aldeguer, C. M. R. (1995). Empathy and the collective good: Caring for one of the others in a social dilemma. *Journal of Personality and Social Psychology, 68,* 619–631.

Batson, C. D., Duncan, B. D., Ackerman, P., Buckley, T., & Birch, K. (1981). Is empathic emotion a source of altruistic motivation? *Journal of Personality and Social Psychology, 40,* 290–302.

Batson, C. D., Klein, T. R., Highberger, L., & Shaw, L. L. (1995). Immorality from empathy-induced altruism: When compassion and justice conflict. *Journal of Personality and Social Psychology, 68,* 1042–1054.

Batson, C. D., O'Quin, K., Fultz, J., Vanderplas, M., & Isen, A. M. (1983). Influence of self-reported distress and empathy on egoistic versus altruistic motivation to help. *Journal of Personality and Social Psychology, 45,* 706–718.

Batson, C. D., Turk, C. L., Shaw, L. L., & Klein, T. R. (1995). Information function of empathic emotion: Learning that we value the other's welfare. *Journal of Personality and Social Psychology, 68,* 300–313.

Baum, A., & Temoshok, L. (1990). Psychosocial aspects of the acquired immunodeficiency syndrome. In L. Temoshok & A. Baum (Eds.), *Psychological perspectives on AIDS: Etiology, prevention, and treatment* (pp. 1–16). Hillsdale, NJ: Erlbaum.

Baumeister, R. F. (1994). Introductions to symposium. *Personality and Social Psychology Bulletin, 20,* 640.

Baumeister, R. F., Chesner, S. P., Sanders, P. S., & Tice, D. M. (1988). Who's in charge here? Group leaders do lend help in emergencies. *Personality and Social Psychology Bulletin, 14,* 17–22.

Baumeister, R. F., Stillwell, A., & Wotman, S. R. (1990). Victim and perpetrator accounts of interpersonal conflict: Autobiographical narratives about anger. *Journal of Personality and Social Psychology, 59,* 994–1003.

Baumeister, R. F., Wotman, S. R., & Stillwell, A. M. (1993). Unrequited love: On heartbreak, anger, guilt, scriptlessness, and humiliation. *Journal of Personality and Social Psychology, 64,* 377–394.

Baumrind, D. (1979). The costs of deception. *IRB: A Review of Human Subjects Research, 6,* 1–4.

Baumrind, D. (1985). Research using intentional deception: Ethical issues revisited. *American Psychologist, 40,* 165–174.

Baxter, D. J., Marshall, W. L., Barbaree, H. E., Davidson, P. R., & Malcolm, P. B. (1984). Deviant sexual behavior: Differentiating sex offenders by criminal and personality history, psychometric measures, and sexual responses. *Criminal Justice and Behavior, 11,* 477–501.

Baxter, L. A. (1990). Dialectical contradictions in relationship development. *Journal of Social and Personal Relationships, 7,* 69–88.

Beall, A. E., & Sternberg, R. J. (1995). The social construction of love. *Journal of Social and Personal Relationships, 12,* 417–438.

Beaman, A. L. (1991). An empirical comparison of meta-analytic and traditional reviews. *Personality and Social Psychology Bulletin, 17,* 252–257.

Beaman, A. L., Cole, M., Preston, M., Klentz, B., & Steblay, N. M. (1983). Fifteen years of the foot-in-the-door research: A meta-analysis. *Personality and Social Psychology Bulletin, 9,* 181–186.

Becker, G., & Becker, C. (1994). The maternal behavior inventory: Measuring the behavioral side of mother-to-infant attachment. *Social Behavior and Personality, 22,* 177–194.

Beckwith, J. B. (1994). Terminology and social relevance in psychological research on gender. *Social Behavior and Personality, 22,* 329–336.

Bell, B. (1991). Loneliness and values. *Journal of Social Behavior and Personality, 6,* 771–778.

Bell, B. (1993). Emotional loneliness and the perceived similarity of one's ideas and interests. *Journal of Social Behavior and Personality, 8,* 273–280.

Bell, B. E., & Loftus, E. F. (1988). Degree of detail of eyewitness testimony and mock juror judgments. *Journal of Applied Social Psychology, 18,* 1171–1192.

Bell, P. A. (1992). In defense of the negative affect escape model of heat and aggression. *Psychological Bulletin, 111,* 342–346.

Bell, P. A., & Fusco, M. E. (1986). Linear and curvilinear relationships between temperature, affect, and violence: Reply to Cotton. *Journal of Social Psychology, 16,* 802–807.

Bell, P. A., & Fusco, M. E. (1990). Heat and violence in the Dallas field data: Linearity, curvilinearity, and heteroscedasticity. *Journal of Applied Social Psychology, 19,* 1479–1482.

Bell, P. A., Baum, A., Green, T. E. F., & Fisher, J. D. (1995). *Environmental psychology* (4th ed.). New York: Holt, Rinehart & Winston.

Bell, P. A., Fisher, J. D., Baum, A., & Green, T. E. (1990). *Environmental psychology* (3rd ed.). New York: Holt, Rinehart and Winston.

Bell, R. A. (1991). Gender, friendship network density, and loneliness. *Journal of Social Behavior and Personality, 6,* 45–56.

Bell, S. T., Kuriloff, P. J., & Lottes, I. (1994). Understanding attributions of blame in stranger rape and date rape situations: An examination of gender, race, identification, and students' social perceptions of rape victims. *Journal of Applied Social Psychology, 24,* 1719–1734.

Belmore, S. M., & Hubbard, M. L. (1987). The role of advance expectancies in person memory. *Journal of Personality and Social Psychology, 53,* 61–70.

Bem, S. L. (1974). The measurement of psychological androgyny. *Journal of Consulting and Clinical Psychology, 42,* 155–162.

Bem, S. L. (1975). Sex role adaptability: One consequence of psychological androgyny. *Journal of Personality and Social Psychology, 31,* 634–643.

Bem, S. L. (1981). Gender schema theory: A cognitive account of sex typing. *Psychological Review, 88,* 354–364.

Bem, S. L. (1983). Gender schema theory and its implications for child development: Raising gender-schematic children in a gender-schematic society. *Signs: Journal of Women in Culture and Society, 8,* 598–616.

Bem, S. L. (1984). Androgyny and gender-schema theory: A conceptual and empirical integration. *Nebraska Symposium on Motivation: Psychology and Gender, 32,* 179–226.

Benson, P. L., Karabenick, S. A., & Lerner, R. M. (1976). Pretty pleases: The effects of physical attractiveness, race, and sex on receiving help. *Journal of Experimental Social Psychology, 12,* 409–415.

Berg, J. H., & McQuinn, R. D. (1989). Loneliness and aspects of social support networks. *Journal of Social and Personal Relationships, 6,* 359–372.

Berkowitz, L. (1987). Mood, self-awareness, and willingness to help. *Journal of Personality and Social Psychology, 52,* 721–724.

Berkowitz, L. (1994). Is something missing? Some observations prompted by the cognitive-neoassociationist view of anger and emotional aggression. In L. R. Huesmann (Rd.), *Aggressive behavior: Current perspectives* (pp. 35–57). New York: Plenum.

Berkowitz, L. (Ed.). (1969). *Roots of aggression.* New York: Atherton.

Berkowitz, L., & Donnerstein, E. (1982). External validity is more than skin deep: Some answers to criticism of laboratory experiments. *American Psychologist, 37,* 245–257.

Berman, M., Gladue, B., & Taylor, S. (1993). The effects of hormones, Type A behavior pattern and provocation on aggression in men. *Motivation and Emotion, 17* 125–138, 182–199.

Bernard, L. C., & Belinsky, D. (1993). Hardiness, stress, and maladjustment: Effects on self-reported retrospective health problems and prospective health center visits. *Journal of Social Behavior and Personality, 8,* 97–110.

Bernath, M. S., & Feshbach, N. D. (1995). Children's trust: Theory, assessment, development, and research directions. *Applied and Preventive Psychology, 4,* 1–19.

Berndt, T. J. (1992). Friendship and friends' influence in adolescence. *Current Directions in Psychological Science, 1,* 156–159.

Berry, D. S., & Brownlow, S. (1989). Were the physiognomists right? Personality correlates of facial babyishness. *Personality and Social Psychology Bulletin, 15,* 266–279.

Berry, D. S., & Zebrowitz-McArthur, L. (1988). What's in a face? Facial maturity and the attribution of legal responsibility. *Personality and Social Psychology Bulletin, 14,* 23–33.

Berscheid, E., Dion, K. K., Hatfield (Walster), E., & Walster, G. W. (1971). Physical attractiveness and dating choice: A test of the matching hypothesis. *Journal of Experimental Social Psychology, 7,* 173–189.

Berscheid, E., Snyder, M., & Omoto, A. M. (1989). The Relationship Closeness Inventory: Assessing the closeness of interpersonal relationships. *Journal of Personality and Social Psychology, 57,* 792–807.

Bersoff, D. (1987). Social science data and the Supreme Court: Lockhart as a case in point. *American Psychologist, 42,* 52–58.

Bettencourt, B. N., & Miller, N. (in press) Sex differences in aggression as a function of provocation: A meta-analysis. *Psychological Bulletin.*

Bienert, H., & Schneider, B. H. (1993). Diagnosis-specific social skills training with peer-nominated aggressive–disruptive and sensitive–isolated preadolescents. *Journal of Applied Developmental Psychology, 26* 182–199.

Bierhoff, H. W., Klein, R., & Kramp, P. (1991). Evidence for the altruistic personality from data on accident research. *Journal of Personality, 59,* 263–280.

Bies, R. J., Shapiro, D. L., & Cummings, L. L. (1988). Voice and justification: Their influence on procedural fairness judgments. *Academy of Management Journal, 31,* 676–685.

Bies, R. J., Shapiro, D. L., & Cummings, L. L. (1988). Causal accounts and managing organizational conflict: Is it enough to say it's not my fault? *Communication Research, 15,* 381–399.

Birkimer, J. C., Lucas, M., & Berkimer, S. J. (1991). Health locus of control and status of cardiac rehabilitation graduates. *Journal of Social Behavior and Personality, 6,* 629–640.

Bishop, G. D. (1987). Lay conceptions in physical symptoms. *Journal of Applied Social Psychology, 17,* 127–146.

Bjorkqvist, K., Lagerspetz, K. M. J., & Kaukiainen, A. (1992). Do girls manipulate and boys fight? Developmental trends in regard to direct and indirect aggression. *Aggressive Behavior, 18,* 117–127.

Bjorkqvist, K., Osterman, K., & Hjelt-Back, M. (1994). Aggression among university employees. *Aggressive Behavior, 20,* 173–184.

Black teens giving up smoking, research finds. (1995, April 19). *Albany Times Union,* p. A-4.

Blake, R. R., & Mouton, J. S. (1984). *Solving costly organizational conflicts.* San Francisco: Jossey-Bass.

Blanck, P. D., Rosenthal, R., Hart, A. J., & Bernieri, F. (1990). The measure of the judge: An empirically based framework for exploring trial judges' behavior. *Iowa Law Review, 75,* 653–684.

Blonston, G. (1993, October 21). New crime wave? Not necessarily so: Statistics don't match America's fears. *Albany Times Union,* pp. A-1, A-9.

Bobo, L. (1983). Whites' opposition to busing: Symbolic racism or realistic group conflict? *Journal of Personality and Social Psychology, 45,* 1196–1210.

Bobocel, D. R., & Meyer, J. P. (1994). Escalating commitment to a failing course of action: Separating the role of choice and justification. *Journal of Applied Psychology, 79,* 360–363.

Bodenhausen, G. F. (1993). Emotion, arousal, and stereotypic judgment: A heuristic model of affect and stereotyping. In D. Mackie & D. Hamilton (Eds.), *Affect, cognition, and stereotyping: Intergroup processes in intergroup perception* (pp. 13–37). San Diego, CA: Academic Press.

Bodenhausen, G. V. (1988). Stereotypic biases in social decision making and memory: Testing process models of stereotype use. *Journal of Personality and Social Psychology, 55,* 726–737.

Bodenhausen, G. V., Kramer, G. P., & Susser, K. (1994). Happiness and stereotypic thinking in social judgment. *Journal of Personality and Social Psychology, 66,* 621–632.

Boehnke, K., Silbereisen, R. K., Eisenberg, N., Reykowski, J., & Palmonari, A. (1989). Developmental pattern of prosocial motivation: A cross-national study. *Journal of Cross-Cultural Psychology, 20,* 219–243.

Bogard, M. (1990). Why we need gender to understand human violence. *Journal of Interpersonal Violence, 5,* 132–135.

Bohren, J. (1993). Six myths of sexual harassment. *Management Review, 18,* 61–63.

Boivin, M., Dodge, K. A., & Coie, J. D. (1995). Individual–group behavioral similarity and peer status in experimental play groups of boys: The social misfit revisited. *Journal of Personality and Social Psychology, 69,* 269–279.

Bond, C. F. (1982). Social facilitation: A self-presentational view. *Journal of Personality and Social Psychology, 42,* 1042–1050.

Boninger, D. S., Krosnick, J. A., & Berent, M. K. (1995). Origins of attitude importance: Self-interest, social identification, and value relevance. *Journal of Personality and Social Psychology, 68,* 61–80.

Bookwala, J., Frieze, I. H., & Grote, N. K. (1994). Love, aggression and satisfaction in dating relationships. *Journal of Social and Personal Relationships, 11,* 625–632.

Booth-Kewley, S., & Vickers, R. R. Jr. (1994). Associations between major domains of personality and health behavior. *Journal of Personality, 62,* 281–298.

Bornstein, R. F. (1994). Dependency as a social cue: A meta-analytic review of research on the dependency–helping relationship. *Journal of Research in Personality, 28,* 182–213.

Bornstein, R. F., & D'Agostino, P. R. (1992). Stimulus recognition and the mere exposure effect. *Journal of Personality and Social Psychology, 63,* 545–552.

Bornstein, R. F., Krukonis, A. B., Manning, K. A., Mastrosimone, C. C., & Rossner, S. C. (1993). Interpersonal dependency and health service utilization in a college student sample. *Journal of Social and Clinical Psychology, 12,* 262–279.

Borrello, G. M., & Thompson, B. (1990). An hierarchical analysis of the Hendrick–Hendrick measure of Lee's typology of love. *Journal of Social Behavior and Personality, 5,* 327–342.

Bossard, J. H. S. (1932). Residential propinquity as a factor in marriage selection. *American Journal of Sociology, 38,* 219–224.

Botha, M. (1990). Television exposure and aggression among adolescents: A follow-up study over 5 years. *Aggressive Behavior, 16,* 361–380.

Bothwell, R. K., & Jalil, M. (1992). The credibility of nervous witnesses. *Journal of Social Behavior and Personality, 7,* 581–586.

Bothwell, R. K., Brigham, J. C., & Malpass, R. S. (1989). Cross-racial identification. *Personality and Social Psychology Bulletin, 15,* 19–25.

Bothwell, R. K., Deffenbacher, K. A., & Brigham, J. C. (1987). Correlation of eyewitness accuracy and confidence: Optimality hypothesis revisited. *Journal of Applied Psychology, 72,* 691–695.

Bottoms, B. L., & Goodman, G. S. (1994). Perceptions of children's credibility in sexual assault cases. *Journal of Applied Social Psychology, 24,* 702–732.

Bouchard, T. J., Jr., Arvey, R. D., Keller, L. M., & Segal, N. L. (1992). Genetic influences on job satisfaction: A reply to Cropanzano and Hames. *Journal of Applied Psychology, 77,* 89–93.

Bourgeois, M. J. (1993). Effects of technicality and access to trial transcripts on verdicts and information processing in a civil trial. *Personality and Social Psychology Bulletin, 19,* 220–227.

Bourgeois, M. J., Horowitz, I. A., & Lee, L. F. (1193) Effects of technicality and access to trial transcripts on verdicts and information processing in a civil trial. *Personality and Social Psychology Bulletin, 19,* 229–227.

Bower, G. H. (1991). Mood congruity of social judgments. In J. P. Forgas (Ed.), *Emotion and social judgments* (pp. 31–55). Oxford: Pergamon Press.

Bowers, L., Smith, P. K., & Binney, V. (1994). Perceived family relationships of bullies, victims and bully/victims in middle childhood. *Journal of Social and Personal Relationships, 11,* 215–232.

Bowlby, J. (1969). *Attachment and loss: Vol. 1. Attachment.* New York: Basic Books.

Bowlby, J. (1979). *The making and breaking of affectional bonds.* London: Tavistock.

Bowlby, J. (1982). *Attachment and loss: Vol. 1. Attachment* (2nd ed.). New York: Basic Books.

Bradbury, T. N., & Fincham, F. D. (1992). Attributions and behavior in marital interaction. *Journal of Personality and Social Psychology, 63,* 613–628.

Bradbury, T. N., Campbell, S. M., & Fincham, F. D. (1995). Longitudinal and behavioral analysis of masculinity and femininity in marriage. *Journal of Personality and Social Psychology, 68,* 328–341.

Brandon, T. H. (1994). Negative affect as motivation to smoke. *Current Directions in Psychological Science, 3,* 33–37.

Branscombe, N. R., & Wann, D. L. (1994). Collective self-esteem consequences of outgroup derogation when a valued social identity is on trial. *European Journal of Social Psychology, 24,* 641–657.

Braza, P., Braza, F., Carreras, M. R., & Munoz, J. M. (1993). Measuring the social ability of preschool children. *Social Behavior and Personality, 21,* 145–158.

Breakwell, G. M., & Fife-Schaw, C. (1992). Sexual activities and preferences in a United Kingdom sample of 16- to 20-year-olds. *Archives of Sexual Behavior, 21,* 271–293.

Brehm, J. W. (1966). *A theory of psychological reactance.* New York: Academic Press.

Brennan, K. A., & Shaver, P. R. (1995). Dimensions of adult attachment, affect regulation, and romantic relationship functioning. *Personality and Social Psychology Bulletin, 21,* 267–283.

Brewer, B. W. (1993). Self-identity and specific vulnerability to depressed mood. *Journal of Personality, 61,* 343–386.

Brewer, M. B., & Caporael, L. R. (1990). Selfish genes vs. selfish people: Sociobiology as origin myth. *Motivation and Emotion, 14,* 237–243.

Brewer, M. B., Ho, H., Lee, J., & Miller, M. (1987). Social identity and social distance among Hong Kong schoolchildren. *Personality and Social Psychology Bulletin, 13,* 156–165.

Brickner, M., Harkins, S., & Ostrom, T. (1986). Personal involvement: Thought provoking implications for social loafing. *Journal of Personality and Social Psychology, 51,* 763–769.

Bringle, R. G., & Bagby, G. J. (1992). Self-esteem and perceived quality of romantic and family relationships in young adults. *Journal of Research in Personality, 26,* 340–356.

Bringle, R. G., & Winnick, T. A. (1992, October). *The nature of unrequited love.* Paper presented at the first Asian Conference in Psychology, Singapore.

Broad, W. J. (1994, April 5). 2 environmental camps feud over noisy ocean experiment. *New York Times,* p. C4.

Broad, W. J. (1995, May 14). Cancer fear is unfounded, physicists say. *New York Times,* p. 19.

Broadstock, M., Borland, R., & Gason, R. (1991). Effects of suntan on judgments of healthiness and attractiveness by adolescents. *Journal of Applied Social Psychology, 22,* 157–172.

Brockner, J. (1992). The escalation of commitment to a failing course of action: Toward theoretical progress. *Academy of Management Review, 17,* 39–61.

Brody, G. H., Neubaum, E., & Forehand, R. (1988). Serial marriage: A heuristic analysis of an emerging family form. *Psychological Bulletin, 103,* 211–222.

Brody, J. E. (1989, August 24). Boning up on possible mental and physical health needs of children who are bound for college. *New York Times,* p. B12.

Brody, J. E. (1994, February 23). Study ties ads for smoking to higher rate for girls in 60's. *New York Times,* p. C12.

Brody, J. E. (1995, May 5). Danish study shows wine aiding longevity. *New York Times,* p. A18.

Brooks-Gunn, J., & Lewis, M. (1981). Infant social perception: Responses to pictures of parents and strangers. *Developmental Psychology, 17,* 647–649.

Brothers, L. (1990). The neural basis of primate social communication. *Motivation and Emotion, 14,* 81–91.

Brown, J. D. (1991). Staying fit and staying well: Physical fitness as a moderator of life stress. *Journal of Personality and Social Psychology, 60,* 555–561.

Brown, J. D., & Dutton, K. A. (1995). The thrill of victory, the complexity of defeat: Self-esteem and people's emotional reactions to success and failure. *Journal of Personality and Social Psychology, 68,* 712–722.

Brown, J. D., Novick, N. J., Lord, K. A., & Richards, J. M. (1992). When Gulliver travels: Social context, psychological closeness, and self-appraisals. *Journal of Personality and Social Psychology, 62,* 717–727.

Brown, J. D., & Rogers, R. J. (1991). Self-serving attributions: The role of physiological arousal. *Personality and Social Psychology Bulletin, 17,* 501–506.

Brown, J. D., & Siegel, J. M. (1988). Attributions for negative life events and depression: The role of perceived control. *Journal of Personality and Social Psychology, 54,* 316–322.

Browne, M. W. (1992, April 14). Biologists tally generosity's rewards. *New York Times,* pp. C1, C8.

Browne, M. W. (1994, December 20). Most precise gauge yet points to global warming. *New York Times,* p. C4.

Bruch, M. A., Hamer, R. J., & Heimberg, R. G. (1995). Shyness and public self-consciousness: Additive or interactive relation with social interaction? *Journal of Personality, 63,* 47–63.

Bruess, C. J. S., & Pearson, J. C. (1993). "Sweet pea" and "pussy cat": An examination of idiom use and marital satisfaction over the life cycle. *Journal of Social and Personal Relationships, 10,* 609–615.

Bryan, J. H., & Test, M. A. (1967). Models and helping: Naturalistic studies in aiding behavior. *Journal of Personality and Social Psychology, 6,* 400–407.

Brylinsky, J. A., & Moore, J. C. (1994). The identification of body build stereotypes in young children. *Journal of Research in Personality, 28,* 170–181.

Buck, R., & Ginsburg, B. (1991). Spontaneous communication and altruism: The communicative gene hypothesis. In M. S. Clark (Ed.), *Prosocial behavior* (pp. 149–175). Newbury Park, CA: Sage.

Buehler, R., & Griffin, D. (1994). Change-of-meaning effects in conformity and dissent: Observing construal processes over time. *Journal of Personality and Social Psychology, 67,* 984–996.

Buehler, R., Griffin, D., & Ross, M. (1994). Exploring the "planning fallacy": Why people underestimate their task completion times. *Journal of Personality and Social Psychology, 67,* 366–381.

Bugental, J. F. T., & Zelen, S. L. (1950). Investigations of the self-concept: I. The W-A-Y technique. *Journal of Personality, 8,* 483–498.

Bukowski, W. M., Hoza, B., & Boivin, M. (1994). Measuring friendship quality during pre- and early adolescence: The development and psychometric properties of the Friendship Qualities Scale. *Journal of Social and Personal Relationships, 11,* 471–484.

Bumpass, L. (1984). Children and marital disruption: A replication and update. *Demography, 21,* 71–82.

Burbank, V. (1987). Female aggression in cross-cultural perspective. *Behavior Science Research, 21,* 70–100.

Burger, J. M. (1986). Increasing compliance by improving the deal: The that's-not-all technique. *Journal of Personality and Social Psychology, 51,* 277–283.

Burger, J. M. (1991). Changes in attributions over time: The ephemeral fundamental attribution error. *Social Cognition, 9,* 182–193.

Burger, J. M. (1992). *Desire for control: Personality, social, and clinical perspectives.* New York: Plenum.

Burger, J. M. (1995). Individual differences in preference for solitude. *Journal of Research in Personality, 29,* 85–108.

Burger, J. M., & Cooper, H. M. (1979). The desirability of control. *Motivation and Emotion, 3,* 381–393.

Burger, J. M., & Palmer, M. L. (1992). Changes in and generalization of unrealistic optimism following experiences with stressful events: Reactions to the 1989 California earthquake. *Personality and Social Psychology Bulletin, 18,* 39–43.

Burger, J. M., & Pavelich, J. L. (1993). Attributions for presidential elections: The situational shift over time. Unpublished manuscript, Santa Clara University.

Burn, S. M., & Oskamp, S. (1986). Increasing community recycling with persuasive communication and public commitment. *Journal of Applied Social Psychology, 16,* 29–41.

Burnstein, E. (1983). Persuasion as argument processing. In M. Brandstatter, J. H. Davis, & G. Stocker-Kriechgauer (Eds.), *Group decision processes.* London: Academic Press.

Burnstein, E., Crandall, C., & Kitayama, S. (1994). Some neo-Darwinian rules for altruism: Weighing cues for inclusive fitness as a function of the biological importance of the decision. *Journal of Personality and Social Psychology, 67,* 773–789.

Burrell, C. (1995, April 24). Number of fatherless children in U.S. quadruples in 45 years. Albany *Times Union,* p. A-8.

Bushman, B. J. (1984). Perceived symbols of authority and their influence on compliance. *Journal of Applied Social Psychology, 14,* 501–508.

Bushman, B. J. (1988). The effects of apparel on compliance: A field experiment with a female authority figure. *Personality and Social Psychology Bulletin, 14,* 459–467.

Buss, A. H. (1961). *The psychology of aggression.* New York: Wiley.

Buss, D. H. (1990). Evolutionary social psychology: Prospects and pitfalls. *Motivation and Emotion, 14,* 265–286.

Buss, D. H. (in press). *Evolutionary psychology.* Boston: Allyn & Bacon.

Buss, D. M. (1988). Love acts: The evolutionary biology of love. In R. J. Sternberg & M. L. Barnes (Eds.), *The psychology of love* (pp. 100–118). New Haven, CT: Yale University Press.

Buss, D. M. (1989). Conflict between the sexes: Strategic interference and the evocation of anger and upset. *Journal of Personality and Social Psychology, 56,* 735–747.

Buss, D. M., & Schmitt, D. P. (1993). Sexual strategies theory: An evolutionary perspective on human mating. *Psychological Review, 100,* 204–232.

Buss, D. M., Larsen, R. J., Westen, D., & Semmelroth, J. (1992). Sex differences in jealousy: Evolution, physiology, and psychology. *Psychological Science, 3,* 251–255.

Butler, A. C., Hokanson, J. E., & Flynn, H. A. (1994). A comparison of self-esteem lability and low trait self-esteem as vulnerability factors for depression. *Journal of Personality and Social Psychology, 66,* 166–177.

Butler, D., & Geis, F. L. (1990). Nonverbal affect responses to male and female leaders: Implications for leadership evaluations. *Journal of Personality and Social Psychology, 58,* 48–59.

Butler, J. M., & Haigh, G. V. (1954). Changes in the relation between self-concepts and ideal concepts consequent upon client-centered counseling. In C. R. Rogers & R. F. Dymond (Eds.), *Psychotherapy and personality change* (pp. 55–75). Chicago: University of Chicago Press.

Butterfield, F. (1992, October 23). Dispute threatens U.S. plan on violence. *New York Times,* p. A8.

Buunk, B. P. (1995). Sex, self-esteem, dependency and extra-dyadic sexual experience as related to jealousy responses. *Journal of Social and Personal Relationships, 12,* 147–153.

Buunk, B. P., Doosje, B. J., Jans, L. G. J. M., & Hopstaken, L. E. M. (1993). Perceived reciprocity, social support, and stress at work: The role of exchange and communal orientation. *Journal of Personality and Social Psychology, 65,* 801–811.

Byrne, D. (1961a). The influence of propinquity and opportunities for interaction on classroom relationships. *Human Relations, 14,* 63–69.

Byrne, D. (1961b). Interpersonal attraction and attitude similarity. *Journal of Abnormal and Social Psychology, 62,* 713–715.

Byrne, D. (1964). Repression–sensitization as a dimension of personality. In B. A. Maher (Ed.), *Progress in Experimental Personality Research, 1,* 169–220.

Byrne, D. (1991). Perspectives on research classics: This ugly duckling has yet to become a swan. *Contemporary Social Psychology, 15,* 84–85.

Byrne, D. (1992). The transition from controlled laboratory experimentation to less controlled settings: Surprise! Additional variables are operative. *Communication Monographs, 59,* 190–198.

Byrne, D., & Blaylock, B. (1963). Similarity and assumed similarity of attitudes among husbands and wives. *Journal of Abnormal and Social Psychology, 67,* 636–640.

Byrne, D., & Buehler, J. A. (1955). A note on the influence of propinquity upon acquaintanceships. *Journal of Abnormal and Social Psychology, 51,* 147–148.

Byrne, D., & Clore, G. L. (1970). A reinforcement–affect model of evaluative responses. *Personality: An International Journal, 1,* 103–128.

Byrne, D., & Fisher, W. A. (1983). *Adolescents, sex, and contraception.* Hillsdale, NJ: Erlbaum.

Byrne, D., & Griffitt, W. (1966). Similarity versus liking: A clarification. *Psychonomic Science, 6,* 295–296.

Byrne, D., & Murnen, S. K. (1988). Maintaining loving relationships. In R. J. Sternberg & M. L. Barnes (Eds.), *The psychology of love* (pp. 293–310). New Haven, CT: Yale University Press.

Byrne, D., & Nelson, D. (1965). Attraction as a linear function of proportion of positive reinforcements. *Journal of Personality and Social Psychology, 1,* 659–663.

Byrne, D., Gouaux, C., Griffitt, W., Lamberth, J., Murakawa, N., Prasad, M. B., Prasad, A., & Ramirez, M., III. (1971). The ubiquitous relationship: Attitude similarity and attraction: A cross-cultural study. *Human Relations, 24,* 201–207.

Byrne, D., Kelley, K., & Fisher, W. A. (1993). Unwanted teenage pregnancies: Incidence, interpretation, and intervention. *Applied and Preventive Psychology, 2,* 101–113.

Cacioppo, J. T., Martzke, J. S., Petty, R. E., & Tassinary, L. G. (1988). Specific forms of facial EMG response index emotions during an interview: From Darwin to the continuous flow hypothesis of affect-laden information processing. *Journal of Personality and Social Psychology, 54,* 52–604.

Cacioppo, J. T., Priester, J. R., & Berntson, G. G. (1993). Rudimentary determinants of attitudes: II. Arm flexion and extension have differential effects on attitudes. *Journal of Personality and Social Psychology, 65,* 5–17.

Cahoon, D. D., & Edmonds, E. M. (1989). Male-Female estimates of opposite-sex first impressions concerning females' clothing styles. *Bulletin of the Psychonomic Society, 27,* 280–281.

Callaci, D. (1993, March 3). The glass is half full. *New York Teacher,* 9–11.

Callan, V. J. (1993). Subordinate manager communication in different sex-dyads: Consequences for job satisfaction. *Journal of Occupational and Organizational Psychology, 66,* 13–27.

Calvert, J. D. (1988). Physical attractiveness: A review and reevaluation of its role in social skill research. *Behavioral Assessment, 10,* 29–42.

Campbell, D. T., & Specht, J. C. (1985). Altruism: Biology, culture, and religion. *Journal of Social and Clinical Psychology, 3,* 33–42.

Campbell, J. D. (1986). Similarity and uniqueness: The effects of attribute type, relevance, and individual differences in self-esteem and depression. *Journal of Personality and Social Psychology, 50,* 281–294.

Campbell, J. D., Chew, B., & Scratchley, L. S. (1991). Cognitive and emotional reactions to daily events: The effects of self-esteem and self-complexity. *Journal of Personality, 59,* 473–505.

Campos, J. J., Barrett, K. C., Lamab, M. E., Goldsmith, H. H., & Stenberg, C. (1983). Socioemotional development. In M. M. Haith & J. J. Campos (Eds.), *Handbook of child psychology: Vol. 2. Infancy and psychobiology* (pp. 783–915). New York: Wiley.

Cann, A., Calhoun, L. G., & Banks, J. S. (1995). On the role of humor appreciation in interpersonal attraction: It's no joking matter. *Humor: International Journal of Humor Research,*

Cannon,W. B., Lewis, J. T., & Britton, S. W. (1927). The dispensability of the sympathetic division of the autonomic nervous system. *Boston Medical Surgery Journal, 97,* 514.

Cantor, N. (1990). Social psychology and sociobiology: What can we leave to evolution? *Motivation and Emotion, 14,* 245–254.

Cappella, J. N., & Palmer, M. T. (1990). Attitude similarity, relational history, and attraction: The mediating effects of kinesic and vocal behaviors. *Communication Monographs, 57,* 161–183.

Caprara, G. V. (1986). Indicators of aggression: The dissipation–rumination scale. *Personality and Individual Differences, 7,* 23–31.

Caprara, G. V. (1987). The disposition–situation debate and research on aggression. *European Journal of Personality, 1,* 1–16.

Caprara, G. V., Barbaranelli, C., Pastorelli, C., & Perugini, M. (1994). Individual differences in the study of human aggression. *Aggressive Behavior, 20,* 291–303.

Carli, L. L., Ganley, R., & Pierce-Otay, A. (1991). Similarity and satisfaction in roommate relationships. *Personality and Social Psychology Bulletin, 17,* 419–426.

Carroll, S. J., Perkowitz, W. T., Lurigio, A. J., & Waver, F. M. (1987). Sentencing goals, causal attributions, ideology, and personality. *Journal of Personality and Social Psychology, 36,* 107–118.

Carron, A. V. (1982). Cohesiveness in sport groups: Interpretations and considerations. *Journal of Sport Psychology, 4,* 123–138.

Carsten, J. M., & Spector, P. E. (1987). Unemployment, job satisfaction, and employee turnover: A meta-analytic test of the Muchinsky model. *Journal of Applied Psychology, 72,* 75–80.

Carter, D. B., & McCloskey, L. A. (1984). Peers and the maintenance of sex-typed behavior: The development of children's conceptions of cross-gender behavior in their peers. *Social Cognition, 2,* 294–314.

Carver, C. S., & Glass, D. C. (1978). Coronary-prone behavior pattern and interpersonal aggression. *Journal of Personality and Social Psychology, 376,* 361–366.

Carver, C. S., Kus, L. A., & Scheier, M. F. (1994). Effects of good versus bad mood and optimistic versus pessimistic outlook on social acceptance versus rejection. *Journal of Social and Clinical Psychology, 13,* 138–151.

Carver, C. S., Pozo, C., Harris, S. D., Noriega, V., Scheier, M. F., Robinson, D. S., Ketcham, A. S., Moffat, F. L., Jr., & Clark, K. C. (1993). How coping mediates the effect of optimism on distress: A study of women with early stage breast cancer. *Journal of Personality and Social Psychology, 65,* 375–390.

Carver, C. S., Reynolds, S. L., & Scheier, M. F. (1994). The possible selves of optimists and pessimists. *Journal of Research in Personality, 28,* 133–141.

Cash, T. F. (1995). Developmental teasing about physical appearance: Retrospective descriptions and relationships with body image. *Social Behavior and Personality, 23,* 123–130.

Cash, T. F., & Derlega, V. J. (1978). The matching hypothesis: Physical attractiveness among same-sex friends. *Personality and Social Psychology Bulletin, 4,* 240–243.

Cash, T. F., & Duncan, N. C. (1984). Physical attractiveness stereotyping among black American college students. *Journal of Social Psychology, 122,* 71–77.

Cash, T. F., & Trimer, C. A. (1984). Sexism and beautyism in women's evaluation of peer performance. *Sex Roles, 10,* 87–98.

Caspi, A., & Herbener, E. S. (1990). Continuity and change: Assortative marriage and the consistency of personality in adulthood. *Journal of Personality and Social Psychology, 58,* 250–258.

Caspi, A., Herbener, E. S., & Ozer, D. J. (1992). Shared experiences and the similarity of personalities: A longitudinal study of married couples. *Journal of Personality and Social Psychology, 62,* 281–291.

Castellow, W. A., Wuensch, K. L., & Moore, C. H. (1990). Effects of physical attractiveness of the plaintiff and defendant in sexual harassment judgments. *Journal of Social Behavior and Personality, 5,* 547–562.

Cavoukian, A., & Doob, A. N. (1980). The effect of a judge's charge and subsequent recharge on judgments of guilt. *Basic and Applied Social Psychology, 1,* 103–114.

Chacko, T. I. (1982). Women and equal employment opportunity: Some unintended effects. *Journal of Applied Psychology, 67,* 119–123.

Chan, C.-J., & Margolin, G. (1994). The relationship between dual-earner couples' daily work mood and home affect. *Journal of Social and Personal Relationships, 11,* 573–586.

Chapman, B. (1992). *The Byrne–Nelson formula revisited: The additional impact of number of dissimilar attitudes on attraction.* Unpublished masters thesis, University at Albany, State University of New York.

Chatterjee, J., & McCarrey, M. (1991). Sex-role attitudes, values, and instrumental-expressive traits of women trainees in traditional vs. non-traditional programmes. *Applied Psychology: An International Review, 40,* 282–297.

Cherek, D. R., Schnapp, W., Gerard Moeller, F., & Dougherty, D. M. (1996). Laboratory measures of aggressive responding in male parolees with violent and nonviolent histories. *Aggressive Behavior 22,* 37–36.

Cheuk, W. H., & Rosen, S. (1992). Helper reactions: When help is rejected by friends or strangers. *Journal of Social Behavior and Personality, 7,* 445–458.

Cheung, C.-k., Lee, J.-j., & Chan, C.-m. (1994). Explicating filial piety in relation to family cohesion. *Journal of Social Behavior and Personality, 9,* 565–580.

Chidester, T. R. (1986). Problems in the study of interracial aggression: Pseudo-interracial dyad paradigm. *Journal of Personality and Social Psychology, 50,* 74–79.

Children's Defense Fund (1992). *The state of America's children, 1992*. Washington, DC: Author.

Christiansen, K., & Knussman, R. (1987). Androgen levels and components of aggressive behavior in men. *Hormones and Behavior, 21*, 170–180.

Christopher, F. S., & Cate, R. M. (1985). Premarital sexual pathways and relationship development. *Journal of Social and Personal Relationships, 2*, 271–288.

Christy, C. A., & Voigt, H. (1994). Bystander responses to public episodes of child abuse. *Journal of Applied Social Psychology, 24*, 824–847.

Christy, P. R., Gelfand, D. M., & Hartmann, D. P. (1971). Effects of competition-induced frustration on two classes of modeled behavior. *Developmental Psychology, 5*, 104–111.

Cialdini, R. B. (1994). Interpersonal influence. In S. Shavitt & T. C. Brock (Eds.), *Persuasion* (pp. 195–218). Boston: Allyn & Bacon.

Cialdini, R. B., & Petty, R. (1979). Anticipatory opinion effects. In B. Petty, T. Ostrom, & T. Brock (Eds.), *Cognitive responses in persuasion*. Hillsdale, NJ: Erlbaum.

Cialdini, R. B., Bauman, D. J., & Kenrick, D. T. (1981). Insights from sadness: A three-step model of the development of altruism as hedonism. *Developmental Review, 1*, 207–223.

Cialdini, R. B., Cacioppo, J. T., Bassett, R., & Miller J. A. (1978). A low-ball procedure for producing compliance: Commitment then cost. *Journal of Personality and Social Psychology, 36*, 463–476.

Cialdini, R. B., Green, B. L., & Rusch, A. J. (1992). When tactical pronouncements of change become real change: The case of reciprocal persuasion. *Journal of Personality and Social Psychology, 63*, 30–40.

Cialdini, R. B., Kallgren, C. A., & Reno, R. R. (1991). A focus theory of normative conduct. *Advances in Experimental Social Psychology, 24*, 201–234.

Cialdini, R. B., Kenrick, D. T., & Baumann, D. J. (1982). Effects of mood on prosocial behavior in children and adults. In N. Eisenberg-Berg (Ed.), *Development of prosocial behavior*. New York: Academic Press.

Cialdini, R. B., Reno, R. R., & Kallgren, C. A. (1990). A focus theory of normative conduct: Recycling the concept of norms to reduce littering in public places, *Journal of Personality and Social Psychology, 58*, 1015–1026.

Cialdini, R. B., Schaller, M., Houlainhan, D., Arps, K., Fultz, J., & Beaman, A. L. (1987). Empathy-based helping: Is it selflessly or selfishly motivated? *Journal of Personality and Social Psychology, 52*, 749–758.

Cialdini, R. B., Vincent, J. E., Lewis, S. K., Catalan, J., Wheeler, D., & Darby, B. L. (1975). Reciprocal concessions procedure for inducing compliance: The door-in-the-face technique. *Journal of Personality and Social Psychology, 31*, 206–215.

Cioffi, D., & Holloway, J. (1993). Delayed costs of suppressed pain. *Journal of Personality and Social Psychology, 64*, 274–282.

Clark, L. F. (1993). Stress and the cognitive–conversational benefits of social interaction. *Journal of Social and Clinical Psychology, 12*, 25–55.

Clark, L. F., & Collins, J. E. II. (1993). Remembering old flames: How the past affects assessments of the present. *Personality and Social Psychology Bulletin, 19*, 399–408.

Clark, M. S., Ouellette, R., Powel, M. C., & Milberg, S. (1987). Recipient's mood, relationship type, and helping. *Journal of Personality and Social Psychology, 53*, 94–103.

Clarke, M. (1990). *Business crime: Its nature and control*. Cambridge, England: Polity Press.

Clarke, M. S. (1991). *Prosocial behavior*. Newbury Park, CA: Sage.

Clary, E. G., & Orenstein, L. (1991). The amount and effectiveness of help: The relationship of motives and abilities to helping behavior. *Personality and Social Psychology Bulletin, 17*, 58–64.

Clement, U., Schmidt, G., & Kruse, M. (1984). Changes in sex differences in sexual behavior: A replication of a study on West German students (1966–1981). *Archives of Sexual Behavior, 13*, 99–120.

Clinton and AIDS. (1994, December 26). *The New Republic, 7*.

Clore, G. L., Schwarz, N., & Conway, M. (1993). Affective causes and consequences of social information processing. In R. S. Wyer & T. K. Srull (Eds.), *Handbook of social cognition* (2nd ed.). Hilldsale, NJ: Erlbaum.

Cohen, S., Doyle, W. J., Skoner, D. P., Fireman, P., Gwaltney, J. M. Jr., & Newson, J. T. (1995). State and trait negative affect as predictors of objective and subjective symptoms of respiratory viral infections. *Journal of Personality and Social Psychology, 68*, 159–169.

Cohen, S., Evans, G. W., Stokols, D., & Krantz, D. (1986). *Behavior, health, and environmental stress*. New York: Plenum.

Cohen, S., Glass, D. C., & Singer, J. E. (1973). Apartment noise, auditory discrimination, and reading ability in children. *Journal of Experimental Social Psychology, 9*, 407–422.

Cohen, S., Kaplan, J. R., Cunnick, J. E., Manuck, S. B., & Rabin, B. S. (1992). Chronic social stress, affiliation, and cellular immune response in nonhuman primates. *Psychological Science, 3*, 301–304.

Cohen, S., Tyrrell, D. A. J., & Smith, A. P. (1993). Negative life events, perceived stress, negative affect, and susceptibility to the common cold. *Journal of Personality and Social Psychology, 64*, 131–140.

Cohn, E. G. (1990). Weather and violent crime: A reply to Perry and Simpson, 1987. *Environment and Behavior, 22*, 280–294.

Coie, J. D., & Cillessen, H. N. (1993). Peer rejection: Origins and effects on children's development. *Current Directions in Psychological Science, 2*, 89–92.

Coleman, L. M., Jussim, L., & Abrams, J. (1987). Students' reactions to teachers' evaluations: The unique impact of negative feedback. *Journal of Applied Social Psychology, 17*, 1051–1070.

Collins, M. A., & Zebrowitz, L. A. (1995). The contributions of appearance to occupational outcomes in civilian and military settings. *Journal of Applied Social Psychology, 25*, 129–163.

Collins, N. L., Dunkel Schetter, C., Lobel, M., & Scrimshaw, S. C. M. (1993). Social support in pregnancy: Psychosocial correlates of birth outcomes and postpartum depression. *Journal of Personality and Social Psychology, 65*, 1243–1258.

Colvin, C. R., Block, J., & Funder, D. C. (1995). Overly positive self-evaluations and personality: Negative implications for mental health. *Journal of Personality and Social Psychology, 68*, 1152–1162.

Compas, B. E., Banez, G. A., Malcarne, V., & Worsham, N. (1991). Perceived control and coping with stress: A developmental perspective. *Journal of Social Issues, 47*(4), 23–34.

Comstock, G. A., & Paik, H. (1991) The effects of television violence on aggressive behavior: A meta-analysis. In: *A preliminary report to the National Research Council on the understanding and control of violent behavior*. Washington, DC: National Research Council.

Condon, J. W., & Crano, W. D. (1988). Inferred evaluation and the relation between attitude similarity and interpersonal attraction. *Journal of Personality and Social Psychology, 54*, 789–797.

Conger, J. A. (1991). Inspiring others: The language of leadership. *Academy of Management Executive, 5*(1), 31–45.

Conlon, K. (1995, February 5). Psychologists study rescuers' motives. *Schenectady Gazette*, p. B4.

Contrada, R. J. (1989). Type A behavior, personality hardiness, and cardiovascular responses to stress. *Journal of Personality and Social Psychology, 57,* 895–903.

Conway, M., Giannopoulos, C., Csank, P., & Mendelson, M. (1993). Dysphoria and specificity in self-focused attention. *Personality and Social Psychology Bulletin, 19,* 265–268.

Conway, M., & Ross, M. (1984). Getting what you want by revising what you had. *Journal of Personality and Social Psychology, 47,* 738–748.

Cook, S. W. (1985). Experimenting on social issues: The case of school desegregation. *American Psychologist, 40,* 452–460.

Cook, S. W., & Pelfrey, M. (1985). Reactions to being helped in cooperating interracial groups: A context effect. *Journal of Personality and Social Psychology, 49,* 1231–1245.

Cook, W. L. (1993). Interdependence and the interpersonal sense of control: An analysis of family relationships. *Journal of Personality and Social Psychology, 64,* 587–601.

Coontz, S. (1992). *The way we never were: American families and the nostalgia trap.* New York: Basic Books.

Cooper, J., & Fazio, R. H. (1984). A new look at dissonance theory. In L. Berkowitz (Ed.), *Advances in experimental social psychology* (Vol. 17, pp. 229–266). New York: Academic Press.

Cooper, J., Hall, J., & Huff, C. (1990). Situational stress as a consequence of sex-stereotyped software. *Personality and Social Psychology Bulletin, 16,* 419–429.

Cooper, J., & Scher, S. J. (1994). Actions and attitudes: The role of responsibility and aversive consequences in persuasion. In T. Brock & S. Shavitt (Eds.), *Persuasion* (pp. 95–111). San Francisco: Freeman.

Costa, P. T. Jr., & McCrae, R. R. (1994). The revised NEO Personality Inventory (NEOP$_T$-R). In R. Briggs & J. M. Cheek (Eds.), *Personality measures: Development and evaluation.* Greenwich, CT: JAI Press.

Costanza, R. S., Derlega, V. J., & Winstead, B. A. (1988). Positive and negative forms of social support: Effects of conversation topics on coping with stress among same-sex friends. *Journal of Experimental Social Psychology, 24,* 182–193.

Cota, A. A., Evans, C. R., Dion, K. L., Kilik, L., & Longman, R. S. (1995). The structure of group cohesion. *Personality and Social Psychology Bulletin, 21,* 572–580.

Cottrell, N. B., Wack, K. L., Sekerak, G. J., & Rittle, R. (1968). Social facilitation of dominant responses by the presence of an audience and the mere presence of others. *Journal of Personality and Social Psychology, 9,* 245–250

Courneya, K. S., & McAuley, E. (1993). Efficacy, attributional, and affective responses of older adults following an acute bout of exercise. *Journal of Social Behavior and Personality, 8,* 729–742.

Cowan, G., & Curtis, S. R. (1994). Predictors of rape occurrence and victim blame in the William Kennedy Smith case. *Journal of Applied Social Psychology, 24,* 12–20.

Cox, M., & Tanford, S. (1989). Effects of evidence and instructions in civil trials: An experimental investigation of rules of admissibility. *Social Behavior, 4,* 31–55.

Cozzarelli, C. (1993). Personality and self-efficacy as predictors of coping with abortion. *Journal of Personality and Social Psychology, 65,* 1224–1236.

Craig, J.-A., Koestner, R., & Zuroff, D. C. (1994). Implicit and self-attributed intimacy motivation. *Journal of Social and Personal Relationships, 11,* 491–507.

Cramer, R. E., McMaster, M. R., Bartell, P. A., & Dragna, M. (1988). Subject competence and minimization of the bystander effect. *Journal of Applied Social Psychology, 18,* 1133–1148.

Crandall, C. S. (1988). Social contagion of binge eating. *Journal of Personality and Social Psychology, 55,* 588–598.

Crandall, C. S. (1994). Prejudice against fat people: Ideology and self-interest. *Journal of Personality and Social Psychology, 66,* 882–894.

Crandall, C. S. (1995). Do parents discriminate against their heavyweight daughters? *Personality and Social Psychology Bulletin, 21,* 724–735.

Crime rate down; murders by teens soar. (1995, May 22). Albany *Times Union,* A-2.

Crocker, J. (1993). Memory for information about others: Effects of self-esteem and performance feedback. *Journal of Research in Personality, 27,* 35–48.

Crocker, J., Cornwell, B., & Major, B. (1993). The stigma of overweight: Affective consequences of attributional ambiguity. *Journal of Personality and Social Psychology, 64,* 60–70.

Crocker, J., Luhtanen, R., Blaine, B., & Broadnax, S. (1994). Collective self-esteem and psychological well-being among white, black, and Asian college students. *Personality and Social Psychology Bulletin, 20,* 503–513.

Crocker, J., & Major, B. (1989). Social stigma and self-esteem: The self-protective properties of stigma. *Psychological Review, 96,* 608–630.

Crocker, J., & Major, B. (1993). *When bad things happen to bad people: The perceived justifiability of negative outcomes based on stigma.* Manuscript submitted for publication.

Cropanzano, R. (Ed.). (1993). *Justice in the workplace* (pp. 79–103). Hillsdale, NJ: Erlbaum.

Crossette, B. (1990, November 26). 1,190 islands in danger: Sea could drown them. *New York Times,* p. A4.

Croyle, R., & Uretsky, M. B. (1987). Effects of mood on self-appraisal of health status. *Health Psychology, 6,* 239–254.

Crusco, A. H., & Wetzel, C. G. (1984). The Midas touch: The effects of interpersonal touch on restaurant tipping. *Personality and Social Psychology Bulletin, 10,* 512–517.

Cruse, D., & Leigh, B. C. (1987). "Adam's Rib" revisited: Legal and non-legal influences on the processing of trial testimony. *Social Behaviour, 2,* 221–230.

Crutchfield, R. A. (1955). Conformity and character. *American Psychologist, 10,* 191–198.

Csikszentmihalyi, M. (1993). Relax? Relax and do what? *New York Times,* p. A25.

Cunningham, J. D., & Antill, J. K. (1994). Cohabitation and marriage: Retrospective and predictive comparisons. *Journal of Social and Personal Relationships, 11,* 77–93.

Cunningham, M. R. (1979). Weather, mood, and helping behavior: Quasi-experiments with the sunshine Samaritan. *Journal of Personality and Social Psychology, 37,* 1947–1956.

Cunningham, M. R. (1986). Measuring the physical in physical attractiveness: Quasi-experiments on the sociobiology of female facial beauty. *Journal of Personality and Social Psychology, 50,* 925–935.

Cunningham, M. R. (1988). Does happiness mean friendliness? Induced mood and heterosexual self-disclosure. *Personality and Social Psychology Bulletin, 14,* 283–297.

Cunningham, M. R. (1989). Reactions to heterosexual opening gambits: Female selectivity and male responsiveness. *Personality and Social Psychology Bulletin, 15,* 27–41.

Cunningham, M. R., Roberts, A. R., Wu, C.-H., Barbee, A. P., & Druen, P. B. (1995). "Their ideas of beauty are, on the whole, the same as ours": Consistency and variability in the cross-cultural perception of female physical attractiveness. *Journal of Personality and Social Psychology, 68,* 261–279.

Cunningham, M. R., Shaffer, D. R., Barbee, A. P., Wolff, P. L., & Kelley, D. J. (1990). Separate processes in the relation of elation and depression to helping: Social versus personal concerns. *Journal of Experimental Social Psychology, 26,* 13–33.

Curtis, R. C., & Miller, K. (1986). Believing another likes or dislikes you: Behavior making the beliefs come true. *Journal of Personality and Social Psychology, 51,* 284–290.

Cutler, B. L., Maran, G., & Narby, D. J. (1992). Jury selection in insanity defense cases. *Journal of Research in Personality, 26,* 165–182.

Cutler, B. L., Penrod, S. D., & Martens, T. K. (1987). Improving the reliability of eyewitness identification: Putting content into context. *Journal of Applied Psychology, 72,* 629–637.

Cutler, B. L., & Wolfe, R. N. (1989). Self-monitoring and the association between confidence and accuracy. *Journal of Research in Personality, 23,* 410–420.

da Gloria, J., Pahlavan, F., Duda, D., & Bonnet, P. (1994). Evidence for a motor mechniasm of pain-induced aggression instigation in humans. *Aggressive Behavior, 20,* 1–7.

Dabbs, J. M., Jr. (1992). Testosterone measurements in social and clinical psychology. *Journal of Social and Clinical Psychology, 11,* 302–321.

Dabbs, J. M., Jr. (1993). Salivary testosterone measurements in behavioral studies. In D. Malamud & L. A. Tabak (Eds.), *Saliva as a diagnostic fluid* (pp. 177–183). New York: New York Academy of Sciences.

Daily, G. C., Ehrlich, A. H., & Ehrlich, P. R. (1994). Optimum human population size. *Population and Environment, 15,* 469–475.

Daley, S. (1983, February 13). Tales of the giant storm: Camaraderie and misery. *New York Times,* pp. 1, 35.

Daly, H. E. (1991). Population and economics: A bioeconomic analysis. *Population and Environment, 12,* 257–263.

Dane, F. C. (1992). Applying social psychology in the courtroom: Understanding stereotypes in jury decision making. *Contemporary Social Psychology, 16,* 33–36.

Darley, J. M. (1991). Altruism and prosocial behavior research: Reflections and prospects. In M. S. Clark (Ed.), *Prosocial behavior* (pp. 312–327). Newbury Park, CA: Sage.

Darley, J. M. (1993). Research on morality: Possible approaches, actual approaches. *Psychological Science, 4,* 353–357.

Darley, J. M., & Batson, C. D. (1973). From Jerusalem to Jericho: A study of situational dispositional variables in helping behavior. *Journal of Personality and Social Psychology, 27,* 100–108.

Darley, J. M., & Latané, B. (1968). Bystander intervention in emergencies. Diffusion of responsibility. *Journal of Personality and Social Psychology, 8,* 377–383.

Daro, D., & McCurdy, K. (1992). *Current trends in child abuse reporting and fatalities: The results of the 1990 annual fifty-state survey.* Chicago: National Center on Child Abuse Prevention Research.

Daubman, K. A. (1993). *The self-threat of receiving help: A comparison of the threat-to-self-esteem model and the theat-to-interpersonal-power model.* Unpublished manuscript, Gettysburg College, Gettysburg, PA.

Davie, M. R., & Reeves, R. J. (1939). Propinquity of residence before marriage. *American Journal of Sociology, 44,* 510–517.

Davis, C., Brewer, H., & Weinstein, M. (1993). A study of appearance anxiety in young men. *Social Behavior and Personality, 21,* 63–74.

Davis, C. G., Lehman, D. R., Wortman, C. B., Silver, R. C., & Thompson, S. C. (1995). The undoing of traumatic life events. *Personality and Social Psychology Bulletin, 21,* 109–124.

Davis, J. H. (1989). Psychology and the law: The last 15 years. *Journal of Applied Social Psychology, 19,* 119–230.

Davis, J. H., Stasson, M., Ono, K., & Zimmerman, S. (1988). Effects of straw polls on group decision making: Sequential voting pattern, timing, and local majorities. *Journal of Personality and Social Psychology, 55,* 918–926.

Davis, J. H., Tinsdale, R. S., Naggao, D. H., Hinsz, W. B., & Robertson, B. (1984). Order effects in multiple decisions by groups: A demonstration with mock juries and trial procedures. *Journal of Personality and Social Psychology, 47,* 1003–1012.

Davis, M. H., & Kraus, L. A. (1989). Social contact, loneliness, and mass media use: A test of two hypotheses. *Journal of Applied Social Psychology, 19,* 1100–1124.

Davis, M. H., Luce, C., & Kraus, S. J. (1994). The heritability of characteristics associated with dispositional empathy. *Journal of Personality, 62,* 369–391.

Davis, S. F., Miller, K. M., Johnson, D., McAuley, K., & Dinges, D. (1992). The relationship between optimism–pessimism, loneliness, and death anxiety. *Bulletin of the Psychonomic Society, 30,* 135–136.

Day, D. V., & Bedian, A. G. (1991). Work climate and Type A status as predictors of job satisfaction: A test of the international perspective. *Journal of Vocational Behavior, 38,* 39–52.

Day, J. D., Borkowski, J. G., Punzo, D., & Howsepian, B. (1994). Enhancing possible selves in Mexican American students. *Motivation and Emotion, 18,* 79–103.

De Vries, H., Backbier, E., Kok, G., & Dijkstra, M. (1995). The impact of social influences in the context of attitude, self-efficacy, intention, and previous behavior as predictors of smoking onset. *Journal of Applied Social Psychology, 25,* 237–257.

de Weerth, C., & Kalma, A. P. (1993). Female aggression as a response to sexual jealousy: A sex role reversal? *Aggressive Behavior, 19,* 265–279.

De Young, R., Boerschig, S., Carney, S., Dillenbeck, A., Elster, M., Horst, S., Kleiner, B., & Thomson, B. (1995). Recycling in multifamily dwellings: Increasing participation and decreasing contamination. *Population and Environment, 16,* 253–267.

DeBono, K. G. (1992). Pleasant scents and persuasion: An information processing approach. *Journal of Applied Social Psychology, 22,* 910–919.

DeBono, K. G., & Packer, M. (1991). The effects of advertising appeal on perceptions of product quality. *Personality and Social Psychology Bulletin, 17,* 194–200.

DeBono, K. G., & Snyder, M. (1995). Acting on one's attitudes: The role of a history of choosing situations. *Personality and Social Psychology Bulletin, 21,* 629–636.

DeJong, W., & Musilli, L. (1982). External pressure to comply: Handicapped versus nonhandicapped requesters and the foot-in-the-door phenomenon. *Personality and Social Psychology Bulletin, 8,* 522–527.

DeLamater, J. (1981). The social control of sexuality. *Annual Review of Sociology, 7,* 263–290.

DePaulo, B. M. (1992). Nonverbal behavior and self-presentation. *Psychological Bulletin, 111,* 230–243.

DePaulo, B. M., & Fisher, J. D. (1980). The costs of asking for help. *Basic and Applied Social Psychology, 1,* 23–35.

DePaulo, B. M., Brown, P. L., Ishii, S., & Fisher, J. D. (1981). Help that works: The effects of aid on subsequent task performance. *Journal of Personality and Social Psychology, 41,* 478–487.

DePaulo, B. M., Dull, W. R., Greenberg, J. M., & Swaim, G. W. (1989). Are shy people reluctant to ask for help? *Journal of Personality and Social Psychology, 56,* 834–844.

DePaulo, B. M., Stone, J. L., & Lassiter, G. D. (1985). Deceiving and detecting deceit. In B. R. Schlenker (Ed.), *The self and social life* (pp. 323–370). New York: McGraw-Hill.

DeSanctis, M., Halcomb, C. G., & Fedoravicius, A. S. (1981). Meteorological determinants of human behavior: A holistic environmental perspective with special reference to air ionization and electrical field effects. Unpublished manuscript, Texas Tech University, Lubbock.

Dean-Church, L., & Gilroy, F. D. (1993). Relation of sex-role orientation to life satisfaction in a healthy elderly sample. *Journal of Social Behavior and Personality, 8*, 133–140.

Deaux, K. (1976). *The behavior of women and men*. Belmont, CA: Brooks/Cole.

Deaux, K. (1993a). Reconstructing social identity. *Personality and Social Psychology Bulletin, 19*, 4–12.

Deaux, K. (1993b). Commentary: Sorry, wrong number—A reply to Gentile's call. *Psychological Science, 4*, 125–126.

Deaux, K., Reid, A., Mizrahi, K., & Ethier, K. A. (1995). Parameters of social identity. *Journal of Personality and Social Psychology, 68*, 280–291.

Delaney, J. (1993) Handcuffing employee theft. *Small Business Report, 18*(7), 29–38.

Dellinger, R. W. (1979). Jet roar: Health problems take off near airports. *Human Behavior, 8*, 50–51.

Demeny, P. (1974). The populations of underdeveloped countries. *Scientific American, 231*(3), 148–159.

Denes-Raj, V., & Epstein, S. (1994). Conflict between intuitive and rational processing: When people behave against their better judgment. *Personality and Social Psychology Bulletin, 66*, 819–829.

Dengerink, H. A., Schnedler, R. W., & Covey, M. K. (1978). Role of avoidance in aggressive responses to attack and no attack. *Journal of Personality and Social Psychology, 36*, 1044–1053.

Deutsch, F. M., & Lamberti, D. M. (1986). Does social approval increase helping? *Personality and Social Psychology Bulletin, 12*, 149–157.

Deutsch, F. M., Zalenski, C. M., & Clark, M. E. (1986). Is there a double standard of aging? *Journal of Applied Social Psychology, 16*, 771–785.

Deutsch, M., & Gerard, H. B. (1955). A study of normative and informational social influences upon individual judgment. *Journal of Abnormal and Social Psychology, 51*, 629–636.

Dexter, H. R., Cutler, B. L., & Moran, G. (1992). A test of voir dire as a remedy for the prejudicial effects of pretrial publicity. *Journal of Applied Social Psychology, 22*, 819–832.

DiMatteo, M. R., Hays, R. D., & Prince, L. M. (1986). Relationships of physicians' nonverbal communication skill to patient satisfaction, appointment noncompliance, and physician workload. *Health Psychology, 5*, 581–594.

Diamond, J. (1993). What are men good for? *Natural History, 102*(5), 26–29.

Dickerson, C. A., Thibodeau, R., Aronson, E., & Miller, D. (1992). Using cognitive dissonance to encourage water conservation. *Journal of Applied Social Psychology, 22*, 841–854.

Diener, E., Wolsic, B., & Fujita, F. (1995). Physical attractiveness and subjective well-being. *Journal of Personality and Social Psychology, 69*, 120–129.

Dion, K. K., & Dion, K. L. (1991). Psychological individualism and romantic love. *Journal of Social Behavior and Personality, 6*, 17–33.

Dion, K. K., & Dion, K. L. (1993). Individualistic and collectivistic perspectives on gender and the cultural context of love and intimacy. *Journal of Social Issues, 49*(3), 53–69.

Dion, K. K., Berscheid, E., & Hatfield (Walster), E. (1972). What is beautiful is good. *Journal of Personality and Social Psychology, 24*, 285–290.

Dion, K. L., & Dion, K. K. (1987). Belief in a just world and physical attractiveness stereotyping. *Journal of Personality and Social Psychology, 52*, 775–780.

Dion, K. L., Dion, K. K., & Keelan, J. P. (1990). Appearance anxiety as a dimension of social-evaluative anxiety: Exploring the ugly duckling syndrome. *Contemporary Social Psychology, 14*, 220–224.

Dipboye, R. L. (1992). *Selection interviews: Process perspectives*. Cincinnati: South-Western.

Ditto, P. H., & Griffin, J. (1993). The value of uniqueness: Self-evaluation and the perceived prevalence of valenced characteristics. *Journal of Social Behavior and Personality, 8*, 221–240.

Dixon, T. M., & Baumeister, R. F. (1991). Escaping the self: The moderating effect of self-complexity. *Personality and Social Psychology Bulletin, 17*, 363–368.

Dodge, K. A., & Coie, J. D. (1987). Social-information-processing factors in reactive and proactive aggression in children's peer groups. *Journal of Personality and Social Psychology, 53*, 1146–1158.

Dodge, K. A., Price, J. M., Bachorowski, J. A., & Newman, J. P. (1990). Hostile attributional biases in severely aggressive adolescents. *Journal of Abnormal Psychology, 99*, 385–392.

Dodge, K.A., Pettit, G. S., McClaskey, C. L., & Brown, M. M. (1986). Social competence in children. *Monographs of the Society for Research in Child Development, 51*(2), 1–85.

Doherty, K., Weigold, M. F., & Schlenker, B. R. (1990). Self-serving interpretations of motives. *Personality and Social Psychology Bulletin, 16*, 485–495.

Dollard, J., Doob, L., Miller, N., Mowerer, O. H., & Sears, R. R. (1939). *Frustration and aggression*. New Haven, CT: Yale University Press.

Donnerstein, E., & Donnerstein, M. (1976). Research in the control of interracial aggression. In R. G. Geen & E. C. O'Neal (Eds.), *Perspectives on aggression*. New York: Academic Press.

Donnerstein, E., & Wilson, D. W. (1976). Effects of noise and perceived control on ongoing and subsequent aggressive behavior. *Journal of Personality and Social Psychology, 34*, 774–781.

Dorian, B. J., Keystone, E., Garfinkel, P. E., & Brown, J. M. (1982). Aberrations in lymphocyte subpopulations and function during psychological stress. *Clinical and Experimental Immunology, 50*, 132–138.

Dougherty, T. W., Turban, D. B., & Callender, J. C. (1994). Confirming first impression in the employment interview: A field study of interviewer behavior. *Journal of Applied Psychology, 79*, 659–665.

Dovidio, J. F., & Gaertner, S. L. (1993). Stereotype and evaluative intergroup bias. In D. M. Mackie & D. L. Hamilton (Eds.), *Affect, cognition, and stereotyping: Interactive processes in group perception*. Orlando, FL: Academic Press.

Dovidio, J. F., Gaertner, S. L., Isen, A. M., & Lowrance, R. (1995). Group representations and intergroup bias: Positive affect, similarity, and group size. *Personality and Social Psychology Bulletin, 21*, 856–865.

Dovidio, J. H., Evans, N., & Tyler, R. B. (1986). Racial stereotypes: The contents of their cognitive representations. *Journal of Experimental Social Psychology, 22*, 22–37.

Downey, J. L., & Damhave, K. W. (1991). The effects of place, type of comment, and effort expended on the perception of flirtation. *Journal of Social Behavior and Personality, 6*, 35–43.

Downs, A. C., & Lyons, P. M. (1991). Natural observations of the links between attractiveness and initial legal judgments. *Personality and Social Psychology Bulletin, 17*, 541–547.

Drachman, D., DeCarufel, A., & Insko, C. A. (1978). The extra credit effect in interpersonal attraction. *Journal of Experimental Social Psychology, 14*, 458–465.

Drigotas, S. M., & Rusbult, C. E. (1992). Should I stay or should I go? A dependence model of breakups. *Journal of Personality and Social Psychology, 62*, 62–87.

Drigotas, S. M., Whitney, G. A., & Rusbult, C. E. (1995). On the peculiarities of loyalty: A diary study of responses to dissatisfaction in everyday life. *Personality and Social Psychology Bulletin, 21,* 596–609.

Driscoll, R., Davis, K. E., & Lipetz, M. E. (1972). Parental interference and romantic love: The Romeo and Juliet effect. *Journal of Personality and Social Psychology, 24,* 1–10.

Drory, A., & Romm, T. (1990). The definition of organizational politics: A review. *Human Relations, 43,* 1133–1154.

Drout, C. E., & Gaertner, S. L. (1994). Gender differences in reactions to female victims. *Social Behavior and Personality, 22,* 267–278.

Duck, S., & Barnes, M. K. (1992). Disagreeing about agreement: Reconciling differences about similarity. *Communication Monographs, 59,* 199–208.

Duck, S., Pond, K., & Leatham, G. (1994). Loneliness and the evaluation of relational events. *Journal of Social and Personal Relationships, 11,* 253–276.

Duggan, E. S., & Brennan, K. A. (1994). Social avoidance and its relation to Bartholomew's adult attachment typology. *Journal of Social and Personal Relationships, 11,* 147–153.

Dumanoski, D. (1990, February 13). Population growth seen as major force in our global environmental problems. *Albany Times Union,* pp. C-1, C-4.

Dunham, R. B., Grube, J. A., & Castaneda, M. B. (1994). Organizational commitment: The utility of an integrative definition. *Journal of Applied Psychology, 79,* 370–380.

Dunn, J. (1992). Siblings and development. *Current Directions in Psychological Science, 1,* 6–11.

Dunn, K. (1993). Fibbers. *The New Republic, 208*(25), 18–19.

Dunning, D., & Stern, L. B. (1994). Distinguishing accurate from inaccurate eyewitness identification via inquiries about decision processes. *Journal of Personality and Social Psychology, 67,* 818–835.

Dutton, D. G., & Aron, A. P. (1974). Some evidence for heightened sexual attraction under conditions of high anxiety. *Journal of Personality and Social Psychology, 30,* 510–517.

Dutton, D. G., & Lake, R. A. (1973). Threat of own prejudice and reverse discrimination in interracial situations. *Journal of Personality and Social Psychology, 28,* 94–100.

Dutton, D. G., Saunders, K., Starzomski, A., & Bartholomew, K. (1994). Intimacy–anger and insecure attachment as precursors of abuse in intimate relationships. *Journal of Applied Social Psychology, 24,* 1367–1386.

Eagly, A. H. (1978). Sex differences in influenceability. *Psychological Bulletin, 85,* 86–116.

Eagly, A. H. (1987). *Sex differences in social behavior: A social-role interpretation.* Hillsdale, NJ: Erlbaum.

Eagly, A. H. (1995). The science and politics of comparing women and men. *American Psychologist, 50,* 145–158.

Eagly, A. H., & Carli, L. (1981). Sex of researchers and sex-typed communications as determinants of sex differences in influenceability: A meta-analysis of social influence studies. *Psychological Bulletin, 90,* 1–20.

Eagly, A. H., & Johnson, B. T. (1990). Gender and leadership style: A meta-analysis. *Psychological Bulletin, 108,* 233–256.

Eagly, A. H., & Steffen, V. J. (1986). Gender and aggressive behavior: A meta-analytic review of the social psychological literature. *Psychological Bulletin, 100,* 309–330.

Eagly, A. H., & Wood, W. (1982). Inferred sex differences in status as a determinant of gender stereotypes about social influence. *Journal of Personality and Social Psychology, 43,* 915–928.

Eagly, A. H., Karau, S. J., & Makhijani, M. G. (1995). Gender and the effectiveness of leaders: A meta-analysis. *Psychological Bulletin, 117,* 125–145.

Eagly, A. H., Makhijani, M. G., & Klonsky, B. G. (1992). Gender and the evaluation of leaders: A meta-analysis. *Psychological Bulletin, 111,* 3–22.

Earley, P. C. (1993). East meets West meets Mideast: Further explorations of collectivistic and individualistic work groups. *Academy of Management Journal, 36,* 319–348.

Ebbeson, E. B., Kjos, G. L., & Konecni, V. J. (1976). Spatial ecology: Its effects on the choice of friends and enemies. *Journal of Experimental Social Psychology, 12,* 508–518.

Edwards, K. (1987). Effects of sex and glasses on attitudes toward intelligence and attractiveness. *Psychological Reports, 60,* 590.

Egbert, J. M. Jr., Moore, C. H., Wuensch, K. L., & Castellow, W. A. (1992). The effect of litigant social desirability on judgments regarding a sexual harassment case. *Journal of Social Behavior and Personality, 7,* 569–579.

Ehrhardt, A. A., Yingling, S., & Warne, P. A. (1991). Sexual behavior in the era of AIDS: What has changed in the United States? *Annual Review of Sex Research, 2,* 25–47.

Eisenberg, N., Fabes, R. A., Schaller, M., Miller, P., Carlo, G., Poulin, R., Shea, C., & Shell, R. (1991). Personality and socialization correlates of vicarious emotional responding. *Journal of Personality and Social Psychology, 61,* 459–470.

Eisenman, R. (1985). Marijuana use and attraction: Support for Byrne's similarity-attraction concept. *Perceptual and Motor Skills, 61,* 582.

Eisenman, R. (1993). Belief that drug usage in the United States is increasing when it is really decreasing: An example of the availability heuristic. *Bulletin of the Psychonomic Society, 31,* 249–252.

Eisenstadt, D., & Leipe, M. R. (1994). The self-comparison process and self-discrepant feedback: Consequences of learning you are what you thought you were not. *Journal of Personality and Social Psychology, 67,* 611–626.

Ekman, P. (1985). *Telling lies.* New York: Norton.

Ekman, P. (1989). The argument and evidence about universals in facial expressions of emotion. In H. Wagner & A. Manstead (Eds.), *Handbook of psychophysiology: Emotion and social behavior* (pp. 143–164). New York: Wiley.

Ekman, P. (1992). Are there basic emotions? *Psychological Review, 99,* 550–553.

Ekman, P., & Friesen, W. V. (1975). *Unmasking the face.* Englewood Cliffs, NJ: Prentice-Hall.

Ekman, P., & Heider, K. (1988). The universality of a contempt expression: A replication. *Motivation and Emotion, 12,* 303–308.

Ekman, P., & Oster, H. (1979). Facial expressions of emotion. *Annual Review of Psychology, 30,* 527–554.

Ekman, P., Davidson, R. J., & Friesen, W. V. (1990). The Duchenne smile: Emotional expression and brain physiology II. *Journal of Personality and Psychology, 58,* 342–353.

Elkin, R., & Leippe, M. (1986). Physiological arousal, dissonance, and attitude change: Evidence for a dissonance–arousal link and "don't remind me" effect. *Journal of Personality and Social Psychology, 51,* 55–65.

Elkins, L. E., & Peterson, C. (1993). Gender differences in best friendships. *Sex Roles, 29,* 497–508.

Ellemers, N., Wilke, H., & van Knippenberg, A. (1993). Effects of the legitimacy of low group or individual status on individual and collective status-enhancement strategies. *Journal of Personality and Social Psychology, 64,* 766–778.

Elliot, A. J., & Devine, P. G. (1994). On the motivational nature of cognitive dissonance: Dissonance as psychological discomfort. *Journal of Personality and Social Psychology, 67,* 382–394.

Ellis, J. B. (1994). Children's sex-role development: Implications for working mothers. *Social Behavior and Personality, 22,* 131–136.

Ellsworth, P. C., & Carlsmith, J. M. (1973). Eye contact and gaze aversion in aggressive encounter. *Journal of Personality and Social Psychology, 33,* 117–122.

Emery, R. E. (1989). Family violence. *American Psychologist, 434,* 321–328.

Emmons, R. A. (1992). Abstract versus concrete goals: Personal striving level, physical illness, and psychological well-being. *Journal of Personality and Social Psychology, 62,* 292–300.

Emmons, R. A., & Colby, P. M. (1995). Emotional conflict and well-being: Relation to perceived availability, daily utilization, and observer reports of social support. *Journal of Personality and Social Psychology, 68,* 947–959.

Ennett, S. T., & Bauman, K. E. (1994). The contribution of influence and selection to adolescent peer group homogeneity: The case of adolescent cigarette smoking. *Journal of Personality and Social Psychology, 67,* 653–663.

Enright, D. J., & Rawlinson, D. (1993). *Friendship.* Oxford, England: Oxford University Press.

Epstein, S. (1983). The unconscious, the preconscious, and the self-concept. In J. Suls & A. Greenwald (Eds.), *Psychological perspectives on the self* (Vol. 2, pp. 220–247). Hillsdale, NJ: Erlbaum.

Epstein S. (in press). An integration of the cognitive and psychodynamic unconscious. *American Psychologist.*

Erber, R. (1991). Affective and semantic priming: Effects of mood on category accessibility and inference. *Journal of Experimental Social Psychology, 27,* 480–498.

Erdley, C. A., & D'Agostino, P. R. (1989). Cognitive and affective components of automatic priming effects. *Journal of Personality and Social Psychology, 54,* 741–747.

Esser, D. (1995, January 3). Frightened son kills his father's rescuer. *Albany Times Union,* pp. A-1, A-5.

Esses, V. M. (1989). Mood as a moderator of acceptance of interpersonal feedback. *Journal of Personality and Social Psychology, 57,* 769–781.

Esses, V. M., & Webster, C. D. (1988). Physical attractiveness, dangerousness, and the Canadian criminal code. *Journal of Applied Social Psychology, 18,* 1017–1031.

Estrada, C. A., Isen, A. M., & Young, M. J. (1995). Positive affect improves creative problem solving and influences reported source of practice satisfaction in physicians. *Motivation and Emotion, 18,* 285–300.

Ethier, K. A., & Deaux, K. (1994). Negotiating social identity when contexts change: Maintaining identification and responding to threat. *Journal of Personality and Social Psychology, 67,* 243–251.

Evans, G. W., Jacobs, S. V., & Frager, N. B. (1982). Behavioral responses to air pollution. *Advances in Environmental Psychology, 4.*

Evans, M. C., & Wilson, M. (1949). Friendship choices of university women students. *Educational and Psychological Measurement, 9,* 307–312.

Fabrigar, L. R., & Krosnick, J. A. (1995). Attitude importance and the false consensus effect. *Personality and Social Psychology Bulletin, 21,* 468–479.

Fajardo, D. M. (1985). Author race, essay quality, and reverse discrimination. *Journal of Applied Social Psychology, 15,* 255–268.

Farnsworth, C. H. (1995, June 4). Canada puts different spin on sensational murder trial. *Albany Times Union,* pp. E-8.

Fazio, R. H. (1989). On the power and functionality of attitudes: The role of attitude accessibility. In A. R. Pratkanis, S. J. Breckler, & A. G. Greenwald (Eds.), *Attitude structure and function* (pp. 153–179). Hillsdale, NJ: Erlbaum.

Fazio, R. H., & Roskos-Ewoldsen, D. R. (1994). Acting as we feel: When and how attitudes guide behavior. In S. Shavitt & T. C. Brock (Eds.), *Persuasion* (pp. 71–93). Boston: Allyn & Bacon.

Fazio, R. H., & Williams, C. J. (1986). Attitude-accessibility as a moderator of the attitude–perception and attitude–behavior relations: An investigation of the 1984 presidential election. *Journal of Personality and Social Psychology, 51,* 505–514.

Fazio, R. H., & Zanna, M. P. (1981). Direct experience and attitude–behavior consistency. In L. Berkowitz (Ed.), *Advances in experimental social psychology* (Vol. 14, pp. 161–202). New York: Academic Press.

Fazio, R. H., Chen, J., McDonel, E. C., & Sherman, S. J. (1982). Attitude accessibility and the strength of the object–evaluation association. *Journal of Experimental Social Psychology, 18,* 339–357.

Fazio, R. H., Sanbonmatsu, D. M., Powell, M. C., & Kardes, F. F. (1986). On the automatic activation of attitudes. *Journal of Personality and Social Psychology, 50,* 229–238.

Feingold, A. (1990). Gender differences in effects of physical attractiveness on romantic attraction: A comparison across five research paradigms. *Journal of Personality and Social Psychology, 59,* 981–993.

Feingold, A. (1992). Gender differences in mate selection preferences: A test of the parental investment model. *Psychological Bulletin, 112,* 125–139.

Feingold, A. (1992). Good-looking people are not what we think. *Psychological Bulletin, 111,* 304–341.

Feingold, A. (1994). Gender differences in personality: A meta-analysis. *Psychological Bulletin, 116,* 412–456.

Feingold, A. J. (1995). *Gender stereotyping for sociability, dominance, character, and mental health: An examination using the bogus stranger paradigm.* Manuscript submitted for publication.

Fekken, G. C., & Jakubowski, I. (1990). Effects of stress on the health of Type A students. *Journal of Social Behavior and Personality, 5,* 473–480.

Feldman, S. P. (1988). Secrecy, information, and politics: An essay in organizational decision making. *Human Relations, 41,* 73–90.

Feldman, S. S., & Nash, S. C. (1984). The transition from expectancy to parenthood: Impact of the firstborn child on men and women. *Sex Roles, 11,* 61–78.

Felmlee, D. H. (1995). Fatal attractions: Affection and disaffection in intimate relationships. *Journal of Social and Personal Relationships, 12,* 295–311.

Fenigstein, A., & Abrams, D. (1993). Self-attention and the egocentric assumption of shared perspectives. *Journal of Experimental Social Psychology, 29,* 287–303.

Ferris, G. R., & Kacmar, K. M. (1992). Perceptions of organizational politics. *Journal of Management, 18,* 93–116.

Ferris, G. R., & King, T. R. (1991). Politics in human resources decisions: A walk on the dark side. *Organizational Dynamics, 20,* 59–71.

Feshbach, S. (1984). The catharsis hypothesis, aggressive drive, and the reduction of aggression. *Aggressive Behavior, 10,* 91–101.

Festinger, L. (1950). Informal social communication. *Psychological Review, 57,* 271–282.

Festinger, L. (1954). A theory of social comparison processes. *Human Relations, 7,* 117–140.

Festinger, L. (1957). *A theory of cognitive dissonance.* Evanston, IL: Row, Peterson.

Festinger, L., & Carlsmith, J. M. (1959). Cognitive consequences of forced compliance. *Journal of Abnormal and Social Psychology, 58*, 203–210.

Festinger, L., Schachter, S., & Back, K. (1950). *Social pressures in informal groups: A study of a housing community.* New York: Harper.

Fichten, C. S., & Amsel, R. (1986). Trait attributions about college students with a physical disability: Circumplex analyses and methodological issues. *Journal of Applied Social Psychology, 16*, 410–427.

Fiedler, F. E. (1994). *Leadership experience and leadership performance.* United States Army Research Institute for the Behavioral and Social Sciences.

Fincham, F. D., & Bradbury, T. N. (1993). Marital satisfaction, depression, and attributions: A longitudinal analysis. *Journal of Personality and Social Psychology, 64*, 442–452.

Fincham, F. D., & Bradbury, T. N. (1992). Assessing attributions in marriage: The relationship attribution measure. *Journal of Personality and Social Psychology, 62*, 457–468.

Fine, M. A., & Kurdek, L. W. (1994). Parenting cognitions in stepfamilies: Differences between parents and stepparents and relations to parenting satisfaction. *Journal of Social and Personal Relationships, 11*, 95–112.

Finn, J. (1986). The relationship between sex role attitudes and attitudes supporting marital violence. *Sex Roles, 14*, 235–244.

Fischer, G. J. (1986). College student attitudes toward forcible date rape: I. Cognitive predictors. *Archives of Sexual Behavior, 15*, 457–466.

Fisher, A. B. (1992, September 21). When will women get to the top? *Fortune,* pp. 44–56.

Fisher, C. D. (1993). Boredom at work: A neglected concept. *Human Relations, 46*, 395–417.

Fisher, H. (1992). *Anatomy of love.* New York: Norton.

Fisher, J. D., Nadler, A., & Whitcher-Alagna, S. (1982). Recipient reactions to aid. *Psychological Bulletin, 91*, 27–54.

Fisher, W. A., Byrne, D., & White, L. A. (1983) Emotional barriers to contraception. In D. Byrne & W. A. Fisher (Eds.), *Adolescents, sex, and contraception* (pp. 207–239). Hillsdale, NJ: Erlbaum.

Fischman, J. (1986, January). Women and divorce: Ten years after. *Psychology Today, 15.*

Fiske, A. P. (1991). The cultural relativity of selfish individualism: Anthropological evidence that humans are inherently sociable. In M. S. Clark (Ed.), *Prosocial behavior* (pp. 176–214). Newbury Park, CA: Sage.

Fiske, S. T. (1993). Social cognition and social perception. In L. W. Porter & M. R. Rosenzweig (Eds.), *Annual Review of Psychology, 44*, 155–194.

Fiske, S. T., & Neuberg, S. L. (1990). A continuum model of impression formation, from category-based to individuating processes: Influence of information and motivation on attention and interpretation. In M. P. Zanna (Ed.), *Advances in experimental social psychology* (Vol. 23). New York: Academic Press.

Fiske, S. T., & Taylor, S. (1991). *Social cognition* (2nd ed.). New York: Random House.

Fiske, S. T., & Taylor, S. E. (1991). *Social cognition.* New York: McGraw-Hill.

FitzGerald, F. (1994, September 2). A manageable crowd. *The New Yorker,* 7–8.

Flannery, D. J., Montemayor, R., Eberly, M., & Torquati, J. (1993). Unraveling the ties that bind: Affective expression and perceived conflict in parent–adolescent interactions. *Journal of Social and Interpersonal Relationships, 10*, 495–509.

Folger, R., & Bies, R. J. (1989). Managerial responsibilities and procedural justice. *Employee Responsibilities and Rights Journal, 2*, 79–90.

Forgas, J. P. (1992). On making sense of odd couples: Mood effects on the perception of mismatched relationships. *Personality and Social Psychology Bulletin, 19*, 59–70.

Forgas, J. P. (1994). Sad and guilty? Affective influences on attributions for simple and serious interpersonal conflict. *Journal of Personality and Social Psychology, 66*, 56–68.

Forgas, J. P. (1994). The role of emotion in social judgments: an introductory review and an affect infusion model (AIM). *European Journal of Social Psychology,* in press.

Forgas, J. P. (1995). Mood and judgment: the Affect infusion model (AIM). *Psychological Bulletin, 21*, 747–765.

Forgas, J. P. (1995). Mood and judgment: The affect infusion model (AIM). *Psychological Bulletin, 117*, 39–66.

Forgas, J. P., & Fielder, K. (1996). Us and them: Mood effects on intergroup discrimination. *Journal of Personality and Social Psychology, 70*, 28–40.

Forge, K. L., & Phemister, S. (1987). The effect of prosocial cartoons on preschool children. *Child Study Journal, 17*, 83–88.

Forston, M. T., & Stanton, A. L. (1992). Self-discrepancy theory as a framework for understanding bulimic symptomatology and associated distress. *Journal of Social and Clinical Psychology, 11*, 103–118.

Forsyth, D. R. (1991). *An introduction to group dynamics,* (2nd ed.). Monterey, CA: Brooks/Cole.

Forsythe, S., Drake, M. F., & Cox, C. E. (1985). Influence of applicant's dress on interviewer's selection decisions. *Journal of Applied Psychology, 70*, 374–378.

Frable, D. E. S. (1993). Dimensions of marginality: Distinctions among those who are different. *Personality and Social Psychology Bulletin, 19*, 370–380.

Fraczek, A. (1985). Moral approval of aggressive acts. A Polish–Finnish comparative study. *Journal of Cross-Cultural Psychology, 16*, 41–54.

Frank, M. G., & Gilovich, T. (1989). Effect of memory perspective on retrospective causal attributions. *Journal of Personality and Social Psychology, 57*, 399–403.

Frankel, A., & Prentice-Dunn, S. (1990). Loneliness and the processing of self-relevant information. *Journal of Social and Clinical Psychology, 9*, 303–315.

Fredrickson, B. L. (1995). Socioemotional behavior at the end of college life. *Journal of Social and Personal Relationships, 12*, 261–276.

Freedman, J. L., & Fraser, S. C. (1966). Compliance without pressure: The foot-in-the-door technique. *Journal of Personality and Social Psychology, 4*, 195–202.

Freudenheim, M. (1992, October 14). Software helps patients make crucial choices. *New York Times,* p. D6.

Fricko, M. A. M., & Beehr, T. A. (1992). A longitudinal investigation of interest congruence and gender concentration as predictors of job satisfaction. *Personnel Psychology, 45*, 99–117.

Friedman, H. S., & Miller-Herringer, T. (1991). Nonverbal display of emotion in public and private: Self-monitoring, personality, and expressive cues. *Journal of Personality and Social Psychology, 61*, 766–775.

Friedman, H. S., Hawley, P. H., & Tucker, J. S. (1994). Personality, health, and longevity. *Current Directions in Psychological Science, 3*, 37–41.

Friedman, H. S., Prince L. M., Riggio, R. E., & DeMatteo, M. R. (1980). Understanding and assessing nonverbal expressiveness: The affective communication test. *Journal of Personality and Social Psychology, 39*, 333–351.

Friedman, H. S., Riggio, R. E., & Casella, D. F. (1988). Nonverbal skill, personal charisma, and initial attraction. *Personality and Social Psychology Bulletin, 14,* 203–211.

Friedman, H. S., Tucker, J. S., Schwartz, J. E., Martin, L. R., Tomlinson-Keasey, C., Wingard, D. L., & Criqui, M. H. (1995). Childhood conscientiousness and longevity: Health behaviors and cause of death. *Journal of Personality and Social Psychology, 68,* 696–703.

Friedman, H. S., Tucker, J. S., Schwartz, J. E., Tomlinson-Keasey, C., Martin, L. R., Wingard, D. L., & Criqui, M. H. (1995). Psychosocial and behavioral predictors of longevity: The aging and death of the "Termites." *American Psychologist, 50,* 69–78.

Friedman, H. S., Tucker, J. S., Tomlinson-Keasey, C., Schwartz, J. E., Wingard, D. L., & Criqui, M. H. (1993). Does childhood personality predict longevity? *Journal of Personality and Social Psychology, 65,* 176–185.

Friedrich, J., Fetherstonhaugh, D., Casey, S., & Gallagher, D. (1996). Argument integration and attitude change: Suppression effects in the integration of one-sided arguments that vary in persuasiveness. *Personality and Social Psychology Bulletin, 22,* 179–191.

Fultz, J., Shaller, M., & Cialdini, R. B. (1988). Empathy, sadness, and distress: Three related but distant vicarious affective responses to another's suffering. *Personality and Social Psychology Bulletin, 14,* 312–325.

Funder, D. C., & Colvin, C. R. (1991). Explorations in behavioral consistency: Properties of persons, situations, and behavior. *Journal of Personality and Social Psychology, 59,* 149–158.

Funder, D. C., & Sneed, C. D. (1993). Behavioral manifestations of personality: An ecological approach to judgmental accuracy. *Journal of Personality and Social Psychology, 64,* 479–490.

Furnham, A. (1990). *The protestant work ethic.* London: Routledge.

Furnham, A., Kirkcaldy, B. D., & Lynn, R. (1994). National attitudes to competitiveness, money, and work among young people: First, second, and third world differences. *Human Relations, 47,* 119–132.

Gabriel, M. T., Critelli, J. W., & Ee, J. S. (1994). Narcissistic illusions in self-evaluations of intelligence and attractiveness. *Journal of Personality, 62,* 143–155.

Gaertner, S. L., & Dovidio, J. F. (1976). The aversive form of racism. In J. F. Dovidio & S. L. Gaertner (Eds.), *Prejudice, discrimination, and racism* (p. 61–89). San Diego, CA: Academic Press.

Gaertner, S. L., Dovidio, J. F., Anastasio, P. A., Bachman, B. A., & Rust, M. C. (1993). The common ingroup identity model: Recategorization and the reduction of intergroup bias. In W. Stroebe & H. Hewstone (Eds.), *European Review of Social Psychology, 4,* 1–26.

Gaertner, S. L., Mann, J., Murrell, A., & Dovidio, J. F. (1989). Reducing intergroup bias: The benefits of recategorization. *Journal of Personality and Social Psychology, 57,* 239–249.

Gaertner, S. L., Mann, J. A., Dovidio, J. F., Murrell, A. J., & Pomare, M. (1990). How does cooperation reduce intergroup bias? *Journal of Personality and Social Psychology, 59,* 692–704.

Gaertner, S. L., Rust, M. C., Dovidio, J. F., Bachman, B. A., & Anastasio, P. A. (1993). The contact hypothesis: The role of a common ingroup identity on reducing intergroup bias. *Small Groups Research, 25*(2), 224–249.

Gaines, S. O. Jr. (1994). Exchange of respect-denying behaviors among male–female friendships. *Journal of Social and Personal Relationships, 11,* 5–24.

Galambos, N. L. (1992). Parent–adolescent relations. *Current Directions in Psychological Science, 1,* 146–149.

Gangestad, S., & Snyder, M. (1985). On the nature of self-monitoring: An examination of latent causal structure. In P. Shaver (Ed.), *Review of Personality and Social Psychology* (Vol. 6, pp. 65–85). Beverly Hills, CA: Sage.

Gangestad, S. W., & Simpson, J. A. (1993). Development of a scale measuring genetic variation related to expressive control. *Journal of Personality, 61,* 133–158.

Garcia, L. T. (1982). Sex role orientation and stereotypes about male–female sexuality. *Sex Roles, 8,* 863–876.

Garcia-Borreguero, D., & Bronisch, T. (1992). Improvement of social phobic symptoms after treatment with brofaromine, a reversible and selective inhibitor of MAO–A. *European Psychiatry, 7,* 93–94.

Gardner, R. M., & Tockerman, Y. R. (1994). A computer–TV methodology for investigating the influence of somatotype on perceived personality traits. *Journal of Social Behavior and Personality, 9,* 555–563.

Garrett, L. (1995). *The coming plague: Newly emerging diseases in a world out of balance.* New York: Farrar, Straus and Giroux.

Geen, R. G. (1968). Some effects of observing violence upon the behavior of the observer. In B. A. Maher (Ed.), *Progress in experimental personality research* (Vol. 8). New York: Academic Press.

Geen, R. G. (1989). Alternative conceptions of social facilitation. In P. B. Paulus (Ed.), *Psychology of group influence* (2nd ed., pp. 10037). New York: Academic Press.

Geen, R. G. (1991). *Human aggression.* Pacific Grove, CA: Brooks/Cole.

Geen, R. G. (1991). Behavioral and physiological reactions to observed violence: Effects of prior exposure to aggressive stimuli. *Journal of Personality and Social Psychology, 40,* 868–875.

Geen, R. G., & Gange, J. J. (1977). Drive theory of social facilitation: Twelve years of theory and research. *Psychological Bulletin, 84,* 1267–1288.

Geier, J. G. (1969). A trait approach to the study of leadership in small groups. *Journal of Communication, 17,* 316–323.

Geller, P. A., & Hobfoll, S. E. (1994). Gender differences in job stress, tedium and social support in the workplace. *Journal of Social and Personal Relationships, 11,* 555–572.

Gentile, D. A. (1993). Just what are sex and gender, anyway? A call for a new terminological standard. *Psychological Science, 4,* 120–122.

George, J. M. (1990). Personality, affect, and behavior in groups. *Journal of Applied Psychology, 75,* 107–116.

George, J. M. (1991). State or trait: Effects of positive mood on prosocial behaviors at work. *Journal of Applied Psychology, 76,* 299–307.

George, J. M. (1995). Leader positive mood and group performance: The case of customer service. *Journal of Applied Social Psychology, 25,* 778–794.

George, J. M., & Brief, A. P. (1992). Feeling good—doing good: A conceptual analysis of the mood at work–organizational spontaneity relationships. *Psychological Bulletin, 112,* 310–319.

Gerard, H. B., Wilhelmy, R. A., & Conolley, E. S. (1968). Conformity and group size. *Journal of Personality and Social Psychology, 8,* 79–82.

Gerrard, M., & Luus, C. A. E. (1995). Judgments of vulnerability to pregnancy: The role of risk factors and individual differences. *Personality and Social Psychology Bulletin, 21,* 160–171.

Gibbons, F. X., Gerrard, M., & McCoy, S. B. (1995). Prototype perception predicts (lack of) pregnancy prevention. *Personality and Social Psychology Bulletin, 21,* 85–93.

Gibbons, F. X., Gerrard, M., Lando, H. A., & McGovern, P. G. (1991). Social comparison and smoking cessation: The role of the "typical smoker." *Journal of Experimental Social Psychology, 27,* 239–258.

Gibbs, N. (1995). In search of the dying. *Time, 145*(22), 44–47.

Gigone, D., & Hastie, R. (1993). The common knowledge effect: Information sharing and group judgment. *Journal of Personality and Social Psychology, 65,* 959–974.

Gilbert, D., & Jones, E. E. (1986). Perceiver-induced constraint: Interpretations of self-generated reality. *Journal of Personality and Social Psychology, 50,* 269–280.

Gilbert, D. T., & Hixon, J. G. (1991). The trouble of thinking: Activation and application of stereotypic beliefs. *Journal of Personality and Social Psychology, 6,* 509–517.

Gilbert, D. T., & Osborne, R. E. (1989). Thinking backward: Some curable and incurable consequences of cognitive busyness. *Journal of Personality and Social Psychology, 54,* 733–740.

Gilbert, D. T., McNulty, S. E., Giuliano, T. A., & Benson, J. E. (1992). Blurry words and fuzzy deeds: The attribution of obscure behavior. *Journal of Personality and Social Psychology, 62,* 18–25.

Gilbert, D. T., Pelham, B. W., & Krull, D. S. (1988). On cognitive busyness: When person perceivers meet persons perceived. *Journal of Personality and Social Psychology, 54,* 733–740.

Gilbert, D. T., Tafarodi, R. W., & Malone, P. S. (1993). You can't not believe everything you read. *Journal of Personality and Social Psychology, 65,* 221–233.

Gilbert, L. A. (1993). *Two careers/one family.* Newbury Park, CA: Sage.

Gillen, B. (1981). Physical attractiveness: A determinant of two types of goodness. *Personality and Social Psychology Bulletin, 7,* 277–281.

Gilovich, T., & Medvec, V. H. (1994). The temporal pattern to the experience of regret. *Journal of Personality and Social Psychology, 67,* 357–365.

Gladue, B. A. (1991). Aggressive behavioral characteristics, hormones, and sexual orientation in men and women. *Aggressive Behavior, 17,* 313–326.

Gladue, B. A., & Delaney, H. J. (1990). Gender differences in perception of attractiveness of men and women in bars. *Personality and Social Psychology Bulletin, 16,* 378–391.

Glass, D. C. (1977). *Behavior patterns, stress, and coronary disease.* Hillsdale, NJ: Erlbaum.

Glass, D. C. (1989). Psychology and health: Obstacles and opportunities. *Journal of Applied Social Psychology, 19,* 1145–1163.

Glass, D. C., Singer, J. E., & Friedman, L. N. (1969). Psychic cost of adaptation to an environmental stressor. *Journal of Personality and Social Psychology, 12,* 200–210.

Gleick, E. (1995, August 21). Out of the mouths of babes. *Time,* 33–34.

Glenn, N. D., & Weaver, C. N. (1988). The changing relationship of marital status to reported happiness. *Journal of Marriage and the Family, 50,* 317–324.

Glick, P. C. (1983). Seventh-year itch. *Medical Aspects of Human Sexuality, 17*(5), 103.

Godfrey, D. K., Jones, E. E., & Lord, C. G. (1986). Self-promotion is not ingratiating. *Journal of Personality and Social Psychology, 50,* 106–115.

Goethals, G. R., & Zanna, M. P. (1979). The role of social comparison in choice shifts. *Journal of Personality and Social Psychology, 37,* 1469–1476.

Goethals, G. R., Cooper, J., & Naficy, A. (1979). Role of foreseen, foreseeable, and unforeseeable behavioral consequences in the arousal of cognitive dissonance. *Journal of Personality and Social Psychology, 37,* 1179–1185.

Gold, J. A., Ryckman, R. M., & Mosley, N. R. (1984). Romantic mood induction and attraction to a dissimilar other: Is love blind? *Personality and Social Psychology Bulletin, 10,* 358–368.

Goldsmith, H. H., & Harman, C. (1994). Temperament and attachment: Individuals and relationships. *Current Directions in Psychological Science, 3,* 53–57.

Goldstein, A. G., Chance, J. E., & Schneller, G. R. (1989). Frequency of eyewitness identification in criminal cases: A survey of prosecutors. *Bulletin of the Psychonomic Society, 27,* 71–74.

Goldstein, M. D., & Strube, M. J. (1994). Independence revisited: The relation between positive and negative affect in a naturalistic setting. *Personality and Social Psychology Bulletin, 20,* 57–64.

Goldstein, W. D., & Strube, M. J. (1994). Independence revisited: The relation between positive and negative affect in a naturalistic setting. *Personality and Social Psychology Bulletin, 20,* 57–64.

Goleman, D. (1991, November 13). All too often, the doctor isn't listening, studies show. *New York Times,* pp. C1, C15.

Goleman, D. (1994, May 11). Seeking out small pleasures keeps immune system strong. *New York Times,* p. C11.

Goleman, D. (1994, November 29). Study finds jurors often hear evidence with a closed mind. *The New York Times,* pp. C1, C12.

Goleman, D. (1994, March 22). The "wrong" sex: A new definition of childhood pain. *New York Times,* C1, C9.

Goleman, D. (1995, August 8). Brain may tag all perceptions with a value. *New York Times,* pp. C1, C10.

Goleman, D. (1995, January 17). Studies point to flaws in lineups of suspects. *The New York Times,* pp. C1, C7.

Gonzalez, R., Ellsworth, P. C., & Pembroke, M. (1993). Response biases in lineups and showups. *Journal of Personality and Social Psychology, 64,* 525–537.

Gordon, C. (1968). Self-conceptions: Configurations of content. In C. Gordon & K. J. Gergen (Eds.), *The self in social interaction. Vol. I. Classic and contemporary perspectives.* New York: Wiley.

Gorman, C. (1992). Danger overhead. *Time, 140*(7), 70.

Gouaux, C. (1971). Induced affective states and interpersonal attraction. *Journal of Personality and Social Psychology, 20,* 37–43.

Gould, D., & Weiss, M. (1981). Effect of model similarity and model self-talk on self-efficacy in muscular endurance. *Journal of Sport Psychology, 3,* 17–29

Govoni, S. J. (1992, February). *To catch a thief.* CFO, 24–32.

Graham, S., & Folkes, V. (Eds.). (1990). *Attribution theory: Applications to achievement, mental health, and interpersonal conflict.* Hillsdale, NJ: Erlbaum.

Grant, P. R. (1993). Ethnocentrism in response to a threat to social identity. *Journal of Social Behavior and Personality, 8,* 143–154.

Grau, P. N. (1985, November/December). Two causes of underachievement: The scapegoat phenomenon and the Peter Pan syndrome. *Cattaraugus-Allegany Teacher's Resource Center,* pp. 47–50.

Graziano, W. G., Jensen-Campbell, L. A., Shebilske, L. J., & Lundgren, S. R. (1993). Social influence, sex differences, and judgments of beauty: Putting the interpersonal back in interpersonal attraction. *Journal of Personality and Social Psychology, 65,* 522–531.

Greeberg, J. (1994). Using socially fair treatment to promote acceptance of a work site smoking ban. *Journal of Applied Psychology, 79,* 288–297.

Greenbaum, P., & Rosenfield, H. W. (1978). Patterns of avoidance in responses to interpersonal staring and proximity: Effects of bystanders on drivers at a traffic intersection. *Journal of Personality and Social Psychology, 36,* 575–587.

Greenberg, J. (1989). Cognitive re-evaluation of outcomes in response to underpayment inequity. *Academy of Management Journal, 32* 174–184.

Greenberg, J. (1990). Employee theft as a reaction to underpayment inequity: The hidden cost of pay cuts. *Journal of Applied Psychology, 75,* 561–568.

Greenberg, J. (1993a). The social side of fairness: Interpersonal and informational classes of organizational justice. In R. Cropanzano (Ed.), *Justice in the workplace* (pp. 79–103). Hillsdale, NJ: Erlbaum.

Greenberg, J. (1993b). Stealing in the name of justice: Informational and interpersonal moderators of theft reactions to underpayment inequity. *Organizational Behavior and Human Decision Processes, 54,* 81–103.

Greenberg, J., & Baron, R. A. (1995). *Behavior in organizations* (5th ed.). Englewood Cliffs, NJ: Prentice-Hall.

Greenberg, J., & Scott, K. S. (in press). Why do workers bite the hands that feed them? Employee theft as a social exchange process. In B. M. Staw & L. L. Cummings (Eds.), *Research in organizational behavior* (Vol. 18). Greenwich, CT: JAI Press.

Greenberg, J., Pyszczynski, T., & Solomon, S. (1982). The self-serving attributional bias: Beyond self-presentation. *Journal of Experimental Social Psychology, 18,* 56–67.

Greenberg, J., Pyszczynski, T., Solomon, S., Pinel, E., Simon, L., & Jordan, K. (1993). Effects of self-esteem on vulnerability-denying defensive distortions: Further evidence of an anxiety-buffering function of self-esteem. *Journal of Experimental Social Psychology, 29,* 229–251.

Greenberg, J., Solomon, S., Pyszczynski, T., Rosenblatt, A., Burling, J., Lyon, D., Simon, L., & Pinel, E. (1992). Why do people need self-esteem? Converging evidence that self-esteem serves an anxiety-buffering function. *Journal of Personality and Social Psychology, 63,* 913–922.

Greenberg, J. A., & Baron, R. (1995). *Behavior in organizations: Understanding and managing the human side of work* (5th ed.). Boston: Allyn & Bacon.

Greenberg, M. A., & Stone, A. A. (1992). Emotional disclosure about traumas and its relation to health: Effects of previous disclosure and trauma severity. *Journal of Personality and Social Psychology, 63,* 75–84.

Greenwald, J. (1993). Here comes the sun. Time, 142(16), 84–85.

Greer, A. E., & Buss, D. M. (1994). Tactics for promoting sexual encounters. *Journal of Sex Research, 31,* 185–201.

Gregerson, H. B., & Black, J. S. (1992). Antecedents to commitment to a parent company and a foreign operation. *Academy of Management Journal, 154,* 461–485.

Grieve, N. (1980). Beyond sexual stereotypes. Androgyny: A model or an ideal? In N. Grieve & P. Grimshaw (Eds.), *Australian women: Feminist perspectives* (pp. 247–257). Melbourne, Australia: Oxford University Press.

Griffin, D., & Bartholomew, K. (1994b). Models of the self and other: Fundamental dimensions underlying measures of adult attachment. *Journal of Personality and Social Psychology, 67,* 430–445.

Griffin, D. W., & Bartholomew, K. (1994a). The metaphysics of measurement: The case of adult attachment. In K. Bartholomew & D. Perlman (Eds.), *Advances in personal relationships: Vol. 5. Attachment processes in adulthood* (pp. 17–52). London: Jessica Kingsley.

Griffin, D. W., & Buehler, R. (1993). Role of construal process in conformity and dissent. *Journal of Personality and Social Psychology, 65,* 657–669.

Groff, D. B., Baron, R. S., & Moore, D. L. (1983). Distraction, attentional conflict, and drivelike behavior. *Journal of Experimental Social Psychology, 19,* 359–380.

Grondahl, P. (1989, December 5). Trees of life: Reforestation begins in the backyard. *Albany Times Union,* pp. C-1, C-12.

Grossman, M., & Wood, W. (1993). Sex differences in intensity of emotional experience: A social role interpretation. *Journal of Personality and Social Psychology, 65,* 1010–1022.

Grusec, J. E. (1991). The socialization of altruism. In M. S. Clark (Ed.), *Prosocial behavior* (pp. 9–33). Newbury Park, CA: Sage.

Gudjonsson, G. H. (1993). Confession evidence, psychological vulnerability and expert testimony. *Journal of Community and Applied Social Psychology, 3,* 117–129.

Gudjonsson, G. H., & Clark, N. K. (1986). Suggestibility in police interrogation: A social psychological model. *Social Behavior, 1,* 83–104.

Guimond, S., & Palmer, D. L. (1990). Type of academic training and causal attributions for social problems. *European Journal of Social Psychology, 20,* 61–75.

Gully, K. J., & Dengerink, H. A. (1983). The dyadic interaction of persons with violent and nonviolent histories. *Aggressive Behavior, 9,* 13–20.

Gunter, B. G., & Gunter, N. C. (1991). Inequities in household labor: Sex role orientation and the need for cleanliness and responsibility as predictors. *Journal of Social Behavior and Personality, 6,* 559–572.

Gur, R. C., Mozley, L. H., Mozley, P. D., Resnick, S. M., Karp, J. S., Alavi, A., Arnold, S. E., & Gur, R. E. (1995). Sex differences in regional glucose metabolism during a resting state. *Science, 267,* 528–531.

Guzzo, R. A., Noonan, K. A., & Elron, E. (1994). Expatriate managers and the psychological contract. *Journal of Applied Psychology, 79,* 617–626.

Hackel, L. S., & Ruble, D. N. (1992). Changes in the marital relationship after the first baby is born: Predicting the impact of expectancy disconfirmation. *Journal of Personality and Social Psychology, 62,* 944–957.

Hackett, R. D., Bycio, P., & Hausdorf, P. A. (1994). Further assessments of Myer and Allen's (1991) three-component model of organizational commitment. *Journal of Applied Psychology, 79,* 15–23.

Hagborg, W. J. (1993). Gender differences on Harter's Self-Perception Profile for Adolescents. *Journal of Social Behavior and Personality, 8,* 141–148.

Halford, W. K., & Sanders, M. R. (1990). The relationship of cognition and behavior during marital interaction. *Journal of Social and Clinical Psychology, 9,* 489–510.

Hall, J. A., & Veccia, E. M. (1990). More "touching" observations: New insights on men, women, and interpersonal touch. *Journal of Personality and Social Psychology, 59,* 1155–1162.

Hallman, W. K., & Wandersman, A. (1992). Attribution of responsibility and individual and collective coping with environmental threats. *Journal of Social Issues, 48*(4), 101–118.

Hamburger, M. E., Hogben, M., McGowan, S., & Dawson, L. J. (1996). Assessing hypergender ideology: Development and initial validation of a gender-neutral measure of adherence to extreme gender role beliefs. *Journal of Research in Personality, 30.*

Hamilton, D. L., & Gifford, R. K. (1976). Illusory correlation in interpersonal perception: A cognitive basis of stereotypic judgments. *Journal of Experimental Social Psychology, 12,* 392–407.

Hamilton, D. L., & Sherman, S. J. (1989). Illusory correlations: Implications for stereotype theory and research. In D. Bar-Tal, C. F. Graumann, A. W. Kruglanski, & W. Stroebe (Eds.), *Stereotyping and prejudice: Changing conceptions* (pp. 59–82). New York: Springer-Verlag.

Hamilton, D. L., Sherman, S. J., & Ruvolo, C. (1990). Stereotype-based expectancies: Effects on information processing and social behavior. *Journal of Social Issues, 46,* 35–60.

Hamilton, G. V. (1978). Obedience and responsibility: A jury simulation. *Journal of Personality and Social Psychology, 36,* 126–146.

Hamilton, J. C., Falconer, J. J., & Greenberg, M. D. (1992). The relationship between self-consciousness and dietary restraint. *Journal of Social and Clinical Psychology, 11,* 158–166.

Hamilton, V. L., Hoffman, W. S., Broman, C. L., & Rauma, D. (1993). Unemployment, distress, and coping: A panel study of autoworkers. *Journal of Personality and Social Psychology, 65,* 234–247.

Hammer, M., & Champy, J. (1993). *Reengineering the corporation: A manifesto for business revolution.* New York: Harper Business.

Hammock, D. S., & Richardson, D. B. A. (1992). Aggression as one response to conflict. *Journal of Applied Social Psychology, 22,* 298–311.

Hammond, W. R., & Yung, B. (1993). Psychology's role in the public health response to assaultive violence among young African-American men. *American Psychologist, 48,* 142–154.

Hans, V., & Vidmar, N. (1982). Jury selection. In N. L. Kerr & R. M. Bray (Eds.), *The psychology of the courtroom* (pp. 39–82). New York: Academic Press.

Hansen, C. H., & Hansen, R. D. (1988). Finding the face in the crowd: An anger superiority effect. *Journal of Personality and Social Psychology, 54,* 917–924.

Harkins, S. (1987). Social loafing and social facilitation. *Journal of Experimental Social Psychology, 23,* 1–18.

Harkins, S., & Szymanski, K. (1989). Social loafing and group evaluation. *Journal of Personality and Social Psychology, 56,* 934–941.

Harmon, M. P., & Coe, K. (1993). Cancer mortality in U.S. counties with hazardous waste sites. *Population and Environment, 14,* 463–480.

Harrigan, J. A., Lucic, K. S., Kay, D., McLaney, A., & Rosenthal, R. (1991). Effect of expresser role and type of self-touching on observers' perceptions. *Journal of Applied Social Psychology, 21,* 585–609.

Harris, M. B. (1993). How provoking! What makes men and women angry? *Journal of Applied Social Psychology, 23,* 199–211.

Harris, M. B. (1994). Gender of subject and target as mediators of aggression. *Journal of Applied Social Psychology, 24,* 453–471.

Harris, M. B. (in press). Aggressive experiences and aggressiveness: Relationship to gender, ethnicity, and age. *Journal of Applied Social Psychology.*

Harris, M. B., (1992). Sex, race, and experiences of aggression. *Aggressive Behavior, 18,* 201–217.

Harris, M. B., Harris, R. J., & Bochner, S. (1982). Fat, four-eyed, and female: Stereotypes of obesity, glasses, and gender. *Journal of Applied Social Psychology, 12,* 503–516.

Hart, A. J. (1995). Naturally occurring expectation effects. *Journal of Personality and Social Psychology, 68,* 109–115.

Hasart, J. K., & Hutchinson, K. L. (1993). The effects of eyeglasses on perceptions of interpersonal attraction. *Journal of Social Behavior and Personality, 8,* 521–528.

Haslam, N. (1994). Mental representation of social relationships: Dimensions, laws, or categories? *Journal of Personality and Social Psychology, 67,* 575–584.

Hastie, R. (Ed.). (1993). *Inside the juror: The psychology of juror decision making.* Cambridge, England: Cambridge University Press.

Hatfield, E. (1988). Passionate and companionate love. In R. J. Sternberg & M. I. Barnes (Eds.), *The psychology of love* (pp. 191–217). New Haven, CT: Yale University Press.

Hatfield, E., & Rapson, R. L. (1992). Similarity and attraction in close relationships. *Communication Monographs, 59,* 209–212.

Hatfield, E., & Rapson, R. L. (1993a). *Love, sex, and intimacy: Their psychology, biology, and history.* New York: HarperCollins.

Hatfield, E., & Rapson, R. L. (1993b). Historical and cross-cultural perspectives on passionate love and sexual desire. *Annual Review of Sex Research, 4,* 67–97.

Hatfield, E., & Sprecher, S. (1986). *Mirror, mirror . . . :* The importance of looks in everyday life. Albany, NY: S.U.N.Y. Press.

Hatfield, E., & Sprecher, S. (1986). Measuring passionate love in intimate relations. *Journal of Adolescence, 9,* 383–410.

Hatfield, E., & Walster, G. W. (1981). *A new look at love.* Reading, MA: Addison-Wesley.

Hatfield, E., Sprecher, S., Pillemer, J. T., Greenberger, D., & Wexler, P. (1989). Gender differences in what is desired in the sexual relationship. *Journal of Psychology and Human Sexuality, 1,* 39–52.

Haub, C. (1991). World and United States population prospects. *Population and Environment, 12,* 297–310.

Hays, R. B. (1989). The day-to-day functioning of close versus casual friendships. *Journal of Social and Personal Relationships, 6,* 21–37.

Hays, R. B., & DiMatteo, M. R. (1984). Toward a more therapeutic physician–patient relationship. In S. Duck (Ed.), *Personal relationships: Vol. 5. Repairing personal relationships* (pp. 1–20). New York: Academic Press.

Hazan, C., & Shaver, P. (1987). Romantic love conceptualized as an attachment process. *Journal of Personality and Social Psychology, 52,* 511–524.

Hazan, C., & Shaver, P. R. (1990). Love and work: An attachment-theoretical perspective. *Journal of Personality and Social Psychology, 59,* 270–280.

Hecht, M. L., Marston, P. J., & Larkey, L. K. (1994). Love ways and relationship quality in heterosexual relationships. *Journal of Social and Personal Relationships, 11,* 25–43.

Heider, F. (1958). *The psychology of interpersonal relations.* New York: Wiley.

Heilbroner, R. L. (1974). *An inquiry into the human prospect.* New York: Norton.

Heilig, G. K. (1994). The greenhouse gas methane (CH_4): Sources and sinks, the impact of population growth, possible interventions. *Population and Environment, 16,* 109–137.

Heilman, M. E., Block, C. J., & Lucas, J. A. (1992). Presumed incompetent? Stigmatization and affirmative action efforts. *Journal of Applied Psychology, 77,* 536–544.

Heilman, M. E., Martell, R. F., & Simon, M. C. (1988). The vagaries of sex bias: Conditions regulating the undervaluation, equivalation, and overvaluation of female job applicants. *Organizational Behavior and Human Decision Processes, 41,* 98–110.

Heinberg, L. J., & Thompson, J. K. (1992). Social comparison: Gender, target importance ratings, and relation to body image disturbance. *Journal of Social Behavior and Personality, 7,* 335–344.

Heine, S. J., & Lehman, D. R. (1995). Cultural variation in unrealistic optimism: Does the West feel more invulnerable than the East? *Journal of Personality and Social Psychology, 68,* 595–607.

Helgeson, V. S. (1992). Moderators of the relation between perceived control and adjustment to chronic illness. *Journal of Personality and Social Psychology, 63,* 656–666.

Helman, D., & Bookspan, P. (1992, February 8). In Big Bird's world, females are secondary. *Albany Times Union,* E-2.

Helson, R., & Roberts, B. (1992). The personality of young adult couples and wives' work patterns. *Journal of Personality, 60,* 575–597.

Henderson, J., & Taylor, J. (1985, November 17). Study finds bias in death sentence: Killers of whites risk execution. *Albany Times Union,* pp. A-19.

Henderson-King, D. H., & Veroff, J. (1994). Sexual satisfaction and marital well-being in the first years of marriage. *Journal of Social and Personal Relationships, 11,* 509–534.

Hendrick, C., & Hendrick, S. S. (1986). A theory and method of love. *Journal of Personality and Social Psychology, 50,* 392–402.

Hendrick, C., Hendrick, S. S., Foote, F. H., & Slapion-Foote, M. J. (1984). Do men and women love differently? *Journal of Social and Personal Relationships, 1,* 177–195.

Hendrick, S. S., & Hendrick, C. (1987). Love and sex attitudes and religious beliefs. *Journal of Social and Clinical Psychology, 5,* 391–398.

Hendrick, S. S., & Hendrick, C. (1993). Lovers as friends. *Journal of Social and Personal Relationships, 10,* 459–466.

Hendrick, S. S., Hendrick, C., & Adler, N. L. (1988). Romantic relationships: Love, satisfaction, and staying together. *Journal of Personality and Social Psychology, 54,* 980–988.

Hendrix, W. H., Steel, R. P., & Schultz, S. A. (1987). Job stress and life stress: Their causes and consequences. *Journal of Social Behavior and Personality, 2,* 291–302.

Henry, W. A. III. (1991). The journalist and the murder. *Time, 138*(15), 86.

Hepworth, J. T., & West, S. G. (1988). Lynchings and the economy: A time-series reanalysis of Hovland and Sears (1940). *Journal of Personality and Social Psychology, 55,* 239–247.

Herbert, J. D. (1995). An overview of the current status of social phobia. *Applied and Preventive Psychology, 4,* 39–51.

Hern, W. M. (1990). Why are there so many of us? Description and diagnosis of a planetary ecopathological process. *Population and Environment, 12,* 9–39.

Hershberger, S. L., Lichtenstein, P., & Knox, S. S. (1994). Genetic and environmental influences on perceptions of organizational climate. *Journal of Applied Psychology, 79,* 24–33.

Herzog, T. A. (1994). Automobile driving as seen by the actor, the active observer, and the passive observer. *Journal of Applied Social Psychology, 24,* 2057–2074.

Hewstone, M., Bond, M. H., & Wan, K. C. (1983). Social factors and social attributions: The explanation of intergroup differences in Hong Kong. *Social Cognition, 2,* 142–157.

Higgins, E. T. (1990). Personality, social psychology, and person–situation relations: Standards and knowledge activation as a common language. In L. A. Pervin (Ed.), *Handbook of personality: Theory and research* (pp. 301–338). New York: Guilford.

Higgins, E. T., & Bargh, J. A. (1987). Social cognition and social perception. *Annual Review of Psychology, 38,* 369–425.

Higgins, E. T., & King, G. (1981). Accessibility of social constructs: Information processing consequences of individual and contextual variability. In N. Cantor & J. Kihlstrom (Eds.), *Personality, cognition, and social interaction* (pp. 69–121). Hillsdale, NJ: Erlbaum.

Higgins, E. T., Rohles, W. S., & Jones, C. R. (1977). Category accessibility and impression formation. *Journal of Experimental Social Psychology, 13,* 141–154.

Hill, C. A. (1987). Affiliation motivation: People who need people but in different ways. *Journal of Personality and Social Psychology, 52,* 1008–1018.

Hill, C. T., Rubin, Z., & Peplau, L. A. (1976). Breakups before marriage: The end of 103 affairs. *Journal of Social Issues, 32,* 147–168.

Hilton, J. L., Klein, J. G., & von Hippel, W. (1991). Attention allocation and impression formation. *Personality and Social Psychology Bulletin, 17,* 548–559.

Hilts, P. J. (1993, July 19). Studies say soot kills up to 60,000 in U.S. each year. *New York Times,* pp. A1, A16.

Hinsz, V. B. (1995). Goal setting by groups performing an additive task: A comparison with individual goal setting. *Journal of Applied Social Psychology, 25,* 965–990.

Hixon, J. G., & Swan, W. B., Jr. (1993). When does introspection bear fruit? Self-reflection, self-insight, and interpersonal choices. *Journal of Personality and Social Psychology, 64,* 35–43.

Hochschild, A. (1989). *The second shift: Inside the two-job marriage.* New York: Viking.

Hogg, M. A., & Hains, S. C. (1996). Intergroup relations and group solidarity: Effects of group identification and social beliefs on depersonalized attraction. *Journal of Personality and Social Psychology, 70,* 25–309.

Hogg, M. A., Cooper-Shaw, L., & Holzworth, D. W. (1993). Group prototypicality and depersonalized attraction in small interactive groups. *Personality and Social Psychology Bulletin, 19,* 452–465.

Hollingsworth, W. G. (1995). Population, immigration, and a believable future. *Population and Environment, 16,* 285–295.

Holtgraves, T., & Grayer, A. R. (1994). I am not a crook: Effects of denials on perceptions of a defendant's guilt, personality, and motives. *Journal of Applied Social Psychology, 24,* 2132–2150.

Holtzworth-Munroe, A., & Jacobson, N. S. (1985). Causal attributions of married couples: When do they search for causes? What do they conclude when they do? *Journal of Personality and Social Psychology, 48,* 1398–1412.

Holtzworth-Munroe, A., & Stuart, G. L. (1994). Typologies of male batterers: Three subtypes and the differences among them. *Psychological Bulletin, 116,* 476–497.

Hope, D. A., Holt, C. S., & Heimberg, R. G. (1995). Social phobia. In T. R. Giles (Ed.), *Handbook of effective psychotherapy* (pp. 227–251). New York: Plenum.

House R. J. (1977). A theory of charismatic leadership. In J. G. Hunt & L. L. Larson (Eds.), *Leadership: The cutting edge* (pp. 189–207). Carbondale, IL: Southern Illinois University Press.

House, R. J., & Podsakoff, P. M. (1994). Leadership effectiveness: Past perspectives and future directions for research. In J. Greenberg (Ed.), *Organizational behavior: The state of the science* (pp. 45–82). Hillsdale, NJ: Erlbaum.

House, R. J., Spangler, W. D., & Woycke, J. (1991). Personality and charisma in the U.S. presidency: A psychological theory of leader effectiveness. *Administrative Science Quarterly, 36,* 364–396.

Hovland, C. I., & Sears, R. R. (1940). Minor studies in aggression: VI. Correlation of lynchings with economic indices. *Journal of Psychology, 9,* 301–310.

Hovland, C. I., & Weiss, W. (1951). The influence of source credibility on communication effectiveness. *Public Opinion Quarterly, 15,* 635–650.

Hovland, C. I., Janis, I. L., & Kelley, H. H. (1953). Communication and persuasion: Psychological studies of opinion change. New Haven, CT: Yale University Press.

Hovland, C. I., Lumsdaine, A. A., & Sheffield, F. D. (1949). *Experiments on mass communications.* Princeton, NJ: Princeton University Press.

Howard, D. J. (1990). The influence of verbal responses to common greetings on compliance behavior: The foot-in-the-mouth effect. *Journal of Applied Social Psychology, 20,* 1185–1196.

Howard, G. S. (1985). The role of values in the science of psychology. *American Psychologist, 40,* 255–265.

Howell, J. M., & Avolio, B. J. (1992). The ethics of charismatic leadership: Submission or liberation? *Academy of Management Executive, 6,* 43–54.

Howell, J. M., & Frost, P. J. (1989). A laboratory study of charismatic leadership. *Organizational Behavior and Human Decision Processes, 43,* 243–269.

Howells, G. N. (1993). Self-monitoring and personality: Would the real high self-monitor please stand up? *Journal of Social Behavior and Personality, 8,* 59–72.

Howes, C. (1989). Friendships in very young children: Definition and functions. In B. H. Schneider, G. Attili, J. Nadel, & R. P. Weissberg (Eds.), *Social competence in developmental perspective* (pp. 127–128). Dordrecht, Netherlands: Kluwer.

Hoyle, R. H. (1993). Interpersonal attraction in the absence of explicit attitudinal information. *Social Cognition, 11,* 309–320.

Hoyle, R. H., & Sowards, B. A. (1993). Self-monitoring and the regulation of social experience: A control-process model. *Journal of Social and Clinical Psychology, 12,* 280–306.

Huang, K., & Uba, L. (1992). Premarital sexual behavior among Chinese college students in the United States. *Archives of Sexual Behavior, 21,* 227–240.

Huesmann, L. R., & Miller, L. S. (1994). Long-term effects of repeated exposure to media violence in childhood. In L. R. Huesmann (Ed.), *Aggressive behavior,* pp. 153–186. New York: Plenum.

Huesmann, L. R. (1988). An information processing model for the development of aggression. *Aggressive Behavior, 14,* 13–24.

Huesmann, L. R. (1994). (Ed.). *Aggressive behavior: Current perspectives.* New York: Plenum.

Huesmann, L. R., & Eron, L. D. (1984). Cognitive processes and the persistence of aggressive behavior. *Aggressive Behavior, 10,* 243–251.

Huesmann, L. R., & Eron, L. D. (1986). *Television and the aggressive child: A cross-national comparison.* Hillsdale, NJ: Erlbaum.

Hughes, C. F., Uhlmann, C., & Pennebaker, J. W. (1994). The body's response to processing emotional trauma: Linking verbal text with autonomic activity. *Journal of Personality, 62,* 565–585.

Hui, C. H., & Triandis, H. C. (1986). Individualism–collectivism: A study of cross-cultural researchers. *Journal of Cross-Cultural Psychology, 17,* 225–248.

Hulin, C. L. (1991). Adaptation, persistence, and commitment in organizations. In M. D. Dunnette & I. M. Hough (Eds.), *Handbook of industrial and organizational psychology* (2nd ed. Vol. 2, pp. 445–506). Palo Alto, CA: Consulting Psychologists Press.

Hummert, M. L., Crockett, W. H., & Kemper, S. (1990). Processing mechanisms underlying use of the balance scheme. *Journal of Personality and Social Psychology, 58,* 5–21.

Humphriss, N. (1989, November 20). Letters. *Time,* 12.

Hyde, J. S., & Plant, E. A. (1995). Magnitude of psychological gender differences: Another side to the story. *American Psychologist, 50,* 159–161.

Ickes, W., Reidhead, S., & Patterson, M. (1986). Machiavellianism and self-monitoring: As different as "me" and "you." *Social Cognition, 4,* 58–74.

Idler, E. L. (1993). Perceptions of pain and perceptions of health. *Motivation and Emotion, 17,* 205–224.

Iffaldano, M. T., & Murchinsky, P. M. (1985). Job satisfaction and job performance: A meta-analysis. *Psychological Bulletin, 72,* 374–381.

Insko, C. A. (1985). Balance theory, the Jordan paradigm, and the West tetrahedron. In L. Berkowitz (Ed.), *Advances in experimental social psychology.* New York: Academic Press.

Isen, A. M. (1984). Toward understanding the role of affect in cognition. In S. R. Wyer & T. K. Srull (Eds.), *Handbook of social cognition* (Vol. 3, pp. 179–236). Hillsdale, NJ: Erlbaum.

Isen, A. M. (1987). Positive affect, cognitive processes, and social behavior. In L. Berkowitz (Ed.), *Advances in experimental social psychology* (Vol. 20), pp. 203–253. New York: Academic Press.

Isen, A. M., & Baron, R. A. (1991). Affect and organizational behavior. In B. M. Staw & L. L. Cummings (Eds.), *Research in organizational behavior* (Vol. 15, pp. 1–53).

Isen, A. M., & Levin, P. A. (1972). Effect of feeling good on helping: Cookies and kindness. *Journal of Personality and Social Psychology, 21,* 384–388.

Istvan, J., & Griffitt, W. (1980). Effects of sexual experience on dating desirability and marriage desirability. *Journal of Marriage and the Family, 43,* 377–385.

Istvan, J., Griffitt, W., & Weidner, G. (1983). Sexual arousal and the polarization of perceived sexual attractiveness. *Basic and Applied Social Psychology, 4,* 307–318.

Izard, C. (1991). *The psychology of emotions.* New York: Plenum.

Izard, C. (1992). Basic emotions, relations among emotions, and emotion–cognition relations. *Psychological Review, 99,* 561–565.

Jackson, L. A., & Grabski, S. V. (1988). Perceptions of fair play and the gender wage gap. *Journal of Applied Social Psychology, 18,* 606–625.

Jackson, L. A., Gardner, P., & Sullivan, L. (1992). Explaining gender differences in self-pay expectations: Social comparison standards and perceptions of fair pay. *Journal of Applied Psychology, 77,* 651–663.

Jacobs, J. R. (1992). Facilitators of romantic attraction and their relation to lovestyle. *Social Behavior and Personality, 20,* 227–234.

Jaffe, Y., Malamuth, N., Feingold, J., & Feshbach, S. (1974). Sexual arousal and behavioral aggression. *Journal of Personality and Social Psychology, 30,* 759–764.

James, D. B., & Kristiansen, C. M. (1985). Women's reactions to miscarriage: The role of attributions, coping styles, and knowledge. *Journal of Applied Social Psychology, 25,* 59–76.

James, W. (1890). *The principles of psychology.* New York: Holt.

James, W. J. (1890). *Principles of psychology.* New York: Holt.

Jamieson, D. W., & Zanna, M. P. (1989). Need for structure in attitude formation and expression. In A. R. Pratkanis, S. J. Breckler, & A. G. Greenwald (Eds.), *Attitude structure and function* (pp. 383–406). Hillsdale, NJ: Erlbaum.

Janis, I. L. (1954). Personality correlates of susceptibility to persuasion. *Journal of Personality, 22,* 504–518.

Janis, I. L. (1982). *Victims of groupthink* (2nd ed.). Boston: Houghton Mifflin.

Jarvis, M. J. (1991). A time for conceptual stock taking. Special issue: Future directions in tobacco research. *British Journal of Addiction, 86,* 632–647.

Jay, S. M., Ozolins, M., Elliott, C. H., & Caldwell, S. (1983). Assessment of children's distress during painful medical procedures. *Health Psychology, 2,* 133–147.

Jeffries, V. (1987). Love: The five virtues of St. Thomas Aquinas. A factor analysis of love of parents among university students. *Sociology and Social Research, 71,* 174–182.

Jeffries, V. (1990). Adolescent love, perception of parental love, and relationship quality. *Family Perspective, 24,* 175–196.

Jeffries, V. (1993). Virtue and attraction: Validation of a measure of love. *Journal of Social and Personal Relationships, 10,* 99–117.

Jemmott, J. B. III, & Magloire, K. (1988). Academic stress, social support, and secretory immunoglobulin. *Journal of Personality and Social Psychology, 55,* 803–810.

Jensen-Campbell, L. A., West, S. G., & Graziano, W. G. (1995). Dominance, prosocial orientation, and female preferences: Do nice guys really finish last? *Journal of Personality and Social Psychology, 68,* 427–440.

Jex, S. M., Cvetanovski, J., & Allen, S. J. (1994). Self-esteem as a moderator of the impact of unemployment. *Journal of Social Behavior and Personality, 9,* 69–80.

Johnson, A. B., & Byrne, D. (1996, March). *Effects of proximity in familiarity and preferences for places of work*. Paper presented at the meeting of the Eastern Psychological Association, Philadelphia.

Johnson, B. T., & Eagly, A. H. (1989). Effects of involvement on persuasion: A meta-analysis. *Psychological Bulletin, 106*, 290–314.

Johnson, D. F., & Pittenger, J. B. (1984). Attribution, the attractiveness stereotype, and the elderly. *Developmental Psychology, 20*, 1168–1172.

Johnson, J. C., Poteat, G. M., & Ironsmith, M. (1991). Structural vs. marginal effects: A note on the importance of structure in determining sociometric status. *Journal of Social Behavior and Personality, 6*, 489–508.

Johnson, K. A., Johnson, J. E., & Petzel, T. P. (1992). Social anxiety, depression, and distorted cognitions in college students. *Journal of Social and Clinical Psychology, 11*, 181–195.

Johnson, K. L., & Edwards, R. (1991). The effects of gender and type of romantic touch on perceptions of relational commitment. *Journal of Nonverbal Behavior, 15*, 43–55.

Johnson, M. P., Huston, T. L., Gaines, S. O., Jr., & Levinger, G. (1992). Patterns of married life among young couples. *Journal of Social and Personal Relationships, 9*, 343–364.

Johnson, R. A. (1993). *Negotiation basics: Concepts, skills, and exercises*. Thousand Oaks, CA: Sage.

Johnson, R. D. (1991). The influence of time-frame for achieving gender neutrality on evaluations of a male-dominated profession. *Journal of Social Behavior and Personality, 6*, 833–842.

Johnston, C., & Short, K. H. (1993). Depressive symptoms and perceptions of child behavior. *Journal of Social and Clinical Psychology, 12*, 164–181.

Johnstone, B., Frame, C. L., & Bouman, D. (1992). Physical attractiveness and athletic and academic ability in controversial–aggressive and rejected–aggressive children. *Journal of Social and Clinical Psychology, 11*, 71–79.

Joiner, T. E. Jr., & Schmidt, N. B. (1995). Dimensions of perfectionism, life stress, and depressed and anxious symptoms: Prospective support for diathesis–stress but not specific vulnerability among male undergraduates. *Journal of Social and Clinical Psychology, 14*, 165–183.

Joiner, T. E., Jr. (1994). The interplay of similarity and self-verification in relationship formation. *Social Behavior and Personality, 22*, 195–200.

Jolly, C. L. (1994). Four theories of population change and the environment. *Population and Environment, 16*, 61–90.

Jones, E. E. (1964). *Ingratiation: A social psychology analysis*. New York: Appleton-Century-Crofts.

Jones, E. E., & Davis, K. E. (1965). From acts to disposition: The attribution process in person perception. In L. Berkowitz (Ed.), *Advances in experimental social psychology* (Vol. 2, pp. 219–266). New York: Academic Press.

Jones, E. E., & McGillis, D. (1976). Corresponding inferences and attribution cube: A comparative reappraisal. In J. H. Har, W. J. Ickes, & R. F. Kidd (Eds.), *New directions in attribution research* (Vol. 1). Morristown, NJ: Erlbaum.

Jones, E. E., & Nisbett, R. E. (1971). *The actor and the observer: Divergent perceptions of the causes of behavior*. Morristown, NJ: General Learning Press.

Jones, M. (1993). Influence of self-monitoring on dating motivations. *Journal of Research in Personality, 27*, 197–206.

Jones, W. H., Carpenter, B. N., & Quintana, D. (1985). Personality and interpersonal predictors of loneliness in two cultures. *Journal of Personality and Social Psychology, 48*, 1503–1511.

Jones, W. H., Hobbs, S. A., & Hockenbury, D. (1982). Loneliness and social skill deficits. *Journal of Personality and Social Psychology, 42*, 682–689.

Josephs, R. A., Markus, H. R., & Tafarodi, R. W. (1992). Gender and self-esteem. *Journal of Personality and Social Psychology, 63*, 391–402.

Judd, C. M., & Krosnick, J. A. (1989). The structural bases of consistency among political attitudes: Effect of political expertise and attitude importance. In A. R. Pratkanis, S. J. Breckler, & A. G. Greenwald (Eds.), *Attitude structure and function* (pp. 99–128). Hillsdale, NJ: Erlbaum.

Judd, C. M., Drake, R. A., Downing, J. W., & Krosnick, J. A. (1991). Some dynamic properties of attitude structures: Context-induced response facilitation and polarization. *Journal of Personality and Social Psychology, 60*, 193–202.

Judd, C. M., Ryan, C. S., & Parke, B. (991). Accuracy in the judgment of in-group and out-group variability. *Journal of Personality and Social Psychology, 61*, 366–379.

Judge, T. A. (1993). Does affective disposition moderate the relationships between job satisfaction and voluntary turnover? *Journal of Applied Psychology, 78*, 395–401.

Judge, T. A., & Watanabe, S. (1993). Another look at the job–life satisfaction relationships. *Journal of Applied Psychology, 78*, 939–948.

Jussim, L. (1991). Interpersonal expectations and social reality: A reflection–construction model and reinterpretation of evidence. *Psychological Review, 98*, 54–73.

Jussim, L., Nelson, T. E., Manis, M., & Soffin, S. (1995). Prejudice, stereotypes, and labeling effects: Sources of bias in person perception. *Journal of Personality and Social Psychology, 68*, 228–246.

Kabanoff, B. (1991). Equity, equality, power, and conflict. *Academy of Management Review, 12*, 9–22.

Kacmar, K. M., Delery, J. E., & Ferris, G. R. (1992). Differential effectiveness of applicant impression management tactics on employment interview decisions. *Journal of Applied Social Psychology, 22*, 1250–1272.

Kagan, J. (1964). Acquisition and significance of sex-typing and sex-role identity. *Review of Child Development Research, 1*.

Kahle, L. R., & Beatty, S. E. (1987). Cognitive consequences of legislating post-purchase behavior: Growing up with the bottle bill. *Journal of Applied Social Psychology, 17*, 828–843.

Kahneman, D., & Miller, D. T. (1986). Norm theory: Comparing reality to its alternatives. *Psychological Review, 93*, 136–153.

Kalichman, S. C., Sarwer, D. B., Johnson, J. R., Ali, S. A., Early, J., & Tuten, J. T. (1993). Sexually coercive behavior and love styles: A replication and extension. *Journal of Psychology & Human Sexuality, 6*, 93–106.

Kameda, T., & Sugimori, S. (1993). Psychological entrapment in group decision making: An assigned decision rule and a group-think phenomenon. *Journal of Personality and Social Psychology, 65*, 282–292.

Kamo, Y. (1993). Determinants of marital satisfaction: A comparison of the United States and Japan. *Journal of Social and Personal Relationships, 10*, 551–568.

Kandel, D. B. (1978). Similarity in real-life adolescent friendship pairs. *Journal of Personality and Social Psychology, 36*, 306–312,

Kanekar, S., Kolsawalla, M. B., & Nazareth, T. (1988). Occupational prestige as a function of occupant's gender. *Journal of Applied Social Psychology, 19*, 681–688.

Kaplan, M. F. (1981). State dispositions in social judgment. *Bulletin of the Psychonomic Society, 18*, 27–29.

Kaplan, M. F., & Miller, C. E. (1987). Group decision making and normative versus informational influence: Effects of type of issue and assigned decision rule. *Journal of Personality and Social Psychology, 53*, 306–313.

Kaplan, R. D. (1992). Continental drift. *New Republic, 207*(27), 15–16, 18, 20.

Karau, S. J., & Williams, K. D. (1993). Social loafing: A meta-analytic review and theoretical integration. *Journal of Personality and Social Psychology, 65,* 681–706.

Karraker, K. H., & Stern, M. (1990). Infant physical attractiveness and facial expression: Effects on adult perceptions. *Basic and Applied Social Psychology,* 11, 371–385.

Kassin, S. M., & Kiechel, K. L. (1996). The social psychology of false confessions: Compliance, internalization, and confabulation. *Psychological Science,* in press.

Kassin, S. M., & McNall, K. (1991). Police interrogations and confessions: Communicating promises and threats by pragmatic implication. *Law and Human Behavior,* 15, 233–251.

Katz, I. M., & Campbell, J. D. (1994). Ambivalence over emotional expression and well-being: Nomothetic and idiographic tests of the stress-buffering hypothesis. *Journal of Personality and Social Psychology,* 67, 513–423.

Katzev, R., & Wang, T. (1994). Can commitment change behavior? A case study of environmental actions. *Journal of Social Behavior and Personality,* 9, 13–26.

Keelan, J. P. R., Dion, K. L., & Dion, K. K. (1994). Attachment style and heterosexual relationships among young adults: A short-term panel study. *Journal of Social and Personal Relationships,* 11, 201–214.

Keinan, G. (1994). Effects of stress and tolerance of ambiguity on magical thinking. *Journal of Personality and Social Psychology,* 67, 48–55.

Keller, L. M., Bouchard, T. J. Jr., Arvey, R. D., Segal, N. L., & Dawis, R. V. (1992). Work values: Genetic and environmental influences. *Journal of Applied Psychology,* 77, 79–88.

Kellerman, J., Lewis, J., & Laird, J. D. (1989). Looking and loving: The effects of mutual gaze on feelings of romantic love. *Journal of Research in Personality,* 23, 145–161.

Kelley, H. H. (1972). Attribution in social interaction. In E. E. Jones et al. (Eds.), *Attribution: Perceiving the causes of behavior.* Morristown, NJ: General Learning Press.

Kelley, H. H., & Michela, J. L. (1980). Attribution theory and research. *Annual Review of Psychology,* 31, 57–501.

Kelley, K., & Byrne, D. (1992). *Exploring human sexuality.* Englewood Cliffs, NJ: Prentice-Hall.

Kelley, K., & Streeter, D. (1992). The role of gender in organizations. In K. Kelley (Ed.), *Issues, theory, and research in industrial/ organizational psychology* (pp. 285–337). Amsterdam: North-Holland.

Kelman, H. C. (1967). Human use of human subjects: The problem of deception in social psychological experiments. *Psychological Bulletin,* 67, 1–11.

Kelman, H. C., & Hovland, C. I. (1953). "Reinstatement" of the communicator in delayed measurement of opinion change. *Journal of Abnormal and Social Psychology,* 48, 327–335.

Kenealy, P., Gleeson, K., Frude, N., & Shaw, W. (1991). The importance of the individual in the 'causal' relationship between attractiveness and self-esteem. *Journal of Community and Applied Social Psychology,* 1, 45–56.

Kenny, D. A., & Kashy, D. A. (1994). Enhanced co-orientation in the perception of friends: A social relations analysis. *Journal of Personality and Social Psychology,* 67, 1024–1033.

Kenrick, D. T., & Gutierres, S. E. (1980). Contrast effects and judgments of physical attractiveness: When beauty becomes a social problem. *Journal of Personality and Social Psychology,* 38, 131–140.

Kenrick, D. T., & Keefe, R. C. (1992). Age preferences in mates reflect sex differences in human reproductive strategies. *Behavioral and Brain Sciences,* 15, 75–133.

Kenrick, D. T., & McFarlane, S. W. (1986). Ambient temperature and horn honking: A field study of the heat/aggression relationship. *Environment and Behavior,* 18, 179–191.

Kenrick, D. T., Groth, G. E., Trost, M. R., & Sadalla, E. K. (1993). Integrating evolutionary and social exchange perspectives on relationships: Effects of gender, self-appraisal, and involvement level on mate selection criteria. *Journal of Personality and Social Psychology,* 64, 951–969.

Kenrick, D. T., Montello, D. R., Gutierres, S. E., & Trost, M. R. (1993). Effects of physical attractiveness on affect and perceptual judgments: When social comparison overrides social reinforcement. *Personality and Social Psychology Bulletin,* 19, 195–199.

Kenrick, D. T., Neuberg, S. L., Zierk, K. L., & Krones, J. M. (1994). Evolution and social cognition: Contrast effects as a function of sex, dominance, and physical attractiveness. *Personality and Social Psychology Bulletin,* 20, 210–217.

Kent, D. (1990). A conversation with Claude Steele. *APS Observer,* 3(3), 11–15, 17.

Kent, R. L., & Moss, S. E. (1994). Effects of sex and gender role on leader emergence. *Academy of Management Journal,* 37, 1335–1346.

Kernis, M. H., Cornell, D. P., Sun, C.-R., Berry, A., & Harlow, T. (1993). There's more to self-esteem than whether it is high or low: The importance of stability of self-esteem. *Journal of Personality and Social Psychology,* 65, 1190–1204.

Kerns, K. A. (1994). A longitudinal examination of links between mother–child attachment and children's friendships in early childhood. *Journal of Social and Personal Relationships,* 11, 379–381.

Kerns, K. A., & Barth, J. M. (1995). Attachment and play: Convergence across components of parent–child relationships and their relations to peer competence. *Journal of Social and Personal Relationships,* 12, 243–260.

Kessler, R. C., Kendler, K. S., Heath, A., Neale, M. C., & Eaves, L. J. (1992). Social support, depressed mood, and adjustment to stress: A genetic epidemiologic investigation. *Journal of Personality and Social Psychology,* 62, 257–272.

Kiesler, C. A, Kiesler, S. B. (1969). *Conformity.* Reading, MA: Addison-Wesley.

Kilham, W., & Mann, L. (1974). Level of destructive obedience as a function of transmitter and executant roles in the Milgram obedience paradigm. *Journal of Personality and Social Psychology,* 29, 696–702.

Kilmann, R. H., & Thomas, R. W. (1977). Developing a forced-choice measure of conflict-handling behavior: The "MODE" instrument. *Educational and Psychological Measurement,* 3, 309–325.

King, L. A. (1993). Emotional expression, ambivalence over expression, and marital satisfaction. *Journal of Social and Personal Relationships,* 10, 601–607.

King, L. A., & Emmons, R. A. (1991). Psychological, physical, and interpersonal correlates of emotional expressiveness, conflict, and control. *European Journal of Social Personality,* 5, 131–150.

Kinsey, A. C., Pomeroy, W., & Martin, C. (1948). *Sexual behavior in the human male.* Philadelphia: W. B. Saunders.

Kinsey, A. C., Pomeroy, W., Martin, C., & Gebhard, P. (1953). *Sexual behavior in the human female.* Philadelphia: W. B. Saunders.

Kirchler, E., & Davis, J. H. (1986). The influence of member status differences and task type on group consensus and member position change. *Journal of Personality and Social Psychology,* 51, 83–91.

Kirkpatrick, L. A., & Epstein, S. (1992). Cognitive–experiential self theory and subjective probability: Further evidence for two conceptual systems. *Journal of Personality and Social Psychology,* 63, 534–544.

Kirkpatrick, S. A., & Locke, E. A. (1991). Leadership: Do traits matter? *Academy of Management Executive, 5*(2), 48–60.

Klagsbrun, F. (1992). *Mixed feelings: Love, hate, rivalry, and reconciliation among brothers and sisters.* New York: Bantam.

Klein, S. B., & Loftus, J. (1988). The nature of self-referent encoding: The contributions of elaborative and organizational processes. *Journal of Personality and Social Psychology, 55,* 5–11.

Klein, S. B., & Loftus, J. (1993). Behavioral experience and trait judgments about the self. *Personality and Social Psychology Bulletin, 16,* 740–745.

Klein, S. B., Loftus, J., & Burton, H. A. (1989). Two self-reference effects: The importance of distinguishing between self-descriptiveness judgments and autobiographical retrieval in self-referent encoding. *Journal of Personality and Social Psychology, 56,* 853–865.

Klein, S. B., Loftus, J., & Plog, A. E. (1992). Trait judgments about the self: Evidence from the encoding specificity paradigm. *Personality and Social Psychology Bulletin, 18,* 730–735.

Klein, S. B., Loftus, J., Trafton, J. G., & Fuhrman, R. W. (1992). Use of exemplars and abstractions in trait judgments: A model of trait knowledge about the self and others. *Journal of Personality and Social Psychology, 63,* 739–753.

Kleinke, C. L. (1986). Gaze and eye contact: A research review. *Psychological Bulletin, 100,* 78–100.

Kleinke, C. L., & Dean, G. O. (1990). Evaluation of men and women receiving positive and negative responses with various acquaintance strategies. *Journal of Social Behavior and Personality, 5,* 369–377.

Kleinke, C. L., Meeker, F. B., & Staneski, R. A. (1986). Preference for opening lines: Comparing ratings by men and women. *Sex Roles, 15,* 585–600.

Klesges, R., Klem, M., Hanson, C., Eck, L., Ernst, J., O'Laughlin, D., Garrot, A., & Rife, R. (1990). The effect of applicant's health status and qualifications on simulated hiring decisions. *International Journal of Obesity, 14,* 527–535.

Klotz, M. L., & Alicke, M. D. (1993). Complaining in close relationships. Manuscript under review.

Knight, G. P., Johnson, L. G., Carlo, G., & Eisenberg, N. (1994). A multiplicative model of the dispositional antecedents of a prosocial behavior: Predicting more of the people more of the time. *Journal of Personality and Social Psychology, 66,* 178–183.

Koehler, S. P., & Willis, F. N. (1994). Traffic citations in relation to gender. *Journal of Applied Social Psychology, 24,* 1919–1926.

Koestner, R., Bernieri, F., & Zuckerman, M. (1992). Self-regulation and consistency between attitudes, traits, and behaviors. *Personality and Social Psychology Bulletin, 18,* 52–59.

Kohlberg, L. (1966). A cognitive-developmental analysis of children's sex-role concepts and attitudes. In E. E. Maccoby (Ed.), *The development of sex differences.* Stanford, CA: Stanford University Press.

Kolata, G. (1995, February 28). Man's world, woman's world? Brain studies point to differences. *New York Times,* C1, C7.

Kolb, D. M., & Bartunek, J. M. (1992). *Hidden conflict in organizations.* Thousand Oaks, CA: Sage

Konovsky, M. A., & Pugh, S. D. (1994). Citizenship behavior and social exchange. *Academy of Management Journal, 37,* 656–669.

Koss, M. P., & Harvey, M. R. (1991). *The rape victim: Clinical and community interventions* (2nd ed.). Newbury Park, CA: Sage.

Koss, M. P., Dinero, T. E., Seibel, C. A., & Cox, S. L. (1988). Stranger and acquaintance rape: Are there differences in the victim's experience? *Psychology of Women Quarterly, 12,* 1–24.

Kotter, J. (1982). *The general managers.* New York: Free Press.

Kowalski, R. M. (1993). Interpreting behaviors in mixed-gender encounters: Effects of social anxiety and gender. *Journal of Social and Clinical Psychology, 12,* 239–247.

Kowalski, R. M., & Brown, K. J. (1994). Psychosocial barriers to cervical cancer screening: Concerns with self-presentation and social evaluation. *Journal of Applied Social Psychology, 24,* 941–958.

Kramer, L., & Baron, L. A. (1995). Intergenerational linkages: How experiences with siblings relate to the parenting of siblings. *Journal of Social and Personal Relationships, 12,* 67–87.

Kraus, S. J. (1995). Attitudes and the prediction of behavior: A meta-analysis of the empirical literature. *Personality and Social Psychology Bulletin, 21,* 58–75.

Kring, A. M., Smith, D. A., & Neale, J. M. (1994). Individual differences in dispositional expressiveness: Development and validation of the emotional expressivity scale. *Journal of Personality and Social Psychology, 66,* 934–949.

Krosnick, J. A. (1988). The role of attitude importance in social evaluation: A study of political preferences, presidential candidate evaluations, and voting behavior. *Journal of Personality and Social Psychology, 55,* 196–210.

Krosnick, J. A. (1989). Attitude importance and attitude accessibility. *Personality and Social Psychology Bulletin, 15,* 297–308.

Krosnick, J. A., & Alwin, D. F. (1989). Aging and susceptibility to attitude change. *Journal of Personality and Social Psychology, 57,* 416–425.

Krosnick, J. A., Betz, A. L., Jussim, L. J., & Lynn, A. R. (1992). Subliminal conditioning of attitudes. *Personality and Social Psychology Bulletin, 18,* 152–162.

Krosnick, J. A., Boninger, D. S., Chuang, Y. C., Berent, M. K., & Carnot, C. G. (1993). Attitude strength: One construct or many related constructs? *Journal of Personality and Social Psychology, 65,* 1132–1151.

Krueger, J., & Clement, R. W. (1994). The truly false consensus effect: An ineradicable and egocentric bias in social perception. *Journal of Personality and Social Psychology, 67,* 596–610.

Kruglanski, A. W., & Mackie D. M. (1991). Majority and minority influence: A judgmental process analysis. In W. Steroebe & M. Hewstone (Eds.), *European review of social psychology* (Vol. 1, pp. 229–261). New York: Wiley.

Krupat, E. (1975). *Psychology is social.* Glenview, IL: Scott Foresman.

Kubany, E. S., Bauer, G. B., Muraoka, M. Y., Richard, D. C., & Read, P. (1995). Impact of labeled anger and blame in intimate relationships. *Journal of Social and Clinical Psychology, 14,* 53–60.

Kuhn, D., Weinstock, M., & Flaton, R. (1994). How well do jurors reason? Competence dimensions of individual variation in a juror reasoning task. *Psychological Science, 5,* 289–296.

Kulik, J. A., & Mahler, H. I. M. (1987). Effects of preoperative roommate assignment on preoperative anxiety and recovery from coronary-bypass surgery. *Health Psychology, 6,* 525–544.

Kunda, Z., Fong, G. T., Sanitioso, R., & Reber, E. (1993). Directional questions direct self-conceptions. *Journal of Experimental Social Psychology, 29,* 63–86.

Kunda, Z., & Oleson, K. C. (1995). Maintaining stereotypes in the face of disconfirmation: Constructing grounds for subtyping deviants. *Journal of Personality and Social Psychology, 68,* 565–579.

Kupersmidt, J. B., DeRosier, M. E., & Patterson, C. P. (1995). Similarity as the basis for children's friendships: The roles of sociometric status, aggressive and withdrawn behavior, academic achievement and demographic characteristics. *Journal of Social and Personal Relationships, 12,* 439–452.

Kurdek, L. A. (1993). The allocation of household labor in gay, lesbian, and heterosexual married couples. *Journal of Social Issues, 49(3),* 127–139.

Kutchinsky, B. (1991). Pornography and rape: Theory and practice? *International Journal of Law and Psychiatry, 14,* 47–64.

Kwon, Y.-H. (1994). Feeling toward one's clothing and self-perception of emotion, sociability, and work competency. *Journal of Social Behavior and Personality, 9,* 129–139.

LaFrance, M., & Hecht, M. A. (1995). Why smiles generate leniency. *Personality and Social Psychology Bulletin, 21,* 207–214.

LaPiere, R. T. (1934). Attitude and actions. *Social Forces, 13,* 230–237.

LaPrelle, J., Hoyle, R. H., Insko, C. A., & Bernthal, P. (1990). Interpersonal attraction and descriptions of the traits of others: Ideal similarity, self similarity, and liking. *Journal of Research in Personality, 24,* 216–240.

Lagerspetz, K. M. J., & Bjorkqvist, K. (1994). Indirect aggression in boys and girls. In L. R. Huesmann (Ed.), *Aggressive behavior: Current perspectives* (pp. 131–147). New York: Plenum.

Laird, J. D. (1984). The real role of facial response in the experience of emotion: A reply to Tourangeua, Ellsworth, and others. *Journal of Personality and Social Psychology, 47,* 909–917.

Lambert, A. J. (1995). Stereotypes and social judgment: The consequences of group variability. *Journal of Personality and Social Psychology, 68,* 388–403.

Lamm, H. & Myers, D. G. (1978). Group-induced polarization of attitudes and behavior. In L. Berkowitz (Ed.), *Advances in experimental social psychology.* New York: Academic Press.

Lander, M. (1992, June 8). Corporate women. *Business Week, 74,* 76–78.

Langer, E., Blank, A., & Chanowitz, B. (1978). The mindlessness of ostensibly thoughtful actions: The role of "placebic" information in interpersonal interaction. *Journal of Personality and Social Psychology, 36,* 635–642.

Langis, J., Sabourin, S., Lussier, Y., & Mathieu, M. (1994). Masculinity, femininity, and marital satisfaction: An examination of theoretical models. *Journal of Personality, 62,* 393–414.

Langlois, J. H., & Roggman, L. A. (1990). Attractive faces are only average. *Psychological Science, 1,* 115–121.

Langlois, J. H., Ritter, J. M., Roggman, L. A., & Vaughn, L. S. (1991). Facial diversity and infant preferences for attractive faces. *Developmental Psychology, 27,* 79–84.

Langlois, J. H., Roggman, L. A., & Musselman, L. (1994). What is average and what is not average about attractive faces? *Psychological Science, 5,* 214–220.

Langlois, J. H., Roggman, L. A., & Rieser-Danner, L. A. (1990). Differential social responses to attractive and unattractive faces. *Developmental Psychology, 26,* 153–159.

Langston, C. A. (1994). Capitalizing on and coping with daily-life events: Expressive responses to positive events. *Journal of Personality and Social Psychology, 67,* 1112–1125.

Langston, C. A., & Cantor, N. (1989). Social anxiety and social constraint: When making friends is hard. *Journal of Personality and Social Psychology, 56,* 649–661.

Larkin, J. C., & Pines, H. A. (1982). No fat persons need apply. *Sociology of Work and Occupations, 6,* 312–327.

Larson, D. G., & Chastain, R. L. (1990). Self-concealment: Conceptualization, measurement, and health implications. *Journal of Social and Clinical Psychology, 9,* 439–455.

Larson, J. H., & Bell, N. J. (1988). Need for privacy and its effects upon interpersonal attraction and interaction. *Journal of Social and Clinical Psychology, 6,* 1–10.

Larson, R. W., Richards, M. H., & Perry-Jenkins, M. (1994). Divergent worlds: The daily emotional experience of mothers and fathers in the domestic and public spheres. *Journal of Personality and Social Psychology, 67,* 1034–1046.

Lasswell, M. E., & Lobsenz, N. M. (1980). *Styles of loving.* New York: Ballantine.

Latané, B., & Darley, J. M. (1968). Group inhibition of bystander intervention in emergencies. *Journal of Personality and Social Psychology, 10,* 215–221.

Latané, B., & Darley, J. M. (1970). *The unresponsive bystander: Why doesn't he help?* New York: Appleton-Century-Crofts.

Latané, B., Williams, K., & Harkins, S. (1979). Many hands make light the work: The causes and consequences of social loafing. *Journal of Personality and Social Psychology, 37,* 822–832.

Latané, B. (1981). The psychology of social impacts. *American Psychologist, 36,* 343–356.

Latest figures: U.S. death rate is lower. (1994, December 16). Associated Press.

Lau, S. (1989). Sex role orientation and domains of self esteem. *Sex Roles, 21,* 415–422.

Lau, S., & Gruen, G. E. (1992). The social stigma of loneliness: Effect of target person's and perceiver's sex. *Personality and Social Psychology Bulletin, 18,* 182–189.

Lauer, J., & Lauer, R. (1985, June). Marriages made to last. *Psychology Today,* 22–26.

Laumann, E. O., Gagnon, J. H., Michael, R. T., & Michaels, S. (1994). *The social organization of sexuality: Sexual practices in the United States.* Chicago: University of Chicago Press.

Law, A., Logan, H., & Baron, R. S. (1994). Desire for control, felt control, and stress inoculation training during dental treatment. *Journal of Personality and Social Psychology, 67,* 926–936.

Lazarus, R. S. (1966). Psychological stress and the coping process. New York: McGraw-Hill.

Lazarus, R. S. (1993). From psychological stress to the emotions: A history of changing outlooks. *Annual Review of Psychology, 44,* 1–21.

Leary, M. R., & Jones, J. L. (1993). The social psychology of tanning and sunscreen use: Self-presentational motives as a predictor of health risk. *Journal of Applied Social Psychology, 23,* 1390–1406.

Leary, M. R., Tambor, E. S., Terdal, S. K., & Downs, D. L. (1995). Self-esteem as an interpersonal monitor: The sociometer hypothesis. *Journal of Personality and Social Psychology, 68,* 518–530.

Leary, W. E. (1988, November 19). Novel methods unlock witnesses' memories. *New York Times,* pp. C1, C15.

Lee, T. W., Ashford, S. J., Walsh, J. P., & Mowday, R. T. (1992). Commitment propensity, organizational commitment, and voluntary turnover: A longitudinal study of organizational entry processes. *Journal of Management, 18,* 15–32.

Lee, Y. T., & Ottati, V. (1993). Determinants of ingroup and outgroup perceptions of heterogeneity: An investigation of Sino-American differences. *Journal of Cross-Cultural Psychology, 25,* 146–158.

Lehman, T. C., Daubman, K. A., Guarna, J., Jordan, J., & Cirafesi, C. (1995, April). *Gender differences in the motivational consequences of receiving help.* Paper presented at the meeting of the Eastern Psychological Association, Boston.

Leippe, M. R., & Romanczyk, A. (1987). Children on the witness stand: A communication/persuasion analysis of jurors' reactions to child witnesses. In S. J. Ceci, M. P. Toglia, & D. F. Ross (Eds.), *Children's eyewitness memory* (pp. 155–177). New York: Springer-Verlag.

Lekic, S. (1995, August 7). Dry times predicted for global water reserves. *Albany Times Union,* p. A-3.

Lemonick, M. D. (1992). The ozone vanishes. *Time, 139*(7), 60–63.

Lemonick, M. D. (1995). Return to the hot zone. *Time, 145*(21), 62–63.

Lerner, Ma. J. (1980). *The belief in a just world: A fundamental delusion.* New York: Plenum Press.

Levenson, R. W. (1992). Autonomic nervous system differences among emotions. *Psychological Science, 3,* 23–27.

Levenson, R. W., Carstensen, L. L., & Gottman, J. M. (1994). The influence of age and gender on affect, physiology, and their interrelations: A study of long-term marriages. *Journal of Personality and Social Psychology, 67,* 56–68.

Levenson, R. W., Ekman, P., & Friesen, W. V. (1990). Voluntary facial action generates emotion-specific autonomic nervous system activity. *Psychophysiology, 27,* 363–384.

Levenson, R. W., Ekman, P., Heider, K., & Friesen, W. V. (1992). Emotion and autonomic nervous system activity in the Minangkabau of West Sumatra. *Journal of Personality and Social Psychology, 62,* 972–988.

Leventhal, G. S., & Anderson, D. (1970). Self-interest and the maintenance of equity. *Journal of Personality and Social Psychology, 15,* 57–62.

Leventhal, A., Nerenz, D. R., & Steele, D. J. (1984). Illness representations and coping with health threats. In A. Baum & J. Singer (Eds.), *Handbook of psychology and health* (pp. 219–252). Hillsdale, NJ: Erlbaum.

Leventhal, G. S., Karuza, J., & Fry, W. R. (1980). Beyond fairness: A theory of allocation preferences. In G. Mikula (Ed.), *Justice and social interaction* (pp. 167–218). New York: Springer-Verlag.

Leventhal, H., Singer, R., & Jones, S. (1965). The effects of fear and specificity of recommendation upon attitudes and behavior. *Journal of Personality and Social Psychology, 2,* 20–29.

Levine, R. V., Martinez, T. S., Brase, G., & Sorenson, K. (1994). Helping in 36 U.S. cities. *Journal of Personality and Social Psychology, 67,* 69–82.

Levinger, G. (1988). Can we picture "love"? In R. J. Sternberg & M. L. Barnes (Eds.), *The psychology of love* (pp. 139–158). New Haven, CT: Yale University Press.

Levy, B., & Langer, E. (1994). Aging free from negative stereotypes: Successful memory in China and among the American deaf. *Journal of Personality and Social Psychology, 66,* 989–997.

Lewin, K., Lippitt, R., & White, R. K. (1939). Patterns of aggressive behavior in experimentally created "social climates." *Journal of Social Psychology, 10,* 271–299.

Leyens, J. P., Camino, L., Parke, R. D., & Berkowitz, L. (1975). Effects of movie violence on aggression in a field setting as a function of group dominance and cohesion. *Journal of Personality and Social Psychology, 32,* 346–360.

Liberman, A., & Chaiken, S. (1992). Defensive processing of personally relevant heath messages. *Personality and Social Psychology Bulletin, 18,* 669–679.

Liden, R. C., & Mitchell, T. R. (1988). Ingratiatory behaviors in organizational settings. *Academy of Management Review, 13,* 572–587.

Liebowitz, M. R., Schneier, F., Campeas, R., Hollander, E., Hatterer, J., Fyer, A., Gorman, J., Papp, L., Davies, S., Gully, R., & Klein, D. F. (1992). Phenelzine vs atenolol in social phobia: A placebo controlled comparison. *Archives of General Psychiatry, 49,* 290–300.

Linden, E. (1992). Rio's legacy. *Time, 139*(25), 44–45.

Lindsay, D. S. (1993). Eyewitness suggestibility. *Current Directions in Psychological Science, 2,* 86–89.

Linville, P. W. (1987). Self-complexity as a cognitive buffer against stress-related illness and depression. *Journal of Personality and Social Psychology, 52,* 663–676.

Linville, P. W., & Fischer, G. W. (1993). Exemplar and abstraction models of perceived group variability and stereotypicality. *Social Cognition, 11,* 92–125.

Linville, P. W., Fischer, G. W., & Salovey, P. (1989). Perceived distributions of the characteristics of in-group and out-group members: Empirical evidence and a computer simulation. *Journal of Personality and Social Psychology, 57,* 165–188.

Linz, D., & Penrod, S. (1992). Exploring the first and sixth amendments: Pretrial publicity and jury decision making. In D. K. Kagehiro & W. S. Laufer (Eds.), *Handbook of psychology and law.* New York: Springer-Verlag.

Linz, D., Donnerstein, E., & Penrod, S. (1988). Effects of long-term exposure to violent and sexually degrading depictions of women. *Journal of Personality and Social Psychology, 55,* 758–768.

Linz, D., Donnerstein, E., & Penrod, S. (1984). The effects of multiple exposure to filmed violence against women. *Journal of Communication, 34,* 130–137.

Lipman-Blumen, J. (1992). Connective leadership: Female leadership styles in the 21st-century workplace. *Sociological Perspectives, 35,* 183–203.

Lippa, R., & Donaldson, S. I. (1990). Self-monitoring and idiographic measures of behavioral variability across interpersonal relationships. *Journal of Personality, 58,* 465–479.

Living memorial. (1992, October 26). *Time, 21.*

Locke, E. A. (1991). *The essence of leadership.* New York: Lexington Books.

Locke, M. (1995, May 25). Love better with age, study says. *Albany Times Union,* p. C-5.

Loftus, E. F. (1992a). *Witness for the defense.* New York: St. Martin's Press.

Loftus, E. F. (1992b). When a lie becomes memory's truth: Memory distortion after exposure to misinformation. *Current Directions in Psychological Science, 1,* 121–123.

Lorenz, K. (1966). *On aggression.* New York: Harcourt, Brace, & World.

Lorenz, K. (1974). *Civilized man's eight deadly sins.* New York: Harcourt, Brace, Jovanovich.

Losch, M., & Cacioppo, J. (1990). Cognitive dissonance may enhance sympathetic tonis, but attitudes are changed to reduce negative affect rather than arousal. *Journal of Experimental Social Psychology, 26,* 289–304.

Lox, C. L., & Rudolph, D. L. (1994). The Subjective Exercise Experiences Scale (SEES): Factorial validity and effects of acute exercise. *Journal of Social Behavior and Personality, 9,* 837–844.

Luks, A. (1988, October). Helper's high. *Psychology Today* pp. 39–40.

Lundberg, G. A., & Beazley, V. (1948). "Consciousness of kind" in a college population. *Sociometry, 11,* 59–74.

Lundberg, J. K., & Sheehan, E. P. (1994). The effects of glasses and weight on perceptions of attractiveness and intelligence. *Journal of Social Behavior and Personality, 9,* 753–760.

Lupfer, M. B., Clark, L. F., & Hutcherson, H. W. (1990). Impact of context on spontaneous trait and situational attributions. *Journal of Personality and Social Psychology, 58,* 239–249.

Lurie, A. (Ed.) (1993). *The Oxford book of modern fairy tales.* Oxford, England: Oxford University Press.

Luten, D. B., Jr. (1991). Population and resources. *Population and Environment, 12,* 311–329.

Luus, C. A., & Wells, G. L. (1994). The malleability of eyewitness confidence: Co-witness and perseverance effects. *Journal of Applied Psychology, 79,* 714–723.

Luus, C. A. E., Wells, G. L., & Turtle, J. W. (1995). Child eyewitnesses: Seeing is believing. *Journal of Applied Psychology, 80,* 317–326.

Lyall, S. (1995, April 30). British watch trial of Simpson. *The New York Times,* p. 9.

Lynn, M., & Mynier, K. (1993). Effects of server posture on restaurant tipping. *Journal of Applied Social Psychology, 23,* 678–685.

Lynn, R. (1991). *The secret of the miracle economy.* London: SAU.

Lynn. R. (1993). Further evidence for the existence of race and sex differences in cranial capacity. *Social Behavior and Personality, 21,* 89–92.

Lyubomirsky, S., & Nolen-Hoeksema, S. (1995). Effects of self-focused rumination on negative thinking and interpersonal problem solving. *Journal of Personality and Social Psychology, 69,* 176–190.

Maas, A., & Clark, R. D. III (1984). Hidden impact of minorities: Fifteen years of minority influence research. *Psychological Bulletin, 95,* 233–243.

MacCoun, R. J., & Kerr, N. L. (1988). Asymmetric influence in mock jury deliberation: Jurors' bias for leniency. *Journal of Personality and Social Psychology, 54,* 21–33.

Macaulay, J. (1970). A shill for charity. In J. Macaulay & L. Berkowitz (Eds.), *Altruism and helping behavior* (pp. 43–59). New York: Academic Press.

Maccoby, E. E. (1990). Gender and relationships: A developmental account. *American Psychologist, 45,* 513–520.

Maccoby, E. E., & Jacklin, C. N. (1974). *The psychology of sex differences.* Stanford, CA: Stanford University Press.

Mack, D., & Rainey, D. (1990). Female applicants' grooming and personnel selection. *Journal of Social Behavior and Personality, 5,* 399–407.

Mackie, D. M., & Worth, L. T. (1989). Processing deficits and the mediation of positive affect in persuasion. *Journal of Personality and Social Psychology, 57,* 27–40.

Mackie, D. M., Allison, S. T., Worth, L. T., & Asuncion, A. G. (1992). The impact of outcome biases on counterstereotypic inferences about groups. *Personality and Social Psychology Bulletin, 18,* 44–51.

Macrae, C. N. (1992). A tale of two curries: Counterfactual thinking and accident-related judgments. *Personality and Social Psychology Bulletin, 18,* 84–87.

Macrae, C. N., & Milne, A. B. (1992). A curry for your thoughts: Empathic effects on counterfactual thinking. *Personality and Social Psychology Bulletin, 18,* 625–630.

Macrae, C. N., Bodenhausen, G. V., Milne, A. B., & Jetten, J. (1994). Out of mind but back in sight: Stereotypes on the rebound. *Journal of Personality and Social Psychology, 67,* 808–817.

Macrae, C. N., Hewstone, M., & Griffiths, R. J. (1993). Processing load and memory for stereotype-based information. *European Journal of Social Psychology, 23,* 77–87.

Macrae, C. N., Milne, A. B., & Bodenhausen, G. V. (1994). Stereotypes as energy-saving devices: A peek inside the cognitive toolbox. *Journal of Personality and Social Psychology, 66,* 37–47.

Maio, G. R., Esses, V. M., & Bell, D. W. (1994). The formation of attitudes toward new immigrant groups. *Journal of Applied Social Psychology, 24,* 1762–1776.

Maisonneuve, J., Palmade, G., & Fourment, C. (1952). Selective choices and propinquity. *Sociometry, 15,* 135–140.

Major, B. (1993). Gender, entitlement, and the distribution of family labor. *Journal of Social Issues, 49*(3), 141–159.

Major, B., & Adams, J. B. (1983). Roles of gender, interpersonal orientation, and self-presentation in distributive justice behavior. *Journal of Personality and Social Psychology, 45,* 598–608.

Major, B., Carnevale, P. J. D., & Deaux, K. (1981). A different perspective on androgyny: Evaluations of masculine and feminine personality characteristics. *Journal of Personality and Social Psychology, 41,* 988–1001.

Major, B., & Deaux, K. (1982). Individual differences in justice behavior. In J. Greenberg & R. L. Cohen (Eds.), *Equity and justice in social behavior.* New York: Academic Press.

Major, B., & Konar, E. (1984). An investigation of sex differences in pay expectations and their possible causes. *Academy of Management Journal, 27,* 777–792.

Major, B., Sciacchitano, A. M., & Crocker, J. (1993). In-group versus out-group comparisons and self-esteem. *Personality and Social Psychology Bulletin, 19,* 711–721.

Malamuth, N. M., & Brown, L. M. (1994). Sexually aggressive men's perceptions of women's communications: Testing three explanations. *Journal of Personality and Social Psychology, 67,* 699–712.

Malle, B. F., & Horowitz, L. M. (1995). The puzzle of negative self-views: An explanation using the schema concept. *Journal of Personality and Social Psychology, 68,* 470–484.

Mallick, S. K., & McCandless, B. R. (1966). A study of catharsis of aggression. *Journal of Personality and Social Psychology, 4,* 591–596.

Mancs, A. I., & Melynk, P. (1974). Televised models of female achievement. *Journal of Applied Social Psychology, 4,* 365–374.

Manolis, M. B., & Milich, R. (1993). Gender differences in social persistence. *Journal of Social and Clinical Psychology, 12,* 385–405.

Marangoni, C., & Ickes, W. (1989). Loneliness: A theoretical review with implications for measurement. *Journal of Social and Personal Relationships, 6,* 93–128.

Marazziti, D., Rotondo, A., Presta, S., Pancioloi-Guadagnucci, M. L., Palego, L., & Conti, L. (1993). Role of serotonin in human aggressive behavior. *Aggressive Behavior, 19,* 347–353.

Marchione, M. (1995, August 14). Discretion needed for loose lips. *Albany Times Union,* p. C-1.

Margalit, M., & Eysenck, S. (1990). Prediction of coherence in adolescence: Gender differences in social skills, personality, and family climate. *Journal of Research in Personality, 24,* 510–521.

Margolick, D. (1994, October 3). Remaking of the Simpson prosecutor. *The New York Times,* p. A10.

Margolin, G., John, R. S., & O'Brien, M. (1989). Sequential affective patterns as a function of marital conflict style. *Journal of Social and Clinical Psychology, 8,* 45–61.

Markman, H. J. (1981). Prediction of marital distress: A 5-year follow-up. *Journal of Consulting and Clinical Psychology, 49,* 760–762.

Marks, N. L., & Miller, H. (1987). Ten years of research on the false-consensus effect: An empirical and theoretical review. *Psychological Bulletin, 8,* 728–735.

Markus, H., & Nurius, P. (1986). Possible selves. *American Psychologist, 41,* 954–969.

Maroney, D., & Golub, S. (1992). Nurses' attitudes toward obese persons and certain ethnic groups. *Perceptual and Motor Skills, 75,* 387–391.

Marsh, H. W. (1993). Relations between global and specific domains of self: The importance of individual importance, certainty, and ideal. *Journal of Personality and Social Psychology, 65,* 975–992.

Marshall, N. L., & Barnett, R. C. (1993). Variations in job strain across nursing and social work specialties. *Journal of Community and Applied Social Psychology, 3,* 261–271.

Martin, B. A., & Murberger, M. A. (1994). Effects of self-esteem and assigned goals on actual and perceived performance. *Journal of Social Behavior Personality, 9,* 81–87.

Martin, C. L. (1987). A ratio measure of sex stereotyping. *Journal of Personality and Social Psychology, 52,* 489–499.

Martin, C. L., & Parker, S. (1995). Folk theories about sex and race differences. *Personality and Social Psychology Bulletin, 21,* 45–57.

Martin, L. L., Tesser, A., & McIntosh, W. D. (1993). Wanting but not having: The effects of unattained goals on thoughts and feelings. In D. M. Wegner & J. W. Pennebaker (Eds.), *Handbook of mental control* (pp. 552–572). Englewood Cliffs, NJ: Prentice-Hall.

Maslach, C., Santee, R. T., & Wade, C. (1987). Individuation, gender role, and dissent: Personality mediators of situational forces. *Journal of Personality and Social Psychology, 53,* 1088–1094.

Mastekaasa, A. (1995). Age variation in the suicide rates and self-reported subjective well-being of married and never married persons. *Journal of Community and Applied Social Psychology, 5,* 21–39.

Masters, R. D. (1991). Individual and cultural differences in response to leaders' nonverbal displays. *Journal of Social Issues, 47,* 151–165.

Masters, R. D., & Sullivan, D. G. (1989). Nonverbal displays and political leadership in France and the United States. *Political Behavior, 11,* 123–156.

Masters, R. D., & Sullivan, D. G. (1990). Facial displays and political leadership in France. *Behavioural Processes, 19,* 1–30.

Matlin, M. W., & Zajonc, R. B. (1968). Social facilitation of word associations. *Journal of Personality and Social Psychology, 10,* 455–460.

Matthews, S. H. (1986). *Friendship through the life course.* Newbury Park, CA: Sage.

Maupin, H. E., & Fisher, R. J. (1989). The effects of superior female performance and sex-role orientation on gender conformity. *Canadian Journal of Behavioral Science, 21,* 55–69.

May, J. L., & Hamilton, P. A. (1980). Effects of musically evoked affect on women's interpersonal attraction and perceptual judgments of physical attractiveness of men. *Motivation and Emotion, 4,* 217–228.

Mayer, J. D., & Hanson, E. (1995). Mood-congruent judgment over time. *Personality and Social Psychology Bulletin, 21,* 237–244.

Mayer, J. D., & Salovey, P. (1995). Emotional intelligence and the construction and regulation of feelings. *Applied and Preventive Psychology, 4,* 197–208.

Mazzella, R., & Feingold, A. (1994). The effects of physical attractiveness, race, socioeconomic status, and gender of defendants and victims on judgments of mock jurors: A meta-analysis. *Journal of Applied Social Psychology, 24,* 1315–1344.

McArthur, L. Z., & Eisen, S. V. (1976). Achievements of male and female storybook characters as determinants of achievement behavior by boys and girls. *Journal of Personality and Social Psychology, 33,* 467–473.

McCabe, M. P. (1987). Desired and experienced levels of premarital affection and sexual intercourse during dating. *Journal of Sex Research, 23,* 23–33.

McCall, M. E., & Struthers, N. J. (1994). Sex, sex-role orientation and self-esteem as predictors of coping style. *Journal of Social Behavior and Personality, 9,* 801–810.

McCann, T. M., & Dipboye, R. L. (1990). The relationship of pre-interview impressions to selection and recruitment outcomes. *Personnel Psychology, 43,* 745–768.

McCanne, T. R., & Anderson, J. A. (1987). Emotional responding following experimental manipulation of facial electromyographic activity. *Journal of Personality and Social Psychology, 52,* 759–768.

McClelland, D. (1976). *The achieving society.* New York: Free Press.

McClelland, D. C. (1986). Some reflections on the two psychologies of love. *Journal of Personality, 54,* 334–352.

McDaniel, M. A., Whetzel, D. L., Schmidt, F. L., & Maurer, S. D. (1994). The validity of employment interviews: A comprehensive review and meta-analysis. *Journal of Applied Psychology, 79,* 599–616.

McDonald, K. A. (1995, March 3). Correlations add new detail to sex study. *The Chronicle of Higher Education,* p. A8.

McDougall, W. (1908). *Introduction to social psychology.* London: Methuen.

McFarland, C., & Buehler, R. (1995). Collective self-esteem as a moderator of the frog-pond effect in reactions to performance feedback. *Journal of Personality and Social Psychology, 68,* 1055–1070.

McGaughey, K. J., & Stiles, W. B. (1983). Courtroom interrogation of rape victims: Verbal response mode use by attorneys and witnesses during direct examination vs. cross-examination. *Journal of Applied Social Psychology, 13,* 78–87.

McGonagle, K. A., Kessler, R. C., & Schilling, E. A. (1992). The frequency and determinants of marital disagreements in a community sample. *Journal of Social and Personal Relationships, 9,* 507–524.

McGuire, A. M. (1994). Helping behaviors in the natural environment: Dimensions and correlates of helping. *Personality and Social Psychology Bulletin, 20,* 45–56.

McHugo, G. J., Lanzetta, J. T., & Bush, L. K. (1987). The effect of attitudes on emotional reactions to expressive displays of political leaders. Unpublished mansucript, Dartmouth College, Hanover, New Hampshire.

McKelvie, S. J. (1993a). Perceived cuteness, activity level, and gender in schematic babyfaces. *Journal of Social Behavior and Personality, 8,* 297–310.

McKelvie, S. J. (1993b). Stereotyping in perception of attractiveness, age, and gender in schematic faces. *Social Behavior and Personality, 21,* 121–128.

McKelvie, S. J., & Coley, J. (1993). Effects of crime seriousness and offender facial attractiveness on recommended treatment. *Social Behavior and Personality, 21,* 265–277.

McKillip, J., & Reidel, S. L. (1983). External validity of matching on physical attractiveness for same and opposite sex couples. *Journal of Applied Social Psychology, 13,* 328–337.

McNulty, S. E., & Swann, W. B., Jr. (1994). Identity negotiation in roommate relationships: The self as architect and consequence of social reality. *Journal of Personality and Social Psychology, 67,* 1012–1023.

McWilliams, S., & Howard, J. A. (1993). Solidarity and hierarchy in cross-sex friendships. *Journal of Social Issues, 49*(3), 191–202.

Mechanic, D. (1983). Adolescent health and illness behavior: Hypotheses for the study of distress in youth. *Journal of Human Stress, 9,* 4–13.

Mednick, M. T., Mednick, S. A., & Mednick, E. V. (1964). Incubation of creative performance and specific associative priming. *Journal of Abnormal and Social Psychology, 69,* 220–232.

Mednick, S. A., Brennan, P., & Kandel, E. (1988). Predispositions to violence. *Aggressive Behavior, 14,* 25–33.

Mehrabian, A., & Piercy, M. (1993a). Positive or negative connotations of unconventionally or conventionally spelled names. *Journal of Social Psychology, 133,* 445–451.

Mehrabian, A., & Piercy, M. (1993b). Affective and personality characteristics inferred from length of first names. *Personality and Social Psychology Bulletin, 19,* 755–758.

Melamed, S., Ben-Avi, I., Luz, J., & Green, M. S. (1995). Objective and subjective work monotony: Effects on job satisfaction, psychological distress, and absenteeism in blue-collar workers. *Journal of Applied Psychology, 80,* 29–42.

Meleshko, K. G. A., & Alden, L. E. (1993). Anxiety and self-disclosure: Toward a motivational model. *Journal of Personality and Social Psychology, 64,* 1000–1009.

Mellers, B. A., Richards, V., & Birnbaum, M. H. (1992). Distributional theories of impression formation. *Organizational Behavior and Human Decision Processes, 51,* 313–343.

Mendolin, M., & Kleck, R. E. (1993). Effects of talking about a stressful event on arousal: Does what we talk about make a difference? *Journal of Personality and Social Psychology, 64,* 283–292.

Metz, M. E., Rosser, B. R. S., & Strapko, N. (1994). Differences in conflict-resolution styles among heterosexual, gay, and lesbian couples. *Journal of Sex Research, 31,* 293–308.

Meyer, D., Leventhal, H., & Gutman, M. (1985). Common-sense models of illness: The example of hypertension. *Health Psychology, 4,* 115–135.

Meyer, J. P., & Allen, N. J. (1991). A three-component conceptualization of organization commitment. *Human Resource Management Review, 1,* 61–89.

Miceli, M. P., & Lane, M. C. (1991). Antecedents of pay satisfaction: A review and extension. In K. Rowland & O. R. Ferris (Eds.), *Research in personnel and human resources management* (Vol. 9, pp. 235–309). Greenwich, CT: JAI Press.

Michael, R. T., Gagnon, J. H., Laumann, E. O., & Kolata, G. (1994). *Sex in America: A definitive survey.* Boston: Little, Brown.

Middlestadt, S. E., Fishbein, M., Albarracin, D., Francis, C., Eustace, M. A., Helquist, M., & Schneider, A. (1995). Evaluating the impact of a national AIDS prevention radio campaign in St. Vincent and the Grenadines. *Journal of Applied Social Psychology, 25,* 21–34.

Mikulincer, M., & Florian, V. (1995). Appraisal of and coping with a real-life stressful situation: The contribution of attachment styles. *Personality and Social Psychology Bulletin, 21,* 406–414.

Mikulincer, M., Florian, V., & Weller, A. (1993). Attachment styles, coping strategies, and posttraumatic psychological distress: The impact of the Gulf War in Israel. *Journal of Personality and Social Psychology, 64,* 817–826.

Milgram, S. (1963). Behavior study of obedience. *Journal of Abnormal and Social Psychology, 67,* 371–378.

Milgram, S. (1965a). Liberating effects of group pressure. *Journal of Personality and Social Psychology, 1,* 127–134.

Milgram, S. (1965b) Some conditions of obedience and disobedience to authority. *Human Relations, 18,* 57–76.

Milgram, S. (1974). *Obedience to authority.* New York: Harper.

Millar, M. G., & Millar, K. U. (1993). Changing breast self-examination attitudes: Influences of repression–sensitization and attitude-message match. *Journal of Research in Personality, 27,* 301–314.

Millar, M. G., & Tesser, A. (1989). The effects of affective-cognitive consistency and thought on the attitude–behavior relation. *Journal of Experimental Social Psychology, 25,* 189–202.

Miller, C. T., Rothblum, E. D., Barbour, L., Brand, P. A., & Felicio, D. (1990). Social interactions of obese and nonobese women. *Journal of Personality, 58,* 365–380.

Miller, C. T., Rothblum, E. D., Brand, P. A., & Felicio, D. M. (1995). Do obese women have poorer social relationships than nonobese women? Reports by self, friends, and coworkers. *Journal of Personality, 63,* 65–85.

Miller, D. T., & Ross, M. (1975). Self-serving biases in attribution of causality: Fact or fiction? *Psychological Bulletin, 82,* 313–325.

Miller, D. T., Turnbull, W., & McFarland, C. (1990). Counterfactual thinking and social perception: Thinking about what might have been. In M. P. Zanna (Ed.), *Advances in experimental social psychology* (Vol. 23). Orlando, FL: Academic Press.

Miller, M. L., & Thayer, J. F. (1989). On the existence of discrete classes in personality: Is self-monitoring the correct joint to carve? *Journal of Personality and Social Psychology, 57,* 143–155.

Miller, N., Maruayama, G., Beaber, R. J., & Valone, K. (1976). Speed of speech and persuasion. *Journal of Personality and Social Psychology, 34,* 615–624.

Miller, R. S. (1991). On decorum in close relationships: Why aren't we polite to those we love? *Contemporary Social Psychology, 15,* 63–65.

Miller, S. N., Brody, D. S., & Summerton, J. (1988). Styles of coping with threat: Implications for health. *Journal of Personality and Social Psychology, 54,* 142–148.

Milner, J. S., Robertson, K. R., & Rogers, D. L. (1990). Childhood history of abuse and adult child abuse potential. *Journal of Family Violence, 2,* 15–34.

Mixon, K. D., Foley, L. A. K., & Orne, K. (1995). The influence of racial similarity on the O. J. Simpson trial. *Journal of Social Behavior and Personality, 10,* 481–490.

Miyake, K., & Zuckerman, M. (1993). Beyond personality impressions: Effects of physical and vocal attractiveness on false consensus, social comparison, affiliation, and assumed and perceived similarity. *Journal of Personality, 61,* 411–437.

Mobley, W. H., Horner, S. O., & Holingsworth, A. T. (1978). An evaluation of precursors of hospital employee turnover. *Journal of Applied Psychology, 63,* 408–414.

Moghaddam, F. M., & Solliday, E. A. (1991). "Balanced multiculturalism" and the challenge of peaceful coexistence in pluralistic societies. *Psychology and Developing Societies, 3,* 51–72.

Monsour, M. (1992). Meanings of intimacy in cross- and same-sex friendships. *Journal of Social and Personal Relationships, 9,* 277–295.

Monsour, M., Betty, S., & Kurzweil, N. (1993). Levels of perspectives and the perception of intimacy in cross-sex friendships: A balance theory explanation of shared perceptual reality. *Journal of Social and Personal Relationships, 10,* 529–550.

Monteith, M. J. (1993). Self-regulation of prejudiced responses: Implications for progress in prejudice-reduction efforts. *Journal of Personality and Social Psychology, 65,* 469–485.

Monteith, M. J. (1996). Affective reactions to prejudice-related discrepant responses: The impact of standard salience. *Personality and Social Psychology Bulletin, 22,* 48–59.

Montepare, J. M., & Zebrowitz-McArthur, L. (1988). Impressions of people created by age-related qualities of their gates. *Journal of Personality and Social Psychology, 55,* 547–556.

Moore, C. H., Wuensch, K. L., Hedges, R. M., & Castellow, W. A. (1994). The effects of physical attractiveness and social desirability on judgments regarding a sexual harassment case. *Journal of Social Behavior and Personality, 9,* 715–730.

Moore, D. (1994). Entitlement as an epistemic problem: Do women think like men? *Journal of Social Behavior and Personality, 9,* 665–684.

Moore, J. S., Graziano, W. G., & Miller, M. G. (1987). Physical attractiveness, sex role orientation, and the evaluation of adults and children. *Personality and Social Psychology Bulletin, 13,* 95–102.

Moore, S., & Rosenthal, D. (1991). Adolescents' perceptions of friends' and parents' attitudes to sex and sexual risk-taking. *Journal of Community and Applied Social Psychology, 1,* 189–200.

Moore, T. (1993, August 16). Millions of volunteers counter image of a selfish society. *Albany Times Union,* p. A-2.

Moran, G., & Cutler, B. L. (1991). The prejudicial impact of pretrial publicity. *Journal of Applied Social Psychology, 21,* 345–367.

More young white women smoking. (1994, November 4). *Albany Times Union,* p. A-17.

Moreland, R. L. (1987). The formation of small groups. In C. Hendrick (Ed.), *Review of Personality and Social Psychology* (Vol. 8, pp. 80–110). Newbury Park, CA: Sage.

Moreland, R. L., & Beach, S. R. (1992). Exposure effects in the classroom: The development of affinity among students. *Journal of Experimental Social Psychology, 28,* 255–276.

Moreland, R. L., & Zajonc, R. B. (1982). Exposure effects in person perception: Familiarity, similarity, and attraction. *Journal of Experimental Social Psychology, 18,* 395–415.

Morey, N., & Gerber, G. L. (1995). Two types of competitiveness: Their impact on the perceived interpersonal attractiveness of women and men. *Journal of Applied Social Psychology, 25,* 210–222.

Morgan, H. J., & Janoff-Bulman, R. (1994). Positive and negative self-complexity: Patterns of adjustment following traumatic versus non-traumatic life experiences. *Journal of Social and Clinical Psychology, 13,* 63–85.

Morgan, R. (1980). Theory and practice: Pornography and rape. In L. Leaderer (Ed.), *Take back the night: Woman on pornography* (pp. 134–140). New York: William Morrow.

Mori, D. L., & Morey, L. (1991). The vulnerable body image of females with feelings of depression. *Journal of Research in Personality, 25,* 343–354.

Morris, K. J. (1985). *Discriminating depression and social anxiety: Self-efficacy analysis.* Unpublished master's thesis, Texas Tech University, Lubbock.

Morris, W. N., Worchel, S., Bois, J. L., Pearson, J. A., Rountree, C. A., Samaha, G. M., Wachtler, J., & Wright, S. I. (1976). Collective coping with stress: Group reactions to fear, anxiety, and ambiguity. *Journal of Personality and Social Psychology, 33,* 674–679.

Morrison, E. W., & Bies, R. J. (1991). Impression management in the feedback-seeking process: A literature review and research agenda. *Academy of Management Review, 16,* 322–341.

Morrow, G. D., Clark, E. M., & Brock, K. F. (1995). Individual and partner love styles: Implications for the quality of romantic involvements. *Journal of Social and Personal Relationships, 12,* 363–387.

Moscovici, S. (1985). Social influence and conformity. In G. Lindzey & E. Aronson (Eds.), *Handbook of social psychology* (3rd ed.). New York: Random House.

Mosher, D. L. (1991). Macho men, machismo, and sexuality. *Annual Review of Sex Research, 2,* 199–247.

Moskowitz, D. S. (1993). Dominance and friendliness: On the interaction of gender and situation. *Journal of Personality, 61,* 387–409.

Moskowitz, G. B., & Roman, R. J. (1992). Spontaneous trait inferences as self-generated primes: Implications for conscious social judgment. *Journal of Personality and Social Psychology, 62,* 728–738.

Moston, S., & Stephenson, G. M. (1993). The changing face of police interrogation. *Journal of Community and Applied Social Psychology, 3,* 101–115.

Muczyk, J. P., & Reimann, B. C. (1987). The case for directive leadership. *Academy of Management Review, 12* 647–687.

Mugny, G. (1975). Negotiations, image of the other and the process of minority influence. *European Journal of Social Psychology, 5,* 209–229.

Mugny, G., & Perez, J. (1991). *The social psychology minority influence.* Cambridge, England: Cambridge University Press.

Mullen, B., & Johnson, C. (1990). Distinctiveness-based illusory correlations and stereotyping: A meta-analytic integration. *British Journal of Social Psychology, 29,* 11–28.

Munsterberg, H. (1907). *On the witness stand: Essays in psychology and crime.* New York: McClure.

Murnen, S. K., & Byrne, D. (1991). The Hyperfemininity Scale: Measurement and initial validation of the construct. *Journal of Sex Research, 28,* 479–489.

Murnighan, K. (Ed.). (1993). *Handbook of social psychology in organizations.* Englewood Cliffs, N.J.

Murray, H. A. (1938). *Explorations in personality.* New York: Oxford University Press.

Murray, S. L., & Holmes, J. G. (1993). Seeing virtues in faults: Negativity and the transformation of interpersonal narratives in close relationships. *Journal of Personality and Social Psychology, 65,* 707–722.

Murray, S. L., & Holmes, J. G. (1994). Storytelling in close relationships: The construction of confidence. *Personality and Social Psychology Bulletin, 20,* 650–663.

Murrell, A. J., & Jones, J. M. (1993). Perceived control and victim derogation: Is the world still just? *Journal of Social Behavior and Personality, 8,* 545–554.

Myers, D. G., & Diener, E. (1995). Who is happy? *Psychological Science, 6,* 10–19.

Nadkarni, D. V., Lundgren, D., & Burlew, A. K. (1991). Gender differences in self-depriving behavior as a reaction to extreme inequity. *Journal of Social Behavior and Personality, 6,* 105–117.

Nadler, A. (1987). Determinants of help-seeking behaviour: The effects of helper's similarity, task centrality and recipient's self-esteem. *European Journal of Social Psychology, 17,* 57–67.

Nadler, A. (1991). Help-seeking behavior: Psychological costs and instrumental benefits. In M. S. Clark (Ed.), *Prosocial behavior* (pp. 290–311), Newbury Park, CA: Sage.

Nadler, A., & Fisher, J. D. (1986). The role of threat to self-esteem and perceived control in recipient reactions to aid: Theory development and empirical validation. *Advances in experimental social psychology, 17,* 81–123.

Nadler, A., Fisher, J. D., Itzhak, S. B. (1983). With a little help from my friend: Effect of a single or multiple acts of aid as a function of donor and task characteristics. *Journal of Personality and Social Psychology, 44,* 310–321.

Nagar, D., & Pandey, J. (1987). Affect and performance on a cognitive task as a function of crowding and noise. *Journal of Applied Social Psychology, 17,* 141–157.

Nahemow, L., & Lawton, M. P. (1975). Similarity and propinquity in friendship formation. *Journal of Personality and Social Psychology, 32,* 205–213.

Narby, D. J., Cutler, B. L., & Moran, G. (1993). A meta-analysis of the association between authoritarianism and jurors' perceptions of defendant culpability. *Journal of Applied Psychology, 78,* 34–42.

Nardi, P. M., & Sherrod, D. (1994). Friendship in the lives of gay men and lesbians. *Journal of Social and Personal Relationships, 11,* 185–199.

National Committee for Prevention of Child Abuse. (1990). *Public attitudes and actions regarding child abuse and its prevention* (Working Paper No. 840). Chicago, IL: National Committee for Prevention of Child Abuse.

National Institute for Occupational Safety and Health, Center for Disease Control and Prevention. "Homicide in the workplace." Document #705003, December 5, 1993.

Nemeth, C. J. (1986). Differential contributions of majority and minority influence. *Psychological Review, 93,* 23–32.

Neto, F. (1992). Loneliness among Portuguese adolescents. *Social Behavior and Personality, 20,* 15–22.

Neuberg, S. L. (1989). The goal of forming accurate impressions during social interaction: attenuating the impact of negative expectancies. *Journal of Personality and Social Psychology, 56,* 374–386.

Neuberg, S. L., Smith, D. M., Hoffman, J. C., & Russell, F. J. (1994). When we observe stigmatized and "normal" individuals interacting: Stigma by association. *Personality and Social Psychology Bulletin, 20,* 196–209.

Neuumn, J. H., & Baron, R. A. (in press). Aggression in the workplace. In Giacalone, R. A., & Greenberg, J. (Eds.), *Antisocial behavior in organizations.* Thousand Oaks, CA: Sage.

Newcomb, M. D., Rabow, J., & Hernandez, A. C. R. (1992). A cross national study of nuclear attitudes, normative support, and activist behavior: Additive and interactive effects. *Journal of Applied Social Psychology 22,* 780–800.

Newcomb, P. R. (1979). Cohabitation in America: An assessment of consequences. *Journal of Marriage and the Family, 41,* 597–603.

Newcomb, T. M. (1956). The prediction of interpersonal attraction. *Psychological Review, 60,* 393–404.

Newcomb, T. M. (1961). *The acquaintance process.* New York: Holt, Rinehart and Winston.

Newcomb, T. M., & Svehla, G. (1937). Intra-family relationships in attitudes. *Sociometry, 1,* 180–205.

Newton, T. L., Kiecolt-Glaser, J. K., Glaser, R., & Malarkey, W. B. (1995). Conflict and withdrawal during marital interaction: The roles of hostility and defensiveness. *Personality and Social Psychology Bulletin, 21,* 512–524.

Nida, S. A., & Koon, J. (1983). They get better looking at closing time around here, too. *Psychological Reports, 52,* 657–658.

Niedenthal, P. M., Setterlund, M. B., & Wherry, M. B. (1992). Possible self-complexity and affective reactions to goal-relevant evaluation. *Journal of Personality and Social Psychology, 63,* 5–16.

Nilchaikovit, T,, Hill, J M , & Holland, J. C. (1993). The effects of culture on illness behavior and medical care: Asian and American differences. *General Hospital Psychiatry, 15,* 41–50.

Nisbett, R. E. (1990). Evolutionary psychology, biology, and cultural evolution. *Motivation and Emotion, 14,* 255–264.

Nisbett, R. E. (1990). Evolutionary psychology, biology, and cultural evolution. *Motivation and Emotion, 14,* 255–264.

Nix, G., Watson, C., Pyszczynski, T., & Greenberg, J. (1995). Reducing depressive affect through external focus of attention. *Journal of Social and Clinical Psychology, 14,* 36–52.

Northwest National Life (1993, October). *Fear and violence in the workplace: A survey documenting the experience of American workers.* Minneapolis, MN: Author.

Norwood, J. L. (1992). Working women: Where have we been? Where are we going? *Population and Environment, 14,* 95–103.

Number of sexually active teens levels off, survey says. (1995, February 24). *Albany Times Union,* A-5.

Number of young U.S. killers triples over past decade. (1996, March 8). *Albany Times Union,* A-4.

O'Connell, P. D. (1988). Pretrial publicity, change of venue, public opinion polls—a theory of procedural justice. *University of Detroit Law Review, 65,* 169–197.

O'Grady, K. E. (1989). Physical attractiveness, need for approval, social self-esteem, and maladjustment. *Journal of Social and Clinical Psycholgy, 8,* 62–69.

O'Leary, S. G. (1995). Parental discipline mistakes. *Current Directions in Psychological Science, 4,* 11–13.

O'Sullivan, C. S., & Durso, F. T. (1984). Effects of schema-incongruent information on memory for stereotypical attributes. *Journal of Personality and Social Psychology, 47,* 55–70.

O'Sullivan, L. F., & Allgeier, E. R. (1994). Disassembling a stereotype: Gender differences in the use of token resistance. *Journal of Applied Social Psychology, 24,* 1035–1055.

O'Sullivan, L. F., & Byers, E. S. (1992). College students' incorporation of initiator and restrictor roles in sexual dating interactions. *Journal of Sex Research, 29,* 435–446.

Oggins, J., Veroff, J., & Leber, D. (1993). Perceptions of marital interaction among black and white newlyweds. *Journal of Personality and Social Psychology, 65,* 494–511.

Ogletree, S. M. (1993). "How do I love thee?" Let me count the valentines. *Social Behavior and Personality, 21,* 129–134.

Ohbuchi, K., Kameda, M., & Agarie, N. (1989). Apology as aggression control: Its role in mediating appraisal of and response to harm. *Journal of Personality and Social Psychology, 56,* 219–227.

Ohbuchi, K. I., & Ogura, S. (1984). The experience of anger (1): The survey for adults and university students with Averill's questionnaire (Japanese). *Japanese Journal of Criminal Psychology, 22,* 15–35.

Ohbuchi, K. I., & Takahashi, Y. (1994). Cultural styles of conflict management in Japanese and Americans: Passivity, covertness, and effectiveness of strategies. *Journal of Applied Social Psychology, 24,* 1345–1366.

Ohbuchi, K. I., Kameda, M., & Agarie, N. (1989). Apology as aggression control: Its role in mediating appraisal of and response to harm. *Journal of Personality and Social Psychology, 56,* 219–227.

Ohlott, P. J., Ruderman, M. N., & McCauley, C. D. (1994). Gender differences in managers' developmental job experiences. *Academy of Management Journal, 37,* 46–67.

Olczak, P. V., Kaplan, M. F., & Penrod, S. (1991). Attorneys' lay psychology and its effectiveness in selecting jurors: Three empirical studies. *Journal of Social Behavior and Personality, 6,* 431–452.

Oliner, S. P., & Oliner, P. M. (1988). *The altruistic personality: Rescuers of Jews in Nazi Europe.* New York: Free Press.

Olivenstein, L. (1992). Cold comfort. *Discover, 13*(8), 18, 20–21.

Oliver, M. B., & Hyde, J. S. (1993). Gender differences in sexuality: A meta-analysis. *Psychological Bulletin, 114,* 29–51.

Olmstead, R. E., Guy, S. M., O'Malley, P. M., & Bentler, P. M. (1991). Longitudinal assessment of the relationship between self-esteem, fatalism, loneliness, and substance use. *Journal of Social Behavior and Personality, 6,* 749–770.

Olson, J. M., & Ross, M. (1988). False feedback about placebo effectiveness:Consequences for the misattribution of speech anxiety. *Journal of Experimental Social Psychology, 24,* 275–291.

Olweus, D. (1986). Aggression and hormones: Behavioral relationship with testosterone and adrenaline. In D. Olweus, J. Block, & M. Radke-Yarrows (Eds.), *Development of antisocial and prosocial behavior* (pp. 51–72). New York: Academic Press.

Omoto, A. M., & Snyder, M. (1995). Sustained helping without obligation: Motivation, longevity of service, and perceived attitude change among AIDS volunteers. *Journal of Personality and Social Psychology, 68,* 671–686.

Orive, R. (1988). Social projective and social comparison of opinions. *Journal of Personality and Social Psychology, 54,* 953–964.

Orlofsky, J. L., & O'Heron, C. A. (1987). Stereotypic and non-stereotypic sex role trait and behavior orientations: Implications for personal adjustment. *Journal of Personality and Social Psychology, 52,* 1034–l042.

Orne, M. T., Soskis, D. A., Dinges, D. F., & Orne, E. C. (1984). Hypnotically induced testimony. In G. L. Wells & E. F. Loftus (Eds.), *Eyewitness testimony: Psychological perspectives* (pp. 171–213). Cambridge, England: Cambridge University Press.

Orpen, C. (1994). The effects of self-esteem and personal control on the relationship between job insecurity and psychological well-being. *Social Behavior and Personality, 22,* 53–56.

Osborne, J. W. (1995). Academics, self-esteem, and race: A look at the underlying assumptions of the disidentification hypothesis. *Personality and Social Psychology Bulletin, 21,* 449–455.

Osterman, K., Bjorkqvist, K., Lagerspetz, K. M. J., Kaukianainen, A., Huesmann, L. W., & Fraczek, A. (1994). Peer and self-estimated aggression and victimization in 8-year-old children from five ethnic groups. *Aggressive Behavior, 20,* 411–428.

Ostroff, C. (1992). The relationship between satisfaction, attitudes and performance: An organizational level analysis. *Journal of Applied Psychology, 77,* 963–974.

Ozone depletion at its most severe, expert says. (1995, August 3). *Albany Times Union,* p. A-13.

Page, D., & Gropp, T. (1995, April). *Pretrial publicity: Attitudinal and cognitive mediators.* Paper presented at the meeting of the Eastern Psychological Association, Boston.

Page, N. R., & Wiseman, R. L. (1993). Supervisory behavior and worker satisfaction in the United States, Mexico, and Spain. *Journal of Business Communication, 30,* 161–180.

Page, R. M. (1991). Loneliness as a risk factor in adolescent hopelessness. *Journal of Research in Personality, 25,* 189–195.

Palys, T. S. (1984). *A content analysis of sexually explicit videos in British Columbia.* Report 15, Working Papers, Department of Psychology, University of British Columbia.

Pan, S. (1993). China: Acceptability and effect of three kinds of sexual publication. *Archives of Sexual Behavior, 22,* 59–71.

Parkes, K. R., & von Rabenau, C. (1993). Work characteristics and well-being among psychiatric health-care staff. *Journal of Community and Applied Social Psychology, 3,* 243–259.

Parrott, W. G. (1991). The emotional experiences of envy and jealousy. In P. Salovey (Ed.), *The psychology of jealousy and envy* (pp. 2–20). New York: Guilford Press.

Passive smoking link found in newborns. (1994, February 23). Associated Press.

Pataki, S. P., Shapiro, C., & Clark, M. S. (1994). Children's acquisition of appropriate norms for friendships and acquaintances. *Journal of Social and Personal Relationships, 11,* 427–442.

Paterson, R. J., & Neufeld, R. W. J. (1995). What are my options? Influences of choice availability on stress and the perception of control. *Journal of Research in Personality, 29,* 145–167.

Patrick, C. J., Bradley, M. M., & Lang, P. J. (1993). Emotion in the criminal psychopath: Startle reflex modulation. *Journal of Abnormal Psychology, 102,* 83–92.

Patterson, C. J. (1994). Lesbian and gay families. *Current Directions in Psychological Science, 3,* 62–64.

Paul, L., Foss, M. A., & Galloway, J. (1993). Sexual jealousy in young women and men: Aggressive responsiveness to partner and rival. *Aggressive Behavior, 19,* 401–420.

Paulhus, D. L., & Bruce, M. N. (1992). The effect of acquaintanceship on the validity of personality impressions: A longitudinal study. *Journal of Personality and Social Psychology, 63,* 816–824.

Paulhus, D. L., Bruce, M. N., & Trapnell, P. D. (1995). Effects of self-presentation strategies on personality profiles and their structure. *Personality and Social Psychology Bulletin, 21,* 100–108.

Paulus, P. B. (Ed.). (1989). *Psychology of group influence* (2nd ed.). Hillsdale, NJ: Erlbaum.

Pearson, K., & Lee, A. (1903). On the laws of inheritance in man: I. Inheritance of physical characters. *Biometrika, 2,* 357–462.

Pedersen, D. M. (1994). Privacy preferences and classroom seat selection. *Social Behavior and Personality, 22,* 393–398.

Pennebaker, J. W., & Beall, S. (1986). Confronting a traumatic event: Toward an understanding of inhibition and disease. *Journal of Abnormal Psychology, 95,* 274–281.

Pennebaker, J. W., Dyer, M. A., Caulkins, R. S., Litowicz, D. L., Ackerman, P. L., & Anderson, D. B. (1979). Don't the girls all get prettier at closing time: A country and western application to psychology. *Personality and Social Psychology Bulletin, 5,* 122–125.

Pennebaker, J. W., Hughes, C. F., & O'Heron, R. C. (1987). The psychophysiology of confession: Linking inhibitory and psychosomatic processes. *Journal of Personality and Social Psychology, 52,* 781–793.

Peplau, L. A., & Perlman, D. (1982). Perspective on loneliness. In L. A. Peplau & D. Perlman (Eds.), *Loneliness: A sourcebook of current theory, research, and therapy.* New York: Wiley.

Peplau, L. A., Hill, C. T., & Rubin, Z. (1993). Sex role attitudes in dating and marriage: A 15-year follow-up of the Boston couples study. *Journal of Social Issues, 49*(3), 31–52.

Perdue, C. W., & Gurtman, M. B. (1990). Evidence for the automaticity of ageism. *Journal of Experimental Social Psychology, 26,* 199–216.

Perez-Pena, R. (1994, October 19). Observers help capture stabbing suspect in New York City. *Albany Times Union,* p. B-2.

Perrewe, P. L., & Anthony, W. P. (1990). Stress in a steel pipe mill: The impact of job demands, personal control, and employee age on somatic complaints. *Journal of Social Behavior and Personality, 5,* 77–90.

Perrine, R. M. (1993). On being supportive: The emotional consequences of listening to another's distress. *Journal of Social and Personal Relationships, 10,* 371–384.

Pessin, J. (1933). The comparative effects of social and mechanical stimulation on memorizing. *American Journal of Psychology, 45,* 263–270.

Peterson, L., & Brown, D. (1994). Integrating child injury and abuse–neglect research: Common histories, etiologies, and solutions. *Psychological Bulletin, 116,* 293–315.

Petkova, K. G., Ajzen, I., & Driver, B. L. (1995). Salience of anti-abortion beliefs and commitment to an attitudinal position: On the strength, structure, and predictive validity of anti-abortion attitudes. *Journal of Applied Social Psychology, 25,* 463–483.

Pettigrew, T. F. (1969). Racially separate or together? *Journal of Social Issues, 24,* 43–69.

Pettigrew, T. F. (1981). Extending the stereotype concept. In D. L. Hamilton (Ed.), *Cognitive processes in stereotyping and intergroup behavior* (pp. 303–331). Hillsdale, NJ: Erlbaum.

Petty, R. E., & Cacioppo, J. T. (1979). Issue involvement can increase or decrease persuasion by enhancing message-relevant cognitive repsonses. *Journal of Personality and Social Psychology, 37,* 1915–1926.

Petty, R. E., & Cacioppo, J. T. (1981). *Attitudes and persuasion: Classic and contemporary approaches.* Dubuque, IA: Wm. C. Brown.

Petty, R. E., & Cacioppo, J. T. (1985). *Communication and persuasion: Central and peripheral routes to attitude change.* New York: Springer-Verlag.

Petty, R. E., & Cacioppo, J. T. (1986). The elaboration likelihood model of persuasion. In L. Berkowitz (Ed.), *Advances in experimental social psychology,* (Vol. 19, pp. 123–205). New York: Academic Press.

Petty, R. E., & Cacioppo, J.T. (1990). Involvement and persuasion: Tradition versus integration. *Psychological Bulletin, 107,* 367–374.

Petty, R. E., Cacioppo, J. T., Strathman, A. J., & Priester, J. R. (1994). To think or not to think: Exploring two routes to persuasion. In S. Shavitt & T. C. Brock (Eds.), *Persuasion* (pp. 113–147). Boston: Allyn & Bacon.

Petty, R. E., Ostrom, T. M., & Brock, T. C. (Eds.). (1981). *Cognitive responses in persuasion.* Hillsdale, NJ: Erlbaum.

Petty, R. E., Unnava, R., & Strathman, A. J. (1991). Theories of attitude change. In T. S. Robertson & H. H. Kassarjian (Eds.), *Handbook of consumer behavior* (pp. 241–280). Englewood Cliffs, NJ: Prentice Hall.

Petty, R. E., Wells, G. L., & Brock, T. C. (1976). Distraction can enhance or reduce yielding to propaganda: Thought disruption versus effort justification. *Journal of Personality and Social Psychology, 34,* 874–884.

Pfeffer, J. (1992). *Managing with power.* Boston: Harvard Business School.

Phelps, E. J. (1981). *The maid of the North.* New York: Holt, Rinehart, & Winston.

Pierce, C. A. (1992). *The effects of physical attractiveness and height on dating choice: A meta-analysis.* Unpublished masters thesis, University at Albany, State University of New York, Albany, NY.

Pierce, C. A., Byrne, D. A., & Aguinis, H. (in press). Attraction in organizations: A model of workplace romance. *Journal of Organizational Behavior.*

Piliavin, J. A., & Unger, R. K. (1985). *The helpful but helpless female: Myth or reality?* In V. E. O'Leary, R. K. Unger, & B. S. Wallston (Eds.), *Women, gender, and social psychology* (pp. 149–189). Hillsdale, NJ: Erlbaum.

Pilisuk, M., & Acredolo, C. (1988). Fear of technological hazards: One concern or many? *Social Behavior, 3,* 17–24.

Pillow, D. R., West, S. G., & Reich, J. W. (1991). Attributional style in relation to self-esteem and depression: Mediational and interactive models. *Journal of Research in Personality, 25,* 57–69.

Pingitore, R., Dugooni, B. L., Tindale, R. S., & Spring, B. (1994). Bias against overweight job applicants in a simulated employment interview. *Journal of Applied Psychology, 79,* 909–917.

Pittman, T. S. (1993). Control motivation and attitude change. In G. Weary, F. Gleicher, & K. L. Marsh (Eds.), *Control motivation and social cognition* (pp. 157–175). New York: Springer-Verlag.

Planalp, S., & Benson, A. (1992). Friends' and acquaintances' conversations: I. Perceived differences. *Journal of Social and Personal Relationships, 9,* 483–506.

Platz, S. G., & Hosch, H. M. (1988). Cross-racial/ethnic eyewitness identification: A field study. *Journal of Applied Social Psychology, 18,* 972–984.

Pleck, J. H., Sonenstein, F. L., & Ku, L. C. (1993). Masculinity ideology: Its impact on adolescent males' heterosexual relationships. *Journal of Social Issues, 49*(3), 11–29.

Plesser-Storr, D. (1995). *Self-presentation by men to attractive and unattractive women: Tactics of ingratiation, blasting, and basking.* Unpublished doctoral dissertation, University at Albany, State University of New York, Albany.

Pliner, P., Chaiken, S., & Flett, G. L. (1990). Gender differences in concern with body weight and physical appearance over the life span. *Personality and Social Psychology Bulletin, 16,* 263–273.

Pliner, P., Hart, H., Kohl, J., & Saari, D. (1974). Compliance without pressure: Some further data on the foot-in-the-door technique. *Journal of Experimental Social Psychology, 10,* 17–22.

Polusny, M. A., & Follette, V. M. (1995). Long-term correlates of child sexual abuse: Theory and review of the empirical literature. *Applied and Preventive Psychology, 4,* 143–166.

Popper, K. (1959). *The logic of scientific discovery.* London: Hutchinson.

Porter, L. S., & Stone, A. A. (1995). Are there really gender differences in coping?: A reconsideration of previous data and results from a daily study. *Journal of Social and Clinical Psychology, 14,* 184–202.

Powell, G. N. (1990). One more time: Do female and male managers differ? *Academy of Management Executive, 4*(3), 68–75.

Powell, G. N., & Butterfield, D. A. (1994). Investigating the "glass ceiling" phenomenon: An empirical study of actual promotions to top management. *Academy of Management Journal, 37,* 68–86.

Powers, P. C., & Geen, R. G. (1972). Effects of the behavior and perceived arousal of a model on instrumental aggression. *Journal of Personality and Social Psychology, 23,* 175–184.

Prager, K. J., & Bailey, J. M. (1985). Androgyny, ego development, and psychosocial crisis. *Sex Roles, 13,* 525–536.

Pratkanis, A. R., & Aronson, E. (1992). *Age of propaganda: The everyday use and abuse of persuasion.* New York: W. H. Freeman.

Pratto, F., & John, O. P. (1991). Automatic vigilance: The attention-grabbing power of negative social information. *Journal of Personality and Social Psychology, 61,* 380–391.

Preston, R. (1995, May 22). Back in the hot zone. *The New Yorker,* 43–45.

Price, D. (1995). Energy and human evolution. *Population and Environment, 16,* 301–319.

Priel, B., Gonik, N., & Rabinowitz, B. (1993). Appraisals of childbirth experience and newborn characteristics: The role of hardiness and affect. *Journal of Personality, 61,* 299–315.

Pritchard, R. D., Dunnette, H. D., & Jorgenson, D. O. (1972). Effects of perceptions of equity and inequity on worker performance and satisfaction. *Journal of Applied Psychology, 56,* 75–94.

Prohaska, T. R., Keller, M. L., Leventhal, E. A., & Leventhal, H. (1987). Impact of symptoms and aging attribution on emotions and coping. *Health Psychology, 6,* 495–514.

Ptacek, J. T., & Dodge, K. L. (1995). Coping strategies and relationship satisfaction in couples. *Personality and Social Psychology Bulletin, 21,* 76–84.

Ptacek, J. T., Smith, R. E., & Dodge, K. L. (1994). Gender differences in coping with stress: When stressor and appraisals do not differ. *Personality and Social Psychology Bulletin, 20,* 421–430.

Ptacek, J. T., Smith, R. E., & Zanas, J. (1992). Gender, appraisal, and coping: A longitudinal analysis. *Journal of Personality, 60,* 747–770.

Pullium, R. M. (1993). Reactions to AIDS patients as a function of attributions about controllability and promiscuity. *Social Behavior and Personality, 21,* 297–302.

Putnam, L. L. (1990). Reframing integrative and distributive bargaining: A process perspective. In B. H. Sheppard, M. H. Bazerman, & R. J. Lewicki (Eds.), *Research on negotiation in organizations* (Vol. 2, pp. 3–30). Greenwich, CT: JAI Press.

Quadrel, M. J., & Lau, R. R. (1989). Health promotion, health locus of control, and health behavior: Two field experiments. *Journal of Applied Social Psychology, 19,* 1497–1521.

Queen Victoria (1981, January). *Medical Aspects of Human Sexuality,* 86.

Quigley, B. M., Johnson, A. B., & Byrne, D. (1995, June). *Mock jury sentencing decisions: A meta-analysis of the attractiveness-leniency effect.* Paper presented at the meeting of the American Psychological Society, New York.

Quinn, R. P., & Staines, G. L. (1979). *The 1976 quality of employment survey.* Ann Arbor, MI: Institute for Social Research.

Radecki-Bush, C., Farrell, A. D., & Bush, J. P. (1993). Predicting jealous responses: The influence of adult attachment and depression on threat appraisal. *Journal of Social and Personal Relationships, 10,* 569–588.

Rahim, M. A. (1983). *Organizational conflict inventories.* Palo Alto, CA: Consulting Psychologists Press.

Rajecki, D. W., McTavish, D. G., Rasmussen, L., Schreuders, M., Byers, D. C., & Jessup, S. K. (1994). Violence, conflict, trickery, and other story themes in TV ads for food for children. *Journal of Applied Social Psychology, 24,* 1685–1700.

Raleigh, M. J., McGuire, M. T., Brammer, G. L., Pollack, D. B., & Yuwiler, A. (1991). Serotonergic mechanisms promote dominance acquisition in adult male vervet monkeys. *Brain Research, 559,* 181–190.

Rall, M. L., Peskoff, F. S., & Byrne, J. J. (1994). The effects of information-giving behavior and gender on the perceptions of physicians: An experimental analysis. *Social Behavior and Personality, 22,* 1–16.

Ramirez, J., Bryant, J., & Zillmann, D. (1983). Effects of erotica on retaliatory behavior as a function of level of prior provocation. *Journal of Personality and Social Psychology, 43,* 971–978.

Randall, D. M., Fedor, D. P., & Longenecker, C. O. (1990). The behavioral expression of organizational commitment. *Journal of Vocational Behavior, 36,* 210–224.

Rathje, W. L. (1991). Once and future landfills. *National Geographic, 179*(5), 116–134.

Raty, H., & Snellman, L. (1992). Does gender make any difference? Common-sense conceptions of intelligence. *Social Behavior and Personality, 20,* 23–34.

Raviv, A. (1993). Radio psychology: A comparison of listeners and non-listeners. *Journal of Community and Applied Social Psychology, 3,* 197–211.

Reed, D., & Weinberg, M. S. (1984). Premarital coitus: Developing and establishing sexual scripts. *Social Psychology Quarterly, 47,* 129–138.

Reesor, K. A., & Craig, K. A. (1988). Medically incongruent chronic pain: Physical limitations, suffering and ineffective coping. *Pain, 32,* 35–45.

Regan, D. T., & Fazio, R. H. (1977). On the consistency between attitudes and behavior: Look to the method of attitude formation. *Journal of Experimental Social Psychology, 13,* 38–45.

Reifman, A. S., Larrick, R. P., & Fein, S. (1991). Temper and temperature on the diamond: The heat–aggression relationship in major league baseball. *Personality and Social Psychology Bulletin, 17,* 580–585.

Reis, H. T., Nezlek, J., & Wheeler, L. (1989). Physical attractiveness in social interaction. *Journal of Personality and Social Psychology, 38,* 604–617.

Reis, T. J., Gerrard, M., & Gibbons, F. X. (1993). Social comparison and the pill: Reactions to upward and downward comparison of contraceptive behavior. *Personality and Social Psychology Bulletin, 19,* 13–20.

Reisman, J. M. (1984). Friendliness and its correlates. *Journal of Social and Clinical Psychology, 2,* 143–155.

Reiss, A. J., & Roth, J. A. (Eds.). (1993). *Understanding and preventing violence.* Washington, DC: National Academy Press.

Reno, R. R., Cialdini, R. B, & Kallgren, C. A (1993). The transsituational influence of social norms. *Journal of Personality and Social Psychology, 64,* 104–112.

Rensberger, B. (1993, November 9). Certain chemistry between vole pairs. *Albany Times Union,* pp. C-1, C-3.

Rentsch, J. R., & Heffner, T. S. (1994). Assessing self-concept: Analysis of Gordon's coding scheme using "Who am I?" responses. *Journal of Social Behavior and Personality, 9,* 283–300.

Revenson, T. A. (1981). Coping with loneliness: The impact of causal attributions. *Personality and Social Psychology Bulletin, 7,* 565–571.

Revicki, D. A., Whitley, T. W., Gallery, M. E., & Allison, E. J. Jr. (1993). Impact of work environment characteristics on work-related stress and depression in emergency medicine residents: A longitudinal study. *Journal of Community & Applied Social Psychology, 3,* 273–284.

Reykowski, J. (1982). Motivation of prosocial behavior. In V. Derlega & J. Grzelak (Eds.), *Cooperation and helping behavior* (pp. 355–375). Orlando, FL: Academic Press.

Rhodewalt, F., & Davison, J., Jr. (1983). Reactance and the coronary-prone behavior pattern: The role of self-attribution in response to reduced behavioral freedom. *Journal of Personality and Social Psychology, 44,* 220–228.

Richardson, D. R., Hammock, G. S., Smith, S. M., Gardner, W., & Signo, M. (1994). Empathy as a cognitive inhibitor of interpersonal aggression. *Aggressive Behavior, 20,* 275–289.

Ridley, M., & Dawkins, R. (1981). The natural selection of altruism. In J. P. Rushton & R. M. Sorrentino (Eds.), *Altruism and helping behavior.* Hillsdale, NJ: Erlbaum.

Riess, M., & Schlenker, B. R. (1977). Attitude change and responsibility avoidance as modes of dilemma resolution in forced-compliance situations. *Journal of Personality and Social Psychology, 35,* 21–30.

Riggio, R. E., & Throckmorton, B. (1988). The relative effect of verbal and nonverbal behavior, appearance, and social skills on valuations made in hiring interviews. *Journal of Applied Social Psychology, 18,* 331–348.

Rind, B. (1196). Effect of beliefs about weather conditions on tipping. *Journal of Applied Social Psychology, 26,* 137–147.

Riordan, C. A. (1978). Equal-status interracial contact: A review and revision of a concept. *International Journal of Intercultural Relations, 2,* 161–185.

Riskind, J. H., & Maddux, J. E. (1993). Loomingness, helplessness, and fearfulness: An integration of harm-looming and self-efficacy models of fear. *Journal of Social and Clinical Psychology, 12,* 73–89.

Riskind, J. H., & Wilson, D. W. (1982). Interpersonal attraction for the competitive person: Unscrambling the competition paradox. *Journal of Applied Social Psychology, 12,* 444–452.

Robberson, N. R., & Rogers, R. W. (1988). Beyond fear appeals: Negative and positive persuasive appeals to health and self-esteem. *Journal of Applied Social Psychology, 18,* 277–287.

Roberts, B. W., & Donahue, E. M. (1994). One personality, multiple selves: Integrating personality and social roles. *Journal of Personality, 62,* 199–218.

Roberts, J. E., & Monroe, S. M. (1992). Vulnerable self-esteem and depressive symptoms: Prospective findings comparing three alternative conceptualizations. *Journal of Personality and Social Psychology, 62,* 804–812.

Roberts, J. V., & Edwards, D. (1989). Contextual effects in judgments of crimes, criminals, and the purposes of sentencing. *Journal of Applied Social Psychology, 19,* 902–917.

Robinson, L. A., Berman, J. S., & Neimeyer, R. A. (1990). Psychotherapy for the treatment of depression: A comprehensive review of controlled outcome research. *Psychological Bulletin, 108,* 30–49.

Rodgers, J. L., Billy, J. O. B., & Udry, J. R. (1984). A model of friendship similarity in mildly deviant behaviors. *Journal of Applied Social Psychology, 14,* 413–425.

Rodin, J., & Salovey, P. (1989). Health psychology. *Annual Review of Psychology, 40,* 533–579.

Rodin, M., & Price, J. (1995). Overcoming stigma: Credit for self-improvement or discredit for needing to improve? *Personality and Social Psychology Bulletin, 21,* 172–181.

Rogers, C. R. (1951). *Client-centered therapy.* Boston: Houghton Mifflin.

Rogers, C. R., & Dymond, R. F. (Eds.). (1954). *Psychotherapy and personality change*. Boston: Houghton Mifflin.

Rogers, M., Miller, N., Mayer, F. S., & Duvall, S. (1982). Personal responsibility and salience of the request for help: Determinants of the relations between negative affect and helping behavior. *Journal of Personality and Social Psychology, 43,* 956–970.

Rogers, R. W. (1980). *Subjects' reactions to experimental deception*. Unpublished manuscript, University of Alabama, Tuscaloosa.

Rogers, R. W., & Ketcher, C. M. (1979). Effects of anonymity and arousal on aggression. *Journal of Psychology, 102,* 13–19.

Romzek, B. S. (1989). Personal consequences of employee commitment. *Academy of Management Journal, 39,* 649–661.

Rosen, K. H., & Stith, S. M. (1995). Women terminating abusive dating relationships: A qualitative study. *Journal of Social and Personal Relationships, 12,* 155–160.

Rosenbaum, M. E. (1986). The repulsion hypothesis: On the non-development of relationships. *Journal of Personality and Social Psychology, 51,* 1156–1166.

Rosenbaum, M. E., & Levin, I. P. (1969). Impression formation as a function of source credibility and the polarity of information. *Journal of Personality and Social Psychology, 12,* 34–37.

Rosenberg, E. L., & Ekman, P. (in press). Conceptual and methodological issues in the judgment of facial expressions of emotion. *Motivation & Emotion*.

Rosener, J. B. (1990). Ways women lead. *Harvard Business Review, 68*(6), 202.

Rosenfield, D., Greenberg, J., Folger, R., & Borys, R. (1982). Effect of an encounter with a black panhandler on subsequent helping for blacks: Tokenism or conforming to a negative stereotype? *Personality and Social Psychology Bulletin, 8,* 664–671.

Rosenhan, D. L., Salovey, P., & Hargis, K. (1981). The joys of helping: Focus of attention mediates the impact of positive affect on altruism. *Journal of Personality and Social Psychology, 40,* 899–905.

Rosenthal, A. M. (1964). *Thirty-eight witnesses*. New York: McGraw-Hill.

Rosenthal, D. A., & Shepherd, H. (1993). A six-month follow-up of adolescents' sexual risk-taking, HIV/AIDS knowledge, and attitudes to condoms. *Journal of Community and Applied Social Psychology, 3,* 53–65.

Rosenthal, E. (1992, August 18). Troubled marriage? Sibling relations may be at fault. *New York Times*, pp. C1, C9.

Rosenzweig, J. M., & Daley, D. M. (1989). Dyadic adjustment/sexual satisfaction in women and men as a function of psychological sex role self-perception. *Journal of Sex and Marital Therapy, 15,* 42–56.

Rosin, H. (1995, June 5). The homecoming. *New Republic*, 21–23, 26.

Roskos-Ewoldsen, D. R., & Fazio, R. H. (1992). The accessibility of source likability as a determinant of persuasion. *Personality and Social Psychology Bulletin 18,* 19–25.

Ross, L. D. (1977). Problems in the interpretation of "self-serving" asymmetries in causal attribution: Comments on the Stephan et al. paper. *Sociometry, 40,* 112–114.

Rotenberg, K. J. (1994). Loneliness and interpersonal trust. *Journal of Social and Clinical Psychology, 13,* 152–173.

Rotenberg, K. J., & Kmill, J. (1992). Perception of lonely and non-lonely persons as a function of individual differences in loneliness. *Journal of Social and Personal Relationships, 9,* 325–330.

Roter, D. L. (1984). Patient question asking in physician–patient interaction. *Health Psychology, 3,* 395–409.

Roth, D. L., Wiebe, D. J., Fillingim, R. B., & Shay, K. A. (1989). Life events, fitness, hardiness, and health: A simultaneous analysis of proposed stress-resistance effects. *Journal of Personality and Social Psychology, 57,* 136–142.

Rothman, A. J., Salovey, P., Antone, C., Keough, K., & Martin, C. D. (1993). The influence of message framing on intentions to perform health behaviors. *Journal of Experimental Social Psychology, 29,* 408–433.

Rotton, J., & Frey, J. (1985). Psychological costs of air pollution: Atmospheric conditions, seasonal trends, and psychiatric emergencies. *Population and Environment, 7,* 3–16.

Rotton, J., & Kelley, I. W. (1985). Much ado about the full moon: A meta-analysis of lunar-lunacy research. *Psychological Bulletin, 97,* 286–306.

Rotton, J., Frey, J., Barry, T., Milligan, M., & Fitzpatrick, M. (1979). The air pollution experience and physical aggression. *Journal of Applied Social Psychology, 9,* 397–412.

Routh, D. K., & Ernst, A. R. (1984). Somatization disorder in relatives of children and adolescents with functional abdominal pain. *Journal of Pediatric Psychology, 50,* 427–437.

Rozin, P., & Nemeroff, C. (1990). The laws of sympathetic magic: A psychological analysis of similarity and contagion. In W. Stigler, R. A. Shweder, & G. Herdt (Eds.), *Cultural psychology: Essays in comparative human development* (pp. 205–232). Cambridge, England: Cambridge University Press.

Rozin, P., Lowery, L., & Ebert, R. (1994). Varieties of disgust faces and the structure of disgust. *Journal of Personality and Social Psychology, 66,* 870–881.

Rozin, P., Markwith, M., & Nemeroff, C. (1992). Magical contagion beliefs and fear of AIDS. *Journal of Applied Social Psychology, 22,* 1081–1092.

Rozin, P., Millman, L., & Nemeroff, C. (1986). Operation of the laws of sympathetic magic in disgust and other domains. *Journal of Personality and Social Psychology, 50,* 703–712.

Rubin, J. Z. (1985). Deceiving ourselves about deception: Comment on Smith and Richardson's "Amelioration of deception and harm in psychological research." *Journal of Personality and Social Psychology, 48,* 252–253.

Rusbult, C. E. (1983). A longitudinal test of the investment model: The development (and deterioration) of satisfaction and commitment in heterosexual involvements. *Journal of Personality and Social Psychology, 45,* 101–117.

Rusbult, C. E., & Martz, J. M. (1995). Remaining in an abusive relationship: An investment model analysis of nonvoluntary dependence. *Personality and Social Psychology Bulletin, 21,* 558–571.

Rusbult, C. E., & Zembrodt, I. M. (1983). Responses to dissatisfaction in romantic involvements: A multidimensional scaling analysis. *Journal of Experimental Social Psychology, 19,* 274–293.

Rusbult, C. E., Morrow, G. D., & Johnson, D. J. (1990). Self-esteem and problem-solving behavior in close relationships. *British Journal of Social Psychology,*

Rusbult, C. E., Onizuka, R. K., & Lipkus, I. (1993). What do we really want?: Mental models of ideal romantic involvement explored through multidimensional scaling. *Journal of Experimental Social Psychology, 29,* 493–527.

Ruscher, J. B., & Hammer, E. D. (1994). Revising disrupted impressions through conversation. *Journal of Personality and Social Psychology, 66,* 530–541.

Rushton, J. P. (1989). Genetic similarity, human altruism, and group selection. *Behavioral and Brain Sciences, 12,* 503–559.

Rushton, J. P. (1989). Genetic similarity in male friendships. *Ethology and Sociobiology, 10,* 361–373.

Rushton, J. P. (1990). Sir Francis Galton, epigenetic rules, genetic similarity theory, and human life-history analysis. *Journal of Personality, 58,* 117–140.

Rushton, J. P., & Nicholson, I. R. (1988). Genetic similarity theory, intelligence, and human mate choice. *Ethology and Sociobiology, 9,* 45–57.

Rushton, J. P., Russell, R. J. H., & Wells, P. A. (1984). Genetic similarity theory: Beyond kin selection. *Behavior Genetics, 14,* 179–193.

Russell, D., Peplau, L. A., & Cutrona, C. E. (1980). The revised UCLA Loneliness Scale: Concurrent and discriminant validity evidence. *Journal of Personality and Social Psychology, 39,* 472–480.

Russell, G. W. (1993). *The psychology of sport.* New York: Springer-Verlag.

Russell, J. A. (1994). Is there universal recognition of emotion from facial expressions? A review of cross-cultural studies. *Psychological Bulletin, 115,* 102–141.

Russo, N. F., Green, B. L., & Knight, G. (1993). The relationship of gender, self-esteem, and instrumentality to depressive symptomatology. *Journal of Social and Clinical Psychology, 12,* 218–236.

Rutkowski, G. K., Gruder, C. L., & Romer, D. (1983). Group cohesiveness, social norms, and bystander intervention. *Journal of Personality and Social Psychology, 44,* 542–552.

Ryan, R. H., & Geiselman, R. E. (1991). Effects of biased information on the relationship between eyewitness confidence and accuracy. *Bulletin of the Psychonomic Society, 29,* 7–9.

Ryckman, R. M., Butler, J. C., Thornton, B., & Lindner, M. A. (1995, April). *Identification and assessment of physique subtype stereotypes.* Paper presented at the meeting of the Eastern Psychological Association, Boston.

Ryckman, R. M., Robbins, M. A., Kaczor, L. M., & Gold, J. A. (1989). Male and female raters' stereotyping of male and female physiques. *Personality and Social Psychology Bulletin, 15,* 244–251.

Ryerson, W. N. (1994). Population communications international: Its role in family planning soap operas. *Population and Environment, 15,* 255–264.

Sadalla, E. K., Kenrick, D. T., & Vershure, B. (1987). Dominance and heterosexual attraction. *Journal of Personality and Social Psychology, 52,* 730–738.

Safir, M. P., Peres, Y., Lichtenstein, M., Hoch, Z., & Shepher, J. (1982). Psychological androgyny and sexual adequacy. *Journal of Sex and Marital Therapy, 8,* 228–240.

Salovey, P. (1992). Mood-induced self-focused attention. *Journal of Personality and Social Psychology, 62,* 699–707.

Salovey, P., Mayer, J. D., & Rosenhan, D. L. (1991). Mood and helping: Mood as a motivator of helping and helping as a regulator of mood. In M. S. Clark (Ed.), *Prosocial behavior* (pp. 215–237). Newbury Park, CA: Sage.

Sanders, G. S. (1983). An attentional process model of social facilitation. In A. Hare, H. Blumberg, V. Kent, & M. Davies (Eds.), *Small groups.* London: Wiley

Sanna, L. J., & Pusecker, P. A. (1994). Self-efficacy, valence of self-evaluation, and performance. *Personality and Social Psychology Bulletin, 20,* 82–92.

Santos, M. D., Leve, C., & Pratkanis, A. R. (1994). Hey buddy, can you spare seventeen cents? Mindful persuasion and pique technique. *Journal of Applied Social Psychology, 24,* 755–764.

Sarason, I. G., Sarason, B. R., & Pierce, G. R. (1994). Social support: Global and relationship-based levels of analysis. *Journal of Social and Personal Relationships, 11,* 295–312.

Sayers, S. L., Baucom, D. H., & Tierney, A. M. (1993). Sex roles, interpersonal control, and depression: Who can get their way? *Journal of Research in Personality, 27,* 377–395.

Schachter, S. (1951). Deviation, rejection, and communication. *Journal of Abnormal and Social Psychology, 46,* 190–207.

Schachter, S. (1959). *The psychology of affiliation.* Stanford, CA: Stanford University Press.

Schachter, S. (1964). The interaction of cognitive and physiological determinants of emotional state. In L. Berkowitz (Ed.), *Advances in experimental social psychology* (Vol. 1, pp. 48–81). New York: Academic Press.

Schachter, S., & Singer, J. E. (1962). Cognitive, social, and physiological determinants of emotional states. *Psychological Review, 69,* 379–399.

Schaefer, J. A., & Moos, R. H. (1993). Relationship, task and system stressors in the health care workplace. *Journal of Community and Applied Social Psychology, 3,* 285–298.

Scheier, M. F., & Carver, C. S. (1987). Dispositional optimism and physical well-being: The influence of generalized outcome expectancies in health. *Journal of Personality, 55,* 169–210.

Scheier, M. F., & Carver, C. S. (1993). On the power of positive thinking: The benefits of being optimistic. *Current Directions in Psychological Science, 2,* 26–30.

Scher, A., & Mayseless, O. (1994). Mothers' attachment with spouse and parenting in the first year. *Journal of Social and Interpersonal Relationships, 11,* 601–609.

Schiaffino, K. M., & Revenson, T. A. (1992). The role of perceived self-efficacy, perceived control, and causal attributions in adaptation to rheumatoid arthritis: Distinguishing mediator from moderator effects. *Personality and Social Psychology Bulletin, 18,* 709–718.

Schleifer, S. J., Keller, S. E., Camerino, M., Thornton, J. C., & Stein, M. (1983). Suppression of lymphocyte function following bereavement. *Journal of the American Medical Association, 250,* 374–377.

Schlenker, B. R. (1980). *Impression management: The self-concept, social identity, and interpersonal relations.* Belmont, CA: Brooks/Cole.

Schmitt, B., Gilovich, T. K., Goore, N., & Joseph, L. (1986). Mere presence and social facilitation: One more time. *Journal of Experimental Social Psychology, 22,* 242–248.

Schneider, B. H. (1991). A comparison of skill-building and desensitization strategies for intervention with aggressive children. *Aggressive Behavior, 17,* 301–311.

Schneider, B. H., Wiener, J., & Murphy, K. (1994). Children's friendships: The giant step beyond peer acceptance. *Journal of Social and Personal Relationships, 11,* 323–340.

Schneider, K. (1991, August 13). Ranges of animals and plants head north. *New York Times,* pp. C1, C9.

Schoenrade, P. A., Batson, C. D., Brandt, J. R., & Loud, R. E. (1986). Attachment, accountability, and motivation to benefit another not in distress. *Journal of Personality and Social Psychology, 51,* 557–563.

Schooler, J. W., & Engstler-Schooler, T. Y. (1990). Verbal overshadowing of visual memories: Some things are better left unsaid. *Cognitive Psychology, 22,* 36–71.

Schooler, J. W., & Loftus, E. F. (1986). Individual differences and experimentation: Complementary approaches to interrogative suggestibility. *Social Behavior, 1,* 105–112.

Schuller, R. A., Smith, V. L., & Olson, J. M. (1994). Jurors' decisions in trials of battered women who kill: The role of prior beliefs and expert testimony. *Journal of Applied Social Psychology, 24,* 316–337.

Schuster, E., & Elderton, E. M. (1906). The inheritance of psychical characters. *Biometrika, 5,* 460–469.

Schwartz, A. E. (1994, December 20). Americans on line seldom fond of disagreement. *Albany Times Union,* p. A-11.

Schwarz, N., Bless, H., Bohner, G. (1991). Mood and persuasion: Affective states influence the processing of persuasive communications. In M. P. Zanna (Ed.), *Advances in experimental social psychology* (Vol. 24, pp. 161–199). San Diego, CA: Academic Press.

Schwarz, N., Bless, H., Strack, F., Klumpp, G., Rittenauer-Schatka, G., & Simons, A. (1991). Ease of retrieval as information: Another look at the availability heuristic. *Journal of Personality and Social Psychology, 61*, 195–202.

Schwarzer, R., Jerusalem, M., & Hahn, A. (1994). Unemployment, social support and health complaints: A longitudinal study of stress in East German refugees. *Journal of Community and Applied Social Psychology, 4*, 31–45.

Schwarzwald, J., Amir, Y., & Crain, R. L. (1992). Long-term effects of school desegregation experiences on interpersonal relations in the Israeli defense forces. *Personality and Social Psychology Bulletin, 18*, 357–368.

Scott, K. P., & Feldman-Summers, S. (1979). Children's reactions to textbook stories in which females are portrayed in traditionally male roles. *Journal of Educational Psychology, 71*, 396–402.

Searcy, E., & Eisenberg, N. (1992). Defensiveness in response to aid from a sibling. *Journal of Personality and Social Psychology, 62*, 422–433.

Sears, D. O. (1988). Symbolic racism. In P. A. Katz & D. A. Taylor (Eds.), *Eliminating racism: Profiles in controversy* (pp. 53–84). New York: Plenum.

Sears, D. O., & Allen, H. M. Jr. (1984). The trajectory of local desegregation controversies and whites' opposition to busing. In N. Miller & M. Brewer (Eds.), *Groups in contact: The psychology of desegregation* (pp. 123–151). Orlando, FL; Academic Press.

Sedikides, C. (1992). Attentional effects on mood are moderated by chronic self-conception valence. *Personality and Social Psychology Bulletin, 18*, 580–584.

Sedikides, C. (1993). Assessment, enhancement, and verification determinants of the self-evaluation process. *Journal of Personality and Social Psychology, 65*, 317–338.

Segal, M. M. (1974). Alphabet and attraction: An unobtrusive measure of the effect of propinquity in a field setting. *Journal of Personality and Social Psychology, 30*, 654–657.

Segrin, C., & Kinney, T. (1995). Social skills deficits among the socially anxious: Rejection from others and loneliness. *Motivation and Emotion, 19*, 1–24.

Seligman, M. E. P. (1975). *On depression, development, and death*. San Francisco: Freeman.

Selye, H. (1956). *The stress of life*. New York: McGraw-Hill.

Seta, C. E., Hayes, N. S., & Seta, J. J. (1994). Mood, memory, and vigilance: The influence of distraction on recall and impression formation. *Personality and Social Psychology Bulletin, 20*, 170–177.

Seta, J. J., Seta, C. E., & Wang, M. A. (1991). Feelings of negativity and stress: An averaging–summation analysis of impressions of negative life experiences. *Personality and Social Psychology Bulletin, 17*, 376–384.

Shakoor, B., & Chalmers, D. (1991). Co-victimization of African American children who witness violence: Effects on cognitive, emotional, and behavioral development. *Journal of the National Medical Association, 83*, 233–237.

Shanab, M. E., & Yahya, K. A. (1977). A behavioral study of obedience in children. *Journal of Personality and Social Psychology, 35*, 530–536.

Shapiro, D. L., Buttner, E. H., & Barry, B. (1995). Explanations: What factors enhance their perceived adequacy? *Organizational Behavior and Human Decision Processes, 58* 346–358.

Shapiro, J. P., Baumeister, R. F., & Kessler, J. W. (1991). A three-component model of children's teasing: Aggression, humor, and ambiguity. *Journal of Social and Clinical Psychology, 10*, 459–472.

Sharabany, R. (1974). Intimate friendship among kibbutz and city children and its measurement. Ph.D. dissertation, Cornell University. No. 74–17–682, Ann Arbor, MI 48106: University Microfilms International.

Sharabany, R. (1994). Intimate friendship scale: Conceptual underpinnings, psychometric properties and construct validity. *Journal of Social and Personal Relationships, 11*, 449–469.

Sharp, M. J., & Gets, J. G. (1996). Substance use as impression management. *Personality and Social Psychology Bulletin, 22*, 60–67.

Sharpe, D., Adair, J. G., & Roese, N. J. (1992). Twenty years of deception research: A decline in subjects' trust? *Personality and Social Psychology Bulletin, 18*, 585–590.

Sharpsteen, D. J. (1991). The organization of jealousy knowledge: Romantic jealousy as a blended emotion. In P. Salovey (Ed.), *The psychology of jealousy and envy* (pp. 31–51). New York: Guilford Press.

Sharpsteen, D. J. (1995). The effects of relationship and self-esteem threats on the likelihood of romantic jealousy. *Journal of Social and Personal Relationships, 12*, 89–101.

Shaver, J. (1993, August 9). America's legal immigrants: Who they are and where they go. *Newsweek*, pp. 20–21.

Shaver, P. R., & Brennan, K. A. (1992). Attachment styles and the "big five" personality traits: Their connections with each other and with romantic relationship outcomes. *Personality and Social Psychology Bulletin, 18*, 536–545.

Shaver, P. R., & Hazan, C. (1994). Attachment. In A. L. Weber & J. H. Harvey (Eds.), *Perspectives on close relationships* (pp. 110–130). Boston: Allyn & Bacon.

Shavitt, S. (1989). Operationalizing functional theories of attitudes. In A. R. Pratkanis, S. J. Breckler, & A. G. Greenwald (Eds.), *Attitude structure and function* (pp. 311–377). Hillsdale, NJ: Erlbaum.

Shavitt, S. (1990). The role of attitude objects in attitude functions. *Journal of Experimental Social Psychology, 26*, 124–148.

Shavitt, S., & Fazio, R. H. (1991). Effects of attribute salience on the consistency between attitudes and behavior predictions. *Personality and Social Psychology Bulletin, 17*, 507–516.

Shaw, J. I., Borough, H. W., & Fink, M. I. (1994). Perceived sexual orientation and helping behavior by males and females: The wrong number technique. *Journal of Psychology and Human Sexuality, 6*, 73–81.

Shaw, L. L., Batson, C. D., & Todd, R. M. (1994). Empathy avoidance: Forestalling feeling for another in order to escape the motivational consequences. *Journal of Personality and Social Psychology, 67*, 879–887.

Shaywitz, B. A., Shaywitz, S. E., Pugh, K. R., Constable, R. T., Skudlarski, P., Fulbright, R. K., Bronen, R. A., Fletcher, J. M., Shankweiler, D. P., Katz, L., & Gore, J. C. (1995). Sex differences in the functional organization of the brain for language. *Nature, 373*(6515) 607–609.

Shechtman, Z. (1993). Group psychotherapy for the enhancement of intimate friendship and self-esteem among troubled elementary-school children. *Journal of Social and Personal Relationships, 10*, 483–494.

Sheeran, P., & Abraham, C. (1994). Unemployment and self-conception: A symbolic interactionist analysis. *Journal of Community & Applied Social Psychology, 4*, 115–129.

Sheldon, W. H., Stevens, S. S., & Tucker, W. B. (1940). *The varieties of human physique*. New York: Harper.

Shenon, P. (1994, May 15). Asia's having one huge nicotine fit. *New York Times*, pp. E1, E16.

Sheppard, B. H., Bazerman M. H., & Lewicki, R. J. (Eds.). *Research on negotiation in organizations*. Greenwich, CT: JAI Press.

Sherif, C. W. (1979). Bias in psychology. In J. A. Sherman & E. T. Beck (Eds.), *The prism of sex: Essays in the sociology of knowledge* (pp. 93–133). Madison: University of Wisconsin Press.

Sherif, M. (1935). A study of some social factors in perception. *Archives of Psychology,* No. 187.

Sherman, J. W., & Klein, S. B. (1994). Development and representation of personality impressions. *Journal of Personality and Social Psychology, 67,* 972–983.

Sherman, S. J., Presson, C. C., & Chassin, L. (1984). Mechanisms underlying the false consensus effect: The special role of threats to the self. *Personality and Social Psychology Bulletin, 10,* 127–138.

Sherman, S. R. (1994). Changes in age identity: Self-perceptions in middle and late life. *Journal of Aging Studies, 8,* 397–412.

Sherman, S. S. (1980). On the self-erasing nature of errors of prediction. *Journal of Personality and Social Psychology, 16,* 388–403.

Shiffrin, R. M. (1988). Attention. In R. C. Atkinson, R. J. Herrnstein, G. Lindzey, & R. D. Luce (Eds.), *Stevens' handbook of experimental psychology: Vol 2. Learning and cognition* (pp. 739–811). New York: Wiley.

Shinn, M., Morch, H., Robinson, P. E., & Neuner, R. A. (1993). Individual, group and agency strategies for coping with job stressors in residential child care programmes. *Journal of Community and Applied Social Psychology, 3,* 313–324.

Shotland, R. I., & Strau, M. K. (1976). Bystander response to an assault: When a man attacks a woman. *Journal of Personality and Social Psychology, 34,* 990–999.

Shotland, R. L., & Goodstein, L. (1983). Just because she doesn't want to doesn't mean its rape: An experimentally causal model of the perception of rape in a dating situation. *Social Psychology Quarterly, 46,* 220–232.

Showers, C. (1992a). Compartmentalization of positive and negative self-knowledge: Keeping bad apples out of the bunch. *Journal of Personality and Social Psychology, 62,* 1036–1049.

Showers, C. (1992b). Evaluative integrative thinking about characteristics of the self. *Personality and Social Psychology Bulletin, 18,* 719–729.

Showers, C., & Ryff, C. D. (1993). Self-differentiation and well-being in a life transition. Manuscript submitted for publication.

Shulman, S., Elicker, J., & Sroufe, L. A. (1994). Stages of friendship growth in preadolescence as related to attachment history. *Journal of Social and Personal Relationships, 11,* 341–361.

Sigall, H., & Ostrove, N. (1975). Beautiful but dangerous: Effects of offender attractiveness and nature of the crime on juridic judgment. *Journal of Personality and Social Psychology, 31,* 410–414.

Sigelman, C. K., Thomas, D. B., Sigelman, L., & Robich, F. D. (1986). Gender, physical attractiveness, and electability: An experimental investigation of voter biases. *Journal of Applied Social Psychology, 16,* 229–248.

Silbereisen, R. K., Boehnke, K., & Reykowski, J. (1986). Prosocial motives from 12 to 18: A comparison of adolescents from Berlin (West) and Warsaw. In R. K. Silbereisen, K. Elferth, & G. Rudinger (Eds.), *Development as action in context* (pp. 137–164). Berlin: Springer.

Sillars, A. L., Folwell, A. L., Hill, K. C., Maki, B. K., Hurst, A. P., & Casano, R. A. (1994). *Journal of Social and Personal Relationships, 11,* 611–617.

Silverstein, R. (1994). Chronic identity diffusion in traumatized combat veterans. *Social Behavior and Personality, 22,* 69–80.

Simmons, D. D., Binney, S. E., & Dodd, B. (1992). Valuing "a clean environment": Factor location, norms, and relation to risks. *Journal of Social Behavior and Personality, 7,* 649–658.

Simon, J. (1989). *The economic consequences of immigration.* New York: Blackwell.

Simon, L., Greenberg, J., & Brehm, J. (1995). Trivialization: The forgotten mode of dissonance reduction. *Journal of Personality and Social Psychology, 68,* 247–260.

Simpson, J. A. (1987). The dissolution of romantic relationships: Factors involved in relationship stability and emotional stress. *Journal of Personality and Social Psychology, 53,* 683–692.

Simpson, J. A., & Gangestad, S. W. (1992). Sociosexuality and romantic partner choice. *Journal of Personality, 60,* 31–51.

Simpson, J. A., & Gangestad, S. W. (1991). Individual differences in sociosexuality: Evidence for convergent and discriminant validity. *Journal of Personality and Social Psychology, 60,* 870–883.

Simpson, J. A., Gangestad, S. W., & Biek, M. (1993). Personality and nonverbal social behavior: An ethological perspective of relationship initiation. *Journal of Experimental Social Psychology, 29,* 434–461.

Simpson, M., & Perry, J. D. (1990). Crime and climate: A reconsideration. *Environment and Behavior, 22,* 295–300.

Singh, D. (1993). Adaptive significance of female physical attractiveness: Role of waist-to-hip ratio. *Journal of Personality and Social Psychology, 65,* 293–307.

Singh, R., & Tan, L. S. C. (1992). Attitudes and attraction: A test of the similarity–attraction and dissimilarity–repulsion hypotheses. *British Journal of Social Psychology, 31,* 227–238.

Sistrunk, F., & McDavid, J. W. (1971). Sex variable in conforming behavior. *Journal of Personality and Social Psychology, 17,* 200–207.

Skelton, J. A., & Strohmetz, D. B. (1990). Priming symptom reports with health-related cognitive activity. *Personality and Social Psychology Bulletin, 16,* 449–464.

Skinner, B. F. (1986). What is wrong with daily life in the Western world? *American Psychologist, 41,* 568–574.

Skolnick, P., & Shaw, J. I. (1994). Is defendant status a liability or a shield? Crime severity and professional relatedness. *Journal of Applied Social Psychology, 24,* 1827–1836.

Skowronski, J. J., & Carlston, D. E. (1989). Negativity and extremity biases in impression formation: A review of explanations. *Psychological Bulletin, 105,* 131–142.

Smeaton, G., & Byrne, D. (1988). The Feelings Scale: Positive and negative affective responses. In C. M. Davis, W. L. Yarber, & S. L. Davis (Eds.), *Sexuality related measures: A compendium* (pp. 88–90). Lake Mills, IA: Graphic Publishing.

Smeaton, G., Byrne, D., & Murnen, S. K. (1989). The repulsion hypothesis revisited: Similarity irrelevance or dissimilarity bias? *Journal of Personality and Social Psychology, 56,* 54–59.

Smeaton, G., Rupp, D., Vig, C., & Byrne, D. (1995). The mediating role of similarity assumptions on the effects of attitude similarity and dissimilarity on attraction and repulsion. Unpublished manuscript, University of Wisconsin–Stout, Menomonie.

Smith, A., & Stansfeld, S. (1986). Aircraft noise exposure, noise sensitivity, and everyday errors. *Environment and Behavior, 18,* 214–226.

Smith, A. J. (1957). Similarity of values and its relation to acceptance and the projection of similarity. *Journal of Psychology, 43,* 251–260.

Smith, D. E., Gier, J. A., & Willis, F. N. (1982). Interpersonal touch and compliance with a marketing request. *Basic and Applied Social Psychology, 3,* 35–38.

Smith, E. R., & Zarate, M. A. (1992). Exemplar-based model of social judgment. *Psychological Review, 99,* 3–21.

Smith, E. R., Byrne, D., & Fielding, P. J. (1995). Interpersonal attraction as a function of extreme gender role adherence. *Personal Relationships, 2* 161–172.

Smith, E. R., Byrne, D., Becker, M. A., & Przybyla, D. P. J. (1993). Sexual attitudes of males and females as predictors of interpersonal attraction and marital compatibility. *Journal of Applied Social Psychology, 23,* 1011–1034.

Smith, K. D., Keating, J. P., & Stotland, E. (1989). Altruism reconsidered: The effect of denying feedback on a victim's status to empathetic witnesses. *Journal of Personality and Social Psychology, 57,* 641–650.

Smith, P. B., & Bond, M. H. (1993). *Social psychology across cultures.* Boston: Allyn & Bacon.

Smith, R. E., Smoll, F. L., & Ptacek, J. T. (1990). Conjunctive moderator variables in vulnerability and resiliency research: Life stress, social support and coping skills, and adolescent sport injuries. *Journal of Personality and Social Psychology, 58,* 360–370.

Smith, S. M., & Shaffer, D. R. (1991). The effects of good moods on systematic processing: "Willing but not able or able but not willing?" *Motivation and Emotion, 15,* 243–280.

Smith, S. M., & Shaffer, D. R. (1991). Celerity and cajolery: Rapid speech may promote or inhibit persuasion through its impact on message elaboration. *Personality and Social Psychology Bulletin, 17,* 663–669.

Smith, S. S., & Richardson, D. (1985). On deceiving ourselves about deception: Reply to Rubin. *Journal of Personality and Social Psychology, 48,* 254–255.

Smith, T. W., & Pope, M. K. (1990). Cynical hostility as a health risk: Current status and future directions. *Journal of Social Behavior and Personality, 5,* 77–88.

Smith, V. I., & Ellsworth, P. C. (1987). The social psychology of eyewitness accuracy: Misleading questions and communicator expertise. *Journal of Applied Psychology, 72,* 294-300.

Smoking rate up for blacks, women. (1993, April 2). *Albany Times Union,* p. A-9.

Smolowe, J. (1992). Where there's smoke. *Time, 140*(21), 59.

Sneddon, I., & Kremer, J. (1992). Sexual behavior and attitudes of university students in Northern Ireland. *Archives of Sexual Behavior, 21,* 295–312.

Snell, W. E. Jr., & Finney, P. D. (1993). Measuring relational aspects of the self: Relational–esteem, relational–depression, and relational–preoccupation. *Contemporary Social Psychology, 17,* 44–55.

Sniffen, M. J. (1991, September 30). Blacks make up 40% of death row. *Albany Times Union,* p. A-3.

Snyder, C. R., & Endelman, J. R. (1979). Effects of degree of interpersonal similarity on physical distance and self-reported attraction: A comparison of uniqueness and reinforcement theory predictions. *Journal of Personality, 47,* 492–505.

Snyder, C. R., & Fromkin, H. L. (1980). *Uniqueness: The human pursuit of difference.* New York: Plenum.

Snyder, M. (1974). Self-monitoring of expressive behavior. *Journal of Personality and Social Psychology, 30,* 526–537.

Snyder, M. (1987). *Public appearances/private realities.* San Francisco: Freeman.

Snyder, M., & DeBono, K. G. (1989). Understanding the functions of attitudes: Lessons from personality and social behavior. In A. R. Pratkanis, S. J. Breckler, & A. G. Greenwald (Eds.), *Attitude structure and function.* Hillsdale, NJ: Erlbaum.

Snyder, M., Gangestad, S., & Simpson, J. A. (1983). Choosing friends as activity partners: The role of self-monitoring. *Journal of Personality and Social Psychology, 45,* 1061–1072.

Snyder, M., & Ickes, W. (1985). Personality and social behavior. In G. Lindzey & E. Aronson (Eds.), *Handbook of social psychology* (3rd ed.) (Vol. 2, pp. 883–947). New York: Random House.

Snyder, M., & Omoto, A. M. (1992a). Volunteerism and society's response to the HIV epidemic. *Current Directions in Psychological Science, 1,* 113–116.

Snyder, M., & Omoto, A. M. (1992b). Who helps and why? The psychology of AIDS volunteerism. In S. Spacapan & S. Oskamp

(Eds.), *Helping and being helped: Naturalistic studies.* Newbury Park, CA: Sage.

Snyder, M., & Simpson, J. A. (1984). Self-monitoring and dating relationships. *Journal of Personality and Social Psychology, 47,* 1281–l291.

Snyder, N. H., & Blair, K. E. (1989). Dealing with employee theft. *Business Horizons,* pp. 27–34.

Solano, C. H., & Koester, N. H. (1989). Loneliness and communication problems: Subjective anxiety or objective skills? *Personality and Social Psychology Bulletin, 15,* 126–133.

Sorenson, K. A., Russell, S. M., Harkness, D. J., & Harvey, J. H. (1993). Account-making, confiding, and coping with the ending of a close relationship. *Journal of Social Behavior and Personality, 8,* 73–86.

Spence, J. T. (1993). Gender-related traits and gender ideology: Evidence for a multifactorial theory. *Journal of Personality and Social Psychology, 64,* 624–635.

Spence, J. T., Helmreich, R., & Stapp, J. (1973). A short version of the Attitudes toward Women Scale (AWS). *Bulletin of the Psychonomic Society, 2,* 219–220.

Spillman, J., & Spillman, L. (1993). The rise and fall of Hugo Munsterberg. *Journal of the History of the Behavioral Sciences, 29,* 322–338.

Sprafkin, J. N., Liebert, R. M., & Poulous, R. W. (1975). Effects of a prosocial televised example on children's helping. *Journal of Personality and Social Psychology, 48,* 35–46.

Sprecher, S., Barbee, A., & Schwartz, P. (1995). "Was it good for you, too?": Gender differences in first sexual intercourse experiences. *Journal of Sex Research, 32,* 3–15.

Sprecher, S., & Duck, S. (1994). Sweet talk: The importance of perceived communication for romantic and friendship attraction experienced during a get-acquainted date. *Personality and Social Psychology Bulletin, 20,* 391–400.

Sprecher, S., Sullivan, Q., & Hatfield, E. (1994). Mate selection preferences: Gender differences examined in a national sample. *Journal of Personality and Social Psychology, 66,* 1074–1080.

Staats, A. W., & Staats, C. K. (1958). Attitudes established by classical conditioning. *Journal of Abnormal and Social Psychology 57,* 37–40.

Staats, A. W., Staats, C. K., & Crawford, H. L. (1962). First order conditioning of meaning and the parallel conditioning of GSR. *Journal of General Psychology, 67,* 159–167.

Stalling, R. B. (1992). Mood and pain: The influence of positive and negative affect on reported body aches. *Journal of Social Behavior and Personality, 7,* 323–334.

Stangor, C., & Ruble, D. N. (1989). Strength of expectancies and memory for social information: What we remember depends on how much we know. *Journal of Experimental Social Psychology, 25,* 18–35.

Stasser, G. (1992). Pooling of unshared information during group discussion. In S. Worchel, W. Wood, & J. H. Simpson (Eds.), *Group process and productivity* (pp. 48–67). Newbury Park, CA: Sage.

Stasser, G., & Hinkle, S. (1994). Research in progress, Miami University, Oxford, Ohio.

Stasser, G., & Stewart, D. (1992). Discovery of hidden profiles by decision-making groups: Solving a problem versus making a judgment. *Journal of Personality and Social Psychology, 63,* 426–434.

Stasser, G., & Titus, W. (1985). Pooling of unshared information in group decision making: Biased information sampling during discussion. *Journal of Personality and Social Psychology, 48,* 1467–1478.

Stasser, G., Taylor, L. A., & Hanna, C. (1989). Information sampling in structured and unstructured discussions of three- and six-person groups. *Journal of Personality and Social Psychology, 57,* 67–78.

Steele, C. M. (1992, April). Race and the schooling of Black Americans. *The Atlantic Monthly, 269*(4), 68–78.

Steele, C. M., Critchlow, B., & Liu, T. J. (1985). Alcohol and social behavior: The helpful drunkard. *Journal of Personality and Social Psychology, 48,* 35–46.

Steele, C. M., Spencer, S. J., & Lynch, M. (1993). Self-image resilience and dissonance: The role of affirmational resources. *Journal of Personality and Social Psychology, 64,* 885–896.

Steffen, V. J., & Eagly, A. H. (1985). Implicit theories about influence style: The effects of status and sex. *Personality and Social Psychology Bulletin, 11,* 191–205.

Stein, R. I., & Nemeroff, C. J. (1995). Moral overtones of food: Judgments of others based on what they eat. *Personality and Social Psychology Bulletin, 21,* 480–490.

Steinhauer, J. (1995, April 10). Big benefits in marriage, studies say. *New York Times,* p. A10.

Stephan, C. W., & Stephan, W. G. (1986). Habla Ingles? The effects of language translation on simulated juror decisions. *Journal of Applied Social Psychology, 16,* 577–589.

Stephan, W. G. (1985). Intergroup relations. In G. Lindzey & E. Aronson (Eds.), *Handbook of social psychology* (Vol. 3, pp. 599–658). New York: Addison-Wesley.

Stern, P. C. (1992). Psychological dimensions of global environmental change. *Annual Review of Psychology, 43,* 269–302.

Sternberg, R. J. (1986). A triangular theory of love. *Psychological Review, 93,* 119–135.

Sternberg, R. J. (1988a). *The triangle of love.* New York: Basic Books.

Sternberg, R. J. (1988b). Triangulating love. In R. J. Sternberg & M. J. Barnes (Eds.), *The psychology of love* (pp. 119–138). New Haven, CT: Yale University Press.

Stevens, W. K. (1992, February 25). Global warming threatens to undo decades of conservation efforts. *New York Times,* p. C4.

Stevens, W. K. (1993a, June 29). Loss of species is worse than thought in Brazil's Amazon. *New York Times,* p. C4.

Stevens, W. K. (1993b, August 26). Scientists startled by a drop in ozone-killing chemicals. *New York Times,* p. A1, A18.

Stevens, W. K. (1994a, April 5). Feeding a booming population without destroying the planet. *New York Times,* pp. C1, C8.

Stevens, W. K. (1994b, September 20). Emissions must be cut to avert shift in climate, panel says. *New York Times,* p. C4.

Stevens, W. K. (1995a, January 27). Global warming resumed in 1994, climate data show. *New York Times,* pp. A1, A13.

Stevens, W. K. (1995b, May 23). More extremes found in weather, pointing to greenhouse gas effect. *New York Times,* p. C4.

Stewart, J. E. II. (1980). Defendant's attractiveness as a factor in the outcome of criminal trials: An observational study. *Journal of Applied Social Psychology, 10,* 348–361.

Stice, E., & Shaw, H. E. (1994). Adverse effects of the media portrayed thin-ideal on women and linkages to bulimic symptomatology. *Journal of Social and Clinical Psychology, 13,* 288–308.

Stiff, J. B., Miller, G. R., Sleight, C., Mongeau, P. I., Gardelck, R., & Rogan, R. (1989). Explanations for visual cue primacy in judgments of honesty and deceit. *Journal of Personality and Social Psychology, 156,* 555–564.

Stinson, L., & Ickes, W. (1992). Empathic accuracy in the interactions of male friends versus male strangers. *Journal of Personality and Social Psychology, 62,* 787–797.

Stocker, C. M., & McHale, S. M. (1992). The nature and family correlates of preadolescents' perceptions of their sibling relationships. *Journal of Social and Personal Relationships, 9,* 179–195.

Stone, A. A., Cox, D., Valdimarsdottir, H., Jandorf, L., & Neale, J. M. (1987). Evidence that secretory IgA antibody is associated with daily mood. *Journal of Personality and Social Psychology, 52,* 988–993.

Stone, A. A., Neale, J. M., Cox, D. S., Napoli, A., Valdimarsdottir, H., & Kennedy-Moore, E. (1994). Daily events are associated with a secretory immune response to an oral antigen in men. *Health Psychology, 13,* 440–446.

Stone, J., Aronson, E., Crain, A. L., Winslow, M. P., & Fried, C. B. (1994). Inducing hypocrisy as a means of encouraging young adults to use condoms. *Personality and Social Psychology Bulletin, 20,* 116–128.

Stoppard, J. M., & Gruchy, C. D. G. (1993). Gender, context, and expression of positive emotion. *Personality and Social Psychology Bulletin, 19,* 143–150.

Stradling, S. G., Crowe, G., & Tuohy, A. P. (1993). Changes in self-concept during occupational socialization of new recruits to the police. *Journal of Community & Applied Social Psychology, 3,* 131–147.

Strauman, T. J., Lemieux, A. M., & Coe, C. L. (1993). Self-discrepancy and natural killer cell activity: Immunological consequences of negative self-evaluation. *Journal of Personality and Social Psychology, 64,* 1042–1052.

Straus, M. A., & Gelles, R. J. (1988). Violence in American families: How much is there and why does it occur? In E. W. Nunnally, C. S. Coleman, & F. M. Cox (Eds.), *Families in trouble* (Series 3, pp. 141–162). Newbury Park, CA: Sage.

Street, R. L. Jr., & Buller, D. B. (1987). Nonverbal response patterns in physician–patient interactions: A functional analysis. *Journal of Nonverbal Behavior, 11,* 234–253.

Strickland, B. R. (1992). Women and depression. *Current Directions in Psychological Sciences, 1,* 132–135.

Stroessner, S. J., & Mackie, D. M. (1993). Affect and perceived group variability: Implications for stereotyping and prejudice. In D. M. Mackie & D. L. Hamilton (Eds.), *Affect, cognition, and stereotyping: Interactive processes in group perception* (pp. 63–86). San Diego, CA: Academic Press.

Stroh, L. K., Brett, J. M., & Reilly, A. H. (1992). All the right stuff: A comparison of female and male managers' career progression. *Journal of Applied Psychology, 77,* 251–260.

Strube, M., Turner, C. W., Cerro, D., Stevens, J., & Hinchey, F. (1984). Interpersonal aggression and the Type A coronary-prone behavior pattern: A theoretical distinction and practical implications. *Journal of Personality and Social Psychology, 47,* 839–847.

Strube, M. J. (1989). Evidence for the Type in Type A behavior: A taxonometric analysis. *Journal of Personality and Social Psychology, 56,* 972–987.

Stycos, J. M. (1995). Population, projections, and policy: A cautionary perspective. *Population and Environment, 16,* 205–219.

Subich, L. M., Cooper, E. A., Barrett, G. V., & Arthur, W. (1986). Occupational perceptions of males and females as a function of sex ratios, salary, and availability. *Journal of Vocational Behavior, 28,* 123–134.

Sugarman, D. B., & Hotaling, G. T. (1989). Dating violence: Prevalence, context, and risk markers. In M. A. Pirog-Good & J. E. Stets (Eds.), *Violence in dating relationships.* New York: Praeger.

Sullivan, D. G., & Masters, R. D. (1988). Happy warriors: Leaders' facial displays, viewers' emotions, and political support. *American Journal of Political Science, 32,* 345–368.

Sullivan, W. (1995, May 2). New theory on ice sheet catastrophe is the direst one yet. *New York Times,* p. C4.

Sulman, F. G., Levy, D., Levy, A., Pfeifer, Y., Saperstein, E., & Tal, E. (1974). Ionometry of hot, dry desert winds (*sharav*) and application of ionizing treatment to weather-sensitive patients. *International Journal of Biometerology, 18,* 393.

Suls, J., & Fletcher, B. (1985). The relative efficacy of avoidant and nonavoidant coping strategies: A meta-analysis. *Health Psychology, 4,* 249–288.

Suls, J., & Rosnow, J. (1988). Concerns about artifacts in behavioral research. In M. Morawski (Ed.), *The rise of experimentation in American psychology* (pp. 163–187). New Haven, CT: Yale University Press.

Suls, J., & Wan, C. K. (1987). In search of the false uniqueness phenomenon: Fear and estimates of social consensus. *Journal of Personality and Social Psychology, 52,* 211–217.

Suls, J., & Wan, C. K. (1989). The effects of sensory and procedural information on coping with stressful medical procedures and pain: A meta-analysis. *Journal of Consulting and Clinical Psychology, 57,* 372–379.

Suls, J., Wan, C. K., & Sanders, G. S. (1988). False consensus and false uniqueness in estimating the prevalence of health-protective behaviors. *Journal of Applied Social Psychology, 18,* 66–79.

Summers, R. J. (1991). The influence of affirmative action on perceptions of a beneficiary's qualifications. *Journal of Applied Social Psychology, 21,* 1265–1276.

Sundstrom, E., & Sundstrom, M. G. (1986). *Work places: The psychology of the physical environment in offices and factories.* London: Cambridge University Press.

Sunnafrank, M. (1992). On debunking the attitude similarity myth. *Communication Monographs, 59,* 165–179.

Sunstein, C. R. (1993). Valuing life. *New Republic, 208*(7), 36–40.

Swann, W. B. Jr., De La Ronde, C., & Hixon, J. G. (1994). Authenticity and positivity strivings in marriage and courtship. *Journal of Personality and Social Psychology, 66,* 857–869.

Swann, W. B. Jr., Griffin, J. J. Jr., Predmore, S. C., & Gaines, B. (1987). Cognitive–affective crossfire: When self-consistency meets self-enhancement. *Journal of Personality and Social Psychology, 52,* 881–889.

Swann, W. B. Jr., Stein-Scrossi, A., & Giesler, R. B. (1992). Why people self-verify. *Journal of Personality and Social Psychology, 62,* 392–401.

Swap, W. C. (1977). Interpersonal attraction and repeated exposure to rewarders and punishers. *Personality and Social Psychology Bulletin, 3,* 248–251.

Swim, J. K. (1994). Perceived versus meta-analytic effect sizes: An assessment of the accuracy of gender stereotypes. *Journal of Personality and Social Psychology, 66,* 21–36.

Swim, J. K., Aikin, K. J., Hall, W. S., & Hunter, B. A. (1995). Sexism and racism: Old-fashioned and modern prejudices. *Journal of Personality and Social Psychology, 68,* 199–214.

Tajfel, H. (1982). *Social identity and intergroup relations.* Cambridge, England: Cambridge University Press.

Tan, D. T. Y., & Singh, R. (1995). Attitudes and attraction: A developmental study of the similarity–attraction and dissimilarity–repulsion hypotheses. *Personality and Social Psychology Bulletin, 21* 975–986.

Tannen, D. (1994). *Talking from 9 to 5.* New York: William Morrow.

Tannen, D. (1995, January 9–15). And rarely the twain shall meet. *Washington Post National Weekly Edition* 25.

Taylor, M. S., Locke, E. A., Lee, C., & Gist, M. E. (1984). Type A behavior and faculty research productivity: What are the mechanisms? *Organizational Behavior and Human Performance, 34,* 402–418.

Taylor, S. E., & Brown, J. D. (1988). Illusion and well-being: A social psychological perspective on mental health. *Psychological Bulletin, 103,* 193–210.

Taylor, S. E., Buunk, B. P., & Aspinwall, L. G. (1990). Social comparison, stress, and coping. *Personality and Social Psychology Bulletin, 16,* 74–89.

Taylor, S. E., Helgeson, V. S., Reed, G. M., & Skokan, L. A. (1991). Self-generated feelings of control and adjustment to physical illness. *Journal of Social Issues, 47,* 91–109.

Taylor, S. P. (1967). Aggressive behavior and physiological arousal as a function of provocation and the tendency to inhibit aggression. *Journal of Personality, 35,* 297–310.

Teens top elderly as victims of crime. (1995, June 1). *Albany Times Union,* p. A-13.

Terman, L. M., & Buttenwieser, P. (1935a). Personality factors in marital compatibility: I. *Journal of Social Psychology, 6,* 143–171.

Terman, L. M., & Buttenwieser, P. (1935b). Personality factors in marital compatibility: II. *Journal of Social Psychology, 6,* 267–289.

Terry, R. L., & Krantz, J. H. (1993). Dimensions of trait attributions associated with eyeglasses, men's facial hair, and women's hair length. *Journal of Applied Social Psychology, 23,* 1757–1769.

Terry, R. L., & Macy, R. J. (1991). Children's social judgments of other children who wear eyeglasses. *Journal of Social Behavior and Personality, 6,* 965–974.

Tetlock, P. E., Peterson, R. S., McGuire, C., Change, S., & Feld, P. (1992). Assessing political group dynamics: A test of the groupthink model. *Journal of Personality and Social Psychology, 63,* 403–425.

Tett, R. P., & Meyer, J. P. (1993). Job satisfaction, organizational commitment, turnover intention, and turnover: Path analyses based on meta-analytic findings. *Personnel Psychology, 46,* 259–293.

The unabomber speaks. (1995, October). *Penthouse, 57–59.*

Thernstrom, S. (1993). Jungle fever. *New Republic, 208*(16), 12, 14.

Thibodeau, R., & Aronson, E. (1992). Taking a closer look: Reasserting the role of the self-concept in dissonance theory. *Personality and Social Psychology Bulletin, 18,* 591–602.

Thomas, K. W. (1988). The conflict-handling modes: Toward more precise theory. *Management Communication Quarterly, 1,* 430–436.

Thompson, D. (1992). The danger in doomsaying. *Time, 139*(10), 61.

Thompson, J. K., & Tantleff, S. (1992). Female and male ratings of upper torso: Actual, ideal, and stereotypical conceptions. *Journal of Social Behavior and Personality, 7,* 345–354.

Thompson, J. M., Whiffen, V. E., & Blain, M. D. (1995). Depressive symptoms, sex and perceptions of intimate relationships. *Journal of Social and Personal Relationships, 12,* 49–66.

Thompson, L. (1990). An examination of naive and experienced negotiators. *Journal of Personality and Social Psychology, 59,* 82–90.

Thompson, L. (1993). Biases in negotiation: An examination of reception and transmission processes. Unpublished manuscript, University of Washington, Seattle.

Thompson, S. C., Nanni, C., & Levine, A. (1994). Primary versus secondary and central versus consequence-related control in HIV-positive men. *Journal of Personality and Social Psychology, 67,* 540–547.

Thompson, S. C., Sobolew-Shubin, A., Galbraith, M. E., Schwankovsky, L., & Cruzen, D. (1993). Maintaining perceptions of control: Finding perceived control in low-control circumstances. *Journal of Personality and Social Psychology, 64,* 293–304.

Thompson, W. C., Cowan, C. L., & Rosenhan, D. L. (1980). Focus of attention mediates the impact of negative affect on altruism. *Journal of Personality and Social Psychology, 38,* 291–300.

Thornton, A., & Freedman, D. (1982) Changing attitudes toward married and single life. *Family Planning Perspectives, 14*(6), 297–303.

Thornton, B. (1992). Repression and its mediating influence on the defensive attribution of responsibility. *Journal of Research in Personality, 26,* 44–57.

Thurstone, L. L. (1982). Attitudes can be measured. *American Journal of Sociology, 33,* 529–544.

Toch, H. (1980). The catalytic situation in the violence equation. *Journal of Applied Social Psychology, 15,* 105–123.

Toch, H. (1985). *Violent men* (rev. ed.). Cambridge, MA: Schenkman.

Toi, M., & Batson, C. D. (1982). More evidence that empathy is a source of altruistic motivation. *Journal of Personality and Social Psychology, 43,* 281–292.

Tomaka, J., & Blascovich, J. (1994). Effects of justice beliefs on cognitive appraisal of and subjective, physiological, and behavioral responses to potential stress. *Journal of Personality and Social Psychology, 67,* 732–740.

Tomaka, J., Blascovich, J., Kelsey, R. M., & Leitten, C. L. (1993). Subjective, physiological, and behavioral effects of threat and challenge appraisal. *Journal of Personality and Social Psychology, 65,* 248–260.

Toobin, J. (1995, July 17). Putting it in black and white. *New Yorker,* 31–34.

Toobin, J. (1995, January 9). True grit. *The New Yorker.* 28–35.

Tooley, V., Brigham, J. C., Maass, A., & Bothwell, R. K. (1987). Facial recognition: Weapon effect and attentional focus. *Journal of Applied Social Psychology, 17,* 845–859.

Topf, M. (1989). Sensitivity to noise, personality hardiness, and noise-induced stress in critical care nurses. *Environment and Behavior, 21,* 717–733.

Torestad, B. (1990). What is anger provoking: A psychophysical study of perceived causes of anger. *Aggressive Behavior, 16,* 9–26.

Townsend, J. M. (1995). Sex without emotional involvement: An evolutionary interpretation of sex differences. *Archives of Sexual Behavior, 24,* 173–206.

Traeen, B., Lewin, B., & Sundet, J. M. (1992). The real and the ideal: Gender differences in heterosexual behaviour among Norwegian adolescents. *Journal of Community & Applied Social Psychology, 2,* 227–237.

Triandis, H. C. (1995). *Individualism & collectivism.* Boulder, CO: Westview.

Triplett, N. (1898). The dynamogenic factors in pacemaking and competition. *American Journal of Psychology, 9,* 507–533.

Trivers, R. (1972). Parental investment and sexual selection. In B. Campbell (Ed.), *Sexual selection and the descent of man, 1871–1971* (pp. 136–179). Chicago: Aldine.

Trobst, K. K., Collins, R. L., & Embree, J. M. (1994). The role of emotion in social support provision: Gender, empathy, and expressions of distress. *Journal of Social and Personal Relationships, 11,* 45–62.

Tucker, P., & Aron, A. (1993). Passionate love and marital satisfaction at key transition points in the family life cycle. *Journal of Social and Clinical Psychology, 12,* 135–147.

Tuckman, B. W., & Sexton, T. L. (1990). The relation between self-beliefs and self-regulated performance. *Journal of Social Behavior and Personality, 5,* 465–472.

Turk, D. C. (1994). Perspectives on chronic pain: The role of psychological factors. *Current Directions in Psychological Science, 3,* 45–48.

Turk, D. C., & Rudy, T. E. (in press). A cognitive–behavioral perspective on chronic pain: Beyond the scalpel and syringe. In C. D. Tollison (Ed.), *Handbook of chronic pain management* (2nd ed.). Baltimore, MD: Williams and Wilkins.

Turner, J. C., Hogg, M. A., Oakes, P. J., Reicher, S. D., & Wetherell, M. S. (1987). *Rediscovering the social group: A self-categorization theory.* Oxford, England: Blackwell.

Turner, M. E., Pratkanis, A. R., & Hardaway, T. J. (1991). Sex differences in reaction to preferential selection: Towards a model of preferential selection as help. *Journal of Social Behavior and Personality, 6,* 797–814.

Tversky, A., & Kahneman, D. (1973). Availability: A heuristic for judging frequency and probability. *Cognitive Psychology, 5,* 207–232.

Tversky, A., & Kahneman, D. (1982). Judgment under uncertainty: Heuristics and biases. In D. Kahneman, P. Slovic, & A. Tversky (Eds.), *Judgment under uncertainty* (pp. 3–20). New York: Cambridge University Press.

Tykocinski, O., Higgins, E. T., & Chaiken, S. (1994). Message framing, self-discrepancies, and yielding to persuasive messages: The motivational significance of psychological situations. *Personality and Social Psychology Bulletin, 20,* 107–115.

Tyler, T. R. (1994). Psychological models of the justice motive: Antecedents of distributive and procedural justice. *Journal of Personality and Social Psychology, 67,* 850–863.

Tyler, T. R., & Schuller, R. A. (1991). Aging and attitude change. *Journal of Personality and Social Psychology, 61,* 689–697.

Type A's lack cholesterol aid, study says. (1992, November 18). *Albany Times Union,* p. A-5.

U.S. Department of Justice. (1994). *Criminal victimization in the United States, 1992.* Washington, DC: Office of Justice Programs, Bureau of Justice Statistics.

U.S. Department of Labor. (1992). *Employment and earnings* (Vol. 39, No. 5: Table A-22). Washington, DC: U.S. Department of Labor.

U.S. birth rate drops as age trends collide. (1995, August 1). *Albany Times Union,* p. A-5.

Uchino, B. N., Kiecolt-Glaser, J. K., & Cacioppo, J. T. (1992). Age-related changes in cardiovascular response as a function of a chronic stressor and social support. *Journal of Personality and Social Psychology, 63,* 839–846.

Uchitelle, L. (1994, November 28). Women in their 50's follow many paths into workplace. *New York Times,* A1, B8.

Udry, J. R. (1980). Changes in the frequency of marital intercourse from panel data. *Archives of Sexual Behavior, 9,* 319–325.

Ullman, C. (1987). From sincerity to authenticity: Adolescents' view of the "true self." *Journal of Personality, 55,* 583–595.

Umpleby, S. A. (1990). The scientific revolution in demography. *Population and Environment, 11,* 159–174.

Unger, R. K. (1994). Alternative conceptions of sex (and sex differences). In M. Haug, R. Whalen, C. Aron, & K. L. Olsen (Eds.), *The development of sex differences and similarities in behavior.* Dordrecht, The Netherlands: Kluwer Academic.

Unger, R. K., & Crawford, M. (1993). Commentary: Sex and gender—The troubled relationship between terms and concepts. *Psychological Science, 4,* 122–124.

Ungerer, J. A., Dolby, R., Waters, B., Barnett, B., Kelk, N., & Lewin, V. (1990). The early development of empathy: Self-regulation and individual differences in the first year. *Motivation and Emotion, 14,* 93–106.

Urbanski, L. (1992, May 21). Study uncovers traits people seek in friends. *The Evangelist,* 4.

van de Vliert, E., & Euwema, M. C. (1994). Agreeableness and activeness as components of conflict behaviors. *Journal of Personality and Social Psychology, 66,* 674–687.

van de Vliert, E., Euwema, M. C., & Huismans, S. E. (1995). Managing conflict with a subordinate or a superior: Effectiveness of conglomerated behavior. *Journal of Applied Psychology, 80,* 271–281.

Van Dyne, L., Graham, J. W., & Dienesch, R. M. (1994). Organizational citizenship behavior: Construct redefinition, measurement, and validation. *Academy of Management Journal, 37,* 765–802.

Van Goozen, S., Frijda, N., & de Poll, N. V. (1994). Anger and aggression in women: Influence of sports choice and testosterone administration. *Aggressive Behavior, 20,* 213–222.

Van Hook, E., & Higgins, E. T. (1988). Self-related problems beyond the self-concept: Motivational consequences of discrepant self-guides. *Journal of Personality and Social Psychology, 55,* 625–633.

Van Lange, P. A. M., & Rusbult, C. E. (1995). My relationship is better than—and not as bad as—yours is: The perception of superiority in close relationships. *Personality and Social Psychology Bulletin, 21,* 32–44.

Van Velsor, E. & Hughes, M. W. (1990). Gender differences in the development of managers: How women managers learn from experience. Technical report no. 145, Center for Creative Leadership, Greensboro, NC.

Van Vianen, A. E. M., & Willemsen, T. M. (1992). The employment interview: The role of sex stereotypes in the evaluation of male and female job applicants in the Netherlands. *Journal of Applied Social Psychology, 22,* 471–491.

Velasques, M., Moberg, D. J., & Cavanaugh, G. F. (1983). Organizational statesmanship and dirty politics: Ethical guidelines for the organizational politician. *Organizational Dynamics, 11,* 65–79.

Vining, J., & Ebreo, A. (1990). What makes a recycler? A comparison of recyclers and nonrecyclers. *Environment and Behavior, 22,* 55–73.

Vinokur, A., & Burnstein, E. (1974). Effects of partially shared persuasive arguments on group-induced shifts: A group problem-solving approach. *Journal of Personality and Social Psychology, 29,* 305–315.

Vogel, D. A., Lake, M. A., Evans, S., & Karraker, K. H. (1991). Children's and adults' sex-stereotyped perceptions of infants. *Sex Roles, 24,* 605–616.

Vrij, A., van der Steen, J., & Koppelaar, L. (1994). Aggression of police officers as a function of temperature: An experiment with the fire arms training system. *Journal of Community and Applied Social Psychology, 4,* 365–370.

Wade, N. (1995, May 14). Microbes into infinity. *New York Times,* p. E4.

Wagner, P. J., & Curran, P. (1984). Health beliefs and physician identified "worried well." *Health Psychology, 3,* 459–474.

Waller, N. G., & Shaver, P. R. (1994). The importance of nongenetic influences on romantic love styles: A twin-family study. *Psychological Science, 5,* 268–274.

Waller, N. G., Kojetin, B. A., Bouchard, T. J. Jr., Lykken, D. T., & Tellegen, A. (1990). Genetic and environmental influences on religious interests, attitudes, and values: A study of twins reared apart and together. *Psychological Science, 1,* 138–142.

Walster, E., & Festinger, L. (1962). The effectiveness of "overheard" persuasive communication. *Journal of Abnormal and Social Psychology, 65,* 395–402.

Walster, E., Walster, G. W., & Berscheid, E. (1978). *Equity: Theory and research.* Boston: Allyn & Bacon.

Walster, E., Walster, G. W., Piliavin, J., & Schmidt, L. (1973). "Playing hard-to-get": Understanding an elusive phenomenon. *Journal of Personality and Social Psychology, 26,* 113–121.

Wardle, J., Bindra, R., Fairclough, B., & Westcombe, A. (1993). Culture and body image: Body perception and weight concern in young Asian and Caucasian British women. *Journal of Community & Applied Social Psychology, 3,* 173–181.

Warm, J. S., Dember, W. N., & Parasuraman, R. (1991). Effects of olfactory stimulation on performance and stress in a visual sustained attention task. *Journal of the Society of Cosmetic Chemists, 42,* 1–12.

Waters, H. F., Block, D., Friday, C., & Gordon, J. (1993, July 12). Networks under the gun. *Newsweek,* 64–66.

Wattenberg, B. J. (1989, February 13). The case for more immigrants. *U.S. News and World Report,* 29–31.

Watts, B. L. (1982). Individual differences in circadian activity rhythms and their effects on roommate relationships. *Journal of Personality, 50,* 374–384.

Wayne, S. J., & Ferris, G. R. (1990). Influence tactics, and exchange quality in supervisor–subordinate interactions: A laboratory experiment and field study. *Journal of Applied Psychology, 75,* 487–499.

Wayne, S. J., & Kacmar, K. M. (1991). The effects of impression management on the performance appraisal process. *Organizational Behavior and Human Decision Processes, 48,* 70–88.

Wayne, S. J., & Liden, R. C. (1995). Effects of impression management on performance ratings: A longitudinal study. *Academy of Management Journal, 38,* 232–260.

Wegener, D. T., & Petty, R. E. (1995). Flexible correction processes in social judgment: The role of naive theories in corrections for perceived bias. *Journal of Personality and Social Psychology, 68,* 36–51.

Wegner, D. M., (1992). You can't always think what you want: Problems in the suppression of unwanted thoughts. In M. P. Zanna (Ed.), *Advances in experimental social psychology* (Vol. 25, pp. 192–225). San Diego, CA: Academic Press.

Wegner, D. M., & Erber, R. (1992). The hyperaccessibility of suppressed thoughts. *Journal of Personality and Social Psychology, 63,* 903–912.

Wegner, D. M. (1992). The premature demise of the solo experiment. *Personality and Social Psychology Bulletin, 18,* 504–508.

Weidner, G., Istvan, J., & McKnight, J. D. (1989). Clusters of behavioral coronary risk factors in employed women and men. *Journal of Applied Social Psychology, 19,* 468–480.

Weigel, R. H., Kim, E. L., & Frost, J. L. (1995). Race relations on prime time television reconsidered: Patterns of continuity and change. *Journal of Applied Social Psychology, 25,* 223–236.

Weigel, R. H., Loomis, J. S., & Soja, M. J. (1980). Race relations on prime time television. *Journal of Personality and Social Psychology, 39,* 884–893.

Weinberg, M. S., Lottes, I. L., & Shaver, F. M. (1995). Swedish or American heterosexual college youth: Who is more permissive? *Archives of Sexual Behavior, 24,* 409–437.

Weinberger, M., Hiner, S. L., & Tierney, W. M. (1987). In support of hassles as a measure of stress in predicting health outcomes. *Journal of Behavioral Medicine, 10,* 19–32.

Weiner, B. (1980). A cognitive (attribution) emotion–action model of motivated behavior: An analysis of judgments of helpgiving. *Journal of Personality and Social Psychology, 39,* 186–200.

Weiner, B., Amirkhan, J., Folkes, V. S., & Verette, J. A. (1987). An attributional analysis of excuse giving: Studies of a naive theory of emotion. *Journal of Personality and Social Psychology, 52,* 316–324.

Weinstein, H., & Rutten, T. (1995, July 7). How does the evidence play after 5 months? *Albany Times Union*, p. A-7.

Weis, D. L. (1983). Affective reactions of women to their initial experience of coitus. *Journal of Sex Research, 19*, 209–237.

Weitzman, L., Eifler, D., Hokada, E., & Ross, C. (1972). Sex-role socialization in picture books for preschool children. *American Journal of Sociology, 77* 1125–1150.

Weldon, E., & Mustari, L. (1988). Felt dispensability in groups of coactors: The effects of shared responsibility and explicit anonymity on cognitive effort. *Organizational Behavior and Human Decision Processes, 41*, 330–351.

Wells, G. L. (1984). The psychology of lineup identification. *Journal of Applied Social Psychology, 14*, 89–103.

Wells, G. L. (1992). Naked statistical evidence of liability: Is subjective probability enough? *Journal of Abnormal and Social Psychology, 62*, 739–752.

Wells, G. L. (1993). What do we know about eyewitness identification? *American Psychologist, 48*, 553–571.

Wells, G. L., & Loftus, E. F. (Eds.). (1984). *Eyewitness testimony: Psychological perspectives*. Cambridge, England: Cambridge University Press.

Wells, G. L., & Luus, C. A. E. (1990). Police lineups as experiments: Social methodology as a framework for properly conducted lineups. *Personality and Social Psychology Bulletin, 16*, 106–117.

Wells, G. L., Luus, C. A. E., & Windschitl, P. D. (1994). Maximizing the utility of eyewitness identification evidence. *Current Directions in Psychological Science, 3*, 194–197.

Werner, C. M., Strube, M. J., Cole, A. M., & Kagehiro, D. K. (1985). The impact of case characteristics and prior jury experience on jury verdicts. *Journal of Applied Social Psychology, 15*, 409–427.

West, S. G., Newsom, J. T., & Fenaughty, A. M. (1992). Publication in JPSP: Stability and change in topics, methods, and theories across two decades. *Personality and Social Psychology Bulletin, 18*, 473–484.

Whaley, K. L., & Rubenstein, T. S. (1994). How toddlers "do" friendship: A descriptive analysis of naturally occurring friendships in a group child care setting. *Journal of Social and Personal Relationships, 11*, 383–400.

Whisman, M. A., & Kwon, P. (1993). Life stress and dysphoria: The role of self-esteem and hopelessness. *Journal of Personality and Social Psychology, 65*, 1054–1060.

Whitbeck, L. B., & Hoyt, D. R. (1994). Social prestige and assortive mating: A comparison of students from 1956 and 1988. *Journal of Social and Personal Relationships, 11*, 137–145.

White, R. K. (1977) Misperception in the Arab-Israeli conflict. *Journal of Social Issues, 33*, 190–221.

Whitley, B. E. Jr. (1993). Reliability and aspects of the construct validity of Sternberg's triangular love scale. *Journal of Social and Personal Relationships, 10*, 475–480.

Whitley, B. E., & Greenberg, M. S. (1986). The role of eyewitness confidence in juror perceptions of credibility. *Journal of Applied Social Psychology, 16*, 387–409.

Wicker, A. W. (1969). Attitudes versus actions: The relationship of verbal and overt behavioral responses to attitude objects. *Journal of Social Issues, 25*, 41–78.

Wiebe, D. J., & McCallum, D. M. (1986). Health practices and hardiness as mediators in the stress–illness relationship. *Health Psychology, 5*, 425–438.

Wiener, Y., Muczyk, J. P., & Martin, H. J. (1992). Self-esteem and job involvement as moderators of the relationship between work satisfaction and well-being. *Journal of Social Behavior and Personality, 7*, 539–554.

Wilder, D. A. (1977). Perception of groups, size of opposition, and social influence. *Journal of Experimental Social Psychology, 13*, 253–268.

Willett, J. B., Ayoub, C. C., & Robinson, D. (1991). Using growth modeling to examine systematic differences in growth: An example of change in the functioning of families at risk of maladaptive parenting, child abuse, or neglect. *Journal of Consulting and Clinical Psychology, 59*, 38–47.

Williams, C. W., & Lees-Haley, P. R. (1993). Perceived toxic exposure: A review of four cognitive influences on perception of illness. *Journal of Social Behavior and Personality, 8*, 489–506.

Williams, D. E., & D'Alessandro, J. D. (1994). A comparison of three measures of androgyny and their relationship to psychological adjustment. *Journal of Social Behavior and Personality, 9*, 469–480.

Williams, G. P., & Kleinke, C. L. (1993). Effects of mutual gaze and touch on attraction, mood, and cardiovascular reactivity. *Journal of Research in Personality, 27*, 170–183.

Williams, J. G., & Solano, C. H. (1983). The social reality of feeling lonely: Friendship and reciprocation. *Personality and Social Psychology Bulletin, 9*, 237–242.

Williams, K. B., Radefeld, P. A., Binning, J. F., & Suadk, J. R. (1993). When job candidates are "hard-" versus "easy-to-get": Effects of candidate availability on employment decisions. *Journal of Applied Social Psychology, 23*, 169–198.

Williams, K. D., & Karau, S. J. (1991). Social loafing and social compensation: The effects of expectations of co-worker performance. *Journal of Personality and Social Psychology, 61*, 570–581.

Williams, K. D., Harkins, S., & Latané, B. (1981). Identifiability as a deterrent to social loafing: Two cheering experiments. *Journal of Personality and Social Psychology, 40*, 303–311.

Williams, K. J., Suls, J., Alliger, G. M., Learner, S. M., & Wan, C. K. (1991). Multiple role juggling and daily mood states in working mothers: An experience sampling study. *Journal of Applied Psychology, 76*, 633–638.

Williamson, G. M., & Clark, M. S. (1989). Providing help and desired relationship type as determinants of changes in moods and self-evaluations. *Journal of Personality and Social Psychology, 56*, 722–734.

Williamson, G. M., & Schulz, R. (1995). Caring for a family member with cancer: Past communal behavior and affective reactions. *Journal of Applied Social Psychology, 25*, 93–116.

Williamson, T. M. (1993). From interrogation to investigative interviewing: Strategic trends in police questioning. *Journal of Community and Applied Social Psychology, 3*, 89–99.

Wills, T. A., & DePaulo, B. M. (1991). Interpersonal analysis of the help-seeking process. In C. R. Snyder & D. R. Forsyth (Eds.), *Handbook of social and clinical psychology* (pp. 357–375). Elmsford, NY: Pergamon Press.

Wills, T. A., DuHamel, K., & Vaccaro, D. (1995). Activity and mood temperament as predictors of adolescent substance use: Test of a self-regulation mediational model. *Journal of Personality and Social Psychology, 68*, 901–916.

Wilson, D. K., Kaplan, R. M., & Schneiderman, L. J. (1987). Framing of decisions and selections of alternatives in health care. *Social Behavior, 2*, 51–59.

Wilson, D. W. (1981). Is helping a laughing matter? *Psychology, 18*, 6–9.

Wilson, E. O. (1975). *Sociobiology*. Cambridge, MA: Harvard University Press.

Wilson, J. P., & Petruska, R. (1984). Motivation, model attributes, and prosocial behavior. *Journal of Personality and Social Psychology, 46*, 458–468.

Wilson, M., Daly, M. & Daniele, A. (1995). Familicide: The killing of spouse and children. *Aggressive Behavior, 21,* 275–291.

Wilson, P. M. (1986). Black culture and sexuality. *Journal of Social Work and Human Sexuality, 4,* 29–44.

Wilson, T. D. (1990). Self-persuasion via self-reflection. In M. Olson & M. P. Zanna (Eds.), *Self-inference processes: The Ontario Symposium* (Vol. 6, pp. 43–67). Hillsdale, NJ: Erlbaum.

Wilson, T. D., & Klaaren, K. J. (1992). Effects of affective expectations on willingness to relive pleasant and unpleasant events. Unpublished data. Cited in Wilson, T. D., & Klaaren, K. J., "Expectation whirl me round": The role of affective expectations in affective experience. In M. S. Clark (Ed.), *Emotion and social behavior* (pp. 1–31). Newbury Park, CA: Sage.

Wilson, T. D., & Kraft, D. (1993). Why do I love thee?: Effects of repeated introspections about a dating relationship on attitudes toward the relationship. *Personality and Social Psychology Bulletin, 19,* 409–418.

Wilson, T. D., & Schooler, J. (1991). Thinking too much: Introspection can reduce the quality of preferences and decisions. *Journal of Personality and Social Psychology, 60,* 181–192.

Wilson, T. D., Lisle, D. J., Kraft, D., & Wetzel, C. G. (1989). Preferences as expectation-driven inferences: Effects of affective expectations on affective experience. *Journal of Personality and Social Psychology, 56,* 519–530.

Winstead, B. A., Derlega, V. J., Montgomery, M. J., & Pilkington, C. (1995). The quality of friendships at work and job satisfaction. *Journal of Social and Personal Relationships, 12,* 199–215.

Wolf, N. (1992). Father figures. *New Republic, 207*(15), 22, 24–25.

Wolf, S., & Bugaj, A. M. (1990). The social impact of courtroom witnesses. *Social Behaviour, 5,* 1–13.

Wolfe, B. M., & Baron, R. A. (1971). Laboratory aggression related to aggression in naturalistic social situation: Effects of an aggressive model on the behavior of college student and prisoner observers. *Psychonomic Science, 24,* 193–194.

Wolfe, D. A. (1991). *Preventing physical and emotional abuse of children.* New York: Guilford Press.

Wolfe, S. (1985). Manifest and latent influence of majorities and minorities. *Journal of Personality and Social Psychology, 48,* 899–908.

Wood, J. V., Giordano-Beech, M., Taylor, K. L., Michela, J. L., & Gaus, V. (1994). Strategies of social comparison among people with low self-esteem: Self-protection and self-enhancement. *Journal of Personality and Social Psychology, 67,* 713–731.

Wood, W. (1982). Retrieval of attitude-relevant information from memory: Effects on susceptibility to persuasion on intrinsic motivation. *Journal of Personality and Social Psychology, 42,* 798–810.

Wood, W., & Stagner, B. (1994). Why are some people easier to influence than others? In S. Shavitt & T. C. Brock (Eds.), *Persuasion* (pp. 149–193). Boston: Allyn & Bacon.

Wood, W., Wong, F. Y., & Cachere, J. G. (1991). Effects of media violence on viewers' aggression in unconstrained social interaction. *Psychological Bulletin, 109,* 371–383.

Worchel, S., & Shackelford, S. L. (1991). Groups under stress: The influence of group structure and environment on process and performance. *Personality and Social Psychology Bulletin, 17,* 640–647.

Wright, P. H. (1984). Self-referent motivation and the intrinsic quality of friendship. *Journal of Social and Personal Relationships, 1,* 115–130.

Wright, R. (1994, November 28). Feminists, meet Mr. Darwin. *The New Republic, 34,* 36–37, 40, 42, 44–46.

Wright, R. (1995, March 13). The biology of violence. *The New Yorker,* 68–77.

Wuensch, K. L., Castellow, W. A., & Moore, C. H. (1991). Effects of defendant attractiveness and type of crime on juridic judgment. *Journal of Social Behavior and Personality, 6,* 713–724.

Wyer, R. S., Jr., & Srull, T. K. (1994). *Handbook of social cognition* (2nd ed). Hillsdale, NJ: Erlbaum.

Wyer, R. S., Jr., Budesheim, T. L., Lambert, A. J., & Swan, S. (1994). Person memory judgment: Pragmatic influences on impressions formed in a social context. *Journal of Personality and Social Psychology, 66,* 254–267

Wyer, R. S. Jr., & Srull, T. K. (Eds.). (1994). *Handbook of social cognition* (2nd ed.) (Vol. 1). Hillsdale, NJ: Erlbaum.

Yamagishi, M., & Yamagishi, T. (1989). *Trust, commitment, and the development of network structures.* Paper presented at the Workshop for the Beyond Bureaucracy Research Project, December 18–21, Hong Kong.

Yamagishi, T. (1988). Exit from the group as an individualistic solution to free rider problem in the United States and Japan. *Journal of Experimental Social Psychology, 24,* 530–542.

Yamagishi, T., & Yamigishi, M. (1994). Trust and commitment in the United States and Japan. *Motivation and Emotion, 18,* 129–166.

Yamaguchi, S., Okamoto, K. & Oka, T. (1985). Effects of coactor's presence: Social loafing and social facilitation. *Japanese Psychological Research, 27,* 215–222.

Yates, S. (1992). Lay attributions about distress after a natural disaster. *Personality and Social Psychology Bulletin, 18,* 217–222.

Yinon, Y., & Landau, M. D. (1987). On the reinforcing value of helping behavior in a positive mood. *Motivation and Emotion, 11,* 83–93.

Yost, J. H., & Weary, G. (1996). Depression and the correspondent inference bias: Evidence for more effortful cognitive processing. *Personality and Social Psychology Bulletin, 22,* 192–200.

Youille, J. C., & Cutshall, J. L. (1986). A case study of eyewitness memory of a crime. *Journal of Applied Psychology, 71,* 291–301.

Youille, J. C., & Tollestrup, P. A. (1990). Some effects of alcohol on eyewitness memory. *Journal of Applied Psychology, 71,* 291–301.

Yovetich, N. A., & Rusbult, C. E. (1994). Accommodative behavior in close relationships: Exploring transformation of motivation. *Journal of Experimental Social Psychology, 30,* 138–164.

Yukl, G. (1981). *Leadership in organizations.* Englewood Cliffs, NJ: Prentice-Hall.

Yukl, G. (1989). *Leadership in organizations* (2nd ed.). Englewood Cliffs, NJ: Prentice-Hall.

Yukl, G. (1994). *Leadership in organizations* (3rd ed.). Englewood Cliffs, NJ: Prentice-Hall.

Yukl, G., & Falbe, C. M. (1991). Importance of different power sources in downward and lateral relations. *Journal of Applied Psychology, 76,* 416–423.

Yukl, G., & Tracey, J. B. (1992). Consequences of influence tactics used with subordinates, peers, and the boss. *Journal of Applied Psychology, 77,* 525–535.

Zaccaro, S. J., & McCoy, M. C. (1988). The effects of task and interpersonal cohesiveness on performance of a disjunctive group task. *Journal of Applied Social Psychology, 18,* 837–851.

Zaccaro, S. J., Foti, R. J., & Kenny, D. A. (1991). Self-monitoring and trait-based variance in leadership: An investigation of leader flexibility across multiple group situations. *Journal of Applied Psychology, 76,* 308–315.

Zajonc, R. B. (1965). Social facilitation. *Science, 149,* 269–274.

Zajonc, R. B. (1968). Attitudinal effects of mere exposure [monograph]. *Journal of Personality and Social Psychology, 9*, 1–27.

Zajonc, R. B., & McIntosh, D. N. (1992). Emotions research: Some promising questions and some questionable promises. *Psychological Science, 3*, 70–74.

Zajonc, R. B., & Sales, S. M. (1966). Social facilitation of dominant and subordinate responses. *Journal of Experimental Social Psychology, 2*, 160–168.

Zajonc, R. B., Adelmann, P. K., Murphy, S. T., & Niedenthal, P. M. (1987). Convergence in the physical appearance of spouses. *Motivation and Emotion, 11*, 335–346.

Zajonc, R. B., Heingartner, A., & Herman, E. M. (1969). Social enhancement and impairment of performance in the cockroach. *Journal of Personality and Social Psychology, 13*, 83–92.

Zajonc, R. B., Murphy, S. T., & Inglehart, M. (1989). Feeling and facial efference: Implications of the vascular theory of emotion. *Psychological Review, 96*, 395–416.

Zammichieli, M. E., Gilroy, F. D., & Sherman, M. F. (1988). Relation between sex-role orientation and marital satisfaction. *Personality and Social Psychology Bulletin, 14*, 747–754.

Zanna, M. P., & Olson, J. M. (1994). The psychology of prejudice. *The Ontario Symposium* (Vol. 7). Hillsdale, NJ: Erlbaum.

Zeitz, G. (1990). Age and work satisfaction in a government agency: A situational perspective. *Human Relations, 43*, 419–438.

Ziller, R. C. (1990). *Photographing the self: Methods for observing personal orientations.* Newbury Park, CA: Sage.

Zillmann, D. (1979). *Hostility and aggression.* Hillsdale, NJ: Erlbaum.

Zillmann, D. (1983). Transfer of excitation in emotional behavior. In J. T. Cacioppo & R. E. Petty (Eds.), *Social psychophysiology: A sourcebook* (pp. 215–240). New York: Guilford Press.

Zillmann, D. (1984). *Connections between sex and aggression.* Hillsdale, NJ: Erlbaum.

Zillmann, D. (1988). Cognition–excitation interdependencies in aggressive behavior. *Aggressive Behavior, 14*, 51–64.

Zillmann, D. (1993). Mental control of angry aggression. In D. M. Wegner & J. W. Pennebaker (Eds.), *Handbook of mental control.* Englewood Cliffs, NJ: Prentice-Hall.

Zillmann, D. (1994). Cognition–excitation interdependencies in the escalation of anger and angry aggression. In M. Potegal & J. F. Knutson (Eds.), *The dynamics of aggression.* Hillsdale, NJ: Erlbaum.

Zillmann, D., & Bryant, J. (1984). Effects of massive exposure to pornography. In N. M. Malamuth and E. Donnerstein (Eds.), *Pornography and sexual aggression.* New York: Academic Press.

Zillmann, D., & Cantor, J. R. (1976). Effects of timing of information about mitigating circumstances on emotional responses to provocation and retaliatory behavior. *Journal of Experimental Social Psychology, 12*, 38–55.

Zillmann, D., Rockwell, S., Schweitzer, K., & Sundar, S. S. (1993). Does humor facilitate coping with physical discomfort? *Motivation and Emotion, 17*, 1–21.

Zimbardo, P. G. (1977). *Shyness: What it is and what you can do about it.* Reading, MA: Addison-Wesley.

Zoglin, R. (1993). The shock of the blue. *Time, 142*(17), 71–72.

Zuber, J. A., Crott, H. W., & Werner, J. (1992). Choice shift and group polarization: An analysis of the status of arguments and social decision schemes. *Journal of Personality and Social Psychology, 62*, 50–61.

Zuckerman, M., DePaulo, B. M., & Rosenthal, R. (1981). Verbal and nonverbal communication of deception. In L. Berkowitz (Ed.), *Advances in experimental social psychology* (Vol. 14, pp. 1–59). New York: Academic Press.

Zuckerman, M., Miyake, K., & Elkin, C. S. (1995). Effects of attractiveness and maturity of face and voice on interpersonal impressions. *Journal of Research in Personality, 29*, 253–272.

Zusne, L., & Jones, W. H. (1989). *Anomalistic psychology: A study of magical thinking* (2nd ed.). Hillsdale, NJ: Erlbaum.

GLOSSARY

Actor–Observer Effect The tendency to attribute our own behavior mainly to situational causes but the behavior of others mainly to internal (dispositional) causes.

Additive Tasks Tasks for which the group product is the sum or combination of the efforts of individual members.

Affect Infusion Model Theory explaining how affect influences social thought and social judgments.

Affect-Centered Model of Attraction Theoretical model of interpersonal attraction proposing that positive and negative interpersonal evaluations are based on positive versus negative emotions, including emotions elicited by cognitive processes.

Affect Our current feelings and moods.

Aggression Machine Apparatus used to measure physical aggression under safe laboratory conditions.

Aggression Behavior directed toward the goal of harming another living being.

Altruism Unselfish concern with the welfare of others.

Altruistic Personality Combination of empathic self-concept, belief in a just world, feelings of social responsibility, internal locus of control, and low egocentrism; increased likelihood of prosocial behavior.

Androgyny In studies of gender, the tendency to report having both traditionally "masculine" and traditionally "feminine" characteristics.

Appearance Anxiety Apprehension or worry about the adequacy of one's physical appearance and about how others evaluate it.

Attachment Style An infant's degree of security in mother–infant interactions, believed to result in a secure, avoidant, or ambivalent attachment style—which affects interpersonal behavior throughout life.

Attitude Accessibility The ease with which specific attitudes can be remembered and brought into consciousness.

Attitude Similarity The extent to which two individuals share the same attitudes about a series of topics.

Attitude-to-Behavior Process Model A model of how attitudes guide behavior that emphasizes the influence of attitudes and stored knowledge (of what is appropriate in a given situation) on one's definition of the present situation; this definition, in turn, influences overt behavior.

Attitudes Lasting evaluations of various aspects of the social world.

Attribution The process through which we seek to identify the causes of others' behavior and so gain knowledge of their stable traits and dispositions.

Augmenting Principle The tendency to attach greater importance to a potential cause of behavior if the behavior occurs despite the presence of other, inhibitory factors.

Automatic Priming Effect that when stimuli of which individuals are not consciously aware alter the availability of various traits or concepts in memory.

Automatic Vigilance The strong tendency to pay attention to undesirable or negative information.

Availability Heuristic Strategy for making judgments on the basis of how easily specific kinds of information can be brought to mind.

Bait-and-Switch Tactic A technique for gaining compliance in which items offered for sale are unavailable or of very low quality. This leads customers to buy a more expensive item that *is* available.

Balance Theory Newcomb's cognitively oriented theory of the relationships among (1) an individual's liking for another person, (2) his or her attitude about a given topic, and (3) the other person's perceived attitude about the same topic.

Balance In Newcomb's theory, the pleasant emotional state that results when two people like each other and agree about a topic of discussion.

Base Rate Fallacy Tendency to ignore or underutilize information relating to base rates—the relative frequency with which events or stimuli actually occur.

Bem Sex-Role Inventory (BSRI) Bem's measure of the extent to which an individual's self-description is characterized by traditional masculinity, a traditional femininity, a mixture of the two (androgyny), or neither (undifferentiated).

Blank-Lineup Control A procedure in which a witness is shown a police lineup that does *not* contain the suspect; helps police ascertain the accuracy of the witness and/or point up the importance of caution.

Body Language Cues provided by the position, posture, and movement of others' bodies or body parts.

Bystander Effect The finding that as the number of bystanders increases, the likelihood of any one bystander helping decreases and more time passes before help does occur.

Cannon–Bard Theory Theory of emotion suggesting that various stimuli elicit both physiological reactions and the subjective reactions we label as emotions.

Catharsis Hypothesis Theory that if angry persons can express their aggressive impulses in relatively safe ways, they will be less likely to engage in more harmful forms of aggression.

Central Route (to persuasion) Attitude change resulting from systematic processing of information presented in persuasive messages.

Charismatic Leadership Leaders who induce high levels of loyalty, respect, and admiration among their followers. (See also *transformational leadership*).

Child Maltreatment Actions that harm children either physically or psychologically.

Classical Conditioning Basic form of learning in which one stimulus, initially neutral, acquires the capacity to evoke reactions through repeated pairing with another stimulus.

Close Friendship A relationship in which friends spend a great deal of time together, interact in a variety of situations, exclude others from the relationship, and provide emotional support to one another.

Cognitive Dissonance Internal state that results when individuals notice inconsistency between two or more of their attitudes or between their attitudes and their behavior.

Cognitive Dissonance An unpleasant state that occurs when individuals discover inconsistencies between two of their attitudes or between their attitudes and their behavior.

Cognitive Perspective (on persuasion) An approach that attempts to understand persuasion by identifying the cognitive processes that play a role in its occurrence.

Cognitive Theories (of aggression) Modern theories suggesting that aggression stems from a complex interplay between cognitive factors, affective states, and additional variables.

Cognitive–Experiential Self-Theory Theory suggesting that our efforts to understand the world around us involve two distinct modes of thought: *intuitive* thought and *deliberate, rational* thought.

Cohesiveness All forces (factors) that cause group members to remain in the group.

Cohesiveness With respect to conformity, the degree of attraction felt by an individual toward an influencing group.

Collective Effort Model An explanation of social loafing suggesting that perceived links between individuals' effort and their outcomes are weaker when they work together with other in a group.

Collective Entrapment Tendency of some groups to cling stubbornly to unsuccessful decisions or policies even in the face of evidence that they are bad ones.

Common Ingroup Identity Model Theory suggesting that to the extent individuals in different groups view themselves as members of a single social entity, positive contacts between them will increase and intergroup bias will be reduced.

Common Knowledge Effect The tendency for information held by most members of a group to exert a stronger impact on the group's final decision than information not held by most members.

Companionate Love Love based on friendship, mutual attraction, common interests, mutual respect, and concern for one another's happiness and welfare.

Complaining In the context of compliance, expressing discontent, dissatisfaction, resentment, or regret as a means of exerting social influence on others.

Compliance A form of social influence involving direct requests from one person to another.

Conflict Actions taken by individuals to block or interfere with others' interests, because of perceptions of incompatible interests and the belief that others may be interfering with the perceiver's interests.

Conformity A type of social influence in which individuals change their attitudes or behavior in order to adhere to existing social norms.

Confounding Confusion that occurs when factors other than the independent variable in an experiment vary across experimental conditions. When confounding occurs, it is impossible to determine whether results stem from the effects of the independent variable or from the other variables.

Consensual Validation The perceived "validation" of one's views about any aspect of the world that is provided whenever someone else holds the same views.

Consensus The extent to which reactions by one person are also shared by others.

Consistency The extent to which an individual responds to a given stimulus or situation in the same way on different occasions (i.e., across time).

Contact Hypothesis Theory that increased contact between members of various social groups can be effective in reducing prejudice between them; seems to be valid only when contact takes under specific favorable conditions.

Converging Operations A principle useful in establishing the validity of research findings. Converging operations suggests that if a particular variable affects some aspect of social behavior by influencing an underlying psychological mechanism, then other variables that influence the same mechanism should produce similar effects on behavior.

Coping Responding to stress in a way that reduces the threat and its effects; includes what a person does, feels, or thinks in order to master, tolerate, or decrease the negative effects of a stressful situation.

Correlational Method Method of research in which a scientist systematically observes two or more variables to determine whether changes in one are accompanied by changes in the other.

Correspondent Inference (theory of) Theory describing how we use others' behavior as a basis for inferring their stable dispositions.

Counterfactual Thinking Tendency to evaluate events by thinking about alternatives to them—"what might have been."

Deadline Technique A technique for increasing compliance in which target persons are told that they have only limited time to take advantage of some offer or to obtain some item.

Debriefing Procedure at the conclusion of a research session in which participants are given full information about the nature of the research and the hypothesis or hypotheses under investigation.

Deception Technique whereby researchers withhold information about the purposes or procedures of a study from persons participating in it.

Decision Making The processes through which individuals or groups combine and integrate available information in order to choose one out of several possible courses of action.

Decision/Commitment In Sternberg's triangular model of love, the cognitive elements involved in the decision to form a relationship and in expressions of continuing commitment to it.

Dependent Variable The variable that is measured in an experiment.

Diffusion of Responsibility Decrease in individual sense of responsibility for taking action in an emergency because of the presence of other bystanders; the greater the number of bystanders, the less likely each individual is to act.

Discounting Principle The tendency to attach less importance to one potential cause of some behavior when other potential causes are also present.

Discrimination Negative behaviors directed toward people who are the object of prejudice.

Disease-Prone Personality Personality type in which the individual responds to stress with negative affect and unhealthy behavior patterns, resulting in physical illness and a shortened life span.

Distinctiveness The extent to which an individual responds in a the same manner to different stimuli or different situations.

Distraction–Conflict Theory Theory suggesting that social facilitation stems from the conflict produced when individuals attempt simultaneously to pay attention to a task and to other persons.

Distributive Justice Fairness Refers to individuals' judgments about whether they are receiving a fair share of available rewards—a share proportionate to their contributions to the group or any social relationship.

Door-in-the-Face Technique A procedure for gaining compliance in which requesters begin with a large request and then, when this is refused, retreat to a smaller one (the one they actually desired all along).

Drive Theories (of aggression) Theories suggesting that aggression stems from external conditions that arouse the motive to harm others; the most famous of these is the frustration–aggression hypothesis.

Drive Theory of Social Facilitation A theory suggesting that the mere presence of others is arousing and increases the tendency to perform dominant responses.

Egoism Exclusive concern with one's own personal welfare.

Elaboration Likelihood Model (of persuasion) A theory suggesting that persuasion can occur in either of two distinct ways, differing in the amount of cognitive effort or elaboration they require.

Emotional Expressiveness The extent to which persons show outward expressions of their inner feelings.

Empathic Joy Hypothesis The proposal that prosocial behavior is motivated by the positive empathetic feelings that result from helping a person in need feel better.

Empathy–Altruism Hypothesis The proposal that at least some prosocial behavior is motivated solely by the desire to help someone who is in need.

Empathy Basically, tendency to respond to another's emotional state with vicarious feelings resembling the emotions of the other; definition has been broadened to include sympathizing, taking the perspective of the other person, and being able to empathize with fictional characters.

Environmental Psychology The research area that concentrates on the interaction between the physical world and human behavior.

Equity Perceived fairness in social exchange. Judgments of equity relate to distributive justice, and involve comparisons, by individuals, of their own outcomes and contributions to those of other person.

Evaluation Apprehension Concern over being evaluated by others; can increase arousal and so contribute to social facilitation.

Evolutionary Social Psychology An area of research that seeks to investigate the potential role of genetic factors in various aspects of social behavior.

Excitation Transfer Theory Theory suggesting that arousal produced in one situation can persist and intensify emotional reactions occurring in later situations.

Experimentation Method of research in which one or more factors (the independent variables) are systematically changed to determine whether such variations affect one or more other factors (dependent variables).

Facial Feedback Hypothesis The suggestion that changes in facial expression can induce shifts in emotions or affective states.

False Consensus Effect The tendency to assume that others behave or think as we do to a greater extent than is actually true.

Familicide Instances in which an individual kills his or her spouse and one or more of his or her children.

Foot-in-the-Door Technique A procedure for gaining compliance in which requesters begin with a small request and then, when this is granted, escalate to a larger one (the one they actually desired all along).

Foot-in-the-Mouth Tactic A procedure for gaining compliance in which the requester establishes some kind of relationship, no matter how trivial, with the target person, thereby increasing this person's feeling of obligation to comply.

Forced Compliance Situations in which individuals are somehow induced to say or do things inconsistent with their true attitudes.

Forensic Psychology Psychological research and theory dealing with legal proceedings and the law.

Forewarning Advance knowledge that one is about to become the target of an attempt at persuasion; often increases resistance to the persuasion that follows.

Framing The specific wording of information, which can influence decision making.

Frustration–Aggression Hypothesis The suggestion that frustration is a very powerful determinant of aggression.

Fundamental Attribution Error The tendency to overestimate the impact of dispositional causes on others' behavior.

Gender Consistency The concept that gender is a basic, enduring attribute of each individual; a concept ordinarily acquired by children between the ages of four and seven.

Gender Identity The sex (male or female) that a person identifies as his or her own; usually, though not always, corresponds corresponds to the person's biological sex.

Gender Stereotypes Stereotypes concerning the traits supposedly possessed by females and males, which distinguish the two genders from each other.

Gender-Stereotype Identification The extent to which an individual identifies the culture's gender stereotypes; masculinity or femininity, as measured by the BSRI.

Gender The attributes, behaviors, personality characteristics, and expectancies associated with a person's biological sex in a given culture; may be based on biology, may be learned, or may represent a combination of biological and cultural determinants.

Genetic Determinism Model The proposal that prosocial behavior is unconsciously motivated by genetic factors that evolved because they enhanced the ability of our ancestors to survive and reproduce; genetic similarity.

Glass Ceiling Barriers based on attitudinal or organizational bias that prevent qualified females from advancing to top-level positions.

Global Warming The probable increase in the temperature of the earth's atmosphere and its oceans brought about partly as a result of various human activities.

Great Person Theory (of Leadership) Theory suggesting that all great leaders share key traits that suit them for positions of authority.

Greenhouse Effect The basis of global warming: gases released into the atmosphere (carbon dioxide, methane, and chlorofluorocarbons) trap the sun's heat, turning the earth into a vast "greenhouse."

Group Polarization The tendency of group members to shift toward more extreme positions than those they initially held as a result of group discussion.

Groupthink The tendency of highly cohesive groups to assume that their decisions can't be wrong: that all members must support the group's decision and ignore information contrary to it.

Hardiness Includes such characteristics as commitment, defining difficulties as challenges, and perceiving oneself as having control over one's life.

Health Psychology The study of how psychological factors influence the origin, prevention, and treatment of physical illness.

Heuristics Rules or principles that allow us to make social judgments rapidly and with reduced effort.

Hostile Aggression Aggression in which the prime objective is to inflict some kind of harm on the victim.

Hostile Attributional Bias Tendency to perceive others' actions as stemming from hostile intent even when this is not clearly the case.

Illusion of Outgroup Homogeneity The tendency to perceive members of outgroups as more similar to one another (more homogeneous) than members of one's own ingroup.

Illusory Correlations Perception of a stronger association between two variables than actually exists; occurs because each variable is distinctive and their apparent correlation is readily entered into and retrieved from memory.

Imbalance In Newcomb's theory, the unpleasant emotional state that results when two people like each other but disagree about a topic of discussion; each is motivated to change some element in the interaction in order to achieve *balance* or *nonbalance*.

Impression Formation The process through which we form impressions of others.

Impression Management (self presentation) Efforts by individuals to produce favorable impressions on others.

Incompatibility Error Mistaken perception by negotiators that their own interests and those of the other side are totally incompatible.

Incompatible Responses In relation to aggression, responses that are incompatible with anger or overt aggression against others.

Independent Variable The factor in an experiment that is systematically varied by the researcher.

Individuation The desire to differentiate oneself from others by emphasizing one's uniqueness or individuality.

Industrial/Organizational Psychologists Psychologists who investigate all aspects of behavior in work settings.

Information Overload Situation in which our ability to process information is exceeded by the amount of information available.

Information Sampling Model A theory of group decision making suggesting that group members are more likely to discuss shared than unshared information; this tendency increases with group size.

Informational Social Influence Social influence based on individuals' desire to be correct (i.e., to possess accurate perceptions of the social world).

Informed Consent Procedure in which research participants are provided with as much information as possible about a research project before deciding whether to participate in it.

Ingratiation A technique for gaining compliance in which requesters first induce target persons to like them, then attempt to change their behavior in some desired manner.

Ingroup Differentiation The tendency to perceive members of our own group as much more different from one another (more heterogeneous) than members of other groups.

Ingroup The social group to which an individual perceives herself or himself as belonging ("us").

Instinct Theory View suggesting that aggression stems from innate tendencies that are universal among members of a given species.

Instrumental Aggression Aggression in which the primary goal is not to harm the victim but rather attainment of some other goal, such as access to valued resources.

Instrumental Conditioning Basic form of learning in which responses that lead to positive outcomes or that permit avoidance of negative outcomes are strengthened.

Interactions (between variables) Instances in which the effects of one variable are influenced by the effects of one or more other variables.

Interdependence The characteristic common to all close relationships—an interpersonal association in which two people influence one another's lives and engage in many joint activities.

Interpersonal Attraction Our evaluation of other people with respect to how much we like or dislike them.

Interpersonal Justice Refers to judgments concerning the considerateness and courtesy individuals are shown by parties responsible for distributing available rewards to members of a group.

Intimacy In Sternberg's triangular model of love, the closeness the two partners feel—the extent to which they are bonded.

James–Lange Theory Theory of emotion contending that emotional experiences result from our perceptions of shifts in bodily states; we become fearful because we notice such physiological reactions as increased heart rate, and so on.

Job Interviews Interviews conducted with applicants for various jobs in order to choose the best job candidates.

Job Satisfaction Attitudes held by individuals about their jobs.

Leadership The process through which leaders influence other group members toward attainment of specific group goals.

Leading Questions Questions asked of witnesses or suspects by police or by attorneys that are worded so as to suggest specific answers.

Legal Authoritarianism Among some jurors, a general tendency to assume the worst about a person accused of a crime.

Leniency Bias Among some jurors, a general tendency to make favorable assumptions about a person accused of a crime.

Less-Leads-to-More Effect The finding that offering individuals small rewards for engaging in counterattitudinal behavior often produces more dissonance, and so more attitude change, than offering larger rewards.

Loneliness The emotional state that results from desiring close interpersonal relationships but being unable to attain them.

Love Several quite different combinations of emotions, cognitions, and behaviors that can be involved in intimate relationships.

Lowball Procedure A technique for gaining compliance in which an offer or deal is changed to make it less attractive to the target person after this person has accepted it.

Magical Thinking Thinking involving assumptions that don't hold up to rational scrutiny—for example, the belief that things that resemble one another share fundamental properties.

Matching Hypothesis The proposal that individuals are attracted to one another as friends, romantic partners, or spouses on the basis of similar attributes—physical attractiveness, age, race, personality characteristics, or social assets of such as wealth, education, or power.

Meta-Analysis Statistical technique for combining data from independent studies in order to determine whether specific variables (or interactions between variables) have significant effects across these studies.

Microexpressions Brief and incomplete facial expressions that occur on individuals' faces very quickly after exposure to a specific stimulus and before active processes can be used to conceal them.

Modeling Basic form of learning in which individuals acquire new forms of behavior through observing others.

Multicultural Perspective A focus on understanding the cultural and ethnic factors that influence social behavior.

Need for Affiliation The motive to seek interpersonal relationships.

Negative State Relief Model The proposal that prosocial behavior is motivated by the desire to reduce uncomfortable negative emotions.

Negotiation A process in which two or more parties to a conflict exchange offers, counteroffers, and concessions in an effort to attain a mutually acceptable agreement.

Noise An unwanted sound, one that brings about a negative affective response.

Nonbalance In Newcomb's theory, the indifferent emotional state that results when two people dislike each other and don't care whether they agree or disagree about a topic of discussion.

Noncommon Effects Effects produced by a particular factor that could not be produced by any other apparent cause.

Nonverbal Communication Communication between individuals that does not involve the content of spoken language but relies instead on an unspoken language of facial expressions, eye contact, and body language.

Normative Social Influence Social influence based on individuals' desire to be liked or accepted by other persons.

Norms Rules within a group indicating how its members should (or should not) behave.

Obedience A form of social influence in which one person obeys direct orders from another to perform some action(s).

Organizational Citizenship Behavior Voluntary behaviors by indiciduals that aid their organizations and that are not related to the formal reward system of their job.

Organizational Commitment Attitudes held by individuals toward their organization, reflecting the extent to which they identify with the company and are unwilling to leave it.

Outgroup Any group other than the one to which individuals perceive themselves belonging

Passion In Sternberg's triangular model of love, the sexual motives and sexual excitement associated with a couple's relationship.

Passionate Love Intense and often unrealistic emotional response to another person; the individuals involved often interpret their feelings as "true love," while observers often label their response as "infatuation."

Peripheral Route (to persuasion) Attitude change that occurs in response to persuasion cues such as the attractiveness, expertise or status of would-be persuaders.

Persuasion Efforts to change others' attitudes.

Physical Attractiveness Combination of facial and bodily characteristics perceived as aesthetically appealing (for example, beautiful or handsome) by others.

Pique Technique A technique for gaining compliance that focuses on gaining target persons' attention and so preventing them from engaging in automatic (mindless) refusal.

Planning Fallacy The tendency to make optimistic predictions concerning how long a given task will take.

Playing Hard to Get Efforts to increase compliance by suggesting that a person or object is scarce and hard to obtain.

Pluralistic Ignorance Bystanders' interpretation of an event, caused by reliance on what others do or say even though no one is sure what is happening; all hold back and act as if there is no problem, then each individual uses this "information" to justify failure to act.

Possible Selves Mental representations of what we might become, or should become, in the future.

Prejudice Negative attitudes toward the members of specific social groups.

Priming Effect that occurs when stimuli or events increase the availability of specific types of information in memory or consciousness.

Procedural Justice Judgments concerning the fairness of the procedures used to distribute available rewards among group members.

Proportion of Similar Attitudes The number of topics on which two individuals hold the same views in relation to the total number of topics on which they compare their views, expressed as a percentage or proportion.

Prosocial Behavior Action that benefit others but have no obvious benefits for the person carrying them out, and which sometimes involve risk for the prosocial person.

Prototypes Mental models of the typical qualities of members of some group or category.

Provocation Actions by others that tend to trigger aggression in the recipient, often because they are perceived as stemming from malicious intent.

Proximity In attraction research, the closeness between two individuals' residences, classroom seats, work areas, and so on; the closer the physical distance, the greater the probability of the individuals' coming into regular contact.

Punishment Delivery of aversive consequences in order to decrease some behavior.

Random Assignment of Participants to Groups A basic requirement for conducting valid experiments. According to this principle, research participants must have an equal chance of being exposed to each level of the independent variable.

Reactance Negative reaction to threats to one's personal freedom; often increases resistance to persuasion.

Realistic Conflict Theory The view that prejudice sometimes stems from direct competition between various social groups over scarce and valued resources.

Recategorizations Shifts in the boundary between an individual's ingroup ("us") and various outgroups ("them"), causing persons formerly viewed as outgroup members now to be seen as belonging to the ingroup.

Repeated Exposure Frequent contact with a stimulus; according to Zajonc's theory, with repeated exposure to any mildly negative, neutral, or positive stimulus, the evaluation of that stimulus becomes increasingly positive.

Representativeness Heuristic Strategy for making judgments based on the extent to which current stimuli or events resemble other stimuli or categories.

Repression A defensive response to threat in which the person attempts to control anxiety by using avoidance mechanisms such as denial and forgetting.

Repulsion Hypothesis Rosenbaum's proposal that attraction is not enhanced by similar attitudes; instead, people initially respond positively to others but are repulsed by the discovery of dissimilar attitudes.

Reverse Discrimination Tendency to evaluate or treat persons belonging to certain groups (especially ones that are the object of ethnic or racial prejudice) more favorably than members of other groups.

Roles The sets of behaviors that individuals occupying specific positions within a group are expected to perform.

Schemas Mental frameworks containing information relevant to specific situations or events, which, once established, help us interpret these situations and what's happening in them.

Selective Avoidance Tendency to direct attention away from information that challenges existing attitudes; increases resistance to persuasion.

Self-Concept One's self-identity, a schema consisting of an organized collection of beliefs and feelings about oneself.

Self-Efficacy A person's evaluation of his or her ability or competency to perform a task, reach a goal, or overcome an obstacle.

Self-Esteem The self-evaluation made by each individual; one's attitude toward oneself along a positive–negative dimension.

Self-Focusing The act of directing attention inward toward oneself as opposed to outward toward the environment.

Self-Healing Personality Personality characterized by enthusiasm, emotional balance, extraversion, alertness, and responsiveness; the individual tends to be energetic, curious, secure, and constructive, and have a relatively lower incidence of physical illness and longer life span.

Self-Monitoring Personality characteristic involving willingness to change one's behavior to fit situations, awareness of one's effect on others, and the ability to regulate one's nonverbal cues and other factors to influence others' impressions.

Self-Monitoring Regulation of one's behavior on the basis of the external situation and the reactions of others (high self-monitoring) or on the basis of internal factors such as beliefs, attitudes, and values (low self-monitoring).

Self-Reference Effect The greater efficacy of cognitive processing of information relevant to the self compared to processing of other types of information.

Self-Serving Bias The tendency to attribute our own positive outcomes to internal causes (e.g., our own traits or characteristics) but negative outcomes or events to external causes (e.g., chance, task difficulty).

Sensitization A defensive response to threat in which the person attempts to control anxiety by using approach mechanisms such as rumination and intellectualization.

Sex Typing Acquisition of the attributes associated with being a male or a female in a given culture.

Sex Maleness or femaleness as determined by genetic factors present at conception that result in anatomical and physiological differences.

Sexism Prejudice based on gender.

Sexual Harassment Unwelcome sexual advances, requests for sexual favors, and other verbal or physical conduct of a sexual nature.

Sexual Jealousy Perception of a romantic relationship by a rival for one's partner.

Sexual Self-Schema The cognitive generalizations about the sexual aspects of oneself that originate in past experience, become manifested in current experience, influence the processing of sexual information, and guide sexual behavior.

Social Categorization The tendency to divide the social world into two separate categories: our ingroup ("us") and various outgroups ("them").

Social Cognition The manner in which we interpret, analyze, remember, and use information about the social world.

Social Comparison Theory Festinger's influential theory of our tendency of a drive to evaluate our opinions and abilities based on comparison with other people and our preference for making comparisons with others similar to ourselves.

Social Comparison The process through which we compare ourselves to others in order to determine whether our view of social reality is or is not correct.

Social Decision Schemes Rules relating the initial distribution of member views to final group decisions.

Social Facilitation Effects upon performance resulting from the presence of others.

Social Identity A person's definition of who he or she is; includes personal attributes (self-concept) along with membership in various (aspects groups shared with others).

Social Influence Efforts by one or more individuals to change the attitudes, beliefs, perceptions, or behaviors of one or more others.

Social Learning View (of prejudice) The view that prejudice is acquired through direct and vicarious experience in much the same manner as other attitudes.

Social Learning View Theory emphasizing that aggressive behaviors are learned either through direct experience and practice or through observation of others.

Social Learning The process through which we acquire new information, forms of behavior, or attitudes from other persons.

Social Loafing Reductions in motivation and effort when individuals work collectively in a group compared to when they work individually or as independent coactors.

Social Norms Rules indicating how individuals are expected to behave in specific situations.

Social Perception The process through which we seek to know and understand other persons.

Social Psychology The scientific field that seeks to understand the nature and causes of individual behavior and thought in social situations.

Social Support Physical and psychological comfort provided by friends and relatives to people facing stress; with social support, people tend to be in better physical health and better able to cope with stress.

Sociobiology A branch of biology that contends that many forms of behavior can be understood within the context of efforts by organisms to pass their genes on to the next generation.

Sociosexuality Personality dimension ranging from an *unrestricted* orientation (willingness to engage in casual sexual interactions) to a *restricted* orientation (willingness to engage in sex only with emotional closeness and commitment).

Staring A form of eye contact in which one person continues to gaze steadily at another regardless of what the recipient does.

Status Social standing or rank within group.

Stereotypes Beliefs to the effect that all members of specific social groups share certain traits or characteristics; stereotypes are cognitive frameworks that strongly influence the processing of incoming social information.

Stigma Any characteristics of a person that some observers perceive negatively.

Straw Poll Procedure in which group members indicate their current preferences regarding a decision in a nonbinding vote.

Stress The response to physical or psychological events perceived by the individual as potentially causing harm or emotional distress.

Subliminal Conditioning (of attitudes) Classical conditioning of attitudes by exposure to stimuli that are below the threshold of conscious awareness.

Superordinate Goals Goals shared by the parties in a conflict or dispute.

That's Not All Technique A technique for gaining compliance in which a requesters offers additional benefits to target persons before they have decided whether to comply with or reject specific requests.

Theories Efforts by scientists in any field to answer the question *Why?* Theories involve attempts to understand why certain events or processes occur as they do.

Theory of Planned Behavior A theory of how attitudes guide behavior suggesting that individuals consider the implications of their actions before deciding to perform various behaviors.

Tokenism Instances in which individuals or groups perform trivial positive actions for people toward whom they feel prejudice, then use these actions as an excuse for refusing more meaningful beneficial behavior.

Transformational Leaders Leaders who exert profound influence over followers by proposing an inspiring vision and through several other techniques. (See also *charismatic leadership*).

Triangular Model of Love Sternberg's conceptualization of love relationships as encompassing three basic components: intimacy, passion, and decision/commitment.

Trivialization A technique for reducing dissonance in which the importance of attitudes or behavior that are inconsistent with each other is cognitively reduced.

Two-Factor Theory Theory of emotion suggesting that in many situations we label our emotional states according to what our inspection of the world around us suggests we *should* be experiencing.

Type A Behavior Pattern Pattern consisting primarily of high levels of competitiveness, time urgency, and hostility.

Type B Behavior Pattern Pattern consisting of the absence of characteristics associated with the Type A behavior pattern.

Ultimate Attribution Error The tendency to make more favorable and flattering attributions about members of one's own group than about members of other groups.

Voir Dire A French term used in law to mean the examination of prospective jurors to determine their competence to serve; both the judge and the opposing attorneys may dismiss certain prospects for specific reasons or for no stated reason.

Workplace Aggression Aggression occurring in work settings.